P9-DTC-118

# Fodor's 95 Canada

PRAISE FOR FODOR'S GUIDES

*"Fodor's guides . . . are an admirable blend of the cultural and the practical."*
—The Washington Post

*"Researched by people chosen because they lived or have lived in the country, well-written, and with good historical sections . . . Obligatory reading for millions of tourists."*
—The Independent, *London*

*"Usable, sophisticated restaurant coverage, with an emphasis on good value."*
—Andy Birsh, Gourmet restaurant columnist, quoted by Gannett News Service

*"Packed with dependable information."*
—Atlanta Journal Constitution

*"Fodor's always delivers high quality . . . thoughtfully presented . . . thorough."*
—Houston Post

*"Valuable because of their comprehensiveness."*
—Minneapolis Star-Tribune

Fodor's Travel Publications, Inc.
New York • Toronto • London • Sydney • Auckland

---

**Fodor's Canada**

**Editor:** Kristen D. Perrault
**Contributors:** Steven K. Amsterdam, Susan Brown, Echo Garrett, Dorothy Guinan, Anto Howard, Arlene Karpan, Robin Karpan, Helga Loverseed, Bevin McLaughlin, Scott McNeely, Peter Oliver, Melissa Rivers, Linda K. Schmidt, Mary Ellen Schultz, Bernard Simon, Alison Stern, Nancy van Itallie, Julie Watson, Ana Watts, Sara Waxman
**Creative Director:** Fabrizio La Rocca
**Cartographer:** David Lindroth
**Illustrator:** Karl Tanner
**Cover Photograph:** Peter Guttman

**Design:** Vignelli Associates

---

# Contents

**Maps and Plans**

# Foreword

We wish to express our gratitude to those who helped prepare this guide: the Canadian Consulate General office in New York, particularly Lois Gerber and Barbara Cartwright; Cathy Graham of Alberta Economic Development and Tourism; the Montréal Convention and Tourism Bureau; the Québec Government Ministry of Tourism, particularly Brian LeCompte, Pauline Roy, and Manon Lefebvre; the Government of Newfoundland and Labrador Department of Development, especially Kay Coxworthy; Dana Ottman of Ontario House in New York; Helen-Jean Newman of the New Brunswick Department of Tourism; the Nova Scotia Department of Tourism, especially Randy Brooks and Lynn McGuinness; also Cathy Quesnelle; Lynda Hanscombe of the PEI Department of Tourism and Parks; the Metropolitan Toronto Convention & Visitors Association; Tourism Vancouver, especially Elvira Quarin; Whistler Resort Association; and the Alberta, Manitoba, and British Columbia Tourism bureaus.

While every care has been taken to ensure the accuracy of the information in this guide, the passage of time will always bring change, and consequently, the publisher cannot accept responsibility for errors that may occur.

All prices and opening times are based on information supplied to us at press time. Hours and admission fees may change, however, and the prudent traveler will avoid inconvenience by calling ahead.

Fodor's wants to hear about your travel experiences, both pleasant and unpleasant. When a hotel or restaurant fails to live up to its billing, let us know and we will investigate the complaint and revise our entries where the facts warrant it. Send your letters to the editors of Fodor's Travel Publications, 201 East 50th Street, New York, NY 10022.

# Highlights'95 and Fodor's Choice

# Highlights '95

**Toronto**  Despite a long recession and cutbacks in municipal services, Toronto can still hold its head high as one of the world's safest, cleanest, and most liveable cities. What's more, its former bland Anglo-Saxon atmosphere has been transformed in recent years by a huge influx of immigrants. Ethnic neighborhoods and restaurants are a fixture of the Toronto scene. Torontonians are especially proud of the back-to-back World Series wins of their Blue Jays baseball team. A Blue Jays game at the impressive SkyDome is a must.

**Montréal**  Montréal's first government-run casino, opened in October 1994, is located on Ile Notre-Dame in the former Palais de la Civilisation, the site of the French pavilion during Expo '67. The casino, a success from the start, cost more than $80 million to set up, and features 65 blackjack, mini-baccarat, and roulette tables; 1,200 slot machines; and a Keno betting room with a draw every five minutes. The casino attracts an average of 10,000 people daily, more on weekends, and houses a gourmet restaurant, Nuances. Further additions are planned for 1995.

**Québec City**  In 1995, Québec City will step back 1,000 years in time to celebrate Médiévales de Québec—a colorful, animated five-day festival in mid-August. Hundreds of actors dressed in period costumes—as troubadours, warriors, artisans, and the like—will invade the Vieille Capitale, and activities will take place at 20 sites throughout the city. A cavalcade will involve some 250 people on horseback who will descend upon Québec from as far as Boston, Massachusetts. This will be the city's second time hosting the festival, which occurs annually, alternating between Québec City and Dinan, France. The event takes place August 9th–13th.

Due to the recession, Québec City saw little development during the past few years, but the few well-invested changes that did occur will grace the city for many years to come. The Château Frontenac—the city's landmark castle hotel—renovated all guest rooms and built a new wing (which includes a health spa) in preparation for its 100th birthday celebration in 1993. And the Capitole, a turn-of-the-century theater that reopened its doors in late 1992 after 20 years in ruin, is more successful than many people had anticipated: Big names like B.B. King, Kenny Rogers, and Québec's own Céline Dion have packed the spot since its opening, and more are expected for 1995.

**Vancouver**  Local Vancouver sightseeing has been improved with two good city tours between March and October. Vancouver Trolleys, like old-fashioned street cars, take you on a guided tour of the city allowing lengthy stopovers at any of 17 designated sightseeing attractions (including Stanley Park, English Bay, Gastown, Robson Street, Granville Island, the Vancouver Museum, Queen

Elizabeth Park, Chinatown) on an all-day, unlimited stop ticket. Gray Line offers a similar narrated tour aboard bright red double-decker buses; passengers get on and off as they choose and are allowed to ride free the following day.

And, once again, Vancouver leads the North American market with three five-star hotels: the Four Seasons, Le Meridien, and the Pan Pacific.

**British Columbia**  BC Ferries has stepped up service, adding two brand new ferries on the Tsawwassen–Swartz Bay route. They are also experimenting with night sailings during the heavy summer travel period on the Horseshoe Bay–Nanaimo route and the Tsawwassen–Nanaimo route. New to the transportation scene is **Victoria Line,** a vehicle ferry service operating daily from May through September between Seattle and downtown Vancouver.

**Canadian Rockies**  In the mountainous outback, an ongoing debate continues regarding trail usage. The Canadian Parks Service currently limits mountain biking, for the most part, to fire roads, while studying the use of bikes on backcountry trails. Park officials are concerned about encounters between bikers and wildlife (especially bears, who are easily surprised by swiftly approaching bikes) and about bikers having trouble getting out of the deep backcountry if their bikes break down. This is all part of a wider and somewhat inevitable conflict of interest between the growing commercial interests in the region and the environmental concerns of the park authorities. Banff, the major town in the Rockies, has now gained limited autonomy from the park's strict bylaws, and already the effects can be seen in the accelerated growth of its downtown area.

**Manitoba, Saskatchewan, Alberta**  The prairie provinces are home to a large part of Canada's native population, and increasingly the Indians are sharing their culture and history with tourists. The largest and most recent project is Wanuskewin Heritage Park, on the outskirts of Saskatoon. Through displays, cultural presentations, demonstrations, and archaeological digs, the park combines the rich history and prehistory of Northern Plains natives with a look at the lives of today. The new First Nations Gallery at the Royal Saskatchewan Museum in Regina uses murals, dioramas, sculptures, portraits, and videos to highlight aboriginal heritage through the ages.

**Ontario**  Don't be surprised at rising admission prices and curtailed services at many Ontario tourist attractions. The debt-burdened provincial government is trying to save every penny it can to bring down its budget deficit. Its search for new revenue sources has led to a softening attitude toward gambling. At press time, the province's first legalized casino was due to open in Windsor during 1994. More may follow in other parts of the province.

**Québec Province**  The ongoing debate about whether or not Québec should secede from the Candian union subsided following the 1992 Canada-wide referendum, when Québec and five other provinces voted against the federal government's plan to rewrite its 125-year-old constitution. The plan would have recognized Québec as a distinct society and given more powers to the provincial governments.

But in Québec the silence was shortlived. The closer the province gets to the next provincial election—to be held in the fall of 1994—the more sovereignty becomes an issue. If the federalist Liberals are reelected, the party will strive to keep Québec within Canada. If the nationalist Parti Québécois takes power, it will hold a referendum within a year—once again asking Québecers to choose between a united Canada and a sovereign Québec.

**Nova Scotia** A historical "grand encampment" (July 28–30) will be just one of the special events celebrating the 250th anniversary of the last siege of Louisbourg, which took place in 1745. Six hundred to 1,000 "troops" will be on hand to reenact the battle at Louisbourg fortress. Other highlights of 1995 include road improvements to the Fleur-de-Lis Trail from St. Peters to Louisbourg, providing an alternative route to Sydney. This new route runs closer to the water, giving access to remote beaches, small harbors, and fishing ports. The province will continue its Village Fair, celebrating small-town hospitality and community spirit.

**Prince Edward Island** Tourists coming to Prince Edward Island by way of the Borden–New Brunswick Ferry will be in a position to view the Island's newest, and probably largest ever, tourist attraction: the causeway being constructed across Northumberland Straight. Summerside is making a name for itself as a sports haven; 1995 marks the first year that the town will act as permanent host for the Canadian Peewee Baseball Championship, bringing in teams from each province. Summerside will also host the Canadian Ladies Hockey Championship during the last week of March. Those who enjoy song more than sport will want to attend the first Maritime Music Festival, a jazz-theme celebration of music, to be held the first weekend in July.

**New Brunswick** About 11 miles west of Fredericton, the **Kings Clear Hotel and Resort** has opened—a new modern hotel, with an interesting history. It is operated by the Malicete Indian Band at Mactaquac, who received government help in building and running the motel as compensation for their voluntary surrender of their traditional net-fishing activity, which was endangering the Atlantic salmon.

The section of the **Trans-Canada Highway** that runs through New Brunswick is being upgraded, with the notable addition of signposts alerting travelers to the existence of special "scenic trails," off-the-beaten-track roads that motorists might otherwise miss.

**Newfoundland and Labrador** In 1993 the province began gearing up for the celebrations to come in 1997, celebrating John Cabot's landing in North America.

**Wilderness Canada** Parks Canada is moving toward opening visitor facilities in two new wilderness areas: **Northern Yukon National Park,** which contains one of the world's largest caribou herds, and **Ellesmere Island National Park,** with its extraordinary polar oasis of plant, animal, and bird life.

# Fodor's Choice

No two people will agree on what makes a perfect vacation, but it's fun and helpful to know what others think. We hope you'll have a chance to experience some of Fodor's Choices yourself in Canada. For detailed information about each entry, refer to the appropriate chapter.

## Toronto

**Attractions** Harbourfront, downtown Toronto

Ontario Science Centre, northeast Toronto

Royal Ontario Museum, Queen's Park

**Shopping** Eaton Centre

Kensington Market/Chinatown

Yorkville Avenue/Bloor Street area

**Cultural Events** Canadian Opera Company at the O'Keefe Centre

National Ballet of Canada at the O'Keefe Centre

Theater at the Royal Alexandra, St. Lawrence Centre, Elgin, and Winter Garden theaters

**Restaurants** Le Bistingo (*$$*)

Centro (*$$$–$$$$*)

Joso's (*$$$–$$$$*)

North 44 (*$$$–$$$$*)

Pronto (*$$$*)

**Hotels** Four Seasons Toronto (*$$$$*)

King Edward (*$$$$*)

Best Western Chestnut Park Hotel (*$$$*)

## Montréal

**Attractions** Pointe-à-Callière Museum of Archaeology and History

Montréal Museum of Fine Arts

Casino de Montréal

**Shopping** Place Montréal Trust

Rue Faubourg Ste-Catherine

Notre-Dame Ouest for antiques

Marché aux puces (flea market), Vieux-Montréal

Les Promenades de la Cathédrale

| | |
|---|---|
| **Cultural Events** | International Jazz Festival |
| | L'Orchestre Symphonique de Montréal |
| | *Juste Pour Rire* (Just for Laughs) Festival |
| **Restaurants** | Les Mignardises (*$$$$*) |
| | Les Trois Tilleuls, Montérégie (*$$$$*) |
| | Milos (*$$$$*) |
| **Hotels** | Le Westin Mont-Royal (*$$$$*) |
| | Ritz-Carlton (*$$$$*) |
| | Hôtel de la Montagne (*$$$*) |
| | Château Versailles (*$$*) |

## Québec City

| | |
|---|---|
| **Attractions** | Château Frontenac |
| | Citadelle |
| | Musée de la Civilisation |
| **Shopping** | Marché du Vieux-Port |
| | La Trois Colombes, Inc. |
| | Quartier Petit-Champlain |
| **Cultural Events** | Bibliothèque Gabrielle-Roy |
| | Grand Théâtre de Québec |
| | Le Théâtre Capitole |
| **Restaurants** | À la Table de Serge Bruyère (*$$$$*) |
| | Aux Anciens Canadiens (*$$$*) |
| | L'Echaudée (*$$*) |
| | Chez Temporel (*$*) |
| **Hotels** | Hilton International Québec (*$$$$*) |
| | Manoir d'Auteuil (*$$$*) |
| | L'Auberge du Quartier (*$$*) |

## Vancouver

| | |
|---|---|
| **Attractions** | Butchart Gardens, Victoria |
| | Dr. Sun-yat Sen Classical Garden, Stanley Park |
| | Granville Public Market, Granville Island |
| | Vancouver Aquarium |
| | Museum of Anthropology |
| | Royal British Columbia Museum, Victoria |

| | |
|---|---|
| **Shopping** | Fourth Avenue (between Burrard and Balsam streets) |
| | Government Street, Victoria |
| | Market Square, Victoria |
| | Robson Street |
| **Restaurants** | Les Deux Gros, Whistler (*$$$*) |
| | Star Anise (*$$$*) |
| | Marina Restaurant, Victoria (*$$–$$$*) |
| | Delilah's (*$$*) |
| | La Rúa Restaurante, Whistler (*$$*) |
| | Phnom Penh (*$*) |
| | Six Mile House, Victoria (*$*) |
| **Hotels** | Hotel Grand Pacific, Victoria (*$$$$*) |
| | Le Chamois, Whistler (*$$$$*) |
| | Le Meridien (*$$$$*) |
| | Ocean Pointe Resort, Victoria (*$$$*) |
| | Wedgewood Hotel (*$$$*) |
| | End Guest House (*$$*) |
| | English Bay Inn (*$$*) |
| | Buchan Hotel (*$*) |

## British Columbia

| | |
|---|---|
| **Attractions** | O'Keefe Historic Ranch, Okanagan Valley |
| | Kilby General Store Museum, Okanagan Valley |
| | Native Heritage Center, Duncan |
| **Great Outdoors** | Adams River Salmon Run, Okanagan Valley |
| | Inside Passage |
| | Naikoon Provincial Park, north of Vancouver Island |
| | Pacific Rim National Park, Vancouver Island |
| **Restaurants** | Sooke Harbour House, Sooke (*$$$$*) |
| | The Aerie, Malahat (*$$$*) |
| | The Mahle House, Nanaimo (*$$*) |
| **Hotels** | The Aerie, Malahat (*$$$$*) |
| | Sooke Harbour House, Sooke (*$$$$*) |
| | Harrison Hot Springs Hotel, Harrison Hot Spring (*$$–$$$$*) |
| | April Point Lodge, Campbell River (*$$$*) |
| | Yellow Point Lodge, Ladysmith (*$–$$$*) |

**Canadian Rockies**

| | |
|---|---|
| **Sights** | The drive along the Icefields Parkway |
| | The view from the Jasper Tramway |
| | Lake Louise and Moraine Lake |
| | Burgess Shale Fossel Beds, Yoho |
| **Sporting Activities** | Mountaineering around the Columbia Icefields and the Bugaboos of the British Columbia Rockies |
| | Horse-pack trips in Kananaskis Country |
| | Skiing at Lake Louise, Nakiska, and Panorama |
| | Heli-skiing and heli-touring in the British Columbia Rockies |
| **Restaurants** | Le Beaujolais, Banff (*$$$$*) |
| | Ristorante Classico, Banff (*$$$$*) |
| | Post Hotel, Lake Louise (*$$$$*) |
| | One-Twelve, Revelstoke (*$$$*) |
| | Emerald Lake Lodge, Yoho (*$$–$$$*) |
| | Barbary Coast, Banff (*$–$$*) |
| **Hotels** | Rimrock Hotel, Banff (*$$$$*) |
| | Chateau Lake Louise (*$$$$*) |
| | Emerald Lake Lodge, Yoho (*$$$*) |
| | Storm Mountain Lodge, Banff (*$$–$$$*) |
| | Kilmorey Lodge, Waterton Lakes (*$$*) |

**Manitoba, Saskatchewan, Alberta**

| | |
|---|---|
| **Attractions** | Alberta Science Centre/Planetarium, Calgary |
| | Devonian Gardens, Calgary |
| | Manitoba Museum of Man and Nature, Winnipeg |
| | Muttart Conservatory, Edmonton |
| | Wanuskewin Heritage Park, Saskatoon |
| | Wascana Waterfowl Park Display Ponds, Regina |
| **Shopping** | Portage Place, Winnipeg |
| | Stephen Avenue Mall, Calgary |
| | Cornwall Centre, Regina |
| | Midtown Plaza, Saskatoon |
| | West Edmonton Mall |
| **Restaurants** | Owl's Nest Dining Room, Calgary (*$$$$*) |
| | Unheardof Dining Lounge, Edmonton (*$$$$*) |

Mieka's, Regina (*$$$*)

Bistro Dansk, Winnipeg (*$$*)

Adonis, Saskatoon (*$*)

Buzzards Café, Calgary (*$*)

Chianti Café, Edmonton (*$*)

**Hotels** Edmonton Hilton (*$$$$*)

The Delta, Regina (*$$$*)

Edmonton House (*$$$*)

Place Louis Riel, Winnipeg (*$$$*)

Westin Hotel, Calgary (*$$$*)

The Patricia, Saskatoon (*$*)

Relax Inn South West, Regina (*$*)

## Province of Ontario

**Attractions** Old Fort William

Maid of the Mist boats

Sainte Marie Among the Hurons

View of Niagara Falls by helicopter

**Restaurants** Elora Mill, Elora (*$$$*)

Inn at the Falls, Bracebridge (*$$$*)

La Brassine, Goderich (*$$*)

**Hotels** Château Laurier, Ottawa (*$$$$*)

Langdon Hall, Cambridge (*$$$$*)

Prince of Wales, Niagara-on-the-Lake (*$$$$*)

Inn at the Falls, Bracebridge (*$$$*)

Millcroft Inn, Alton (*$$$*)

Kettle Creek Inn, Port Stanley (*$$–$$$*)

## Province of Québec

**Sights** Basilica of Ste-Anne de Beaupre

Bonaventure Island, the Gaspé Peninsula

**Restaurants** L'Eau à la Bouche, Ste-Adèle (*$$$$*)

Chatel Vienna, Ste-Agathe (*$$–$$$*)

**Hotels** Auberge la Pinsonnière, Cap-à l'Aigle (*$$$$*)

Manoir Hovey, North Hatley (*$$$$*)

Auberge la Maison Otis, Baie-St-Paul (*$$$$*)

Hostellerie Les Trois Tilleuls, St. Marc sur Richelieu ($$$–$$$$)

Hôtel Cap-aux-Pierres, Ile aux Coudres ($$)

## Nova Scotia

**Sights**  Fortress Louisbourg, Cape Breton Island

Cape Breton Highlands National Park

The Citadel, Halifax

Peggy's Cove

**Restaurants**  Amherst Shore Country Inn, Amherst ($$$)

The Braeside Inn, Pictou ($$$)

MacAskill's Restaurant, Dartmouth ($$$)

Old Man Morias, Halifax ($$)

**Hotels**  The Pines Resort Hotel, Digby ($$$)

Ramada Renaissance, Dartmouth ($$$)

## Prince Edward Island

**Attractions**  Annual musical *Anne of Green Gables* at Confederation Centre of the Arts, Charlottetown

Prince Edward Island National Park/Green Gables, Cavendish

Province House, Charlottetown

**Restaurants**  The Griffon Room, Charlottetown ($$$)

Inn at Bay Fortune, Bay Fortune ($$$)

Claddagh Room Restaurant, Charlottetown ($$–$$$)

Kelly's, Victoria Row, Charlottetown ($$)

Lobster suppers in New Glasgow, New London, and Hope River ($$)

**Hotels**  Dalvay-by-the-Sea, Grand Tracadie ($$$$)

Prince Edward Hotel and Convention Centre, Charlottetown ($$$$)

Inn at Bay Fortune, Bay Fortune ($$$)

West Point Lighthouse, West Point ($$)

## New Brunswick

**Attractions**  Acadian Village, Grande Anse, near Caraquet

Kings Landing Historical Settlement, Prince William, near Fredericton

**Shopping**  Craft and antiques shops of St. Andrews and Gagetown

Mulhouse Country Classics, Fredericton

| | |
|---|---|
| **Restaurants** | Cy's, Moncton (*$$*) |
| **Hotels** | Hotel Beausejour, Moncton (*$$$*) |
| | Marshlands Inn, Sackville (*$$–$$$*) |
| | Shadow Lawn Country Inn, Saint John (*$$–$$$*) |
| | Chez Françoise, Shediac (*$–$$*) |

## Newfoundland and Labrador

| | |
|---|---|
| **Attractions** | L'Anse aux Meadows, northern tip of Newfoundland |
| | Signal Hill, St. John's |
| | Gros Morne Mountain, Gros Morne National Park |
| **Shopping** | NONIA, St. John's, for crafts |
| **Restaurants** | The Cellar, Baird's Cove (*$$$*) |
| | Stone House, Kenna's Hill (*$$$*) |
| **Hotels** | Hotel Newfoundland, St. John's (*$$$*) |
| | Compton House Bed & Breakfast, St. John's (*$$*) |
| | Prescott House Bed & Breakfast, St. John's (*$$*) |

## Wilderness Canada

| | |
|---|---|
| **Attractions** | Klondike Gold Fields, Dawson City |
| | Prince of Wales Northern Heritage Centre, Yellowknife |
| | S. S. *Klondike*, Whitehorse |
| | Virginia Falls, Nahanni National Park |
| **Lodges** | Edgewater Hotel, Whitehorse (*$$$*) |
| | Inconnu Lodge, Yukon wilderness (*$$$*) |
| | Westmark Inn, Dawson City (*$$*) |

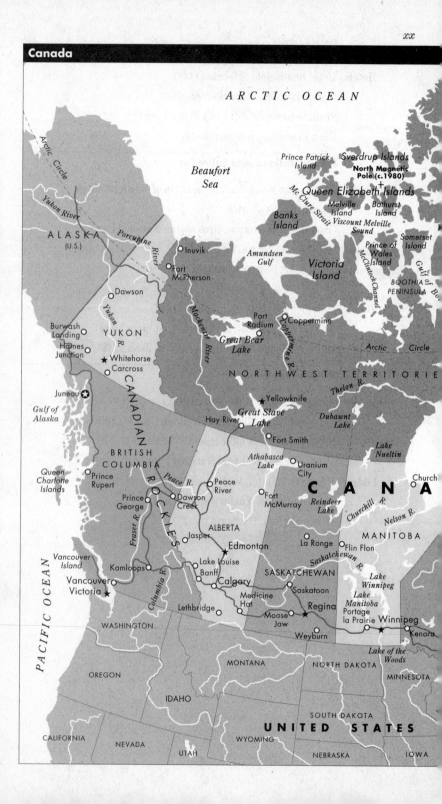

Ellesmere Island
Devon Island
ancaster Sound
ithia
S
Southampton Island

GREENLAND
(Denmark)

ICELAND

Denmark Strait

Baffin Bay

Baffin Island

Davis Strait

Prince Charles Island

*Foxe Basin*

Lake Amadjuak
Iqaluit
Lake Harbour
*Hudson Strait*

Cape Chidley

Labrador Sea

Coats Island
Mansel Island
Ivujivik

*Ungava Bay*

Nain

NEWFOUNDLAND

Battle Harbour

Hudson Bay

**D    A**

Belcher Islands

LABRADOR

Schefferville
Goose Bay

Gander

Fort Severn

Labrador City

St. John's

Severn R.

Fort George

QUEBEC

*James Bay*

Sept-Iles
Anticosti Island

Newfoundland

Moosonee

*Lake Mistassini*

*GASPÉ PENINSULA*

*Gulf of St. Lawrence*

ST. PIERRE AND MIQUELON
(France)

ONTARIO

Rimouski

PRINCE EDWARD ISLAND

*Lake Nipigon*

Chicoutimi

Sydney

Cochrane

Ste-Agathe-Des-Monts

NEW BRUNSWICK

Charlottetown

Thunder Bay

Timmins

Trois-Rivières

Québec City

Fredericton

NOVA SCOTIA

*Lake Superior*

Sudbury

North Bay

Montréal

Saint John

Halifax

Sault Ste. Marie

Ottawa

St. Lawrence

MAINE

*Bay of Fundy*

N

ATLANTIC OCEAN

WISCONSIN

*Lake Huron*

Toronto

*Lake Ontario*

VT.

N.H.

MICHIGAN

*Lake Michigan*

Niagara Falls

NEW YORK

MASSACHUSETTS

CONN.  R.I.

ILLINOIS

INDIANA

OHIO

*Lake Erie*

PENNSYLVANIA

N.J.

0          400 miles

0          600 km

# World Time Zones

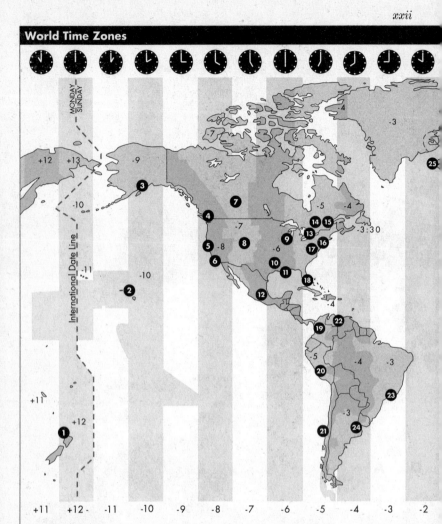

Numbers below vertical bands relate each zone to Greenwich Mean Time (0 hrs.).
Local times frequently differ from these general indications,
as indicated by light-face numbers on map.

# Introduction

By Bob
Levin

Originally
from
Philadelphia,
Pennsylvania,
Maclean's
Foreign
Editor Bob
Levin moved
to Toronto in
October 1985.
He traveled
from coast to
coast for this
article on an
American's
impressions
of Canada.

I have not seen any moose. No wolves, no musk-oxen, no cuddly little seals. Even from the cockpit of a small propeller plane, 1,500 feet over the mazelike Mackenzie Delta in the icebound Arctic, I spotted not a single furry polar bear lumbering out of hibernation to complete the picture. "Foxes have been coming right up into the town," advised Ronald Knoller, who runs a general store in the tiny Arctic settlement of Aklavik. "You see them running around, and they've tangled with dog teams." But not when I was there. I did see an impressive elk in Banff National Park, trotting casually by the roadside, but for me Canada's wildlife has consisted mostly of squawking seagulls and mischievous raccoons in my Toronto neighborhood. And maybe that is just as well: It has forced an American, newly arrived, to avoid at least the "moose" half of the hated moose-and-Mounties cliché. While trying to discover the real Canada—especially the one beyond Toronto, which, as non-Torontonians are quick to argue, is not *really* Canada—I have had to focus on its people.

And this is what I have found: most Canadians—regardless of what the media say—are not sitting around worrying about what a Canadian is. Nor do they conform to that other set of stereotypes, the ones Canadians are supposed to hold about themselves. Where are all those pallid, self-doubting people when so many of the ones I have met are colorful, confident, and passionately in love with their land?

All right, I admit it, a few tepid types may reside in Toronto. They certainly show up for baseball games, clapping with the politeness of long-ago tennis fans and mouthing that most insipid of fight songs, "Okay, okay, Blue Jays." In fact, to my mind there is something curiously passionless about the city as a whole, an urban success story boasting everything but a soul. It is kinder, gentler, cleaner, and certainly safer than any U.S. city its size—my visiting American friends invariably find it wonderful and cannot understand its New York–like, love-to-hate-it place in the Canadian national consciousness. My own feelings fall closer to the American view. But "I love Toronto" could never be the city's slogan—no, I *like* Toronto sums it up perfectly.

It has been on trips outside the city, to the more far-flung sectors of this most resolutely regional of nations, that I have found Canada at its more extreme, independent, quirky—even romantic, as un-Canadian a word as that is supposed to be. One snow-swept morning in Pouch Cove, a fishing-village-turned-suburb north of St. John's, Newfoundland, I visited William Noseworthy in his white clapboard house high on Noseworthy's Hill. Blue-eyed and ruddy-cheeked, Noseworthy sat in the kitchen by a wood stove, distractedly smoking a cigarette. He was 66 and had just retired the year before after four decades of fishing, but he still stared out the window at the North Atlantic. "There's something that draws you to it," he said in the rich accent of "the Rock."

His son, 31-year-old Barry, sipping a Labatt's beer, recalled that once, when he was 13, his father caught him whistling in a boat. "He was going to throw me overboard," said Barry. "It's just bad luck." William explained: "You don't whistle on the water. You wouldn't dare. You wouldn't launch your boat on Friday either. They're just superstitions, maybe. But several years ago, someone launched a big fishing trawler on a Friday, and she was lost on a Friday, and all the crew members, too." A minute later, William pulled out a shiny red accordion and played a jig, tapping his foot, but his eyes never left the water.

**N**ewfoundland was also a place to sample Canadian regionalism at its most craggy and entrenched. The province's inshore fishermen claim that their very way of life is endangered by declining cod catches, which they blame on offshore trawling, often by foreigners. And they blame Ottawa for not looking out for their interests—even 40 years after joining Confederation, the old refrain still comes quickly to some residents' lips: "A Newfoundlander first, a Canadian second." But in a Pouch Cove twine store, where four diehard fishermen repaired their cod traps while country music drawled from a tape player, Frank Noseworthy, a slim, mustachioed cousin of Barry, said that he rejected the Newfoundlanders-first sentiment—and would far rather be Canadian than American. "In the States," he said, "them that's got it, gets more; them that don't, gets less. The Canadian government's more generous toward people that don't have."

Noseworthy has met many American tourists and he has not been impressed. "They come in their flashy cars," he said, "putting on airs. They seem to think they're a superior race, but I haven't seen one that's superior to me yet." He poked at the broken twine with his knife. He had one more thing to say, a point of both resentment and pride. "Some of the worst are Newfoundlanders who moved to the States. They forget their roots. They're sort of looking down their noses, instead of appreciating that there are people here trying to maintain their heritage."

Canada has hardly cornered the market on regionalism. A divided United States fought a horrific civil war in the 1860s, and as a northerner who has lived down South, I can attest to the fact that, to some southerners, the old resentments have not gone with the wind. But the United States also has the Melting Pot, the American Dream, the Pledge of Allegiance, the Hollywood-enhanced legends of Davy Crockett and even Ronald Reagan—an ever-enlarging collection of nationalistic symbols, myths, and heroes that bind the country together. Like glue, they may sometimes seem sticky and malodorous, but they do the job.

On the other hand, Canadians, writes Toronto author June Callwood, "have never created a myth that would unify them into nationhood"—except for Québec francophones. The question of Québec nationalism has arisen wherever I have gone in Canada. Much of the sentiment seems to reflect that of Pouch Cove's William Noseworthy, who said, "They're always looking for special treatment—if they want to get out of Canada, let 'em get out."

In the office of Daniel Latouche, a political scientist and a former adviser to René Lévesque, the separatist Québec premier who died in 1987, I asked whether Québecers had a special affinity for Americans—whether, as Callwood implies, the two share a romantic vision of themselves. "There is a belief here," he replied, "that there are only two kinds of North Americans— Americans and Québecers. Two kinds of people who tried to build what North America is all about. One is much bigger, the other one lost. But both have a dream."

That is the kind of language an American can understand. But it may be a sign of American myopia that few people south of the international border, I suspect, would immediately include Québecers in such a continent-wide club of dreams. In fact, the Québec issue is quite literally foreign to Americans. The closest U.S. equivalent is the current push by Spanish-speakers in some states for official bilingualism; English-speakers have reacted heatedly, and 17 states have now declared English to be their official language. But the Hispanics are mostly recent immigrants, not a cofounding people like Québec francophones—and no American can seriously imagine Florida trying to secede from the union.

In a 37th-floor Montréal office looking out toward the frozen St. Lawrence, I asked commercial lawyer Ronald Montcalm whether there was anything binding the English and French together, any mutual myths or heroes. Montcalm thought about it and smiled. "Our hockey teams—boy, that's Canada's game." I would recall that answer on a plane the next day, when the Edmonton Oilers were on board and a steady stream of young autograph-seekers were interrupting their card game, and center Craig MacTavish talked about how "we're not the biggest country population-wise but we produce the best hockey players." But in Montcalm's office, hockey seemed more than just a sport—it was the great unifier. "At one point," the lawyer said, "Québec ultranationalists were talking about having our own team. The argument against that is, 'Hey, you've got to have Mario Lemieux and Wayne Gretzky on the same team or the Russians will beat us.'"

No Canadian region has left a more indelible impression on me than the North. The frontier is among the most enduring of American symbols, and while the American West was settled long ago, the Canadian North still lies empty and alluring—a distant dreamscape reachable by Boeing 737. Last March, I visited Inuvik, Northwest Territories, a government-built town on the east side of the Mackenzie Delta. It is a place of fur-trimmed parkas and brightly colored houses, with a church shaped like an igloo and a bar called The Zoo.

But, more traditionally, it also has an RCMP detachment, a CBC office, and a Hudson's Bay Co. store. "Twelve hundred miles from anywhere," said Mayor John Hill, "and here's small-town Canada—at least the way the bureaucrats decided it would be." Which raises the question: How can a country whose government knows exactly what a Canadian town should look like—and can create one from scratch 200 kilometers (124 miles) north of the Arctic Circle—have such a famously chronic identity crisis?

For me, Inuvik aroused feelings of ambivalence as sharp as its –30°C (–22°F) cold. On the one hand, there is the exhilarating remoteness of the place and the upbeat attitudes of many immigrants to the area— prominent businesspeople who came originally from Scotland, Germany, Greece, even Lebanon. "You've got to have the balls to come and get started in business here," noted Hill, a British transplant. "But once you have, the competitiveness isn't as intense as it would be in, say, Edmonton." On the other hand, there is a local native population with profound problems. I am suspicious of snap impressions. I also know that Americans bear their own shame over their appalling treatment of natives, and I know that, for all the historic wrongs native people have suffered in Canada, they have now organized to elect legislators, fight for land claims, and combat social ills. But in the North, the despairing side of the picture is as obvious as stray beer cans. Inuvik's RCMP Cpl. John de Jong explained that at least 80% of local crimes are alcohol-related. "These are not what you'd call social drinkers," said de Jong. "They drink until the liquor is gone and then they search for more. Then we end up having to look after them one way or the other."

The natives' problems go beyond alcohol—the suicide rate among the Inuit of the Northwest Territories is four times the national average. "There's a lot of grief," confirmed Diane Nelson, a program coordinator with the Canadian Mental Health Association office in Inuvik. "This country is hard to live in, just trying to survive. People get drunk and wander off and die of hypothermia. They fall through the ice. There's a lot of tragedy in their lives." One Métis woman told me that her brother and sister had both died alcohol-related deaths—and that her father and several relatives had sexually abused her from the age of 6 to 17. "It puts you through hell," she said. However, she has managed to get on with her life—she is married and a college graduate.

The social workers and educators in town talked of culture shock—of native people thrust abruptly into the space age and paying the price emotionally; of old amusements like berry-picking and sliding and new ones like watching ever-present videos. In some places the old ways are still evident. One day I traveled the ice road, a slick, winter-only passage on the frozen Mackenzie, more than four feet thick, lined with scrubby bush and spindly black spruce—and speed-limit signs. The Richardson Mountains gleamed in the distance. The buzz of snowmobiles announced the onset of a town. Aklavik, a largely native settlement on the delta's west side, is a motley collection of wood houses, prone to erosion and flooding. Inuvik was designed to replace it, but many residents simply refused to leave. "This was supposed to be a ghost town," recalled Dorothy McLeod, a 59-year-old Métis. "But it's such a good place for hunting and trapping and fishing—you can almost live off the land. In Inuvik, you live out of the stores."

**M**aybe I was just seizing on hopeful signs; or maybe, like many whites, I tend to romanticize natives and their intense ties to the land. But later, when I thought of Aklavik, I thought also of the Newfoundland fishermen, clinging to a dwindling life in the boats, and of the French nationalists, fighting to preserve their language and culture— and I thought how they would have understood Dorothy Mc-Leod, trying to hold on to the old ways.

Canadians share a collective guilt over the plight of the natives, but they take an often-justified pride in their treatment of other minorities. To an American, Canada's vaunted multiculturalism is, like Québec nationalism, simply a foreign concept. It is also an attractive one, although the gap between theory and practice is sometimes hard to ignore.

What is happening in Vancouver is a case in point. The trouble in Canada's Pacific paradise surrounds home-buyers from Hong Kong, which will become part of mainland China in 1997. The newcomers have cash on hand and have helped to drive up housing prices beyond the range of many Vancouverites, touching off a frenzied real estate boom. Never mind that the overwhelming majority of new British Columbians come not from Hong Kong but from such foreign locales as Alberta and Ontario—public perception has focused on the Asians. "There's always an element of anxiety about change," said Mayor Gordon Campbell. "But with a certain percentage there's clearly an element of racism as well."

Vancouver is undergoing a kind of tolerance test—one that, to some residents, lies at the very core of what it means to be Canadian. "I think Canada is developing some uniqueness," said Saintfield Wong, program coordinator of the Chinese Cultural Centre in Vancouver's Chinatown. "We're more receptive to new ideas—Canada's culture *is* multiculturalism." In his gift shop down the street, however, Harry Con expressed some doubts. The national president of Chinese Freemasons in Canada, Con maintained that multiculturalism keeps Canadians too tied to their old countries. "Everybody sends money home," he said. "Italians, Chinese. Whatever happens over there, people volunteer to help. But if the government here wants to raise taxes, we give them hell. So who loves Canada?"

Dwight Chan plainly does. Chan emigrated from Hong Kong in 1974 and now, at 39, he is a successful Vancouver real estate broker who understands the city's attractions to foreigners— the ocean and mountains, the mild climate, the patently laid-back lifestyle. I asked him, though, whether there is anything to tie newcomers to the country at large; even if current fears dissipate and the latest immigrants end up feeling as welcome as he does, is there, in American terms, such a thing as the Canadian Dream? After a moment's reflection, Chan said, "The Canadian Dream is probably a healthy, stable, and secure way of living, rather than the American Dream of big money. It's to have time to enjoy your life, to play, to travel. This country allows me to do all that, and that feels good to me."

Canada continues to defy easy definition. I have crossed and recrossed time zones, sampled caribou and cod's tongue, and gathered a startling variety of mental images that, like the country itself, may not add up to a coherent whole but certainly make a pretty picture. Canada is *not* the United States—that much is abundantly clear, even if Arctic-dwellers *can* watch Detroit news on television—and its ingrained regionalism is one of its most telling traits. Travel anywhere outside of Ontario, it seems, and over and over people say, as Vancouver's Mayor Campbell did: "We're very proud to be Canadians. But there is a strong sense that the central government does not recognize we're here." Americans say nasty things about Washington, too, but when their government launches an invasion of Grenada, they swiftly rally around.

In general, Canadians also strike me as more outward-looking than Americans. They did not, after all, grow up being told that they already live in the greatest country on earth. "Americans are like TV evangelists," maintained Roger Bill, an Indiana native who is now the Newfoundland-based Atlantic field producer for CBC Radio's *Sunday Morning* show. "They really believe theirs is the best way and everyone else should follow. Canadians aren't nearly so arrogant." They do, however, take a palpable pride in place, with a decided prejudice toward the small, friendly, and relaxed. "I wouldn't live in the States, or in Toronto or Montréal," said Richard Harvey, a high-school principal from Upper Gullies, Newfoundland. "You couldn't pay me enough." I have heard Inuvik people say the same about Yellowknife—and Aklavik people say the same about Inuvik.

I only wish Canadians would say it louder, that they would boast—with the kind of cheerful cockiness I saw at the Calgary Olympics—of a nation vast, varied, scenic, wealthy, safe, fairminded, and infinitely appealing. I wish they would make an epic movie or two about it, one with endless prairies and dazzling mountains and heroic characters hell-bent on, say, building a railroad clear to the Pacific. I wish they would brag about the CBC and national health insurance, too, and I wish, if they really want to dispel the moose-and-Mounties image, that they would stop making that ubiquitous line of postcards picturing furry seals and polar bears and saying simply, "Canada." But then, I am afraid I sound very much like an American. Only a Canadian can really sum it all up. As Montréal lawyer Montcalm put it, "Funny country, eh?"

# 1 Essential Information

# Before You Go

## Government Tourist Offices

**In the United States** Contact the tourism department of the province or territory you plan to visit: **Tourism British Columbia** (Parliament Buildings, Victoria, BC V8V 1X4, tel. 800/663–6000), **Alberta Tourism** (10155 102 St., 3rd floor, Edmonton, AB T5J 4L6, tel. 800/661–8888), **Tourism Saskatchewan** (1919 Saskatchewan Dr., Regina, SK S4P 3V7, tel. 800/667–7191), **Travel Manitoba** (Dept. 20, 155 Carlton St., 7th floor, Winnipeg, MB R3C 3H8, tel. 800/665–0040, ext. 20), **Ontario Ministry of Culture, Tourism, and Recreation** (77 Bloor St. W., 9th floor, Toronto, Ont. M7A 2R9), **Tourisme Québec** (C.P. 979, Montréal, Qué. HC3 2W3, tel. 800/363–7777), **Tourism New Brunswick** (Box 12345, Fredericton, NB E3B 5C3, tel. 800/561–0123), **Nova Scotia Dept. of Tourism and Culture** (Box 456, Halifax, NS B3J 2R5, tel. 800/341–6096), **Prince Edward Island Dept. of Economic Development and Tourism** (Quality Services Division, Box 940, Charlottetown, PEI C1A 7M5, tel. 800/565–0267), **Newfoundland and Labrador Dept. of Tourism and Culture**, Box 8700, St. John's, NF A1B 4K2, tel. 800/563–6353), **Tourism Yukon** (Box 2703, Whitehorse, YK Y1A 2C6, tel. 403/667–5340), and **Northwest Territories Tourism** (Box 1320, Yellowknife, NWT X1A 2L9, tel. 800/661–0788).

**U.S. Government Travel Briefings** The U.S. Department of State's **Citizens Emergency Center** issues Consular Information Sheets, which cover crime, security, and health risks as well as embassy locations, entry requirements, currency regulations, and other routine matters. For the latest information, stop in at any passport office, consulate, or embassy; call the interactive hotline (tel. 202/647–5225); or, with your PC's modem, tap into the Bureau of Consular Affairs' computer bulletin board (tel. 202/647–9225).

**In the United Kingdom** Contact the **Canadian High Commission Department of Tourism**, Canada House, Trafalgar Square, London SW1Y 5BJ, tel. 071/258–6346; or **Québec Tourism** (59 Pall Mall, London SW1Y 5JH, tel. 071/930–8314), **B.C. House** (1 Regent St., London, SW1Y 4N5, tel. 071/930–6857), **Alberta House** (1 Mount St., Berkeley Square, London, W1Y 5AA, tel. 071/491-3430).

## Tours and Packages

Should you buy your travel arrangements to Canada packaged or do it yourself? There are advantages either way. Buying packaged arrangements saves you money, particularly if you can find a program that includes exactly the features you want. You also get a pretty good idea of what your trip will cost from the outset. Generally, you have two options: fully escorted tours and independent packages.

Escorted tours are most often via motorcoach, with a tour director in charge. They're ideal if you don't mind having limited free time and traveling with strangers. Your baggage is handled, your time rigorously scheduled, and most meals planned. Escorted tours are therefore the most hassle-free way to see a destination, as well as generally the least expensive. Independent packages allow plenty of flexibility. They normally include airline travel and hotels, with certain options available, such as sightseeing, car rental, and excursions. Independent packages are usually more expensive than escorted tours, but your time is your own.

Travel agents are your best source of recommendations for both tours and packages. They will have the largest selection, and the cost to you is the same as buying direct. Whatever program you ultimately choose, be sure to find out exactly what is included: taxes, tips, transfers, meals, baggage handling, ground transportation, entertainment, excursions, sports or recreation (and rental equipment if necessary). Ask about the level of hotel used, its location, the size of its rooms, the kind of beds, and the amenities, such as pool, room service, or programs for children, if they're important to you. Find out the operator's cancellation penalties. Nearly everyone charges them, and the only way to avoid it is to buy trip-cancellation insurance (*see* Trip Insurance, *below*). Also ask about the single supplement, a surcharge assessed to solo travelers. Some operators do not make you pay it if you agree to be matched up with a roommate of the same sex, even if one is not found by departure time. Remember that a program that has features you won't use, whether for rental sporting equipment or discounted museum admissions, may not be the most cost-wise choice for you.

**Fully Escorted Tours**
Escorted tours are usually sold in three categories: deluxe, first-class, and tourist or budget class. Some operators specialize in one category, while others offer a range.

Top operators include **Maupintour** (Box 807, Lawrence, KS 66044, tel. 913/843–1211 or 800/255–4266) and **Tauck Tours** (11 Wilton Rd., Westport, CT 06881, tel. 203/226–6911 or 800/468–2825) in the deluxe category; **Brendan Tours** (15137 Califa St., Van Nuys, CA 91411, tel. 818/985–9696 or 800/421–8446), **Domenico Tours** (751 Broadway, Bayonne, NJ 07002, tel. 201/823–8687 or 800/554–8687), **Gadabout Tours** (700 E. Tahquitz Way, Palm Springs, CA 92262, tel. 619/325–5556 or 800/952–5068), **Globus** (5301 South Federal Circle, Littleton, CO 80123, tel. 303/797–2800 or 800/221–0090), and **Princess Tours** (2815 Second Ave., Suite 400, Seattle, WA 98121, tel. 206/728–4215 or 800/426–0442) in the first-class category. In the budget category try **Cosmos Tourama,** a sister company of Globus (*see above*).

Most itineraries are jam-packed with sightseeing, so you see a lot in a short amount of time (usually one place per day). To judge just how fast-paced the tour is, review the itinerary carefully. If you are in a different hotel each night, you will be getting up early each day to head out, travel to your next destination, do some sightseeing, have dinner, and go to bed, then you'll start all over again. If you want some free time, make sure it's mentioned in the tour brochure; if you want to be escorted to every meal, confirm that any tour you consider does that. Also, when comparing programs, be sure to find out if the motorcoach is air-conditioned and has a rest room on board. Make your selection based on price and stops on the itinerary.

**Independent Packages**
Independent packages are offered by airlines, tour operators who may also do escorted programs, and any number of other companies from large, established firms to small, new entrepreneurs. Contact **Air Canada** (tel. 800/776–3000), **American Airlines Fly Away Vacations** (tel. 800/321–2121), **Delta Dream Vacations** (tel. 800/872–7786), **Supercities** (139 Main St., Cambridge, MA 02142, tel. 617/621–9988 or 800/333–1234), **United Vacations** (tel. 800/328–6877), and **USAir Vacations** (tel. 800/428–4322).

Their programs come in a wide range of prices based on levels of luxury and options—in addition to hotel and airfare, sightseeing, car rental, transfers, admission to local attractions, and other extras. Note that when pricing different packages, it sometimes pays to purchase the same arrangements separately, as when a rock-bottom promotional airfare is being offered, for example. Again, base your choice on what's available at your budget for the destinations you want to visit.

**Special-Interest Travel**  Special-interest programs may be fully escorted or independent. Some require a certain amount of expertise, but most are for the average traveler with an interest and are usually hosted by experts in the subject matter. When the program is escorted, it enjoys the advantages and disadvantages of all escorted programs; because your fellow travelers are apt to be passionate or knowledgeable about the subject, they can prove as enjoyable a part of your travel experience as the destination itself. The price range is wide, but the cost is usually higher—sometimes a lot higher—than for ordinary escorted tours and packages because of the expert guiding and special activities.

*Adventure*  Contact the **American Wilderness Experience** (Box 1486, Boulder, CO 80306, tel. 303/494–2992 or 800/444–0099) and **Tauck Tours** (*see above*), for its several tours to Athabasca Glacier and the Cariboo Mountains. **Mountain Madness** (4218 S.W. Alaska, Suite 206, Seattle, WA 98116, tel. 206/937–8389) specializes in mountain treks and ice climbing in the Rockies.

*Bicycling*  **Backroads** (1516 5th St., Suite L101, Berkeley, CA 94710, tel. 510/527–1555 or 800/462–2848) has trips to Banff, Lake Louise, and the Saskatchewan River. **Bike Centennial** (Box 8308, Missoula, MT 59802, tel. 406/721–1776) will help you map out a solitary route to Jasper or Banff, and **Classic Adventures** (Box 153-P, Hamlin, NY 14464, tel. 716/964–8488 or 800/777–8090) has hiking and biking tours to Prince Edward Island, Nova Scotia, and Québec.

*Canoeing*  **Battenkill Canoe, Ltd.** (Box 65, Arlington, VT 05250, tel. 802/362–2800) tours offer paddling in whitewater or more relaxed scenic trips, with lodgings at country inns or secluded riverside campsites throughout eastern Canada.

*Cruises*  **Commodore Cruise Line** (800 Douglas Rd., Suite 600, Coral Gables, FL 33134, tel. 305/446–4400 or 800/237–5361) explores coastal Nova Scotia and Prince Edward Island and the St. Lawrence. **Royal Viking Line** (95 Merrick Way, Coral Gables, FL 33134, tel. 305/445–0515 or 800/422–8000) calls at Charlottetown (Prince Edward Island), Halifax (Nova Scotia), Saint John (New Brunswick), and Montréal. **Holland America Line** (300 Elliott Ave. W, Seattle, WA 98119, tel. 206/281–3535 or 800/426–0327) and **Princess Cruises** (Box 60010, Los Angeles, CA 90060, tel. 213/553–1666 or 800/421–5522) operate Inside Passage cruises between Vancouver, BC, and Alaska. **St. Lawrence Cruise Lines** (253 Ontario St., Kingston, ON K7L 2Z4, tel. 800/267–7868) has two replica steamships that cruise the St. Lawrence and Saguenay rivers.

*Fall Foliage*  Contact **Domenico Tours** (*see* Fully Escorted Tours, *above*), **Parker Tours** (218–14 Northern Blvd., Bayside, NY 11361, tel. 718/428–7800 or 800/833–9600), or **Trieloff Tours** (24301 El Toro Rd., Suite 140, Laguna Hills, CA 92653, tel. 800/248–6877 or 800/432–7125 in CA).

*Horseback Riding*  **FITS Equestrian** (685 Lateen Rd., Solvang, CA 93463, tel. 805/688–9494) will arrange horseback rides into the untouched wilderness of British Columbia's Coast Range.

*Nature/ Environmental*  **Questers Worldwide Nature Tours** (275 Park Ave. S, New York, NY 10010, tel. 212/673–3120) provide opportunities to learn about wildlife while you travel. **Earthwatch** (680 Mount Auburn St., Watertown, MA 02272, tel. 617/926–8000) recruits volunteers to serve in its EarthCorps as short-term assistants to scientists on research expeditions. **National Audubon Society** (700 Broadway, New York, NY 10003 tel. 212/979–3066) has a natural history-oriented Maritime Canada cruise around the Thousand Islands on the Nantucket Clipper.

*Skiing*   **Air Canada** (*see above*) and **United Vacations Ski Packages** (tel. 800/525–2052) have skiing programs to both eastern and Rockies resort areas.

*Whale*   **Oceanic Society Expeditions** (Fort Mason Center, Bldg. E, San
*Watching*   Francisco, CA 94123, tel. 415/441–1106 or 800/326–7491) offers a program in July that includes snorkeling with the belugas in the mouth of the Churchill River.

## When to Go

When to go will depend on your itinerary and your interests. In the maritime provinces of **Nova Scotia, New Brunswick,** and **Prince Edward Island,** the weather is relatively mild, though snow can remain on the ground well into spring and fog is common year-round. In **Newfoundland** and **Labrador** temperatures vary widely; winter days can be about 32°F (0°C) in St. John's—and as low as –50°F (–45°C) in Labrador and on the west coast. **Québec** and **Ontario** have hot, steamy summers and severe winters, with snow lasting from mid-December to mid-March. The whole of eastern Canada enjoys blooming springs and brilliant autumns.

Farther west, in **Manitoba, Saskatchewan,** and **Alberta,** summers are short but sunny, and marked by an occasional heavy shower. In winter, snowfall here is light, but temperatures stay low. Southern **British Columbia** has warmer winters and mild summers. Though the weather fluctuates because of the mountain ranges—the Coast Mountains and the eastern chain of the Rockies—the coastal region has the country's mildest winters, with rainfall almost inevitable. Summers here are fairly sunny, but seldom oppressively hot. The best time to visit **northern Canada** is during its short but surprisingly warm summer. The area—which includes the northern parts of the provinces of British Columbia, Alberta, Saskatchewan, Manitoba, Ontario, and Québec, as well as the **Yukon** and **Northwest Territories**—is like Siberia in winter, with devastating cold and dangerous windchill.

*Climate*   The sheer size of Canada—about half the area of the former Soviet Union and larger than China—makes it difficult to generalize. The following are average daily maximum and minimum temperatures for a number of Canada's major cities.

| *Calgary* | **Jan.** | 23F | – 5C | **May** | 61F | 16C | **Sept.** | 63F | 17C |
|---|---|---|---|---|---|---|---|---|---|
| | | 2 | –17 | | 37 | 3 | | 39 | 4 |
| | **Feb.** | 29F | – 2C | **June** | 67F | 19C | **Oct.** | 54F | 12C |
| | | 8 | –13 | | 44 | 7 | | 30 | – 1 |
| | **Mar.** | 34F | 1C | **July** | 74F | 23C | **Nov.** | 38F | 3C |
| | | 14 | –10 | | 49 | 9 | | 17 | – 8 |
| | **Apr.** | 49F | 9C | **Aug.** | 72F | 22C | **Dec.** | 29F | – 2C |
| | | 27 | – 3 | | 47 | 8 | | 8 | –13 |

| | | | | | | | | | |
|---|---|---|---|---|---|---|---|---|---|
| Edmonton | Jan. | 14F | −10C | May | 63F | 17C | Sept. | 62F | 17C |
| | | − 3 | −19 | | 41 | 5 | | 41 | 5 |
| | Feb. | 22F | − 6C | June | 69F | 21C | Oct. | 52F | 11C |
| | | 4 | −16 | | 48 | 9 | | 32 | 0 |
| | Mar. | 31F | − 1C | July | 74F | 23C | Nov. | 32F | 0C |
| | | 13 | −11 | | 53 | 12 | | 17 | − 8 |
| | Apr. | 49F | 9C | Aug. | 71F | 22C | Dec. | 21F | − 6C |
| | | 29 | − 2 | | 50 | 10 | | 5 | −15 |

| | | | | | | | | | |
|---|---|---|---|---|---|---|---|---|---|
| Halifax | Jan. | 33F | 1C | May | 58F | 14C | Sept. | 67F | 19C |
| | | 20 | − 7 | | 41 | 5 | | 53 | 12 |
| | Feb. | 33F | 1C | June | 67F | 19C | Oct. | 58F | 14C |
| | | 19 | − 7 | | 50 | 10 | | 44 | 7 |
| | Mar. | 39F | 4C | July | 73F | 23C | Nov. | 48F | 9C |
| | | 26 | − 3 | | 57 | 14 | | 36 | 2 |
| | Apr. | 48F | 9C | Aug. | 73F | 24C | Dec. | 37F | 3C |
| | | 33 | 1 | | 58 | 13 | | 25 | 4 |

| | | | | | | | | | |
|---|---|---|---|---|---|---|---|---|---|
| Montréal | Jan. | 23F | − 5C | May | 65F | 18C | Sept. | 68F | 20C |
| | | 9 | −13 | | 48 | 9 | | 53 | 12 |
| | Feb. | 25F | − 4C | June | 74F | 23C | Oct. | 57F | 14C |
| | | 12 | −11 | | 58 | 14 | | 43 | 6 |
| | Mar. | 36F | 2C | July | 79F | 26C | Nov. | 42F | 6C |
| | | 23 | − 5 | | 63 | 17 | | 32 | 0 |
| | Apr. | 52F | 11C | Aug. | 76F | 24C | Dec. | 27F | − 3C |
| | | 36 | 2 | | 61 | 16 | | 16 | − 9 |

| | | | | | | | | | |
|---|---|---|---|---|---|---|---|---|---|
| Ottawa | Jan. | 20F | − 7C | May | 65F | 18C | Sept. | 68F | 20C |
| | | 4 | −16 | | 44 | 7 | | 49 | 9 |
| | Feb. | 23F | − 5C | June | 75F | 24C | Oct. | 57F | 14C |
| | | 6 | −14 | | 54 | 12 | | 39 | 4 |
| | Mar. | 34F | 1C | July | 80F | 27C | Nov. | 41F | 5C |
| | | 18 | − 8 | | 58 | 14 | | 29 | − 2 |
| | Apr. | 51F | 11C | Aug. | 77F | 25C | Dec. | 25F | − 4C |
| | | 33 | 1 | | 56 | 13 | | 12 | −11 |

| | | | | | | | | | |
|---|---|---|---|---|---|---|---|---|---|
| Québec City | Jan. | 20F | − 7C | May | 62F | 17C | Sept. | 66F | 19C |
| | | 6 | −14 | | 43 | 6 | | 49 | 9 |
| | Feb. | 23F | − 5C | June | 72F | 22C | Oct. | 53F | 12C |
| | | 8 | −13 | | 53 | 12 | | 39 | 4 |
| | Mar. | 33F | 1C | July | 78F | 26C | Nov. | 39F | 4C |
| | | 19 | − 7 | | 58 | 14 | | 28 | − 2 |
| | Apr. | 47F | 8C | Aug. | 75F | 24C | Dec. | 24F | − 4C |
| | | 32 | 0 | | 56 | 13 | | 12 | −11 |

| | | | | | | | | | |
|---|---|---|---|---|---|---|---|---|---|
| Toronto | Jan. | 30F | − 1C | May | 64F | 18C | Sept. | 71F | 22C |
| | | 18 | − 8 | | 47 | 8 | | 54 | 12 |
| | Feb. | 32F | 0C | June | 76F | 24C | Oct. | 60F | 16C |
| | | 19 | − 7 | | 57 | 14 | | 45 | 7 |
| | Mar. | 40F | 4C | July | 80F | 27C | Nov. | 46F | 8C |
| | | 27 | − 3 | | 62 | 17 | | 35 | 2 |
| | Apr. | 53F | 12C | Aug. | 79F | 26C | Dec. | 34F | 1C |
| | | 38 | 3 | | 61 | 16 | | 23 | − 5 |

| *Vancouver* | Jan. | 42F | 6C | **May** | 60F | 16C | **Sept.** | 65F | 8C |
| | | 33 | 1 | | 47 | 8 | | 52 | 11 |
| | Feb. | 45F | 7C | **June** | 65F | 18C | **Oct.** | 56F | 13C |
| | | 36 | 2 | | 52 | 11 | | 45 | 7 |
| | Mar. | 48F | 9C | **July** | 70F | 1C | **Nov.** | 48F | 9C |
| | | 37 | 3 | | 55 | 13 | | 39 | 4 |
| | Apr. | 54F | 12C | **Aug.** | 70F | 21C | **Dec.** | 43F | 6C |
| | | 41 | 5 | | 55 | 13 | | 35 | 2 |

*Information* For current weather conditions for cities in the United States and
*Sources* abroad, plus the local time and helpful travel tips, call the **Weather
Channel Connection** (tel. 900/932–8437; 95¢ per minute) from a
touch-tone phone.

## Government Holidays

Though banks, schools, and government offices close for national
holidays, many stores remain open. As in the United States, certain
holidays are observed on the Monday nearest the actual date, creating a long weekend.

**National** National holidays for 1995 are: New Year's Day (January 1), Good
**Holidays** Friday (April 14), Easter Monday (April 17), Victoria Day (May 22),
Canada Day (July 1), Labor Day (September 4), Thanksgiving (October 9), Remembrance Day (November 11), Christmas (December
25), and Boxing Day (December 26).

**Provincial** **Alberta:** Heritage Day (August 7). **British Columbia:** British Colum-
**Holidays** bia Day (August 7). **New Brunswick:** New Brunswick Day (August
7). **Manitoba, Northwest Territories, Ontario, Saskatchewan,** and
**Nova Scotia:** Civic Holiday (August 7). **Newfoundland** and **Labrador:**
St. Patrick's Day (March 17), St. George's Day (April 26), Discovery
Day (June 21), Orangeman's Day (July 12). **Québec:** St. Jean
Baptiste Day (June 24). **Yukon:** Discovery Day (August 21).

## Festivals and Seasonal Events

You're likely to find a festival or special event whenever you travel
around Canada, in winter and summer alike. Contact tourist boards
to see what's in the offing for the time you'll be visiting, and inquire
about any advance tickets you may need. The following are some of
the top events.

**Alberta** **January:** Jasper Winter Festival in Jasper and Marmot Basin fea-
tures dog sledding, skating, ice sculpting, and other events.
**February:** Calgary Winter Festival is a 10-day celebration of
Calgary's Olympic spirit, featuring winter sports and ice sculpting.
**April:** Silver Buckle Rodeo at Red Deer attracts cowboys from all
over North America.
**May:** Edmonton International Children's Festival draws profession-
al musicians, mimes, jugglers, clowns, puppeteers, and singers
worldwide; at the Red Deer Annual Westerner Spring Quarter
Horse Show, horses compete from western Canada and the United
States.
**June:** Jazz City International Festival in Edmonton features 10 days
of jazz concerts, workshops, club dates, and free outdoor events;
Ponoka 58th Annual Stampede professional rodeo attracts partici-
pants from across the continent; Banff Festival of the Arts (through
August) showcases nearly 1,000 young artists in music, opera,
dance, drama, comedy, and visual arts.
**July:** Ukrainian Pysanka Festival in Vegreville celebrates with cos-

tumes and traditional singing and dancing; Calgary Exhibition and Stampede is one of the most popular Canadian events and includes 10 days of Western showmanship, hot-air balloon races, chuckwagon races, agricultural shows, crafts exhibits, and Indian dancing; Edmonton's Klondike Days celebrate the town's early frontier community with pancake breakfasts, gambling casinos, gold panning, and raft races.

**August:** Fringe Theatre Festival, in Edmonton, is regarded as one of the largest festivals for alternative theater in North America.

**September:** Spruce Meadows Masters' Tournament, Calgary, is an international horse-jumping competition at one of North America's leading equestrian centers.

**British Columbia**

**January–February:** The Polar Bear Swim on New Year's Day in Vancouver is said to bring good luck all year. Skiing competitions take place at most alpine ski resorts throughout the province.

**March–April:** Pacific Rim Whale Festival celebrates the spring migration of gray whales with guided tours by whale experts and accompanying music and dancing; the Vancouver International Wine Festival is held; Terrific Jazz Party, in Victoria, has 20 top international Dixieland bands.

**May:** Cloverdale Rodeo in Surrey is rated sixth in the world by the Pro Rodeo Association; Vancouver Children's Festival features free open-air stage performances.

**June:** Canadian International Dragon Boat Festival, in Vancouver, includes entertainment, exotic foods, and the ancient "awakening the dragons" ritual of long, slender boats decorated with huge dragon heads. Whistler Summer Festivals, through September, feature daily street entertainment and a variety of music festivals at the international ski and summer resort.

**July:** Each year, Harrison Festival of the Arts focuses on different ethnic music, dance, and theater, such as African, Caribbean, and Central American; Vancouver Sea Festival celebrates the city's nautical heritage with the World Championship Bathtub Race, sailing regattas, and windsurfing races.

**August:** Squamish Days Loggers Sports Festival features loggers from around the world competing in a series of incredible logging feats; the Abbotsford International Airshow is three days of flight performances and a large-aircraft display; Pacific National Exhibition in Vancouver has parades, exhibits, sports, entertainment, and logging contests.

**October:** The Vancouver International Film Festival is held; Okanagan Wine Festivals occur in the Okanagan-Similkameen area; cars race through downtown Vancouver in the PGA Indy Car World Series.

**December:** The Carol Ships, sailboats full of carolers and decorated with colored lights, ply the waters of the Vancouver harbor.

**Manitoba**

**February:** Festival du Voyageur, in St. Boniface, Winnipeg, celebrates the history of the region's early fur traders.

**March:** Royal Manitoba Winter Fair in Brandon.

**June:** Red River Exhibition, in Winnipeg, features lumberjack contests, body-building shows, and an international band festival; Winnipeg International Children's Festival provides top national and international children's entertainment and activities.

**July:** Winnipeg Folk Festival takes place in Birds Hill Park, 24 kilometers (15 miles) northeast of Winnipeg, and features performers singing country, bluegrass, folk, Acadian music, and jazz on 10 stages scattered throughout the park; Manitoba Stampede and Exhibition in Morris is an agricultural fair with rodeos and chuckwagon races.

**August:** Folklorama is considered the largest multicultural festival in the world, with more than 40 pavilions throughout Winnipeg; National Ukrainian Festival, in Dauphin, offers costumes, artifacts, exhibits, fiddling contests, dancing, and workshops; Icelandic Festival, in Gimli, gathers the largest Icelandic community outside of Iceland; Pioneer Days, in Steinbach, celebrates the heritage of the Mennonites with demonstrations of threshing and baking, a parade, a horse show, a barbecue, and Mennonite foods.

**New Brunswick**

**June:** Festival Moncton highlights internationally acclaimed and regional artists.

**July:** Loyalist Days Festival, in Saint John, celebrates the town's founding with parades, dancing, and sidewalk festivities; the Shediac Lobster Festival takes place in the town that calls itself the Lobster Capital of the World; there's an Irish festival in Chatham; St. Andrews Summer Arts Festival runs throughout July and August.

**August:** Miramichi Folk Song Festival, in Newcastle, features fiddling competitions, casinos, beer gardens, and a parade; Foire Brayonne, in Edmundston, is Canada's largest French festival outside of Québec; Festival by the Sea, in Saint John, attracts more than 200 entertainers from across Canada and includes cultural and ethnic performances; Acadian Festival, at Caraquet, celebrates the region's Acadian heritage with folk singing and indigenous food; the Chocolate Festival in St. Stephen includes suppers, displays, and children's events.

**Newfoundland and Labrador**

**June:** Opening of rainbow trout and salmon fishing seasons; St. John's Day commemorates the city's birthday and includes a parade, street dance, concerts, and sporting and cultural events in St. John's.

**July:** Humber Valley Strawberry Jamboree; Musicfest in Stephenville celebrates music ranging from rock and roll to traditional Newfoundland music; the Hangashore Folk Festival in Corner Brook; the Exploits Valley Salmon Festival in the Grand Falls area; the Fish, Fun and Folk Festival in Twillingate; the Conception Bay Folk Festival in Carbonear; Signal Hill Tattoo in St. John's runs through August and re-enacts the final battle of the Seven Years' War between the British and the French in 1762.

**August:** The Festival of Flight in Gander celebrates this town as the aviation "Crossroads of the World," with dances, parades, and a folk festival; *Une Longue Veillée* folk festival of western Newfoundland's French heritage features traditional musicians, singers, and dancers in Cape St. George; the St. John's Regatta, St. John's; the Newfoundland and Labrador Folk Festival in St. John's; the Labrador Straits Bakeapple Folk Festival in southern Labrador.

**September:** Humber Valley Agricultural Home and Handicraft Exhibition in Deer Lake.

**December:** First Night is a nonalcoholic New Year's Eve celebration featuring dozens of activities and concerts in St. John's.

**Nova Scotia**

**May:** Apple Blossom Festival, in Annapolis Valley, includes dancing, parades, and entertainment.

**July:** Antigonish Highland Games, staged annually since 1861, has Scottish music, dance, and such ancient sporting events as the caber toss; Nova Scotia International Tattoo in Halifax has entertainment and competitions; Nova Scotia Bluegrass and Oldtime Music Festival at Ardoise.

**August:** Mahone Bay Wooden Boat Festival; Nova Scotia Fisheries Exhibition and Fishermen's Reunion in Lunenburg; Lunenburg

Folk Harbour Festival; Festival of Scottish Fiddling in St. Anns; Scallop Days in Digby.

**September:** Shearwater International Air Show.

**Ontario**  **February:** Ontario Winter Carnival Bon Soo in Sault Ste. Marie; Winterlude-Bal de Neige, Ottawa, encourages ice-sculpting, snow-shoe races, ice boating, and other wintertime activities.

**April:** Maple Syrup Festival in Elmira; Shaw Festival in Niagara-on-the-Lake (through November) presents plays by George Bernard Shaw and his contemporaries.

**May:** Stratford Festival, in Stratford, features performances of many of Shakespeare's plays through the beginning of November; Folk Arts Festival, in St. Catharines; the Canadian Tulip Festival, in Ottawa, heralds the season with 3 million blossoming tulips.

**June:** Metro International Caravan is an ethnic fair in Toronto; International Festival of Native Arts features dancers, crafts booths, and entertainment in Toronto; Changing of the Guard begins at Ottawa's Parliament Buildings (through August).

**July:** Canada Day celebrations in Ottawa have entertainment and fireworks; Queen's Plate Thoroughbred horse race takes place in Toronto; Blueberry Festival in Sudbury; Molson INDY race in Toronto; Caribana draws on the riches of Toronto's West Indian community for this Caribbean festival.

**August:** Glengarry Highland Games, in Maxville, is North America's largest Highland Gathering; Six Nations Native Pageant is an Iroquois celebration and exhibit of the tribe's culture and history in Brantford; Royal Canadian Henley Regatta, in St. Catharines, is the largest rowing regatta in North America; Canadian National Exhibition, in Toronto, features air shows, entertainment, and exhibits.

**September:** The Canadian Open Golf Championship is in Oakville; Festival of Festivals is Toronto's international film festival; Niagara Grape and Wine Festival in St. Catharines.

**October:** Oktoberfest, in Kitchener–Waterloo, attracts more than half a million enthusiasts to its many beer halls and tents.

**November:** The Royal Agricultural Winter Fair, in Toronto, is the largest indoor agricultural fair and equestrian competition in the world.

**Prince**  **June:** Charlottetown Festival Theatre (through September) offers a
**Edward Island**  series of concerts and musicals.

**July:** Rollo Bay Fiddle Festival; Summerside Lobster Carnival, in Summerside, is a week-long feast of lobster.

**August:** Highland Games, in Belfast, is a gathering of Scotsmen for games and celebrations; Annual Community Harvest Festival in Kensington; Old Home Week in Charlottetown.

**September:** Festival Acadien de la Region Evangeline is an agricultural fair with Acadian music, a parade, and lobster suppers, at Wellington Station.

**Québec**  **January:** La Fête des Neiges winter carnival in Montréal.

**February:** Winter Carnival, in Québec City, is an 11-day festival of winter sports competitions, ice-sculpture contests, and parades.

**April:** Sugaring-off parties throughout the province celebrate the beginning of the maple syrup season.

**June:** Molson Grand Prix, with some of the world's best drivers, takes place on the Gilles-Villeneuve Race Track, in Montréal; International Jazz Festival in Québec; International Children's Folklore Festival takes place in Beauport, Québec.

**July:** Festival International de Jazz de Montréal features more than 1,000 jazz musicians from all over the world for this 10-day series;

Québec International Summer Festival offers entertainment in the streets and parks of old Québec City; Juste pour Rire (Just for Laughs) comedy festival features comics from around the world, in French and English; Drummondville World Folklore Festival brings troupes from more than 20 countries to perform in the streets and parks; Festival Orford features international artists performing at Orford Park's music center (through August); Matinée Ltd. International will spotlight best male tennis players in Montréal in 1995.

**August:** Montréal World Film Festival; Hot Air Balloon Festival in Saint-Jean-sur-Richelieu is the biggest gathering of hot air balloons in Canada.

**September:** Québec International Film Festival in Québec City.

**October:** Festival of Colors, throughout the province.

**Saskatchewan**

**March:** Winter Festival in Meadow Lake is a three-day festival with a minor hockey tournament, family snowmobile rally, dance, children's events, Jam Can curling, and sled races.

**May:** International Band and Choral Festival, in Moose Jaw, attracts 7,000 musicians, 100 bands, and 25 choral groups; Vesna Festival, in Saskatoon, is the world's largest Ukrainian cabaret, with traditional Ukrainian food and crafts.

**June:** Frontier Days Regional Fair and Rodeo, in Swift Current, is a community fair and exhibit with parades, horse show, and rodeo; Mosaic, in Regina, is a festival of cultures from around the world.

**July–August:** Buffalo Days Exhibition, in Regina, features rides, a grandstand show, dancing, livestock judging, and horse racing; Big Valley Jamboree, in Craven, is a four-day country-music festival; the "Trial of Louis Riel," in Regina, one of Canada's longest running stage shows, re-enacts the events surrounding the North West Rebellion of 1885; Shakespeare on the Saskatchewan Festival, in Saskatoon, has productions in tents on the banks of the South Saskatchewan River.

**Wilderness Canada**

**February:** The Yukon Sourdough Rendezvous, in Whitehorse, features dog-team races, leg wrestling, log sawing, snowshoe races, local arts and crafts, and talent contests.

**June:** The Midnight Sun Golf Tournament in Yellowknife tees off at midnight on the first day of summer.

**July:** Yukon International Festival of Storytelling, Whitehorse, features storytellers from all over the circumpolar North.

**August:** Dawson City commemorates the Klondike gold strike with the Discovery Days festival, with parades, raft and canoe races, baseball tournaments, and dances.

## What to Pack

**Clothing**

How you pack will depend on when you go and what you plan to do. Layering is the best defense against Canada's cold winters; a hat, scarf, and gloves are essential. For summer travel, loose-fitting natural-fiber clothes are best; bring a wool sweater and light jacket. If you're planning to spend time in Canada's larger cities, pack both casual clothes for day touring and more formal wear for evenings out. If your visit includes a stay at a large city hotel, bring a bathing suit in any season to take advantage of the indoor pool.

**Miscellaneous**

If you plan on camping or hiking in the deep woods during the summer, particularly in northern Canada, insect repellent is a must, especially in June, which is blackfly season.

Bring an extra pair of eyeglasses or contact lenses. If you have a health problem that may require you to purchase a prescription drug, pack enough to last the duration of the trip, or have your doctor write a prescription using the drug's generic name, since brand names vary from country to country. And don't forget to pack a list of the addresses of offices that supply refunds for lost or stolen traveler's checks.

**Luggage** Free airline baggage allowances depend on the airline, the route,
*Regulations* and the class of your ticket. In general, on domestic flights and on international flights between the United States and foreign destinations, you are entitled to check two bags—neither exceeding 62 inches, or 158 centimeters (length + width + height), or weighing more than 70 pounds (32 kilograms). A third piece may be brought aboard as a carryon; its total dimensions are generally limited to less than 45 inches (114 centimeters), so it will fit easily under the seat in front of you or in the overhead compartment. There are variations, so ask in advance. In the United States the Federal Aviation Administration (FAA) gives airlines broad latitude to limit carry-on allowances and tailor them to different aircraft and operational conditions. Charges for excess, oversize, or overweight pieces vary, so inquire before you pack.

*Safeguarding* Before leaving home, itemize your bags' contents and their worth in
*Your Luggage* case they go astray. To minimize that risk, tag them inside and out with your name, address, and phone number. (If you use your home address, cover it so that potential thieves can't see it.) At check-in, make sure that the tag attached by baggage handlers bears the correct three-letter code for your destination. If your bags do not arrive with you, or if you detect damage, immediately file a written report with the airline before you leave the airport.

## Money Matters

American money is readily accepted in much of Canada (especially in communities near the border), and traveler's checks and major U.S. credit cards are accepted in larger cities and resorts.

**Traveler's** Traveler's checks are preferable in metropolitan centers, although
**Checks** you'll need cash in rural areas and small towns. The most widely recognized are **American Express, Citicorp, Diners Club, Thomas Cook,** and **Visa,** which are sold by major commercial banks. Both American Express and Thomas Cook issue checks that can be counter-signed and used by you or your traveling companion. Typically the issuing company or the bank at which you make your purchase charges 1% to 3% of the checks' face value as a fee. Some foreign banks charge as much as 20% of the face value as the fee for cashing travelers' checks in a foreign currency. Buy a few checks in small denominations to cash toward the end of your trip, so you won't be left with excess foreign currency. Record the numbers of checks as you spend them, and keep this list separate from the checks.

**Currency** Banks offer the most favorable exchange rates. If you use currency
**Exchange** exchange booths at airports, rail and bus stations, hotels, stores, and privately run exchange firms, you'll typically get less favorable rates, but you may find the hours more convenient.

You can get good rates and avoid long lines at airport currency-exchange booths by getting a small amount of currency at **Thomas Cook Currency Services** (630 5th Ave., New York, NY 10111, tel. 212/757–6915 or 800/223–7373 for locations in major metropolitan areas throughout the U.S.) or **Ruesch International** (tel. 800/424–2923 for locations) before you depart. Check with your travel agent to be sure that the currency of the country you will be visiting can be imported.

## Getting Money from Home

**Cash Machines**  Many automated-teller machines (ATMs) are tied to such international networks as **Cirrus** and **Plus.** You can use your bank card at ATMs away from home to withdraw money from an account and get cash advances on a credit-card account if your card has been programmed with a personal identification number, or PIN. Check in advance on limits on withdrawals and cash advances within specified periods. Ask whether your bank-card or credit-card PIN number will need to be reprogrammed for use in the area you'll be visiting. Four digits are commonly used overseas. Note that Discover is accepted only in the United States. On cash advances you are charged interest from the day you receive the money from ATMs as well as from tellers. Although transaction fees for ATM withdrawals abroad will probably be higher than fees for withdrawals at home, Cirrus and Plus exchange rates tend to be good.

For specific Cirrus locations in the United States and Canada, call 800/424–7787 and press the area code and first three digits of the number you're calling from (or the calling area where you want an ATM).

**Wiring Money**  You don't have to be a cardholder to send or receive a **MoneyGram from American Express** for up to $10,000. Go to a MoneyGram agent in retail and convenience stores and American Express travel offices, pay up to $1,000 with a credit card and anything over that in cash. You are allowed a free long-distance call to give the transaction code to your intended recipient, who needs only present identification and the reference number to the nearest MoneyGram agent to pick up the cash. MoneyGram agents are in more than 70 countries (call 800/926–9400 for locations). Fees range from 3% to 10%, depending on the amount and how you pay.

You can also use **Western Union.** To wire money, take either cash or a cashier's check to the nearest office or call and use your MasterCard or Visa. Money sent from the United States or Canada will be available for pickup at agent locations in Canada within minutes. Once the money is in the system it can be picked up at any one of 22,000 locations (call 800/325–6000 for the one nearest you).

## Canadian Currency

The units of currency in Canada are the Canadian dollar (C$) and the cent, in almost the same denominations as U.S. currency—the $1 bill is no longer used; instead it has been replaced by a $1 coin ($2, $5, $10, $20, 1¢, 5¢, 10¢, 25¢, etc.). The use of $2 paper currency is common here although rare in the United States. At press time the exchange rate was C$1.38 to US$1 and C$2.09 to £1. The Canadian dollar has decreased significantly in value relative to the U.S. dollar in recent months.

## What It Will Cost

Throughout this guide, unless otherwise stated, prices are quoted in Canadian dollars.

With some exceptions, most food prices are higher in Canada than in the United States, but lower than in much of Western Europe. The biggest expense of the trip will be accommodations, but a range of choices, from economy to deluxe, is available in metropolitan areas, the country, and in resort areas.

**Sample Prices** The following prices are for Toronto (prices in other cities and regions are often lower): A soda (pop) costs $1–$1.25; a glass of beer, $3–$6; a sandwich, $3.50–$6; a taxi, as soon as the meter is turned on, $2.20, and $1 for every kilometer; a movie, about $8. (*See* Staying in Canada, GST and Sales Tax, *below*).

## Passports and Visas

**U.S. Citizens** Because of the volume of border traffic between Canada and the United States, entry requirements are fairly simple. Citizens and legal residents of the United States do not need a passport or a visa to enter Canada, but proof of citizenship (a birth certificate, valid passport, or voter registration card) and proof of identity may be requested. Naturalized U.S. residents should carry their naturalization certificate or "green card." U.S. residents entering Canada from a third country must have a valid passport, naturalization certificate, or "green card." For more information, contact the **Canadian Embassy** (501 Pennsylvania Ave. NW, Washington, DC 20001, tel. 202/682–1740).

**U.K. Citizens** Citizens of the United Kingdom need a valid passport to enter Canada for stays of up to six months; all visitors must have a return ticket out of Canada. Applications for new and renewal passports are available from main post offices as well as at the six passport offices, located in Belfast, Glasgow, Liverpool, London, Newport, and Peterborough. You may apply in person at all passport offices, or by mail to all except the London office. Children under 16 may travel on a parent's passport when accompanying them. All passports are valid for 10 years. Allow a month for processing.

## Customs and Duties

**On Arrival** American and British visitors may bring in the following items duty-free: 200 cigarettes, 50 cigars, and two pounds of tobacco; 1 bottle (1.14 litres or 40 imperial ounces) of liquor, or 24 355-milliliter (12-ounce) bottles or cans of beer for personal consumption; gifts up to the value of $60 per gift. A deposit is sometimes required for trailers (refunded upon return). Cats and dogs must have a certificate issued by a licensed veterinarian that clearly identifies the animal and certifies that it has been vaccinated against rabies during the preceding 36 months. Plant material must be declared and inspected. With certain restrictions (some fruits and vegetables), visitors may bring food with them for their own use, providing the quantity is consistent with the duration of the visit.

**Returning Home**
**U.S. Customs** Provided you've been out of the country for at least 48 hours and haven't already used the exemption, or any part of it, in the past 30 days, you may bring home US$400 worth of foreign goods duty-free. So can each member of your family, regardless of age; and your exemptions may be pooled, so one of you can bring in more if another brings in less. A flat 10% duty applies to the next US$1,000 of goods; above US$1,400, the rate varies with the merchandise. (If the 48-hour or 30-day limits apply, your duty-free allowance drops to US$25, which may not be pooled.) Please note that these are the *general* rules, applicable to most countries, including Canada.

Travelers 21 or older may bring back 1 liter of alcohol duty-free, provided the beverage laws of the state through which they reenter the United States allow it. In addition, 100 non-Cuban cigars and 200 cigarettes are allowed, regardless of your age. Antiques and works of art more than 100 years old are duty-free.

Gifts valued at less than US$50 may be mailed to the U.S. duty-free, with a limit of one package per day per addressee (do not send alcohol or tobacco products, nor perfume valued at more than US$50). These gifts do not count as part of your exemption, unless you bring them home with you. Mark the package "Unsolicited Gift" and include the nature of the gift and its retail value on the outside.

For a copy of "Know Before You Go," a free brochure detailing what you may and may not bring back to the United States, rates of duty, and other pointers, contact the **U.S. Customs Service** (Box 7407, Washington, DC 20044, tel. 202/927–6724).

*U.K. Customs*   From countries outside the EU, such as Canada, you may import duty-free 200 cigarettes, 100 cigarillos, 50 cigars or 250 grams of tobacco; 1 liter of spirits or 2 liters of fortified or sparkling wine; 2 liters of still table wine; 60 milliliters of perfume; 250 milliliters of toilet water; plus £136 worth of other goods, including gifts and souvenirs.

For further information or a copy of "A Guide for Travellers," which details standard customs procedures as well as what you may bring into the United Kingdom from abroad, contact **HM Customs and Excise** (Dorset House, Stamford St., London SE1 9PY, tel. 071/928–3344).

## Traveling with Cameras, Camcorders, and Laptops

**Film and Cameras**   If your camera is new or if you haven't used it for a while, shoot and develop a few rolls of film before leaving home. Store film in a cool, dry place—never in the car's glove compartment or on the shelf under the rear window.

Airport security X-rays generally aren't harmful to film with ISO below 400. To protect your film, carry it with you in a clear plastic bag and ask for a hand inspection. Such requests are honored at U.S. airports, up to the inspector abroad. Don't depend on a lead-lined bag to protect film in checked luggage—the airline may increase the radiation to see what's inside. Call the Kodak Information Center (tel. 800/242–2424) for details.

**Camcorders**   Before your trip, put camcorders through their paces, invest in a skylight filter to protect the lens, and check all the batteries.

**Videotape**   Unlike still-camera film, videotape is not damaged by X-rays. However, it may well be harmed by the magnetic field of a walk-through metal detector. Airport security personnel may want you to turn the camcorder on to prove that that's what it is, so make sure the battery is charged.

**Laptops**   Security X-rays do not harm hard-disk or floppy-disk storage, but you may request a hand-check, at which point you may be asked to turn on the computer to prove that it is what it appears to be. (Check your battery before departure.) Most airlines allow you to use your laptop aloft except during takeoff and landing (so as not to interfere with navigation equipment). For international travel, register your foreign-made laptop with U.S. Customs as you leave the country. If your laptop is U.S.-made, call the consulate of the country you'll be visiting to find out whether it should be registered with customs upon arrival. Before departure, find out about repair facilities at your destination.

## Language

Canada's two official languages are English and French. Though English is widely spoken, it may be useful to learn a few French phrases if you plan to travel to the province of Québec or to the French Canadian communities in the maritime provinces (Nova Scotia, New Brunswick, and Prince Edward Island), northern Manitoba, and Ontario. Canadian French, known as Québecois or *joual*, is a colorful language often quite different from that spoken in France.

Canada, like the United States, has been settled by successive influxes of immigrants, from the British, Scottish, Irish, and French to the Germans, Scandinavians, Ukrainians, and Chinese. Many of these groups maintain their cultural identity through their native language, and ethnic daily and weekly newspapers are common. Immigration since the 1960s accounts for Asians, Arabs, East Indians, Italians, Hispanics, and Caribbean blacks. The native population of Canada now comprises less than 1% of the total population, yet it is possible to hear the languages of Native Canadians where these groups reside.

---

## Insurance

**U.S. Residents** Most tour operators, travel agents, and insurance agents sell specialized health-and-accident, flight, trip-cancellation, and luggage insurance as well as comprehensive policies with some or all of these features. But before you make any purchase, review your existing health and homeowner policies to find out whether they cover expenses incurred while traveling.

*Health-and-Accident Insurance* Specific policy provisions of supplemental health-and-accident insurance for travelers include reimbursement for $1,000 to $150,000 worth of medical and/or dental expenses caused by an accident or illness during a trip. The personal-accident, or death-and-dismemberment, provision pays a lump sum to your beneficiaries if you die or to you if you lose one or both limbs or your eyesight; the lump sum awarded can range from $15,000 to $500,000. The medical-assistance provision may reimburse you for the cost of referrals, evacuation, or repatriation and other services, or it may automatically enroll you as a member of a particular medical-assistance company (*see* Assistance Companies, *above*).

*Flight Insurance* Often bought as a last-minute impulse at the airport, flight insurance pays when a plane crashes a lump sum to either a beneficiary if the insured dies or sometimes to a surviving passenger who loses eyesight or a limb; it supplements the airlines' coverage described in the limits-of-liability paragraphs on your ticket. Charging an airline ticket to a major credit card often automatically entitles you to coverage and may also embrace travel by bus, train, and ship.

*Baggage Insurance* In the event of loss, damage, or theft on international flights, airlines' liability is US$20 per kilogram for checked baggage (roughly about US$640 per 70-pound bag) and US$400 per passenger for unchecked baggage. On domestic flights, the ceiling is US$1,250 per passenger. Excess-valuation insurance can be bought directly from the airline at check-in for about $10 per $1,000 worth of coverage. However, you cannot buy it at any price for the rather extensive list of excluded items shown on your airline ticket.

*Trip Insurance* **Trip-cancellation-and-interruption insurance** protects you in the event you are unable to undertake or finish your trip, especially if your airline ticket, cruise, or package tour does not allow changes or cancellations. The amount of coverage you purchase should equal the cost of your trip should you, a traveling companion, or a family member fall ill, forcing you to stay home, plus the nondiscounted one-way airline ticket you would need to buy if you had to return home early. Read the fine print carefully, especially sections defining "family member" and "preexisting medical conditions." **Default or bankruptcy insurance** protects you against a supplier's failure to deliver. Such policies often do not cover default by a travel agency, tour operator, airline, or cruise line if you bought your tour and the coverage directly from the firm in question. Tours packaged by one of the 33 members of the United States Tour Operators Association (USTOA, 211 E. 51 St., Suite 12B, New York, NY 10022; tel. 212/750–7371), which requires members to maintain $1 million each in an account to reimburse clients in case of default, are likely to present the fewest difficulties. Even better, pay for travel arrangements with a major credit card, so that you can refuse to pay the bill if services have not been rendered—and let the card company fight your battles.

*Comprehensive Policies*
Companies supplying comprehensive policies with some or all of the above features include **Access America, Inc.** (Box 90315, Richmond, VA 23230, tel. 800/284–8300); **Carefree Travel Insurance** (Box 310, 120 Mineola Blvd., Mineola, NY 11501, tel. 516/294–0220 or 800/323–3149); **Tele-Trip** (Mutual of Omaha Plaza, Box 31762, Omaha, NE 68131, tel. 800/228–9792); **The Travelers Companies** (1 Tower Sq., Hartford, CT 06183, tel. 203/277–0111 or 800/243–3174); **Travel Guard International** (1145 Clark St., Stevens Point, WI 54481, tel. 715/345–0505 or 800/826–1300); and **Wallach and Company, Inc.** (107 W. Federal St., Box 480, Middleburg, VA 22117, tel. 703/687–3166 or 800/237–6615).

**U.K. Residents**
Most tour operators, travel agents, and insurance agents sell specialized policies covering accident, medical expenses, personal liability, trip cancellation, and loss or theft of personal property. You can also purchase an annual travel-insurance policy valid for every trip you make during the year in which it's purchased (usually only trips of less than 90 days). Make sure you will be covered if you have a preexisting medical condition or are pregnant.

For advice by phone or a free booklet, "Holiday Insurance," that sets out what to expect from a holiday-insurance policy and gives price guidelines, contact the **Association of British Insurers** (51 Gresham St., London EC2V 7HQ, tel. 071/600–3333; 30 Gordon St., Glasgow G1 3PU, tel. 041/226–3905; Scottish Providence Bldg., Donegall Sq. W, Belfast BT1 6JE, tel. 0232/249176; call for other locations).

## Car Rentals

All major car-rental companies are represented in Canada, including **Alamo** (tel. 800/327–9633); **Avis** (tel. 800/331–1212, 800/879–2847 in Canada); **Budget** (tel. 800/527–0700); **Hertz** (tel. 800/654–3001, 800/263-0600 in Canada); **National** (tel. 800/227–7368), affiliated with **Tilden Rent-a-Car** (tel. 514/842–9445). In cities, rates range from about $50 per day for an economy car to $70 for a large car; weekly rates range from $190 to $350. Unlimited mileage rentals are available only in limited areas. This does not include the 7% GST tax.

**Requirements**
Any valid state or national driver's license is acceptable. If you have rented in the United States, be sure to keep the rental contract with

you to indicate that use in Canada is authorized by the rental agency.

**Extra Charges** Picking up the car in one city or country and leaving it in another may entail substantial drop-off charges or one-way service fees. The cost of a collision or loss-damage waiver (*see below*) can be high, also. Fill the tank when you turn in the vehicle to avoid being charged for refueling at what you'll swear is the most expensive pump in town.

**Cutting Costs** Major international companies have programs that discount their standard rates by 15%–30% if you make the reservation before departure (anywhere from 24 hours to 14 days), rent for a minimum number of days (typically three or four), and prepay the rental. Ask about these advance-purchase schemes when you call for information. More economical rentals may come as part of fly/drive or other packages, even bare-bones deals that combine only the rental plus an airline ticket (*see* Tours and Packages, *above*).

Several companies that operate as wholesalers—they that do not own their own fleets but rent in bulk from those that do—offer advantageous rates to their customers. Rentals through such companies must be arranged and paid for before you leave the United States. Among them is **Auto Europe** (Box 1097, Camden, ME 04843, tel. 207/236–8235 or 800/223–5555, in Canada, 800/458–9503). You won't see these wholesalers' deals advertised; they're even better in summer, when business travel is down. Always ask whether the prices are guaranteed in U.S. dollars or foreign currency and if unlimited mileage is available. Find out about any required deposits, cancellation penalties, and drop-off charges, and confirm the cost of the Collision Damage Waiver.

**Insurance and Collision Damage Waiver** Until recently, standard rental contracts included liability coverage (for damage to public property, injury to pedestrians, and so on) and coverage for the car against fire, theft, and collision damage with a deductible. Due to law changes in some states and rising liability costs, several car rental agencies have reduced the type of coverage they offer. Before you rent a car, find out exactly what coverage, if any, is provided by your personal auto insurer. Don't assume that you are covered. If you do want insurance from the rental company, secondary coverage may be the only type offered. You may already have secondary coverage if you charge the rental to a credit card. Only Diner's Club (tel. 800/234–6377) provides primary coverage in the United States and worldwide.

## Rail Passes

Although **VIA Rail,** Canada's major passenger carrier, has made considerable cuts in its services, it is still possible to travel coast to coast on its trains. The **Canrailpass** allows 12 days of coach-class travel within a 30-day period; sleeping cars are available, but they sell out very early and must be reserved at least a month in advance during the high season (June 1–Sept. 30) when the pass is C$510 for adults age 25–60, C$460 for travelers under 25 or over 60. Low season rates (Oct. 1–Dec. 14 and Jan. 6–May 31) are C$349 for adults and C$319 for youth and senior citizens. The pass is not valid during the Christmas period (Dec. 15–Jan. 5). The Canrailpass must be purchased prior to arrival in Canada; for more information and reservations, contact VIA Rail (tel. 800/665–0200 in the United States) or Compass Travel (Box 113, Peterborough, PE1 1LE, tel. 0733/51780, in the United Kingdom).

## Student and Youth Travel

Travel
Agencies

**Council Travel Services (CTS),** a subsidiary of the nonprofit Council on International Educational Exchange (CIEE), specializes in low-cost travel arrangements abroad for students and is the exclusive U.S. agent for several discount cards. Also newly available from CTS are domestic air passes for bargain travel within the United States. CIEE's twice-yearly *Student Travels* magazine is available at the CTS office at CIEE headquarters (205 E. 42nd St., 16th Floor, New York, NY 10017, tel. 212/661–1450) and in Boston (tel. 617/266–1926), Miami (tel. 305/670–9261), Los Angeles (tel. 310/208–3551) and at 43 branches in college towns nationwide (free in person, $1 by mail). **Campus Connections** (1100 E. Marlton Pike, Cherry Hill, NJ 08034, tel. 800/428–3235) specializes in discounted accommodations and airline fares for students. The **Educational Travel Centre** (438 N. Frances St., Madison, WI 53703, tel. 608/256–5551) offers low-cost domestic and international airline tickets, mostly for flights departing from Chicago, and rail passes. Other travel agencies catering to students include **TMI Student Travel** (1146 Pleasant St., Watertown, MA 02172, tel. 617/661–8187 or 800/245–3672), and **Travel Cuts** (187 College St., Toronto, Ont. M5T 1P7, tel. 416/979–2406).

Discount
Cards

For discounts on transportation and on museum and attractions admissions, buy the **International Student Identity Card** (ISIC) if you're a bona fide student, or the **International Youth Card** (IYC) if you're under 26. In the United States the ISIC and IYC cards cost US$15 each and include basic travel accident and sickness coverage. Apply to **CIEE** (*see* address *above*, tel. 212/661–1414; the application is in *Student Travels*). In Canada the cards are available for C$15 each from **Travel Cuts** (*see above*). In the United Kingdom they cost £5 and £4 respectively at student unions and student travel companies, including Council Travel's London office (28A Poland St., London W1V 3DB, tel. 071/437–7767).

Hosteling

A **Hostelling International** (HI) membership card is the key to more than 6,000 hostels in 70 countries; the sex-segregated, dormitory-style sleeping quarters, including some for families, go for US$7 to US$20 a night per person. Membership is available in the United States through **Hostelling International/American Youth Hostels** (AYH, 733 15th St. NW, Washington, DC 20005, tel. 202/783–6161), the American link in the worldwide chain, and costs US$25 for adults 18–54, US$10 for those under 18, US$15 for those 55 and over, and US$35 for families. Volume 2 of the *Guide to Budget Accommodation* lists hostels in Asia and Australia as well as in Canada and the United States (US$13.95 including postage). HI membership is available in Canada through **Hostelling International–Canada** (205 Catherine St., Suite 400, Ottawa, Ont. K2P 1C3, tel. 613/748–5638) for C$26.75, and in the United Kingdom through the **Youth Hostel Association of England and Wales** (Trevelyan House, 8 St. Stephen's Hill, St. Albans, Herts. AL1 2DY, tel. 0727/55215) for £9.

## Traveling with Children

Publications
Newsletter

*Family Travel Times,* published 10 times a year by **Travel With Your Children** (TWYCH, 45 W. 18th St., 7th Floor Tower, New York, NY 10011, tel. 212/206–0688; annual subscription $55), covers destinations, types of vacations, and modes of travel. TWYCH also publishes *Cruising with Children* and *Skiing with Children*.

| | |
|---|---|
| Books | *Traveling with Children—And Enjoying It,* by Arlene K. Butler (US$11.95 plus US$3 shipping; Globe Pequot Press, Box 833, Old Saybrook, CT 06475, tel. 800/243–0495, in CT, 800/962–0973), helps plan your trip with children, from toddlers to teens. Also from Globe Pequot is *Recommended Family Resorts in the United States, Canada, and the Caribbean,* by Jane Wilford with Janet Tice (US$12.95). |
| Tour Operators | **Grandtravel** (6900 Wisconsin Ave., Suite 706, Chevy Chase, MD 20815, tel. 301/986–0790 or 800/247–7651) offers international and domestic tours for people traveling with their grandchildren. The catalogue, as charmingly written and illustrated as a children's book, positively invites armchair traveling with lap-sitters aboard. **Rascals in Paradise** (650 5th St., Suite 505, San Francisco, CA 94107, tel. 415/978–9800, or 800/872–7225) specializes in programs for families. |
| Getting There Air Fares | On international flights, the fare for infants under 2 not occupying a seat is generally 10% of the accompanying adult's fare; children ages 2–11 usually pay half to two-thirds of the adult fare. On domestic flights, children under 2 not occupying a seat travel free, and older children currently travel on the "lowest applicable" adult fare. |
| Baggage | In general, infants paying 10% of the adult fare are allowed one carry-on bag, not to exceed 70 pounds or 45 inches (length + width + height) and a collapsible stroller; check with the airline before departure, because you may be allowed less if the flight is full. The adult baggage allowance applies for children paying half or more of the adult fare. |
| Safety Seats | The FAA recommends the use of safety seats aloft and details approved models in the free leaflet **"Child/Infant Safety Seats Recommended for Use in Aircraft"** (available from the Federal Aviation Administration, APA–200, 800 Independence Ave. SW, Washington, DC 20591, tel. 202/267–3479). Airline policy varies. U.S. carriers allow FAA-approved models bearing a sticker declaring their FAA approval. Because these seats are strapped into a regular passenger seat, they may require that parents buy a ticket even for an infant under 2 who would otherwise ride free. Foreign carriers may not allow infant seats, may charge the child's rather than the infant's fare for their use, or may require you to hold your baby during take-off and landing, thus defeating the seat's purpose. |
| Facilities Aloft | Some airlines do provide other services for children, such as children's meals and freestanding bassinets (to those sitting in seats at the bulkhead, where there's enough legroom). Make your request when reserving. The annual February/March issue of *Family Travel Times* gives details of the children's services of dozens of airlines (US$10; *see above*). "Kids and Teens in Flight" (free from the U.S. Department of Transportation, tel. 202/366–2220) offers tips for children flying alone. |
| Lodging | Although most major hotels in Canada welcome children, the policies and programs they offer are usually limited to a free stay for children under a certain age when sharing a room with their parents. For example, the Sheraton Hotels worldwide offer a free stay to children under the age of 17. At Best Westerns, the age limit ranges from 12 to 16, depending on the hotel. Baby-sitting services can often be arranged at the front desk of most hotels. In addition, priority for connecting rooms is often given to families. Inquire about programs and discounts when you make your reservation. |

## Hints for Travelers with Disabilities

**Organizations** **Canadian Paraplegic Association National Office** (520 Sutherland
*In Canada* Dr., Toronto, Ont., M4G 3U9, tel. 416/422–5640) provides information about touring in Canada.

*In the United* Several organizations provide travel information for people with
*States* disabilities, usually for a membership fee, and some publish newsletters and bulletins. Among them are the **Information Center for
Individuals with Disabilities** (Fort Point Pl., in MA, 27–43 Wormwood St., Boston, MA 02210, tel. 617/727–5540 or, in MA, 800/462–
5015 between 11 and 4, or leave message; TDD 617/345–9743); **Mobility International USA** (Box 10767, Eugene, OR 97440, tel. and
TDD 503/343–1284, fax 503/343–6812), the U.S. branch of an international organization based in Britain (*see below*) and present in 30
countries; **MossRehab Hospital Travel Information Service** (1200 W.
Tabor Rd., Philadelphia, PA 19141, tel. 215/456–9603, TDD 215/
456–9602); the **Travel Industry and Disabled Exchange** (TIDE, 5435
Donna Ave., Tarzana, CA 91356, tel. 818/368–5648, fax 818/344–
0078); and **Travelin' Talk** (Box 3534, Clarksville, TN 37043, tel. 615/
552–6670, fax 615/552–1182).

*In the United* Main information sources include the **Royal Association for Disabili-
*Kingdom* ty and Rehabilitation** (RADAR, 25 Mortimer St., London W1N
8AB, tel. 071/637–5400), which publishes travel information for the
disabled in Britain, and **Mobility International** (228 Borough High
St., London SE1 1JX, tel. 071/403–5688), the headquarters of an international membership organization that serves as a clearinghouse
of travel information for people with disabilities.

**Travel** **Flying Wheels Travel** (143 W. Bridge St., Box 382, Owatonna, MN
**Agencies** 55060, tel. 507/451–5005 or 800/535–6790) is a travel agency specia-
**and Tour** lizing in domestic and worldwide cruises, tours, and independent
**Operators** travel itineraries for people with disabilities. Adventurers should
contact **Wilderness Inquiry** (1313 5th St. SE, Minneapolis, MN
55414, tel. and TDD 612/379–3838), which orchestrates action-
packed trips like white-water rafting, sea kayaking, and dog sledding.

**Publications** In addition to the fact sheets, newsletters, and books mentioned
above are several free publications available from the Consumer Information Center (Pueblo, CO 81009): "New Horizons for the Air
Traveler with a Disability," a U.S. Department of Transportation
booklet describing changes resulting from the 1986 Air Carrier Access Act and those still to come from the 1990 Americans with Disabilities Act (include Department 608Y in the address), and the
Airport Operators Council's *Access Travel: Airports* (Dept. 5804),
which describes facilities and services for people with disabilities at
more than 500 airports worldwide.

*Travelin' Talk Directory* (*see* Organizations, *above*) was published
in 1993. This 500-page resource book ($35) is packed with informa-
tion for travelers with disabilities. Twin Peaks Press (Box 129, Vancouver, WA 98666, tel. 206/694–2462 or 800/637–2256) publishes the
*Directory of Travel Agencies for the Disabled* ($19.95), listing more
than 370 agencies worldwide and *Wheelchair Vagabond* ($14.95), a
collection of personal travel tips. Add $2 per book for shipping.

## Hints for Older Travelers

**Organizations** The **American Association of Retired Persons** (AARP, 601 E St. NW,
Washington, DC 20049, tel. 202/434–2277) provides independent

travelers who are members of the AARP (open to those age 50 or older; $8 per person or couple annually) with the Purchase Privilege Program, which offers discounts on lodging, car rentals, and sightseeing, and the AARP Motoring Plan, which furnishes domestic trip-routing information and emergency road-service aid for an annual fee of $39.95 per person or couple ($59.95 for a premium version). AARP also arranges group tours, cruises, and apartment living through AARP Travel Experience from American Express (400 Pinnacle Way, Suite 450, Norcross, GA 30071, tel. 800/927–0111 or 800/745–4567).

Two other organizations offer discounts on lodgings, car rentals, and other travel products, along with such nontravel perks as magazines and newsletters: the **National Council of Senior Citizens** (1331 F St. NW, Washington, DC 20004, tel. 202/347–8800; membership US$12 annually) and **Mature Outlook** (6001 N. Clark St., Chicago, IL 60660, tel. 800/336–6330; US$9.95 annually).

Note: Mention your senior-citizen identification card when booking hotel reservations for reduced rates, not when checking out. At restaurants, show your card before you're seated; discounts may be limited to certain menus, days, or hours. If you are renting a car, ask about promotional rates that might improve on your senior-citizen discount.

**Educational Travel** The nonprofit **Elderhostel** (75 Federal St., 3rd Floor, Boston, MA 02110, tel. 617/426–7788) has offered inexpensive study programs for people 60 and older since 1975. Held at more than 1,800 educational institutions in the United States, Canada, and 45 countries, courses cover everything from marine science to Greek myths and cowboy poetry. Participants generally attend lectures in the morning and spend the afternoon sightseeing or on field trips; they live in dorms on the host campuses. Fees for programs in the United States and Canada, which usually last one week, run about US$300, not including transportation.

**Tour Operators** **Saga International Holidays** (222 Berkeley St., Boston, MA 02116, tel. 800/343–0273), which specializes in group travel for people over 60, offers a selection of variously priced tours and cruises covering five continents. If you want to take your grandchildren, look into **Grandtravel** (*see* Traveling with Children, *above*).

**Discounts** **VIA Rail Canada** (tel. 800/665–0200) offers those 60 and over a 10% discount on basic transportation for travel any time and with no advance-purchase requirement. This 10% discount can also apply to off-peak reduced fares that have advance-purchase requirements.

**Publications** *The 50+ Traveler's Guidebook: Where to Go, Where to Stay, What to Do* by Anita Williams and Merrimac Dillon ($12.95; St. Martin's Press, 175 Fifth Ave., New York, NY 10010) is available in bookstores and offers many useful tips. "The Mature Traveler" (Box 50820, Reno, NV 89513, tel. 702/786–7419; $29.95), a monthly newsletter, contains many travel deals for older travelers.

## Hints for Gay and Lesbian Travelers

**Organizations** The **International Gay Travel Association** (Box 4974, Key West, FL 33041, tel. 305-292-0217 or 800/999–7925 or 800-448-8550), which has 700 members, will provide you with names of travel agents and tour operators who specialize in gay travel. The **Gay & Lesbian Visitors Center of New York Inc.** (135 W. 20th St., 3rd Floor, New York, NY 10011, tel. 212/463–9030 or 800/395–2315; $100 annually) mails a monthly newsletter, valuable coupons, and more to its members.

**Tour Operators and Travel Agencies** The dominant travel agency in the market is **Above and Beyond** (3568 Sacramento St., San Francisco, CA 94118, tel. 415/922–2683 or 800/397–2681). Tour operator **Olympus Vacations** (8424 Santa Monica Blvd., Suite 721, West Hollywood, CA 90069; tel. 310/657–2220 or 800/965–9678) offers all-gay and lesbian resort holidays. **Skylink Women's Travel** (746 Ashland Ave., Santa Monica, CA 90405, tel. 310/452–0506 or 800/225-5759) handles individual travel for lesbians all over the world and conducts two international and five domestic group trips annually.

**Publications** The premiere international travel magazine for gays and lesbians is **Our World** (1104 N. Nova Rd., Suite 251, Daytona Beach, FL 32117, tel. 904/441–5367; $35 for 10 issues). **Out & About** (tel. 203/789-8518 or 800/929–2268; $49 for 10 issues) is a 16-page monthly newsletter with extensive information on resorts, hotels, and airlines that are gay-friendly.

### Further Reading

**Fiction** Mordecai Richler is well known as the author of *The Apprenticeship of Duddy Kravitz,* a novel set in Montréal, which was made into a movie. His various collections of essays are also worth exploring. Margaret Atwood, a prolific poet and novelist, is also regarded as a stateswoman of sorts in her native Canada. Her novel *Cat's Eye* is set in northern Canada and Toronto. Alice Munro writes about small-town life in Ontario in *The Progress of Love. Northern Lights,* by Howard Norman, focuses on a child's experiences growing up in Manitoba and, later, Toronto. Howard Engel's mystery series features the adventures of Bennie Cooperman, a Toronto-based detective. *The Suicide Murders* is an especially compelling novel from the series. Jack Hodgin's *Spit Delaney's Island* is peopled with loggers, construction workers and other rural Canadians. *Peace Shall Destroy Many* is Rudy Wiebe's account of a Mennonite community in Manitoba. Joy Kogawa's first novel, *Obasan,* tells about the Japanese community of Canada during World War II. *Medicine River* is a collection of short stories by Native American writer Thomas King, who was one of the authors, along with Cheryl Calver and Helen Hoy, of *The Native in Literature,* about the image of Native Americans in literature. For an excellent view of New Brunswick, especially the famed salmon-fishing region called the Miramichi, look for the humorous books *The Americans Are Coming* and *The Last Tasmanian* by local author Herb Curtis.

**Nonfiction** *Canada North* is by Farley Mowat, as is *Never Cry Wolf,* his humorous account of a naturalist who goes to a remote part of Canada to commune with wolves. Andrew Malcolm gives a cultural and historical overview of the country in *The Canadians.* Stephen Brook's *The Maple Leaf Rag* is a collection of idiosyncratic travel essays. *Why We Act Like Canadians: A Personal Exploration of Our National Character,* by Pierre Burton, is one of many popular nonfiction books by Burton focusing on Canada's history and culture. *Short History of Canada,* by Desmond Morton, is a recent historical account of the country.

# Arriving and Departing

### From North America by Plane

Flights are either nonstop, direct, or connecting. A **nonstop** flight requires no change of plane and makes no stops. A **direct** flight stops at least once and can involve a change of plane, although the flight number remains the same; if the first leg is late, the second waits. This is not the case with a **connecting** flight, which involves a different plane and a different flight number.

**Airports and Airlines** You can fly nonstop to Canada from most major U.S. cities; every major U.S. airline has nonstop service. The major international hubs are Montréal, Toronto, and Vancouver, but international flights also fly into Halifax, Calgary, and Edmonton. Some of the major airlines serving these hubs are **American** (tel. 800/433–7300), **Continental** (tel. 800/525–0280), **Delta** (800/221–1212), **Northwest** (tel. 800/225–2525), **United** (tel. 800/722–5243), and **USAir** (tel 800/428–4322).

**Flying Time** **To Montréal:** 1½ hours from New York, 2 hours from Chicago, 6 hours from Los Angeles, 6½ hours from London. **To Toronto:** 1½ hours from New York and Chicago, 4½ hours from Los Angeles. **To Calgary:** 5½ hours from New York, 3½ hours from Toronto, 4 hours from Los Angeles. **To Vancouver:** 6½ hours from Montréal, 4 hours from Chicago, 2½ hours from Los Angeles.

**Cutting Flight Costs** The Sunday travel section of most newspapers is a good source of deals. When booking, particularly through an unfamiliar company, call the Better Business Bureau or your local or state Consumer Protection Bureau to find out whether any complaints have been registered against the company, pay with a credit card if you can, and consider trip-cancellation and default insurance (*see* Insurance, *above*).

**Promotional Airfares** Less expensive fares, called promotional or discount fares, are round-trip and involve restrictions, which vary according to the route and season. You must usually buy the ticket—commonly called an APEX (advance purchase excursion) when it's for international travel—in advance (7, 14, or 21 days are usual), although some of the major airlines have added no-frills, cheap flights to compete with new bargain airlines on certain routes.

With the major airlines the cheaper fares generally require minimum- and maximum-stays (for instance, over a Saturday night or at least 7 and no more than 30 days). Airlines generally allow some return date changes for a $25 to $50 fee, but most low-fare tickets are nonrefundable. Only a death in the family would prompt the airline to return any of your money if you cancel a nonrefundable ticket. However, you can apply an unused nonrefundable ticket toward a new ticket, again with a small fee. The lowest fare is subject to availability, and only a small percentage of the plane's total seats will be sold at that price. Contact the U.S. Department of Transportation's Office of Consumer Affairs (I–25, Washington, DC 20590, tel. 202/366–2220) for a copy of "Fly-Rights: A Guide to Air Travel in the U.S." *The Official Frequent Flyer Guidebook* by Randy Petersen ($14.99 plus $3 shipping; 4715-C Town Center Dr., Colorado Springs, CO 80916, tel. 719/597–8899 or 800/487-8893, 800/485-8893) yields valuable hints on getting the most for your air travel dollars.

**Consolidators** Consolidators or bulk-fare operators—"bucket shops"—buy blocks of seats on scheduled flights that airlines anticipate they won't be able to sell. They pay wholesale prices, add a markup, and resell the seats to travel agents or directly to the public at prices that still undercut the airline's promotional or discount fares (higher than a charter ticket but lower than an APEX ticket, and usually without the advance-purchase restriction). Moreover, some consolidators sometimes give you your money back. Carefully read the fine print detailing penalties for changes and cancellations. If you doubt the reliability of a company, call the airline once you've made your booking and confirm that you do, indeed, have a reservation on the flight.

*Charter Flights*  Charters usually have the lowest fares and the most restrictions. Departures are limited and seldom on time, and you can lose all or most of your money if you cancel. (The closer to departure you cancel, the more you lose, although sometimes you will be charged only a small fee if you supply a substitute passenger.) The charterer may legally cancel the flight for any reason up to 10 days before departure; within 10 days of departure, the flight may be canceled only if it is physically impossible to operate it. The charterer may also revise the itinerary or increase the price after you have bought the ticket, but if the new arrangement constitutes a "major change," you have the right to a refund. Before buying a charter ticket, read the fine print for the company's refund policy and details on major changes. Money for charter flights is usually paid into a bank escrow account, the name of which should be on the contract. If you don't pay by credit card, make your check payable to the escrow account (unless you're dealing with a travel agent, in which case, his or her check should be payable to the escrow account). The U.S. Department of Transportation's Office of Consumer Affairs (I–25, Washington, DC 20590, tel. 202/366–2220) can answer questions on charters and send you its "Plane Talk: Public Charter Flights" information sheet.

Charter operators may offer flights alone or with ground arrangements that constitute a charter package. You typically must book charters through your travel agent. One good source is **Charterlink** (988 Sing Sing Rd., Horseheads, NY 14845, tel. 607/739–7148 or 800/221–1802), a no-fee charter broker that operates 24 hours a day.

*Discount*    Travel clubs offer their members unsold space on airplanes, cruise
*Travel Clubs*  ships, and package tours at nearly the last minute and at well below the original cost. Suppliers thus receive some revenue for their "leftovers," and members get a bargain. Membership generally includes a regular bulletin or access to a toll-free telephone hot line giving details of available trips departing anywhere from three or four days to several months in the future. Packages tend to be more common than flights alone, so if airfares are your only interest, read the literature before joining. Reductions on hotels are also available. Clubs include **Discount Travel International** (114 Forrest Ave., Suite 203, Narberth, PA 19072, tel. 215/668–7184; US$45 annually, single or family), **Entertainment Travel Editions** (Box 1014, Trumbull, CT 06611, tel. 800/445–4137; $28-$48 annually), **Great American Traveler** (Box 27965, Salt Lake City, UT 84127, tel. 800/548–2812; $29.95 annually), **Moment's Notice** (425 Madison Ave., New York, NY 10017, tel. 212/486–0503; US$45 annually, single or family), **Privilege Card** (3391 Peachtree Rd. NE, Suite 110, Atlanta, GA 30326, tel. 404/262–0222 or 800/236–9732; domestic annual membership $49.95, international, $74.95), **Travelers Advantage** (CUC Travel Service, 49 Music Sq. W, Nashville, TN 37203, tel. 800/548–1116; US$49 annually, single or family), and **Worldwide Discount Travel Club** (1674 Meridian Ave., Miami Beach, FL 33139, tel. 305/534–2082; US$50 annually for family, US$40 single).

**Enjoying**   Fly at night if you're able to sleep on a plane. Because the air aloft is
**the Flight**  dry, drink plenty of beverages while on board; remember that drinking alcohol contributes to jet lag, as do heavy meals. Sleepers usually prefer window seats to curl up against; restless passengers ask to be on the aisle. Bulkhead seats, in the front row of each cabin, have more legroom, but since there's no seat ahead, trays attach

awkwardly to the arms of your seat, and you must stow all posses-
sions overhead. Bulkhead seats are usually reserved for people with
disabilities, the elderly, and people traveling with babies.

**Smoking** Smoking is now banned on all domestic flights of less than six hours
duration in the United States, and on all Canadian flights, including
flights to and from Europe and the Far East. The U.S. ban also applies to domestic segments of international flights aboard U.S. and
foreign carriers.

## From the United States by Car

Drivers must have proper owner registration and proof of insurance
coverage, which is compulsory in Canada. The Canadian Non-Resi-
dent Inter-Provincial Motor Vehicle Liability Insurance Card, available from any U.S. insurance company, is accepted as evidence of
financial responsibility anywhere in Canada. Minimum insurance
requirement in Canada is $200,000, except in Québec where the min-
imum is $50,000. For more information, contact the Insurance Bu-
reau of Canada (181 University Ave., Toronto, Ont., M5H 3M7, tel.
416/362–2301). If you are driving a car that is not registered in your
name, carry a letter from the owner that authorizes your use of the
vehicle. (*See also* Getting around by Car, *below.*) The U.S. Interstate Highway System leads directly into Canada: I–95 from Maine
to New Brunswick; I–91 and I–89 from Vermont to Québec; I–87
from New York to Québec; I–81 and a spur off I–90 from New York to
Ontario; I–94, I–96, and I–75 from Michigan to Ontario; I–29 from
North Dakota to Manitoba; I–15 from Montana to Alberta; and I–5
from Washington state to British Columbia. Most of these connections hook up with the Trans-Canada Highway within a few miles.
There are many smaller highway crossings between the two countries as well.

From Alaska, take the Alaska Highway (from Fairbanks), the Klondike Highway (from Skagway), and the Top of the World Highway
(to Dawson City).

## From the United States by Train, Bus, and Ship

**By Train** **Amtrak** (tel. 800/872–7245) has service from New York to Montréal,
New York and Buffalo to Toronto, and Chicago to Toronto. Amtrak's
*Montrealer* departs from New York's Pennsylvania Station at 8:25 PM
and arrives in Montréal the next day at about 10:45 AM. Sleepers are
highly recommended for the overnight trip but must be booked well in
advance. The *Montrealer* is the only Amtrak train to Canada that requires reservations.

A second Amtrak train to Montréal leaves New York from Pennsylvania Station in the morning and takes 10½ hours; the trip from New
York to Toronto (passing through Buffalo) takes 11 hours and 45
minutes; travel from Chicago to Toronto takes 12 hours. In addition
to these direct routes, there are connections from many major cities.
At press time, Amtrak was scheduled to start daily rail service between Seattle and Vancouver by the end of 1994, providing connections in Seattle with Amtrak's U.S.-wide network and in Vancouver
with VIA Rail's Canadian trans-continental routes.

**By Bus** **Greyhound** (tel. 800/231–2222) has the most widespread bus service
to Canada, and you can get from almost any point in the United
States to any point in Canada on its extensive network. One of the
longest routes, from New York to Vancouver via Seattle, takes about
3½ days.

**By Ship** You can take a car ferry between the state of Washington and Vancouver Island or Maine and Nova Scotia (*see* Essential Information in individual chapters). Many Canadian cities are also accessible by water on private yachts and boats. Local marine authorities can advise you about the necessary documentation and procedure.

### From the United Kingdom by Plane

**Airlines** The major carriers between Great Britain and Canada are **Air Canada** (tel. 081/759–2331 in the London area, or 0800/181313 elsewhere), **British Airways** (tel. 081/897–4000), and **Canadian Airlines International** (tel. 071/930–3501). Air Canada has the most flights and serves the most cities, with at least one flight a day to Toronto, Vancouver, and Montréal from Heathrow, and considerably more at peak periods. Air Canada also flies to Calgary, Edmonton, Halifax, and St. John's from Heathrow; to Toronto from Birmingham and Manchester; and to Calgary, Halifax, Toronto, and Vancouver from Prestwick (Glasgow). British Airways has as many as 23 flights a week to Canada from Heathrow, serving Montréal, Toronto, and Vancouver. Canadian Airlines International serves Calgary, Edmonton, Ottawa, and Vancouver from London Gatwick, has at least one flight a day to Toronto, and has service from Manchester to Toronto.

# Staying in Canada

## Getting Around

**By Plane** **Air Canada** (tel. 800/776–3000) operates in every province. The other major domestic carrier is **Canadian Airlines International** (tel. 800/426–7000). Regularly scheduled flights to every major city and to most smaller cities are available on Air Canada or Canadian Airlines International or the domestic carriers associated with them: **Air Alliance** serves Québec; **Air Atlantic** flies in the Atlantic region; **Air BC** serves British Columbia and Alberta with new extended service out of Portland and Seattle; **Air Nova** serves Atlantic Canada; **Air Ontario** serves the Ontario region; and **First Air** includes a flight from Ottawa to New York. These airlines can be contacted at local numbers within each of the many cities they serve. Check with the territorial tourist agencies for charter companies and with the District Controller of Air Services in the territorial (and provincial) capitals for the locations of air bases that allow private flights and for regulations.

**By Train** Transcontinental rail service is provided by **VIA Rail Canada** (tel. 800/665–0200). If you're planning on traveling to several major cities in Canada, the train may be your best bet. Routes run across the country as well as within individual provinces, with the exception of the Northwest Territories and the Yukon, Newfoundland, and Prince Edward Island.

You can choose either sleeping-car or coach accommodations on most trains. Both classes allow access to dining cars. Sleeping-car passengers can enjoy comfortable parlor cars, drawing rooms, bedrooms, and roomettes. First-class seats, sleeping-car accommodations, and Dayniter seats between Ontario, Québec, and the maritime provinces require reservations. VIA has a new "Silver and Blue" service on its transcontinental trains that provides first-class "cruise" comfort and amenities including exclusive use of their dome car. **Rocky Mountain Railtours** (*see* Compass Travel, *below*) operates spectacular two-day, all daylight rail trips through the Canadian Rockies to the west coast. In the United Kingdom, **Compass Travel** (Box 113, Peterborough, PE1 1LE, tel. 0733/51780) represents both VIA Rail and Rocky Mountain Railtours.

**By Bus** The bus is an essential form of transportation in Canada, especially if you want to visit out-of-the-way towns that do not have airports or rail lines. Two major bus companies, **Greyhound** (222 1st Ave. SW, Calgary, AB, T2P 0A6, tel. 403/265–9111) and **Voyageur** (505 E Boulevard Maisonneuve H2L 1Y4, Montréal, tel. 514/843–4231), offer interprovincial service. In the United Kingdom, contact **Greyhound World Travel Ltd.,** Sussex House, London Road, E. Grinstead, West Surrey, RHI9 1LD (tel. 0342/317317).

**By Car** Canada's highway system is excellent. It includes the Trans-Canada Highway, the longest highway in the world, which runs about 5,000 miles from Victoria, British Columbia, to St. John's, Newfoundland, using ferries to bridge coastal waters at each end. The second-longest Canadian highway, the Yellowhead Highway, follows the old Indian route from the Pacific Coast and over the Rockies to the prairies. North of the population centers, roads become fewer and less developed.

You are required to wear seat belts (and use infant seats) except in the Yukon Territory. Some provinces have a statutory requirement to drive with vehicle headlights on for extended periods after dawn and before sunset. In the Yukon, the law requires headlights on at all times while driving on territory highways.

Speed limits vary from province to province, but they are usually within the 90–100 kph (50–60 mph) range outside the cities. The price of gasoline varies more than the speed limit, from 40¢ to 72¢ a liter. (There are 3.8 liters in a U.S. gallon, 4.5 liters in a Canadian Imperial gallon.) Distances are now always shown in kilometers, and gasoline is always sold in liters. The Imperial gallon is seldom used.

Foreign driver's licenses are valid in Canada. The International Driving Permit is also valid but must be accompanied by the visitor's state or national driver's license. Members of the Automobile Association of America (AAA) can contact the **Canadian Automobile Association** (1775 Courtwood Crescent, Ottawa, Ont. K2C 3J2, tel. 613/226–7631; emergency road service, tel. 800/336–4357). Members of the Automobile Association of Great Britain, the Royal Automobile Club, the Royal Scottish Automobile Club, the Royal Irish Automobile Club and the automobile clubs of the Alliance Internationale de Tourisme (AIT) and Fédération Internationale de l'Automobile (FIA) are entitled to all the services of the CAA on presentation of a membership card.

**By Ferry** Car ferries provide essential transportation on both the east and west coasts of Canada. **Marine Atlantic** (Box 250, North Sydney, NS B2A 3M3, tel. 902/794–5700 or 800/341–7981) operates ferries between Nova Scotia and Newfoundland; New Brunswick and Prince Edward Island; New Brunswick and Nova Scotia; and also between Portland, Maine, and Nova Scotia. On the west coast, the **British Columbia Ferry Corporation** (1112 Fort St., Victoria, BC V8V 4V2, tel. 604/656–0757) operates 38 ships among 42 ports of call. Other ferries also operate between the state of Washington and British Columbia's Vancouver Island.

## Telephones

Phones work as they do in the United States. Drop 25¢ in the slot and dial; pay phones accept American coins, unlike U.S. phones, which spit out Canadian money. There are no problems dialing direct to the United States; U.S. telephone credit cards are accepted. For directory assistance, dial 1, the area code, and 555–1212. To place calls outside Canada and the United States, dial "0" and ask for the overseas operator.

## Mail

**Postal Rates**   In Canada you can buy stamps at the post office or from automatic vending machines in most hotel lobbies, railway stations, airports, bus terminals, many retail outlets, and some newsstands. Within Canada, postcards and letters up to 30 grams cost 46¢; between 30 grams and a kilogram, the cost is $3.75. Letters and postcards to the United States cost 52¢ for up to 30 grams, and $3.40 for up to 250 grams. Prices include GST.

International mail and postcards run 92¢ for up to 30 grams, and $2.10 for up to 100 grams.

**Telepost** is a fast "next day or sooner" service that combines the CN/CP Telecommunications network with letter-carrier delivery service. Messages may be telephoned to the nearest CN/CP Public Message Centre for delivery anywhere in Canada or the United States. Telepost service is available 24 hours a day, seven days a week, and billing arrangements may be made at the time the message is called in. **Intelpost** allows you to send documents or photographs via satellite to many Canadian, American, and European destinations. This service is available at main postal facilities in Canada, and is paid for in cash.

Visitors may have mail sent to them c/o General Delivery in the town they are visiting, for pickup in person within 15 days, after which it will be returned to the sender.

## Tipping

Tips and service charges are not usually added to a bill in Canada. In general, tip 15% of the total bill. This goes for waiters, waitresses, barbers and hairdressers, taxi drivers, etc. Porters and doormen should get about 50¢–$1 a bag ($1 or more in a luxury hotel). For maid service, $1 a day is sufficient ($2 in luxury hotels).

## Opening and Closing Times

Stores, shops, and supermarkets are usually open Monday through Saturday from 9 to 6—although in major cities, supermarkets are often open from 7:30 AM until 9 PM. Blue laws are in effect in much of Canada, but a growing number of provinces have stores with limited Sunday hours, usually from noon to 5 (shops in areas highly frequented by tourists are usually open on Sunday). Retail stores are generally open on Thursday and Friday evenings, most shopping malls until 9 PM. Most banks in Canada are open Monday through Thursday from 10 to 3, and from 10 to 5 or 6 on Friday. Some banks are open longer hours and are also open on Saturday morning. All banks are closed on national holidays. Drugstores in major cities are often open until 11 PM, and convenience stores are often open 24 hours a day, seven days a week.

## GST and Sales Tax

A countrywide goods and services tax of 7% (GST) applies on virtually every transaction in Canada except for the purchase of basic groceries. Nonresidents can get a full GST refund on any purchase taken out of the country and on short-term accommodations (but not on food, drink, tobacco, car or motorhome rentals, or transportation); rebate forms, which must be submitted within 60 days of leaving Canada, may be obtained from certain retailers, duty-free shops, customs officials, or Revenue Canada (Visitor's Rebate Program, Ottawa, Ont. K1A 1J5, tel. in Canada 800/668-4748). Instant rebates are provided by some duty-free shops when leaving Canada, and most provinces do not tax goods that are shipped directly by the vendor to the purchaser's home. You'll need your sales slips.

In addition to the GST, all provinces except Alberta, the Northwest Territories, and the Yukon levy a sales tax from 5% to 12% on most items purchased in shops, on restaurant meals, and sometimes on hotel rooms. Alberta and Ontario charge 5% tax on hotel rooms, for example; British Columbia adds 8%; and New Brunswick, 11%. Nova Scotia and Newfoundland offer a sales-tax rebate system similar to the federal one; call the provincial toll-free information lines for details (*see* Government Tourist Offices, *above*).

---

## Shopping

**Antiques** On the whole, prices for antiques are lower in Canada than in the United States. Shops along Montréal's rue Sherbrooke Ouest stock everything from ancient maps to fine crystal; Vieux-Montréal and the rue Notre-Dame sell antiques and collectibles ranging from Napoléonic-period furniture to 1950s bric-a-brac. Toronto's offerings are equally eclectic, although priced higher than elsewhere in Canada. (But for comparison's sake, consider that many Toronto antiques dealers send their wares to New York City, where the price is doubled before it goes on the sales floor.) The Yorkville area, with its European collections, caters to interior designers, although the markets at Lansdowne and Harbourfront are livelier and have wider selections. Antiques shopping is a respectable pastime in Vancouver as well, and Victoria offers some of the best buys in antique silver in the shops clustered on Fort Street.

**Arts and Crafts** Sweaters, silver objects, pottery, and Acadian crafts can be found in abundance in New Brunswick. For pewter, head for Fredericton. For woven items, visit the village of St. Andrews. In Québec, check out the wood carvings. The Mennonite communities of Ontario sell their handmade quilts each May at the Mennonite Relief sale. Prices can run to $2,000 for a large quilt.

**Native Canadian Art** Interest has grown in the highly collectible art and sculpture of the Inuit, usually rendered in soapstone. For the best price and a guarantee of authenticity, purchase Inuit and other native crafts in the province where they originate. Many styles are now attributed to certain tribes and are mass-produced for sale in galleries and shops miles away from their regions of origin. At the very top galleries you can be assured of getting pieces done by individual artists, though the prices will be higher than in the provinces of origin. The Canadian government has registered the symbol of an igloo as a mark of a work's authenticity. Be sure this Canadian government sticker or tag is attached before you make your purchase. Many galleries and shops in the west also carry work done by Native Canadians of the Northwest, who have revived their ancient art. They are known for their highly stylized masks, totem poles, and canoes. Themes and images from nature, such as whales, bears, wolves, and eagles, are prominent in their work. Bright colors and geometric patterns distinguish their woven products: blankets, wall hangings, and clothing.

In and around Calgary you can find ceremonial headdresses, clothing, and tools made by the nomadic Plains tribes. Algonkian and Iroquoian art survives mainly in the museums of eastern Canada and in the gift shops of some of the reservations in Ontario.

**Maple Syrup**　Eastern Canada is famous for its sugar maples. The trees are tapped in early spring, and the sap is collected in buckets to be boiled down into maple syrup. This natural confection is sold all year. Avoid the tourist shops and department stores; for the best prices and information, stop at farm stands and markets in the provinces of Québec, Ontario, and New Brunswick. A small can of syrup costs about $6–$9.

## National Parks

Banff, the country's first national park, was established in 1885, and since then the national park system has grown to encompass 34 national parks and 112 national historic sites. Because of Canada's eagerness to preserve its environment, new lands are continually being added to this network. Almost every park offers camping—either primitive camping or campsites with various facilities that can accommodate recreational vehicles. Hiking trails weave their way through each of the parks. Among the most popular preserves are Fundy National Park in New Brunswick and several Rocky Mountain parks. Environment Canada (Inquiry Center, Ottawa, Ont. K1A 0H3, tel. 819/997–2800) publishes *Canada's National Parks* and *Canada's National Historic Sites*, with descriptions and other key information.

## Participant Sports and Outdoor Activities

**Biking**　Eastern and western Canada offer some of the best bicycling terrain. In the east, bikers favor the Gaspé Peninsula in Québec and the surrounding Atlantic provinces. The terrain varies from very hilly around the Gaspé to flat on Prince Edward Island, and varied in New Brunswick and Nova Scotia. A western tour might include the area around the Rocky Mountains and on through British Columbia. Some cities, such as Vancouver and Ottawa, have bike trails marked throughout town. Write to the provincial tourist boards for road maps (which are more detailed than the maps available at gas stations) and information on local cycling associations.

**Boating**　With so much coastline—on the Atlantic and Pacific, the Great Lakes, major rivers, and thousands of smaller lakes—boating is extremely popular throughout Canada. Boat rentals are widely available, and provincial tourism departments can provide lists of companies.

**Camping**　Canada's 2,000-plus campgrounds range from simple roadside turnoffs with sweeping mountain vistas to fully equipped facilities with groomed sites, trailer hookups, recreational facilities, and vacation village atmosphere. Many of the best sites are in Canada's national and provincial parks, with nominal overnight fees. Commercial campgrounds offer more amenities, such as electrical and water hookups, showers, and even game rooms and grocery stores. They cost more and are—some think—antithetical to the point of camping: getting a little closer to nature. Contact tourist offices for listings.

**Canoeing and Kayaking**  Your degree of expertise and experience will dictate where you will canoe. Beginners will look for waterways in more settled areas; the pros will head north to the streams and rivers that flow into the Arctic Ocean. Provincial tourist offices and the federal Department of Northern Development and Indian Affairs (Ottawa, Ont. K1A OH4, tel. 819/997–0002) can be of assistance, especially in locating an outfitter to suit your needs. You can also contact the **Canadian Recreational Canoeing Association** (5–1029 Hyde Park Rd., London, Ont. N0M 1Z0, tel. 519/473–2109).

**Fishing**  Anglers can find their catch in virtually any region of the country, though restrictions, seasons, license requirements, and bag limits vary from province to province. In addition, a special fishing permit is required to fish in all national parks; it can be obtained at any national park site, for a nominal fee. **Newfoundland** offers cod, mackerel, salmon, and sea trout in the Atlantic and speckled trout and rainbow trout in its other waters. The waters surrounding **Prince Edward Island** have some of the best deep-sea tuna fishing. **Nova Scotia** has some of the most stringent freshwater restrictions in Canada, but the availability of Atlantic salmon, speckled trout, and striped bass makes the effort worthwhile. Salmon, trout, and black bass are abundant in the waters of **New Brunswick,** and although many salmon pools in the streams and rivers are leased to private freeholders, either individuals or clubs, fly fishing is still readily available for visitors. The lakes of **Québec** hold trout, bass, pike, and landlocked salmon, called ouananiche (pronounced *Wah*-nah-nish). Just about every kind of North American freshwater game fish is available in some part of **Ontario. Manitoba** and **Saskatchewan** offer lake trout, brook trout, pike, grayling, walleye, Hudson Bay salmon, and smallmouth bass. They also offer a winter fishing season, but some areas require a guide. **Alberta** is considered a paradise for sportfishers, with its trout in streams; its pike, walleye, and perch in lakes; and its grayling, goldeye, and whitefish in rivers. **British Columbia** is unparalleled for salmon, but only two of the five species may be taken in nontidal waters. **Northwest Territories** offers Arctic char, lake trout, and grayling in the Great Bear and Great Slave lakes.

**Golf**  Every province has something for the duffer, but British Columbia and Ontario dominate the golf scene. Ontario has nearly 400 golf courses. British Columbia also has many golf courses, and Victoria's mild weather makes it especially appealing to golfers. Because public courses are often overcrowded, if you are a member of a golf club, check to see if it has a reciprocal playing arrangement with any of the private clubs in the areas that you will be visiting.

**Hiking**  Miles and miles of trails weave through all of Canada's national and provincial parks. Write to the individual provincial tourist offices (*see* Essential Information in individual chapters) or the Inquiry Center for the National Parks Department (*see* National Parks, *above*).

**Horseback Riding**  This sport is popular out West, especially in places like Banff National Park in Alberta, which has many outfitters that can arrange week-long trips on the park's trails. Contact the park's information center (tel. 403/762–3324) for more details. There are a growing number of working ranches in Alberta and British Columbia that offer horseback vacations.

**Hunting** As with fishing, hunting is governed by federal, provincial, and territorial laws. You will need a hunting license from each province or territory in which you plan to hunt. A federal permit is required for hunting migratory game birds and is available at most Canadian post offices. Weapons of any type are prohibited in many of Canada's provincial parks and reserves and adjacent areas, and no hunting is permitted in Canada's national parks. Guides are required in many places and are available almost everywhere. Provincial tourist offices can provide specific information.

**Mountain Climbing** Offering mountain climbers a challenge are the summits of Banff and Jasper national parks in Alberta and the provincial park of Mt. Robson and Yoho National Park in British Columbia. Mountain climbing should not be undertaken lightly. Write to the Inquiry Center (*see* National Parks, *above*) for more information about these parks or contact mountaineering organizations listed in individual chapters.

**Scuba Diving** More than 3,000 shipwrecks lie off the coast of Nova Scotia, making it particularly attractive to divers. The provincial Department of Tourism can provide details on the location of wrecks and where to buy or rent equipment. In Ontario, the Fathom Five National Marine Park has been established at the tip of Georgian Bay's Bruce Peninsula. Here 20 known wrecks can be explored in exceptionally clear waters. A wealth of sea life makes diving in coastal areas of British Columbia particularly attractive. Contact **Dive B.C.** (707 Westminster Ave., Powell River, BC V8A 1C5, tel. 604/485–6267).

**Skiing** Skiing is probably the most popular winter sport in Canada. For downhill skiing there are slopes in every province, but those in Québec, Alberta, and British Columbia are the best. Alberta and British Columbia also offer heli-skiing trips. For cross-country skiing, almost any provincial or national park will do. (*See* the individual chapters.)

**Whale Watching** The shores off British Columbia are some of the best places to observe whales, seals, and other natural wildlife. Day-long and sometimes week-long boat trips are offered. In the Pacific Ocean, along Vancouver Island, migrating whales pass on their way to California breeding grounds in the fall and come back in the spring. On the Atlantic coast, the waters around Newfoundland offer excellent whale watching, and giant humpback, right whales, finback, and minke whales can be seen in the Bay of Fundy. Boat trips are available from New Brunswick and Nova Scotia. The St. Lawrence River estuary, particularly near the mouth of the Saguenay River, is another important whale-watching area.

**White-Water Rafting** There are opportunities for rafting in almost every province, but the white waters of Ontario and British Columbia are especially inviting for thrill seekers. Commercial rafting companies offer a variety of trip packages.

**Winter Sports** Canadians flourish in winter, as the range of winter sports attests. In addition to the sports already mentioned, at the first drop of a snowflake Canadians will head outside to ice-skate, toboggan, snowmobile, dogsled, snowshoe, and ice-fish.

## Spectator Sports

**Baseball** If you're missing a bit of Americana, don't fret. Baseball has been a favorite in Canada since the major leagues expanded into Montréal in 1969 with the Montréal Expos, and the Toronto Blue Jays formed a World Series–caliber club. The Toronto Blue Jays won the World Series in 1992 (the first time a non–U.S. team played in and won the baseball championship) and again in 1993. Minor league teams compete in Vancouver, Edmonton, Calgary, Lethbridge, and Medicine Hat.

**Curling**  For a true taste of Canadian sportsmanship you might want to watch a curling match, which is not unlike a shuffleboard game on ice. Two teams of four players each compete by sliding large polished granite stones toward the center of a bullseye, or "house."

**Football**  The Canadian Football League plays the game its own way, allowing three downs, a 110-yard field, and 12 players per side. Teams are located in Toronto, Ottawa, Hamilton, Winnipeg, Regina, Calgary, Edmonton, and Vancouver. The CFL has recently expanded into the U.S. cities of Sacramento, CA, and Las Vegas, NV.

**Hockey**  Officially, Canada's national sport is lacrosse, but ice hockey is the national favorite. It's played by children and professionals alike, with leagues and teams organized everywhere. The National Hockey League teams in Canada include the Vancouver Canucks, Calgary Flames, Winnipeg Jets, Edmonton Oilers, Toronto Maple Leafs, Ottawa Senators, Montréal Canadiens, and Québec Nordiques. The season runs from October to April.

**Rodeos and Horse Racing**  Alberta is rodeo country. The biggest and most famous event is the Calgary Stampede held every year in July. Thoroughbred racing during the spring, summer, and fall takes place in Ontario, Manitoba, Saskatchewan, Alberta, and British Columbia.

## Dining

The earliest European settlers of Canada—the British and the French—bequeathed a rather bland diet of meat and potatoes. But though there are few really distinct national dishes here, except in Québec, the strong ethnic presence in Canada makes it difficult not to have a good meal. This is especially true in the larger cities, where Greek, Italian, Chinese, Indian, and other immigrants operate restaurants. In addition, each province is well known for various specialties. **Ontario** is famous for its cheeses, while seafood usually heads the menu at restaurants in **British Columbia, Newfoundland, Nova Scotia, New Brunswick,** and **Prince Edward Island.** Fiddleheads, curled young fern fronds picked in the spring, often accompany dishes in the maritime provinces of New Brunswick, Nova Scotia, and Prince Edward Island. Leave your vegetarian tendencies at home when visiting **Alberta** and **Saskatchewan,** where the meals invariably center on thick steaks and roasts. In some areas of Canada, especially in the plains, you may be lucky enough to find some Native treats, such as venison, pheasant, and buffalo meat accompanied by fiddlehead ferns in the spring or wild rice. And vestiges of what the European settlers learned from the Native Americans is evident in the hearty ingredients that make up the French Canadian cuisine, which thrives in **Québec.** To enjoy the best of the province's hearty meat pies and pâtés, head to Québec City; Montréal dining tends to be more classic French than French Canadian.

## Lodging

Aside from the quaint hotels of Québec, Canada's range of accommodations more closely resembles that of the United States than Europe. In the cities you'll have a choice of luxury hotels, moderately priced modern properties, and smaller older hotels with perhaps fewer conveniences but a bit more charm. Options in smaller towns and in the country include large, full-service resorts; small, privately owned hotels; roadside motels; and bed-and-breakfast establishments. Canada's answer to the small European family-run hotel is the mom-and-pop motel, but even though Canada is as attuned to automobile travel as the United States, you won't find these motels as frequently. Even here you'll need to make reservations at least on the day on which you're planning to pull into town.

**Chain Hotels** There are two advantages to staying at a chain hotel. The first is that you'll be assured of standard accommodations, your own bathroom, and a range of services at the front desk. The second is the ease with which you can get information and make or change reservations, since most chains have toll-free booking numbers.

The major hotel chains in Canada include **Best Western International** (tel. 800/528–1234, in the U.K., 081/541–0033), **CP (Canadian Pacific) Hotels & Resorts** (tel. 800/828–7447, in the U.K., 071/798–9866), **Delta Hotels** (tel. 800/877–1133, in the U.K., 071/937–8033), **Four Seasons Hotels** (tel. 800/332–3442, in the U.K., 081/941–7941), **Holiday Inns** (tel. 800/465–4329, in the U.K., 071/722–7755), **Howard Johnson Hotels** (tel. 800/654–2000, in the U.K., 081/688–1640), **Radisson Hotels** (tel. 800/333–3333, in the U.K., 0992/441517), **Ramada** (tel. 800/228–2828, in the U.K., 071/235–5264), **Sheraton** (tel. 800/325–3535, in the U.K., 0800/353535), **Travelodge** (tel. 800/255–3050, in the U.K., 0345/404040), and **Westin Hotels** (tel. 800/228–3000, in the U.K., 071/408–0636).

**Room Rates** Expect accommodations to cost more in summer, peak tourist season, than in the off-season. But don't be afraid to ask about special deals and packages when reserving. Big city hotels that cater to business travelers often offer weekend packages, and many city hotels offer rooms at up to 50% off in winter. If you're planning to visit a major city or resort area during the high season, book well in advance. Also be aware of any special events or festivals that may coincide with your visit and block every room for miles around. For resorts and lodges, consider the winter ski-season high as well and plan accordingly (*See* GST and Sales Tax, *above*).

**Bed-and-Breakfasts and Country Inns** One way to save on lodging and spend some time with a native Canadian is to stay at a bed-and-breakfast establishment. They are gaining in popularity and are located in both the country and the cities. Every provincial tourist board either has a listing of B&Bs or can refer you to an association that will help you secure reservations. Rates range from $20 to upwards of $70 a night and include a Continental or a full breakfast. Because most bed-and-breakfasts are in private homes, you might not have your own bathroom. And some B&B hosts lock up early. Be sure to ask about your host's policies. Room quality varies from home to home as well, so don't be bashful about asking to see a room before making a choice. **Fodor's** guide *Canada's Great Country Inns* lists wonderful places to stay from coast to coast—from unpretentious houses with something special to the elegant Relais & Châteaux (*see below*). You can buy it in most bookstores or ask to have it ordered.

**Farm Vacations** Vacations on working farms and ranches are one way to enjoy the Canadian countryside. Depending on the size of the farm and the farmer's preferences, you'll be able to observe or even participate in daily activities. These stays include breakfast and some offer other meals and special family rates. For more information about farm vacations, contact the **Canadian Country Vacations Association** (525 Kylemore Ave., Winnipeg, Manitoba R3L 1B5, tel. 204/475-6624).

**Dorms and Hostels** There are a few alternatives to camping for those on a budget. Among them are hostels, which are open to young and old, families, and singles (*see* Student and Youth Travel, *above*) and university campuses, which open their dorms to travelers for overnight stays from May through August.

**Relais &** Canada has 11 members of this prestigious association where rates
**Châteaux** run from $150 to $450 a night. Many of these small hotels and inns once served as private estates to the Canadian wealthy. One property is set in a wildlife preserve in the Algonquin Park in Ontario; another is in the countryside, just 30 minutes from Montréal. Reservations must be made directly with each property; for a complete list contact **Relais & Châteaux** (tel. 800/743–8033; 800/677–3524 for reservations).

**Home** You can find a house, apartment, or other vacation property to ex-
**Exchange** change for your own by becoming a member of a home-exchange organization, which then sends you its annual directories listing available exchanges and includes your own listing in at least one of them. Arrangements for the actual exchange are made by the two parties to it, not by the organization. For more information contact the **International Home Exchange Association** (IHEA, 41 Sutter St., Suite 1090, San Francisco, CA 94104, tel. 415/673–0347 or 800/788–2489). Principal clearinghouses: **HomeLink International** (Box 650, Key West, FL 33041, tel. 800/638–3841), with thousands of foreign and domestic listings, publishes four annual directories plus updates; the $50 membership includes your listing in one book. **Intervac International** (Box 590504, San Francisco, CA 94159, tel. 415/435–3497) has three annual directories; membership is $62, or $72 if you want to receive the directories but remain unlisted. **Loan-a-Home** (2 Park La., Apt. 6E, Mount Vernon, NY 10552, tel. 914/664–7640) specializes in long-term exchanges; there is no charge to list your home, but the directories cost $35 or $45 depending on the number you receive.

**Apartment** If you want a home base that's roomy enough for a family and comes
**and Villa** with cooking facilities, a furnished rental may be the solution. It's
**Rentals** generally cost-wise a good solution, too, although not always—some rentals are luxury properties (economical only when your party is large). Home-exchange directories do list rentals—often second homes owned by prospective house swappers—and there are services that can not only look for a house or apartment for you (even a castle if that's your fancy) but also handle the paperwork. Some send an illustrated catalogue and others send photographs of specific properties, sometimes at a charge; up-front registration fees may apply.

Among the companies are **Property Rentals International** (1 Park West Circle, Suite 108, Midlothian, VA 23113, tel. 804/378–6054 or 800/220–3332) and **Rent a Home International** (7200 34th Ave. NW, Seattle, WA 98117, tel. 206/789–9377 or 800/488–7368). **Hideaways International** (15 Goldsmith St., Box 1270, Littleton, MA 01460, tel. 508/486–8955 or 800/843–4433) functions as a travel club. Membership (US$99 yearly per person or family at the same address) includes two annual guides plus quarterly newsletters; rentals are arranged directly between members, not by the club staff.

**Provincial** There is no national government rating system for hotels, but many
**Ratings** provinces rate their accommodations. For example, in British Columbia and Alberta, a blue Approved Accommodation decal on the window or door of a hotel or motel indicates that it has met provincial hotel association standards for courtesy, comfort, and cleanliness. Ontario's voluntary rating system boasts about 1,000 Ontario properties.

## Credit Cards

The following credit card abbreviations are used throughout this guide: AE, American Express; D, Discover; DC, Diners Club; MC, MasterCard; V, Visa. It's a good idea to call ahead to check current credit-card policies.

# 2 Toronto

*By Allan
Gould*

*Updated by
Bernard
Simon*

A joke popular in the neighboring province of Québec between the wars went "First prize, one week in Toronto. Second prize, two weeks in Toronto. Third prize, three weeks in Toronto." Toronto was a deadly city, right into the 1950s, at which time its half-million citizens used to rush off to Detroit (a four-hour drive to the southwest) and Buffalo (90 minutes to the south, around Lake Ontario) for a good time. Today, of course, the rushing is in the opposite direction.

Like many cities around the world, Toronto has had some tough breaks over the past five years, including rising unemployment, upscale restaurants going out of business, and the new, brutal 7% federal goods and services tax, alias GST, shaking businesses and tourism to the core. (In many cases, that 7% is tacked on to the already steep 8% provincial [Ontario] sales tax.) Indeed, international studies often rate Toronto as among the most expensive cities in the Western Hemisphere. However expensive Toronto may be for those who live here, though, it need not be oppressively so for visitors, who can benefit from the city's numerous free events, special hotel packages, and the rebate of much of the GST. What's more, in 1994 the local economy had started to pick up again. Canada's biggest city—buoyed by two back-to-back World Series wins by the local Blue Jays and the arrival of a brand-new National Basketball League franchise—was regaining the vibrance which marked its heady growth in the 1980s.

Much of Toronto's excitement is explained by its ethnic diversity. Nearly two-thirds of the 3.2 million people who now live in the metropolitan area were born and raised somewhere else. Half a million Italians live here, as does the largest Chinese community in Canada and the biggest Portuguese colony in North America. What this has meant to Toronto is the rather rapid creation of a vibrant mix of cultures that has echoes of turn-of-the-century New York City—but without the slums, crowding, disease, and tensions.

Still, to give to its burgeoning ethnic population all, or even most, of the credit for Toronto's becoming a cosmopolitan, world-class city in just a few decades would be a kind of reverse racism, and not totally correct, either. Much of the thanks must be given to the so-called dour Scots who set up the banks, built the churches, and created the kind of solid base for a community that would come to such a healthy fruition in the four decades following World War II. Toronto is clearly this country's center of culture, commerce, and communications—"New York run by the Swiss," according to Peter Ustinov.

Toronto has gained the nickname Hollywood North, because dozens of major films have been made in this city, especially over the past decade, from *Moonstruck* to *Used People*, and from David Cronenberg's *Dead Ringers* and *Naked Lunch* to such TV series as *Top Cops, Class of '96, Road to Avalon*, and many more. Indeed, it is hard to walk about the city nowadays without tripping over a movie crew and a number of famous people. But since this is Canada—and Toronto—you'll probably all apologize sweetly.

# Essential Information

## Arriving and Departing by Plane

**Airports and
Airlines**  Flights into Toronto land at the **Lester B. Pearson International Airport,** so named in 1984 to honor Canada's Nobel Peace Prize–winning prime minister from nearly three decades ago. It's commonly

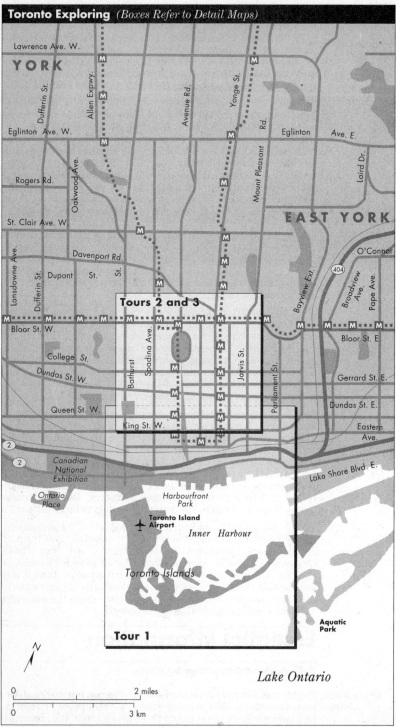

**Toronto Exploring** *(Boxes Refer to Detail Maps)*

YORK

Lawrence Ave. W.

Dufferin St.

Allen Expwy.

Avenue Rd.

Yonge St.

Eglinton Ave. W.

Rogers Rd.

Oakwood Ave.

St. Clair Ave. W.

Lansdowne Ave.

Dufferin St.

Dupont St.

Davenport Rd.

Eglinton Ave. E.

Laird Dr.

EAST YORK

O'Connor

Bayview Ext.

404

Broadview Ave.

Pape Ave.

Mount Pleasant Rd.

**Tours 2 and 3**

Bloor St. W.

Spadina Ave.

Jarvis St.

College St.

Dundas St. W.

Bathurst

Queen St. W.

King St. W.

Parliament St.

Bloor St. E.

Gerrard St. E.

Dundas St. E.

Eastern Ave.

2

Canadian National Exhibition

Ontario Place

Lake Shore Blvd. E.

Harbourfront Park

Toronto Island Airport

Inner Harbour

Toronto Islands

Aquatic Park

**Tour 1**

Lake Ontario

N

0                    2 miles

0                    3 km

called "the Toronto airport" or "Malton" (after the once-small town where it was built, just northwest of the city). The impact of the recession on airline traffic, and long-overdue improvements to the airport itself make a visitor's arrival a less traumatic experience than it was three or four years ago. The cavernous Terminal 3, which opened in 1991 and is used mainly by Canadian Airlines International, American Airlines, and United Airlines, is seldom congested these days. The once-dreary Terminal 2, the home of Air Canada and USAir, among others, has also undergone a facelift. Terminal 1, which was built in 1964, shows its age; but at least the peak-hour pandemonium is a thing of the past. Airlines using Terminal 1 include Northwest and Delta. One annoyance at Terminal 3, the only one of the three terminals which is privately-owned, is that a C$1 fee is charged for baggage carts.

Toronto is served by **American** (tel. 800/433–7300), **Delta** (tel. 800/843–9378), **Northwest** (tel. 800/225–2525), **United** (tel. 800/241–6522), **USAir** (tel. 800/428–4322), **Air Canada** (tel. 800/422–6232), **Canadian Airlines International** (tel. 800/387–2737), as well as more than a dozen European carriers with easy connections to many U.S. cities. **Air Ontario,** affiliated with Air Canada (tel. 416/925–2311), flies from the small, downtown Island Airport to and from Ottawa, Montréal, London, Ontario, and Newark. It is a good alternative to Pearson International for those staying downtown and making trips to these cities.

**Between the Airport and Center City** Although Pearson is not far from the downtown area (about 32 kilometers, or 18 miles), the drive can take well over an hour during Toronto's weekday rush hours (7–9 and 3:30–6:30). Taxis and limos to a hotel or attraction near the lake typically cost $30 or more. Airport cabs have fixed rates to different parts of the city. You have little choice but to pay the full fare from the airport, but it is often possible to negotiate a lower fare from downtown, where airport cabs have to compete with regular city cabs for business. It is illegal for city cabs to pick up passengers at the airport, unless they are specifically called—a time-consuming process, but sometimes worth the wait.

Many airport and downtown hotels offer free buses from each of Toronto's three terminals. Travelers on a budget should consider the express coaches offered by **Grey Coach** (tel. 416/393–7911), which link the airport to three subway stops in the southwest and north-central areas of the city. Buses depart several times each hour, from 8 AM to 11:30 PM. Fares average $6–$7. Even better is the service to and from several downtown hotels, which operates every 30 minutes from 6 AM to midnight daily and costs approximately $11.

Should you be renting a car at the airport, be sure to ask for a street map of the city. Highway 427 runs south, some 5.8 kilometers (3.6 miles) to the lakeshore. Here you pick up the Queen Elizabeth Way (QEW or Queen E) east to the Gardiner Expressway, which runs east into the heart of downtown. If you take the QEW west, you'll find yourself swinging around Lake Ontario, toward Hamilton, Niagara-on-the-Lake, and Niagara Falls.

## Arriving and Departing by Train, Bus, and Car

**By Train** **Amtrak** (tel. 800/872–7245) runs a daily train to Toronto from Chicago (a 12-hour trip), and another from New York City (11 hours). From Union Station you can walk underground to many hotels—a real boon in inclement weather.

**By Bus** **Greyhound** (tel. 416/393–7911) has regular bus service into Toronto from all over the United States and Canada. From Detroit, the trip takes five hours; from Buffalo, two to three hours; from Chicago and New York City, 11 hours. Buses arrive at 610 Bay Street, just above Dundas Street.

**By Car** Drivers should have proper owner registration and proof of insurance coverage. There is no need for an international driver's license; any valid one will do. You may be asked several questions at the border crossing, none of them terribly personal or offensive: your place of birth; your citizenship; your expected length of stay. Every fourth or fifth car may be searched, and this can increase the wait at peak visiting times to 30 minutes. A recent explosion of cross-border shopping finds thousands of Canadians shuttling across the border every month to take advantage of lower gas, food, and even appliance prices, so expect those Detroit–Windsor and Buffalo–Fort Erie crossings to take even longer, especially on weekends and holidays. It's true, however, that the popularity of cross-border shopping has declined along with the slide of the Canadian dollar to less than 80¢ (American), but gas, cigarettes, and many other items are still much cheaper on the U.S. side.

The wonderfully wide Highway 401—it reaches up to 16 lanes as it slashes across Metro Toronto from the airport on the west almost as far as the zoo on the east—is the major link between Windsor, Ontario (and Detroit), and Montréal, Québec. It's also known as the Macdonald-Cartier Freeway but is really never called anything other than "the 401." There are no tolls, but be warned: In weekday rush hours the 401 can become dreadfully crowded, even stop-and-go. Plan your trips to avoid these times.

Those who are driving from Buffalo, New York, or Niagara Falls should take the Queen Elizabeth Way, which curves up along the western shore of Lake Ontario, eventually turns into the Gardiner Expressway, and flows right into the downtown core.

Yonge Street, which begins at the Lakefront, is called Highway 11 once you get north of Toronto and continues all the way to the Ontario–Minnesota border, at Rainy River. At 1,896.2 kilometers (1,178.3 miles), it is the longest street in the world (as noted in the *Guinness Book of World Records*). We trust that you are duly impressed.

## Getting Around

Most of Toronto is laid out on a grid pattern. The key street to remember is Yonge Street (pronounced "young"), which is the main north–south artery. Most major cross streets are numbered east and west of Yonge Street. In other words, if you are looking for 180 St. Clair Avenue West, you want a building a few blocks *west* of Yonge Street; 75 Queen Street East is a block or so *east* of Yonge Street.

At press time, the fare for buses, streetcars, and trolleys was $2 in exact change, but 10 adult tickets/tokens cost $13, which lowers the price per journey a bit. All fares will undoubtedly have risen at least a nickel or dime during 1994, since prices did not change in 1993—the first time in a dozen years. Children (2–13) pay only 50¢ in exact change, and may purchase eight tickets for $2.50. Two-fare tickets are available for $3 for adults. Visitors who plan to stay in Toronto for more than a month should consider the **Metropass**, a photo-identity card that costs $67 for adults plus $2.75 extra for the photo (and, yes, probably a few dollars more than that, as of January 1995).

Families should take advantage of the so-called **Day Pass.** It costs $5 and is good for unlimited travel for one person, Monday–Friday after 9:30 AM, and all day Saturday. On Sunday and holidays, it's good for up to six persons (maximum two adults) for unlimited travel. For information on how to take public transit to any street or attraction in the city call 416/393–INFO from 7 AM to 11:30 PM. A very useful **Ride Guide** is published by the Toronto Transit Commission each year. It shows nearly every major place of interest and how to reach it by public transit. These guides are available in most subways and many other places around the city. The subways stop at 2 AM, but the Toronto Transit Commission runs bus service from 1 to 5:30 AM on most major streets, including King, Queen, College, Bloor, Yonge, and as far north as Sheppard, Finch, and Steeles.

**By Subway** The Toronto Transit Commission runs one of the safest, cleanest, most trustworthy systems of its kind anywhere. There are two major subway lines, with 60 stations along the way: the **Bloor/Danforth Line,** which crosses Toronto about 4.8 kilometers (3 miles) north of the Lakefront, from east to west, and the **Yonge/University/Spadina Line,** which loops north and south, like a giant "U," with the bottom of the "U" at Union Station. Tokens and tickets are sold in each subway station and at hundreds of convenience stores along the many routes of the TTC. Get your transfers just after you pay your fare and enter the subway; you'll find them in machines on your way down to the trains.

**By Bus** All buses and streetcars accept exact change, tickets, or tokens. Paper transfers are free; pick one up from the driver at the time that you pay your fare.

**By Taxi** The meter begins at $2.20, and includes the first .2 kilometer. Each additional .2 kilometer is 20¢—as is each additional passenger in excess of four. The waiting time "while under engagement" is 20¢ for every 33 seconds—and in one of the horrible traffic jams, this could add up. Still, it's possible to take a cab across downtown Toronto for $6–$8. The largest companies are **Beck** (tel. 416/467–0067), **Co-op** (tel. 416/364–8161), **Diamond** (tel. 416/366–6868), **Metro** (tel. 416/363–5611), and **Royal** (tel. 416/785–3322). For more information, call the Metro Licensing Commission (tel. 416/392–3000).

**By Car** Pedestrian crosswalks are sprinkled throughout the city; they are marked clearly by overhead signs and very large painted Xs. All a pedestrian has to do is stick out a hand, and cars (hopefully!) screech to a halt in both directions. Right turns on red lights are nearly always permitted, except where otherwise posted. You must come to a complete stop before making the turn.

## Important Addresses and Numbers

**Tourist Information** The **Metropolitan Toronto Convention & Visitors Association** has its office at Queen's Quay Terminal (207 Queen's Quay W, Suite 509, M5J 1A7, tel. 416/203–2500 or 800/363–1990). Booths providing brochures and pamphlets about the city and its attractions, as well as accommodations, are set up in the summer outside the Eaton Centre, on Yonge Street just below Dundas Street, and outside the Royal Ontario Museum.

The **Traveller's Aid Society** is not just for the down-and-out. This is a nonprofit group whose 130 volunteers can recommend restaurants and hotels, and distribute subway maps, tourist publications, and Ontario sales tax rebate forms. *In Union Station, Room B23 on the basement level and also on the Arrivals level; tel. 416/366–7788.*

*Open daily 9–9. In Terminal I at Pearson Airport, Arrivals level,*
*past Customs, near Area B; tel. 416/676–2868. Open daily 9 AM–*
*10 PM. In Terminal 2, between International and Domestic Arrivals,*
*tel. 416/676–2869. Open daily 9 AM–10 PM. In Terminal 3, Arrivals*
*level, near the International side; tel. 416/612–5890. Open daily 9 AM–*
*10 PM.*

**Consulates** The **Consulate General of the United States** (360 University Ave.,
just north of Queen St., M56 1S4, tel. 416/595–0228).

The **British Consulate General** (777 Bay St., at the corner of College
St., M56 2G2, tel. 416/593–1267).

For all other consulates—there are dozens of countries represented
in Toronto—look up "Consulate Generals" in the white pages of the
phone book.

**Emergencies** Dial 911 for **police** and **ambulance.**

*Doctors and* Check the Yellow Pages or ask at your hotel desk. Also, call **Dial-a-**
*Dentists* **Doctor** (tel. 416/756–6259), or the **Dental Emergency Service** (tel.
416/967–5649).

*24-hour* **Pharma Plus Drugmart** (Church St. and Wellesley Ave., tel. 416/
*Pharmacies* 924–7760); **Lucliff Place** (700 Bay St., tel. 416/979–2424); **Shoppers
Drug Mart** (2500 Hurontario St., Mississauga, tel. 416/568–3201).

*Road* The **CAA** (the Canadian version of AAA) has 24-hour road service
*Emergencies* (tel. 416/222–5222).

The following gas stations and auto-repair shops are open 24 hours:
**Texaco Stations** (153 Dundas St. W, behind New City Hall; 333 Davenport, just south of Casa Loma; and 601 Eglington Ave. E, west of
the Ontario Science Center); **Cross Town Service Center** (1467 Bathurst St., at St. Clair Ave. W), well known and respected for both gas
and repairs; **Jim McCormack Esso** (2901 Sheppard Ave. E), in the
Scarborough area, heading toward the Metro Zoo; **Guido's Esso**
(1104 Albion Rd.), not far from the airport; and **Bill's Service Station**
(2272 Lakeshore Blvd. W), close to the QEW.

## Guided Tours

**Orientation** **Toronto Harbour and Islands Boat Tours** are provided by **York-Han-
nover Tour and Travel** (tel. 416/364–2412) on attractive, sleek, Am-
sterdam-style touring boats, with competent tour guides. The
hourly tour visits the Toronto Islands, with lovely views of the Toronto cityscape. Boats leave from the Queen's Quay Terminal from
early May through mid-October, daily noon–5. Tours leave as late as
7:15 PM during the summer. Other boats depart from the Harbour Castle Westin. At press time, prices were $9.95 adults, $7.95 students and
senior citizens, $5.95 children ages 4–14, $21.95 families, but rates may
increase, so call ahead.

**Toronto Tours** (tel. 416/869–1372 or 416/868–0400) also provides
one-hour boat tours of the Toronto harborfront for similar prices
from mid-May through October. It also runs an informative 90-min-
ute tour aboard a restored 1920s trolley car, which goes by both city
halls, and through the financial district and the historic St. Lawrence market area.

**Gray Line Sightseeing Bus Tours** (tel. 416/367–8747) runs tours during the high season that leave from the Bus Terminal (Bay and
Dundas Sts.) and spend 2½ hours visiting such places as Eaton Centre, both city halls, Queen's Park, the University of Toronto,
Yorkville, Ontario Place, and Casa Loma—the latter, for a full hour.

These charming tours cost about $18 for adults, $12 for children under 12, and run April through November.

In winter, city bus tours are provided by **Niagara Tours** (tel. 416/868–0400). These tours, lasting 1½ hours, drive past the above attractions, but do not stop. Adult fares are $19.50 (incl. GST), $14.95 children under 12. Pickup at all major downtown hotels.

**Downtown Toronto Walking Tour** (tel. 416/922–7606) is just that—the closest look possible at central Toronto, with the emphasis on architecture. The 2- to 2½-hour tours take place daily Tuesday–Sunday between May and October, starting in front of Old City Hall on the northeast corner of Bay and Queen streets. Starting times vary, so call in advance. Price: $10 (incl. GST).

**Special-Interest Tours**

**Antours** (tel. 416/424–4403) provides several tours of Niagara-on-the-Lake, which include lunch and major performances at the Shaw Festival. The **Toronto Stock Exchange** (tel. 416/947–4700), the largest fully-automated stock exchange in North America, has tours of its visitors' center, Tuesday through Friday at 2 PM. The **Bruce Trail Association** (tel. 416/690–4453) arranges day and overnight hikes around Toronto and environs.

# Exploring Toronto

Well, now you're in Toronto, and probably in the downtown area. It's rather confusing, isn't it? But once you establish that Lake Ontario runs along the south of the city, and that the fabulous Harbourfront complex is there, as well as the ferry to the lovely Toronto Islands, you are well on your way to orienting yourself.

Imagine the downtown area of Toronto as a large rectangle. The southern boundary is, as you already know, Lake Ontario. The western edge, shooting north to Bloor Street (the northern edge) and beyond, is Spadina Avenue, near the foot of which stands the CN Tower, Harbourfront, and the spectacular new SkyDome Stadium. Just west of the rectangle along the waterfront are the Canadian National Exhibition grounds, site of the enormous annual fair, and Ontario Place, an amusement park built on man-made islands. On the east side of downtown, running from the lakefront north for hundreds of miles (believe it or not), is Yonge Street, which divides the city in half. University Avenue, a major road that parallels Yonge Street, for some reason changes its name to Avenue Road at the corner of Bloor Street, next to the Royal Ontario Museum. A further note: College Street, legitimately named, since many of the University of Toronto's buildings run along it, becomes Carlton Street where it intersects Yonge Street, then heads east.

## Highlights for First-time Visitors

**Casa Loma,** Tour 3: Academia, Culture, Commercialism, Crassness
**CN Tower,** Tour 1: Waterfront, the Financial District, and the Underground City
**Eaton Centre,** Tour 2: From Eaton Centre to the City Halls and the Far and Middle East
**Harbourfront and Toronto Islands,** Tour 1: Waterfront, the Financial District, and the Underground City
**McMichael Canadian Art Collection,** *see* Off the Beaten Track
**Metro Toronto Zoo,** *see* What to See and Do with Children
**Ontario Science Centre,** *see* What to See and Do with Children
**Royal Ontario Museum,** Tour 3: Academia, Culture, etc.

## Tour 1: Waterfront, the Financial District, and the Underground City

*Numbers in the margin correspond to points of interest on the Tour 1 map.*

Since, as we noted, Toronto has a waterfront as its southernmost border, it seems logical that we begin there. And it shouldn't be too hard to get there, since it's just south of Union Station, which is the terminus of both the University Avenue/Spadina Avenue and Yonge Street subways. Until quite recently, Toronto was notoriously negligent about its waterfront. The Gardiner Expressway, Lakeshore Boulevard, and a network of rusty rail yards stood as hideous barriers to the natural beauty of Lake Ontario.

Just over a decade ago the various levels of government—city, Metro, provincial (Ontario), and federal (Ottawa)—began a struggle to change this unfortunate situation. By that time, most of the area just south of the Gardiner Expressway and Lakeshore Boulevard was overflowing with grain silos, various warehouses, and unattractive (and unsweet-smelling) towers of malt, used by local breweries.

Part of the answer was the building of a very handsome hotel, the Harbour Castle Westin, and an attractive tower of condominiums at the foot of Yonge Street on Harbourfront. The hotel has an exterior, glassed-in elevator that offers guests a view of the waterfront and the Toronto Islands. These buildings are now just part of a phalanx of hotels, condominiums, shopping malls, and recreational and cultural attractions that stretch for almost a mile along the lakefront west of Yonge Street *(see below)*.

**Toronto Islands ❶** Just behind the giant Harbour Castle Westin is the debarkation point for ferries to the **Toronto Islands,** surely one of the highlights of any trip to the city—especially from May to October. It takes only eight minutes for the quaint little ferries to chug across the tiny bay. The islands make up a pleasant park area with numerous attractions, including a unique view of the Toronto skyline.

The four thin, curved, tree-lined islands—Centre, Ward's, Algonquin, and Hanlan's Point—have been attracting visitors since 1833, four years before Victoria became queen and just a year before the town of York changed its name to Toronto. And the more than 550 acres of parkland are irresistible, especially during the hot summer months.

The beaches on Ward's tend to be the least crowded. They're also the cleanest, and there have been problems with the cleanliness of Lake Ontario's water over the past decade. Except for the hottest days in August, the Great Lake tends to be uncomfortably chilly, so bring appropriate clothing. You'll be wise to rent a bike for an hour or more and work your way across the interconnected islands.

If you are traveling with children, Centre Island is certainly the one to check out first. A few hundred yards from the ferry docks lies **Centreville,** an amusement park that's supposed to be a turn-of-the-century children's village. The concept works wondrously well: True, the pizza, fries, and hot dogs are barely edible—pack a lunch!—but on the little Main Street there are charming shops, a town hall, a little railroad station, and more than a dozen rides, including a restored 1890s merry-go-round with more than four dozen hand-carved animals. And there's no entrance fee to the modest, 14-acre amusement park, although you'll have to pay a nominal charge for each ride or buy an all-day pass. Perhaps most enjoyable for children is the free **Far Enough Farm,** which is near enough to walk to. It has all kinds of animals to pet and feed, ranging from piglets to geese, cows to birds. *Tel. 416/203–0405. Open 10:30–8 weekends only Apr. 30–May 15 and Sept. 10–25; daily Victoria Day (mid-May)–Labor Day.*

All transportation on these islands comes to you compliments of your feet: No cars are allowed anywhere. Your nostrils will wonder at the lack of exhaust fumes, while your feet will wonder why you insist on walking all the way along the boardwalk from Centre to Ward's Island (2½ kilometers, or 1½ miles).

Once you've arrived, you'll find **Gibraltar Lighthouse,** built back in 1808, the oldest monument in the city that is still standing on its original site. Right next to it is a pond stocked with rainbow trout, and a concession for buying bait and renting rods.

Encircling the islands are sandy beaches; the best ones are on the southeast tip of Ward's, the southernmost edge of Centre, and the west side of Hanlan's. There are free changing rooms near each of these areas, but no facilities for checking your clothes. Swimming in the various lagoons and channels is prohibited. The winter can be bitterly cold on the islands, but snowshoeing and cross-country skiing, with downtown Toronto over your shoulder, will be irresistible to many. In the summer, there are rowboat and canoe rentals, tennis courts, gardens, playgrounds, and a wildlife sanctuary.

The ferries run irregularly during the winter: every half hour or so until 10 or 11 AM, and every hour or so thereafter. In the summer, the ferries leave three times an hour at the foot of Bay Street. The cost is $3 adults, $1.50 students and senior citizens, $1 children under 15. For a recording giving the schedule and prices, call 416/392–8193; for other information, call 416/392–8186.

**Harbourfront**
**❷**

Back at the ferry docks on the mainland, your next move should be to **Harbourfront.** This is a trip that is well worth planning for: Check *Now* magazine, *Eye Weekly* magazine, the Thursday edition of the *Toronto Star,* and Saturday's *Globe and Mail* to see what concerts, dances, art shows, and festivals are taking place, and build your visit around them.

Harbourfront is within walking distance of Union Station. Drivers should head for the foot of Bay Street or Spadina Avenue, and park in one of the many lots. There's also a streetcar that swings around from Union Station to Harbourfront, and on to Spadina Avenue.

For many years, as we said, Toronto had good reason to be ashamed of its God-given, man-taken-away waterfront. Today, Harbourfront has become a 100-acre culture and recreation center, drawing more than 3 million visitors each year. Stretching from just west of the Harbour Castle Westin for nearly a mile to Bathurst Street, the complex has become the scene of fabulous entertainment, exquisite buildings, glorious attractions—a true match for San Francisco's Pier 39 and Baltimore's Inner Harbor. Sadly, there have been numerous problems with funding this wonderful concept: All three levels of government—federal, provincial, and local—are fighting over who should pay and what may have to be closed. Still, even if some of Harbourfront's attractions are lost in the bureaucratic flip-flop, this will remain one of Toronto's best tourist spots.

Highlights are many. The **Queen's Quay Terminal** is a must: The 57-year-old food warehouse was transformed in 1983, at a cost of more than $60 million, into a magnificent eight-story structure with de-

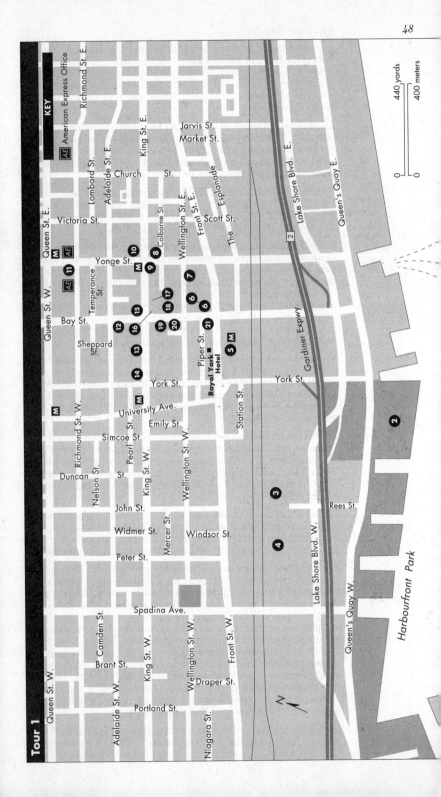

Tour 1

KEY

AE American Express Office

Richmond St. E.

Jarvis St.
Market St.

Lombard St.
Adelaide St. E.
Church          St.
King St. E.
The Esplanade
Front St. E.
Scott St.
Wellington St. E.
Colborne St.
Lake Shore Blvd. E.
Queen's Quay E.

Victoria St.
Queen St. E.
M AE
M AE

Yonge St.

10
8
9
11

Temperance St.
7
17
18
6
15
16
6
12
19 20
21
Bay St.
Sheppard St.
13
5 M
14
York St.
Piper St.
Royal York Hotel
Station St.
York St.
Gardiner Expwy.

University Ave.
M
M
Emily St.
Richmond St. W.
Simcoe St.
Pearl St.
Duncan St.
Nelson St.
King St. W.
John St.
Wellington St. W.
Widmer St.
Mercer St.
Windsor St.
Peter St.

3
Rees St.
2
4

Lake Shore Blvd. W.

Spadina Ave.

Camden St.
Brant St.
King St. W.
Wellington St. W.
Front St. W.
Adelaide St. W.
Draper St.
Niagara St.
Portland St.
Queen St. W.

N

Queen's Quay W.

Harbourfront Park

440 yards
400 meters
0
0

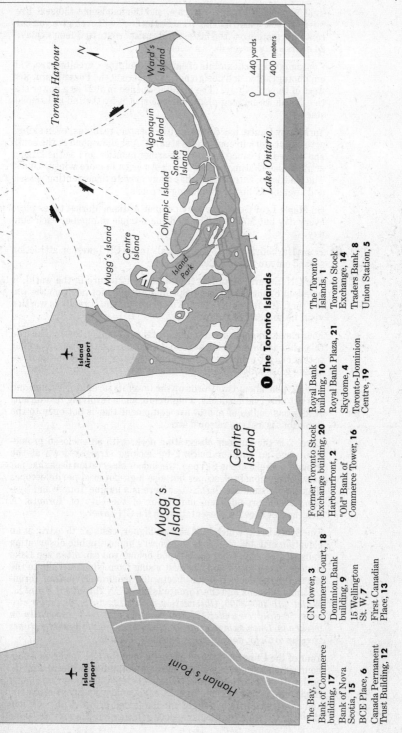

**1 The Toronto Islands**

| | |
|---|---|
| The Bay, **11** | Royal Bank building, **10** |
| Bank of Commerce building, **17** | Royal Bank Plaza, **21** |
| Bank of Nova Scotia, **15** | Skydome, **4** |
| BCE Place, **6** | Toronto-Dominion Centre, **19** |
| Canada Permanent Trust Building, **12** | |
| CN Tower, **3** | The Toronto Islands, **1** |
| Commerce Court, **18** | Toronto Stock Exchange, **14** |
| Dominion Bank building, **9** | Traders Bank, **8** |
| 15 Wellington St. W, **7** | Union Station, **5** |
| First Canadian Place, **13** | |
| Former Toronto Stock Exchange building, **20** | |
| Harbourfront, **2** | |
| "Old" Bank of Commerce Tower, **16** | |

lightful specialty shops, eateries, and the handsome 450-seat Premiere Dance Theatre. The "Traffic Hotline" will even give you current information on "the fastest and easiest route to Queen's Quay," 24 hours a day, seven days a week (tel. 416/203–0510).

Contemporary art exhibits of painting, sculpture, architecture, video, photography, and design now take place at the **Power Plant,** just west of Queen's Quay. (The building opened in 1927 as a power station for an ice-making plant; you can spot it by the tall red smokestack.)

**York Quay Centre** has concerts, live theater, readings, even skilled artisans at work in open crafts studios. A shallow pond at the south end is used for canoe lessons in warmer months, and as the largest artificial ice-skating rink in North America in more wintry times. The Nautical Centre nearby has many private firms renting vessels and offering sailing and canoeing lessons.

On **Maple Leaf Quay,** the very popular **Antique Market** takes place every day but Monday. The 70 dealers triple in number each Sunday.

❸ From Harbourfront, it's a short walk to the **CN Tower,** an attraction second only to Eaton Centre.

The CN Tower, the tallest freestanding structure in the world, is found on Front Street, near Spadina Avenue, not far from the waterfront. It's fully 1,815 feet, 5 inches high, and it really is worth a visit, if the weather is clear.

Four elevators zoom up the outside of the $57 million tower. The ride takes but a minute, going at 20 feet a second, a rate of ascent similar to that of a jet-plane takeoff. But each elevator has only one floor-to-ceiling glass wall, preventing vertigo.

The **Skypod,** about two-thirds up the tower, is seven stories high and has two observation decks, a nightclub, and a revolving restaurant. It also has oodles of microwave equipment that is not open to the public but is its true raison d'être.

Level 2 is the **outdoor observation deck,** with an enclosed promenade, and an outdoor balcony for looking straight down at the ground. Level 3 of the Skypod, the **indoor observation deck,** has not only conventional telescopes but also high-powered peritelescopes that almost simulate flight. Also here is a unique Tour Wand System, which provides an audio tour of the City of Toronto. A minitheater shows a presentation on the CN Tower.

The **Space Deck,** which is 33 stories higher, costs $2.25 extra; at an elevation of 1,465 feet, it is the world's highest public observation gallery. But even from the Skypod below, you can often see Lake Simcoe to the north and the mist rising from Niagara Falls to the south. All the decks provide spectacular panoramic views of Toronto, Lake Ontario, and the Toronto Islands. *CN Tower, 301 Front St. W, tel. 416/360–8500. Observation deck: $12 adults, $8 senior citizens, $6 children under 13. Peak visiting hrs: 11–4, especially on weekends. Open summer, daily 10 AM–midnight; fall–winter, times vary up to an hr, depending on season (call ahead).*

**Tour of the Universe,** located at the base of the CN Tower, is a one-hour simulated space shuttle journey to Jupiter in the year 2019, with a 64-screen Multivision Wall that briefs you on your upcoming flight, laser "inoculation," an InterPlanetary Passport souvenir, and a too-brief ride in a flight simulator that provides physical motion to match the spectacular special-effects film. It's very well done and a good attraction to combine with the CN Tower visit. *Tel. 416/ 868–6937. Admission: $8 adults, $7 senior citizens, $6 children 5– 12. Note: 3-ft-height requirement.*

Also at the base of the CN Tower is **Q-Zar,** a live-action, laser-tag game of strategy played in an arena of pulsating music, lighting, and special effects. *Admission: $8 adults, $7 senior citizens, $6 children 5–12. Combination prices are available for the various CN Tower attractions.*

❹ In the shadow of the CN Tower is one of Toronto's newest—and already one of its most famous—landmarks. **SkyDome,** home of the Blue Jays, is the world's only stadium with a fully retractable roof. Toronto has lost no opportunity to honor its World Series–winning baseball team—the official address of SkyDome is 1 Blue Jays Way. One way to see the huge 52,000-seat stadium is to buy tickets for a Blue Jays game or one of the many other events that take place there. These have included cricket matches, Wrestlemania, monster truck races, Peter Pan on Ice, and even the opera *Aïda.* Visitors can also take a one-hour walking tour (including a 15-minute film), given daily on the hour between 10AM and 4PM. The tours are not available, however, when daytime events are scheduled. *Tel: 416/341–2770. Admission: $6 adults, $4 children, and senior citizens.*

**Financial District** ❺ On the south side of Front Street, between Bay and York streets (and across from the handsome Royal York Hotel), **Union Station** is a most historic building, though it is of this century. It was designed back in 1907, when trains were still as exciting as space shuttles are today, and it was opened in 1927 by the Prince of Wales. Try to imagine the awe of the immigrants who poured into Toronto between the wars by the tens of thousands, staring up at the towering ceiling of Italian tile or leaning against one of the 22 pillars, each 40 feet tall and weighing 75 tons. Walk along the lengthy concourse and study the mellow reflection in its walls. Get a sense of the beauty of the light flooding through the high, arched windows at each end of the mammoth hall.

As you come out of Union Station, walk back to Yonge Street and the beautiful building at the northwest corner of Front Street. Formerly a branch of the Bank of Montreal, the building is now home to the **Hockey Hall of Fame,** the world's biggest collection of hockey artifacts, displays, and memorabilia. The 13 zones include one where visitors can take shots at a computer-generated goalie; another is a precise replica (right down to the trainer's whirlpool) of the Montréal Canadiens' dressing room. There's also a store that carries an array of hockey jerseys, skates, and other apparel, as well as souvenirs. *Concourse Level, BCE Pl., tel. 416/360–7765. Admission: $7.50 adults, $5.50 children under 13 and senior citizens. Open Mon.–Wed. 9–6, Thurs. and Fri. 9–9:30, Sat. 9–6, Sun. 10–6.*

❻ Built around the old bank is one of the two towers of the striking new **BCE Place,** with its exquisite, huge Galleria, completed in mid-1992, which, as one architectural critic wrote, "brings a new level of sophistication to the interior spaces of the city's core." Just steps north is a shabby row of shops, which are among the oldest surviving commercial buildings in the city. Many of the original Georgian facades have been drastically altered, but the one- and two-story structures give you a sense of the scale of buildings from the 1850s and are the last remnants of the early business community of the then-brand-new city of Toronto.

Make a left turn at the first intersection, which is Wellington Street
**7** West. **Number 15** is the oldest building on this walk, an elegant stone
bank designed in the Greek Revival style.

Head back a few steps to Yonge Street and go north again. On the
northeast corner of Yonge and Colborne streets, at 67 Yonge Street,
**8** is **Traders Bank,** the first "skyscraper" of the city when it went up in
1905–06, complete with an observation deck. The next building to
the north, built in 1913, is owned by **Canadian Pacific,** the famous
company whose transcontinental railroad literally helped build a
country.

**9** At the southwest corner of King and Yonge streets is the **Dominion
Bank building,** erected in 1913 by the same architects who designed
the voluptuous Bank of Montreal. This classic Chicago-style skyscraper has a marble and bronze stairway leading to the opulent
banking hall on the second floor. There you can enjoy the marble
floor, marble walls, and the ornate plaster ceiling, which features
the coats of arms of the then nine Canadian provinces.

**10** On the northeast corner is the original **Royal Bank building,** also
built in 1913. Note the distinctive cornice, the overhanging roof, the
decorative pattern of sculpted ox skulls above the ground-floor windows, and the classically detailed leaves at the top of the Corinthian
columns.

Farther north along Yonge Street, at Richmond Street West, is the
**11** original Simpsons department store, now **The Bay.** Built in 1895, it
was one of the city's first buildings with a steel-frame construction.
There are attractive terra-cotta decorations in the section closest to
Yonge Street, which went up in 1908; the part along Richmond
Street, near Bay Street, added in 1928, is a fine example of the Art
Deco style, popular between the two world wars.

Continue a few steps west to Bay Street, a name synonymous with
finance and power in Canada, as Wall Street is in the United States.
Head south (left), back toward the lakefront. Just south of Adelaide
**12** Street, on the west side of Bay Street, is the **Canada Permanent
Trust Building** (320 Bay St.). Built in the very year of the stock market crash (and we don't mean the 1987 one), it's a skyscraper in the
New York wedding-cake style. Look up at the ornate stone carvings
both on the lower stories and on the top, where carved, stylized
faces peer down to the street below. Walk through the imposing
vaulted entrance, with its polished brass doors, and note that even
the elevator doors in the foyer are embossed brass. The spacious
banking hall has a vaulted ceiling, marble walls and pillars, and a
marble floor with mosaic borders.

Turn right (west) along King Street, and on your right is the first of
the towering bank buildings that have defined Toronto's skyline
**13** over the past two decades. This is **First Canadian Place** (100 King St.
W), built in the early 1970s. Its 72 stories were deliberately faced
with white marble to contrast with the black of the Toronto-Dominion Centre, to the south, and with the silver of the Commerce Court
Tower, diagonally opposite.

Farther along you come to the second phase of the project, opened in
**14** 1983, which houses the ultramodern **Toronto Stock Exchange (TSE).**
The Exchange Tower (2 First Canadian Pl.) has a Visitor's Center,
where you can learn about the securities industry through colorful
displays, or even join in daily presentations. The attractions are
many: a 140-seat auditorium, an educational audio-visual presentation, and a real-time stock-quotation terminal. *Tel. 416/947–4700.*

*Admission free. Open weekdays 9–4:30. Public tour Tues.–Fri. at 2.*

⑮ On the northeast corner of King and Bay streets (44 King St. W) is the **Bank of Nova Scotia.** Built between 1949 and 1951, and partially replaced by the recently completed Scotia Tower just to the east, it has sculptural panels inspired by Greek mythology above the large, exterior windows. In the lobby, there are reliefs symbolizing four regions of Canada and a brightly colored gilded plaster ceiling. The original stainless steel–and–glass stairway with marine motifs is attractive, as are the marble counters and floors. The north wall relief depicts some of the industries and enterprises financed by the bank.

⑯ On the southeast corner of King and Bay streets is the "Old" **Bank of Commerce Tower,** which for a third of a century was the tallest building in the British Commonwealth. The base has bas-relief carvings, and marvelous animal and floral ornamentation around the vaulted entrance. Because the top is set back, you must look up to see the huge, carved human heads adorning all four sides of the building.

⑰ The **Bank of Commerce Building** (25 King Street W) was built during the two years following the stock market crash of 1929, but the hard times didn't prevent the creation of a stunning interior of marble floors, limestone walls, and bronze vestibule doors decorated with masks, owls, and animals. In the alcoves on each side of the entrance are murals that trace the history of transportation. The bronze elevator doors are richly decorated and the vaulted banking hall is lit by period chandeliers.

⑱ Just south of the "old tower", at 243 Bay Street, is **Commerce Court,** the bank's 57-story stainless-steel sister. And due west, just across Bay Street, also on the south side of King Street, are the five black
⑲ towers of the **Toronto-Dominion Centre,** the first International-style skyscrapers built in Toronto, thanks to the "less is more" man, Mies van der Rohe. Two of the towers went up in the mid-1960s, and they are starkly plain and stripped of ornament. The only decoration consists of geometric repetition, and the only extravagance is the use of rich materials, such as marble counters and leather-covered furniture. The Aetna Tower, which is part of the T-D Centre, houses the Toronto-Dominion Bank's **Gallery of Inuit Art,** one of the finest of its kind in Canada. *79 Wellington St., tel. 416/982–8473. Admission: free. Open weekdays 8–6, weekends 10–4.*

⑳ Immediately south of the T-D Centre towers, at 234 Bay Street, is the **former Toronto Stock Exchange building,** which, for close to half a century, was the financial hub of Toronto. Built in 1937 of polished pink granite and smooth buff limestone, it's a delightful example of Art Deco design. The stainless-steel doors are a wonder, as is the wise and witty stone frieze carved above them. Don't miss the hilarious social commentary up there—the banker with the top hat marching behind the laborer, his hand sneaking into the worker's pocket.

㉑ Walk south another block to the northwest corner of Bay and Front streets: There, in all its golden glory, is the **Royal Bank Plaza,** built in 1976 and already a classic of its kind. Be sure to go into the 120-foot-high banking hall and admire the lovely hanging sculpture by Jesus Raphael Soto.

**Underground City** The origins of Toronto's **Underground City**—purportedly the largest pedestrian walkway in the world, and more than four times the size of Montréal's—go back over a generation. One can walk—and shop, eat, and browse—without ever seeing the light of day, from beneath Union Station to the Royal York Hotel, the Toronto-Dominion Centre, First Canadian Place, the Sheraton Centre, the Eaton Centre, and the Atrium-on-Bay. Altogether, it extends through nearly 3 miles of tunnels and seven subway stops.

Enter the subterranean community from anywhere between Dundas Street on the north and Union Station on the south, and you'll encounter everything from art exhibitions to buskers (the city actually auditions young musicians and licenses the best to perform throughout its subway system and elsewhere) to walkways, fountains, and trees growing as much as two stories high. Because up to 50% of the complex lies underneath Toronto's multibillion-dollar Financial District, you will keep bumping into men and women in business suits, browsing or on lunch breaks.

### Tour 2: From Eaton Centre to the City Halls and the Far and Middle East

*Numbers in the margin correspond to points of interest on the Tours 2 and 3 map.*

From the corner of Yonge and Queen streets, one can begin a tour that will include several of this city's most popular attractions, as well as some of its most interesting neighborhoods. One of these, Eaton Centre, is closed on Sunday, while others thrive on what is still considered the Lord's Day in the province of Ontario. Still, the following walking/driving tour describes a very pleasant day in the central and western portions of Toronto's downtown.

**Eaton Centre and City Hall**
**㉒**

**Eaton Centre,** a 3-million-square-foot building that extends along the west side of Yonge Street all the way from Queen Street up to Dundas Street (with subway stops at each end), has quickly become the number-one tourist attraction of Toronto. Even people who rank shopping with the flu will be charmed, even dazzled, for this is a very beautiful environment indeed. From its graceful glass roof, arching 127 feet above the lowest of the mall levels, to Michael Snow's exquisite flock of fiberglass Canada geese floating poetically in the open space of the Galleria, to the glass-enclosed elevators, porthole windows, and nearly two dozen long and graceful escalators, there are plenty of good reasons for visiting the Eaton Centre.

Galleria Level 1 contains two food courts; popularly priced fashions; photo, electronics, and record stores; and much "convenience" merchandise. Level 2 is directed to the middle-income shopper, while Level 3, suitably, has the highest elevation, fashion, and prices. **Eaton's,** one of Canada's classic department-store chains, has a nine-floor branch here. At the southern end of Level 3 is a skywalk that connects the Centre to the seven-floor **The Bay** department store across Queen Street.

Dozens of restaurants, from snack to full-service, can be found here. A 17-theater cinema complex—the initial unit of the now international Cineplex chain—is located at the Dundas Street entrance. *Tel. 416/598–2322 for Eaton Centre information. Open weekdays 10–9, Sat. 9:30–6, Sun. 1–5.*

Exit the Eaton Centre at Queen Street and walk just one long block west to Toronto's city halls. Yes, the plural is correct.

**㉓**
**㉔**
**Old City Hall** is the very beautiful building at the northeast corner of Queen and Bay streets, sweetly coexisting with the futuristic **New City Hall,** just across the street, on the west side. The creator of the

old one, which opened in 1899, was none other than E.J. Lennox, who would later design Casa Loma. It was considered one of North America's most impressive municipal halls in its heyday, and since the opening of its younger sister, it has been the site for the provincial courts, county offices, and thousands of low-cost marriages. Note the hideous gargoyles above the front steps, which were apparently the architect's witty way of mocking certain politicians of the time. The great stained-glass window as you enter is attractive, and the handsome old structure stands in delightful contrast to its daring and unique sibling.

The New City Hall was the result of a massive international competition in 1958. The winning presentation by Finnish architect Viljo Revell was very controversial: two towers of differing height, and curved! But there was and is a logic to it all: An aerial view of the New City Hall shows a circular council chamber sitting like an eye between the two tower "eyelids." Within months of its opening in 1965, the New City Hall became a symbol of a thriving city.

Annual events at the New City Hall include the Spring Flower Show in late March; the Toronto Outdoor Art Exhibition early each July, and the Cavalcade of Lights from late November through Christmas each year, when more than 100,000 sparkling lights are illuminated across both city halls. *Tel. 416/392–7341; TDD 416/392–7354. Underground garage for 2,400 cars. Open weekdays 8:30–4:30. Free 30-min guided tours. Cafeteria open daily 7:30–4.*

**Chinatown and the Museums** Just north of the New City Hall begins Toronto's main **Chinatown,** which is the largest in all of North America. There are more than 100,000 Chinese living in the city, which is remarkable, considering that just over a century ago there was only one—Sam Ching, who ran a hand laundry on Adelaide Street. Today, Chinatown covers much of the area around Spadina Avenue from Queen Street to College Street, running along Dundas Street nearly as far east as Bay Street.

One of the best times to explore Chinatown is on a Sunday, when, up and down Spadina Avenue and along Dundas Street, Chinese music blasts from storefronts, cash registers ring, abacuses clack, and bakeries, markets, herbalists, and restaurants do their best business of the week. But whatever day you wander, we recommend that you start on Elizabeth Street, just north of the New City Hall, and walk north to Dundas Street, east toward Bay Street, then turn back and walk west to Spadina Avenue. You will be thrilled by the diversity, the excitement, the liveliness—the sheer foreignness of it all.

On Dundas Street, you'll pass shops selling reasonably priced silk blouses and antique porcelain, silk kimonos for less than half the price elsewhere, lovely sake sets, and women's silk suits. Huge Chinese characters hang over the **52nd Division police station,** a large building on the west side of Simcoe Street, just south of Dundas Street. Many of the banks still have abacuses, for those who prefer the 4,000-year-old "hand-held calculators" to modern ones.

**26** Turn south off Dundas Street to the **Ontario College of Art** (100 McCaul St.), one of the major colleges of animation, design, advertising art, tapestry, glassblowing, sculpture, and painting in Canada. Directly across the street is **Village by the Grange** (89 McCaul St.), an apartment and shopping complex with more than a hundred shops selling everything from ethnic fast food to serious art. It's a perfect example of wise, careful blending of the commercial and the residential.

## Tour 2

Art Gallery of Ontario, **28**

Eaton Centre, **22**

52nd Division police station, **25**

Kensington Market, **29**

New City Hall, **24**

Old City Hall, **23**

Ontario College of Art, **26**

Village by the Grange, **27**

## Tour 3

Campbell House, **30**

Casa Loma, **48**

The Colonnade, **45**

George R. Gardiner Museum of Ceramic Art, **41**

Hart House, **32**

Hazelton Lanes, **47**

Knox College, **34**

McLaughlin Planetarium, **42**

Medical Sciences Building, **35**

Metropolitan Toronto Library, **46**

Ontario Legislative Bulding, **38**

Parliament Buildings, **39**

Public and Community Relations Office, **36**

Queen's Park, **37**

Royal Ontario Museum, **40**

Sigmund Samuel Canadiana Collection, **43**

University College, **33**

University of Toronto, **31**

Yorkville, **44**

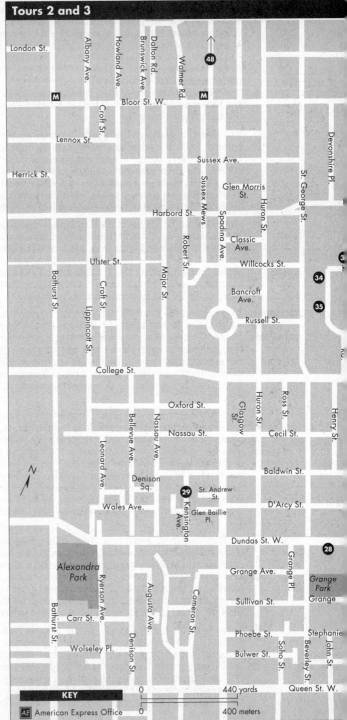

## Tours 2 and 3

London St.

Albany Ave.

Howland Ave.

Brunswick Ave.

Dalton Rd.

Walmer Rd.

Bloor St. W.

Croft St.

Lennox St.

Herrick St.

Sussex Ave.

Sussex Mews

Glen Morris St.

St. George St.

Devonshire Pl.

Harbord St.

Spadina Ave.

Huron St.

Classic Ave.

Robert St.

Ulster St.

Willcocks St.

Bathurst St.

Croft St.

Lippincott St.

Major St.

Bancroft Ave.

Russell St.

College St.

Oxford St.

Glasgow St.

Huron St.

Ross St.

Henry St.

Bellevue Ave.

Nassau Ave.

Nassau St.

Cecil St.

Leonard Ave.

Denison Sq.

Baldwin St.

St. Andrew St.

D'Arcy St.

Wales Ave.

Kensington Ave.

Glen Baillie Pl.

Dundas St. W.

*Alexandra Park*

Ryerson Ave.

Augusta Ave.

Cameron St.

Grange Ave.

Grange Pl.

*Grange Park*

Grange

Sullivan St.

Bathurst St.

Carr St.

Denison St.

Phoebe St.

Soho St.

Beverley St.

Stephanie

John St.

Wolseley Pl.

Bulwer St.

Queen St. W.

**KEY**

AE American Express Office

0   440 yards

0   400 meters

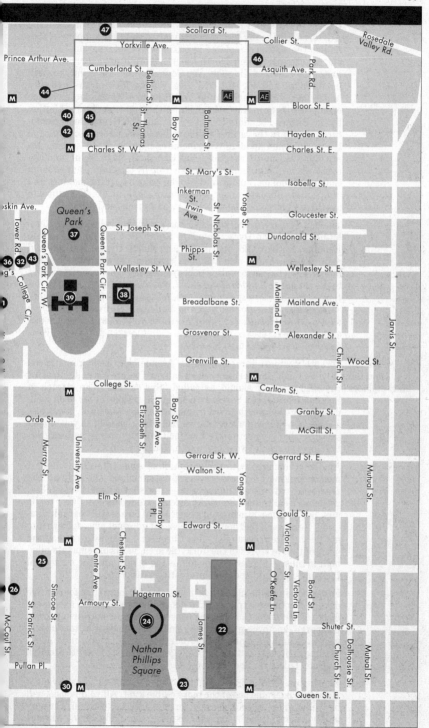

**28** Return to Dundas Street and head west to the newly reopened **Art Gallery of Ontario.** From extremely modest beginnings in 1900, the AGO is now in the big league in terms of exhibits and support. A $50-million renovation completed in 1992 has won international acclaim and put the AGO among North America's top 10 art galleries. International exhibits of King Tut, Van Gogh, Turner, Judy Chicago, William Blake, and Picasso will give you an idea of the gallery's importance, image, and profile. In 1993, the AGO was chosen as one of only two stops in North America for the first travelling exhibition by the Barnes Foundation's art collection. The **Henry Moore Sculpture Centre** has the largest public collection of Moore's sculpture in the world. The **Canadian Wing** includes major works by such northern lights as Emily Carr, Cornelius Krieghoff, David Milne, and Homer Watson. Visitors of any age can drop by the Anne Tannenbaum Gallery School on Sunday and explore painting, print-making, and sculpture in Toronto's most spectacular studio space. The museum arranges numerous other workshops and special activities.

The Art Gallery of Ontario also has a growing collection of Rembrandt, Hals, Van Dyck, Hogarth, Reynolds, Chardin, Renoir, de Kooning, Rothko, Oldenburg, Picasso, Rodin, Degas, Matisse, and many others. And it also has **The Grange,** a historic house just behind the AGO, a perfect place to browse, either before or after a visit to the art gallery. *317 Dundas St. W, 3 blocks west of St. Patrick station on the University subway line, tel. 416/979–6649. Admission: $7.50 adults, $4 senior citizens and students, children under 12 free with a paying adult, $15 families (up to 6 members). Two-for-one admission Fri. evening. Open Thurs. and weekends 10–5:30, Wed. and Fri. 10–10, holidays 10–5:30.*

**Spadina and the Marketplaces** Toronto's widest street, **Spadina Avenue,** has been pronounced "Spa-*dye*-nah" for a century and a half, and we are too polite to point out that it really should be called "Spa-*dee*-na." The stretch of Spadina from Queen Street to College Street has never been fashionable, or even worth a visit by most tourists. Way back, it was just a collection of inexpensive stores, factories that sold to you wholesale if you had connections, ethnic food and fruit stores, and eateries that gave you your two cents' worth, usually plain.

And so it remains, with the exception of some often first-class, if modest-looking, Chinese restaurants sprinkled throughout the area. Each new wave of immigrants—Jewish, Chinese, Portuguese, East and West Indian, South American—added its own flavor to the mix, but Spadina-Kensington's basic bill of fare is still "bargains galore." Here you'll find gourmet cheeses at gourmet prices, fresh (no, not fresh-frozen) ocean fish, fine European kitchenware at half the price of that in stores in the Yorkville area, yards of remnants piled high in bins, designer clothes minus the labels, and the occasional rock-and-roll night spot and interesting greasy spoon.

For any visitor who plans to be in Toronto for more than four or five days, a few hours exploring the ins and outs of Spadina's garment district, between College and Queen streets, could bring great pleasure—and even greater bargains. Park your car at the lot just west of Spadina Avenue on St. Andrew's Street (a long block north of Dundas Street), or take the College or Queen streetcar to Spadina Avenue. (Also, *see* Shopping, *below*.)

**29** **Kensington Market** is a delightful side tour off Spadina Avenue. Here, the bargains are of the more edible kind. All your senses will be titillated by this old, steamy, smelly, raucous, colorful, European-style marketplace. Come and explore, especially during warmer weather, when the goods pour out into the narrow streets: Russian rye breads, barrels of dill pickles, fresh fish on ice, mountains of cheese, bushels of ripe fruit, and crates of chickens and rabbits that will have your children both giggling and horrified. Jewish and Eastern European stores sit side by side with Portuguese, Caribbean, Latin American, and East Indian stores—with Vietnamese, Japanese, and Chinese establishments sprinkled throughout. Most shops are open every day except Sunday, from as early as 6 AM.

Afterward, you can rest in **Bellevue Square** (corner of Denison Square and Augusta Place), a lovely little park with shady trees, benches, and a wading pool and playground for children.

## Tour 3: Academia, Culture, Commercialism, Crassness

University Avenue, running from Front Street for about 3 miles north to Bloor Street, where it changes its name to Avenue Road and continues north, is one of Toronto's few mistakes. It's horribly boring, with hospital after office building after insurance company after office building. Yet it is still an interesting start for a healthy walk, because it does have lovely flower beds and fountains in a well-maintained strip along its middle. Still, you may wish to drive this part of the tour, or take the subway, which runs underneath University Avenue all the way from Union Station to Bloor Street.

**30** One highlight is **Campbell House** (northwest corner of Queen Street and University Avenue), the stately Georgian mansion of Sir William Campbell, the sixth chief justice of Upper Canada. Built in 1822 and tastefully restored with elegant 18th- and early 19th-century furniture, it is one of Toronto's most charming "living museums." Costumed hostesses will tell you about the social life of the upper class of the period. *Tel. 416/597-0227. Admission: $2.50 adults, $1.25 students and senior citizens, children under 5 free. Guided tours available. Open Oct.–mid-May, weekdays 9:30–11:30 and 2:30–4:30; summer, weekdays 9:30–11:30 and 2:30–4:30, weekends noon–4:30.*

**31** College Street is the southern boundary of the **University of Toronto,** which dates to 1827, when King George IV signed a charter for a "King's College in the Town of York, Capital of Upper Canada." The Church of England had control then, but by 1850 the college was proclaimed nondenominational, renamed the University of Toronto, and put under the control of the province. And then, in a spirit of good Christian competition, the Anglicans started Trinity College, the Methodists began Victoria, and the Roman Catholics begat St. Michael's; by the time the Presbyterians founded Knox College, the whole thing was almost out of hand.

But not really: The 17 schools and faculties are now united, and they welcome anyone who can pass the entrance exams and afford the tuition. The architecture is interesting, if uneven. Enter the campus just behind the Provincial Legislature buildings, where Wellesley Street ends. Go under the bridge, past the guardhouse (whose keeper will not let you pass if you are in an automobile), and turn right, around King's College Circle.

**32** At the top of the circle is **Hart House,** a Gothic-style student center built during the teens of this century by the Masseys—the folks who brought us Massey-Ferguson farm equipment, Massey Hall, Vincent Massey (a governor-general of Canada), and Raymond Massey, the actor. It was once an all-male enclave; today, anyone may visit the Great Hall and the library, both self-conscious imitations of Oxford and Cambridge. Check out the dining hall for its stained-glass windows as well as its food, which is cheap and rather good.

 As you continue around King's College Circle, you'll see on your right the Romanesque **University College,** built in 1859. Next is **Knox College,** whose Scottish origins are evident in the bagpipe music that escapes from the building at odd hours. It's been training ministers since 1844, although the building was erected more recently, in 1915.

You may well wish to tip your hat to the **Medical Sciences Building,** which is no beauty but is where, in 1921, Drs. Banting, Best, and others discovered the insulin that has saved the lives of tens of millions of diabetics around the world.

There is lots more to see and do around the main campus of the University of Toronto. Visit the **Public and Community Relations Office** (Room 133S, 27 King's College Circle, tel. 416/978–2021), across the field from Hart House, and pick up free maps of the school grounds. Guided one-hour walking tours are held on summer weekdays, setting out from the map room of Hart House at 10:30, 12:30, and 2:30 (tel. 416/978–5000).

Back at College Street and University Avenue, you can see the Victorian structure of the Legislature buildings to the north, with Queen's Park just north of them.

**Queen's Park**  There are a number of meanings to **Queen's Park,** for the native Torontonian as well as the visitor. The term can refer to the charming circular park just a few hundred yards south of the Royal Ontario Museum (on University Avenue, just below Bloor Street). This is a grand place to rest your feet after a long day of shopping or visiting the Royal Ontario Museum. But Queen's Park also refers to the **Ontario Legislative Building,** which is home to part of the provincial government. The mammoth building was opened back in 1893, and is really quite extraordinary, with its rectangular towers, triangular roofs, and circular and oval glass.

The **Parliament Buildings** look grotesque to some, with their pink exterior and heavy, almost Romanesque quality. But a close look will show the beautifully complex detail carved in the stone, and on the inside there are huge, lovely halls that echo half a millennium of English architecture. The long hallways are hung with hundreds of oils by Canadian artists, most of which capture scenes of the province's natural beauty. Should you choose to take one of the frequent (and free) tours, you will see the chamber where the 130 elected representatives from across Ontario, called MPPs (Members of Provincial Parliament), meet on a regular basis. There are two heritage rooms—one each for the parliamentary histories of Great Britain and Ontario—filled with old newspapers, periodicals, and pictures. And the lobby holds a fine collection of minerals and rocks of the province. On the lawn in front of the Parliament buildings, facing College Street, are many statues, including one of Queen Victoria and one of Canada's first prime minister, Sir John A. Macdonald. *Tel. 416/965–4028. Guided tours from mid-May to Labor Day, daily on the hr 9–4, weekends every half hr 9–11:30 and 1:30–4; frequent tours the rest of the year; also at 6:45 PM when evening sessions are held. University Ave. subway, Queen's Park stop. There are parking lots in the area and metered parking around Queen's Park Circle.*

Just to the north of Queen's Park is the world-class **Royal Ontario Museum.** Once labeled "Canada's single greatest cultural asset" by the Canada Council, the museum floundered throughout much of its existence, which began in 1912 (on the day the *Titanic* sank). It never stopped collecting—always with brilliance—reaching more than 6 million items altogether. But by the 1970s, the monstrous building had leaky roofs, no climate control, and little space to display its glorious treasures. Today, thanks to a major fund-raising effort that brought in $80 million, the museum has the space it needs, and when expansion is completed sometime before the end of the century, the ROM will be the second-largest museum in North America, after New York's Metropolitan Museum of Art.

What makes the ROM unique is the fact that science, art, and archaeology exhibits are all under one roof. The **Dinosaur Collection** will stun children and adults alike. The **Evolution Gallery** has an ongoing audiovisual program on Darwin's theories of evolution. The **Roman Gallery** has the most extensive collection of Roman artifacts in Canada. And the **European Musical Instruments Gallery** has a revolutionary audio system and more than 1,200 instruments dating back to the late 16th century. The **Discovery Gallery** allows children (over age 6) to handle objects from the ROM's collections and to study them, using microscopes, ultraviolet light, and magnifying glasses.

The **Bat Cave,** opened in early 1988, contains 4,000 freeze-dried and artificial bats in a lifelike presentation. Piped-in narration directs visitors on a 15-minute walk through a dimly lit replica of an 8-foot-high limestone tunnel in Jamaica, filled with sounds of dripping water and bat squeaks. In early 1992, the brilliant **Ancient Egypt Gallery** reopened, joined with a brand-new **Nubia Gallery**—the only one in North America. *110 Queens Park, tel. 416/586–5549. Admission: $7 adults, $4 students and senior citizens, children under 4 free, $15 family (up to 6 members). Senior citizens free Tues. (including Gardiner Museum and planetarium shows); all others free Tues. after 4:30. Open late May–Labor Day, Sun., Mon., Wed., and Fri. 10–6, Tues. and Thurs. 10–8; Labor Day–mid-May, Sun., Wed., and Fri. 10–6, Tues. and Thurs. 10–8; closed Jan. 1. Discovery Gallery hrs vary; call ahead. University subway to Museum stop; parking is expensive.*

**㊶** The **George R. Gardiner Museum of Ceramic Art** has now merged with the ROM, meaning that it costs not a penny more to visit a magnificent $25 million collection of rare European ceramics. The collection features 17th-century English delftware and 18th-century yellow European porcelain. Don't miss the museum's gift shop, which stocks many unusual items. *Across University Ave. from ROM. Open Tues.–Sun. 10–5.*

**㊷** Just south of the ROM is the **McLaughlin Planetarium,** which attracts some 250,000 visitors a year. There are four new 45-minute star shows each year. Open since 1986 is the **Astrocentre,** which has hands-on exhibits, computer terminals designed for both adults and children, and an animated model of the star system. *Tel. 416/586–5736. Admission: $5.50 adults, $3.50 students and senior citizens, $2.75 children 6–18. Senior citizens free on Tues. Open same hrs as ROM, plus evening hrs for star shows. Tel. 416/586–5751 for taped description of current night sky.*

A five-minute walk south of the planetarium will bring you to the **㊸** **Sigmund Samuel Canadiana Collection** (part of the ROM) of early Canadian furnishings, glassware, silver, and six room settings of 18th- and 19th-century furniture. *14 Queen's Park Crescent W, on the northwest corner of University Ave. and College St. Open Tues.–Sat. 10–5, Sun. 1–5.*

After so much culture, you may wish to enjoy one of the most dynamic and expensive areas of Toronto—**Yorkville.** Some call it
Toronto's Rodeo Drive; others call it Toronto's Fifth Avenue. One
thing is certain: These blocks are packed with specialty shops, ritzy
restaurants, and high-price stores specializing in designer clothes,
furs, and jewels.

**The Colonnade,** on the south side of Bloor Street, a few doors east of
University Avenue, has recently undergone a $10 million face-lift.
In addition to several levels of luxury residential apartments and
private offices, it also has two floors of stores selling quality leather
goods, perfumes, jewelry, and European apparel. Take a walk to the
upper floor for a fascinating visit to **The Bata Shoe Museum Collection,** the only such exhibition in North America. Some artifacts displayed here are more than 4,000 years old and are from nearly every
country in the world. Arranged in three main galleries, the museum
features the interactive Shoe Discovery Centre; the Highlights Gallery, boasting famous people's footwear; and the Feature Gallery, in
which North American footwear is displayed. Items such as pressu-
rized sky-diving boots, iron-spiked shoes used for crushing chest-
nuts, and smugglers clogs are just a few of the 4,500 pieces in this
collection. *Tel. 416/924–7463. Admission to museum: $3 adults, $1
students, senior citizens, and children, $6 families. Open Tues.–
Sun. 11–6.*

A block north of Bloor and Yonge streets is the magnificent **Metropolitan Toronto Library.** Arranged around a tall, wide interior atrium, the library gives a fabulous sense of open space. It was designed
by one of Canada's most admired architects, Raymond Moriyama,
who also created the Ontario Science Centre. Browsers will appreciate that fully one-third of the more than 1.3 million books—spread
across 28 miles of shelves—are open to the public. In the many audio
carrels, with headphones, you may listen to any one of more than
10,000 albums. The **Arthur Conan Doyle Room** houses the finest public collection of Holmesiana anywhere, with records, films, photos,
books, manuscripts, and letters. *789 Yonge St., just steps north of
Bloor St., tel. 416/393–7000. Open May–Sept., Mon.–Thurs. 9–9,
Fri. 9–6, Sat. 9–5; Oct.–Apr., Sun. 1:30–5. To get an answer to any
question, on any subject, tel. 416/393–7131.*

On the east side of Avenue Road, two blocks north of Bloor Street, is
a don't-miss shopping area—**Hazelton Lanes** (tel. 416/968–8600).
Offering everything from Swiss chocolates to Hermès silks and
Giorgio Armani's latest fashions, this is a wonderful, magical paean
to capitalism. And in 1989 it doubled, in size and glory, with the addition of some 80 new stores. But be warned—prices here are as
high as they get in Toronto.

**Casa Loma** (1 Austin Terr.; on Spadina Ave., south of St. Clair Ave.;
and near the St. Clair West subway stop) is an honest-to-goodness
20th-century castle, with 98 rooms; two towers; secret panels; long,
creepy passageways; and some of the best views of Toronto—all just
a short distance from the heart of the city. The medieval-style castle
was built shortly before World War I by Sir Henry Pellatt, a soldier
and financier who spent more than $3 million to construct his dream.
The architect E.J. Lennox, who also designed Toronto's Old City
Hall and King Edward Hotel, created a remarkable structure;
Toronto's "house on the hill" is a real treat. There are no more
guided tours of Casa Loma—you now get automatic tape record-
ings. That's all for the best, because you can drift through at your
own speed while the children rush off to the stables or towers. You'll
have walked a good mile by the time you're done, so wear sensible

shoes. *Tel. 416/923–1171. Admission: $8 adults, $4.50 senior citizens and children 6–16. Open daily 10–4. Closed Dec. 25 and Jan. 1.*

## What to See and Do with Children

**Free Attractions**

The **ferry boat** to the **Toronto Islands** and **Far Enough Farm** (*see* Tour 1, *above*).

The **David Dunlap Observatory** in Richmond Hill, just north of Metro Toronto, and the **McLaughlin Planetarium** (*see* Tour 3, *above*).

**Harbourfront** nearly always has free events and activities, from painting and sculpting to concerts and plays.

**Ontario Place,** just west of Harbourfront, is a waterfront entertainment complex built on three man-made islands that contains something for everyone: the **Cinesphere,** a dome with a six-story movie screen that shows Imax and 70mm films; several shows in pods that float above the water; the *Haida,* a World War II destroyer that's fun to explore; the outdoor **Forum,** where nightly concerts take place; various eateries; and **Children's Village,** with water games, slides, puppet shows, clowns, magicians, and a children's theater. *South of Lakeshore Blvd. (across from CNE grounds), tel. 416/314–9900. Admission free. Open mid-May–mid-Sept., daily. Bumper boats, pedal boats, Cinesphere, and concerts have nominal admission fees.*

**Modestly Priced Attractions**

**Apple, strawberry,** and **raspberry picking** are available within a short drive of downtown Toronto. Try **Al Ferri's** (15 minutes west of the airport, near the corner of Mississauga Road and Steeles Avenue; tel. 416/455–8202). Check out Ferri's astonishingly wonderful Macoun apples—like Red Delicious merged with MacIntosh. If Al Ferri's is full or picked out, as it sometimes is, drive farther along the same road to one of the many other fruit farms in the area.

The **Art Gallery of Ontario's** hands-on room and Henry Moore sculpture that children love to climb are popular attractions; and the fascinating, historic **Grange** house is another affordable option (*see* Tour 2, *above*).

In **Casa Loma,** children can explore the secret passages and towers of this 20th-century castle (*see* Tour 3, *above*).

**More Expensive Attractions**

The **Ontario Science Centre** is a stunningly successful blend of education and entertainment that should not be missed. It has free movies and thrilling space, communications, laser, and electricity exhibits, and an irresistible new exhibit called Challenger. Also, be sure to check out the marvelous permanent exhibit called The Sport Show. *770 Don Mills Rd., about 11 km (7 mi) from downtown. Take the Yonge St. subway from downtown to the Eglinton station and Eglinton East bus to the Don Mills Parkway stop. Tel. 416/696–3127 or 416/429–4100. Admission: $7.50 adults, $5.50 youths 13–17, $3 children 5–12, children under 5 free, $17 families (up to 8 members: 2 adults and 6 children). Free Fri. after 4 PM. Parking $2. Open Sun.–Thurs. and Sat. 10–6, Fri. 10–9.*

**Black Creek Pioneer Village** is as good a reproduction as you'll find of a rural Victorian community in the 1860s. Roblin's Mill, powered by a big wooden water wheel, grinds wheat as it was done 130 years ago. At the weaver's shop, a costumed interpreter explains the magic of the loom. At other artisans' shops scattered around the village, you can watch blacksmiths, clock makers, gunsmiths, and broom makers at their trade. *1000 Murray Ross Pkwy. (near Jane St. and Steeles Ave.), North York, M3J 2P3, tel. 416/736–1733. Admission:*

*$7 adults, $4.50 senior citizens, $3 children 5–14. Open mid-Mar.–
late Dec., daily 10–4:30. Closed Dec. 25.*

The **Young People's Theatre** (tel. 416/862–2222) often has excellent
fare, as do **Roy Thomson Hall** (tel. 416/593–4828) and the **Minkler
Auditorium** (tel. 416/491–8877).

**The Metro Toronto Zoo** was built for animals, not people. The Rouge
Valley, just east of Toronto, was an inspired choice of site when it
was built in the 1960s, with its varied terrain, from river valley to
dense forest, where mammals, birds, reptiles, and fish have been
grouped according to where they live in the wild. In most of the regions, you'll find remarkable botanical exhibits in enclosed, climate-
controlled pavilions. Don't miss the 3-ton banyan tree in the Indo-
Malayan Pavilion, the fan-shape traveler's palm from Madagascar in
the African Pavilion, or the perfumed flowers of the jasmine vines in
the Eurasian Pavilion. The "round-the-world tour" takes about
three hours and is suitable for any kind of weather, because most of
the time is spent inside pavilions. It's been estimated that it would
take four full days to see everything in the Metro Zoo, so study the
map you'll get at the zoo entrance and decide in advance what you
wish to see most.

For younger children, there is the delightful Littlefootland, a special area that allows contact with tame animals, such as rabbits and
sheep. In the winter, cross-country skiers follow groomed trails
that skirt the animal exhibits. Lessons and rentals are available.
There is an electrically powered train that moves silently among the
animals without frightening them. It can accommodate wheelchairs
(available free inside the main gate), and all pavilions have ramp access. For those on a very tight budget, the zoo is free if you show up
the last hour of the day, which is enough time to give you a taste of
this very impressive, world-class zoo. *Meadowvale Rd., just north of
Highway 401, in Scarborough, a 30-min drive from downtown; or
take Bus 86A from the Kennedy subway station. Tel. 416/392–5900.
Admission: $9.75 adults, $7 senior citizens and children 12–17, $5
children 5–11. Free parking in winter; parking Mar.–Oct. $4. Open
daily 9:30–4:30. Closed Dec. 25.*

**Cullen Gardens and Miniature Village** is located in Whitby, a 35-min-
ute drive east of downtown Toronto along Highway 401. Owned by
the family that runs one of Toronto's best-known garden-store
chains, the complex aptly stretches across 25 acres of carefully-
tended gardens and includes 140 miniature 1/12-scale buildings. Activities continue throughout the year, from a tulip festival in May, to
a rose festival June–July, and a winter carnival in late December
and early January. *300 Taunton Rd. W, Whitby L1N 5R5, tel. 905/
668–6606. Admission: $8.95 adults, $6.95 students and senior citizens, $3.95 children 3–12. Open daily 10–8 (open until 10 PM during
summer months). Closed January–Easter.*

## Off the Beaten Track

**Watching the Italian promenade.** St. Clair Avenue West, running
from Bathurst Street to Dufferin Street and beyond, remains the
heart of this city's vibrant Italian community. On many evenings,
especially Sunday, the street is filled with thousands of men and
women promenading between *gelaterie*, eyeing each other, and generally enjoying their neighbors.

**Greektown on a Sunday.** The Danforth (Bloor Street east of the Don
Valley Parkway) has great Greek restaurants, gift shops, and hun-

dreds of Greek Canadians promenading. Welcome to the Mediterranean!

There's no hotel more romantic than the **Guild Inn** (2010 Guildwood Pkwy., tel. 416/261–3331), and no view of Toronto more wonderful than from **Centre Island at sunset.**

A 45-minute drive north of downtown, in the village of Kleinburg, is the superb **McMichael Canadian Art Collection.** The landscape paintings of Canada's Group of Seven artists, and extensive collections of Inuit and Native art are only part of the McMichael's charm. The gallery is set in 100 acres of woodland, with strategically placed windows so that visitors can appreciate the scenery even as they admire the art. *10365 Islington Ave., Kleinburg (west of Hwy. 400, and north of Major Mackenzie Dr.), tel. 905/893–1121. Admission: $6 adults, $3 students and senior citizens, $13 families. Open Tues.–Sun. 10–4.*

# Shopping

Toronto prides itself on having some of the finest shopping in North America; and, indeed, most of the world's name boutiques can be found here. There's also a large artistic and crafts community, with many art galleries, custom jewelers, clothing designers, and artisans selling everything from sophisticated glass sculpture to Native art, traditional crafts, antiques, quilts, wood carvings, and pine furniture.

Local food items include wild rice, available in bulk or in gift packages, and maple syrup in jars or cans.

The biggest sale day of the year is Boxing Day, the first business day after Christmas, when nearly everything in the city is half-price. As winter fades, clothing prices tend to drop even further. Summer sales start in late June and continue through August.

**Bargaining** Shoppers can haggle at flea markets, including the Harbourfront Antique Market, and perhaps in the Chinatown and Kensington Market/Spadina Avenue areas. In some small boutiques, where the owner is in attendance, you may be able to negotiate for a better price than what you see on the ticket.

**Refund Information** Visitors, including Canadians from other provinces, can receive a refund on the GST and on the 8% Ontario sales tax for purchases over $100 (*see* GST and Sales Tax in Staying in Canada, *above*).

## Shopping Districts

The **Yorkville Avenue/Bloor Street area** is where you'll find the big fashion names, fine leather goods, important jewelers, some of the top private art galleries, upscale shoe stores, and discount china and glassware. Streets to explore include Yorkville Avenue, Cumberland Street, and Scollard Street, all running parallel to Bloor Street, and Hazelton Avenue, running north from Yorkville Avenue near Avenue Road. Hazelton Lanes, between Hazelton Avenue and Avenue Road, and the adjacent York Square are among the most chi-chi shopping areas in Canada, and they are headquarters for café society during the brief annual spell of warm weather.

On **Bloor Street** you'll find such wonderful stores as **Zoe,** with haute couture designs; **The Bay,** a department store with elegant, high-fashion designer clothes for men and women; **Holt Renfrew,** possibly the most stunning store in Toronto, with marble, chrome, glass, and glittering fashions for both sexes; **Eddie Bauer,** selling sturdily made and cleverly designed clothing, equipment, and accessories for all sports; **Harry Rosen** for men; **Georg Jensen;** and such shoe shops as **Boutique Quinto** and **David's.** Très expensive, and très good.

The **Eaton Centre** is a very large galleria-style shopping center downtown, on Yonge Street between Queen and Dundas streets. With scores of large and small stores and restaurants, all sheltered from the weather, it's one of the city's major tourist attractions. Generally speaking, the lower levels are lower priced and the higher levels are more expensive.

**Queen Street West,** starting just west of University Avenue and continuing past Spadina Avenue, creeping ever westward past Bathurst Street, is a trendy area near the Ontario College of Art. Here, you'll find young, hip designers; new and used-book bookstores; vintage clothes; two comic-book stores, including the biggest in North America (**Silver Snail,** No. 367; see also Dragon Lady Comic Shop at No. 200); and the more progressive private galleries.

**Harbourfront** includes an antiques market that's Canada's biggest on Sunday, when there are about 200 dealers (390 Queen's Quay W, tel. 416/260–2626; open Tues.–Fri. 11–6, Sat. 10–6, Sun. 8–6). The **Queen's Quay Terminal** is a renovated warehouse that now houses a collection of unique boutiques, craft stalls, patisseries, and so on; it's a great place to buy gifts. There's frequent streetcar service from Union Station, but it's a fairly easy walk. Parking is expensive.

**Spadina Avenue,** from Wellington Street north to College Street, has plenty of low-price clothing for the whole family, as well as fur and leather factory outlets. **Winner's,** south of King Street, is a good discount outlet for women and children. **Evex Luggage Centre,** 369 Spadina Avenue, south of College, has good discount luggage, handbags, and leather accessories.

Downtown Toronto has a vast underground maze of shopping warrens that burrow in between and underneath the office towers. The tenants of the **Underground City** are mostly the usual assortment of chain stores, and the shopping is rather dull; also, directions are poorly marked. The network runs roughly from the Royal York Hotel near Union Station north to the Eaton Centre.

## Department Stores

The major department stores have branches around the city and flagship stores downtown. They accept major credit cards and have liberal return policies. However, service tends to be very slow and uninformed compared with that of boutiques, and the stores generally lack the cachet of such American stores as Bloomingdale's or Macy's. The big names are **Eaton's,** in the Eaton Centre, and **The Bay** (The Hudson's Bay Company), on Yonge Street between Queen and Richmond streets and at Yonge and Bloor streets.

## Specialty Shops

**Antiques and Galleries** Yorkville is the headquarters of the establishment antiques dealers. There are several other pockets around town, including a strip along Queen Street East, roughly between Sherbourne and George streets.

**The Allery** (322½ Queen St. W, tel. 416/593–0853) specializes in antique prints and maps. **Art Metropole** (788 King St. W, tel. 416/367–

2304) specializes in limited-edition, small-press, or self-published artists' books from around the world. **Ballenford Architectural Books** (98 Scollard St., tel. 416/960–0055) has Canada's largest selection of architectural titles and a gallery with usually interesting exhibits of architectural drawings and related work. **Jane Corkin Gallery** (179 John St., north of Queen St., tel. 416/979–1980) specializes in photography. In the same building is **Isaacs Gallery,** owned by Av Isaacs, godfather of many of the established Canadian artists. The more avant-garde galleries include **Cold City** (30 Duncan St.), **YYZ** (1087 Queen St. W), and **Mercer Union** (333 Adelaide St. W). Also check out **Toronto Photographers Workshop** and the other galleries at 80 Spadina Avenue, where you'll usually find at least one opening on a Saturday afternoon. **Prime Canadian Crafts** (52 Bacal St., tel. 416/593–5750) has an ever-changing array of merchandise. **Quasi Modo** (789 Queen St. W, next door to Dufflet Pastries, tel. 416/366–8370) has a quirky collection of 20th-century furniture and design. You never know what will be on display: vintage bicycles, Noguchi lamps, a corrugated cardboard table by Frank Gehry. **20th Century** (23 Beverley St., just north of Queen St., tel. 416/598–2172) is for serious collectors of 20th-century design, particularly furniture, lamps, jewelry, and decorative arts. Many of the pieces are museum quality, and the owners are extremely erudite.

**Books**    Toronto is rich in bookstores selling new books, used books, bestsellers, and remainders. If you just need a current magazine or a paperback for the plane, there are the ubiquitous chains—Coles, Classic Bookshops, and W. H. Smith. Otherwise, try:

The **Albert Britnell Book Shop** (765 Yonge St., just north of Bloor St., tel. 416/924–3321) has been a Toronto legend since 1893, with a marvelous, British ambience and great browsing.

The **Book Cellar** (1560 Yonge St., above St. Clair Ave., tel. 416/967–5577; 142 Yorkville Ave., near Avenue Rd., tel. 416/925–9955) offers a fine choice of classical records, as well as international political and intellectual journals.

**Book City** has three locations (501 Bloor St. W, near Honest Ed's, tel. 416/961–4496; Carrot Common, 348 Danforth Ave., near Chester Station, tel. 416/469–9997; and 2350 Bloor St. W., tel. 416/766–9412). It's strong on good remaindered books and has a knowledgeable staff.

**Edward's Books and Art,** one of the loveliest minichains in the city, now at four locations (356 Queen St. W, near Spadina Ave., tel. 416/593–0126; 2179 Queen St. E, in The Beaches, tel. 416/698–1442; 170 Bloor St. W, in the Park Plaza Hotel, tel. 416/961–2428; and 2200 Yonge St., south of Eglinton Ave., tel. 416/487–5431), advertises huge discounts on best-sellers and remainders in every Saturday's *Globe and Mail.* All are open Sunday.

**Longhouse Book Shop** (497 Bloor St. W, just west of Bathurst St., tel. 416/921–9995) stocks only Canadian titles, handsomely shelved or piled high on pine tables: more than 20,000 back titles and new publications.

**Bob Miller Book Room** (180 Bloor St. W, just northwest of the ROM, tel. 416/922–3557) has the best literature section in the city and a staff that has been with Bob for decades.

**Pages Books and Magazines** (256 Queen St. W, tel. 416/598–1447) has a wide selection of international and small-press literature; fashion and design books and magazines; and books on film, art, and literary criticism. This is one astoundingly intellectual bookstore!

**This Ain't the Rosedale Library** (483 Church St., south of Wellesley Ave., tel. 416/929–9912) stocks the largest selection of baseball books in Canada, as well as a good selection of fiction, poetry, photography, design, rock, and jazz books.

**Writers & Co.** (2005 Yonge Street near Davisville, a few blocks south of Eglinton, tel. 416/481–8432) is arguably Canada's finest literary bookstore, with hard-to-find poets, essayists, and world novelists. If you have been looking for a rare Caribbean poetry collection, a Swedish play in translation, or an Asian novella, this is the store to visit. It's a marvelous place, and they'll be happy to order any book for you.

**Clothing**   Queen Street West is well known for its stores catering to the young, hip, and zany. Among those in the neighborhood are: **Fab Gear** (No. 275); **290 Ion** (No. 290); **Fashion Crimes** (No. 395); **Boomer** (No. 309) for men; and **I.X.L.** (No. 202). Yonge Street is also a popular area for clothes shopping. Stores here include a branch of I.X.L (No. 535) and **B Scene** (No. 584).

**Brown's** (1975 Avenue Rd., south of Hwy. 401, tel. 416/489–1975) provides classic clothing for short men and women. There's also a store for men only (545 Queen St. W, tel. 416/368–5937). An offshoot is **Muskat & Brown** (2528 Yonge St., tel. 416/489–4005) for petite women.

**Fetoun** (97 Scollard St., tel. 416/923–3434) is one of the latest high-fashion emporiums for the nouveau riche. If you go to a lot of charity balls, this is the place to shop.

**Linda Lundstrom,** (Street Level, 2 First Canadian Pl., tel. 416/391–2838) is an award-winning designer of high-fashion, winter clothing. This is the place to buy an eye-catching parka.

**Food Markets**   **Kensington Market** (northwest of Dundas St. and Spadina Ave.) is an outdoor market with a vibrant ethnic mix. Saturday is the best day to go, preferably by public transit, because parking is difficult.

**St. Lawrence Market** (Front St. and Jarvis St., tel. 416/392–7219) is best early on Saturday, when, in addition to the permanent indoor market on the south side of Front Street, there's a farmer's market in the building on the north side. The historic south market was once Toronto's city hall, and it fronted the lake before extensive landfill projects were undertaken.

**Gift Ideas**   **The Guild Shop** (140 Cumberland St., tel. 416/921–1721) is an outlet for a wide variety of Canadian artists, in the broadest sense of the word. Soapstone carvings from Inuit communities in the Arctic, aboriginal paintings from British Columbia and Ontario, and even woollen ties from Nova Scotia are among the items for sale. Even if you don't buy anything, the Guild Shop is worth a visit for an appreciation of indigenous Canadian arts and crafts.

**Bragg** (446 Queen St., west of Spadina Ave., tel. 416/264–0756) has an amusing assortment of vintage bric-a-brac, china, cards, and jewelry.

**Arts-on-King** (169 King St. E, tel. 416/777–9617) is a bright and spacious store with a varied selection of glass, ceramic, wood, and other creations. Established artists have exhibits in the Loft Galleries.

**Filigree** (1210 Yonge St., tel. 416/961–5223) has a good assortment of linens, as well as drawer liners, silver frames, and other Victorian pleasures. In the neighborhood are other gift shops selling fine glass and antiques.

Jewelry **Secrett Jewel Salon** (150 Bloor St. W, tel. 416/967–7500) is a reputable source of unusual gemstones and fine new and estate jewelry; local gemologists consider it the best in town.

# Sports and Fitness

## Participant Sports

Contact the Ministry of Tourism and Recreation (Queen's Park, Toronto, Ont. M7A 2R2) for pamphlets on various activities. For information on sports activities in the province, call 800/268–3735 from anywhere in the continental United States and Canada (except the Northwest Territories and the Yukon). In Toronto, contact Ontario Travel (tel. 416/314–4008).

A number of fine **conservation areas** circle Metro Toronto, many less than a half-hour from downtown. Most have large swimming areas, sledding, and cross-country skiing, as well as skating, fishing, and boating. Contact the Metro Conservation Authority (tel. 416/661–6600) and ask for a pamphlet.

Bicycling There are more than 29 kilometers (18 miles) of street bike routes cutting across the city and dozens more along safer paths through Toronto's many parks. Bikes can be rented on the Toronto Islands. The **Martin Goodman Trail** is a 19-kilometer (12-mile) strip that runs along the waterfront all the way from the Balmy Beach Club in the east end out past the western beaches southwest of High Park.

**Metro Parks Department** (tel. 416/392–8186) has maps that show bike (and jogging) routes that run through Toronto parkland. **Ontario Cycling** (tel. 416/495–4141) has maps, booklets, and information. Maps are available at most local bike shops.

Boating Grenadier Pond, in High Park, Centre Island, Ontario Place, Harbourfront, and most of the Conservation Areas surrounding Metro Toronto rent canoes, punts, and/or sailboats.

Fishing One does not have to go very far from downtown Toronto to catch trout, perch, bass, walleye, salmon, muskie, pike, and whitefish. Contact Communication Services, Wildlife Information, Ministry of Natural Resources (Queen's Park, Toronto M7A 1W3, tel. 416/314–2225).

Within Metro Toronto itself, fishing is permitted in the trout pond at Hanlan's Point on Toronto Island, as well as in Grenadier Pond in High Park. And the salmon fishing just off the Scarborough Bluffs, in Toronto's east end, is extraordinary.

There are more than 100 charter boats on Lake Ontario (about $60 for a half-day). Contact **Ontario Travel** (tel. 416/314–0944). Be warned, though: Some fish caught in this province have such high levels of mercury in them that you can take your temperature at the same time that you eat them. It's sad, but water pollution (including acid rain) has taken its toll upon the edibility of many fish in Ontario.

Golf The season lasts only from April to late October. The top course is **Glen Abbey** (tel. 416/844–1800), where the Canadian Open Championships is held in late summer. Cart and greens fees will cost up to $75 on weekends, but this course is a real beauty.

Less challenging courses—but much closer to the heart of the city— are the **Don Valley Golf Course** (Yonge St., tel. 416/392–2465); just south of Highway 401 and the **Flemingdon Park Golf Club** (Don Mills

Rd. and Eglinton Ave., tel. 416/429–1740). For other courses, contact Metro Parks (tel. 416/406–5587) or Ontario Travel (tel. 416/314–0944).

**Horseback** There is one stable within the city limits. **SunnyBrook Stables**
**Riding** (Leslie St. and Eglinton Ave., tel. 416/444–4044), in Sunnybrook Park, has an indoor arena, an outdoor ring, and about 19 kilometers (nearly 12 miles) of bridle trails through the Don Valley.

**Hotel Health** Nearly every major hotel in the Metro Toronto area has a decent in-
**Facilities** door swimming pool; some even have indoor/outdoor swimming pools. The best include the **Sheraton Centre,** at Queen and Bay streets, and the **Inn on the Park,** at Eglinton Avenue near Leslie Street. Many also have health clubs, with saunas and Nautilus equipment.

**Ice Skating** Toronto operates some 30 outdoor artificial rinks and 100 natural-ice rinks—and all are free! Among the most popular are in Nathan Phillips Square, in front of the New City Hall, at Queen and Bay streets; down at Harbourfront, which has Canada's largest outdoor artificial ice rink; College Park, at Yonge and College streets; Grenadier Pond, within High Park, at Bloor and Keele streets; and inside Hazelton Lanes, that classy shopping mall on the edge of Yorkville, on Avenue Road, just above Bloor Street. For details on any city rink, call 416/392–1111.

**Jogging** The **Martin Goodman Trail** (*see* Bicycling, *above*) is ideal. Also try the boardwalk of The Beaches in the east end, High Park in the west end, the Toronto Islands, or any of Toronto's parks.

**Sailing** This can be a breeze, especially between April and October. Contact the **Ontario Sailing Association** (tel. 416/495–4240). The **Royal Canadian Yacht Club** has its summer headquarters in a beautiful Victorian mansion on Centre Island (tel. 416/967–7245).

**Skiing** Try Toronto's parks and ravines; High Park; the lakefront along the
*Cross-country* southern edge of the city; Tommy Thompson Park; Toronto Islands; and Centennial Park, in the western borough of Etobicoke, only a 20-minute drive from downtown. Check the yellow pages for ski-equipment rentals; there are many places.

*Downhill* Although there are a few places where one can get a taste of this sport within Metro Toronto, such as **Earl Bales Park,** on Bathurst Street, just south of Sheppard Avenue, and **Centennial Park Ski Hill** (tel. 416/394–8754), in Etobicoke the *best* alpine hills are a good 45–60 minutes north of the city. These include **Blue Mountain Resorts** (tel. 416/869–3799) in Collingwood, the **Caledon Ski Club** (tel. 519/927–5221) in Caledon, **Glen Eden Ski Area** (tel. 905/878–5011) in Milton, **Hidden Valley** (tel. 705/789–2301) in Huntsville, **Hockley Valley Resort** (tel. 519/942–0754) in Orangeville, **Horseshoe Valley** (tel. 705/835–2790) in Barrie, and **Snow Valley Ski Resort** (tel. 905/366–7669), just outside Barrie. Call 416/314–0998 for daily reports on lifts and surface conditions.

**Sleigh Riding** **Black Creek Pioneer Village** (tel. 416/661–6610 or 416/661–6600),
**and** north of 401 along Highway 400, at Steeles Avenue, is open winter
**Tobogganing** weekends 10–5 for skating, tobogganing, and horse-drawn sleigh rides. The best parks for tobogganing include **High Park,** in the west end, and **Winston Churchill Park,** at Spadina and St. Clair avenues, just two blocks from Casa Loma: It is sheer terror.

**Tennis** The city provides dozens of courts, all free, and many of them flood-lit. Parks with courts open from 7 AM to 11 PM, in season, include the famous High Park in the west end; Stanley Park, on King Street West, three blocks west of Bathurst Street; and Eglinton Park, on Eglinton Avenue West, just east of Avenue Road. A number of indoor courts are open throughout the winter months. Call the **Ontario Tennis Association** (tel. 416/495–4215).

## Spectator Sports

**Auto Racing**  For the past several years, the **Molson Indy** (tel. 416/260–4639) has been roaring around the Canadian National Exhibition grounds, including the major thoroughfare of Lakeshore Boulevard, for three days in mid-July. You'll pay more than $85 for a three-day "red" reserved seat, but general admission for the qualifying rounds, the practice rounds, and the Indy itself can be as cheap as $10–$20, depending upon the day.

Less than a half-hour drive away is the **Cayuga International Speedway** (tel. 905/765–5305), where international stock-car races are held from May through September.

**Baseball**  The **Toronto Blue Jays,** whose home is the SkyDome, have developed into one of baseball's most dynamic teams. Indeed, their back-to-back World Series wins in 1992 and 1993 still have the whole city buzzing. The Jays have the most costly tickets in the major leagues, ranging from rotten $5 seats (nicknamed nose-bleeds) up to ones that cost $11, $15, and $19.50, and they usually sell out every single home game, so plan way ahead of your Toronto visit. *For ticket information, tel. 416/341–1111.*

**Canoeing and Rowing**  One of the world's largest **canoeing and rowing regattas** is held every July 1, as it has been for more than a century, on Toronto Island's Long Pond. *Canoe Ontario, tel. 416/495–4180.*

**Football**  The Canadian Football League has teetered near extinction in recent years, but was given a new lease on life when it expanded into such un-Canadian locations as Sacramento, California, in 1993. The **Toronto Argonauts,** which are partly owned by hockey superstar Wayne Gretzky, have been as erratic as the league itself. The Argos play their home games at the SkyDome. Americans might find the three downs and 110-yard field to be rather quaint, but the game is much like their own. *Tel. 416/595–1131 for tickets and information.*

**Golf**  The permanent site of the **Canadian Open** golf championship is Glen Abbey, a course designed by Jack Nicklaus. This tournament is one of golf's Big Five and is always played in late summer. *Less than a 45-min drive west, along the Queen Elizabeth Way (QEW). Tel. 416/844–1800.*

**Hockey**  The **Toronto Maple Leafs** play 40 home games each season (Oct.–Apr.), usually on Wednesday and Saturday nights, in the big, ugly Maple Leaf Gardens. There are always tickets available at each game—at least from scalpers in front of the stadium on Carlton Street, a half-block east of the corner of Yonge and College streets. Call the office (tel. 416/977–1641) at 9 AM sharp on the day of the game you wish to see.

**Horse Racing**  The **Greenwood** track, built in 1874, is where the best trotters and pacers do their stuff at three annual meetings. *Tel. 416/675–6110.*
**Harness Racing**  *Spring gathering runs Jan.–mid-Mar.; summer meeting, late May–Sept.; brief winter meeting, last 2 wks in Dec.*

**Thoroughbred Racing**  There are four major racetracks handled by the Ontario Jockey Club (tel. 416/675–6110).

**Greenwood Race Track** is one of the premier harness tracks in North America and is the home of many of Canada's greatest trotting and pacing events, including the North American Cup. It is located in the city's east end, a 10-minute streetcar ride from downtown, at Woodbine Avenue and Queen Street East, near the lakeshore. *Tel. 416/698–3131. Winter meeting runs late Oct.–early Dec.; spring meeting runs mid-Mar.–late Apr.*

**Woodbine Race Track** is the showplace of thoroughbred racing in Canada. Horses run late Apr.–late Oct. *Located 30-min northwest of downtown Toronto, not far from the airport, at Hwy. 27 and Rexdale Blvd., tel. 416/675–6110.*

**Mohawk** is in the heart of Ontario's standardbred breeding country, and it features a glass-enclosed, climate-controlled grandstand and other attractive facilities. *A 30-min drive west of Toronto, along Hwy. 401, past the town of Milton, tel. 905/854–2255.*

**Fort Erie,** in the Niagara tourist region, is one of the most picturesque racetracks in the world, with willows, manicured hedges, and flower-bordered infield lakes. It has racing on the dirt as well as on grass, with the year's highlight being the Prince of Wales Stakes, the second jewel in Canada's Triple Crown of Racing. 230 Catherine St., *tel. 905/871–3200 from Toronto, 716/856–0293 from Buffalo.*

**Royal Horse Show** This highlight of Canada's equestrian season is part of the Royal Winter Fair each November. *The CNE grounds, Dufferin St., by the waterfront, tel. 416/393–6400.*

**Soccer** Although Toronto keeps getting and losing and getting a professional soccer team, one can catch this exciting sport, as well as collegiate football, in the very handy **Varsity Stadium.** *Bloor St. W at Bedford, 1 block west of Royal Ontario Museum and University Ave., tel. 416/978–7389.*

# Dining

*By Sara Waxman*

*Restaurant critic for the Financial Post and the Toronto Sun, Sara Waxman is the author of three best-selling cookbooks and a Toronto restaurant guide.*

The restaurant scene is in a state of perpetual motion. Is it the recession that causes all those openings and closings, or is everyone searching for that elusive, perfect little restaurant? Still, more new restaurants opened than closed this year in Toronto.

The formal haute cuisine establishments have all but faded into Toronto's gastronomic history, making way for bistros, cantinas, tavernas, trattorias, tapas bars, noodle bars, wine bars, and smart cafés. No new steak house has opened in a decade. Meanwhile, the cuisines of the world have appeared on Toronto's doorstep. Recipes need no passports to cross borders. Little Italy, three different Chinatowns, Little India, and of course, the cooking of Southeast Asia—a tidal wave of Korean, Vietnamese, Laotian, Thai, and Malaysian restaurants—are taking our taste buds by storm with their assertive, clean flavors: chili, ginger, lemongrass, coconut, lime, and tamarind.

Toronto's brilliant young chefs recognize that when most customers start requesting "sauce on the side," the public's collective taste is changing; those with vision are looking over their shoulders toward California for a more creative marriage of fresh-market ingredients.

Highly recommended restaurants in each category are indicated with a star ★.

| Category | Cost* |
|----------|-------|
| $$$$ | over $40 |
| $$$ | $30–$40 |
| $$ | $20–$30 |
| $ | under $20 |

*per person without tax, tip, or drinks*

## Cafés

**$$** **Studio Café.** At this well-lit, comfortable café—a combination hotel
**★** coffee shop, restaurant, and contemporary glass-and-art gallery—
you can experience a full Japanese breakfast; order nutritionally
balanced selections lower in calories, sodium, and fat (try the exu-
berant presentation of chicken stir fry with Shanghainese noodles);
and indulge in such trend-setting pastas as three-cheese rigatoni
with oven-roasted plum tomato. The homey braised lamb shank with
buttermilk mashed potatoes, and the applewood smoked salmon
sandwich with cream cheese on pumpernickel prove that there's
something good here for every taste. For the kids, there's spaghetti
Italiano, Hot Diggety Dog, and more. *Four Seasons Hotel, 21 Ave-
nue Rd. (north of Bloor St.), tel. 416/964–0411. Reservations ad-
vised. Dress: casual but neat. AE, DC, MC, V.*

**$** **Future Bakery & Café.** A European-style bakery has blossomed into
a small chain of cafeterias supplied by their own dairy. Old Europe-
an recipes have remained: beef borscht, buckwheat cabbage rolls,
and potato cheese *varenycky* slathered with thick sour cream. This
place is beloved by students for its generous portions, by homesick
Europeans hungry for goulash and knishes, by the cheesecake-and-
coffee crowd, by health-conscious foodies looking for fruit salad with
homemade yogurt and honey, and by people-watchers looking for
people worth watching from 7 AM to 1 AM. *1535 Yonge St., tel. 416/
944–1253; 438 Bloor St. W, tel. 416/922–5875; 2199 Bloor St. W, tel.
416/769–5020; 739 Queen St. W, tel. 416/368–4235; St. Lawrence
Market, 95 Front St. E, tel. 416/366–7259. No reservations. Dress:
casual. MC, V.*

**$** **Masquerade Caffe Bar.** An eclectic array of red, yellow, blue, and
green sofas, chairs, and banquettes fills this Fellini-esque environ-
ment. The Harlequin pattern of the bar is echoed in the red-on-red
walls. Murano glass mosaics add sparkle to the huge primary color
stoves. The daily changing Italian menu may include roasted onion
soup with pesto croutons; exotic lettuce salad with tuna, cheese, ol-
ives, marinated mushrooms; a seafood or vegetable antipasto; saf-
fron and porcini risotto; divine mushroom-filled ravioli; or a choice of
panini—Italian sandwiches on homemade breads with scrumptious
meat, cheese, and veggie fillings. Zabaglione—eggs, marsala wine,
and a bit of sugar whipped to a thick, frothy cream and poured over
fresh berries—is a knockout dessert. *BCE Place, Front and Yonge
Sts., tel. 416/363–8971. No reservations. Dress: casual but neat.
AE, DC, MC, V.*

## Chinese

**$$** **Roppongi.** Recessed lighting in a charcoal gray room with unusual
tables of brushed metals, and deep, comfortable banquettes give
this restaurant in a downtown office tower an air of sophistication.
Although Chinese cuisine is served, owner Athena Ho and several of

74

## Toronto Dining

Auberge
du Pommier, **27**
Bistro 990, **14**
Centro, **25**
Chinese
Vegetarian
House, **5**
Cuisine of
India, **20**
Future Bakery
& Café, **22**
Giovanna
Trattoria, **3**
Grano, **24**
Il Fornello, **9**
Il Posto, **18**
Joso's, **17**
Jump Café &
Bar, **11**
KitKat Bar &
Grill, **7**
Le Bistingo, **8**
Masquerade
Caffe Bar, **12**
Movenpick, **10**
Nami, **13**
North 44, **26**
Otago, **23**
Prego, **15**
Pronto, **28**
Renaissance
Café, **1**
Roppongi, **6**
Splendido, **2**
Studio Café, **19**
Thai Magic, **21**
Vanipha
Lanna, **16**
Wah Sing, **4**

Lowther Ave.

Albany Ave.

Howland Ave.

Madison Ave.

Bloor St. W.

Lennox St.

Borden St.

Brunswick Ave.

Sussex Ave

Sussex Mews

Huron St.

St. George St.

Harbord St.

Spadina Ave.

Ulster St.

Croft St.

Lippincott St.

Major St.

Robert St.

Willcocks St.

Russell St.

Euclid Ave.

College St.

Oxford St.

Huron St.

Henry St.

Nassau St.

Cecil St.

Palmerston Blvd.

Markham St.

Bathurst St.

Bellevue Ave.

Nassau Ave.

Baldwin St.

D'Arcy St.

Dundas St. W.

Grange
Park

Alexandra
Park

Denison St.

Augusta Ave.

Sullivan St.

Beverley St.

Robinson St.

Carr St.

Wolseley St.

Bulwer St.

Soho St.

Tecumseth St.

Richmond St. W.

Spadina Ave.

Bathurst St.

Adelaide St. W.

Peter St.

Widmer St.

John St.

KEY

AE American Express Office

0        440 yards

0        400 meters

King St. W.

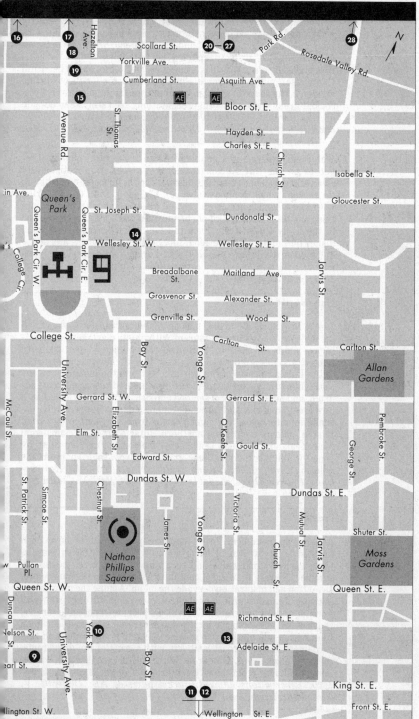

her staff speak Japanese, and the restaurant is named after an upscale area of Tokyo. The waiters are adept at discovering exactly what you'd like to eat. Savor the crisp rolled pancakes stuffed with juicy duck meat, mushrooms, and green onions, or try the extravagant "flying fish" dish—deep fried fish with fried wonton "sails"— that makes heads turn as it's brought to your table, or the beautiful Cantonese "goldfish-swimming-in-a-pond" entrée—minced shrimp molded in the shape of goldfish, steamed, and arranged in a circle on cooked greens. Such fanciful presentations are rarely seen outside of Asia. Karaoke begins at 10 PM. *230 Richmond St. W, tel. 416/977–6622. Reservations advised. Dress: casual but neat. AE, DC, MC, V. Closed Sat. and Sun. lunch.*

$ **Wah Sing.** Just one of a jumble of Asian restaurants clustered together on the tiny Kensington Market street, this meticulously clean and spacious restaurant has two-for-the-price-of-one lobsters (in season, which is almost always). Chopped, shell on, and fried with black-bean sauce or ginger and green onion, they're scrumptious and tender. Or try giant shrimp Szechuan-style, or choose one of the lively Queen crabs from the tank. Chicken and vegetarian dishes for landlubbers are good, too. Service is pleasant, and at the end of your meal there's a juicy, sliced orange for dessert. *41 Baldwin St., tel. 416/596–1628. Reservations required for 7 or more. Dress: casual. AE, MC, V.*

## Fish/Seafood

$$$–$$$$ **Joso's.** Joso Spralja—artist, musician, and restaurateur—has filled
★ his midtown, two-story restaurant with objets d'art: sensual paintings of nudes and the sea, stylized busts of women, signed celebrity photos, and intriguing wall hangings. The kitchen prepares dishes of the Dalmatian side of the Adriatic Sea, and the international artistic community who frequent the place adore the magnificent, unusual, and healthy array of seafood and fish. *Risotto carajoi* is Joso's own creation of rice and sea snails simmered in an aggressively seasoned tomato sauce. Try tiger prawns from Vietnam, porgy from Boston, salmon trout from northern Ontario, or baby clams from New Zealand. The dish that seems most often carried aloft by speed-walking servers is flame-grilled prawns, their charred tails pointing skyward. *202 Davenport Rd., tel. 416/925–1903. Reservations required. Dress: casual but neat. AE, DC, MC, V. Closed Sat. lunch, Sun.*

## French

$$$–$$$$ **Auberge du Pommier.** Two groundskeepers' cottages have been merged to create this French country restaurant with murals, whitewashed stone walls, and rough hewn ivy-covered beams. In summer, flowers in massive containers show their glorious colors. Invention and inspiration pervade the menu. Among the unusual appetizers is warm soufflé of goat cheese served on bitter greens with a creamy cider vinaigrette. The waiters provide impeccable service; they're well versed in the intricacies of serving soy-roasted salmon fillet with a julienne of crisp sesame vegetables and sweet-and-tart cardamom sauce, or roast lamb loin with a crust of sun-dried tomatoes and black olives. Dinner at this beautiful spot is worth the 20-minute cab ride from the city center. *4150 Yonge St., tel. 416/222–2220. Reservations advised. Jacket advised. AE, DC, MC, V. Closed Sat. lunch, Sun.*

**$$$ Bistro 990.** A superior kitchen combined with bistro informality make this a favorite restaurant for the 90s. Start dinner with steamed Prince Edward Island string cultured mussels with a red tomato curry and cilantro, or Provençal fish soup with rouille and garlic croutons; move on to traditional Bavette steak, grilled rare and served with frites and bordelaise or roquefort sauce; or pan-roasted half chicken with garlic, mashed potatoes, and rosemary. Pasta might be fusilli with peppers, tomatoes, olives, basil, and parmesan. The purist kitchen uses artesian spring water for all stocks and homemade breads. Country-style desserts such as apple and sun-dried cherry crumble, and lemon tart, are not grand, just wonderful. Faux stone walls stencilled with Cocteau-esque designs, sturdily upholstered chairs, and a tiled floor create an ambiance where a jacket and tie is easily as acceptable as casual clothes. *990 Bay St., tel. 416/921–9990. Reservations advised. Dress: casual but neat. AE, DC, MC, V. Closed Sat. lunch, Sun.*

**$$ Le Bistingo.** In this true bistro on Queen Street—Toronto's answer to the Left Bank—George Gurnon stands "en garde" in the dining room, while co-owner Claude Bouillet commands in the kitchen. Persimmon walls are hung with an arresting exhibit of Bouillet's own photographs; oak bar and floors gleam. Filled with attractive habitués, this place exudes the spirit of France. The food is superior. Try the steaming tureen of intensely flavored fish soup with croutons and rouille, or ovals of fresh goat cheese whisked with hot pepper flakes and chives; and whether the entrée is calves liver with onions, a half roast chicken with sweet garlic cloves, or grilled red snapper with a ragout of littleneck clams and shrimp, don't deprive yourself of warm apple tart with ice cream for dessert. *349 Queen St. W, tel. 416/598–3490. Reservations advised. Dress: casual. AE, MC, V. Closed Sat. lunch, Sun.*

**$$ Otago.** The room is simply done—nothing that might interfere with its raison d'être: the personal, innovative, French cuisine of chef-owner Vaughan Chittock. Knowledgeable servers in blue jeans and casual shirts complement the unpretentious tone set by the young New Zealander. Appetizers and salads are visually stunning. Silken ovals of chicken liver terrine melt on the tongue, splashed with bitter chocolate dressing and textured with tiny frozen grapes that create explosions of flavor in the mouth. The lamb is outstanding. Sometimes it's a pan-roasted rack, served with a slice of sirloin, sweet breads, kidney, and tongue all bound with a rich Merlot wine sauce; sometimes the roast comes on sweet tomato confit with a dark coriander sauce. Chicken is scented with cinnamon, partnered with roasted walnuts and morels. Desserts such as coconut rum soufflé with crème anglaise heart are what sweet fantasies are made of. *1995 Yonge St., tel. 416/486–7060. Reservations advised. Dress: casual but neat. AE, DC, MC, V. Closed Sat. lunch, Sun.*

## Indian

**$$ Cuisine of India.** It's fascinating to see Chef Shishir Sharma at work in the glass-walled, open kitchen of his casually-styled, unassuming, suburban restaurant. He slaps a ball of dough with his hands, thrusts it onto a smooth, round rock, and lowers it into the depths of the tandoor oven. Moments later, the puffy, crusty, buttery-center *naan* is ready to eat. Sharma has mastered the art of blending spices, herbs, and roots with other ingredients and achieves a delicate balance of flavors and visual appeal. He lifts a whole salmon trout from it's marinade, fits it onto a forged steel skewer, and plunges it deep into the tandoor. A whole leg of lamb for two, halved chicken breasts, and giant shrimp can all be ordered oven-baked, too. Vegans can also enjoy elaborate dinners here. The vegetable dishes are diverse in their seasonings, and come with fragrant basmati rice. It's worth the 20-minute taxi ride from the city center to enjoy this exquisite cuisine. *5222 Yonge St., tel. 416/229-0377. Reservations required. Dress: casual but neat. AE, DC, MC, V.*

### Italian

**$$$–$$$$**    **Centro.** The facade of etched glass, granite, and marble shouts hard-
★    edge. But inside it's as warm as the folksy blow-ups of owner Franco Prevedello's home town of Asolo, in northern Italy. Massive columns that seem to hold up a bright blue ceiling, and salmon-color walls lined with comfortable banquettes help to create an intimate space of this 182-seat restaurant. Many would say this is Toronto's best restaurant; regardless, it *is* the trendsetter. Every detail—from the variety of homemade breads to the incredible desserts, from the coat check to the valet parking—is overseen by Franco. You can be sure that he's tasted the ricotta and spinach gnocchi with a ragout of scallion and herb-seasoned sweetbreads, and he's approved the peppered linguine with clams, basil, and pancetta. The 2-inch-thick veal chop grilled over mesquite tingles with Sicilian seasoning; poached Atlantic salmon nestles gently in a bowl of elegant risotto and asparagus. The menu doesn't just change with each season, it seems to get better. *2472 Yonge St., tel. 416/483-2211. Reservations required. Jacket advised. AE, DC, MC, V. Closed Sun.*

**$$$–$$$$**    **Il Posto.** Foodies, socialites, and the who's who of the business world recognize the sophistication and ingenuity of Piero Maritano's kitchen and wife Nella's charm in the dining room. In this rather plain space tucked into the hip of Hazelton Lanes, they serve simple, traditional, excellent Italian dishes. An iced trolley of fresh fish and seafood is wheeled over for your choosing, or you may want the perfectly grilled veal chop, liver with fresh sage leaves, or angel hair pasta with a whole lobster. The signature desserts are peeled whole oranges marinated in Grand Marnier, and cake layered with fresh bananas and chocolate, topped with fluffy Italian meringue. In summer, the flower-filled outdoor patio is a people-watchers delight. *148 Yorkville Ave., tel. 416/968-0469. Reservations advised. Jacket advised. AE, DC, MC, V. Closed Sun.*

**$$$**    **Prego.** Tucked into a chic shopping passage between the glitz of the Renaissance Plaza and the timeworn stones of the gracefully aging Church of the Redeemer, this see-and-be-seen Italian eatery is a busy spot. Come summer, when the outdoor patio is in full bloom, it's filled with the who's who of the city's highly visible film and television industry which has earned Toronto the name "Hollywood North." The menu has evolved into a concise litany of everyone's favorites: stone roasted half chicken with herbs; homemade *agnolotti* (round ravioli) with stuffings like beet with burned butter sauce or butternut squash with tomato and fresh basil; pasta with sauces that are oil-based, tomato-based, or cream-based. And there's a vast display of cold antipasti including marinated vegetables and savory tortes. Chef Massimo strolls through the contemporary, muralled room, checking to see who's eating what. Next door at Enoteca della Piazza, a design award-winning wine bar, the chic and cheerful sip wine from a list of several hundred labels and nibble on *affettati misti* (thin slices of dry cured meats), smoked chicken, and marinated eggplant. *150 Bloor St. W, tel. 416/920-9900. Reservations advised. Dress: casual but neat. AE, DC, MC, V. Closed Sun.*

**$$$ Pronto.** On the cutting edge of innovative, modern, Italian cuisine, this glitzy black, mirror-and-chrome restaurant has the look of Milan. The menu marries the sunny flavors of California with solid Italian tradition and includes pan-fried oyster mushrooms on red oak lettuce laced with white truffle olive oil, and sophisticated pastas like lemon fettucine with mussels and roasted garlic. A brace of boneless jumbo quails, charred to the color of mahogany, comes with whole roasted cloves of garlic, sweet and crisp snow pea vines, and drunk sour sun-dried cherries. But the kitchen has not lost sight of rustic tradition, and shines with homey dishes such as braised lamb shank served in a massive bowl with flageolets and greens. The trend of the future, using vegetable purées as sauces is an idea whose time has come, and not surprising, it has come from Pronto. *692 Mount Pleasant Rd., tel. 416/486–1111. Reservations required. Dress: casual but neat. AE, D, MC, V.*

**$$$ Splendido.** This latest in a series of slick, upbeat Italian restaurants is immensely popular with television, music, and film industry types. Chef-partner Arpi Magyar presents a Cal-Ital sparkling, contemporary menu. The chef coaxes ricotta and potato into plump gnocchi and serves it with splashes of white truffle oil and chives as an appetizer or main course; he roasts farm-raised chicken in a wood-burning oven, and perches it on a levain bread salad, textured with currants and pine nuts. Rack of lamb is baked with honey mustard and comes partnered with homey garlic potato purée. Casual, sophisticated good taste meets the eye at every turn. Walls in warm shades of orange and blue are hung with artist Helen Lucas's glorious, oversize flower paintings, mirrors are anything but square, and a glass wall marked "Cucina" separates the open kitchen from the dining room. The bar is popular for nightcaps. *88 Harbord St., tel. 416/929–7788. Reservations advised. Dress: casual but neat. AE, DC, MC, V.*

**$$ ★ Grano.** What started as a bakery and takeout antipasto bar has grown into a joyful collage of the Martella family's Italy. Come for animated talk, good food, and great bread in these lively rooms with faux ancient plaster walls, wooden tables, and bright chairs. There's a small espresso bar to perch at while you wait for a table or takeout. Choose, if you can, from 40 delectable vegetarian dishes and numerous meat and fish antipasti. Lucia's homemade gnocchi and ravioli are divine, as are the *tiramisù* (lady fingers soaked in rum and espresso and mixed with chocolate bits, mascarpone cheese, whipped cream, and beaten egg whites) or white chocolate and raspberry pie. *2035 Yonge St., tel. 416/440–1986. Dress: casual. AE, DC, MC, V. Closed Sun.*

**$$ KitKat Bar & Grill.** Walls are crammed with autographed memorabilia, and the kitchen is built around a massive tree. It all seems quite natural in this eclectic and eccentric Southern Italian eatery. Since it's in the middle of the theater district, pre- and post-theater hours are really busy. Choose from window tables in the front, perch at the long bar, enjoy the privacy of an old-fashioned wooden booth, or sit at a picnic table in the rear. Portions are enormous. An antipasto platter for two is a meal; pastas, seafood, roast chicken, and grilled steak are all delectable. Owner Al Carbone welcomes everyone like long lost family. *297 King St. W, tel. 416/977–4461. Reservations advised. Dress: casual but neat. AE, DC, MC, V. Closed Sat. lunch, Sun.*

**$ Giovanna Trattoria.** Yes, there really is a Giovanna, and can she cook! You'll thoroughly enjoy something as simple as a half roast chicken on a crisp Tuscan bread salad. This is but one of the new and delightful eateries recently opened during the renaissance of Little Italy on College Street. Walls are hung with works depicting the wine god Bacchus in various stages of enjoyment, and flowers are everywhere. Large groups with compatible tastebuds would do well to order family-style: enormous platters of homemade fettucine marinara, or farfalle with artichokes and red-pepper cream sauce, or fusilli with prosciutto. Giovanna's cooking is light, traditional, and generous. Try the rabbit braised in traditional Italian style, paired with polenta; the succulent, grilled whole red snapper; or the veal paillard splashed with lemon and herbs. *637 College St., tel. 416/ 538–2098. Reservations advised. Dress: casual. AE, DC, MC, V.*

$ ★ **Il Fornello.** Pizza afficionados especially love Il Fornello's 10-inch, thin-crust pie, baked in a wood-burning oven. Orchestrate your own medley from over 100 traditional and exotic toppings that include braised onion, capicolla (spicy Italian sausage), pancetta, provolone, calamari, escargots, mussels, eggplant, and anchovies. A bottle of extra-virgin, herbal olive oil graces each table. Pastas, veal dishes, and salads are available, too. Wheat-free pizza crust and dairy-free cappuccino are now on the menu—your taste buds won't know the difference. Customer clamor prompted the opening of more venues. *55 Eglinton Ave. E, tel. 416/486–2130; 86 Bloor St. W, tel. 416/588– 5658; 214 King St. W, tel. 416/977–2855; 1560 Yonge St., tel. 416/920– 8291; 486 Bloor St. W, tel. 416/588–9358; 1968 Queen St. E, tel. 416/ 691–8377; 1218 St. Clair Ave. W, tel. 416/658–8511. Reservations accepted. Dress: casual. AE, D (only at King St. W), MC, V.*

## Japanese

$$$ **Nami.** In this large, attractive, downtown restaurant, diners can choose to eat at the sushi bar, in tatami rooms with non-traditional wells under the tables, or at the *robatayaki*—a cooking grill surrounded by an eating counter. Watch the chef douse soft shell crabs with a special sauce and put them on the grill. Scallops, shrimp, Atlantic salmon, mackerel, and ocean perch sizzle on skewers. At the sushi bar, it's a thrill to watch the chef at work: He slaps a bit of rice on his palm, tops it with a spicy condiment, a shred of vegetable, and a cap of toro, yellowtail, or maguro tuna. In seconds, he hand-rolls cornets of salmon skin, and if sea urchin is at hand, he ties it into a neat packet with a ribbon of green onion. Each sushi design is as personal as a signature. Special $22 dinner combos at a table or booth include soup, salad, tempura, chicken yakitori (served on skewers) or a beef or salmon teriyaki dish, rice, and dessert. *55 Adelaide St. E, tel. 416/362–7373. Reservations advised. Dress: casual but neat. AE, DC, MC, V. Closed Sat. lunch, Sun.*

## Mixed Menu

$$$–$$$$ ★ **North 44.** A foyer of brushed steel nuggets outlined in black, a steel compass showing Toronto's longitude imbedded in a gorgeous marble floor, textured walls hung with mirrored sconces holding exotic arrangements of fresh ginger and lilies—can Chef Marc McEwen's dishes meet the standards of this singular decor? Yes. Your tastebuds will thrill to appetizers like cherry-wood–smoked Atlantic salmon with crisp potato artichoke rosti, scallion dressing, and fresh horseradish; and who could decline a nibble of crisp tortilla spring rolls plump with barbecued chicken, vegetables, and plum mustard chili dip? The kitchen grills Atlantic salmon to perfection, tops it with a honey mustard crust, and partners it with sesame bokchoy greens and crispy leeks. Winning combinations are spaghettini

with seared scallops, grilled calamari, shrimp and sweet tomato fondue, or pan-fried gnocchi with grilled mahogany quail. Caramelized apple-pecan layer cake or crème brûlée with berries are worth every luscious calorie. In the rear, a delightful private dining room seating 12–15 people has a wraparound mural of the view from a Venetian canal. *2537 Yonge St., tel. 416/487–4897. Reservations advised. Dress: casual but neat. AE, DC, MC, V. Closed Sun. dinner.*

**$$$ Jump Café & Bar.** Look up through the atrium and you'll see that you're surrounded by towering skyscrapers and "Big Apple" ambiance. Try to get a table at the glass wall that abuts the interior courtyard, which, from May to September, becomes a vast flower- and fountain-filled patio. The East meets West menu with Italian top notes is refreshing, with appetizers such as Mediterranean octopus with tuscan bean salad, charred artichokes and leek in spiced olive oil, and crispy duck spring roll with cucumber noodles. The chef's pasta of the moment is orecchiette with spinach, forest mushrooms, roasted garlic, prosciutto, and fresh rosemary. From 5 PM to 7 PM, a smartly dressed, downtown office crowd packs the bar. *Court Level, Commerce Court E, Yonge and Wellington Sts., tel. 416/363–3400. Reservations advised. Dress: casual but neat. AE, DC, MC, V. Closed Sat. lunch, Sun.*

## Swiss

**$$ Movenpick.** Swiss hospitality, an eager-to-please staff, and a cosmopolitan atmosphere make this downtown restaurant all things to all people. Among the dinner specialties are *Zurcher G'Schnatzlets*, the famous Swiss dish of thinly sliced veal and mushrooms in a creamy white wine sauce served with rosti (pan-fried) potatoes; *Kasseler*, a thick, smoked, juicy pork-chop grilled to perfection and served with braised savoy cabbage; and Red Wine herring from Iceland marinated in wine and selected spices. The Swiss Farmers Sunday Brunch ($19.80 per person), a vast buffet of food stations, is particularly popular. You can have your eggs with ham, sausage, bacon, or rosti potatoes. Cheeses, breads, juices, cereals, and accompaniments are displayed in abundance. You can also sample more salads than you bargained for, with raw and marinated vegetables, and a variety of smoked fish and soup. Cold cuts include traditional smoked turkey and black forest ham as well as Bundnerfleish, a Swiss salt-cured, air-dried beef. Roast chicken, leg of lamb, and beef roasts are complimented by sautéed vegetables and fresh pastas. A dessert table with fresh fruits, Swiss cakes, tarts, and flans satisfies your sweet tooth. *165 York St., tel. 416/366–5234. Dress: casual but neat. AE, DC, MC, V.*

## Thai

**$$ Thai Magic.** Bamboo trellises, cascading vines, fish and animal carvings, and a shrine to a voluptuous mermaid goddess make a magical setting for coolly saronged waiters and hot-and-spicy Thai food. Hurricane Kettle is a dramatic presentation of fiery seafood soup. Whole coriander lobster sparkles with flavor, while chicken with cashews and whole dried chilies is for the adventurous. If you're in the mood for Thai, this is certainly a pretty place to indulge. *1118 Yonge St., tel. 416/968–7366. Reservations required. Dress: casual. AE, MC, V. Closed Sat. lunch, Sun.*

**$ Vanipha Lanna.** Every night this tidy, colorful restaurant is
★ crowded with people who don't care if they're sitting almost cheek to

cheek with strangers, or how long they have to wait for their food. They can't get enough of the clean, bright flavors, grease-free cooking, and lovingly garnished Lao-Thai presentations. The bamboo steamer of dumplings with minced chicken and seafood, sticky rice in a raffia cylinder, and chicken and green beans stir-fried in lime sauce are exceptional. Rice is served from a huge silver tureen. Everything here is made from scratch. *471 Eglinton Ave. W, tel. 416/484–0895. Reservations advised. Dress: casual but neat. MC, V. Closed Sun.*

## Vegetarian

**$  Chinese Vegetarian House.** The owner of this sparkling clean restaurant is well versed in vege-trivia and the delights of dim-sum. He's fashioned a vegetarian menu to suit downtown Kensington Market's melting pot neighborhood, including pressed wheat gluten that tastes like barbecued pork, wonton soup afloat with plump dumplings, an eight-vegetable stir fry with organic brown rice, and bean curd rolls on a sizzling plate. *39 Baldwin St., tel. 416/599–6855. Reservations accepted. Dress: casual. No credit cards. Closed weekend lunch, Mon.*

**$  Renaissance Café.** The good vegetarian food here comes from influences around the globe: Mexican nachos, Lebanese baba ghanouj (garlicky eggplant purée), Italian pesto pizza and lasagna, Indonesian rice and stir fries, Greek *spanakopita* (spinach pie), West Indian roti (spicy meat- or vegetable-filled pastries), and soup of the day with an all-you-can-eat salad bar. A seat by the window in this quaint corner café lends a good view of the busy passing parade. *509 Bloor St. W, tel. 416/968–6639. Reservations accepted. Dress: casual. AE, MC, V.*

# Lodging

Places to stay in this cosmopolitan city range, as one might expect, from luxurious hotels to budget motels to a few dozen bed-and-breakfasts. Prices are cut over weekends and during quiet times of the year (many Toronto hotels drop their rates a full 50% in January and February). Due to the recession and stiff competition, hotels in all price ranges have struggled to fill their rooms over the past few years. Wherever you stay in Toronto, you should be able to bargain for a lower-than-standard rate. You can insist on corporate prices or demand special deals, and you should nearly always get your request granted, as long as rooms are available.

**Accommodation Toronto** (tel. 416/629–3800), a service of the Hotel Association of Toronto, is an excellent source for finding the room and price you want. Don't forget to ask about family deals and special packages. You might also try the **Metropolitan Bed & Breakfast** (615 Mt. Pleasant Rd., Suite 269, Toronto M4S 3C5, tel. 416/964–2566, fax 416/537–0233) registry service, which has 33 city and suburban homes on its books.

Highly recommended properties in each category are indicated by a star ★.

| Category | Cost* |
|---|---|
| $$$$ | over $175 |
| $$$ | $125–$175 |

| $$ | $70–$125 |
|---|---|
| $ | under $70 |

*All prices are for a standard double room, excluding taxes and optional service charge.*

## $$$$

**Four Seasons Toronto.** It's hard to imagine a hotel that is more exclusive than the Four Seasons. The location is ideal: on the edge of Yorkville, a few meters from the Royal Ontario Museum. The 380 units are tastefully appointed. Maids come twice a day, and there are comfortable bathrobes, oversize towels, fresh flowers, and a fine indoor/outdoor pool. Even the special family rates, however, will not drop the cost much below $200 a night. Its restaurants include the Studio Café, the Lobby Bar, La Serre, for dinner only, and the formal dining room, Truffles. *21 Avenue Rd., M5R 2G1, a block north of Bloor St., tel. 416/964–0411 or 800/332–3442, fax 416/964–1489. 380 rooms. Facilities: indoor/outdoor pool, 4 restaurants. AE, DC, MC, V.*

**Harbour Castle Westin.** This was a Hilton International hotel until 1987, when Westin and Hilton suddenly switched ownership of their major downtown Toronto hotels. A favorite with conventioneers, this accommodation is located just steps from Harbourfront and the Toronto Islands ferry. It's a bit inconvenient to the city's amenities except for those directly on the lakeshore, but it enjoys the best views of any hotel in the city. There's a shuttle bus service as well as frequent public transportation to downtown business and shopping, and the swimming pool, squash courts, and health club are among the best in town. Its 900 rooms are well appointed and tastefully modern, and the frequent family and weekend rates help bring its regular price down by as much as a third. Its Regatta restaurant is open all day, and the revolving Lighthouse restaurant, atop the 37th floor, is open for lunch and dinner. And what a view! *1 Harbour Sq., M5J 1A6, tel. 416/869–1600 or 800/228–3000, fax 416/869–0573. 900 rooms. Facilities: pool, squash courts, health club, 2 restaurants, shuttle bus. AE, DC, MC, V.*

**The King Edward.** The grande dame of downtown Toronto hotels is the beauty built in 1903 but entirely remodelled in the early 80s. The 315-room "King Eddie" is now a member of the worldwide Forte chain, and still has an air of understated elegance, with its vaulted ceiling, marble pillars, and palm trees. Among its guests have been the Duke of Edinburgh, Margaret Thatcher, and Charles de Gaulle. A highlight of the King Eddie is the Chef's Table: for $100 per person, executive chef John Higgins will prepare an eight-course meal for a table of up to eight people, right next to the stoves in his kitchen. After the meal, he'll give you a full kitchen tour. If you'd rather not eat in the kitchen, the hotel's two restaurants, Chiaro's and the Café Victoria, are favorites among Toronto power brokers—but be warned, at the King Eddie neither the accommodation nor the food comes cheap. *37 King St. E, M5C 1E9, tel. 416/863–9700, fax 416/ 367–5515. 315 rooms. Facilities: 2 restaurants. AE, DC, MC, V.*

**Park Plaza Hotel.** It may lack a pool, but this hotel has one of the best locations in the city: a short distance from the Royal Ontario Museum, Queen's Park, and the Yorkville shopping area. The 350 units are well appointed in a plush, old-fashioned way, and they seem to coast by on their old-shoe familiarity to regular Toronto visitors who have been staying in them since the days when there was much less choice. The Roof Restaurant was once described by novel-

**Toronto Lodging**

Sherbourne St.

Pembroke St.

George St.

Allan Gardens

Carlton St.

Jarvis St.

Mt. Pleasant Rd.

Gloucester St.

Bloor St. E.

Hayden St.

Charles St. E.

Isabella St.

Asquith Ave.

AE

AE

Cumberland St.

St. Nicholas St.

Charles St. W.

St. Mary's St.

Phipps St.

St. Thomas St.

St. Joseph St.

Wellesley St. E.

Maitland Ave.

St.

Wood St.

Alexander St.

Maitland St.

Church St.

Mutual St.

Gerrard St. E.

Grancy St.

McGill St.

Dundas St. E.

Mutual St.

Shuter St.

Wellesley St. W.

Breadalbane St.

Grosvenor St.

Grenville St.

Yonge St.

Gerrard St. W.

Walton St.

Edward St.

Gould St.

Bond St.

O'Keefe St.

**5**

**6**

Bay St.

Elizabeth St.

Dundas St. W.

James

Wellesley St. W.

Queen's Park Cir. E.

Queen's Park

Queen's Park Cir. W.

College St.

University Ave.

Elm St.

Orde St.

Murray St.

Armoury St.

Chestnut St.

**7**

**4**

Avenue Rd.

**3**

Hoskin Ave.

Tower Rd.

College Cir.

King's Cir.

King's College Rd.

Henry St.

St. Patrick St.

McCaul St.

Grange Rd.

Grange Park

Devonshire Ave.

George St.

**2**

Huron St.

Sussex Ave.

Willcocks St.

Russell St.

Cecil St.

Baldwin St.

D'Arcy St.

Ross St.

Huron St.

Beverley St.

Grange Pl.

Sullivan St.

Bloor St. W.

Spadina Ave.

Sussex Mews

Robert St.

Major St.

Harbord St.

Brunswick Ave.

Howland Ave.

Croft St.

Ulster St.

Lippincott St.

Bathurst St.

Oxford St.

Nassau St.

Nassau Ave.

Bellevue Ave.

Leonard Ave.

Denison Av

Ryerson Ave.

Carr St.

Alexandra Park

**1**

Lennox St.

Herrick St.

College St.

N

Markham St.

Palmerston Blvd.

Euclid Ave.

Dundas St. W.

Robinson St.

Clinton St.

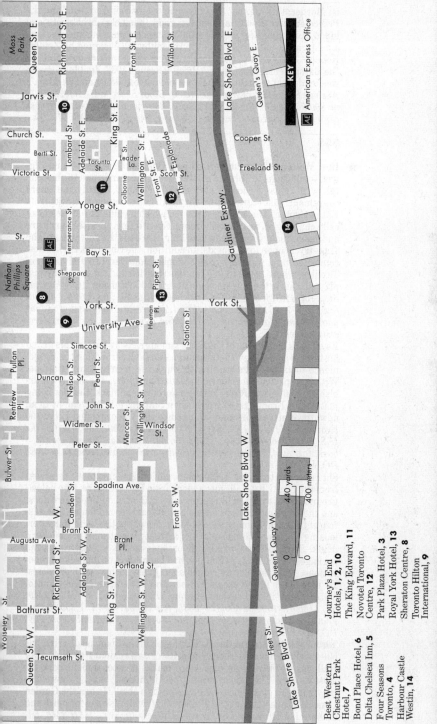

KEY

AE American Express Office

Best Western
Chestnut Park
Hotel, **7**

Bond Place Hotel, **6**

Delta Chelsea Inn, **5**

Four Seasons
Toronto, **4**

Harbour Castle
Westin, **14**

Journey's End
Hotels, **1, 2, 10**

The King Edward, **11**

Novotel Toronto
Centre, **12**

Park Plaza Hotel, **3**

Royal York Hotel, **13**

Sheraton Centre, **8**

Toronto Hilton
International, **9**

ist Mordecai Richler as "the only civilized place in Toronto," and the Prince Arthur Room is open for good (business) breakfasts and lunch. Additions now include a 550-seat ballroom, a business center, a palm court, and a restaurant in the lobby, all designed by Zeidler Roberts Partnership, the same architects who were responsible for the Eaton Centre and Ontario Place. Through 1993, double rooms on weekends cost as little as $109, and include breakfast and parking. *4 Avenue Rd., M5R 2E8, at the cnr. of Bloor St. W, tel. 416/924–5471 or 800/268–4927, fax 416/929–4031. 350 rooms. Facilities: fitness center, 3 restaurants, ballroom, business center. AE, DC, MC, V.*

## $$$

★ **Best Western Chestnut Park Hotel.** One of the newest—and biggest—additions to Toronto's hotel scene, this handsome 16-floor hotel with glass-enclosed atrium lobby could hardly be more convenient: just steps behind City Hall and a few short blocks from Eaton Centre. The 522 guest rooms, which include 21 for the physically challenged, are all well decorated with finely crafted furniture and desks; many have queen- and king-size beds. Its restaurant, **The Tapestry,** is open for all meals. In addition, the Chestnut Park is now connected by a walkway from the mezzanine level to a Museum of Textiles, where some 15,000 textiles from around the world are displayed. This is the only museum of its kind in Canada. *108 Chestnut St., M5G 1R3, just north of Nathan Phillips Sq., tel. 416/977–5000, fax 416/977–9513. 522 rooms. Facilities: restaurant, heated indoor pool, sauna, Jacuzzi, health club and gymnasium, children's creative center. AE, DC, MC, V.*

**Royal York Hotel.** One of Canada's famous railway hotels, this grand hostelry was built by the Canadian Pacific Railroad for the convenience of passengers passing through the nearby train stations. With its spacious corridors and bustling lobby, the newly-refurbished, 1,408-room Royal York is a Toronto landmark. Besides being just across Front Street from Union Station, it is convenient to all downtown attractions and is linked to the Underground City. *100 Front St. W, M5J IE3, tel. 416/368–2511 or 800/828–7447 (in the U.S.), fax 416/368–2884. 1,1408 rooms. Facilities: 7 restaurants, 5 bars, lap pool, fitness center including sauna and masseuse. AE, DC, MC, V.*

**Sheraton Centre.** This 1,430-room conventioneer's tower is across from the New City Hall, just a block from Eaton Centre. The below-ground level is part of Toronto's labyrinth of shop-lined corridors, and there are more shops on the ground and second floors. The restaurants' reach seems to exceed their grasp, but the Long Bar, overlooking Nathan Phillips Square, is a great place to meet friends for a drink. There's a no-smoking floor and various special rates and packages. As of 1992, $47 million had been spent on marvelous renovations, with completely refurbished guest rooms and bathrooms, six new floors in the exclusive Sheraton Towers, and 15 new, automated check-in and cashier stations. *123 Queen St. W, M5H 2M9, tel. 416/361–1000 or 800/325–3535, fax 416/947–4874. 1,430 rooms. Facilities: indoor/outdoor pool, hot tub, sauna, workout room. AE, DC, MC, V.*

**Toronto Hilton International.** This hotel, in the financial district, has 600 newly-renovated rooms, and its close proximity to New City Hall, major businesses, and more makes it a convenient base for most visitors. The indoor/outdoor pool is modest, but the view of the city from the glass-enclosed elevators is a thrill. It has the **Garden Court** lobby restaurant and Trader Vic's, which is open for lunch and dinner. *145 Richmond St. W and University Ave., M5H 3M6, tel.*

*416/869–3456, fax 416/869–3187. 600 rooms. Facilities: restaurant, pool. AE, DC, MC, V.*

---

## $$

**Delta Chelsea Inn.** Toronto's biggest hotel is this 1,600-room giant. It's especially popular with tour groups and out-of-town business people, and it features a year-round activity center with supervised children's programs. This vast hotel is a couple of short blocks north of the Eaton Centre, and half a block from the busy Bay Street bus route. However, it is a little farther from a subway station than most other downtown hotels. *33 Gerard St. W, M5G 1Z4, tel. 416/595–1975 or 800/877-1133 (USA), fax 416/585–4375. 1,600 rooms. Facilities: 2 pools, Jacuzzi, sauna, fitness center. AE, DC, MC, V.*

**Novotel Toronto Centre.** This moderately priced hotel—part of a popular French chain—opened in December 1987. There are 266 modest, modern rooms on nine floors in the heart of downtown, within walking distance of Harbourfront and the CN Tower. *45 The Esplanade, M5E 1W2, tel. 416/367–8900 or 800/221–4542, fax 416/360–8285. 266 rooms. Facilities: restaurant, indoor pool, whirlpool, exercise room, sauna. AE, DC, MC, V.*

**Valhalla Inn.** If you prefer a suburban setting, where hotels typically offer greater value for money than downtown, this property has two convenient locations, depending on your sightseeing priorities. One is set on spacious grounds in the western borough of Etobicoke, just off Highway 427 and a five-minute drive from the international airport. The other is located on Highway 7 in the town of Markham, a 35-minute drive north of downtown. *1 Valhalla Inn Rd., Etobicoke M9H 1S0, tel. 416/239–2391, fax 416/239–8764. 235 rooms. Facilities: 3 restaurants, pool, sauna, fitness center. 50 E. Valhalla Dr., Markham, L3R 0A3, tel. 416/477–2010, fax 905/477–2026. 202 rooms. Facilities: restaurant, pool, sauna, fitness center.*

---

## $

**Bond Place Hotel.** If you plan to spend your money on shopping rather than on your accommodation, this is a good choice for a place to stay—just two blocks from the Eaton Centre. This 286-room hotel has clean, spacious rooms with color TV, but few other frills. The Garden Café serves breakfast, lunch, and dinner, but you'll find a wider variety of food at the Eaton Centre. The Bond Place is also a few minutes walk from the Elgin, Pantages, and Winter Garden theaters. Several floors are set aside for non-smoking guests. Lower rates apply in winter months. *65 Dundas St. E, M5B 2G8, tel. 416/362–6061 or 800/268–9390, fax 416/360–6406. 286 rooms. Facilities: restaurant. AE. DC. MC. V.*

**Journey's End Hotels.** This is a rapidly growing chain that offers three convenient Toronto locations. The airport hotel costs about $100 for up to four people, with 10% off for corporate travelers and senior citizens; the two downtown locations charge only about $60 on weekend nights. These latter-mentioned lodgings are an easy walk from many of the sights. Don't expect original antiques here, but all rooms are spotlessly clean and quite pleasant, and some locations have restaurants. No pools or saunas or convention rooms, but the prices are so low, how can you complain? *All locations: tel. 800/668–4200; in Toronto, 416/624–8200. 262 Carlingview Dr., M9W 5G1, near Hwy. 427 (airport), fax 416/674–3088; 258 suites. 280 Bloor St. W, M5S 1V8, few blocks west of Avenue/University, fax 416/968–2265; 214 rooms. 111 Lombard St., M5C 2T9, near Queen and*

*Jarvis, fax 416/367–3470; 196 rooms. Facilities: each location has informal restaurant. AE, DC, MC, V.*

**Toronto Bed & Breakfast.** More than two dozen private homes are affiliated with this service, most of them scattered across Metro Toronto. Rooms cost as little as $50 a night and include breakfast. *Tel. 416/961–3676.*

# The Arts and Nightlife

## The Arts

Toronto is not only Canada's capital of the lively arts, but has become the most important theater city in the English-speaking world, after New York and London. True, Winnipeg has a very fine ballet, and Montréal's orchestra is superb. But no other city in Canada, and few in North America, can compete with the variety of music, opera, dance, and theater found in Toronto.

The best places to get information on cultural happenings are in the Thursday editions of the *Toronto Star*, the Saturday *Globe and Mail*, the free weeklies *Now* and *Eye Weekly*, and *Toronto Life*. For half-price tickets on the day of a performance, don't forget the **Five Star Tickets booth,** located in the Royal Ontario Museum lobby during the winter and, at other times, at the corner of Yonge and Dundas streets, outside the Eaton Centre. The museum booth is open daily 10–7, the Yonge and Dundas booth is open—in good weather—Monday–Saturday noon–7:30, and Sunday 11–3. Tickets are sold for cash only, all sales are final, and a small service charge is added to the price of each ticket. The booth outside the Eaton Centre also gives out piles of superb brochures and pamphlets on the city.

**Concert Halls and Theaters** The **Roy Thomson Hall** (just below the CN Tower) has become since 1982 the most important concert hall in Toronto. It is the home today of the Toronto Symphony and the Toronto Mendelssohn Choir, one of the world's finest choral groups. It also hosts orchestras from around the world and popular entertainers from Liza Minnelli to Anne Murray. *60 Simcoe St., at cnr. of King Street W, a block west of University Ave., tel. 416/593–4828. Tickets $20–$60 (best rows H and J in the orchestra and row L upstairs). Rush seats are sold the day of a performance, 2 hrs before show time. Tours of the stunning structure take place Mon.–Sat. 12:30 PM (cost: $3, but call; it is subject to cancellation. Tel. 416/593–4822, ext. 363. On Wed. at 12:30 you can tour the impressive organ for $5).*

**Massey Hall** has always been cramped and dingy, but its near-perfect acoustics and its handsome, U-shape tiers sloping down to the stage have made it a happy place to hear the Toronto Symphony, or almost anyone else in the world of music, for almost a century. The nearly 2,800 seats are not terribly comfortable, but it remains a venerable place to catch the greats and near-greats. *178 Victoria St. at Shuster, a few feet east of the Eaton Centre, tel. 416/593–4828. Best seats are rows G–M center and balcony rows 32–50.*

The **O'Keefe Centre** has become the home of the Canadian Opera Company and the National Ballet of Canada. It is also home to visiting comedians, pre-Broadway musicals, rock stars, and almost anyone else who can fill it. When it was built in 1960, the O'Keefe Centre's 3,167 seats made it the largest concert hall on the continent. *1 Front St. E, a block east of Union Station, tel. 416/872–2262.*

*Tickets $20–$50. Try for seats close to A47–48; avoid the very front rows, such as AA, BB, etc.*

About 50 yards east of the O'Keefe is the **St. Lawrence Centre for the Arts.** Since 1970, it has been presenting everything from live theater to string quartets and forums on city issues. The main hall, the luxuriously appointed **Bluma Appel Theatre,** hosts the often brilliant productions of the **Canadian Stage Company** and **Theater Plus.** Classical and contemporary plays are often on a level with the best of Broadway and London's West End. *Front St. at cnr. of Scott St., tel. 416/366–7723. Tickets $20–$45. Try for rows E–N, seats 1–10.*

The **Royal Alexandra** has been the place to be seen in Toronto since its opening in 1907. The plush red seats, gold brocade, and baroque swirls and curlicues all make theatergoing a refined experience. It's astonishing to recall that all this magnificence was about to be torn down in the 1960s, but was rescued by none other than "Honest Ed" Mirvish of discount-store fame. He not only restored the theater to its former glory but also made it profitable. *260 King St. W, tel. 416/872–3333. Tickets $35–$75 (more for major musicals). Student tickets as low as $15. Avoid rows A and B; try for rows C–L center. For musicals, try the first rows of the first balcony.*

**Classical Concerts** The **Toronto Symphony,** now over 65 years old, is not about to retire. Since 1922, with conductors of the quality of Seiji Ozawa, Walter Susskind, Sir Thomas Beecham, and Andrew Davis, it has achieved world acclaim. Maestro Jukka-Pekka Sarasti is scheduled to replace Maestro Gunther Herbig as music director in the 1994/95 season. When the TS is home, it presents about three concerts weekly from September to May in Roy Thomson Hall (*see above*) and a miniseason each summer at Ontario Place. Tickets cost $16–$35.

The **Toronto Mendelssohn Choir** often guests with the Toronto Symphony. This 180-singer group, going since 1894, has been applauded worldwide, and its *Messiah* is handeled well every Christmas (no, we couldn't resist that). *For program information, tel. 416/598–0422; for tickets, Roy Thomson Hall.*

**Opera** Since its founding in 1950, the **Canadian Opera Company** has grown into the largest producer of opera in Canada. Each year, at Toronto's O'Keefe Centre, more than 150,000 people attend the season of seven operas, with such world-class performers as Joan Sutherland, Grace Bumbry, Martina Arroyo, Marilyn Horne, and Canada's own Louis Quilico and Maureen Forrester. The COC also performs mini-operas in a tent during the summer, at Harbourfront. *Tel. 416/363–8231 or 416/393–7469.*

**Dance** **National Ballet of Canada** made its official debut in 1951. In less than four decades, the company has done some extraordinary things, with such principal dancers as Karen Kain, Frank Augustyn, Kevin Pugh, and Owen Montague all wowing the Russians at the Moscow competitions. Performances November, February, and May at the O'Keefe Centre (*see above*); in summer at Ontario Place Office, tel. 416/362–1041, 416/872–1111, or 416/872–2277. Tickets cost $15–$55.

**Toronto Dance Theatre,** its roots in the Martha Graham tradition, tours Canada and has played major festivals in England, Europe, and the United States. *Most performances are in the Premiere Dance Theatre, at Harbourfront, 235 Queen's Quay W, tel. 416/973–4000.*

**Theater** There are more than four dozen performing spaces in Toronto; we will mention only a handful of the most prominent.

The **Young People's Theatre,** the only theater center in the country devoted solely to children, does not condescend or compromise its dramatic integrity. *165 Front St. E, near Sherbourne, tel. 416/862–2222.*

The **Elgin** and **Winter Garden Theaters** are two recently renovated old vaudeville places, stacked upon each other. (The Elgin, downstairs, has about 1,500 seats; the Winter Garden is some 500 seats smaller; both are stunningly attractive.) *189 Yonge St., just north of Queen, tel. 416/870–8000.*

**Second City,** just east of the heart of downtown, has been providing some of the best comedy in North America since its owner Andrew Alexander bought the rights to the name for one dollar. Among those who have cut their teeth on the Toronto stage are the late Gilda Radner, Dan Aykroyd, Martin Short, Andrea Martin, Catherine O'Hara, and the late John Candy. Shows can be seen alone or in a dinner-theater package. *Old Firehall Theatre, 110 Lombard St., cnr. of Jarvis St., tel. 416/863–1111.*

When planning your trip to Toronto, consider contacting the **North York Performing Arts Centre** (5040 Yonge St., tel. 416/872–2222)— situated less than a half-hour's drive north of the waterfront, and close to the North York subway stop—to see the wildly acclaimed Hal Prince production of the classic American musical **Show Boat;** the forever-running **Phantom of the Opera** at the stunning **Pantages Theatre** downtown; and **Miss Saigon,** which should run a long time at the new **Prince of Wales Theatre,** next to the Royal Alex. Expect good seats to run close to $100 each, but these Broadway-quality productions are worth paying for.

Next to Second City, **Yuk-Yuk's Komedy Kabaret** has always been the major place for comedy in Toronto. This is where the zany comedian Howie Mandel and the inspired impressionist Jim Carrey got their starts, and where such comic luminaries as George Carlin, Rodney Dangerfield, Robin Williams, and Mort Sahl have presented their best routines. *1280 Bay St., just above Bloor St., 2335 Yonge St., just above Eglinton Ave. and 5165 Dixie, just above Eglinton, tel. 416/967–6425. Cover charge: $7 and up. Yonge St. location closed Sun.*

**Mysteriously Yours . . .** should be of special interest to murder-mystery buffs. On Thursday, Friday, and Saturday evenings, a "despicable crime" is perpetrated at the Royal York Hotel. The mystery begins to unravel during dinner (cocktails at 6:30) and is solved after dinner, by 10. The complete dinner and mystery costs $50–$60 per person, including tax and tip. Call Brian Caws at 416/486–7469 or 800/NOT–DEAD.

**Film** Every September since 1976, Toronto has been holding a world-class film festival, called—with no great modesty—**The Festival of Festivals** (tel. 416/966–4217). Whether retrospectives of the films of Marguerite Duras, Jean-Luc Godard, and Max Ophuls, or tributes to the careers of Martin Scorsese, Robert Duvall, and John Schlesinger, this is the time for lovers of film.

Toronto is one of the film capitals of the world, and you can often catch a movie here that is not showing anywhere else—or even available on video.

**Carlton Cinemas,** part of the Cineplex chain, shows rare, important films from around the world in nearly a dozen screening rooms. *20 Carlton St., just steps east of the College St. subway, tel. 416/979–FILM.*

**Nightlife**

Jazz Clubs   A few blocks east of Eaton Centre is **George's Spaghetti House** (290 Dundas St. E, corner of Sherbourne St., tel. 416/923–9887), the oldest jazz club in the city. The music starts at 8:30 PM, with the world-famous Moe Koffman (of "Swinging Shepherd Blues" fame) performing one week each month. (For Moe, and on weekends, you'll need reservations.) George's has a modest cover charge and a decent Italian menu.

**Chick 'n Deli** has long been one of the great jazz places in Toronto. A casual atmosphere prevails, and the lack of dress code helps with the neighborhood-bar ambience. There's a dance floor and dark wood everywhere, giving it a publike feel. It's also famous for wings and live music; the former half-price, Monday and Tuesday until 9, the latter playing at 9 PM most nights, and 7:30 on Sunday. Check out the occasional jazz shows, and Sunday brunch—all you can eat for less than $10. *744 Mount Pleasant Rd., near Eglinton Ave., tel. 416/489–3363 or 416/489–7931.*

**Top O' The Senator,** this city's first club exclusively for jazz, has the atmosphere of a between-the-wars lounge. With its long wooden bar and towering dark-blue ceilings, this is one fabulous place. *249 Victoria St., tel. 416/364–7517.*

Rock and   Most major international recording companies have offices in Toron-
Popular Music   to, so the city is a regular stop for top musical performers of today, whether Frank Sinatra, Billy Joel, Whitney Houston, Sting, or Bruce Springsteen. Tickets ($15–$40) can usually be booked through **Ticketmaster** (tel. 416/872–1111).

Major venues include the **SkyDome** (tel. 416/341–3663), on Front Street; **Maple Leaf Gardens** (60 Carlton Street, tel. 416/977–1641), a block east of Yonge Street and the College Street subway stop; the **O'Keefe Centre** (Yonge and Front streets, tel. BASS, 416/872–2262); and **Exhibition Stadium** (tel. 416/393–6000 at the CNE grounds). **Ontario Place** (tel. 416/965–7711) has pop, rock, and jazz concerts all summer at a nominal cost. We say "nominal" because you may pay around $10 to see/hear a fabulous singer or group (or orchestra or ballet corps) that would cost you $25–$50 elsewhere. This is one of the loveliest and least expensive places for concerts in all of Toronto.

**Kingswood Music Theatre,** next to Canada's Wonderland, also has important rock and pop concerts during the warmer months. *Hwy. 400, 10 min north of Hwy. 401, tel. 416/832–8131. Admission usually less than $10 above the cost of Canada's Wonderland.*

**The Phoenix Concert Theatre** has a wide variety of music, with DJs from local radio stations broadcasting live on Monday (classic rock) and Saturday (alternative music). *410 Sherbourne St., tel. 416/323–1251. Cover charge: $8 after 10 PM on weekends, less expensive earlier in the evening.*

A major showcase for more daring arts in Toronto has long been **The Rivoli,** along the Queen Street "mall." A place for new, local artists not yet established enough to have their own gallery showings, the back room functions as a club, with theater happenings, "new music" (progressive rock and jazz), comedy troupes with very funny improvisations twice a month, and more. *332 Queen St. W, just west of University Ave., tel. 416/597–0794. No dress code. Cover charge: $5–$10. Closed Sun.*

Rhythm and   **Network,** an entertainment lounge specializing in name acts of the
Blues   quality of The Stylistics, Junior Walker, and Goodman and Brown.

It's a supper club and show, with the cover and buffet combined at a reasonable $20 or so. The only dress code is "no jeans," and there is a dance floor. The clientele is urban professionals in their early thirties; the decor is modern—brass, black, polished oak. *138 Pears Ave., near Davenport Rd., tel. 416/323–0164.*

**Albert's Hall** has been called one of the top 25 bars in all of North America, in spite of its shabby decor. It features top blues bands. The crowd is older and more laid-back than downstairs, in the Brunswick, but it's still noisy and friendly—and loud. *481 Bloor St. W, near Spadina Ave., tel. 416/964–2242. Cover charge on weekends; closed Sun.*

**Dancing** The area bounded by Front, Adelaide, Peter, and John streets has become the center of Toronto's club and bar scene in recent years. Popular venues include **Club Max** (52 Peter St., tel. 416/597–1567) and the **Loose Moose Tap & Grill,** (220 Adelaide St. W, tel. 416/971–5252). In 1993, hockey superstar Wayne Gretzky opened **Wayne Gretzy's** (41 Peter St., tel 416/979–7825), a sports bar and restaurant. DJs play '60s music (downstairs) and '90s music (upstairs) in a four-story century-old funhouse named **Big Bop.** Thursday night is Ladies' Night, with no cover for women. In rebellion against the New York School of Glitzy, there is no chrome or mirrors—just a deliberate effort to be campy, vibrant, and unpretentious. The clientele is 18–25. It's a true meat market, but it doesn't pretend to be otherwise. Capacity is 800, and jeans are de rigueur. Many international stars walk in, but the owner insists that it's no big deal. (No big deal? Jack Nicholson. William Hurt. Matt Dillon!) *651 Queen St. W, tel. 416/366–6699. Open weekends to 3 AM.*

**Barracuda,** on the same gigantic warehouse site as the former Copa, has to be seen to be believed. Besides the music and the dancing, there are indoor batting cages and indoor beach volleyball. Local radio stations broadcast live on weekends. *21 Scollard St., tel. 416/921–4496. Cover charge: $2.50 weeknights, $4 weekends.*

**Heartbreak Hotel** is all concrete and steel, and was known as the **Boom Boom Room,** one of Toronto's best rock-and-roll dance places, until the late 1980s. Here you can hear and dance to heavy metal or more trendy beats, with the worst sexism showing in the prices: "Guys $5, Girls $3." Ages range from 19 to 30, so beware. *650½ Queen St. W, 2 blocks west of Bathurst, tel. 416/368–6468. Open Wed.–Sat. 9 PM–2 AM.*

**StiLife** caters to an older (25–35) crowd and to rapidly aging 40-year-olds. The decor is metallic and modular, with all the furnishings custom-made. The art is aided by sophisticated lighting. No jeans or sneakers. A DJ provides dance music, and the clientele is Yorkville-ish, with many clothing designers, other restaurant owners, etc. Check out the bathrooms—you'll find out why. *217 Richmond St. W, tel. 416/593–6116. Closed Sun. Cover charge: $6–$15.*

**Lounges** Up on the 51st floor of the ManuLife Centre, **The Aquarius Lounge** is the highest piano lounge in the city. The busy time in the summer is Thursday–Saturday after 8:30 PM, but there's a high turnover, so the wait is never too long. In the winter, the lines begin as early as 8 PM. Its romantic atmosphere makes this a marvelous place for a date. No shorts, but jeans are allowed. *55 Bloor St. W, at Bay St., tel. 416/967–5225.*

The **Consort Bar,** in the King Edward Hotel, features swing jazz on Thursday, Friday, and Saturday evenings, and Sunday afternoon. A tray of mouth-watering pastries is sometimes on display at the doorway to help tempt you inside. *37 King St. East, tel. 416/863–9700.*

In the classy Four Seasons Hotel is **La Serre,** which looks like a library in a mansion: plush and green, with lots of brass and dark wood. It has a stand-up piano bar and a pianist worth standing for. Drinks, coffees, and teas are all expensive, but what can you expect in one of the costliest hotels in the country? Weekdays attract a business crowd, weekends bring out the couples. *Avenue Rd. and Yorkville Ave., tel. 416/964–0411.*

The **Park Plaza Roof Lounge** has been used as a setting in the writings of such Canadian literary luminaries as Margaret Atwood and Mordecai Richler. The decor used to be plush, in an older European style, with chandelier, marble tables, and waiters in red jackets. It remains an important hangout for the upper-middle class businesspeople, professional, and, *bien sur,* literary types. It was renovated in 1990, but it's still gorgeous and tasteful. *In the Park Plaza Hotel, Avenue Rd. and Bloor St., tel. 416/924–5471.*

# 3 Montréal

*By Patricia Lowe*

*Updated by Helga Loverseed*

"Plus ça change, plus c'est la même chose," like other travel clichés, no longer applies to Montréal, which marked its 350th anniversary in 1992. For years, as Québec's largest city and the world's second-largest French-speaking metropolis, Montréal clung to an international reputation attained in the heyday of former Mayor Jean Drapeau, who brought his beloved hometown the 1967 World's Fair (Expo '67), the Métro subway, its Underground City, and the 1976 Summer Olympics. During his nearly three decades in power, Drapeau's entrepreneurial spirit added pizzazz to this transportation and financial capital at the gateway to the St. Lawrence Seaway.

But with the arrival of a nationalist provincial government in 1976, the mayor and Montréal were forced to rest on their laurels as the province agonized over its place in Canada. Separation from the rest of the country was seriously considered. The provincial government passed the controversial Bill 101, which makes French the official language of business and public communication. For the city it was a wrenching ideological change; the only difference that visitors saw was that English or bilingual billboards and public signs were replaced by French ones. Bill 101 was replaced by the more conciliatory Bill 178 in January, 1994, which permits English and other languages to be used in certain public areas and on road signs.

Nearly 60% of the province's population opted in 1980 to remain in the federal family, but a decade later, French-speaking Québecois' old animosities regarding English Canada were rekindled when former Prime Minister Mulroney attempted to unite all 10 provinces through a constitutional agreement called the Meech Lake accord. However, the legislatures of two provinces did not ratify the accord. In 1992, Mulroney came up with a more elaborate plan, this time allowing the Canadian people to decide in a referendum. On October 26, six provinces rejected a deal that would have radically changed the country's 125-year-old constitution. Today the problem remains unresolved.

The melding of old and new architecture that characterizes this city is no more apparent than in the flamboyant office tower of La Maison des Coopérants. Even though the design of this 35-story pink glass structure imitates the Gothic-style Christ Church Cathedral it overshadows, it was not what the earnest French missionaries who founded Montréal envisioned. What today is a metropolis of 3.1 million—some 15% of English mother tongue—began as 54 dedicated souls from France who landed on Montréal island in 1642 to convert the Indians to Christianity.

For nearly 200 years city life was confined to a 95-acre walled community, today's Vieux-Montréal and a protected historic site. Ville-Marie became a fur-trading center, the chief embarkation point for the voyageurs setting off on discovery and trapping expeditions. This business quickly usurped religion as the settlement's raison d'être, along with its role as a major port at the confluence of the St. Lawrence and Ottawa rivers.

The Old Montréal of the French regime lasted until 1760, when, during one of the battles of the Seven Years' War, British troops easily forced the poorly fortified and demoralized city to surrender. The Treaty of Paris ended the war in 1763, and Québec became one of Great Britain's most valuable colonies. British and Scottish settlers poured in to take advantage of Montréal's geography and economic potential. When it was incorporated as a city in 1832, it was a leading colonial capital of business, finance, and transportation.

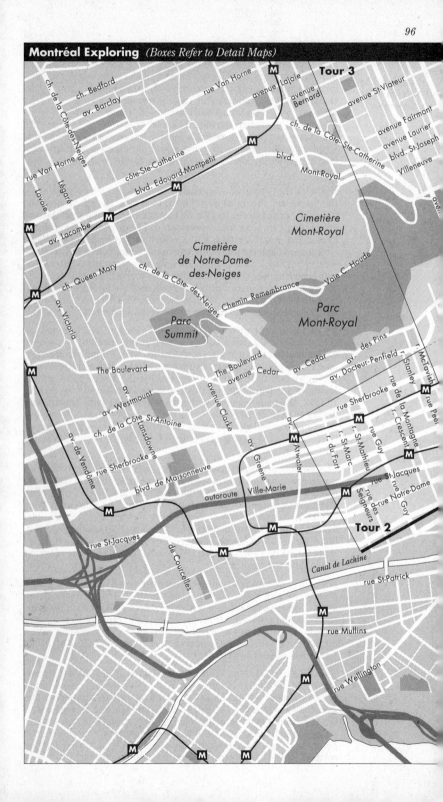

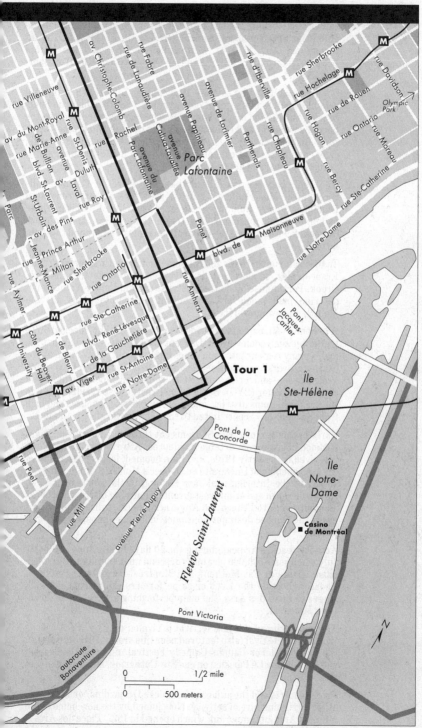

Montréal is still Canada's transport hub: It is home to the national railway and airline, the largest private rail company (Canadian Pacific), Canada's version of Amtrak (VIA Rail), Air Canada, the International Air Transport Association (IATA), and the United Nations' International Civil Aviation Organization (ICAO) on Sherbrooke.

Solidly established by the late 19th century, downtown today still reminds visitors of its grand old days, particularly along rue Sherbrooke, the lifeline of chic Montréal. The busy flower-lined stretch between rues Guy and University takes in the de la Montagne–Crescent–Bishop–Mackay sector, where sophisticated restaurants, cafés, and bars share canopied facades with haute-couture salons, antiques shops, and art galleries.

Rue Peel, between rue Sherbrooke and Place du Canada, rolls through the Montréal most tourists visit. The recently renovated Dominion Square Building is the art deco home of tourism offices and information bureaus. Bus tours, taxi guides, and *calèches* (horse-drawn carriages) all depart from some point around this public park.

To the east, rue St-Denis and the surrounding Latin Quarter attract Francophiles; a more ethnic flavor characterizes the Chinese, Greek, Portuguese, and other districts around Prince Arthur's pedestrian mall, boulevard St-Laurent (known to locals as "the Main"), and avenue du Parc.

A bohemian atmosphere pervades rue Prince Arthur, blocked off to traffic between boulevard St-Laurent and Carré St-Louis. What the mall's many restaurants sometimes lack in quality they make up for in ethnic diversity—Chinese, Greek, Italian, Polish, Québecois, and Vietnamese—and price, especially at establishments where you supply the liquor (BYO). Some 12,000 Portuguese residents live in the area's St-Louis district, and their bright pastel houses and lush front gardens have contributed to the neighborhood's renaissance.

Early in this century, rue St-Denis cut through a bourgeois neighborhood of large, comfortable residences. After a period of decline, it revived in the early 1970s, and then boomed, largely as a result of the 1969 opening of Université du Québec's Montréal campus and the launch of the International Jazz Festival in the summer of 1980. Rows of French and ethnic restaurants, charming bistros, and chess hangouts cater to Franco and Anglo academics; stylish intellectuals prowl the Québec designer boutiques, antiques shops, and art galleries.

Activity reaches its peak during the 10 days in late June and early July when some 500,000 jazz buffs descend upon the city to hear such music giants as Pat Metheny and Montréal-born Oscar Peterson. Theaters hosting the 1,000 or so performers range from sidewalk stages to Place des Arts, the main performing arts center in downtown Montréal.

The popularity of the jazz festival is rivaled only by the August's World Film Festival (also featured near this area at Place des Arts), the lively Just For Laughs Comedy Festival in the St-Denis area, and the Cinéma Le Parisien on rue Ste-Catherine, among other venues.

Place des Arts and the adjacent Complexe Desjardins constitute another intriguing hive of activity. Now joined by the new home of the Musée d'Art Contemporain, which opened in 1992, Place des Arts is really three separate halls built around a sweeping plaza overlooking rue Ste-Catherine.

One often-overlooked sector of the city requires a Métro ride but is worth the fare for a varied tour of Olympic and de Maisonneuve parks, the Château Dufresne Decorative Arts Museum, the Botanical Garden, and the Biodome—all located at or near the corner of boulevard Pie-IX (Métro station of the same name) and rue Sherbrooke Est.

This triangle in the east end is distinguished by the flying-saucer design of the Olympic Stadium, completed by the world's "tallest inclined tower." The stadium's latest attraction is the funicular cable car that speeds sightseers to its observation deck for a spectacular view of the island of Montréal.

# Essential Information

### Arriving and Departing by Plane

**Airports**  Montréal is served by two airports: **Dorval International,** 22½ kilometers (14 miles) west of the city, handles domestic and most U.S. flights; **Mirabel International,** 54½ kilometers (34 miles) northwest of the city, is a hub for the rest of the international trade.

**Airlines**  From the United States: **Air Canada** (tel. 514/393–3333 or 800/361–8620) has nonstop service from New York, Miami, and Tampa; nonstop from Boston via Air Canada's connector airline, **Air Alliance;** direct service is available from Los Angeles and San Francisco. **American Airlines** (tel. 800/433–7300) has nonstop service from Chicago with connections from the rest of the United States. **British Airways** (tel. 514/287–9133; in Québec province, 800/668–1059) has nonstop service from Detroit to Montréal. **Canadian Airlines International,** (tel. 514/847–2211; in Canada, 800/363–7530; in U.S., 800/426–7000) formerly CP Air, has a nonstop charter from Fort Lauderdale and direct or connecting service from Hawaii and Los Angeles. **Delta Air Lines** (tel. 514/337–5520, in Québec Province, 800/361–1970; in U.S., 800/221–1212) has nonstops from Boston, Hartford, Connecticut, and Miami and connecting service from most major U.S. cities. **USAir** (tel. 800/428–4322) has services from Buffalo and Syracuse, New York, and from Pittsburgh.

**Flying Time**  From New York, 1½ hours; from Chicago, two hours; from Los Angeles, 6½ hours (with a connection).

**Between the Airports and Center City**  Dorval Airport is about a 20- to 30-minute drive from downtown Montréal, and Mirabel International is about a 45-minute drive away.

*By Taxi*  A taxi from Dorval to downtown will cost $25. The taxi rates from Mirabel to the center of Montréal average $56, depending on traffic, and you can count on about the same cost for a taxi between the two airports. All taxi companies in Montréal must charge the same rates by law. It is best to have Canadian money with you, because the exchange rate for U.S. dollars is at the driver's discretion.

*By Bus*  **Autobus Connaisseur** (tel. 514/934–1222) provides a much cheaper alternative into town from Mirabel. For $14 a van will take you into the city, with stops at Le Reine Elizabeth (Queen Elizabeth)—next to Gare Centrale—and the Voyageur bus station. It runs every hour from 4 AM until noon and 8 PM until 2 AM, and every half hour between 12:30 and 7:30. Bus service between Mirabel and Dorval is also available for $12, every hour from 9:20 AM until 11:20 AM and 8:20 PM until 11:20 PM. Between 11:40 AM and 8 PM the bus runs every 20 minutes.

**Grayline** (tel. 514/934–1222) offers bus transportation between Dorval and downtown Montréal for $9. On weekdays it runs every 20 minutes between 7:30 AM and 12:30 AM; on weekends every half hour between 7:30 AM and 12:30 AM.

## Arriving and Departing by Train, Bus, and Car

**By Train** The Gare Centrale (Central Station), on rue de la Gauchetière between rues University and Mansfield (behind La Reine Elizabeth—Queen Elizabeth Hotel—on boulevard René-Lévesque Ouest), is the rail terminus for all trains from the United States and from other Canadian provinces. It is connected by underground passageway to the Métro's Bonaventure stop (schedule information, tel. 514/871–1331).

**Amtrak** (tel. 800/USA–RAIL) runs the overnight *Montrealer* (reservations necessary), which gives travelers in the Northeast the option of day or night transportation. It has a dining car with snacks and full dinners. Sleepers are available; make reservations well in advance. The unreserved *Adirondack* departs New York's Penn Station every morning and takes 10½ hours to reach Montréal. It has a snack car but no dinner service or sleepers. A round-trip ticket on either train is cheaper than two one-way fares, except during major holidays.

**VIA Rail** (tel. 514/871–1331; in Québec province, 800/361–5390; in the United States, 800/561–3949) connects Montréal by train with all the major cities of Canada, including Québec City, Halifax, Ottawa, Toronto, Winnipeg, Edmonton, and Vancouver.

**By Bus** **Greyhound** has coast-to-coast service and serves Montréal with buses arriving from and departing for various cities in North America. **Voyageur** and **Voyageur-Colonial** service destinations primarily within Québec and Ontario. **Vermont Transit** (tel. 514/842–2281) also serves Montréal via Boston, New York, and other points in New England. Both lines use the city's downtown bus terminal, Terminus Voyageur (tel. 514/842–2281), which connects with the Berri-UQAM Métro station in downtown.

**By Car** Montréal is accessible from the rest of Canada via Trans-Canada Highway 401, which enters the city from the east and west via Highways 20 and 40. The New York State Thruway (I–87) becomes Highway 15 at the Canadian border, and then it's 47 kilometers (30 miles) to the outskirts of Montréal. U.S. I–89 becomes two-lane Route 133 at the border, which is Highway 10 at St-Jean. From I–91 from Boston, you must take Highways 55 and 10 to reach Montréal. At the border you clear Canadian Customs, so be prepared with proof of citizenship and your vehicle's ownership papers. On holidays and during the peak summer season, expect waits of a half hour or more at the major crossings.

Once you're in Québec, the road signs will be in French (this will change as Bill 178 takes effect), but they're designed so you shouldn't have much trouble understanding them. The speed limit is posted in kilometers; on highways the limit is 100 kph (about 62 mph). There are extremely heavy penalties for driving while intoxicated, and drivers and front-seat passengers must wear over-the-shoulder seat belts. Gasoline is sold in liters (3.75 liters equal 1 U.S. gallon), and lead-free is called *sans plomb*. If you're traveling in winter, remember that your car may not start on extra-cold mornings unless it has been kept in a heated garage. All Montréal parking signs are in French, so brush up on your *gauche* (left) and *droit* (right).

You should be aware that Montréal police have a diligent tow-away and fine system for cars double-parked or stopped in no-stopping zones in downtown Montréal during rush hours and business hours. The penalty will cost between $35 and $40. If your car is towed away while illegally parked, it will cost an additional $35 to retrieve it. New York State, Maine, and Ontario residents should drive with extra care in Québec: Traffic violations in the province (and vice versa) are entered on their driving records.

## Getting Around

**By Métro and Bus**  You should be armed with a few maps to see Montréal, but you won't need a car; public transit will do quite well, thank you. The Métro is clean, quiet (it runs on rubber wheels), and safe, and it's heated in winter and cooled in summer. Métro hours are from 5:30 AM to 12:58 AM Monday through Friday, 5:30 AM to 1:28 AM on Saturday, and 5:30 AM to 1:58 AM on Sunday. The Blue Line runs daily from 5:30 AM to 11 PM. Trains run as often as every three minutes on the most crowded lines. The Métro is also connected to the 29 kilometers (18 miles) of the Underground City, so you may not need to go outside during bad weather. Each of the 65 Métro stops has been individually designed and decorated; Berri-UQAM has stained glass, and at Place d'Armes a small collection of archaeological artifacts is exhibited. The stations between Snowdon and Jean-Talon on the Blue Line are worth a visit, particularly Outremont, with its glass-block design. Each station connects with one or more bus routes, which cover the rest of the island. The STCUM (Société de Transport de la Communauté Urbaine de Montréal) administers both the Métro and the buses, so the same tickets and transfers are valid on either service. You should be able to go within a few blocks of anywhere in the city on one fare. At press time rates were: $1.75; six tickets, $7; monthly pass, $43.

Free maps may be obtained at Métro ticket booths. Try to get the *Carte Réseau* (system map); it's the most complete. Transfers from Métro to buses are available from the dispenser just beyond the ticket booth inside the station. Bus-to-bus and bus-to-Métro transfers may be obtained from the bus driver. Information on reaching your destination can be had by dialing 514/AUTOBUS (288–6287).

**By Taxi**  Taxis in Montréal all run on the same rate: $2.25 minimum and $1 a kilometer (at press time). They're usually prompt and reliable, although they may be hard to find on rainy nights after the Métro has closed. Each carries on its roof a white or orange plastic sign that is lit when available and off when occupied.

## Important Addresses and Numbers

**Tourist Information**  **Greater Montreal Convention and Tourism Bureau,** 1555 rue Peel, Suite 600, Montréal, Québec H3A 1X6 (tel. 514/844–5400 or 800/363–7777) or **Tourisme-Québec** (tel. 514/873–2015).

Stop by the downtown headquarters for Info-Touriste, the home of Tourisme-Québec (tel. 514/873–2015 or 800/363–7777), on the north side of Square Dorchester. It's run by the Greater Montreal Convention and Tourism Bureau, and is open daily, June 10–Labor Day, 8:30–7:30; Labor Day–June 9, 9–6. Info-Touriste also operates a smaller tourist information center at 174 rue Notre-Dame Est (tel. 514/873–2015) in Vieux-Montréal, at the corner of Place Jacques-

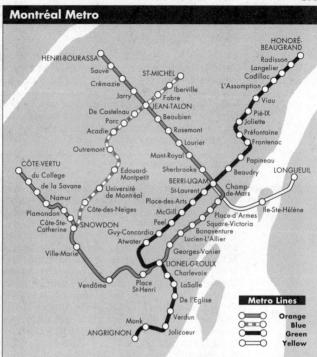

## Montréal Metro

HONORÉ-BEAUGRAND

HENRI-BOURASSA

Sauvé

ST-MICHEL

Crémazie — Iberville

Jarry — Fabre

JEAN-TALON

De Castelnau — Beaubien

Parc

Acadie — Rosemont

Outremont — Laurier

Mont-Royal

Radisson
Langelier
Cadillac
L'Assomption

Viau

Pié-IX
Joliette
Préfontaine
Frontenac

Papineau

CÔTE-VERTU
du Collège
de la Savane

Edouard-Montpetit
Sherbrooke
BERRI-UQAM
Université St-Laurent
de Montréal
Place-des-Arts

Beaudry
Champ-de-Mars

LONGUEUIL

Namur

Côte-des-Neiges
McGill
Peel
Guy-Concordia
Atwater

Place-d'Armes
Square-Victoria
Bonaventure
Lucien-L'Allier

Ile-Ste-Hélène

Plamondon
Côte-Ste-Catherine
SNOWDON

Ville-Marie

Georges-Vanier

LIONEL-GROULX
Charlevoix

Vendôme
Place
St-Henri
LaSalle

De l'Eglise

Monk
Verdun

ANGRIGNON
Jolicoeur

### Metro Lines

- Orange
- Blue
- Green
- Yellow

Cartier, and is open Labor Day–mid-May, daily 9–1 and 2–5; mid-May–Labor Day, daily 9–7.

**Consulates** **United States** (1155 St-Alexandre, Métro Place des Arts, tel. 514/398–9695).

**United Kingdom** (1155 rue University, Métro McGill, tel. 514/866–5863).

**Emergencies** Dial 911 to reach the **police, fire,** and **ambulance.**

*Doctors and Dentists* The U.S. Consulate cannot recommend specific doctors and dentists but does provide a list of various specialists in the Montréal area. Call in advance (tel. 514/398–9695) to make sure the consulate is open.

**Dental clinic** (tel. 514/342–4444) open 24 hours, Sunday emergency appointments only; **Montréal General Hospital** (tel. 514/937–6011); the **Québec Poison Control Centre** (800/463–5060); **Touring Club de Montréal-AAA, CAA, RAC** (514/861–7111).

*Late-night Pharmacies* Many pharmacies are open weeknights until 11 PM, weekends until 10, including: **Jean Coutu** (501 Mt. Royal E, tel. 514/521–3481; 5510 Côte-des-Neiges, tel. 514/344–8338).

**Travel Agencies** **American Express** (1141 boul. de Maisonneuve O, tel. 514/284–3300). **Thomas Cook** (1155 rue University, Suite 314, tel. 514/398–0555).

## Opening and Closing Times

**Banks** are open weekdays from 10 to 4, with some banks open until 5 on weekdays (until 8 on Thursday) and on Saturday morning. Many Montréal banks also have 24-hour banking-machine services.

A law that passed in December 1992 allows shops to stay open weekdays 9–9 and weekends 9–5. However, many merchants close Monday–Wednesday evenings and on Sunday. You'll find many specialty service shops closed on Monday, particularly in predominantly French neighborhoods. Stores in designated tourist zones, such as Vieux-Montréal, remain open on Sunday.

## Guided Tours

**Orientation**  **Gray Line** (tel. 514/934–1222) has nine different tours of Montréal in the summer, and one tour during the winter. It offers pickup service at the major hotels, or you may board the buses at Info-Touriste (1001 Square Dorchester).

**Amphi Tour Ltée** (tel. 514/386–1298) offers a unique tour of Vieux-Montréal (Old Montréal) and the Vieux-Port (Old Port) on both land and water in an amphibious bus. The one-hour tours run from May 1 to October 31.

**Boat Tours**  **Montreal Harbour Cruises** (tel. 514/842–3871) runs two-hour and day-long harbor cruises daily, between May 1 and mid-October. Vessels have room for up to 400 passengers, and evening dinner cruises are available. Boats leave several times a day from the Clock Tower Pier at the foot of rue Berri in the Vieux-Port next to Vieux-Montréal (Métro Champs-de-Mars).

**Calèche Rides**  Open horse-drawn carriages—fleece-lined in winter—leave from Place Jacques-Cartier, Square Dorchester, Place d'Armes and rue de la Commune. An hour-long ride is about $50 (tel. 514/653–0751).

# Exploring Montréal

*By Andrew Coe*

*Updated by Dorothy Guinan*

When you explore Montréal, there will be very little to remind you that it's an island. It lies in the St. Lawrence River roughly equidistant (256 kilometers, or 160 miles) from Lake Ontario and the point where the river widens into a bay. For its entire length, the St. Lawrence is flanked by flat, rich bottomland for 48 kilometers (30 miles) or more on each side. The only rise in the landscape is the 233-meter (764-foot) Mont Royal, which gave Montréal its name. The island itself is 51 kilometers (32 miles) long and 14 kilometers (9 miles) wide and is bounded on the north by the narrow Rivière des Prairies and on the south by the St. Lawrence. Aside from Mont Royal, the island is relatively flat, and because the majority of attractions are clustered around this hill, most tourists don't visit the rest of the island.

Head to the Mont Royal Chalet Belvedere (lookout) for a panoramic view of the city. You can drive most of the way, park, and walk ½ kilometer (¼ mile) or hike all the way up from avenues Côte-des-Neiges or Côte des Pins. If you look directly out—southeast—from the belvedere, at the foot of the hill will be the McGill University campus and, surrounding it, the skyscrapers of downtown Montréal. Just beyond, along the banks of the St. Lawrence, are the stone houses of Vieux-Montréal. Hugging the opposite banks are the Iles Ste-Hélène and Notre-Dame (St. Helen's and Notre-Dame islands), sites of La Ronde amusement park, the Biosphere, the Montréal Casino, acres of parkland, and the Lac de l'Ile Notre-Dame public beach.

There are a host of attractions that you can see on all-day and half-day trips. The most popular are the amusement park complex on Ile St-Hélène and the Olympic Stadium and its neighbor, the Botanical Garden. The 500 forested acres of Parc du Mont-Royal are busy with joggers and strollers year-round, and skaters in winter. Beyond the city limits are the Eastern Townships and the Laurentians for day trips or weekends in the country.

Montréal is easy to explore. Street signs, subways, and bus lines are clearly marked. The city is divided by a grid of streets roughly aligned east–west and north–south. (This grid is tilted about 40 degrees off—to the left of—true north, so west is actually southwest and so on.) North–south street numbers begin at the Fleuve St-Laurent (St. Lawrence River) and increase as you head north. East–west street numbers begin at boulevard St-Laurent, which divides Montréal into east and west halves. The city is not so large that seasoned walkers can't see all the districts around the base of Mont Royal on foot.

## Highlights for First-time Visitors

**Botanical Garden/Olympic Park complex** (*see* Parks and Gardens, *below*)
**Historic Montréal,** Tour 1: Vieux-Montréal
**Mont Royal** (*see* Parks and Gardens, *below*)
**Rue St-Denis,** Tour 3: St-Denis, Prince Arthur, and North
**Rue Sherbrooke Ouest,** Tour 2: Downtown Montréal

## Tour 1: Vieux-Montréal (Old Montréal)

*Numbers in the margin correspond to points of interest on the Tour 1: Vieux-Montréal map.*

The Fleuve St-Laurent was the highway on which the first settlers arrived in 1642. Just past the island of Montréal are the Lachine Rapids, a series of violent falls over which the French colonists' boats could not safely travel. It was natural for them to build their houses just above the rapids, near the site of an old Iroquois settlement on the bank of the river nearest Mont Royal. In the mid-17th century Montréal consisted of a handful of wood houses clustered around a pair of stone buildings, the whole flimsily fortified by a wood stockade. For the next three centuries this district—bounded by rues Berri and McGill on the east and west, rue St-Antoine on the north, and the river to the south—was the financial and political heart of the city. Government buildings, the largest church, the stock exchange, the main market, and the port were there. The narrow but relatively straight streets were cobblestone and lined with solid, occasionally elegant houses, office buildings, and warehouses—also made of stone. Exiting the city meant using one of four gates through the thick stone wall that protected against Indians and marauding European powers. Montréal quickly grew past the bounds of its fortifications, however, and by World War I the center of the city had moved toward Mont Royal. The new heart of Montréal became Dominion Square (now Square Dorchester). For the next two decades Vieux-Montréal, as it became known, was gradually abandoned, the warehouses and offices emptied. In 1962 the city began studying ways to revitalize Vieux-Montréal, and a decade of renovations and restorations began.

Today, Vieux-Montréal is a center of cultural life and municipal government, if not of commerce and politics. Most of the summer activities revolve around Place Jacques-Cartier, which becomes a pedestrian mall with street performers and outdoor cafés spilling out of restaurants. This lovely square is a good place to view the fireworks festival, and it's adjacent to the Vieux-Port exhibition grounds and the docks for the harbor cruises. Classical music concerts are staged all year long at the Notre-Dame Basilica, which possesses one of the finest organs in North America, and plays are staged in English by the Centaur Theatre in the old stock-exchange building. This district has six museums devoted to history, religion, and decorative and fine arts.

To begin your tour of Vieux-Montréal, take the Métro to the Place d'Armes station, beneath the Palais des Congrès convention center, and walk 1½ blocks south on rue St-Urbain to **Place d'Armes.** In the 1600s, Place d'Armes was the site of battles with the Iroquois and later became the center of Montréal's "Upper Town." In the middle of the square is a statue of Paul de Chomedey, Sieur de Maisonneuve, the founder of Montréal. In 1644 he was wounded here in a battle with 200 Indians. Historians recently uncovered a network of tunnels beneath the square; they connected the various buildings, and one tunnel ran down to the river. These precursors of the Underground City protected the colonists from the extremes of winter weather and provided an escape route should the city be overrun. Unfortunately, the tunnels are too small and dangerous to visit. Calèches are available at the south end of the square.

The north side of the square is dominated by the **Bank of Montréal,** an impressive building with Corinthian columns, built in 1847 (remodeled by renowned architects McKim, Mead & White in 1905), that houses a small, interesting numismatics museum. *129 rue St-Jacques. Admission free. Open weekdays 9–5.*

The office building to the west of the square is the site of the old Café Dillon, a famous gourmet restaurant frequented by members of the fur traders' Beaver Club (*see Dining, below*). Two extremely important edifices form the south end of Place d'Armes: the Sulpician Seminary, the oldest building in Montréal, and the imposing Notre-Dame Basilica.

The first church called Notre-Dame was a bark-covered structure built within the fort in 1642, the year the first settlers arrived. Three times it was torn down and rebuilt, each time in a different spot, each time larger and more ornate. The enormous (3,800-seat) neo-Gothic **Notre-Dame Basilica,** which opened in 1829, is the most recent. The twin towers, named Temperance and Perseverance, are 227 meters (69 feet) high, and the western one holds one of North America's largest bells, the 12-ton Gros Bourdon. The interior of the church was designed in medieval style by Victor Bourgeau, with stained-glass windows, a stunning blue vault ceiling with gold stars, and pine and walnut wood carving in traditional Québec style. The church has many unique features: It is rectangular rather than cruciform in shape; it faces south rather than east; the floor slopes down 4 meters (1¼ feet) from back to front; and it has twin rows of balconies on each side. The Casavants, a Québec family, built the 6,800-pipe organ, one of the largest on the continent. Notre-Dame has particularly excellent acoustics and is often the site of Montréal Symphony (tel. 514/842–9951) concerts, notably, Handel's *Messiah* during the week before Christmas and the Mozart Plus Festival in July. Behind the main altar is the Sacré-Coeur Chapel, which was destroyed by fire in 1978 and rebuilt in five different styles. Also in

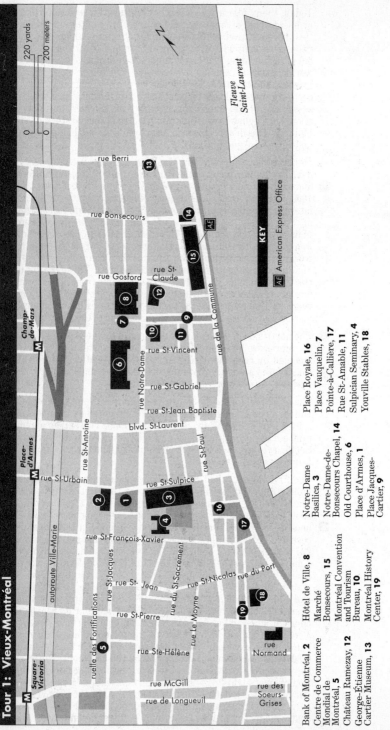

# Tour 1: Vieux-Montréal

220 yards
200 meters

*Fleuve Saint-Laurent*

**KEY**

AE American Express Office

Bank of Montréal, **2**
Centre de Commerce Mondial de Montréal, **5**
Château Ramezay, **12**
George-Étienne Cartier Museum, **13**

Hôtel de Ville, **8**
Marché Bonsecours, **15**
Montréal Convention and Tourism Bureau, **10**
Montréal History Center, **19**

Notre-Dame Basilica, **3**
Notre-Dame-de-Bonsecours Chapel, **14**
Old Courthouse, **6**
Place d'Armes, **1**
Place Jacques-Cartier, **9**

Place Royale, **16**
Place Vauquelin, **7**
Pointe-à-Callière, **17**
Rue St-Amable, **11**
Sulpician Seminary, **4**
Youville Stables, **18**

the back of the church is a small museum of religious paintings and historical objects. *116 rue Notre-Dame O. Basilica: tel. 514/849–1070. Open Labor Day–June 24, daily 7–6; June 25–Labor Day, daily 7 AM–8 PM. Guided tours daily (except Sun. morning) May–June 24, 9–4; June 24–Labor Day, 8:30–4:30; Labor Day–mid-Oct., 9–4. Museum: tel. 514/842–2925. Admission: $1 adults, 50¢ children. Open weekends 9:30–5.*

**❹** The low, more retiring stone building behind a wall to the west of the basilica is the **Sulpician Seminary.** This is Montréal's oldest building, built in 1685, and is still a residence for the Sulpician order (unfortunately, it's closed to the public). For almost two centuries, until 1854, the Sulpicians were *the* political power in the city, because they owned the property rights to the island of Montréal. They were also instrumental in recruiting and equipping colonists for New France. The building itself is considered the finest, most elegant example of rustic 17th-century Québec architecture. The clock on the roof over the main doorway is the oldest (pre-1701) public timepiece in North America. Behind the seminary building is a small garden, another Montréal first.

**❺** Take a right on rue St-François-Xavier to rue St-Jacques and turn left to reach the new **Centre de Commerce Mondial de Montréal** (World Trade Centre of Montréal), an ambitious block-long complex that combines old and new. It's home to the new Inter-Continental Hotel in Montréal, a retail mall, and office space. Developers of this innovative complex have gambled that they can attract businesses back from downtown to rue St-Jacques, which, when it was known as St. James Street, was the financial center of Canada.

Moving back toward the Basilica, visit **rue St-Sulpice,** the first street in Montréal. On the eastern side of the street there's a plaque marking where the Hôtel-Dieu, the city's first hospital, was built in 1644. Now cross rue St-Sulpice—the Art Deco **Aldred Building** sits on the far left corner—and take rue Notre-Dame Est. One block farther, just past boulevard St-Laurent, on the left, rises the black-glass-sheathed **Palais de Justice** (1971), which houses the higher courts for both the city and the province. (Québec's legal system is based on the Napoleonic Code for civil cases and on British common law for criminal cases.)

**❻** The large domed building at 155 rue Notre-Dame Est is the classic revival–style **Old Courthouse** (1857), now municipal offices. Across the street, at 160 rue Notre-Dame Est, is the **Maison de la Sauvegarde** (1811), one of the oldest houses in the city and now home to the European sausage restaurant, Chez Better (*see* Dining, be-

**❼** *low*). The Old Courthouse abuts the small **Place Vauquelin,** named after the 18th-century naval hero who is memorialized by a statue in its center. North of this square is **Champs-de-Mars,** the former site of a colonial military parade ground and now a public park. The or-

**❽** nate building on the east side of Place Vauquelin is the Second Empire–style **Hôtel de Ville** (City Hall, 1878). On July 24, 1967, French President Charles de Gaulle stood on the central balcony of the hotel and made his famous *"Vive le Québec libre"* speech.

**❾** You are in a perfect spot to explore **Place Jacques-Cartier,** the heart of Vieux-Montréal. This two-block-long square opened in 1804 as a municipal market, and every summer it is transformed into a flower market. The 1809 monument at the top of the square celebrates Lord Nelson's victory at Trafalgar. At the western corner of rue Notre-Dame is a small building (1811), site of the old Silver Dollar Saloon, so named because there were 350 silver dollars nailed to the

**⓾** floor. Today it's the home of the **Greater Montreal Convention and Tourism Bureau** (*see* Important Addresses and Numbers, *above*). Both sides of the square are lined with two- and three-story stone buildings that were originally homes or hotels.

**Time Out** **Le St-Amable** (188 rue St-Amable, tel. 514/866–3471) features a businessmen's lunch weekdays from noon to 3, but you don't have to be an executive or even be dressed like one to sample such classics as fresh poached salmon or grilled New Zealand lamb chops.

**⓫** In the summer, the one-block **rue St-Amable** becomes a marketplace for local jewelers, artists, and craftspeople. From the bottom of Place Jacques-Cartier you can stroll out into the **Port of Montreal Exhibition Ground,** where from summer through the Winter Carnival there is always something going on. At the foot of boulevard St-Laurent and rue de la Commune are the port's major exhibitions: **Images du Futur, IMAX Super Cinema,** and **Expotec.**

Retrace your steps to the north end of Place Jacques-Cartier, then continue east on rue Notre-Dame. At the corner of rue St-Claude on **⓬** the right is **Château Ramezay** (1705), built as the residence of the 11th governor of Montréal, Claude de Ramezay. In 1775–76 it was the headquarters for American troops seeking to conquer Canada. Benjamin Franklin stayed here during that winter occupation. One of the most elegant colonial buildings still standing in Montréal, the château is now a museum, and it has been restored to the style of Governor de Ramezay's day. The ground floor is furnished like a gentleman's residence of New France, with dining room, bedroom, and office. *280 rue Notre-Dame E, tel. 514/861–3708. Admission: $5 adults, $3 students and senior citizens, $10 families. Visitors using wheelchairs are advised to reserve 1 day in advance. Open Tues.– Sun. 10–4:30.*

At the end of rue St-Paul are two houses built by Sir George-Étienne Cartier, a 19th-century Canadian statesman. They recently have **⓭** been opened as the **George-Étienne Cartier Museum.** Downstairs displays focus on the political career of this Québec-born Father of Canadian Confederation. Upstairs rooms are furnished as they would have been in the 1850s and 1860s when the Cartiers lived here. *458 rue Notre-Dame E, tel. 514/283–2282. Admission free. Open summer, daily 9–5; fall–winter, Wed.–Sun. 10–noon and 1–5.*

One block back on rue St. Paul is rue Bonsecours, one of the oldest streets in the city. At the end of rue Bonsecours is the small but **⓮** beautiful **Notre-Dame-de-Bonsecours Chapel.** Marguerite Bourgeoys, who was canonized in 1983, helped found Montréal and dedicated this chapel to the Virgin Mary in 1657. It became known as a sailor's church, and small wood models of sailing ships are suspended from the ceiling just above the congregation. In the basement there is a small, strange museum honoring the saint that includes a story of her life modeled by little dolls in a series of dioramas. A gift shop sells Marguerite Bourgeoys souvenirs. From the museum you can climb to the rather precarious bell tower (beware of the slippery metal steps in winter) for a fine view of Vieux-Montréal and the port. *400 rue St-Paul E, tel. 514/845–9991. Admission: $2 adults, 50¢ children. Chapel and museum open May–Oct., Tues.– Sun. 9–4:30; Nov.–Apr., Tues.–Sun. 10:30–2:30.*

At the corner of rues St-Paul and Bonsecours is the historic **Maison du Calvet,** now a charming café. Double back and head west on rue **⓯** St-Paul. The long, large, domed building to the left is the **Marché**

**Bonsecours** (1845), for many years Montréal's main produce, meat, and fish market and now municipal offices. The market has been transformed into a permanent cultural center with temporary exhibits on Montréal.

**Rue St-Paul** is the most fashionable street in Vieux-Montréal. For almost 20 blocks it is lined with fine restaurants, shops, and even a few nightclubs. Québecois handcrafts are a specialty here, with shops at 88, 136, and 272 rue St-Paul Est. **L'Air du Temps,** at 191 rue St-Paul Ouest, is one of the city's top jazz clubs. Nightly shows usually feature local talent, with occasional international name bands. Take rue St-Paul eight short blocks west of Place Jacques-Cartier, and you will come to **Place Royale,** the site of the first permanent settlement in Montréal.

Behind the Old Customs House you will find **Pointe-à-Callière,** a small park that commemorates the settlers' first landing. A small stream used to flow into the St. Lawrence here, and it was on the point of land between the two waters that the colonists landed their four boats on May 17, 1642. After they built the stockade and the first buildings at this site, the settlement was almost washed away the next Christmas by a flood. When it was spared, de Maisonneuve placed a cross on top of Mont Royal as thanks to God. The new **Pointe-à-Callière Museum of Archaeology and History** has been built around the excavated remains of structures dating back to Montréal's beginnings, including the city's first Catholic cemetery. The museum is a labyrinth of stone walls and corridors, illuminated by spotlights and holograms of figures from the past. An audiovisual show gives a historical overview of the area. *350 Place Royale, tel. 514/872–9150. Admission: $6 adults, $5 senior citizens, $4 students, children under 12 free. Open June 24–Sept. 5, Tues.–Sun. 10–8; Sept. 6–June 23, Tues.–Sun. 10–5.*

A 1½-block walk down rue William takes you to the **Youville Stables** on the left. These low stone buildings enclosing a garden were originally built as warehouses in 1825 (they never were stables). A group of businesspeople renovated them in 1968, and the buildings now house offices, shops, and a restaurant.

Across rue William from the stables is the **Montréal History Centre.** Visitors to this high-tech museum are led through a series of audiovisual environments depicting the life and history of Montréal. *335 Place d'Youville, tel. 514/872–3207. Admission: $4.50 adults, $2.75 senior citizens and students 6–17, children under 6 free (Jan. 5–Apr.); $4.50 adults, $3 senior citizens and students 6–17, children under 6 free (May–Dec.). Open Jan. 5–May 2, Tues.–Sun. 10–5; May 3–July 4, daily 9–5; July 5–Sept. 6, daily 10–6; Sept. 7–Dec. 12, Tues.–Sun. 10–5.*

## Tour 2: Downtown

*Numbers in the margin correspond to points of interest on the Tour 2: Downtown Montréal map.*

Downtown is a sprawling 30- by 8-block area bounded by avenue Atwater and boulevard St-Laurent on the west and east, respectively, avenue des Pins on the north, and rue St-Antoine on the south.

After 1700, Vieux-Montréal wasn't big enough for the rapidly expanding city. In 1701 the French administration signed a peace treaty with the Iroquois, and the colonists began to feel safe about building outside Montréal's fortifications. The city inched northward, toward Mont Royal, particularly after the English conquest in 1760. By the end of the 19th century, rue Ste-Catherine was the main commercial thoroughfare, and the city's elite built mansions on the slope of the mountain. Since 1960 city planners have made a concerted effort to move the focus eastward. With the opening of Place des Arts (1963) and the Complexe Desjardins (1976), the city center shifted in that direction. It hasn't landed on any one corner yet, although some Montréalers will tell you it's at the intersection of avenue McGill College and rue Ste-Catherine.

A major development of the past 30 years is the inauguration of the **Underground City,** an enormous network of passages linking various shopping and office complexes. These have served to keep the retail trade in the downtown area, as well as to make shoppers and workers immune to the hardships of the Canadian winter.

Our tour of downtown begins at the McGill Métro station. The corner of rue University and boulevard de Maisonneuve has recently been the center of intensive development. Two huge office buildings, **2020 University** and **Galleries 2001,** with malls at street and basement levels, rise from the north side of the intersection. The southwest  corner, indeed the entire block, is taken up by **Eaton** (*see* Shopping, *below*), one of the Big Three department stores in the city. Aside from many floors of mid-priced clothing and other merchandise, the real attraction of Eaton is the ninth-floor art deco dining room.

**Time Out**    **Eaton le 9e** was modeled after the dining room of the luxury liner *Ile-de-France,* Lady Eaton's favorite cruise ship. Elegant marble columns hold up the ceiling, and the walls are decorated with two art deco murals featuring willowy ladies at leisure. The patrons are usually shoppers, of course, dining on pasta, fish, and meat dishes. The service is practical and fast; the decor's the thing. *677 rue Ste-Catherine O, tel. 514/284–8421. AE, MC, V. Open Mon.–Wed. 11:30–3, Thurs. and Fri. 11:30–3 and 4:30–7, Sat. 11:30–3.*

Eaton is connected to the **Eaton Centre** shopping complex via passageways; it is also linked to the McGill Métro and Les Promenades de la Cathédrale and La Baie (The Bay) eastward, and Place Montréal Trust westward.

 Across rue University from Eaton stands **Christ Church Cathedral** (1859), the main church of the Anglican Diocese of Montréal. In early 1988 this building was a sight. Plagued by years of high maintenance costs and declining membership, the church fathers leased their land and air rights to a consortium of developers for 99 years. All the land beneath and surrounding the cathedral was removed, and the structure was supported solely by a number of huge steel stilts. The glass 34-story office tower behind the cathedral, **La Maison des Coopérants,** and Les Promenades de la Cathédrale retail complex beneath it, are the products of that agreement.

**Place Ville-Marie** is an office, retail, and mall complex that signaled a new era for Montréal when it opened in 1962. It was the first link in the huge chain of the Underground City, which meant that people could have access to all the services of the city without setting foot outside. It was also the first step Montréal took to claiming its place as an international city. The labyrinth that is the Underground City now includes six hotels, thousands of offices, 30 movie theaters, more than 1,000 boutiques, hundreds of restaurants, and almost 18 kilometers (10.8 miles) of passageways.

From Place Ville-Marie head south via the passageways toward **Le Reine Elizabeth (Queen Elizabeth)** hotel. You can reach the **Gare**

# Tour 2: Downtown Montréal

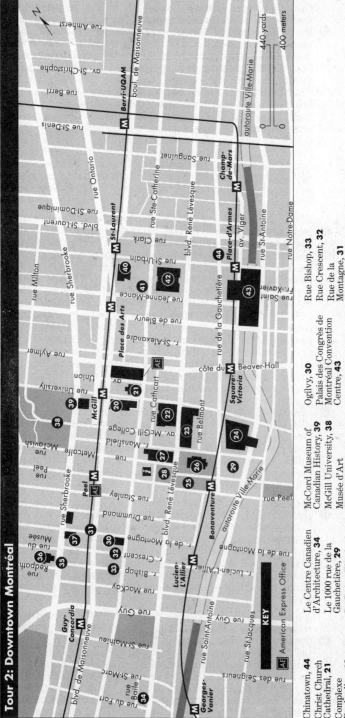

Chinatown, **44**
Christ Church Cathedral, **21**
Complexe Desjardins, **42**
Eaton, **20**
Holt Renfrew, **37**

Le Centre Canadien d'Architecture, **34**
Le 1000 rue de la Gauchetière, **29**
Le Reine Elizabeth (Queen Elizabeth), **23**
Mary Queen of the World Cathedral, **26**

McCord Museum of Canadian History, **39**
McGill University, **38**
Musée d'Art Contemporain, **41**
Musées des Beaux-Arts de Montréal, **36**

Ogilvy, **30**
Palais des Congrès de Montréal Convention Centre, **43**
Place Bonaventure, **24**
Place des Arts, **40**
Place du Canada, **25**
Place Ville-Marie, **22**

Rue Bishop, **33**
Rue Crescent, **32**
Rue de la Montagne, **31**
Square Dorchester, **28**
Square Mile, **35**
Sun Life Building, **27**

**KEY**

**AE** American Express Office

**Centrale (Central Railway Station)** just behind the hotel. Trains from the United States and the rest of Canada arrive here. Then fol-
➋➍ low the signs marked "Métro/Place Bonaventure" to **Place Bonaventure,** the largest commercial building in Canada. On the lower floors there are shops and restaurants, then come exposition halls and of-fices, and finally the whole thing is topped by the Bonaventure Hilton International (*see* Lodging, *below*) and 2½ acres of gardens. From here take the route marked "Place du Canada," which will bring you to the mall in the base of the **Le Château Champlain** (*see* Lodging, *below*). This building is known as the Cheesegrater be-cause of its rows and rows of half-moon-shape windows. Our explora-tion of this leg of the Underground City will end at **Windsor Station** (follow the signs). This was the second railway station built in Mont-réal by the Canadian Pacific Railway Company. Windsor Station, with its massive rustic stone exterior holding up an amazing steel-and-glass roof over an arcade, was designed in 1889 by New York ar-chitect George Price.

Exit at the north end of Windsor Station and cross the street to the
➋➎ park known as **Place du Canada.** In the center of the park there is a statue to Sir John A. Macdonald, Canada's first prime minister.
➋➏ Then cross the park and rue de la Cathédrale to the **Mary Queen of the World Cathedral** (1894), which you enter on boulevard René-Lévesque. This church is modeled after St. Peter's Basilica in Rome. Victor Bourgeau, the same architect who did the interior of Notre-Dame in Vieux-Montréal, thought the idea of the cathedral's design terrible but completed it after the original architect proved incom-petent. Inside there is even a canopy over the altar that is a minia-ture copy of Bernini's *baldacchino* in St. Peter's. The massive gray granite edifice across boulevard René-Lévesque from the cathedral
➋➐ is the **Sun Life Building** (1914), at one time the largest building in the British Commonwealth. During World War II much of England's fi-nancial reserves and national treasures were stored in Sun Life's vaults. The park that faces the Sun Life building just north of boule-
➋➑ vard René-Lévesque is **Square Dorchester,** for many years the heart of Montréal. Until 1870 a Catholic burial ground occupied this block (and there are still bodies buried beneath the grass), but with the rapid development of the area, the city fathers decided to turn it into a park. The statuary of Square Dorchester includes a monument to the Boer War in the center and a statue of the Scottish poet Robert Burns near rue Peel.

In the large skyscraper just south of Square Dorchester is an indoor
➋➒ skating rink, **Le 1000 rue de la Gauchetière,** that is open year-round. Located in the 1000 rue de la Gauchetière office tower, the $5 million rink is bathed in natural light and surrounded by a host of amenities, such as cafés, a food court, and a winter garden. It's open to all levels of skaters, and skate rentals and lockers are available. There are also a regular program of ice shows, Saturday-night skating to rock music, and skating lessons. *1000 rue de la Gauchetière, tel. 514/499–2001.*

A block north of Square Dorchester is rue Ste-Catherine, the main retail shopping street of Montréal. Three blocks west, at 1307 rue
➌➊ Ste-Catherine Ouest and rue de la Montagne, is **Ogilvy,** the last of the Big Three department stores. The store has been divided into individual name boutiques that sell generally pricier lines than does La Baie or Eaton. Most days at noon a bagpiper plays Scottish airs
➌➊ as he circumnavigates the ground floor. **Rue de la Montagne,** and
➌➋ ➌➌ rues **Crescent** and **Bishop,** the two streets just west of it, constitute the heart of Montréal's downtown nightlife and restaurant scene.

This area once formed the playing fields of the Montréal Lacrosse and Cricket Grounds, and later it became an exclusive suburb lined with millionaires' row houses. Since then these three streets between rues Sherbrooke and Ste-Catherine have become fertile ground for trendy bars, restaurants, and shops ensconced in those old row houses.

**34** While you're in the vicinity, take in one of downtown's newest attractions, **Le Centre Canadien d'Architecture (Canadian Centre for Architecture)**, just four blocks west at rue St-Marc on rue Baile. The lifelong dream of its founding director, Phyllis Lambert (of the Bronfman fortune), the CCA opened in May 1989 and houses one of the world's premier architectural collections. *1920 rue Baile, tel. 514/939-7000. Admission free to children under 12 and Thurs. evening to adults; otherwise, $5 adults, $3 senior citizens and students. Group rates available. Open Wed. and Fri. 11–6, Thurs. 11–8, weekends 11–5. Reservations required.*

**35** Now that you're in the mood for historic pursuits, backtrack to rues Ste-Catherine and Bishop. By walking two blocks north on rue Bishop to rue Sherbrooke, you enter a very different environment: the exclusive neighborhood known as the **Square Mile.**

**36** Directly across the street from the end of rue Bishop is the **Musée des Beaux-Arts de Montréal (Montreal Museum of Fine Arts)**, the oldest established museum in Canada (1860). The present building was completed in 1912 and holds a large collection of European and North American fine and decorative art; ancient treasures from Europe, the Near East, Asia, Africa, and America; art from Québec and Canada; and Native American and Eskimo artifacts. From June through October there is usually one world-class exhibition, such as the inventions of Leonardo da Vinci or the works of Marc Chagall.

The Museum of Fine Arts has a gift shop, an art-book store, a restaurant and cafeteria, and a gallery from which you can buy or rent paintings by local artists. *1380 rue Sherbrooke O, tel. 514/285–1600. Admission: permanent collection, $4.75 adults, $3 students, $1 children 12 and under and senior citizens; visiting exhibitions, $9.50 adults, $4.75 students and senior citizens, $2 children 12 and under; audio guides, $4. Open Tues., Thurs., Fri., and Sun. 11–6; Wed. and Sat. 11–9.*

**37** Walking east on rue Sherbrooke brings you to the small and exclusive **Holt Renfrew** department store, perhaps the city's fanciest, at the corner of rue de la Montagne (*see* Shopping, *below*). A few blocks farther east along rue Drummond stands the **Ritz-Carlton,** the grande dame of Montréal hotels. It was built in 1912 so the local millionaires' European friends would have a suitable place to stay. Take a peek in the elegant Café de Paris restaurant. It's Montréal's biggest power dining spot, and you just might see the prime minister dining here. (For more on the Ritz-Carlton and its restaurants, *see* Lodging and Dining sections, *below*.) The Ritz-Carlton's only real competition in town is the modern and elegant **Le Westin Mont-Royal** two blocks west at rues Sherbrooke and Peel. Just beyond this hotel **38** on the other side of the street begins the grassy **McGill University** campus. James McGill, a wealthy Scottish fur trader, bequeathed the money and the land for this institution, which opened in 1828 and is perhaps the finest English-language school of higher education in the nation. The student body numbers 15,000, and the university is best known for its medical and engineering schools.

**39** Just across rue Sherbrooke from the campus is the **McCord Museum of Canadian History.** The quality and extent of the McCord collections, which date primarily from the 18th century, make it one of the best history museums in Canada. The collections document the environment of Canadian native peoples and feature costumes and textiles, decorative arts, paintings, prints and drawings, and the 700,000-print-and-negative Notman Photographic Archives, which highlights 19th-century life in Montréal. The McCord is the only museum in Canada with a permanent costume gallery. There are guided tours (call for times), a reading room and documentation center, a gift shop and bookstore, and a tearoom. *690 rue Sherbrooke O, tel. 514/398–7100. Admission: $5 adults, $3 senior citizens, $2 students, $8 families, $3 per person in groups, children under 12 free. Open Tues., Wed., and Fri. 10–6; Thurs. 10–9; weekends 10–5. Closed Mon., except statutory holidays.*

Turn right on rue University and walk a block to the McGill Métro station. Take the train one stop in the direction of Honoré-Beaugrand to the Place des Arts station.

Montréal's Métro opened in 1966 with well-designed stations—many decorated with works of art—and modern trains running on quiet pneumatic wheels. Today there are 65 stations on four lines with 65 kilometers (40 miles) of track. The 759 train cars carry more

**40** than 700,000 passengers a day. When you exit at **Place des Arts,** follow the signs to the theater complex of the same name. From here you can walk the five blocks to Vieux-Montréal totally underground. Place des Arts, which opened in 1963, is reminiscent of New York's Lincoln Center in that it is a government-subsidized complex of three very modern theaters. The largest, Salle Wilfrid Pelletier, is the home of the Orchestre Symphonique de Montréal (Montreal Symphony Orchestra), which has won international raves under the baton of Charles Dutoit. The Orchestre Métropolitain de Montréal, Grands Ballets Canadiens, and the Opéra du Québec also stage productions here.

**41** The complex also houses the **Musée d'Art Contemporain,** the city's modern art museum, which moved here from Cité du Havre in 1991. The museum's large permanent collection represents works by Québecois, Canadian, and international artists in every medium. The museum often features weekend programs, with many child-oriented activities, and almost all are free. There are guided tours, though hours vary and groups of more than 15 are asked to make a reservation. *185 rue Ste-Catherine O, tel. 514/847–6226. Admission: $4.75 adults, $3.75 senior citizens, $2.75 students, children under 12 free. Wed. evenings free. Open Tues. and Thurs.–Sun. 11–6, Wed. 11–9.*

**42** While still in Place des Arts, follow the signs to the **Complexe Desjardins.** Built in 1976, this is another office building, hotel, and mall development along the lines of Place Ville-Marie. The luxurious Meridien Hotel (*see* Lodging, *below*) rises from its northwest corner. The large galleria space is the scene of all types of performances, from lectures on Japanese massage techniques to pop music, as well as avid shopping in the dozens of stores. The next development south is the **Complexe Guy-Favreau,** a huge federal office building named after the Canadian Minister of Justice in the early

**43** '60s. If you continue in a straight line, you will hit the **Palais des Congrès de Montréal Convention Centre** above the Place d'Armes Métro stop. But if you take a left out of Guy-Favreau onto rue de la

**44** Gauchetière, you will be in **Chinatown,** a relief after all that artificially enclosed retail space.

The Chinese first came to Montréal in large numbers after 1880, following the construction of the transcontinental railroad. They settled in an 18-block area between boulevard René-Lévesque and avenue Viger to the north and south, and near rues Hôtel de Ville and Bleury on the east and west, an area that became known as Chinatown, where there are many restaurants, food stores, and gift shops.

## Tour 3: St-Denis, Prince Arthur, and North

*Numbers in the margin correspond to points of interest on the Tour 3: St-Denis, Prince Arthur, and North map.*

After a long day of fulfilling your touristic obligations at the historical sites and museums of downtown and Vieux-Montréal, it's good to relax and indulge in some primal pleasures, such as eating, shopping, and nightlife. For these and other diversions, head to the neighborhoods east and north of downtown. Our tour begins in the Latin Quarter, the main student district, then wends its way north.

The southern section of this area, around the base of rue St-Denis, was one of the city's first residential neighborhoods, built in the 19th century as the city burst the bounds of Vieux-Montréal. Then known as Faubourg St-Laurent, it was the home of many wealthy families. The lands to the north of present-day rue Sherbrooke were mostly farms and limestone quarries.

Begin at the **Berri-UQAM** Métro stop, perhaps the most important in the whole city, because three lines intersect here. This area, particularly along **rue St-Denis** on each side of boulevard de Maisonneuve, is known as the **Latin Quarter** and is the site of the **Université du Québec à Montréal** and a number of other educational institutions. Rue St-Denis is lined with cafés, bistros, and restaurants that attract the academic crowd. On rue Ste-Catherine there are a number of low-rent nightclubs popular with avant-garde rock-  and-roll types. Just west of rue St-Denis you find the **Cinémathèque Québecoise**, a museum and repertory movie house. For $3 you can visit the permanent exhibition on the history of filmmaking equipment and see two movies. The museum also houses one of the largest cinematic reference libraries in the world. *335 boul. de Maisonneuve O, tel. 514/842–9763. Admission free; movies $3. Library, museum, and theater open June–Aug., weekdays 12:30–4:30; Sept.–May, Mon. and Fri. 12:30–5, Tues.–Thurs 12:30–8:30.*

 Around the corner and half a block north on rue St-Denis stands the 2,500-seat **Théâtre St-Denis,** the second-largest auditorium in Montréal (after Salle Wilfrid Pelletier in Place des Arts). Sarah Bernhardt and numerous other famous actors have graced its stage. It currently is the main site for the summertime concerts of the Montréal International Jazz Festival. On the next block north you see the Beaux Arts **Bibliothèque Nationale du Québec** (1915), a library that houses Québec's official archives (1700 rue St-Denis; open Tues.–Sat. 9–5). If you have a lot of money and some hours set aside for dining, try **Les Mignardises** at 2035–37 rue St-Denis just south of rue Sherbrooke (*see* Dining, *below*).

Continue north on rue St-Denis past rue Sherbrooke. On the right, above the Sherbrooke Métro station, is the **Hôtel de l'Institut,** the hands-on training academy of the government *hôtelier* school. To the  left is the small **Square St-Louis,** once considered among the most beautiful in Montréal; unfortunately, now it is a haven for neighborhood panhandlers. In its heyday, this was the focal point of the com-

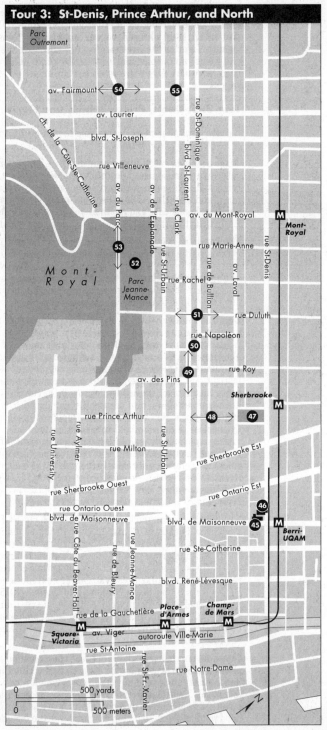

**Tour 3:  St-Denis, Prince Arthur, and North**

munity, and the surrounding neighborhood takes its name from the once grand square. Originally a reservoir, these blocks became a park in 1879 and attracted upper-middle-class families and artists to the area. French Canadian poets were among the most famous creative people to occupy the houses back then, and the neighborhood is the home today for Montréal painters, filmmakers, musicians, and writers. On the wall of 336 Square St-Louis you can see—and read, if your French is good—a long poem by Michel Bujold.

**48** **Rue Prince Arthur** begins at the western end of Square St-Louis. In the '60s the young people who moved to the neighborhood transformed the next few blocks into a small hippie bazaar of clothing, leather, and smoke shops. It remains a center of youth culture, although it's much tamer and more commercial. In 1981 the city turned the blocks between avenue Laval and boulevard St-Laurent into a pedestrian mall. Hippie shops live on today as inexpensive Greek, Vietnamese, Italian, Polish, and Chinese restaurants and boîtes of the singles-bar variety.

**49** When you reach **boulevard St-Laurent,** take a left and stroll south on the street that cuts through Montréal life in a number of ways. First, this is the east–west dividing street; like the Greenwich meridian, boulevard St-Laurent is where all the numbers begin. The street is also lined with shops and restaurants that represent the incredible ethnic diversity of Montréal. Until the late 19th century this was a neighborhood first of farms and then of middle-class Anglophone residences. It was on boulevard St-Laurent in 1892 that the first electric tramway was installed that could climb the slope to Plâteau Mont-Royal. Working-class families, who couldn't afford a horse and buggy to pull them up the hill, began to move in. In the 1880s the first of many waves of Russian-Jewish immigrants escaping the pogroms arrived and settled here. Boulevard St-Laurent became known as the Main, as in "main street," and Yiddish was the primary language spoken along some stretches. The Russian Jews were followed by Greeks, Eastern Europeans, Portuguese, and, most recently, Latin Americans.

The 10 blocks north of rue Sherbrooke are filled with delis, junk stores, restaurants, luncheonettes, and clothing stores, as well as fashionable boutiques, bistros, cafés, bars, nightclubs, bookstores, and galleries exhibiting the work of the latest wave of "immigrants" to the area—gentrifiers and artists. The block between rues Roy and Napoléon is particularly rich in delights. Just east at 76 rue Roy is **Waldman's Fish Market,** reputed to be the largest wholesale/retail fish market in North America. **Warshaw's Supermarket** at 3863 boulevard St-Laurent is a huge Eastern European–style emporium that sells all sorts of delicacies.

A few doors up the street from Warshaw's—at No. 3895—is **50** **Schwartz's Delicatessen.** Among the many contenders for the "smoked-meat king" title in Montréal, Schwartz's is most frequently at the top. Smoked meat is just about all it serves, but the meat comes in lean, medium, or fatty cuts. The waiters give you your food and take your money, and that's that.

A block north is **Moishe's** (*see* Dining, *below*), home of the best, but priciest, steaks in Montréal as well as the noisiest atmosphere. The **51** next corner is **rue Duluth,** where merchants are seeking to re-create rue Prince Arthur. If you take a walk to the right all the way to rue St-Denis, you will find Greek and Vietnamese restaurants and boutiques and art galleries on either side of the street. A left turn on rue **52** Duluth and a three-block walk brings you to **Parc Jeanne-Mance,** a flat, open field that's a perfect spot for a picnic of delicacies purchased on the Main. The park segues into the 2 wooded, hilly square kilometers (494 acres) of **Parc Mont-Royal.**

**53** **Avenue du Parc** forms the western border of Parc Jeanne-Mance. To get there either cut through the park or take a left on avenue du Mont-Royal at the north end. No. 93 avenue du Mont-Royal Ouest is the home of **Beauty's,** a restaurant specializing in bagels, lox, pancakes, and omelets. Expect a line weekend mornings. Turn right and head north to **avenue Laurier.** All along this avenue, from Côte Ste-Catherine to boulevard St-Laurent, are some of the fanciest fur stores, boutiques, pastry shops, and jewelers in the city. For a quick chocolate eclair bracer or two, go to **Le Nôtre,** at 1050 avenue Laurier O, a branch of the Parisian shop of the same name.

**Time Out**    **La Petite Ardoise** is a casual, slightly arty café that serves soups, quiches, sandwiches, and more expensive daily specials. The onion soup is lovingly overdosed with cheese, bread, and onions. Whether it's breakfast, lunch, or dinner, the best accompaniment for your meal is a big, steamy bowl of creamy café au lait. This café is a perfect place to take a breather from shopping. *222 av. Laurier O, tel. 514/495–4961. AE, MC, V. Open daily 8 AM–midnight, later on weekends.*

The next three blocks of avenue du Parc form the heart of the Greek district. Try **Symposium,** at No. 5334, or the neighboring **Milos** at 5357 avenue du Parc (*see* Dining, *below*) for some of the best Greek appetizers, grilled seafood, and atmosphere you'll find in this hemisphere.

**54** **Avenue Fairmount,** a block north of avenue Laurier, is the site of two small but internationally known culinary landmarks. The **Fairmount Bagel Factory,** at 74 avenue Fairmount Ouest, claims to make the best bagels in the world.

Half a block east, on the corner of avenue Fairmount and rue Clark, **55** stands the famous **Wilensky's Light Lunch** (*see* Dining, *below*). Moviegoers will recognize this Montréal institution from *The Apprenticeship of Duddy Kravitz,* based on the Mordecai Richler novel of the same name. Lunch is all that's served here, and it certainly is light on the wallet. A couple of dollars will get you a hot dog or a bologna, salami, and mustard pretzel-roll sandwich with a strawberry soda. Books are available for perusing. The atmosphere is free.

## Parks and Gardens

*Numbers in the margin correspond to points of interest on the Olympic Park and Botanical Garden map.*

Of Montréal's three major parks, **Lafontaine** is the smallest (the other two are Parc Mont-Royal and Ile Ste-Hélène). Parc Lafontaine, founded in 1867, is divided into eastern and western halves. The eastern half is French style; the paths, gardens, and lawns are laid out in rigid geometric shapes. There are two public swimming pools on the north end, along rue Rachel. In the winter the park is open for ice skating. The western half is designed on the English system, in which the meandering paths and irregularly shaped ponds follow the natural contours of the topography. Pedal boats can be rented for a paddle around one of two man-made lakes. Its band shell is the site of many free outdoor summertime concerts, performances by dance and theater groups, and film screenings. Take the Métro to the Sherbrooke station and walk eight blocks east along rue Cherrier until avenue Parc Lafontaine. *3933 av. Parc Lafontaine, tel. 514/872–6211. Open dialy 9 AM–10 PM.*

The giant, mollusk-shape **Olympic Stadium** and the tilted tower that supports the roof are probably the preeminent symbols of modern Montréal. Planning for the Olympic Stadium complex began in 1972, and construction in the old Parc Maisonneuve started soon afterward. The Olympics took place in 1976, but the construction of the stadium's roof and tower was not completed until 1989. Many Montréalers were proud of what they had—at least until the summer of 1991, when a 55-ton concrete beam in the stadium came crashing to the ground, and the stadium was forced to close for several months. The Olympic Park includes the 70,000-seat **Olympic Stadium**, the **Olympic Tower**, six swimming pools, the **Aréna Maurice-Richard**, and the Olympic Village. Daily guided tours (tel. 514/252–8687) of the entire complex leave from Tourist Hall at 11, 12:40, 2, and 3:40; two are in English, two are in French. Perhaps the most popular visitor activity is a ride up to the tilted tower's observatory on the Funicular, the exterior cable car. The two-level cable car holds 90 people and takes two minutes to climb the 270 meters (890 feet) to the observatory, from which you can see up to 80 kilometers (50 miles) on clear days.

The **Biodôme,** in the former Olympic Park Velodrome, opened in June of 1992. This natural sciences museum combines four ecosystems—the boreal forest, tropical forest, polar world, and St. Lawrence River—under one climate-controlled dome. Visitors follow protected pathways through each environment, observing indigenous flora and fauna of each of the ecosystems. Animals from the former zoo at Angrignon Park and the now closed aquarium on Ile Ste-Hélène have been incorporated into this center. *4777 av. Pierre-de-Coubertin, tel. 514/868–3000. Admission: $8.50 adults, $6 senior citizens over 65 and students, $4.25 children 6–17, children under 5 free. Open June 18–Sept. 9, daily 9–8; Sept. 10–June 17, daily 9–6.*

If you've brought your swimsuit and towels, take a dip at the **Aquatic Center** (tel. 514/252–4622 for hours). There are also a cafeteria and a souvenir shop on the grounds. You can reach the **Olympic Park** via the Pie-IX or Viau Métro stations (the latter is nearer the stadium entrance).

Continuing your back-to-nature experience, cross rue Sherbrooke to the north of the Olympic Park (or take the free shuttle bus) to reach the **Botanical Garden** (closest Métro stop is Pie-IX). Founded in 1931, this garden is said to be one of the largest in the world. During the summer you can visit the 73 hectares (181 acres) of outdoor gardens—a favorite is the poisonous-plants garden; the 10 exhibition greenhouses are open year-round. There are more than 26,000 species of plants here. When the 5-acre **Montréal-Shanghai Dream Lake Garden** opened here in June 1991, it became the site of the largest Chinese garden outside Asia. The authentic Ming-style garden has seven elegant pavilions, including a large exhibition hall featuring changing exhibitions and a 30-foot rockery around a central reflecting pool. There is also an impressive collection of penjings or Chinese bonsais (miniature trees). A **Japanese Garden** and its pavilion, where guests may join a formal tea ceremony, are next to the Dream Lake. The **Insectarium,** a bug-shape building, houses more than 250,000 insect specimens collected by Montréal entomologist Georges Brossard. *4101 rue Sherbrooke E, tel. 514/872–1400. Admission to the greenhouses and the Insectarium May–Oct.: $7*

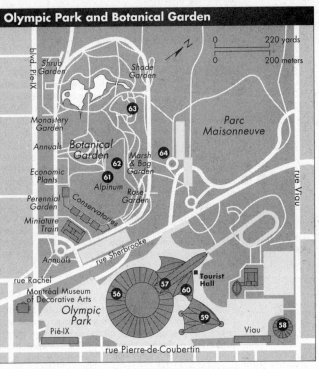

**Olympic Park and Botanical Garden**

*adults, $3.50 children 6–17, $5 senior citizens; Nov.–Apr.: $5 adults, $2.50 children 6–17, $3.50 senior citizens.*

**Ile Ste-Hélène** (along with Ile Notre-Dame, the former site of the Expo '67 World's Fair), opposite Vieux-Montréal in the middle of the St. Lawrence River, draws big crowds, particularly during the warm months. You can reach it via either the de la Concorde or Jacques-Cartier bridges, via the Métro to the Ile Ste-Hélène station, or by city bus (summer only) from downtown. Ile Ste-Hélène is a wooded, rolling park perfect for picnicking in the summer and cross-country skiing and ice skating during the snow season. The former 1967 World's Fair site on the island has been upgraded. Buckminster Fuller's biosphere (the world's largest geodesic dome when the famous architect and engineer built it for Expo '67, but since ravaged by fire) is scheduled to reopen in 1995 as a permanent water and environment interpretation center.

**La Ronde** was created as part of the Expo celebration. This world-class amusement park boasts a huge new roller coaster (the second-highest in the world), water slides with incredible drops, an international circus, Ferris wheels, boat rides, and rides, rides, rides. La Ronde is also the site of the annual Benson & Hedges International Fireworks Competition, on Saturday or Sunday nights during June and July. A ticket, which includes a reserved seat for the show and an amusement park pass, costs $22.75. *Ile Ste-Hélène, tel. 514/872–6222 or 800/361–7178 for La Ronde; 514/790–1245 or 800/361–4595 for fireworks. Admission: $19.25 adults, $9.50 children, $44.50 families. Open May and early June, weekends; mid-June–Aug., Sun.–Thurs. 11 AM–midnight, Fri. and 11 AM–1 AM.*

A stroll back along the north side of the island brings you to the **Old Fort** just under the Jacques-Cartier Bridge. This former British arsenal has been turned into the **David M. Stewart Museum** and a dinner theater called **Le Festin du Gouverneur.** The latter is a re-creation of a 17th-century banquet, complete with balladeers and comedy skits. In the military museum are displays of old firearms, maps, scientific instruments, uniforms, and documents of colonial times. During the summer the parade ground is the scene of mock battles—cannons and all—by the Compagnie Franche de la Marine and bagpipe concerts by the 78th Fraser Highlanders. *Tel. 514/861–6701. Admission: $3 adults, $2 children and senior citizens. Open summer, Wed.–Mon. 10–6; winter, Wed.–Mon. 10–5.*

In mid-June, **Ile Notre-Dame** is the site of the Molson Grand Prix du Canada, a top Formula I international circuit auto race at the Gilles Villeneuve Race Track.

Just west of de la Concorde Bridge is the futuristic **Casino de Montréal.** Since it opened in October 1993, the government-owned gaming hall—the site of the French Pavilion during Expo '67—has been a roaring success. Over 10,000 people a day stream in to try their hand at the 65 gaming tables and more than 1,200 slot machines. Restaurants and gift shops are on the premises. *1 av. du Casino, tel. 514/392–2746 or 800/665–2274. Admission (minimum age is 18) and parking free. No jeans, shorts, or jogging shoes. Open daily 11 AM–3 AM.*

Another former Expo building, the Québec Pavilion, opened a **Dinasaurium** in June 1994. Visitors enter a time tunnel to take a "safari" through landscapes depicting Earth 200 million years ago, complete with giant beasts. Hands-on exhibits, interpretive talks, and dinosaur films are part of the program. *Tel. 514/861–3462 for hours and admission fees.*

Ile Notre-Dame is also site of the city's only natural beach on **Lac de l'Ile Notre-Dame.** Opened in the summer of 1990, it was an immediate success and is now packed on every hot, sunny day. Just a Métro stop away (Ile Ste-Hélène Métro) from downtown, the beach is an oasis, with clear lake water filtered by a treatment system that relies on aquatic plants, and an inviting stretch of lawn and trees rimmed with sand. Lifeguards are on duty; there is a shop that rents swimming and boating accessories, and there are picnic areas and a restaurant on the premises. There is also a moderate admission fee.

The **Parc Mont-Royal,** the finest in the city, is not easy to overlook. These 494 acres of forest and paths at the heart of the city were designed by Frederick Law Olmsted, the celebrated architect of New York's Central Park. He believed that communion with nature could cure body and soul. The park is designed following the natural topography and accentuating its features, as in the English mode. You can go skating on Beaver Lake in the winter, visit one of the two lookouts and scan the horizon, or study the park interpretation center in the chalet at the Mont Royal belvedere. Horse-drawn transport is popular year-round: sleigh rides in winter and calèche rides in summer. On the eastern side of the hill stands the 30-meter (100-foot) steel cross that is the symbol of the city.

## Shrines

**St. Joseph's Oratory,** on the northwest side of Mont Royal, is a Catholic shrine on a par with Lourdes or Fatima. Take the blue Métro line to the Côte-des-Neiges station, then walk three blocks uphill on the chemin de la Côte-des-Neiges. You can't miss the enormous church up on the hillside. Brother André, a member of the Society of the Brothers of the Holy Cross, constructed a small chapel to St. Joseph, Canada's patron saint, in 1904. Brother André was credited with a number of miracles and was beatified in 1982. His chapel became a pilgrimage site, the only one to St. Joseph in the world (St. Joseph is the patron saint of healing). The dome is among the world's largest, and while the interior is of little aesthetic interest, there is a small museum dedicated to the life of the Holy Family and containing many displays, including thousands of crutches discarded by the formerly disabled faithful. From early December through February the museum features a display of crèches (nativity scenes) from all over the world. Carillon, choral, and organ concerts are held weekly at the oratory during the summer, and you can still visit Brother André's original chapel and tomb at the side of the massive basilica. *3800 chemin Queen Mary, tel. 514/733–8211. Open Sept.–May, daily 6 AM–9:30 PM; June–Aug., daily 6 AM—10 PM.*

## Montréal for Free

**The Saidye Bronfman Centre** hands-on fine arts school has openhouse activities, gallery exhibitions, and public affairs lectures (*see* Off the Beaten Track, *below*).

Classical and pop concerts, dance performances, and theater are held at **Parc de Lafontaine,** rue Rachel.

Picnic in **Parc Mont-Royal,** sail miniature boats in its Beaver Lake during the summer, and skate on it during the winter (*see* Parks and Gardens, *above*).

Bicycle along Montréal's waterfront to the Lachine Canal, atop its mountain, or through the Vieux-Port (*see* Participant Sports, *below*).

**Le Centre Canadien d'Architecture** is free on Thursday evening (*see* Tour 2, *above*).

## What to See and Do with Children

**Biodôme de Montréal** at Olympic Park (*see* Parks and Gardens, *above*).

At the Old Fort on Ile Ste-Hélène, now the site of the **David M. Stewart Museum,** mock battles, military drills, military-history exhibitions, and bagpipe concerts take place all summer long (*see* Parks and Gardens, *above*).

**Dow Planetarium.** The heavens are reproduced with the aid of a giant Zeiss projector on the inside of the planetarium's vaulted dome. *1000 rue St-Jacques, tel. 514/872–4530. Admission: $4 adults, $2.50 children and senior citizens; prices may vary. Open Tues.–Sun. 12:30–8:30.*

**Images du Futur** has futuristic art and science exhibits, and interactive displays highlighting new technologies—laser images, holograms, computer graphics, videos and electronic music. *Vieux-Port at boul. St-Laurent and rue de la Commune, tel. 514/849–1612. Open mid-May–mid-Sept., daily 10 AM–11 PM.*

**IMAX Super Cinema** shows films on a seven-story-tall screen. Next to Images du Futur is **Expotec,** a hands-on scientific exhibition. *Vieux-Port, Shed No. 7, tel. 514/496–IMAX for information, 514/*

*790–1245 for tickets. Admission: $11.50 adults, $9.50 students and senior citizens, $7 children; prices may vary. Open daily 10–10.*

**The Botanical Garden's Insectarium** (*see* Parks and Gardens, *above*).

**La Ronde's Amusement Park** (*see* Parks and Gardens, *above*).

**Olympic Tower.** Zoom up the "tallest-inclined-tower-in-the-world" on the funicular for a 50-mile panorama of Montréal and its environs (*see* Parks and Gardens, *above*).

Indoor skating year-round at the **Le 1000 rue de la Gauchetière** (*see* Tour 2, *above*).

## Off the Beaten Track

Just two blocks west of Victoria and the Métro Côte-Ste-Catherine station is the Saidye Bronfman Centre. This multidisciplinary institution has long been recognized as a focus of cultural activity for the Jewish community in particular and for Montréal as a whole. The center was a gift from the children of Saidye Bronfman in honor of their mother's lifelong commitment to the arts. In fact, the Mies van der Rohe-inspired building was originally designed by Mrs. Bronfman's daughter, Montréal architect Phyllis Lambert. Accessible by car, just one block east of the Décarie Expressway and about four blocks north of chemin Queen Mary, the center is well worth the trip.

Many of its activities, such as gallery exhibits, lectures on public and Jewish affairs, performances, and concerts, are free to the public. The center, open year-round, is home to the Yiddish Theatre Group, one of the few Yiddish companies performing today in North America. The theater also stages English works, often by local playwrights. Many an artist has passed through the doors of the center's School of Fine Arts. *5170 Côte Ste-Catherine, tel. 514/739–2301; box office 514/739–7944. Admission to gallery free; theater ticket prices vary. Open Mon.–Thurs. 9–9, Fri. 9–3, Sun. 10–5. Closed Jewish holidays.*

Accessible by Métro and bus is **Maison Saint-Gabriel,** which dates back to 1668, when it served as a boarding school for Les Filles du Roy—the young women, many of them orphans, who were brought over to New France to marry the predominantly male settlers. Here Montréal's first teacher (and Canada's first female saint), Marguerite Bourgeoys, patiently trained the "King's wards" to take on their duties as wives and mothers. The house was renovated in 1960. A typical "habitant" farmhouse, it displays furnishings and household objects from the 17th, 18th, and 19th centuries, as well as a kitchen much like the one Les Filles would have learned to bake in before setting off for their new homes. You can see the exhibits by guided tour only mid-April to mid-December. It is advisable to call beforehand. *2146 Place Dublin (Square-Victoria Métro, then transfer to Bus 61), tel. 514/935–8136. Admission: $3 adults, $2 students 8–16 and senior citizens. Tours Tues.–Sat., 1:30 and 3; Sun. 1:30, 2:30, and 3:30.*

# Shopping

*By Patricia Lowe*

Montréalers *magasinent* (go shopping) with a vengeance, so it's no surprise that the city has 160 multifaceted retail areas encompassing some 7,000 stores.

Visitors usually reserve at least one day to hunt for either exclusive fashions along rue Sherbrooke or bargains at the Vieux-Montréal flea market. But there are specific items that the wise shopper seeks out in Montréal.

Montréal is one of the fur capitals of the world. Close to 85% of Canada's fur manufacturers are based in the city, as are many of their retail outlets: **Alexandor** (2025 rue de la Montagne), **Shuchat** (402 boul. de Maisonneuve O), **Grosvenor** (400 boul. de Maisonneuve O), **McComber** (440 boul. de Maisonneuve O), and **Birger Christensen at Holt Renfrew** (1300 rue Sherbrooke O) are a few of the better showrooms.

Fine English bone china, crystal, and woolens are more readily available and cheaper in metropolitan stores than in their U.S. equivalents, thanks to Canada's tariff status as a Commonwealth country. There are three **Jaeger** boutiques (Holt Renfrew, Centre Rockland in the town of Mount Royal, and Centre Fairview in the West Island) selling classical woolen sweaters, along with $700 pure-wool suits. Collectors of china and crystal will find reasonable prices at **Caplan Duval** (Côte-St-Luc's Cavendish Mall and Montréal's Plaza Côte-des-Neiges), which offers an overwhelming variety of patterns.

Today, only dedicated connoisseurs can uncover real treasures in traditional pine Canadiana, but scouting around for Québec *antiquités* and art can be fun and rewarding, especially along increasingly gentrified rue Notre-Dame Ouest.

The Montréal area has six major retail districts: the city center (or downtown), Vieux-Montréal, rue Notre-Dame Ouest, the Plâteau Mont-Royal–St-Denis area, the upper St-Laurent–Laurier Ouest areas of Outremont, and the city of Westmount.

Just about all stores, with the exception of some bargain outlets and a few selective art and antiques galleries, accept major credit cards. Buy your Canadian money at a bank or exchange bureau beforehand to take advantage of the latest rates on the dollar. Most purchases are subject to a federal goods and services tax of 7% as well as a provincial tax of 8%.

If you think you might be buying fur, it is wise to check with your country's customs officials before leaving to find out which animals are considered endangered and cannot be imported. Do the same if you think you might be buying Eskimo carvings, many of which are made of whalebone and ivory and cannot be brought into the United States.

(For general opening times, *see* Opening and Closing Times in Essential Information, *above*.)

## City Center

Central downtown is Montréal's largest retail district. It takes in rue Sherbrooke, boulevard de Maisonneuve, rue Ste-Catherine, and the side streets between them. Because of the proximity and variety of shops, it's the best shopping bet for visitors in town overnight or over a weekend.

**Faubourg Ste-Catherine** Several complexes have added glamour to the city-center shopping scene. A good place to start is the **Faubourg Ste-Catherine,** Montréal's answer to Boston's Quincy Market. At the corner of rues Ste-Catherine Ouest and Guy, it is a vast bazaar housed in a former parking and auto-body garage abutting the Grey Nuns' convent grounds. Three levels of clothing and crafts boutiques, as well as food counters selling fruits and vegetables, pastry, baked goods, and meats, surround the central atrium of tiered fountains and islands of café tables and chairs where food-fair kiosks sell such snacks as egg rolls, pizza, souvlaki, and sushi. This is the place to pick up Québec maple syrup and maple candy, at the pine-decorated boutique at street level, or a fine French wine, about $30, at the government-run **Société d'Alcools du Québec.** Prices at most stores are generally reasonable here, especially if you're sampling the varied ethnic cuisine at any of the snack counters.

**Les Cours Mont-Royal** Continuing east on rue Ste-Catherine, the *très élégant* **Les Cours Mont-Royal** dominates the east side of rue Peel between this main shopping thoroughfare and boulevard de Maisonneuve. This mall caters to expensive tastes, but even bargain hunters find it an intriguing spot for window shopping.

**Place Montréal Trust** Just two blocks away, **Place Montréal Trust** at McGill College is the lively entrance to an imposing glass office tower. Shoppers, fooled by the aqua and pastel decor, may think they have stumbled into a California mall. Prices at the 110 outlets range from hundreds (for designs by **Alfred Sung,** haute couture at **Gigi** or **Rodier,** or men's high fashion at **Bally**) to mere dollars (for sensible cotton T-shirts, or beef-and-kidney pies or minced tarts at the British dry goods and food store **Marks & Spencer**). These imported goodies share the floor space with moderately ticketed ladies' suits, menswear, lingerie, and children's clothing.

Les Cours Mont-Royal and Place Montréal Trust compete with the **Centre Eaton** and **Les Promenades de la Cathédrale.** All four of these centers are linked to the Underground City retail network. Always a favorite with visitors, the nearly 29-kilometer (17.4-mile) "city below" draws large crowds to its shop-lined corridors honeycombing between Les Promenades de la Cathédrale, Place Ville-Marie, Place Bonaventure, and Complexe Desjardins.

**Les Promenades de la Cathédrale** Nestled between Eaton and La Baie department stores, this underground retail complex is popular with Montréalers. Its unusual location makes it a sightseeing adventure as well: It's connected to the McGill Métro and located directly beneath the stately and historic Christ Church Cathedral. A highlight (some say a travesty) of the retail mall's design is the replication of architectural details found in the cathedral above. Among its 150 boutiques and chain stores, Les Promenades boasts Canada's largest Linen Chest outlet, with hundreds of bedspreads and duvets draped over revolving racks plus aisles of china, crystal, linen, and silver.

**Place Ville-Marie** Weatherproof shopping began in 1962 beneath the 42-story cruciform towers of Place Ville-Marie on boulevard René-Lévesque (formerly Dorchester Boulevard) at rue University. (Take the corridor from Centre Eaton, south, to Place Ville-Marie.) A recent renovation has opened Place Ville-Marie up to the light, creating a more cheerful ambience as well as adding stores.

Stylish women head to Place Ville-Marie's 100-plus retail outlets for the clothes: haute couture at **Tristan, Iseut, JC Creations, Cactus,** and **Danier.** Traditionalists will love **Aquascutum.** More affordable clothes shops include **Dalmy's, Marie Claire, Reitman's,** and, for shoes, **Mayfair, Brown's, François Villon,** and **French.**

**Place Bonaventure** From here it's an easy underground trip through Gare Centrale (the train station) to Place Bonaventure's mall beneath one of Canada's largest commercial buildings. It houses some 120 stores, ranging from the trendy (**Au Coton** and **Bikini Village**) to the exclusive (**Armand Boudrias** boutique). There are also a number of fun shops: **Aldo** for trendy leather wear; and **Ici-Bas** for outrageous hose.

**Complexe**
**Desjardins**
Still in the downtown area but a bit farther east on boulevard René-Lévesque is Complexe Desjardins. It's a fast ride via the Métro at Bonaventure station; just get off at Place des Arts and follow the tunnels to Desjardins' multitiered atrium mall. Filled with splashing fountains and exotic plants, Desjardins exudes a Mediterranean joie de vivre, even when it's below freezing outside. Roughly 80 stores include budget outlets like Le Château for fashion as well as the exclusive Redeor, where wool and jersey-knit ensembles start at about $150.

**Department**
**Stores**
**Eaton** is the city's leading department store and part of Canada's largest chain. Founded in Toronto by Timothy Eaton, the first Montréal outlet appeared in 1925. It now sells everything—from the art decorating the top-floor restaurant entrance to zucchini loaves in the basement bakery. The main restaurant is an unusual art deco replica of the dining room aboard the old *Ile-de-France* ocean liner, once Lady Eaton's favorite cruise ship.

The nearby sandstone building housing **La Baie** opened in 1891, although the original Henry Morgan Company that founded it moved to Montréal in 1843. Morgan's was purchased in 1960 by the Hudson Bay Company, which was founded in 1670 by famous Montréal voyageurs and trappers Radisson and Grosseilliers. La Baie is known for its Hudson Bay red-, green-, and white-stripe blankets and duffel coats. It also sells the typical department store fare.

Exclusive **Holt Renfrew,** at 1300 rue Sherbrooke Ouest, is known for its furs. The city's oldest store, it was established in 1837 as Henderson, Holt and Renfrew Furriers and made its name supplying coats to four generations of British royalty. When Queen Elizabeth II married Prince Phillip in 1947, Holt's created a priceless Labrador mink as a wedding gift. Holt's carries the exclusive and pricey line of furs by Denmark's Birger Christensen, as well as the haute-couture and prêt-à-porter collections of Yves St-Laurent.

Around the corner and two blocks down rue de la Montagne, at **Ogilvy** (1307 rue Ste-Catherine O), a kilted piper regales shoppers every day at noon. An institution with Montréalers since 1865, the once-homey department store has undergone a miraculous face-lift. Fortunately, it has preserved its delicate pink glass chandeliers and still stocks traditional apparel—Aquascutum, Jaeger, tweeds for men, and smocked dresses for little girls.

This area—bounded by rues Sherbrooke and Ste-Catherine, and rues de la Montagne and Crescent—also boasts antiques and art galleries as well as designer salons. Rue Sherbrooke is lined with an array of art and antiques galleries as well as tony clothing stores. Rue Crescent is a tempting blend of antiques, fashions, and jewelry boutiques displayed beneath colorful awnings.

## Vieux-Montréal

The second major shopping district, historic Vieux-Montréal, can be a tourist trap, but a shopping spree there can be a lot less expensive and more relaxing than shopping downtown. Both rues Notre-Dame and St-Jacques, from rue McGill to Place Jacques-Cartier, are lined with low to moderately priced fashion boutiques, garish souvenir shops slung with thousands of Montréal T-shirts, and shoe stores.

Along the edge of Vieux-Montréal is Montréal's rejuvenated waterfront, the Vieux-Port, which hosts a sprawling flea market, the **Marché aux Puces,** on Quai King Edward (King Edward Pier). Dealers and pickers search for secondhand steals and antique treasures as they prowl through the huge hangar that is open Wednesday through Sunday from spring through early fall.

## Notre-Dame Ouest

The place for antiquing is the city's third shopping sector, beginning at rue Guy and continuing west to avenue Atwater (a five-minute walk south from the Lionel-Groulx Métro station). Once a shabby strip of run-down secondhand stores, this area has blossomed beyond its former nickname of Attic Row. It now has the highest concentration of antiques, collectibles, and curiosity shops in Montréal. Collectors can find Canadian pine furniture—armoires, cabinets, spinning wheels, rocking chairs—for reasonable prices here. Consider a Sunday tour, beginning with brunch at **Salon de Thé Ambiance,** a charming restaurant that also sells antiques (No. 1874).

## Plateau Mont-Royal and St-Denis

Popular with students, academics, and journalists, this easterly neighborhood embraces boulevard St-Laurent, the longtime student ghetto surrounding the Prince Arthur mall, St-Denis and its Latin Quarter near the Université du Québec à Montréal campus, and the Plateau district. Plateau Mont-Royal and St-Denis attract a trendier, more avant-garde crowd than the determined antiquers along Notre-Dame.

Boulevard St-Laurent—dubbed "the Main" because it divides the island of Montréal into east and west—has always been a lively commercial artery. It was first developed by Jewish merchants who set up shop here in the early 1900s. Cutting a broad swath across the island's center, this long boulevard has an international flavor, with its mélange of stores run by Chinese, Greek, Latin American, Portuguese, Slav, and Vietnamese immigrants. Lower boulevard St-Laurent is lined with discount clothing and bric-a-brac stores, secondhand shops, electronics outlets, and groceries selling kosher meats, Hungarian pastries, Peking duck, and natural foods.

While boulevard St-Laurent's personality is multi-ethnic, rue St-Denis's is distinctly French. (Both are lengthy arteries, so make use of Bus 55 for boulevard St-Laurent, Buses 31 and 30 along rue St-Denis.) More academic in makeup, the boulevard has awnings that shelter bookstores (mostly French), art galleries, antiques stores, and a range of boutiques.

## Upper St-Laurent and Laurier Ouest

Upper boulevard St-Laurent (for our purposes, roughly from avenue du Mont-Royal north to rue St-Viateur), intersecting with avenue Laurier Ouest and climbing the mountain to rue Bernard, has blossomed into one of Montréal's chicest *quartiers* in recent years. It's not entirely surprising, given that much of this area lies within or adjacent to Outremont, traditionally the enclave for wealthy Francophone Montréalers, with restaurants, boutiques, nightclubs, and bistros catering to the upscale visitor. In addition, the influx of a new generation of multi-ethnic professionals, artists, and entrepreneurs is making its mark on the area. It now rivals St-

Denis, downtown, and Laurier Ouest as a cultural hot spot, and it is reminiscent of New York City's SoHo.

Avenue Laurier Ouest, from boulevard St-Laurent to chemin de la Côte-Ste-Catherine, is roughly an eight-block stretch; you'll criss-cross it many times as you explore its Québec-style shops, which carry everything from crafts and clothing to books and paintings.

### Square Westmount and Avenue Greene

Visitors with time to shop or friends in the elegant residential neighborhood of Westmount, a separate municipality in the middle of the island of Montréal, should explore Square Westmount and adjacent avenue Greene. Next door to downtown, these malls are on the Angrignon Métro line, easily accessible via the Atwater station, which has an exit at Square Westmount. Just follow the tunnel to this mall's 90 or so exclusive shops.

The square's plaza opens onto avenue Greene's two-block shopping area, which is lined with trees and flowers. Its redbrick row houses and even the renovated old post office are home to a wealth of boutiques and shops.

# Sports and Fitness

The range of sporting activities available in Montréal is testament to Montréalers' love of the outdoors. With world-class skiing in the Laurentians and the Eastern Townships less than an hour away and dozens of skating rinks within the city limits, they revel in winter. When the last snowflake has melted, they store away skis, poles, and skates and dust off their bikes, tennis rackets, and fishing poles. And year-round they watch the pros at hockey matches, baseball games, car races, and tennis tournaments.

### Participant Sports

**Bicycling** The island of Montréal—except for Mont Royal itself—is quite flat, and there are more than 20 cycling paths around the metropolitan area. Among the most popular are those on Ile Ste-Hélène, along the Lachine Canal, and in Angrignon and Vieux-Port parks. You can rent 10-speed bicycles at **Cyclo-Touriste** at the Centre Info-Touriste (1001 Sq. Dorchester, tel. 514/393–1528).

Parks Canada conducts guided cycling tours along the historic **Lachine Canal** (1825) every summer weekend. For more details, call 514/283–6054 or 514/637–7433.

**Golf** For a complete listing of the many golf courses in the Montréal area, call **Tourisme-Québec** at 514/873–2015.

**Hunting and Fishing** Québec's rich waters are filled with fish, but before you begin your chase, you need to purchase a license from the Ministère des Loisirs, de la Chasse et de la Pêche or from an authorized agent. The lakes and rivers around Montréal teem with fish, and a number of guides offer day trips. For complete information, call **Tourisme-Québec** (tel. 514/873–2015).

**Ice Skating** There are at least 195 outdoor and 21 indoor rinks in the city. You'll probably find one in the nearest park. Call parks and recreation (tel. 514/872–6211).

**Jogging** Montréal became a runner's city following the 1976 Olympics. There are paths in most city parks, but for running with a panoramic view, head to the dirt track in **Parc du Mont-Royal** (take rue Peel, then the steps up to the track).

**Rafting**  Montréal is the only city in the world where you can step off a downtown dock and minutes later be crashing through Class V white water in a sturdy aluminum jet boat. The Lachine Rapids, just south of Vieux-Montréal, were responsible for the founding of Montréal. The roiling waves were too treacherous for the first settlers to maneuver, so they founded Ville-Marie, the forerunner of Vieux-Montréal. Modern voyageurs suit up for the 45-minute jet-boat trip in multiple layers of wool and rain gear, but it's nearly impossible to stay dry— or to have a bad time. *Lachine Rapids Tours Ltd., 105 rue de la Commune, Vieux-Montréal, tel. 514/284-9607. 5 trips daily, departing from Quai Victoria May–Sept., 10, noon, 2, 4, and 6. Trips are narrated in French and English and reservations are necessary. Rates: $45 adults, $40 senior citizens, $35 children 13–18, $25 children 6– 12. Special group and family rates are available.*

**Skiing**  For the big slopes you'll have to go northwest to the Laurentians or
*Downhill*  south to the Eastern Townships, an hour or two away by car. There is a small slope in Parc du Mont-Royal. Pick up the Ski-Québec brochure at one of the Tourisme-Québec offices.

*Cross-country*  Trails crisscross most of the city's parks, including Notre-Dame and Ile Ste-Hélène, Angrignon, Maisonneuve, and Mont-Royal.

**Squash**  You can reserve court time for this fast-paced racquet sport at **Nautilus Centre St-Laurent Côte-de-Liesse Racquet Club** (8305 chemin Côte-de-Liesse, tel. 514/739-3654).

**Swimming**  There is a large indoor pool at the **Olympic Park** (Métro Viau, tel. 514/252-4622) and another at the **Centre Sportif et des Loisirs Claude-Robillard** (1000 av. Emile Journault, tel. 514/872-6900). The outdoor pool on Ile Ste-Hélène is an extremely popular (and crowded) summer gathering place, open June–Labor Day. The new city-run beach at Ile Notre-Dame is the only natural swimming hole in Montréal (tel. 514/872-6211).

**Tennis**  There are public courts in the Jeanne-Mance, Kent, LaFontaine, and Somerled parks. For details, call Montréal Sports and Recreation (tel. 514/872-6211).

**Windsurfing**  Sailboards and small sailboats can be rented at **L'École de Voile de
**and Sailing**  Lachine** (2105 boul. St-Joseph, Lachine, tel. 514/634-4326) and the **Société de l'Ile Notre-Dame** (Ile Notre-Dame, tel. 514/872-6093).

## Spectator Sports

**Baseball**  The National League **Montréal Expos** play at the Olympic Stadium from April through September. For information and reservations, call 514/253-3434 or 800/463-9767.

**Cycling**  **Le Tour de l'Ile de Montréal** has made the *Guinness Book of World Records* for attracting the greatest number of participants. More than 30,000 amateur cyclists participate in "North America's most important amateur cycling event" each June, wending their way 70 kilometers (38 miles) through the streets and parks of Montréal (514/847-8687).

**Grand Prix**  The annual **Molson Grand Prix du Canada,** which draws top Formula 1 racers from around the world, takes place every June at the Gilles Villeneuve Race Track on Ile Notre-Dame (tel. 514/392-0000 for tickets, tel. 514/392-4731 for information).

**Hockey** The **Montréal Canadiens,** winners of 23 Stanley Cups, meet National Hockey League rivals at the Forum (2313 rue Ste-Catherine O, tel. 514/932–2582) from October to April.

# Dining

The promise of a good meal is easily satisfied in Montréal. Les Montréalais don't "eat out"; they "dine." And they are passionate about dining. The city has more than 4,500 restaurants of every price representing more than 75 ethnic groups. It has such culinary institutions as Les Mignardises, Le Paris, and the Beaver Club, which emphasize classic cuisine and tradition. Delicatessens such as Briskets, Schwartz's, and Wilensky's are mainstays for budget dining. In between there are ethnic eateries featuring the foods of China, Greece, India, Morocco, and Italy. Then there are the ubiquitous inexpensive fast-food outlets and coffee shops. But above all, Montréal is distinguished by the European ambience of its restaurants. Catch a glimpse of the eateries' terraces from midday to 2 PM for a look at the hours that Montréal diners take most seriously. Each of the city's well-known bistros is more Parisian than the last. The challenge of dining in Montréal is choosing from among the thousands of restaurants and the varieties of inexpensive fast-food outlets and coffee shops.

Many expensive French and Continental restaurants offer two options, which can be a blessing or a burden to your wallet. Either choice guarantees you a great meal. Instead of ordering à la carte—you select each dish—you can opt for the table d'hôte or the *menu de dégustation.* The table d'hôte is a complete two- to four-course meal chosen by the chef. It is less expensive than a complete meal ordered à la carte and often offers interesting special dishes. It also may take less time to prepare. If you want to splurge with your time and money, indulge yourself with the *menu de dégustation,* a five- to seven-course dinner executed by the chef. It usually includes, in this order, salad, soup, a fish dish, sherbet, a meat dish, dessert, and coffee or tea. At the city's finest restaurants, this menu for two and a good bottle of wine can cost $170 and last three or four hours. But it's worth every cent and every second.

Montréal restaurants are refreshingly relaxed. Although many of the hotel restaurants require a jacket and tie, neatness (no torn T-shirts and scruffy jeans) is appreciated in most other restaurants. Lunch hour is generally from noon to 2:30 and dinner from 6 to 11 or midnight. (Montréalers like to dine late, particularly on summer weekends.) Some restaurants are closed on Sunday or Monday. Because there is no consistent annual closing among Montréal eateries—some will take time off in August, while others will close around Christmas and January—call ahead to avoid disappointment.

Highly recommended restaurants in each price category are indicated by a star ★.

| Category | Cost* |
|----------|-------|
| $$$$ | over $30 |
| $$$ | $20–$30 |

| $$ | $10–$20 |
| --- | --- |
| $ | $5–$10 |

*\*per person without tax (combined GST of 7% and provincial tax of 4% on all meals), service, or drinks*

## Chinese

**$$–$$$**  **Zen.** At press time this mod establishment in the basement of Le Westin Mont-Royal (*see* Lodging, *below*) was offering a $19 fixed-price menu that should not be missed. Called the Zen Experience, the meal is a kind of all-you-can-eat extravaganza, except that instead of helping yourself to a buffet of precooked dishes, you are presented with a menu of 41 items and asked to select one at a time until you can't possibly eat any more. The food is delicate Chinese with some Thai, Malaysian, and Indonesian dishes mixed in for variety. Try the fillet of chicken with crispy spinach, eggplant croquettes with sweet-and-sour sauce, and Mother Ma's shredded zucchini with spicy garlic sauce. This is very fine Chinese cuisine, and you'll pay for it. Check to make sure the Zen Experience is still being offered. *Le Westin Mont-Royal, 1050 Sherbrooke St. W, tel. 514/499–0801. Reservations advised. Dress: casual but neat. AE, DC, MC, V.*

**$$**  **Cathay Restaurant.** Hong Kong investors, fearful of their city's future, are pouring money into Montréal's Chinatown, among other Chinatowns in North America. They're opening slick, Hong Kong–style restaurants and competing with the older Chinese eateries. The consumer wins in these restaurant wars. The 15-year-old Cathay was remodeled and expanded in 1985, and is now the most popular and largest dim sum restaurant in the city. The two floors are both huge rooms with institutional dropped ceilings and the usual red and gold Chinese stage decorations. From 11 AM to 2:30 PM, waitresses emerge from the kitchen pushing carts laden with steaming beef dumplings in bamboo steamers, spicy cuttlefish, shrimp rice noodles, bean-curd rolls, and on and on. *73 rue de la Gauchetière O, Chinatown, tel. 514/866–3131. Reservations accepted. Dress: casual. AE, MC, V.*

## Continental

**$$$**  **Nuances.** One of the best and classiest new restaurants is in, of all
★  places, the Casino de Montréal. Gaming halls aren't normally known for their elegance and good taste, but this establishment is not only ritzy, its menu is sophisticated. The setting, too, is stunning: Diners sit amidst burnished rosewood paneling and dusky pink upholstery and drapes, eating off pretty Bosch and Villeroy porcelain plates displayed on a sea of starched white linen. The clientele is as elegant as the decor. The casino has a strict dress code; high rollers turn up in gowns and tuxedos. Less flamboyant types can get away with a jacket and tie. Starters include a sautée of fresh foie gras served on a bed of braised cabbage, a heavenly mussel soup flavored with pesto, and venison paté encased in filo pastry. The main dishes include coriander flavored rabbit stuffed with scampi, medaillions of salmon topped with a scallop mousse, and smoked duck with cardamom sauce. More conservative diners can opt for tenderloin of beef, veal chops, or roast rack of lamb. *1 av. de Casino, tel. 514/392–2708. Reservations required. Jacket and tie required. AE, DC, MC, V. Closed weekend lunch.*

# Montréal Dining

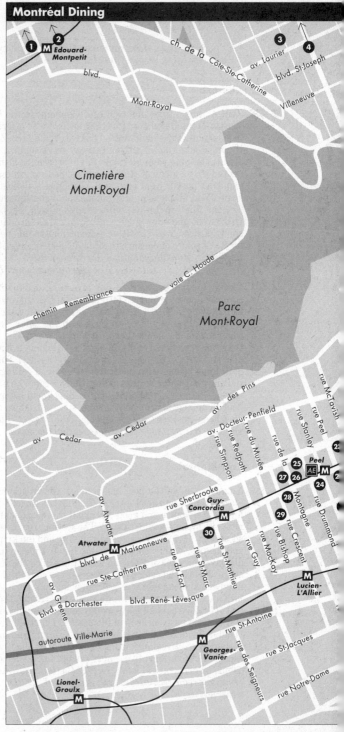

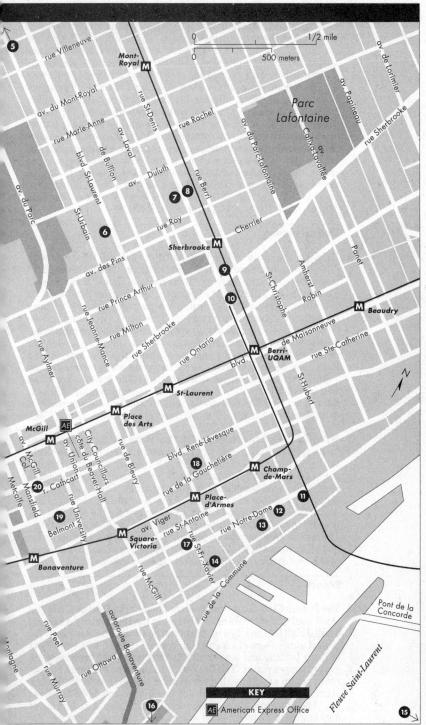

rue Villeneuve

Mont-
Royal M

av. du Mont-Royal

rue Marie-Anne

rue St-Denis

de Bullion

av. du Parc

St-Urbain

blvd St-Laurent

av. Laval

av. Duluth

rue Rachel

rue Berri

Parc
Lafontaine

av. du Parc-Lafontaine

av. Calixa-Lavallée

av. Papineau

av. de Lorimier

rue Sherbrooke

**7** **8**

**6**

rue Roy

Cherrier

Sherbrooke M

av. des Pins

rue Prince Arthur

rue Jeanne-Mance

rue Milton

rue Sherbrooke

rue Aylmer

**9**

**10**

rue Ontario

St-Christophe

Amherst

Robin

Panet

Beaudry M

de Maisonneuve

rue Ste-Catherine

Berri-
UQAM M

blvd.

St-Hubert

St-Laurent M

Place
des Arts M

McGill M

AE

av. Union

côte du Beaver-Hall

City Councillors

rue de Bleury

blvd. René-Lévesque

**18**

rue de la Gauchetière

Champ-
de-Mars M

**11**

McGill Col.

r. Cathcart

av. McGill

rue University

rue Mansfield

Metcalfe

**20**

**19**

Belmont

av. Viger

Square-
Victoria M

Place-
d'Armes M

rue St-Antoine

rue Notre-Dame

**17**

**12**

**13**

rue St-Xavier

**14**

Bonaventure M

rue McGill

autoroute Bonaventure

rue de la Commune

Pont de la
Concorde

rue Peel

rue Ottawa

Montagne

rue Murray

**16**

**KEY**

AE American Express Office

Fleuve Saint-Laurent

**15**

1/2 mile

500 meters

**5**

**$ La Charade.** A short walk east from City Hall on rue Notre-Dame Est, this storefront restaurant is a gathering place for civil servants and some of the more budget-minded city councillors. The restaurant is cozy, and the food, although not gourmet fare, is plentiful and varied, served by a pleasant staff. The menu features Italian and French dishes, with a sprinkling of such other choices as paella with a tangy tomato sauce, and chicken or shrimp brochettes. The accent is definitely on pasta, offering five or six different linguine selections, and there are a hearty veal Parmesan, one of the tastier dishes, and *coq au vin*, a hefty portion of chicken stewed in a thick wine sauce with onions and mushrooms. Lighter eaters may sample seafood stews of *moules* (mussels) and shrimp or a Caesar salad. The table d'hôte offers a choice of meals with soup, a main course, and coffee, many of which come to less than $15 (excluding taxes). Of course, ordering up a carafe of house wine or a bottle of imported beer adds to the bill. *358 rue Notre-Dame E (Champ-de-Mars Métro), tel. 514/861–8756. Dress: casual. MC, V.*

## Delicatessens

**$ Bens.** On the menu of this large, efficient deli, all the items with "Bens" in the name are red or are covered in red: "Bens Cheesecake" is smothered in strawberries; "Bens Ice Cold Drink" is the color of electric cherry juice; and the specialty, the "Big Ben Sandwich," is two slices of rye bread enclosing a seductive, pink pile of juicy smoked meat (Montréal's version of corned beef). According to Bens lore, the founder, Ben Kravitz, brought the first smoked-meat sandwich to Montréal in 1908. The rest, as they say, is history. A number of the walls are devoted to photos of celebrities who have visited Bens. The decor is strictly '50s, with yellow and green walls and vaguely art deco, institutional furniture. The waiters are often wisecracking characters but are nonetheless incredibly efficient. Beer, wine, and cocktails are served. *990 boul. de Maisonneuve O, downtown, tel. 514/844–1000. No reservations. Dress: casual. MC, V.*

**$ Wilensky's Light Lunch.** Since 1932 the Wilensky family has served up its special: Italian-American salami on a kaiser roll, generously slathered with mustard. Served hot, it's a meal in itself. You can also get hot dogs or a grilled sandwich, which comes with a marinated pickle and an old-fashioned sparkling beverage. The regulars at the counter are among the most colorful in Montréal. A visit here is a must. This neighborhood haunt was a setting for the film *The Apprenticeship of Duddy Kravitz*, from the novel by Mordecai Richler. The service does not prompt one to linger, but the prices make up for it. *34 Fairmount O, tel. 514/271–0247. No reservations. Dress: casual. No credit cards. No liquor license. Closed weekends.*

## French

**$$$$ The Beaver Club.** Early fur traders started the Beaver Club in a shack during Montréal's colonial days. In the 19th century it became a social club for the city's business and political elite. It still has the august atmosphere of a men's club devoted to those who trap: Pelts of bear, buffalo, and beaver still line the walls with members' engraved copper plates. The Beaver Club is a gourmet French restaurant open to anyone with a reservation who arrives in the proper attire. Master chef John Cordeaux has a large and devoted following. The luncheon table d'hôte includes such dishes as terrine of duckling with pistachios and onion, and cranberry compote. For more mundane tastes, the restaurant also specializes in such meaty dishes as roast prime rib of beef au jus. The Beaver Club always offers one or two low-fat, low-salt, low-calorie plates. The waiters are veteran (Charles, the maître d', has worked here for more than 20 years), and the service is as excellent as the food. *La Reine Elizabeth, 900 boul. René-Lévesque O, downtown, tel. 514/861–3511. Reservations required. Jacket and tie required. AE, D, DC, MC, V.*

$$$$ **Le Lutetia.** This magnificent restaurant is worth a little detour, if only for the piano bar happy hour. The plethora of styles—rococo, renaissance, empire, fin de siècle, and baroque—is a spectacle in itself. This outrageously romantic restaurant is the perfect choice for a tête-à-tête by candlelight. The French cuisine, sometimes nouvelle, sometimes classic, is always served under a silver cover. Behind their glass partition, the cooks busy themselves and give the clientele an appetizing show, even at the busiest moments. The *menu gastronomique* changes each week according to the market and the seasons. The menu changes frequently as well, with such creative dishes as shrimp with fennel in puff pastry, ballotine of pheasant in a brioche dough, noisettes of veal *périgourdine* (with truffles), or medaillions of beef with coarse mustard, all preceding the cheese or the dessert cart. There is a very good wine list and champagne. *1430 rue de la Montagne, tel. 514/288–5656. Reservations advised. Dress: casual but neat. Terrace on the roof in summer. AE, D, DC, MC, V.*

$$$$ **Les Halles.** Definitely French, this restaurant took its name from
★ the celebrated Parisian market. Its old-France character is enhanced by mirrors and typical bistro inscriptions, and fussy waiters, with their white aprons and towels on their arms, seem to come straight out of a '40s French film. The wine cellar is exceptional and contains about 250 different bottles, with prices ranging from $20 to $540 a bottle. The menu shows a lot of imagination without ignoring the classics: Grapefruit Marie-Louise with scallops and lobster, poêlée d'escargots, or duck with pears sit comfortably beside the chef's ventures into nouvelle cuisine, such as his lobster with ginger and coconut. The desserts are classic, delicious, and remarkably fresh. The Paris-Brest, a puff pastry with praline cream inside, is one of the best in town. *1450 rue Crescent, tel. 514/844–2328. Reservations advised. Dress: casual but neat. AE, DC, MC, V. Closed Sun. lunch, Mon. lunch, and some holidays.*

$$$$ **Les Mignardises.** Chef Jean-Pierre Monnet used to run the kitchen
★ at Les Halles. Now that he has his own place, his talents are given free range. Les Mignardises is considered the finest and certainly the most expensive restaurant in town. You enter via the bar and climb up one flight to the simple, elegant dining room decorated with copper pans hanging from the exposed-brick walls. The dining area holds only about 20 tables, so reservations are a must. If your wallet is full, you can choose the six-course *menu de dégustation* ($68.50). But if you're on a budget, it's still possible to enjoy a full meal. The three-course table d'hôte lunch menu allows you to sample such delicious dishes as fish salad on gazpacho or marinated duck breast with vinegar sauce. In the evening, the chef's creations include *panaché de poisson* (salmon and lotte served with a tangy lime sauce) and *noisette de faux filet* (tender beef medaillions in sherry wine). The presentation always takes a back seat to the taste. As you would expect, the wine list is large and pricey. The waiters and waitresses are prompt, knowledgeable, and friendly. *2035–37 rue St-Denis, near Berri and Sherbrooke métros, tel. 514/842–1151. Reservations required. Dress: casual, but no jeans or T-shirts. AE, DC, MC, V.*

**$$$ Auberge le Vieux St-Gabriel.** Established in a big stone house in 1754, this restaurant claims to be part of the oldest inn in North America. The interior is lined with rough stone walls, and enormous old beams hold up the ceilings. The fare is hearty yet unadventurous French, with a bit of local Québecois flavor: You may want to start off with the maple smoke salmon, followed by sautéed shrimp on a bed of buttered leeks, although the rack of lamb seasoned with fresh thyme is the chef's specialty. For the brave diner, the Unforgettable 1754 is an old-fashioned Québecois experience: a steaming bowl of pea soup à la Canadienne for starters, then tortière (meat pie), baked beans, pigs knuckles, and homemade ketchup. The restaurant seats close to 500 people, but you'd never guess it because there are so many separate dining rooms. *426 rue St-Gabriel, Vieux-Montréal, tel. 514/878-3561. Reservations advised. Dress: casual but neat. AE, DC, MC, V. Closed Sat. lunch.*

**$$$ Le Café de Paris.** This restaurant, a study in atmosphere, seats patrons at large, well-spaced tables in a room ablaze with flowers and with light streaming through the French windows. Renovated in 1991, the Ritz garden, with its picturesque duck pond, is open for summer dining alfresco. Inside or outside the waiters provide perfect, unobtrusive service. The menu opens with a selection of fresh caviar flown in from Petrossian's in New York City. You can choose from such classics as calf sweetbreads with a slightly bitter endive sauce or the flambéed fillet of buffalo with green peppercorns. At meal's end the waiter will trundle over the dessert cart; the crème brûlée with raisins is a favorite. The wine list includes everything from reasonably priced bottles to extremely expensive vintages. The table to the right rear of the dining room as you enter is where the prime minister dines when in town. If the prime minister is not there, you are likely to see other national political and financial figures supping or schmoozing among the tables. *Hôtel Ritz-Carlton, 1228 rue Sherbrooke O, tel. 514/842-4212. Reservations required. Jacket required at lunch and dinner. AE, D, DC, MC, V.*

**$$$ Le Cercle.** Le Cercle has the power look. The choicest seats are on a raised circular platform, encircled by a white Hellenistic colonnade. In these impressive surroundings Québec's political and business leaders dine on first-class nouvelle cuisine. Many must suffer from high blood pressure, because the menu features "alternative cuisine" dishes with reduced salt, cholesterol, and calories. The grilled lamb chops with mint dressing are not on this list. If you are on a budget, stop in for lunch and have the onion soup with a ham and cheese sandwich on French bread. Power breakfasts start at 6:30 AM. The standard of service here, as in the rest of the hotel, is high. The wine list is expensive and excellent, of course. *Le Westin Mont-Royal, 1050 rue Sherbrooke O, tel. 514/284-1110. Reservations advised. AE, DC, MC, V.*

**$$$ Toqué.** One of the zaniest restaurants on the Montréal scene, this eatery has been a hit from the moment it opened its doors in the spring of '93. Its name means "a bit crazy." Montréalers call it *flyée*, an expression meaning "slightly off the wall." Both descriptions fit the bill. Its appeal lies not just in its market-fresh ingredients whipped into dazzling combinations and colors, but also in its stark, futuristic decor. Toqué looks like a cross between an art gallery and an airport terminal, but the ambience is funky and eccentric. Passersby along the trendy St-Denis are stopped short by the sight of Toqué's chefs preparing food behind a wall of plate glass. The young and innovative chef-owner, thirty-something Normand Laprise, who trained with Jean-Pierre Bulloux of Dijon, France, is considered to be one of the best chefs in the city. Such entrées as venison medaillions, swordfish steaks, smoked salmon, and warm fois gras are flavored with such fresh ingredients as red peppers, raspberry vinaigrette, thinly shredded leeks, celery roots, and Québec goat cheese. The portions don't look big but they are supringly filling. *3842 rue St-Denis, tel. 514/499–2084. Reservations required at least a day ahead. Dress: casual. MC, V. Closed Sun.*

**$$–$$$** **L'Express.** The crowd is elbow to elbow, and the animated atmos-
**★** phere is reminiscent of a Paris train station. L'Express has earned the title "best bistro in town." Popular media figures come here to be seen, a task made easier by the mirrored walls. The atmosphere is smoky, and the noise level at its peak on weekend evenings. The cuisine is always impeccable, the service is fast, and the prices are very good. L'Express has one of the best and most original wine cellars in town. Wine and champagne are available by the glass as well as by the bottle. The steak tartare with french fries, the salmon with sorrel, the calves' liver with tarragon, the first course of chicken livers with pistachios, or even the modest smoked salmon are all marvelous year-round. There are specials of the day to give the many regulars a change of pace. Jars of gherkins and fresh *baguettes*, cheeses aged to perfection, and quality eaux-de-vie make the pleasure last longer. *3927 rue St-Denis, tel. 514/845–5333. Reservations required. Dress: casual but neat. AE, DC, MC, V.*

**$$** **Bonaparte.** This classical French eatery is situated in the heart of Vieux-Montréal, a stone's throw from the Centaur, Montréal's English language theater. Piped Mozart serenades diners surrounded by exposed brick walls hung with pictures of soldiers from Napoléon's era. Chef Nicolas Carrere comes from Paris and prepares French dishes that, while traditional, have a light touch. Starters include fresh oysters (when in season) served on a bed of ice, salmon smoked on the premises, and game pâté with pistachios. The entrées run the gamut from tuna steak marinated in Vermouth, to veal sweetbreads served with wine sauce. *443 rue St-François-Xavier, tel. 514/844–4368. Reservations required (except winter). Dress: casual. AE, MC, V. Closed Sat. morning.*

## Greek

**$$$$** **Milos.** Nets, ropes, floats, and lanterns—the usual cliché symbols of the sea—hang from Milos's walls and ceilings. The real display, however, is in the refrigerated cases and on the beds of ice in the back by the kitchen, fresh fish from all over the world: octopus, squid, and shrimp; crabs, oysters, and sea urchins; lamb chops, steaks, and chicken; and vegetables, cheese, and olives. The seafood is flown in from wholesalers in Nova Scotia, New York, Florida, and Athens. A meal can start out with chewy, tender, hot octopus, or, if you're adventurous, the cool and creamy roe scooped from raw sea urchins. The main dish at Milos is usually fish—pick whatever looks freshest—grilled over charcoal and seasoned with parsley, capers, and lemon juice. It's done to a turn and is achingly delicious. The fish are priced by the pound, and you can order one large fish to serve two or more. The bountiful Greek salad (enough for two) is a perfect side dish or can be a meal itself. For dessert you might try the traditional baklava, or for something lighter, the fresh fruit plate. The waiters are professional but not always knowledgeable about the array of exotic seafood available. Milos is a healthy walk from Métro Laurier. You can also take Bus 51 from the same Métro stop and ask the driver to let you off at avenue du Parc; Milos is halfway up the block to the right. *5357 av. du Parc, tel. 514/272–3522. Reservations required. Dress: casual. AE, MC, V.*

### Indian

**$$–$$$  Le Taj.** One of the rare Indian restaurants in town in which the decor
and the music are appropriate. The cuisine of the north of India is
honored here, less spicy and more refined than that of the south. The
tandoori ovens seal in the flavors of the grilled meat and fish, the
*naan* bread comes piping hot to the table, and behind a glass partition the cook retrieves the skewers from the hot coals with his bare
hands, just like an experienced fakir. There are a few vegetarian
specialties on the menu; for example, the *taj-thali*, consisting of len-
tils, chili *pakoras*, *basmati* rice, and *saag panir*—spicy white
cheese with spinach. The tandoori quail and the nan stuffed with
meat go well together, as does a whole series of dry curries, from
lamb to chicken and beef with aromatic rice. A nine-course buffet is
served daily at lunch for under $10. The desserts, coconut ice cream,
or mangoes (canned) are sometimes decorated with pure silver
leaves. The tea scented with cloves is delicious; it cleans the palate,
warms in winter, and cools in summer. *2077 rue Stanley, tel. 514/
845–9015. Reservations advised weekend. Dress: casual but neat.
AE, MC, V.*

### Italian

**$$$  Bocca d'Oro.** This Italian restaurant next to Métro Guy has a huge
menu offering a wide variety of appetizers, pastas, veal, and vege-
tarian dishes. One pasta specialty is *tritico di pasta*, which is one
helping each of spinach ravioli with salmon and caviar, shellfish ma-
rinara, and spaghetti primavera. A good choice from the dozen or so
veal dishes is scaloppine *zingara* (with tomatoes, mushrooms, pick-
les, and olives). The *tajiolini misteriosi* combines pasta, avocado,
and shrimp in white wine. With the dessert and coffee, the waiters
bring out a big bowl of walnuts for you to crack at your table (nut-
crackers provided). The two floors of dining rooms are decorated
with brass rails, wood paneling, and paintings, and Italian pop songs
play in the background. The staff is extremely friendly and profes-
sional; if you're in a hurry, they'll serve your meal in record time.
*1448 rue St-Mathieu, downtown, tel. 514/933–8414. Reservations
advised. Dress: casual but neat. AE, DC, MC, V. Closed Sun.*

**$$  Pizzaiole.** The wood-fired oven pizzas have had no respite since they
started to appear in Montréal in the beginning of the 1980s.
Pizzaiole, the pioneer in the field, is still by far the best. The two
branches have somewhat adopted the same fresh decor emphasizing
the brick oven, but the clientele and the ambience of the rue Crescent location are a bit younger. In both places, there are about 20
possible combinations, without counting the toppings and extras
that personalize a pizza in no time at all. Whether you choose a simple tomato-cheese or a ratatouille on a whole-wheat crust, all the
pizzas are made to order and brought immediately to the table. The
calzone, a turnover filled with a variety of meats and cheeses, is
worth the trip. Try the thirst-quenching Québec-brewed Boréale
beer on tap, or the local St. Ambroise bottled beer. *Two locations:
1446-A rue Crescent, tel. 514/845–4158; 5100 rue Hutchison, tel.
514/274–9349. Dress: casual. AE, DC, MC, V.*

### Japanese

**$$$–$$$$  Katsura.** This cool, elegant Japanese restaurant introduced sushi to
Montréal and is the haunt of businesspeople who equate raw food
with power. If you're with a group or just want privacy, you can re-

serve a tatami room closed off from the rest of the restaurant by rice-paper screens. The sushi chefs create an assortment of raw seafood delicacies, as well as their own delicious invention, the Canada roll (smoked salmon and salmon caviar) at the sushi bar at the rear. Sushi connoisseurs may find some offerings less than top quality. The service is excellent, but if you sample all the sushi, the tab can be exorbitant. *2170 rue de la Montagne, downtown between Peel and Guy métros, tel. 514/849–1172. Reservations required, but you might get a seat at the sushi bar without them. Dress: casual but neat. AE, DC, MC, V. Closed weekend lunch.*

## Lebanese

**$ Basha.** The neon lights along gaudy rue Ste-Catherine and the ebb and flow of the crowd make this fast-food restaurant an entertaining spot for a quick evening bite. Bistro chairs and bare tables make up the utilitarian decor, and diners pick up plastic trays and choose their kebabs and falafels from the cafeteria-style counter. The menu, with prices as low as $2 and $3, includes beef and lamb shish-kebab sandwiches and platters, chicken brochettes, a daily falafel special, and a "Basha" grill platter. Open until 3 AM on weekends and until midnight during the week, this is one of the city's night-owl meccas; Montréalers stop by after a late movie for sticky, sweet Arab pastries and coffee. *930 rue Ste-Catherine O, level 2 (McGill or Peel Métro), tel. 514/866–4272. There is another downtown location at 2140 rue Guy, tel. 514/932–6682. Dress: casual. No credit cards.*

## Sausages

**$ Chez Better.** The rustic fieldstone walls of historic Maison Sauvegarde create a fitting ambience for this North American branch of a popular European sausage house. Although the decor—exposed stone walls, casement windows, dimmed lighting—is upscale, the limited nature of the menu keeps prices down, to only $3.25 (excluding taxes) in the case of the "Better Special," a satisfying sandwich of one mild sausage on freshly baked bread. It's a convenient refueling stop for visitors touring Vieux-Montréal, only a few steps from Place Jacques-Cartier and the Info-Touriste center on rue Notre-Dame Est. This Notre-Dame restaurant is the most elegant of the five "Betters," although all serve the same wide variety of sausages, imported beers, and rich desserts. Service is politely efficient and the noontime crowd lively; dining is more subdued in the evenings. *160 rue Notre-Dame E (Champ-de-Mars Métro), 5400 chemin Côte-des-Neiges, 1310 boul. de Maisonneuve, 4382 boul. St-Laurent, and 1430 rue Stanley; tel. 514/861–2617. Dress: casual. AE, MC, V.*

## Seafood

**$$$ Chez Delmo.** This stretch of rue Notre-Dame is halfway between the courts and the stock exchange, and at lunchtime Chez Delmo is filled with professionals gobbling oysters and fish. The first room as you enter is lined with two long, dark, wood bars, which are preferred by those wishing a fast lunch. Above one is a mural depicting a medieval feast. In the back is a more sedate and cheerful dining room. In either room the dining is excellent and the seafood fresh. A good first course, or perhaps a light lunch, is the seafood salad, a delicious mix of shrimp, lobster, crab, and artichoke hearts on a bed of Boston lettuce, sprinkled with a scalliony vinaigrette. The poached salmon with hollandaise is a nice slab of perfectly cooked fish with potatoes and broccoli. The lobsters and oysters are priced according to market rates. Chez Delmo was founded at the same address in 1910. The service is efficient and low-key. *211–215 rue Notre-Dame O, Vieux-Montréal, tel. 514/849–4061. Dinner reservations advised. Dress: casual but neat. AE, DC, MC, V. Closed Sun., 2 wks in midsummer, and Christmas week.*

## Steaks

**$$$ Moishe's.** A paradise for carnivores, Moishe's is the last place to receive dietetic advice. The meat portions are as large as a pound, which will no doubt wreak havoc with your cholesterol level. Rib steak, T-bone, and filet mignon are all grilled on wood and presented with dill-scented pickles, cole slaw, and french fries or baked potato. The meat, imported from the western United States, is juicy and tender, marbled and delectable, and aged 21 days in the restaurant's cold chambers. Moishe's grouchy service, its white aluminum-siding exterior and dark interior (reminiscent of an all-male private club), and its bland desserts don't seem to frighten away the real meat eaters. For those with a smaller appetite, the portions can be shared, but it will cost you an additional $4 and the waiter's reproachful look. *3961 boul. St-Laurent, tel. 514/845–3509. Reservations required for parties of 3 or more. Dress: casual. AE, DC, MC, V.*

**$ Le Tramway.** The cheery, fire-engine-red facade of this steak and burger restaurant draws diners off rue Ste-Catherine, especially in winter, when the lanterns inside glow a warm welcome. Once you're aboard, the Tramway is a trip back some 50 years to a time when streetcars, not the Métro, ferried people around downtown Montréal. Interior decorations are refashioned memorabilia: old lamp fixtures, former fare boxes that now hold plants, and overhead racks now used as shelves above the shiny, red banquettes. A reasonably priced menu concentrates on juicy hamburgers, although there is a "jumbo" smoked-meat sandwich with dill pickle and fries and a great thick Polish sausage garnished with sauerkraut and salad, all under $10. There are a few more expensive selections, such as the charbroiled prime-rib steak and filet mignon, so this streetcar is a desirable choice for family diners with varying tastes and appetites. *1122 rue Ste-Catherine O, tel. 514/875–6300. No reservations. Dress: casual. AE, DC, MC, V.*

## Tearooms

**$–$$ La Chartreuse.** This tiny tearoom, in the Viennese tradition, has big surprises in store. Although it's best known for its scrumptious desserts, the tearoom serves quiches, salads, and soups as well. Mouthwatering and filling cakes including *rigo iancsi*, a Hungarian cake smothered in chocolate sauce, and the gâteau autrichien au café, a cake with nuts and whipped cream, are exhibited on the counter. The espresso and cappuccino complement the desserts, and the coffee is served with liqueurs, chocolate, cinnamon, or cream (whipped or not). Mozart is played discreetly in the background. *3439 rue St-Denis, tel. 514/842–0793. No reservations. Dress: casual. No credit cards. Closed Mon.*

## Restaurants near Montréal

**$$$$ La Sucrerie de la Montagne.** On the road to Rigaud in the direction of Ottawa, maple syrup flows from carafes year-round and seasons the plates of pork and beans, *tourtière*, maple-glazed ham, omelet soufflés, and crêpes cooked over wood fires at this old-fashioned sugar hut. Even the bread is baked on the premises in the old brick ovens fired with maple wood. Everything in this young maple grove is intended to re-create the atmosphere of the sugar season: from the sap flowing in the snow (in season) to the workhorses to men collecting the sap bucket by bucket. Pierre Faucher, the owner of this immense sugar cabin, who looks more like a lumberjack than a restaurateur, greets the Sunday passersby as well as the buses overflowing with Japanese tourists in the middle of July. An old-fashioned general store sells Québec handcrafts and maple syrup. During the sugaring season (March–mid-April) a complete meal costs $28 adults, $14 children 8–12, $8 children 3–7; off-season it costs $30 for lunch and $40 for dinner for adults. Ask about reduced rates for children. *300 rang St-Georges, Rigaud (Rte. 40, exit 17), tel. 514/451–5204. Reservations required. Dress: casual. AE, MC, V.*

**$$$$ ★** **Les Trois Tilleuls.** In Saint Marc sur Richelieu, 30 minutes southeast of town, you can lunch or dine on delectable food right on the Râivière Richelieu. This small romantic inn, one of the Relais et Châteaux chain, has a terrace on the river and a large, airy dining room. Chef Roger Robin specializes in cream of onion soup, sweetbreads, and game dishes made with rabbit, quail, and venison. You can stay overnight in one of the two dozen rooms, or splurge for the palatial royal suite. *290 rue Richelieu, Saint Marc sur Richelieu, tel. 514/584–2231, fax 514/584–3146. Reservations required. Dress: casual but neat. AE, DC, MC, V.*

**$$$** **Le Mitoyen.** North of the city, in the small village of Ste-Dorothée (today part of the city of Laval), is this great French restaurant that leans resolutely in favor of nouvelle cuisine. People come mainly from Montréal to taste the inventions of the self-taught chef. The meticulously decorated old house with the red roof is a haven for gourmands. Although it changes along with the seasons, the menu will always include such delicious creations as galette of smoked salmon, sweetbreads ragout with artichoke hearts, guinea hen with sherry wine vinegar, and quail with juniper berries in puff pastry. All are heavenly. For dessert, the maple nougat glacé or the poached pears in red wine and pepper end the meal elegantly. *652 Pl. Publique Ste-Dorothée, Laval (Rte. 13 N), tel. 514/689–2977. Reservations required. Dress: casual but neat. AE, MC, V. Closed Mon. and lunch Tues.–Sat.*

# Lodging

On the island of Montréal alone there are 22,000 rooms available in every type of accommodation, from world-class luxury hotels to youth hostels, from student dormitories to budget executive motels. Keep in mind that during peak season (May–August) it may be difficult to find a bed without reserving, and most, but not all, hotels raise their prices. Rates often drop from mid-November to early April. Throughout the year a number of the better hotels have two-night, three-day, double-occupancy packages that offer substantial discounts.

If you arrive in Montréal without a hotel reservation, the tourism information booths at either airport can provide you with a list of hotels and room availability. You must, however, make the reservation yourself. There are no information booths at the Voyageur bus terminal, but the Gare Centrale is directly behind Le Reine Elizabeth hotel.

The following list is composed of recommended lodgings in Montréal for various budgets. The rates quoted are for a standard double room in May 1993; off-season rates are almost always lower.

Highly recommended hotels in each price category are indicated by a star ★.

| Category | Cost* |
|----------|-------|
| $$$$ | over $160 |
| $$$ | $120–$160 |
| $$ | $85–$120 |
| $ | under $85 |

**All prices are for a standard double room, excluding an optional service charge.*

## Downtown

$$$$ **Bonaventure Hilton International.** This 393-room Hilton—situated atop a Métro station, the Place Bonaventure exhibition center, and a mall crowded with shops and restaurants—rises 17 stories. From the outside the massive building is uninviting, but the kind staff inside warms things up. When you exit the elevator, you find yourself in a spacious reception area flanked by an outdoor swimming pool (heated year-round) and 2½ acres of gardens, complete with ducks. Also on this floor is a complex of three restaurants and a nightclub that features well-known international entertainers. Le Castillon is the flagship restaurant, known for its three-course, 55-minute businessperson's lunch. On Sunday, there's a special theme menu. All rooms have fully stocked minibars and black-and-white TVs in the bathrooms. The furnishings are a bit dowdy, but comfortable. The Bonaventure has excellent access to the Métro station of the same name beneath it and to all the shops at Place Ville-Marie through the Underground City. *1 Pl. Bonaventure, H5A 1E4, tel. 514/878–2332 or 800/445–8667, fax 514/878–1442. 393 rooms. Facilities: 3 restaurants, nightclub, health club with sauna, pool, rooftop garden, gift shop, shopping mall, 24-hr room service. AE, D, DC, MC, V.*

$$$$ **Hôtel du Parc.** Half a block away from the acres of greenery in Parc du Mont-Royal is this perfectly located hotel, which caters mostly to a corporate clientele. Rooms are large, and the decor is modern and well maintained. From the lobby you can descend to a shopping mall with many stores and movie theaters. The nightlife of rue Prince Arthur is six blocks away. *3625 av. du Parc, H2X 3P8, tel. 514/288–6666, in Canada, 800/363–0735; in U.S., 800/448–8355; fax 514/288–2469. 358 rooms, 20 suites. Facilities: restaurant, café-bar, health club, squash courts, 2 pools, tennis court, no-smoking floors, gift shop. AE, D, DC, MC, V.*

$$$$ **Hotel Inter-Continental Montréal.** This first Inter-Continental property in Montréal, built in 1991, brings hotel luxury to Vieux-Montréal. The 24-story hotel is linked to the World Trade Centre, the block-long retail and office development that combines old and new in the former financial heart of the city, close to Vieux-Montréal attractions and the Palais des Congrès convention center. Le Continent, the elegant restaurant located in the main lobby, serves international cuisine, and there are also two bars, including Chez Plume, at ground level. The rooms are done in soft pastel colors, and match the Victorian flavor of the banquet center in the Nordheimer Build-

ing next door. The interior of the hotel makes rich use of granite and wood paneling. Other facilities include minibars and refrigerators in rooms, 12 meeting rooms, twice-daily maid service, complimentary shoe shine, a daily newspaper, and a ballroom once frequented by actress Sarah Bernhardt. *360 rue St-Antoine O, H2Y 3X4, tel. 514/ 987–9900, in U.S., 800/327–0200; in Canada, 800/361–3600; fax 514/874–8550. 335 rooms, 22 suites. Facilities: restaurant, health club with sauna, indoor pool, cable TV, 24-hr room service. AE, DC, MC, V.*

**$$$$** **Hôtel Vogue.** One of Montréal's newest and most elegant hotels, the Vogue opened in late 1990, happily surprising everyone who remembered this building as a drab office tower. Now beautifully transformed, with tall windows and a facade of polished rose granite and deep aqua trim, this hotel is chic, sophisticated, and in the heart of downtown, right across rue de la Montagne from Ogilvy department store. The lobby's focal point, the L'Opéra Bar, boasts an expansive bay window. Room furnishings are decorated in striped silk, and double-, queen-, and king-size beds are draped with satiny duvets. Fax machines and multiline telephones in rooms appeal to business travelers. Bathrooms come with Jacuzzis, televisions, and phones. The Société Café on the lobby level is a favorite among downtowners. *1425 rue de la Montagne, H3G 1Z3, tel. 514/285–5555 or 800/465–6654, fax 514/849–8903. 148 rooms, 6 suites. Facilities: restaurant, bar, exercise room. AE, D, DC, MC, V.*

**$$$$** **Le Centre Sheraton.** In a huge 37-story complex well placed between the downtown business district and the restaurant streets of Crescent and Bishop, this Sheraton offers a wide variety of services to both the business and tourist crowds. It's also a favorite with international entertainment celebrities. There are two restaurants, two bars, an indoor pool, a health club, and indoor parking. The elite, five-story Towers section is geared toward business travelers. The Sheraton caters to conventions, so expect to encounter such groups when you stay here. Though the decor is beige and unremarkable (once inside you could be in any large, modern hotel in any North American metropolis), the location's the thing. *1201 boul. René-Lévesque O, H3B 2L7, tel. 514/878–2000 or 800/325–3535, fax 514/ 878–3958. 824 rooms, 40 suites. Facilities: 2 restaurants, 2 bars, health club with whirlpool and sauna, indoor pool, unisex beauty parlor, gift shop. AE, D, DC, MC, V.*

**$$$$** **Le Meridien.** This Air France property rises 12 stories from the center of the Complexe Desjardins, a boutique-rich mall in the middle of the plushest stretch of the Underground City. The hotel caters to businesspeople and tourists who want ultramodern European style and convenience. Le Meridien is designed on a plan of circles of privilege within these already-exclusive surroundings. For instance, within Le Café Fleuri French restaurant there's a chicer, pricier enclave called Le Club. There are no-smoking floors and an indoor pool, sauna, and whirlpool facility. And if the atmosphere ever seems too confining, you can always burst out the door and go to Chinatown, a five-minute walk away. *4 Complexe Desjardins, C.P. 130, H5B 1E5, tel. 514/285–1450 or 800/543–4300, fax 514/285–1243. 572 rooms, 28 suites. Facilities: 3 restaurants, business center, piano bar, indoor pool, sauna, whirlpool, nearby YMCA and YWCA, baby-sitting services located in complex with shops and boutiques. AE, D, DC, MC, V.*

**$$$$** **Le Westin Mont-Royal.** Service and hospitality make this establish-
★ ment stand out among Montréal's best hotels. The shiny brass entrance opens onto a small lobby with a usually busy concierge desk and a discreet reception counter. The clientele here is primarily corporate, and the large rooms are decorated to serve that market:

Auberge de
Jeunesse
Internationale de
Montréal, **14**
Bonaventure
Hilton
International, **21**
Château
Versailles, **2**
Delta
Montréal, **17**
Holiday Inn
Crowne
Plaza, **18**
Hotel Inter-
Continental
Montréal, **26**
Hôtel de la
Montagne, **4**
Hôtel
du Parc, **15**
Hôtel Radisson
des Gouverneurs
de Montréal, **22**
Hôtel Vogue, **5**
Howard Johnson
Hôtel Plaza, **16**
La Citadelle, **19**
Le Centre
Sheraton, **9**
Le Château
Champlain, **10**
Le Meridien, **23**
Le Nouvel
Hôtel, **3**
Le Reine
Elizabeth (Queen
Elizabeth), **20**
Le Royal
Roussillon, **24**
Le Shangrila
Best Western, **11**
Le Westin
Mont-Royal, **12**
Lord Berri, **25**
McGill Student
Apartments, **13**
Ritz-Carlton, **6**
Université de
Montréal
Residence, **1**
YMCA, **8**
YWCA, **7**

## Montréal Lodging

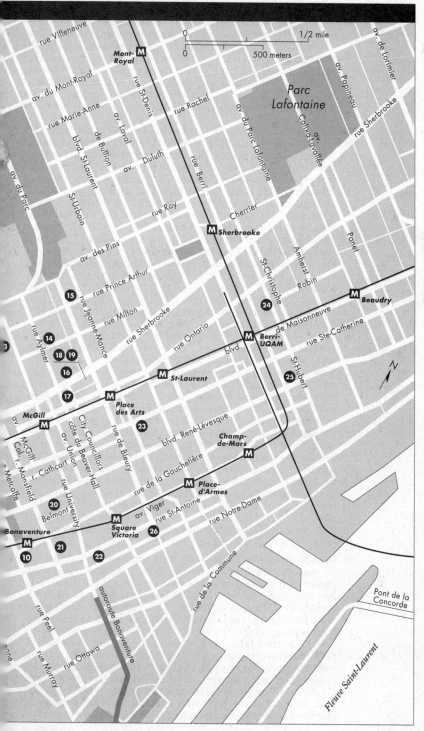

floral chintzes, plush carpeting, and English traditional furnishings. Even the least expensive room has a bathroom telephone, minibar, hair dryer, and safe. For stress control, the hotel has a well-equipped health club, a heated outdoor swimming pool with a swimming tunnel connecting it to the building, a whirlpool, and two saunas. Two of the city's best restaurants are located here—Le Cercle and Zen. *1050 rue Sherbrooke O, H3A 2R6, tel. 514/284–1110 or 800/332–3442, fax 514/845–3025. 300 rooms, including 29 suites. Facilities: 2 restaurants, lounge, health club, heated outdoor pool, 24-hr room service.*

**$$$$** **Le Reine Elizabeth.** If the Ritz-Carlton is a stately old cruise ship,
★ then Le Reine Elizabeth, also called the Queen Elizabeth, is a battleship. Massive and gray, this Canadian Pacific hotel sits on top of the Gare Centrale train station in the very heart of the city, beside Mary Queen of the World Catholic Cathedral and across the street from Place Ville-Marie. The lobby is a bit too much like a railway station—hordes march this way and that—to be attractive and personal, but upstairs the rooms are modern, spacious, and spotless, especially in the more expensive Entrée Gold section. All the latest gadgets and other trappings of luxury are present. The hotel is home to the Beaver Club (*see* Dining, *above*), a flagship restaurant that is considered an institution. There's a cheaper restaurant, too, as well as four lounges. Conventions are a specialty here. *900 boul. René-Lévesque O, H3B 4A5, tel. 514/861–3511 or 800/441–1414, fax 514/954–2256. 929 rooms, 81 suites. Facilities: 4 restaurants, 2 bars-lounges, beauty salon, boutiques, gift shops. AE, D, DC, MC, V.*

**$$$$** **Ritz-Carlton.** This property floats like a stately old luxury liner
★ along rue Sherbrooke. It was opened in 1912 by a consortium of local investors who wanted a hotel where their rich European friends could stay and indulge their champagne-and-caviar tastes. Since then many earthshaking events have occurred here, including the marriage of Elizabeth Taylor and Richard Burton. Power breakfasts, lunches, and dinners are the rule at the elegant Café de Paris, and the prime minister and others in the national government are frequently sighted eating here. A less heady atmosphere prevails at the Ritz-Carlton's two other excellent restaurants. Guest rooms are a successful blend of Edwardian style—some suites have working fireplaces—with such modern accessories as electronic safes. Careful and personal attention are hallmarks of the Ritz-Carlton's service. Even if you're not a guest, stop by the Ritz's Hotel Courtyard during the summer for afternoon tea and to see the duck pond, a Ritz tradition since 1912. *1228 rue Sherbrooke O, H3G 1H6, tel. 514/842–4212 or 800/223–6800, fax 514/842–3383. 201 rooms, 39 suites. Facilities: restaurant, bar, piano bar, gift shop, barber shop, and 24-hr room service. AE, DC, MC, V.*

**$$$** **Delta Montréal.** The French-style Delta is making a bid to break into the ranks of Montréal's world-class hotels. Many of the spacious guest rooms have balconies and excellent views of the city. The Le Bouquet restaurant and the piano lounge are designed like 19th-century Parisian establishments, with dark wood paneling and brass chandeliers. The cuisine is Continental and not above trendy touches like grilling over mesquite. The Delta has the most complete exercise and pool facility in Montréal. There are indoor and outdoor pools, two international squash courts, an exercise room, a sauna, and a whirlpool. The innovative Children's Creative Centre lets your children play (under supervision) while you gallivant around town. *475 av. President-Kennedy, H3A 2T4, tel. 514/286–1986 or 800/268–1133, fax 514/284–4306. 443 rooms, 10 suites. Facilities: restaurant; jazz bar (which also serves lunch weekdays); indoor and outdoor* *pools; health club with whirlpool, sauna, squash courts, aerobics classes; children's center; gift shop; pinball and video-game rooms. AE, DC, MC, V.*

**$$$ Holiday Inn Crowne Plaza.** The flagship of the Holiday Inn chain's downtown Montréal hotels, the Crowne Plaza could just as well have been plopped down in Las Vegas or Atlanta. On the other hand, one doesn't stay in Holiday Inns for originality of design. This hotel *does* sparkle: It is constantly being upgraded, and has the largest indoor pool of the city's hotels, in addition to a health club, café-restaurant, and two bars. It has two suites, a penthouse, and two business floors. Popular for conventions, this hotel is near Métro McGill, rue Sherbrooke shopping, and downtown. *420 rue Sherbrooke O, H3A 1B4, tel. 514/842–6111 or 800/465–4329, fax 514/842–9381. 478 rooms, 6 suites. Facilities: café-restaurant, 2 bars, indoor pool, health club with sauna and whirlpool, unisex beauty parlor, gift shop. AE, D, DC, MC, V.*

**$$$ Hôtel de la Montagne.** Upon entering the reception area you'll be
★ greeted by a naked, butterfly-winged nymph who rises out of a fountain. An enormous crystal chandelier hangs from the ceiling and tinkles to the beat of disco music played a little too loudly. The decor resembles Versailles rebuilt with a dash of art nouveau and is reminiscent of a mid-'70s discothèque. The rooms are tamer, large, and comfortable. As for the food, it's excellent, especially in the main restaurant—Le Lutetia—known as one of the best and most innovative gourmet eateries in Montréal (*see* Dining, *above*). Tea and cocktails are served in the two lobby bars on each side of the hall, and a tunnel connects the hotel to Thursday's/Les Beaux Jeudis, a popular singles bar, restaurant, and dance club all rolled into one. Clientele is a truly bilingual mixture of French-speaking Montréalers stopping by for a drink and Torontonians in town on business. If you're staying elsewhere, the reception area is at least worth a visit. *1430 rue de la Montagne, H3G 1Z5, tel. 514/288–5656 or 800/361–6262, fax 514/288–9658. 135 rooms. Facilities: 2 restaurants, disco-bar, pool. AE, D, DC, MC, V.*

**$$$ La Citadelle.** There's a small pack of hotels on rue Sherbrooke, all of them convenient to Place des Arts, shopping, and the financial district; La Citadelle, a Clarion Hotel property, is one of them. This relatively small business hotel offers both four-star elegance in a low-key atmosphere and service, along with all the features of its better-known brethren: minibars, in-room movies, a small health club with an indoor pool, etc. There's also a passable French restaurant, C'est La Vie. *410 rue Sherbrooke O, H3A 1B3, tel. 514/844–8851 or 800/465–6654, fax 514/844–0912. 180 rooms. Facilities: restaurant; lounge; health club with Nautilus, sauna, and steam room; indoor pool; gift shop. AE, DC, MC, V.*

**$$$ Le Château Champlain.** In the heart of downtown Montréal, at the southern end of Place du Canada, is this 36-floor skyscraper with distinctive half moon–shape windows. The decor inside is formal, with only 20 rooms per floor. A number of floors are reserved for nonsmokers. Underground passageways connect the Champlain with the Bonaventure Métro station, the Bonaventure Hilton International, and Pl. Ville-Marie. *1 Pl. du Canada, H3B 4C9, tel. 514/878–9000 or 800/268–9411, fax 514/878–6761. 510 rooms, 46 suites. Facilities: 3 restaurants, lounge, health club with sauna and whirlpool, large indoor pool, gift shops. AE, DC, MC, V.*

**$$$ Le Shangrila Best Western.** If you're a frequent traveler to Montréal, you may want to try something different: an Oriental-style hotel. The hotel's decor from reception to restaurant to rooms is modern, with an amalgam of Korean, Chinese, Japanese, and Indian motifs and artwork. In addition to special corporate-class extras, such as a lounge for buffet breakfasts and snacks, there are also pluses for the fitness fanatic: more than 10 health rooms—private rooms with exercise facilities. For your hunger pangs, there's a large Szechuan-style restaurant, Dynastie de Ming, on the lobby level. During the week the clientele is corporate; on weekends most of the guests are tourists from the United States and Ontario. Le Shangrila is situated across the street from Le Westin Mont-Royal on rue Sherbrooke, one block from Métro Peel. *3407 rue Peel, H3A 1W7, tel. 514/288–4141 or 800/361–7791, fax 514/288–3021. 146 rooms, 17 suites. Facilities: café, restaurant, bar, business lounge, gift shop, salon. AE, D, DC, MC, V.*

$$ ★ **Château Versailles.** The excellently situated, small, charming hotel occupies a row of four converted mansions on rue Sherbrooke Ouest. The owners have decorated it with many antique paintings, tapestries, and furnishings; some rooms have ornate moldings and plaster decorations on the walls and ceilings. Each room also has a full bath, TV, and air-conditioning. The reception area is designed to look like a European pension. Across the street, at 1808 rue Sherbrooke, the Villeneuve family has added a former apartment hotel as an annex to the original town houses. Called La Tour Versailles, it offers 107 larger, more Spartan rooms—at the same reasonable price—and a restaurant run by Christien Lévêque, former chef at the Ritz. It's aptly called the Champs-Élysées. The staff is extremely helpful and friendly. The Versailles is unassuming, not too expensive, and classy. *1659 rue Sherbrooke O (near Métro Guy-Concordia), H3H 1E3, tel. 514/933–3611 or 800/361–3664, fax 514/933–7102. 70 rooms in Château, 105 rooms and 2 suites in La Tour. Facilities: breakfast room in the Château, restaurant in La Tour. AE, DC, MC, V.*

$$ ★ **Hôtel Radisson des Gouverneurs de Montréal.** Abutting the stock exchange, this property rises above a stunning three-story atrium-reception area and is especially attractive to the convention crowds. It's centrally located and is near the Place Bonaventure, the western fringe of Vieux-Montréal, and the Métro Square Victoria (accessible via an underground passage). Amenities include the usual health club and pool facilities, a more exclusive floor for higher-paying guests, and a shopping arcade on the underground level. Most outstanding, however, are the restaurants. The Tour de Ville on the top floor is the city's only revolving restaurant, and its bar has live jazz nightly. Chez Antoine, an art nouveau–style bistro, serves gourmet salads and sandwiches. *777 rue University, H3C 3Z7, tel. 514/879–1370 or 800/361–8155, fax 514/879–1761. 692 rooms, 23 suites. Facilities: 2 restaurants, bar, health club with spa and steam room, indoor pool, gift shop. AE, DC, MC, V.*

$$ **Howard Johnson Hôtel Plaza.** This medium-size, medium-price hotel, next to the McGill campus, caters to the business trade and families. Exercise machines and a spa with sauna have been added, and the lobby was redone. The decor of the restaurant is Italianate, with lots of brass and marble and with bay windows overlooking the street. There's also a terrace for summer dining outdoors. The Hôtel Plaza is handy to downtown business and shopping areas. *475 rue Sherbrooke O, H3A 2L9, tel. 514/842–3961 or 800/446–4656, fax 514/842–0945. 200 rooms. Facilities: restaurant, café. AE, DC, MC, V.*

$$ **Le Nouvel Hôtel.** The Nouvel Hôtel is what hotel managers like to call a "new concept"—in its four towers it has studios and 2½-room apartments. It's not very classy, but it's brightly colored and functional. Le Nouvel Hôtel is near the restaurant district, five or six blocks from the heart of downtown and two blocks from the Guy-Concordia Métro station. *1740 boul. René-Lévesque O, H3H 1R3, tel. 514/931–8841 or 800/363–6063, fax 514/931–3233. 126 rooms, 60*

2½-room units. *Facilities: restaurant, bar, gift shop, pool. AE, DC, MC, V.*

**$$ Lord Berri.** Next to the Université du Québec à Montréal, the Lord Berri is a new, moderately priced hotel convenient to the restaurants and nightlife of rue St-Denis. It offers some of the services of its more expensive competition: minibars, in-room movies, and no-smoking floors. The Il Cavaliere restaurant serves Italian food and is popular with a local clientele. The Berri-UQAM Métro stop is a block away. *1199 rue Berri, H2L 4C6, tel. 514/845–9236 or 800/363–0363, fax 514/849–9855. 154 rooms. Facilities: restaurant, gift shop. AE, DC, MC, V.*

**$ Le Royal Roussillon.** This hotel is adjacent to the Terminus Voyageur bus station (buses park directly beneath one wing of the hotel), and some of the bus station aura seems to rub off on the Roussillon: It's a little dingy. But if you're stumbling after a long bus ride and want somewhere to stay *now*, the Rousillon's rooms are large and clean, the service is friendly, and the price is right. It's also handy to the Berri-UQAM Métro station. *1600 rue St-Hubert, H2L 3Z3, tel. 514/849–3214, fax 514/849–9812. 147 rooms. Facilities: restaurant. AE, DC, MC, V.*

**$ YMCA.** This clean Y is downtown, next to Peel Métro station. Book at least two days in advance. Women should book seven days ahead because there are fewer rooms with showers for them. Anyone staying summer weekends must book a week ahead, as well. *1450 rue Stanley, H3A 2W6, tel. 514/849–8393, fax 514/849–7821. 331 rooms, 429 beds. AE, MC, V.*

**$ YWCA.** Very close to dozens of restaurants, the Y is right downtown, one block from rue Ste-Catherine. Although men can eat at the café, the overnight facilities and health club are for women only. If you want a room with any amenities you must book in advance. *1355 boul. René-Lévesque, H3G 1P3, tel. 514/866–9941, fax 514/861–1603. 107 rooms, some with sink and bath. Facilities: café, gym, pool, sauna, whirlpool, weight room, fitness classes. MC, V.*

## McGill University Area

**$ Auberge de Jeunesse Internationale de Montréal.** The youth hostel near the McGill campus in the student ghetto charges $15 for members, $19 for non-Canadian nonmembers, and $17 for Canadian nonmembers, per night per person. Reserve early during the summer tourist season. *3541 rue Aylmer, H2X 2B9, tel. 514/843–3317. 112 beds. Facilities: rooms for 4–12 people (same sex); a few rooms available for couples and families. MC,V.*

**$ McGill Student Apartments.** From mid-May to mid-August, when McGill is on summer recess, you can stay in its dorms on the grassy, quiet campus in the heart of the city. Nightly rates: $27.50 students; $36.50 nonstudents (single rooms only). *3935 rue University, H3A 2B4, tel. 514/398–6367. 1,000 rooms. Facilities: campus swimming pool and health facilities (visitors must pay to use them).*

## Université de Montréal Area

**$ Université de Montréal Residence.** The university's student housing accepts visitors from May 9 to August 22. It's on the other side of Mont Royal, a long walk from downtown and Vieux-Montréal, but there's the new Université de Montréal Métro stop right next to the campus. Nightly rates: $21 students per night, $100 students per week, $31 nonstudents per night. *2350 boul. Édouard-Montpetit,*

*H3C 3J7, tel. 514/343-6531. 1,171 rooms. Facilities: campus sports center with pool and gym (visitors must pay to use it). AE, MC, V.*

## Bed-and-Breakfasts

**Bed and Breakfast à Montréal.** Most of the more than 50 homes are downtown or in the elegant neighborhoods of Westmount and Outremont. Some of them can be quite ritzy. Others are less expensive, but all provide breakfast and a wealth of information about the city. *Contact: Marian Kahn, Box 575, Snowdon Station, Montréal H3X 3T8, tel. 514/738-9410. Single $35-$55, double $55-$105. AE, MC, V accepted for deposits only; the balance must be paid with cash or traveler's checks.*

**Downtown B&B Network.** This organization will put you in touch with 75 homes and apartments, mostly around the downtown core and along rue Sherbrooke, that have one or more rooms available for visitors. These homes generally are clean, lovingly kept up, and filled with antiques. Even during the height of the tourist season, this organization has rooms open. *Contact: Bob Finkelstein, 3458 av. Laval (at rue Sherbrooke), Montréal H2X 3C8, tel. 514/289-9749. Single $25-$40, double $35-$55. AE, MC, V.*

# The Arts and Nightlife

The entertainment section of the *Gazette*, the English-language daily paper, is a good place to find out about upcoming events in Montréal. The Friday weekend guide has an especially good list of all events at the city's concert halls, theaters, clubs, dance spaces, and movie houses. Other publications listing what's on include *The Mirror, Hour, Scope,* and *Voir* (in French), distributed free at restaurants and other public places.

For tickets to major pop and rock concerts, shows, festivals, and hockey and baseball games, go to the individual box offices or call Admission (tel. 514/790-1245). Ticketron outlets are located in La Baie department store and in all Provigo supermarkets. Place des Arts tickets may be purchased at its box office underneath the Salle Wilfrid-Pelletier, next to the Métro station.

## The Arts

Music    The **Orchestre Symphonique de Montréal** has gained world renown under the baton of Charles Dutoit. When not on tour its regular venue is the Salle Wilfrid-Pelletier at the Place des Arts. The orchestra also gives Christmas and summer concerts in the Notre-Dame Basilica and pop concerts at the Arena Maurice Richard in the Olympic Park. For tickets and program information, call 514/842-9951. Also check the *Gazette* listings for its free summertime concerts in Montréal's city parks. Montréal's other orchestra, the **Orchestre Métropolitain de Montréal** (tel. 514/598-0870), also stars at Place des Arts most weeks during the October-May season. McGill University, at Pollack Concert Hall (tel. 514/398-4547) and Redpath Hall (tel. 514/398-8993), is also the site of many classical concerts. The most notable are given by the **McGill Chamber Orchestra,** which also occasionally plays at Place des Arts with guest artists. **L'Opéra de Montréal,** founded in 1980, stages four productions a year at Place des Arts (tel. 514/985-2222).

The 20,000-seat **Montréal Forum** (tel. 514/932-6131) and the much larger Olympic Stadium are where rock and pop concerts are staged. More intimate concert halls include the **Théâtre St-Denis** (1594 rue St-Denis, tel. 514/849–4211) and the **Spectrum** (318 rue Ste-Catherine O, tel. 514/861–5851).

**Theater**
French-speaking theater lovers will find a wealth of dramatic productions. There are at least 10 major companies in town, some of which have an international reputation. Best bets are productions at **Théâtre d'Aujourd'hui** (3900 rue St. Denis, tel. 514/282–3900), **Théâtre du Nouveau Monde** (84 rue Ste-Catherine O, tel. 514/861–0563), and **Théâtre du Rideau Vert** (4664 rue St-Denis, tel. 514/844–1793). Anglophones have less to choose from, unless they want to chance the language barrier. **Centaur Theatre,** the best-known English theatrical company, stages productions in the Beaux Arts–style former stock exchange building at 453 rue St-François-Xavier in Vieux-Montréal (tel. 514/288–3161). English-language plays can also be seen at the **Saidye Bronfman Centre** at 5170 chemin de la Côte Ste-Catherine (tel. 514/739–7944). Michel Tremblay is Montréal's premier playwright, and all of his plays are worth seeing, even if in the English translation. Touring companies of Broadway productions can often be seen at the completely renovated and expanded **Théâtre St-Denis** on rue St-Denis (tel. 514/849–4211), as well as at Place des Arts (tel. 514/842– 2112)—especially during the summer months.

**Dance**
Traditional and contemporary dance companies thrive in Montréal, though many take to the road or are on hiatus in the summer. Among the best known are **Ballets Classiques de Montréal** (tel. 514/866–1771); **Les Grands Ballets Canadiens,** the leading Québec company (tel. 514/849–8681); **O Vertigo Danse** (tel. 514/251–9177); **Montréal Danse** (tel. 514/845–2031); **LaLaLa Human Steps** (tel. 514/288–8266); **Les Ballets Jazz de Montréal** (tel. 514/982–6771); **Margie Gillis Fondation de Danse** (tel. 514/845–3115); and **Tangente** (tel. 514/525–5584)—a nucleus for many of the more avant-garde dance troupes. When not on tour, many of these artists can be seen at Place des Arts or at any of the Maisons de la Culture (tel. 514/872–6211) performance spaces around town. Montréal's dancers have a brand-new downtown performance and rehearsal space, the Agora Dance Theatre, affiliated with the Université de Montréal dance faculty (840 rue Chérrier E, tel. 514/525–1500). Check newspaper listings for details. Every other September (that is, in the odd-numbered years, such as 1995), the **Festival International de Nouvelle Danse** brings "new" dance to various venues around town. Tickets for this event always sell quickly.

## Nightlife

**Bars and Clubs**
Elegant dinner-theater productions have revitalized Montréal's English theater. Prices range from about $12 for the show alone to more than $50 for the show and dinner (not including drinks—which can run up to about $6.50 each—tips, or tax). **La Diligence** (tel. 514/731–7771) has two dinner theaters and a solid reputation for presenting polished performances of popular productions—usually Broadway hits, as well as light musical comedies and plays in English. **Le Festin du Gouverneur,** at the old fort on Ile Ste-Hélène (tel. 514/879–1141), offers a unique dinner-theater experience. Light operatic airs, beautifully rendered as a merry 17th-century frolic in the military barracks mess hall, are served up with copious amounts of food and drinks. Great for group outings.

*Classical*
For classical music, drop by the Bar de Vieux Montréal (tel. 514/499–9403), at 408 rue St. Francois-Xavier.

*Jazz*  Montréal has a very active local jazz scene. The best-known club is Vieux-Montréal's **L'Air du Temps** (191 rue St-Paul O, tel. 514/842–2003). This small, smoky club presents 90% local talent and 10% international acts from 5 PM on into the night. There's a cover charge Thursday through Saturday. Downtown, duck into **Biddle's** (tel. 514/842–8656), at 2060 rue Aylmer, where bassist Charles Biddle holds forth most evenings when he's not appearing at a local hotel. Bernard Primeau's Trio is an upscale club that is also a restaurant serving ribs and chicken. There's a cover charge for the big acts. You also might try **Le Grand Café** (tel. 514/849–6955) at 1720 rue St-Denis, and **Quai des Brumes Dancing** (tel. 514/499–0467) at 4481 rue St-Denis.

*Rock*  Rock clubs seem to spring up, flourish, then fizzle out overnight. **Club Soda** (tel. 514/270–7848), at 5240 avenue du Parc, the granddaddy of them all, sports a neon martini glass complete with neon effervescence outside. Inside it's a small hall with a stage, three bars, and room for about 400 people. International rock acts play here, as does local talent. It's also a venue for the comedy and jazz festivals. Open seven nights from 8 PM to 3 AM; admission ranges from nothing up to $20, depending. **Foufounes Électriques** (tel. 514/845–5484)—which translates as "electric buttocks"—at 97 rue Ste-Catherine Est in the Latin Quarter is the downscale, more avant-garde competitor of Club Soda. Foufounes is the center for the local band scene and also attracts up-and-coming acts from the United States. There's a "quiet" section for conversation and a "loud" section for music and dancing. Open weekdays 1 PM–3 AM, weekends 7 PM–3 AM; admission varies. Other clubs include **Déjà Vu** (1224 rue Bishop, tel. 514/866–0512), **Station 10** (2071 rue Ste-Catherine O, tel. 514/934–0484), **Back Street Rock Bar** (382 rue Mayor, tel. 514/987–7671), and **L'Ours Qui Fume**—The Smoking Bear (2019 rue St-Denis, tel. 514/845–6998).

**Discos**  Montréalers are as into discos as you could imagine. The newest and the glitziest is **Metropolis** (59 rue Ste-Catherine Est, tel. 514/288–2020). The crowd is young, primarily French-speaking, and clad in black. It's open on weekends only, and costs $5 on Friday, $8 on Saturday. If a band is appearing, the admission fee is more. **Bowling Bar** (4428 boul. St-Laurent, tel. 514/285–8869) is particularly popular with the thirty-something crowd, and any kind of music goes—funk, rave, heavy metal. **L'Opera** (3523A boul. St-Laurent, tel. 514/284–7793) is *the* place to people-watch and to be seen, wearing the appropriate gear, of course—leather, plunging necklines, and minis. Other popular discothèques include the **Hard Rock Café** (1458 rue Crescent, tel. 514/987–1420) and the **Crocodile** (636 rue Cathcart, tel. 514/866–4979).

# 4 Québec City

*By Alice H. Oshins*

*Updated by Dorothy Guinan*

An excursion to French-speaking Canada is incomplete without a visit to Québec City, located in one of the most beautiful natural settings in North America. The Vieille Ville (Old City) measures 11 square kilometers (7 square miles) and is a lot of ground to cover. This well-preserved part of town is a small and dense place, steeped in four centuries of history and French tradition. Once you begin to explore firsthand the 17th- and 18th-century buildings, the ramparts that once protected the city, and the numerous parks and monuments, you will soon realize how much there is to see.

The oldest municipality in Québec province, Québec City was the first settlement of French explorers, fur trappers, and missionaries in the 17th century, who came here to establish the colony of New France. Today it still resembles a French provincial town in many ways, with its family-oriented residents with strong ties to their past. More than 95% of its metropolitan population of 650,000 are French-speaking. Québec City is also a fortified city, the only one in North America, an attribute that led UNESCO to declare it a World Heritage treasure.

Québec City is huddled on a cliff above the St. Lawrence River, at a point where the body of water narrows; this strategic location forged its historic destiny as a military stronghold. When Winston Churchill visited Québec City in the early 1940s, he named it "Gibraltar of North America" because of its position at the gateway to the continent. The city's military prominence paved the way for its leading political role, first as the French colony's administrative center and eventually as the capital of Québec province.

In 1535, French explorer Jacques Cartier first came upon what the Algonquin Indians called "Kebec," meaning "where the river narrows." New France, however, was not actually founded in the area of what is now Québec City until 1608, when another French explorer, Samuel de Champlain, recognized the military advantages of the location and set up a fort. Along the banks of the St. Lawrence, on the spot now called Place Royale, this fort developed into an economic center for fur trade and shipbuilding. Twelve years later, de Champlain realized the French colony's vulnerability to attacks from above and expanded its boundaries to the top of the cliff, where he built the fort Château St-Louis on the site of the present-day Château Frontenac.

During the early days of New France, the French and British fought for control of the area. In 1690, when an expedition led by Admiral Sir William Phipps arrived from England, Comte de Frontenac, New France's most illustrious governor, issued his famous statement, "Tell your lord that I will reply with the mouth of my cannons."

England was determined to conquer New France. The French constructed walls and other military structures and had the advantage of the defensive position on top of the cliff, but they still had to contend with Britain's naval supremacy. On September 13, 1759, the British army, led by General James Wolfe, scaled the colony's cliff and took the French troops led by Général Louis-Joseph Montcalm by surprise. The British defeated the French in a 20-minute battle on the Plains of Abraham, and New France came under English rule.

The British brought their mastery of trade to the region. During the 18th century, Québec City's economy prospered because of the success of the fishing, fur trading, shipbuilding, and timber industries. In order to further protect the city from invasion, the British continued to expand upon the fortifications left by the French. Defensive structures that were built included a wall encircling the city and a star-shape citadel, both of which still enhance the city's urban landscape. The city remained under British rule until 1867, when the Act of Confederation united several Canadian provinces (Québec, Ontario, New Brunswick, and Nova Scotia) and designated Québec City the capital of the province of Québec.

During the mid-19th century, the economic center of eastern Canada shifted west from Québec City to Montréal and Toronto. Today government is Québec City's main business: About 30,000 civil-service employees work and live in the area. Office complexes continue to appear outside the older portion of town; modern malls, convention centers, and imposing hotels now cater to an established business clientele.

Despite the period of British rule, Québec City has remained a center of French Canadian culture. It is home to Université Laval (Laval University), a large Catholic institution that grew out of Séminaire de Québec (Québec Seminary), founded in 1663 by French bishop François de Montmorency Laval; today Laval has a sprawling campus in the suburb of Sainte-Foy. Québec City also has several theaters, including the Grand Théâtre de Québec, where local artists perform plays that deal directly with French Canadian culture. The Québec government has completely restored many of the centuries-old buildings of Place Royale, one of the oldest districts on the continent. The city's ancient stone churches and homes, as well as its cultural institutions, such as Musée de Québec and Musée de la Civilisation, are firmly rooted in French Canadian society.

Québec City is a wonderful place in which to wander on foot. Its natural beauty is world renowned. You're bound to enjoy the view from Parc Montmorency (Montmorency Park), where the Laurentian Mountains jut majestically over the St. Lawrence River. Even more impressive vistas are revealed if you walk along the walls or climb to the city's highest point, Cap Diamant (Cape Diamond). Several blissful days may be spent investigating the narrow cobblestone streets of the historic Old City, browsing for local arts and crafts in the boutiques of quartier Petit-Champlain, or strolling the Terrasse Dufferin promenade along the river. When you've worked up an appetite, you can stop to indulge in one of the many reliable cafés and restaurants, with a choice of French, Québecois, and international fare. If you've had enough of the past, another vibrant, modern part of town beckons beyond the city gates. And if you're tired of walking you can always board a calèche (horse-drawn carriage) near the city gates or hop on the ferry across the St. Lawrence River to Lévis for a thrilling view of the Québec City skyline. What follows will help you uncover some of the secrets of this exuberant, romantic place.

# Arriving and Departing

### By Plane

Airports/
Airlines

Québec City has one airport, **Québec City International Airport,** located in the suburb of Sainte-Foy, approximately 19 kilometers (12 miles) from downtown. Few U.S. airlines fly directly to Québec City. You usually have to stop in Montréal or Toronto and take one of the regional and commuter airlines, such as Air Canada's **Air Alliance** (tel. 418/692–0770) or **Canadian Airlines International** (tel. 418/

# Metropolitan Québec City Exploring *(Boxes Refer to Detail Maps)*

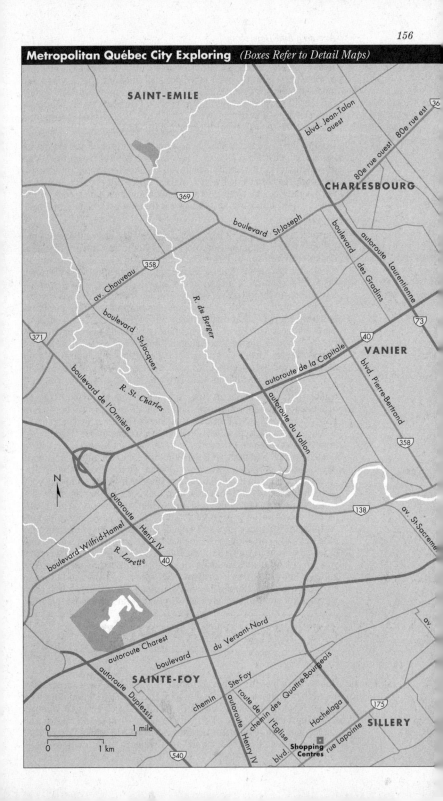

SAINT-EMILE

blvd. Jean-Talon
ouest

36

80e rue ouest
80e rue est

CHARLESBOURG

369

boulevard   St-Joseph

boulevard
des Gradins

autoroute   Laurentienne

358

av. Chauveau

boulevard   St-Jacques

R. du Berger

73

371

boulevard de l'Ormière

R. St. Charles

40

autoroute de la Capitale

VANIER

blvd. Pierre-Bertrand

autoroute du Vallon

358

N

autoroute   Henry IV

138

av. St-Sacreme.

boulevard   Wilfrid-Hamel

R. Lorette

40

autoroute Charest

du Versant-Nord

av.

boulevard

Ste-Foy

SAINTE-FOY

autoroute Duplessis

chemin

autoroute   Henry IV

route de   l'Église

chemin des Quatre-Bourgeois

Hochelaga

175

SILLERY

rue Lapointe

blvd.

**Shopping
Centres**

0        1 mile

0        1 km

540

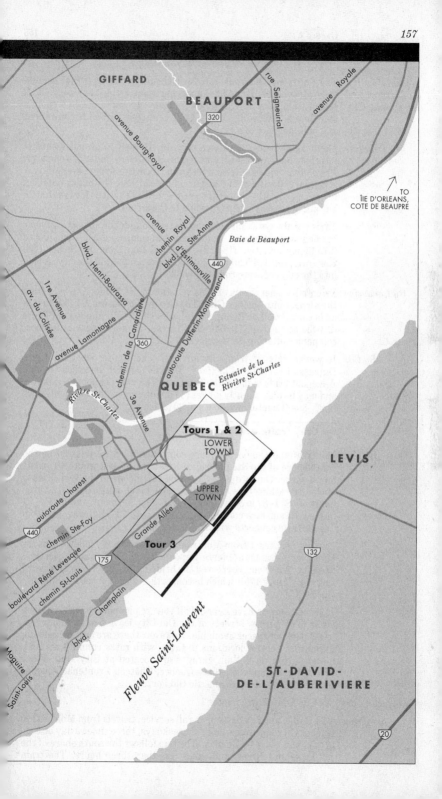

692–1031). Air Alliance offers a direct flight between Newark, New Jersey, and Québec City seven days a week.

**Between the Airport and Québec City**
The ride from the airport into town should be no longer than 30 minutes. Most hotels do not have an airport shuttle, but they will make a reservation for you with a bus company. If you're not in a rush, a shuttle bus offered by Maple Leaf Tours (*see below*) is convenient and half the price of a taxi.

*By Bus* **Maple Leaf Tours** (240 3ième rue, tel. 418/649–9226) has a shuttle bus that runs from the airport to hotels and costs under $10 one way. The shuttle makes several trips to and from the airport every day. A schedule is posted at the airport. Stops include the major hotels in town, and any other hotel upon request. Reservations for the shuttle bus are necessary when traveling to the airport.

*By Taxi* Taxis are always available immediately outside the airport exit near the baggage claim area. Some local taxi companies are **Taxi Québec** (975 8ième av., tel. 418/522–2001) and **Taxi Coop de Québec** (496 2ième av., tel. 418/525–5191), the largest company in the city. A ride into the city costs approximately $25.

*By Limousine* Private limo service is expensive, starting at $50 for the ride from the airport into Québec City. Try **Groupe Limousine A-1** (30 chemin de la Cornière, Lac Beauport, tel. 418/849–7473). **Maple Leaf Tours** (240 3ième rue, tel. 418/649–9226) acts as a referral service for local companies offering car service.

*By Car* If you're driving from the airport, take Route 540 (Autoroute Duplessis) to Route 175 (boul. Laurier), which becomes Grande Allée and leads right to the Old City. The ride is about 30 minutes and may be only slightly longer (45 minutes or so) during rush hours (7:30–8:30 AM into town, and 4–5:30 PM leaving town).

## By Car, Train, and Bus

**By Car** Montréal and Québec City are connected by Autoroute 20 on the south shore of the St. Lawrence River and by Autoroute 40 on the north shore. On both highways, the ride between the two cities is about 240 kilometers (150 miles) and takes approximately three hours. U.S. I–87 in New York, U.S. I–89 in Vermont, and U.S. I–91 in New Hampshire connect with Autoroute 20. Highway 401 from Toronto also connects with Autoroute 20.

Driving northeast from Montréal on Autoroute 20, follow signs for Pont Pierre-Laporte (Pierre-Laporte Bridge) as you approach Québec City. After you've crossed the bridge, turn right onto boulevard Laurier (Route 175), which becomes the Grande Allée leading into Québec City.

It is necessary to have a car only if you are planning to visit outlying areas. The narrow streets of the Old City leave few two-hour metered parking spaces available. However, there are several parking garages at central locations in town, with rates running approximately $10 a day. Main garages are located at City Hall, Place d'Youville, Complex G, Place Québec, Château Frontenac, Québec Seminary, rue St-Paul, and the Old Port.

*Rental Cars* *See* Car Rentals in Chapter 1.

**By Train** **VIA Rail,** Canada's passenger rail service, travels from Montréal to Québec City four times daily on weekdays, three times a day on Saturday, and twice on Sunday. The trip follows the south shore of the St. Lawrence River, and takes less than three hours. The train makes a stop in Sainte-Foy and has first-class service available. Tickets must be purchased in advance at any VIA Rail office or travel agent. The basic one-way rate is about $40. At certain periods throughout the year, that price is reduced to $23. Reservations must be made at least five days in advance. The discount is not offered on Friday, Sunday, or holidays. First-class service costs about $65 each way. *Tel. 418/692–3940; in Québec City and in Sainte-Foy, 800/ 361–5390; in Québec province, tel. 800/361–5390.*

The train arrives in Québec City at the 19th-century **Gare du Palais** (450 rue de la Gare du Palais, tel. 418/524–6452), in the heart of the Old City.

**By Bus** **Voyageur Inc.** provides regular service from Montréal to Québec City daily, departing hourly 6 AM–9 PM, with an additional bus at 11 PM. The cost of the three-hour ride is $35 one way. A round-trip costs $50, if you return within 10 days and do not travel on Friday. Senior citizens travel for $25 each way. You can only purchase tickets at the terminal; tickets are not sold on the bus.

*Bus Terminals* **Montréal:** Voyageur Terminal (505 boul. de Maisonneuve E, tel. 514/ 842–2281).

**Québec:** Downtown Terminal (225 boul. Charest E, tel. 418/524– 4692); Sainte-Foy Terminal (2700 boul. Laurier, tel. 418/651–7015).

# Staying in Québec City

## Getting Around

Walking is the best way to explore Québec City. The Old City measures 11 square kilometers (7 square miles), and most historic sites, hotels, and restaurants are located within the walls or a short distance outside. City maps are available at tourist information offices.

**By Bus** The public transportation system in Québec City is dependable, and buses run frequently. You can get to anywhere in Québec City and the outlying areas, although you may be required to transfer. The city's transit system, **Commission de Transport de la Communauté Urbaine de Québec (CTCUQ)** (tel. 418/627–2511) runs buses approximately every 15 or 20 minutes that stop at major points around town. The cost is $1.80, children under 5 free; you'll need exact change. All buses stop in Lower Town at Place Jacques-Cartier or outside St-Jean Gate at Place d'Youville in Upper Town. Transportation maps are available at tourist information offices.

**By Taxi** Taxis are stationed in front of major hotels, including the Château Frontenac, Hilton International, Loews Le Concorde, and Hôtel des Gouverneurs, as well as in front of Hôtel de Ville (City Hall) along rue des Jardins and Place d'Youville outside St-Jean Gate. For radio-dispatched cars, try **Taxi Coop de Québec** (tel. 418/525–5191) and **Taxi Québec** (tel. 418/522–2001). Passengers are charged an initial $2.25, plus $1 for each kilometer.

**By Limousine** Groupe Limousine A-1 (30 chemin de la Cornière, Lac Beauport, tel. 418/849–7473) has 24-hour service.

## Important Addresses and Numbers

**Tourist Information** **Québec City Region Tourism and Convention Bureau** has two tourist information centers:

**Québec City:** 60 rue d'Auteuil, tel. 418/692–2471. Open June–early September, daily 8:30–8; early September–mid-October, daily 8:30–5:30; mid-October–mid-April, weekdays 9–5; mid-April–May, weekdays 8:30–5:30.

**Sainte-Foy:** 3005 boul. Laurier (near the Québec and Pierre-Laporte bridges), tel. 418/651–2882. Open June–August, daily 8:30–8; September–mid-October, daily 8:30–6; mid-October–mid-April, daily 9–5; mid-April–May, daily 8:30–6.

**Québec Government Tourism Department:** 12 rue Ste-Anne (Place d'Armes), tel. 418/643–2280 or 800/363–7777. Open fall–winter, daily 9–5; summer, daily 8:30–7:30.

**U.S. Consulate** The consulate (2 Place Terrasse Dufferin, tel. 418/692–2095) faces the Governors Park near the Château Frontenac.

**Emergencies** **Police and fire,** tel. 418/691–6911; **provincial police,** tel. 418/623–6262.

*Medical Care* **Hôtel-Dieu Hospital** (11 côte du Palais, tel. 418/691–5042) is the main hospital inside the Old City; **Jeffrey Hale Hospital** (1250 chemin Sainte-Foy, tel. 418/683–4471) is opposite St. Sacrament Church.

**24-hour Medical Service** (tel. 418/687–9915).

**Distress Center** (tel. 418/683–2153).

**24-hour Poison Center** (tel. 418/656–8090).

*Dental Service* 1175 rue Lavigerie, Room 100, Sainte-Foy, tel. 418/653–5412; weekends, tel. 418/656–6060. Open Monday and Tuesday 8–8, Wednesday and Thursday 8–5, Friday 8–4.

*Pharmacy* **Pharmacie Brunet** (Les Galeries Charlesbourg, 4266 1ière av., north of Québec City in Charlesbourg, tel. 418/623–1571) is open daily, 24 hours a day.

**Traffic** Tel. 418/643–6830.

**Weather** Tel. 418/648–7766.

**English-language Bookstore** **La Maison Anglaise** (Place de la Cité, Sainte-Foy, tel. 418/654–9523).

**Travel Agencies** **Inter-Voyage** (1095 rue de l'Amérique française, tel. 418/524–1414) is located on the first floor of the Édifice Bon Pasteur (Bon Pasteur Building), on the corner of rue St-Amable and rue de l'Amérique française, near the Parliament. It's open weekdays 8:30–5:30.

## Opening and Closing Times

Most banks are open Monday through Wednesday 10–3 and close later on Thursday and Friday. **Bank of Montreal** (Place Laurier, 2700 boul. Laurier, Sainte-Foy, tel. 418/525–3786) is open on Saturday 10–3. For currency exchange, **Banque d'Amérique** (24 côte de la Fabrique, tel. 418/694–1937) is open late June–August, weekdays 9–6, weekends 9–5; September–late June, weekdays 9–5, weekends 10–4.

Museum hours are typically 10–5, with longer evening hours during summer months. Most are closed on Monday.

Shopping hours are Monday through Wednesday 9:30–5:30, Thursday and Friday 9:30–9, and Saturday 9:30–5. Stores tend to stay open later during summer months.

During the winter, many attractions and shops change their hours; visitors are advised to call ahead.

## Guided Tours

**Orientation Tours By Bus** The three major touring companies—Gray Line, Maple Leaf, and Visite Touristique de Québec—offer similar full- and half-day guided bus tours in English. Tours cover such sights as Québec City, Montmorency Falls, and Sainte-Anne-de-Beaupré; combination city and harbor cruise tours are also available. Québec City tours operate year-round; other excursions to outlying areas may operate only in the summer.

Tickets for **Gray Line** (720 rue des Rocailles; departure from Château Frontenac terrace, tel. 418/622–7420) bus tours can be purchased at most major hotels or at the kiosk at Terrasse Dufferin at Place d'Armes. Tours run year-round and cost $13–$70 adults, half-price children 5–12.

**Maple Leaf Sightseeing Tours** (240 3ième rue, tel. 418/649–9226) offers guided tours in a minibus. Call for a reservation, and the company will pick you up at your hotel. Prices are $20–$91, with reduced rates for children under 12.

**Visite Touristique de Québec** (C.P. 246, Québec, tel. 418/653–9722) gives tours (in English or French) in a panoramic bus, and charges $20–$39, children 6–14 half-price, children under 6 free.

Smaller companies offering tours include **La Tournée du Québec Inc.** (tel. 418/831–1385) and **Fleur de Lys** (418/831–0188).

**By Ferry** The Québec–Lévis ferry makes a 15-minute crossing of the St. Lawrence River to the town of Lévis. The first ferry leaves daily at 6:30 AM from the pier at rue Dalhousie, across from Place Royale. Crossings run every half hour from 7:30 AM until 6:30 PM, then hourly until 2:30 AM, with a final crossing at 3:45 AM. *Tel. 418/644–3704. Cost: $1.25 adults, 75¢ children 5–11 and senior citizens.*

**By Horse-drawn Carriage** Hire a calèche on rue d'Auteuil between the St-Louis and Kent gates from **André Beaurivage** (tel. 418/687–9797). The cost is about $50 without tax or tip for a 45-minute tour of the Old City. Some drivers talk about Québec's history and others don't. So if you want a storyteller, ask in advance.

**Special-Interest Tours Boat Trips** **Beau Temps, Mauvais Temps** (22 rue du Quai, Suite 101, Sainte-Pétronille, Île d'Orléans, tel. 418/828–2275) offers two river cruises that stop to tour neighboring islands. Boats depart from piers at Saint-Laurent on Île d'Orléans, and Pier 19 at Vieux-Port, in Québec. The boat trip to Île-aux-Grues costs $72 for adults, with reduced rates for children. The trip to Grosse-Île costs $65 for adults; children under 12 are not accepted. Both trips include a light lunch.

**Croisières AML Inc.** (Pier Chouinard, 10 rue Dalhousie, across the street from the funicular, tel. 418/692–1159) runs cruises on the St. Lawrence River aboard the MV *Louis-Jolliet*. One- to three-hour cruises from May through mid-October cost $13–$24 for adults, half-price for children 5 and over, 10% discount for senior citizens.

**Île d'Orléans** **Beau Temps, Mauvais Temps** (*see above*) has guided tours of Île d'Orléans by bus, walking tours of the island's historic manors and churches, and trips to a maple-sugar hut.

**Walking Tours** **Baillairgé Cultural Tours, Inc.** (2216 chemin du Foulon, Sillery, tel. 418/658–4799; 51 rue des Jardins, 2nd Floor, tel. 418/692–5234) has a 2½-hour walking tour, "Québec on Foot," from late June through

September at 9:30 AM and 2 PM daily. The tour leaves from 2 côte de la Fabrique and includes sights in both the Upper and Lower towns. The cost is about $12 adults, children under 12 free.

# Exploring Québec City

Québec City's split-level landscape divides the Upper Town on the cape from the Lower Town, along the shores of the St. Lawrence. If you look out from the Terrasse Dufferin boardwalk in Upper Town, you will see the rooftops of Lower Town buildings directly below. Separating these two sections of the city is steep and precipitous rock, against which were built the city's more than 25 *escaliers* (staircases). Today you can also take the *funiculaire* (funicular), a cable car that climbs and descends the cliff between Terrasse Dufferin and the Maison Jolliet in Lower Town.

With the exception of some of the outlying suburbs, most of Québec City's historic area will interest tourists. The first two tours offered here focus primarily on the oldest sections of town, while the third tour strays off the beaten path to provide a glimpse of the modern part of the city.

## Tour 1: Upper Town

*Numbers in the margin correspond to points of interest on the Tours 1 and 2: Upper and Lower Towns map.*

This tour visits the most prominent buildings of Québec City's earliest inhabitants, who came from Europe in the 17th century to set up political, educational, and religious institutions. Upper Town became the political capital of the colony of New France and, later, of British North America. It was also the place where the religious orders first set down their roots: The Jesuits founded the first school for priests in 1635; the Ursuline nuns, a school for girls in 1639; and the Augustine nuns, the first hospital in 1639. Historic buildings, with thick stone walls, large wood doors, glimmering copper roofs, and majestic steeples, compose the heart of the city.

Begin this tour where rue St-Louis meets rue du Fort at Upper Town's most central location, **Place d'Armes.** For centuries, this square seated on a cliff has been a meeting place for parades and military events. It is bordered by government buildings; at its west side, the majestic **Ancien Palais de Justice** (Old Courthouse), a Renaissance building from 1887, replaced the original 1650 courthouse, which was smaller and situated farther from the square. The present courthouse stands on land that was occupied by a church and convent of the Recollet missionaries (Franciscan monks), who in 1615 were the first order of priests to arrive in New France. The Gothic fountain at the center of Place d'Armes pays tribute to their arrival.

The colony's former treasury building, **Maison Maillou,** at 17 rue St-Louis, possesses architectural traits typical of New France: a sharply slanted roof, dormer windows, concrete chimneys, shutters with iron hinges, and limestone walls. Built between 1736 and 1753, it marks the end of rue du Trésor, the road colonists took on their way to pay rent to the king's officials. Maison Maillou is not open to tourists and is now used as the location for the Québec City Chamber of Commerce offices.

You are now within a few steps east of Québec City's most celebrated landmark, **Château Frontenac** (1 rue des Carrières, tel. 418/692–

3861), once the administrative and military headquarters of New France. The imposing green-turreted castle with its slanting copper roof owes its name to the Comte de Frontenac, governor of the French colony between 1672 and 1698. Looking at the magnificence of the château, you can see why Frontenac said, "For me, there is no site more beautiful nor more grandiose than that of Québec City."

Samuel de Champlain, who founded Québec City in 1608, was responsible for Château St-Louis, the first structure to appear on the site of the Frontenac; it was built between 1620 and 1624 as a residence for colonial governors. In 1784, Château Haldimand was constructed here, but it was demolished in 1892 to make way for Château Frontenac. The latter was built as a hotel in 1893, and it was considered to be remarkably luxurious at that time: Guest rooms contained fireplaces, private bathrooms, and marble fixtures, and a special commissioner traveled to England and France in search of antiques for the establishment. The hotel was designed by New York architect Bruce Price, who also worked on Québec City's **Gare du Palais** (Rail Station) and other Canadian landmarks, such as Montréal's Windsor Station. The Frontenac was completed in 1925 with the addition of a 20-story central tower. Owned by Canadian Pacific Hotels, it has accumulated a star-studded guest roster, including Queen Elizabeth, Madame Chiang Kai-shek, Ronald Reagan, and François Mitterrand, as well as Franklin Roosevelt and Winston Churchill, who convened here in 1943 and 1944 for two wartime conferences. As you head to the boardwalk behind the Frontenac, notice the glorious bronze statue of Samuel de Champlain, situated where he built his residence. The statue's steps are made of des Vosges granite, and the pedestal consists of Château-Landon stone, the same material used for the Arc de Triomphe in Paris.

❸ Walk south along the boardwalk called the **Terrasse Dufferin** for a panoramic view of the St. Lawrence River, the town of Lévis on the opposite shore, Île d'Orléans, and the Laurentian Mountains. The wide boardwalk, with an intricate wrought-iron guardrail, was named after Lord Dufferin, who was governor of Canada between 1872 and 1878 and who had this walkway constructed in 1878. At its western tip begins the **Promenade des Gouverneurs,** which skirts along the cliff and leads up to Québec's highest point, Cap Diamant (Cape Diamond), and also to the Citadel.

❹ As you pass to the southern side of the Frontenac, you will come to a small park called **Jardin des Gouverneurs** (Governors' Park), which is bordered by three streets of old manors. During the French regime, the public area served as a garden for the governors who resided in Château St-Louis. The park's Wolfe-Montcalm Monument, a 50-foot obelisk, is unique in that it pays tribute to both a winning (English) and a losing (French) general. The monument recalls the 1759 battle on the Plains of Abraham, which ended French rule of New France. British General James Wolfe lived only long enough to hear of his victory; French Général Louis-Joseph Montcalm died shortly after Wolfe with the knowledge that the city was lost. *Admission free. Open daily.*

On the southeast corner of the park is the **U.S. Consulate** (2 Place Terrasse Dufferin). On the south side of the park is **avenue Ste-Geneviève,** lined with well-preserved Victorian homes dating from 1850 to 1900 that have been converted to quaint old-fashioned inns.

❺ Make your way to the north side of the park and follow rue Mont Carmel until you come to another small park landscaped with footpaths and flower beds, **Cavalier du Moulin.** The former stone wind-

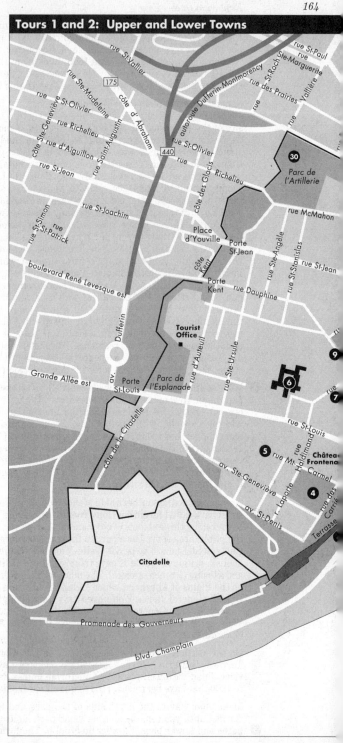

## Tours 1 and 2: Upper and Lower Towns

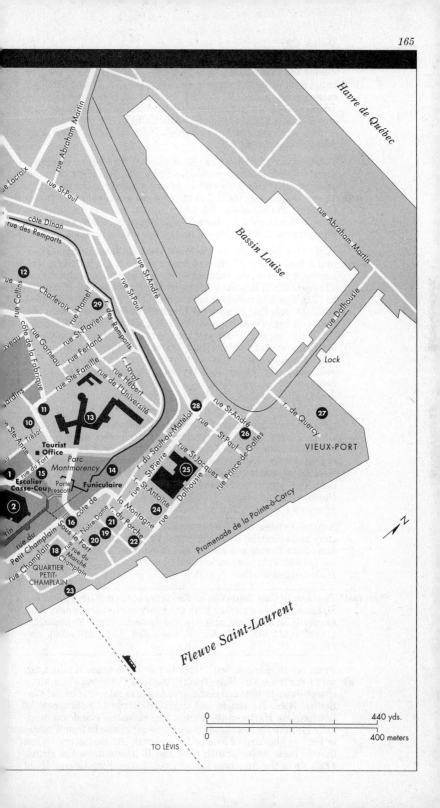

Havre de Québec

rue Abraham Martin

rue St-Paul

rue Lacroix

côte Dinan

rue des Remparts

Bassin Louise

rue Abraham Martin

rue St-André

rue St-Paul

rue Dalhousie

12

rue Collins

Charlevoix

rue Hamel

29

r. des Remparts

côte de la Fabrique

rue Garneau

rue St-Flavien

rue Ferland

rue Ste-Famille

rue Laval

rue Hébert

rue de l'Université

Lock

Jardins

11

13

rue St-André

28

rue St-Paul

r. de Quercy

27

10

Ste-Anne

Trésor

rue St-Jacques

26

VIEUX-PORT

Tourist
Office

Parc
Montmorency

14

r. du Sault-au-Matelot

rue St-Pierre

St-Paul

rue St-Antoine

rue Prince-de-Galles

rue Dalhousie

1

15

rue du Fort

Porte
Prescott

Funiculaire

25

Escalier
Casse-Cou

2

côte de la Montagne

24

Promenade de la Pointe-à-Carcy

rue du
Petit Champlain

Sous le Fort

16

Notre-Dame

21

r. du Porche

19

22

N

18

rue du
Marché-
Champlain

rue
Champlain

QUARTIER
PETIT-
CHAMPLAIN

23

Fleuve Saint-Laurent

0          440 yds.

0          400 meters

TO LÉVIS

mill, which became part of the French fortifications, was considered during the 17th century to be located on the outskirts of town because most of the city was situated below the cliff. The windmill was strategically placed so that its cannons could destroy the Cap-Diamant Redoubt (situated near Promenade des Gouverneurs) and the St-Louis Bastion (near St-Louis Gate) in the event that New France was captured by the British. *Admission free. Open May–Nov., daily 7 AM–9 PM.*

Retrace your steps down rue Mont Carmel, turn left on rue Haldimand and left again on rue St-Louis; then make a right on rue du Parloir until it intersects with a tiny street called rue Donnacona. At 12 rue Donnacona, you'll find the **Couvent des Ursulines** (Ursuline Convent), the site of North America's oldest teaching institution for girls, which is still a private school. Founded in 1639 by two French nuns, the convent has many of its original walls still intact.

Within the convent walls, the **Musée des Ursulines** (Ursuline Museum) is housed in the former residence of one of the founders, Madame de la Peltrie. The museum offers an informative perspective on 120 years of the Ursulines' life under the French regime, from 1639 to 1759. Exhibits tell of the early days of New France. For instance, you'll discover that because the Ursulines were without heat in winter, their heavy clothing sometimes weighed as much as 20 pounds. You'll also see why it took an Ursuline nun nine years of training to attain the level of a professional embroiderer; the museum contains magnificent pieces of ornate embroidery, such as altar frontals with gold and silver threads intertwined with precious jewels. *12 rue Donnacona, tel. 418/694–0694. Admission: $2.50 adults, $1.25 students, $1.50 senior citizens, $5.75 families. Open Jan.–Nov., Tues.–Sat. 9:30–noon and 1:30–4:40, Sun. 12:30–5:15.*

At the same address is the **Chapelle des Ursulines** (Ursuline Chapel), where French Général Montcalm was buried after he died in the 1759 battle. The chapel's exterior was rebuilt in 1902, but the interior contains the original chapel, which is the work of sculptor Pierre-Noël Levasseur, accomplished between 1726 and 1736. The votive lamp here was lit in 1717 and has never been extinguished. *12 rue Donnacona. Admission free. Open May–Oct., Tues.–Sat. 9:30–noon and 1:30–4:40, Sun. 12:30–5:15.*

Next to the museum at the **Centre Marie-de-l'Incarnation** are a bookstore and an exhibit on the life of the Ursulines' first superior, who came from France and cofounded the convent. *10 rue Donnacona, tel. 418/692–1569. Admission free. Open Feb.–Nov., Tues.–Sat. 10–11:30 and 2–4:30, Sun. 2–4:30.*

**Time Out**  The neon-lit **Café Taste-Vin,** on the corner of rue des Jardins and rue St-Louis, shares a kitchen with the gourmet restaurant next door; sample delicious salads, pastries, and desserts. *32 rue St-Louis, tel. 418/692–4191. AE, DC, MC, V. Open Feb.–Oct., daily 7:30 AM–11 PM.*

From rue Donnacona, walk north to rue des Jardins. Within a few yards you'll see the **Holy Trinity Anglican Cathedral.** This stone church dates to 1804 and is the first Anglican cathedral outside the British Isles. Its simple and dignified facade is reminiscent of London's St. Martin-in-the-Fields. The cathedral's land was originally given to the Recollet fathers (Franciscan monks from France) in 1681 by the king of France for a church and monastery. When Québec came under British rule, the Recollets made the church available to the Anglicans for services. Later, King George III of

England ordered construction of the present cathedral, with an area set aside for members of the royal family. A portion of the north balcony still remains exclusively for the use of the reigning sovereign or her representative. The church houses precious objects donated by George III. The oak benches were imported from the Royal Forest at Windsor. The cathedral's impressive rear organ has more than 2,500 pipes. *31 rue des Jardins, tel. 418/692–2193. Admission free. Open June–Aug., daily 9–9; Sept.–mid-Oct., weekdays 9–3.*

The building on the corner of rue des Jardins and rue Ste-Anne is one of Québec City's finest Art Deco structures. Geometric patterns of stone and wrought iron decorate the interior of the **Hôtel Clarendon** (57 rue Ste-Anne, tel. 418/692–2480). Although the Clarendon dates back to 1866, it was reconstructed with its current Art Deco decor in 1930.

More Art Deco can be found next door at 65 rue Ste-Anne, the 15-story **Edifice Price** (Price Building). The city's first skyscraper was built in 1929 and served as the headquarters of the Price Brothers Company, the lumber company founded in Canada by Sir William Price. Today it is owned by the provincial government and houses the offices of Québec City's mayor. Don't miss the interior: Exquisite copper plaques depict scenes of the company's early pulp and paper activities, while the two artfully carved maple-wood elevators are '30s classics.

Head back on rue Ste-Anne past the Holy Trinity Anglican Cathedral and continue straight on this street until it becomes a narrow, cobblestone thoroughfare lined with boutiques and restaurants. During the summer, the activity here starts buzzing early in the morning and continues until late at night. Stores stay open, artists paint, and street musicians perform as long as there is an audience, even if it's one o'clock in the morning.

Turn left into a narrow alley called **rue du Trésor,** where hundreds of colorful prints, paintings, and other artworks are on display. You won't necessarily find masterpieces here, but this walkway is a good stop for a souvenir sketch or two. During the French regime people came to this street to pay rent to the crown; the royal treasury stood at the end of the street, at Maison Maillou.

At the bottom of rue du Trésor, turn left on rue Buade. When you reach the corner of côte de la Fabrique, you'll see the **Basilique Notre-Dame-de-Québec** (Our Lady of Québec Basilica), with the oldest parish in North America, dating to 1647. The basilica has been rebuilt on three separate occasions: in the early 1700s, when François de Montmorency Laval was the first bishop; in 1759, after cannons at Lévis fired upon it during the siege of Québec, and in 1922, after a fire. This basilica has a somber ambience despite its ornate interior, which includes a canopy dais over the episcopal throne, a ceiling of clouds decorated with gold leaf, richly colored stained-glass windows, and a chancel lamp that was a gift of Louis XIV. Perhaps the solemn mood here may be attributed to the basilica's large and famous crypt, which was Québec City's first cemetery; more than 900 people are interred here, including 20 bishops and four governors of New France. The founder of Québec City, Samuel de Champlain, is believed to be buried somewhere near the basilica. Archaeologists have been searching for his tomb for more than 40 years. *16 rue Buade, tel. 418/692–2533. Admission free. Open daily 8–6.*

The basilica marks the beginning of Québec City's Latin Quarter, which extends to the streets northwest of Québec Seminary (rue

Buade, rue des Remparts, côte de la Fabrique, and côte du Palais) as far as rue St-Jean. This district was deemed the Latin Quarter because Latin was once a required language course at the seminary and was spoken among the students. Although Latin is no longer compulsory and Québec Seminary–Laval University has moved out to a larger campus in Sainte-Foy, students still cling to this neighborhood.

Head down côte de la Fabrique and turn right when it meets rue Collins. The cluster of old stone buildings sequestered at the end of the street is the **Monastère des Augustines de l'Hôtel-Dieu de Québec** (Augustine Monastery). Augustine nuns arrived from Dieppe, France, in 1639 with a mission to care for the sick in the new colony, and they established the first hospital north of Mexico, the **Hôtel-Dieu Hospital,** which is the large building west of the monastery. The **Musée des Augustines** (Augustine Museum) is housed in hospital-like quarters with large sterile corridors leading into a ward that features a small exhibit of antique medical instruments used by the Augustines, such as an 1850 microscope and a pill-making device from the 17th century.

Upon request, the Augustines also offer guided tours of the chapel (1800) and the cellars used by the nuns as a hiding place beginning in 1659, during bombardments by the British. *32 rue Charlevoix, tel. 418/692–2492. Admission free. Open Tues.–Sat. 9:30–11:30 and 1:30–5, Sun. 1:30–5.*

---

**Time Out**    For a crusty white or whole-wheat croissant, try **Croissant Plus** (50 rue Garneau, tel. 418/692–4215).

---

Retrace your steps on Collins Street and côte de la Fabrique. When you reach rue Ste-Famille on the left, you will find the wrought-iron entrance gates of the **Séminaire de Québec** (Québec Seminary). Behind these gates lies a tranquil courtyard surrounded by austere stone buildings with rising steeples; these structures have housed classrooms and student residences since 1663. The seminary was founded by François de Montmorency Laval, the first bishop of New France, to train priests of the new colony. In 1852 the seminary became Université Laval (Laval University), the first Catholic university in North America. The university eventually outgrew these cramped quarters; in 1946, Laval moved to a larger, modern campus in the suburb of Sainte-Foy. The Musée du Séminaire (*see below*) offers guided tours of the seminary during the summer. *1 côte de la Fabrique.*

Head north across the courtyard to the **Musée du Séminaire** (Seminary Museum). Housed in a former student residence, the museum focuses on the three centuries of the seminary's existence, until 1940. It emphasizes European secular and religious works of art; there are more than 400 landscape and still-life paintings dating as far back as the 15th century. The museum also houses a showcase of scientific instruments that were acquired through the centuries for the purposes of research and teaching. A former chapel has been renovated and now holds an exhibit of elegant religious and secular antique silver. The museum also has a rare collection of Canadian money that was used in colonial times. *9 rue de l'Université, tel. 418/692–2843. Admission: $3 adults, $1.50 students, $1 children under 16, $2 senior citizens, $6 families; Tues. free. Open June–Sept., daily 10–5:30; Oct.–May, Tues.–Sun. 10–5.*

Then visit the Québec Seminary's **Chapelle Extérieure** (Outer Chapel), at the seminary's west entrance. The small Roman-style chapel was built in 1888, after the fire destroyed the first chapel, built in 1750. In 1950 a memorial crypt of Laval was added here. The chapel is open in the summer only, and follows the same schedule as the museum (*see above*).

Now exit the seminary from the east at rue de l'Université and head south to côte de la Montagne, where **Parc Montmorency** (Montmorency Park) straddles the hill between Upper Town and Lower Town. This park marks the spot where Canada's first wheat was grown in 1618 and where the nation's first legislation was passed in 1694. A monument stands in tribute to Louis Herbert, a former apothecary and the first Canadian farmer, who cleared and tilled this area's land.

In 1688, Monseigneur de Saint-Vallier, the second bishop of New France, had his residence, the first episcopal palace, built here. In 1792 the palace's chapel became the seat of the first parliament of Lower Canada. The chapel was demolished in 1833, and a new legislative building was constructed that served as Québec's parliament until 1883, when it was destroyed by fire. A park monument commemorates Georges-Étienne Cartier, a French Canadian political leader and a father of the 1867 Confederation.

Take the **Escalier Frontenac** (Frontenac Stairway) up to the north end of the Terrasse Dufferin. You may be out of breath, but the climb is worth it for the 30-minute recap on the six sieges of Québec City at the **Musée du Fort** (Fort Museum). This museum's sole exhibit is a sound-and-light show with a model of 18th-century Québec that reenacts the region's most important battles, including the Battle of the Plains of Abraham and the 1775 attack by American generals Arnold and Montgomery. *10 rue Ste-Anne, tel. 418/692–2175. Admission: $4.75 adults, $3.75 senior citizens, $2.75 students. Open June–Aug., daily 10–6; Apr.–May, Sept.–Oct., daily 10–5; Nov.–Mar., weekdays 11–3, weekends 11–5.*

As you exit from the museum, head southeast to the funicular booth along Terrasse Dufferin. Ride the funicular ($1.10) to Lower Town to begin Tour 2.

## Tour 2: Lower Town

New France began to flourish in the streets of Lower Town along the banks of the St. Lawrence River. These streets became the colony's economic crossroads, where furs were traded, ships came in, and merchants established their residences.

Despite the status of Lower Town as the oldest neighborhood in North America, its narrow and time-worn thoroughfares have a new and polished look. In the '60s, after a century of decay as the commercial boom moved west and left Lower Town an abandoned district, the Québec government committed millions of dollars to restore the area to the way it had been during the days of New France. Today modern boutiques, restaurants, galleries, and shops catering to tourists occupy the former warehouses and residences.

Begin this tour on the northern tip of rue du Petit-Champlain at **Maison Louis-Jolliet** (16 rue du Petit-Champlain, tel. 418/692–1132), which houses the lower station of the funicular and a souvenir shop. Built in 1683, this home was used by the first settlers of New France as a base for further westward explorations. It was in 1672, however, that Louis Jolliet—the first Canadian born in Québec to make history—discovered the Mississippi River. A monument commemorating this discovery stands in the park next to the house. At the north side of the house is **Escalier Casse-Cou** (Breakneck Steps), the city's first iron stairway. Its steepness is ample evidence of how it got its name. Its ambitious 1893 design was by Charles Baillairgé, a city architect and engineer, and it was built on the site of the original 17th-century stairway that linked Upper Town and Lower Town during the French regime. Today tourist shops, quaint boutiques, and restaurants are situated at various levels.

**17** Heading south on **rue du Petit-Champlain,** the city's oldest street, you'll notice the cliff on the right that borders this narrow thoroughfare, with Upper Town situated on the heights above. Rue du Petit-Champlain retains its size from when it was the main street of a harbor village, replete with trading posts and the homes of rich merchants. In 1977 artists, craftspeople, and private investors decided to initiate a revival of the street; today it consists of pleasant boutiques and cafés. The best buys here are the ceramics, wood carvings, and jewelry done by local artists. Natural-fiber weaving, Inuit carvings, hand-painted silks, and enameled copper crafts are some of the local specialties for sale.

At the point where rue du Petit-Champlain intersects with boulevard Champlain, make a U-turn to head back north on rue Champlain. One block farther, at the corner of rue du Marché-Champlain,
**18** you'll find **Maison Chevalier,** an annex of the ethnographic Civilization Museum. This old stone house was built in 1752 for shipowner Jean-Baptiste Chevalier. It was restored in 1959, adding two 17th-century buildings to the original structure. Inside you will find the original wood beams and stone fireplaces, and an exhibit of 18th-century furniture. *50 rue du Marché-Champlain, tel. 418/643–2158. Admission free. Open late May–late June, Tues.–Sun. 10–5; late June–early Sept., daily 10–5; early Sept.–early Oct., Tues.–Sun. 10–5.*

East of Maison Chevalier, take rue Notre-Dame, which leads direct-
**19** ly to **Place Royale,** formerly the heart of New France. This cobblestone square is encircled by buildings with steep Normandy-style roofs, dormer windows, and several chimneys. These were once the homes of wealthy merchants. Until 1686 the area was called Place du Marché, but its name was changed when a bust of Louis XIV, *"le Roi Soleil"* (the Sun King), was erected at its center.

During the late 1600s and early 1700s, when Place Royale was continually under threat of attacks from the British, the colonists progressively moved to higher and safer quarters atop the cliff in Upper Town. Yet after the French colony fell to British rule in 1759, Place Royale flourished again with shipbuilding, logging, fishing, and fur trading.

The small stone church at the south side of the Place Royale is the
**20** **Église Notre-Dame-des-Victoires** (Our Lady of Victory Church), the oldest church in Québec, dating to 1688. It was built on the site of Samuel de Champlain's first residence, which also served as a fort and trading post. However, the church had to be completely restored on two occasions: after a fire in 1759 and more recently in 1969. It got its name from two French victories against the British: one in 1690 against Admiral William Phipps and another in 1711 against Sir Hovendon Walker. The interior contains copies of such European masters as Van Dyck, Rubens, and Boyermans; its altar resembles the shape of a fort. A scale model suspended from the ceiling represents *Le Brezé,* the boat that transported French soldiers to New France in 1664. The side chapel is dedicated to Sainte-Geneviève, the guardian saint of Paris. *Place Royale, tel. 418/692–1650.*

*Admission free. Open mid-May–Sept., daily 9–4, except during Mass (Sun. 9:30, 11, and noon; May–Oct., Sat. 7 PM), marriages, and funerals; Oct.–mid-May, Tues.–Sat. 8:30–noon.*

㉑ Turn to the northwest corner of the square to the cool, dark, and musty cellars of the **Maison des Vins,** a former warehouse dating to 1689; here the Québec Société des Alcools sells more than 1,000 kinds of rare and vintage wines, which range in price from $10 to $1,000. *1 Pl. Royale, tel. 418/643–1214. Admission free. Open Tues. and Wed. 9:30–5:30, Thurs. and Fri. 9:30–9, Sat. 9:30–5.*

㉒ On the east side of Place Royale, take rue de la Place, which leads to an open square, **Place de Paris,** a newcomer to these historic quarters. Looming at its center is a black-and-white geometric sculpture, Dialogue avec l'Histoire (Dialogue with History), a gift from France positioned on the site where the first French settlers landed. Paris Mayor Jacques Chirac inaugurated the square in August 1987 with Québec City's Mayor Jean Pelletier. Its French counterpart is the Place du Québec, inaugurated in 1984 at St-Germain-des-Prés in Paris.

㉓ At this point of the tour you may conveniently catch the 15-minute **Lévis–Québec ferry** to the opposite shore of the St. Lawrence River. The boat docks a block south on rue Dalhousie; we recommend that you take the ferry for the opportunity of an unprecedented view of Québec City's skyline, with the Château Frontenac and the Québec Seminary high above the cliff. The view is even more impressive at night. *First ferry leaves at 6:30 AM. Crossings run every ½ hr between 7:30 AM and 6:30 PM, every hr between 7:30 PM and 2:30 AM, with a final crossing at 3:45 AM. Cost: $1.25 adults, 75¢ children and senior citizens.*

**Time Out**   **Café Loft,** located in a converted garage on rue Dalhousie between Place de Paris and the Civilization Museum, offers delectable desserts, such as a pyramid-shape chocolate cake. Grab an inviting *baguette* sandwich and equally scrumptious quiches and salads. *49 rue Dalhousie, tel. 418/692–4864. AE, DC, MC, V. Open Mon.–Thurs. 11–11, Fri. 11 AM–1 AM, Sat. 9 AM–1 AM, Sun. 9 AM–11 PM.*

㉔ Next door to the Café Loft you will notice the new diorama, **Explore.** This 30-minute sound-and-light show works on the same principle as the one at the Musée du Fort (*see* Tour 1), except that it uses more modern diorama technology. The show tells the story of Québec and the age of exploration, opening with the native Indians and leading up to Cartier's entrance into the St. Lawrence River. *63 rue Dalhousie, tel. 418/692–2175. Admission: $4.75 adults, $3.75 senior citizens, $2.75 students. Open June–Aug., daily 10–6; Apr.–May, Sept., and Oct., daily 10–5; Nov.–Mar., weekdays 11–3, weekends 11–5.*

㉕ Continue north on the rue Dalhousie until you come to the **Musée de la Civilisation** (Civilization Museum). Wedged into the foot of the cliff, this spacious museum, with its striking limestone and glass facade, has been artfully designed to blend into the city landscape. Architect Moshe Safdie skillfully incorporated three historic buildings into the museum's modern structure: the house Estèbe, the site of the First Bank of Québec, and the Maison Pagé-Quercy. Many of the materials that were used to construct the newer portions of the museum are native to Québec province. The building's campanile echoes the shape of church steeples throughout the city.

The museum, which opened officially in 1988, houses innovative, entertaining, and sometimes playful exhibits devoted to aspects of Québec's culture and civilization. Several of the shows, with their imaginative use of artwork, video screens, computers, and sound, will appeal to both adults and children. An excellent permanent exhibition, "Memoires" ("Memories"), considers both Québec's history and French Canadian society today. In addition, there are dance, music, and theater performances and a good boutique for high-quality souvenirs. Guides are available in the exhibition rooms. *85 rue Dalhousie, tel. 418/643–2158. Admission: $5 adults, $4 senior citizens, $3 students; children under 16 free; Tues. free in winter. Open late June–early Sept., Thurs.–Tues. 10–7, Wed. 10–9; early Sept.–late June, Tues. and Thurs.–Sun. 10–5, Wed. 10–9.*

**26** Across the street you'll find the **Naturalium**, Québec's new natural sciences museum. It features a fascinating showcase of 100,000 insects and arthropods; most are preserved, however some—like tarantulas and cockroaches—are very much alive. It houses over 800 preserved mammals, including some realistic portrayals of animals in nature. There are also 500 fossils and numerous minerals on display. The collection belongs to Georges Brossard, a self-taught entomologist and biologist.

One permanent exhibit, "Le Monde" ("The World"), is devoted to explaining the reproduction, nutrition, habitat, and social organization of living creatures. Another focuses on the Saint Lawrence River's fauna, and the constant struggle against its harsh environment. Also, visitors may drop by the laboratory to witness the procedure used to prepare the specimens for display. *84 rue Dalhousie, tel. 418/692–1515. Admission: $6.00 adults, $4.50 senior citizens over 60, $4 children 5–17, under 5 free. Open late June–early Sept., daily 10–9; early Sept.–late June, daily 10–5.*

**27** From rue Dalhousie, head east toward the river to the **Vieux-Port de Québec** (Old Port of Québec). The breezes here from the St. Lawrence provide a cool reprieve on a hot summer's day. The old harbor dates to the 17th century, when ships first arrived from Europe bringing supplies and settlers to the new colony. At one time this port was among the busiest on the continent: Between 1797 and 1897, Québec shipyards turned out more than 2,500 ships, many of which passed the 1,000-ton mark. Yet Québec City's port saw a rapid decline after steel replaced wood and the channel to Montréal was deepened to allow larger boats to reach a good port upstream. In 1984, the 72-acre port was restored with a $100 million grant from the federal government; today it encompasses several parks. You can stroll along the riverside promenade, where merchant and cruise ships are docked. At its northern end, where the St. Charles meets the St. Lawrence, a lock protects the marina in the Louise basin from the generous tides of the St. Lawrence. Because Québec City is close to the Atlantic Ocean, it is susceptible to tides, which can range from 9 to 16 feet. At the northwest area of the port, an exhibition center, **Port de Québec in the 19th Century,** presents the history of the port in relation to the lumber trade and shipbuilding. *100 rue St-André, tel. 418/648–3300.*

The port's northwestern tip features the **Marché du Vieux-Port** (Farmer's Market), where farmers come from the countryside to sell their fresh produce. *Admission free. Open May–Oct., daily 8–8.*

**28** You are now in the ideal spot to explore Québec City's **antiques district.** One block south from rue St-André, antiques boutiques cluster along rue St-Pierre and rue St-Paul (*see* Shopping, *below*). Rue St-

Paul was formerly part of a business district where warehouses, stores, and businesses once abounded. After World War I, when shipping and commercial activities plummeted, the street consisted mainly of empty warehouses and offices. In 1964, the low rent and commercial nature of the area attracted several antiques dealers, who set up shops along rue St-Paul. Today numerous cafés, restaurants, and art galleries have turned this area into one of the town's more fashionable sections.

Walk west along rue St-Paul and turn left onto a steep brick incline called côte Dambourges; when you reach côte de la Cantonerie, take the stairs back on the cliff to rue des Remparts. Continue approximately a block west along rue des Remparts until you come to the last building in a row of purple houses. **Maison Montcalm** was the home of French Général Louis-Joseph Montcalm from 1758 until the capitulation of New France. A plaque dedicated to the general is situated on the right side of the house.

Continue west on rue des Remparts and turn left on rue de l'Arsenal, which brings you to the **Parc de l'Artillerie** (Artillery Park). This National Historic Park is a complex of 20 military, industrial, and civilian buildings, so situated to guard the St. Charles River and the Old Port. Its earliest buildings served as headquarters for the French garrison and were taken over in 1759 by the British Royal Artillery soldiers. The defense complex was used as a fortress, barracks, and cartridge factory during the American siege of Québec in 1775 and 1776. The area was converted to an industrial complex providing ammunition for the Canadian army from 1879 until 1964, when it became a historic park. *2 rue d'Auteil, tel. 418/648–4205. Admission: $3 adults, $1.50 children 6–16, senior citizens and children under 6 free, $6 families. Open late June–early Sept., daily 10–5.*

One of the three buildings you may visit is a former **powder house**, which in 1903 became a shell foundry. The building houses a detailed model of Québec City in 1808, rendered by two surveyors in the office of the Royal Engineers Corps, Jean-Baptiste Duberger of Québec and John By of England. The wood model was intended to show British officials (it was sent to England in 1813) the strategic importance of Québec so that more money would be provided to expand the city's fortifications. The model, which details the city's houses, buildings, streets, and military structures, is an accurate portrayal of Québec during the early 19th century. *Open early Sept.–early May, daily 1–5; early May–early Sept., daily 10–5.*

The **Dauphine Redoubt** (*dauphine* is "heir apparent" in English) was named after the son of Louis XIV and was constructed from 1712 to 1748. It served as a barracks for the French garrison until 1760, when it became an officers' mess for the Royal Artillery Regiment. When the British called their soldiers back to England in 1871, it became a residence for the Canadian Arsenal superintendent. *Open late June–early Sept., daily 10–5.*

The **Officers' Quarters** building, a dwelling for Royal Artillery officers until 1871 when the British army departed, is now a museum for children, with shows on military life during the British regime. *Open late June–early Sept., daily 10–5.*

## Tour 3: Outside the City Walls

*Numbers in the margin correspond to points of interest on the Tour 3: Outside the City Walls map.*

In the 20th century, Québec City grew into a modern metropolis outside the city walls and its historic confines. In this tour, you will see a glimpse of modern-day Québec City and explore neighborhoods typically left off the tourist track.

**❸❶** Start close to St-Louis Gate at **Parc de l'Esplanade** (Esplanade Park), the site of a former military drill and parade ground. In the 19th century, this area was a clear and uncluttered space surrounded by a picket fence and poplar trees. Today you'll find the completely renovated **Poudrière de l'Esplanade** (Powder Magazine), which the British constructed in 1820; it houses a model depicting the evolution of the wall surrounding the Old City. *100 rue St-Louis, tel. 418/648-7016. Admission free. Open Apr., daily 1–5; May–Oct., daily 10–5.*

Esplanade Park is also the starting point to walk the city's 4.6 kilometers (3 miles) of walls; in the summer, guided tours begin here. The French began building ramparts along the city's natural cliff as early as 1690 to protect themselves from British invaders. But by 1759, when the British gained control of New France, the walls were still incomplete; the British took a century to finish them.

From the Powder Magazine, head south on Côte de la Citadelle, **❸❷** which leads directly to the **Citadelle** (Citadel). Built at the city's highest point, the Citadel is the largest fortified base in North America still occupied by troops. The 25-building fortress was intended to protect the port, prevent the enemy from taking up a position on the Plains of Abraham, and provide a last refuge in case of an attack. The French had constructed previous structures on this site based on plans of Québec engineer Gaspard Chaussegros de Léry, who came to the region in 1716.

Having inherited incomplete fortifications, the British sought to complete the Citadel to protect themselves against retaliations from the French. As fate would have it, by the time the Citadel was completed in 1832, the invasions and attacks against Québec City had ended.

Since 1920 the Citadel has served as a base for the Royal 22nd Regiment. A collection of firearms, uniforms, and decorations from the 17th century is housed in the **Royal 22nd Regiment Museum,** located in the former powder house, built in 1750. If weather permits, you may witness the Changing of the Guard, an elaborate ceremony in which the troops parade before the Citadel in the customary red coats and black fur hats. *Côte de la Citadelle, tel. 418/648-3563. Guided tours only. Admission: $4 adults, $2 students under 18; free for people with disabilities. Open mid-Mar.–Apr., daily 10–3; May and June, daily 9–4; July–early Sept., daily 9–6; early Sept.–Oct., daily 9–4; Nov.–early Feb. and mid-Feb.–mid-March, groups only (reservations required); early Feb.–mid-Feb., daily 10–2. Changing of the Guard: mid-June–Labor Day, daily 10. Tattoo: July and Aug., Tues., Thurs., and weekends 7 PM (for visitors on 6 PM tour only).*

Retrace your steps back down côte de la Citadelle to Grande Allée. **❸❸** Continue west until you come to the Renaissance-style **Parliament Buildings,** which mark the area known as **Parliament Hill,** headquarters of the provincial government. The constitution of 1791 designated Québec City the capital of Lower Canada until the 1840 Act of Union that united both Upper and Lower Canada and made Montréal the capital. In 1867, the Act of Confederation, uniting Québec, Ontario, New Brunswick, and Nova Scotia, made Québec City the capital of Québec province. Today the government is the biggest em-

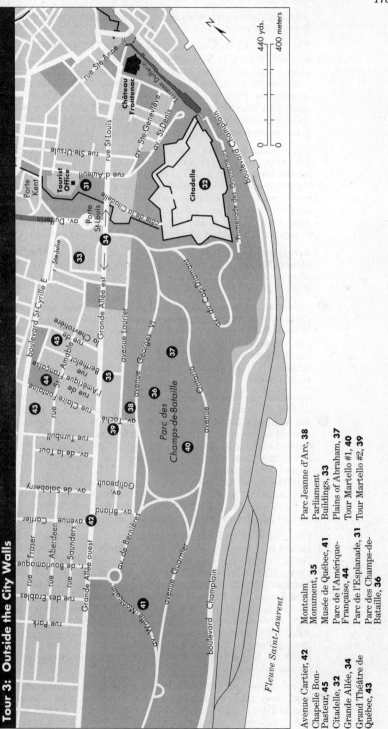

# Tour 3: Outside the City Walls

Avenue Cartier, **42**
Chapelle Bon-
Pasteur, **45**
Citadelle, **32**
Grande Allée, **34**
Grand Théâtre de
Québec, **43**

Montcalm
Monument, **35**
Musée de Québec, **41**
Parc de l'Amérique-
Française, **44**
Parc de l'Esplanade, **31**
Parc des Champs-de-
Bataille, **36**

Parc Jeanne d'Arc, **38**
Parliament
Buildings, **33**
Plains of Abraham, **37**
Tour Martello #1, **40**
Tour Martello #2, **39**

175

ployer in Québec City, with about 30,000 civil servants working and living in the area.

The Parliament Buildings, erected between 1877 and 1884, are the seat of **L'Assemblée Nationale** (the National Assembly) of 125 provincial representatives. Québec architect Eugène-Étienne Taché designed the classic and stately buildings in the late 17th-century Renaissance style of Louis XIV, with four wings set in a square around an interior court. In front of the Parliament, statues pay tribute to important figures of Québec history: Cartier, de Champlain, de Frontenac, Wolfe, and Montcalm.

The Parliament offers a 30-minute tour (in English or French) of the President's Gallery, the National Assembly Chamber, and the Legislative Council Chamber. The chamber of the 125-member National Assembly is decorated in green, white, and gold—colors that correspond to the House of Commons in both London and Ottawa. *Cnr. of av. Dufferin and Grande Allée E, door 3, tel. 418/643–7239. Admission free. Guided tours Jan.–May and Sept.–Nov., weekdays 9–4:30; late June–Aug., daily 9–4:30. Reservations required.*

Across from the Parliament on the south side of Grande Allée is the **Manège Militaire,** a turreted granite armory built in 1888, four years after the Parliament Buildings. It was also designed by Taché. It is still a drill hall for the 22nd Regiment.

**㉞** Continue along **Grande Allée,** Québec City's version of the Champs-Elysées, with its array of trendy cafés, clubs, and restaurants. One of the oldest streets, Grande Allée was the route people took from outlying areas to sell their furs in Québec City. The street actually has four names: in the old city, it is rue St-Louis; outside the walls, Grande Allée; farther west, chemin St-Louis; and farther still, boulevard Laurier.

One block after the armory, on your left (the south side of Grande Allée) you'll come to Place Montcalm. If you turn left, you'll be facing
**㉟** the **Montcalm Monument.** France and Canada joined together to erect this monument honoring Louis-Joseph Montcalm, who claimed his fame by winning four major battles in North America—but his most famous battle was the one he lost, when the British conquered New France on September 13, 1759. Montcalm was north of Québec City at Beauport when he learned that the British attack was imminent. He quickly assembled his troops to meet the enemy and was wounded in battle in the leg and stomach. Montcalm was carried into the walled city, where he died the next morning.

Continue south on Place Montcalm to one of North America's larg-
**㊱** est and most scenic parks, **Parc des Champs-de-Bataille** (Battlefields Park). This 250-acre area of gently rolling slopes offers unparalleled
**㊲** views of the St. Lawrence River. West of the citadel are the **Plains of Abraham,** the site of the famous 1759 battle that decided the fate of New France. The Plains of Abraham were named after the river pilot Abraham Martin, who arrived in 1620 and owned several acres here. *A free shuttle bus circles the Plains of Abraham, with 11 stops. Also, a free guided bus tour of the Plains of Abraham is offered, leaving from the Battlefield Park Interpretation Center (Pavillon Baillargé, Musée de Québec, tel. 418/648–4071) mid-June–Aug. Telephone for departure times.*

Take avenue Laurier, which runs parallel to Battlefields Park, a
**㊳** block west until you come to a neatly tended garden called **Parc Jeanne d'Arc** (Joan of Arc Park); it is abundant with colorful flowers and is centered on an equestrian statue of Jeanne d'Arc. A symbol of

courage, this statue stands in tribute to the heroes of 1759 near the place where New France was lost to the British. The park also commemorates the Canadian national anthem *Oh Canada;* it was played here for the first time on June 24, 1880.

**39** If you continue west on avenue Laurier, you'll see a stone oval defense tower, **Tour Martello #2** (Martello Tower), on the north corner of avenue Taché and avenue Laurier. This is the second of four Martello towers built in the early 19th century around Québec City to slow the enemy's approach to the city. At the left, toward the south **40** end of the park, stands **Tour Martello #1,** which was built between 1802 and 1810.

Of the 16 Martello towers in all of Canada, four were built in Québec City because the British government feared an invasion after the American Revolution. Tour #3 was located near Jeffery Hale Hospital in order to guard westward entry to the city, but it was demolished in 1904. Tour #4 is located on rue Lavigueur overlooking rivière St-Charles (St. Charles River). Towers 1 and 2 are open to the public; the first exhibits the history of the four structures, the second has an astrology display.

Continue a block west on rue de Bernières and then follow avenue George V along the outskirts of Battlefields Park until it intersects with avenue Wolfe-Montcalm. You'll come to the tall **Wolfe Monument,** which marks the place where the British general died. Wolfe landed his troops less than 2 miles (about 3 kilometers) from the city's walls; the 4,500 English soldiers scaled the cliff and opened fire on the Plains of Abraham. Wolfe was mortally wounded in battle and was carried behind the lines to this spot.

**41** Turn left on avenue Wolfe-Montcalm for a leisurely stroll through the **Musée de Québec** (Québec Museum). This neoclassical beaux-arts showcase houses the finest collection of Québec art. With one of the largest acquisition budgets of Canada's museums, it possesses more than 18,000 traditional and contemporary pieces. The portraits done by artists well known in the area, such as Ozias Leduc (1864–1955) and Horatio Walker (1858–1938), are particularly notable; some locals find paintings of their relatives on the walls here. The museum's very formal and dignified building in Battlefields Park was designed by Wilfrid Lacroix and erected in 1933 to commemorate the tricentennial anniversary of the founding of Québec. The museum recently received $22.4 million from the provincial government to renovate the original building, incorporating the space of a nearby, abandoned prison dating to 1867. A hallway of cells, with the iron bars and courtyard still intact, has been preserved as part of a permanent exhibition of the prison's history. *1 av. Wolfe-Montcalm, tel. 418/643–2150. Admission: $4.75 adults, $3.75 senior citizens, $2.75 students, children under 16 free. Open June–Aug., Thurs.–Tues. 10–5:45, Wed. 10–9:45; Sept.–May, Tues. and Thurs.–Sun. 10–5:45, Wed. 10–9:45.*

From the museum head north on avenue Wolfe-Montcalm, turning right on Grande Allée and walking a block until you reach avenue Cartier. At 115 Grande Allée Ouest is the **Krieghoff House.** This typical Québec home with its bell-shape roof and dormer windows is closed to tourists, but it's worth noting for its former owner, Cornelius Krieghoff, who lived there from 1858 to 1860. One of Canada's most famous landscape painters, Krieghoff was among the first to depict Québec scenery. Born in Amsterdam in 1815, he served in the American army, married a French Canadian in 1839, and settled in Québec in 1852.

**42** Head north on **avenue Cartier** to indulge in the pleasures offered by the many good restaurants, clubs, and cafés lining the block. On the east side, stroll through the food mall, **Alimentation Petit-Cartier** (1191 avenue Cartier, tel. 418/524–3682). Here you'll find a supermarket and shops that sell French delicacies—cheeses, pastries, breads, and candies. Some of the better stores are **Boulangerie La Mère-Michele,** for breads and pastries such as petit fours, and **Le Vrac du Quartier,** where you can buy everything from spices to cookies in amounts you measure yourself. The mall also houses three restaurants: Café Rousseau, Le Piazetta, and Le Graffiti (*see* Dining, *below*).

**Time Out**  On the east side of avenue Cartier is **Café Krieghoff,** named after the 19th-century painter who lived nearby. Grab a newspaper, play a game of chess, drink some of the best coffee in town, and complement it with quiche, a croissant, or dessert. *1089 av. Cartier, tel. 418/522–3711. MC, V. Open Sun.–Wed. 7 AM–midnight, Thurs.–Sat. 7 AM–1 AM.*

If you continue north along avenue Cartier, the first major intersection is boulevard St-Cyrille Est. Turn right and walk two blocks to **43** the concrete modern building of the **Grand Théâtre de Québec,** a center for the city's performing arts and home of the music school, La Conservatoire de Musique de Québec. Opened in 1971, the theater incorporates two main halls, both named after 19th-century Canadian poets. The "Grande Salle" of Louis-Frechette, named after the first Québec poet and writer to be honored by the French Academy, holds 1,800 seats and is used for concerts, opera, and theater. The "Petite Salle" of Octave-Crémazie, used for experimental theater and variety shows, derives its name from the poet who stirred the rise of Québec nationalism in the mid-19th century.

As the complex was being constructed, Montréal architect Victor Prus commissioned Jordi Bonet, a Québec sculptor, to work simultaneously on a three-wall mural. The themes depicted in the three sections are death, life, and liberty. Bonet wrote "La Liberté" on one wall to symbolize the Québecois' struggle for freedom and cultural distinction. The theater has a full repertoire in the winter, but no shows in the summer. *269 boul. St-Cyrille E, tel. 418/646–0609. Guided tours offered daily 9–5. Reservations required.*

High-waving flags east of the Grand Théâtre are displayed in the **44** **Parc de l'Amérique-Française,** dedicated to places in North America with a French-speaking population. Québec's own Fleur de Lys leads the way. The colors of blue and white, an emblem of Sun King Louis XIV, constitute a reminder of Québec's French origins, culture, and language. Inaugurated in 1985 by Québec Prime Minister Réne Lévesque, the park also flies flags from Acadia, British Columbia, Louisiana, Manitoba, Saskatchewan, and Ontario.

Take rue Claire-Fontaine a block south, turn left on rue St-Amable, and then left again on rue de la Chevrotière. On the west side of the **45** street you'll see the **Chapelle Bon-Pasteur** (Bon-Pasteur Chapel), which is surrounded by modern office complexes. This slender church with a steep sloping roof was designed by Charles Baillargé in 1868. Its ornate interior in a baroque style has carved wood designs painted elaborately in gold leaf. The chapel houses 32 religious paintings done by the nuns of the community from 1868 to 1910. Classical concerts are performed here between October and June. *1080 rue de la Chevrotière, tel. 418/641–1069 or 418/648–9710. Ad-*

*mission free. Open May–Sept., Tues.–Sun. 1–4; Oct.–Apr., by reservation only; musical artists' Mass Sun. at 10:45.*

Across rue de la Chevrotière is the entrance of a large, gray concrete modern office tower called **Anima G** (Complex G), Québec's tallest office building. The structure, 31 stories high, has by far the best view of the city and the environs. An express elevator ascends to the observation gallery on top. *1037 rue de la Chevrotière, tel. 418/644–9841. Admission free. Open late Jan.–early Dec., weekdays 10–4, weekends and holidays 1–5.*

## What to See and Do with Children

**Aquarium du Québec** (Québec Aquarium). The aquarium, situated above the St. Lawrence River, houses more than 300 species of marine life, including reptiles, exotic fish, and seals from the lower St. Lawrence River. A wooded picnic area makes this spot ideal for a family outing. The Québec City transit system, Commission de Transport de la Communauté Urbaine de Québec (CTCUQ) (tel. 418/659–5264), runs buses here. *1675 av. des Hôtels, Sainte-Foy, tel. 418/659–5266. Admission: $5 adults, $1 children under 14, $4.25 senior citizens, $10 families. Open daily 9–5.*

**Jardin Zoologique du Québec** (Québec Zoological Gardens). Children usually enjoy going to zoos, but this one is especially scenic because of the DuBerger River, which traverses the grounds. About 250 animal species reside here, including bears, wildcats, primates, and birds of prey. Children will enjoy the farm and the horse-drawn carriage rides. The zoo is situated 11 kilometers (7 miles) west of Québec City on Route 73. Québec Urban Community Transit (tel. 418/627–2511) operates buses here. *8191 av. du Zoo, Charlesbourg, tel. 418/622–0312. Admission: (May–Oct.) $7 adults, $1 children under 14, $5 senior citizens, $14 families; (Nov.–Apr.) $4.25 adults, $1 children under 14, $3 senior citizens, $8 families. Open May–Oct., daily 9:30–6; Nov.–Apr., daily 9:30–5.*

**Parc Cartier-Brébeuf.** Stretched along the north bank of the St. Charles River, this national historic park commemorates the area where French explorer Jacques Cartier spent his first winter in Canada (1535–36); it also pays tribute to Father Jean de Brébeuf, founder of the Jesuit Order in New France. A replica of the *Grande Hermine*, the ship Cartier used on his second expedition to America, is stationed here. Playgrounds and 9 kilometers (5½ miles) of walking paths are available. *175 rue de l'Espinay, tel. 418/648–4038. Admission free. Call ahead for hrs.*

**Parc de l'Artillerie** (Artillery Park). This 20-building complex near St-Jean Gate has for centuries played an important part in the city's defense structures. The Officers' Quarters, barracks for Royal Artillery officers until 1871, has a special program for children designed to show how the military lived when Québec was a British colony, from 1759 to 1867. Children's toys and educational games are also available. *2 rue d'Auteil, tel. 418/648–4205. Admission: $3 adults, $1.50 children 6–16, $6 families, senior citizens and children under 6 free. Open late June–early Sept., daily 10–5.*

**Parc du Porche.** This playground has ladders and swings in a historic setting just outside Place Royale (between rue du Porche and rue de l'Union). *Admission free. Open daily.*

# Shopping

Shopping is European-style along the fashionable streets of Québec City. The boutiques and specialty shops clustered along narrow streets (such as rue du Petit-Champlain, or rue Buade and rue St-Jean in the Latin Quarter) are located within one of the most striking historic settings on the continent.

Prices in Québec City tend to be on a par for the most part with those in Montréal and other North American cities, so you won't have much luck hunting for bargains. When sales occur, they are usually listed in the French daily newspaper, *Le Soleil*.

Stores are generally open Monday through Wednesday 9:30–5:30, Thursday and Friday until 9, and Saturday until 5. During the summer, shops may be open seven days a week, and most have later evening hours.

## Shopping Centers

The mall situated closest to the Old City is **Place Québec** (5 Place Québec, tel. 418/529–0551), near the National Assembly. This multilevel shopping complex and convention center with 40 stores is connected to the Hilton International. **Alimentation Petit-Cartier** (1191 av. Cartier, tel. 418/524–3682), located off Grande Allée and a 15-minute walk from St-Louis Gate, is a food mall for gourmets, with everything from utensils to petits fours.

Other shopping centers are approximately a 15-minute drive west along Grande Allée. **Place Sainte-Foy** (2450 boul. Laurier, Sainte-Foy, tel. 418/653–4184) has 120 specialty stores. Next door is **Place de la Cité** (2600 boul. Laurier, Sainte-Foy, tel. 418/657–6920), with 120 boutiques. And finally there is the massive **Place Laurier** (2700 boul. Laurier, Sainte-Foy, tel. 418/653–9318), with more than 350 stores.

**Quartier Petit-Champlain** (tel. 418/692–2613) in Lower Town is a pedestrian mall with some 40 boutiques, local businesses, and restaurants. This popular district is the best area to find native Québec arts and crafts, such as wood sculptures, weaving, ceramics, and jewelry. Recommended stores in the area are **Poten-Ciel** (27 rue du Petit-Champlain, tel. 418/692–1743) for ceramics and **Pauline Pelletier** (38 rue du Petit-Champlain, tel. 418/692–4871) for porcelain.

## Department Stores

Large department stores can be found in the malls of the suburb of Sainte-Foy, but some have outlets inside Québec City's walls.

**Holt Renfrew & Co., Ltd.** (Place Sainte-Foy, Sainte-Foy, tel. 418/656–6783), one of the city's more exclusive stores, carries furs, perfume, and tailored designer collections for men and women.
**La Baie** (Place Laurier, Sainte-Foy, tel. 418/627–5959) is Québec's version of the Canadian Hudson's Bay Company conglomerate, founded in 1670 by Montréal trappers Pierre Radisson and Medard de Groseillers; the company established the first network of stores in the Canadian frontier. Today, La Baie carries both men's and women's clothing and household wares.
**Simons** (20 côte de la Fabrique, tel. 418/692–3630), one of Québec City's oldest family stores, used to be the city's only source for fine

British woolens and tweeds, and now the store has added a large selection of designer clothing, linens, and other household items.

## Food and Flea Markets

**Marché du Vieux-Port** enables farmers from the Québec countryside to sell their fresh produce in the Old Port near rue St-André, from May through October, 8–8.

**Rue du Trésor** hosts a flea market near the Place d'Armes that features sketches, paintings, and etchings by local artists. Fine portraits of the Québec City landscape and region are plentiful. Good, inexpensive souvenirs also may be purchased here (*see* Tour 1, *above*).

## Specialty Stores

Antiques    Québec City's antiques district is located in the area of rue St-Paul and rue St-Pierre, across from the Old Port. French Canadian, Victorian, and art deco furniture, along with clocks, silverware, and porcelain, are some of the rare collectibles that can be found here. Authentic Québec pine furniture, characterized by simple forms and lines, is becoming increasingly rare and costly.

**L'Héritage Antiquités** (110 rue St-Paul, tel. 418/692–1681) specializes in precious Québecois furniture from the 18th century.

**Antiquités Zaor** (112 rue St-Paul, tel. 418/692–0581), the oldest store on rue St-Paul, is still the best place in the area to find excellent English, French, and Canadian antiques. The floor upstairs houses a fine collection of Québec wood furniture.

Art    **Aux Multiples Collections** (43 rue Buade, tel. 418/692–4298) and **Galerie Brousseau et Brousseau** (Château Frontenac, 1 rue des Carrières, tel. 418/694–1828) feature a good selection of Inuit art done by Canada's native people, as well as such antique furniture and accessories as sculpted wood ducks.

**Galerie Madeleine Lacerte** (1 côte Dinan, tel. 418/692–1566), situated in Lower Town, sells contemporary art and sculpture.

Books    English-language books are difficult to find in Québec. One of the city's first bookstores, **Librarie Garneau** (24 côte de la Fabrique, tel. 418/692–4262), is centrally located near City Hall and carries mostly volumes in French. Other popular bookstores in the city include **La Maison Anglaise** (Place de la Cité, Sainte-Foy, tel. 418/654–9523), with the best selection of English-language titles in the area, and **Classic Bookshop** (Place Laurier, boul. Laurier, tel. 418/653–8683).

Clothing    **François Côté Collections** (35 rue Buade, tel. 418/692–6016) is a chic boutique with fashions for men.

**La Maison Darlington** (7 rue Buade, tel. 418/692–2268) carries well-made woolens, dresses, and suits for women by fine names in couture.

**Louis Laflamme** (Place Québec, tel. 418/523–6633) has a large selection of stylish men's clothes.

Crafts    **Les Trois Colombes Inc.** (46 rue St-Louis, tel. 418/694–1114) sells hand-made items. You will find two floors filled with such goods as clothing made from hand-spun fabric, Indian and Inuit carvings, jewelry, pottery, and paintings.

Fur    Fur trade has been an important industry for centuries in the area. Québec City is a good place to purchase high-quality furs at fairly reasonable prices. Since 1894, one of the best furriers in town has been **Jos Robitaille** (Place Sainte-Foy, Sainte-Foy, tel. 418/650–

6185). The department store **J.B. Laliberté** (Mail Centre-Ville, tel. 418/525–4841) also carries furs.

Gifts **Collection Lazuli** (774 rue St-Jean, tel. 418/525–6528) features a tasteful selection of unusual art objects, gifts, and jewelry from around the world.

Jewelry **Bijouterie Louis Perrier** (48 rue du Petit-Champlain, tel. 418/692–4633) has Québec-made gold and silver jewelry. Exclusive jewelry can also be found at **Zimmermann** (46 côte de la Fabrique, tel. 418/692–2672).

# Sports and Fitness

Two parks are central to Québec City: the 250-acre Battlefields Park, with its panoramic views of the St. Lawrence River, and Cartier-Brébeuf Park, which runs along the St. Charles River. Both are favorite spots for such outdoor sports as jogging, biking, and cross-country skiing. Scenic rivers and mountains close by (no more than 30 minutes by car) make this city ideal for the sporting life. For information about sports and fitness, contact **Québec City Region and Convention Bureau** (60 rue d'Auteuil, Québec G1R 4C4, tel. 418/692–2471) or **Québec City Bureau of Parks and Recreation** (65 rue Ste-Anne, 5th Floor, Québec, G1R 4S9, tel. 418/691–6278).

## Participant Sports

Bicycling Short bike paths along rolling hills are found in Battlefields Park, located at the south side of the city. The best bet for a longer ride over flat terrain is the path north of the city skirting the St. Charles River; this route can be reached from Third Avenue near the Marie de l'Incarnation Bridge. Paths along the côte de Beaupré, beginning at the union of the St. Charles and St. Lawrence rivers, are especially scenic. They begin northeast of the city at rue de la Verandrye and boulevard Montmorency and continue 10 kilometers (6 miles) along the coast to Montmorency Falls.

Bicycles can be rented at **Location Petit Champlain** (94 rue du Petit-Champlain, tel. 418/692–2817).

Boating Lakes around the Québec City area have facilities for boating and canoeing. Take Route 73 north of the city to Saint-Dunstan de Lac Beauport, then take Exit 157, boulevard du Lac, to **Lac Beauport** (tel. 418/849–2821), one of the best nearby resorts. Boats and boards can be rented at **Campex** (8 chemin de l'Orrée, Lac Beauport, tel. 418/849–2236) for canoeing, kayaking, and windsurfing. You can also rent boats in **Lac St-Joseph**, 40 kilometers (25 miles) northwest of Québec City, at **La Vigie** (tel. 418/875–2727).

Fishing Permits are needed for hunting and fishing in Québec. They are available from the **Ministry of Recreation, Hunting, and Fishing** (Place de la Capitale, 150 boul. Réné Levesque E, tel. 418/643–3127). The ministry also publishes a pamphlet on fishing regulations that is available at tourist information offices.

**Réserve Faunique des Laurentides** (tel. 418/848–2422) is a wildlife reserve with good lakes for fishing, approximately 48 kilometers (30 miles) north of Québec City via Route 73.

Golf The Québec City region has 18 golf courses, and several are open to the public. Reservations during summer months are essential. **Club de Golf de Cap Rouge** (4600 rue St-Felix, tel. 418/653–9381) in Cap Rouge, with 18 holes, is one of the closest courses to Québec City.

**Club de Golf de Beauport** (3533 rue Clemenceau, tel. 418/663–1578), a nine-hole course, is 20 minutes by car via Route 73 N. **Parc du Mont Sainte-Anne** (Rte. 360, C.P. 653 Beaupré, tel. 418/827–3778), a half-hour drive north of Québec, has one of the best 18-hole courses in the region.

**Health and Fitness Clubs**  One of the city's most popular health clubs is **Club Entrain** (Place de la Cité, 2600 boul. Laurier, tel. 418/658–7771). Facilities include a weight room with Nautilus, a sauna, a whirlpool, aerobics classes, and racquetball and squash courts.

Nonguests at **Hôtel Radisson des Gouverneurs** (690 boul. Rêné Levesque E, tel. 418/647–1717) can use the health club facilities, which include weights, a sauna, a whirlpool, and an outdoor heated pool, for a $5 fee.

**Hilton International Québec** (3 Place Québec, tel. 418/647–2411) has a smaller health club with weights, a sauna, and an outdoor pool available to nonguests for a $10 fee.

Pool facilities cost $2.25 at the **YMCA** (855 av. Holland, tel. 418/683–2155).

**Hiking/Jogging**  The Parc Cartier-Brébeuf, north of the Old City along the banks of the St. Charles River, has about 13 kilometers (8 miles) of hiking trails. For more mountainous terrain, head 19 kilometers (12 miles) north via Route 73 to Lac Beauport. **Villages des Sports** (1860 boul. Valcartier, Val Cartier, tel. 418/844–3725), a man-made sports complex 24 kilometers (15 miles) from downtown on Route 371, has 16 kilometers (10 miles) of trails. For jogging, Battlefields Park and Parc Cartier-Brébeuf are the most popular places in the area.

**Horseback Riding**  **Jacques Cartier Excursions** (978 av. Jacques Cartier N, Tewkesbury, tel. 418/848–7238), also known for rafting, offers summer and winter horseback riding. An excursion includes an hour of instruction and three hours of riding; the cost is $49 on weekends and $35 weekdays in spring and fall, and $55 on weekends and $39 on weekdays in winter.

**Rafting**  Jacques Cartier River, about 48 kilometers (30 miles) northwest of Québec City, provides good rafting; the waterway flows south from Laurentian Park 56 kilometers (35 miles) from Québec City into the St. Lawrence River.

**Jacques Cartier Excursions** (978 av. Jacques Cartier N, Tewkesbury, G0A 4P0, tel. 418/848–7238) offers rafting trips on the Jacques Cartier River. Tours originate from Tewkesbury, a half-hour drive from Québec City, from May through September. A half-day tour costs $55 on weekends, $39 on weekdays. A full day costs $68 on weekends, $49 on weekdays. Wet suits cost $12 extra. In the winter, snow-rafting excursions are available, and include a two-hour sleigh ride and all-day mountain sliding in river rafts. The total cost is $49.

**Nouveau Monde, Expeditions en Rivière** (C.P. 100, chemin de la Rivière Rouge, Calumet, J0V 1B0, tel. 800/361–5033) has excursions on the Jacques Cartier River from mid-May through September. A 3-hour excursion costs $44. Reserve one month in advance for weekends, two weeks in advance for weekdays.

**Skating**  The ice-skating season runs December through March. There is a 3.8-kilometer (2.4-mile) stretch for skating along the St. Charles River, between the Samson and Marie de l'Incarnation bridges, January through March, depending on the ice. Rentals and changing rooms are nearby. *Skating hours: weekdays noon–10, weekends 10–10.*

Place d'Youville, just outside St-Jean Gate, has an outdoor skating rink open from November to April. Nighttime skating can be done at **Villages des Sports** (1860 boul. Valcartier, Val Cartier, tel. 418/844–3725).

**Skiing** Numerous trails exist for cross-country skiing enthusiasts. Battle-
*Cross-country* fields Park on Québec City's south side, which you can access on Place Montcalm, has scenic marked trails. For information, call **Québec City Bureau of Parks and Recreation** (tel. 418/691–6278). Lac Beauport, 19 kilometers (12 miles) north of the city, has more than 20 marked trails (250 kilometers; 155 miles). Contact **Les Sentiers du Moulin** (99 chemin du Moulin, tel. 418/849–2778). **Parc du Mont Sainte-Anne** (Rte. 360, C.P. 400 Beaupré, G0A 1E0, tel. 418/827–4561), which is 40 kilometers (25 miles) northeast of Québec City, has 235 kilometers (141 miles) of cross-country trails. Contact **Rang Saint-Julien** (tel. 418/827–4561, ext. 408) for more information.

*Downhill* Four alpine ski resorts, all with night skiing, are located within a 30-minute drive of Québec City. **Parc du Mont Sainte-Anne** (Rte. 360, C.P. 400 Beaupré, G0A 1E0, tel. 418/827–4561) is the largest resort in eastern Canada, with 50 downhill trails, 12 lifts, and a gon-
dola. **Stoneham** (1420 av. Hibou, Stoneham, Québec, G0A 4P0, tel. 418/848–2411) is known for its long, easy slopes with 25 downhill runs and 10 lifts. Two smaller alpine centers can be found at Lac Beauport: 14 trails at **Mont St-Castin** (82 chemin le Tour du Lac, Box 1129, Lac Beauport, Québec G0A 2C0, tel. 418/849–6776) and 24 trails at **Le Relais** (1084 boul. du Lac, Box 280, Lac Beauport, Québec G0A 2C0, tel. 418/849–1851). Upon request, most major hotels arrange skibus service for guests for a fee.

A municipal bus service, **Skibus** (tel. 418/627–2511), is offered on weekends. It leaves from Place Laurier (2700 boul. Laurier, Sainte-
Foy) at 8 AM for Stoneham and Mont Sainte-Anne and returns once a day (at 4:05 from Stoneham, and at 4:15 from Mont Sainte-Anne). The cost each way is $3.50 for Stoneham and $4 for Mont Sainte-Anne.

**Visite Touristique de Québec** (tel. 418/653–9722) offers a bus service to Mont Sainte-Anne and Stoneham. For Mont Sainte-Anne, it leaves from major hotels in Québec daily between 7:30 AM and 8:30 AM and returns at 4:30 PM. For Stoneham, it leaves from major hotels daily between 7:45 AM and 8:45 AM, and returns at 4:30 PM. It costs $7 each way. Telephone for reservations.

Brochures about ski centers in Québec are available at Québec Tourism and Convention Bureaus or by phoning 800/363–7777.

**Tennis** At **Montcalm Tennis Club** (901 boul. Champlain, Sillery, tel. 418/687–1250), south of Québec City in Sillery, four indoor and seven outdoor courts are open daily from 8 AM to 10 PM. Twelve indoor courts are also available at **Tennisport** (6280 boul. Hammel, Ancienne Lorette, tel. 418/872–0111).

## Spectator Sports

Tickets for sporting events can be purchased at **Colisée de Québec** (Québec Coliseum; 2205 av. du Colisée, tel. 418/523–3333 or 800/463–3333) or through Billetech, whose main outlet is at the **Grand Théâtre de Québec** (269 boul. René Levesque E, tel. 418/643–8131). Other outlets are at Bibliothèque Gabrielle-Roy, Palais Montcalm, La Baie department store (Place Laurier, Sainte-Foy, tel. 418/627–

5959), and Provigo supermarkets. The outlet hours vary depending on the location.

**Harness Racing**  Horse racing is on view at the racetrack **Hippodrome de Québec.** *C.P. 2053, Parc de l'Exposition, tel. 418/524–5283. Admission: $2.25 adults, $1.25 senior citizens, children under 12 free.*

**Hockey**  A National Hockey League team, the Québec Nordiques, plays at the **Colisée de Québec** (Québec Coliseum). *2205 av. du Colisée, Parc de l'Exposition, tel. 418/523–3333 or 800/463–3333. Open Oct.– Mar., daily.*

# Dining

Québec City reveals its French heritage most obviously in its cuisine. You'll discover a French touch in the city's numerous cafés and brasseries and in the artful presentation of dishes at local restaurants. Most dining establishments usually have a selection of dishes à la carte, but you'll often experience more creative specialties by opting for the table d'hôte, a two- to four-course meal chosen daily by the chef. At dinner, many restaurants will offer a *menu de dégustation*, a five- to seven-course dinner of the chef's finest creations.

Although many visitors will find a gourmet meal in their price range, budget-conscious diners may want to try out the more expensive establishments during lunchtime. Lunch usually costs about 30% less than dinner, and many of the same dishes are available. Lunch is usually served 11:30 through 2:30; dinner, 6:30 until about 11. You should tip about 15% of the bill.

Québec City is the best place in the province to sample French Canadian cuisine, composed of robust, uncomplicated dishes that make use of the region's bounty of foods, including fowl and wild game (caribou, quail, venison), maple syrup, and various berries and nuts. Because Québec has a cold climate for a good portion of the year, it has a traditionally heavy cuisine, with such specialties as *cretons* (pâtés), *tourtière* (meat pie), and *tarte au sucre* (maple-syrup pie).

Highly recommended restaurants in each price category are indicated by a star ★.

| Category | Cost* |
| --- | --- |
| $$$$ | over $30 |
| $$$ | $20–$30 |
| $$ | $10–$20 |
| $ | under $10 |

*per person, excluding drinks, service, 7% federal sales tax, and 4% provincial sales tax*

### $$$$

★  **A la Table de Serge Bruyère.** This restaurant has put Québec on the map of great gastronomic cities. The city's most famous culinary institution serves classic French cuisine presented with plenty of crystal, silver, and fresh flowers and with relentless attention to detail. Only one sitting is offered each night. Chef Serge Bruyère came to Québec City from Lyons, France, and worked at various restau-

## Dining

À la Table de Serge Bruyère, **19**

Aux Anciens Canadiens, **23**

Café de la Paix, **22**

Casse-Crepe Breton, **16**

Chalet Suisse, **21**

Chez Temporel, **20**

Gambrinus, **32**

L'Apsara, **11**

L'Astral, **5**

Le Café de la Terrasse, **28**

Le Cochon Dingue, **30**

Le Graffiti, **4**

Le Marie Clarisse, **31**

Le Paris Brest, **7**

Le Saint-Amour, **12**

L'Echaudée, **33**

Les Frères de la Côte, **18**

Mille Feuille, **15**

Paparazzi, **2**

## Lodging

Château Bonne Entente, **1**

Château Frontenac, **29**

Château de la Terrasse, **27**

Hilton International Québec, **10**

Hôtel du Théâtre, **14**

Hôtel Loews Le Concorde, **6**

Hôtel Radisson Gouverneurs Québec, **9**

L'Auberge du Quartier, **3**

L'Auberge Saint-Louis, **24**

Le Château de Pierre, **25**

L'Hôtel du Vieux Québec, **17**

Manoir d'Auteuil, **13**

Manoir des Remparts, **34**

Manoir Lafayette, **8**

Manoir Sainte-Geneviève, **26**

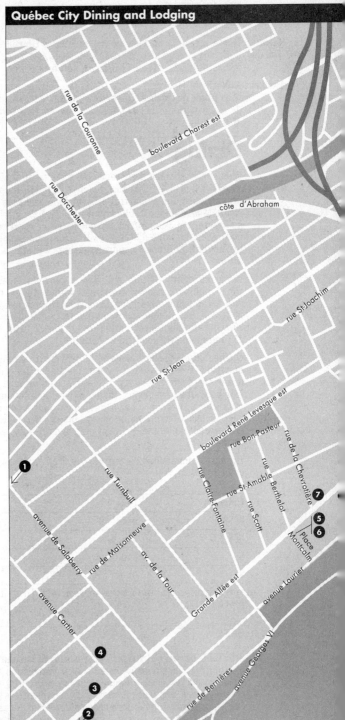

## Québec City Dining and Lodging

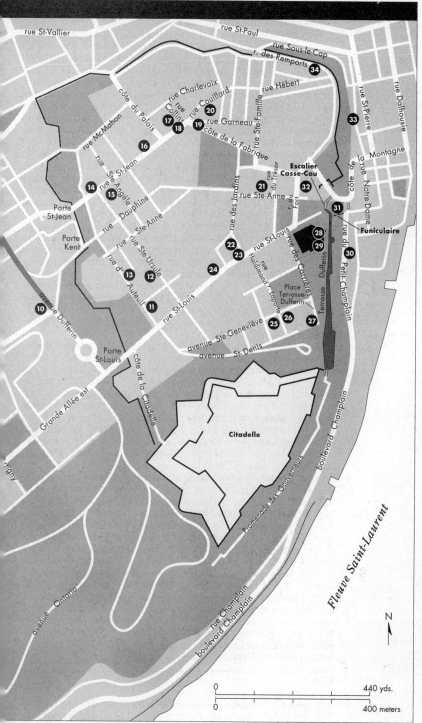

rue St-Vallier

rue St-Paul

rue Sous-le-Cap

r. des Remparts

**34**

rue St-Pierre

rue Dalhousie

côte du Palais

rue Charlevoix

rue Couillard

**20**

rue Collins

**17**

**18**

**19**

rue Garneau

côte de la Fabrique

rue McMahon

**16**

rue Ste-Famille

rue Hébert

**33**

côte de la Montagne

rue St-Jean

rue Ste-Angèle

**14**

**15**

rue Dauphine

rue Ste-Anne

rue des Jardins

**Escalier Casse-Cou**

rue du Trésor

**21**

**32**

côte de la Notre-Dame

Porte St-Jean

**Funiculaire**

rue Ste-Anne

r. du Fort

**31**

Porte Kent

rue Ste-Ursule

**22**

**23**

rue St-Louis

**28**

**29**

rue du Petit-Champlain

rue d'Auteuil

**13**

**12**

**24**

rue Haldimand

rue des Carrières

**30**

**11**

Terrasse Dufferin

**10**

rue St-Louis

Place Terrasse Dufferin

avenue Dufferin

rue J.-Laporte

Porte St-Louis

côte de la Citadelle

avenue Ste-Geneviève

**25**

**26**

**27**

avenue St-Denis

Grande Allée est

boulevard Champlain

**Citadelle**

Promenade des Gouverneurs

avenue Ontario

*Fleuve Saint-Laurent*

rue Champlain

boulevard Champlain

N

| 0 | | | 440 yds. |

| 0 | | | 400 meters |

rants until he opened his own in 1980. The *menu gourmand* is a five-course meal for about $50. The extensive wine list starts at $26 and goes up to $800. Wine is also available by the glass. Specialties include scampi in puff pastry with fresh tomatoes, scallop stew with watercress, and duckling supreme with blueberry sauce. In 1984, Bruyère expanded inside the restaurant's old 1843 Livernois building and created a minimall with a European-style tearoom, a contemporary piano bar, and a food store—all serving gourmet treats from his celebrated kitchen. If A la Table de Serge Bruyère is out of your price range, **A la Petite Table** in the food mall is less formal and less expensive, with such dishes as seafood terrine and pork with tarragon sauce. *1200 rue St-Jean, tel. 418/694–0618. Reservations required. Jacket required. AE, DC, MC, V. No lunch weekends.*

**Café de la Paix.** An evening spent at this local favorite takes you back to a dining experience in Paris circa 1930. The tables could not get closer nor the lights dimmer amid the art deco extravagance of lamps in Venetian glass, wood sculpted in geometric patterns, and stained-glass windows. The food is on a par with other fine restaurants in the city, but there are hints that the chefs are relying on their reputations (the restaurant dates from 1952). The table d'hôte includes such tasty dishes as pheasant with peaches. Salmon comes with four sauces: raspberry vinegar, hollandaise, tarragon, or mustard. The meat entrées, including filet mignon and leg of lamb, are also recommended. You choose your dessert from a cart; try the fresh fruit and the chocolate truffle cake. The service is prompt and attentive. Private dining rooms are available on the second floor. *44 rue des Jardins, tel. 418/692–1430. Reservations advised. Dress: casual but neat. AE, DC, MC, V. No lunch Sun. in winter.*

**Le Marie Clarisse.** Wood-beam ceilings, stone walls, sea-blue decor, and a lit fireplace make this dining spot one of the coziest in town. Housed in an ancient building on the bottom of the Breakneck Steps near Place Royale, Le Marie Clarisse is well known for its unique seafood dishes, such as halibut with nuts and honey and scallops with port and paprika. Occasionally, the menu includes a good game dish, such as caribou with curry. The *menu du jour* has about seven entrées to choose from; dinner includes soup, salad, dessert, and coffee. Wines are served from the restaurant's cellar. *12 rue du Petit-Champlain, tel. 418/692–0857. Reservations required. Dress: casual but neat. AE, DC, MC, V. Closed Sun. and lunch Sat.*

★ **Le Saint-Amour.** This restaurant has all the makings of a true haute-cuisine establishment without having a pretentious atmosphere. A light and airy atrium, with a retractable roof for outdoor dining in summer, creates a relaxed dining ambience. Chef Jean-Luc Boulay continues to educate himself by taking various courses in France; his studies pay off in the creation of such specialties as stuffed quails in port sauce and salmon with light chive mousse. Sauces here are light, with no flour or butter. The *menu de dégustation* has nine courses, and the *menu gastronomique* has seven courses. If you plan to order one of these two menus, it's a good idea to mention this when making your reservation. Wines can be ordered by the glass to complement courses. The chef's true expertise shines when it comes to his diverse dessert menu. Try the nougat ice cream with fresh figs or the three-chocolate cake. Better yet, order the Saint-Amour assortment of desserts. *48 rue Ste-Ursule, tel. 418/694–0667. Reservations advised. Dress: casual but neat. AE, DC, MC, V.*

**$$$**

★ **Aux Anciens Canadiens.** This establishment is named after a book by Philippe-Aubert de Gaspé, who once resided here. The house dates back to 1675 and has four dining rooms with different themes. The *vaisselier* (dish room) is bright and cheerful, with colorful antique dishes, a fireplace, and an antique stove. Another room displays guns from the French regime. Come for the authentic French Canadian cooking; hearty specialties include duck in maple glaze and lamb with blueberry wine sauce. The restaurant also serves the best caribou drink in town. (Caribou is a local beverage made with sweet red wine and whiskey, and is known for its kick.) *34 rue St-Louis, tel. 418/692–1627. Reservations advised. Dress: casual. AE, DC, MC, V.*

**L'Astral.** This circular restaurant on the 29th floor of the Hôtel Loews Le Concorde revolves high above Battlefields Park and the Old City. The food is not the best in town, but the views are excellent. The modern and uninspired decor does not detract from the view, either; there's no room for anything besides the dining tables next to large windows and the vast buffet of salads, meat, and poultry dishes. Sunday brunch consists of more than 45 items ($21 adults, $9 children under 12). *1225 Pl. Montcalm, tel.418/647–2222. Reservations advised. Dress: casual but neat. AE, DC, MC, V.*

**Le Graffiti.** A good alternative to Old City dining, this restaurant, housed in a modern gourmet food mall, serves the cuisine of Provence. It's a romantic setting, with dark mahogany-paneled walls and large bay windows that look out onto the passersby along avenue Cartier. The distinctive menu includes such dishes as scampi spiced with basil and red pepper, and chicken liver mousse with pistachios. The reasonably priced table d'hôte comes with soup, appetizer, entrée, dessert, and coffee. Desserts are made fresh each day. *1191 av. Cartier, tel. 418/529–4949. Reservations advised. Dress: casual but neat. AE, DC, MC, V.*

★ **Gambrinus.** This comfortable restaurant offers excellent Continental cuisine in two elegant, mahogany-paneled, plant-filled dining rooms with windows facing the street. The reliable menu includes a range of meat, fish, and pasta entrées, with such specialties as pheasant supreme with fruit, seafood in puff pastry with saffron, and rack of lamb with basil. The table d'hôte is a good bet and provides generous portions and delectable desserts. Service here is unrushed and thoroughly professional. Gambrinus is conveniently located near rue du Trésor and the Château Frontenac. *15 rue du Fort, tel. 418/692–5144. Reservations advised. Dress: casual but neat. AE, DC, MC, V. No lunch weekends.*

★ **Le Paris Brest.** This busy restaurant on Grande Allée serves a gregarious crowd attracted to its tastefully prepared French dishes. Its angular halogen lighting and soft yellow walls add a fresh, modern touch to this historic building. Traditional fare, such as *escargots au Pernod* (snails with Pernod) and steak tartare, are presented artistically. Popular dishes served here include lamb with herbs from Provence and beef Wellington. A la carte and main-course dishes are accompanied by a generous side platter of vegetables. Wine prices range from $22 to $250. *590 Grande Allée E, tel. 418/529–2243. Reservations advised. Dress: casual but neat. AE, DC, MC, V.*

## $$

**Chalet Suisse.** This large chalet close to Place d'Armes serves Swiss cuisine. Fondues are a mainstay, and there are 25 different ones to choose from; the Gruyère and the chocolate fondues are two of the tastiest house specialties. Another popular dish is *raclette*, a Swiss dish with melted cheese, served with bread and potatoes as well as such diverse flavorings as onions, pickles, and ham. The spacious chalet looms three stories high with clichéd murals of alpine scenes. In the summer, there are umbrella-shaded café tables outside. *32 rue Ste-Anne, tel. 418/694–1320. Reservations accepted. Dress: casual. AE, DC, MC, V.*

**L'Apsara.** The Cambodian family that owns this restaurant near the St-Louis Gate excels at using both subtle and tangy spices to create unique flavors that are ideal for those seeking a reprieve from French fare. Decor combines Western and Eastern motifs, with flowered wallpaper, Oriental art, and small fountains. Innovative dishes from Vietnam, Thailand, and Cambodia include such starters as *fleur de pailin* (a rice paste roll filled with fresh vegetables, meat, and shrimp) or *mou sati* (pork kebabs with peanut sauce and coconut milk). The assorted miniature Cambodian pastries are delicious with tea served from a little elephant container. *71 rue d'Auteuil, tel. 418/694–0232. Reservations accepted. Dress: casual. AE, MC, V.*

**Le Café de la Terrasse.** This restaurant, housed in the landmark Château Frontenac, does not share the hotel's opulence, but it does offer a view along Terrasse Dufferin and the St. Lawrence River. You can try the businessperson's breakfast buffet of fruits, omelets, and croissants and an à la carte lunch menu of salads and sandwiches. Standard but dependable Continental dishes are served during the lunch and dinner buffets. *Château Frontenac, 1 rue Carrières, tel. 418/692–3861. Reservations accepted. Dress: casual but neat. AE, DC, MC, V.*

★ **L'Echaudée** (Whitewash). This chic black-and-white bistro attracts a mix of business and tourist clientele because of its location between the financial and antiques districts in Lower Town. The modern decor features a stark dining area with a mirrored wall and a stainless-steel bar where you dine atop high stools. Lunch offerings include *cuisse de canard confit* (duck confit) with french fries and fresh seafood salad. The three-course brunch for Sunday antiques shoppers includes giant croissants and a tantalizing array of desserts. *73 Sault-au-Matelot, tel. 418/692–1299. Weekend reservations advised. Dress: casual. AE, DC, MC, V. Closed Sun. and Mon. dinners Sept.–May.*

**Paparazzi.** The story goes like this: two Québecers were dining in Napa Valley, California. They were so impressed by chef Suzanne Sylvester, they convinced her to pack up her Harley Davidson and move to Québec City. In 1993, after four months of study in southern Italy, the threesome opened the Paparazzi, an Italian restaurant located about a 15-minute drive west of the Old City. Its sleek, bistro ambiance—bare wooden tables, halogen lighting, wrought iron accents—competes with many of the finer dining establishments in town, but without the high prices. The menu is imaginative, and changes twice a year. Specialties include the pizza paparazzi, with wild mushrooms, fresh tomatoes, and a mix of cheeses. Choose from a list of interesting desserts. *1365 av. Maguire, Sillery, tel. 418/683–8111. Reservations advised. Dress: casual. AE, DC, MC, V.*

## $

**Casse-Crêpe Breton.** Crêpes in generous proportions are served in this small, square, diner-style restaurant on rue St-Jean. From a menu of 15 ingredients, pick your own chocolate or fruit combinations, or design a larger meal with cheese, ham, and vegetables. The tables surround three round hot plates at which you watch your creations being made. Crêpes made with two to five ingredients cost under $5. *1136 rue St-Jean. tel. 418/692-0438. No reservations. Dress: casual. No credit cards. Open weekdays 7:30 AM-11 PM, weekends 7:30 AM-midnight.*

★ **Chez Temporel.** Tucked behind rue St-Jean and côte de la Fabrique, this homey café is an experience *très français.* The aroma of fresh coffee fills the air. The rustic decor incorporates wooden tables, chairs, and benches, and a tiny staircase winds to an upper level. Croissants are made in-house; the staff will fill them with Gruyère and ham or anything else you want. Try the equally delicious croque-monsieur and quiche Lorraine. *25 rue Couillard, tel. 418/694-1813. No reservations. Dress: casual. No credit cards. Open 7 AM-1 AM.*

**Le Cochon Dingue.** Across the street from the ferry in Lower Town is this cheerful café (whose name translates to "The Crazy Pig"), with sidewalk tables and indoor dining rooms, which artfully blend the chic and the antique. Black-and-white checkerboard floors contrast with ancient stone walls that are typical of the oldest sections of town. Café fare includes dependably tasty homemade quiches, thick soups, and such desserts as fresh raspberry tarte and maple-sugar pie. *46 boul. Champlain, tel. 418/692-2013. Reservations accepted. Dress: casual. AE, MC, V. Open weekdays 7 AM-11 PM, weekends 8 AM-midnight.*

**Les Frères de la Côte.** This pizza house, although located in the heart of the tourist district, is a favorite for many locals—including some provincial politicians. The friendly, boisterous atmosphere flows from its doors into the foyer, where you will find hundreds of snapshots documenting happy dining experiences. On the menu, you'll find 17 kinds of pizza, but there is also a full range of other dishes—like pasta with blue cheese, lamb with herbes de province, or grilled spicy Italian sausage with fries. For dessert, try the apple pie served with an orange, caramel glaze, and cream. And when it comes time to leave, don't overlook the tempting basket of homemade bread for sale. *1190 rue St-Jean, tel. 418/692-5445. Reservations advised. Dress: casual. AE, MC, V.*

**Mille Feuille.** In the heart of the Latin Quarter is this vegetarian restaurant situated in a well-preserved, historic building that dates to 1782. The daily menu offers three or four creative dishes, such as cabbage leaves stuffed with brown rice and vegetables and topped with rich tomato sauce and fresh Parmesan cheese, and Greek-style pizza with black olives. All dishes are served with soup and salad. On Saturday and Sunday a "health brunch" is served from 9 AM to 3 PM, and costs about $6. *32 rue Sainte-Angèle, tel. 418/692-2147. May close during winter months. Also at 1405 chemin Ste.-Foy (a 10-min drive west of the city), tel. 418/681-4520. Reservations accepted. Dress: casual. MC, V.*

# Lodging

With more than 35 hotels within its walls, Québec City has a range of lodging options. Landmark hotels stand as prominent as the city's most historic sites; modern high rises outside the ramparts offer spectacular views of the Old City. Also, visitors can immerse themselves in the city's historic charm by staying in one of the many old-fashioned inns where no two rooms are alike.

Whichever kind of accommodations you choose, be sure to make a reservation during peak season, from May through September. If you are planning to visit during the summer or at the time of the Winter Carnival in February, you may have trouble finding a room without one. During busy times, hotel rates usually rise 30%. From November through April, many of the city's lodgings offer discount weekend packages and other promotions.

Highly recommended properties in each price category are indicated by a star ★.

| Category | Cost* |
| --- | --- |
| $$$$ | over $140 |
| $$$ | $85–$140 |
| $$ | $50–$85 |
| $ | under $50 |

*All prices are for a standard double room, excluding 7% federal sales tax, 4% provincial sales tax, and an optional service charge.*

### $$$$

★ **Château Frontenac.** Towering above the St. Lawrence River, the Château Frontenac is indisputably Québec City's most renowned landmark. Although the Frontenac can no longer claim to be the city's top-rated hotel, the mystique of staying at "the Château" endures. Its public rooms—from the intimate piano bar to its 700-seat ballroom, reminiscent of the Versailles Hall of Mirrors—have the opulence of years gone by, and almost all the guest rooms offer excellent views. You must make a reservation in advance, as the average booking rate is 80% a year. A five-year, $60 million renovation was completed in 1993, in time for the hotel's 100th birthday. A new wing of rooms was added, as was a long-awaited health spa. The Frontenac has one of the finer restaurants in town, Le Champlain, where classic French cuisine is served by waiters dressed in traditional French costumes. The ground floor has several luxury shops and a restaurant, Le Café de la Terrasse (*see* Dining, *above*). *1 rue des Carrières, G1R 4P5, tel. 418/692–3861 or 800/441–1414, fax 418/692–1751. 610 rooms. Facilities: 3 restaurants, 2 bars, health spa, indoor pool. AE, DC, MC, V.*

★ **Hilton International Québec.** Just outside St-Jean Gate, the Hilton rises from the shadow of Parliament Hill as the city's finest luxury hotel. It has such spacious facilities and efficient services that it could easily cater exclusively to the convention crowd. Instead, it has adapted its renowned comfort and dependable service to tourists. The sprawling atrium lobby is flanked with a bar and an open-air restaurant, and it offers the added convenience of being connected with the mall, Place Québec, which offers 40 shops and boutiques. Ultramodern rooms with pine furniture have tall windows so that rooms on upper floors offer fine views of the Old City. *3 Pl. Québec, G1K 7M9, tel. 418/647–2411 or 800/445–8667, fax 418/647–6488. 565 rooms, 36 suites. Facilities: restaurant, piano bar, pool, health club, sauna, whirlpool. AE, DC, MC, V.*

**Hôtel Radisson Gouverneurs Québec.** Opposite the Parliament Buildings, this large, full-service establishment is part of a Québec chain. Formerly called Auberge des Gouverneurs when it opened in 1975, the hotel has upgraded its light and spacious rooms by furnishing them with luminous pastel decor, wood furniture, and marble bathrooms. VIP floors were designed to lure the business traveler, but there is also plenty of room for tourists. The hotel occupies the first 12 floors of a tall office complex; views of the Old City are limited to the higher floors. There's a year-round outdoor swimming pool, perfect for use even when the weather is frigid. *690 boul. René Levesque E, G1R 5A8, tel. 418/647–1717 or 800/333–3333, fax 418/647–2146. 377 rooms with private bath. Facilities: restaurant, piano bar, health club, heated outdoor pool, sauna, whirlpool. AE, DC, MC, V.*

★ **Hôtel Loews Le Concorde.** When Le Concorde was built in 1974, the shockingly tall concrete structure went up with controversy because it was taking the place of 19th-century Victorian homes. Yet of all the modern hotels outside the city gates, tourists will probably find that Le Concorde occupies one of the most convenient locations for city touring and nightlife. Inside the hotel there's almost as much going on as at the cafés and restaurants along the nearby Grande Allée; Le Concorde houses the revolving restaurant L'Astral (*see* Dining, *above*), a sidewalk café, and a bar. Rooms have good views of Battlefields Park, and nearly all have been redone in modern decor combined with traditional furnishings. Amenities for business travelers have expanded; one of the new VIP floors is reserved for female executives. *1225 Pl. Montcalm, G1R 4W6, tel. 418/647–2222 or 800/463–5256; in the U.S., tel. 800/23–LOEWS; fax 418/647–4710. 424 rooms. Facilities: 2 restaurants, bar, heated outdoor pool, health club, sauna, whirlpool. AE, DC, MC, V.*

## $$$

**Château Bonne Entente.** If you have a car, you may want to stay at this sprawling resort located 10 minutes from the airport and 20 minutes from the walled city. The hotel is more commonly called "The Other Château," the country cousin of the urban Frontenac. It was a private mansion until 1940, when it became a hotel; a $7 million renovation several years ago has helped this establishment become a popular spot for the well-heeled. In 1993, a spa and exercise room—known as the relaxarium—was added. In the newer section, rooms are decorated in contemporary style with fine wood, plush carpeting, and all the modern amenities. The other rooms are furnished with antiques, and a rustic atmosphere prevails. The property encompasses 11 acres of land with a main complex as well as separate cottage rooms in back. *3400 chemin Ste-Foy, Sainte-Foy G1X 1S6, tel. 418/653–5221 or 800/463–4390, fax 418/653–3098. 163 rooms. Facilities: restaurant, bar, spa, pool, tennis court, trout fishing in back pond, ice-skating in winter, full day care. AE, DC, MC, V.*

**Le Château de Pierre.** Built in 1853 and converted from a private residence in 1960, this tidy Victorian manor on a picturesque street has kept its English origins alive. The high-ceiling halls have ornate chandeliers. The rooms are imaginatively decorated with floral themes, and each usually has some special added feature—a balcony, fireplace, or vanity room—to lend some extra charm. Rooms in the front face imposing old stone buildings across the way that date from the English regime. *17 av. Ste-Geneviève, G1R 4A8, tel. 418/694–0429, fax 418/694–0153. 15 rooms with private bath and air-conditioning. MC, V.*

**L'Hôtel du Théâtre.** There's much history that accompanies this hotel, located in the Capitole Building just outside the St-Jean Gate. In 1903 this property opened as an avant-garde theater, then, in the 1920s—the era of silent films—it became a movie house, and some 12 years ago the doors closed in ruin. However, in 1992 the hotel came back to life, following a $15 million restoration, which transformed this historic building into an exclusive 40-room lodging, Italian bistro, and an elaborate 1920s cabaret-style dinner theater (*see* Arts and Nightlife, *below*). A glitzy show-biz theme is prevalent throughout the hotel, with stars on carpets, doors, and keys. Rooms are small and simple, highlighted with a few rich details. Ceilings are painted within sculpted moldings with a blue-and-white sky motif; beds are adorned with white down-filled comforters, and plush terry-cloth bathrobes await guests in every room. *972 rue St-Jean, G1R 1R5, tel. 418/694–4040, fax 418/694–1916. 40 rooms. Facilities: restaurant, bar, theater. AE, MC, V.*

**L'Hôtel du Vieux Québec.** Located in the heart of the Latin Quarter on rue St-Jean, this hotel's brick exterior is surrounded by more striking historic structures. The establishment was once an apartment building and still has the long-term visitor in mind. The interior design is simple, featuring sparsely decorated but comfortable rooms decorated in pastel colors. The hotel recently added five new rooms on the main floor, overlooking Québec's busy main street. Many rooms have a full kitchenette with a stove, cabinets, a sink, and a refrigerator; all have cable TV. Dishes and cooking utensils can be rented for $10. Some rooms are air-conditioned. *1190 rue St-Jean, G1R 1S6, tel. 418/692–1850, fax 418/692–5637. 42 units with private bath. AE, MC, V.*

★ **Manoir d'Auteuil.** Originally a private home, this lodging is one of the more lavish manors in town, artfully revamped at great expense. An ornate sculpted iron banister wraps around four floors; guest rooms feature detailed trimmings in mahogany and marble and blend modern design with the art deco structure. Each room differs in shape and design; one room was formerly the residence's chapel, while another has become a duplex with a luxurious marble bathroom on the second floor. Some rooms look out onto the wall between the St-Louis and St-Jean gates. A complimentary Continental breakfast awaits guests each morning. *49 rue d'Auteuil, G1R 4C2, tel. 418/694–1173, fax 418/694–0081. 16 rooms with private bath. AE, MC, V.*

**Manoir Sainte-Geneviève.** This quaint and elaborately decorated hotel dating from 1880 stands near the Château Frontenac, on the southwest corner of the Jardin des Governeurs. A plush Victorian ambience is created with fanciful wallpaper and rooms decorated with precious stately English manor furnishings, such as marble lamps, large wooden bedposts, and velvet upholstery; you'll feel as if you are staying in a secluded country inn. A hidden porch facing the Citadel is perfect for relaxing and soaking in the atmosphere of Upper Town. Service here is personal and genteel. One suite on the ground floor has a private entrance. *13 av. Ste-Geneviève, G1R 4A7, tel. and fax 418/694–1666. 9 rooms with private bath; 7 rooms have air-conditioning, color TV. No credit cards.*

## $$

**Château de la Terrasse.** Although this four-story inn may not have the same charm as others in the city, it does have something that the others in the area lack: a view of the St. Lawrence River. However, only half of the rooms face the river; others in the rear look out onto the backs of buildings. While the interior hints at having once possessed a refined and elegant decor, with its high ceilings and stained glass lining the large bay windows, the furnishings these days are plain and unremarkable. *6 Pl. Terrasse Dufferin, G1R 4N5, tel. 418/694–9472, fax 418/694–0055. 18 rooms with private bath. V.*

★ **L'Auberge du Quartier.** This small, amiable inn, situated in a house dating from 1852, will please those seeking moderately priced lodging with a personal touch. Proprietors Lise Provost and Pierre Couture are highly attentive to their guests' needs. The cheerful rooms, without phones or televisions, are modestly furnished but well maintained; two of them have fireplaces. A suite of rooms on the third floor can accommodate a family at a reasonable cost. This is one of the few inns in the area that offers a tasty Continental breakfast—warm croissants, homemade banana bread, cheese, preserves, strong coffee, and fresh fruit. A 20-minute walk west from the Old City, L'Auberge du Quartier is convenient to avenue Cartier and Grande Allée nightlife; joggers can use Battlefields Park across the street. *170 Grande Allée O, G1R 2G9, tel. 418/525–9726. 13 rooms, 11 with private bath. Free parking. AE, DC, MC, V.*

**L'Auberge Saint-Louis.** If you're looking for convenience, this inn's central location on the main street of the city can't be beat. A lobby resembling a European pension and tall staircases lead to small guest rooms with comfortable but bare-bones furniture. The ultrabudget room on the fourth floor is just big enough for a bed. The service here is friendly and hospitable. Most guest rooms share floor bathrooms or have a semibathroom. *48 rue St-Louis, G1R 3Z3, tel. 418/692–2424, fax 418/692–3797. 27 rooms, 13 with private bath. MC, V.*

**Le Manoir Lafayette.** In 1882, this gray stone building was a lavish, private home; over a century later, it is a simple hotel. Considering the location on Grande Allée—a street crowded with restaurants and trendy bars—the clean, comfortable accommodations are reasonably priced. The lobby is open and welcoming, with floral sofas surrounding a fireplace and television. In 1992 the hotel underwent a massive renovation, adding 53 rooms to the existing 14. Rooms in the new wing—although fresher— resemble those in the old part: each is quite small, with high ceilings, wooden furniture, floral spreads and drapes, a television, and phone. Rooms facing Grande Allée may be noisy; older rooms cost a little less. *661 Grande Allée E, G1R 2K4, tel. 418/522–2652 or 800/363–8203, fax 418/522–2652. 67 rooms. Facilities: bistro, baby-sitting. AE, DC, MC, V.*

## $

**Manoir des Remparts.** There's nothing fancy about this hotel, which is on a residential street bordering the north side of Québec City's natural cliff. But this manor offers just enough to attract the budget-conscious traveler: spacious and clean rooms with basic old-time furnishings. The halls are well lighted and considered large for a residence in the Old City. Guest rooms have private bath or share a bath on the floor but don't have telephones or televisions. A Continental breakfast, which includes croissants, cereal, juice, and coffee, is included in the price of the room. *3½ rue des Remparts, G1R 3R4, tel. 418/692–2056, fax 418/692–1125. AE, MC, V.*

**Bed-and-Breakfasts**

Québec City has a large number of bed-and-breakfast and hostel accommodations. To guarantee a room during peak season, be sure to
reserve in advance. **Québec City Tourist Information** (60 rue
d'Auteuil, G1R 4C4, tel. 418/692–2471) has B&B listings. **Bed and
Breakfast–Bonjour Québec** (450 rue Champlain, G1K 4J3, tel. 418/
524–0524) has several B&Bs to choose from. Prices range from $45
for a single room to $75 for a double. Apartments are available start-
ing at $75.

# The Arts and Nightlife

For a place its size, Québec City boasts a wide variety of cultural
events, from the reputable Québec Symphony Orchestra to several
small theater companies. The arts scene changes significantly depending on the season. From September to May, a steady repertoire
of concerts, plays, and performances is presented in theaters and
halls around town. In summer, indoor theaters close to make room
for several outdoor stages.

For arts and entertainment listings in English, consult the *Québec
Chronicle-Telegraph,* published on Wednesday. Each day in the
French-language daily newspaper, *Le Soleil,* listings appear on a
page called "Où Aller à Québec" ("Where to Go in Québec"). *Voilà
Québec* and *Hospitalité Québec* are bilingual quarterly entertain-
ment guides distributed free in tourist information areas.

Tickets for most shows can be purchased through **Billetech,** whose
main outlet is the Grand Théâtre de Québec (269 boul. René
Levesque E, tel. 418/643–8131). Other outlets are located at
Bibliothèque Gabrielle-Roy, Colisée, Implanthéâtre, Palais Montcalm, Salle Albert-Rousseau, La Baie department store (Place Laurier, tel. 418/627–5959), and Provigo supermarkets. Outlet hours
vary, depending on the location.

## The Arts

Dance  **Grand Théâtre de Québec** (269 boul. René Levesque E, tel. 418/643–
8131) presents a dance series with both Canadian and international
companies. Dancers also appear at Bibliothèque Gabrielle-Roy,
Salle Albert-Rousseau, and the Palais Montcalm (*see* Theater, *below*).

Film  Most theaters present French films and American films dubbed into
French. Two popular theaters are **Cinéma de Paris** (966 rue St-Jean,
tel. 418/694–0891) and **Cinéma Place Charest** (500 rue du Pont, tel.
418/529–9745). **Cinémas Sainte-Foy** (Place Sainte-Foy, Sainte-Foy,
tel. 418/656–0592) almost always features films in English. **Le Clap**
(2360 chemin Ste.-Foy, Ste.-Foy, tel. 418/650–2527) offers a repertoire of foreign, off-beat, and art films.

Music  **L'Orchestre Symphonique de Québec** (Québec Symphony Orchestra)
is Canada's oldest. It performs at Louis-Frechette Hall in the **Grand
Théâtre de Québec** (269 boul. René Levesque E, tel. 418/643–8131).
**Bibliothèque Gabrielle-Roy** (350 rue St-Joseph E, tel. 418/529–
0924). Classical concerts are performed at the Auditorium Joseph
Lavergne. Tickets must be purchased in advance at the library.
**Colisée de Québec** (2205 av. du Colisée, Parc de l'Exposition, tel.
418/691–7211). Popular music concerts are often booked here.

**Theater**  All theater productions are in French. The following theaters schedule shows from September through April:

**Grand Théâtre de Québec** (269 boul. René Levesque E, tel. 418/643–8131). Classic and contemporary plays are staged by the leading local theater company, le Théâtre du Trident (tel. 418/643–5873).

**Palais Montcalm** (995 Pl. d'Youville, tel. 418/670–9011). This municipal theater outside St-Jean Gate presents a broad range of productions.

**Salle Albert-Rousseau** (2410 chemin Ste-Foy, Sainte-Foy, tel. 418/659–6710). A diverse repertoire, from classical to comedy, is staged here.

**Théâtre Capitole** (972 rue St-Jean, tel. 418/694–4444). This recently restored turn-of-the-century cabaret-style theater offers a diverse repertoire of classical and pop music, plays, and comedy shows.

**Théâtre de la Bordée** (1143 rue St-Jean, tel. 418/694–9631). This local company presents small-scale productions.

**Théâtre Périscope** (2 rue Crémazie E, tel. 418/529–2183). This multipurpose, experimental theater stages about 200 presentations a year, including performances for children.

*Summer*  **Place d'Youville** (tel. 418/670–9011). During the summer, open-air
*Theater*  concerts are presented here, just outside St-Jean Gate. Recent renovations have made this spot quite enjoyable.

## Nightlife

Nightlife in Québec City is centered on the clubs and cafés of rue St-Jean, avenue Cartier, and Grande Allée. In the winter, evening activity is livelier toward the end of the week, beginning on Wednesday. But as the warmer temperatures set in, the café-terrace crowd emerges, and bars are active seven days a week. Most bars and clubs stay open until 3 AM.

**Bars and**  **Le Central** (1200 rue St-Jean, tel. 418/694–0618). At this stylish pi-
**Lounges**  ano bar at Serge Bruyère's restaurant complex, you can order from the restaurant's sophisticated haute-cuisine menu.

**Le Pub Saint-Alexandre** (1087 rue St-Jean, tel. 418/694–0015). This popular English-style pub, formerly a men-only tavern, is a good place to look for your favorite brand of beer. There are approximately 135 different kinds.

**Vogue** and **Sherlock Holmes** (1170 d'Artigny, tel. 418/529–9973). You'll find mainly Yuppies at these two bars stacked one on top of the other. Sherlock Holmes is a pub-restaurant downstairs; for dancing, try Vogue upstairs.

**Disco**  **Chez Dagobert** (600 Grande Allée E, tel. 418/522–0393). You'll find a little bit of everything—live rock bands to loud disco—at this large and popular club.

**Merlin** (1179 av. Cartier, tel. 418/529–9567). This one-room disco is packed nightly. It's a favorite Québecois hangout.

**Folk, Jazz,**  **Chez Son Père** (24 St-Stanislas, tel. 418/692–5308). French Canadian
**and Blues**  folk songs fill this smoky pub on the second floor of an old building in the Latin Quarter. Singers perform every Wednesday through Friday night.

**Le d'Auteuil** (35 rue d'Auteuil, tel. 418/692–2263). Rhythm and blues, jazz, and blues emanate from this converted church across from Kent Gate.

**L'Emprise at Hôtel Clarendon** (57 rue Ste-Anne, tel. 418/692–2480). The first jazz bar in Québec City is the preferred spot for enthusiasts. The art deco decor sets the mood for Jazz Age rhythms.

# Excursion 1: Côte de Beaupré

As legend tells it, when explorer Jacques Cartier first gained sight of the north shore of the St. Lawrence River in 1535, he exclaimed, *"Quel beau pré!"* ("What a lovely meadow!"), because the area was the first inviting piece of land he had spotted since leaving France. Today this fertile meadow, first settled by French farmers, is known as Côte de Beaupré (Beaupré Coast), stretching 40 kilometers (25 miles) from Québec City to the famous pilgrimage site of Sainte-Anne-de-Beaupré. The impressive Montmorency Falls are located midway between these two points.

## Tourist Information

**Beaupré Coast Interpretation Center,** housed in the old mill Petit-Pré, built in 1695, features displays on the history and development of the region. *7007 av. Royale, Château-Richer, tel. 418/824–3677. Admission: $1. Open late June–Labor Day, daily 9–noon and 1–5.*
**Beau Temps, Mauvais Temps,** offers guided bus tours of the Côte de Beaupré. *22 rue du Quai, Suite 101, Saint-Pétronille, Ile d'Orléans, tel. 418/828–2275.*
The offices of the **Québec City Region Tourism and Convention Bureau** (tel. 418/692–2471) can provide information on tours of the Côte de Beaupré (*see* Staying in Québec City, *above*).

## Guided Tours

Québec City touring companies, such as **Gray Line** (tel. 418/622–7420) and **Maple Leaf Sightseeing Tours** (tel. 418/649–9226), lead day excursions along the Côte de Beaupré, with stops at Montmorency Falls and the Sainte-Anne-de-Beaupré Basilica.

## Arriving and Departing

**By Car** To reach Montmorency Falls, take Route 440 (Dufferin-Montmorency Autoroute) northeast from Québec City. Approximately 9.6 kilometers (6 miles) east of the city is the exit for Montmorency Falls. To drive directly to Sainte-Anne-de Beaupré, continue northeast on Route 440 for approximately 29 kilometers (18 miles) and exit at Sainte-Anne-de-Beaupré.

An alternative way to reach Sainte-Anne-de-Beaupré is to take Route 360 or avenue Royale. Take Route 440 from Québec City, turn left at d'Estimauville, and right on boulevard des Chutes until it intersects with Route 360. Also called "le chemin du Roi" (the King's Road), this panoramic route is one of the oldest in North America, winding 30 kilometers (18.8 miles) along the steep ridge of the Côte de Beaupré. The road borders 17th- and 18th-century farmhouses, historic churches, and Normandy-style homes with half-buried root cellars. Route 360 goes past the Sainte-Anne-de-Beaupré Basilica.

## Montmorency Falls

Begin this excursion with a visit to **Montmorency Falls.** The Montmorency River, named after Charles de Montmorency who was a governor of New France, cascades over a coastal cliff and is one of the most beautiful sights in the province. The falls, which are actually 50% higher than the wider Niagara Falls, measure 83 meters (274 feet) in height. During very cold weather conditions, the falls' heavy spray freezes and forms a giant loaf-shape ice cone known to Québecois as the Pain du Sucre (Sugarloaf); this phenomenon attracts sledders and sliders from Québec City. In the warmer months, a park in the river's gorge leads to an observation terrace that is continuously sprayed by a fine drizzle from water pounding onto the cliff rocks. The top of the falls can be observed from avenue Royale. *Admission free. Open daily.*

**Time Out** **Restaurant Baker** (8790 av. Royale, Château-Richer, tel. 418/824–4478), on the way to Sainte-Anne-de Beaupré on Route 360, is a good, old-fashioned rustic restaurant that serves such hearty traditional French Canadian dishes as meat pie, pea soup, pâtés, and maple-sugar pie.

### Basilique Sainte-Anne-de-Beaupré

The monumental and inspiring **Basilique Sainte-Anne-de-Beaupré** (Sainte-Anne-de-Beaupré Basilica) is located in a small town with the same name. The basilica has become a popular attraction as well as an important shrine: More than half a million people visit the site each year.

The French brought their devotion to Saint Anne with them when they sailed across the Atlantic to New France. In 1650, Breton sailors caught in a storm vowed to erect a chapel in honor of this patron saint at the exact spot where they would land. The present-day neo-Roman basilica constructed in 1923 was the fifth to be built on the site where the sailors first touched ground.

According to local legend, Saint Anne was responsible over the years for saving voyagers from shipwrecks in the harsh waters of the St. Lawrence. Tributes to her miraculous powers can be seen in the shrine's various mosaics, murals, altars, and church ceilings. A bas-relief at the entrance depicts Saint Anne welcoming her pilgrims, and ceiling mosaics represent details from her life. Numerous crutches and braces posted on the back pillars have been left by those who have felt the healing powers of Saint Anne.

The basilica, which is in the shape of a Latin cross, has two granite steeples jutting from its gigantic structure. Its interior has 22 chapels and 18 altars, as well as round arches and numerous ornaments in the Romanesque style. The 214 stained-glass windows by Frenchmen Auguste Labouret and Pierre Chaudière, finished in 1949, tell a story of salvation through personages who were believed to be instruments of God over the centuries. Other features of the shrine include intricately carved wood pews decorated with various animals and several smaller altars (behind the main altar) that are dedicated to different saints.

The original wood chapel built in the village of Sainte-Anne-de-Beaupré during the 17th century was situated too close to the St. Lawrence and was swept away by flooding of the river. In 1676, the chapel was replaced by a stone church that was visited by pilgrims for more than a century, but this structure was also demolished in 1872. The first basilica, which replaced the stone church, was destroyed by a fire in 1922. The following year architects Maxime Rosin from Paris and Louis-N. Audet from Québec province designed the basilica that now stands. *10,018 av. Royale, Sainte-Anne-de-Beaupré, tel. 418/827–3781. Admission free. Reception booth open mid-May–mid-Oct., daily 8:30–7:30. Tours daily in summer at 1 PM start at the information booth at the southwest corner of the courtyard outside the basilica. Guided tours during the off-season (Sept.–mid-May) can be arranged by phoning in advance.*

Across the street from the basilica on avenue Royale is the **Commemorative Chapel,** designed by Claude Bailiff and built in 1878. The memorial chapel was constructed on the location of the transept of a stone church built in 1676 and contains the old building's foundations. Among the remnants housed here are the old church's bell dating from 1696, an early 18th-century altar designed by Vezina, a crucifix sculpted by François-Noël Levaseur in 1775, and a pulpit designed by François Baillargé in 1807.

# Excursion 2: Ile d'Orléans

**Ile d'Orléans,** an island slightly downstream in a northeasterly direction from Québec City, exemplifies the historic charm of rural Québec province with its quiet, traditional life-style. A drive around the island will take you past stone churches that are among the oldest in the region and centuries-old houses amid acres of lush orchards and cultivated farmland. Horse-drawn carriages are still a means of transport. Ile d'Orléans is also an important marketplace that provides fresh produce daily for Québec City; roadside stands on the island sell a variety of local products, such as crocheted blankets, woven articles, maple syrup, homemade bread and jams, and fruits and vegetables.

The island was discovered at about the same time as Québec City in 1535. Explorer Jacques Cartier noticed an abundance of vines on the island and called it the "Island of Bacchus," after the Greek god of wine. In 1536, Cartier renamed the island in honor of the duke of Orléans, son of the king of France, François I. Long considered part of the domain of Côte de Beaupré, the island was not given its seignorial autonomy until 1636, when it was bought by La Compagne des Cents Associés, a group formed by Louis XIII to promote settlement in New France.

Ile d'Orléans, about 9 kilometers (5 miles) wide and 34 kilometers (21 miles) long, is now composed of six small villages. These villages have sought over the years to remain relatively private residential and agricultural communities; the island's bridge to the mainland was built only in 1935.

## Important Addresses and Numbers

**Tourist Information**  **Beau Temps, Mauvais Temps** has a tourist office located in Sainte-Pétronille. *22 rue du Quai, suite 101, tel. 418/828–2275. Open Feb.– May, weekdays 8:30–4; June–Sept., daily 8:30–8; Oct.–Jan., will respond to messages left on answering machine.*

The island's **Chamber of Commerce** operates a tourist information kiosk situated at the west corner of côte du Pont and chemin Royal. *490 côte du Pont, Saint-Pierre, tel. 418/828–9411. Open June–Sept., daily 10–7; Oct.–May, weekdays (no fixed schedule).*

**Medical Clinic**  **Centre Médical** (1015 rte. Prévost, Saint-Pierre, tel. 418/828–2213) is the only medical clinic on the island.

## Guided Tours

**Beau Temps, Mauvais Temps** (22 rue du Quai, suite 101, Sainte-Pétronille, Ile d'Orléans, tel. 418/828–2275) offers guided walking tours of three villages: Sainte-Pétronille, Saint-Jean, and Saint-Laurent. River excursions departing from Saint-Laurent are available from mid-May–mid-September. In addition, the company is a referral service for lodging.

Beau Temps, Mauvais Temps also sells dinner-theater packages, which include a meal at one of the island's restaurants, followed by a play at one of three theaters on Ile d'Orléans and Ancienne Lorette. *Available mid-May–Labor Day. Cost: Wed. and Thurs. $45–$60, Fri.–Sun. $47–$62.*

Québec City touring companies, including **Maple Leaf Sightseeing Tours** (tel. 418/649–9226), **Gray Line** (tel. 418/622–7420), and **Visite Touristiques de Québec** (tel. 418/653–9722) offer full- and half-day bus tours of the western tip of the island, combined with sightseeing along the Côte de Beaupré.

Any of the offices of the **Québec City Region Tourism and Convention Bureau** can provide information on tours and accommodations on the island (*see* Staying in Québec City, *above*).

## Arriving and Departing

**By Car**  Ile d'Orléans has no public transportation; cars are the only way to get to and around the island, unless you take a guided tour (*see* Guided Tours, *above*). Parking on the island is never a problem; you can always stop and explore the villages on foot. The main road, chemin Royal (Route 368), extends 67 kilometers (40 miles) through the island's six villages; street numbers along chemin Royal begin at No. 1 for each municipality.

From Québec City, take Route 440 (Dufferin-Montmorency Autoroute) northeast. After a drive of approximately 10 kilometers (7 miles) take the bridge, Pont de l'Ile d'Orléans, to reach the island. Before you get to the island's only traffic light, turn right heading west on chemin Royal to begin the exploring tour, *below*.

## Exploring Ile d'Orléans

*Numbers in the margin correspond to points of interest on the Ile d'Orléans map.*

Start your tour heading west on chemin Royal to **Sainte-Pétronille**, the first village to be settled on the island. Founded in 1648, the community was chosen in 1759 by British General James Wolfe for his headquarters. With 40,000 soldiers and a hundred ships, the English bombarded French-occupied Québec City and Côte de Beaupré.

During the late-19th century, the English population of Québec developed Sainte-Pétronille into a resort village. This section is considered by many to be the island's most beautiful area, not only because of the spectacular views it offers of Montmorency Falls and Québec City but also for the stylish English villas and exquisitely tended gardens that can be seen from the roadside.

On the left at 20 chemin Royal is the **Plante family farm,** where you can stop to pick apples (in season) or buy some of the island's fresh fruits and vegetables.

**1** Farther along on the right is the **Maison Gourdeau de Beaulieu House** (137 chemin Royal), the island's first home, built in 1648 for Jacques Gourdeau de Beaulieu, who was the first seigneur of Sainte-Pétronille. Today this white building with blue shutters is still owned by his descendants. Over the years, the house has been remodeled and it now incorporates both French and Québecois styles. Its thick walls and dormer windows are characteristic of Breton architecture, but its sloping bell-shape roof, designed to protect buildings from large amounts of snow, is typically Québecois.

**2** After you descend an incline, turn right beside the river on the tiny street called **rue Horatio-Walker,** named after the 19th-century painter known for his landscapes of the island. Walker lived on this street from 1904 until his death in 1938. Around the corner are his home and studio, where exhibits of his paintings are held during the summer. *Open by reservation with Beau Temps, Mauvais Temps (tel. 418/828-2275).*

Rue Horatio-Walker was also the place where people crossed the St. Lawrence by an ice path in the winter to go from the island to the mainland before the bridge was built in 1935.

Farther along chemin Royal, at the border of Sainte-Pétronille and Saint-Laurent, look for a large boulder situated in the middle of nowhere. The **roche à Maranda,** named after the owner of the property where the rock was discovered in the 19th century, is one of the oldest rock formations in the world. When the glaciers melted in 9000 BC, the land at the foot of the Laurentian mountains (today the Côte de Beaupré) was flooded and formed the Sea of Champlain. As the waters receded, the island detached itself from the land, and such rocks as this one rolled down with glacial water from the Laurentians, onto lower land.

**3** As you approach the village of Saint-Laurent, you'll find the **studio of blacksmith Guy Bel** (2200 chemin Royal, tel. 418/828-9300), a talented and well-known local craftsman who has done the ironwork restoration for Québec City. He was born in Lyons, France, and studied there at the École des Beaux Arts. In the summer, you can watch him hard at work; his stylish candlesticks, mantels, and other ironworks are for sale.

**Saint-Laurent,** founded in 1679, is one of the island's maritime villages. Until as late as 1935, residents here used boats as their main means of transportation. Next to the village's marina stands the **4** tall, inspiring **Saint-Laurent Church.** Built in 1860, it was erected on the site of an 18th-century church that, because of its poor construction, had to be torn down. One of the church's procession chapels is a miniature stone replica of the church. *1532 chemin Royal. Admission free. Open summer, daily.*

Ile d'Orléans is known for its superb fruits, and you won't find better strawberries anywhere else in the province. There are about two dozen spots where you can pick your own. One of the larger fields, **5** **Domaine de l'Auto-Cueillette** (211 chemin Royal), is located in Saint-Laurent. You can buy a basket for picking for around 50¢; a full basket of strawberries will cost about $5.

**Time Out**   **Moulin de Saint-Laurent** is an early 18th-century stone mill. Dine here in the herb-and-flower garden out back. Scrumptious snacks, such as quiches, bagels, and salads, are available at the café-terrace. *754 chemin Royal, tel. 418/829-3888. AE, DC, MC, V. Closed Nov.-Apr.*

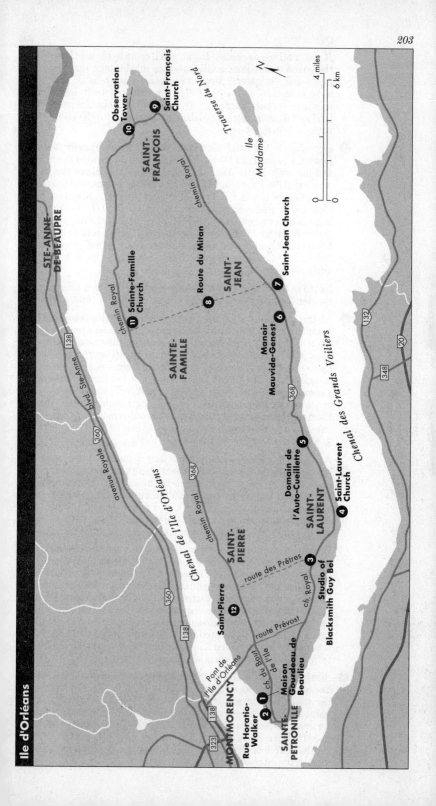

Ile d'Orléans

If you continue on chemin Royal, you'll come to the southern side of the island, **Saint-Jean,** a village whose inhabitants were once river pilots and navigators. Most of its small, homogeneous row homes were built close to the river between 1840 and 1860. Being at sea most of the time, the sailors did not need large homes and plots of land as did the farmers. The island's sudden drop in elevation is most noticeable in Saint-Jean.

❻ Saint-Jean's beautiful Normandy-style manor, **Manoir Mauvide-Genest,** was built in 1734 for Jean Mauvide—surgeon to Louis XV—and his wife, Marie-Anne Genest. Most notable about this house, which still has its original thick walls, ceiling beams, and fireplaces, is the degree to which it has held up over the years, in spite of being targeted by English guns during the 1759 siege of Québec City. The home is a pleasure to roam; all rooms are furnished with original antiques from the 18th and 19th centuries. It also offers an exhibit on French architecture and a downstairs restaurant that serves French cuisine. *1451 chemin Royal, tel. 418/829–2630. Open June–Aug., daily 10–5; Sept.–mid-Oct., weekends 10–5.*

North of the manor stands **Théâtre Paul-Hébert,** an indoor summer theater founded five years ago by an actor who lives on the island.

❼ At the opposite end of the village, you'll see **Saint-Jean Church,** a massive granite structure with large red doors and a towering steeple built in 1749. The church bears a remarkable resemblance to a ship; it is big and round and appears to be sitting right on the St. Lawrence River. Paintings of the patron saints of seamen line the interior walls. The church's cemetery is also intriguing, especially if you can read French. Back in the 18th century, piloting the St. Lawrence was a dangerous profession; the boats could not easily handle the rough currents. The cemetery tombstones recall the tragedies of lives lost in these harsh waters. *2001 chemin Royal, tel. 418/829–3182. Admission free. Open summer, daily.*

As you leave Saint-Jean, chemin Royal mounts the incline and
❽ crosses **route du Mitan.** In old French, *mitan* means "halfway." This road, dividing the island in half, is the most direct route from north to south. It is also the most beautiful on the island, with acres of tended farmland, apple orchards, and maple groves. If you're running out of time and want to end the tour here, take route du Mitan, which brings you to Saint-Pierre and the bridge to the mainland.

When you come to 17th-century farmhouses separated by sprawling open fields, you know you've reached the island's least-toured and most rustic village, **Saint-François.** At the eastern tip of the island, this community is the one situated farthest from the St. Lawrence River and was originally settled mainly by farmers. Saint-François is also the perfect place to visit one of the island's *cabanes à sucre* (maple-sugaring huts) found along chemin Royal. Stop at a hut for a tasting tour; sap is gathered from the maple groves and boiled until it turns to a syrup. When it is poured on ice, it tastes like a delicious toffee. The maple season is late March through April.

❾ Straight on chemin Royal is **Saint-François Church,** built in 1734 and one of eight provincial churches dating from the French regime. At the time the English seized Québec in 1759, General Wolfe knew Saint-François to be among the better strategic points along the St. Lawrence. Consequently, he stationed the British troops here and used the church as a military hospital. In May 1988, a fatal car crash set the church on fire. Although it is in the process of being rebuilt, most of the interior treasures were lost.

⑩ About a mile down the road is a picnic area with a wood **observation tower** situated for perfect viewing of the majestic St. Lawrence at its widest point, 10 times as wide as it is near Québec City. During the spring and autumn months, you can observe wild Canadian geese here.

Heading west on chemin Royal, you'll come to one of the island's earliest villages, Sainte-Famille, which was founded in 1661. The scenery is exquisite here; there are abundant apple orchards and strawberry fields with a view of Côte de Beaupré and Mont Sainte-Anne in the distance. But the village also has plenty of man-made historic charm; it has the area's highest concentration of stone houses dating from the French regime.

⑪ Take a quick look at **Sainte-Famille Church,** which was constructed in 1749, later than some of the others on the island. This impressive structure is the only church in the province to have three bell towers at the front. Its ceiling was redone in the mid-19th century with elaborate designs in wood and gold. The church also holds a famous painting, *L'Enfant Jésus Voyant la Croix,* done in 1670 by Frère Luc (Father Luc), who was sent from France to decorate churches in the area. *3915 chemin Royal. Admission free. Open summer, daily.*

⑫ The next village situated on the north side of the island, **Saint-Pierre,** was established a bit later than Sainte-Famille, in 1679. Its church, though, is older—dating back to 1717—and is officially the oldest on the island. **Saint-Pierre Church** is no longer open for worship, but it was restored during the 1960s and is open to tourists. Many of its original components are still intact, such as benches with compartments below, where hot bricks and stones were placed to keep people warm during winter services. *1243 chemin Royal. Admission free. Open summer, daily.*

Because Saint-Pierre is situated on a plateau with the island's most fertile land, the village has long been the center of traditional farming industries. The best products grown here are potatoes, asparagus, and corn, and the many dairy farms have given the village a renowned reputation for butter and other dairy products. At 2370 chemin Royal is the former home of Felix Leclerc, one of the many artists who have made the island their home. Leclerc, the father of Québecois folk singing, lived here until he died in August 1988.

If you continue west on chemin Royal, just up ahead are the bridge back to the mainland and Route 440.

## Dining and Lodging

For price categories, *see* Québec City Dining and Lodging, *above.*

**Dining** **La Goéliche.** The first rule of the kitchen is that only the freshest
**$$$** ingredients from the island's farms can be used. The menu is classic French and depends upon the fruits and vegetables in season. Lunch is a moderately priced à la carte selection of salads, quiches, and omelets. The evening's menu is more expensive and features such specialties as quail with red vermouth and chicken with pistachio mousseline. The desserts, such as maple syrup mousse with strawberry syrup, have a regional flavor. This rustic inn has a romantic dining room with windows overlooking the St. Lawrence River and a view of Québec City. *22 chemin du Quai, Sainte-Pétronille, tel. 418/828–2248. Reservations advised. Dress: casual but neat. MC, V. Closed Jan.*

**$$$** **L'Atre.** After you park your car, you'll take a horse-drawn carriage to a 17th-century Normandy-style house furnished with Québecois pine antiques. True to the establishment's name, which means "hearth," all the traditional dishes are cooked and served from a fireplace. The menu emphasizes hearty fare, such as beef Bourguignon and *tourtière* (meat pie), with maple-sugar pie for dessert. La Grande Fête (The Big Feast) is a nine-course dinner that costs about $60. Half way through the meal, guests visit the attic for a nip of maple syrup liqueur. *4403 chemin Royal, Sainte-Famille, tel. 418/829-2474. Reservations required. Dress: casual but neat. AE, MC, V. Open mid-May-mid-Oct.; occasionally in winter; call ahead.*

**Lodging** **Auberge le Chaumonot.** This medium-size hotel in rural Saint-
**$$** François is right near the St. Lawrence River's widest point. The inn's large bay windows capitalize on the view of the river and neighboring islands, but the decor is uninspired, with simple wood furniture of the island. The service here is efficient and friendly. The restaurant serves Continental cuisine, with table d'hôte and à la carte menus. *425 chemin Royal, Saint-François, G0A 3S0, tel. 418/ 829-2735. 8 rooms with private bath and air-conditioning. Facilities: restaurant, pool. AE, MC, V. Closed Nov.-Apr.*

**$$** **La Goéliche.** This 1890 Victorian country inn stands just steps away from the St. Lawrence River in the village of Sainte-Pétronille. Québecois antiques decorate light and spacious rooms with their original wood floors. Rooms are on the second and third floors, and half of them look out across the river to Québec City. The rooms have no television, but they do have phones. *22 chemin du Quai, Sainte-Pétronille, G0A 4C0, tel. 418/828-2248. 22 rooms, 18 with private bath. Facilities: 2 restaurants. MC, V.*

You can get to know the island by staying at one of its 30 bed-and-breakfasts. Reservations are necessary. The price for a room, double occupancy, runs about $45-$90. **Beau Temps, Mauvais Temps** (tel. 418/828-2275) is a referral service for these accommodations.

# 5 Vancouver

Updated by
Melissa
Rivers

Vancouver is a young city, even by North American standards. While three to four hundred years of settlement may make cities like Québec and Halifax historically interesting to travelers, Vancouver's youthful vigor attracts visitors to its powerful elements that have not yet been ground down by time. Vancouver is just over a hundred years old; it was not yet a town in 1870, when British Columbia became part of the Canadian confederation. The city's history, such as it is, remains visible to the naked eye: Eras are stacked east to west along the waterfront like some century-old archaeological dig—from cobbled, late-Victorian Gastown to shiny postmodern glass cathedrals of commerce grazing the sunset.

The Chinese were among the first to recognize the possibilities of Vancouver's setting. They came to British Columbia during the 1850s seeking the gold that inspired them to name the province *Gum-shan*, or Gold Mountain. They built the Canadian Pacific Railway that gave Vancouver's original townsite a purpose—one beyond the natural splendor that Royal Navy Capt. George Vancouver admired during his lunchtime cruise around its harbor on June 13, 1792. The transcontinental railway, along with its Great White Fleet of clipper ships, gave Vancouver a full week's edge over the California ports in shipping tea and silk to New York at the dawn of the 20th century.

Vancouver's natural charms are less scattered than in other cities. On clear days, the mountains appear close enough to touch. Two 1,000-acre wilderness parks lie within the city limits. The salt water of the Pacific and fresh water direct from the Rocky Mountain Trench form the city's northern and southern boundaries.

Bring a healthy sense of reverence when you visit: Vancouver is a spiritual place. For its original inhabitants, the Coast Salish peoples, it was the sacred spot where the mythical Thunderbird and Killer Whale flung wind and rain all about the heavens during their epic battles—how else to explain the coast's occasional climatic fits of temper? Devotees of a later religious tradition might worship in the sepulchre of Stanley Park or in the polished, incense-filled quiet of St. James Anglican Church, designed by English architect Sir Adrian Gilbert Scott and perhaps Vancouver's finest building.

Vancouver has a level of nightlife possible only in a place where the finer things in life have never been driven out to the suburbs and where sidewalks have never rolled up at 5 PM. There is no shortage of excellent hotels and restaurants here either. But you can find good theater, accommodations, and dining almost anywhere these days. Vancouver's *real* culture consists of its tall fir trees practically downtown and its towering rock spires close by, the ocean at your doorstep, and people from every corner of the earth all around you.

# Essential Information

### Arriving and Departing by Plane

**Airport and Airlines**
*International Airports*

**Vancouver International Airport** is on an island about 14 kilometers (9 miles) south of downtown. The main terminal building has three levels: departures, international arrivals, and domestic arrivals; a small south terminal building services flights to secondary destinations within the province. **American Airlines** (tel. 800/433–7300), **Delta** (tel. 604/221–1212), **Horizon Air** (800/547–9308), and **United** (tel. 800/241–6522) fly into the airport. The two major domestic airlines are **Air Canada** (tel. 800/776–3000) and **Canadian Airlines** (tel. 800/426–7000).

*Other Facilities*   Air BC (tel. 604/688-5515) offers 30-minute harbor-to-harbor service (downtown Vancouver to downtown Victoria) several times a day. Planes leave from near the Bayshore Hotel. Helijet Airways (tel. 604/273–1414) has helicopter service from downtown Vancouver to downtown Victoria. The heliport is near Vancouver's Pan Pacific Hotel.

**Between the Airport and Downtown**   The drive from the airport to downtown is 20–45 minutes, depending on the time of day. Airport hotels offer free shuttle service to and from the airport.

*By Bus*   The **Airport Express** (tel. 604/261–2299) bus leaves the domestic arrivals level of the terminal building every 15 minutes in summer and every 30 minutes in winter, stopping at major downtown hotels and the bus depot. It operates from 5:30 AM until 12:30 AM. The fare is $8.25 one-way and $14 round-trip.

*By Taxi*   Taxi stands are in front of the terminal building on domestic and international arrivals levels. Taxi fare to downtown is about $24. Area cab companies are Yellow (tel. 604/681–3311) and Black Top (tel. 604/681–2181).

*By Limousine*   Limousine service from **Airlimo** (tel. 604/273–1331) costs about the same as a taxi to downtown: The current rate is about $28.

## Arriving and Departing

**By Car**   From the south, I–5 from Seattle becomes **Highway 99** at the U.S.–Canada border. Vancouver is a three-hour drive from Seattle. Avoid border crossings during peak times: holidays and weekends.

Highway 1, the **Trans-Canada Highway,** enters Vancouver from the east. To avoid traffic, arrive after rush hour (8:30 AM).

**By Ferry**   **BC Ferries** operates two major ferry terminals outside Vancouver. From Tsawwassen to the south (an hour's drive from downtown), ferries sail to Victoria and Nanaimo on Vancouver Island and through the Gulf Islands (the small islands between the mainland and Vancouver Island). From Horseshoe Bay (30 minutes north of downtown), ferries sail a short distance up the coast and to Nanaimo on Vancouver Island. Call 604/277–0277 for departure and arrival times.

**By Train**   The Pacific Central Station (1150 Station St.) is the hub for rail, bus, and SkyTrain service. The **VIA Rail** (tel. 800/561–8630) station is at Main Street and Terminal Avenue. VIA provides trans-continental service through Jasper to Toronto three times a week. Passenger trains leave the **BC Rail** (tel. 604/631–3500) station in North Vancouver for Whistler and the interior of British Columbia. There is no Amtrak service from Seattle.

**By Bus**   **Greyhound Lines** (tel. 604/662–3222) is the biggest bus line servicing Vancouver. The Pacific Central Station (1150 Station St.) is the depot. **Quick Shuttle** (tel. 604/244–3744 or 800/665-2122 in the U.S.) bus service runs between Vancouver and Seattle six times a day.

## Getting Around

**By Car**   Although no freeways cross Vancouver, rush-hour traffic is not yet horrendous. The worst rush-hour bottlenecks are the North Shore

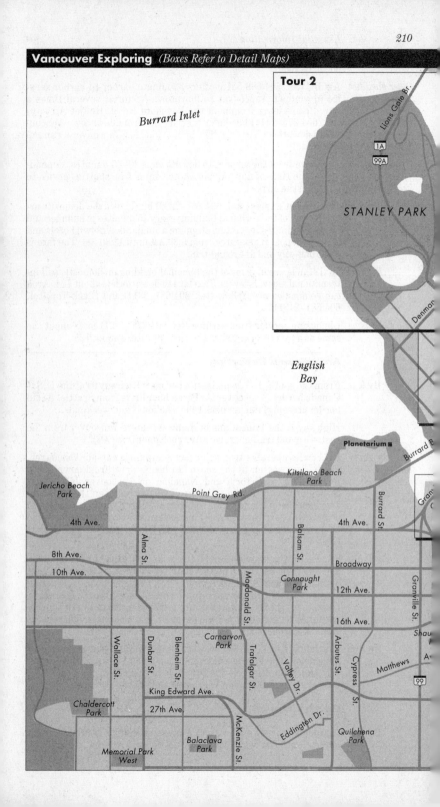

**Tour 2**

Lions Gate Br.

1A

99A

STANLEY PARK

Denman

*Burrard Inlet*

*English Bay*

Planetarium■

Burrard B

*Kitsilano Beach Park*

*Jericho Beach Park*

Point Grey Rd.

Burrard St.

4th Ave.

4th Ave.

Gran

Balsam St.

Alma St.

8th Ave.

10th Ave.

Broadway

Connaught Park

Macdonald St.

12th Ave.

Granville St.

16th Ave.

Shau

Carnarvon Park

Wallace St.

Dunbar St.

Blenheim St.

Trafalgar St.

Valley Dr.

Arbutus St.

Cypress St.

Matthews

A

99

Chaldercott Park

King Edward Ave.

27th Ave.

McKenzie St.

Eddington Dr.

Quilchena Park

Memorial Park West

Balaclava Park

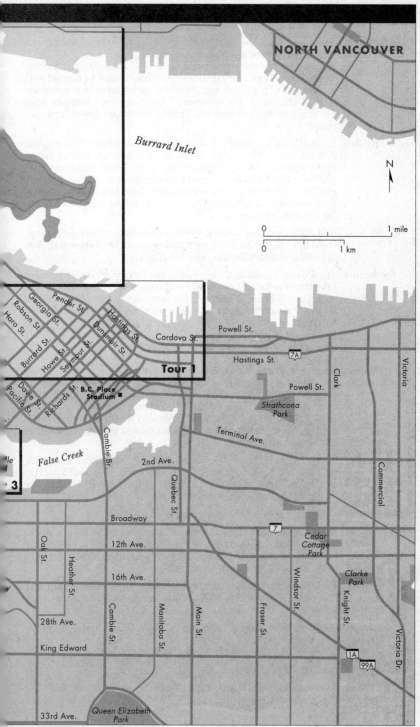

NORTH VANCOUVER

Burrard Inlet

N

0                    1 mile
0                    1 km

Pender St.
Georgia St.
Robson St.
Haro St.
Hastings St.
Dunsmuir St.
Cordova St.
Burrard St.
Howe St.
Seymour St.
Davie St.
Richards St.
Pacific St.

**Tour 1**

Powell St.
Hastings St.  7A
Powell St.
Clark
Victoria

B.C. Place
Stadium

Strathcona
Park

Terminal Ave.

False Creek

3

2nd Ave.

Quebec St.

Broadway

7

Cedar
Cottage
Park

Clarke
Park

Commercial

Oak St.

Heather St.

12th Ave.

16th Ave.

Windsor St.

Knight St.

Victoria Dr.

28th Ave.

King Edward

Cambie St.

Manitoba St.

Main St.

Fraser St.

1A
99A

33rd Ave.

Queen Elizabeth
Park

Cambie Br.

bridges, the George Massey Tunnel on Highway 99 south of Vancouver, and Highway 1 through Coquitlam and Surrey.

**By Rapid Transit** Vancouver has a one-line, 25-kilometer (15-mile) rapid transit system called **SkyTrain**, which travels underground downtown and is elevated for the rest of its route to New Westminster and Surrey. Trains leave about every five minutes. Tickets must be carried with you as proof of payment, and are sold at each station from machines; correct change is not necessary. You may use transfers from SkyTrain to SeaBus and BC Transit buses (*see below*) and vice versa.

**By Bus** Exact change is needed to ride the buses: $1.50 adults, 75¢ for senior citizens and children 5–13. Books of 25 tickets are sold at convenience stores and newsstands; look for a red, white, and blue "Fare Dealer" sign. Day passes, good for unlimited travel after 9:30 AM, cost $4.50 for adults. They are available from fare dealers and any SeaBus or SkyTrain station. Transfers are valid for 90 minutes and allow travel in both directions.

**By Taxi** It is difficult to hail a cab in Vancouver; unless you're near a hotel, you'd have better luck calling a taxi service. Try **Yellow** (tel. 604/681–3311) or **Black Top** (tel. 604/681–2181).

**By SeaBus** The **SeaBus** is a 400-passenger commuter ferry that crosses Burrard Inlet from the foot of Lonsdale (North Vancouver) to downtown. The ride takes 13 minutes and costs the same as the transit bus. With a transfer, connection can be made with any BC Transit bus or SkyTrain.

## Important Addresses and Numbers

**Tourist Information** **Vancouver Travel Infocentre** (200 Burrard St., tel. 604/683–2000) provides maps and information about the city and is open in summer, daily 8–6; in winter, weekdays 8:30–5, Saturday 9–5. A kiosk in Pacific Centre Mall is open daily in summer, Monday–Saturday 9:30–5, Sunday noon–5; in winter, Monday–Saturday 9–5. Eaton's department store downtown also has a tourist information counter that is open all year.

**Embassies** There are no embassies in Vancouver, only consulates and trade commissions: **United States** (1075 W. Pender St., tel. 604/685–4311) and **United Kingdom** (800–1111 Melville St., tel. 604/683–4421). For a complete listing, see the Yellow Pages.

**Emergencies** Call 911 for **police, fire department,** and **ambulance.**

*Hospitals and Clinics* **St. Paul's Hospital** (1081 Burrard St., tel. 604/682–2344), a downtown hospital, has an emergency ward. **Medicentre** (1055 Dunsmuir St., lower level, tel. 604/683–8138), a drop-in clinic on the lower level of the Bentall Centre, is open weekdays.

*Dentist* The counterpart to Medicentre is **Dentacentre** (1055 Dunsmuir St., lower level, tel. 604/669–6700), which is next door and is also open weekdays.

*Late-night Pharmacy* **Shopper's Drug Mart** (1125 Davie St., tel. 604/685–6445) offers 24-hour service daily.

*Road Emergencies* **BCAA** (tel. 604/293–2222) has 24-hour emergency road service for members of AAA or CAA.

**Travel Agencies** **American Express Travel Service** (1040 W. Georgia St., tel. 604/669–2813), **Hagen's Travel** (185–1200 W. 73rd Ave., tel. 604/684–2448), and **P. Lawson Travel** (409 Granville St., Suite 150, tel. 604/682–4272).

## Opening and Closing Times

**Banks** traditionally are open Monday–Thursday 10–3 and Friday 10–6, but many banks have extended hours and are open on Saturday, particularly outside of downtown.

**Museums** are generally open 10–5, including Saturday and Sunday. Most are open one evening a week as well.

**Department store** hours are Monday–Wednesday and Saturday 9:30–6, Thursday and Friday 9:30–9, and Sunday noon–5. Many smaller stores are also open Sunday. Robson Street and Chinatown are particularly good for Sunday shopping.

## Guided Tours

**Orientation** **Gray Line** (tel. 604/879-3363), the largest tour operator, offers the 3½-hour Grand City bus tour year-round. Departing from the Sandman Inn in summer and the Plaza of Nations in winter, the tour includes Stanley Park, Chinatown, Gastown, English Bay, and Queen Elizabeth Park and costs about $31. During the spring, summer, and fall, **Westcoast City and Nature Sightseeing** (tel. 604/451–5581) accommodates up to 24 people in vans that run a 3½-hour City Highlights Tour for $27 (pickup available from any downtown location). Using minibuses, **Vance Tours** (tel. 604/941–5660) offers a similar tour (3½ hours, $32) that includes a visit to the University of British Columbia, and a shorter city tour (2½ hours, $30).

The **Vancouver Trolley Company** (tel. 604/451-5581) runs turn-of-the-century–style trolleys through Vancouver from April to October on a 1½-hour narrated tour of Stanley Park, Gastown, English Bay, the Vancouver Museum, Granville Island, Queen Elizabeth Park, Science World, and Chinatown, among other sights. A day pass allows you to complete one full circuit, getting off and on as often as you like. Start the trip at any of the sights and buy a ticket on board. It's a perfect way to deal with a rainy day in Vancouver. Adult fare is $15, children's $7. Between June and September, **Gray Line** (tel. 604/879–3363) offers a similar narrated tour aboard double-decker buses; passengers get on and off as they choose and are allowed to ride free the following day if they haven't had their fill. Adult fare is $17, children's $8.

North Shore tours usually include any or several of the following: a gondola ride up Grouse Mountain, a walk across the Capilano Suspension Bridge, a stop at a salmon hatchery, the Lonsdale Quay Market, and a ride back to town on the SeaBus. Half-day tours cost anywhere from $30–$45 and are offered by **Landsea Tours** (tel. 604/255–7272), **Harbour Ferries** (tel. 604/687–9558), **Gray Line** (tel. 604/879–3363), and **Pacific Coach Lines** (tel. 604/662–7575).

**Air Tours** Tour the mountains and fjords of the North Shore by helicopter for $175 per person (minimum of three people) for 50 minutes: Vancouver Helicopters (tel. 604/270–1484) flies from the Harbour Heliport downtown. Or see Vancouver from the air for $65 for 30 minutes: Harbour Air's (tel. 604/688–1277) seaplanes leave from beside the Bayshore Hotel.

**Boat Tours** The Royal Hudson, Canada's only functioning steam train, heads along the mountainous coast up Howe Sound to the logging town of Squamish. After a break to explore, you sail back to Vancouver via the MV *Britannia*. This highly recommended excursion costs about $55, takes 7 hours, and is organized by **Harbour Ferries** (tel. 604/687–9558). Reservations are necessary.

The **SS** *Beaver* (tel. 604/682–7284), a replica of a Hudson Bay fur-trading vessel that ran aground here in 1888, offers two trips. One is the Harbour Sunset Dinner Cruise, a three-hour trip with a barbecue dinner; the other is a four-hour daytime trip up Indian Arm with salmon for lunch. Each is under $50 and reservations are necessary for both.

**Harbour Ferries** (tel. 604/687–9558) takes a 1½-hour tour of Burrard Inlet in a paddlewheeler, and costs under $20.

**Fraser River Connection** (tel. 604/525–4465) will take you on a six-hour tour of a fascinating working river—past log booms, tugs, and houseboats. Between May and October, ride from New Westminster to Fort Langley, aboard a convincing replica of an 1800s-era paddlewheeler, for about $25.

**Personal Guides**   **Early Motion Tours** (tel. 604/687–5088) covers Vancouver in a Model-A Ford convertible that comfortably seats about four people. For about $60, up to four people can take an hour-long trip around downtown, Chinatown, and Stanley Park.

**AAA Horse & Carriage** (tel. 604/681–5115) has a 50-minute tour of Stanley Park, along the waterfront, and through a cedar forest and a rose garden for about $10.

# Exploring Vancouver

The heart of Vancouver—which includes the downtown area, Stanley Park, and the West End high-rise residential neighborhood—sits on a peninsula bordered by English Bay and the Pacific Ocean to the west; by False Creek, the inlet home to Granville Island, to the south; and to the north by Burrard Inlet, the working port of the city, past which loom the North Shore mountains. The oldest part of the city—Gastown and Chinatown—lies at the edge of Burrard Inlet, around Main Street, which runs north–south and is roughly the dividing line between the east side and the west side. All the avenues, which are numbered, have east and west designations.

### Highlights for First-time Visitors

**Chinatown,** Tour 1: Downtown Vancouver
**English Bay,** Tour 2: Stanley Park
**Granville Island,** Tour 3: Granville Island
**Stanley Park,** Tour 2: Stanley Park

### Tour 1: Downtown Vancouver

*Numbers in the margin correspond to points of interest on the Tour 1: Downtown Vancouver map.*

❶ You can logically begin your downtown tour in either of two ways. If you're in for a day of shopping, amble down **Robson Street** (*see* Shopping, *below*), where you'll find any item from souvenirs to high fashions, from espresso to sushi.

❷ If you opt otherwise, start at **Robson Square,** built in 1975 and designed by architect Arthur Erickson to be the gathering place of downtown Vancouver. The complex, which functions from the outside as a park, encompasses the Vancouver Art Gallery and govern-

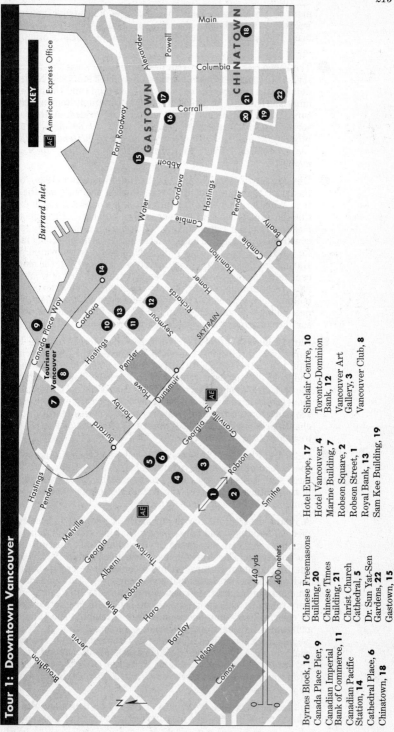

# Tour 1: Downtown Vancouver

**KEY**

**AE** American Express Office

Burrard Inlet

GASTOWN

CHINATOWN

Main
Powell
Alexander
Columbia
Carrall
Port Roadway
Abbott
Water
Cordova
Hastings
Pender
Cambie
Beatty
Hamilton
Homer
Richards
SKYTRAIN
Seymour
Granville St
Dunsmuir
Howe
Hornby
Burrard
Georgia
Robson
Smithe
Nelson
Comox
Haro
Barclay
Thurlow
Bute
Jervis
Broughton
Alberni
Melville
Canada Place Way
Tourism Vancouver

440 yds
400 meters

N

Byrnes Block, **16**
Canada Place Pier, **9**
Canadian Imperial Bank of Commerce, **11**
Canadian Pacific Station, **14**
Cathedral Place, **6**
Chinatown, **18**

Chinese Freemasons Building, **20**
Chinese Times Building, **21**
Christ Church Cathedral, **5**
Dr. Sun Yat-Sen Gardens, **22**
Gastown, **15**

Hotel Europe, **17**
Hotel Vancouver, **4**
Marine Building, **7**
Robson Square, **2**
Robson Street, **1**
Royal Bank, **13**
Sam Kee Building, **19**

Sinclair Centre, **10**
Toronto-Dominion Bank, **12**
Vancouver Art Gallery, **3**
Vancouver Club, **8**

ment offices and law courts that have been built under landscaped walkways, a block-long glass canopy, and a waterfall that helps mask traffic noise. An ice-skating rink and restaurants occupy the below-street level.

❸ The **Vancouver Art Gallery** that heads the square was a neoclassical-style 1912 courthouse until Erickson converted it in 1980. Notice the detail: lions that guard the majestic front steps and the use of columns and domes—features borrowed from ancient Roman architecture. In back of the old courthouse, a more modest staircase now serves as a speakers' corner. *750 Hornby St., tel. 604/682–5621. Admission: $5 adults, $2.50 students and senior citizens; free Thurs. eve. Open Mon., Wed., Fri., and Sat. 10–5; Thurs. 10–9; Sun. noon–5.*

❹ Directly across Hornby Street is the **Hotel Vancouver** (1939), one of the last of the railway-built hotels. (The last one built was the Chateau Whistler, in 1989.) Reminiscent of a medieval French castle, this château style has been incorporated into hotels throughout almost every major Canadian city. With the onset of the depression, construction was halted here, and the hotel was finished only in time for the visit of King George VI in 1939. It has been renovated twice: During the 1960s it was unfortunately modernized, but the more recent refurbishment is more in keeping with the spirit of what is the most recognizable roof on Vancouver's skyline. The exterior of the building has carvings of malevolent gargoyles at the corners, an ornate chimney, Indian chiefs on the Hornby Street side, and an assortment of grotesque mythological figures.

❺ **Christ Church Cathedral** (1895), across the street from the Hotel Vancouver, is the oldest church in Vancouver. The tiny church was built in a Gothic style with buttresses and pointed arched windows and looks like the parish church of an English village. By contrast, the cathedral's rough-hewn interior is that of a frontier town, with Douglas-fir beams and carpenter woodwork that offers excellent acoustics for the frequent vespers, carol services, and Gregorian chants presented here. *690 Burrard St., tel. 604/682–3848. Open weekdays 10–4.*

❻ **Cathedral Place,** on the corner of Hornby and Georgia streets, is a spectacular office tower adjacent to Christ Church Cathedral. Three large sculptures of nurses at the corners of the building are replicas of the statues that graced the Art Deco Georgia Medical-Dental Building, the site's previous structure.

A restored terra-cotta arch—formerly the front entrance to the medical building—and frieze panels showing scenes of individuals administering care now grace the **Canadian Craft Museum,** across the courtyard. The Craft Museum, which opened in 1992, is one of the first national cultural facilities dedicated to craft—historical and contemporary, functional and decorative. Craft embodies the human need for artistic expression in everyday life, and examples here range from elegantly carved utensils with decorative handles to colorful hand-spun and hand-woven garments. The three-level museum offers exhibits, workshops, lectures, and the Museum Shop, which specializes in, of course, Canadian crafts. The restful courtyard is a quiet place to take a break. *639 Hornby St., tel 604/ 687–8266. Admission: $4 adults, $2 senior citizens and students, children under 12 free. Open Mon.–Sat. 9:30–5:30, Sun. and holidays noon–5.*

Cathedral Place also is the site of the **Sri Lankan Gem Museum,** which opened in 1993. The museum features a floor of 9,000 polished agates set in aggregate, and some $5 million worth of gemstones, including moonstones, rubies, lapis, diamonds, garnets, jade, and emeralds. Many of the gems are from Sri Lanka. *925 W. Georgia St., tel. 604/662–7708. Admission: $3.50 (proceeds go to the Vancouver Symphony Orchestra). Open Mon.–Sat. 10:30–5:30.*

**❼** The **Marine Building** (1931), at the foot of Burrard Street, is Canada's best example of Art Deco architecture. Terra-cotta bas-reliefs depict the history of transportation: Airships, biplanes, steamships, locomotives, and submarines are figured. These motifs were once considered radical and modernistic adornments, because most buildings were still using classical or Gothic ornamentation. From the east, the Marine Building is reflected in bronze by 999 West Hastings, and in silver from the southeast by the Canadian Imperial Bank of Commerce. Stand on the corner of Hastings and Hornby streets for the best view of the Marine Building.

A nice walk is along Hastings Street—the old financial district. Until the period between 1966 and 1972, when the first of the bank towers and underground malls on West Georgia Street were developed, this was Canada's westernmost business terminus. The temple-style banks, businessmen's clubs, and investment houses survive as evidence of the city's sophisticated architectural advances prior to

**❽** World War I. The **Vancouver Club,** built between 1912 and 1914, was a gathering place for the city's elite. Its architectural design is reminiscent of private clubs in England that were inspired by Italian Renaissance palaces. The Vancouver Club is still the private haunt of some of the city's businessmen. *915 W. Hastings St., tel. 604/685–9321.*

**❾** The foot of Howe Street, north of Hastings, is **Canada Place Pier.** Originally built on an old cargo pier to be the off-site Canadian pavilion in Expo '86, Canada Place was later converted into Vancouver's Trade and Convention Center. It is dominated at the shore end by the luxurious Pan Pacific Hotel (*see* Lodging, *below*), with its spectacular three-story lobby and waterfall. The convention space is covered by a fabric roof shaped like 10 sails, which has become a landmark of Vancouver's skyline. Below is a cruise ship facility, and at the north end are an Imax theater, a restaurant, and an outdoor performance space. A promenade runs along the pier's west side with views of the Burrard Inlet harbor and Stanley Park. *999 Canada Pl., tel. 604/688–8687.*

---

**Time Out**   Across the street and accessible via an enclosed walkway is the luxurious **Waterfront Centre Hotel,** a 23-story glass structure that opened in 1992. The lobby, lounge, and restaurant offer stunning views of Burrard Inlet; at night, the casual Herons Lounge is filled with the sounds of piano music. Weather permitting, you can enjoy the view from the patio outside Herons Restaurant, where the menu offers local and regional Pacific Rim specialties. *900 Canada Place Way, tel. 604/691-1991.*

---

Just next door to the Waterfront Centre Hotel is the **Tourism Vancouver Infocentre** (200 Burrard St., tel. 604/683-2000), with brochures and personnel to answer questions, as well as an attractive Northwest Coast native art collection.

**❿** Walk back up to Hastings and Howe streets to the **Sinclair Centre.** Vancouver's outstanding architect, Richard Henriquez, has knitted four government office buildings (built 1905–1939) into an office-retail complex. The two Hastings Street buildings—the 1905 post office with the elegant clock tower and the 1913 Winch Building—are linked with the Post Office Extension and Customs Examining Warehouse to the north. Painstaking and very costly restoration involved finding master masons—the original terrazzo suppliers in Europe—and uncovering and refurbishing the pressed-metal ceilings.

Walking a bit farther up Hastings, at Granville Street, will reveal one of Vancouver's oldest and most impressive charter banks, the

**⓫** former **Canadian Imperial Bank of Commerce** headquarters (1906–1908); the columns, arches, and details are of typically Roman influ-

**⓬** ence. The **Toronto–Dominion Bank,** one block east, is of the same style but was built in 1920.

Backtrack directly across from the CIBC on Hastings Street to the

**⓭** more Gothic **Royal Bank.** It was intended to be half of a symmetrical building that was never completed, due to the depression. Striking, though, is the magnificent hall, ecclesiastical in style, reminiscent of a European cathedral.

**⓮** At the foot of Seymour Street is the **Canadian Pacific Station,** the third and most pretentious of three Canadian Pacific Railway passenger terminals. Constructed in 1912–1914, this terminal replaced the other two as the western terminus for Canada's transcontinental railway. After Canada's railways merged, the station became obsolete until a 1978 renovation turned it into an office-retail complex and SeaBus terminal. Murals in the waiting rooms show passengers what kind of scenery to expect on their journeys across Canada.

From Seymour Street, pick up Water Street, on your way to

**⓯** **Gastown.** Named after the original townsite saloon keeper, "Gassy" Jack Deighton, Gastown is where Vancouver originated. Deighton arrived at Burrard Inlet in 1867 with his Indian wife, a barrel of whiskey, and few amenities. A statue of Gassy Jack stands on the north side of Maple Tree Square, the intersection of five streets, where he built his first saloon.

When the transcontinental train arrived in 1887, Gastown became the transfer point for trade with the Orient and was soon crowded with hotels and warehouses. The Klondike gold rush encouraged further development until 1912, when the "Golden Years" ended. The 1930s–1950s saw hotels being converted into rooming houses and the warehouse district shifting elsewhere. The area gradually became unattended and run-down. However, both Gastown and Chinatown were declared historic areas and have been revitalized.

**⓰** The **Byrnes Block** building was constructed on the corner of Water and Carrall streets (the site of Gassy Jack's second saloon) after the 1886 Great Fire. The date is just visible at the top of the building above the door where it says "Herman Block," which was its name for a short time. The extravagantly detailed Alhambra Hotel that was situated here was luxury class for the time, at a cost of a dollar a night.

Tucked behind 2 Water Street are **Blood Alley** and **Gaoler's Mews.** Once the site of the city's first civic buildings—the constable's cabin and courthouse, and a two-cell log jail—today the cobblestone street with antique streetlighting is the home of architectural offices.

**⓱** The **Hotel Europe** (1908–1909), a flatiron building at Powell and Alexander streets, was billed as the best hotel in the city and was Vancouver's first reinforced concrete structure. Designed as a functional commercial building, the hotel lacks ornamentation and fine detail, a style unusually utilitarian for the time.

From Maple Tree Square, walk three blocks up Carrall Street to
⓲ Pender Street, where **Chinatown** begins. There was already a sizable Chinese community in British Columbia because of the 1858 Cariboo gold rush in central British Columbia, but the biggest influx
from China occurred in the 1880s, during construction of the Canadian Pacific Railway, when 15,000 laborers were imported. The Chinese were among the first inhabitants of Vancouver, and some of the
oldest buildings in the city are in Chinatown.

Even while doing the hazardous work of blasting the railbed through
the Rocky Mountains, the Chinese were discriminated against. The
Anti-Asiatic Riots of 1907 stopped growth in Chinatown for 50
years, and immigration from China was discouraged by more and
more restrictive policies, climaxing in a $500 head tax during the
1920s.

In the 1960s the city council was planning bulldozer urban renewal
for Strathcona, the residential part of Chinatown, and freeway connections through the most historic blocks of Chinatown were
charted. Fortunately, the plans were halted, and today Chinatown
is an expanding, vital district fueled by investment from Vancouver's most notable newcomers—immigrants from Hong Kong. It
is best to view the buildings in Chinatown from the south side of
Pender Street, where the Chinese Cultural Center stands. From
here you'll get a view of important details that adorn the upper stories. The style of architecture in Vancouver's Chinatown is patterned
on that of Canton and won't be seen in any other Canadian cities.

The corner of Carrall and East Pender streets, now the western
boundary of Chinatown, is one of the neighborhood's most historic
⓳ spots. Standing at 8 West Pender Street is the **Sam Kee Building**,
recognized by *Ripley's Believe It or Not!* as the narrowest building
in the world, at just 6 feet wide. The 1913 structure still exists, with
its bay windows overhanging the street and a basement that bur-
rows under the sidewalk.

⓴ The **Chinese Freemasons Building** (1901) at 1 West Pender Street has
two completely different styles of facades: The side facing Chinatown displays a fine example of Cantonese-imported recessed balconies; on the Carrall Street side, the standard Victorian style
common throughout the British Empire is displayed. It was in this
building that Dr. Sun Yat-sen hid for months from the agents of the
Manchu dynasty while he raised funds for its overthrow, which he
accomplished in 1911.

㉑ Directly across Carrall Street is the **Chinese Times Building**, constructed in 1902. Inside, there is a hidden mezzanine floor from
which police officers could hear the clicking sounds of clandestine
mah-jongg games played after sunset. Attempts by vice squads to
enforce restrictive policies against the Chinese gamblers proved
fruitless, because police were unable to find the players, who were
hidden on the secret floor.

㉒ Planning for the **Chinese Cultural Center** and **Dr. Sun Yat-sen Gardens** (1980–1987) began during the late 1960s; the first phase was
designed by James Cheng, a former associate of Arthur Erickson.
The cultural center has exhibition space, classrooms, and meeting
rooms. The Dr. Sun Yat-sen Gardens, located behind the cultural
center, were built by 52 artisans from Suzhou, the Garden City of
the People's Republic. The gardens incorporate design elements
and traditional materials from several of that city's centuries-old
private gardens and are the first living classical Chinese gardens
built outside China. As you walk through the gardens, remember

that no power tools, screws, or nails were used in the construction. Free guided tours are offered throughout the day; telephone for times. *Dr. Sun Yat-sen Gardens. 578 Carrall St., tel. 604/689–7133. Admission: $3.50 adults, $2.50 senior citizens and students, $7 families. Open May–Sept., daily 10–8; Oct.–Apr., daily 10–4:30.*

## Tour 2: Stanley Park

*Numbers in the margin correspond to points of interest on the Tour 2: Stanley Park map.*

A 1,000-acre wilderness park just blocks from the downtown section of a major city is a rarity but is one of Vancouver's major attractions. In the 1860s, due to a threat of American invasion, the area that is now Stanley Park was designated a military reserve (though it was never needed). When the city of Vancouver was incorporated in 1886, the council's first act was to request that the land be set aside for a park. In 1888 permission was granted and the grounds were named Stanley Park after Lord Stanley, then governor general of Canada (the same person after whom hockey's Stanley Cup is named).

An afternoon in Stanley Park gives you a capsule tour of Vancouver that includes beaches, the ocean, the harbor, Douglas fir and cedar forests, and a good look at the North Shore mountains. The park sits on a peninsula, and along the shore is a pathway 9 kilometers (5½ miles) long called the seawall. You can walk or bicycle all the way around or follow the shorter route suggested below.

Bicycles are for rent at the foot of Georgia Street near the park entrance. Cyclists must ride in a counterclockwise direction and stay on their side of the path. A good place for pedestrians to start is at
**㉓** the foot of Alberni Street beside **Lost Lagoon.** Go through the underpass and veer right to the seawall.

**㉔** The old wood structure that you pass is the **Vancouver Rowing Club,** a private athletic club (established 1903); a bit farther along is the
**㉕** **Royal Vancouver Yacht Club.**

**㉖** About ½ kilometer (⅓ mile) away is the causeway to **Deadman's Island,** a former burial ground for the local Salish Indians and the early settlers. It is now a small naval training base called the HMCS
**㉗** *Discovery* that is not open to the public. Just ahead is the **Nine O'Clock Gun,** a cannonlike apparatus that sits by the water's edge. Originally used to alert fishermen to a curfew ending weekend fishing, it now automatically signals every night at 9.

**㉘** Farther along is **Brockton Point** and its small but functional lighthouse and foghorn. The **totem poles,** which are situated more inland, make a popular photo spot for tourists. Totem poles were not carved in the Vancouver area; they were brought to the park from the north coast of British Columbia and were carved by the Kwakiutl and Haida peoples late in the last century. These cedar poles with carved animals, fish, birds, or mythological creatures were like family coats-of-arms or crests.

**㉙** At kilometer 3 (mile 2) is **Lumberman's Arch,** a huge log archway dedicated to the workers in Vancouver's first industry. Beside the arch is an asphalt path that leads back to Lost Lagoon, for those who want a shorter walk. (It's about a third of the distance.) This path
**㉚** also leads to the **Vancouver Public Aquarium.** Walk through the humid Amazon rain-forest gallery, with its piranhas, giant cockroaches, alligators, tropical birds, and jungle vegetation. Other

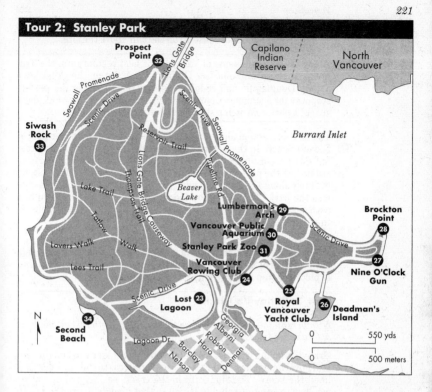

## Tour 2: Stanley Park

displays show the underwater life of coastal British Columbia, the Canadian arctic, and other areas of the world. The Clamshell Gift Shop next to the aquarium is one of the best spots in town for high-quality souvenirs and gifts, most with an emphasis on natural history. *Aquarium, tel. 604/682-1118. Admission: $9.50 adults, $8.25 senior citizens and youths, $6.25 children 5-12, $27 families. Open summer, daily 9:30-8; winter, daily 10-5:30. Clamshell open July-Labor Day, daily 9:30-8; Labor Day-June, daily 10-5:30.*

**31** Next to the aquarium is the **Stanley Park Zoo**, a friendly place, easily seen in an hour or two. Except for the polar bears, most of the animals are small—monkeys, seals, exotic birds, penguins, and playful otters.

About 1 kilometer (¾ mile) farther is the **Lions Gate Bridge**—the halfway point of the seawall. On the other side of the bridge is **32 Prospect Point,** where cormorants build their seaweed nests along the cliff's ledges. The large black diving birds are recognized by their long necks and beaks; when not nesting, they often perch atop floating logs or boulders. Another remarkable bird found along the park's shore is the beautiful great blue heron, which reaches up to 4 feet tall and has a wing span of 6 feet. The heron preys on passing fish in the waters here; the oldest heron rookery in British Columbia is in the trees around the zoo.

Continuing around the seawall you will come to the **English Bay** side and the beginning of sandy beaches. The imposing rock just offshore **33** is **Siwash Rock.** Legend tells of a young Indian who, about to become a father, bathed persistently to wash his sins away so that his son could be born pure; for his devotion he was blessed by the gods and immortalized in the shape of Siwash Rock. Two small rocks, said to be his wife and child, are just up on the cliff above the site.

**Time Out** Along the seawall is one of Vancouver's best restaurants, the **Teahouse at Ferguson Point** (*see* Dining *below*). Set on the great lawn among Douglas fir and cedar trees, the restaurant is the perfect stopover for a summer weekend lunch or brunch. If you want just a snack, a park concession stand is also at Ferguson Point.

The next attraction along the seawall is the large saltwater pool at **Second Beach.** In the summer it is a children's pool with lifeguards, but during winter the pool is drained and skateboarders perform stunts. At the pool you can take a shortcut back to Lost Lagoon, by walking along the perpendicular road behind the pool, which cuts into the park. The wood footbridge that's ahead will lead you to a path along the south side of the lagoon and to your starting point at the foot of Alberni or Georgia street.

If you continue along the seawall, it will emerge out of the park into a high-rise residential neighborhood, the **West End.** You can walk back to Alberni Street along Denman Street, where there are plenty of places to stop for coffee, ice cream, or a drink.

### Tour 3: Granville Island

*Numbers in the margin correspond to points of interest on the Tour 3: Granville Island map.*

Granville Island was just a sandbar until World War I, when the federal government dredged False Creek for access to the sawmills that lined the shore. The sludge from the creek was heaped up onto a sandbar to create Granville Island so that it could house the much-needed industrial- and logging-equipment plants for British Columbia. By the late 1960s, however, many of the businesses that had once flourished on Granville Island had deteriorated. Buildings were rotted, rat-infested, and dangerous. In 1971, the federal government bought up leases from businesses that wanted to leave, and offered an imaginative plan to refurbish the island. A public market was introduced, and marine activities and artisans' studios were supported. The opposite shore of False Creek was the site of the 1986 World's Fair and is now part of the largest urban redevelopment plan in North America.

The small island has no residents except for a small houseboat community. Most of the previously used industrial buildings and tin sheds have been retained but are painted in upbeat reds, yellows, and blues. Through a committee of community representatives, the government regulates the types of businesses that settle on Granville Island; most of the businesses permitted here involve food, crafts, marine activities, and the arts.

To access Granville Island on foot, make the 15-minute walk from downtown Vancouver to the south end of Thurlow Street. From a dock behind the Vancouver Aquatic Center, the Granville Island ferry leaves every six minutes for the short trip across False Creek to the Granville Island Public Market. These pudgy boats are a great way to see the sights on False Creek, but for a longer ferry ride, go to the Maritime Museum (1905 Ogden St., tel. 604/257–8300), where visitors can board the wheelhouse of a tugboat and chart the coastal waters of British Columbia. For more information, call Granville Island Ferries (tel. 604/684–7781).

Another way to reach the island is to take a 20-minute ride on a BC Transit (tel. 604/261–5100) bus. Take a UBC, Granville, Arbutus, Cambie, or Oak bus from downtown to Granville and Broadway, and transfer to Granville Island Bus 51 or False Creek Bus 50 from Gastown or stops on Granville Street for direct service to Granville Island. Parking is limited, but if you must take a car, go early in the week and early in the day to avoid crowds. Parking is free for one to three hours; paid parking is available in garages on the island, provided you can find a space.

**35** The ferry to Granville Island will drop you off at the **Granville Island Public Market,** where food stalls are enclosed in the 50,000-square-foot building. Since the government allows no chain stores, each outlet is unique, and most are of good quality. You probably won't be able to leave the market without a snack, espresso, or fixings for a lunch out on the wharf. Don't miss the charcoal-grilled oysters from **Sea-kist,** fish chowder or bouillabaisse from the **Stock Market,** fresh fudge at **Olde World Fudge,** or smoked salmon from the **Salmon Shop.** Year-round you'll see mounds of raspberries, strawberries, blueberries, and more exotic fruits like persimmons and lychees. You'll find plenty of outdoor seating on the water side of the market. *Public Market, tel. 604/666–6477. Open June–Aug., daily 9–6; Sept.–May, Tues.–Sun. and Mon. holidays 9–6.*

**36** The **Granville Island Information Centre,** kitty-corner to the market, is a good place to get oriented. Maps are available, and a slide show depicts the evolution of Granville Island. Ask here about special-events days; perhaps there's a boat show, outdoor concert, dance performance, or some other happening. *1592 Johnston St., tel. 604/666–5784. Open daily 8–6.*

Continue walking south on Johnston Street, beginning a clockwise loop tour of the island. Next is **Ocean Cement,** one of the last of the island's former industries; its lease does not expire until the year 2004.

**37** Next door is the **Emily Carr College of Art and Design.** Just inside the front door, to your right, is the **Charles H. Scott Gallery,** which hosts contemporary multimedia exhibits. *1399 Johnston St., tel. 604/687–2345. Admission free. Open daily noon–5.*

Past the art school, on the left, is one of the only **houseboat communities** in Vancouver; others have been banned by the city because of problems with sewage and property taxes. The owners of this community appealed the ban and won special status. Take the boardwalk that starts at the houseboats and continues partway around the island.

As you circle around to Cartwright Street, stop in **Kakali** at number 1249, where you can watch the fabrication of fine handmade paper from such materials as bluejeans, herbs, and sequins. Another unusual artisan on the island is the **glassblower** at 1440 Old Bridge Street, around the corner.

The next two attractions will make any child's visit to Granville Island a thrill. First, on Cartwright Street, is the children's **water**
**38** **park,** with a wading pool, sprinklers, and a fire hydrant made for children to shower one another. A bit farther down, beside Isadora's
**39** restaurant, is the **Kids Only Market,** with two floors of small shops selling toys, arts-and-crafts materials, dolls, records and tapes, chemistry sets, and other sorts of kid stuff. *Water park: 1318 Cartwright St., tel. 604/665–3425; admission free; open June–Aug., dai-*

## Tour 3: Granville Island

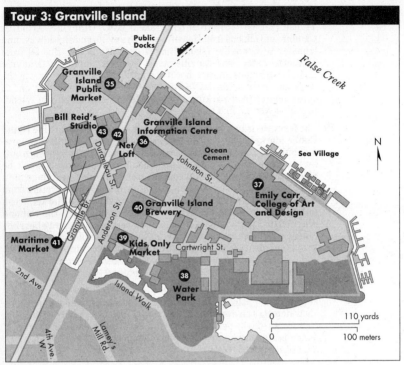

False Creek

Granville Island Public Market **35**

Bill Reid's Studio **43** **42**

Granville Island Information Centre **36**

Net Loft

Ocean Cement

Sea Village

N

**37** Emily Carr College of Art and Design

Johnston St.

**40** Granville Island Brewery

Maritime Market **41**

**39** Kids Only Market

Cartwright St.

**38** Water Park

Island Walk

Anderson St.

Granville Br.

Duranleau St.

2nd Ave.

4th Ave. W.

Lamey's Mill Rd.

| 0 | 110 yards |
| 0 | 100 meters |

*ly 10–6. Kids Only Market: 1496 Cartwright St., tel. 604/689–8447; open Mon.–Thurs. 10–6, Fri.–Sun. 10–9.*

**40** At the **Granville Island Brewery,** across the street, you can take a half-hour tour every afternoon; at the end of the tour, sample the Granville Island lager that is produced here and sold locally in most restaurants. *1441 Cartwright St., tel. 604/687–2739. Admission free. Tours weekdays at 1, weekends at 1 and 3.*

Cross Anderson Street and walk down Duranleau Street. On your left, the scuba-diving pool in **Adrenalin Sports** marks the start of the **41** **Maritime Market,** a string of businesses all geared to the sea. The first walkway to the left, Maritime Mews, leads to marinas and dry docks. There are dozens of outfits in the Maritime Market that charter boats (with or without skippers) or run cruise-and-learn trips. Another way to take to the water is by kayak. Take a lesson or rent a kayak from **Ecomarine Ocean Kayak Center** (1668 Duranleau St., tel. 604/689–7575).

**Time Out** **Bridges** (1696 Duranleau St., tel. 604/687–4400), in the bright yellow building across from the market, is a good spot to have lunch, especially on a warm summer's day. Eat on the spacious deck that looks out on the sailboats, fishing boats, and other water activities.

The last place to explore on Granville Island is the blue building next **42** to Ecomarine on Duranleau Street, the **Net Loft.** The loft is a collection of small, high-quality stores, including a bookstore, crafts store–gallery, kitchenware shop, postcard shop, custom-made hat shop, handmade paper store, British Columbian native Indian gallery, do-it-yourself jewelry store, and more.

**❹** Behind Blackberry Books, in the Net Loft complex, is **Bill Reid's studio,** belonging to British Columbia's most respected Haida Indian carver. His *The Raven and the First Men,* which took five carvers more than three years to complete, is in the Museum of Anthropology (*see* Other Museums, *below*); Reid's Pacific Northwest Coast Indian artworks are world renowned. Although you can't visit the studio, there are large windows to peer through.

Since you have come full circle, you can either take the ferry back to downtown Vancouver or stay for dinner and catch a play at the **Arts Club** (tel. 604/687–1644) or the **Waterfront Theater** (tel. 604/685–6217).

## Other Museums

The **Maritime Museum** traces the history of marine activities on the west coast. Permanent exhibits depict the port of Vancouver, the fishing industry, and early explorers; the model ships on display are a delight. Traveling exhibits vary but always have a maritime theme. Guided tours are led through the double-masted schooner *St. Roch,* the first ship to sail in both directions through the treacherous Northwest Passage. A changing variety of restored heritage boats from different cultures are moored behind the museum, and a huge Kwakiutl totem pole stands out front. *North foot of Cypress St., tel. 604/257–8300. Admission: $5 adults, $2.50 children, students, and senior citizens, $10 families. Open spring–fall, daily 10–5; winter, Tues.–Sun. 10–5. Access via Granville Island Ferries.*

The **Museum of Anthropology,** focusing on the arts of the Pacific Northwest Indians, is Vancouver's most spectacular museum. It's situated on the campus of the University of British Columbia and housed in an award-winning glass-and-concrete structure designed by Arthur Erickson. In the Great Hall are large and dramatic totem poles, ceremonial archways, and dugout canoes—all adorned with carvings of frogs, eagles, ravens, bears, and salmon. Also showcased are exquisite carvings of gold, silver, and argillite (a black stone found in the Queen Charlotte Islands), as well as masks, tools, and costumes from many other cultures. The museum contains a ceramics wing, which houses about 600 pieces from 15th- to 19th-century Europe. *6393 N.W. Marine Dr., tel. 604/822–3825. Admission: $5 adults, $2.50 students 6–18 and senior citizens, $10 families; free Tues. Open Tues. 11–9, Wed.–Sun. 11–5.*

**Science World** is in a gigantic shiny dome that was built for Expo 86 for an Omnimax Theater—the world's largest dome screen. The hands-on museum encourages visitors to touch and participate in the theme exhibits. A special gallery, the Search Gallery, is aimed at younger children, as are the fun-filled demonstrations given in Center Stage. *1455 Quebec St., tel. 604/268–6363. Admission to Science World: $7 adults, $4.50 senior citizens and children. Admission to Omnimax is $9; discounted admission to both. Open weekdays 10–5, weekends 10–6.*

**Vancouver Museum** displays permanent exhibits that focus on the city's early history and native art and culture. Life-size replicas of an 1897 Canadian Pacific Railway passenger car, a trading post, and a Victorian parlor, as well as a real dugout canoe are highlights. Also on the site are the Planetarium and Observatory (*see* Off the Beaten Track, *below*). *1100 Chestnut St., tel. 604/736–7736. Admission: $5 adults, $2.50 senior citizens and children. Open winter, Tues.–Sun. 10–5; summer, daily 10–5.*

## Other Parks and Gardens

**Nitobe Garden** is a small (2.4-acre) garden that is considered the most authentic Japanese garden outside Japan. The circular path around the park symbolizes the cycle of life and provides a tranquil view from every direction. In April and May cherry blossoms are the highlight, and in June the irises are magnificent. *1903 West Mall, Univ. of B.C., tel. 604/822–6038. Admission: $2 adults, $1.25 senior citizens and students, free Wed. and every day Oct. 11–Mar. 17. Open summer, daily 10–dusk; winter, weekdays 10–dusk; call for exact closing times.*

**Pacific Spirit Park** (4915 W. 16th Ave., tel. 604/224–5739) is a 1,000-acre park that is bigger and more rugged than Stanley Park. Pacific Spirit's only amenities are 61 kilometers (30 miles) of trails, a few washrooms, and a couple of signboard maps. Go for a wonderful walk in the west coast woods—it's hard to believe that you are only 15 minutes from downtown Vancouver.

**Queen Elizabeth Park** has lavish gardens and lots of grassy picnicking spots. Illuminated fountains; the botanical Bloedel Conservatory, with tropical and desert zones and 35 species of free-flying tropical birds; and other facilities including 20 tennis courts, lawn bowling, pitch and putt, and a restaurant are on the grounds. *Cambie St. and 33rd Ave., tel. 604/872–5513. Admission to conservatory: $3 adults, $1.50 senior citizens and students, $6 families. Open Apr.–Sept., weekdays 9–8, weekends 10–9; Oct.–Mar., daily 10–5.*

**Van Dusen Botanical Garden** was a 55-acre golf course but is now the grounds of one of the largest collections of ornamental plants in Canada. Native and exotic plant displays include the shrubbery maze and the rhododendrons in May and June. For a bite to eat, stop into Sprinklers Restaurant (tel. 604/261–0011), on the grounds. *5251 Oak St. at 37th Ave., tel. 604/266–7194. Admission: $4.50 adults, $2.25 senior citizens and children 13–18, $9 families; half-price off-season. Garden open 10–dusk.*

## Vancouver for Free

Among the public galleries and museums that offer free admission, the **Vancouver Art Gallery** (750 Hornby St., tel. 604/682–5621) is free on Thursday evening; the **Museum of Anthropology** (6393 N.W. Marine Dr., tel. 604/822–3825) is free every Tuesday; and the **Vancouver Museum** (1100 Chestnut St., tel. 604/736–7736) is free on the first Thursday evening of every month (it is also free every Tuesday for senior citizens).

The **University of British Columbia Botanical Garden** and **Nitobe Garden** (tel. 604/822–6038), a well-established Japanese garden also at UBC, are free on Wednesday and all winter.

Video documentaries, photographs, costumes, and an array of sporting equipment are displayed at the **B.C. Sports Hall of Fame and Museum** (B.C. Place Stadium, 777 Pacific Blvd. S, tel. 604/687–5523). There's a high-tech, hands-on participation gallery, so bring tennis shoes; admission is free year-round during museum hours (Wed.–Sun., 9–5).

In North Vancouver, the **Lynn Canyon Suspension Bridge** (off Peters Rd. in Lynn Canyon Park, North Vancouver, tel. 604/987–5922) and the **Capilano Fish Hatchery** in the Regional Park (Capilano Regional

Park, 4500 Capilano Park Rd., tel. 604/666–1790) are both free of charge (*see* Off The Beaten Path, *below*).

## What to See and Do with Children

Take your pint-size chef out to Sunday brunch at **Griffin's** (900 W. Georgia St., tel. 604/662–1900), the bistro-style restaurant in the Hotel Vancouver, where the little ones don small-person–size aprons and make their own pancakes and churn ice cream.

**Stanley Park Zoo** (*see* Tour 2: Stanley Park, *above*).

The **miniature steam train** in Stanley Park, just five minutes northwest of the aquarium, is a big hit with children as it chugs through the forest.

**Splashdown Park** (Hwy. 17, just before the Tsawwassen Ferry causeway, tel. 604/943–2251), 38 kilometers (24 miles) outside Vancouver, is a giant waterslide park with 11 slides (for toddlers to adults), heated water, picnic tables, and minigolf.

**Richmond Nature Park** (No. 5 Rd. exit from Hwy. 99, tel. 604/273–7015), with its displays and games in the Nature House, is geared toward children. Guides answer questions and give tours. Since the park sits on a natural bog, rubber boots are recommended if it's been wet, but a boardwalk around the duck pond makes some of the park accessible to strollers and wheelchairs.

**Maplewood Farms** (405 Seymour River Pl., tel. 604/929–5610), a 20-minute drive from downtown Vancouver, is set up like a small farm, with all the barnyard animals for children to see and pet. Cows are milked every day at 1:15.

**Kids Only Market** (*see* Tour 3: Granville Island, *above*).

**The Planetarium** (1100 Chestnut St., tel. 604/736–3656), on the same site as the Vancouver Museum in Vanier Park, has astronomy shows each afternoon and evening, and laser rock music shows later in the night.

**Science World** (*see* Other Museums, *above*).

**Vancouver Aquarium** (*see* Tour 2: Stanley Park, *above*).

## Off the Beaten Track

On the North Shore you can get a taste of the mountains and test your mettle at the **Lynn Canyon Suspension Bridge** (off Peters Rd. in Lynn Canyon Park, North Vancouver, tel. 604/987–5922), which hangs 170 feet above Lynn Creek. Also on the North Shore is the **Capilano Fish Hatchery** in the Regional Park (Capilano Regional Park, 4500 Capilano Park Rd., tel. 604/666–1790), with exhibits about salmon.

If the sky is clear, the telescope at the **Gordon Southam Observatory** (1100 Chestnut St., in Vanier Park, tel. 604/738–2855) will be focused on whatever stars or planets are worth watching that night. While you're there, visit the planetarium on the site. Open on clear Friday, Saturday, Sunday, and holiday evenings.

**Rock and Roll Heaven** (19 Water St., tel. 604/685–8841), formerly the Beatles Museum, exhibits memorabilia from Jimi Hendrix, Jim Morrison, the Beatles, and other rock icons. Admission is $4, and the museum is open daily 11–6, Sunday noon–6.

# Shopping

Unlike many cities where suburban malls have taken over, Vancouver has a downtown area that is still lined with individual boutiques and specialty shops. Stores are usually open daily and on Thursday and Friday nights, and Sunday noon to 5.

## Shopping Districts

The immense **Pacific Center Mall,** in the heart of downtown, connects Eaton's and The Bay department stores, which stand at opposite corners of Georgia and Granville streets. Pacific Center is on two levels and is mostly underground.

A new commercial center has developed around **Sinclair Center** (*see* Tour 1, *above*), which caters to sophisticated and upscale tastes.

On the opposite side of Pacific Center is **Robson Street,** stretching from Burrard to Bute streets and chockablock with small stores and cafés. Vancouver's liveliest street is not only for the fashion-conscious, it also provides many excellent corners for people-watching.

Two other shopping districts, one on **West 41st Avenue** between West Boulevard and Larch Street in Kerrisdale and the other on **West 10th** from Discovery Street west, are both in upscale neighborhoods and have high-quality shops and restaurants.

**Fourth Avenue,** from Burrard to Balsam streets, offers an eclectic mix of stores (from sophisticated women's clothing to surfboards).

In addition to the Pacific Center Mall, **Oakridge Shopping Center** at Cambie Street and 41st Avenue has chic, expensive stores that are fun to browse.

**Ethnic Districts** Chinatown (*see* Tour 1, *above*)—centered on Pender and Main streets—is an exciting and animated place for restaurants, exotic foods, and distinctive architecture.

Commercial Drive (around East 1st Avenue) is the heart of the Italian community, here called **Little Italy.** You can sip cappuccino in coffee bars where you may be the only one speaking English, or buy sun-dried tomatoes, real Parmesan, or an espresso machine.

The **East Indian shopping district** is on Main Street around 50th Avenue. Curry houses, sweet shops, grocery stores, and sari shops abound.

A small **Japantown** on Powell Street at Dunlevy Street is made up of grocery stores, fish stores, and a few restaurants.

## Department Stores

The biggest department stores in Vancouver, **Eaton's, Holt Renfew,** and **The Bay,** are Canadian-owned and located downtown and at most malls.

## Flea Markets

A huge flea market (703 Terminal Ave., tel. 604/685–0666), with more than 300 stalls, is held weekends and holidays from 8 to 4. It is easily accessible from downtown via SkyTrain, if you exit at the Main Street station.

## Auctions

On Wednesday at noon and 7 PM, auctions are held at **Love's** (1635 W. Broadway, tel. 604/733–1157). **Maynard's** (415 W. 2nd Ave., tel. 604/ 876–6787) has home furnishings auctions on Wednesday at 7 PM. Phone for times of art and antiques auctions.

## Specialty Stores

**Antiques** A stretch of antiques stores runs along Main Street from 19th to 35th avenues. On 10th Avenue near Alma are a few antiques stores that specialize in Canadiana, including **Folkart Interiors** (3715 W. 10th Ave.) and **Old Country Antique Co.** (3720 W. 10th Ave.). Also try **Canada West** (3607 W. Broadway). For very refined antiques, see **Artemis** (321 Water St.) in Gastown. For Oriental rugs, go to Granville Street between 7th and 14th avenues.

**Art Galleries** There are many private galleries throughout Vancouver. The best of them are **Buschlen-Mowatt** (1445 W. Georgia St., tel. 604/682–6004), **Diane Farris** (1565 W. 7th Ave., tel. 604/737–2629), **Equinox** (2321 Granville St., tel. 604/736–2405), and the **Heffel Gallery** (2247 Granville St., tel. 604/732–6505). Call all galleries before visiting to make sure they are open.

**Books** The best general bookstores are **Duthie's,** located downtown (919 Robson St.) and near the university (4444 W. 10th Ave.), and **Blackberry Books** (1663 Duranleau St.) on Granville Island.

Specialty bookstores include **The Travel Bug** (2667 W. Broadway) and **World Wide Books and Maps** (736A Granville St., downstairs) for travel books, **Vancouver Kidsbooks** (3083 W. Broadway), **Sportsbooks Plus** (230 W. Broadway), **Pink Peppercorn** (2686 W. Broadway) for cookbooks, and **William McCarley** (213 Carrall St.) for design and architecture.

Most of the secondhand and antiquarian dealers, such as **William Hoffer** (60 Powell St.) and **Colophon Books** (407 W. Cordova St., upstairs), are in the Gastown area. A block or two away are **McLeod's** (455 W. Pender St. and around the corner at 432 Richards St.), and **Ainsworth's** (321 W. Pender St.). **Lawrence Books** (3591 W. 41st Ave.) is out of the way but is probably the best used-books bookstore in town.

**Children's Stores** An unusual children's store worth checking out is **The Imagination Market** (528 Powell St.), an oddball warehouse-type store selling recycled industrial goods for arts-and-crafts materials: barrels of metallic plastic, feathers, fluorescent-colored paper, buttons, bits of Plexiglas, and other materials by the bagful.

**Clothing** **Men** Several high-quality men's clothing stores are in the business district: **Edward Chapman** (750 W. Pender St.) sells the conservative look; **E.A. Lee** (466 Howe St.) is stylish; **Leone** (757 W. Hastings St.) is ultrachic.

A few blocks away, at Pacific Center, are **Harry Rosen, Eddie Bauer,** and **Holt Renfrew.** If your tastes are traditional, don't miss **George Straith** (900 W. Georgia St.) in the Hotel Vancouver.

On Robson Street, a more trendy shopping area, are **Boy's Co.** (No. 1080) and **Club Monaco** (No. 1153), for casual wear.

There are numerous fine men's clothing shops outside downtown Vancouver including **Boboli** (2776 Granville St.), which sells Italian imports, and, in Kerrisdale, **Finn's** (2159 W. 41st Ave.) and **S. Lampman** (2126 W. 41st Ave.).

*Women* For women's fashions, visit **E.A. Lee** (466 Howe St.), **Wear Else?** (789 W. Pender St.), **Leone** (757 W. Hastings St.), and the more conservative **Chapy's** (833 W. Pender St.), all in the business district.

On Robson Street, look for **Margareta** (No. 948), **Alfred Sung** (No. 1143), **Club Monaco** (No. 1153), and a lingerie shop, **La Vie en Rose** (No. 1001). The two blocks between Burrard and Bute have six shoe stores.

Two expensive and very stylish import stores in South Granville are **Boboli** (2776 Granville St.) and **Bacci** (2788 Granville St.). Nearby, one of the largest and best shoe stores in town is **Freedman Shoes** (2867 Granville St.).

On the west side **Enda B.** (4346 W. 10th Ave.) and **Wear Else?** (2360 W. 4th Ave.) are the largest and best stores for high-quality fashions, but there's also **Bali Bali** for the more exotic (4462 W. 10th Ave.) and **Zig Zag** (4424 W. 10th Ave.) for fashion accessories.

*Gifts* Want something special to take home from British Columbia? The best places for good-quality souvenirs are the Vancouver Art Gallery (750 Hornby St.) and the Clamshell Gift Shop at the aquarium in Stanley Park. The Salmon Shop in the Granville Island Public Market will wrap smoked salmon for travel. In Gastown, Haida and Salish Indian art is available at Images for a Canadian Heritage (164 Water St.). Near Granville Island Leona Lattimer's (1590 W. 2nd Ave.) shop is built like an Indian longhouse and is full of Indian arts and crafts ranging from cheap to priceless.

# Sports and the Outdoors

## Participant Sports

*Biking* **Stanley Park** (*see* Tour 2 in Exploring Vancouver, *above*) is the most popular spot for family cycling. Rentals are available here from **Bayshore Bicycles** (745 Denman St., tel. 604/688–2453) or **Stanley Park Rentals** (1798 W. Georgia, tel. 604/681–5581).

Another biking route is along the north or south shores of **False Creek**. Rent bikes at **Granville Island Bike Rentals** (1496 Cartwright, tel. 604/669–2453) on Granville Island.

*Fishing* You can fish for salmon all year in coastal British Columbia. **Sewell's Marina Horseshoe Bay** (6695 Nelson St., Horseshoe Bay, tel. 604/921–3474) organizes a daily four-hour trip on Howe Sound or has hourly rates on U-drives. **Bayshore Yacht Charters** (1601 W. Georgia St., tel. 604/691–6936) has a daily five-hour fishing trip; boats are moored five minutes from downtown Vancouver. **Island Charters** (Duranleau St., Granville Island, tel. 604/688–6625) arranges charters or boat shares and supplies all gear.

*Golf* Lower Mainland golf courses are open all year. **Fraserview Golf Course** (tel. 604/327–3717), a spacious course with fairways well defined by hills and mature conifers and deciduous trees, is the busiest course in the country. Fraserview is also the most central, about 20 minutes from downtown. **Seymour Golf and Country Club** (tel. 604/929–5491), on the south side of Mt. Seymour, on the North Shore, is a semiprivate club that is open to the public on Monday and Friday. One of the finest public courses in the country is **Peace Portal** (tel. 604/538–4818), near White Rock, a 45-minute drive from downtown.

| | |
|---|---|
| **Health and Fitness Clubs** | Both the **YMCA** (955 Burrard St., tel. 604/681–0221) and the **YWCA** (580 Burrard St., tel. 604/683–2531) downtown have drop-in rates that let you participate in all activities for the day. Both have pools, weight rooms, and fitness classes; the YMCA has racquetball, squash, and handball courts. Another recommended club is **Tower Courts Racquet and Fitness Club** (1055 Dunsmuir St., lower level, tel. 604/689–4424), with racquetball courts, weight rooms, and aerobics. |

**Hiking**    **Pacific Spirit Park** is a 1,000-acre wilderness park with 48 kilometers (30 miles) of hiking trails (*see* Other Parks and Gardens in Exploring Vancouver, *above*).

The **Capilano Regional Park** (*see* Off the Beaten Track in Exploring Vancouver, *above*), on the North Shore, provides a scenic hike.

**Jogging**    The seawall around **Stanley Park** (*see* Tour 2 in Exploring Vancouver, *above*) is 9 kilometers (5½ miles) and gives an excellent minitour of the city. A shorter run of 4 kilometers (2½ miles) in the park is around **Lost Lagoon.**

**Skiing**   *Cross-country*    The best cross-country skiing is at **Cypress Bowl Ski Area** (tel. 604/926–6007).

*Downhill*    Vancouver is two hours away from **Whistler/Blackcomb** (Whistler Resort Association, tel. 604/685–3650; snow report, tel. 604/687–7507), one of the top ski spots in North America.

There are three ski areas on the North Shore mountains, close to Vancouver, with night skiing. The snow is not as good as at Whistler, and the runs are generally used by novice, junior, and family skiers or those who want a quick ski after work. **Cypress Bowl** (tel. 604/926–5612; snow report, tel. 604/926–6007) has the most and the longest runs; **Grouse Mountain** (tel. 604/984–0661; snow report, tel. 604/986–6262) has extensive night skiing, restaurants, and bars; and **Mt. Seymour** (tel. 604/986–2261; snow report, tel. 604/879–3999) is the highest in the area, so the snow is a little better.

**Water Sports**   *Kayaking*    Rent a kayak from **Ecomarine Ocean Kayak Center** (tel. 604/689–7575) on Granville Island (*see* Tour 3 in Exploring Vancouver, *above*).

*Rafting*    The Thompson, the Chilliwack, and the Fraser are the principal rafting rivers in southwestern British Columbia. The Fraser River has whirlpools and big waves, but for frothing white water, try the Thompson and Chilliwack rivers. Trips range from three hours to several days. Some well-qualified outfitters that lead trips are **Kumsheen** (Lytton, tel. 604/455–2296; in British Columbia, 800/482–2269), **Hyak Wilderness Adventures** (Vancouver, tel. 604/734–8622), and **Canadian River Expeditions** (Vancouver, tel. 604/738–4449).

*Sailing*    Several charter companies offer a cruise-and-learn vacation, usually to the Gulf Islands. **Sea Wing Sailing Group, Ltd.** (Granville Island, tel. 604/669–0840) offers a five-day trip teaching the ins and outs of sailing.

*Windsurfing*    Boards can be rented at **Windsure Windsurfing School** (Jericho Beach, tel. 604/224–0615) and **Windmaster** (English Bay Beach, tel. 604/685–7245).

## Spectator Sports

The **Vancouver Canucks** (tel. 604/254–5141) of the National Hockey League play in the Coliseum October–April. The **Canadians** (tel.

604/872–5232) play baseball in an old-time outdoor stadium in the Pacific Coast League; their season runs April–September. The **B.C. Lions** (tel. 604/583–7747) football team scrimmages at the B.C. Place Stadium downtown June–November. The Vancouver Eighty-Sixers (tel. 604/299–0086) play soccer in Swangard Stadium from late April through early September. Tickets are available from Ticketmaster (tel. 604/280–4444).

## Beaches

An almost continuous string of beaches runs from Stanley Park to the University of British Columbia. Children and hardy swimmers can take the cool water, but most others prefer to sunbathe; these beaches are sandy, with grassy areas running alongside. Note that liquor is prohibited in parks and on beaches. For information on beaches, call the **Parks Department of the City of Vancouver** (tel. 604/ 681–1141).

**Kitsilano Beach.** Kits Beach, with a lifeguard, is the busiest of them all—transistor radios, volleyball games, and sleek young people are ever present. The part of the beach nearest the Maritime Museum is the quietest. Facilities include a playground, tennis courts, heated saltwater pool (good for serious swimmers to toddlers), concession stands, and many nearby restaurants and cafés.

**Point Grey Beaches.** Jericho, Locarno, and Spanish Banks begin at the end of Point Grey Road. This string of beaches has a huge expanse of sand, especially in the summer and at low tide. The shallow water here is warmed slightly by the sun and the sand and so is best for swimming. Farther out, toward Spanish Banks, you'll find the beach becomes less crowded, but the last concession stand and washrooms are at Locarno. If you keep walking along the beach just past Point Grey, you'll hit Wreck Beach, Vancouver's nude beach. It is also accessible from Marine Drive at the university, but there is a fairly steep climb from the beach to the road.

**West End Beaches.** Second Beach and Third Beach, along Beach Drive in Stanley Park, are large family beaches. Second Beach has a guarded saltwater pool. Both have concession stands and washrooms. Farther along Beach Drive, at the foot of Jervis Street, is Sunset Beach, a surprisingly quiet beach, considering the location. A lifeguard is on duty, but there are no facilities.

# Dining

Vancouver offers the visitor a diverse gastronomical experience; restaurants—from the bustling downtown area to trendy beachside neighborhoods—have enticing locales in addition to succulent cuisine. A new wave of Chinese immigration and Japanese tourism has brought a proliferation of upscale Chinese and Japanese restaurants, offering dishes that would be at home in their own leading cities. Restaurants featuring Pacific Northwest fare—including such homegrown regional favorites as salmon and oysters, accompanied by British Columbia and Washington State wines—have become some of the city's leading attractions.

Highly recommended restaurants in each price category are indicated by a star ★.

| Category | *Cost |
|----------|-------|
| $$$$ | over $40 |
| $$$ | $30—$40 |
| $$ | $20—$30 |
| $ | under $20 |

*per person, including appetizer, entrée, and dessert; excluding drinks, service, and sales tax*

**American** **Isadora's.** Not only does Isadora's offer good coffee, a menu that ranges from samosas to lox and bagels, and children's specials, but there is also an inside play area packed with toys. Rest rooms with changing tables accommodate families. In the summer, the restaurant opens onto Granville Island's waterpark, so children can entertain themselves. Service can be slow, but Isadora's staff is friendly. The restaurant is now no-smoking. *1540 Old Bridge St., Granville Island, tel. 604/681–8816. Reservations required for 6 or more. Dress: casual. DC, MC, V. Closed Mon. dinner Sept.–May.* $

**Nazarre BBQ Chicken.** The best barbecued chicken in several hundred miles comes from this funky storefront on Commercial Drive. Owner Gerry Moutal massages his chickens for tenderness before he puts them on the rotisserie and bastes them in a mixture of rum and spices. Chicken comes with roasted potatoes and a choice of mild, hot, extra hot, or hot garlic sauce. You can eat in, at one of four rickety tables, or take out. *1859 Commercial Dr., tel. 604/251–1844. No reservations. Dress: casual. No credit cards.* $

**Cambodian/** **Phnom Penh Restaurant.** A block away from the bustle of Keefer
**Vietnamese** Street, the Phnom Penh is part of a small cluster of Southeast Asian
★ shops on the fringes of Chinatown. Simple, pleasant decor abounds: arborite tables, potted plants, and framed views of Ankor Wat on the walls. The hospitable staff serves unusually robust Vietnamese and Cambodian fare, including crisp, peppery garlic prawns fried in the shell and slices of beef crusted with ground salt and pepper mixed in the warm beef salad. The decor in the new Broadway location is fancier and the food is every bit as good as at East Georgia Street. *244 E. Georgia St., tel. 604/682–5777; 955 W. Broadway, tel. 604/734–8898. No lunch reservations; dinner reservations advised for 5 or more. Dress: casual. DC, MC. Closed Tues.* $

**Chinese** **Kirin Mandarin Restaurant.** Fish swim in tanks set into the slate
★ green walls, part of the lavish decorations of this restaurant serving a smattering of northern Chinese cuisines. Dishes include Shanghai-style smoked eel, Peking duck, and Szechuan hot-and-spicy scallops. Kirin is just two blocks from most of the major downtown hotels. *1166 Alberni St., tel. 604/682–8833. Reservations advised. Dress: casual but neat. AE, DC, V.* $$

**The Pink Pearl.** In the world of Cantonese restaurants, biggest may very well be best: This 650-seat restaurant certainly wins the prize in Vancouver. The huge, noisy room features tanks of live seafood—crab, shrimp, geoduck, oysters, abalone, rock cod, lobsters, and scallops. Menu highlights include clams in black-bean sauce, crab sautéed with five spices (a spicy dish sometimes translated as crab with peppery salt), and Pink Pearl's version of crispy-skinned chicken. Arrive early for dim sum on the weekend if you don't want to be caught in the lineup. *1132 E. Hastings St., tel.604/253–4316. Reservations advised. Dress: casual. AE, DC, MC, V.* $$

**Szechuan Chongqing.** Although fancier Szechuan restaurants can be found, the continued popularity of this unpretentious, white-table-

234

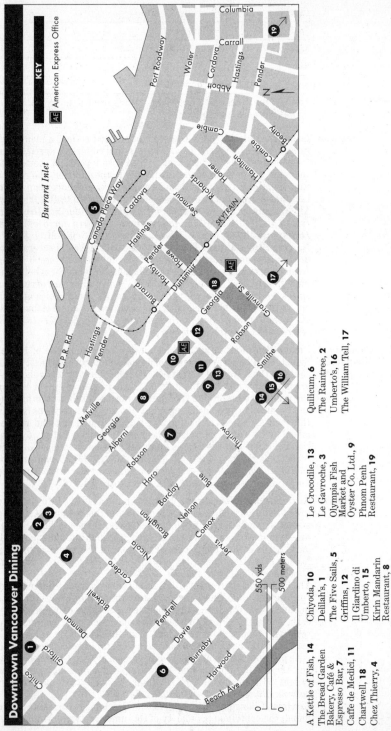

# Downtown Vancouver Dining

**KEY**

AE American Express Office

A Kettle of Fish, 14
The Bread Garden
Bakery, Café &
Espresso Bar, 7
Caffe de Medici, 11
Chartwell, 18
Chez Thierry, 4

Chiyoda, 10
Delilah's, 1
The Five Sails, 5
Griffins, 12
Il Giardino di
Umberto, 15
Kirin Mandarin
Restaurant, 8

Le Crocodile, 13
Le Gavroche, 3
Olympia Fish
Market and
Oyster Co. Ltd., 9
Phnom Penh
Restaurant, 19

Quilicum, 6
The Raintree, 2
Umberto's, 16
The William Tell, 17

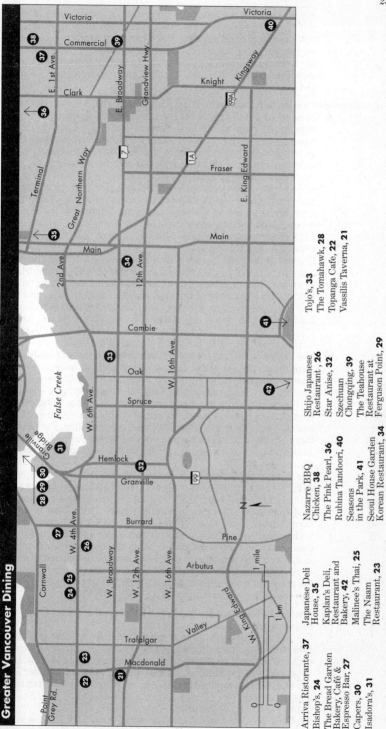

# Greater Vancouver Dining

Victoria
Commercial
E. 1st Ave.
Clark
E. Broadway
Grandview Hwy.
Knight
Kingsway
Victoria
Terminal
Great Northern Way
Fraser
E. King Edward
2nd Ave.
Main
Main
12th Ave.
Cambie
W. 16th Ave.
Oak
W. 16th Ave.
Spruce
False Creek
Granville Bridge
W. 6th Ave.
Hemlock
Granville
Burrard
Pine
W. 4th Ave.
W. Broadway
W. 12th Ave.
W. 16th Ave.
Arbutus
Cornwall
Trafalgar
Macdonald
Point Grey Rd.
W. King Edward
Valley

N

1 mile
1 km
0
0

Arriva Ristorante, **37**
Bishop's, **24**
The Bread Garden
Bakery, Café &
Espresso Bar, **27**
Capers, **30**
Isadora's, **31**

Japanese Deli
House, **35**
Kaplan's Deli,
Restaurant and
Bakery, **42**
Malinee's Thai, **25**
The Naam
Restaurant, **23**

Nazarre BBQ
Chicken, **38**
The Pink Pearl, **36**
Rubina Tandoori, **40**
Seasons
in the Park, **41**
Seoul House Garden
Korean Restaurant, **34**

Shijo Japanese
Restaurant, **26**
Star Anise, **32**
Szechuan
Chongqing, **39**
The Teahouse
Restaurant at
Ferguson Point, **29**

Tojo's, **33**
The Tomahawk, **28**
Topanga Cafe, **22**
Vassilis Taverna, **21**

cloth restaurant in a revamped fried-chicken franchise speaks for itself. Try the Szechuan-style fried green beans, steamed and tossed with spiced ground pork, or the Chongqing chicken—a boneless chicken served on a bed of spinach cooked in dry heat until crisp, giving it the texture of dried seaweed and a salty, rich, and nutty taste. *2808 Commercial Dr., tel. 604/254-7434. Reservations advised. Dress: casual. AE, MC, V. $*

**Continental**
★ **Chartwell.** Named after Sir Winston Churchill's country home (a painting of which hangs over the green marble fireplace), the flagship dining room at the Four Seasons Hotel (*see* Lodging, *below*) looks like an upper-class British club. Floor-to-ceiling dark wood paneling, deep leather chairs to sink back in and sip claret, plus a quiet setting make this the city's top spot for a power lunch. The chefs cook robust, inventive Continental food with lighter offerings and a variety of low-calorie, low-fat entrées. Favorites, including tomato basil soup with gin, rack of lamb, and a variety of salmon offerings, are repeated on the seasonal menu. There is a fine array of wines to compliment every dish. *791 W. Georgia St., tel. 604/844-6715. Reservations advised. Jacket advised. AE, DC, MC, V. Closed weekend lunch. $$$*

**Seasons in the Park.** Seasons has a commanding view over the park gardens to the city lights and the mountains beyond. A comfortable room with lots of light wood, white tablecloths, and deep-pile carpeting, this restaurant in Queen Elizabeth Park serves a conservative Continental menu with such standards as grilled salmon with fresh mint and roast duck with orange ginger sauce. *Queen Elizabeth Park, tel. 604/874-8008. Reservations advised. Dress: casual but neat. AE, MC, V. Closed Dec. 25. $$$*

★ **The Teahouse Restaurant at Ferguson Point.** The best of the Stanley Park restaurants is perfectly poised for watching sunsets over the water, especially from its newer wing, a glassed-in room with a conservatorylike ambience. Although the teahouse has a less innovative menu than its sister restaurant, Seasons in the Park, certain specialties, such as the cream of carrot soup, lamb with herb crust, and the perfectly grilled fish, don't need any meddling. For dessert, there's baked Alaska. *Ferguson Point in Stanley Park, tel. 604/669-3281. Reservations required. Dress: casual but neat. AE, MC, V. Closed Dec. 25. $$$*

**The William Tell.** Silver underliners, embossed linen napkins, and a silver flower vase on each table set the tone of Swiss luxury. The William Tell's well-established reputation for excellent Continental food continues at its quarters on the main floor of the Georgian Court Hotel. Chef John Rogers offers sautéed veal sweetbreads with red onion marmalade and marsala sauce and such Swiss specialties as *Zurcher Geschnezeltes* (thinly sliced veal with mushrooms in a light white wine sauce) and *Buendnerfleisch* (paper-thin slices of air-dried beef). Professional and discreet service contributes to the restaurant's excellence. *765 Beatty St., tel. 604/688-3504. Reservations advised. Jacket advised. AE, DC, MC, V. $$$*

**Deli/Bakery**
**The Bread Garden Bakery, Café & Espresso Bar.** What began as a croissant bakery has taken over two neighboring stores and is now the ultimate Kitsilano 24-hour hangout. Salads, quiches, elaborate cakes and pies, giant muffins, and cappuccino bring a steady stream of the young and fashionable. You may be subjected to an irritatingly long wait in line here, or, for that matter, at any of its other locations popping up around the city; quality is suffering with the rapid expansion. *1880 W. 1st Ave., tel. 604/738-6684; 812 Bute St., tel. 604/688-3213. No reservations. Dress: casual. MC, V. $*

**Kaplan's Deli, Restaurant and Bakery.** Tucked into a minimall on

Oak Street (the road that leads to the Tsawwassen ferries and Seattle), Kaplan's is the traveler's last chance for authentic Jewish deli food before leaving town. Eat in at booths, or take your chopped liver, chopped herring, lox, and homemade corned beef with you. Vegetarian dishes are now available as well. The bakery makes justly famous cinnamon buns. *5775 Oak St., tel. 604/263–2625. No reservations. Dress: casual. MC, V. Closed Jewish holidays. $*

**East Indian** **Rubina Tandoori.** If one must single out the best East Indian food in
★ the city, then Rubina Tandoori, 20 minutes from downtown, ranks as a top contender. The large menu spans most of the subcontinent's cuisines, and the especially popular *chevda* (East Indian salty snack) gets shipped to fans all over North America. Maître d' Shaffeen Jamal has a phenomenal memory for faces. Nonsmokers get the smaller, funkier back room with the paintings of coupling gods and goddesses; smokers get the slightly more subdued new room. *1962 Kingsway, tel. 604/874–3621. Weekend reservations advised. Dress: casual. DC, MC, V. Closed lunch Sat.–Wed., Sun. $$*

**French** **Le Gavroche.** Time has stood still in this charming turn-of-the-
★ century house, where a woman dining with a man will be offered a menu without prices. Featuring classic French cooking, lightened—but by no means reduced—to nouvelle cuisine, Le Gavroche's menu also includes such simple listings as smoked salmon with blinis and sour cream. Other options may be as complex as smoked pheasant breast on a puree of celeriac, shallots, and wine with a light truffle sauce. The excellent wine list stresses Bordeaux. No reservations are necessary after 9:30, when the late-dessert menu is offered. Tables by the front window promise mountains-and-water views. *1616 Alberni St., tel. 604/685–3924. Weekend reservations advised. Jacket and tie advised. AE, MC, V. Closed lunch, Sun., and holidays. $$$*

**Chez Thierry.** This cozy bistro on the Stanley Park end of Robson Street adds pizzazz to a celebration: Owner Thierry Damilano stylishly slashes open champagne bottles with a sword on request. For the past 18 years, he has worked together with chef Francois Launay in creating country-style French fare. Try watercress and smoked salmon salad; fresh tuna grilled with artichokes, garlic, and tomatoes; or filet mignon with a creamy cognac dijon black pepper sauce; and apple tarte Tatin for dessert. During the week the intimate dining room promises a relaxing meal; on the weekend, however, with every one of the 16 tables jammed, the restaurant gets noisy. *1674 Robson St., tel. 604/688–0919. Reservations advised. Dress: casual. AE, DC, MC, V. Closed lunch and Dec. 24–26. $$*

★ **Le Crocodile.** Diners are no longer packed as tight as sardines since Le Crocodile moved into its roomier new location off Burrard Street, which seats up to 85. Chef Michael Jacob still manages to serve extremely well cooked, simple food at reasonable prices. His Alsatian background shines with the caramelly, sweet onion tart. Anything that involves innards is superb, and even such old standards as duck à l'orange are worth ordering here. In addition to the overpriced specialty wine list is another with over 150 more affordable selections. *100–909 Burrard St., tel. 604/669–4298. Reservations required. Dress casual. AE, DC, MC, V. Closed Sat. lunch and Sun. $$*

**Greek** **Vassilis Taverna.** The menu in this family-run restaurant, located in the heart of the city's small Greek community, is almost as conventional as the decor: checked tablecloths and mandatory paintings of white fishing villages and the blue Aegean Sea. At Vassilis, though, even standards become memorable due to the flawless preparation.

The house specialty is a deceptively simple *kotopoulo* (a half-chicken, pounded flat, herbed, and charbroiled); the lamb fricassée with artichoke hearts and broad beans in an egg-lemon sauce is more complicated, though not necessarily better. Save room for a *navarino*, a creamy custard square topped with whipped cream and ground nuts. *2884 W. Broadway, tel. 604/733–3231. Weekend reservations advised. Dress: casual. AE, DC, MC, V. Closed Mon. and weekend lunch. $$*

**Health Food**
★ **Capers.** Hidden in the back of the most lavishly handsome health food store in the Lower Mainland, Capers (open for breakfast, lunch, and dinner) drips with earth-mother chic: wood tables, potted plants, and heady smells from the store's bakery. Breakfast starts at 8. Eggs and bacon? Sure, but Capers serves free-range eggs and bacon with no additives. Feather-light blueberry pancakes crammed with berries star here. The view of the water compensates for service that can be slow and forgetful. *2496 Marine Dr., W. Vancouver, tel. 604/925–3316; 2285 W. 4th, tel. 604/739–6685. No reservations. Dress: casual. MC, V. Closed Sun. dinner. $*

**The Naam Restaurant.** Vancouver's oldest alternative restaurant is now open 24 hours, so those needing to satisfy a late-night tofu-burger craving, rest easy. The Naam has left its caffeine- and alcohol-free days behind and now serves wine, beer, cappuccino, and wicked chocolate desserts, along with the vegetarian stir-fries. Wood tables and kitchen chairs provide a homey atmosphere. On warm summer evenings, the outdoor courtyard at the back of the restaurant welcomes diners. *2724 W. 4th Ave., tel. 604/738–7151. Reservations required for 7 or more. Dress: casual. MC, V. $*

**Italian**
★ **Caffe de Medici.** You'll need to shift gears as you leave the stark concrete walls of the Robson Galleria behind and step into this elegant restaurant with its ornate molded ceilings, rich green velvet curtains and chair coverings, and portraits of the de Medici family. But after a little wine, an evening's exposure to courtly waiters, and a superb meal, you may begin to wish the outside world conformed more closely to this peaceful environment. Although an enticing antipasto table sits in the center of the room, consider the *Bresaola* (air-dried beef marinated in olive oil, lemon, and pepper) as a worthwhile appetizer. Try the rack of lamb in a mint, mustard, and Martini & Rossi sauce. Any of the pastas is a safe bet. *1025 Robson St., tel. 604/669–9322. Reservations advised. Jacket advised. AE, D, DC, MC, V. Closed weekend lunch. $$$*

**Il Giardino di Umberto, Umberto's.** First came Umberto's, a Florentine restaurant serving classic northern Italian food, installed in a century-old Vancouver home at the foot of Hornby Street. Then, next door, Umberto Menghi built Il Giardino, a sunny, light-splashed restaurant styled after a Tuscan house. A young, moneyed crowd goes to Il Giardino for braided breast of pheasant with polenta and reindeer fillet with crushed peppercorn sauce. Fish is treated either Italian style—sea bass or salmon grilled and served with sun-dried tomatoes, black olives, and pine nuts—or with a taste of the Far East, as in yellowfin tuna grilled with wasabi butter. *Il Giardino, 1382 Hornby St., tel. 604/669–2422. Umberto's, 1380 Hornby St., tel. 604/687–6316. Reservations advised. Dress: casual but neat. AE, DC, MC, V. Umberto's closed Mon. lunch; Il Giardino closed weekend lunch. $$$*

**Arriva Ristorante.** Commercial Drive Italian restaurants, like Chinese restaurants in Chinatown, are best looked at with a skeptical eye. The best of the breed are elsewhere, and what's left is often found cranking out North Americanized travesties of the home country's food. Arriva is one Little Italy restaurant that's worth the drive, and it's a welcome find if you've spent the day shopping in Italian groceries. There's a version of spaghetti and meatballs on the menu, ziti with spicy squid sauce, and a fusilli with wild game—"Bambi and Bugs Bunny," as the waiters have affectionately coined it. The antipasto plate includes a heaping order of octopus, shrimp, roasted red peppers, cheese, sausage, and fat lima beans in an herby marinade. Don't miss the orange sherbet served in a hollowed-out orange for dessert. *1537 Commercial Dr., tel. 604/251–1177. Reservations advised. Dress: casual. AE, DC, MC, V. Closed weekend lunch. $$*

**Griffin's.** Sunday brunch here was rated as top entertainment in 1992 by the daily newspaper, *The Province.* The ambience is fun, energetic, and kid-oriented: Kids in aprons (provided by the restaurant) whip up their own pancakes and take turns churning ice cream for dessert. The rest of the week the emphasis is on the adult crowd. This brasserie uniquely blends the charm of old Italy with the flair of sophisticated design and fresh, regional ingredients. Squash-yellow walls, bold black-and-white tiles, and splashy food art by Mary Frances Tuck enhance Griffin's liveliness. The hotel's gargoyles are repeated in stenciling on the walls and in the red, yellow, and green carpet. The brasserie features an open kitchen that prepares inspirational cuisine, including such buffet selections as convict bread, a round loaf stuffed with soft, fresh goat cheese, olives, tomatoes, and peppers in olive oil; smoked salmon; chicken pasta al pesto; and baked Pacific black cod with herbed crumbs. There's a pizza buffet on Saturday. *900 W. Georgia St., tel. 604/662–1900. Reservations advised. Dress: casual. AE, DC, MC, V. $$*

**Japanese** **Tojo's.** Hidekazu Tojo is a sushi-making legend here. His handsome
★ blond-wood tatami rooms, on the second floor of a new green-glass tower in the hospital district on West Broadway, provide proper ambience for intimate dining, but Tojo's 10-seat sushi bar stands as the centerpiece. With Tojo presiding, it is a convivial place for dinner and offers a ringside seat for watching the creation of edible art. Although tempura and teriyaki dinners will satisfy, the seasonal menu is more exciting. In October, ask for *dobbin mushi,* a soup made from pine mushrooms that's served in a teapot. In spring, try salad made from scallops and pink cherry blossoms. *777 W. Broadway, No. 202, tel. 604/872–8050. Weekend reservations advised. Dress: casual but neat. AE, DC, MC, V. Closed lunch and Sun.; Dec. 24–26 and Jan. 1 and 2. $$$*

**Chiyoda.** The robata bar curves like an oversize sushi bar through Chiyoda's main room: On one side are the customers and an array of flat baskets full of the day's offerings; on the other side are the robata chefs and grills. There are 35 choices of things to grill, from squid, snapper, and oysters to eggplant, mushrooms, onions, and potatoes. The finished dishes, dressed with sake, soy, or *ponzu* sauce, are dramatically passed over on the end of a long wooden paddle. If Japanese food means only sushi and tempura to you, check this out. *1050 Alberni St., tel. 604/688–5050. Reservations accepted. Dress: casual. AE, MC, V. Closed weekend lunch. $$*

**Shijo Japanese Restaurant.** Shijo has an excellent and very large sushi bar, a smaller robata bar, tatami rooms, and a row of tables overlooking bustling Fourth Avenue. The epitome of modern urban Japanese chic is conveyed through the jazz music, handsome lamps with a patinated bronze finish, and lots of black wood. Count on creatively prepared sushi, eggplant *dengaku* topped with light and dark miso paste and broiled, and shiitake *foil yaki* (fresh shiitake mushrooms cooked in foil with *ponzu* sauce). *1926 W. 4th Ave., tel.*

604/732–4676. Reservations advised. Dress: casual. AE, MC, V. Closed weekend lunch. $$

**Japanese Deli House.** The least expensive sushi in town is served in this high-ceilinged main floor room of a turn-of-the-century building on Powell Street, once the heart of Vancouver's Japantown. Along with the standard sushi-bar menu, Japanese Deli House makes a pungent but tender hot ginger squid appetizer from baby squid caught off the Thai coast, and a geoduck appetizer in mayonnaise worth wandering off the beaten path for. The food is especially fresh and good if you can make it an early lunch: Nigiri-zushi and sushi rolls are made at 11 AM for the 11:30 opening. *381 Powell St., tel. 604/ 681–6484. Reservations for 10 or more. Dress: casual. No credit cards. Closed Sun. and Mon. dinners. $*

**Korean** **Seoul House Garden Korean Restaurant.** The shining star in a desperately ugly section of East Broadway, Seoul House is a bright restaurant, decorated in Japanese style, that serves a full menu of Japanese and Korean food. The best bet is the Korean barbecue, which you cook at your table. A barbecue dinner of marinated beef, pork, chicken, or fish comes complete with a half-dozen side dishes—kimchi, salads, stir-fried rice, and pickled vegetables—as well as soup and rice. Service can be chaotic in this very popular restaurant. *36 E. Broadway, tel. 604/874–4131. Reservations advised. Dress: casual. MC, V. Closed Sun. lunch. $*

**Mexican** **Topanga Cafe.** Arrive before 6:30 or after 8 PM to avoid waiting in line for this 40-seat Kitsilano classic. The California-Mexican food hasn't changed much in the 16 years the Topanga has been dishing up fresh salsa and homemade tortilla chips. Quantities are still huge and prices are low. Kids can color blank menu covers while waiting for food; a hundred or more of the clientele's best efforts are framed on the walls. *2904 4th Ave., tel. 604/733–3713. No reservations. Dress: casual. MC, V. Closed Sun. $*

**Nouvelle** **Bishop's.** John Bishop established Vancouver's most influential restaurant in 1985 by serving West Coast Continental cuisine with an emphasis on British Columbia seafood. Penne with grilled eggplant, roasted peppers, and basil pasta cohabit the menu with medallions of venison, rack of lamb, and roasted duck breast. The small white rooms—their only ornament some splashy, expressionist paintings—are favored by Pierre Trudeau and by Robert De Niro when he's on location in Vancouver. *2183 W. 4th Ave., tel. 604/738–2025. Reservations required. Dress: casual but neat. AE, DC, MC, V. Closed first wk in Jan. and weekend lunch. $$$*

★ **Delilah's.** Cherubs dance on the ceiling, candles flicker on the tables, and martini glasses clink in toast, but this incredibly popular restaurant is simply too crowded and noisy to be romantic. Under the direction of chef Peg Montgomery, the nouvelle California cuisine is delicious, innovative, and beautifully presented; not surprisingly, portions are small. The fresh daily menu lets you choose two- or five-course prix fixe dinners. Try the salmon in strawberry peppercorn sauce and the pecan-crusted pork loin; there are also dozens of martini concoctions to experience. Reservations are not accepted, and patrons have been known to line up before the restaurant even opens for dinner. *Buchan Hotel, 1906 Haro St., tel. 604/ 687–3424. No reservations. Dress: casual but neat. DC, MC, V. Closed lunch and Dec 24–27. $$*

**Pacific** **The Five Sails.** On the fourth floor of the Pan Pacific Hotel, this spe-
**Northwest** cial occasion restaurant affords a stunning panoramic view of Canada Place, Lions Gate bridge, and the lights of the north shore twinkling across the bay. Austrian chef Dorfler Ernst, a past mem-

ber of the Canadian Culinary Olympic team, has a special flare for presentation, from the swan-shape butter served with breads early in the meal to the chocolate ice-cream bonbon served on a bed of dry ice at the end. Pacific Rim best describes the broad-reaching menu that includes New Zealand venison in black currant sauce, scallop tempura with wasabi-papaya sauce, and such old favorites as medallions of B.C. salmon or Saltspring lamb. *Pan Pacific Hotel, 300–999 Canada Pl., tel. 604/662–8211. Reservations advised. Jacket advised. AE, DC, MC, V. Closed lunch and Dec. 24, 26, and Jan. 1. $$$$*

★ **Star Anise.** When Sammy Lalji and Adam Busby, top performers from the highly regarded Bishop's, left to open their own restaurant, they built a faithful following in record time. Their superior skills in attentive service, imaginative presentation, and excellent preparation of Pacific Northwest cuisine with French flare shine in this intimate, no-smoking location just off Granville on the west side of town. Don't miss the cilantro and Dungeness crab cakes with fried ginger threads, rouille, and guafrette potatoes frequently repeated on the seasonal menu; spot prawn raviolis, grilled pork chops, and the carrot and ginger mousse are also good choices. The extensive wine list features an array of fine international and West Coast choices. Weekend brunch is a real treat here. *1485 W. 12th Ave., tel. 604/737–1485. Reservations advised. Dress: casual but neat. AE, DC, MC, V. Closed Dec. 25, 26 and Jan. 1. $$$*

**Quilicum.** Only a few blocks from English Bay, this downstairs "longhouse" serves the original Northwest Coast cuisine: bannock bread, baked sweet potato with hazelnuts, alder-grilled salmon, and soapberries for dessert. Try the authentic but odd dish—oolichan grease—that's prepared from candlefish. Native music is piped in, and Northwest Coast Indian masks (for sale) peer out from the walls. *1724 Davie St., tel. 604/681–7044. Reservations advised. Dress: casual. AE, MC, V. Closed lunch Sat.–Tues. $$*

★ **The Raintree.** This cool, spacious restaurant offers a local menu and wine list, which features vintages from British Columbia, Washington, and Oregon. Raintree bakes its own bread, makes luxurious soups, and offers such old favorites as a slab of apple pie for dessert. The kitchen, focusing on healthy cuisine, teeters between willfully eccentric and exceedingly simple; specials could include Queen Charlotte abalone and side-stripe shrimps, stir-fried with scallions and spinach in chamomile essence; and grilled lamb chops with a mint and pear purée. Main courses change daily depending on market availability. Leon's Bar and Grill, on the ground floor, stocks local beers and a respectable number of single-malt scotches. The pub-food menu includes organic-beef burgers and vegetarian chili. *1630 Alberni St., tel. 604/688–5570. Weekend reservations advised. Dress: casual. AE, DC, MC, V. Closed weekend lunch and Dec. 24–26. $$*

**The Tomahawk.** North Vancouver was mostly trees in 1926, when the Tomahawk first opened. Over the years, the original hamburger stand grew and mutated into part Northwest Coast Indian kitsch museum, part gift shop, and part restaurant. Renowned for its Yukon breakfast—five slices of back bacon, two eggs, hash browns, and toast—the Tomahawk also serves gigantic muffins, excellent French toast, and pancakes. The menu switches to oysters, trout, and burgers named after Indian chiefs for lunch and dinner. *1550 Philip Ave., tel. 604/988–2612. No reservations. Dress: casual. AE, MC, V. $*

**Seafood** **A Kettle of Fish.** Since opening in 1979, this family-run restaurant at
★ the foot of Burrard bridge has developed a strong local following; de-

pend on getting top quality seafood here. The menu varies daily according to market availability, but there are generally 15 fresh seafoods to choose from that are either grilled, sautéed, poached, barbecued, or blackened Cajun-style according to your preference. The B.C. salmon and the seafood combo plate are always good choices. *900 Pacific St., tel. 604/682–6853. Reservations accepted. Dress: casual. AE, DC, MC, V. $$*

**Olympia Fish Market and Oyster Co. Ltd.** Some of the city's best fish-and-chips are fried in this tiny shop located behind a fish store in the middle of the Robson Street shopping district. The choice is halibut, cod, prawns, calamari, and whatever's on special in the store, served with homemade coleslaw and genuine—never frozen—french fries. *1094 Robson St., tel. 604/685–0716. No reservations. Dress: casual. DC, V. $*

**Thai** **Malinee's Thai.** The city's most consistently interesting Thai food
★ can be found in this typically Southeast Asian–style room, tapestries adorning the walls. The owners, two Canadians who lived for several years in Thailand, can give you detailed descriptions of every dish. Steamed fish with ginger, pickled plums, and red chili sauce is on the regular menu; a steamed whole red snapper marinated in oyster sauce, ginger, cilantro, red pepper, and lime juice is a special worth ordering when available. *2153 W. 4th Ave., tel. 604/737–0097. Reservations advised. Dress: casual. AE, DC, MC, V. Closed lunch. $$*

# Lodging

The hotel industry has become a major business for Vancouver, a fairly young city that hosts a lot of Asian businesspeople and others who are used to an above-average level of service. Although by some standards pricey, properties here are highly competitive, and you can expect the service to reflect this trend.

*Note:* At press time, the new **Radisson at Wall Centre** (1000 Burrard St., tel. 604/663–9255) was about to open. Although we were unable to visit the property, reports have been glowing.

Highly recommended lodgings in each price category are indicated by a star ★.

| Category | Cost* |
| --- | --- |
| $$$$ | over $180 |
| $$$ | $140–$180 |
| $$ | $90–$140 |
| $ | under $90 |

*\*All prices are for a standard double room for two, excluding 10% provincial accommodation tax, 15% service charge, and 7% GST.*

**$$$$** **Four Seasons.** This bustling 28-story hotel is adjacent to the Vancouver Stock Exchange and is attached to the Pacific Centre shopping mall. Standard rooms are average in size; roomier corner deluxe or deluxe Four Seasons rooms are recommended. Expect tasteful and stylish decor in the rooms and hallways. A huge sun deck and indoor-outdoor pool are part of the complete health club facilities. Service is outstanding, and the Four Seasons has all the amenities. The formal dining room, Chartwell (*see* Dining, *above*), is one of the best in the city. *791 W. Georgia St., V6C 2T4, tel. 604/689–9333; in*

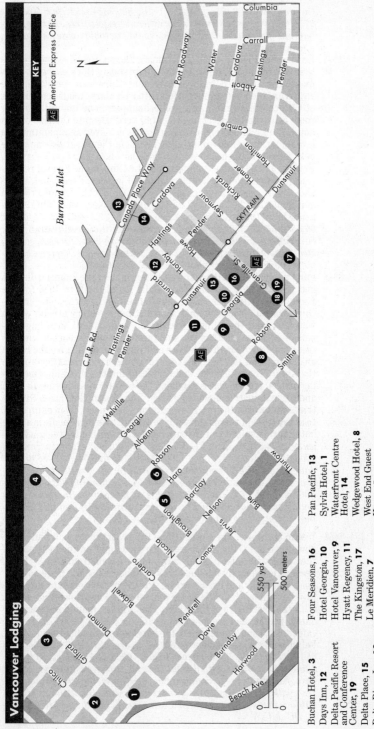

# Vancouver Lodging.

**KEY**

AE American Express Office

Burrard Inlet

Buchan Hotel, **3**
Days Inn, **12**
Delta Pacific Resort
  and Conference
  Center, **19**
Delta Place, **15**
Delta River Inn, **18**
English Bay Inn, **2**

Four Seasons, **16**
Hotel Georgia, **10**
Hotel Vancouver; **9**
Hyatt Regency, **11**
The Kingston, **17**
Le Meridien, **7**
O'Doul's, **6**

Pan Pacific, **13**
Sylvia Hotel, **1**
Waterfront Centre
  Hotel, **14**
Wedgewood Hotel, **8**
West End Guest
  House, **5**
Westin Bayshore, **4**

*Canada, 800/268–6282; in the U.S., 800/332–3442; fax 604/844–6744. 317 rooms, 68 suites. Facilities: 2 restaurants, bar, indoor-outdoor pool, sun deck, weight room, aerobics classes, sauna, Jacuzzi. AE, DC, MC, V.*

**\$\$\$\$** **Le Meridien.** This property feels more like an exclusive guest house
★ than a large hotel: Its lobby has sumptuously thick carpets, enormous displays of flowers, and elegant European furniture. The rooms are even better, furnished with rich, dark woods reminiscent of 19th-century France. Bathrobes, slippers, and umbrellas in the room attest to the attention to detail here. Despite the size of this hotel, the Le Meridien in Vancouver has achieved and maintained a level of intimacy and exclusivity. The Café Fleuri serves one of the best Sunday brunches in town (plus a chocolate buffet on Thursday, Friday, and Saturday evenings), and Le Club, a fine French restaurant, is a special-occasion place. Lots of leather, dark wood, wingback chairs, and a fireplace give the Gerard bar the feel of a refined gentlemen's club. The tiny La Boulangerie Bakery, added in 1993, is a new hit in town. *845 Burrard St., V6Z 2K6, tel. 604/682–5511, fax 604/682–5513. 350 doubles, 47 suites. Facilities: restaurant; café; bar; bakery; business center; health club with pool, Jacuzzi, sauna, steam room, tanning bed, masseuse, salon, weights, exercise equipment; adjoining apartment hotel. AE, D, DC, MC, V.*

**\$\$\$\$** **Pan Pacific.** Canada Place sits on a pier right by the financial district and houses the luxurious Pan Pacific Hotel (built in 1986 for the Expo), the Vancouver Trade and Convention Centre, and a cruise-ship terminal. The lobby has a dramatic three-story atrium with a waterfall, and the lounge, restaurant, and café all have huge expanses of glass, so that you are rarely without a harbor view or mountain backdrop. Earthtones and Japanese detail give the rooms an understated elegance. Make sure you get a room that looks out on the water. The hotel's fine dining restaurant, the Five Sails (*see* Dining *above*), offers what is arguably the best panoramic view in town and an imaginative menu to match. The health club has a \$15 fee that's well worth the price; everything you'll need, from equipment to attire (except tennis shoes), is provided. The Pan Pacific is a busy hotel better suited to conventions than an intimate weekend getaway. *300–999 Canada Pl., V6C 3B5, tel. 604/662–8211; in Canada, 800/663–1515; in the U.S., 800/937–1515; fax 604/685–8690. 467 doubles, 39 suites. Facilities: 3 restaurants; bar; health club with indoor track, sauna, steam room, whirlpools, tanning beds, state-of-the-art aerobics equipment, weights, massage and Shiatsu; sports lounge with wide-screen TV; squash, racquetball, and paddle-tennis courts; heated outdoor pool. AE, DC, MC, V.*

**\$\$\$–\$\$\$\$** **Westin Bayshore.** The closest thing to a resort that you'll find in the downtown area, the Bayshore is perched right on the best part of the harbor. Because it is only a five-minute walk from Stanley Park, because of the truly fabulous view, and because of its huge outdoor pool, sun deck, and grassy areas, it is the perfect place to stay during the summer, especially for a family. The new tower has rooms with the best views of the water; rooms in the main wing were updated in 1994, and are now comparable in contemporary style. The café is okay, and Trader Vic's, the hotel's dining room, is a pleasant, Polynesian-style experience. *1601 W. Georgia St., V6G 2V4, tel. 604/682–3377 or 800/228–3000; fax 604/691–6959. 484 doubles, 33 suites, 2 floors for persons with disabilities. Facilities: restaurant, café, 2 bars, free shuttle service downtown, boutiques, bicycle rentals, marina with fishing and sailing charters, health club with indoor and outdoor pools, Jacuzzi, sun deck, masseur, sauna, pool table. AE, D, DC, MC, V.*

**\$\$\$ Delta Pacific Resort & Conference Center.** It's not a view or a shoreline that makes this place (five minutes from the airport) a resort, it's the facilities on the 14-acre site: three swimming pools (one indoor), four all-year tennis courts with a pro (matching list for partners), an outdoor fitness circuit, squash courts, aqua-exercise classes, outdoor volleyball nets, golf practice nets, a play center for children, summer camps for 5- to 12-year-olds, and a playground; at press time, a tubular water slide was being added. In spite of the hotel's enormity, the atmosphere is casual and friendly. There are two guest-room towers and a few low-rise buildings for convention facilities. The resort was renovated in 1993, so guest rooms are modern with contemporary decor and a pleasant blue and green color scheme. The Japanese restaurant is expensive and not the best value. *10251 St. Edwards Dr., V6X 2M9, tel. 604/278–9611; in Canada, 800/268–1133; in the U.S., 800/877–1133; fax 604/276–1122. 460 doubles, 4 suites. Facilities: restaurant, café, bar, sauna, shuttle to airport and shopping center, gift shop, baby-sitting. AE, DC, MC, V.*

**\$\$\$ Delta Place.** This 18-story hotel was built in 1985 by the luxurious Hong Kong Mandarin chain but was sold to Delta Hotels in 1987. Although the rates went down, the surroundings did not change: The lobby is still restrained and tasteful—one has to look for the registration desk, which is tucked off to the right. A slight Oriental theme is given to the rich furnishings in light oak or dark mahogany. Most rooms have small balconies, and the studio suites—roomier, and only slightly more expensive than a standard room—are recommended. The business center has secretarial services, work stations, cellular phones for rent, and small meeting rooms. The restaurant and bar are adequate. The hotel's location is perfect; the business and shopping district is a five-minute walk away. *645 Howe St., V6C 2Y9, tel. 604/687–1122; in Canada, 800/268–1133; in the U.S., 800/877–1133; fax 604/643–7267. 181 doubles, 16 suites. Facilities: restaurant, bar, squash and racquetball courts, lap pool, weight room, sauna, whirlpool, massage. AE, DC, MC, V.*

**\$\$\$ Delta Vancouver Airport Hotel and Marina.** On the edge of the Fraser River, this hotel is just two minutes from the airport. Rooms on the south side get the best view. Although renovations began in 1990, the River Inn still has a way to go to compete with others in the price range. The hotel's draw lies in its proximity to the airport and its attachment to the marina, which organizes fishing charters so there are things for guests to do here. Food does not seem to be a priority with Delta. *3500 Cessena Dr., V7B 1C7, tel. 604/278–1241; in Canada, 800/268–1133; in the U.S., 800/877–1133; fax 604/276–1975. 415 doubles, 4 suites. Facilities: 2 restaurants, 2 lounges, jogging route, pool, free shuttle to airport, gift shop, extensive health club at nearby Delta Pacific Resort. AE, DC, MC, V.*

**\$\$\$ Hotel Vancouver.** The copper roof of this grand château-style hotel
★ dominates Vancouver's skyline. The hotel itself, opened in 1939 by the Canadian National Railway, commands a regal position in the center of town across from the art gallery and Cathedral Place. Even the standard guest rooms lend an air of prestige with mahogany furniture, TVs in armoires, attractive linens, and the original, deep bathtubs. Entrée Gold suites, with French doors, graceful wingback chairs, and fine mahogany furniture take up two floors, and come with extra services and amenities, including complimentary breakfast in a private, luxurious lounge. Spectacular views at the Roof Restaurant set the mood for fine dining and dancing to live entertainment nightly. Reservations are a must for Griffin's, the hotel's popular bistro-style restaurant. *900 W. Georgia St., V6C 2W6, tel. 604/684–3131 or 800/441–1414, fax 604/662–1937. 466 doubles,*

*42 suites, rooms for guests with disabilities. Facilities: 2 restaurants; 2 bars; two-line telephones; health club with lap pool, exercise machines, tanning bed; sun deck. AE, DC, MC, V.*

**$$$ Hyatt Regency.** The 34-story hotel, which opened in 1973, completed an $11 million renovation in 1992. The Hyatt's standard rooms are spacious and have been decorated in deep, dramatic colors and dark wood. Ask for a corner room with a balcony on the north or west side. The lobby, with its four-story atrium, can't escape the feel of a large convention hotel. For a small fee, the Regency Club gives you the exclusivity of one floor accessed by keyed elevators, your own concierge, a private lounge with a stereo and large TV, complimentary breakfast, 5 PM hors d'oeuvres, and evening pastries. Robes and special toiletries are also in the Regency Club rooms. For a hotel restaurant, Fish & Co. is unusually casual, with a fun atmosphere and good food. The Gallery Lounge is one of the most pleasant in town. Health club facilities include outdoor heated pool, saunas, exercise machine, and access to a nearby fitness center with racquetball and squash courts. *655 Burrard St., V6C 2R7, tel. 604/683–1234 or 800/233–1234, fax 604/689–3707. 612 doubles, 34 suites. Facilities: restaurant, café, 2 bars, health club, in-room safes. AE, D, DC, MC, V.*

**$$$ O'Doul's.** Conveniently situated on a lively street with loads of shops and restaurants, O'Doul's is only a five-minute walk from both the heart of downtown and Stanley Park. Public areas are very well maintained, and to insure extra security guests must use their room keys to operate the elevators. The rooms aren't what you'd expect, either: The decor is modern, with pastel color schemes. Deluxe rooms (with king-size beds) face Robson Street and are worth the price, especially off-season, when rates plummet. *1300 Robson St., V6E 1C5, tel. 604/684–8461 or 800/663–5491, fax 604/684–8326. 119 doubles, 11 suites. Facilities: 3 telephones in each room, pool, whirlpool, steam rooms, exercise machines, free parking. AE, D, DC, MC, V.*

**$$$ Waterfront Centre Hotel.** This dramatically elegant, 23-story glass hotel opened in 1991 across from Canada Place, the Convention Centre, and the cruise-ship terminal—all of which can be reached from the hotel by an enclosed walkway. Views from the caramel-color lobby and many of the guest rooms are of Burrard Inlet; other guest rooms look out onto the mountains. The Entrée Gold floor has a lounge, terrace, and includes a concierge, board room, shoe-shine service, deluxe breakfast, cocktail-hour canapes, and honor bar. All guest rooms are attractively furnished with contemporary artwork, minibars, and armoires concealing the TV. A pleasant place for guests to enjoy a drink is Herons Lounge, off of the lobby area. But as the evening progresses, the activity usually moves into Herons Restaurant, where a West Coast ambience prevails and guests can watch their meals being prepared in the open kitchen and rotisserie. Sunday here is relaxed and elegant, as a live string quartet entertains during a lavish brunch that includes imaginative dishes and decadent desserts. The property's health club includes a whirlpool, enclosed walkway to an outdoor heated pool, a variety of exercise equipment, a steam room, and massage services. *900 Canada Place Way, V6C 3L5, tel. 604/691–1991 or 800/441–1414, fax 604/691–1999. 460 doubles, 29 suites. Facilities: restaurants, health club, whirlpool, heated outdoor pool, steam room, massage. AE, D, DC, MC, V.*

**$$$ Wedgewood Hotel.** This hotel upholds its reputation for being a
★ small, elegant property run by an owner who fervently cares about her guests. The intimate lobby is decorated in fine detail with polished brass, beveled glass, a fireplace, and tasteful artwork. All the extra touches are here, too: nightly turndown service, afternoon ice

delivery, dark-out drapes, flowers growing on the balcony, terry-cloth robes, and morning newspaper. No tour groups or conventions stop here; the Wedgewood's clients are almost exclusively corporate, except on weekends, when the place turns into a couple's retreat. It's a treasure. *845 Hornby St., V6Z 1V1, tel. 604/689–7777 or 800/663–0666, fax 604/688–3074. 60 doubles, 33 suites. Facilities: restaurant, bar, in-room safe, fitness room. AE, D, DC, MC, V.*

**$$ Days Inn.** For the businessperson looking for a bargain, this location is tops. The six-story hotel, which opened as the Abbotsford in 1920, is the only moderately priced hotel in the business core. Recent renovations of the guest rooms and the lobby have made this accommodation even more agreeable. Although it's a basic hotel, rooms are bright, clean, and functional; standard units are very large, but there is no room service and few amenities. Suites 310, 410, 510, and 610 have a harbor view. The Bombay Bicycle Club bar is a favorite with businesspeople. *921 W. Pender St., V6C 1M2, tel. 604/681–4335, fax 604/681–7808. 74 doubles, 11 suites. Facilities: restaurant, 2 bars, no-smoking rooms, free overnight parking. AE, D, DC, MC, V.*

**$$ English Bay Inn.** This newly renovated 1930s Tudor house is one
★ block from the ocean and Stanley Park in a quiet residential part of the West End. The guest rooms—each with private bath—have wonderful sleigh beds (in all but one room) with matching armoires, Ralph Lauren linen, and alabaster lighting fixtures. The third-floor suite with fireplace is outfitted for romance. The common areas of this no-smoking inn are generous and elegantly furnished: The sophisticated but cozy parlor has wingback chairs, a fireplace, and French doors opening onto the front garden. A small, sunny English country garden graces the back of the inn. Breakfast is served in a rather formal dining room furnished with a Gothic dining room suite, a fireplace, and a late 17th-century grandfather clock. *1968 Comox St., V6G 1R4, tel. 604/683–8002. 4 rooms, 1 suite. Facilities: free off-street parking, afternoon sherry. AE, V.*

**$$ Hotel Georgia.** This handsome 12-story hotel, built in 1927, has such Old World features as a dark-wood-paneled lobby, ornate brass elevators, and a subdued, genteel atmosphere. Although it's lacking in extra amenities, the Georgia is a reliable and satisfactory deal. Rooms are small but well furnished, with nothing worn around the edges. Executive rooms have an almost separate seating area; rooms facing the art gallery have the best views. From this hotel (situated across from the Four Seasons) it's a five-minute walk to the business district. *801 W. Georgia St., V6C 1P7, tel. 604/682–5566 or 800/663–1111, fax 604/682–8192. 310 doubles, 4 suites. Facilities: restaurant, 3 bars. AE, DC, MC, V.*

**$$ West End Guest House.** Judge this lovely Victorian house, built in
★ 1906, by its gracious front parlor, cozy fireplace, and early 1900s furniture rather than by its bright pink exterior. Most of the small but extraordinarily handsome rooms have high brass beds, antiques, gorgeous linens, and dozens of old framed pictures of Vancouver. However, avoid the basement rooms. All units have phones, TVs, modern bathrooms, and newly papered walls. There's a veranda for people-watching, and a back deck for sunbathing. A full breakfast is included and can be served in bed. The inn's genial host, Evan Penner, has learned that it is the little things that make the difference, including a predinner glass of sherry, duvets and feather mattress-pads, terry bathrobes, hand-knit slippers, turn-down service, and a goodnight tart. The inn is in a residential neighborhood that is a 15-minute walk from Stanley Park and two minutes from Robson Street. This is a no-smoking establishment. *1362 Haro*

*St., V6E 1G2, tel. 604/681–2889, fax 604/688–8812. 7 rooms. Facilities: off-street parking. AE, D, MC, V.*

$ ★ **Buchan Hotel.** This three-story 1930s building is conveniently set in a tree-lined residential street a block from Stanley Park, a block from shops and restaurants on Denman Street, and a 15-minute walk from the liveliest part of Robson Street. The hallways appear a bit institutional, but the rooms are bright and clean. Furnishings, in good condition, consist of a color TV and a wood-grained arborite desk and chest of drawers. The rooms are small and the bathrooms tiny; none of the rooms have phones. You have to park on the street, but with this location you probably won't use your car much. Rooms on the east side are brightest and overlook a park; front corner rooms are the biggest. The pension-style rooms with shared bath down the hall are perhaps the most affordable accommodations in downtown. A popular basement restaurant with an eclectic menu is open for dinner. Since 1993, this has been a no-smoking hotel. *1906 Haro St., V6G 1H7, tel. 604/685–5354 or 800/668–6654, fax 604/685–5367. 60 rooms, 30 with private bath. Facilities: TV lounge, laundry room, in-room ceiling fans, bike storage room. AE, DC, MC, V.*

$ **The Kingston.** The Kingston is a small budget hotel in a location convenient for shopping. It is an old-style, four-story hotel, with no elevator—the type of establishment you'd find in Europe. The Spartan rooms are small and immaculate and share a bathroom down the hall. All rooms have phones but no TVs. Rooms on the south side are brighter. Continental breakfast is included. *757 Richards St., V6B 3A6, tel. 604/684–9024, fax 604/684–9917. 60 rooms, 7 with bath. Facilities: sauna, coin-op laundry, TV lounge, free nighttime parking. AE, MC, V.*

$ **Sylvia Hotel.** Perhaps the Sylvia Hotel is the best bargain in Vancouver, but don't count on staying here June–August unless you've booked six months ahead. What makes this hotel so popular are its low rates and near-perfect location: about 25 feet from the beach, 200 feet from Stanley Park, and a 20-minute walk from downtown. Vancouverites are particularly fond of the eight-story ivy-covered brick hotel—it was once the tallest building in the West End and the first to open a cocktail bar in the city, in 1954. It's part of the local history and was declared a protected heritage building in the 1970s. Rooms are unadorned and have worn, plain furnishings that have probably been around for more than 20 years—not much to look at, but the view—particularly on the south and west sides—and price make it worthwhile. Suites are huge, and all have kitchens, making this a perfect family accommodation. There is little difference between the old and new wings. *1154 Gilford St., V6G 2P6, tel. 604/681–9321. 97 doubles, 18 suites. Facilities: restaurant, lounge–bistro, parking. AE, DC, MC, V.*

# The Arts and Nightlife

For information on events, look in the entertainment section of the *Vancouver Sun;* Thursday's paper has listings in the **"What's On"** column, and there's the **Arts Hotline** (tel. 604/684–ARTS). For tickets, book through **Ticketmaster** (tel. 604/280–3311).

## The Arts

**Theater** The **Vancouver Playhouse** (Hamilton St. at Dunsmuir, tel. 604/872–6622) is the most established venue in Vancouver. The **Arts Club Theatre** (tel. 604/687–1644), with two stages on Granville Island

(1585 Johnston St.) and performances all year, is the most active. Both feature mainstream theatrical shows. **Carousel Theater** (tel. 604/669–3410), which performs off-off Broadway shows at the Waterfront Theatre (1405 Anderson St.) on Granville Island, and **Touchstone** (tel. 604/687–8737), at the Firehall Theater (280 E. Cordova St.), are smaller but lively companies. The **Back Alley Theatre** (751 Thurlow St., tel. 604/688–7013) hosts Theatresports, a hilarious improv event. The **Vancouver East Cultural Centre** (1895 Venables St., tel. 604/254–9578) is a multipurpose performance space that always hosts high-caliber shows.

**Music** The **Vancouver Symphony Orchestra** (tel. 604/684–9100) and the **CBC Orchestra** (tel. 604/662–6000) play at the restored **Orpheum Theatre** (601 Smithe St.). Choral groups like the **Bach Choir** (tel. 604/921–8012), the **Cantata Singers** (no phone), and the **Vancouver Chamber Choir** (tel. 604/738–6822) play a major role in Vancouver's classical music scene. The **Early Music Society** (tel. 604/732–1610) performs Medieval, Renaissance, and Baroque music throughout the year and hosts the Vancouver Early Music Summer Festival, one of the most important early music festivals in North America. Concerts by the **Friends of Chamber Music** (no phone) and the **Vancouver Recital Society** (tel. 604/736–6034) are always of excellent quality.

**Vancouver Opera** (tel. 604/682–2871) stages four productions a year, usually in October, January, March, and May, at the **Queen Elizabeth Theatre** (600 Hamilton St.). Productions are high caliber with both local and imported talent.

**Dance** Watch for **Ballet British Columbia's** (tel. 604/669–5954) Dance Alive! series, presenting visiting or local ballet companies (from the Kirov to Ballet BC). Most performances by these companies can be seen at the Orpheum or the Queen Elizabeth Theatre (*see above*). Local modern dance companies worth seeing are **Karen Jamison, Judith Marcuse,** and **JumpStart.**

**Film** Two theaters have distinguished themselves by avoiding the regular movie fare: **Ridge Theatre** (3131 Arbutus St., tel. 604/738–6311), which generally plays foreign films and rerun double-bills, and **Pacific Cinématèque Pacifique** (1131 Howe St., tel. 604/688–3456), which goes for even more esoteric foreign and art films. The **Vancouver International Film Festival** (tel. 604/685–0260) is held during September and October in several theaters around town.

## Nightlife

**Bars and Lounges** The **Gérard Lounge** (845 Burrard St., tel. 604/682–5511) at Le Meridien Hotel is probably the nicest in the city because of its fireplaces, wingback chairs, dark wood, and leather; this venue is commonly known as the Polo Club of the north. For spectacular views, head up to the **Roof Lounge** (900 W. Georgia St., tel. 604/684–3131), in the Hotel Vancouver, where a pianist plays nightly. The **Bacchus Lounge** (845 Hornby St., tel. 604/689–7777) in the Wedgewood Hotel is stylish and sophisticated. The **Gallery Lounge** (655 Burrard St., tel. 604/687–6543) in the Hyatt is a genteel bar, with lots of windows that let in the sun and provide views of the action on the bustling street. The **Garden Court** (791 W. Georgia St., tel. 604/689–9333) in the Four Seasons is bright and airy with greenery and a waterfall, plus big soft chairs you won't want to get out of. For a more lively atmosphere, try **Joe Fortes** (777 Thurlow St., 604/669–1940), **Soho Café and Billiards** (1144 Homer, tel. 604/688–1180) in Yaletown, or **Night Court** (801 W. Georgia St., tel. 604/682–5566) in the Georgia Hotel.

The **English Bay Café** (1795 Beach Ave., tel. 604/669–2225) is the place to go to catch the sunset over English Bay. **La Bodega** (1277 Howe St., tel. 604/684–8815), beneath the Château Madrid, is a popular Spanish tapas bar.

Two bars on Granville Island catering to the after-work crowd are **Bridges** (tel. 604/687–4400), near the Public Market, and the upscale **Pelican Bay** (tel. 604/683–7373), in the Granville Island Howard Johnson Plaza, at the other end of the island. The **Backstage Lounge** (1585 Johnston St., tel. 604/687–1354), behind the main stage at the Arts Club Theatre, features one of the largest selections of scotches in town, and is the hangout for local and touring musicians and actors.

**Music** While discos come and go, lines still form every weekend at **Rich-**
*Discos* **ard's on Richards** (1036 Richards St., tel. 604/687–6794) for live and taped Top-40 music.

*Jazz* A jazz and blues hot line (tel. 604/682–0706) gives you current information on concerts and clubs. **Carnegie's** (1619 W. Broadway, tel. 604/733–4141), and the **Alma Street Café** (2505 Alma St., tel. 604/222–2244), both restaurants, are traditional venues with good mainstream jazz. The **Glass Slipper** (185 E. 11th Ave., tel. 604/877–0066) has mainstream to contemporary jazz with a more underground atmosphere.

*Rock* The **Town Pump** (66 Water St., tel. 604/683–6695) is the main venue for local and touring rock bands. The **Soft Rock Café** (1925 W. 4th Ave., tel. 604/736–8480) is decidedly more upscale. There's live music with dinner. The **86th Street Music Hall** (750 Pacific Blvd., tel. 604/683–8687) serves up big-name bands. The **Commodore Ballroom** (870 Granville St., tel. 604/681–7838), a Vancouver institution, has been restored to its original, Art Deco style and offers live music ranging from B.B. King to zydeco bands.

**Casinos** A few casinos have been licensed recently in Vancouver, and proceeds go to local charities and arts groups. No alcohol is served. Downtown there are the **Royal Diamond Casino** (535 Davie St., tel. 604/685–2340) and the **Great Canadian Casino** (2477 Heather St., tel. 604/872–5543) in the Holiday Inn.

**Comedy** **Yuk Yuks** (750 Pacific Blvd., tel. 604/687–5233) is good for a few laughs. **Punchlines Comedy Theatre** (15 Water St., tel. 604/684–3015), another fun place, is in Gastown.

# Excursion to Victoria

## Important Addresses and Numbers

**Tourist** **Tourism Victoria** (1175 Douglas St., Suite 710, Victoria V8W 2E1,
**Information** tel. 604/382–2127 or 800/663–3883).

**Emergencies** Dial 911 in Victoria.

**Hospitals** **Victoria General Hospital** (35 Helmcken St., tel. 604/727–4181).

**Late-night** All-night pharmacies are virtually unknown in British Columbia,
**Pharmacies** even in the largest cities, although some pharmacies do offer after-hours emergency numbers. Generally, emergency prescriptions can be filled through major hospitals. **McGill and Orme Pharmacies** (649 Fort St., tel. 604/384–1195) could provide assistance.

### Arriving and Departing by Plane

**Airports and Airlines** **Victoria International Airport** serves Victoria. **Air Canada** (tel. 604/360–9074; in the U.S., 800/776–3000) and **Canadian Airlines International** (tel. 604/382–6111; in the U.S., 800/426–7000) are the two dominant carriers. **Air B.C.** (tel. 604/360–9074; in the U.S., 800/776–3000) provides both airport-to-airport and harbor-to-harbor service from Vancouver to Victoria at least hourly. Both flights take about 35 minutes. Air B.C. is the major regional line and runs daily flights between Seattle and Victoria. **Helijet Airways** (tel. 604/382–6222) helicopter service is available from downtown Vancouver to downtown Victoria.

### Arriving and Departing by Car, Bus, and Boat

**By Car** The TransCanada Highway, Route 1, runs south from Nanaimo to Victoria. Route 14 connects Sooke to Port Renfrew, on the West Coast of Vancouver Island, with Victoria.

**By Bus** **Greyhound** (tel. 800/231–2222) connects destinations throughout British Columbia with cities and towns throughout the Pacific North Coast.

**By Boat** **BC Ferries** (tel. 604/656–0757) travel year-round from Tsawwassen, just south of Vancouver, to Swartz Bay, a 30-minute trip by car or bus from Victoria.

Direct passenger and vehicle service between Seattle and Victoria is available May 21–September 18 on the **Royal Victorian**, operated by **Victoria Line** (tel. 604/480–5555), a subsidiary of B.C. Ferries. Outfitted to carry 192 cars and 1,000 passengers, the ship will make one round-trip daily, departing Victoria at 7:30 AM and returning from Seattle at 1 PM. One-way fares for car and driver are $49, and round-trip is $90. Tickets for additional passengers or foot passengers cost $25 one-way, and $45 round-trip. Reservations are advised for those traveling with a vehicle.

There is year-round passenger service (closed Christmas) between Victoria and Seattle via the *Victoria Clipper* (tel. 800/888–2535).

**Washington State Ferries** (tel. in Victoria, 604/381–1551; in Seattle, 206/464–6400) make year-round daily crossings between Sidney, just north of Victoria, and Anacortes, WA. **Black Ball Transport** (tel. in Victoria, 604/386–2202; in Seattle, 206/622–2222) operates between Victoria and Port Angeles, WA.

### Getting Around

For the most part, Victoria is a walker's city; most of its main attractions are downtown or just a few blocks from the core. Attractions on the outskirts of downtown can easily be reached by bus or a short cab ride (though taxis can be alarmingly expensive). In the summer you have the added option of horse-drawn carriage, bicycle, boat, or double-decker bus tours.

**By Bus** The **BC Transit System** (tel. 604/382–6161) runs a fairly extensive service throughout Victoria and the surrounding areas, with an all-day pass that costs $4 for adults, $3 for students and senior citizens. Passes are sold at many outlets in downtown Victoria, including Eaton Centre.

## Guided Tours

**Tally-Ho Horsedrawn Tours** (tel. 604/479–1113) offers visitors a get-acquainted session with downtown Victoria that includes Beacon Hill Park.

## Exploring Victoria

*Numbers in the margin correspond to points of interest on the Downtown Victoria map.*

Victoria, originally Fort Victoria, was the first European settlement on Vancouver Island and is the oldest city on Canada's west coast. It was chosen in 1842 by James Douglas to be the Hudson's Bay Company's most western outpost, and it became the capital of British Columbia in 1868. Today it's a compact seaside town laced with tea shops and gardens. Though it's quite touristy during the high summer season, it's also at its prettiest, with flowers hanging from turn-of-the-century building posts and strollers feasting on the beauty of Victoria's natural harbor.

**1** A logical place to begin this tour is at the **Visitors Information Centre,** located on the waterfront. *812 Wharf St., tel. 604/382–2127. Open July and Aug., daily 9–9; May, June, and Sept., daily 9–7; Oct.–Apr., daily 9–5.*

**2** Just across the way is the **Empress Hotel,** which originally opened in 1908, and is a symbol both of the city and of the Canadian Pacific Railway. Designed by Francis Rattenbury, whose works dot Victoria, the property is another of the great châteaux built by Canadian Pacific, the still-current owners who also built the Château Frontenac in Québec City, Château Laurier in Ottawa, and Château Lake Louise in Alberta. The $45 million face-lift was a hot topic of discussion in traditional Victoria, though not all of the comments have been positive: For contrast, take a pleasant stroll through the modern, elegantly designed Victoria Conference Centre at the south end of the Empress. Criticism aside, the ingredients that made the 483-room hotel a tourist attraction in the past are still alive. Stop in for tea—served at hour-and-a-half intervals during the afternoon. *721 Government St., tel. 604/384–8111. No jeans, shorts, or T-shirts.*

Around the corner from the Empress is **Miniature World,** on Humboldt Street, where small replicas of people, trains, and historic events are displayed. The exhibit seems at times like a mix of fact and fiction, with the models laid out so delicately. *649 Humboldt St., tel. 604/385–9731. Admission: $6.75 adults, $5.75 children 12–17, $4.75 children 4–11, people with disabilities with escort free. Open mid-June–mid-Sept., daily 8:30 AM–10 PM; mid-Sept.–mid-June, daily 9–5.*

A short walk around the harbor leads you to the old CPR Steamship Terminal, also designed by Rattenbury and completed in 1924. To-
**3** day it is the **Royal London Wax Museum,** housing more than 250 wax figures, including replicas of Queen Victoria, Elvis, and Marilyn Monroe. *470 Belleville St., tel. 604/388–4461. Admission: $6.75 adults, $6.25 students, $5.00 senior citizens, $3.00 children 6–12. Open May–Aug., daily 9–9; Sept.–Apr., daily 9–5.*

**4** Next to the wax museum is the **Pacific Undersea Gardens,** where more than 5,000 marine specimens are on display in their natural habitat. You'll also see performing scuba divers and a giant Pacific octopus. Unfortunately, there are no washrooms, and the site is not

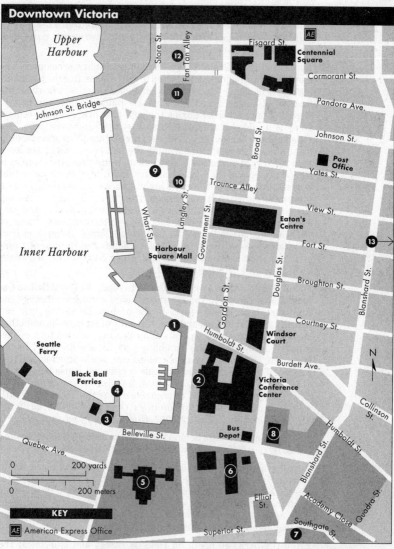

# Downtown Victoria

Upper Harbour

Store St.

Fan Tan Alley

Fisgard St.

**12**

**11**

Johnson St. Bridge

**9**

**10**

Trounce Alley

Centennial Square

Cormorant St.

Pandora Ave.

Johnson St.

Post Office

Yates St.

View St.

Eaton's Centre

Fort St.

**13** →

Inner Harbour

Wharf St.

Langley St.

Government St.

Harbour Square Mall

Gordon St.

Broad St.

Douglas St.

Blanshard St.

Broughton St.

Courtney St.

**1**

Humboldt St.

Windsor Court

Seattle Ferry

Black Ball Ferries

**4**

**3**

**2**

Victoria Conference Center

Burdett Ave.

N

Belleville St.

Bus Depot

**8**

Collinson St.

Quebec Ave.

0        200 yards

0        200 meters

**5**

**6**

Elliot St.

Blanshard St.

Humboldt St.

Academy Close

Quadra St.

**KEY**

*AE* American Express Office

Superior St.

Southgate St.

**7**

wheelchair accessible. *490 Belleville St., tel. 604/382–5717. Admission: $6 adults, $5.50 senior citizens, $4.50 children 12–17, $2.75 children 5–11. Open Oct.–May, daily 10–5; summer, daily 9–9. Closed Dec. 25. Shows run about every 45 min.*

**❺** Across Belleville Street is the **Parliament Buildings** complex. The stone-exterior building, completed in 1897, dominates the inner harbor and is flanked by two statues: Sir James Douglas, who chose the location of Victoria, and Sir Matthew Baille Begbie, the man in charge of law and order during the gold-rush era. Atop the central dome is a gilded statue of Captain George Vancouver, who first sailed around Vancouver Island; a statue of Queen Victoria stands in front of the complex; and outlining the building at night are more than 3,000 lights. Another of Rattenbury's creations, the complex is a good example of the rigid symmetry and European elegance that characterize much of the city's architecture. The public can watch the assembly, when it's in session, from the galleries overlooking the Legislative Chamber. Tour guides discuss the history and government of British Columbia and the architectural significance of the building. *501 Belleville St., tel. 604/387–3046. Admission free. Tours run several times daily and are conducted in at least 4 languages in summer and 3 in winter. Open Sept.–June, weekdays 8:30–5; summer, daily 8:30–5:30.*

**❻** Follow Belleville Street one block east to reach the **Royal British Columbia Museum.** Here you can spend hours wandering through the centuries, back 12,000 years. In the prehistoric exhibit, you can actually smell the pines and hear the calls of mammoths and other ancient wildlife. Other exhibits allow you to explore a turn-of-the-century town, with trains rumbling past. In the Kwakiutl Indian Bighouse, the smell of cedar envelops you, while piped-in potlatch songs tell the origins of the genuine ceremonial house before you. *675 Belleville St., tel. 604/387–3014. Admission: free Mon., Oct.–Apr.; otherwise $5 adults, $3 students and senior citizens, $2 children 6–18 and people with disabilities. Open Sept.–June, daily 10–5:30; July and Aug., daily 9:30–7. Closed Dec. 1 and Jan. 1.*

The **Newcombe Theatre** behind the museum presents slide talks and films. *Tel. 604/387–5822. Admission varies with event.*

A walk east on Belleville Street to Douglas Street will lead you to **❼** **Beacon Hill Park,** a favorite place for joggers, walkers, and cyclists. The park's southern lawns offer one of the best views of the Olympic Mountains and the Strait of Juan de Fuca. There are also lakes, walking paths, abundant flowers, a wading pool, petting zoo, and an outdoor amphitheater for Sunday-afternoon concerts.

From the park, go north on Douglas Street and stop off at the **❽** **Crystal Gardens.** Opened in 1925 as the largest salt water swimming pool in the British Empire, this glass-roof building—now owned by the provincial government—is home to flamingos, macaws, 75 varieties of other birds, hundreds of blooming flowers, and monkeys. At street level there are several boutiques and Rattenbury's Restaurant, one of Victoria's well-frequented establishments. *713 Douglas St., tel. 604/381–1213. Admission: $5 adults, $3 children 6–16 and senior citizens; discounted admission in winter. Open Oct.–Apr., daily 10–5:30; summer, daily 9–9.*

From Crystal Gardens continue north on Douglas Street to View **❾** Street, then west to **Bastion Square,** with its gas lamps, restaurants, cobblestone streets, and small shops. This is the spot James Douglas chose as the original Fort Victoria in 1843 and the original Hudson's Bay Company trading post. Today fashion boutiques and restaurants occupy the old buildings. While you're here, you may want to stop in at what was Victoria's original courthouse but is now  the **Maritime Museum of British Columbia.** Dugout canoes, model ships, Royal Navy charts, photographs, uniforms, and ship's bells chronicle Victoria's seafaring history. A seldom-used 100-year-old cage lift, believed to be the oldest in North America, ascends to the third floor. In 1995, however, a new museum is scheduled to open and replace this facility. *28 Bastion Sq., tel. 604/385–4222. Admission: $5 adults, $4 seniors, $3 children 11–18, $2 children 6–10. Open daily 9:30–4:30. Closed Dec. 25 and Jan. 1.*

West of Government Street, between Pandora Avenue and Johnson Street, is **Market Square,** offering a variety of specialty shops and boutiques and considered one of the most picturesque shopping districts in the city. At the turn of the century this area—once part of Chinatown—provided everything a visitor desired: food, lodging, entertainment. Today the square has been restored to its original, pre-1900s character.

Just around the corner from Market Square is Fisgard Street, the heart of one of the oldest **Chinatown**s in Canada. It was the Chinese who were responsible for building much of the Canadian Pacific Railway in the 19th century, and their influences still mark the region. If you enter Chinatown from Government Street, you'll walk under the elaborate **Gate of Harmonious Interest,** made from Taiwanese ceramic tiles and decorative panels. Along the street, merchants display fragile paper lanterns, embroidered silks, imported fruits, and vegetables. **Fan Tan Alley,** situated just off Fisgard Street, holds claim not only to being the narrowest street in Canada but also to having been the gambling and opium center of Chinatown, where mahjongg, fantan, and dominoes games were played.

A 15-minute walk or a short drive east on Fort Street will take you to Joan Crescent, where **Craigdarroch Castle** stands. This lavish mansion was built as the home of British Columbia's first millionaire, Robert Dunsmuir, who oversaw coal mining for the Hudson's Bay Company. (He died before the castle's completion in about 1890.) Converted into a museum depicting turn-of-the-century life-style, the castle is strikingly authentic, with elaborately framed landscape paintings, stained-glass windows, carved woodwork—precut in Chicago for Dunsmuir and sent by rail—and rooms for billiards and smoking. The location offers a wonderful view of downtown Victoria from the fifth-floor tower; guided tours are given. *1050 Joan Crescent, Victoria, tel. 604/592–5323. Admission: $5.50 adults, $4.50 students, children under 12 by donation. Open mid-June–Aug., daily 9–7:30; Sept.–Dec. and Apr.–mid-June, daily 10–5.*

## What to See and Do with Children

**Anne Hathaway's Cottage,** tucked away in a unique English village complex, is a full-size replica of the original thatched home in Stratford-Upon-Avon, England. The building and the 16th-century antiques inside are typical of Shakespeare's era. The Olde England Inn, on the grounds, is a pleasant spot for tea or a traditional English-style meal. You can also stay ($74–$198; AE, DC, MC, V) in one of the 50 antiques-furnished rooms, some complete with four-poster beds. *429 Lampson St., Victoria, V9A 5Y9, tel. 604/388–4353. Admission: $6 adults, $3.75 senior citizens and children 8–17, children under 8 free. Open June–Sept., daily 9–9; Oct.–May, daily 10–4. Guided tours leave from inn in winter and from cottage in summer. From downtown Victoria, take Munro bus to door.*

**Pacific Undersea Gardens** (*see* Exploring Victoria, *above*).

**Swan Lake Christmas Hill Nature Sanctuary.** This 23-acre lake, set within 110 acres of open fields and wetlands out Blanshard Street, is 10 minutes from downtown. From the 1½-mile chip trail and floating boardwalk, birders can spot a variety of waterfowl in winter and nesting birds in the tall grass. Children will enjoy the displays and games in the nature house. *3873 Swan Lake Rd. (take Bus 70 or 75), tel. 604/479–0211. Admission free. Nature House open weekdays 8:30–4; weekends and holidays noon–4.*

## Off The Beaten Track

**Butchart Gardens,** situated on the 130-acre Ross estate about 21 kilometers (13 miles) north of downtown Victoria, grows more than 700 varieties of flowers and has Italian, Japanese, and English rose gardens. During the summer, many of the exhibits are illuminated at night. Once a limestone quarry, the grounds were transformed in 1904 when Canadian cement pioneer Robert Butchart began building bridges and walkways and planting shrubs and flowers on the 50-acre (20-hectare) site. The grounds are lighted with beautiful displays during the Christmas season. Also on the premises are a gift shop, teahouse, and restaurants. *800 Benvenuto Ave., Victoria, tel. 604/652–5256. Admission: $11 adults, $5.75 children 13–17, $1.50 children under 13, excluding GST; discounted rates in winter.*

At the turnoff to Butchart Gardens is **Butterfly World Victoria**, a 1,200-square-foot greenhouse providing a tropical home to more than 60 brilliantly colorful species of butterfly along with canaries, finches, turtles, and fish. *Box 130 Benvenuto Ave., Brentwood Bay V0S 1A0, tel. 604/652–7811. Admission: $6.50 adults, $5.50 senior citizens, $4.50 children 13–17, $3.50 children 3–12, $21.50 families. Open Mar. and Oct.–Dec., daily 10–4; Apr.–Sept., daily 10–5.*

## Shopping

Shopping in Victoria is easy: Virtually everything can be found in the downtown area, beginning at the Empress and walking north along Government Street. In succession you'll hit **Roger's Chocolates** (tel. 604/384–7021), for fine chocolates; **George Straith Ltd.** (tel. 604/384–6912), for woolens; **Edinburgh Tartan Shop** (tel. 604/388–9312), for traditional Scottish plaids, woolens, and accessories; **Alcheringa Gallery** (tel. 604/383–8224) for good-quality Indian art; **Munro's Books** (tel. 604/382–2464), for the best selection of Victoriana in the city; and **Old Morris Tobacconist, Ltd.** (tel. 604/382–4811), for unusual pipe tobacco blends.

On the block of Douglas Street behind the Empress are such shops as the exclusive **G. Gagliano of Florence** (tel. 604/656–4114), with beautiful Italian leather goods; **LeJame Fashions** (tel. 604/386-2232), with clothing designed and manufactured in Victoria; and the **Stephen Lowe Art Gallery** (tel. 604/384-3912). Handy, also, is the **Currency Exchange,** which is open daily. The **Eaton Centre** at Government and Fort streets is both a department store and a series of small boutiques, with a total of 140 shops and restaurants. **Market Square,** between Johnson and Pandora, has three stories of specialty shops.

At last count, Victoria had 60-plus **antiques shops** specializing in coins, stamps, estate jewelry, rare books, crystal, china, furniture, or paintings and other works of art. A short walk on Fort Street going away from the harbor will take you to **Antique Row** between

Blanshard and Cook streets. **Waller Antiques** (tel. 604/388–6116) and **Newberry Antiques** (tel. 604/388–7732) offer a wide selection of furniture and collectibles. You will also find antiques on the west side of Government Street near the **Old Town.**

A 10-minute drive (or the No. 1 or No. 2 bus) from downtown out Fort Street to Oak Bay Avenue will take you to one of the few residential shopping areas that is not a mall. The **Oak Bay Village** is great for browsing, buying, or an afternoon *cuppa'*. Start at the corner of Oak Bay and Foul Bay and work your way east toward the water.

## Sports and Outdoor Activities

Golf   Though **Victoria Golf Club** (1110 Beach Dr., Victoria, tel. 604/598–4321) is private, it's open to other private-club members. This windy course is the oldest (built in 1893) in British Columbia and offers a spectacular view of the Strait of Juan de Fuca. Located 20 minutes from downtown, Victoria's newest public course, the **Olympic View Golf Club** (643 Latoria Rd., tel. 604/474–3673), offers both challenging and forgiving tees and stunning views of the Strait of Juan de Fuca and the Olympic Mountains. **Uplands Golf Club** (3300 Cadboro Bay Rd., Victoria, tel. 604/592–1818) is a flat, semiprivate course (it becomes public after 2). **Cedar Hill Municipal** (1400 Derby Rd., Victoria, tel. 604/595–3103) is a public course with up-and-down terrain. **Royal Oak Golf Club** (540 Marsett Pl., Victoria, tel. 604/658–1433) is the newest nine-hole course in the area. **Gorge Vale Golf Club** (1005 Craigflower Rd., Victoria, tel. 604/386–3401) is a semiprivate course but is open to the public. It has punitive traps and a deep gorge that eats up golf balls. **Glen Meadows Golf and Country Club** (1050 McTavish Rd., Sidney, tel. 604/656–3921), situated near the ferry terminal, is a semiprivate course that's open to the public at select times.

Whale   Three resident pods of orca (killer) whale travel in the waters
Watching   around Vancouver Island and are the primary focus of nature-watching charter boat tours that depart Victoria from May to October. June and July are actually the best time to see the whales, and harbor seal, sea lion, porpoise, and marine bird sightings are a safe bet anytime. These two to three-hour Zodiac (an inflatable boat powered by outboard motor) excursions cost around $70 (half-price for children). **Five Star Charters** (tel. 604/386–3253) and **Seacoast Expeditions** (tel. 604/477–1818) are the top operators.

## Dining and Lodging

Dining   For prices *see* Dining chart for Vancouver, *above*.

**Chez Daniel.** One of Victoria's old standbys, Chez Daniel offers dishes that are rich, though the nouvelle influence has found its way into a few of the offerings. The interior, following a burgundy color scheme, seems to match the traditional caloric cuisine. The wine list is varied, and the menu has a wide selection of basic dishes: rabbit, salmon, duck, steak. This is a restaurant with a romantic atmosphere in which you will want to linger. *2524 Estevan Ave., tel. 604/592–7424. Reservations advised. Jacket advised. AE, MC, V. Closed lunch and Sun. and Mon. $$$*

**Chez Pierre.** Established in 1973, this is the oldest French restaurant in Victoria, and the intimate, rustic decor creates a pleasant ambience. House specialties include *canard à l'orange* (duckling in orange sauce), rack of lamb, and British Columbia salmon. Although a tourist destination, this downtown restaurant has managed to maintain its high quality over the years. *512 Yates, tel. 604/388–7711. Reservations advised. Dress: casual but neat. AE, MC, V. Closed lunch and Sun. $$–$$$*

★ **The Marina Restaurant.** This lovely, round restaurant overlooking the Oak Bay Marina would be a good choice for a romantic meal, but it's so popular with the locals that it's always crowded and a bit noisy. If you go without a reservation, you'll be lucky to get a seat at the oval oyster bar, but they serve the full menu here as well. Best bets on the imaginative menu are the grilled marlin in citrus sesame vinaigrette, the crab served with drawn butter and an Indonesian hot-and-sour sauce, and the roasted chicken breast basted in a balsamic glaze. Choose from over 250 wines to compliment the meal, and save room for the Chocolate Fetish, a feast for two that includes chocolate crème brûlée, white chocolate and Cointreau parfait, truffle torte with white chocolate sauce, warm milk chocolate soufflé, and mousse. *1327 Beach Dr., tel. 604/598–8555. Reservations advised. Dress: casual but neat. AE, DC, MC, V. Closed Dec. 24 and 25. $$–$$$*

**Camilles.** This restaurant is romantic, intimate, and one of the few West Coast–cuisine restaurants in Victoria. Such house specialties as chicken Napoli, papaya brochettes (prawns wrapped around chunks of papaya in a lime and jalapeño marinade), and phyllo-wrapped salmon (fresh fillet of salmon in phyllo pastry) are all served in generous portions. Camilles also has an extensive wine cellar. *45 Bastion Sq., tel. 604/381–3433. Reservations advised. Dress: casual but neat. MC, V. Closed lunch and Mon. $$*

★ **La Ville d'Is.** This historic brick building houses one of the best seafood restaurants in Victoria. Both the quality and price are right. Run by Michel Duteau, a Brittany native, the restaurant is cozy and friendly, with an outside café open May–October. An extensive, imaginative wine list features bottles from the Loire Valley that go well with the seafood, rabbit, lamb, and New York strip steak specials. Try the *perche de la Nouvelle Zélande* (orange roughie in muscadet with herbs) or lobster soufflé for a unique taste. *26 Bastion Sq., tel. 604/388–9414. Reservations advised. Dress: casual but neat. AE, DC, MC, V. Closed Sun. and Jan. $$*

★ **Pagliacci's.** If you want Italian food, Pagliacci's is a must. Dozens of pasta dishes, quiches, veal, and chicken in marsala sauce with fettuccine are standard. The pastas are freshly made in-house. You'll dine surrounded by orange walls covered with photos of Hollywood movie stars. *1011 Broad St., tel. 604/386–1662. No reservations. Dress: casual. MC, V. $$*

**Blethering Place.** The menu points out that "blethering" is Scottish for "voluble, senseless talking." You might spot a bit of that going on in this clubby, neighborhood restaurant populated by dignified ladies sipping afternoon tea and blethering over crumpets, tarts, and scones. Later, neighborhood families stroll in for a dinner of steak-and-kidney pie, East Indian curries, and wonderfully rich desserts. Wines from British Columbia are featured. *2250 Oak Bay Ave., tel. 604/598–1413. Dress: casual but neat. AE, MC, V. $–$$*

**Don Mee's.** A large neon sign signals guests to Don Mee, a traditional Chinese restaurant. The long, red staircase leads to an expansive, comfortable restaurant for Szechuan and Cantonese entrées, such as sweet-and-sour chicken, almond duck, and bean curd with broccoli. *538 Fisgard St., tel. 604/383–1032. Reservations accepted. Dress: casual. AE, DC, MC, V. $–$$*

**Le Petite Saigon.** This intimate café-style restaurant offers a quiet dining experience with beautifully presented meals and a fare that is primarily Vietnamese, with a touch of French. The crab, asparagus, and egg swirl soup is a specialty of the house, and combination meals are cheap and tasty. *1010 Langley St., tel. 604/386–1412. Dress: casual. AE, MC, V. Closed Sat. lunch and Sun. $–$$*

**Cafe Mexico.** Hearty portions of Mexican food, such as *pollo chipolte* (grilled chicken with melted cheddar and spicy sauce, on a bed of rice) are served at this spacious, redbrick dining establishment, situated just off the waterfront. Bullfight ads and cactus plants decorate the restaurant and reinforce its character and Mexican theme. *1425 Store St., tel. 604/386–5454. Reservations accepted. Dress: casual. AE, DC, MC, V. $*

**Periklis.** Standard Greek cuisine is offered in this warm, taverna-style restaurant, but there are also steaks and ribs on the menu. On the weekends you can enjoy Greek and belly dancing, but brace yourself for the hordes of people who come for the entertainment. *531 Yates St., tel. 604/386–3313. Reservations accepted. Dress: casual. Closed weekend lunch fall–spring and Sun. lunch summer. AE, MC, V. $*

**Siam.** The Thai chefs at Siam, located one block south of the McPherson Playhouse, work wonders with both hot and mild Thai dishes. The *Phad Thai Goong* (fried rice noodles with prawns, tofu, peanuts, eggs, bean sprouts and green onions) and *Panang* (choice of meat in curry and coconut milk) are particularly good options. Mirrored walls give this small, simple restaurant a feeling of space, and there is a well-stocked bar with a variety of beer suited to the spices used here. *1314 Government St., tel. 604/383–9911. Reservations accepted. Dress: casual. MC, V. $*

★ **Six-Mile-House.** This 1855 carriage house is a Victoria landmark. The brass, carved oak moldings and stained glass set a festive mood for the evening. The menu constantly changes but always includes seafood selections and burgers. Try the cider or one of the many international beers offered. *494 Island Hwy., tel. 604/478–3121. Reservations accepted. Dress: casual. DC, MC, V. $*

**Lodging**

| Category | Cost* |
| --- | --- |
| $$$$ | over $180 |
| $$$ | $110–$180 |
| $$ | $70–$110 |
| $ | under $70 |

*All prices are for a standard double room for two, excluding 10% provincial accommodation tax, service charge, and 7% GST.*

**The Bedford Hotel.** This European-style hotel, located in the heart of downtown, is reminiscent of San Francisco's small hotels, with personalized service and strict attention to details. Rooms are in earth colors, and many have goose-down comforters, fireplaces, and whirlpool bathtubs. Meeting rooms and small conference facilities are also available, making this a good businessperson's lodging. An extensive breakfast is included in the room rate. *1140 Government St., V8W 1Y2, tel. 604/384–6835 or 800/665–6500, fax 604/386–8930. 40 rooms. Facilities: restaurant, pub. AE, MC, V. $$$$*

**Chateau Victoria.** Wonderful views are to be had from the upper rooms and rooftop restaurant of this 19-story hotel, situated across from Victoria's new Conference Centre, near the inner harbor and the Royal British Columbia Museum. Rooms are fairly standard in size, and some have balconies or sitting areas and kitchenettes. *740 Burdett Ave., V8W 1B2, tel. 604/382–4221 or 800/663–5891, fax 604/ 380–1950. 178 rooms. Facilities: restaurant, lounge, indoor pool,* *whirlpool, meeting rooms, courtesy vans to ferry, access to health club, free parking. AE, D, DC, MC, V. $$$$*

**The Empress Hotel.** This is Victoria's dowager queen with a face-lift. First opened in 1908, the hotel underwent a $45 million dollar renovation in 1989 that enhanced its Edwardian charm, updated existing guest rooms, and added some 45 new ones. Stained glass, carved archways, and hardwood floors are used effectively. The Empress dominates the inner-harbor area and is the city's primary meeting place for politicians, locals, and tourists. From the Lobby Lounge, guests can have a splendid view of the harbor. Afternoon tea has been a tradition here since 1908, but it's so popular today that reservations are a must. The Bengal Lounge is full of colonial charm from British India, including a stuffed Bengal tiger, overhead fans, and mosquito netting. *721 Government St., V8W 1W5, in Canada, tel. 604/384–8111 or 800/441–1414, fax 604/381–4334. 483 rooms. Facilities: restaurant, café, 2 lounges, afternoon tea, conference center, indoor pool, sauna, health club, in-room movies, cable TV, Christmas discount, family discount. AE, D, DC, MC, V. $$$$*

★ **Abigail's.** A Tudor country inn with gardens and crystal chandeliers, Abigail's is not only lovely but also conveniently located four blocks east of downtown. All guest rooms are prettily detailed in contemporary colors. Down comforters, together with Jacuzzis and fireplaces in some, add to the pampering atmosphere. There's a sense of elegant informality about this no-smoking hotel, noticed especially in the guest library and sitting room, where you'll want to spend an hour or so relaxing over evening hor d'oeuvres. Breakfast, included in the room rate, is served from 8 to 9:30 in the downstairs dining room. *906 McClure St., V8V 3E7, tel. 604/388–5363, fax 604/361–1905. 16 rooms. MC, V. $$$–$$$$*

**The Beaconsfield Inn.** Built in 1875 and restored in 1984, the Beaconsfield has retained its Old World charm. Dark mahogany wood appears throughout the house; down comforters and some canopy beds and claw-foot tubs adorn the rooms, reinforcing the Edwardian style of this residentially situated inn. Some of the rooms have fireplaces and whirlpool bathtubs. An added plus is the guest library and conservatory/sun room. Full breakfast, with homemade croissants or scones, and afternoon tea as well as evening sherry are included in the room rates. This is a no-smoking property. *998 Humboldt St., V8V 2Z8, tel. 604/384–4044, fax 604/361–1908. 10 rooms, 1 suite. Facilities: library, whirlpool tubs. MC, V. $$$–$$$$*

**Oak Bay Beach Hotel.** This Tudor-style hotel in Oak Bay, on the southwest side of the Saanich Peninsula, is well removed from the bustle of downtown. There's a wonderful atmosphere here, though; the hotel, situated oceanside, overlooks the Haro Strait and catches the setting sun. The interior decor is as dreamy as the grounds, with antiques and flower prints decorating the rooms. The restaurant, Tudor Room by the Sea, is average, but the bar with its cozy fireplace is truly romantic. *1175 Beach Dr., V8S 2N2, tel. and fax 604/598–4556. 51 rooms. Facilities: restaurant, pub, yacht for cruises, access to health club. AE, DC, MC, V. $$$–$$$$*

**Dashwood Manor.** If you want a quiet place with a great view, this is it. Located on the waterfront next to Beacon Hill Park, this Heritage Tudor mansion, built in 1912 on property once owned by Governor Sir James Douglas, offers panoramic views of the Strait of Juan de Fuca and the Olympic Mountains. This B&B lacks some of the charm that many offer because the parlor and dining rooms have been made into guest quarters. The only place for guests to congregate is in the tiny office, where sherry or wine is offered in the afternoon. Three guest rooms have fireplaces, and all rooms come with a fully stocked frig in the kitchenette; breakfast is "make your own." *1*

*Cook St., V8V 3W6, tel. 604/385–5517, fax 604/385–1760. 14 rooms. AE, MC. $$$*

★ **Holland House Inn.** Two blocks from the inner harbor, legislative buildings, and ferry terminals, this no-smoking hotel has a sense of casual elegance. Some of the individually designed rooms have original fine art created by the owner, and some have four-poster beds and fireplaces. All rooms have private baths, and all but two have their own balconies. A gourmet breakfast is included in room rates. You'll recognize the house by the picket fence around it. *595 Michigan St., V8V 1S7, tel. 604/384–6644, fax 604/384–6117. 10 rooms. Facilities: lounge. AE, DC, MC, V. $$$*

★ **Hotel Grand Pacific.** This is one of Victoria's newest and finest hotels, with a lot of mahogany woodwork and an elegant ambience. Overlooking the harbor, and adjacent to the legislative buildings, the hotel accommodates business and vacationing people looking for comfort, convenience, and great scenery; all rooms have terraces, with views of either the harbor or the Olympic Mountains. The health club is elaborate, equipped with Nautilus, racquetball-squash courts, and sauna. *450 Québec St., V8V 1W5, tel. 604/386–0450 or 800/663–7550, fax 604/383–7603. 149 rooms. Facilities: restaurant, lounge, sauna, whirlpool, fitness center, 2 racquetball-squash courts, aerobics classes, massage, convention facilities, free underground parking, indoor pool. AE, D, DC, MC, V. $$$*

**Mulberry Manor.** This Tudor mansion is a special place for a number of reasons: It is the last building to have been designed by Victoria architect Simon McClure; the grounds were designed and, until recently, maintained by a gardener at the world-famous Butchart Gardens; the manor has been restored and decorated to magazine-cover perfection with antiques, sumptuous linens, and tile baths. Hosts Susan and Tony Temple are charming and provide gourmet breakfasts with homemade jams and great coffee. *611 Foul Bay Rd., V8S 1H2, tel. 604/370–1918, fax 604/370–1968. 3 rooms, 1 suite. MC, V. $$$*

★ **Ocean Pointe Resort.** Set across the "blue bridge" from downtown Victoria, the resort opened in the summer of 1992 on the site of an old shingle mill and an area once claimed by the Songhees natives. Public rooms and half of the guest rooms offer romantic evening views of downtown Victoria and the parliament buildings, bedecked with some 3,000 twinkling lights. Guest rooms are spacious and some come with floor-to-ceiling windows and small balconies. The property offers a rich cache of amenities, including hydrotherapy, micronized marine algae body wrap, massages, aerobics, and beauty treatments in the spa. There are salads, sandwiches, and a variety of buffet items in the Boardwalk Restaurant and Brasserie; Pacific Northwest and Continental entrées, along with low-calorie, low-fat spa cuisine are served in the Victorian Restaurant. *45 Songhees Rd., Victoria V9A 6T3, tel. 604/360–2999 or 800/667–4677, fax 604/360–1041. 213 rooms, 37 housekeeping suites w/kitchens. Facilities: 2 restaurants, lounge–piano bar, 2 tennis courts, whirlpool, sauna, exercise room, indoor pool, squash and racquetball court, beauty salon. Reservations advised in Victorian Restaurant. AE, DC, MC, V. $$$*

**Victoria Regent Hotel.** Originally built as an apartment house, this is now a posh, condo-living hotel that offers views of the harbor or city. The outside is plain, with a glass facade, but the interior is sumptuously decorated with warm earth tones and modern furnishings; each suite has a living room, dining room, deck, kitchen, and one or two bedrooms with bath. *1234 Wharf St., V8W 3H9, tel. 604/386–2211 or 800/663–7472, fax 604/386–2622. 47 rooms, including*

*32 suites. Facilities: restaurant, free parking, laundromat. AE, D, DC, MC, V. $$$*

**Admiral Motel.** Located on the Victoria harbor and along the tourist strip, this motel is right where the action is, although it is relatively quiet in the evening. If you're looking for basic, clean lodging, the Admiral is just that. The amicable owners take good care of the newly refurbished rooms, and small pets are permitted. *257 Belleville St., V8V 1X1, tel. and fax 604/388–6267. 29 rooms, 23 with kitchens. Facilities: cable TV, free parking, laundry. AE, D, MC, V. $–$$*

**The Cats Meow.** Travelers on a tight budget will appreciate The Cat's Meow, a small youth hostel located just across the bridges in Victoria West. Operated by bubbly Daphne Cuthill and resident meow Rufus, the hostel offers two baths, two showers, two kitchens, and a TV room. Laundry service and breakfast are available at nominal extra cost; Daphne also arranges discounted day trips. It's only a 15-minute walk to downtown. *422 Wilson St., V9A 3G5, tel. and fax 604/380–1157. 5 dorms with 26 beds. No credit cards. $*

## The Arts and Nightlife

**The Arts**  The **Art Gallery of Greater Victoria** is considered one of Canada's fin-
*Galleries*  est art museums and is home both to large collections of Chinese and Japanese ceramics and other art and to the only authentic Shinto shrine in North America. The gallery hosts about 40 different temporary exhibitions yearly. *1040 Moss St., Victoria, tel. 604/384–4101. Admission: $3 adults, $1.50 students and senior citizens, children under 12 free; free Thurs. after 5, though donations are accepted. Open Mon.–Wed., Fri., and Sat. 10–5; Thurs. 10–9; Sun. 1–5.*

The **Emily Carr Gallery** (under the auspices of the Greater Victoria Gallery) presents the art of and films about this renowned artist, who was a contemporary of the Group of Seven. *1107 Wharf St., Victoria, tel. 604/384–3130.*

Among the numerous commercial galleries, the **Fran Willis North Park Gallery** (200–1619 Store St., tel. 604/381–3422) is a good bet. In a gorgeously restored warehouse near the waterfront, it shows contemporary paintings and sculpture by local artists; music is performed from time to time. For a further look at what's going on in Victoria's art scene, try the **Winchester Galleries** (tel. 604/595–2777), the **Nunavut Gallery** (tel. 604/598–1344), and the **Barton Leir Gallery** (tel. 604/383–6477).

*Music*  The **Victoria Symphony** has a winter schedule and a summer season, playing in the recently refurbished **Royal Theatre** (805 Broughton St., Victoria, tel. 604/386–6121) and at the **University Centre Auditorium** (Finnerty Rd., Victoria, tel. 604/721–8480). The **Pacific Opera Victoria** performs three productions a year in the 900-seat **McPherson Playhouse** (3 Centennial Sq., tel. 604/386–6121), adjoining the Victoria City Hall. The **Victoria International Music Festival** (tel. 604/736–2119) features internationally acclaimed musicians, dancers, and singers each summer from the first week in July through late August.

The **Victoria Jazz Society** (tel. 604/388–4423) organizes an annual **JazzFest International** in late June, which in the past has featured such jazz, blues, and world-beat artists as Dizzy Gillespie, Frank Morgan, Ellis Marsalis, and Aster Aweke.

For listings of clubs and restaurants featuring jazz during the year, call **Jazz Hotline** (604/658–5255).

Theater Live theater can be seen at the **Belfry Theatre** (1291 Gladstone Ave., Victoria, tel. 604/385–6815), **Phoenix Theatre** (Finnerty Rd., tel. 604/721–8000) at the University of Victoria, **Langham Court Theatre** (805 Langham Ct., tel. 604/384–2142), and **McPherson Playhouse** (3 Centennial Sq., tel. 604/386–6121).

Nightlife In addition to live music, darts, and brewery tours, **Spinnakers Brew Pub** (308 Catherine St., tel. 604/384–0332) features plenty of B.C. microbrews, including five of their own concoction. **Harpo's** (15 Bastion Sq., tel. 604/385–5333) has live rock, blues, and jazz, with visits from internationally recognized bands. For dancing, head to **Merlin's Cabaret** (1208 Wharf St., tel. 604/381–2331), where a younger crowd moves on two dance floors to taped techno and Top-40.

# Excursion to Whistler

## Important Addresses and Numbers

Tourist Contact the **Whistler Resort Association** (4010 Whistler Way, Whis-
Information tler V0N 1B4; in Whistler, tel. 604/932–3928; reservations, tel. 604/932–4222; in the U.S. and Canada, tel. 800/944–7853). There is an information booth (tel. 604/932–2394) in Whistler Village at the front door of the Conference Center; hours fluctuate, so call before visiting.

A provincial government **Travel Infocentre** (tel. 604/932–5528) is on the main highway, about 1½ kilometers (1 mile) south of Whistler.

Emergencies Dial 0 for **police, ambulance,** or **poison control.**

## Arriving and Departing by Car

By Car Driving time from Seattle to Vancouver is about three hours. Whistler is 1½–2 hours north of Vancouver via Route 99, the Sea-to-Sky Highway.

## Getting Around

By Bus **Maverick Coach Lines** (tel. in Vancouver 604/662–8051, in Whistler 604/932–5031) has buses leaving every couple of hours from the bus depot in downtown Vancouver. The bus stops at Whistler Village and the fare is less than $15 one way. During ski season, the last bus leaves Whistler at 10 PM.

**Perimeter Bus Transportation** (tel. 604/261–2299) has daily service, November–April and June–September from Vancouver Airport to Whistler. Reservations are necessary 24 hours in advance; the ticket booth is on the Arrivals level of the airport.

By Train **BC Rail** (tel. 604/984–5246) travels north from Vancouver to Whistler along a beautiful route. The Vancouver Bus Terminal and the North Vancouver Station are connected by bus shuttle.

## Exploring Whistler

If you think of skiing when you hear mention of **Whistler,** British Columbia, you're thinking on track. Whistler and Blackcomb mountains, part of the Whistler Resort Association, are the two biggest ski mountains in North America and are consistently ranked the first- or second-best ski destinations on the continent. There's winter and summer glacier skiing, the longest vertical drop in North

America, and the most advanced lifts in the world. At the base of the mountains is Whistler Village—a small community of lodgings, restaurants, pubs, gift shops, and boutiques. With more than 60 hotels, most of which are arranged within a five-minute walk between the mountains, the site is frenzied with activity. Culinary options within the village range from burgers to French, Japanese to deli cuisine; and nightly entertainment runs the gamut from sophisticated piano bars to casual pubs.

In the winter, the village buzzes with skiers taking to the slopes in vibrantly colored attire, but as the scenery changes from winter's snow-white to summer's lush-green landscapes, the mood of Whistler changes, too. Things seem to slow down a bit, and the resort sheds some of its competitive edge and welcomes a more relaxed, slower-paced environment. Even the local golf tournaments and the triathlon are interspersed with Mozart and bluegrass festivals.

New developments in this rapidly growing resort include **Whistler North**, with still more boutiques, condo hotels, and dining outlets, and **Glacier Creek Lodge**, a visually stunning 5.6 million dollar addition on Blackcomb Mountain that expands the dining options on the mountain.

Adjacent to the area is the 31,579-hectare (78,000-acre) **Garibaldi Provincial Park,** with dense mountainous forests splashed with hospitable lakes and streams. But even if you don't want to roam much farther than the village, there are five lakes for canoeing, fishing, swimming, and windsurfing, and many nearby hiking and mountain-bike trails.

No matter what the season, though, Whistler Village is very accessible to the pedestrian—in fact, it is a pedestrian-only village. Anywhere you want to go within the resort is at most five minutes away, and parking lots are just outside the village. The bases of Whistler and Blackcomb mountains are also just at the edge; in fact, you can ski right into the lower level of the Chateau Whistler Hotel, and all 2,700 of the village's hotel rooms are less than 1,000 feet from the lifts.

If you are interested in a tour of the area, **Alpine Adventure Tours** (tel. 604/932–2705) has a Whistler history tour of the valley and a Squamish day trip.

## Scenic Drives

Completion of a new highway opened the **Coast Mountain Circle,** linking Vancouver to Cariboo Country. This 702-kilometer (435-mile) route takes in spectacular Howe Sound, the deep-water port of Squamish, Whistler Resort, and Pemberton Valley before heading back to Vancouver through scenic Fraser Canyon and Harrison Hot Springs. The loop makes a comfortable two- to three-day journey. For more information contact the **Tourism Association of Southwestern B.C.** (204-1755 W. Broadway, Vancouver V6J 4S5, tel. 604/739–9011 or 800/667–3306, fax 604/739–0153).

## Sports and the Outdoors

**Canoeing and Kayaking** You'll see lots of canoes and kayaks at the many lakes and rivers near Whistler. If you want to get in on the fun, rentals are available at Alta Lake at both **Lakeside Park** and **Wayside Park.** Another spot that's perfect for canoeing is the **River of Golden Dreams,** either from Meadow Park to Green Lake or upstream to Twin Bridges.

Kayakers looking for a thrill may want to try **Green River** from Green Lake to Pemberton. Call **Whistler Outdoor Experience** (tel. 604/932–3389) or **Sea to Sky Kayaking** (tel. 604/938–1233) for equipment or guided trips.

**Fishing**  **Whistler Backcountry Adventures** (tel. 604/938–1410) or **Whistler Fishing Guides** (tel. 604/932–4267) will take care of anything you need—equipment, guides, and transportation. All five of the lakes around Whistler are stocked with trout, but the area around **Dream River Park** is one of the most popular fishing spots. Slightly farther afield, try **Cheakamus Lake, Daisy Lake,** and **Callaghan Lake.**

**Golf**  Arnold Palmer designed the par-72 championship **Whistler Golf Course** (tel. 604/932–4544), which is said to be a "good four-iron shot from the village." The course is very scenic, fairly flat, and challenging for the experienced, but pleasant for beginners. The equally scenic **Chateau Whistler Golf Club** (4612 Blackcomb Way, tel. 604/938–8000) designed by Robert Trent Jones II and nestled at the foot of the mountain on the opposite side of Whistler Village, was ranked the best new course in Canada by Golf Digest in 1993.

**Skiing**  Whistler Resort has more than 200 runs along with hotels and res-
*Downhill*  taurants, and, like Whistler, is in the process of rapidly expanding. The vertical drops and elevation at **Blackcomb** and **Whistler** mountains are, perhaps, the most impressive features to skiers. Blackcomb has a 5,280-foot vertical drop, North America's longest, while Whistler comes in second, with a 5,020-foot drop. The top elevation is 7,494 feet on Blackcomb and 7,160 on Whistler. These mountains also have the most advanced ski-lift technology: Blackcomb has a 26,350-skier-per-hour lift capacity, while Whistler's capacity is 22,295 skiers per hour. Blackcomb and Whistler have more than 100 marked trails each and receive an average of 450 inches of snow per year; Blackcomb is open June–August for summer glacier skiing. **Whistler Ski School** (tel. 604/932–3434) and **Blackcomb Ski School** (tel. 604/932–3141) offer lessons to skiers of all levels.

*Heli- and*  In Whistler, **Mountain Heli-Sports** (tel. 604/932–2070 or 604/932–
*Snowcat Skiing*  3512), **Tyax Heli-Skiing** (tel. 604/932–7007), and **Whistler Heli-Ski-ing** (tel. 604/932–4105) have day trips with up to four glacier runs, or 12,000 vertical feet of skiing for experienced skiers; the cost is about $350.

---

## Dining and Lodging

**Dining**  For prices *see* Dining chart for Vancouver, *above.*

**Il Caminetto Di Umberto; Trattoria di Umberto; Settebello's.** Umberto Menghi is Vancouver's best-known restaurateur because of his fabulously successful Italian restaurants. Now there are three in Whistler. Il Caminetto and the Trattoria are in the village, and Settebello's is in Whistler Creek, about 3 kilometers (2 miles) south. Umberto offers home-style Italian cooking in a relaxed atmosphere; he specializes in such pasta dishes as crab-stuffed cannelloni or a four-cheese lasagna. The Trattoria has a Tuscan-style rotisserie, highlighting a pasta dish served with a tray of chopped tomatoes, hot pepper, basil, olive oil, anchovies, and Parmesan so that you can mix it as spicy and flavorful as you like. Settebello's specialty is lean grilled beef and chicken, and Il Caminetto, perhaps the best restaurant in the Whistler area, is known for its veal, osso buco, and zabaglione. *Il Caminetto: 4242 Village Stroll, tel. 604/932–4442; Trattoria: Mountainside Lodge, tel. 604/932–5858; Settebello's:*

*Whistler Creek Lodge, tel. 604/932–3000. Dinner reservations advised. Dress: casual but neat. AE, DC, MC, V. $$$*

★ **Les Deux Gros.** The name means "the two fat guys," which may explain the restaurant's motto, "Never trust a skinny chef." Portions of the country French cuisine are generous indeed. The spinach-and-warm-duck salad, steak tartare, juicy rack of lamb, and salmon Wellington are all superbly crafted and presented, and the service is friendly but unobtrusive. Located just southwest of the village, this is the spot for that special romantic dinner; request one of the prime tables by the massive stone fireplace. *1200 Alta Lake Rd., tel. 604/932–4611. Dinner only. Reservations advised. Dress: casual but neat. AE, MC, V. $$$*

**The Wildflower Cafe.** Although this is the main dining room of the Chateau Whistler, it's an informal, comfortable restaurant. Huge picture windows overlook the ski slopes and let in the bright sun reflected off the snow. The rustic effect of the Chateau Whistler lobby continues in the Wildflower—more than 100 antique wood birdhouses decorate the room, and chairs and tables have that farmhouse look. Although there is an à la carte menu that focuses on Northern Italian cuisine, the restaurant features terrific breakfast, lunch, and dinner buffets that may include fresh crêpes and omelets, sweet potato-and-parsnip soup, barbecued salmon, smoked halibut, artichoke-and-mushroom salad, pepper salad, seafood pâté, pasta in a spicy tomato sauce, and cold meats. *Chateau Whistler Hotel, tel. 604/938–8000. Dinner reservations advised. Dress: casual. AE, D, DC, MC, V. $$$*

★ **La Rúa Restaurante.** One of the newest and brightest additions to the Whistler dining scene is La Rúa, located on the ground floor of Le Chamois (*see below*). Reddish flagstone floors and sponge-painted walls, a wine cellar behind a wrought iron door, modern oil paintings, and sconce lighting give the restaurant an intimate, Mediterranean ambiance. Favorites from the Continental menu include Asian prawns, rack of lamb, and grilled swordfish with spicy, sweet corn salsa. Start with the filling black-bean soup and end with the pleasing tiramisu. *4557 Blackcomb Way, tel. 604/932–5011. Reservations advised. Dress: casual. AE, DC, MC, V. Closed lunch Mon.–Thurs., first 3 wks in Nov. $$*

**Lodging** All lodgings can be booked through the **Whistler Resort Association** (tel. 604/932–4222 or 800/944–7853); summer rates are greatly discounted.

For prices *see* Lodging chart for Victoria, *above*.

★ **Le Chamois.** Sharing the prime ski-in, ski-out location at the base of the Blackcomb runs is this elegant, new luxury hotel. Of the 62 spacious guest rooms with convenience kitchens, the most popular are the studios with Jacuzzi tubs set in front of the living room's bay windows overlooking the slopes and lifts. Guests can keep an eye on the action also from the glass elevators and the heated outdoor pool. *4557 Blackcomb Way, tel. 604/932–8700; in the U.S. and Canada 800/777–0185; fax 604/938–1888. 62 suites and studios. Facilities: restaurant, deli, outdoor heated pool, Jacuzzi, fitness room, laundry room, complimentary ski locker, free parking, shuttle to village, rooms equipped for people with disabilities. AE, DC, MC, V. $$$$*

**Chateau Whistler.** Whistler's most extravagant hotel is a large and friendly looking fortress, just outside the village. It was built and run by Canadian Pacific. It is the same style as the Banff Springs Hotel and the Jasper Park Lodge; the marvelous lobby is filled with rustic Canadiana, handmade Mennonite rugs, enormous fireplaces, and enticing overstuffed sofas. Floor-to-ceiling windows in the lounge, the health club, and the Wildflower Cafe overlook the base of Blackcomb Mountain. It's possible to schuss from there right into the basement of the hotel. The standard rooms are called premier and are average, but the suites are fit for royalty, with specially commissioned quilts and artwork, complemented by antique furnishings. Both the Wildflower Cafe (*see* Dining, *above*) and La Fiesta, a tapas bar, are very good choices for a meal. The resort added an extensive spa facility in late 1993; ask about reasonably priced retreat packages and summer rates that drop by 50%. *4599 Chateau Blvd., Box 100, V0N 1B0, tel. 604/938–8000; in the U.S. and Canada 800/441–1414; fax 604/938–2055. 307 doubles, 36 suites. Facilities: 2 restaurants, bar, indoor-outdoor pool, indoor and outdoor whirlpools, saunas, steam rooms, massage, shiatsu, aromatherapy, hydrotherapy, weight room, 3 tennis courts, golf course, rooms equipped for people with disabilities, no-smoking rooms, small pets allowed. AE, D, DC, MC, V. $$$$*

**Pension Edelweiss.** The Edelweiss is one of seven charming and very European bed-and-breakfasts around Whistler, and it's within walking distance of Whistler Village. Rooms have that crisp, northern European spic-and-span feel, in keeping with the Bavarian chalet style of the house; all have private baths and some have balconies and telephones. A romantic room with fireplace and private entrance was added in 1993. Each morning a different breakfast (included in room rate) is served: Scandinavian, American, French, German. A bus stop just outside provides easy access to Whistler Village. *7162 Nancy Greene Way, Box 850, tel. 604/932–3641 or 800/665–1892 (Whistler B&B Inns), fax 604/932–3776. 8 rooms, 1 suite. Facilities: sauna, hot tub, occasional dinners. AE, MC, V. $$*

# 6 British Columbia

*By Ray
Chatelin*

*Updated by
Melissa
Rivers*

Canada's third-largest province (only Québec and Ontario are bigger), British Columbia occupies almost 10% of Canada's total surface area, stretching from the Pacific Ocean to the provinces of Alberta, Saskatchewan, and Manitoba, and from the U.S. border to the Yukon and Northwest Territories. It spans more than 360,000 square miles, making it larger than every American state except Alaska.

But size alone doesn't account for British Columbia's popularity as a vacation destination. Even easterners, content in the fact that Ontario and Québec form the industrial heartland of Canada, admit that British Columbia is the most spectacular part of the nation, with salmon-rich waters, abundant coastal scenery, and stretches of snow-capped peaks.

The region's natural splendor has ironically become the source of one of its more serious conflicts. For more than a century, logging companies have depended on the abundant supply of British Columbia wood, and whole towns are still centered on the industry. But environmentalists and many residents see the logging industry as a threat to the natural surroundings. Compromises have been achieved in recent years, but the issue is far from resolved.

The province used to be very British and predictable, reflecting its colonial heritage, but no longer. Vancouver, for example, has become an international city whose relaxed lifestyle is spiced by a rich and varied cultural scene embracing large Japanese, Chinese, Italian, and Greek communities. Even Victoria, which clings with restrained passion to British traditions and lifestyles, has undergone an international metamorphosis in recent years.

No matter how modern the province, evidence remains of the earliest settlers, Pacific Coast natives (Haida, Kwakiutl, Nootka, Salish, and others), who occupied the land for more than 12,000 years before the first Europeans arrived en masse in the late 19th century.

But material proof of their heritage may not be enough for today's native residents, who often face social barriers that have kept them from the mainstream of the province's rich economy. Although some have gained university educations and have fashioned careers, many are just now beginning to make demands on the nonnative population. In dispute are thousands of square miles of land claimed as aboriginal territory, some of which is located within such major cities as Vancouver, Prince George, and Prince Rupert.

Although the issue of ownership remains inconclusive, testimony of British Columbia's roots is apparent throughout the province, from small-town boutiques to big-city dining establishments. Native arts, such as wood-carved objects and silver-etched pendants, fetch top dollar from visitors and residents alike, and native Canadian restaurants prepare authentic culinary delights from traditional recipes.

# Essential Information

## Important Addresses and Numbers

**Tourist
Information**

For information concerning the province contact **Discover British Columbia** (Ministry of Tourism, Parliament Buildings, Victoria V8V 1X4, tel. 604/663-6000 in B.C. or 800/663-6000 in the U.S.). More than 140 communities in the province have **Travel Infocentres**.

The principal regional tourist offices are: **Tourism Association of Southwestern B.C.** (204–1755 W. Broadway, Vancouver V6J 4S5, tel. 604/739–9011 or 800/667–3306, fax 604/739–0153); **Tourism Association of Vancouver Island** (302–45 Bastion Sq., Victoria V8W 1J1, tel. 604/382–3551, fax 604/382–3532); **Okanagan–Similkameen Tourist Association** (104–515 Hwy. 97 S, Kelowna V1Z 3J2, tel. 604/769–5959, fax 604/861–7493); **High Country Tourist Association** (2–1490 Pearson Pl., Kamloops V2C 6H1, tel. 604/372–7770, fax 604/828–4656); **North By Northwest Tourism** (3840 Alfred Ave., Box 1030, Smithers V0J 2N0, tel. 604/847–5227, fax 604/847–7585); **Rocky Mountain Visitors Association** (495 Wallinger Ave., Box 10, Kimberley V1A 2Y5, tel. 604/427–4838, fax 604/427–3344); **Prince Rupert Convention and Visitors Bureau** (100 McBride St., Box 669 CMG, Prince Rupert V8J 3S1, tel. 604/624–5637); **Kootenay Country Tourist Association** (610 Railway St., Nelson V1L 1H4, tel. 604/352–6033, fax 604/352–1656); **Cariboo Chilcotin Coast Tourist Association** (190 Yorston St., Box 4900, Williams Lake V2G 2V8, tel. 604/392–2226 or 800/663–5885, fax 604/392–2838); **Peace River Alaska Highway Tourist Association** (9908 106th Ave., Box 6850, Fort St. John V1J 4J3, tel. 604/785–2544, fax 604/785–4424).

**Emergencies**  Dial **911** in Vancouver and Victoria; dial **0** elsewhere in the province for **police, ambulance,** or **poison control.**

**Hospitals**  British Columbia has hospitals in virtually every town, including: in Prince George, **Prince George Regional Hospital** (2000 15th Ave., tel. 604/565–2000 or for emergencies, 604/565–2444); in Chilliwack, **Chilliwack General Hospital** (45600 Menholm, tel. 604/795–4141); in Kamloops, **Royal Inland Hospital** (311 Columbia St., tel. 604/374–5111); in Kelowna, **Kelowna General Hospital** (2268 Pandosy St., tel. 604/862–4000).

**Late-night Pharmacies**  All-night pharmacies are virtually unknown in British Columbia, even in the largest cities, although some pharmacies do offer after-hours emergency numbers. Generally, emergency prescriptions can be filled through major hospitals. The following is a list of some pharmacies that could provide assistance: in Prince George, **Hart Drugs** (3789 W. Austin Rd., tel. 604/962–9666); in Kamloops, **Kipp-Mallery I.D.A. Pharmacy** (273 Victoria St., tel. 604/372–2531); in Hope, **Pharmasave Drugs** (235 Wallace St., tel. 604/869–2486).

---

## Arriving and Departing by Plane

**Airports and Airlines**  British Columbia is served by **Victoria International Airport** and **Vancouver International Airport.** Domestic airports are in most cities. **Air Canada** (tel. 604/688–5515 in Vancouver, 800/776–3000 in the U.S.) and **Canadian Airlines International** (tel. 604/279–6611 in Vancouver, 800/426–7000 in the U.S.) are the two dominant carriers. **Air B.C.** (tel. 604/688–5515 in Vancouver, 604/360–9074 in Victoria, 800/776–3000 in the U.S.) is the major regional line and runs daily flights between Seattle and Victoria.

---

## Arriving and Departing by Car, Bus, and Boat

**By Car**  Driving time from Seattle to Vancouver is about 2½ hours. From other Canadian regions, there are three main routes leading into British Columbia: through Sparwood, in the south, take Highway 3; from Jasper and Banff, in the central region, travel on Route 1 (Trans-Canada) or Highway 5; and through Dawson Creek, in the north, follow Highways 2 and 97.

By Bus   Greyhound (tel. 800/231–2222, 604/662–3222 in Vancouver, 206/624–
3456 in Seattle) connects destinations throughout British Columbia
with cities and towns throughout the Pacific North Coast.

By Boat   There is year-round passenger service (closed Christmas) between
Victoria and Seattle via the *Victoria Clipper* (tel. 800/888–2535, 206/
448–5000 in Seattle, 604/382–8100 in Victoria).

Washington State Ferries (tel. 604/381–1551 in Victoria, 206/464–
6400 in Seattle) cross daily, year-round, between Sidney, just north
of Victoria, and Anacortes, WA. Black Ball Transport (tel. 604/386–
2202 in Victoria, 206/622–2222 in Seattle) operates between Victoria and Port Angeles, WA.

Direct passenger and vehicle service between Seattle and Victoria
is available May 21–September 18 on the *Royal Victorian,* operated
by Victoria Line (tel. 604/480–5555), a subsidiary of B.C. Ferries.
Outfitted to carry 192 cars and 1,000 passengers, the ship will make
one round-trip daily, departing Victoria at 7:30 AM and returning
from Seattle at 1 PM. One-way fares for car and driver are $49, and
round-trip is $90. Tickets for additional passengers or foot passengers
cost $25 one-way, and $45 round-trip. Reservations are advised for
those traveling with a vehicle.

## Getting Around

By Air   Harbour Air (tel. 604/627–1341 in Prince Rupert, 604/637–5355 in
*Queen*   Sandspit) runs scheduled floatplanes between Sandspit, Masset,
*Charlotte*   Queen Charlotte City, and Prince Rupert daily except Christmas,
*Islands*   Boxing Day (Dec. 26), and New Year's Day.

Air B.C. provides both airport-to-airport and harbor-to-harbor
service from Vancouver to Victoria at least hourly. Both flights take
about 35 minutes.

*Vancouver*   Helijet Airways (tel. 604/273–1414 or 604/382–6222) helicopter serv-
*Island*   ice is available from downtown Vancouver to downtown Victoria.

By Car   Major roads in British Columbia, and most secondary roads, are
paved and well engineered. Mountain driving is slower but more scenic. There are no roads on the mainland coast once you leave the populated areas of the southwest corner near Vancouver.

*Car Rentals*   Most major agencies, including Avis, Budget, and Hertz, service cities throughout the province (*see* Renting and Leasing Cars in Chapter 1).

By Bus   Greyhound Lines of Canada (tel. 800/231–2222 or 604/388–5248)
*North of*   serves the area north of Vancouver with hundreds of stops in the
*Vancouver*   province, including the municipalities of Prince Rupert, Terrace,
*Island*   and Smithers.

*Vancouver*   Pacific Coach Lines (tel. 800/661–1725) operates daily connecting
*Island*   service between Victoria and Vancouver via B.C. Ferries. Island
Coach Lines (tel. 604/385–4411) serves the Vancouver Island area.
Maverick Coach Lines (tel. 604/662–8051) services Nanaimo from
Vancouver, via B.C. Ferries (*see below*).

By Ferry   B.C. Ferries (tel. 604/277–0277 in Vancouver, 604/656–0757 in Victoria, 604/753–6626 in Nanaimo) provides frequent year-round passenger and vehicle service between Vancouver and Vancouver
Island, from Tsawwassen (south of Vancouver) to Swartz Bay;
Tsawwassen to Nanaimo; and Horseshoe Bay (north of Vancouver)
to Nanaimo. There are eight round-trips daily between Tsawwassen–Nanaimo and Horseshoe Bay–Nanaimo, and at least eight

round-trips per day between Tsawwassen–Swartz Bay (additional sailings during the summer, on weekends, and during holiday periods). B.C. Ferries also provides service to the northern and southern Gulf Islands; the Sunshine Coast; through the Inside Passage between Port Hardy and Prince Rupert; and from Prince Rupert to the Queen Charlotte Islands. When traveling with a vehicle during summer months, plan to arrive at the terminal well in advance of the scheduled sailing time. For schedule information call the numbers above for a 24-hour recorded message.

**By Train**  **BC Rail** (tel. 604/984–5246 or 604/631–3500 in Vancouver, 604/564–9080 in Prince George) travels from Vancouver to Prince George, a route of 747 kilometers (463 miles), and offers daily service to Whistler. **Via Rail** (tel. 800/561–8630 in B.C.) provides service between Prince Rupert and Prince George.

*Vancouver*  **Esquimalt & Nanaimo Rail Liner** (450 Pandora Ave., Victoria V8W
*Island*  3L5, tel. 604/383–4324; in B.C., 800/561–8630) makes the round-trip from Victoria's Pandora Avenue Station to Courtenay; schedules vary seasonally.

## Guided Tours

**Orientation**  The following operators offer tours throughout the province: **Classic Holidays Tour & Travel** (102–75 W. Broadway, Vancouver V5Y 1P1, tel. 604/875–6377), **Klineburger Worldwide Travel** (800 S. Michigan St., Seattle, WA 98108-2651, tel. 206/763–4009), and **Sea to Sky** (1928 Nelson Ave., W. Vancouver V7V 2P4, tel. 604/922–7339).

**Special-Interest**  A few Vancouver Island–based companies that conduct whale-
**Tours**  watching tours are: **Subtidal Adventures** (Box 253, Ucluelet V0R
*Nature Tours*  3A0, tel. 604/726–7336), **Inter-Island Excursions** (Box 393, Tofino V0R 2Z0, tel. 604/725–3163), **Jamie's Whaling Station** (Box 590, Tofino V0R 2Z0, tel. 604/725–3919), **Tofino Sea-Kayaking Company** (Box 620, Tofino, VOR 2Z0, tel. 604/725–4222), and, near Port Hardy, **Stubbs Island Charters** (Box 7, Telegraph Cove V0N 3J0, tel. 604/928–3185).

**Ecosummer Expeditions** (1516 Duranleau St., Vancouver V6H 3S4, tel. 604/669–7741) runs ecological tours of the Queen Charlotte Islands.

# Exploring British Columbia

When traveling by car, keep in mind that more than three-quarters of British Columbia is mountainous terrain. Trips that appear relatively short may take longer, especially in the northern regions and along the coast, where roads are often narrow and winding. In certain areas—most of the uninhabited west coast of Vancouver Island, for example—roads do not exist.

Within British Columbia, there is a vast range of climates, largely a result of the province's size, its mountainous topography, and its border on the Pacific. Vancouver Island, surrounded by Pacific waters, experiences relatively mild winters and summers (usually above 32°F winter, below 80°F summer), although it rains frequently in winter. Likewise, the northern coast around Prince Rupert and the Queen Charlotte Islands has wet winter months and few extremes in temperature. But as you move inland, especially toward the Peace River region in the north, the climate becomes much colder. In the southern interior, the Okanagan Valley has an arid climate, with temperatures dropping below the freezing level in winter and sometimes reaching 90° F during the summer.

## Highlights for First-time Visitors

**Kilby General Store Museum,** Tour 3: Okanagan Valley and Environs
**Mintner Gardens,** Tour 3: Okanagan Valley and Environs
**Naikoon Provincial Park,** Tour 2: North of Vancouver Island
**O'Keefe Historic Ranch,** Tour 3: Okanagan Valley and Environs
**Pacific Rim National Park,** Tour 1: Vancouver Island

## Tour 1: Vancouver Island

Vancouver Island, the largest island on the west coast, stretches 450 kilometers (280 miles) from Victoria in the south to Cape Scott, although 97% of the population live between Victoria and Campbell River (halfway up the island); 50% of them live in Victoria itself. Geographically, the differences between the east and west are impressive. The western side is wild, often inhospitable, with just a handful of small settlements. Virtually all of the island's human habitation is on the eastern coast, where the weather is gentler and the topography is low-lying.

The cultural heritage of the island is from the Kwakiutl, Nootka, and Coastal Salish native groups. Native art and cultural centers flourish throughout the region, especially in the lower section of the island. These centers enable visitors to catch a glimpse of contemporary native culture.

Mining, logging, and tourism are the important island industries. But environmental issues, such as logging practices by British Columbia's lumber companies, are becoming important to islanders—both native and nonnative. Residents are working to reach a happy coexistence with the island's wilderness and its economy, which is dependent on industrial development and tourism.

*Numbers in the margin correspond to points of interest on the Vancouver Island map.*

**❶** Beginning your driving tour from Victoria (*see* Chapter 5), take Highway 14 west to **Sooke** (26 miles, or 42 kilometers, west of Victoria), a logging, fishing, and farming community. **East Sooke Park,** on the east side of the harbor, offers 3,500 acres of beaches, hiking trails, and meadows dotted with wildflowers. You can also visit the **Sooke Region Museum and Travel Infocentre,** with displays of Salish and Nootka crafts, artifacts from 19th-century Sooke, barbecued salmon and strawberry shortcake on the front lawn during the summer, and plenty of information about the region. *2070 Phillips Rd., Box 774, V0S 1N0, tel. 604/642–6351. Admission free; donations accepted. Open summer, daily 9–6; winter, Tues.–Sun. 9–5. Closed Dec. 25 and 26.*

**Time Out** **Seventeen Mile House** (5121 Sooke Rd., Sooke, tel. 604/642–5942) is on the road to Sooke from Victoria. Stop here for British pub fare, a beer, or fresh local seafood. Built as a hotel, the house is an education in turn-of-the-century island architecture.

The adventurous can continue on Highway 14 west and pick up the logging road from Port Renfrew back to the east coast, although conditions on the gravel road may be hazardous, especially on weekdays with the trucks rolling by. The more reliable route backtracks to Victoria, then follows the Trans-Canada Highway up the eastern

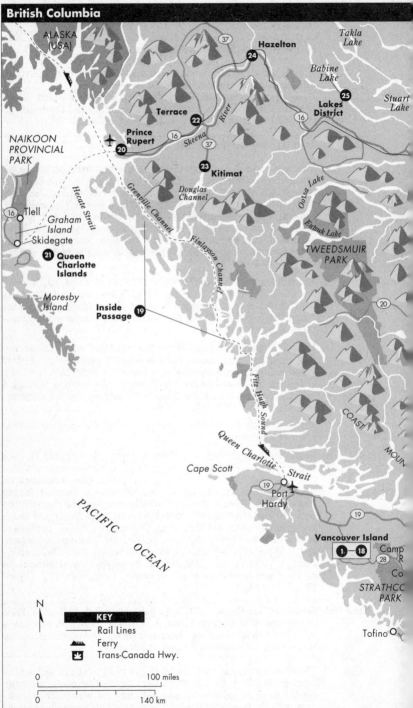

# British Columbia

ALASKA
(USA)

Takla
Lake

37

**Hazelton**
24

Babine
Lake

25

**Lakes
District**

Stuart
Lake

**Terrace**
22

16

Skeena
River

37

**Prince
Rupert**
20

*NAIKOON
PROVINCIAL
PARK*

23 **Kitimat**

Douglas
Channel

Ootsa Lake

*Hecate Strait*

*Grenville Channel*

Tlell
16

*Graham
Island*

Skidegate

Eutsuk Lake

*TWEEDSMUIR
PARK*

21 **Queen
Charlotte
Islands**

*Moresby
Island*

*Finlayson Channel*

**Inside
Passage**
19

20

*Fitz Hugh Sound*

*Queen Charlotte*

*Cape Scott*

Strait

*COAST
MOUN*

19 Port
Hardy

19

**Vancouver Island**

1 — 18
Camp
R

28

Co

*STRATHCC
PARK*

Tofino

N

## KEY

—— Rail Lines

⛴ Ferry

⛨ Trans-Canada Hwy.

0        100 miles

0        140 km

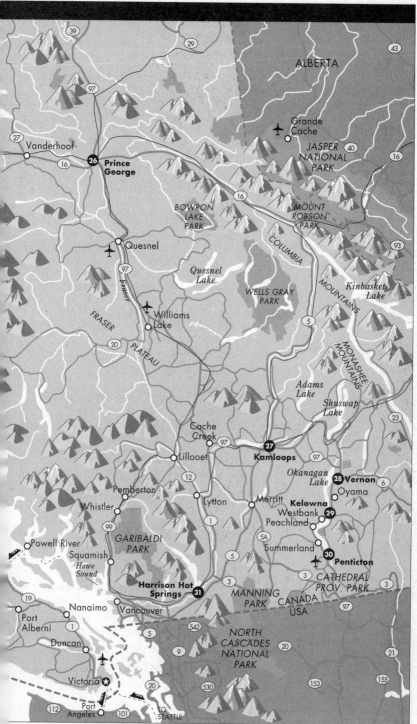

ALBERTA

39

29

43

97

27

Vanderhoof

16

26 **Prince George**

JASPER NATIONAL PARK

40

16

Grande Cache

BOWRON LAKE PARK

16

MOUNT ROBSON PARK

93

Quesnel

97

Quesnel Lake

WELLS GRAY PARK

COLUMBIA

Kinbasket Lake

Fraser

FRASER

Williams Lake

20

PLATEAU

5

MOUNTAINS

MONASHEE MOUNTAINS

Adams Lake

Shuswap Lake

23

Cache Creek

97

Kamloops 27

97

Okanagan Lake

28 **Vernon**

6

Lillooet

12

Oyama

Pemberton

Lytton

Merritt

**Kelowna**

Westbank

29

Whistler

1

Peachland

99

5A

GARIBALDI PARK

Summerland

Powell River

5

30 Penticton

Squamish

Howe Sound

3

CATHEDRAL PROV. PARK

3

19

**Harrison Hot Springs** 31

MANNING PARK

CANADA

Nanaimo

Vancouver

USA

97

Port Alberni

1

542

Duncan

5

NORTH CASCADES NATIONAL PARK

20

21

9

Victoria

153

112

20

530

155

Port Angeles

101

TO SEATTLE

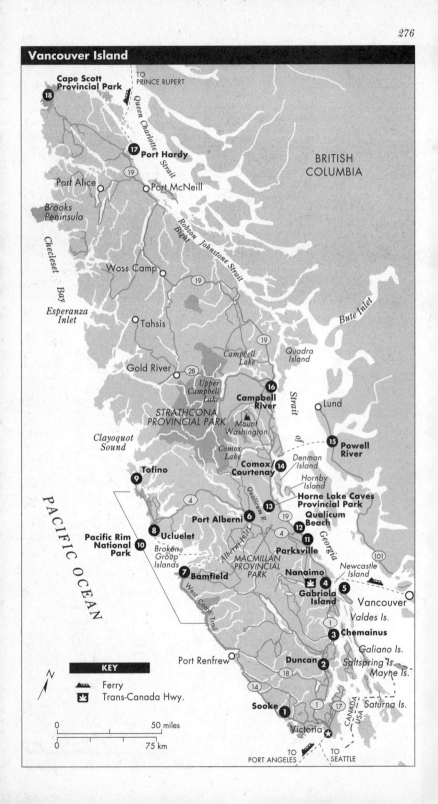

coast toward Nanaimo, the mid-island B.C. Ferries terminal point. ❷ On your way you'll pass through the town of **Duncan** (about 60 kilometers, or 37 miles, north of Victoria), nicknamed City of Totems for the many totem poles that dot the small community. The two carvings behind the City Hall are worth a short trip off the main road.

Duncan is also home to the **Native Heritage Centre.** Covering 13 acres of land on the banks of the Cowichan River, the center features a native bighouse, theater, occasional interpretive dance presentations, an arts-and-crafts gallery that focuses on carvings and weaving traditions, and native fare served in the Bighouse Restaurant. *200 Cowichan Way, Duncan, tel. 604/746–8119. Admission: $6.75 adults, $6.25 senior citizens and students, $2 children 6–12, children 5 and under free, $16 families. Open mid-May–mid Oct., daily 9:30–5:30; mid-Oct.–mid-May, daily 10:30–4:30.*

Also in Duncan is the **B.C. Forest Museum.** More a park than a museum, the attraction spans more than 40 hectares (100 acres), combining indoor and outdoor exhibits that focus on the history of forestry in British Columbia. You ride an original steam locomotive around the property and over an old wood trestle bridge. The exhibits feature logging and milling equipment. *RR 4 Trans-Canada Hwy., tel. 604/746–1251, fax 604/746–1487. Admission: $6 adults, $5 senior citizens and children 13–18, $3 children 6–12, children 5 and under free. Open May–Sept., daily 9:30–6; off-season, by appointment.*

❸ Just north of Duncan, the small town of **Chemainus** has become known recently for the bold epic murals that decorate its landscape. Once dependent on the lumber industry, the town began to revitalize in the early 1980s when its mill closed down. Since then, more than 25 murals depicting local historical events have been painted around town by international artists. Restaurants, shops, cafés, and coffee bars have added to the town's growth. Footsteps on the sidewalk lead you on a self-guided tour of the murals.

❹ **Nanaimo,** across the strait of Georgia from Vancouver, is about an hour's drive from Victoria. Throughout the Nanaimo region, petroglyphs (rock carvings) representing humans, birds, wolves, lizards, sea monsters, and supernatural creatures can be found. The **Nanaimo District Museum** (100 Cameron St., tel. 604/753–1821) will give you information about local carvings. Eight kilometers (5 miles) south of town is the **Petroglyph Provincial Park,** where designs estimated to have been carved thousands of years ago can be seen along the marked trails that begin at the parking lot.

Nanaimo is a convenient departure point for other island activities. ❺ A 20-minute ferry ride leaves from town for **Gabriola Island,** a rustic, rural island with lodging; and a 10-minute ferry takes you to **Newcastle Island,** where you can picnic, ride your bicycle, walk on trails leading past old mines and quarries, and wait for glimpses of deer, rabbits, and eagles.

As you continue north on Highway 19, you have the option of taking Highway 4 west to Port Alberni and the lower west-coast towns. ❻ **Port Alberni** is about an 80-kilometer (49-mile) drive from Nanaimo and is mainly a pulp- and sawmill town and a stopover for those on the way to Ucluelet and Tofino, though fishermen will want to take advantage of the salmon-rich waters. While you're here, consider taking a breathtaking trip down the Alberni Inlet to Barkley Sound aboard the *Lady Rose,* a Scottish ship, built in 1937. The *Lady Rose* leaves the Argyle Street dock Tuesday, Thursday, and Saturday (and Friday and Sunday in July and August) for the four-hour cruise ❼ to **Bamfield,** a remote village of about 200. Bamfield's seaside boardwalk affords an uninterrupted view of ships heading up the inlet to Port Alberni. Oddly, for a place this small, it is well equipped to handle overnight visitors. The west coast is invaded every summer by fishermen, kayakers, scuba divers, and hikers. Bamfield is also a good base from which to take boating trips to the Broken Group Islands and hikes along the West Coast Trail (*see below*). From early June to mid-September the *Lady Rose* and *Francis Barkley* sail for Ucluelet on Monday, Wednesday, and Friday. It's a unique trip and deserves all the accolades it receives. Most of the trips, to both Bamfield and Ucluelet, stop at the Broken Group Islands, but call ahead to make sure. *Argyle St. dock, tel. 604/723–8313 or 800/663–7192 for reservations Apr.-Sept. Bamfield fare: $36; Broken Group Islands fare: $38; Ucluelet fare: $40. Sailings depart daily at 8 AM.*

North of Bamfield are Ucluelet and Tofino—the whale-watching capitals of Canada, if not of the whole west coast of North America. The two towns are quite different in character, though both are relaxed in the winter and swell to several times their sizes in summer.

**❽ Ucluelet,** which in the native language means "people with a safe landing place," is totally focused on the sea. Fishing, water tours, and whale-watching are the primary activities. Whale-watching is big business, with a variety of charter companies that take tourist boats to greet the 20,000 gray whales that pass within a very short distance of Ucluelet on their migration to the Bering Sea every March–May. Sometimes the migrating whales can even be seen from the Ucluelet shore.

**❾ Tofino,** on the other hand, is more commercial, with beachfront resorts, motels, and several unique bed-and-breakfast establishments. But the surrounding area remains natural. You can walk along the beach discovering caves, cruise around the ancient forests of Meares Island, or take an hour-long water taxi to the hot springs north of town.

**❿** Ucluelet and Tofino bookend the Long Beach section of the **Pacific Rim National Park** (Box 280, Ucluelet, V0R 3A0, tel. 604/726–7721, fax 604/726–4720), the first national marine park in Canada. The park itself comprises three separate areas—Long Beach, the Broken Group Islands, and the West Coast Trail. Each accommodates a specific interest.

The unit of **Long Beach** gets its name from an 11-kilometer (7-mile) strip of hard-packed white sand strewn with twisted driftwood, shells, and the occasional Japanese glass fishing float. The beach is a favorite spot during the summer, and you often have to fight heavy traffic along the twisting 85 kilometers (53 miles) of Highway 4 from Port Alberni.

The 100 islands of the **Broken Group Islands** can be reached only by boat. Many commercial charter tours are available from Ucluelet, which rests at the southern end of Long Beach, and from Bamfield and Port Alberni. The islands are alive with sea lions, seals, and whales. The sheltered lagoons of Gibraltar, Jacques, and Hand islands offer protection and good boating conditions, but go with a guide.

The third element of the park is the **West Coast Trail** (*see* Hiking, *below*), which stretches along the coast from Bamfield to Port Renfrew. After the SS *Valencia* ran aground in 1906, killing all but 30 of the crew and passengers, the Canadian government constructed the lifesaving trail to help future victims of shipwrecks reach safe ground. The trail remains, with demanding bogs, steep slopes and gullies, cliffs (with ladders), slippery boardwalks, and insects. Although it presents many obstacles for hikers, the rewards are the panoramic views of the sea, dense rain forest, sandstone cliffs with waterfalls, and wildlife that includes gray whales and seals.

Heading back to the east coast from Port Alberni, stop off at **Cathedral Grove,** located in MacMillan Provincial Park on Highway 4. Walking trails lead you past Douglas fir trees and western red cedars, some about 800 years old. Their remarkable height creates a spiritual effect, as though you were gazing at a cathedral ceiling. Another stop along the way is **Butterfly World** (Alberni Hwy., Box 36, Coombs, V0R 1M0, tel. 604/248–7026), an enclosed tropical garden housing a massive collection of exotic, free-flying tropical butterflies.

**⑪** At the junction of Highways 4 and 19 is **Parksville**—one of the east island's primary resort areas with lodges and waterfront motels catering to families, campers, and boaters. In **Rathtrevor Provincial Park** (tel. 604/248–9449), 1½ kilometers (about 1 mile) south of Parksville, high tide brings ashore the warmest ocean water in British Columbia. Swimmers should time their visits accordingly.

**⑫** Just 12 kilometers (7 miles) north of Parksville is **Qualicum Beach,** known largely for its salmon fishing and opportunities for beachcombing along the long, sandy beaches. The nonprofit **Old School House Gallery and Art Centre** (122 Fern Rd. W, tel. 604/752–6133), with nine working studios, shows and sells the work of local artists and artisans.

**⑬** Continue north, then head west off the highway and follow signs for about 15 kilometers (9 miles) to Horne Lake and the **Horne Lake Caves Provincial Park.** Three of the six caves are open at all times. If you decide to venture in, bring along a flashlight, warm clothes, and a hard hat, and be prepared to bend and even crawl. Riverbend Cave, spanning 383 meters (1,259 feet), requires ladders and ropes in some parts, and can only be explored with a guided tour. Spelunking lessons and tours are offered for all levels, from beginner to advanced. *Tel. 604/248–3931. Fees for tours vary depending on ability level. Reservations suggested for tours.*

Between the Horne Lake turnoff and the twin cities of Comox and Courtenay is tiny Buckley Bay, where ferries leave for **Denman Island,** with connecting service to **Hornby Island.** Denman offers old-growth forests and long sandy beaches, while Hornby's spectacular beaches have earned it the nickname the Undiscovered Hawaii of British Columbia. Many artists have settled on the islands, establishing studios for pottery, jewelry, wood carving, and sculpture.

**⑭** **Comox** and **Courtenay** are near **Strathcona Provincial Park** and are commonly used as a base for anyone skiing Mt. Washington in the winter. Strathcona, the largest provincial park on Vancouver Island, encompasses **Mt. Golden Hinde,** at 2,200 meters (7,218 feet) the island's highest mountain; and **Della Falls,** Canada's highest waterfall, reaching 440 meters (1,443 feet). The park's multitude of lakes and 161 campsites attract summer canoers, fishermen, and wilderness campers, and the **Strathcona Park Lodge and Outdoor Education Center,** well known for its wilderness-skills programs, provides information on the park's facilities. *Education Center, Hwy. 28, on Upper Campbell Lake, about 45 km (28 mi) west of Hwy. 19, Box 2160, Campbell River, V9W 5C9, tel. 604/286–3122. Hours vary; call ahead.*

**⑮** From Comox, you can take a 75-minute ferry east across the Strait of Georgia to **Powell River,** a city established around the MacMillan pulp-and-paper mill, which opened in 1912. Renowned as a year-round salmon-fishing destination, the mainland's Sunshine Coast town has 30 regional lakes that offer exceptional trout fishing, as well. For information contact **Powell River Travel Info Center** (4690 Marine Dr., tel. 604/485–4701).

**16** **Campbell River** is ringed by shopping centers that make it look like a free-zoned mess. But people don't come here for the aesthetics, they come for the fish; some of the biggest salmon ever caught on a line have been landed just off the coast at Campbell River. At the mouth of the town's namesake, you can try for membership in Campbell River's Tyee Club, which would allow you to fish in a specific area, and possibly land a giant chinook. Requirements for membership in the club include registering and landing a tyee (a spring salmon weighing 30 pounds or more). Coho salmon and cutthroat trout are also plentiful in the river. *Travel Information Center, 1235 Shoppers Row (Island Hwy.), Box 400, Campbell River, V9W 5B6, tel. 604/287–4636. Open late June–Labor Day, daily 8–6; Labor Day–mid-June, weekdays 9–5.*

Pods of resident Orcas live nearby year-round in Johnstone Strait; and in Robson Bight they like using the beaches to rub against. Because of their presence, Robson Bight has been made into an ecological preserve: Whales there must not be disturbed by human observers. Some of the island's best whale-watching tours, however, are conducted nearby, out of Telegraph Cove, a village built on pilings over water.

**17** Farther north is **Port Hardy**, the departure and arrival point for B.C. Ferries going through the Inside Passage to and from Prince Rupert, the coastal port serving the Queen Charlotte Islands. During the summer the town can be crowded, so book your accommodations well in advance.

If you choose to continue to the northernmost point on Vancouver Island, drive about 60 kilometers (about 37 miles) on logging roads **18** to reach **Cape Scott Provincial Park,** a wilderness camping region designed for well-equipped and experienced hikers. At Sand Neck, a strip of land that joins the cape to the mainland of the island, you can see both the eastern and western shores at once.

## Tour 2: North of Vancouver Island

*Numbers in the margin correspond to points of interest on the British Columbia map.*

**19** The 274-nautical-mile **Inside Passage,** between Port Hardy on northern Vancouver Island and Prince Rupert, is a sheltered marine highway that follows a series of natural channels behind protective islands along the green-and-blue shaded British Columbia coast. The undisturbed landscape of rising mountains and humpbacked islands has a prehistoric look that leaves an indelible impression.

After a short segment in the open ocean, the 410-foot MV *Queen of the North* ducks in behind Calvert Island into Fitz Hugh Sound. From there, its route is protected from ocean swells all the way through Finlayson and Grenville channels, which are flanked by high, densely wooded mountains that rise steeply, in places, from narrow gorges. The *Queen of the North* carries up to 800 passengers and 157 vehicles, and takes 15 hours (almost all in daylight during summer sailings) to make the Port Hardy to Prince Rupert trip. The ship has plenty of deck space plus lounge areas, a self-serve cafeteria, and a satisfactory restaurant that offers a plentiful buffet. Day-use cabins are available for an additional fee. Children can play in the Captain Kids Room. *British Columbia Ferry Corporation, 1112 Fort St., Victoria V8V 4V2, tel. 604/386–3431. Cost varies according to cabin, vehicle, and season. Reservations required for the cruise and advised for hotel accommodations at ports of call. Oct.–Apr. sailings are once weekly; May sailings twice-weekly; June–Sept. sailings daily, departing on alternate days from Port Hardy and Prince Rupert; departure time 7:30 AM, arrival time 10:30 PM. Schedule and fares subject to change.*

An alternative to the ferry cruise along the Inside Passage is one of the more expensive luxury-liners that sail along the B.C. coast (*see* Chapter 1) from Vancouver to Alaska.

**20** **Prince Rupert,** the final stop on the B.C. Ferries route through the Inside Passage, is about 750 air kilometers (465 miles) northwest of Vancouver, though it takes more than 20 hours to drive the mountainous 1,500 kilometers (936 miles). Prince Rupert has a mild but wet climate, so take rain gear.

The town lives off fishing, fish processing, logging, saw- and pulp-mill operations, and deep-sea shipping. A gondola ride to the top of Mt. Hays, located just outside the downtown area, offers magnificent views on a clear day of the industrial harbor, the Queen Charlotte Islands, and the mountains of Alaska. You can ski Mt. Hays during the winter and picnic in the summer. Prince Rupert is also a place where British Columbia's cultural heritage is quite evident. The **Museum of Northern British Columbia** has one of the province's finest collections of coastal native art, some artifacts dating back 10,000 years. Native artisans carve totem poles in the carving shed and, during the summer, the museum runs a 2½-hour boat tour of the harbor and Metlakatla native village. *1st Ave. and McBride St., Prince Rupert, tel. 604/624–3207. Admission free; donations accepted. Open Sept.–May, Mon.–Sat. 10–5; June–Aug., Mon.–Sat. 9–9, Sun. 9–5.*

From Prince Rupert you can continue on to explore either the Alaskan Panhandle, the Queen Charlotte Islands, or interior British Columbia. If you wish to proceed north through the Alaskan waterways to Skagway, board the **Alaska Marine Highway System ferry** (tel. in Prince Rupert, 604/627–1744 or 800/642–0066), which docks alongside the *Queen of the North* in Prince Rupert. Alaska ferries travel this route four times a week in the summer, twice a week the rest of the year.

**21** A popular vacation destination, the **Queen Charlotte Islands,** or Misty Islands, though once the remote preserve of the Haida natives, is now easily accessible by ferry. Today the Haida make up only one sixth of the population, but they continue to infuse the island with a sense of the Haida past and contribute to the logging and fishing industries, and to tourism, as well. Haida elders lead tours—an essential service if you want to reach the isolated, abandoned villages. Though the region has become a popular tourist destination, limited accommodations make it necessary to reserve guest rooms well in advance.

The *Queen of Prince Rupert* (tel. 604/386–3431), a B.C. Ferries ship, sails six times a week between late May and September (three times a week the rest of the year), and can easily accommodate recreational vehicles. Crossing the Hecate Strait from Prince Rupert to Skidegate, near Queen Charlotte on Graham Island, takes about six hours. Schedules vary and reservations are required, so call ahead. The **MV** *Kwuna,* another B.C. Ferries ship, connects

Skidegate Landing to Alliford Bay on Moresby Island, with 12 20-minute sailings daily. Access to smaller islands off Graham Island (the northernmost and largest of the group of 150) and Moresby Island is by boat or air; plans should be made in advance through a travel agent.

In the Queen Charlottes, there are 150 kilometers (93 miles) of paved road, most of it on Graham Island, connecting Queen Charlotte in the south to Masset in the north. Some of the other islands are laced with gravel roads, most of which can be accessed with any sturdy car or RV. The rugged, rocky west coast of the archipelago faces the ocean; the east coast has many broad sandy beaches. Throughout, the mountains and shores are often shrouded in fog and rain-laden clouds, adding to the mysteriousness of the islands.

**Naikoon Provincial Park** (tel. 604/557–4390), in the northeast corner of Graham, preserves a large section of the unique wilderness found here, where low-lying swamps, pine and cedar forests, lakes, beaches, trails, and wildlife combine to create an intriguing environment. Take the 5-kilometer (3-mile) walk from the Tlell Picnic Site to the beach, and on to the bow section of the old wooden shipwreck of the *Pezuta*, a 1928 log-hauling vessel. On the southern end of Graham Island, the **Queen Charlotte Islands Museum** has a small but impressive display of Haida totem poles, masks, and carvings of both silver and argillite (a hard black slate). There is also a natural-history exhibit, which gives interesting background on the wildlife of the islands. *Box 1373, Skidegate V0T 1S1, tel. 604/559–4643. Admission: $2.50 adults; children 13 and under free. Open Apr.–late Oct., weekdays 9–5, weekends 1–5; winter, Wed.–Sun. 1–5.*

If you have time on Graham Island, drive up to Old Massett on the northern coast, site of the **Ed Jones Haida Museum.** Exhibits here include totems and artifacts. Nearby, artists sell their work from their homes. South of Graham, in and around South Moresby National Park Reserve, lie most of the better-known abandoned Haida villages, which are accessible by water. Visiting some of the villages requires at least several days travel time, and lots of planning for the wilderness. You (or your tour) need to contact Parks Canada (tel. 604/559–8818) before you go.

For more information on the Queen Charlotte Islands, contact the **Queen Charlotte Islands Travel Information Center** (Box 337, Queen Charlotte V0T 1S0, tel. 604/559–4742, fax 604/559–8188).

To see interior British Columbia, take Highway 16 east from Prince Rupert. En route you'll pass through or near such communities as **㉒ Terrace,** with a hot-springs complex at the Mt. Layton Resort, skiing at Shames Mountain, and excellent fishing in the Skeena River; **㉓** and **Kitimat** (on Highway 37, south of Terrace), at the head of the **㉔** Douglas Channel, where the fishing is superb. At **Hazelton,** a town rich in the culture of the Gitksan and Wet'suwet'en peoples you must visit **'Ksan,** just outside town, a re-created Gitksan village. The brightly painted community of six longhouses is a replica of the one that stood on the same site when the first explorers arrived during the last century. The **National Exhibition Centre and Museum** displays works and artifacts from the Upper Skeena River region. A workshop, often used by 'Ksan artists, is open to the public, and three other longhouses can be visited on a 45-minute tour: One features contemporary masks and robes, another has song-and-dance dramas in the summer. A gift shop and museum are on the grounds. *National Exhibition Centre: Box 333, Hazelton, V0J 1Y0, tel. 604/ 842–5723; admission free; open year-round, Thurs.–Mon. 10:30–*

*4:30. 'Ksan Indian Village: Box 326, Hazelton, V0J 1Y0, tel. 604/
842–5544; admission $5.50 adults, $3.50 senior citizens, $3 stu-
dents, $2 children 5–12; open May–mid-Oct., daily 9–6; mid-Oct.–
Apr., Thurs.–Mon. 9–5. Tours given May–mid-Oct., on the hour.*

**㉕** North of Highway 16 you pass by the serene **Lakes District,** which is
popular for camping, fishing, and water sports, before coming to
**㉖** **Prince George** (Tourism Prince George, 1198 Victoria St., V2L 2L2,
tel. 604/562–3700), British Columbia's third-largest city. This provincial hub contains the Fraser-Ft. George Regional Museum (tel.
604/562–1612), a railroad museum (tel. 604/563–7351; open late
May–Labor Day), and the Prince George Native Art Gallery (tel.
604/562–7385). From Prince George you can turn south on Highway
97 for Kamloops and the Okanagan Valley (*see* Scenic Drives, *below*),
or you can continue on Highway 16, then on Highway 5 for a longer
(some say even more spectacular) route to the same place.

## Tour 3: Okanagan Valley and Environs, Including Rainbow and High Country

The Okanagan Valley is part of a highland plateau between the Cascade range of mountains on the west and the Monashee mountains on
the east. Though small in size (only 3% of the province's total land
mass), the area contains the interior's largest concentration of people. Dominating the valley is Okanagan Lake, a vacation hot-spot
for tourists from the west coast and Alberta. In summer months it
can be difficult to find rooms. The largest towns along the lake are
Vernon at the north end, Kelowna in the middle, and Penticton at
the south. Between, and along the lake, are the recreational and
resort communities of **Summerland, Peachland, Westbank,** and
**Oyama,** which are popular tourist destinations and have camping facilities, motels, and cabins. Favorite local lore tells of the legendary
Ogopogo, a snakelike creature that inhabits the lake between
Peachland and Summerland.

The valley is the fruit-growing capital of Canada, producing apricots, cherries, pears, plums, apples, and peaches. A visit to the region from mid-April through early June promises to jolt your senses
with the brightness and fragrance of the spring blossoms.

**㉗** We arrive in the valley by way of **Kamloops** (which is officially a part
of High Country, not Okanagan), a convenient passageway from
Fraser Canyon and Thompson Valley, and a stop on the Canadian Pacific Railroad. The town is 50 minutes northeast of Vancouver by air
and 425 kilometers (260 miles) by road and is surrounded by 500
lakes, which provide an abundance of trout, Dolly Varden, and
kokanee. During late September and October, however, attention
turns to the sockeye salmon, when thousands of these fish—intent
on breeding—return home to their birth waters in Adams River
(only 65 kilometers, or 40 miles, east of Kamloops off the Trans-Canada Highway).

Once every four years—the last time was 1994—the sockeye run
reaches a massive scale, as more than a million salmon pack the waters and up to 500,000 visitors come to observe. The **Roderick Haig-
Brown Conservation Area,** which protects the 11-kilometer (7-mile)
stretch of Adams River, is the best place to watch.

Wildlife enthusiasts will also enjoy the **Kamloops Wildlife Park** (Box
698, Kamloops, V2C 5L7, tel. 604/573–3242), a 55-acre compound
housing 71 species in fairly natural habitats. Canyon hiking trails, a

miniature railway, and adjacent waterslides provide something for everyone.

Vernon, Kelowna, and Penticton, running south along Highway 97, like to believe each has a distinct personality, but local rivalries aside, the towns are actually one large unit. Okanagan Lake is their glue, offering recreation, lodging, and restaurants.

**28** Of the three, **Vernon** is the least dependent on tourism, organized instead around forestry and agriculture. The city borders on two other lakes besides Okanagan, the most enticing of which is Kalamalka Lake. The **Kalamalka Lake Provincial Park** has warm waters, and some of the most scenic viewpoints and hiking trails in the region. Twelve kilometers (7.5 miles) north of Vernon, the **O'Keefe Historic Ranch** gives visitors a window on cattle-ranch life at the turn of the century. The O'Keefe house is a late-19th-century Victorian mansion opulently furnished with original antiques. On the 50 acres (20 hectares) are a Chinese cooks' house, St. Ann's Church, a blacksmith shop, a reconstructed general store, and a display of the old Shuswap and Okanagan Railroad. Also featured are a contemporary restaurant and gift shop. New additions include a ranching gallery in the musuem, and a reproduction stagecoach offers rides around the grounds. *9830 Hwy. 97, 12 km (8 mi) north of Vernon, tel. 604/542–7868. Admission: $4.75 adults, $3.75 senior citizens and children 13–18, $2.75 children 6–12; family and group rates available. Open mid-May–mid-Oct., daily 9–5.*

**29** **Kelowna,** the largest city in the Okanagan, is home to **Father Pandosy's Mission,** the first nonnative settlement in the region, founded in 1859. *3685 Benvouline Rd., tel. 604/860–8369. Admission free; donations accepted. Open daily 8–dusk.*

Kelowna is the geographic center of the valley's wine industry, with **Calona Wines Ltd.** (1125 Richter St., tel. 604/762–3332), British Columbia's oldest and biggest winemaker. Also around Kelowna are smaller but more intimate wineries, including **Gray Monk Estate Winery** (1051 Camp Rd., 8 km, or 5 mi, west of Winfield, off Hwy. 97, tel. 604/766–3168), and **Cedarcreek Estate Winery** (5445 Lakeshore Rd., 12 km, or 7.5 mi, south of Kelowna, off Hwy. 97 on the corner of Pandosy and Lakeshore Rds., tel. 604/764–8866).

**30** **Penticton** is the most tourist-oriented of the three. While its winter population is about 25,000, its population in summer nears 130,000. An 11-kilometer (5-mile) drive south on Highway 97 takes you to the **Okanagan Game Farm** (tel. 604/497–5405), with more than 650 species of wild animals from around the world. Farther south, off Highway 3 and along the U.S. border, **Cathedral Provincial Park** (tel. 604/494–0321) features 82,000 acres (33,198 hectares) of lakes and rolling meadows, teeming with mule deer, mountain goats, and California bighorn sheep. To reach the main part of the park, either take the steep, eight-hour hike, or arrange (and pay in advance) for the Cathedral Lake Resort (in the park, tel. 604/499–5848, fax 604/499–5266) to transport you by four-wheel drive. There are 16 campsites in the park.

Winding farther south, Highway 3 connects with the Trans-Canada Highway (Highway 1), which parallels the Fraser River through the region known as **Rainbow Country.** A glimpse through the mists above roiling **Hell's Gate,** off Highway 1 in Fraser Canyon, hints at how the region got its name. An airtram carries visitors across the foaming canyon, above the fishway, where millions of sockeye salmon fight their way upriver to spawning grounds four times a year— April, July, August, and October. In addition to interpretive displays on the life cycle of the salmon, you'll find a fudge factory, gift shop, and restaurant at the lower airtram terminal. *Box 129, Hope, tel. 604/867–9277. Admission: $8.50 adults, $7.50 senior citizens, $5 children 6–14, $22 families. Open mid-Apr.–mid-June and mid-Sept.–mid-Oct,, Mon.–Thurs. 9–5 and Fri.–Sun. 9–7; mid-June–early Sept., daily 9–7.*

Continue southwest on Highway 1 to the well-signed **Minter Gardens** at Exit 135 in Rosedale. This 27-acre compound contains 11 beautifully presented theme gardens—Chinese, rose, English, fern, fragrance, and more—along with aviaries and ponds. There are playgrounds and a giant evergreen maze to entertain the kids. *52892 Bunker Rd., Rosedale, tel. 604/794–7191 or 800/661–3919 in Canada. Admission: $7.50 adults, $6.50 senior citizens, $3.50 children 6–12, children 5 and under free, $20 families. Open Apr.–Oct., daily 9–dusk.*

It's hard to miss the **Trans-Canada Waterslides,** just across the highway. This tremendously popular waterpark features slides with such names as Kamikaze, Cannonball, Super Heroes, Black Hole, and Flash Flood, along with wave and soaking pools, snack bars, and sunbathing areas to provide plenty of warm-weather fun. *Bridal Falls Rd., Rosedale, tel. 604/794–7455. Admission: $12 adults, $8.50 children 4–12, children 3 and under free. Open mid-May–mid-June, weekends 10–8, mid-June–early Sept., daily 10–9.*

**③** The same exit also leads to **Harrison Hot Springs,** a small resort community at the southern tip of picturesque Harrison Lake. Vacationers flock here to relax and rejuvenate in this almost pristine natural setting. Mountains surround the 64-kilometer (40-mile) lake that is ringed by pretty beaches and provides a broad range of outdoor activities to enjoy, in addition to the hot springs. Located across from the beach in the large building to the left of the Harrison Hot Springs Hotel is a spring-fed public pool. *100 Esplanade, Harrison Hot Springs, tel. 604/796–2244. Admission: $6 adults, $4 senior citizens and children, under 5 free; unlimited-entry day passes $9 adults, $6 children. Open spring–fall, Sun.–Thurs. 8 AM–9 AM, Fri. and Sat. 8 AM–10 PM; winter, Sun.–Thurs. 9–9, Fri. and Sat. 8 AM–10 PM.*

A tour of the **Kilby General Store Museum,** a heritage attraction in nearby Harrison Mills, takes you back in time to the British Columbia of the 1920s. Visitors tour the general store and hotel of T. Kilby, a pioneer of the area, and chat with the shopkeeper, sniff whatever is simmering on the wood-burning stove, and tramp through the orchards, stockroom, fueling station, barn, and dairy house on the grounds. This is a fine slice of living history. *215 Kilby Rd. (1.6 km [1 mi] off Hwy. 7 on north shore of Frazer River; follow signs), Harrison Mills, tel. 604/796–9576. Admission: $3.50 adults and senior citizens, $1.50 children 7–16, children 6 and under free. Open May–June and Labor Day–mid-Oct., Thurs.–Mon. 11–5; July and Aug., daily 11–5; mid-Oct.–Nov. 1, daily 9:30–4:30.*

## Scenic Drives

The **Gold Rush Trail** is a 640-kilometer (400-mile) route along which the frontiersmen traveled in search of gold in the 19th and early 20th centuries. The interior British Columbia trail begins just below Prince George in the north, and extends to Lillooet in the south, but juts off at points in between. Following the route you can travel through Quesnel, Williams Lake, Wells, Barkerville, along the Fraser Canyon, and Cache Creek. Most towns and communities through which the trail passes have re-created villages, history museums, or historic sites that help to tell the story of the gold rush era. For more information contact the **Cariboo Chilcotin Coast Tourist Association** (Box 4900, Williams Lake V2G 2V8, tel. 604/392–2226; in U.S. 800/663–5885, fax 604/392–2838).

Completion of a new highway opened the **Coast Mountain Circle,** linking Vancouver to Cariboo Country. This 702-kilometer (435-mile) route takes in spectacular Howe Sound, the deep-water port of Squamish, Whistler Resort, and Pemberton Valley before heading back to Vancouver through scenic Fraser Canyon and Harrison Hot Springs. The loop makes a comfortable two- to three-day journey. For more information contact the **Tourism Association of Southwestern B.C.** (204–1755 W. Broadway, Vancouver V6J 4S5, tel. 604/739–9011 or 800/667–3306).

# Shopping

**Okanagan Valley**
The **Okanagan Pottery Studio** (tel. 604/767–2010), located on Highway 97 in Peachland, sells handcrafted ceramics.

**Geert Maas Sculpture Gardens, Gallery, and Studio.** World-class sculptor Geert Maas exhibits his art in an indoor gallery and a 1-acre garden, in the hills above Kelowna. Maas, who works in bronze, stoneware, and mixed media, creates distinctive abstract figures with a round and fluid quality. He also sells medallions, original paintings, and etchings. *R.R. 1250 Reynolds Rd., Kelowna, V1Y 7P9, tel. 604/860–7012. Admission free. Call for hours.*

**Prince Rupert**
Native art and other local crafts are available at **Studio 9** (516 3rd Ave. W, tel. 604/624–2366).

**Queen Charlotte Islands**
The Haida carve valuable figurines from the hard, black slate called argillite. The specific variety used by the Haidas is found only on the islands. Their works can be found at the **Adams Family House of Silver** (tel. 604/626–3215), in Old Masset, behind the Ed Jones Haida Museum, and at **Joy's Island Jewellers** (tel. 604/559–4742) in Queen Charlotte. Other island specialties are silk-screen prints and silver jewelry.

**Vancouver Island**
Duncan is the home of Cowichan wool sweaters, handknitted by the Cowichan people. A large selection is available from **Hills Indian Crafts** (tel. 604/746–6731) and **Big Foot Trading Post** (tel. 604/748–1153), both on the main highway, about 1½ kilometers (1 mile) south of Duncan. Also check out **Modeste Wool Carding** (2615 Modeste Rd., Duncan, tel. 604/748–8983), about a half mile off the highway.

# Sports and Outdoor Activities

**Canoeing and Kayaking**
Canoeing and kayaking are favorite ways to explore the miles of extended, interconnected waterways and the breathtaking coastline of British Columbia. The **Inside Passage, Queen Charlotte Strait, Strait of Georgia,** and the other island-dotted straits and sounds that border the mainland provide fairly protected sea-going from Washington State to the Alaskan border, with numerous marine parks to explore along the way. Another particular favorite among paddlers is the **Powell Forest Canoe Route,** a 60-kilometer (45-mile) circuit of 12 lakes connected by streams, rivers, and well-maintained portage trails.

For rentals on Vancouver Island, contact **Tofino Sea-Kayaking Company** (Box 620, Tofino, tel. 604/725–4222) and **Stubbs Island Charters** (Box 7, Telegraph Cove, tel. 604/928–3185). On the mainland, try **Clipper Canoes** (1717 Salton Rd., Box 115, Abbotsford, tel. 604/853–9320) or **Lavington Rental** (5562 Hwy. 6, Vernon, tel. 604/542–4788). For multiple-day guided canoe or kayak trips, contact **Okanagan Canoe Holidays** (R.R. 1, 2910 N. Glenmore Rd., Kelowna V1Y 7P9, tel. and fax 604/762–8156) or **Mount Robson Adventure Holidays** (Box 687, Valemount V0E 2Z0, tel. 604/566–4386).

**Fishing** Miles of coastline and thousands of lakes, rivers, and streams bring more than 750,000 fishermen to British Columbia each year. The waters of the province hold 74 species of fish (25 of them sport fish), including Chinook salmon and rainbow trout. A saltwater-fishing license for one day costs $3.75 for Canadian residents and non-Canadians, and is available at virtually every fishing lodge and sporting-goods outlet along the coast. Annual licenses are about $11 for non-B.C. Canadians and $38 for non-Canadians.

For updated fishing information and regulations, contact the **B.C. Fish Branch** (Ministry of Environment, 810 Blanshard St., Victoria V8V 1X5, tel. 604/387–4573). For a guide to saltwater fishing, contact the **Department of Fisheries and Oceans** (Recreational Fisheries Div., Station 415, 555 W. Hastings St., Vancouver V6B 5G3, tel. 604/666–3271).

**Golf** There are more than 200 golf courses in British Columbia, and the figure is growing. The province is now an Official Golf Destination of the PGA Tour in Canada and of the American PGA Tour. Greens fees are about $20–$40. The topography in British Columbia tends to be mountainous, and many courses have fine views as well as treacherous approaches to greens.

*Okanagan Valley and Environs* The Okanagan has a central tee-time booking service for out-of-town golfers that lists all of the Okanagan/Interior British Columbia courses below. *Box 342, Westbank V0H 2A0, tel. 604/764–4118, call collect. Open May 15–Oct. 15, weekdays 9–5; leave message if no answer.*

**Gallaghers Canyon Golf and Country Club** (4320 McCulloch Rd., Kelowna, tel. 604/861–4240) is one of the most challenging semi-private courses in British Columbia, with long, rolling, and twisting fairways. **Kelowna Golf and Country Club** (1297 Glenmore Dr., Kelowna, tel. 604/763–2736) is a private club that favors straight drivers; visitors are welcome but advised to avoid weekends. **Osoyoos Golf and Country Club** (62 Ave. off Hwy. 99, Osoyoos, tel. 604/495–7003) provides a green setting in the dry, parched hills; only two of the 12 par fours on the course are under 350 yards. Visitors are welcome. **Penticton Golf and Country Club** (799 Eckhardt Ave. W, Penticton, tel. 604/492–8727) has 10 acres of water hazards, challenging traps, and bunkers; it is a semi-private club that welcomes visitors. The relatively new **Predator Ridge Golf Resort** (360 Commonage Rd., Vernon, tel. 604/542–3436) is a very challenging public course. **Rivershore Golf Club** (off Old Shuswap Rd., Kamloops, tel. 604/573–4622) is a Robert Trent Jones–designed course and is one of British Columbia's longest, at 7,007 yards. Visitors are welcome. **Salmon Arm Golf Course** (3400 Hwy. 97B, Salmon Arm, tel. 604/832–4727) welcomes visitors to its hilly terrain. **Shadow Ridge Golf Club** (3770 Bullman Rd., Kelowna, tel. 604/765–7777) is a relatively new course, set in a valley and surrounded by orchards. **Summerland Golf and Country Club** (2405 Mountain Rd., Summerland, tel. 604/494–9554) is slightly off the beaten track but has two distinctly different nines with the front nine clear and the back nine cut through a pine forest. **Twin Lakes Golf and Country Resort** (Hwy. 3A, Kaleden, tel. 604/497–5359) has an on-site RV park.

*Vancouver Island*  Golf is also very popular on Vancouver Island, and there are many good courses to choose from, including: the **Glen Meadows Golf Club** (1050 McTavish Rd., Sidney, tel. 604/656–3136) on the Saanich Peninsula; the **Morningstar Golf Course** (525 Lowery Rd., Parksville, tel. 604/248–8161) not far from Nanaimo; and the **Long Beach Golf Course** (Pacific Rim Hwy., Tofino, tel. 604/725–3332) on the west side of the island.

**Hiking**  One of the most challenging hikes in British Columbia is along the **West Coast Trail** (*see* Exploring, Tour 1) in Pacific Rim National Park (tel. 604/726–7721, fax 604/726–4720), on Vancouver Island. The demanding 77-kilometer (47-mile) trail is for experienced hikers and follows part of the coast known as the "Graveyard of the Pacific" because of the large number of shipwrecks that have occurred there. It can be traveled only on foot, takes an average of six days to complete, and is open from May to late September. A permit is necessary to hike this trail; reservations are available from March through September.

In the Okanagan Valley, hikers will enjoy exploring the railbeds, trestles, tunnels, and abandoned stations of the **Kettle Valley Railway** network, stretching along Lake Okanagan between Penticton and Kelowna. The going is mild; just remember to make enough noise to let the rattlesnakes and bears know you're coming. The Visitors Bureaus for Kelowna (tel. 604/861–1515) and Penticton (tel. 604/493–4055) can provide maps and information.

Virtually all of British Columbia's provincial parks have fine hiking trail networks; the **Ministry of Parks** (1610 Mt. Seymour Rd., N. Vancouver V7G 1L3, tel. 604/924–2200) offers detailed information.

*Heli-hiking*  Heli-hiking is very popular in this province; helicopters deliver hikers to high alpine meadows and verdant mountain tops that have remained virtually untouched because of their inaccessibility. **Highland Helicopter** (1685 Tranmer, Agassiz V0M 1K0, tel. 604/796–9610) and **Mount Robson Adventure Holidays** (Box 687, Valemount V0E 2Z0, tel. 604/566–4386) can provide further information.

**Rafting**  With such beautiful rivers as Adams, Clearwater, Fraser, Illecillewaet, and Thompson interlacing the High Country, Okanagan Valley, and Fraser Canyon, there is a diverse range of rafting trips from which to choose. Operators such as **Mount Robson Adventure Holidays** (Box 687, Valemount V0E 2Z0, tel. 604/566–4386), **Fraser River Raft Expeditions Ltd.** (Box 10, Yale V0K 2S0, tel. 604/863–2336), **Hyak Wilderness Adventures** (1975 Maple St., Vancouver V6J 3S9, tel. 604/734–8622), and **Alpine Rafting Company** (Box 1409, Golden V0A 1H0, tel. 604/344–5016) provide options ranging from lazy half-day floats to exhilarating white-water journeys of up to a week.

**Skiing**  British Columbia has hundreds of kilometers of groomed cross-country (Nordic) ski trails in the provincial parks and more than 40 cross-country resorts. Most downhill destinations have carved out Nordic routes along the valleys, and there are literally thousands more trails in unmanaged areas of British Columbia.
*Cross-country*

For cross-country enthusiasts, two of the finest facilities in the province are **Posthill Lake Lodge** (Box 854, Kelowna V1Y 7P5, tel. 604/860–1655) just east of Kelowna and **Manning Park Resort** (Manning Park V0X 1R0, tel. 604/840–8822) en route to the Okanagan, about

200 kilometers (124 miles) east of Vancouver. Manning Park also has downhill facilities, which are just as popular as the Nordic program. On Vancouver Island, **Mt. Washington** and **Mt. Cain Alpine Park** (*see below*) have Nordic facilities, as do **Apex Alpine, Big White,** and **Silver Star Mountain Resort** (*see below*) in the Okanagan Valley.

*Downhill* With more than half the province situated higher than 4,200 feet above sea level, new downhill courses are constantly opening. At the moment, more than 40 major resorts have downhill facilities.

On Vancouver Island, **Mt. Washington Ski Resort Ltd.** (Box 3069, Courtenay V9N 5N3, tel. 604/338–1386), with more than 40 runs and an elevation of 5,200 feet, is the largest ski area on the island, and the third-largest in terms of visitors, in the province. Located in the Comox Valley, it's a modern, well-organized mountain with snowpack averaging 472 inches a year. It also has 36 kilometers (22 miles) of double track–set Nordic trails. Other island ski areas are **Forbidden Plateau** (Box 3268, Courtenay V9N 5N4, tel. 604/334–4744), located near Mt. Washington, with 15 runs and a fall of 1,150 feet; and **Mt. Cain** (Box 1225, Port McNeill V0N 2R0, tel. 604/949–9496), on the northern part of the island near the community of Sayward off Highway 19, with 16 runs and a fall of 1,500 feet.

The Okanagan Valley region, four hours east by car from Vancouver, or one hour by air, offers some of the best ski bargains in the province. **Big White Ski Resort** (Box 2039, Station R, Kelowna V1X 4K5, tel. 604/765–3101) is the highest ski area in British Columbia, though Whistler has a longer free fall. The resort has more than 50 runs, and, like Whistler, is in the process of rapidly expanding. **Silver Star Mountain Resort** (Box 2, Silver Star Mountain V0E 1G0, tel. 604/542–0224), with more than 65 runs, offers well-lighted night skiing. The complete village at the base of the mountain has enough hotels to accommodate more than 725 people. **Apex Alpine** (Box 1060, Penticton V2A 7N7, tel. 604/492–2800) has 45 runs and is the largest ski resort in South Okanagan. On-mountain condominiums—many for rent—can accommodate a total of 350.

Kootenay Country (*see* Canadian Rockies, Chapter 7), a southeastern section of British Columbia that includes the Rockies, Purcells, Selkirks, and Monashees, features two major resorts: **Whitewater** (Box 60, Nelson V1L 5P7, tel. 604/354–4944), with more than 20 runs and a lot of powder skiing; and **Red Mountain Resorts** (Box 670, Rossland V0G 1Y0, tel. 604/362–7700), which spans two mountains and three mountain faces, and has 30 marked runs.

The resorts in the High Country reflect British Columbia's most diverse topographical area. At 3,100 feet of vertical drop, **Sun Peaks Resort at Tod Mountain** (Box 869, Kamloops V2C 5M8, tel. 604/578–7222) has 61 runs. On-mountain accommodations are limited to private condominium rentals and a bed-and-breakfast that accommodates up to 32 people. **Mt. Mackenzie** (Box 1000, Revelstoke V0E 2S0, tel. 604/837–5268) has 26 runs and offers deep-powder skiing. Revelstoke, located 5 kilometers (3 miles) from the base, has a wide selection of lodging.

*Heli- and* Heli-skiing operators are often located at well-established resorts,
*Snowcat Skiing* taking clients into otherwise inaccessible deep-powder regions of the mountains. Others operate as independents and offer accommodations, dining, and recreational facilities in their deluxe lodges. Some companies offer Snowcat skiing, in which an enclosed all-terrain vehicle takes you into the wilderness areas.

In Kootenay Country, try **Kootenay Helicopter Skiing** (Box 717, Nakusp V0G 1R0, tel. 604/265–3121; in B.C., Alberta, and the U.S., 800/663–0100). With accommodations at Kuskanax Lodge, they run seven-day packages to and from Kelowna, Spokane, WA, and Castlegar. **Selkirk Tangiers Helicopter Skiing** (Box 1409, Golden V0A 1H0, tel. 604/344–5016 or 800/663–7080, fax 604/344–5016) runs three-, six-, and seven-day all-inclusive packages in the Selkirk and Monashee mountains from their base in Revelstoke.

In the High Country, **Cat Powder Skiing** (Box 1479, Revelstoke V0E 2S0, tel. 604/837–9489) organizes two-, three-, and five-day, all-inclusive packages that run into the Selkirks and on the upper slopes of Mt. MacKenzie in Revelstoke.

# Dining and Lodging

### Dining

Throughout British Columbia you'll find a variety of cuisines, from Vancouver Island's seafood places to interior British Columbia's wild game-oriented menus. Prices vary from location to location, but ratings reflect the categories listed on the dining chart.

| Category | Cost* |
| --- | --- |
| $$$$ | over $35 |
| $$$ | $25–$35 |
| $$ | $15–$25 |
| $ | under $15 |

*per person, excluding drinks, service, and 7% GST, in Canadian dollars*

Highly recommended restaurants in each price category are indicated by a star ★.

### Lodging

The lodging possibilities across the region are as diverse as the restaurant menus. Accommodations range from bed-and-breakfast inns and rustic cabins to deluxe chain hotels. In the cities, especially, there is an abundance of accommodations, but once you get off the beaten track, guest rooms are often a rare commodity and may require advance booking.

| Category | Cost* |
| --- | --- |
| $$$$ | over $125 |
| $$$ | $90–$125 |
| $$ | $50–$90 |
| $ | under $50 |

*All prices are for a standard double room, excluding 7% GST. Prices are in Canadian dollars.*

Highly recommended lodgings in each price category are indicated by a star ★.

## Vancouver Island

**Campbell River Dining ★**

**Royal Coachman Inn.** This is another of those informal, blackboard-menu restaurants that dot the landscape of the island. The menu, which changes daily, is surprisingly daring for what is essentially a high-end pub, and the inn draws crowds nightly, especially on Tuesday and Saturday (prime rib nights). Come early for both lunch and dinner to avoid a wait. *84 Dogwood St., tel. 604/286-0231. No reservations. Dress: casual. AE, MC, V. $-$$*

**Dining and Lodging**

**Tsa-Kwa-Luten Lodge.** This resort, operated by members of the Kwakiutl tribe, offers authentic Pacific Coast native food and cultural activities. It is located on a high bluff amid 1,100 acres of forest on Quadra Island, a 10-minute ferry ride from Campbell River. Each room in the main lodge has a sea view from a deck or patio; many have a fireplace and loft. There are also four beachfront cabins with fireplace, whirlpool tub, kitchen facilities, and private veranda. Guests are invited to take part in traditional dances in the resort's lounge, which resembles a longhouse, and to visit nearby petroglyphs to make rubbings. *Box 460, Quathiaski Cove, VOP 1NO, tel. 604/285-2042 or 800/665-7745, fax 604/285-2532. 26 rooms, 4 cabins. Facilities: restaurant, lounge, fitness room, sauna, hot tub, mountain bikes, guided salmon fishing. AE, DC, MC, V. $$$$*

**★ April Point Lodge and Fishing Resort.** Operated for 50 years by the friendly Peterson family, it comes as no surprise that April Point Lodge has developed a tremendous reputation and whopping amount of repeat business among vacationers. Spread across a point of Quadra Island, and stretching into Discovery Passage across from Campbell River, the 1944 cedar lodge is surrounded by refurbished fishermen's cabins and guest houses that have been added over the years. For the most part, the accommodations are tidy and comfortable rather than fancy; most have kitchen facilities, fireplaces, and sun decks, and a few are equipped with Jacuzzi baths and hot tubs. Kwakiutl and Haida art adorn the comfortable lounge and dining room where fine regional cuisine is served. Native feasts on the beach on warm summer nights are especially memorable, with spitted salmon roasted over an open fire; fresh steamed scallops, prawns, and clams; and one of the wines from the extensive cellar. *1000 April Point Rd., Box 1, V9W 4Z9, tel. 604/285-2222, fax 604/285-2411. 33 units. Facilities: restaurant, lounge, gift shop, gym, pool, nature trails, bikes marina, sea plane dock, salmon charters and nature tours available. AE, D, DC, MC, V. Some units closed Oct.–Apr. $$$*

**Comox/ Courtenay Dining ★**

**The Old House Restaurant.** This split-character restaurant offers both formal and casual dining, in a restored 1938 home with large cedar beams and a stone fireplace. Upstairs, among linen and fresh flowers, you select from an innovative Continental menu, with a delightful chateaubriand as the house specialty. Downstairs, where it is decidedly more informal, you can order sandwiches, pastas, and salads. *1760 Riverside La., Courtenay, tel. 604/338-5406. Reservations advised upstairs; no reservations downstairs. Dress: casual but neat upstairs; casual downstairs. AE, D, DC, MC, V. $$*

**Lodging**

**The Greystone Manor.** This no-smoking bed-and-breakfast, set in a 70-year-old house with period furnishings, looks out on Comox Harbor, where a playful colony of seals is often visible from the house. The antiques, wood stove, and wood paneling add to the hospitable, cozy feel of this inn. Breakfast, which includes fresh fruit, muffins, and fruit pancakes, is enough to keep you filled most of the day. *4014 Haas Rd. (Site 684–C2, RR 6), Courtenay V9N 8H9, tel. 604/338-*

*1422. 4 rooms share 2 baths. Facilities: garden, walking trails. MC, V. $$*

★ **The Kingfisher.** Located five minutes south of Courtenay, this hotel is situated among trees and overlooks the Strait of Georgia. Solid furnishings, clean white-stucco walls, a bright lobby with lots of greenery, and rooms with mountain and ocean views offer a nice change from the majority of plain accommodations lining the main drag. *4330 S. Island Hwy. (Site 672, RR 6), Courtenay V9N 8H9, tel. 604/338–1323. 30 units. Facilities: restaurant, lounge, tennis court, pool, sauna, whirlpool. AE, D, DC, MC, V. $$*

**Malahat**
*Dining and Lodging*
★ **The Aerie.** The million-dollar view of Finlayson Arm and the Gulf Islands persuaded Austrians Leo and Maria Schuster to build their small, luxury resort. In this Mediterranean-style villa, some plush rooms have a patio; others have whirlpool tubs tucked into window nooks to take advantage of the scenery. The dining room is open to the public for stunning dinner views and outstanding cuisine. The maple-smoked salmon, pheasant consommé, medallions of venison in morel sauce, and crème brûlée with fruit sorbet are more than worth the short drive from Victoria. *600 Ebedora La., V0R 2L0, tel. 604/743–7115 or 604/743–4055, fax 604/743–4766. 8 rooms, 14 suites. Facilities: restaurant, indoor pool, indoor and outdoor hot tubs, sauna, tennis court, exercise room, library, heli-pad, nature trails. Reservations advised for restaurant. AE, MC, V. $$$–$$$$*

**Nanaimo**
*Dining*
★ **The Mahle House.** This casually elegant place serves innovative Northwest cuisine, such as braised rabbit with Dijon mustard and red wine sauce. Twelve items adorn the regular menu, including a succulent carrot and ginger soup, and a catch of the day. Care to detail, an intimate setting, and a new addition to the three country-style rooms make this one of the finest dining experiences in the region. *Cedar and Heemer Rds., tel. 604/722–3621. Reservations advised. Dress: casual but neat. MC, V. Closed lunch and Mon. and Tues. $$*

★ **The Grotto.** A perennial favorite, the Grotto is a Nanaimo institution that specializes in a variety of seafood. The restaurant is set against a waterfront background, and dining here is relaxed and casual. Try the spare ribs, garlic prawn pasta, or the seafood platter—zum-zum—that's big enough for two. *1511 Stewart Ave., tel. 604/753–3303. Reservations accepted. Dress:casual. AE, MC, V. Closed lunch. $–$$*

*Dining and Lodging*
**Best Western Dorchester Hotel.** Upbeat Mediterranean tones of champagne, ochre, and teal replace the old drab blue exterior of the Dorchester. Once the Nanaimo Opera House, this elegant hotel overlooking the harbor has a distinctive character, with gold knockers on each of the doors, winding hallways, and a spacious library. The rooms are small but exceptionally comfortable, and most have views of the harbor. *70 Church St., V8R 5H4, tel. 604/754–6835 or 800/528–1234, fax 604/754–2638. 70 rooms. Facilities: restaurant, meeting rooms, lounge, library, rooftop patio. AE, D, DC, MC, V. $$–$$$*

★ **Yellow Point Lodge.** Yellow Point is a very popular resort area on a spit of land south of Nanaimo, east of Ladysmith. Rebuilt in 1986 after a fire destroyed the original, the lodge lost almost nothing in ambience and gained a great deal: Nine larger rooms have better facilities (all have private baths and are available year-round). Situated on a rocky knoll overlooking the Stuart Channel are beach cabins, field cabins, a range of different-size cottages, and beach barracks for the hardy (closed mid-October to mid-April; cabins, cottages, and barracks have no running water and share a central bathhouse). Beach cabins can be private and include tree-trunk beds and wood-burning stoves; beach barracks are not as sound, and noises carry from unit to unit, but the location along the shore makes them popular. One hundred eighty acres of land provides plenty of strolling and exploring. Three full meals and snacks are included in the rate. *Yellow Point Rd., RR 3, Ladysmith V0R 2E0, tel. 604/245–7422. 50 rooms. Facilities: restaurant (for guests only), 2 tennis courts, seawater pool, hot tub, sauna, canoes, kayaks, mountain bikes. MC, V. $–$$$*

**Dining and Lodging**

**La Coast Bastion Inn.** This hotel is conveniently located downtown near the ferry terminal, train, and bus stations. All rooms with balconies have views of the old Hudson's Bay fort and the ocean and are modernly furnished. The three eating–entertainment establishments are located within the hotel. *11 Bastion St., V9R 2Z9, tel. 604/753–6601 or 800/663–1144 in the U.S., fax 604/753–4155. 179 rooms. Facilities: restaurant, lounge, Irish deli/pub, gift shop, boutique, convention rooms, sauna, hot tub, gym. AE, DC, MC, V. $$$–$$$$*

**Parksville**
**Dining and Lodging**

**Beach Acres Resort Hotel.** For a family vacation, this collection of cottages set in the woods facing the Georgia Strait is both charming and practical. Each unit has one or two bedrooms, living room, kitchen, fireplace, and storage areas. *1015 E. Island Hwy., V9P 2E4, tel. 604/248–3424, fax 604/248–6145 or 800/663–7309 in B.C. and Alberta. 75 cottages. Facilities: restaurant, indoor pool, sauna, whirlpool, playground, 3 tennis courts, health club. AE, DC, MC, V. 1-wk minimum July–Aug. $$$$*

**The Roadhouse Inn.** This Swiss chalet, set on 3 acres, is central to four of the region's golf courses. There are a limited number of rooms, but all are comfortable. *1223 Smithers Rd., V9P 2C1, tel. 604/248–2912. 6 rooms. Facilities: restaurant. MC, V. $–$$*

**Port Hardy**
**Dining and Lodging**

**Glen Lyon Inn.** All of the rooms have a full ocean view of Hardy Bay and, like most area motels, have clean, modern amenities. Eagles are often on the premises, eyeing the water for fish to prey on. It's a short ride from the inn to the ferry terminal. *6345 Hardy Bay Rd., Box 103, V0N 2P0, tel. 604/949–7115, fax 604/949–7415. 29 rooms. Facilities: restaurant, lounge, nearby marina, boat launch. AE, D, DC, MC, V. $*

**Sidney**
**Lodging**
★

**Borthwick Country Manor.** Flower boxes and awnings adorn the windows of this Tudor home, built in 1979 on Vancouver Island's Saanich Peninsula. It is ideally located in the quiet countryside within minutes of Victoria, Butchart Gardens, the airport, and Washington and British Columbia ferries. Owners Ann and Brian Reid, originally from England, concentrate on providing an English experience for guests, from afternoon tea to a hearty English-style breakfast of eggs, sausage, bacon, muffins, fried tomatoes, and home-made jams. Rooms are cheerful, with coordinated floral comforters, shams, and curtains. French doors lead to the backyard, with gardens to admire and a hot tub to enjoy. Smokey, the Reid's watch cat, is friendly. *9750 Ardmore Dr., RR 2, V8L 3S1, tel. 604/656–9498. 5 rooms. Facilities: hot tub, fishing charters available. MC, V. $$–$$$*

**Sooke**
**Dining and Lodging**
★

**Sooke Harbour House.** This original 1931 clapboard farmhouse-turned-inn has three suites, a 10-room addition, and a dining room—all of which exude elegance. One of the finest restaurants in British Columbia, it is well worth the trip to Sooke, from Victoria. The seafood is just-caught fresh, and the herbs, picked from some 200 varieties, are grown on the property. Four chefs in the kitchen guarantees an abundance of creative dishes. On a nice summer evening you may want to sit on the terrace, where you can catch a glimpse of the sea mammals that play by the spit of land in front of the restaurant. Equally exquisite are the romantic guest rooms, with natural wood and white finishes adding to each unit's unique theme. Rooms range from the Herb Garden Room—decorated in shades of mint, with French doors opening onto a private patio—to the Longhouse Room, complete with Native American furnishings. All units, with fireplaces and either ocean or mountain views, come with fresh flowers, a decanter of port, and wet bars that include herbal teas and cookies. Breakfast and lunch are included in your room rate, but you must make a reservation for your meals. Likewise, nonguests must make reservations for dinner. Hosts Fredrica and Sinclair Philip have been paying attention to details here since 1979. *1528 Whiffen Spit Rd., RR 4, V0S 1N0, tel. 604/642–3421, fax 604/ 642–6988. 13 rooms. Facilities: restaurant. Closed lunch except for hotel guests. Dress: casual but neat. AE, MC, V. $$$$*

**Ocean Wilderness.** This large 1940s log cabin sits on five forested, beachfront acres, 13 kilometers (8 miles) west of Sooke. Owner Marion Rolston added seven guest rooms in a rough cedar addition in 1990, then divided the two larger suites during a 1993 renovation for a total of nine rooms. This auction buff has furnished her home with a fine collection of Victorian antiques. Romantic canopies and ruffled linens on high beds dominate the spacious guest rooms, which have sitting areas with views of either the Strait of Juan de Fuca or the pretty gardens in the back. Just outside, stepping stones lead to a hot tub housed in a Japanese-style gazebo near a winding path that descends to the beach cove where seals make their summer home. *109 W. Coast Rd., RR 2, V0S 1N0, tel. and fax 604/646–2116. 9 rooms. Facilities: private decks or patios, hot tub, hiking trails, meal service available. MC, V. $$–$$$*

**Ucluelet/Tofino**

*Dining*

**Whale's Tale.** This is a no-frills, dark but warmly decorated down-to-earth place where the cooking and the rustic decor go hand-in-hand. The view isn't much, but the cedar-shingle building, set on pilings, shakes with a good gust of wind. The menu is highlighted by prime rib and a variety of local seafood. *1861 Peninsula Rd., Ucluelet, tel. 604/726–4621. Dress: casual. MC, V. Closed lunch and Nov.–Jan. $$*

★ **The Wickaninnish Restaurant.** Before the Canadian government acquired this wonderful wood building for its interpretive center, it was a unique inn. It is still a restaurant, with an ambience—the beach setting, combined with the building's glass exterior and stone-and-beam interior, accented by a stone fireplace—that cannot be matched anywhere else in the area. Seafood is the primary choice here—especially the West Coast chowder—but if you order the stir-fry, you won't be disappointed. *On Long Beach, 16 km (11 mi) north of Ucluelet, tel. 604/726–7706. Reservations advised for 7 or more. Dress: casual. AE, MC, V. Closed mid-Oct.–mid-Feb. $$*

*Lodging*

**Canadian Princess Fishing Resort.** If old ships are to your liking, book a berth on this converted survey ship which has 36 comfortable, but hardly opulent, staterooms. Each offers one to four berths, and all share washrooms; for something a bit more spacious, request the captain's cabin. Roomier than the ship cabins and complete with more contemporary furnishings are the resort's deluxe shoreside rooms. Promising an unusual experience, this Spartan resort provides the bare necessities—mostly to the many fishermen who flock here during the summer. *The Boat Basin, Box 939, Ucluelet V0R 3A0, tel. 604/726–7771 or 800/663–7090, fax 604/726–7121. 36* *shoreside and 36 ship-sleeping units. Facilities: 10 charter boats. AE, DC, MC, V. $$–$$$*

★ **Chesterman's Beach Bed and Breakfast.** This is one of several small, romantic bed-and-breakfasts located on the beach, but the front yard—the rolling ocean surf—makes this one unique. You can while away the hours just walking the beach, searching the tidal pools, or—from March to October—watching whales migrate. The self-contained suite in the main house and the separate Lookout Suite are romantic, cozy, and unique; both have comfortable beds and a view of the beach. The self-sufficient one-bedroom garden cottage offers no ocean view but accommodates up to four; it's a good option for a family vacation. Owner Joan Dublanko makes hot muffins every morning. *1345 Chesterman's Beach Rd., Tofino V0R 2Z0, tel. 604/725–3726. 1 room, 2 suites. Facilities: bikes, surfboards, beach. V. $$–$$$*

**Pacific Sands Beach Resort.** Just a mile north of Pacific Rim National Park is this rustic resort with motel suites and individual two-bedroom cottages. The motel rooms are basic with modern furnishings, but fireplaces make them seem cozier. Some of the rooms in the new, three-story addition have Jacuzzi tubs. Pacific Sands is close to Long Beach golf course and is on the ocean. *1421 Pacific Rim Hwy., Box 237, Tofino V0R 2Z0, tel. 604/725–3322 or 800/565–2322, fax 604/725–3155. 54 rooms and 10 cottages. AE, MC, V. $$–$$$*

## North of Vancouver Island

**Prince Rupert**
*Dining*

**Smile's Seafood Café.** If you don't mind walking among the fish-processing plants by the railway, you'll find this place a real change of pace. It has been a mainstay of Prince Rupert since 1935 and has succeeded because it provides small-town friendly service along with its seafood menu. Favorites include the halibut cheeks and the fisherman's platter. *113 George Hills Way, tel. 604/624–3072. No reservations. Dress: casual. MC, V. $$*

*Lodging*

**Highliner Inn.** This modern high-rise near the waterfront is conveniently situated and relatively well priced. It's in the heart of the downtown shopping district and is only one block from the airline terminal building. Ask for a room with a private balcony and view of the harbor. *815 1st Ave. W, V8J 1B3, tel. 604/624–9060, fax 604/627–7759. 96 rooms. Facilities: restaurant, lounge, convention rooms, beauty salon, laundromat. AE, DC, MC, V. $$*

*Dining and*
*Lodging*
★

**Crest Motor Hotel.** It may surprise you to find a four-diamond AAA hotel in this small community, but this warm, modern hotel is probably the finest in the north. It's one block away from the two shopping centers but is situated on a bluff overlooking the harbor. The pleasantly decorated restaurant has brass rails, beam ceilings, and a waterfront view, and specializes in seafood; particularly outstanding are the salmon dishes. *222 1st Ave. W, V8J 3P6, tel. 604/624–6771; in Canada, 800/663–8150; fax 604/627–7666. 103 rooms. Facilities: restaurant, lounge, coffee shop, hot tub, fitness room. Reservations required for restaurant. Dress: casual but neat. AE, D, DC, MC, V. $$–$$$*

**Queen**
**Charlotte**
**Islands**
*Lodging*

**Alaska View Lodge.** On a clear day, you can step onto your porch at this bed-and-breakfast and see the mountains of Alaska in the distance. The lodge is bordered by a long stretch of sandy beach on one side and by woods on the other. Eliane and Charly Feller, both European by origin, offer simple beach-house rooms with few of the amenities you're likely to find in a Hilton; but the private balconies more than compensate. For an additional cost, Eliane makes a three-course dinner, using classical recipes based on Queen Charlotte fare, such as home-smoked salmon, scallops, and Dungeness crab; plenty of advance notice is necessary for dinners. *Tow Hill Rd., Box 227, Masset V0T 1M0, tel. 604/626–3333 or 800/661–0019 in Canada. 4 rooms. No credit cards. $$*

**Spruce Point Lodge.** This cedar-sided building, encircled by a balcony, attracts families and couples because of its inexpensive rates and down-home feel. Like most Queen Charlotte accommodations, this one is more rustic than luxurious and features locally-made pine furnishings that go with the northern-woods motif. For the money you get a Continental breakfast and an occasional seafood barbecue, with a menu that depends on the daily catch. Kayakers and hikers on a budget should ask about the bunk rooms, usually available at a low nightly rate. *609 6th Ave., Queen Charlotte V0T 1S0, tel. and fax 604/559–8234. 7 rooms. MC, V. $*

*Dining and Lodging*   **Tlell River House.** The smell of fresh-cut wood welcomes you into this new, secluded lodge overlooking the Tlell River. From the property in the middle of the woods, it's only a few hundred feet to the beach (and the shipwreck of the *Pezuta*). The rooms are decorated with all-wood paneling, floral curtains, and thick down comforters; many have views of the river. The restaurant serves excellent seafood and a variety of deliciously rich cheesecakes. *Beitush Rd., just south of the Tlell River Bridge on Hwy. 16, Box 56, Tlell V0T 1Y0, tel. 604/ 557–4211 or 800/667–8906 in Canada, fax 604/557–4622. 10 rooms. Facilities: restaurant, lounge, meeting room, laundromat, boat rentals, guided fishing trips. MC, V. $$*

## Okanagan Valley and Environs Including Rainbow and High Country

*Harrison Hot Springs Dining*   **The Black Forest.** Ask the locals where to dine and they'll send you here, a charming Bavarian dining room on Harrison Village Esplanade, overlooking the lake. It comes as no surprise that the specialties here are German standards, from schnitzels to Black Forest cake, with a few Continental dishes (mainly steaks and seafood) thrown in for good measure. Hearty German beer and an array of wines round out the selection. *180 Esplanade, tel. 604/796–9343. Reservations advised. Dress: casual but neat. AE, MC, V. Closed lunch. $$–$$$*

*Dining and Lodging*
★   **Harrison Hot Springs Hotel.** Ever since fur traders and gold miners discovered the soothing hot springs in the late 1800s, Harrison has been a favored stopover spot. The St. Alice Hotel, built in 1896 to accommodate these weary travelers, was destroyed by fire, and from its ashes rose the Harrison Hot Springs Hotel in the 1920s. The property has continued to grow over the decades, and, for the most part, you can tell from the decor when sections were built. The most reasonably priced rooms located in the original building and west tower are dated, with worn furnishings, fixtures, and carpets; those in the new east tower (added in 1989) are much more modern and plush, with a heftier price tag. The long list of amenities and scenic lakeside location give the hotel a resort feel; plans to add a PGA-rated 18-hole golf course are under way. Bring a robe to make the trip from your room to the indoor hot spring-fed pools or heated outdoor pool. *100 Esplanade, Harrison Hot Springs V0M 1K0, tel. 604/ 796–2244; in the Pacific Northwest, 800/663–2266; fax 604/796–9374. 290 rooms, 16 cottages. Facilities: 2 restaurants, lounge, 2 indoor pools, outdoor pool, saunas, 3 tennis courts, 9-hole executive golf course, games room, gift shops, beauty salon, health club, com-*

*plimentary afternoon tea, bike rentals, hiking trails. Reservations advised for restaurants. Dress: neat. AE, D, DC, MC, V. $$–$$$*

**Kamloops**
*Dining and*
*Lodging*
★

**Lac le Jeune Resort.** With 160 kilometers (99 miles) of cross-country skiing, a lake stocked with trout, and a restaurant that serves robust helpings, this resort is a good choice for those who want to experience the outdoors. The rustic, self-sufficient cabins are perfect for families because of their ample size and amenities, and pets are permitted. There are also comfortable, spacious rooms in the main lodge, with no phones or televisions to distract from the beauty of the setting. *Off Coquihala Hwy., 29 km (18 mi) southwest of Kamloops, Box 3215, Kamloops V2C 6B8, tel. 604/372–2722 or 800/561–5253, fax 604/372–8755. 28 rooms, 4-plex chalet, 6 cabins. Facilities: restaurant, lounge, meeting room, gift shop, theater, games room, indoor whirlpool, sauna, boat and ski rentals. AE, D, DC, MC, V. $$–$$$$*

**Kelowna**
*Dining*

**Papillon.** This contemporarily furnished restaurant features a Continental menu that offers pasta, seafood, and steak. While seafood is not necessarily the specialty here, the prawns and scallops Caribbean is superb and highly recommended. The wine list includes a wide selection of imported and local wines that work nicely with the meals. *375 Leon Ave., tel. 604/763–3833. Reservations advised. Dress: casual but neat. AE, DC, MC, V. Closed weekend lunch. $$–$$$*

*Dining and*
*Lodging*

**Hotel Eldorado.** In 1989, the owners bought the old Eldorado Arms, built in 1926, and floated it by barge to its present location. Shortly thereafter, the old property burned down, but a new Eldorado has been built in its place, with much of the old-style charm intact. Rooms tend to be small and cozy, with light carpets, floral patterns, and antique furnishings; many have balconies affording superb views of Okanagan Lake. The Eldorado Dining Room has earned a fine reputation, serving fresh rack of lamb and seafood dishes. Ask for a seat on the waterfront patio. *500 Cook Rd., V1W 3G9, tel. 604/763–7500, fax 604/861–4779. 20 rooms. Facilities: restaurant, lounge, conference room, marina, whirlpool tub suite. Dress: casual but neat. AE, MC, V. $$$*

*Dining and*
*Lodging*
★

**Lake Okanagan Resort.** This well-acclaimed Hotels and Resorts property is a popular, self-contained destination on the west side of Okanagan Lake. All rooms have either kitchens or kitchenettes and range in size from one-room suites in the main hotel to spacious three-room chalets situated around the 300 acres. The resort shows some signs of age, particularly in the worn floors; but functional furnishings, wood-burning fireplaces, perfect views of the lake, and all the resort activities make this a good choice. Try to book one of the Lakeside Terrace rooms, renovated in 1993. *2751 Westside Rd., V1Y 8B2, tel. 604/769–3511 or 800/663–3273, fax 604/769–6655. 150 rooms. Facilities: restaurant, café, poolside lounge, hot tub and sauna, 3 pools, par-3 9-hole golf course, 7 tennis courts, stables, marina, scuba shop, pro shop, hiking and biking trails, nature and dinner cruises. AE, D, DC, MC, V. $$$$*

**Merritt**
*Dining and*
*Lodging*
★

**Corbett Lake Country Inn.** The locals want to keep this one a secret, but not owner Peter McVey, a French-trained chef. His restaurant offers a different fixed menu every night; favorites include rack of lamb and chateaubriand. The six single cabins (with extra beds) and two duplexes are comfortable and basic (though one duplex renovated in 1993 could now be considered deluxe), and there are also three rooms in the main lodge. Fly-fishing for rainbow trout is a big attraction here. Small pets are allowed. *Off Hwy. 5A, 11 km (6.8 mi)* *south of Merritt, Box 327, V0K 2B0, tel. 604/378–4334. 10 cabins, 3 rooms. Facilities: boat rentals. Reservations required for restaurant. Dress: casual. V. Closed mid-Jan.–Apr. and Oct. 15–Dec. 23. $$*

**Penticton**
*Dining*
★
**Granny Bogner's.** Perhaps the owners got a bit carried away with the homey theme: flowing lace curtains, Oriental rugs, wood chairs, cloth-covered tables, and waitresses in long skirts. But the food at this mostly Continental restaurant is excellent and prepared meticulously to order. The poached halibut and roasted duck have contributed to the widely held belief that this is the best restaurant in the Okanagan. *302 Eckhardt Ave. W, tel. 604/493–2711. Reservations advised. Dress: casual. AE, MC, V. Closed lunch; Sun. and Mon.; and Jan. $$–$$$*

*Lodging*
**Coast Lakeside Resort.** On the shore of Okanagan Lake, the inn is both a peaceful retreat and right in the center of the action. The waterfront offers relaxation, and the nearby Penticton Golf and Country Club invites a competitive round of golf. Vancouver businesspeople love this place for its comfort and convention facilities. The newly renovated rooms are bright and airy, and half of them have lake views. *21 Lakeshore Dr. W, V2A 7M5, tel. 604/493–8221 or 800/663–1144, fax 604/493–0607. 204 rooms. Facilities: 2 restaurants, lounge, beauty salon, 2 tennis courts, volleyball, windsurfing, sailing, waterskiing, indoor pool, health club, sauna, hot tub, games room, shuffleboard, masseuse. AE, DC, MC, V. $$$$*

**Riordan House.** When John and Donna Ortiz bought and restored the former Tiffin Tea House/Riordan Restaurant for their residence, they didn't expect to give guided tours to the newly spiffed-up 1921 house. But people seemed to like the place, built by a Prohibition rum-runner and furnished now with family antiques, so the Ortizes bowed to the inevitable and opened it as a bed-and-breakfast. One bedroom has a fireplace and one a sitting area; all look out on the surrounding hills. The Continental breakfast stars home-baked croissants, scones, muffins, and a selection of seasonal fruit; box lunches are packed on request (and Granny Bogner's is 60 paces away). Lake Okanagan is only a short walk, and you can drift on a rubber raft down the canal that connects it with Skaha Lake. *689 Winnipeg St., V2A 5N1, tel. 604/493–5997 or 604/490–7017. 3 rooms share 3 baths. Facilities: airport pickup, shuttle to lake beach, robes and slippers. MC, V. $–$$*

**Silver Star**
**Mountain**
*Dining*
★
**Craigellachie Dining Room.** The home-cooked meals in the dining room of the Putnam Station Hotel are filling rather than fancy. Soups and sandwiches are on the lunch menu, while old favorites like barbecue ribs, lasagne, pork chops, steaks, and pastas are offered in the evenings. The daily three-course special is generally a good deal. *Silver Star Mountain Resort, Box 4, Silver Star Mountain, tel. 604/542–2459. Reservations accepted. Dress: casual. AE, MC, V. $$*

*Dining and*
*Lodging*
★
**Vance Creek Hotel.** Looking more like the set of a spaghetti Western than a modern hotel, the Vance Creek enjoys a prime location in the heart of the *Gaslight*-era-theme village resort, atop Silver Star Mountain. Rooms are simple, with coordinated decor, long vanities in the entryway, and boxy bathrooms. Those on the first floor are popular with families because they are equipped with kitchenettes, bunk beds for the kids, and private entrances that open outside the hotel. Willow furniture and fireplaces add a touch more comfort to suites in the annex completed in 1993. *Silver Star Mountain Resort, Box 3, Silver Star Mountain V0E 1G0, tel. 604/549–5191, fax 604/549–5177. 84 rooms. Facilities: 2 restaurants, lounge, bar, hot tubs,*

*ski locker, meeting room, resort amenities including hiking and biking trails, indoor pool, horseback riding, bike and in-line skate rentals. Reservations accepted in restaurants. Dress: casual. Closed mid-Apr.–mid-May. AE, D, MC, V. $$$*

★ **Silver Lode Inn.** To complete the alpine experience on Silver Star Mountain, head to the Silver Lode Restaurant for raclette or fondue. Owners Max Schlaepfer and Trudi Amstutz, originally from Berne, Switzerland, serve hearty helpings of the real thing in the cheerful restaurant of their inn. No-frills rooms offer the basic comforts and are the most reasonably priced in the village. *Silver Star Mountain Resort, Box 5, Silver Star Mountain V0E 1G0, tel. 604/549–5105; fax 604/549–2163. Facilities: restaurant, bar, lounge, ski locker, hot tub, meeting room, resort amenities including hiking and biking trails, indoor pool, horseback riding, bike and Rollerblade rentals. Reservations accepted in restaurant. Dress: casual. AE, MC, V. $$–$$$*

**Vernon** **Intermezzo.** This intimate Italian restaurant combines dim lighting,
**Dining** high-backed chairs, olive-green wall paneling, and a lounge with a fireplace. The effect is formal and old-European, although the service is anything but stiff. Owner Jean DeLisle offers standard veal, fish, and pasta dishes, and an excellent selection of wines, as displayed in the wood cabinet of the main dining room. *3206 34th Ave., Box 22, Vernon V1T 6M1, tel. 604/542–3853. Reservations accepted. Dress: casual but neat. AE, MC, V. $*

**Lodging** **Village Green Hotel.** This hotel offers access to four golf courses and to the Silver Star Ski Resort, just 22 kilometers (14 miles) away. The bright, pleasant decor and reasonable prices make this hotel a good alternative to the other accommodations that line Highway 97. The rooms are spacious and the service is personal and friendly. *4801 27th St., V1T 4Z1, tel. 604/542–3321, fax 604/549–4252. 138 rooms. Facilities: restaurant, coffee shop, gift shop, lounge, night club, 4 tennis courts, volleyball, indoor and outdoor pools, sauna, hot tub, shuttle to ski resort and golf courses. AE, D, DC, MC, V. $$*

# 7 The Canadian Rockies

*By Peter Oliver*

*Updated by Anto Howard*

Comparing mountains is a subjective and imprecise business. Yet few would argue that the 640-kilometer (400-mile) stretch of the Canadian Rockies easily ranks as one of the most extravagantly beautiful ranges on earth. With little standing between the mountains and the Alberta prairie, the Rockies etch on the horizon an abrupt and stony line of chaotic grandeur that can be seen from 100 kilometers (60 miles) away to the east. Behind the prairie, granite walls rise thousands of feet above evergreen forests and glacially carved basins.

The peak that best epitomizes the character of the Canadian Rockies is Mt. Robson, which, at 3,954 meters (12,931 feet), is the highest of them all. A colossus of tumbling glaciers and cliff walls, usually shrouded in storm clouds, Mt. Robson creates its own irascible climate zone: The rush of avalanches down its flanks has triggered wind blasts well over 320 kilometers (200 miles) an hour.

In this region, keeping mountain ranges straight can be tedious. The Columbia Mountains, a series of parallel ranges just west of the Rockies, are often lumped together with the Rockies (as in fact they are in this chapter). This makes logistical sense when visiting the region for at least two good reasons: first, because the Columbias are in close proximity to the Rockies, and second, because many recreational activities that are prohibited in the national parks of the Rockies (notably helicopter-assisted skiing and hiking) are allowed in the Columbias.

However, this is the sort of travel-guide gerrymandering that undoubtably gives geologists fits. In fact, geologically speaking, the actual Rockies rise along the Continental Divide and are, at about 60 million years old, relative youngsters as mountains go. The Columbias, by comparison, were first formed about 180 million years ago and consist of four sub-ranges: the Cariboos to the north and, farther south, the Purcells, Selkirks, and Monashees, from east to west, respectively.

Measured against the U.S. Rockies, the Rockies and Columbias of Canada are not exceptionally high; elevations generally average 600–900 meters (about 2,000–3,000 feet) lower than those in Colorado, for example. Still, the Rockies and Columbias seem higher. For one thing, they start at a much lower elevation. The Columbia River Valley (or "trench," as it is often called) separating the Rockies and Columbias is surprisingly low at only about 600 meters (2,000 feet) high on average. By comparison, valley elevations in the Colorado Rockies typically range between 2,100 and 2,800 meters (about 7,000–9,000 feet). In addition, the tree line—the approximate elevation above which trees generally can't grow—is lower. In the Canadian Rockies, the tree line is at about 2,000 meters (6,500 feet), but Colorado's tree line usually starts above 3,000 meters (9,750 feet).

While glaciers in the United States have all but disappeared (except for those in Alaska and the mountains of the Pacific Northwest), they are still a common sight in Canada. Glacier National Park in the Columbias, for example, has more than 400 glaciers, covering 10% of the park's territory. The pale glacial blue strikes a dramatic balance against the blue-gray granite, the deep green of fir, spruce, and larch forests, and the panchromatic sweep of wildflowers. The glacial melt also feeds high-mountain lakes with mineral-rich silt deposits that tint the waters emerald green and cobalt blue, colors that change with the moods of the weather and the seasons.

Recognizing early the region's exceptional natural beauty, the Canadian government began shielding the area from human development and resource exploitation in the 1880s. In 1885, the government created a park preserve around the Cave and Basin Hot Springs in Banff. Two years later, Canada's first national park, Rocky Mountain Park (later Banff National Park), was officially established. Lands that would later become Yoho National Park and Glacier National Park in the Columbias were first set aside in 1886.

Today, approximately 25,000 square kilometers (roughly 10,000 square miles)—an area larger than the state of New Hampshire—are protected in seven national parks in the Rockies and the Columbias. Because they were protected early on, the parks of the Rockies—Waterton Lakes, Banff, Kootenay, Yoho, and Jasper—have remained relatively untouched by human development. The only significant clusters of human settlement are the town centers of Banff, Jasper, and Waterton Lakes, and the area around Lake Louise. Several thousand more square kilometers are also protected as wilderness areas and provincial parks, most notably Mt. Robson and Mt. Assiniboine provincial parks and Kananaskis Country.

# Essential Information

## Important Addresses and Numbers

**Tourist Information** The three major sources of tourism information are **Alberta Tourism** (Main Level, Commerce Building, City Centre, 10155 102 St., Edmonton, AB T5J 4L6, tel. 800/661–8888), **Discover British Columbia** (Parliament Bldgs., Victoria, BC V8V 1X4, tel. 800/663–6000), and **Canadian Heritage Parks Canada** (Information Services, Box 2989, Station M, Calgary, AB T2P 3H8, tel. 403/292–4401). Parks Canada information is also available at the **Parks Information Center** (Box 900, 224 Banff Ave., Banff, AB T0L 0C0, tel. 403/762–1550). Specify particular interests when requesting information; all the organizations have an extensive list of maps and publications. It's best to call the Information Office first, but if need be (e.g., for current weather conditions or camping availability), you can also contact individual offices of the four contiguous Rockies parks directly: **Banff** (tel. 403/762–1500), Jasper (tel. 403/852–6161), **Kootenay** (tel. 604/347–9615), or **Yoho** (tel. 604/343–6324). For local information in Banff, contact the **Banff–Lake Louise Tourism Bureau** (Suite 375, 317 Banff Ave., AB T0L 0C0, tel. 403/762–0270) or the **Town of Banff** (229 Bear St., Banff, AB T0L 0C0, tel. 403/762–1200); in Jasper, **Jasper Tourism and Commerce** (Box 98, Jasper, AB T0E 1E0, tel. 403/852–3858); in Kananaskis Country, **Kananaskis Country** (Suite 100, 1011 Glenmore Trail SW, Calgary, AB T2V 4R6, tel. 403/297–3362); in Waterton Lakes, **Waterton Lakes National Park** (Superintendent, Waterton Park, AB T0K 2M0, tel. 403/859–2224) or **Waterton Park Chamber of Commerce** (Box 55, Waterton Park, AB T0K 2M0, tel. 403/859–2203); in Revelstoke and Glacier Parks, **Mount Revelstoke and Glacier National Parks** (Park Superintendent, Box 350, Revelstoke, BC V0E 2S0, tel. 604/837–5155); and in the British Columbia Rockies, the **Rocky Mountain Visitors Association** (Box 10, Kimberley, BC V1A 2Y5, tel. 604/427–4838).

**Emergencies** Throughout Alberta and British Columbia **911** is the number for **police** or **ambulance.** For any extended trip into the backcountry, always register with the nearest park warden's office.

## Arriving and Departing by Plane

Calgary is the most common gateway for travelers arriving by plane. Those who plan to visit only Jasper and northern park regions may prefer to use Edmonton as a gateway city. Both cities have international airports served by several major carriers; the Calgary flight schedule is somewhat more extensive.

Airports and Airlines
**Calgary International Airport** and **Edmonton International Airport** serve the British Columbia Rockies region. (For airline information, *see* Arriving and Departing by Plane in Chapter 8.)

**Air Canada** and **Canadian Air** have daily flights to and from Cranbrook's airport, in southern British Columbia; most of these flights connect with flights through Vancouver International Airport and the international airports in Calgary and Edmonton.

## Arriving and Departing by Car, Train, and Bus

By Car
Route 1, the Trans-Canada Highway, is the principal east–west route into the region. Banff is 128 kilometers (80 miles) west of Calgary on Route 1 and 858 kilometers (515 miles) east of Vancouver. The other major east–west routes are Route 16 to the north, the main highway between Edmonton and Jasper, and Route 3 to the south. The main routes from the south are Route 89 (Route 2 in Canada), which enters Canada east of Waterton Lakes National Park from Montana, and Route 93, also from Montana, which provides access to the British Columbia Rockies.

By Train
**Rocky Mountaineer Railtours** (tel. 800/665–7245) offers service connecting Vancouver, Kamloops, Banff, Jasper, and Calgary. **VIA Rail** (tel. 800/361–3677) trains stop in Jasper, with connecting overnight runs to and from Toronto, Edmonton, Vancouver, and Jasper. Call for schedules.

By Bus
**Greyhound Lines** (call local listing) provides regular service to Calgary, Edmonton, and Vancouver, with connecting service to Jasper and Waterton Lakes. **Brewster Transportation and Tours** (tel. 800/661–1152) offers service between the Calgary International Airport and Banff, Jasper, and Lake Louise. **Laidlaw Transportation** (tel. 403/762–9102) also operates between Calgary Airport and the Banff–Lake Louise area.

## Getting Around

A fee is charged to all vehicles entering the national parks. A day pass is $5; a four-day pass, $10; and an annual pass, for any stay longer than four days, $30. You are permitted to leave and reenter the park for the duration of the pass without additional charge.

By Car
Unless you plan to go, literally, off the beaten path (in Kananaskis Country or in the Columbias; vehicles aren't permitted off major roadways in the national parks), a special vehicle (e.g., a four-wheel-drive vehicle) is not necessary. Major roadways are well maintained. Keep in mind, however, that snow arrives in early fall and remains until late spring. When traveling between October and April, stay informed of local road conditions, especially if you're traveling over mountain passes or along the Icefields Parkway (Route 93). A few roads, such as Route 40 over Highwood Pass in Kananaskis Country, are closed during the winter.

*Rental Cars*
Car-rental outlets are located at the Calgary and Edmonton airports, as well as in Banff, Jasper, and Cranbrook. Daily rentals for

sightseeing are available but should be reserved well ahead of time, especially in summer.

## Guided Tours

**Orientation Bus Tours**

**Brewster Transportation and Tours** (Box 1140, Banff, AB T0L 0C0, tel. in Banff, 403/762–6700; in Jasper, 403/852–3332; in Calgary, 403/221–8242; or 800/661–1152) offers half-, full-, and multiday sightseeing tours of the parks. The longer tours travel from Calgary to Vancouver and back. Prices start at about $30 per person.

**Tauck Tours** (11 Wilton Rd., Box 5027, Westport, CT 06881, tel. 203/226–6911) and **Holland American Westours** (300 Elliot Ave. W, Seattle, WA 98119, tel. 206/281–3535) conduct multiday bus tours through the region. Some Tauck Tours include heli-hiking options.

**Boat Tours**

**Minnewanka Boat Tours** (Box 2189, Banff, AB T0L 0C0, tel. 403/762–3473) offers 1½-hour tours in summer ($20 adult, $10 children) on Lake Minnewanka, near Banff.

**Maligne Lake Scenic Cruises** (Box 280, 626 Connaught Dr., Jasper, AB T0E 1E0, tel. 403/852–3370) runs 1½-hour tours on Maligne Lake, near Jasper, from mid-May through September ($29 adults, $14.50 children).

**Scenic Boat Cruises** (Box 126, Waterton, AB T0K 2M0, tel. 403/859–2362) offers half- and full-day cruises of Waterton Lake, some with hiking options.

**Auto Tours**

Audiocassette tapes for self-guided auto tours of the parks are produced by **Inc. Auto Tape Tours** and **Rocky Mountain Tape Tours**. Tapes can be rented or purchased at news or gift shops in Banff, Lake Louise, and Jasper.

**Heli-Tours**

**Canmore Helicopters** (Box 2069, Canmore, AB T0L 0M0, tel. 403/678–4802) is located 20 minutes southeast of Banff and provides year-round, guided "flightseeing" tours (20–60 minutes) above the valleys of the Banff, Lake Louise, and Kananaskis areas. They also combine tours with heli-picnics–barbecues which make it a half- or full-day event. Prices begin at $75.

**Special-Interest Tours**

**Seasonal Tours**

**Challenge Enterprises** (1300 Railway Ave., Box 2008, Canmore, AB T0L 0M0, tel. 403/678–2628) has a variety pack of tour options, including fishing, rafting, and cycling trips in summer, as well as snowmobiling, ice fishing, and dogsledding tours in winter.

**Kingmik Expeditions** (Box 227, Lake Louise, AB T0L 1E0, tel. 403/522–3525) specializes in dogsledding tours through the mountains and across the frozen waters of Lake Louise. You can even have a go at being the musher; tours range from half- to five-day outings with prices starting at $55 per sled (2 adults per sled).

For hiking, mountaineering, or backcountry ski tours, **Banff Alpine Guides** (Box 1025, Banff, AB T0L 0C0, tel. 403/678–6091) organizes tours according to weather conditions. Bookings can be arranged for private groups. The **Canadian School of Mountaineering** (Box 723, Canmore, AB T0L 0M0, tel. 403/678–4134) offers tours and instruction for mountaineering (in summer and winter) and backcountry skiing. Andre Fabbri of **Canadian Tourism Consultants** (Box 1877, Banff, AB T0L 0C0, tel. 403/762–3359) customizes guided tours—hiking or vehicle—that can include backcountry areas. In the Jasper area, the **Jasper Climbing School and Mountaineering Service** (Box 452, Jasper, AB T0E 1E0, tel. 403/852–3964) has guided hiking and

**Performing Arts** The **Jasper Activity Centre** (303 Pyramid Ave., tel. 403/852–3381) hosts local troupes performing theater, music, and dance productions throughout the year.

The **Jasper Summer Theatre** (Giekie and Miette Sts., tel. 403/852–5325) stages shows from June through August, at the Anglican Church Hall.

At the **Wild Horse Theater** (Fort Steele, BC V0B 1N0, tel. 604/426–6923), in Fort Steele, college presentations are staged from late June to mid-September.

**Film** Both the **Lux Cinema** (in the Wolf and Bear Mall, tel. 403/762–8595) in Banff and **Chaba Movie Theater** (on Connaught Dr., tel. 403/852–4749) in Jasper play major Hollywood movies and the selection changes each week. The Cannes award-winning **"Challenge of the Canadian Rockies"** (narrated by Peter Ustinov) plays every night in summertime at the Challenge Theater (tel. 403/852–4728) on Connaught Drive in Jasper.

**Music** The **Jasper Folk Festival** takes place on the first weekend in August and Canadian folk music is played in the center of the town fields, and at other venues throughout town.

During the summer months, Bavarian bands in Kimberley strike up with oompah music on the Platzl, especially when festivals are in swing. The **Old Time Accordion Championships,** in early July, is a Kimberley musical highlight.

In late summer, the Royal Canadian Mounted Police perform their precision **Musical Ride at Fort Steele** (tel. 604/426–6923).

## Nightlife

Like many activities in the Canadian Rockies, nightlife, too, is an outdoor event. In summer darkness doesn't fall until after 10 PM, so an after-dinner hike, sail, or even nine holes of golf is possible. As for the bar scene, keep in mind that the drinking age is 18, and expect a boisterous and youthful clientele at many of the drinking holes in Jasper and especially in Banff.

For cocktails and socializing, the big hotels—the **Banff Springs Hotel, Chateau Lake Louise, Jasper Park Lodge,** and the **Lodge at Kananaskis**—have lounges or dining rooms with entertainment and dancing (*see* Lodging, *above*).

In Banff, **Wild Bill's** (Banff Ave. and Caribou St., tel. 403/762–0333) is a cowboy bar with live music and the place for two-steppers to strut their stuff. If you prefer rock and roll with your drink, try **Back Alley** (137 Banff Ave., tel 403/762–8434) and **Barbary Coast** (119 Banff Ave., tel. 403/762–4616).

In Canmore, local folk kick back at **Sherwood House** (738 8th St., tel. 403/678–5211), which occasionally has live bands on weekends.

In Jasper, the **Athabasca Hotel's** nightclub (510 Patricia St., tel. 403/852–3386) features dancing to Top–40 music and live bands. The **Whistle Stop** (in the Whistler Inn, on Connaught Dr., tel. 403/852–3361) is a local haunt with the decor—dartboad included—and ambience of a British pub.

Also in Jasper, the **Astoria Hotel** (404 Connaught, tel. 403/852–3351) is known for a happy hour that can become crowded and raucous.

# 8 Manitoba Saskatchewan Alberta

*By Theodore Fischer*

*Updated by Robin and Arlene Karpan*

Between the wilds of western Ontario and the eastern slopes of the Rockies lie Canada's three prairie provinces: Manitoba, Saskatchewan, and Alberta. This is Canada's heartland: the principal source of such solid commodities as wheat, oil, and beef. These provinces are also the home of a rich stew of ethnic communities that make the area unexpectedly colorful and cosmopolitan.

The term "prairie provinces" is a bit of a misnomer, as most of this region (the northern half of Alberta and Saskatchewan, and the northern two-thirds of Manitoba) consists of sparsely populated expanses of lakes, rivers, and forests. Most of northern Saskatchewan and Manitoba belong to the Canadian Shield, with a foundation of Precambrian rock that is some of the oldest in the world. The fertile plains of the south are home to Canada's agricultural heartland, where wheat is still king, but other crops, as well as livestock, help boost the economy. The landscape is quite diverse, with farms and ranches interspersed with wide river valleys, lakes, rolling hills, badlands, and even dry hills of sand.

The Prairies' history is quite significant, dating from 75 million years ago when dinosaurs roamed what was then semitropical swampland; 12,000 years ago the first human settlers crossed the Bering Strait from Asia. In the 17th century European fur traders began arriving, and in 1670 the British Crown granted the Hudson's Bay Company administrative and trading rights to "Rupert's Land," a vast territory whose waters drained into Hudson Bay. A hundred years later, the North West Company went into direct competition by building outposts throughout the area. From this fur-trading tradition arose the Métis—mostly French-speaking offspring of Indian women and European traders who followed the Roman Catholic religion but adhered to a traditional Indian lifestyle.

By 1873 the North West Mounted Police was established in Manitoba, just six years after the formation of the Canadian government. In 1874, the Mounties began their march west: Their first chores included resolving conflicts between the Indians and American whiskey traders and overseeing the orderly distribution of the free homesteads granted by the Dominion Lands Act of 1872. The Mounties played a role in the North West Rebellion—a revolt by Métis, who feared that the encroachment of western settlement would threaten their traditions and freedom. Although the Métis eventually succumbed, and their leader, Louis Riel, was hanged in 1885, Riel is now hailed as a martyr of the Métis and a statue of him stands on the grounds of Manitoba's Legislature Building.

Railroads arrived in the 1880s and with them a torrent of immigrants seeking free government land. An influx of farmers from the British Isles, Scandinavia, Holland, Germany, Eastern Europe, Russia, and especially Ukraine, plus persecuted religious groups, such as the Mennonites, Hutterites, Mormons, and Jews, transformed the prairies into a rich wheat-growing breadbasket and cultural mosaic that is still very much in evidence today. In 1947, a big oil strike transformed Edmonton and Calgary into gleaming metropolises full of "blue-eyed Arabs."

The people of the prairie provinces are relaxed, reserved, and irascibly independent. They maintain equal suspicion toward "Ottawa" (big government) and "Toronto" (big media and big business). To visitors, the people of this region convey a combination of Western openness and Canadian-style courtesy: no fawning, but no rudeness. Visitors also find exceptional outdoor recreational facilities—a spectrum of historical attractions that focuses on Mounties,

Métis, dinosaurs, and railroads; excellent accommodations and cuisine at reasonable (but not low) prices; and quiet, crowdless expanses of extraordinarily wide open spaces.

# Essential Information

## Important Addresses and Numbers

**Tourist**
**Information**
*Manitoba*

**Travel Manitoba** (Dept. 2036, 7th Floor, 155 Carlton St., Winnipeg, Man., R3C 3H8, tel. 204/945–3777 or 800/665–0040) distributes a free road map and several useful brochures. The office is open weekdays 8:30–4:30.

**Manitoba Travel Information Centers** are located just inside the Manitoba border along major routes. The centers are open mid-May through early September from 8 AM to 9 PM.

*Saskatchewan*

**Tourism Saskatchewan** (Saskatchewan Trade & Convention Centre, 1919 Saskatchewan Dr., Regina, Sask. S4P 3V7, tel. 800/667–7191) can provide you with brochures and maps of attractions, accommodations, and parks inside and outside the province. The main office is open weekdays 8–7, Saturday 10–4.

**Information centers** are located in cities throughout the province, and in the summer along major highways leading into the province.

*Alberta*

**Alberta Tourism** (Box 2500, Edmonton, Alb., T5J 2Z4, tel. in Edmonton, 403/427–4321; in Alberta, 800/222–6501; in the United States and Canada, 800/661–8888) distributes extremely comprehensive and useful free promotional literature. The office is open weekdays 9–4:30.

## Arriving and Departing by Plane, Bus, and Train

**By Plane**

**Air Canada** has direct or connecting service from Boston, New York, Chicago, San Francisco, and Los Angeles to Winnipeg, Regina, Saskatoon, Calgary, and Edmonton. Commuter affiliates serve other U.S. and Canadian destinations. U.S. airlines serving the prairie provinces include **Northwest** to Winnipeg; **American, Delta,** and **United** to Calgary; and **American, Delta,** and **Northwest** to Edmonton.

**By Bus**

**Greyhound Lines** (consult local directory) and local bus companies provide service from the United States, other parts of Canada, and throughout the prairie provinces.

**By Train**

There is no rail service between the United States and the prairie provinces.

**VIA Rail** trains (from New York and Connecticut, tel. 800/361–3677; from the Atlantic seaboard, 800/561–3949; from the Midwest, 800/387–1144; from the western United States, 800/665–0200), connect eastern Canada and the west coast through Winnipeg–Saskatoon–Edmonton.

## Getting Around

**By Car**

Two main east–west highways link the major cities of the prairie provinces. The Trans-Canada Highway (Route 1), mostly a four-lane divided freeway, runs through Winnipeg, Regina, and Calgary on its nationwide course. The two-lane Yellowhead Highway (Route 16) branches off the Trans-Canada Highway west of Winnipeg and heads northwest toward Saskatoon, Saskatchewan, and Edmonton,

Alberta. Traveling north–south, four-lane divided freeways connect Saskatoon–Regina (Route 11) and Edmonton–Calgary (Route 2).

From the United States, interstate highways cross the Canadian border, and two-lane highways continue on to major prairie province cities. From Minneapolis, I–94 and then I–29 connect to Highway 75 at the Manitoba border south of Winnipeg. Driving distance between Minneapolis and Winnipeg is 691 kilometers (432 miles). A main route to Alberta is I–15 north of Helena, Montana, which connects to Highways 2, 3, and 4 to Calgary. Calgary is 690 kilometers (425 miles) from Helena; it's also 670 kilometers (419 miles) from Seattle, via the Trans-Canada Highway.

# Winnipeg

With a population of more than 600,000, Winnipeg ranks as Canada's seventh-largest city and the largest population center between Toronto and Calgary. Though geographically isolated, this provincial capital has become a center for both commerce and culture, boasting a symphony orchestra, ballet and opera companies, a lively theater scene, and a thriving community of local and native artists.

The first stop on the great Canadian land rush of the late-19th century, Winnipeg is still home to descendants of the original French and British settlers, and it has distinct neighborhoods of Ukrainians, Jews, Italians, Mennonites, Hungarians, Portuguese, Poles, and Chinese. Unlike the boom-and-bust towns farther west, Winnipeg has enjoyed steady growth, with a diversified economy based on manufacturing, banking, transportation, and agriculture. Winnipeg looks like the cosmopolitan centers of midwestern America—Minneapolis, Milwaukee, Chicago—with a downtown area filled with cast-iron buildings and established neighborhoods of older homes along curving, tree-lined streets.

Originally, buffalo-hunting Plains Indians were the only inhabitants of the area that was franchised by the British Crown to the Hudson's Bay Company. That was until Pierre Gaultier de Varennes established in 1738 a North West Company fur-trading post at the junction of the Red and Assiniboine rivers. Lord Selkirk, a Scot, brought a permanent agricultural settlement in 1812; Winnipeg was incorporated as a city in 1873; and soon after, in 1886, the Canadian Pacific Railroad arrived, bringing a rush of European immigrants. Winnipeg boomed as a railroad hub, a center of the livestock and grain industries, and a principal market city of western Canada.

## Important Addresses and Numbers

**Tourist Information**
The **Government Tourist Reception Office** (Broadway and Osborne St., tel. 204/945–3777 or 800/665–0040), housed in the Manitoba Legislative Building, is open May–Labor Day, daily 8:30 AM–9 PM; Labor Day–April, weekdays 8:30–4:30. **Tourism Winnipeg** (320-25 The Forks Market Road, tel. 204/943–1970) is open weekdays 8:30–4:30; and there's an airport location (tel. 800/665–0204) that's open 8 AM–10 PM.

**Emergencies**
Dial 911 for **fire, police, ambulance,** or **poison control.**

**Hospital**
Emergency rooms are located at the **Health Sciences Centre** (700 William Ave., tel. 204/787–3167 general emergency; tel. 204/787–2306 children's emergency), **Winnipeg Municipal Hospital** (1 Morley

354

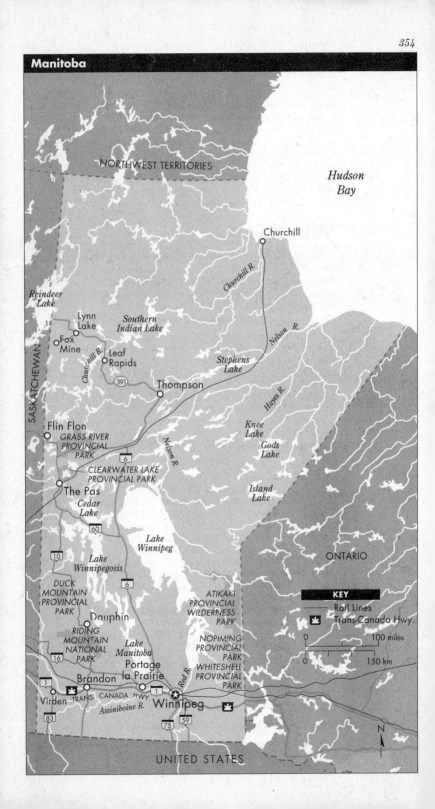

# American Express offers Travelers Cheques built for two.

Cheques *for Two*℠ from American Express are the Travelers Cheques that allow either of you to use them because both of you have signed them. And only one of you needs to be present to purchase them.

Cheques *for Two* are accepted anywhere regular American Express Travelers Cheques are, which is just about everywhere. So stop by your bank, AAA* or any American Express Travel Service Office and ask for Cheques *for Two*.

**Travelers Cheques**

# Pack light.
## Take the one number you need for any kind of call, anywhere you travel.

Checking in with your family back home? Calling for a tow truck? When you're on the road, the phone you use might not accept your calling card. Or you might get overcharged by an unknown telephone company. Here's the solution: dial 1 800 CALL ATT.[sm] You'll get flawless AT&T service, competitive calling card prices, and the lowest prices for collect calls from any phone, anywhere. Travel light. Just bring along this one simple number: 1 800 CALL ATT.

Ave., tel. 204/452–3411), and **Misericordia General Hospital** (99 Cornish Ave., tel. 204/788–8188).

| | |
|---|---|
| **Late-night Pharmacy** | **Metro Drugs** (905 Corydon Ave., tel. 204/453–8331) is open until 9 PM. |

## Arriving and Departing by Plane

**Winnipeg International Airport** is served by Northwest, Air Canada, Canadian Airlines International, and several commuter airlines. Because the airport is only about 8 kilometers (5 miles) away, taxi fare downtown runs about $10–$12. Some airport-area hotels provide complimentary airport shuttles.

## Getting Around

**By Bus** The **City of Winnipeg Transit System** (tel. 204/986–5700) operates an extensive network of buses throughout the city and metropolitan area. Adult fare is $1.30 exact change, 70¢ for senior citizens and children; transfers are free.

**By Taxi** Taxis—relatively expensive by U.S. standards—can be found outside downtown hotels or summoned by phone. Car services are **Unicity** (tel. 204/947–6611) and **Duffy's Taxi** (tel. 204/775–0101).

## Guided Tours

**Boat Tours** Several lines ply the Red and Assiniboine rivers between May and mid-October. The ***Paddlewheel River Rouge*** (tel. 204/942–4500) offers a variety of cruises (dining, dinner-dance, evening), combining sailings with double-decker bus tours.

**Train Tours** The **Prairie Dog Central Steam Train** (tel. 204/832–5259) plies a 58-kilometer (36-mile) route from the CNR St. James Station (1661 Portage Ave.) to Grosse Isle on Sunday, from mid-May through September, departing at 11 AM and 3 PM.

**Walking Tours** Walking tours of the turn-of-the-century Exchange District begin at the Manitoba Museum of Man & Nature (190 Rupert Ave., tel. 204/943–3139 or 204/956–2830) during July and August.

## Exploring Downtown Winnipeg

*Numbers in the margin correspond to points of interest on the Downtown Winnipeg map.*

It's somewhat difficult to get one's bearings in Winnipeg. The downtown area is located just north of the junction of the Red and Assiniboine rivers, and its streets interconnect at skewed angles with the curving rivers, creating diagonal streets in all directions. Much of downtown Winnipeg is linked by a network of enclosed overhead pedestrian overpasses and underground concourses. The intersection of Portage Avenue and Main Street is the focal point of the city, with Portage Avenue (Hwy. 1) the principal artery heading west and Main Street (Hwy. 52) heading north. South of Winnipeg, the main drag is Pembina Highway (Hwy. 42). Streets in St. Boniface, east of the Red River, are labeled in French—evidence of the community's ethnic heritage.

Begin at the southeast corner of downtown Winnipeg at the tourist information center (*see* Important Addresses and Numbers, *above*),  housed in the **Legislative Building.** The classic Greek-style structure made of local Tyndall stone contains the offices of Manitoba's pre-

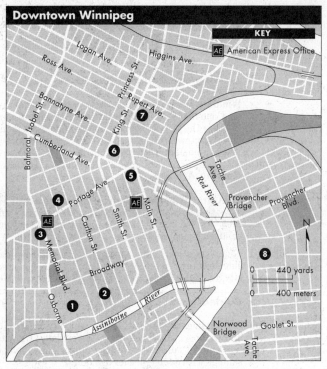

mier and members of the cabinet, as well as the chamber where the legislature meets. The 240-foot dome supports Manitoba's symbol, Golden Boy—a gold-sheathed statue with a sheaf of wheat under his left arm and the torch of progress in his right hand. Along the grounds and gardens surrounding the riverside stand statues that celebrate Manitoba's ethnic diversity, including Scotland's Robert Burns, Iceland's Jon Sigurdson, Ukrainian poet Taras Ahevchenko, and Métis leader and "Father of Manitoba" Louis Riel.

**2** Walk east on Broadway and south on Carlton Street to **Dalnavert,** a Queen Anne Revival–style house built in 1895 for Sir Hugh John Macdonald, who became premier of Manitoba. Costumed guides escort visitors around the premises. *61 Carlton St., tel. 204/943–2835. Admission: $3.21 adults, $2.14 senior citizens, $1.50 students, $1 children 5–12. Open June–Aug., daily 10–6; Sept.–Dec., daily noon–5; Jan. and Feb., weekends noon–5; Mar.–May, daily noon–5.*

Back at the Legislature, head north on Osborne Street past the stately The Bay store (the legacy of the Hudson's Bay Company) to **3** the **Winnipeg Art Gallery.** The gallery, which owns the world's largest collection of Inuit sculpture and art, also houses contemporary Canadian art and sculpture. *300 Memorial Blvd., tel. 204/786–6641. Admission: $3 adults, $2 senior citizens and students, $5 families, children under 12 free; free Wed. Open mid-June–Labor Day, Thurs.–Tues. 10–5, Wed. 10–9; Sept.–early June, Tues. and Thurs.–Sun. 11–5, Wed. 11–9.*

Turn east at the north end of the Winnipeg Art Gallery to Portage Avenue. The north side of Portage between Balmoral and Carlton

**④** streets is occupied by sprawling **Portage Place,** an indoor mall encompassing 150 stores (*see* Shopping, *below*).

**Time Out** Winnipeg's oldest restaurant, the 1918 **Chocolate Shop** (268 Portage Ave., tel. 204/942–4855), serves generous sandwiches for lunch and more ambitious entrées at dinnertime. Teacups and tarot cards are read 1–9.

Continue east on Portage Avenue to Main Street and what's reputed to be the windiest intersection in the world. Five floors above the **⑤** breeze, visit the **Winnipeg Commodity Exchange,** the oldest and largest futures exchange in Canada, and observe the controlled chaos of wild men (and a few women) involved in the buying and selling of grains, cooking oils, gold, and silver. *360 Main St., tel. 204/949–0495. Open weekdays 9:30–1:20.*

Below-ground is **Winnipeg Square,** an underground concourse with shops and fast-food stores. Emerge to street level on the north side **⑥** of Portage Avenue and into the **Exchange District**—a concentration of renovated warehouses, banks, and insurance companies that were built during Winnipeg's turn-of-the-century boom period but now stand as a thriving nightlife spot. On Sunday, from May through October, attention focuses on **Old Market Square Park** (King St. and Bannatyne Ave.), a new marketplace bursting with fresh produce, fish, crafts, and street performers.

**⑦** Continue north on Main Street to Rupert Avenue and **Centennial Centre,** site of a concert hall, the **Manitoba Museum of Man and Nature,** and the dazzling **Manitoba Planetarium.** Exhibits at the museum focus on prehistoric Manitoba, local wildlife, the native peoples of the region, and the exploration of Hudson Bay. Downstairs, the planetarium presents a variety of cosmic adventures in the multimedia **Star Theater;** 60 interactive multisensory exhibits in Touch the Universe explain laws of nature. *190 Rupert Ave., tel. 204/943–3139 (museum), tel. 204/943–3142 (planetarium). Admission: museum $3.50 adults, $2.50 students, senior citizens, and children 4–12; planetarium $4 adults, $2.50 students, senior citizens, and children 4–12; Touch the Universe $2.50 adult, $2 students, $2.75 senior citizens and children 4–12; all three $7.50 adults, $5.50 students, $4.50 senior citizens and children 4–12. Open mid-May–early Sept., daily 10–6; Sept.–mid-May, Tues.–Thurs. 10–6, weekends noon–6.*

**St. Boniface,** about 2½ kilometers (1½ miles) away, can be reached by crossing the Provencher Bridge and turning right onto Avenue Tache. The largest French community in western Canada was founded as Fort Rouge in 1783 and became an important fur-trading outpost for the North West Company. Upon the arrival of Roman Catholic priests, the settlement was renamed St. Boniface. Remnants of a 1908 basilica that survived a 1968 fire can be seen outside **⑧** the perimeter of the present **St. Boniface Cathedral** (av. de la Cathedral and av. Tache, tel. 204/233–7304), built in 1972. The grave of Louis Riel, the St. Boniface native son who led the Métis rebellion, is in the churchyard.

Housed in the oldest (1846) structure in Winnipeg and the largest oak log building in North America, the **St. Boniface Museum** tells the French and Métis side of Manitoba history. Artifacts include an altar crafted from papier-mâché, the first church bell in western Canada, and a host of innovative household gadgets. The museum re-opens in 1995 after being closed for structural repairs; call ahead to confirm opening date. *494 av. Tache, tel. 204/237–4500. Admis-*

*sion free, but donations accepted. Open mid-May–Sept., daily 9–9; Sept.–mid-May, weekdays 9–5, weekends and holidays 10–5.*

You can see Canadian and foreign coins rolling off the presses at the **Royal Canadian Mint,** 6.4 kilometers (4 miles) southeast of downtown off Highway 1 or by Bus 50, available on the east side of Fort Street between Portage and Graham avenues on weekdays. *520 Lagimodière Blvd. (at the Trans-Canada Hwy.), Winnipeg, R2J 3E7, tel. 204/257–3359. Admission: $2. Tours run 9–3, mid-May–mid-Sept.*

## Other Points of Interest

About 48 kilometers (30 miles) southeast of Winnipeg is the town of **Steinbach,** populated with nearly 10,000 descendants of Mennonites who fled religious persecution in late-19th-century Europe. Note the large number of automobile dealerships: Manitoban car buyers flock here because of the Mennonite reputation for making square deals.

In the **Mennonite Heritage Village,** a 40-acre museum, guides demonstrate blacksmithing, wheat grinding, and old-time housekeeping chores while conversing in the Mennonite Low German dialect. During the Pioneer Days festival in early August, everyone wears costumes and demonstrates homespun crafts. An authentic and extremely low-priced restaurant serves Mennonite specialties, such as borscht, pirogies, and *ukrenky* (cheese or potato torte). *Hwy. 12, 2 km (1¼ mi) north of Steinbach, tel. 204/326–9661. Admission: $2 adults, $1 students and senior citizens, 75¢ children grades 1–6. Open May and Sept., Mon.–Sat. 10–5, Sun. noon–5; June–Aug., Mon.–Sat. 9–7, Sun. noon–7.*

**Lower Fort Garry,** built in 1830, is the oldest stone fort remaining from the Hudson's Bay Company fur-trading days. Nowadays, costumed employees describe daily tasks and recount thrilling journeys by York boat, the "boat that won the west." Beaver, raccoon, fox, and wolf pelts hang in the fur loft as a reminder of the bygone days. *Hwy. 9, 32 km (20 mi) north of Winnipeg, tel. in Winnipeg, 204/983–6341; in Selkirk, 204/482–6483. Admission: $3.25 adults, $1.50 children 5–16. Grounds open year-round in daylight hours. Buildings open mid-May–Sept. 2, daily 10–6.*

**Gimli,** the largest Icelandic community outside the homeland, was once the center of the independent state of New Iceland. A giant Viking statue proclaims allegiance to the far-off island; the **Gimli Historical Museum,** on the Gimli harbor waterfront, preserves the ethnic heritage of early Ukrainian and Icelandic settlers and records the history of the Lake Winnipeg commercial fishing industry. *Hwy. 9, Gimli harbor area, tel. 204/642–5317. Admission: $1.25 adults, 75¢ children, $3 families, senior citizens free. Open mid-May–June, Wed.–Sun. 10–5; July and Aug., daily, 10–6.*

## City and Provincial Parks

**Assiniboine Park,** situated in Winnipeg along the river of the same name, encompasses 376 acres of cycling paths, picnic areas, playgrounds, a miniature railway, formal English and French gardens, a conservatory, and a cricket pitch. **Assiniboine Zoo,** also on the grounds, houses more than 1,200 species in reasonably natural settings. *Assiniboine Park and Zoo, tel. 204/986–6921. Admission to zoo: $3 adults, $2.75 senior citizens, $1.50 youths 13–17, $1 children 2–12, children under 2 free, $7.50 families. Open daily 10 AM–dusk.*

**The Forks National Historic Site,** at the junction of the Red and Assiniboine rivers, is where Winnipeg began 6,000 years ago. Today, the 56 acres host a playground, riverside promenade, small boat dock, amphitheater, and archaeological excavations. The promenade has recently been extended, and interpretive programs are available. *At the confluence of the Red and Assiniboine rivers, tel. 204/983–2007. Open Victoria Day–Labor Day, daily 9:30–6; Labor Day–Victoria Day, weekdays 8–4:30.*

**Grand Beach Provincial Park** is on the eastern shore of Lake Winnipeg, the seventh-largest lake in North America. On summer weekends, crowds flock here from Winnipeg for the white-powder sand, the grass-crowned 30-foot dunes, and a lagoon that makes birdwatchers' dreams come true. **Grand Marais** is the service area at the southern portal to the park. *Hwy. 12, 87 km (54 mi) northwest of Winnipeg, tel. 204/754–2212. Open May–Sept., daily.*

**Hecla Provincial Park,** about a 2½-hour drive from Winnipeg, is a densely wooded archipelago named for the Icelandic volcano that drove the area's original settlers to Canada. The park is located on the central North American flyway, and 50,000 waterfowl summer here. **Moose Tower** is a good spot in the early morning and evening to view moose and other wildlife. The original 1880s Hecla Icelandic Fishing Village is restored near **Gull Harbour,** the tourist center of the park and site of the luxurious **Gull Harbour Resort** (tel. 204/475–2354), complete with a marina, hiking trails, and a devilishly difficult golf course. *Hecla Provincial Park, Hwy. 8, 175 km (109 mi) north of Winnipeg, tel. 204/378–2945. Open May–Sept., daily.*

**Spruce Woods Provincial Heritage Park** encompasses, among rolling hills of spruce and basswood, the desertlike Spirit Sands, a 16-square-kilometer (10-square-mile) tract of cactus-filled sand dunes. Walk the self-guided trail through the dunes, but keep your eyes peeled for lizards and snakes! Your final destination will be **Devil's Punch Bowl,** a dramatic pit dug out by an underground stream. You can also tour the park in a horse-drawn covered wagon. *Hwy. 5, 180 km (114 mi) west of Winnipeg, tel. 204/827–2543. Open May–Sept., daily.*

**Whiteshell Provincial Park,** a 2,590-square-kilometer (1,550-square-mile) tract on the edge of the Canadian Shield, encompasses 200 lakes that offer some of the best northern-pike, perch, walleye, and lake-trout fishing in western Canada. The **Falcon Lake** area has a shopping center, a golf course, tennis courts, a very good beach, a sailing club, and top-grade accommodations in the 34-room **Falcon Lake Resort & Club** (tel. 204/349–8400). **Beaver Creek** trail is a short walk to such wilderness denizens as beaver and deer. Farther on, **West Hawk Lake** (or Crater Lake)—formed a few thousand years ago by a falling meteor—is 111 meters (365 feet) deep and full of feisty smallmouth bass. Scuba divers love it. *Whiteshell Provincial Park, Hwy. 1E, 143 km (89 mi) from Winnipeg, tel. 204/369–5232. Open daily 8 AM–11 PM.*

## What to See and Do with Children

**Assiniboine Park and Zoo** (*see* City and Provincial Parks, *above*).

**Fort Whyte Center for Environmental Education** (1961 McCreary Rd., Winnipeg, tel. 204/989–8355) makes use of several cement quarries and the 200 acres of land around them to re-create the natural habitats of Manitoba's lakes and rivers. Self-guided nature trails and an interpretive center explain all.

**Fun Mountain Water Slide Park** (Rte. 1, east at Murdock Rd., Winnipeg, tel. 204/255–3910), located about 13 kilometers (8 miles) east of downtown, includes bumper boats, a mammoth hot tub, rides, and a playground.

**Manitoba Children's Museum** (109 Pacific Ave., Winnipeg, tel. 204/957–0005) is western Canada's first hands-on museum for children, and it shows them how to operate a grain elevator, put on a circus, understand their senses, and much more.

**Manitoba Museum of Man and Nature/Planetarium** (*see* Exploring Downtown Winnipeg, *above*).

**Skinner's Wet n' Wild Waterslide Park** (Hwy. 44, Lockport, tel. 204/757–2623) has four big slides, two kiddie slides, and many other damp attractions.

## Shopping

**Malls and Shopping Districts**  Downtown shopping is dominated by **Portage Place** (Portage Ave. between Balmoral and Carlton Sts.) and **Eaton Place** (bounded by Graham Ave., Hargrave St., St. Mary Ave., and Donald St.), two malls with numerous stores, fast-food joints, and movie theaters.

Across the Assiniboine River, the **Osborne Village** area (Osborne St. between River and Corydon Aves.) has 150 trendy boutiques and specialty shops, cafés, restaurants, and crafts shops.

**Art and Crafts**  The **Crafts Guild of Manitoba** (183 Kennedy St., tel. 204/943–1190) features works by Manitoba carvers, weavers, and jewelers. **Northern Images** (#216 393 Portage Ave., tel. 204/942–5501; Airport Executive Centre, 1790 Wellington Ave., tel. 204/788–4806) markets the work of the Inuit and Dene members of the NWT Co-operative, which owns the stores. For more Indian art, check out the **Great Canadian Print Company** (75 Albert St., tel. 204/942–1002) or **The Upstairs Gallery** (266 Edmonton St., tel. 204/943–2734) for prints, drawings, wall hangings, and sculpture.

## Sports

**Participant Sports**
*Bicycling and Jogging*  Most public parks in Manitoba have marked biking and jogging paths. For information on routes, pick up maps from **Travel Manitoba** (*see* Important Addresses and Numbers in Essential Information, *above*).

*Health and Fitness Clubs*  Drop-in rates and a full slate of classes and equipment are available at **Body Options** (1604 St. Mary's Rd., Winnipeg, tel. 204/255–6600) and **Bodyworks** (2 Donald St., Winnipeg, tel. 204/477–1691).

**Spectator Sports**
*Basketball*  The **Winnipeg Thunder** (tel. 204/956–4667) of the National Basketball League play home games at the **Winnipeg Arena** (1430 Maroons Dr., Winnipeg).

*Football*  The **Winnipeg Blue Bombers** (tel. 204/784–2583) of the Canadian Football League play home games at the Winnipeg Arena.

*Hockey*  The **Winnipeg Jets** (tel. 204/982–5387) confront National Hockey League opposition between October and April at the Winnipeg Arena.

*Horse Racing*  **Assiniboia Downs** (3975 Portage Ave. at Perimeter Hwy. W, Winnipeg, tel. 204/885–3330) hosts thoroughbred racing May–October.

Soccer   The **Winnipeg Fury** of the Canadian Soccer League play a May–September schedule at **Winnipeg Soccer Complex** (1465 Maroons Rd., Winnipeg, tel. 204/475–3879).

## Dining and Lodging

Dining   Although places specializing in generous helpings of Canadian beef still dominate the scene, restaurants throughout the prairie provinces now tastily reflect the region's ethnic makeup and offer a wide variety of cuisine to fit every price range.

Highly recommended restaurants in each price category are indicated by a star ★.

| Category | Cost* |
|----------|-------|
| $$$$ | over $25 |
| $$$ | $20–$25 |
| $$ | $15–$20 |
| $ | under $15 |

*three-course dinner, per person, excluding drinks, service, and taxes*

Dining   **Le Beaujolais.** This sophisticated, bright spot in the French St. Boniface district presents waiters in black tie; a softly lit ambience with French blue, coral, and burgundy decor; fresh-cut flowers; and a menu that combines classic French with lighter nouvelle cuisine. Fresh salmon with herb vinaigrette is the recommended seafood; tournedos with green peppercorns, veal with Roquefort and leeks, and rack of lamb are other entrée suggestions. Save room for dessert. *131 Provencher Blvd., tel. 204/237–6306. Reservations advised. Jacket advised. AE, DC, MC, V. $$$$*

**Restaurant Dubrovnik.** The setting is a romantic Victorian town house, with seating on an enclosed veranda overlooking the Assiniboine River. An extensive menu blends Continental specialties, such as rack of lamb, breast of duck, and pheasant, with southern Yugoslavian dishes. Two good dishes to try are the *gibanica* (feta cheese in phyllo pastry) and the *muckalica* (pork, lamb, chicken, and sausage casserole). A lengthy wine list is available. *390 Assiniboine Ave., tel. 204/944–0594. Reservations advised. Jacket required. AE, MC, V. Closed Sun. $$$$*

**Victor's.** Located in the elegant Marlborough Inn (*see* Lodging, *below*), with its rich wood paneling and chandeliers, Victor's serves Continental cuisine for those who want a stylish, upscale evening. Joanna's Café, in the same hotel, is a more casual dining spot and one that's appropriate for before- or after-dinner drinks. In both restaurants, poppyseed cake is a must for dessert. *331 Smith St., tel. 204/947–2751. Reservations advised. Jacket advised. AE, DC, MC, V. Closed Sun. $$$$*

**Amici.** The sophisticated and posh downtown *ristorante* is the local avatar of *cucina nuova*, the Italian version of nouvelle cuisine. Clever pastas and such dishes as roast quail on radicchio and chicken stuffed with goat cheese are served in a second-floor dining room that's divided by partitions of frosted glass. Downstairs, the Bombolini Wine Bar serves many simpler dishes at lower prices. *326 Broadway, tel. 204/943–4997. Reservations advised. Jacket advised for Amici; casual for Bombolini. AE, DC, MC, V. Closed Sun. $$$*

★ **Bistro Dansk.** Wood tables, bright red chairs, and strains of classical music convey a cozy European air. Dinner entrée selections mingle Danish specialties like *frikadeller* (meat patties), and salmon topped with crab, with such dishes as roast chicken. A less expensive lunch menu features a vast variety of open-face sandwiches. *63 Sherbrook St., tel. 204/775–5662. Reservations advised. Dress: casual. DC, V. Closed Sun. $$*

**Picasso's.** It may be named after a Spanish painter, but this is a Portuguese restaurant, featuring outstanding seafood. On the street level it's a bustling neighborhood café; upstairs there's a subdued atmosphere where white tablecloths, candlelight, and soft music prevail. Try the salmon or Arctic char; Portuguese favorites are paella, octopus stew, and steak Picasso. *615 Sargent Ave., tel. 204/775–2469. Reservations advised. Dress: casual. AE, DC, MC, V. $$*

★ **d'8 Schtove.** The name is Mennonite for "the eating room," and, true to its name, the menu features heavyweight servings of soup, salads, and Mennonite concoctions, usually involving meat, potatoes, onions, and vegetables. Try the *klopz* (ground-beef-and-pork meatballs) or *wrenikje* (cottage-cheese pierogies). The new south-side location is bright and immaculately clean, and it looks spacious, although you may still have to wait for a table. Service is quick and friendly. *1842 Pembina Hwy., tel. 204/275–2294. No reservations. Dress: casual. AE, DC, MC, V. $*

**Homer's.** This good-time, downtown place, with a definite Mediterranean atmosphere, has been one of the city's favorite Greek restaurants for more than 15 years. Greek specialties include roast leg of lamb and moussaka, but Homer's is also famous for ribs, steak, seafood, pasta, and fresh hot bread. In the summer ask to be seated outdoors on the patio. *520 Ellice Ave., tel. 204/788–4858. Reservations advised. Dress: casual. AE, DC, MC, V. $*

**Kelekis.** This north-end shrine has purveyed legendary burgers, hot dogs, and fries for more than 60 years. Decor includes a photo montage of family history and autographed photos of celebrities. Breakfast, lunch, and dinner are served daily. *1100 Main St., tel. 204/582–1786. No reservations. Dress: casual. No credit cards. $*

**Mandarin.** The Sargent Avenue Mandarin is a crowded, 12-table, west-side place with unique and reasonably exotic northern Chinese dishes. Complete Gourmet Delight Dinners include soup, dumplings, entrées, and dessert. Wine is the only alcohol served. The River Mandarin, a spin-off, has a slightly different menu, a calmer pace, and a full liquor license. *Mandarin, 613 Sargent Ave., tel. 204/775–7819; River Mandarin, 252 River Ave., tel. 204/284–8963. Reservations advised. Dress: casual. AE, MC, V. $*

**Lodging** Highly recommended lodgings in each price category are indicated by a star ★.

| Category | Cost* |
|----------|-------|
| $$$$ | over $150 |
| $$$ | $75–$150 |
| $$ | $50–$75 |
| $ | under $50 |

*All prices are for a standard double room, excluding taxes.*

**Lodging**  **Holiday Inn Airport/West.** This bright and sumptuous modern prop-
★ erty is located on the Trans-Canada Highway's western approach to Winnipeg, near the airport, racetrack, and shopping areas. Rooms

are large, with modern earthtone furnishings. Executive suites, decorated in blue and green, are a bit fancier than standard units. The atrium is a lush setting for the pool and poolside lounge. *2520 Portage Ave., R3J 3T6, tel. 204/885–4478 or 800/465–4329, fax 204/ 831–5734. 210 rooms. Facilities: 2 restaurants, lounge, indoor pool, sauna, exercise room. AE, DC, MC, V. $$$*

**Holiday Inn Crowne Plaza.** Winnipeg's largest hotel, this Holiday Inn is 17 stories high and connects to the Convention Centre. Rooms, having recently undergone a renovation, are decorated in pastels and have pleasant modern furnishings—some rooms overlook the skylighted pool. Ticker's lobby bar is a lively spot for a rendezvous. *350 St. Mary Ave., R3C 3J2, tel. 204/942–0551 or 800/465–4329, fax 204/943–8702. 406 rooms; no-smoking rooms available. Facilities: 3 restaurants, lounge, cabaret, indoor and outdoor pools, sauna, whirlpool, exercise room. AE, DC, MC, V. $$$*

**Hotel Fort Garry.** Built in 1913 and known far and wide as the Grand Castle, the old railroad hotel has been completely renovated and has resumed its role as one of Winnipeg's gathering places. Located on the south edge of downtown, near Union Station, the hotel and its hushed spacious lobby are furnished with inviting armchairs and original marble, brass, and crystal finishes. Large guest rooms still have classic, dark wood furnishings and floral wallpapers. *222 Broadway, R3C 0R3, tel. 204/942–8251 or 800/665–8088, fax 204/ 956–2351. 246 rooms. Facilities: 2 restaurants, lounge, cabaret. AE, DC, MC, V. $$$*

★ **Place Louis Riel.** This luxury-class bargain is a converted apartment building that has 255 contemporary suites with living rooms, dining areas, and fully equipped kitchens. Though all rooms are up-to-date, the suites on the upper floors facing west are preferred because of their view of the Parliament Building. The supreme downtown location—adjacent to Eaton Place mall—is only one of the hotel's highlights. *190 Smith St., R3C 1J8, tel. 204/947–6961; in Canada, 800/665–0569; fax 204/947–3029. 255 suites; no-smoking suites available. Facilities: restaurant/lounge, free parking. AE, DC, MC, V. $$$*

**Travelodge Hotel Downtown Winnipeg.** Positioned at the low end of the expensive range, this high-rise venture of Canada's oldest budget chain is in a strategically desirable location, next to the bus depot and adjacent to the Bay and Winnipeg Art Gallery. Rooms on the south side look out on the Legislative Building, and north-side rooms overlook the city. Guest rooms have subdued modern furnishings in either neutral or pastel colors. *360 Colony St., R3B 2P3, tel. 204/786–7011 or 800/661–9563, fax 204/772–1443. 157 rooms; no-smoking rooms available. Facilities: restaurant, indoor pool, whirlpool. AE, DC, MC, V. $$$*

★ **Westin Hotel Winnipeg.** The top luxury hotel is located near Winnipeg's hub—Portage and Main streets—and is connected by the skywalk to office buildings and Portage Place Mall. The 21st-floor rooftop indoor pool makes a dramatic setting for a swim. Chimes offers a contemporary setting for light meals. Other restaurants include the elegant Velvet Glove Dining Room, and Café Express for quick meals at affordable prices. *2 Lombard Pl., R3B 0Y3, tel. 204/957–1350 or 800/228–3000, fax 204/956–1791. 350 rooms; no-smoking rooms available. Facilities: 3 restaurants, lounge, indoor pool, sauna, whirlpool, fitness center. AE, DC, MC, V. $$$*

★ **Charter House.** Half the refurbished rooms in this five-story low-rise on the south side of downtown have balconies. Furnishings are contemporary motel style, and the atmosphere is quite friendly. The Rib Room is a popular, moderately priced place for dinner. *330 York Ave., R3C 0N9, tel. 204/942–0101; in Manitoba, 204/942–0101* *or 800/782–0175, fax 204/956–0685. 90 rooms; no-smoking rooms available. Facilities: 2 restaurants, lounge, pool. AE, DC, MC, V. $$*

**Gordon Downtowner Motor Hotel.** There's nothing fancy here, but it's a good deal on the edge of downtown, a block from the Portage Place mall. Most rooms are decorated in dusty rose with gray carpeting. Two-room suites, modernly furnished, are the best bargains. *330 Kennedy St., R3B 2M6, tel. 204/943–5581. 40 rooms. Facilities: restaurant, pub, free parking. AE, DC, MC, V. $$*

**Journey's End.** This south-side lodging is a reliable choice. The rooms are an adequate size and are furnished in contemporary style, with rose or beige carpets, dusty rose and earthtone accessories. There is no charge for local phone calls, and morning coffee is free. *3109 Pembina Hwy., R3T 4R6, tel. 204/269–7390 or 800/668–4200, fax 204/261–7565. 80 rooms. AE, DC, MC, V. $$*

**Marlborough Inn.** This ornate, 1914 Gothic structure in the Financial District has vaulted ceilings and a stained-glass window, and is home to Joanna's Café and Victor's (*see* Dining, *above*). The public areas and guest rooms have been recently renovated. The lounge provides an intimate setting for guests. In the spacious lobby, with its marble floors, high ceilings, and wood paneling, there are soft and comfortable sofas. *331 Smith St., R3B 2G9, tel. 204/942–6411, 204/942–2017, or 800/667–7666, fax 204/942–2017. 121 rooms. Facilities: 2 restaurants, lounge. AE, DC, MC, V. $$*

**Assiniboine Gordon Inn on the Park.** This two-story hotel and motor inn is adjacent to a park on the west side, not far from the airport. Rooms are modern and large, albeit somewhat overwrought with masculine dark wood and bold designs. *1975 Portage Ave., R3J 0J9, tel. 204/888–4806. 48 rooms. Facilities: restaurant, lounge, disco. AE, MC, V. $*

## The Arts and Nightlife

The Arts
*Theater*
One of Canada's most acclaimed regional theaters, the **Manitoba Theatre Centre**, produces serious plays from many sources on the 785-seat **Mainstage** (174 Market Ave., Winnipeg, tel. 204/942–6537) and more experimental work in the **MTC Warehouse Theatre** (140 Rupert Ave., Winnipeg, tel. 204/942–6537). The **Prairie Theatre Exchange** focuses on local playwrights in an attractive facility in the Portage Place mall (Portage Ave. and Carlton St., Winnipeg, tel. 204/942–5483).

*Music and Dance*
Winnipeg's principal venue for serious music, dance, and pop concerts is the magnificent 2,263-seat Centennial Concert Hall in the **Manitoba Centennial Centre** (555 Main St., Winnipeg, tel. 204/956–1360). From September to mid-May it is the home of the **Winnipeg Symphony Orchestra** (tel. 204/949–3999); the **Royal Winnipeg Ballet** (tel. 204/956–2792 or 800/667–4792) performs there in October, December, March, and May; and the **Manitoba Opera** (tel. 204/942–7479) presents three operas a year—in November, February, and May. Throughout the year, pop concerts take place at the center.

The **Winnipeg Art Gallery** (300 Memorial Blvd., tel. 204/786–6641) features jazz, blues, chamber music, and contemporary groups. For contemporary dance and new music, check out **Le Rendez-Vous** (768 av. Tache, tel. 204/233–9214 or 204/237–7692) in St. Boniface. Other performance spaces include **Pantages Playhouse Theatre** (180 Market Ave. E, tel. 204/986–3003) and the **Winnipeg Convention Centre** (375 York Ave., tel. 204/956–1720).

*Film* In Winnipeg, the best places to find imports, art films, oldies, and midnight cult classics are at **Cinémathèque** (100 Arthur St., Winnipeg, tel. 204/942–6795) and **Cinema 3** (585 Ellice Ave., Winnipeg, tel. 204/783–1097). The **WAG** (Winnipeg Art Gallery, 300 Memorial Blvd., Winnipeg, tel. 204/786–6641) also has a cinema series.

*Nightlife* **Hy's Steak Loft** (216 Kennedy St., Winnipeg, tel. 204/942–1000) is
*Bars and Clubs* convenient for cocktails and has a late-evening piano bar. A most convincingly British pub in the Exchange District is **The King's Head** (120 King St., Winnipeg, tel. 204/957–1479).

*Casinos* Play blackjack, baccarat, la boule, and roulette at the Crystal Casino (7th Floor, Hotel Fort Garry, 222 Broadway Ave., Winnipeg, tel. 204/957–2600), daily.

*Comedy* Try **Rumors Comedy Club** (2025 Corydon Ave., Winnipeg, tel. 204/488–4520) or the **Comedy Oasis** (531 St. Mary's Rd., Winnipeg, tel. 204/231–1463), just for laughs.

*Music* Country-and-western music fans flock to Winnipeg's **Golden Nugget** (1155 Main St., Winnipeg, tel. 204/589–6308) and the **Palomino Club** (1133 Portage Ave., Winnipeg, tel. 204/772–0454). The hardest-rocking places in town are the **Spectrum** (176 Fort St., Winnipeg, tel. 204/943–6487) and the **Albert** (48 Albert St., Winnipeg, tel. 204/943–8750). A more sedate dance floor comes alive after 9 PM in **Windows Lounge** in the Sheraton Winnipeg (161 Donald St., Winnipeg, tel. 204/942–5300).

# Regina

Regina was originally dubbed Pile O'Bones, in reference to the remnants left by years of buffalo hunting, but it was renamed after the Latin title of Queen Victoria, the reigning monarch in 1883. It was at this time that the railroad arrived and the city became the capital of the Northwest Territories. The Mounties made it their headquarters. When the province of Saskatchewan was formed in 1905, Regina was chosen as its capital. At the beginning of the 20th century, immigrants from the British Isles, Eastern Europe, and the Far East rushed in to claim parcels of river-fed prairie land for $1 per lot. Oil and potash were discovered in the 1950s and 1960s, and Regina became a major agricultural and industrial distribution center as well as the head office of the world's largest grain-handling cooperative.

The centerpiece of this city of 185,000 is Wascana Centre, created by expanding meager Wascana Creek into the broad Wascana Lake and surrounding it with 2,000 acres of parkland. This unique multipurpose site contains the city's major museums, the Saskatchewan legislature, the University of Regina campus, and all the amenities of a big-city park and forest preserve.

## Important Addresses and Numbers

*Tourist* **Tourism Regina** (Box 3355, Regina, Sask. S4P 3H1, tel. 306/789–
*Information* 5099) has an information center on the Trans-Canada Highway (Rte. 1) on the eastern approach to the city and is open Victoria Day–Labor Day, 8–6; Labor Day–Victoria Day, weekdays 8:30–4:30. The **Tourism Saskatchewan** information center (Saskatchewan Dr. and Rose St., tel. 306/787–2300) is open weekdays 8–7, Saturday 10–4.

**Emergencies** Dial 911 for emergency **fire, police,** or **ambulance service.**

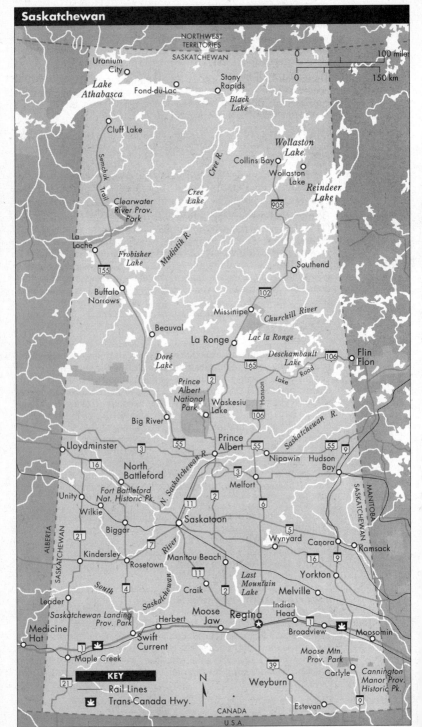

# Saskatchewan

NORTHWEST TERRITORIES

SASKATCHEWAN

0 — 100 miles
0 — 150 km

Uranium City

*Lake Athabasca*

Fond-du-Lac

Stony Rapids

*Black Lake*

Cluff Lake

*Cree R.*

*Wollaston Lake*

Collins Bay

Wollaston Lake

*Reindeer Lake*

Semchuk Trail

Clearwater River Prov. Park

*Cree Lake*

905

La Loche

*Frobisher Lake*

*Mudjatik R.*

155

Southend

Buffalo Narrows

102

Beauval

Missinipe

*Churchill River*

Doré Lake

La Ronge

*Lac la Ronge*

*Deschambault Lake*

106

Flin Flon

165

Hanson Lake Road

Prince Albert National Park

2

Big River

Waskesiu Lake

106

MANITOBA

SASKATCHEWAN

Prince Albert

*Saskatchewan R.*

Lloydminster

55

55

55

Nipawin

Hudson Bay

9

16

North Battleford

3

*N. Saskatchewan R.*

Melfort

3

Fort Battleford Nat. Historic Pk.

11

2

6

Unity

Saskatoon

Wilkie

5

Biggar

Wynyard

Canora

16

Kamsack

ALBERTA

SASKATCHEWAN

21

Kindersley

7

*River*

Manitou Beach

9

Rosetown

11

Yorkton

4

*South*

Craik

2

Melville

Leader

*Saskatchewan*

*Last Mountain Lake*

Indian Head

*Saskatchewan Landing Prov. Park*

Herbert

Moose Jaw

Regina

1

Broadview

Moosomin

Medicine Hat

Swift Current

*Moose Mtn. Prov. Park*

Maple Creek

39

Carlyle

*Cannington Manor Prov. Historic Pk.*

21

**KEY**

N

Weyburn

9

— Rail Lines

Trans-Canada Hwy.

Estevan

CANADA

U.S.A.

**Hospitals**  Emergency rooms are located at **Regina General Hospital** (1140 14th Ave., tel. 306/359–4444), **Plains Health Centre** (4500 Wascana Pkwy., tel. 306/584–6211), and **Pasqua Hospital** (4101 Dewdney Ave., tel. 306/359–2222).

**Late-night Pharmacy**  **Bi-Rite Drugs** locations (Northgate Mall, tel. 306/777–8010; Broad St. and 14th Ave., tel. 306/757–8100; Gordon Rd. and Albert St., tel. 306/777–8040; and Victoria Square, tel. 306/777–8060) are open until midnight.

## Arriving and Departing by Plane

**Regina Airport,** located 8 kilometers (5 miles) southwest of downtown, is served by Air Canada, Canadian Airlines International, and several Canadian commuter airlines. Cabs charge about $7 for the 10- to 15-minute ride downtown.

## Getting Around

**By Bus**  **Regina Transit's** (tel. 306/777–7433) 19 bus routes serve the metropolitan area daily except Sunday. The fare is $1.10 for adults, 65¢ for students, 55¢ for children 5–14.

**By Taxi**  Taxis are easy to find outside major hotels, or they can be summoned by phone. Call **Regina Cabs** (tel. 306/543–3333), **Capital Cab** (tel. 306/781–7777), or **Co-op Taxis** (tel. 306/586–6555).

## Guided Tours

**Classic Carriage Service** (tel. 306/543–9155) offers horse-drawn carriage rides around the city during summer and horse-drawn sleigh and hayrides around Wascana Park during winter. Both tours accommodate 15–20 people and cost $60–$75 per hour.

## Exploring Regina

*Numbers in the margin correspond to points of interest on the Regina map.*

Streets in Regina run north–south; avenues, east–west. The most important north–south artery is Albert Street (Rte. 6); Victoria Avenue is the main east–west thoroughfare. The Trans-Canada Highway (Route 1) bypasses the city to the south and east.

**❶**  Begin at the northwest corner of **Wascana Centre,** at the **Royal Saskatchewan Museum.** A time line traces local history from prehistory through the dinosaur era to today. The **Earth Sciences Gallery** depicts 2 billion years of Saskatchewan geological history, while the **First Nations Gallery** highlights aspects of native life and history. The museum is home to Canada's first animated dinosaur, "Megamunch." *College Ave. and Albert St., tel. 306/787–2815. Admission free. Open May–Sept. 2, daily 9–8:30; Sept. 3–Apr., daily 9–4:30.*

Continue south on Albert Street past **Speakers Corner** where, as in London's Hyde Park, free speech is volubly expressed. Turn left on

**❷**  Legislative Drive, to the quasi-Versailles-style **Legislative Building.** "The Ledge" was built in 1908–1912, with local Tyndall stone on the exterior and an interior composed of 34 types of marble from all over the world. As you tour the Legislative Assembly Chamber, note the huge picture of Queen Elizabeth—a reminder that Canada retains a technical allegiance to the monarchy. *Legislature Dr., tel. 306/787–*

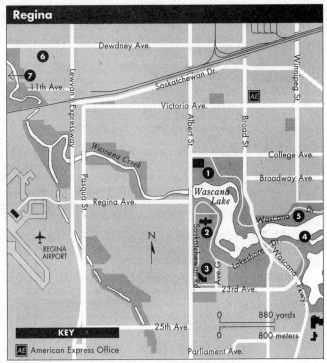

*5357. Admission free. Open Victoria Day–Labor Day, daily 8–9; winter, daily 8–5. Free tours leave on ½-hr.*

❸ Take Saskatchewan Road (west of the Legislature) south to the new location of the **MacKenzie Art Gallery,** which displays 19th- and 20th-century European art, and Canadian historical and contemporary works, with a special emphasis on western Canadian art. The popular Prairie Artists Series allows emerging Saskatchewan artists to display recent work. For three nights a week in August, a stage becomes the courtroom setting for "The Trial of Louis Riel." Riel led rebellions of the Métis against the new Canadian government in the 1870s and 1880s and was tried in Regina (and ultimately hanged) for treason. *3475 Albert St., tel. 306/522–4242. Admission free. Open Fri.–Tues. 11–6, Wed. and Thurs. 11–10.*

❹ Continuing along Saskatchewan Road, turn north on Avenue G and then east on Lakeshore Drive to the **Wascana Waterfowl Park Display Ponds,** a boardwalk constructed over a marsh and accompanied by display panels that help identify the more than 60 breeds of migrating waterfowl found here. *Lakeshore Dr., tel. 306/522–3661. Admission free. Open daily 9–9. Guided tours available (if there is a group) June–Sept., daily at 3.*

❺ Return to Broad Street (Wascana Parkway), cross the bridge to Wascana Drive, and head toward Winnipeg Street and the **Saskatchewan Science Centre,** housed in the refurbished City of Regina powerhouse, now called the Powerhouse of Discovery. Hands-on exhibits encourage visitors to build bubbles, juggle hot-air balloons, make voice prints, and take apart human bodies. Demonstrations of biological, geological, and astronomical phenomena take place on the hour. Located in the complex is the **Kramer IMAX Theatre,** which screens breathtaking films several times daily on a five-story screen. *Science center: Winnipeg St. and Wascana Dr., tel. 306/352–5811. Admission: $5.50 adults; $3.75 senior citizens 60 and over and youths 6–18 years, children under 6 free. Open May–June, Mon.–Thurs. 9–6, Fri. 9–8, Sat. 10–8, Sun. 10–6; July–Aug., daily 10–8; Sept.–Apr., Tues–Fri. 9–4, Sat. noon–8, Sun. noon–6. Closed Mon. holidays. IMAX admission: $6.50 adults, $4.50 senior citizens and children 6–18, $3 children under 6. Call 306/522-IMAX for showtimes and details.*

**Time Out**    The Edgewater Café at the Science Centre serves fine French cuisine.

A car or bike will be necessary to continue this tour. Return to Broad Street and take it north to Dewdney Avenue, then head west

**❻** to the **Government House.** Between 1891 and 1945 this was the lavish home of Saskatchewan's lieutenant governors. *4607 Dewdney Ave., tel. 306/787–5726. Admission free. Open Oct.–Mar., Tues.–Fri. 1–4, Sun. 1–5; Apr.–June and Sept., Tues.–Sat. 1–4, Sun. 1–5; July and Aug., Tues.–Fri. 1–4, Sun. 1–5.*

**❼** Continue west on 11th Avenue to the **Royal Canadian Mounted Police Training Academy,** the Mounties' only training center. Visitors can tour the grounds and nondenominational RCMP Chapel, a converted cookhouse originally built in 1883 and considered Regina's oldest building. Try to arrive about 12:45 weekdays for the stirring Sergeant Major's parade on Parade Square (in Drill Hall during winter and inclement weather). In July and August, the spectacular Sunset Retreat Ceremony takes place Tuesday evening; try to arrive by 6:30. On the grounds is the **Centennial Museum,** featuring exhibits and mementos of the Mounties (originally the North West Mounted Police). The order's proud history is revealed by weaponry, uniforms, photos, and oddities, such as Sitting Bull's rifle case and tobacco pouch. *11th Ave. W, tel. 306/780–5838. Admission free. Open June–mid-Sept., daily 8–6:45; mid-Sept.–May, daily 10–4:45.*

### Other Points of Interest

**Cannington Manor Historic Park,** just south of Moose Mountain Provincial Park (*see* National and Provincial Parks, *below*), preserves the 1880s lifestyles of this experimental aristocratic Victorian settlement. Abandoned after 15 years, what remains to be seen are the original manor house, a church, shops, and a museum housed in the original schoolhouse. *Hwy. 603, 16 km (10 mi) northeast of Manor, tel. 306/787–9573. Donations accepted. Open late May–early Sept., daily 10–6.*

**Moose Jaw,** Saskatchewan's third-largest city (population 35,000), is a prosperous railroad and industrial center, renowned as a wide-open Roaring '20s haven for American gangsters. It is said that Al Capone visited here from Chicago, on the old Soo Line train. Today, Moose Jaw's most prominent citizen is Mac the Moose, an immense sculpture that greets travelers alongside the visitor information center (Rte. 1 east of Rte. 2, tel. 306/692–6414) on the Trans-Canada Highway.

A stop at the information center can direct you to other Moose Jaw attractions, including the **Moose Jaw Zoo** (7th Ave. SW, tel. 306/691–0111), with more than 50 North American species and exotic animals, in addition to the amusement park, surrounded by a log fortress. The **Western Development Museum** (50 Diefenbaker Dr., tel. 306/693–6556), which focuses on air, land, water, and rail transportation, presents the "Snowbirds Gallery" devoted to Canada's air demonstration team, the Snowbirds, who are stationed at the nearby Armed Forces base. **The Moose Jaw Art Museum** (Crescent Park, Athabasca St. and Langdon Crescent, tel. 306/692–3144), displays Indian art and small farm implements. While there, pick up *A Walking Tour of Downtown Moose Jaw* ($1.50), a guide to the city's notable and notorious landmarks. As you drive around Moose Jaw notice the giant historical murals that cover the exterior walls of many downtown buildings.

## National and Provincial Parks

**Grasslands National Park** is located between Val Marie and Killdeer in southwestern Saskatchewan. The Frenchman River Valley, part of which is within the Grasslands, was the first portion of mixed grass prairie in North America to be set aside as a park, and is famous for strange land formations and badlands. Colonies of black-tailed prairie dogs are the most numerous of the many animal species found here. Interpretive and visitor services are limited at this time. Tent camping is permitted, and electrical hook-ups are provided; all sites cost $10 per night. *Box 150, Val Marie, Sask. S0N 2T0, tel. 306/298–2257. Park office open June–Aug., daily 8–6; Sept.–May, weekdays 8–4:30. Information center open late May–early Sept., daily 8–6.*

**Moose Mountain Provincial Park** is 401 square kilometers (155 square miles) of rolling poplar and birch forest that forms a natural refuge for moose and elk and a wide variety of birds. A 24-kilometer (15-mile) gravel road accesses moose and elk grazing areas (best times: early morning and early evening). The park supplements wildlife experiences with beaches, golf, tennis, and riding horses. There are 330 campsites available; ⅓ have electric hook-ups. The Kenosee Inn (Kenosee Village, S0C 2S0, tel. 306/577–2099) is a 30-room accommodation on the park grounds. *Hwys. 9 and 209, tel. 306/577–2131; 306/577–2144 for camping reservations. Admission: $6/day per car, senior citizen drivers free. Camping fees: $14 per night w/electricity; $12 w/o electricity. Open daily.*

A 50-kilometer (31-mile) drive north on Highway 4, from Swift Current, will bring you to **Saskatchewan Landing Provincial Park** (tel. 306/375–2434). The 54-square-kilometer (21-square-mile) natural preserve is situated at the point where Indians and pioneers forded the South Saskatchewan River en route to northern Saskatchewan. Campsites, picnic facilities, and an interpretive center are on hand. *Hwy. 4, tel. 306/375–2434. Admission: $6/day per car, senior citizen drivers free. Camping fees: mid-Sept.–mid-May, $8 w/electricity; $7 w/o electricity; mid-May–mid-Sept., $14 w/electricity; $12 w/o electricity. Open daily.*

## What to See and Do with Children

**RCMP Training Academy** and **Centennial Museum** (*see* Exploring Regina, *above*).

**Royal Saskatchewan Museum** (*see* Exploring Regina, *above*).

**Saskatchewan Science Centre** (*see* Exploring Regina, *above*).

**Tee Off Park.** This is a family-fun complex with year-round indoor miniature golf and, between June and September, a walk-through maze and kiddieland rides. *3310 Pasqua St., Regina, tel. 306/586–4585. Admission: $3 golf, $3 maze, $1.50–$3 for rides. Open weekdays 3–9, weekends 1–9.*

**Maxwell's Amusements.** Go-karts, miniature golf, bumper boats, waterslides, and a games alley attract children and adults by the hordes. *Hwy. 1 E, tel. 306/789–2585 or 306/569–8333. Admission: free, rides cost extra. Open June–Aug., daily 11–10; Apr., May, Sept., and Oct., reduced hrs.*

## Shopping

**Malls**  Cornwall Centre (11th Ave. and Saskatchewan Dr.), located downtown, is an indoor mall with more than 100 shops, including Eaton's and Sears. Indoor passages connect to the Galleria (11th Ave. and Saskatchewan Dr.), an indoor mall with more than 50 stores. Other major malls include Victoria Square Mall (223 Victoria Ave. E), Northgate Mall (Albert St. N and 9th Ave. N), with more than 80 stores, and Southland Mall (Albert St. S and Gordon Rd.), which also has more than 80 stores.

**Art and Antiques**  The **Strathdee Shoppes** (Dewdney Ave. and Cornwall St.) consist of arts, crafts, antiques, and specialty stores—plus a food court. The **Antique Mall** (1175 Rose St., tel. 306/525–9688) encompasses 28 antiques, art, and collectibles sellers. Also featuring arts and crafts are **Patchworks** (3026 13th Ave., tel. 306/522–0664), **Sarah's Corner** (1853 Hamilton St., tel. 306/565–2200), and **Affinity's Antiques** (1178 Albert St., tel. 306/757–4265).

## Sports

**Participant Sports**  **Wascana Place** (2900 Wascana Dr., Regina, tel. 306/522–3661) provides maps of the many jogging, biking, and hiking trails in **Wascana Centre.** The Devonian Pathway—8 kilometers (about 5 miles) of paved trails that follow Wascana Creek and pass through six city parks—is a favorite of walkers, joggers, and cyclists. Rent bikes within Wascana Centre at the **Wascana Pool** (2211 College Ave., Regina, tel. 306/777–7921).

*Bicycling and Jogging*

*Health and Fitness Clubs*  The **Regina Sportplex & Lawson Aquatic Centre** (1717 Elphinstone St., Regina, tel. 306/777–7156 for fieldhouse; tel. 306/777–7323 for aquatic center) encompasses a pool and diving well, a 200-meter track, tennis and badminton courts, weight rooms, a sauna, a whirlpool, and drop-in aerobic and aquacize sessions.

**Spectator Sports**  Check out this incredibly popular local sport at the **Curlodrome** (Exhibition Park, Lewvan Expwy. and 11th Ave., Regina, tel. 306/352–9809).

*Curling*

*Football*  The **Saskatchewan Roughriders** (tel. 306/525–2181) of the Canadian Football League play their home games at Taylor Field.

*Hockey*  The **Regina Pats** play other Western Hockey League (minor league) teams in the **Agridome** (Exhibition Park, Lewvan Expwy. and 11th Ave., Regina, tel. 306/522–5604).

*Horse Racing*  **Queensbury Downs Raceway** (Exhibition Park, Lewvan Expwy. and 11th Ave., Regina, tel. 306/781–9310) hosts Thoroughbred or standardbred racing in the summer and televised racing year-round.

**Dining and Lodging**

For price categories, *see* Winnipeg Dining and Lodging, *above*.

**Dining**
★

**Mieka's.** Chef Mieka Wiens learned her craft at the Cordon Bleu; her art-filled walls and sleek contemporary furniture certainly reflect outside influence. The menus of this downtown café change with the season but always include imaginative combinations of fresh seafood and meat, local produce, spices, and liquors. There are also creative sandwiches, unusual salads, and a terrific cheesecake. *1810 Smith St., tel. 306/522–6700. Reservations advised. Dress: casual. DC, MC, V. Closed Sun. $$$*

**Bartleby's.** This good-time downtown "dining emporium and gathering place" is a veritable museum of western memorabilia, musical instruments, and old-time carnival games. Victorian lampshades and heavy leather armchairs further convey the whimsical tone. Karioke music at night adds a bit of fun. The menu features big sandwiches and western beef, especially prime rib. *1920 Broad St., tel. 306/565–0040. Reservations advised. Dress: casual. AE, DC, MC, V. $$*

**C.C. Lloyd's.** Locals esteem the fine service and casual elegance of the dining room in the downtown Chelton Inn. The decor evokes the atmosphere of Manhattan circa 1930, and the menu features such international classics as rack of lamb, chicken en croûte dijonnaise, fillet of beef Madeira, shrimp Provençal, and a variety of tasty steaks. *1907 11th Ave., tel. 306/569–4650. Reservations advised. Jacket advised. AE, MC, V. $$*

**Brewsters.** The copper kettle and shiny fermentation tanks are proudly prominent in Saskatchewan's first brew pub. This full mash brewery has 11 in-house concoctions on tap, as well as a large selection of imports and domestic beers, wine, and spirits. The menu consists of pub snacks and a full-service menu. *Victoria East Plaza, 1832 Victoria Ave. E, tel. 306/761–1500. No reservations. Dress: casual. AE, MC, V. $*

**Simply Delicious.** Everything is homemade in this small country-style café. Specialties include cinnamon buns, fresh pies, chicken noodle and vegetable soups, several salads, and specialty coffees. *826 Victoria Ave., tel. 306/352–4929. No reservations. Dress: casual. No credit cards. $*

**Lodging**
★

**The Delta Regina.** This modern downtown property has a dramatic multilevel, sun-filled lobby that's graced by abundant foliage and a charming waterfall. A second-floor oasis is the perfect setting for such water-theme pastimes as a soothing soak in the whirlpool or, for the children, a dip in either the kiddie or standard pool. Rooms are airy and modernly furnished in light colors and dusty rose. *1818 Victoria Ave., S4P 0R1, tel. 306/569–1666 or 800/268–1133, fax 306/525–3550. 251 rooms. Facilities: 2 restaurants, lounge, pub, underground heated parking, indoor pool, sauna, whirlpool, games room. AE, DC, MC, V. $$$*

**Hotel Saskatchewan Radisson Plaza.** This one-time railway hotel built in 1927 was recently restored to its former grandeur. Rooms are decorated in an early 1930s style, with lots of wood and lace curtains. Every afternoon in the Victoria Room, high tea is served, and fine dining is offered every evening in the Cortlandt Hall Dining Room. For a light lunch or evening cocktails visit the cozy and casually elegant Monarch Lounge. *2125 Victoria Ave., S4P 0S3, tel. 306/522–7691 or 800/333–3333, fax 306/757–5521. 215 rooms; no-smoking rooms available. Facilities: 2 restaurants, lounge, indoor spa pool, steam room, health club. AE, DC, MC, V. $$$*

**Ramada Hotel.** The tallest building in Saskatchewan, Regina's newest and most luxurious hotel rises 25 stories over the city and is attached to the Saskatchewan Trade & Convention Centre. Rooms are furnished in subtle pastels and have modern amenities. The pool has a three-story waterslide, and there's a Tourism Saskatchewan information center in the lobby. *1919 Saskatchewan Dr., S4P 4H2, tel. 306/525–5255 or 800/268–8998, fax 306/781–7188. 255 rooms; no-smoking rooms available. Facilities: 2 restaurants, lounge, indoor pool, waterslide, whirlpool. AE, DC, MC, V. $$$*

**Regina Inn.** A plant-filled lobby welcomes you into this modern downtown hotel, where all the guest rooms—decorated with blues, grays, and browns—have balconies overlooking either Broad or Victoria streets. On the ground floor is the Lauderdale Bar and Grill, the local hot spot. *1975 Broad St. at Victoria Ave., S4P 1Y2, tel. 306/525–6767 or 800/667–8162, fax 306/352–1858. 237 rooms. Facilities: 2 restaurants, lounge, nightclub, indoor parking, 2 outdoor hot tubs, weight room. AE, DC, MC, V. $$$*

**Regina Travelodge Hotel.** The hotel's convenient location, on Regina's main thoroughfare and close to downtown, is the biggest draw for its guests. The other feature is the well-known waterslide complex on the property. In the evenings the pub, the Blarney Stone, is a fun place to grab a beer or soda. *4177 Albert St., S4S 3R6, tel. 306/586–3443 or 800/255–3050, fax 306/586–9311. 200 rooms. Facilities: restaurant, pub, indoor pool and waterslide complex, hot tub. AE, DC, MC, V. $$$*

**Chelton Inn.** This property, situated in the heart of downtown, is one of Regina's biggest bargains. The inn is an older property, but its rooms have been modernized and are downright huge. Contemporary, light wood furnishings match the earthtones that are used in the dry goods and fabrics. Service is particularly friendly. The cuisine in C.C. Lloyd's (*see* Dining, *above*) is among the best in town. *1907 11th Ave., S4P 0J2, tel. 306/569–4600 or 800/667–9922, fax 306/569–3531. 56 rooms. Facilities: restaurant, coffee shop, lounge. AE, DC, MC, V. $$*

★ **Landmark Inn.** This three-story property on the south side of town has large, modern rooms and a unique indoor-outdoor waterslide. Rooms, decorated in pastel greens and white, are light and airy and have modern furnishings. *4150 Albert St. (Hwy. 6), S4S 3R8, tel. 306/586–5363; in Saskatchewan, 800/667–9811; elsewhere in Canada, 800/667–8191; fax 306/586–0901. 188 rooms; no-smoking rooms available. Facilities: restaurant, lounge, indoor pool, waterslide, sauna, whirlpool, games room. AE, DC, MC, V. $$*

★ **Relax Inn South West.** This is a dependable accommodation, with average-size, well-furnished rooms, and Saskatchewan's largest private indoor pool. *4025 Albert St. (Hwy. 6), S4S 3R6, tel. 306/586–2663 or 800/667–3529, fax 306/584–1345. 105 rooms. Facilities: indoor pool. AE, DC, MC, V. $*

## The Arts and Nightlife

**The Arts** On a theater-in-the-round stage inside the old Regina City Hall, the
*Theater* **Globe Theatre** (1801 Scarth St., Regina, tel. 306/525–9553) offers classics and contemporary Saskatchewan works from October to April. **Regina Little Theatre** (Regina Performing Arts Centre, 1077 Angus St., Regina, tel. 306/352–5535 or 306/543–7292) presents lighthearted original productions.

*Music and* Two theaters in the **Saskatchewan Centre of the Arts** (Wascana Cen-
*Dance* tre, 200 Lakeshore Dr., Regina, tel. 306/565–0404) are venues for the Regina Symphony, pop concerts, dance performances, and Broadway musicals and plays.

**Nightlife**

*Bars and Clubs* **Caper's,** in the Ramada Hotel (1919 Saskatchewan Dr., Regina, tel. 306/525–5255), is where local movers and shakers mingle with visitors from the convention center next door.

*Music* **The Pump** (641 Victoria Ave. E, tel. 306/522–0977) features Canadian and American country-and-western bands. **Delbert's** (1433 Hamilton St., tel. 306/757–ROCK) is known for high energy rock and roll. **Longbranch Saloon** (1400 McIntyre St., tel. 306/525–8336) specializes in country and western music.

## Excursion from Regina: Swift Current to Cypress Hills Provincial Park

West of Regina, the square townships and straight roads of the grain-belt prairie farms gradually give way to the arid rolling hills of the upland plains ranches.

The Trans-Canada Highway skirts the edge of the Missouri Coteau—glacial hills that divide the prairie from the dry western plain—on its way west to **Swift Current** (174 kilometers, or 108 miles). Swift Current (population 16,000), cultivates its western image during Frontier Days Regional Fair and Rodeo (*see* Festivals and Seasonal Events in Chapter 1). Further depicting Swift Current are the exhibits at the **Swift Current Museum,** where pioneer and Indian artifacts and exhibits of local natural history are displayed. *105 Chaplin St., tel. 306/778–2775. Admission free. Open July and Aug., daily 2–5 and 7–9; June and Sept.–mid-Oct., weekends and Mon. 2–5, Tues.–Fri. 7–9; mid-Oct.–May, Sun. and Mon. 2–5.*

A recent addition to Swift Current is the **Canadian Country Music Hall of Fame** with its portraits, memorabilia, and artifacts of North American country music. An art gallery features artwork on nature and western themes. *1100 Fifth Ave. NE, tel. 306/773–7854. Admission: $4 adults, $3 senior citizens, children under 13 free. Open summer, daily 9–9; winter, weekdays 9–5, weekends 9–7.*

Along the next 128-kilometer (80-mile) stretch of the Trans-Canada Highway, the road skirts the southern edge of the **Great Sand Hills.** These desertlike remnants of a huge glacial lake now abound with such native wildlife as pronghorn antelope, mule deer, coyote, jackrabbit, and kangaroo rats. Heading south on Highway 21 will bring you into **Maple Creek,** a self-styled "old cow town," with a number of preserved Old West storefronts. Saskatchewan's oldest museum, the **Old Timer's Museum,** features pictures and artifacts of Mounties, early ranchers, and Indians. *218 Jasper St., tel. 306/662–2474. Admission: $2 adults, 50¢ children, preschoolers free. Open June–Sept., daily 9–5; Oct., Apr., and May, weekdays 1–4.*

Drive south on Highway 21 for another 27 kilometers (17 miles) to **Cypress Hills Provincial Park,** which is open year-round. Cypress Hills consists of two sections, a Centre Block and a West Block, which are about 25 kilometers (16 miles) apart and separated by nonpark land. The larger West Block abuts the border with Alberta and is connected to Alberta's Cypress Hills Provincial Park. Within the Centre Block, the Cypress Hills plateau, rising more than 4,000 feet above sea level, is covered with spruce, aspen, and lodgepole pines that were erroneously identified as cypress by early European explorers. From Lookout Point you have a 50-mile-range (80-kilometer-range) view of Maple Creek and the hills beyond. In addition to the wildlife and flora that abound in the park, there is Cypress Four Seasons Resort (*see* Lodging, *below*), complete with a golf course, tennis courts, campgrounds, riding stables, and a full complement of winter sports. Maps are available at the Administrative Building near the park entrance. *Cypress Hills Provincial Park, Hwy. 21, tel. 306/662–4411. Admission: $6/day per car, senior citizen drivers free. Open daily.*

A rough gravel road connects the Cypress Hills Centre Block plateau with the West Block plateau. During wet weather, take Highway 21 north to Maple Creek and Highway 271 southwest to the West Block.

The two blocks share the same plant life, animal life, and scenic vistas, but the West Block also encompasses **Fort Walsh National Historic Park.** The original fort was built by the Mounties in 1875 to establish order between the "wolfers" (whiskey traders) and the Assiniboine Indians. Fort Walsh remained the center of local commerce until its abandonment in 1883. Today, free bus service is available between the **Visitor Reception Centre** and the reconstructed fort itself, Farwell's Trading Post, and a picnic area. No private vehicles are permitted beyond the parking area. *Ft. Walsh, Hwy. 271, 55 km (34 mi) southwest of Maple Creek, tel. 306/662–2645. Admission free. Open mid-May–mid-Oct., daily 9–5.*

**Dining**  For rates, *see* Winnipeg Dining and Lodging, *above.*

*Cypress Hills*  **Cypress Four Seasons Resort.** This resort is located within the Centre Block of Cypress Hills Provincial Park, and its restaurant is a bright and woodsy place with picture windows that overlook the forest. The standard Canadian fare is more successful than the Chinese dishes on the menu. *Box 1480, Maple Creek, tel. 306/662–4477. No reservations. Dress: casual. MC, V. $$*

*Swift Current*  **Wong's Kitchen.** This longtime area favorite features fine Canadian food and an even better Oriental menu: Dry garlic ribs are the star attraction. Count on live entertainment nightly. *Hwy. 1, S. Service Rd., tel. 306/773–6244. Reservations advised. Dress: casual. AE, MC, V. $$*

**Lodging**  **Cypress Four Seasons Resort.** It's not part of the Four Seasons chain,
*Cypress Hills*  but the rooms here are new, comfortable, modern, and right in the middle of a lodgepole pine forest. Either pastels or earthtones adorn the rooms, which are contemporary and have basic amenities. *Box 1480, Maple Creek, S0N 1N0, tel. 306/662–4477. 35 rooms; cabins and condos. Facilities: restaurant, lounge, indoor pool, whirlpool. MC, V. $$*

*Swift Current*  **Horseshoe Lodge.** It's conveniently situated along the Trans-Canada Highway service road, yet the rooms still have fine views of the surrounding countryside. The cocktail lounge is a popular meeting spot, and the restaurant features solid Canadian cooking. *Mobile Rte. 35, Hwy. 1E, S9H 3X6, tel. 306/773–4643. 49 rooms. Facilities: 2 restaurants, lounge, pool. AE, DC, MC, V. $*

# Saskatoon

Saskatchewan's largest city is Saskatoon (population 186,000), nicknamed "City of Bridges" because seven spans cross the South Saskatchewan River that cuts the city in half diagonally. Saskatoon was founded in 1882 when a group of Ontario Methodists were granted 200,000 acres to form a temperance colony. Teetotaling Methodists controlled only half the land, however, and eventually the influence of the other "half" turned the town "wet." The coming of the railroad in 1890 made it the major regional transportation hub, but during the 20th century it became known for its three major resources: potash, oil, and wheat. Saskatoon today is the high-tech hub of Saskatchewan's agricultural industry and is also home to the University of Saskatchewan—a major presence in all aspects of local life.

## Important Addresses and Numbers

**Tourist Information**    **Tourism Saskatoon** (310 Idylwyld Dr. N, Box 369, Saskatoon, Sask. S7K 3L3, tel. 306/242–1206) is open weekdays 8:30–5 year-round. In summer, information booths are set up at various points along the highway.

**Emergencies**    Dial 911 for **police, fire, ambulance, poison,** and **emergency** services.

**Hospitals**    Emergency rooms include **City Hospital** (Queen St. and 6th Ave. N, tel. 306/242–6681), **Royal University Hospital** (University Grounds, tel. 306/244–2323), and **St. Paul's Hospital** (1702 20th St. W, tel. 306/ 382–3220).

**Late-night Pharmacy**    **Shoppers Drug Mart** stores (2410 22nd St. W, tel. 306/382–5005; 610 Taylor St. E, at Broadway Ave., tel. 306/343–1608) are open until midnight.

## Arriving and Departing by Plane

**Saskatoon Airport,** 7 kilometers (4½ miles) northwest of downtown, is served by Canadian Airlines International, Air Canada, and Canadian commuter carriers. Taxis to the downtown area cost about $9.

## Getting Around

**By Bus**    **Saskatoon Transit** (tel. 306/975–3100) buses offer convenient service to points around the city. The fare is $1.10 for adults, 65¢ for students, 55¢ for children 5–12.

**By Taxi**    Taxis are plentiful, especially outside downtown hotels, but they are fairly expensive. For service, call **United Yellow Cab** (tel. 306/652– 2222), **Blueline Taxi** (tel. 306/653–3333), or **Saskatoon Radio Cab** (tel. 306/242–1221).

## Guided Tours

**W.W. Northcote River Cruises** (tel. 306/665–1818; tours run June– Aug., daily 10–8) depart on the hour for 11-kilometer (7-mile) tours of the South Saskatchewan River.

## Exploring Saskatoon

*Numbers in the margin correspond to points of interest on the Saskatoon map.*

Reasonably compact for a Western city, Saskatoon proper is easily accessible to drivers and cyclists. Idylwyld Drive divides the city into east and west; 22nd Street divides the city into north and south. The downtown area and the Spadina Crescent are located on the west side of the South Saskatchewan River. Begin exploring at  **Meewasin Valley Centre,** a small museum that traces Saskatoon history back to temperance-colony days. Meewasin is Cree for "beautiful valley," and this is a fitting place to embark upon the **Meewasin Valley Trail,** a 17-kilometer (10-mile) biking and hiking trail along

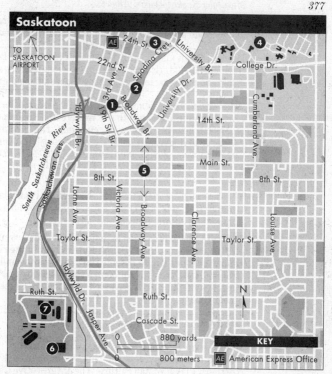

both banks of the beautiful South Saskatchewan River. *Meewasin Valley Centre, 402 3rd Ave. S, tel. 306/665–6888. Admission free. Open weekdays 9–5, weekends 10:30–5.*

**②** Follow Spadina Crescent north along the river and past the **Delta Bessborough** (*see* Lodging, *below*), the most prominent old building in the Saskatoon skyline. A few blocks farther north is the **③** **Ukrainian Museum of Canada,** which celebrates—through photos, costumes, textiles, and of course the famous *pysanky* (Easter eggs)—the rich history of the Ukrainian people who make up 10% of Saskatchewan's population. *910 Spadina Crescent E, tel. 306/244–3800. Admission: $2 adults, $1 senior citizens, 50¢ children. Open Mon.–Sat. 10–5, Sun. 1–5, and holidays.*

From Spadina Crescent, head east over the river via the University **④** Bridge to the **University of Saskatchewan,** which occupies a 2,550-acre site overlooking the river. The university grounds are among the most picturesque in Canada, and they house several museums and galleries including the Natural Sciences Museum, Little Stone School House, Museum of Antiquities, Biology Museum, and Gordon Snelgrove Gallery. A highlight is the **Right Hon. John G. Diefenbaker Centre** (tel. 306/966–8384; open weekdays 9:30–4:30 and weekends and holidays 12:30–5), a museum, art gallery, and working archives commemorating Canada's 13th prime minister. The center explores Diefenbaker's life and times. Two replica rooms represent the Privy Council Chamber and the prime minister's Ottawa office where he served in the late 1950s and early 1960s.

Exit the campus, head west on College Drive, and then pick up University Drive, lined with grand old homes. University Drive eventu-

**⑤** ally becomes **Broadway Avenue,** the city's oldest business district and location of more than 150 shops, restaurants, and a cinema.

**Time Out** Unpretentious and entirely too small, **Calories** (721 Broadway Ave., tel. 306/665–7991) is a crowded but delicious place to stop for cheesecakes and pastries, ice cream, sandwiches, and superb coffee.

**⑥** Take Broadway Avenue south to 8th Street; then head west to Lorne Avenue and south to the **Western Development Museum.** One of Saskatchewan's four such museums, the Saskatoon branch is called "1910 Boomtown" and re-creates early 20th-century life in the Canadian west. *2610 Lorne Ave. S, tel. 306/931–1910. Admission: $4 adults, $3.50 senior citizens, $1.50 children 5–12. Open summer, daily 9–5; winter, call for hours.*

**⑦** The museum is part of the **Saskatoon Prairieland Exhibition Grounds** (tel. 306/931–7149), a vast plot that encompasses space for agricultural shows, rodeos, and horse races.

To return to downtown Saskatoon, take the scenic route: Head north on Lorne Avenue, then west on Ruth Street to the river. Follow St. Henry Avenue, Taylor Street, Herman Avenue, and Saskatchewan Crescent past the fine old homes that overlook one of the prettier stretches of the South Saskatchewan River. Cross over the 19th Street Bridge.

### Other Points of Interest

**Wanuskewin Heritage Park,** just a few kilometers north of Saskatoon, is a relatively new complex, which portrays 6,000 years of Northern Plains Indian culture. The Interpretive Centre has an archaeological laboratory, displays, films, and hands-on activities. Outside walking trails take you to archaeological sites, including a medicine wheel, tipi rings, bison kills and pounds, habitation sites, and stone cairns. *R.R. 4, Saskatoon, S7K 3J7, tel. 306/931–6767. Admission: $5 adults, $4.25 senior citizens, $2 children 5–12, $12 families. Open Victoria Day–Labor Day, daily 9–9; Labor Day–Victoria Day, daily 9–5.*

**Batoche National Historic Site,** 100 kilometers (60 miles) northeast of Saskatoon, is a large historic park and the center of Métis heritage. It was here that the Métis under Louis Riel fought and lost their last battle against the Canadian militia in 1885. The site includes a visitor center, displays, historic church and rectory, and walking trails taking you by many of the battle sites. Take Highway 11 north of Saskatoon and follow the signs to the park. *Tel. 306/423–6227. Admission to park free; to film: $1.50 adults, $.75 children, senior citizens and children under 6 free. Open July and Aug., daily 10–6; May, June, Sept., and Oct., daily 9–5.*

**Prince Albert,** 141 kilometers (88 miles) north of Saskatoon, is Saskatchewan's fourth-largest city (population 34,000), the center of the lumber industry, and the self-proclaimed "Gateway to the North." It's a prosperous modern city straddling the North Saskatchewan River, and the most interesting attractions are downtown. Pick up a walking-tours pamphlet at the **Prince Albert Historical Museum,** housed in an old firehouse. *River St. and Central Ave., tel. 306/764–2992. Admission: $1 adults, 50¢ children. Open mid-May–Aug., Mon.–Sat. 10–6, Sun. 10–9.*

The **Western Development Museum** in North Battleford, 138 kilometers (86 miles) northwest of Saskatoon, presents a re-created 1920s farming village, complete with homes, offices, churches, and a Mountie post. The museum also exhibits vintage farming tools and provides demonstrations of agricultural skills used. *Hwys. 16 and 40, tel. 306/445–8033. Admission: $4 adults, $3.50 senior citizens, $1.50 children 5–12. Call for hrs of operation.*

While in North Battleford, visit the **Allen Sapp Gallery**, which features the paintings of Cree Indian artist Allen Sapp. The gallery is rare in that it is devoted to the work of a living artist. *1901 100th St., tel. 306/445–3304. Admission free. Open May–Sept., daily 1–5; Sept.–May, Wed.–Sun. 1–5.*

For a refreshing, revitalizing 124-kilometer (77-mile) getaway from Saskatoon, take Routes 16 and 365 southeast, to **Manitou Beach**. Fifty years ago the town of Manitou Beach was a world-famous spa nicknamed the "Carlsbad of Canada." The mineral water in Little Manitou Lake is said to be three times saltier than the ocean and dense enough to make anyone float. Today, **Manitou Springs Mineral Spa** (open year-round) attracts vacationers as well as sufferers of arthritis, rheumatism, and skin disorders to the spa resort. *Hwy. 365, Manitou Beach, tel. 306/946–3949.*

## National and Provincial Parks

**Fort Battleford National Historic Site** pays tribute to the role of mounted police in the development of the Canadian west. The fort was established in 1876 as the North West Mounted Police headquarters for the District of Saskatchewan. Costumed guides explain day-to-day life at the post, and an interpretive center has exhibits relating to the history of the Mounted Police and lifestyles of Indians and settlers. *Central Ave., tel. 306/937–2621. Admission free. Open July and Aug., daily 9–6; May, June, Sept., and Oct., daily 9–5.*

**Prince Albert National Park**, 220 kilometers (137 miles) north of Saskatoon, encompasses nearly a million acres of wilderness and waterways and is divided into three landscapes: wide-open fescue grassland, rolling wooded parkland, and dense boreal forest.

In addition to hiking trails, the park has three major campgrounds, with more than 500 sites, plus rustic campgrounds and primitive sites in the back country. Pick up maps and information at the visitor center in **Waskesiu**, a townsite with restaurants, motels, and stores within the park.

The **Nature Centre**, located inside the visitor center, can help to orient you to the plant and animal life of the area. Hiking along the marked trails, you have a good chance of spotting moose, deer, bear, elk, and red fox. Canoes, rowboats, and powerboats can be rented from Waskesiu Lake Marina. Lodging in Waskesiu includes the Lakeview Hotel (Lakeview Dr., Box 26, S0J 2Y0, tel. 306/663–5311), a year-round accommodation. *Prince Albert National Park, off Hwy. 2, tel. 306/663–5322. Admission: $5/day per car; $10 for 4 days. Open daily. Waskesiu Lake Visitor Center, Rtes. 263 and 264, tel. 306/663–5322. Open May–Sept., daily 8 AM–10 PM; Oct.–Apr., weekdays 8–4:30.*

## What to See and Do with Children

**Forestry Farm Park and Zoo** (off Attridge Dr. in NE Saskatoon, tel. 306/975–3382) has more than 300 animals and spotlights such species native to Saskatchewan as deer, wolf, bear, coyote, and fox. The park encompasses barbecue areas, nature displays, cross-country ski trails, and sports fields.

**Kinsmen Park** (Spadina Crescent and 25th St., Saskatoon, tel. 306/975–3366) is a riverside amusement park and a children's play village.

**Wanuskewin Heritage Park** (*see* Exploring Saskatoon, *above*).

**Western Development Museum** (*see* Exploring Saskatoon, *above*).

## Shopping

Malls and Shopping Districts
**Midtown Plaza** (22nd St. and 1st Ave., tel. 306/652–9366) and **Scotia Centre Mall** (123 2nd Ave., tel. 306/665–6120) are enclosed malls located downtown. The area around **Broadway Avenue**, between 8th and 12th streets east of the river, has 150 boutiques and services.

Specialty Stores
**Trading Post Limited** (226 2nd Ave. S, tel. 306/653–1769) carries an extensive and reasonably priced selection of Inuit and Indian crafts and Canadian foodstuffs—including Saskatoon berry products. Local crafts are also available at **Handmade House** (710 Broadway Ave., tel. 306/665–5542) and the **Homespun Craft Emporium** (212 3rd Ave. S, tel. 306/652–3585).

## Sports

Participant Sports
*Bicycling and Jogging*
The **Meewasin Valley Trail** (tel. 306/665–6888) is a gorgeous 15-kilometer (10-mile) biking and jogging trail along both banks of the South Saskatchewan River in Saskatoon. You can obtain information about the trail by calling 306/665–6888.

*Health and Fitness Clubs*
The **Riverraquet Athletic Club** (322 Saguenay Dr., Saskatoon, tel. 306/242–0010) has racquetball and squash courts, a weight room, aerobics classes, minigolf, and beach volleyball in summer. The **Saskatoon Field House** (University of Alberta, 2020 College Dr., Saskatoon, tel. 306/975–3354) has tennis courts, a weight room, a gymnastics area, an indoor track, a fitness dance area, and drop-in fitness classes.

Spectator Sports
*Hockey*
The **Saskatoon Blades** play Canadian Hockey League (minor league) matches at **Saskatchewan Place** (3515 Thatcher Ave., Saskatoon, tel. 306/938–7800). The **Saskatoon Slam** of the National Basketball League plays at Saskatchewan Place, as well.

*Horse Racing*
**Marquis Downs Racetrack** (Prairieland Exhibition Centre, enter on Ruth St., Saskatoon, tel. 306/242–6100) has Thoroughbred and harness racing from early May through mid-October.

## Dining and Lodging

For price categories, *see* Winnipeg Dining and Lodging, *above*.

Dining
**R.J. Willoughby's.** The lush, tropical, pink-and-green color scheme of the Holiday Inn's main dining room is enhanced by copious groves of bamboo and foliage. The menu features Continental preparations plus themed evenings with specialty buffets (prime rib on Wednesday, pasta on Friday, seafood on Sunday). The Sunday Brunch, which features an impressive array including custom-made omelettes and flambé fruit, is very popular. *Holiday Inn, 90 22nd St. E, tel. 306/665–7576. Reservations advised. Jacket advised. AE, DC, MC, V. $$$*

**St. Tropez Bistro.** This sophisticated bistro is a short stroll from downtown hotels, and offers intimate French-bistro decor, with blue-and-pink florals, candle-lit tables, and imaginative preparations that change daily. Veal, fish, pasta, quiche, and outstanding homemade bread are often on the menu. A tasty specialty is the blackened chicken. For dessert, try the chocolate fondue. *243 3rd Ave. S, tel. 306/652–1250. Reservations advised. Dress: casual. AE, MC, V. Closed Sun. $$*

**Saskatoon Station Place.** The station is newly built, but the railroad cars and decorative antiques are fascinatingly authentic. The newspaper-style menu headlines Canadian prime rib and steaks, seafood, and Greek specialties, such as Greek ribs and souvlakia. *221 Idylwyld Dr. N, tel. 306/244–7777. Reservations advised. Dress: casual. AE, MC, V. $$*

★ **Adonis.** By day such Middle Eastern dishes as falafel and hummus, are served cafeteria-style. At night, tablecloths and candles transform the room into a romantic setting for couscous, dolmades, steak Andalousia, and other Mediterranean delights. It's one of Saskatoon's few outdoor cafés and a great place for breakfast. *101 3rd Ave. S, tel. 306/652–9598. No reservations. Dress: casual. AE, MC, V. $*

**Lydia's.** This Broadway Avenue restaurant is divided into a dining room with a warm, relaxed atmosphere, and a neighborhood pub in back. Menu specialties include beef kebab, chicken Kiev, chicken brochettes, and a range of pastas. Choose from several cheesecakes for dessert. The pub features a full menu selection as well as pub snacks. *650 Broadway Ave., tel. 306/652–8595. Dress: casual, MC, V, DC. $*

**Taunte Maria's.** This is a Mennonite restaurant, which is to suggest a menu of hearty soups, huge farmer's sausages, potato salad, homemade bread, and noodles steeped in gravy. The decor, too, reflects the Mennonite tradition: simple, functional, and comfortable. *Try* to save room for Ho-Ho Cake (chocolate cake with cream filling and chocolate icing) or bread pudding with ice cream. Taunte Maria's is convenient to the airport. *51st St. and Faithfull Ave., tel. 306/931–3212. No reservations. Dress: casual. MC, V. Closed Sun. $*

**Lodging**
★ **Delta Bessborough.** Saskatoon's grand old landmark, opened in 1935, looks like a castle and dominates the skyline from its riverfront setting. The hotel has recently been restored and upgraded with modern amenities, but still retains the grand appearance. *601 Spadina Crescent E, S7K 3G8, tel. 306/244–5521 or 800/268–1133, fax 306/653–2458. 227 rooms; no-smoking rooms available. Facilities: 2 restaurants, 2 lounges, indoor and outdoor pools, sauna, whirlpool. AE, DC, MC, V. $$$*

**Ramada Renaissance.** Saskatoon's newest luxury property has a prime riverfront location downtown and 19 floors of classically styled, ample-size rooms. Units are large, and the peach, gray, and pastel colors make them bright and airy; for still more atmosphere, request a river view. The elaborate Waterworks Recreation Complex encompasses an indoor pool, whirlpool, sauna, and two three-story water slides. *405 20th St. E, S7K 6X6, tel. 306/665–3322 or 800/228–9898, fax 306/665–5531. 291 rooms; no-smoking rooms available. Facilities: 2 restaurants, lounge, indoor pool, sauna, whirlpool, water slides. AE, DC, MC, V. $$$*

**Sheraton Cavalier.** Located downtown opposite Kiwanis Park, this eight-story property features unusually large rooms that face either the city or the river, and an elaborate water-sports complex. Benedict's Dining Room is the place for elegant dining, while Windows Café is more informal and offers a view of the river from every table. Lorenzo's Lounge is a piano bar featuring nightly music. The Barley Bin is a sophisticated but chummy pub. *612 Spadina Crescent E, S7K 3G9, tel. 306/652–6770 or 800/325–3535, fax 306/244–1739. 250* *rooms; no-smoking rooms available. Facilities: 2 restaurants, pub, 2 indoor pools, water slides, sauna, whirlpool, games room. AE, DC, MC, V. $$$*

**Travelodge.** This sprawling property near the airport has two flora-filled indoor pool complexes. Rooms come in a great variety of sizes and shapes, and many have balconies overlooking the pool. The Aloha Gardens offers informal poolside dining; the Heritage Dining Room is the place for fine dining. *106 Circle Dr. W, S7L 4L6, tel. 306/242–8881 or 800/255–3050, fax 306/665–7378. 220 rooms; no-smoking rooms available. Facilities: 2 restaurants, lounge, bar, 2 indoor pools, water slides, sauna, whirlpools, games room. AE, DC, MC, V. $$*

**Colonial Square Motel.** This pink-stucco, two-story motel opened in 1989, east of the river, along a fast-food strip. Rooms are furnished in pastel colors and have two queen-size beds or a double bed plus pullout sofa. Across the parking lot is the Venice Pizza House and Lounge. *1301 8th St. E, S7H 0S7, tel. 306/343–1676 or 800/667–3939, fax 306/956–1313. 80 rooms; no-smoking rooms available. Facilities: restaurant, lounge. AE, MC, V. $*

★ **Patricia Hotel.** Situated in the center of downtown, this older hotel is conveniently located and will appeal to anyone looking for a bargain. There's a dining room called Karz Kafe and a lounge. *345 2nd Ave. N, tel. 306/242–8861, fax 306/242–8861. 45 rooms. Facilities: restaurant, lounge. MC, V. $*

## The Arts and Nightlife

**The Arts**
*Theater*
Saskatoon's oldest professional theater, **25th Street Theatre Centre** (420 Duchess St., Saskatoon, tel. 306/664–2239), produces mostly works by Canadian playwrights, as well as **The Fringe Festival** every summer. **Persephone Theatre** (2802 Rusholme Rd., Saskatoon, tel. 306/384–7727) presents six plays and musicals a year. **Gateway Players** (709 Cumberland St., Saskatoon, tel. 306/653–1200) presents five productions from October through April. **Nightcap Productions** (tel. 306/653–2300) offers "Shakespeare on the Saskatchewan" in a riverside tent in July and August, as well as midnight improvisational comedy at the Broadway Theatre (715 Broadway Ave., Saskatoon, tel. 306/652–6556). Each summer Saskatoon is home to the popular **Saskatchewan Jazz Festival,** when jazz musicians from around the world play more than 125 performances throughout the city.

*Music and Dance*
The **Saskatoon Symphony** (tel. 306/665–6414) performs an October–April season at **Saskatoon Centennial Auditorium** (35 22nd St. E, Saskatoon, tel. 306/644–9777). When the symphony isn't in concert, the 2,003-seat auditorium hosts ballet, rock and pop concerts, comedians, musical comedies, and opera. The **Mendel Art Gallery** (950 Spadina Crescent E, Saskatoon, tel. 306/975–7610) has a regular concert program, and the **Saskatoon Jazz Society** performs in its permanent space, **The Bassment** (245 3rd Ave. S, Saskatoon, tel. 306/652–1421).

*Nightlife*
*Bars and Clubs*
**One Up** (410 22nd St. E, Saskatoon, tel. 306/244–7770) is a civilized rooftop place with great river views. Saskatoon's businesspeople interface with traveling executives at **Caper's Lounge** (405 20th St. E, Saskatoon, tel. 306/665–3322) in the Ramada Renaissance. See top rock groups at **Bud's On Broadway** (817 Broadway Ave., Saskatoon, tel. 306/244–4155) and **Amigos** (632 10th St. E, Saskatoon, tel. 306/652–4912). The **Artful Dodger** (100–119 4th Ave. S, Saskatoon, tel. 306/653–2577) is a pub with live entertainment. Go out to **Texas T**

(3331 8th St. E, Saskatoon, tel. 306/373–8080) for country sights and sounds around the city's largest dance floor.

# Calgary

With the eastern face of the Rockies as its backdrop, Calgary's crisp concrete-and-steel skyline seems to rise from the plains as if by sheer force of will. In fact, all the elements in the great saga of the Canadian West—Mounties, Indians, railroads, cowboys, oil—have converged to create a city with a brand-new face and a surprisingly traditional soul.

Calgary, Gaelic for "preserved pasture at the harbor," was founded in 1875 at the junction of the Bow and Elbow rivers as a North West Mounted Police post. The Canadian Pacific Railroad arrived in 1883, and ranchers established major spreads on the plains surrounding the town. Incorporated as a city in 1894, Calgary grew quickly, and by 1911 its population had reached 43,000.

The major growth came with the oil boom in the 1960s and 1970s, when most Canadian oil companies established their head offices in the city. Today, Calgary is a city of more than 720,000 mostly easy-going and downright neighborly people. It is Canada's third-largest center for corporate head offices. Downtown is still evolving, but Calgary's planners have made life nice by connecting most of the buildings with Plus 15, a network of enclosed walkways 15 feet above street level.

## Important Addresses and Numbers

**Tourist Information**
The main **Calgary Convention & Visitors Bureau** (237 8th Ave. SE, T2G 0K8, tel. 403/263–8510 or 800/661–1678) is open daily 8–5 in summer, varying hours the rest of the year. There is also a walk-in Visitor Service Centre at the base of the Calgary Tower.

**Emergencies**
Dial 911 for all emergencies; **police,** tel. 403/266–1234; **poison center,** tel. 403/670–1414.

**Hospitals**
Emergency rooms are located at **General Hospital** (841 Centre Ave. E, tel. 403/268–9111), **Foothills Hospital** (1403 29th Ave. NW, tel. 403/670–1110), **Alberta Children's Hospital** (1820 Richmond Rd. SW, tel. 403/229–7211), and **Rocky View Hospital** (7007 14th St. SW, tel. 403/541–3000).

**Late-night Pharmacy**
The **Super Drug Mart** (504 Elbow Dr. SW, tel. 403/228–3338) is open daily until midnight.

## Arriving and Departing by Plane

**Calgary International Airport** is 20 minutes northeast of the city center. Airlines serving Calgary include Air Canada, Canadian Airlines International, Air BC, American, Delta, United, and KLM. Taxis make the 20-minute trip for about $16.

## Getting Around

**By Car**
Although many attractions are located in the downtown area and can be reached on foot, a car is advisable for visiting outlying attractions. From June through September visitors can obtain a three-day **Visitor Car Park** permit offering "hassle-free" parking at street-level city meters. The permit is free at the **Calgary Convention & Visitors Bureau** (*see above*).

# Alberta

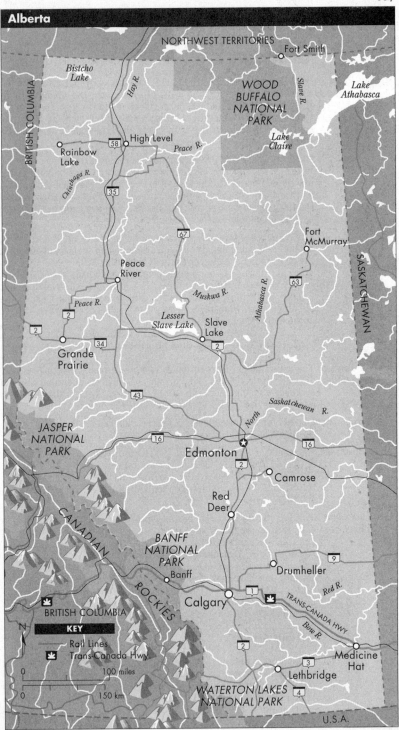

NORTHWEST TERRITORIES

Fort Smith

*Bistcho Lake*

WOOD BUFFALO NATIONAL PARK

*Slave R.*

*Lake Athabasca*

BRITISH COLUMBIA

*Hay R.*

58 High Level

*Peace R.*

*Lake Claire*

Rainbow Lake

*Chinchaga R.*

35

67

Fort McMurray

63

*Athabasca R.*

SASKATCHEWAN

Peace River

2 *Peace R.*

*Muskwa R.*

*Lesser Slave Lake*

Slave Lake

2

34

Grande Prairie

43

*Saskatchewan   R.*

*North*

JASPER NATIONAL PARK

16

Edmonton

2

16

Camrose

CANADIAN

Red Deer

BANFF NATIONAL PARK

Drumheller

9

*Red R.*

Banff

ROCKIES

Calgary

1

TRANS-CANADA HWY

BRITISH COLUMBIA

**KEY**

— Rail Lines
🍁 Trans-Canada Hwy

N

*Bow R.*

Medicine Hat

2

3

Lethbridge

4

WATERTON LAKES NATIONAL PARK

0 ___ 100 miles
0 ___ 150 km

U.S.A.

**By Bus/LRT**  Calgary Transit (206 7th Ave. SW, tel. 403/276–7801) operates a comprehensive bus system and light rail transit system (the **"C-Train"** or **"LRT"**) throughout the area. Fares are $1.50 for adults, 90¢ for children 6–14. Books of 10 children's tickets are $8.50; 10 adults' tickets $12. A CT Day Pass good for unlimited rides costs $4 adults, $2.50 children. The C-Train has lines running northwest (Brentwood), northeast (Whitehorn), and south (Anderson) from downtown.

**By Taxi**  Taxis are fairly expensive, at $2.05 for the "drop" and about $1 for each additional mile. Major taxi services are **Checker** (tel. 403/299–9999), **Yellow Cab** (tel. 403/974–1111), **Red Top** (tel. 403/974–4444), **Associated Cabs** (tel. 403/299–1111), and **Co-op** (tel. 403/531–8294).

## Guided Tours

Several companies offer tours of Calgary and environs, although none operate on regular schedules. Call the **Calgary Convention and Visitors Bureau** (tel. 800/661–1678) for up-to-date information.

## Exploring Calgary

*Numbers in the margin correspond to points of interest on the Downtown Calgary and Greater Calgary maps.*

In the Calgary grid pattern, numbered streets run north–south in both directions from Centre Street, and numbered avenues run east–west in both directions from Centre Avenue.

**①** Begin your downtown walking tour at **Calgary Tower**, a 190-meter (626-foot), scepter-shape edifice that affords great views of the city's layout, the surrounding plains, and the face of the Rockies rising 80 kilometers (50 miles) west. A flame on top is lit for special occasions; the revolving **Panorama Dining Room** provides refreshment. *9th Ave. and Centre St. S, tel. 403/266–7171. Admission: $3.75 adults, $2.50 senior citizens and children 13–17, $1.75 children 6–12. Open weekdays and Sat. 7:30 AM–11:30 PM, Sun. 7:30 AM–10:30 PM.*

**②** Take the "Plus 15" walkway (it is 15 feet above street level) over 9th Avenue Southwest to **Glenbow Museum**, Calgary's premier showcase of both art and history. Along with traveling exhibits, the Glenbow has comprehensive displays devoted to Alberta's native (Indian and Inuit) inhabitants, early European settlers, and later-day pioneers. The mineralogy collection and cache of arms and armor are superb. *130 9th Ave. SE, tel. 403/264–8300; tel. 403/237–8988 for hours and exhibit information. Admission: $3 adults, $2 students 13–17, $1 senior citizens. Sat. $1. Open Tues.–Sun. 10–6.*

**③** Take the Plus 15 walkway over 1st Street Southeast to the **Calgary Centre for the Performing Arts** (tel. 403/294–7444), a complex of three theater spaces, a concert hall, and shopping area. The center was pieced together with the historic Calgary Public Building (1930) and the Burns Building (1913). Come at night for a performance (*see* The Arts and Nightlife, *below*), or take a one-hour walking tour at noon most weekdays.

**④** Step outside into **Olympic Plaza** (7th Ave. SE and Macleod Trail SE), site of the Olympic medals presentation. The Plaza is a popular year-round venue for city festivals, arts, and entertainment. Public skating takes place during the winter.

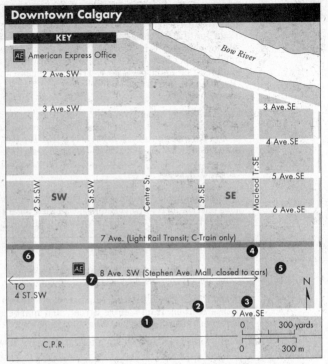

**Downtown Calgary**

KEY

AE American Express Office

**5** You're not likely to overlook the **Municipal Building** (8th Ave. SE and Macleod Trail), an angular mirror-walled structure that reflects city landmarks. One of the most stunning reflections is **City Hall**, a stately 1911 sandstone building that still houses the mayor's office and some city offices.

Seventh Avenue Southeast is closed to cars to make room for the C-Train, Calgary's light rail system. Hop on for a free ride (along 7th Avenue downtown only) to the center of the downtown shopping dis-
**6** trict. Literally, the top attraction of the area is **Devonian Gardens**, above Toronto Dominion Square. The 2½-acre enclosed roof garden has 20,000 mostly tropical plants, nearly a mile of lush walkways, a sculpture court, and playground. Accessed by a glass-enclosed elevator just inside the 8th Avenue door, the Devonian Gardens has a reflecting pool that turns into a skating rink during winter and a small stage for musical performances year-round. *Between 2nd and 3rd Sts., and 7th and 8th Aves. SW. Admission free. Open daily 9–9.*

Seventh Avenue Southeast, between Macleod Trail and 4th Street
**7** Southwest, is a pedestrian-only shopping area called **Stephen Avenue Mall**. Shops, nightclubs, and restaurants occupy the ground floors of Calgary's oldest structures, mostly sandstone buildings erected after an 1886 fire destroyed almost everything older.

**Time Out** While shopping downtown, take a breather at the **Elephant & Castle Pub and Restaurant** (751 3rd St. SW, tel. 403/265–3555), located at the base of Eaton's Centre off Stephen Avenue Mall. Enjoy traditional pub fare in an imported British atmosphere. Choose among full dinners, finger food, and a health-conscious light menu.

Alberta Science Centre/ Planetarium, **14**

Calgary Chinese Cultural Centre, **15**

Calgary Zoo Botanical Gardens and Prehistoric Park, **10**

Canada Olympic Park, **16**

Deane House, **9**

Fort Calgary, **8**

Heritage Park, **12**

Museum of the Regiments, **13**

Stampede Park, **11**

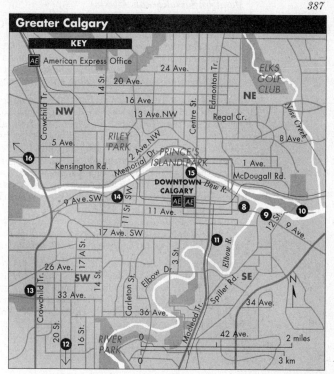

**Greater Calgary**

**KEY**

AE American Express Office

**8** You'll need a car to continue from here. Head on to **Fort Calgary,** at the confluence of the Bow and Elbow rivers. Established in 1875 by the North West Mounted Police, the fort was to subdue Montana whiskey traders who raised havoc among the Indians. In the 40-acre park in the valley occupied by Fort Calgary, a line of stumps traces the outline of the original post, and an ultracontemporary interpretive center traces the history of area Indians, Mounties, and white settlers. The **Deane House** (809 9th Ave. SE, tel. 403/269–7747), situated directly across the 9th Avenue Bridge, is the renovated 1906 post commander's house; it has free tours and a tearoom serving light meals. *Ft. Calgary Interpretive Centre, 750 9th Ave. SE, tel. 403/290–1875. Admission free. Open daily 9–5.*

**9**

**10** Continue east on 9th Avenue, turn north on 12th Street, and cross the bridge to St. George's Island and the **Calgary Zoo Botanical Gardens and Prehistoric Park,** with more than 1,400 animals in natural settings. A relatively new area is the Canadian Wild's section that replicates endangered Canadian nature ecosystems. The Prehistoric Park displays dinosaur replicas in a bygone natural habitat. *1300 Zoo Rd. NE, tel. 403/232–9372. Admission: $7.50 adults, $4.75 senior citizens, $3.75 children 2–15; Tues. $5 adults, senior citizens free. Open 9 AM; closing time seasonally adjusted.*

**11** Head south and west to Olympic Way and **Stampede Park** (17th Ave. and 2nd St. SE, tel. 403/261–0101), the focus each July of the world-famous Calgary Exhibition and Stampede (*see* Festivals and Seasonal Events in Chapter 1). Throughout the year the Roundup Centre, Big Four Building, and Agriculture Building host trade shows; the Olympic Saddledome has concerts and Calgary Flames hockey games; and the Grandstand is the site of Thoroughbred and harness racing (*see* Sports, *below*). Visitors can wander the grounds, take free one-hour tours of the **Olympic Saddledome** (tel. 403/261–0400), and visit the free **Grain Academy** in Roundup Centre, an interesting little museum that proudly proclaims itself "Canada's only grain interpretive centre." *Grain Academy in Stampede Park, tel. 403/263–4594. Admission free. Open weekdays 10–4, Sat. noon–4.*

 Follow Macleod Trail past a strip of fast-food outlets, motels, and shopping centers and go west on Heritage Drive to **Heritage Park,** where more than 100 authentic structures from all over western Canada have been collected in a parklike setting beside Glenmore Reservoir. The "neighborhoods," inhabited by costumed staff, range from an 1850s fur-trading post to a 1910-era town. Steam trains, horse-drawn buses, and paddle-wheel steamers provide transportation, and North America's only antique amusement park re-creates bygone thrills. Theme snacks—sarsaparilla, beef jerky, fresh apple pie—abound. *1900 Heritage Dr. SW, tel. 403/259–1900. Admission: $6 adults, $5 senior citizens, $3 children 3–16. Open late May–June, weekdays 10–4, weekends 10–6; July–Sept. 2, daily 10–6; Sept. 3–early Oct., weekends and holidays 10–5.*

East across Glenmore Reservoir, turn north on Crowchild Trail to reach the **Museum of the Regiments** (4520 Crowchild Trail SW, tel. 403/240–7674), which depicts the history of Calgary-based regiments dating back to 1900. Slightly further north on Crowchild Trail is the **Naval Museum of Alberta** (1820 24th St. SW, tel. 403/242–0002). This is Canada's second largest naval museum, focusing on the role of the Prairie Provinces in the Navy. *Both museums open July 1–Labor Day, daily 10–6; Labor Day–June 30, daily 10–4. Admission free.*

Continuing north on Crowchild Trail, turn east on 9th Avenue Southwest and then north again on 11th Street Southwest to the **Alberta Science Centre/Planetarium.** The Science Centre in the lower chamber has more than 35 hands-on exhibits of scientific marvels, such as holograms, frozen shadows, and laser beams; user-friendly demonstrations are given Friday– Sunday. Up in the planetarium, the 360-degree Star Chamber presents educational Star Shows with children's matinees on weekends, Laser Shows on Friday through Sunday nights. Imaginative combinations of special effects, magic tricks, and old-time show-biz make performances fascinating for all ages. *701 11th St. SW, tel. 403/221–3700. Admission: Science Centre, $5.50 adults, $4.25 senior citizens and youth 17 and under; Science Centre and Planetarium (including shows), $8 adults, $6.50 senior citizens and youth 17 and under. Open daily 9–9.*

Head east on 9th Avenue, then north on 6th Street SW and watch for signs to the **Calgary Chinese Cultural Centre.** This ornate multi-million dollar centre is located in the heart of Chinatown beside the Bow River. The focal point is the Hall of Prayers of the Temple Heaven, with column details and paintings that include 561 dragons and 40 phoenixes. It also houses a cultural museum, craft store, herbal medicine store, and 330-seat Chinese restaurant. *197 1st St. SW, tel. 403/262–5071. Admission to Centre free. Admission to museum: $2 adults, $1 senior citizens and children. Open daily 9:30–9.*

From the Chinese Cultural Centre, head west on 6th Avenue, and follow the signs to the Crowchild Trail north to 16th Avenue Northwest (Rte. 1) and then head west about 8 kilometers (5 miles) to **Canada Olympic Park,** site of the 1988 Winter Olympics and a year-round attraction. A one-hour bus tour goes over, under, around, and through the 70- and 90-meter ski jumps, bobsled, and luge tracks (in summer you have the option of walking down the slopes). In winter the slopes are open to the public (lessons available). Visitors can experience Olympic-size thrills on the one-minute Tourist Bobsleigh Ride ($100) and slightly briefer Tourist Luge Ride ($12); safety equipment is provided. Premises include a day lodge with a cafeteria, and the **Olympic Hall of Fame,** a collection of Olympic memorabilia and video displays. The highlight here is the scarifying four-man bobsled simulator. *Trans-Canada Hwy. W (Rte. 1) at Bowfort Rd. NW, tel. 403/286–2632. Admission: Bus or self-guided tour, $6.95 adults, $3.75 senior citizens, students, and children. Hall of Fame, $3.50 adults, $2.50 senior citizens, students, and children. Tour and Hall of Fame, $9.10 adults, $4.85 senior citizens, students, and children. Park open mid-June–Sept. 2, daily 7 AM– 9 PM; Sept. 3–mid-June, daily 8 AM–9 PM; Hall of Fame open daily 10–5.*

## What to See and Do with Children

**Alberta Science Centre/Planetarium** (see Exploring Calgary, *above*).

**Calaway Park** (Rte. 1, 10 km, or 6 mi, west of Calgary, tel. 403/240– 3822). Western Canada's largest outdoor amusement park also has live entertainment, mini-golf, driving range, maze, petting farm, food outlets, and shops. There's a new RV park and campground, which costs $19 per night for a full-service site; $16 per night for a bare site.

**Calgary Zoo Botanical Gardens and Prehistoric Park** (*see* Exploring Calgary, *above*).

**Canada Olympic Park** (*see* Exploring Calgary, *above*).

**Heritage Park** (*see* Exploring Calgary, *above*).

## Shopping

**Malls and Shopping Districts**
Calgary's premier shopping areas are located in the center of the downtown area, and you can wander through various shopping centers connected by indoor walkways. Major complexes include **Bankers Hall,** with exclusive specialty shops, restaurants, and cinemas; **Scotia Centre,** with fashion, accessory, and other retail outlets; **Penny Lane Mall** in renovated, early 20th-century buildings; and **Toronto Dominion Centre,** which is home to the indoor park—Devonian Gardens—as well as more than 100 stores. For outdoor shopping, the six-block stretch of 8th Avenue Southwest, between 3rd Street Southwest and Macleod Trail Southeast, has been turned into the traffic-free **Stephen Avenue Mall.**

**Specialty Stores**
**Uptown 17** and **Kensington** are trendy shopping districts just outside the city center along 17th Avenue Southwest, and feature several craft shops, antiques stores, boutiques, galleries, cafés, and coffee shops.

## Sports

**Participant Sports**
*Bicycling and Jogging*
Calgary has about 200 kilometers (120 miles) of bicycling and jogging paths, most of which wind along rivers and through city parks. Maps are available at visitor centers (*see* Important Addresses and Numbers in Calgary, *above*) and bike shops. Rent bikes at **Sports Rent** (4424 16th Ave. NW, Calgary, tel. 403/292–0077).

Health and  Three **Leisure Centre** water parks in Calgary have wave pools and
Fitness Clubs  water slides, plus gymnasiums and training facilities; Southland
and Family have racquetball and squash courts. *Village Square Leisure Centre, 2623 56th St. NE, tel. 403/280–9714; Family Leisure Centre, 11150 Bonaventure Dr. SE, tel. 403/278–7542; Southland Leisure Centre, 2000 Southland Dr. SW, tel. 403/251–3505. Rates and hrs vary.*

Just south of downtown, the striking white-dome **Lindsay Park Sports Centre** (2225 Macleod Trail SW, Calgary, tel. 403/233–8393) encompasses a 50-meter natatorium, a 200-meter track, racquetball and squash courts, and a weight room.

**Spectator**  The **Calgary Stampeders** of the Canadian Football League play home
**Sports**  games in **McMahon Stadium** (1817 Crowchild Tr. NW, tel. 403/289–
*Football*  0205) throughout the season, which runs July–November.

*Hockey*  The **Calgary Flames** play National Hockey League matches October–April at the **Olympic Saddledome** (17th Ave. and 2nd St. SE, Calgary, tel. 403/261–0475) in Stampede Park.

*Horse Racing*  There's racing year-round (except March) in **Stampede Park** (17th Ave. and 2nd St. SE, Calgary, tel. 403/261–0101). Thoroughbreds race April–May and September–November; trotters May–September and December–February. **Spruce Meadows** (just south and west of the Calgary city boundary, tel. 403/254–3200) is one of the world's finest show-jumping facilities, with major competitions held June–September.

---

## Dining and Lodging

For price categories, *see* Winnipeg Dining and Lodging, *above*.

**Dining**  **Owl's Nest Dining Room.** Plush armchairs and dark-wood booths ex-
★  press the subdued confidence of a restaurant long proclaimed the best in town. Standards are maintained, and all dishes are served with impeccable Continental flair. Alberta beef entrées are still ample and tender; British Columbia salmon is memorably fresh; the wine list is still exhaustive. *Westin Hotel, 320 4th Ave. SW, tel. 403/266–1611. Reservations advised. Jacket advised. AE, DC, MC, V. $$$$*

**Cannery Row Restaurant.** This cozy eatery is housed in a former warehouse, whose decor consists of exposed piping, brick walls, hardwood floors, and high ceilings. Fresh creole and Cajun dishes make good use of the seafood that's flown in. The crowds are entertained here by live New Orleans–style jazz bands and special dining events that are organized sporadically throughout the year. *317 10th Ave. SW, tel. 403/269–8889. Reservations needed for lunch. Dress: casual. AE, DC, MC, V. $$$*

**Hy's Steak House.** This is where Calgary (and Edmonton, Winnipeg, Toronto, etc.) goes for immense portions of charcoal-broiled steaks, fresh seafood, chicken, and a huge selection of wines. Wood paneling and earthy decor are components of a sedate Victorian ambience. *316 4th Ave. SW, tel. 403/263–2222. Reservations advised. Jacket advised. AE, DC, MC, V. Closed Sun. $$$*

**Silver Dragon.** A Chinatown institution for more than 20 years, the huge L-shape dining room is softened by carpeting and delicate Chinese paintings. The menu includes standard beef, pork, and poultry dishes but shines on concoctions of rock cod, crab, abalone, cuttlefish, and other seafood. Dim sum lunch is featured daily. *106 3rd Ave. SE, tel. 403/264–5326. No reservations. Dress: casual. AE, DC, MC, V. $$$*

**Billy MacIntyre's Cattle Company.** This Western restaurant serves up authentic Alberta-style home cooking, following the recipes used by Alberta ranchers in the early 1900s. Try the baby-back ribs. *Two locations in Calgary: #500, 3630 Brentwood Rd. NW, tel. 403/282–6614; 7104 Macleod Tr. S, tel. 403/252–2260. Reservations for groups only. Dress: casual. AE, DC, MC, V. $$*

★ **Buzzards Cafe.** This lively European-style downtown café serves 70 wines by the bottle or glass and the exclusive home brew, Buzzard Breath Ale. Wine-theme prints and posters adorning the walls remind you of the original attraction to this place. Food selections include 8-ounce Alberta beef Buzzard Burgers, pub grub, and low-priced entrées, such as teriyaki chicken and fettuccine Alfredo. In summer, dine out on the patio. Adjoining the café is Bottlescrew Bill's Old English Pub. *140 10th Ave. SW, tel. 403/264–6959. No reservations. Dress: casual. AE, DC, MC, V. $*

**Kaos Café.** Rapidly becoming Calgary's premiere jazz club, this relaxed New York–style café specializes in a jazzy selection of entrées, coffees, and desserts. The large outdoor patio is a pleasant choice in summer. The Saturday and Sunday brunches are popular. *718 17 Ave. SW, tel. 403/228–9997. Reservations advised. Dress: casual. AE, DC, MC, V. $*

**Lodging** **Delta Bow Valley.** The bright, 24-story high-rise occupies a relatively quiet street on the southern edge of downtown. Decent-size contemporary rooms, with rose-and-green furnishings, have good views on upper floors. For the brightest and most colorful units, request a room with a northern exposure. The sunny lobby—decorated in pink tones and with lush foliage—is an uplifting addition to an already lively setting. *209 4th Ave. SE, T2G 0C6, tel. 403/266–1980 or 800/268–1133, fax 403/266–0007. 400 rooms. Facilities: 2 restaurants, lounge, indoor pool, saunas, exercise room, no-smoking floors. AE, DC, MC, V. $$$$*

★ **The Palliser.** The downtown area of every Canadian city has a grand old railroad hotel, and the Palliser is Calgary's. This landmark, built in 1914, was recently restored to its former grandeur. Guest rooms are tastefully appointed with classic furnishings, ornate moldings, and high ceilings. *133 9th Ave. SW, T2P 2M3, tel. 403/262–1234 or 800/268–9411, fax 403/260–1260. 406 rooms. Facilities: restaurant, bar, exercise room, no-smoking floor. AE, DC, MC, V. $$$$*

**Radisson Plaza Hotel.** This is a business-class hotel with a convenient location in the heart of downtown, connected to the Calgary Convention Centre. Also surrounding the property are the Glenbow Museum and the Calgary Centre for Performing Arts, which provide executive and leisure guests nearby options for their spare time. The warm, inviting lobby leads to the clean pastel-and-maroon-tone rooms. *110 9th Ave., T2G 5A6, tel. 403/266–7331 or 800/661–7776, fax 403/262–8442. 387 rooms. Facilities: 2 restaurants, 2 lounges, indoor pool, sauna, fitness club, racquetball arrangements at nearby club, no-smoking floors. AE, DC, MC, V. $$$$*

**Sheraton Cavalier.** This recently renovated northeast Calgary hotel features a lobby decorated with pale colors, lots of plants, and a large marble water fountain. It's furnished with comfortable couches and chairs arranged around marble coffee tables. **Barlow's Lounge** hosts live entertainment from Thursday through Saturday. For sports fans, there's **Henry's Pub,** the hotel's sports bar with large TV screens. One other highlight is the **Oasis River Country,** on the second floor of the hotel, which has two 200-foot water slides and a recreation and exercise area. *2620 32nd Ave. NE, T1Y 6B8, tel. 403/291–0107 or 800/325–3535, fax 403/291–2834. 307 rooms; no-*

*smoking rooms available. Facilities: restaurant, bar, indoor pool. AE, DC, MC, V. $$$$*

★ **Westin Hotel.** Calgary's Plus 15 pedway system connects this luxury high-rise in the midst of downtown to most other important structures. Rooms in the Tower Section, especially, are large and decorated with tasteful contemporary furniture and pastel and neutral tones. The rooftop pool is one of this lodging's unique attractions. The Owl's Nest restaurant (*see* Dining, *above*) is one of the best dining spots in town. For lighter meals stop into the Lobby Court, which features Fitness Buffet breakfasts. *320 4th Ave. SW, T2P 2S6, tel. 403/266–1611 or 800/228–3000, fax 403/265–7908. 525 rooms, no-smoking rooms available. Facilities: 2 restaurants, 2 lounges, indoor pool, fitness club, sauna. AE, DC, MC, V. $$$$*

**Carriage House.** This unique, locally owned property, almost 10 kilometers (6 miles) south of City Centre, has a lobby with fish tanks, caged songbirds, and a waterfall. Room decor is comfortably mismatched. Nighttime entertainment options include a disco and rock club, country and rock saloon, and an English pub. Guests get discounts at nearby Family Leisure Centre (*see* Sports, *above*). *9030 Macleod Trail S, T2H 0M4, tel. in U.S. (call collect) 403/253–1101; or 800/661–9566; fax 403/259–2414. 175 rooms, no-smoking rooms available. Facilities: 2 restaurants, 3 lounges, heated outdoor pool, indoor whirlpool and sauna. AE, DC, MC, V. $$$*

**Prince Royal Inn.** Calgary's bargain inn has quite a lot going for it within its 28 floors: downtown and convenient location, all-suite (studios, one-, and two-bedrooms) accommodations with fully equipped kitchens, free parking, free Continental breakfast, and a health club. It's a great deal for families. *618 5th Ave. SW, T2P 0M7, tel. 403/263–0520; in Canada, 800/661–1592; fax 403/262–9991. 300 suites. Facilities: restaurant, bar, health club with sauna, exercise equipment, convenience store, florist, dry cleaner, no-smoking floors. AE, DC, MC, V. $$*

**Ramada Inn Airport.** This convenient and comfortable property is on the northeast side of town a few minutes from Calgary International Airport. Bright rooms are large, have standard furnishings, and are tastefully decorated with a rose-and-mauve scheme. *1250 McKinnon Dr. NE, T2E 7T7, tel. 403/230–1999 or 800/661–5095, fax 403/277–2623. 168 rooms; no-smoking rooms available. Facilities: restaurant, bar, indoor pool, sauna, sun deck. AE, DC, MC, V. $$*

## The Arts and Nightlife

Tickets for events at the Calgary Centre for the Performing Arts, Jubilee Auditorium, and Olympic Saddledome are available at Ticketmaster outlets at Calgary Centre box office, The Bay, Sears, or by telecharge (tel. 403/270–6700 or 403/266–8888).

**The Arts**
*Theater*

Calgary's showcase theater facility is the **Calgary Centre for the Performing Arts** (205 8th Ave. SE, Calgary, tel. 403/294–7455), with three modern auditoriums in two contiguous historic buildings. Productions by resident Alberta Theatre Projects (ATP) of principally Canadian playwrights are highly recommended. More than 20 local companies use the stage of the **Pumphouse Theatre** (2140 9th Ave. SW, Calgary, tel. 403/263–0079). The **University of Calgary Theatre** (Reeve Theatre, 2500 University Drive NW, Calgary, tel. 403/220–4900) features classic and contemporary works.

*Music and Dance*

**Calgary Philharmonic Orchestra** (tel. 403/294–7420) Concerts, chamber groups, and a broad spectrum of music and dance shows are performed in the 1,755-seat Jack Singer Concert Hall in the **Calgary Centre for the Performing Arts** (205 8th Ave. SE, Calgary, tel. 403/

294–7455). The larger **Jubilee Auditorium** (1415 14th Ave. NW, Calgary, tel. 403/297–8000) hosts the Alberta Ballet company and a variety of classical music, opera, dance, pop, and rock concerts. Concerts are also performed at **University of Calgary Theatres** (2500 University Dr. NW, Calgary, tel. 403/220–4900).

**Nightlife** **Loose Moose** (2003 McKnight Blvd. NE, Calgary, tel. 403/291–5682)
*Bars and Clubs* features competitive "Theatresports" and all sorts of fun and games.

*Casinos* In Calgary, play blackjack, roulette, and wheel of fortune at **River Park Casino** (1919 Macleod Trail S, Calgary, tel. 403/269–6771), **Cash Casino Place** (4040B Blackfoot Trail SE, Calgary, tel. 403/287–1635), **Tower Casino** in Tower Centre, and **Frontier Casino** in the Big Four Building in Stampede Park.

*Comedy* The Calgary outpost of **Yuk Yuk's** (Blackfoot Inn, 5940 Blackfoot Trail, Calgary, tel. 403/258–2028), Canada's comedy chain, has name performers from Canada and the United States. **Jester's** (239 10th Ave. SE, Calgary, tel. 403/269–6669) has comedians and Wednesday-night open mikes.

*Music* The Casablanca-style **Cafe Calabash** (107 10A St. NW, Calgary, tel. 403/270–2266) has live jazz every night but Sunday. For Western sights and sounds, head for **Ranchman's** (9615 Macleod Trail S, Calgary, tel. 403/253–1100) or the **Longhorn Dance Hall** (9631 Macleod Trail S, Calgary, tel. 403/258–0528). The **Rocking Horse Saloon** (24 7400 Macleod Trail S, Calgary, tel. 403/255–4646) also features country music every night but Sunday. **Sole Luna** (739 2nd Ave. SW, tel. 403/264–5100) has nightly dancing amidst a Mediterranean-style decor.

---

## Excursion from Calgary: Southern Alberta

Head east on the Trans-Canada Highway (Route 1) out of Calgary and enter the vast Canadian prairie of seemingly endless expanses of flat country in every direction. About 20 kilometers (12 miles) east of Calgary, turn north on Highway 9 and drive 120 kilometers (75 miles) to Drumheller, a coal-mining center for several years. The town is situated in the rugged valley of the Red Deer River, where millions of years of wind and water erosion exposed the "strike" that produced what amounts to present-day Drumheller's major industry: dinosaurs.

The barren lunar landscape of stark badlands and eerie rock cylinders (called hoodoos) may seem an ideal setting for the herds of dinosaurs that stalked the countryside 75 million years ago, but in fact, when the dinosaurs were here the area had a semitropical climate and verdant marshlands not unlike the Florida Everglades. You learn this and more geological and paleontological history of Alberta at the **Royal Tyrrell Museum of Paleontology.** Participate in hands-on exhibits and meet the local hero, Albertosaurus, a smaller, fiercer version of Tyrannosaurus rex that was the first dino discovered around here. *Hwy. 838, 6 km (4 mi) west of Drumheller, tel. 403/823–7707; in Calgary, 403/294–1992. Admission: $5.50 adult, $2.25 children 7–17, $13 families. Tues. free. Open mid-May–early Sept., daily 9–9; mid-Sept.–mid-May, Tues.–Sun. 10–5.*

Capitalizing on its rich paleontological past, Drumheller has a number of dinosaur-related businesses. **Reptile World** (Hwy. 9, tel. 403/823–TOAD) boasts a crowd-pleasing collection of poisonous snakes; the **Homestead Antique Museum** (Hwy. 838, tel. 403/823–2600) packs 4,000 Indian artifacts, medical instruments, period clothing, and other items of Canadiana into a roadside quonset hut; **Ollie's Rock & Fossil Shop** (off Hwy. 575, tel. 403/823–7625) depicts life-size dinosaurs in a badlands setting and sells a vast selection of fossils, bones, rocks, and petrified wood. No visit to Drumheller is complete without a family portrait beside the comic-book Tyrannosaurus rex guarding the Highway 9 bridge over the Red Deer River.

Continuing the dinosaur tour of Alberta requires a 142-kilometer (90-mile) drive south from Drumheller on Highway 56. Go east on the Trans-Canada Highway (Route 1), north at Brooks on Highway 873, east on Highway 544, and follow the signs to **Dinosaur Provincial Park,** a 15,000-acre park encompassing Canada's baddest badlands. Soft sedimentary rock was deposited by 72-million-year-old rivers and sculpted into starkly fascinating shapes by melting waters of the Ice Age that occurred a mere 14,000 years ago. Incessant wind, water, and frost erosion have exposed one of the world's most important collections of fossilized bones. Roads access some *in situ* fossil sites; two looped interpretive trails lead to more, with guided tours on weekends. During summer, 90-minute bus tours explore backcountry areas from which visitors are otherwise restricted. The cacti bloom from June through August. The **Royal Tyrrell Museum of Paleontology Field Station** in the park offers a concise orientation to the prehistoric world. Note: Since concessions are limited, bring a lunch to eat in one of the picnic areas. *Hwy. 544, Patricia, 48 km (30 mi) northeast of Brooks, tel. 403/378–4587. Admission free. Tyrrell Field Station open mid-May–early Sept., daily 9–9; Sept.– mid-May, Wed.–Sun. 10–5.*

**Medicine Hat** lies about 95 kilometers (60 miles) southeast of Patricia on the Trans-Canada Highway. Roadside views consist of small well pumps and storage tanks amid endless expanses of "prairie wool," principally spear and blue grama grass. There is much local lore concerning the origin of the name Medicine Hat, but one legend tells of a battle waged between Cree and Blackfoot Indians: The Cree fought bravely until their medicine man deserted, losing his headdress in the South Saskatchewan River. The site's name, "Saamis," meaning "medicine man's hat," was later translated by white settlers into Medicine Hat.

Medicine Hat is a prosperous and scenic city built on high banks overlooking the South Saskatchewan River. Alberta's fifth-largest city's wealth derives from vast deposits of natural gas below, some of which gets piped up to fuel quaint gas lamps in the turn-of-the-century downtown area. Prosperity is similarly communicated by the striking glass-sided **Medicine Hat City Hall.** *1st St. SE and 6th Ave. SE, tel. 403/529–8100. Open weekdays 8:30–4:30. Guided group and self-guided tours available.*

But Medicine Hat's greatest achievement was turning the land alongside the South Saskatchewan River and Seven Persons Creek into parkland and environmental preserves interconnected by 15 kilometers (9⅓ miles) of walking, biking, and cross-country ski trails. Detailed trail maps are available at the **Tourist Information Centre** (8 Gehring Rd. SW, tel. 403/527–6422). Other Medicine Hat attractions include a half-mile of falling water at **Riverside Waterslide** (Hwy. 1 and Power House Rd., tel. 403/529–6218) and **Echo Dale Regional Park** (Holsom Rd. off Hwy. 3, tel. 403/529–6225), the riverside setting for swimming, boating, fishing, a 1900s farm, and an historic coal mine.

Head west out of Medicine Hat toward **Lethbridge** on Crowsnest Highway (Rte. 3). Lethbridge, Alberta's third-largest city, is an

1870s coal boomtown that is now the center of agriculture, oil, and gas. The main attraction, **Fort Whoop-Up,** part of the **Indian Battle Park,** is a reconstruction of a southern Alberta whiskey fort. Along with weapons, relics, and a 15-minute audiovisual historical presentation, Fort Whoop-Up has wagon-train tours of the river valley and other points of local historical interest. *Indian Battle Park, Whoop-Up Dr. and Oldman River, tel. 403/329–0444. Fort Whoop-Up admission free. Wagon-train tour 50¢. Open late May–Labor Day, Mon.–Sat. 10–6, Sun. 2–8; off-season, call for hrs.*

**Henderson Lake Park,** 3 kilometers (2 miles) east on the other side of downtown Lethbridge, is filled with lush trees, a golf course, baseball stadium, tennis courts, a swimming pool, and a 60-acre man-made lake. Alongside the lake, **Nikka Yuko Japanese Gardens** is a tranquil setting for manicured trees and shrubs, miniature pools and waterfalls, a teahouse, and pebble designs constructed in Japan and reassembled alongside Henderson Lake. *Henderson Lake Park, Mayor Magrath Dr. and S. Parkside Dr., tel. 403/320–3020; Gardens, tel. 403/328–3511. Admission: $2.50 adults, $1.25 senior citizens and students 12 and over. Open mid-May–mid-June, daily 9–5; mid-June–Aug., daily 9–8; Sept.–early Oct., daily 9–5.*

Travel west along Highway 3 for 50 kilometers (31 miles) to **Fort Macleod.** Southern Alberta's oldest settlement, the installation was founded by the Mounties in 1874 to maintain order among the farmers, Indians, whiskey vendors, and ranchers beginning to settle here. The wood-frame buildings (pre-1900) and the more recent sandstone-and-brick buildings have established this as Alberta's first historic area. For information about guided and self-guided tours, visit the information booth (tel. 403/553–2500) beside Fort Macleod Museum. An authentic reconstruction of the 1874 fort, **Fort Macleod Museum** grants almost equal exhibitory weight to settlers, Indians, old North West Mounted Police, and today's Royal Canadian Mounted Police. *25th St., tel. 403/553–4703. Admission: $3 adults, $2.50 senior citizens, $1 students 13–18, 50¢ children 6–12. Open May–June 14 and Sept. 3–Oct. 15, daily 9–5; June 15–Sept. 2, daily 9–7.*

**Head-Smashed-In Buffalo Jump** is about a 15-minute drive from Fort Macleod. Take Highway 3 west and follow signs. A large interpretive center is built into the side of a cliff and explains how Plains Indians herded buffalo over the edge to their death, so the natives could later harvest meat and fur from the carcasses. On the site are museum displays that describe the tradition and offer some insight into the life and customs of the Plains Indians, especially the Blackfoot. Also, walking trails are available, and tours are given by native guides. *On Hwy. 785, 16 km (9 mi) northeast of Fort Macleod; tel. 403/553–2731. Admission: $5.50 adults, $2.25 children 7–17, $13 families; free Tues. Open May 15–Labor Day, daily 9–8; Labor Day–May 14, Tues.–Sun. 9–5.*

**Dining**    For rates, *see* Winnipeg Dining and Lodging, *above.*

*Lethbridge*    **Cafe Martinique.** This locally renowned fine dining spot, located in the El Rancho Motor Hotel, specializes in aged steaks and chateaubriand made with tender Alberta beef. For something lighter in a more informal setting, try the El Rancho coffee shop, on the same property. Live music and dancing take place most nights. *526 Mayor Magrath Dr., tel. 403/327–5701. Reservations advised. Jacket advised. AE, DC, MC, V. $$$*

**Sven Eriksen's Family Restaurant.** Tasty versions of Canadian prairie standards, including chicken and an especially good prime rib, are cooked up at this homey, colonial-style eatery. "Family Restaurant" label not withstanding, there's a full bar. *1715 Mayor Magrath Dr., tel. 403/328–7756. Reservations advised, especially on weekends. Dress: casual. AE, MC, V. $$*

**Lodging** **Lethbridge Lodge Hotel.** This modern-day lodge has great Oldman
*Lethbridge* River views and a pleasant tropical indoor courtyard filled with exotic plants, a swimming pool, whirlpool, waterfall, and chairs for lounging. The hotel boasts two restaurants: At the more formal **Anton's** the waitstaff is dressed in tuxedos and reservations are needed. *320 Scenic Dr., T1J 4B4, tel. 800/661–1232 or 403/328–1123. 190 rooms; no-smoking rooms available. Facilities: restaurant, lounge, indoor pool, whirlpool. AE, MC, V. $$*

**Parkside Inn.** This comfortable nearly 40-year-old hotel is a good bargain, and is conveniently located across the street from a golf course and within walking distance of Henderson Lake Park and the Japanese Gardens. Renovated in the last two years, the lobby is done in muted burgundies and blues, while rooms are styled in grays and rusts. The hotel's tavern has live country-and-western music on weekends and the lounge features video lottery machines. *1009 Mayor Magrath Dr., T1K 2P7, tel. 403/328–2366. 65 rooms; no-smoking rooms available. Facilities: restaurant, lounge. AE, MC, V. $*

*Medicine Hat* **Medicine Hat Lodge.** Although it's situated on the edge of town adjacent to a shopping mall, this hotel has several rooms with inward views of the indoor pool, whirlpool, and huge, curving water slide. The Atrium Dining Room serves fine Continental meals. J.D.'s is a hotel country-and-western spot. *1051 Ross Glen Dr. SE, T1B 3T8, tel. 403/529–2222 or 800/661–8095. 190 rooms; no-smoking rooms available. Facilities: 2 restaurants, 2 lounges, indoor pool, whirlpool, water slide, steam room. AE, DC, MC, V. $$*

# Edmonton

Lucky Edmonton is a recidivist boomtown that never seems to go bust. The first boom arrived in 1795, when the North West Company and Hudson's Bay Company both established fur-trading posts in the area. Boom II came in 1897, when Edmonton became principal outfitter on the overland "All Canadian Route" to the Yukon goldfields; as a result, Edmonton was named capital when the province of Alberta was formed in 1905. The latest and greatest of booms began on February 13, 1947, when oil was discovered in Leduc, 40 kilometers (25 miles) to the southwest. More than 10,000 wells were eventually drilled within 100 kilometers (62 miles) of the city and with them fields of refineries and supply depots. By 1965 Edmonton had solidified its role as the "oil capital of Canada."

More interesting is how wisely Edmonton has spread the wealth to create a beautiful and livable city. Shunning the uncontrolled development of some other oil boomtowns, Edmonton turned its great natural resource, the North Saskatchewan River Valley, into a 27-kilometer (17-mile) greenbelt of parks and recreational facilities. With a population of 850,000, Edmonton is the largest northerly city in the Americas and the fifth-largest city in Canada. It is also Canada's largest city in land area—681 hectares (270 square miles). As the seat of the Alberta government and home to the University of Alberta, Edmonton has an unusually sophisticated atmosphere that has generated many fine restaurants and a thriving arts community. Its premier attraction, the West Edmonton Mall, is a year-round drawing card for shoppers and families, complete with facilities ranging from an amusement park to a shopping center and hotel, from a cinema complex to a water park.

## Important Addresses and Numbers

**Tourist Information**
An **Edmonton Tourism Information Centre** (97th St. and Jasper Ave., tel. 403/496–8400 or 800/463–4667) is located downtown at the Edmonton Convention Centre. The office is open mid-May–September, daily 8:30–4:30; September–mid-May, weekdays 8:30–4:30. Other offices are open around Edmonton; for locations and times call the above number.

**Emergencies**
Dial 911 for **police, fire, ambulance,** and **poison center.**

**Hospitals**
Emergency rooms are located at the **Royal Alexandra Hospital** (10240 Kingsway Ave., tel. 403/477–4111) and **University of Alberta Hospitals** (8440 112th St., tel. 403/492–8822).

**Dentists**
For 24-hour dental care, contact **Denta Care** (472 Southgate Shopping Centre, 111th St. and 51st Ave., tel. 403/434–9566).

**Late-night Pharmacy**
**Mid-Niter Drugs** (11408 Jasper Ave., tel. 403/482–1171) is open until midnight. **Shoppers Drug Mart** (8210–109 St. tel. 403/433–3121) is open 24 hours.

## Arriving and Departing by Plane

Edmonton has two airports, though most international flights and long-haul domestic flights use **Edmonton International Airport.** Short-haul flights, mainly to neighboring provinces, use **Edmonton Municipal Airport,** just north of downtown. Along with the major Canadian airlines (Air Canada, Canadian Airlines International, Air BC, NWT Air), Edmonton is served by American, Delta, and Northwest.

Taxi rides from Edmonton International can be costly, but **The Grey Goose Airporter** (tel. 403/463–7520) provides frequent service between the airport and major downtown hotels. Fare is $11 one way, $18 round-trip. Grey Goose also provides service between Edmonton International and Edmonton Municipal Airport or West Edmonton Mall ($11 one way, $18 round-trip).

## Getting Around

**By Bus/LRT**
Edmonton Transit (tel. 403/421–INFO) operates a comprehensive system of buses throughout the area and a light rail transit (**LRT**) line from downtown to the northeast side of the city. The fare is $1.35 for adults, 80¢ for senior citizens and children 6–16; transfers are free. Adult fares are $1.60 during weekday rush hours. Buses operate from 5:30 AM to 2 AM. The LRT is free in the downtown area (between Churchill and Grandin stations) weekdays 9–3 and Saturday 9–6. The **Downtown Information Centre** above Central LRT Station (100A St. and Jasper Ave.) provides free information, timetables, and maps, weekdays 9–5.

**By Taxi**
Taxis tend to be costly: $2 for the first 105 meters, and 10¢ for each additional 105 meters. Cabs may be hailed on the street, but phoning is recommended. Call **Alberta Co-op Taxi** (tel. 403/425–8310), **Checker** (tel. 403/455–2211), or **Yellow** (tel. 403/462–3456).

## Guided Tours

From early May to early October three **Royal Tours** (tel. 403/488–9090) itineraries hit the high points of Edmonton. **Klondike Jet Boats** (tel. 403/486–0896) ply the North Saskatchewan River, May–October. **North Saskatchewan Riverboat Company** (tel. 403/424–2628) operates up to six cruises per day, May–October.

## Exploring Downtown Edmonton

*Numbers in the margin correspond to points of interest on the Downtown Edmonton map.*

The Edmonton street system is a straight grid with numbered streets running north–south and numbered avenues running east–west. Meeting at the center are 100th Street and 100th Avenue; Edmontonians often use the last digit or two as shorthand for the complete number: the Inn on 7th is on 107th Street; the 9th Street Bistro can be found on 109th Street. Edmonton's "main drag" is Jasper Avenue, which runs east–west through the center of downtown.

The city's striking physical feature, where most recreational facilities are located, is the broad green valley of the North Saskatchewan River, running diagonally northeast–southwest through the city center. The downtown area lies just north of the river, between 95th and 109th streets.

**❶** Start exploring downtown Edmonton at the **Edmonton Convention Centre** (9797 Jasper Ave., tel. 403/421–9797), a most unconventional building filled with surprises. On street level the building houses the **Edmonton Tourism Information Centre** (*see* Important Addresses and Numbers, *above*), a repository of useful brochures and advice. It's all literally downhill from here, since the Centre has been built onto a slope with various terraced levels accessed by glass-enclosed escalators with great views of the North Saskatchewan River valley. On the Pedway Level check out the **Canadian Country Music Hall of Honor,** actually a wall filled with plaques memorializing such good old boys as Hank Snow, Wilf Carter, and Orval "The Canadian Plowboy" Prophet.

Head west along Jasper Avenue and turn north on 99th Street to the **Civic Centre,** a six-block area that incorporates many of Edmonton's **❷** major institutions; Civic Centre structures surround **Sir Winston Churchill Square.** The largest theater complex in Canada, the **Citadel Theatre** (*see* Arts and Nightlife, *below*) houses five different venues (plus workshops and classrooms) and an indoor garden with waterfall. Across 99th Street the **Edmonton Public Library** (7 Sir Winston Churchill Sq., tel. 403/423–2331) augments books and art exhibits with a lively round of activities in the Children's Art Department.

Continue north on 99th Street. As you cross 102nd Avenue, glance east at **Chinatown Gate,** a symbol of friendship between Edmonton and sister city Harbin, China; it spans the portal to Edmonton's meager Chinatown. The new City Hall is more than a place for civic government. This architectural showcase features a grand staircase, a large art exhibition space, and a 200-foot tower with an enor-**❸** mous 23-bell carillon. Across 99th Street is the **Edmonton Art Gallery,** site of more than 30 yearly exhibits of classical and contemporary art from Canada and the rest of the world. *2 Sir Winston Churchill Sq., tel. 403/422–6223. Admission: $3 adults, $1.50 senior citizens and youths, children 12 and under free; free Thurs. after 4.*

# Downtown Edmonton

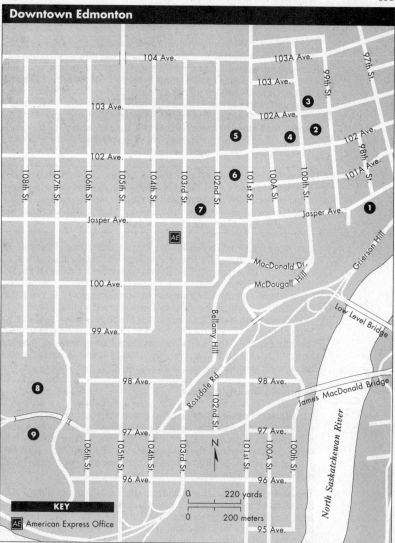

Alberta Government
Centre, **8**

Alberta Legislature
Building, **9**

The Bay, **7**

Eaton Centre, **5**

Edmonton Art
Gallery, **3**

Edmonton Convention
Centre, **1**

Edmonton Centre, **4**

ManuLife Place
and City Centre
Building, **6**

Sir Winston Churchill
Square, **2**

**KEY**

AE American Express Office

*Open Mon.–Wed. 10:30–5, Thurs. and Fri. 10:30–8, weekends and holidays 11–5.*

Directly west of Churchill Square begins a maze of multilevel shopping malls, department stores, cinemas, and office buildings—all climatically controlled and interconnected by a network of tunnels and second-floor pedways. Go south on 100th Street to find **Edmonton Centre;** head west on 102nd Avenue to **Eaton Centre,** with a miniature golf course in the middle of the mall; south of 102nd Avenue are the shops of **ManuLife Place and City Centre Building;** and on 102nd Street you'll find the domain of one of Canada's most powerful institutions, **The Bay,** contemporary retail descendant of the Hudson's Bay Company (*see* Shopping, *below*).

**Time Out** For a change of scenery, exit briefly to **Boardwalk Market** (102nd Ave. and 103rd St., tel. 403/424–5570). The bright and airy renovated historic block encompasses an indoor market with everything from Mongolian beef to steamed clams and pastries, all accompanied by a lively assemblage of street entertainers.

Emerging from The Bay on Jasper Avenue, enter the LRT station at 103rd or 104th Street for the ride to Grandin Station and the seat of the Alberta government. The **Alberta Government Centre** (109th St. and 97th Ave.) encompasses several hectares of carefully manicured gardens and fountains highlighted by the Government Greenhouse (tel. 403/427–7445). The **Alberta Legislature Building** is a stately 1912 Edwardian structure overlooking the river on the site of an early trading post. Frequent free tours of the building help to explain the intricacies of the Albertan and Canadian systems of government. *109th St. and 97th Ave., tel. 403/427–7362. Admission and tours free. Open May–Sept., weekdays 9–8:30, weekends 9–4:30.*

### Other Points of Interest

The **Muttart Conservatory** is one of the most important botanical facilities in North America. Separate greenhouses each contain flora of a different climate: arid, tropical, temperate. A show pavilion features special seasonal floral displays. *9626 96A St., tel. 403/496–8755. Admission: $4 adults, $3 senior citizens and youths 13–18, $2 children. Open Sun.–Wed. 11–9, Thurs.–Sat. 11–6.*

The **Old Strathcona Historic Area** (the area surrounding 104th Street and 82nd Avenue) is a district of restored houses and shops built mainly when Strathcona Town amalgamated with Edmonton, in 1912. The low buildings and wide streets have a decidedly Old West air, and Old Strathcona is a good place to get out and wander. For a more determined exploration, pick up a walking tour map at the Old Strathcona Foundation. *8331 104th St., tel. 403/433–5866. Open weekdays 8:30–4:30.*

The **Provincial Museum of Alberta** hosts exhibits concerning paleontology, geological evolution, native crafts and life, and pioneer settlement. Displays of Canadian wildlife in near-natural settings are especially informative. *12845 102nd Ave., tel. 403/453–9100. Admission: $3.25 adults, $1.25 children 7–17, $8 families. Open May–Sept., daily 9–8; Oct.–Apr., Tues.–Sun. 9–5.*

The **Edmonton Space and Science Centre** explores the heavens with a stunning variety of high-tech techniques. Standing exhibits and a fascinating science shop are always of interest, but the star attractions include laser-light concerts and IMAX films of an appropriately celestial nature. *11211 142nd St., tel. 403/451–7722. Admission:*

*$6 adults, $4 children 4–12, $18 families; IMAX $7 adults, $4.50 children, $20 families. Combination tickets: $11.25 adults, $7.25 children, $32 families. Senior citizens 65 years and older get discount. Open June–Sept., Sun.–Thurs. 10–10, Fri. and Sat. 10 AM–11 PM; Oct.–May, Tues.–Thurs. 10–10, Fri. and Sat. 10 AM–11 PM, Sun. 10–10.*

**Fort Edmonton Park,** Canada's largest historic park (158 acres), is home to an authentic re-creation of several periods in Edmonton history. There is a fur press in the 1846 Hudson's Bay Company fort; blacksmith shop, saloon, and jail along 1885 Street; photo studios and a firehouse on 1905 Street; and relatively modern conveniences on 1920 Street. Horse wagon, streetcar, stagecoach, and pony rides are available. *Whitemud and Fox Drs., tel. 403/496–8787. Admission: $6.25 adults, $4.75 senior citizens and youths 13–17, $3 children 12 and under, $18.50 families. Open mid-May–June, weekdays 10–4, weekends 10–6; July–early Sept., daily 10–6; Sept., Mon.–Sat. 11–2, Sun. and holidays 10–6; closed Oct.–mid-May.*

**West Edmonton Mall,** acclaimed by the *Guinness Book of World Records* as the world's largest mall, is Edmonton's preeminent attraction. Its sheer magnitude and variety transform it from a mere shopping center to an indoor city with high-rent districts, blue-collar strips, and hidden byways waiting to be discovered. The credentials shout for themselves. There are 800 stores and services, including 11 major department stores, 19 movie theaters, and 110 places to eat; but the mall also contains an amusement park, an ice-skating rink, a replica of Columbus's ship the *Santa Maria*, an 18-hole miniature-golf course, the Deep Sea Adventure submarine ride and dolphin show, the 5-acre World Waterpark water amusement park, a luxury hotel (*see* Lodging, *below*), auto dealerships, a playhouse, a bingo parlor, a chapel, and casino. If you don't feel like walking the Mall, rent an electric scooter or hitch a ride on a rickshaw. *8770 170th St., tel. 403/444–5200. Admission: Amusement Park, day pass $19.95 adults, $9 senior citizens, $15.95 children under 48 inches, $49.95 families of up to 4; individual ride tickets 95¢ (rides cost 1–7 tickets). World Waterpark, day pass $18.95 adults, $7.95 senior citizens, $15.95 children 3–10, $49.95 families of up to 5. Deep Sea Adventure, $10 adults, $5.00 senior citizens and children 3–10, $35 families. Open mid-June–early Sept., Mon.–Sat. 10–10, Sun. 11–7; early Sept.–mid-June, Mon.–Thurs. noon–8, Fri. and Sat. 10–10, Sun. 11–7.*

## What to See and Do with Children

**Edmonton Space and Science Centre** (*see* Other Points of Interest, *above*).

**Fort Edmonton Park** (*see* Other Points of Interest, *above*).

**Old Strathcona Model and Toy Museum** (8603 104th St., tel. 403/433–4512) features models made of paper.

**Valley Zoo** (134th St. and Buena Vista Rd., tel. 403/496–7275) is a small but imaginative zoo in riverside Laurier Park that places exotic species in well-known storybook settings.

**William Hawrelak Park** (off Groat Rd., just south of North Saskatchewan River, tel. 403/428–3559) invites children only—or adults in their company—to fish in this rainbow trout-stocked pond. Park includes paddleboats and adventure playground.

**West Edmonton Mall** (*see* Other Points of Interest, *above*).

**Whitemud Drive Amusement Park** (7411 51st Ave., tel. 403/465–1190) amuses with go-carts, bumper-boats, miniature golf, and batting cages.

**Wild Waters Waterslide Park** (21515 103rd Ave., tel. 403/447–4476) offers lots of wet fun on the western edge of the city.

## Shopping

**Malls and Shopping Districts**
In the heart of **downtown,** between 100th and 103rd streets, is a complex of shopping centers (Eaton Centre, 120 stores; ManuLife Place, 65 stores; Edmonton Centre, 140 stores) and department stores (The Bay, Eaton's) connected by tunnels or second-level pedways. **West Edmonton Mall** (87th Ave. and 170th St.; *see* Other Points of Interest, *above*) has 800 retail establishments, including such department stores as Sears, The Bay, Eaton's, Zeller's, Ikea (furniture), and Canadian Tire. **Strathcona Square** (8150 105th St., tel. 403/424–6060) in the Old Strathcona Town (*see* Other Points of Interest, *above*) 1913-era post office has been converted into a cheerful market filled with restaurants and enticing boutiques. **High Street/124th Street** (along 124th and 125th streets between 102nd and 109th avenues) is an outdoor shopping area full of boutiques, bistros, bookstores, and galleries.

## Sports

**Participant Sports**
*Bicycling and Jogging*
The North Saskatchewan River valley is the longest stretch of urban parkland in Canada. For information about jogging and cycling trails call the **River Valley Outdoor Centre** (10125 97th Ave., tel. 403/496–7275).

*Health and Fitness Clubs*
The Kinsmen Sports Centre (9100 Walterdale Rd., tel. 403/496–7300) and Mill Woods Recreation Centre (7207 28th Ave., tel. 403/428–2888) have swimming pools and a variety of facilities for the entire family.

**Spectator Sports**
*Hockey*
The **Edmonton Oilers** play National Hockey League hockey October–April at the **Northlands Coliseum** (118th Ave. and 74th St., tel. 403/471–2191).

*Horse Racing*
**Northlands Park** (112th Ave. and 74th St., tel. 403/471–7378) hosts harness racing from early March to mid-May and from mid-September through November. Thoroughbred racing occupies the summer months, mid-May through early September.

## Dining and Lodging

For price categories, *see* Winnipeg Dining and Lodging, *above*.

**Dining**
**La Boheme.** Resting on the historic east-side Gibbard Block is this fittingly splendid restaurant that presents classic French cuisine, prepared with invention and served with solicitous care. The setting features Edwardian pressed-tin ceilings and a French provincial fireplace surrounded by Voltaire chairs. Specialties include lamb sausages, pâté maison, and daily concoctions of fresh fish. The restaurant is part of a bed-and-breakfast. *6427 112th Ave., tel. 403/474–5693. Reservations advised. Jacket advised. AE, MC, V. $$$$*

★ **Unheardof Dining Lounge.** Hardly "unheard of" any longer, this is an extremely popular restaurant in an antiques-filled old house. The seven-course prix-fixe dinner changes weekly but is likely to feature game in autumn, poultry or beef the rest of the year. Dinners begin with a light pâté and are punctuated by surprising salads and re-freshing sorbets. Desserts, especially the Danish cream-cheese cheesecake, are light and delicious. *9602 82nd Ave., tel. 403/432–0480. Reservations required. Jacket advised. AE, MC, V. Closed lunch Tues.–Sat. $$$$*

**Bistro Praha.** Table lamps and paintings of Praha (Prague) street scenes make this European-style café feel as homey as Grandma's living room. Background music is classical, clientele mainly urban young professional. The menu includes such Eastern European fa-vorites as cabbage soup and Wiener schnitzel. A rich selection of desserts and a choice from 12 brands of tea make this a perfect stop for snacks. *10168 100A St. at Jasper Ave., tel. 403/424–4218. No res-ervations. Dress: casual. AE, DC, MC, V. $$$*

**La Spiga.** Admirable Northern Italian cuisine is served in a flower-filled 1913 home that feels more like Montréal than the western plains. Menu highlights include rack of lamb with grappa, breast of chicken with fresh tomato, and various renditions of veal. Portions are large and accompanied by fettuccine; the wine list is long. *10122 125 St., at 102nd Ave., tel. 403/482–3100. Reservations advised. Jacket advised. AE, MC, V. Closed lunch and Sun. $$$*

**Bourbon Street.** This is actually an assemblage of moderately priced restaurants situated around a cul-de-sac on the main floor of West Edmonton Mall. "Exterior" decor features New Orleans street lamps and wrought-iron balconies. **Café Orleans** serves such Cajun/Creole dishes as jambalaya and oysters. **Sherlock Holmes** is an En-glish pub with imported draft beer and such dishes as Mrs. Hudson's Home Made Pies. **Albert's** has deli fare including the Montréal favor-ite, smoked meat. Other spots include **Zambelli's Pizza & Steak House, Pacific Fish Co.** (*see below*), and, for belly-up-to-the-bar drinking, the **Bourbon Street Saloon.** *West Edmonton Mall, 8770 170th St., Entrance 6. No reservations. Dress: casual. AE, MC, V. $$*

**Pacific Fish Company.** Three locations satisfy landlocked Edmon-ton's appetite for fresh seafood with daily fly-ins. Order oysters Rockefeller and whiskey shrimp as appetizers, and anything charbroiled over mesquite turns out fine. Decor varies slightly, but count on the deck flooring, corrugated walls, and nets dangling overhead. *10020 101A Ave., tel. 403/422–0282; Argyll Plaza, 6258 99th St., tel. 403/437–7472; West Edmonton Mall, Bourbon St., En-trance 6, tel. 403/444–1905. Reservations advised. Dress: casual. AE, MC, V. $$*

★ **Chianti Café.** This extremely popular spot occupies part of the main floor of Strathcona Square, a converted post office in the lively Old Strathcona District. A mostly young crowd gathers for square meals featuring tasty shellfish appetizers, more than 20 varieties of pasta, a couple dozen veal dishes, and a discriminating selection of des-serts. Be prepared to wait for seating on weekend evenings. *10501 82nd Ave., tel. 403/439–9829. No reservations. Dress: casual. AE, DC, MC, V. $*

**Mongolian Food Experience.** The "experience" is selecting from a vast buffet of raw meat (lamb, beef, turkey), vegetables (mush-rooms, scallions, sprouts, cabbage), and exotic sauces and then hav-ing the chef barbecue it for you. Non-"experience" dishes, such as Szechuan beef, lemon chicken, and moo shoo pork, are also avail-able. Decor is bright and unpretentious. *10160 100A St., tel. 403/426–6806; 12520 102nd Ave., tel. 403/452–7138. Reservations ad-vised. Dress: casual. AE, MC, V. $*

**Vi's.** In summer, this old house has outdoor seating on a deck over-looking the river; in winter, tables are warmed by a blazing fire. All year the menu emphasizes the basics: hearty soups, fresh salads, extravagant sandwiches, and desserts—with special mention for chocolate pecan pie. Try Vi's for Sunday brunch. *9712 111th St., tel. 403/482–6402. Dress: casual. AE, MC, V. $*

**Lodging** **Edmonton Hilton.** Formerly the Four Seasons, and a Hilton Interna-
★ tional property since 1988, this financial-district luxury high-rise connects by second-level passageways to five major office buildings and two shopping centers. Rooms—all with bay windows and blue-and-gray color schemes—are decorated with sophistication and include marble tabletops, walnut furniture, and accents of brass. Mezzanine-level Patisserie serves a bargain Loonie Breakfast (coffee and muffin for a buck), and The Rose and Crown is an authentic English pub, perfect for throwing darts and drinking draft beers. *10235 101st St., T5J 3E9, tel. 403/428–7111 or 800/268–9275, fax 403/441–3098. 312 rooms. Facilities: 4 restaurants, 2 lounges, indoor pool, whirlpool, saunas, access to exercise room and squash and racquetball courts, no-smoking floors. AE, DC, MC, V. $$$$*

**Howard Johnson Plaza Hotel.** The renovated property on a quiet street a few blocks from downtown features a lobby and fair-size guest rooms with old-style flair: richly appointed cherry-wood furniture and a warm, cozy ambience. Some rooms have balconies, and almost all have MovieBars—a unit that includes TV, VCR, minibar, and snacks. A selection of videotapes is for rent in the lobby. Room rates include breakfast buffet. *10010 104th St., T5J 0Z1, tel. 403/423–2450. 138 rooms. Facilities: restaurant, lounge, indoor pool, sauna, exercise room, no-smoking floors. AE, DC, MC, V. $$$*

★ **Edmonton House.** The building's cylindrical design creates oddly shaped but large and comfortable one- and two-bedroom and executive suites. All units have balconies with views of the skyline or river valley, and kitchens are fully equipped (down to a toaster). A small mezzanine-level convenience store supplies basic essentials. Weekend and long-term rates are available. *10205 100th Ave., T5J 4B5, tel. 403/424–5555 or 800/661–6562, fax 403/425–5485. 293 suites. Facilities: restaurant, lounge, underground parking, complimentary shuttle service to West Edmonton Mall, indoor pool, sauna, fitness center, games room, no-smoking floors. AE, DC, MC, V. $$$*

**Fantasyland Hotel & Resort.** This important component of massive West Edmonton Mall (*see* Other Points of Interest, *above*) has regular and theme rooms; the latter include Victorian coach rooms, where guests sleep in open carriages; Roman rooms, with classic round beds; truck rooms, where the bed is the back of a pickup; and Polynesian rooms, with catamaran beds and waterfalls. All theme rooms have Jacuzzis, and non-theme quarters are comfortable and tidy. *17700 87th Ave., T5T 4V4, tel. 403/444–3000 or 800/661–6454, fax 403/444–3294. 334 rooms, 125 theme rooms. Facilities: 2 restaurants, lounge, shopping mall with 800 shops, 5-acre water park, miniature golf course, indoor amusement park. AE, DC, MC, V. $$$*

**Inn on 7th.** Edmonton shorthand provides the name for this cheerful property on 107th Street. The foliage-filled lobby features Paul Bunyan–size easy chairs. A former Holiday Inn now run by the Courtyard Inn chain, this hotel caters to tourists and government employees. Rooms are comfortably modern; the location is convenient. *10001 107th St., T5J 1J1, tel. 403/429–2861 or 800/661–7327, fax 403/426–7225. 180 rooms. Facilities: restaurant, lounge, deli, no-smoking floors. AE, DC, MC, V. $$$*

**Westin Hotel.** The brown block structure in the heart of downtown has large, comfortable rooms that are tastefully decorated with attractive artwork. The atrium lobby, with a decorative mobile, trees, and plants, conveys comfort and luxury; beige-and-pastel rooms, in keeping with the hotel's outward appearance, are equally sophisticated, down to the Caswell and Massey toiletries. The experienced staff speaks a total of 29 languages. Some of the finest food in the downtown area can be found in The Carvery. *10135 100th St., T5J 0Z1, tel. 403/426–3636 or 800/228–3000, fax 403/428–6060. 420 rooms. Facilities: 2 restaurants, 2 lounges, indoor pool, sauna, whirlpool, no-smoking floors. AE, DC, MC, V. $$$*

**West Harvest Inn.** This clean, modern three-story hotel catering to families is on the western edge of town and is only five minutes away from West Edmonton Mall. Rooms in the new wing are slightly larger and more expensive than those in the older wing, but all are comfortable. Grainfield's family restaurant is located on the premises; Xian Chinese restaurant is next door. *17803 Stony Plain Rd. (Rte. 16), T5S 1B4, tel. 403/484–8000 or 800/661–6993. 162 rooms. Facilities: restaurant, lounge. AE, MC, V. $$*

**Travelodge.** This budget chain operates two clean and functional motels: Travelodge West is located on the edge of town, not far from West Edmonton Mall, while Travelodge South is on the road to the airport. *18320 Stony Plain Rd., T5S 1A7, tel. 403/483–6031 or 800/661–9563, 227 rooms; no-smoking rooms available. 10320 45th Ave. S, T6H 5K3, tel. 403/436–9770, 222 rooms; no-smoking rooms available. Facilities: restaurant, lounge, indoor pool, whirlpool. AE, DC, MC, V. $*

**YMCA of Edmonton.** This Y has an outstanding location: in the heart of downtown adjacent to Edmonton Centre shopping mall. Rooms are small and spare but carpeted and cheerfully furnished. Singles and couples are invited to stay for $25–$29 a night. All facilities are available to overnight guests. *10030 102A Ave., T5J 0G5, tel. 403/421–9622. 113 rooms, 30 with bath. Facilities: cafeteria, indoor pool, fitness center, weight room, running track, racquetball courts. MC, V. $*

## The Arts and Nightlife

Tickets for events in Edmonton are available from Ticket Master located in Edmonton Centre, Champions in West Edmonton Mall, and Sears stores, or call 403/451–8000 to telecharge tickets to most events.

**The Arts**  Edmonton has 13 professional theater companies. The paramount
*Theater*  facility is the glass-clad downtown **Citadel Theatre Complex** (99th St. and 101A Ave., tel. 403/425–1820), where four theaters mingle esoteric works and classics. **Northern Light Theater** (Kaasa Theatre, Jubilee Auditorium, 118th Ave. and 74th St., tel. 403/471–1586) takes chances that usually succeed.

*Music and*  The **Edmonton Opera** (tel. 403/424–4040), **Edmonton Symphony Or-
*Dance*  chestra** (tel. 403/428–1414), and **Alberta Ballet Company** (tel. 403/428–6839) all perform in the **Northern Alberta Jubilee Auditorium** at the University of Alberta (87th Ave. and 114th St., tel. 403/427–9622).

*Film*  Edmonton's **Metro Cinema** (NFB Theatre, Canada Place, 9700 Jasper Ave., tel. 403/425–9212) presents classics, imports, and brave new films on weekend nights. The **Edmonton Film Society** screens an ambitious program at a theater in the **Provincial Museum of Alberta** (12845 102nd Ave., tel. 403/427–1730). The **Princess Theatre** (10337 Whyte Ave., tel. 403/433–5785), an old-time movie house in Old Strathcona district, presents revivals, experiments, and foreign films.

**Nightlife**
*Bars and Clubs* The **Rose & Crown** English-style pub in the Edmonton Hilton (10235 101st St., tel. 403/428–7111) is a popular downtown gathering place with dart boards and a huge selection of beers. **Elephant & Castle Pubs** are pleasant watering holes in downtown Edmonton's Eaton Centre (tel. 403/424–4555) and the West Edmonton Mall (tel. 403/444–3555).

*Casinos* Roulette, blackjack, and wheel of fortune action usually takes place in Edmonton between noon and midnight daily except Sunday at the **Casino ABS Downtown** (10161 112th St., tel. 403/428–6679), **Casino ABS South** (7055 Argyll Rd., tel. 403/466–0199), and the **Palace Casino** at the West Edmonton Mall (tel. 403/444–1246).

*Comedy* Edmonton boasts a branch of **Yuk Yuk's** at West Edmonton Mall (tel. 403/481–9857).

*Music* The **Sidetrack Cafe** (10333 112th St., tel. 403/421–1326) features top-name entertainers, big-screen telecasts of sports events, Variety Night on Sunday, and the Monday-night Comedy Bowl. **Yardbird Suite** (10203 86th Ave., tel. 403/432–0428) is Edmonton's premier jazz showcase. **Club Malibu** (10310 85th Ave., tel. 403/432–7300) blasts out Top–40 hits in a converted armory. **Goose Loonies** (9933 Argyll Rd., tel. 403/438–5571) has two levels of lights, lasers, and loudness. **Cook County Saloon** (8010 103rd St., tel. 403/432–0177) has mellow honky-tonk ambience and country-and-western music.

# 9 Province of Ontario

*By David E. Scott*

*Updated by Bernard Simon*

Ontario is an Iroquoian word variously interpreted as: beautiful lake, beautiful water, or rocks standing high beside the water (the last an apparent reference to Niagara Falls). Ontario is Canada's second-largest province—from east to west the traveler will cross 2,080 kilometers (1,300 miles) and one time zone. However, only 10 million people live in this vast area, and 90% of them are within a narrow strip just north of the U.S. border.

Ontario is Canada's most urbanized province; half of its population lives in four cities whose boundaries have spread to such an extent that they almost adjoin. Metropolitan Toronto has more than 2 million people. To the east, Oshawa has 175,000 people and heavily populated suburbs. South and west of Toronto are Hamilton with 550,000 people and St. Catharines with 290,000. Half of Ontario's population is British, but successive waves of immigrants over the past century have turned the province into a mini-United Nations. Thunder Bay contains the largest settlement of Finns outside Finland. Toronto has half a million Italians, the largest Chinese community in Canada, and the biggest Portuguese colony in North America. More recent arrivals include thousands of West Indians, Vietnamese, Somalis, South Africans, and east Europeans giving Ontario—Toronto in particular—a cosmopolitan flavor that rivals New York and Chicago.

The towns and cities of northern Ontario are strung along the railway lines that brought them into being. And the discovery of immense deposits of gold, silver, uranium, and other minerals by railway construction gangs sparked mining booms that established such communities as Sudbury, Cobalt, and Kirkland Lake, which continue to owe their existence to mining.

Ontario has the most varied landscape of any Canadian province. The most conspicuous topographical feature is the Niagara Escarpment, which runs from Niagara to Tobermory at the tip of the Bruce Peninsula in Lake Huron. The northern 90% of Ontario is covered by the Canadian Shield, worn-down mountain ranges of the world's oldest rock, reaching only 682 meters (2,183 feet) above sea level at their highest point. On James Bay, January temperatures range from 14°C to 28°C (7°F to 15°F).

East of Hamilton toward Niagara Falls is a narrow strip along the south shore of Lake Ontario in a partial rain shadow of the Niagara Escarpment. The climate, moderated in winter by Lakes Ontario and Erie, allows the growing of tender fruits and grapes, making it Canada's largest wine-producing area.

You could spend a lifetime exploring this enormous province and still not see it all. But by using three cities—Ottawa, Sault Ste. Marie, and Toronto—as bases for one- and two-day excursions, you can see all the major sights and some special little corners that even many Ontarians don't know about.

# Essential Information

## Important Addresses and Numbers

**Tourist Information**
*Ontario*

Ontario has a wealth of excellent and free tourist information. From within Canada or the continental United States (except Yukon, Northwest Territories, and Alaska) dial 800/668–2746, 8–8 daily, mid-May–Labor Day, and 8–4:30 weekdays the rest of the year. Or write to the **Ministry of Culture, Tourism and Recreation** (77 Bloor

St. W, Toronto, Ont. M7A 2R9). When requesting information, specify your areas of interest: antiquing, boating, camping, fishing, dining, hiking, etc. There is literature available on the entire province. Free booklets on accommodations, camping, country inns, marinas, cruises, antiques markets, and more can all be obtained. The ministry has an especially useful service for visitors eager to see the province's magnificent fall colors at their finest. By calling 800/ONTARIO between early September and late October, visitors can obtain information on where to view the autumn leaves—a sight not to be missed.

This same information is also available from Travel Information Centers at every major entry point by road and at dozens of Regional Travel Information Centers province-wide.

*Hamilton* **Greater Hamilton, Regional Municipality of Hamilton–Wentworth** (127 King St. E, Hamilton, Ont. L8N 1B1, tel. 905/546–2666 or 800/263–8590).

*Kingston* **Kingston District Chamber of Commerce** (209 Wellington St., Kingston, Ont. K7K 2Y6, tel. 613/548–4453).

*Kitchener* **Kitchener and Waterloo Chamber of Commerce** (Box 2367, 67 King St. E, Kitchener, Ont. N2H 6L4, tel. 519/742–4760).

*Midland* **Midland Chamber of Commerce** (208 King St., Box 158, Midland, Ont. L4R 4K8, tel. 705/526–7884).

*Niagara Falls* **Niagara Falls, Canada Visitor and Convention Bureau** (5433 Victoria Ave., Niagara Falls, Ont. L2G 3L1, tel. 905/356–6061 or 800/563–2557).

*Ottawa* **Ottawa Tourism and Convention Authority** (Ottawa–Carleton Centre, 2nd Floor, 111 Lisgar St., Ottawa, Ont. K2P 2L7, tel. 613/237–5150 or 800/465–1867).

*Peterborough* **Greater Peterborough Chamber of Commerce** (175 George St. N, Peterborough, Ont. K9J 3G6, tel. 705/748–9771).

*Sault Ste. Marie* **Hospitality & Travel** (99 Foster Dr., 3rd Floor, Sault Ste. Marie, Ont. P6A 5N1, tel. 705/759–5432).

*Windsor* **Convention and Visitors Bureau of Windsor, Essex County, and Pelee Island** (333 Riverside Dr. W, Suite 103, Windsor, Ont. N9A 5K4, tel. 519/255–6530).

**Emergencies** Dial 911 for **police, fire,** or **ambulance** anywhere in Ontario. The main hospitals in Ottawa are **Ottawa General Hospital** (tel. 613/737–7777) and **Ottawa Civic Hospital** (tel. 613/761–4000). **Shoppers Drug Mart** (1460 Merivale Rd., tel. 613/224–7270) is open 24 hours a day. The main hospitals in Sault Ste. Marie are **General Hospital** (tel. 705/759–3333) and **Plummer Memorial Public Hospital** (tel. 705/759–3434). Also available for emergency service is **Group Health Centre** (240 McNabb St., tel. 705/759–1234). There are no 24-hour pharmacies in Sault Ste. Marie, but **Shoppers Drug Mart** (tel. 705/949–2143) in the Cambrian Mall is open seven days a week.

**Telephones** The 416 area code in southern Ontario was split into two separate codes, 416 and 905. The 416 code now applies only to numbers in metropolitan Toronto. However, calls classified as local before the split have remained local.

## Arriving and Departing by Plane

**Airports and Airlines** Toronto, the area's major city, is served by most major international airlines. *See* Chapter 2 for details.

**Ottawa International Airport** (tel. 613/998–3151), 18 kilometers (12 miles) from downtown, is served by **Air Canada** (tel. 800/776–3000), **First Air** (tel. 800/468–8292), **Canadian Airlines International** (tel. 800/426–7000), **Delta Airlines** (tel. 800/221–1212), **KLM** (tel. 800/ 777–5553), **Lufthansa** (tel. 800/645–3880), and **USAir** (tel. 800/428– 4322).

## Arriving and Departing by Car, Train, and Bus

**By Car** The **Macdonald–Cartier Freeway,** known as Highway 401, is Ontario's major highway link. It runs from Windsor in the southwest through Toronto, along the north shore of Lake Ontario, and along the north shore of the St. Lawrence River to the Québec border west of Montréal. The **Trans-Canada Highway** follows the west bank of the Ottawa River from Montréal to Ottawa and on to North Bay. From North Bay to Nipigon at the northern tip of Lake Superior, there are two Trans-Canada highways, and from just west of Thunder Bay to Kenora, near the Manitoba border, another two. For 24-hour road-conditions information anywhere in Ontario, call 416/235–1110 or 800/268–0637.

**By Train** Ontario is served by cross-Canada **VIA Rail** (tel. 800/361–1235 outside Toronto, Kingston, London, Windsor, Hamilton; within those cities check local listings) service and connects with **Amtrak** (tel. 800/872–7245) service at Windsor (Detroit) and Fort Erie (Buffalo). VIA Rail operates frequent trains on the Windsor–London–Toronto–Kingston–Montréal corridor and the Ottawa rail station at the southeastern end of town (200 Tremblay Rd., tel. 613/244–8289; in Canada, 800/361–1235).

**By Bus** **Voyageur Colonial Bus Lines** (265 Catherine St., tel. 613/238–5900) offers frequent service from Montréal and Toronto to Ottawa, including some express buses.

## Getting Around

**By Taxi** Major cab companies, such as **Blue Line** (tel. 613/238–1111) and **Diamond** (tel. 613/235–1821), operate in and around Ottawa. Cabs are also plentiful in other major cities.

**By Bus** **OC Transpo** (tel. 613/741–4390) serves the metropolitan region of Ottawa–Carleton on the Ontario side of the Ottawa River. It operates buses on city streets and on the Transitway, a system of bus-only roads. All bus routes in downtown Ottawa meet at the Rideau Centre (Rideau St. between Nicholas and Sussex and the Mackenzie King Bridge).

**By Car** A valid driver's license from any country is good in Ontario for up to three months. Ontario is a no-fault province, and minimum liability insurance is $200,000. If you're driving across the Ontario border, either bring the policy or the vehicle registration forms and a free Canadian Non-Resident Insurance Card from your insurance agent. If you're driving a borrowed car, also bring a letter of permission signed by the owner. Driving motorized vehicles (including boats, all-terrain vehicles, and motor bikes) while impaired by alcohol is taken seriously in Ontario and results in heavy fines or imprisonment, or both. You can be convicted for refusing to take a Breathalyzer test. The threshold for impaired driving amounts to roughly the equivalent of one drink an hour. Radar warning devices are not permitted in Ontario even if they are turned off and are just in transit to other provinces. Police can seize them on the spot, and heavy fines may be imposed. Seat belts must be worn by adults and children weighing more than 18 kg (40 lb), if the car is designed with them; infants from birth to 9 kg (20 lb) must travel in a rear-facing child restraint system; children 9–18 kg (20–40 lb) must travel in a safety seat.

Studded tires and window coatings that do not allow a clear view of the vehicle interior are forbidden in Ontario. Right turns on red lights are permitted unless otherwise noted. Pedestrians crossing at designated crosswalks have the right of way.

## Guided Tours

**Ottawa**
*City Tours*
The **Gray Line** (tel. 613/748–4426) operates frequent, two-hour, 50-kilometer (31-mile) orientation tours from mid-May through October. Fares: $15 adults, $13 senior citizens, $7 children. **Picadilly Bus Tours** (tel. 613/235–7674) has a regular schedule of 1¾-hour tours in double-decker London buses to Ottawa's major sites, May 1 through October 31.

*Boat Tours*
**Paul's Boat Lines Limited** (tel. 613/235–8409) offers seven 75-minute cruises daily on the Rideau Canal and four 90-minute cruises daily on the Ottawa River from mid-May to mid-October. Canal boats dock across from the National Arts Centre; river cruise boats dock at the Bytown Museum at the foot of the Ottawa Locks on the Rideau Canal. **Ottawa Riverboat Company** (tel. 613/562–4888) operates two-hour sightseeing tours on the Ottawa River from May through October. The SS *Bytown Pumper* (tel. 613/737–6601) is a wood-burning steamboat that offers tours on the Rideau River from mid-May to mid-October. It has an 1897 engine in a 1903 hull. Cruises depart daily at 10, noon, 2, and 4 from Hog's Back Marina Park; dinner cruises are available (call ahead because the boat is sometimes chartered for the evening).

**Niagara Falls**
*City Tours*
**Double Deck Tours** (tel. 905/295–3051) touches all the bases in its 4½- to 5-hour tours in double-decker English buses, which include most of the major sights of Niagara Falls. The tours operate daily from mid-May through October. The fare of $34.90 for adults and $18.40 for children 6–12 includes GST and admissions to Table Rock Scenic Tunnels, Maid of the Mist, and a trip in the Niagara Spanish Aero Car. A shorter tour does not stop at attractions to which admission is charged, and costs $14 for adults and $7 for children. The **Niagara Parks Commission** operates People Mover System, consisting of semiarticulated air-conditioned buses, on a loop route between its public parking lot above the falls at Rapids View Terminal (well signposted) and the Niagara Spanish Aero Car parking lot about 8 kilometers (5 miles) downriver. With a day's pass (available at any booth on the system: $3 adults, $1.50 children 6–12) you can get on and off as many times as you wish at the well-marked stops along the route.

*Boat Tours*
**Maid of the Mist Steamboat Company Ltd.** (tel. 905/358–5781) operates small cruise boats that pass so near the American and Horseshoe Falls that passengers are outfitted with hooded rainslickers. The boats sail frequently between mid-May and the third week in October. *Admission: $8.65 adults, $5 children 6–12.*

*Air Tours*
**Niagara Helicopters Ltd.** (tel. 905/357–5672) takes you on a nine-minute flight over the Giant Whirlpool, up the Niagara Gorge, and past the American Falls and then banks around the curve of the Horseshoe Falls for a never-to-be-forgotten thrill—if you can keep your eyes open! *$65 per adult, $120 per two adults, $25 children 2–12 (cost includes GST). Open daily 9 AM–½-hr after sunset.*

**Sault Ste. Marie City Tours**   **Hiawathaland Tours** (tel. 705/759–6200) operates three city tours by double-decker bus and a wilderness tour by minivan to Aubrey Falls from June 15 to October 15. A 75-minute evening tour is also available.

*Boat Tours*   **Lock Tours Canada** (tel. 705/253–9850) runs two-hour excursions through the 21-foot-high Soo Locks, the 16th and final lift for ships bound for Lake Superior from the St. Lawrence River. Tours aboard the 200-passenger MV *Chief Shingwauk* or 156-passenger MV *Bon Soo* leave from the Norgoma Dock just downriver from the Holiday Inn, May 15–October 15 and up to eight times daily July 1–Labor Day. *$14 adults, $7 children 5–12, $10.50 youngsters 13–18.*

*Train Tours*   The **Agawa Canyon Train** or the **Snow Train** (tel. 705/254–4331)—the name varies with the seasons—runs from Sault Ste. Marie to Mile 114 in summer, and to Mile 120 in winter. Trains operate daily June 5–October 15 and on weekends only January–March. Trains leave Sault Ste. Marie at 8 AM in summer and 8:30 AM in winter and return at 5 PM. *$44 adults, $22 children 6–18, $7.80 children under 6.*

The **Choo-Choo Steam Train Company** runs a 75-minute excursion along the Gatineau River between Hull and Wakefield, in Québec (*see* Guided Tours in Chapter 10).

# Exploring Ontario

## Highlights for First-time Visitors

**Canada's best bird/butterfly-watching,** Tour 4: Fort Erie–Windsor
**Changing of the Guard in front of the Parliament Buildings,** Tour 1: Ottawa
**Fort Wellington,** Tour 2: Ottawa–Kawartha Lakes
**Hamilton's Castle,** Tour 5: Niagara Falls–London
**Mennonite country,** Tour 5: Niagara Falls–London
**Niagara's Horseshoe Falls,** Tour 5: Niagara Falls–London
**Old Fort Henry,** Tour 2: Ottawa–Kawartha Lakes
**Ontario's grand canyons,** Tour 6: Sault Ste. Marie–Thunder Bay
**Polar Bear Express to the Gateway to the Arctic,** Tour 8: Moosonee and Moose Factory Island
**Shaw Festival,** Tour 5: Niagara Falls–London
**Stratford's Shakespeare Festival,** Tour 5: Niagara Falls–London
**Upper Canada Village,** Tour 2: Ottawa–Kawartha Lakes
*See* also, Highlights for First-time Visitors in Toronto, Chapter 2.

## Tour 1: Ottawa

*Numbers in the margin correspond to points of interest on the Lower Ontario Province, Downtown Ottawa, and Greater Ottawa and Hull maps.*

Canadians are taught in school that it was Queen Victoria's fault their capital is inconveniently situated off the main east–west corridor along the U.S. border. But the facts are that politicians of the day were no more capable of making an unpopular decision than many who have followed them. They dithered, from 1841 to 1857, trying to decide among five possible sites, including Québec City, Montréal, Cobourg, Kingston, and Ottawa. In 1857 they passed the buck to Buckingham Palace, and Queen Victoria got them off the hook.

She chose Ottawa for five reasons, all valid at the time: The site was politically acceptable to both Canada east and Canada west. It was also centrally located, reassuringly remote from the hostile United States, and industrially prosperous. And it had a naturally beautiful setting at the confluence of the Ottawa and Rideau rivers.

Three decades earlier, when Colonel John By and his Royal Engineers arrived to build a canal from Ottawa to Kingston, there were only a few scattered settlers at what is now Ottawa. The waterway was to ensure a protected supply route from Montréal to the Great Lakes in the event of a repeat of the War of 1812 against the Americans. Between 1826 and 1832 the canal was hacked through 200 kilometers (125 miles) of swamp, rock, and lakes whose different levels were overcome by locks.

By established his canal headquarters at what is now Ottawa, and the population growth was immediate as men arrived with their families, seeking employment on the biggest construction project on the continent. The settlement, then called Bytown, grew rapidly and fast became a rowdy, rough-and-tumble backwoods town. The Ottawa River then was used for floating timber to Montréal—each spring lumberjacks tied their rafts of timber to the shore and celebrated their release from isolated lumber camps in the taverns and brothels of Bytown.

By 1837, when its population had reached 2,400, Bytown was declared by the attorney general of Upper Canada to be a town. Government moved slowly even then, and it was not legally incorporated until 1850. Five years later, when the population had reached 10,000, Bytown became a city and was farsightedly given the name Ottawa, an Indian name meaning "a place for buying and selling."

Construction started on the Parliament Buildings in 1859. The buildings are magnificent, but their location in the mid-1850s earned Ottawa the nickname "Westminster in the Wilderness." More recently, perhaps because of their neo-Gothic towers and spires—or possibly because of legislation passed inside them— some refer to Parliament Hill as "Disneyland on the Rideau."

As early as 1899, federal politicians were concerned with more than just the grounds around the Parliament Buildings, known as "the Hill." A variety of commissions and committees and plans have become today's National Capital Commission (NCC). The NCC works with all municipalities within the 2,903-square-kilometer (1,800-square-mile) National Capital Region, which includes neighboring Hull and a big chunk of Québec, to coordinate development in the best interests of the region. The result is a profusion of beautiful parks, bicycle paths, jogging trails, and the world's longest skating rink, a 6-kilometer (4-mile) stretch of the Rideau Canal kept cleared and smooth from January to March and provided with heated huts, food concessions, and skate-sharpening and rental services.

Ottawa's population is only 570,000 (another 180,000 live across the river in Hull), but parking is at a premium. This is also a tricky city for the first-time visitor to negotiate by car: One wrong turn, it seems, and you're on one of five bridges across the Ottawa River to ❶ Hull. Therefore, much of your **Ottawa** sightseeing will be on foot.

❷ Begin at the **Parliament Buildings.** Like London's Buckingham Palace, these striking buildings will be passed by visitors moving around Ottawa whether they plan to visit them or not. What you see on the Hill is similar to what opened in 1867, but the only part not destroyed by fire in 1916 was the 1876 Library of Parliament behind

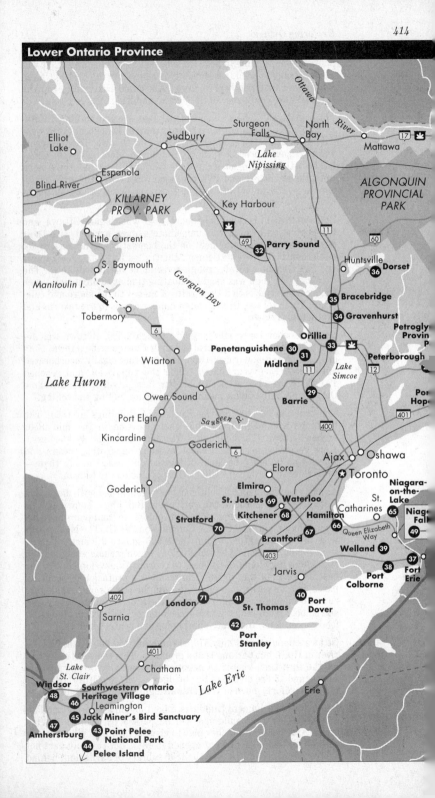

**Lower Ontario Province**

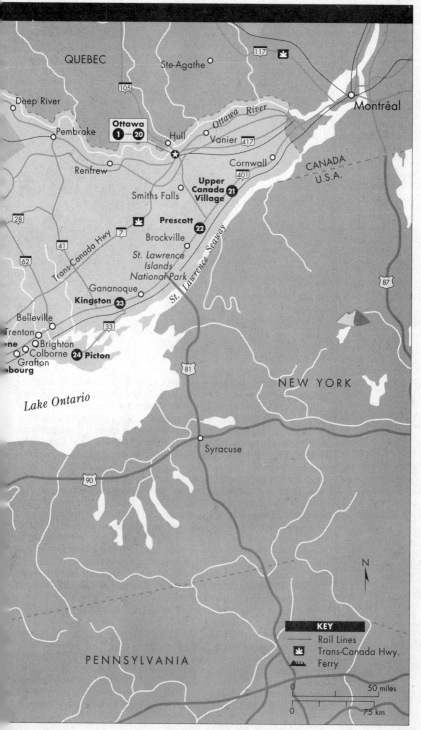

QUEBEC

Ste-Agathe

117

Montréal

Deep River

105

Ottawa River

Pembroke

Ottawa
1 — 20

Hull

Vanier
417

Renfrew

Cornwall
401

CANADA
U.S.A.

Smiths Falls

Upper
Canada
Village
21

28

Prescott
22

7

Brockville

Trans-Canada Hwy

41

St. Lawrence
Islands
National Park

62

Gananoque

St. Lawrence Seaway

87

Kingston
23

Belleville

33

Trenton

Brighton

ne

Colborne

Picton
24

Grafton

bourg

81

NEW YORK

Lake Ontario

Syracuse

90

N

PENNSYLVANIA

**KEY**
— Rail Lines
⬇ Trans-Canada Hwy.
⛴ Ferry

0        50 miles

0

75 km

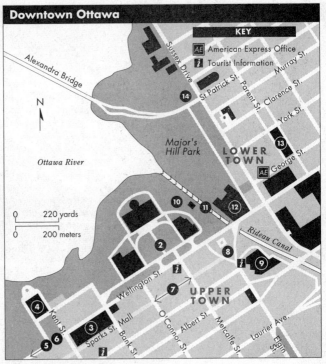

**Downtown Ottawa**

KEY

AE American Express Office

i Tourist Information

the Centre Block and the northwest wing. There are three massive
buildings on a promontory overlooking the Ottawa River, though
none face it. The **Centre Block** is where the Senate and House of
Commons, the two houses of Parliament, work to shape the laws of
the land. The central **Peace Tower** houses a Memorial Chamber with
an Altar of Sacrifice, which houses the names of 66,651 Canadians
killed during active service in World War I and 44,895 Canadians
who died in World War II. There is also a 53-bell carillon whose bells
individually range from 10 pounds to 11 tons, and together weigh 60
tons. Concerts are performed by the **Dominion Carillonneur** (tel.
613/992–4793) daily from 12:30–12:45. North (toward the river) of
the Centre Block and reached from it is the **Library of Parliament**,
which escaped the fire of 1916 but was damaged in its own fire in
1952. A statue of a young Queen Victoria is the centerpiece of the
many-sided chamber, whose walls are lined with books, many of
them priceless, and carved wooden galleries restored from the 1952
fire. In front of, and to either side of, the Parliament Buildings are
the **East Block** and **West Block**. The East Block has four historic
rooms open to the public: the original Governor General's office restored to the period of Lord Dufferin, 1872–1878; the offices of Sir
John A. Macdonald and Sir George-Étienne Cartier, Fathers of the
Confederation in 1867; and the Privy Council Chamber. The West
Block, originally designed to house the civil service, has been converted to offices for parliamentarians and is not open to the public.
The Parliament Buildings are surrounded by 29 acres of lawns that
contain statues of famous Canadians. *Tel. 613/992–4793. Open sum-
mer, daily 9–8:30; winter, daily 9–4:30. Free 20-min tours given in
English or French every ½-hr. To avoid waiting in busy summer*

*period, visitors may make same-day reservations for tours at white Infotent east of Centre Block.*

There's lots of room to stand and no charge for the colorful **Changing of the Guard ceremony** that takes place in front of the Peace Tower at 10 AM daily, June 22–August 25, weather permitting. The Ceremonial Guard brings together two of Canada's most historic regiments, the Canadian Grenadier Guards and the Governor General's Foot Guards.

Against the backdrop of the imposing Parliament Buildings, a half-hour **Sound and Light Show** highlights Canada's history. There's bleacher seating, and the shows are free. Shows are daily from early July through Labor Day, and four nights a week from early May through June and in September. In summer there are two shows daily, English first, followed by French. Check dates and times with the Public Information Office (tel. 613/992–4793).

**❸** Turn right onto Wellington Street and walk past Bank Street to the **Bank of Canada,** inside which is the **Currency Museum.** The ancestors of the credit card are all here: bracelets made from elephant hair, cowrie shells, whale's teeth, and what is believed to be the world's largest coin. Here, too, of course, is the most complete collection of Canadian notes and coins. *245 Sparks St., tel. 613/782–8914. Admission: $2 adults, children under 7 free, $3 families; Tues. free. Open May–Sept., Mon–Sat. 10:30–5, Sun. 1–5; Sept.–May, Tues.–Sat. 10:30–5, Sun. 1–5.*

**❹** Turn right onto Kent Street to the **Supreme Court.** It was established in 1875, and in 1949 it became the ultimate court of appeal in the land. The nine judges sit only in Ottawa in three sessions each year in their stately art deco building. *Kent and Wellington Sts., tel. 613/995–4406 ext.327. Free tours May–Aug., daily 9–5; Sept.–Apr., by appt.*

**❺** At the end of Wellington Street is the **Garden of the Provinces,** which commemorates confederation with the emblems of Canada's 10 **❻** provinces and two territories. Across from the park is the **National Archives of Canada** and the **National Library of Canada.** The archives, Canada's oldest cultural institution, contains more than 60 million manuscripts and government records, 1 million maps, and about 11 million photographs. The National Library collects, preserves, and promotes the published heritage of Canada and exhibits books, paintings, maps, and photographs. *395 Wellington St., tel. 613/995–5138 for archives; 613/992–9988 for library. Admission free. Open daily 9 AM–10:30 PM.*

**❼** Return toward Parliament Hill via **Sparks Street Pedestrian Mall,** where the automobile has been banished and browsers wander among fountains, rock gardens, sculptures, and outdoor cafés. **❽** Emerging from the mall, you'll face **Confederation Square** and the **National War Memorial** honoring the 66,651 Canadian dead of World War I.

**❾** Adjacent to the square stands the **National Arts Centre,** a huge theater complex designed around the repetitive motif of the hexagon. The complex includes an opera hall, a theater, a studio theater, and a salon for readings and concerts. The center has its own orchestra, and touring companies offer more than 900 performances a year. Its canal-side café, **Le Cafe,** spills outside in warm weather and is popular for a meal or drink. *53 Elgin St., tel. 613/996–5051. Admission free. 30- to 40-min tours depart from the main lobby May 1–Aug. 31, daily at noon, 1:30, and 3; Sept.–Apr., Tues., Thurs., and Sat. (Sun. to the end of Oct.).*

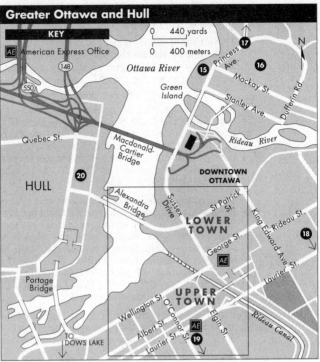

⑩ Ottawa's oldest building, now the **Bytown Museum,** houses a collection of 3,500 artifacts of Colonel By and Ottawa memorabilia at the
⑪ **Rideau Locks** between The Hill and Ottawa's grand hotel, the
⑫ **Château Laurier Hotel** (*see* Lodging, *below*). By built the stone building in 1826, and it was his commissariat for payroll monies and supplies during construction of the canal. *Tel. 613/234–4570. Admission: $2.25 adults, $1.10 students and senior citizens, 50¢ children, $5.50 families. Open mid-May–mid-Oct., Mon. and Wed.–Sat. 10–4, Sun. 2–5; Apr.–mid-May and mid-Oct.–Nov., weekdays 10–4.*

Between the Château Laurier Hotel and the Rideau Canal is the **Museum of Contemporary Photography,** which opened in 1992. The museum has 158,000 images, shown in changing exhibitions. There's a 50-seat theater and a boutique. *1 Rideau Canal, tel. 613/990–8257. Admission: $2.50 adults, $1.25 senior citizens, full-time students and donors free. Free Thurs. Open Fri.–Tues. 11–5, Wed. 4–8, Thurs. 11–8.*

There has been a farmers' market here since 1840 with fresh produce, maple products, and flowers; surrounding the market stalls are permanent specialty food shops, some well over 100 years old. In
⑬ **Byward Market** there are cafés, restaurants, patios, boutiques, and bars, and the area hops day and night.

⑭ The **National Gallery of Canada,** a magnificent glass-towered temple to art, reflects the Parliament Buildings in its modern mirror-and-granite facade. The gallery contains the most comprehensive collection of Canadian art. Inside is the reconstructed Rideau Convent Chapel, a classic example of 19th-century French Canadian architecture with the only neo-Gothic fan-vaulted ceiling on the continent. The building has three restaurants and a large bookstore with publications on the arts. *380 Sussex Dr., tel. 613/990–1985. Admission: $5 adults, $3 senior citizens, students and children under 18 free. Free Thurs. Closed Mon. and holidays in winter.*

It's best to continue the tour by car or bicycle as Sussex Drive skirts the Ottawa River above limestone bluffs. Sussex Drive is Ottawa's embassy row. On your left look out for Earlsmere, the elegant residence of the British high commissioner. The sprawling dark-brown building a little farther on the right is the Lester B. Pearson Building, named for the former prime minister who was Canada's only winner of the Nobel Peace Prize. The building houses the Department of External Affairs. An address known to most Canadians, 24 Sussex Drive, is the official **residence of the prime minister.** Don't try parking near the mansion; security is tight. The best way to view the mansion is by slowing down your car as you pass the gates, though all you'll get is a glimpse of a couple of roof gables and some expensive landscaping.

**⑯** Government House, also known as **Rideau Hall,** has been the official residence of the governor-general of Canada since 1865. Visiting heads of state, royalty, and the monarch stay here while on official business. The 1830 mansion has a ballroom, and there are a skating rink and a cricket pitch. Sentries of the Canadian Grenadier Guards and the Governor General's Foot Guards are posted outside the main gate of Rideau Hall from late June through August. Free walking tours of the grounds are conducted year-round, but days and times change frequently according to season. *1 Sussex Dr., tel. 613/993–0311.*

**⑰** Follow Sussex Drive past Rideau Hall to the Rockcliffe Driveway and then signs that say 4 kilometers (2½ miles) to the **National Aviation Museum** at Rockcliffe Airport. There are more than 100 aircraft in this collection, from a replica of the Silver Dart that made the first powered flight in Canada through World War I Sopwiths. *Tel. 613/993–2010 or 800/463–2038. Admission: $5 adults, $4 students and senior citizens, $1.75 children 6–15, $10 families. Free Thurs. Open May–Aug., Mon. holidays, Fri.–Sun., Tues., and Wed. 9–5, Thurs. 9–9; Sept.–Apr., Mon. holidays and Tues.–Sun. 9–5, Thurs. 9–8.*

**⑱** Don't plan on scampering through the **National Museum of Science and Technology** collections in half an hour. There are permanent displays of printing presses, antique cars, steam locomotives, and agricultural machinery, and there are ever-changing exhibits, many of which are hands-on, or "minds-on." Take the St. Laurent Boulevard South exit from the Queensway. The entrance is 1.6 kilometers (1 mile) south off Lancaster Road. *1867 St. Laurent Blvd., tel. 613/991–3044. Admission: $5 adults, $4 senior citizens and students, $1.75 children 6–15, $10 families. Free Thurs. 5–9. Open May–Aug., Mon. holidays, Fri.–Sun., Tues., and Wed. 9–5, Thurs. 9–9; Sept.–Apr., Mon. holidays and Tues.–Sun. 9–5, Thurs. 9–8.*

**⑲** **The Canadian Museum of Nature** collection used to be called the National Museum of Natural Sciences, and some of the collection has gone across the river to Hull to help fill galleries in the enormous Canadian Museum of Civilization (*see below*). But there's lots of interest left in this grand old building that was briefly the seat of government in 1916 after the Parliament Buildings burned. The dinosaur collection is fabulous, and so are the stuffed birds and animals in simulated habitats. *McLeod St. at Metcalfe, tel. 613/996–*

*3102. Admission: $4 adults, $3 students, $2 children 6–16 and senior citizens, $12 families. Half price on Thurs. until 5, free 5–8. Open May–Aug., Fri.–Wed. 10–5, Thurs. 10–8; Sept.–Apr., Fri.–Wed. 10–5, Thurs. 10–8.*

**㉒** Although the **Canadian Museum of Civilization** is not in Ontario, it is definitely considered part of the Ottawa scene, literally, because visitors can see it on the other side of the Ottawa River from behind the Parliament Buildings on the Hill. This immense, modernistic building on the Québec shore of the Ottawa River features galleries, displays, films, lectures, theaters, and exhibitions chronicling thousands of years of Canadian history. In the Grand Hall, six native longhouses, towering totem poles, and life-size reconstructions of Canadian historic scenes help you travel through time. Special exhibitions throughout the year are offered for an additional admission fee at Cineplus, the first theater to project the larger-than-life Imax and Omnimax. *100 Laurier St., Hull, tel. 819/776–7000. Admission to the museum: $4.50 adults, $3 students and senior citizens, children 15 and under free, free Thurs. 5–8; Cineplus, tel. 819/776–7010. Prices change depending on the program, but are usually $7 adults, $5 students and senior citizens, and children. Open May–Sept., daily 9–5, Thurs. 9–8; Sept.–Apr., Tues.–Sun. Closed Dec. 25 and Jan. 1.*

## Tour 2: Heritage Highway

From Ottawa, Highway 31 runs southeast about 75 kilometers (46 miles) to scenic Highway 2 at Morrisburg. One of the province's major tourist attractions is 11 kilometers (7 miles) west by Highway 2 or Highway 401. Eight villages disappeared under rising waters when the St. Lawrence Seaway opened in 1959, but their best historic buildings were moved to a new village called **Upper Canada Village,** a faithful re-creation of an Ontario community from the 1800s. The village occupies 66 acres of the 2,000-acre **Crysler's Farm Battlefield Memorial Park,** a site that figured prominently in the War of 1812. Such newfangled gadgets as radios, walkie-talkies, and tape players are banned in this throwback to the days of the United Empire Loyalists. The village has three mills, two farms, two churches, two hotels, and 25 other buildings. A leisurely tour takes three to four hours. There are more than 150 staff people on the site, all in early 1800s costume, to answer questions. The Village Store is open year-round and sells Canadian crafts and village-made bread, cheese, and flour. Willard's Hotel, licensed for beer and wine, serves lunches, full-course meals, and teas. Two-day passes are available (at reduced rates). *Hwy. 2 E, tel. 613/543–3704. Admission: $9/$13.75 for two days adults, $6/$9 students, $5.50/$7.75 senior citizens, $3.75/$5.75 children 6–12. Open mid-May–mid-Oct., daily 9:30–5; winter, open for special events only.*

**㉒** Head west on Highway 2 about 40 kilometers (25 miles) to **Prescott** and its second fort, Fort Wellington, built by the British in 1813 to protect goods and troops moving between Montréal and Upper Canada after the outbreak of the War of 1812. The fort was never attacked and was completed in 1814, the year the war ended. The Ottawa–Kingston Rideau Canal eliminated its need and it was abandoned. In 1837 rebellion broke out in Upper and Lower Canada, and the British built a new and stronger Fort Wellington on the site. The buildings are furnished in the 1846 period. *370 Vankoughnet St., tel. 613/925–2896. Admission free. Open mid-May–Aug., daily 10–6; Sept.–mid-Oct., daily 10–5; mid-Oct–mid-May, by reservation only.*

Ontario's oldest barracks building is one block west of Fort Wellington at 356 East Street and open daily in July and August as a museum. Lunches and dinners at **Stockade Barracks and Hospital Museum** feature historic menus year-round. By prior arrangement, groups of 15–40 can have five- or six-course meals of 1812-style dishes served by mess waiters in military uniforms. *356 East St., tel. 613/925–4894. Admission: $2 adults, children under 12 free, families $5.*

**㉓** **Kingston's** imposing architecture has been impressing visitors since 1673, when LaSalle chose the location as the site for a meeting between Governor Frontenac and the Iroquois. Before the meeting, Frontenac built a stockaded fort to impress the Indians and thus tap into the fur trade. Thanks to misguided American strategy, Kingston survived the War of 1812 almost totally unscathed. Many of its beautiful limestone buildings remain in mint condition today. From 1841 to 1844, Kingston was the capital of the province of Canada; today the gorgeous, cut-limestone city hall dominates the city's downtown core, facing a riverfront park. Tours are given weekdays in the summer, but visitors can wander through the lobby area any time of the year.

The city occupied a strategic site at the junction of the St. Lawrence River and Rideau Canal system, and four Martello towers still guard the harbor. The **Royal Military College of Canada** features a museum in Fort Frederick, the largest of the Martello towers. The museum contains the internationally renowned Douglas Arms Collection, which includes the small-arms collection of General Porfirio Díaz, president of Mexico from 1886 to 1912. *Off Hwy. 2, just east of Kingston, tel. 613/541–6663 or 613/541–6652. Admission free. Open last weekend in June–Labor Day, daily 10–5.*

The massive **Fort Henry** was built during the War of 1812 to repel a possible American invasion, which never came. Students in period military costume guide visitors through, hold parades, and recreate the pomp and pageantry of an era past. *Hwys. 2 and 15, tel. 613/542–7388. Admission: late May–mid-Oct., $9 adults, $5 senior citizens, $5.85 students, $3.80 children 6–12; mid-Oct.–mid-May, $3.40 adults, $1.75 senior citizens, students, and children. Open daily 9–5.*

Locals nicknamed it Tea Caddy Castle, Molasses Hall, and Pekoe Pagoda, but Canada's first prime minister, Sir John A. Macdonald, who lived in the house for a year, called it **Bellevue** because of its view over the St. Lawrence River. Today the 1840 house is a National Historic Park site restored and furnished to the 1848 period when Macdonald lived there. *35 Centre St., tel. 613/545–8666. Admission free. Open May–Nov., daily 9–6; Dec.–Apr., daily 10–5.*

All you'd ever want to know about steam engines and their history— and then some—is available on display in the **Pump House Steam Museum** (23 Ontario St., tel. 613/546–4696), the restored Victorian-style 1849 municipal water-pumping station. All the exhibits run on steam (only between mid-May and Labor Day), and the collection is believed to be the largest in the world. Models range from miniatures to an 1897-model Toronto-built engine with a 9-ton flywheel. The **Marine Museum of the Great Lakes at Kingston** (55 Ontario St., tel. 613/542–2261), under the same management, features a rambling display area at the historic former Kingston Drydock that traces Great Lakes shipping since 1678. The 3,000-ton, 210-foot retired icebreaker, the *Alexander Henry*, is also on tour from mid-May to mid-October. Summer visitors can rent a stateroom and sleep aboard. Tickets are available for one, two, or all three of these attractions. *Admission: $3.75/$5.25/$6.25 adults, $2.25/$3.25/$4.75 senior citizens and children. Both museums open Apr.–Dec., daily 10–5; Jan.–Mar., weekdays 10–4.*

Kingston is the birthplace of organized ice hockey—the first league game was played in the city in 1885. So it seems fitting that the city is also home to an **International Hockey Hall of Fame,** a shrine to puck-chasing. (Canada's other Hockey Hall of Fame opened as a bigger venue in Toronto in 1993.) *York and Alfred Sts., 1 block north of Princess St. (Hwy. 2), tel. 613/544–2355. Admission: $2.14 adults, $1.61 senior citizens and students, children under 12 free, $4.28 families. Open mid-June–mid-Sept., daily 10–5; late Sept.–early June, weekends and by appt.*

Highway 2 or 401 will take you to **Belleville,** but consider Highway 33, which will take you past Kingston's Gothic penitentiary at Collins Bay to Picton in the island county of Prince Edward. A free, 10-minute ferry ride (service every 15 minutes in summer) lands you at Glenora on the island, and it's 9 kilometers (6 miles) to Picton, the county seat.

㉔ **Picton** is a serene town of 4,300 with fine old buildings and strong associations with Sir John A. Macdonald, Canada's first prime minister, who practiced law at the 1834 county courthouse that is still in use. Within the town is the **Macaulay Heritage Park,** which sits on about 15 acres of land and includes picnic facilities, the Macaulay House, and the County Museum. Tours of the park and town's attractions are available by prior arrangement and may include a visit to the jail, where a double gallows is kept handy (although it hasn't been used since 1884). *Tel. 613/476–3833. Admission to house: $2 adults, children free. House open weekdays 10–4:30.*

New Englanders wandering the island might find themselves wondering if they had ever left home—so similar are the scenery and the pages of history that brought both regions into being. The island was one of the earliest parts of Ontario to be settled after the American Revolution, and the Loyalist influence remained dominant for generations. The first of these settlers landed at Adolphustown Reach from Bateaux on June 16, 1784, and village locals nicknamed the landing area the Plymouth Rock of Ontario. The earliest burial ground in the district is located here, and the Loyalist church erected in 1822 is still used as a parish meeting hall.

㉕ About an hour west of Belleville, or 90 minutes from Picton, are the towns of **Cobourg** and **Port Hope,** both richly endowed with mansions originally built as summer homes by Americans. Again, the traveler has the choice of the four-lane Highway 401 or Highway 2, which is closer to the shore of Lake Ontario and wanders through the pretty communities of **Brighton, Colborne,** and **Grafton.** Cobourg is another community that expected to be chosen as the provincial capital. It was passed over, but not before the town just about bankrupted itself building the magnificent **Victoria Hall,** officially opened in 1860 by the young Prince of Wales, later King Edward VII. The hall was used for town council meetings, formal balls, and concerts on the second floor; a courtroom modeled after London's Old Bailey was located on the ground floor. Today's visitor can take a free tour of some of the 41 rooms in the building. *55 King St. W, tel. 905/372–5831. Admission free. Guided tours in summer or by prior arrangement.*

㉖ From Port Hope, take Highway 28 for about 40 kilometers (25 miles) into the Kawartha lakes region to reach the small city of **Peter-**

**borough,** home of Trent University and 70,000 people. High notes in Peterborough are the signature lift locks on the Trent-Severn Waterway, which are among the world's highest, and Centennial Fountain in Little Lake, which at 250 feet is the highest jet fountain in Canada. The lift lock on the Trent Canal system was built in 1904. In less than 10 minutes it lifts boats, and the water they're floating in, 65 feet straight up. The lock and the Trent Canal operate mid-May–mid-October; slides and films at a visitor center explain their mechanism. *Hunter St. E, tel. 705/745–8389. Admission free. Open June–Sept., daily 9–6; Oct.–June, daily 9–5 (call ahead).*

 Southeast of Peterborough, around the town of **Keene,** are several attractions. **Serpent Mounds Provincial Park** is 13 kilometers (9 miles) southeast of Peterborough on the shores of Rice Lake. About 2,000 years ago a nomadic native tribe buried its dead in nine earth mounds, the largest of which is shaped like a 200-foot-long serpent. An interpretation center explains the site and displays artifacts. *Tel. 705/295–6879. Admission: $5 per vehicle, $15.25 to camp overnight. Open mid-May–mid-Oct., daily.*

On the way to the park, about 3 kilometers (2 miles) north of the village of Keene is the well-signed **Lang Pioneer Village,** with its museum and 26 pioneer buildings. There are displays and demonstrations of pioneer arts and crafts in the summer. *Tel. 705/295–6694. Admission, including GST: $6 adults, $4.50 students, $5 senior citizens, $2.75 children under 14, $13.75 families. Open mid-May–mid-Oct., weekdays 11–5, Sat. 1–5, Sun. 1–6; museum gallery open daily (except Dec. 25), 1–5.*

Canada's largest concentration of native rock carvings was found at the east end of Stoney Lake, outside the hamlet of Stonyridge, in 1954. The site, 50 kilometers (31 miles) northwest of Peterborough, is now within **Petroglyphs Provincial Park.** The well-preserved symbols and figures, which are carved on a flat expanse of white marble almost 70 feet wide, are encased in a protective building. The more than 900 carvings are believed to be of Algonquin spirit figures. *East of Hwy. 28 on Northey's Bay Rd., tel. 705/877–2552. Admission: $6 per vehicle, $3 for senior citizens. Open mid-May–mid-Oct., daily.*

Stoney Lake is also one of Ontario's most popular locations for weekend cottages. Drive along the lakeside roads for a glimpse of the cottages, some of which would more aptly be described as mansions.

## Tour 3: North of Toronto to the Lakes

**Barrie,** a city of almost 80,000 on the shores of Lake Simcoe, is about 75 kilometers (46 miles) north of Toronto on the four-lane Highway 400. A winter carnival attracts ice fishermen, dogsled racers, and ice motorcyclists. From late June through Labor Day, there's informal theater in Gryphon Theatre at Georgian College and harness racing at Barrie Raceway.

More than a dozen artists have studios in the Barrie area—most of the work spaces are attached to their homes. Among those studios worth a visit is the home of Henni Stoffregen who sells lampshades, placemats, cards, and numerous other items made from pressed wild flowers, leaves, and grasses. *Concession 2 and Mill St., near Hillsdale, tel. 705/835–3296. For studio tour maps call Chris Symes: tel. 705/329–0842.*

From just north of Barrie, take Highways 400 and 93 about 50 kilometers (30 miles) to the towns of **Penetanguishene** (known locally

**③** as Penetang) and **Midland** in a small corner of northern Simcoe County known as Huronia. This 30- by 60-kilometer (20- by 40-mile) area was the scene of some of the most grisly episodes in North American history. Each town sits on a snug, safe harbor at the foot of two bays that lead out to Georgian Bay.

Just 5 kilometers (3 miles) east of Midland on Highway 12, visitors can explore a complete reconstruction of **Sainte-Marie among the Hurons.** Jesuit missionaries built the Sainte-Marie mission at this spot in 1639. The Jesuits preached Christianity, and the Hurons—also called Wendat—taught the French settlers how to survive in the harsh climate. By 1648 the mission was home to one-fifth of the European population of New France. The villagers built Ontario's first hospital, farm, school, and social service center here and constructed a canal from the Wye River. A combination of disease and Iroquois attacks led to the mission's demise. Twenty-two structures, faithfully reproduced from a scientific excavation, including an Indian longhouse and wigwam, can now be toured. The canal is working again; staff in period costume saw timber, repair shoes, sew clothes, and grow vegetables. *Tel. 705/526–7838. Admission: $5.75 adults, $3.50 students, $3.25 senior citizens, children under 6 free. Open Apr.–mid-Oct., daily 10–4:30; winter, by appt.*

On a hill overlooking Sainte-Marie is **Martyr's Shrine,** a twin-spired stone cathedral built in 1926 to honor the eight missionaries who died in Huronia (the name given to the area originally); in 1930 five of the priests were canonized by the Roman Catholic church. The grounds include a theater, souvenir shop, cafeteria, and picnic area. *Tel. 705/526–3788. Open Victoria Day–mid-Oct., daily.*

The best artifacts from several hundred archaeological digs in the area are displayed at **Huronia Museum and Gallery of Historic Huronia** in Little Lake Park in Midland. Behind the museum and gallery building is **Huron Indian Village,** a full-scale replica of a 16th-century Huron Indian village. *Little Lake Park, tel. 705/526–2844. Admission to museum and village: $5 adults, $3.50 students, $4.50 senior citizens. Open Jan.–late May, weekdays 9–5; late May–mid-Oct., Mon.–Sat. 9–5, Sun. 10–5.*

**Cruises** leave from the town docks of both Midland and Penetang to explore the 30,000 island region of Georgian Bay from May to Thanksgiving (Canadians observe this on the second Monday in October). From Midland town dock the 215-passenger MS *Miss Midland* (tel. 705/526–0161 or 800/461–1767 in Ontario) offers one to four 2½-hour sightseeing cruises. From the Penetang town dock, the 200-passenger MS *Georgian Queen* (tel. 705/549–7795) takes passengers on three-hour tours of the islands, from late May through Thanksgiving. The cruises leave once daily at 2 PM.

**③** From Penetang or Midland, it's 110 kilometers (68 miles) by Highways 12 and 69 to **Parry Sound.** Here Canada's largest, $3 million sightseeing cruise ship, the *Island Queen*, offers a more extensive three-hour cruise of Georgian Bay, one to two times daily, depending on season. There's free parking at the town dock. *9 Bay St., tel. 705/746–2311. Admission: $15 adults, $7.50 children. Operates June–Thanksgiving.*

From mid-July to mid-August, Festival of the Sound (tel. 705/746–2410) is held. Jazz, popular music, classical piano, and show tunes are performed in the auditorium of Parry Sound High School and aboard the *Island Queen*.

33 **Orillia,** about 35 kilometers (21 miles) north of Barrie on Highway 11 at the junction of Highway 12, will be recognized by readers of Canada's greatest humorist, Stephen Leacock, as Mariposa, the "little town" he described in *Sunshine Sketches of a Little Town.* The writer's former summer home is now a museum, the **Stephen Leacock Memorial Home.** In the Mariposa Room, characters from the book are matched with the Orillia residents who inspired them. *Off Hwy. 12B in the east end of Orillia (well signposted), tel. 705/326–9357. Admission: $4 adults, $3.50 senior citizens, $1 youths 15–18, 50¢ children under 15. Open Apr. 16–mid-June and Labor Day–Dec. 15, daily 10–2 and by appt.; mid-June–Labor Day, daily 10–5.*

North along Highway 11, rolling farmland suddenly changes to lakes and pine trees amid granite outcrops of the Canadian Shield. This region, called Muskoka, is the playground of folks who live in the highly urbanized areas in and on either side of Toronto. 34 **Gravenhurst,** 39 kilometers (24 miles) north of Orillia, is a town of fewer than 6,000 and the birthplace of Canada's least-known hero—least known in Canada, that is. In China, Norman Bethune's name is almost as well known as Wayne Gretzky's is in Canada. Bethune is remembered for his heroic work in China as a field surgeon and medical educator. The **Bethune Memorial House,** an 1880-vintage frame home, has become a shrine of sorts to Chinese diplomats visiting North America. *235 John St., tel. 705/687–4261. Admission free. Open June–Labor Day, daily 10–6; Labor Day–May, 10–5. Closed winter holidays.*

The RMS *Segwun* (the initials stand for Royal Mail Ship) is the sole survivor of a fleet of steamships that once provided transportation through the Muskoka Lakes. The 128-foot boat, built in Scotland and assembled in Gravenhurst in 1887, carries 99 passengers on cruises from early June to early October. Cruises range from 90 minutes to two days in length (passengers dine aboard but sleep in one of Muskoka's grand resorts). Reservations are strongly recommended. *Muskoka Lakes Navigation and Hotel Company Limited, 820 Bay St., Sagama Park, Gravenhurst P1P 1G7, tel. 705/687–6667.*

35 Just 11 kilometers (8 miles) north of Gravenhurst outside **Bracebridge** is **Santa's Village and Mister Rudolph's Funland.** After letting Santa know what they'd like to find under the Christmas tree, youngsters can delight in the Kris Kringle Riverboat, the Candy Cane Express Train, minibikes, bumper boats, paddleboats, or pony rides, to name a few. Mister Rudolph's Funland is for children 12 and older and offers go-karts, batting cages, in-line skating, 18-hole mini-putt and an indoor activity center with video games. *Santa's Village, west of Bracebridge, well signposted, tel. 705/645–2512. Admission: $13.98 adults, $8.13 senior citizens and children 2–4; unlimited rides all day. Open mid-June–Labor Day, daily 10–6. Mister Rudolph's Funland open late May–mid-June and Labor Day–Thanksgiving, weekends 10–10; mid-June–Labor Day, daily 10–10.*

36 **Dorset** is a pretty village on a narrows between two bays of the Lake of Bays, about 40 kilometers (25 miles) east of Huntsville by Highways 60 and 35. The village is home to **Robinson's General Store** (tel. 705/766–2415), which makes the modest claim "Voted Canada's Best Country Store." Voting was by the editors of *Canadian Living* magazine, but visitors are not likely to question the choice. With the exception of the World War II years, the store, established in 1921, has been open continuously and operated by a Robinson. You'll find everything here from moose-fur hats to stoves and pine furniture.

You can circle back to Toronto on scenic Highway 35 or make Dorset a circle tour from Huntsville around the Lake of Bays.

If you have more time at your disposal, take Highway 60 northeast from Huntsville to **Algonquin Park.** Stretching across 7,600 square kilometers of lakes, forests, rivers, and cliffs, Algonquin is a hiker's, canoeist's, and camper's paradise. But don't be put off if you're not the athletic or rough-outdoors sort. About a third of all visitors to Algonquin come for the day to visit a museum, walk one of the 14 interpretive trails, or enjoy a swim or a picnic. Swimming is especially good at Lake of Two Rivers, about halfway between the west and east gates along Highway 60. A morning drive through the park in May or June is often rewarded by a sighting of moose, which are attracted to the highway by the slightly salty water in roadside ditches. Wolf-howling expeditions, led by a park naturalist, take place in August. The drive back to Toronto takes about four hours. Alternatively, once you reach the east gate of the park, you're only two to three hours northwest of Ottawa. *Algonquin Provincial Park, Box 219, Whitney K0J 2M0, tel. 705/633–5572.*

## Tour 4: Fort Erie and West to Windsor

**37** **Fort Erie** is at the extreme southeast tip of the Niagara Peninsula, 155 kilometers (95 miles) south of Toronto and just across the International Peace Bridge over the Niagara River from Buffalo, New York. It's a drab, boom-or-bust town of fast-food chains, taverns, and gas stations whose profits rise or fall with the exchange rate between Canadian and U.S. dollars. The heavy American influx to the area is not without historic irony; the last American presence on Canadian soil took place here at the end of the War of 1812.

**Old Fort Erie,** situated at the south end of Fort Erie, has been reconstructed as it existed before it was destroyed at the end of the War of 1812. The Old Fort's colorful and bloody history reveals that thousands of soldiers lost their lives within sight of the earthworks, drawbridges, and palisades. The fort itself was destroyed in 1779 and again in 1803 by spectacular storms that drove masses of ice ashore at the foot of Lake Erie. Visitors are conducted through the display rooms by guards in period uniforms of the British army. During summer the guards stand sentry duty, fire the cannon, and demonstrate drill and musket practice. *Tel. 905/871–0540. Admission: $3.50 adults, $3.15 senior citizens, $2 students, $9 family. Open mid-May–mid-Sept., daily.*

The town's other major attraction, the **Fort Erie Race Track,** opened in 1897, but it is one of the most modern—and picturesque—tracks in North America. Glass-enclosed dining lounges overlook a 1-mile dirt track and a seven-furlong turf course. Also in view are gardens, ponds, and waterways. *Tel. 905/871–3200. Open May–Sept., Fri.–Mon. for 1 PM race; Oct., Fri.–Sun. for 1 PM race.*

**38** Lake Erie's **Port Colborne,** or "The Ports," is about 30 kilometers (20 miles) west of Fort Erie by Highway 3 (at the south end of the Welland Canal—*see* Tour 5, *below*). There's no admission charge to **Port Colborne Historical and Marine Museum,** a six-building complex where afternoon tea is served (at a price) from Arabella's Tea Room. *280 King St., tel. 905/834–7604. Admission free. Open May–Dec., daily noon–5.*

**39** About 10 kilometers (6 miles) north of Port Colborne is the industrial city of **Welland.** For years the city was bypassed by the 14–16 million tourists who visit Niagara Falls annually, so in 1988 Welland initiated its Festival of Arts Murals. There now are 27 giant murals on downtown buildings; the longest is 130 feet, and the tallest is three stories high. Visitors can pick up a free mural tour map from **Welland Tourism** (32 E. Main St., tel. 905/735–8696) or from brochure racks at City Hall and in local restaurants and hotels. *Festival of Arts, 800 Niagara St. N, tel. 905/788–3000.*

From Welland, Highway 3 wanders west through rolling farm country occasionally slashed by a river emptying into Lake Erie. At **Jarvis,** 80 kilometers (50 miles) west, turn south on Highway 6 to **(40) Port Dover,** home of the world's largest fleet of freshwater fishing boats. It's a pretty beach resort town where freshwater fish is served up steamy and golden at a number of restaurants.

**Time Out**    The **Erie Beach Motor Hotel** (19 Walker St., tel. 519/583–1391) dining rooms have developed a following since the Schneider family opened the first one in 1946. For those not eager to dig into a platter of local perch or pickerel, steak or shrimp are on the menu, as well as a variety of draft beers by the glass or pitcher.

Take Highway 24 north to Simcoe to rejoin Highway 3 westbound. **(41) St. Thomas's** first buildings went up in 1810, over a decade and a half ahead of the first building in London, 28 kilometers (17 miles) north. For all its premature cosmopolitanism, its population has leveled at 29,000, while London's has hit the 310,000 mark. Note the **statue of Jumbo,** the Barnum and Bailey circus elephant, killed there in a freak railway accident in 1885. The monument is a 10%-larger-than-life-size statue of the largest elephant ever in captivity. Adjacent to the Jumbo monument is a railway caboose, summer office of the St. Thomas Chamber of Commerce, and a gift shop for Jumbo kitsch. *538 Talbot St., tel. 519/631–1981; monument, tel. 519/631–8188. Chamber office open year-round 8:30–5; monument office open May–Labor Day, daily 9–9.*

About 15 kilometers (10 miles) south of St. Thomas is the summer **(42)** resort town of **Port Stanley,** with a fine brown sand beach and the boutiques, snack bars, and kitsch stands that survive on vacationers following the sun.

It isn't hauled by a steam engine anymore, but the London and Port Stanley Railroad (L&PS) still packs in travelers. The operation has proven so popular the little train now runs year-round and its trackage has been doubled. The railroad was built in 1856 between London and Port Stanley and intended as a main trade link between Canada and the United States. The trade didn't materialize, but the railroad survived on excursion traffic until 1957. Railroad buffs restored some passenger cars and repaired the line to Union, in 1992 extending it to St. Thomas. You can take a 45-minute excursion to Union year-round, or—from June through October—a two-hour round-trip to St. Thomas. *Port Stanley Railway Station, tel. 519/ 782–3730. Round-trip fares to Union: $6.50 adults, $6.25 senior citizens, $3.75 children under 12; to St. Thomas: $11 adults, $10 senior citizens, $5.50 children.*

From Port Stanley/St. Thomas the fastest way to cover the 150 kilometers (95 miles) to the extreme southwest corner of Ontario is on Highway 401, but it's a flat, straight, and deadly dull trip. The two-lane Highway 3 is a better choice—it follows the shore of Lake Erie and passes through a number of towns and villages. In summer and fall, vegetable stands sprout like mushrooms along this route, offering fresh locally grown fruits and vegetables.

**Point Pelee** juts into Lake Erie, serving as a rest stop for migrating
**43** birds and butterflies. The southern tip of the point, **Point Pelee National Park,** has the smallest dry land area of any Canadian national
park, yet it manages to draw more than half a million visitors every
year. There's no overnight camping, and there are a lot of other rules
and regulations to observe because the park is home to a number of
endangered species of plants and reptiles. Drive slowly to the visitor
center, 5 kilometers (3 miles) inside the park, where there are exhibits, slide shows, and a keen, knowledgeable staff to answer questions. Seven hundred kinds of plants and 347 species of birds have
been recorded here. A propane-powered, open-sided train operates
from the center to the tip of Point Pelee, the southernmost part of
the Canadian mainland. September in Pelee is the best time to see
monarch butterflies resting before they head 3,350 kilometers
(2,100 miles) south to winter in the Sierra Madre of Mexico. It is also
among the best locations in North America for bird-watching, especially during spring and fall migrations. In September, groups of
birders bedecked with camera lenses the size of rocket launchers
and clanking with binoculars, tape recorders, video equipment, and
even CB radios converge on the park and on the hotels, highways,
motels, and restaurants of nearby Leamington, an otherwise quiet
town of 23,000. *Tel. 519/322–2365. Admission: $5 per vehicle Apr.–
Labor Day, free rest of the year. Open daily 6 AM–10 PM.*

**44** **Pelee Island** is a small, flat island, roughly 13 by 6 kilometers (8 by 4
miles), at the west end of Lake Erie, served spring through fall by
ferry boats that link it with Kingsville and Leamington in Ontario
and Sandusky in Ohio. In winter there are scheduled flights from
Windsor. Ferries land at either West Dock or Scudder Dock, the
main communities on the island. The permanent population is 270,
but in summer that quadruples as vacationers, mostly from Ohio,
cram into 200 private cottages. At the end of October and beginning
of November, 700 hunters arrive to fill 18,000 pheasants with buckshot. The island has raised pheasants for hunters since 1932, a business that helps reduce taxes. There's usually someone to inform
visitors about Pelee's biggest industry, the pheasant farm in the
middle of the island, and explain why the chicks wear what look like
sunglasses. (It's so they can't peck one anothers' eyes out.) Pelee Island is not the most southerly place in Canada—that honor belongs
to neighboring Little Middle Island—but Pelee *is* south; it's on the
same latitude as northern California and northern Spain.

From the community of **West Dock** you can see **Perry's Victory and
International Peace Monument,** a 352-foot-high monument commemorating American commander Captain Oliver Hazard Perry,
who won control of Lake Erie at Put-in-Bay Island, Ohio, in 1813 by
sailing straight into the British fleet while firing broadside, succinctly reporting: "We have met the enemy and they are ours."

From Leamington, take Highway 18 west to Kingsville and then follow Division Road north to Essex County Road 29. The road to **Jack
**45** Miner's Bird Sanctuary** is well signposted. Jack Miner was an avid
hunter who realized no species could survive both its natural enemies *and* man. In 1904 he dug ponds, planted trees, and introduced
four Canada geese with clipped wings to the ponds. That number
grew to the 50,000 that now winter here. From 1910 to 1940 Miner
lectured on conservation and convinced kings and presidents of its
need, thus earning him the Order of the British Empire in 1943. His
former home is now a trust, open year-round except Sunday. No admission is charged and nothing is sold on the grounds. A two-story
museum in the former stables has a wealth of Miner memorabilia,

and at a pond beside the house you can feed far-from-shy geese and ducks with free feed. At 3 and 4 PM daily, including Sunday, the birds are flushed for "air shows," circling wildly overhead until they feel it's safe to land. The best times to view migrations are late March, October, and November. *On Essex County Rd. 29, 5 km (3 mi) north of Kingsville, tel. 519/733–4034. Admission free. Open daily (museum closed Sun.)*

The **John R. Park Homestead and Conservation Area,** 8 kilometers (5 miles) west of Kingsville, is a pioneer village anchored by one of Ontario's few examples of American Greek Revival architecture, an 1842 home. The 10 buildings include the house of John R. Park, a shed built with no nails, a smokehouse, icehouse, outhouse, blacksmith shop, sawmill, and livestock stable. *County Rd. 50 at Iler Rd., tel. 519/738–2029. Admission: $2.50 adults, $2 children, $9 families. Open July–Labor Day, daily 10–5; Oct.–mid-May, Sun.–Fri. 10–4, when special events are held.*

**46** The turn-of-the-century **Southwestern Ontario Heritage Village** has 20 historic buildings on 54 wooded acres. Volunteers in period dress show visitors how pioneers baked, operated weaving looms, and dipped candles. The **Transportation Museum of the Historic Vehicle Society of Ontario, Windsor Branch,** features a fine collection of travel artifacts, from snowshoes to buggies to vintage automobiles. The gem of the collection is the world's only 1893 Shamrock. This adorable two-seater was the second effort at a workable prototype built by the Mira Brothers. When this one didn't run properly, either, the brothers abandoned their brief career as auto manufacturers. *About halfway bet. Kingsville and Essex on County Rd. 23, tel. 519/776–6909. Open Apr.–Nov., Wed.–Sun. 11–5; July and Aug., daily 11–5.*

**47** The riverside parks in the quiet town of **Amherstburg** are great venues for watching the procession of Great Lakes shipping. **Navy Yard Park,** with flower beds ringed by old anchor chains, has benches overlooking Bois Blanc Island and the narrow main shipping channel.

**Fort Malden** was the British base in the War of 1812, when Detroit was captured, though its history goes back to 1727, when a Jesuit mission began occupying lands in the area. Now the fort is an 11-acre National Historic Park, which includes remains of the original earthworks, restored barracks, a military pensioner's cottage, two exhibit buildings, and picnic facilities. *Tel. 519/736–5416. Admission free. Open winter, daily 10–5; June–Labor Day, daily 10–6.*

The **North American Black Historical Museum** tells of daring escapes by U.S. slaves and the Underground Railroad system many used to flee to Canada. Between 1800 and 1860, 30,000–50,000 slaves made the pilgrimage to Canada, the Promised Land, and many of those crossed the Detroit River at Amherstburg because it was the narrowest point. An 1848-vintage church and log cabin contain exhibits, artifacts, and biographies. *227 King St., tel. 519/736–5433. Admission: $3 adults, $1 children and senior citizens, families $7. Open Wed.–Fri. 10–5, weekends 1–5.*

**48** **Windsor,** long an unattractive industrial city that hosted Ford, General Motors, and Chrysler manufacturing plants, has become an attractive place to visit. The riverfront has pretty parks, some with fountains and statues, all overlooking the spectacular Detroit skyline. The cities are linked by the Ambassador Bridge and the Windsor–Detroit Tunnel. If you're traveling by car, start your visit at the

Convention and Visitors Bureau (80 Chatham St. E), where you can get a free date-stamped parking pass for use during your stay.

The **Art Gallery of Windsor** features changing displays of contemporary and historic Canadian and foreign art. However, a strange thing happened to the gallery in 1993: Its exhibits were temporarily moved to a local shopping mall, to make way for Ontario's first casino. The Art Gallery will move back to its own building when a permanent site for the casino is completed, probably sometime during 1996. *Temporary address: 3100 Howard Ave., tel. 519/969–4494. Admission free. Open Tues.–Wed. and Sat. 11–5; Sun. 11–5:30, Thurs. and Fri. 11–9.*

The **Francois Baby House: Windsor's Community House** is a collection of area artifacts displayed in the 1812 house where the Battle of Windsor, the final incident in the Upper Canada Rebellion, was fought in 1838. *254 Pitt St., tel. 519/253–1812. Admission free. Open Tues.–Sat. 10–5, Sun. 2–5.*

Farmers, butchers, and bakers from southwestern Ontario sell their fresh produce at **Windsor City Market,** which rents space to more than 100 permanent vendors. *Chatham St. E, between MacDougall and Market Sts., tel. 519/255–6260. Open Tues.–Thurs. 7–4, Fri. 7–6, Sat. 5 AM–4 PM. Some stalls open Mon. and Tues.*

**Willistead Manor** is the former home of Edward Chandler Walker, second son of Hiram, who founded Walker's Distillery in 1858. The 15-acre estate is now a city park, and tours of the manor are available. Work on the mansion was completed in 1906, and no expense was spared building the 36-room spread designed in the 16th-century Tudor-Jacobean style of an English manor house. *Niagara St. at Kildare Rd., tel. 519/255–6545 or 519/255–6270. Admission: $2.75 adults, $2.25 senior citizens, $1.25 children. Open for tours Sept.– June, 1st and 3rd Sun. of each month, 1–4 (last tour at 3:30); July and Aug., Sun.–Wed., 1–4 (last tour at 3:30).*

Since 1959, Windsor and Detroit have combined their national birthday parties (Canada Day, July 1; and Independence Day, July 4) into a massive bash called **International Freedom Festival.** The two-week party includes nonstop entertainment with more than 100 special events on both sides of the river and a spectacular fireworks display, billed as the largest in North America. *Tel. 519/255–6530.*

---

## Tour 5: Niagara and West to London

There is probably no natural attraction exploited as thoroughly as the falls at **Niagara.** You can fly above the falls in a helicopter; get almost directly underneath them by boat; go around them on bridges; or go behind them in a tunnel. The first travel writer to visit Niagara Falls more than 300 years ago wrote, "The universe does not afford its parallel. The roar of them can be heard 15 leagues away" (a distance of 72 kilometers, or 45 miles). And explorer and missionary Father Louis Hennepin described their height as 600 feet—when in fact they are 176 feet high. When Europeans read Hennepin's 1678 accounts, they ranked Niagara among the Seven Wonders of the World. Despite Hennepin's gross exaggerations and the crass commercialism that is much in evidence, few have ever been disappointed by a visit to the falls. About 12 million tourists visit each year. Daredevils have been drawn to Niagra Falls since 1828: Eight people have survived plunging over the falls in a variety of contraptions, and the list of those who perished in the attempt is a long one. Fines for performing illegal stunts on property owned by the Niagara Parks Commission (NPC) have been raised to $10,000, but the stunt-lovers keep on coming.

*Numbers in the margin correspond to points of interest on the Niagara Falls map.*

The NPC was formed in 1885 to preserve the area around the falls. Beginning with a small block of land, the NPC has gradually acquired most of the land fronting on the Canadian side of the Niagara River, from Niagara-on-the-Lake to Fort Erie. This 56-kilometer (35-mile) riverside drive is a 3,000-acre ribbon of parkland lined with parking areas, picnic tables, and barbecue pits, and the public is welcome to use the facilities at no charge. The NPC's **Greenhouse and Plant Conservatory** (tel. 905/356–4699), just south of the Horseshoe Falls, is open daily year-round.

Visitors are also welcome at the **NPC School of Horticulture** several miles north of (downriver from) the falls, on the Niagara Parkway. The school has been graduating professional gardeners since 1936, and students display their expertise with flowers and shrubbery.

From the school it's a short distance (downriver) to one of the world's largest **floral clocks.** Its 40-foot-wide "living" face is planted in a different design each year.

Heading back upriver, there are trails maintained by the NPC in the **Niagara Glen.** A **bicycle trail** that parallels the Niagara Parkway from Fort Erie to Niagara-on-the-Lake winds between beautiful homes on one side and the river, with its abundant bird life, on the other. There are free band concerts on summer Sundays at **Queenston Heights Park, Queen Victoria Park,** and **Old Fort Erie** (*see* Tour 4, *above*), as well as **Rainbow Bridge Carillon** recitals. And don't forget to catch the free colored illumination of the falls 365 nights a year.

The **Festival of Lights** runs from the end of November to the third week of February. It started in Niagara Falls, Ontario, in 1981, and now stretches the length of the Niagara Parkway between Fort Erie and Niagara-on-the-Lake. The city claims a lot of superlatives during this period: world's largest Christmas tree (the Skylon Tower), world's largest gift (Your Host Motor Inn decorated to look like a giant gift-wrapped box), world's largest candle (the Minolta Tower), etc. The festival started with massive corporate displays, but the idea caught on with smaller businesses and private residents. There are now so many displays that tours are offered ranging from 2½ to 3½ hours.

*Maid of the Mist* **boats** have been operating since 1846, when they were wooden-hulled, coal-fired steamboats. Nowadays, passengers are issued hooded rain slickers for the 30-minute trip because the three modern boats get so close to both falls that the spray is heavy. *Boats leave from the foot of Clifton Hill, tel. 905/358–5781. Admission: $8.65 adults, $5 children 6–12. Open mid-May–late Oct., daily. Late June–Labor Day, boats leave as often as every 15 min 9:45–7:45; off-season, boats leave every 30 min weekdays 9:45–7:45.*

At **Table Rock Scenic Tunnels** your admission ticket includes use of rubber boots and a hooded rain slicker. You walk to an observation plaza just under the lip of the falls, and from there a tunnel takes you almost to the middle of the falls and behind the wall of crashing water. *Tours begin at Table Rock House in Queen Victoria Park, tel. 905/354–1551. Admission: $5.25 adults, $4.75 senior citizens, $2.65 children 6–12. Open mid-June–Labor Day, daily 9–11; Labor Day–early June, daily 9–5. Closed Dec. 25.*

# Niagara Falls

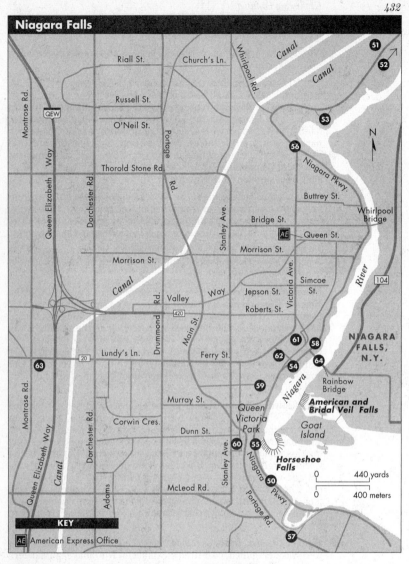

**KEY**

AE American Express Office

**56** The **Niagara Spanish Aero Car,** a cable car that crosses the Whirlpool Basin in the Niagara Gorge, has been operating since 1918. This trip is not for the fainthearted; when you're swinging high above the roiling whirlpool, those cables seem awfully thin. **The Great Gorge Adventure** involves taking an elevator to the bottom of the Niagara Gorge where you can walk a boardwalk beside the roaring torrent of the Niagara River. There the gorge is forced between sheer cliffs as it enters the Giant Whirlpool. *On River Rd., 3 km (2 mi) north of the falls, tel. 905/354–5711. Aero Car admission: $4.50 adults, $4.05 senior citizens, $2.25 children 6–12. Great Gorge Adventure admission: $4.25 adults, $3.85 senior citizens, $2.15 children. Open June–Labor Day, daily 9–9; Labor Day–mid-Oct., shorter hrs, weather permitting. The NPC sells an Explorer Passport for admission to Table Rock Scenic Tunnels, Spanish Aero Car, and the GreatGorge adventure for a 10% savings: $12.60 adults, $6.35 children 6–12.*

**57** **Marineland,** a theme park with marine shows, wildlife displays, and rides, is located 1½ kilometers (1 mile) south of the falls. The daily marine show includes performing dolphins, harbor seals, and sea lions. Children can pet and feed a herd of 500 deer and get nose-to-nose with North American freshwater fish. Among the many rides is the world's largest steel roller coaster. Marineland is signposted from Niagara Parkway or reached from the Queen Elizabeth Way by exiting at McLeod Road (Exit 27). *7657 Portage Rd., tel. 905/356–9565 for recording or 905/356–8250. Admission: $19.95 adults, $16.95 children 4–9 and senior citizens. In winter rides are closed and prices drop more than 50%. Open mid-May–June, daily 10–5; June–Aug., daily 9–6; Sept., daily 10–5.*

**58** The **Niagara Falls Museum** claims to be North America's oldest museum and is chockablock with everything from stuffed birds to an excellent display of Egyptian mummies. It houses the Daredevil Hall of Fame and displays barrels and other contraptions in which people have gone over the falls. There are 26 galleries on four floors and 700,000 exhibits, so gauge your time accordingly—this museum is well worth two hours of browsing. *5651 River Rd., tel. 905/356–2151. Admission: $5.75 adults, $5 senior citizens, $3.75 students, $2.75 children 5–10. Open mid-June–Labor Day, daily 8:30–11; Labor Day–mid-June, daily 10–5.*

Three towers and a huge Ferris wheel offer **panoramic views** of the falls and surrounding area, as does Niagara Helicopters Ltd. (*see* Guided Tours, *above*). The view of the Horseshoe Falls is best from

**59 60 61** the **Skylon Tower** or **Minolta Tower** (at the base of which is a reptile display and aquarium), but the **Kodak Tower** at Maple Leaf Village has the best view over the American Falls, Niagara Gorge, and the rapids above the falls. You can also get a good look over all the falls from atop North America's largest Ferris wheel at **Maple Leaf Village Amusement Park.**

*Skylon Tower, 520 feet above ground level, 5200 Robinson St. (directly above the Horseshoe Falls), tel. 905/356–2651. Admission: $5.95 adults, $4.95 senior citizens, $3.50 children 6–12, $16.95 families (2 adults, 2 children). For dining, elevator rate is $2 adults, $1 children and senior citizens. Open mid-June–Labor Day, daily 8–1; Labor Day–early June, daily 10–9.*

*Minolta Tower, 325 feet above ground level, 6732 Oakes Dr., tel. 905/356–1501. Admission to tower only: $5.95 adult, $4.95 students 5–18 and senior citizens.*

*Maple Leaf Village and Kodak Tower: The tower is 360 feet above ground level; the top of the Ferris wheel is 175 feet above ground lev-*

*el; 5685 Falls Ave., tel. 905/371–0288. Admission to the village is free. Admission to tower and daredevil exhibit: $5.50 adults, $3.50 senior citizens, $1.50 children under 12. Single ride on Ferris wheel: $3.30, children under 3 free. Open mid-May–mid-Oct., daily 10:30–4; summer, daily 10–6:30.*

**㉒ Clifton Hill,** almost directly opposite the American falls, is probably the most touristy corner of Niagara Falls. Sometimes referred to as "Museum Alley," this area encompasses the Guinness World of Records Museum, Ripley's Believe It Or Not Museum, Louis Tussaud's Waxworks Museum, The Haunted House, The Funhouse, The House of Frankenstein and Super Star Recording (where you can record the musical number of your choice), Movieland Wax Museum, Criminals Hall of Fame Wax Museum, the Elvis Presley Museum, and the That's Incredible Museum.

**㉓ White Water Water Park** offers just about every means of getting wet there is, including Canada's biggest water slide, two hot tubs, and a wave pool. If you arrive within the first hour of the day, you'll receive $1 off the admission price. *7430 Lundy's La., tel. 905/357–3380. Admission: $13.95 adults, $10.95 children, senior citizens free. Open June–Labor Day, daily 10–8.*

**㉔ Ride Niagara** is a relatively new attraction, open since 1991. The ride is divided into three portions: a theater presentation, an elevator ride down to the tunnel, and the shuttle that's located near the falls and simulates plunging down the rapids in a barrel. The entire event takes about 20–25 minutes. *5755 River Rd., tel. 905/374–7433. Admission: $7.95 adults, $6.95 youths 13–18 and senior citizens, $4.25 children 5–12, children 3–5 free. Not recommended for children under 3. Open daily; call for hrs.*

Some of the Niagara Peninsula's 13 **wineries** are on the Niagara Parkway between Niagara Falls and Niagara-on-the-Lake (*see below*), or on Highway 55 from the Queen Elizabeth Way. As the quality of Ontario wines has improved in recent years (and it has!), winemakers have stepped up their marketing and promotional activities. Look for the Wine Regions Welcome Centre (Casablanca Blvd., Grimsby; open July, Fri. 3–8, Sat. 9–5, Sun. 10–3), located just off the Queen Elizabeth Way East.

For a map of the wine region, including locations of individual wineries and details of summer events, write: Wine Regions of Ontario (35 Maywood Ave., St. Catharine's, Ont. L2R 1C5, tel. 905/570–8758). Several wineries offer tours, and the product may be sampled and bought; for exact times call ahead. The best-known wineries include **Château des Charmes Wines Ltd.** (tel. 905/262–4219), **Hillebrand Estates Winery** (tel. 905/468–7123), **Iniskillin Wines** (tel. 905/468–3554), **Konzelmann Winery** (tel. 905/935–2866), **Reif Winery** (tel. 905/468–7738), and **Willowbank Estate Wines** (tel. 905/468–4219).

*Numbers in the margin correspond to points of interest on the Lower Ontario Province map.*

**㉕** The Victorian town of **Niagara-on-the-Lake,** 15 kilometers (10 miles) north of Niagara Falls (downriver), is one of Ontario's showplaces. Stately homes sit back from tree-shaded streets, well apart from their neighbors. Though most are at least a century old, their modern-day owners maintain their original charm by keeping rose trellises freshly painted and brass door knockers gleaming. A dozen lovely inns here, some a century and a half old, make this a perfect getaway for Torontorians and tourists worn down by the neon of this village's southern neighbor. Any proposed new business is screened

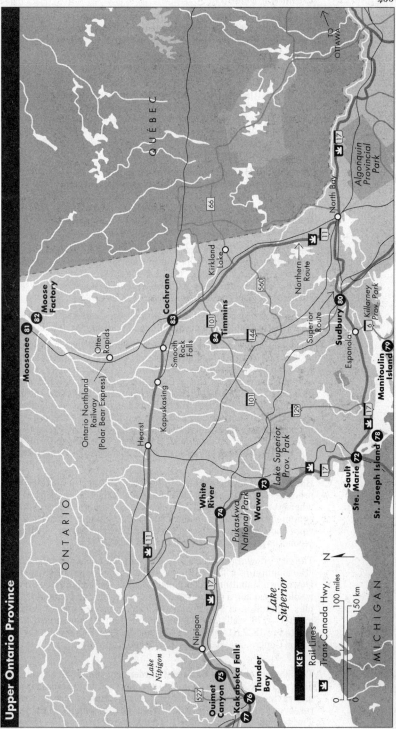

**Upper Ontario Province**

QUÉBEC

ONTARIO

TO OTTAWA

17 Algonquin Provincial Park

North Bay

111

66

Kirkland Lake

560

Northern Route

Sudbury **80**

Superior Route

Killarney Prov. Park

6

Espanola

17 Manitoulin Island **79**

**78**

Cochrane **83**

Smooth Rock Falls

Timmins **84**

101

144

101

129

17

Lake Superior Prov. Park

**72** Sault Ste. Marie

St. Joseph Island

Moosonee **81**

**82** Moose Factory

Otter Rapids

Ontario Northland Railway (Polar Bear Express)

Kapuskasing

Hearst

111

White River **74**

**73** Wawa

Pukaskwa National Park

17

17

Nipigon

527

Ouimet Canyon **75**

Kakabeka Falls **76**

**77** Thunder Bay

Lake Nipigon

Lake Superior

MICHIGAN

N

**KEY**

Rail Lines

Trans-Canada Hwy.

0    100 miles

0  150 km

by the village council to ensure that no chrome, glass, or neon-girdled atrocity will mar the Victorian character. There's no room on these tiny roads for the invasion of motor homes, campers, and buses that occurs each summer, so be prepared for long traffic snarls. The best way to experience the town at any time of year is to stroll.

Don't miss the **Niagara Apothecary,** a pharmacy museum on the main street, across from the 1848 courthouse, which replicates the pharmacy that first opened here in 1866. The serving counters are solid planks of walnut, and the crystal chandeliers are reproductions of original gasoliers. *5 Queen St., tel. 905/962–4861. Admission free. Open mid-May–Labor Day, daily noon–6.*

The **Niagara Historical Society Museum,** built in 1906, houses a collection of artifacts from prehistory through the arrival of the Loyalists and the War of 1812. *43 Castlereagh St., tel. 905/468–3912. Admission: $2.50 adults, $1.50 students, 50¢ children under 12. Open May–Oct., daily 10–5; Jan. and Feb., weekends 1–5; Mar.–Apr. and Nov.–Dec., daily 1–5.*

The British **Fort George** was fully restored in 1939. Today soldiers in period dress perform drills and musical programs on the parade square. *Niagara Pkwy., tel. 905/468–4257. Admission: $2.75 adults, $1.25 youths 6–16, $7 families, children under 6 and senior citizens free. Open late May–Oct., daily 9:30–4:30.*

The event that has really put Niagara-on-the-Lake on the map is the **Shaw Festival** (*see* The Arts and Nightlife, *below,* for details).

The **Niagara Peninsula** is Ontario's fruit basket. From mid-summer to late fall, fruit and vegetable stands proliferate along the highways and byways, and there are several farmers' markets along the Queen Elizabeth Way. One of the best displays of fruits and vegetables is on Lincoln County Road 55 between Niagara-on-the-Lake and the Queen Elizabeth Way, the route you'll take to Hamilton. **Harvest Barn Market,** marked by a red-and-white-stripe awning, not only features regional fruits and vegetables but also tempts with a bakery offering sausage rolls, tiny loaves of bread, and fruit pies. You can test the market's wares at the picnic tables, where knowledgeable locals have lunch.

**66** **Hamilton** is Canada's steel capital—the Dofasco and Stelco mills produce 60% of Canada's iron and steel. This isn't the sort of city where you'd expect to find 2,700 acres of gardens and exotic plants, a symphony orchestra, a modern and active theater, 45 parks, a 100-voice choir and an opera company. But they're all here in Ontario's second-largest city and Canada's third-busiest port.

The city's downtown is on a plain between the harbor and the base of "the mountain," a 250-foot-high section of the Niagara Escarpment. Downtown Hamilton is a potpourri of glass-walled high rises, century-old mansions, a convention center, coliseum, and shopping complex. Hamilton is also home to Canada's largest indoor farmers' market—176 stalls spread over more than 20,000 square feet—started in 1837. Its new home adjoins Jackson Square and the new Eaton Centre. *Tel. 905/546–2096. Open Tues., Thurs., and Sat. 7–6; Fri. 9–6.*

The 50-year-old **Royal Botanical Gardens** encompass five major gardens and 48 kilometers (30 miles) of trails that wind across marshes and ravines, past the world's largest collection of lilac, 2 acres of roses, and all manner of shrubs, trees, plants, hedges, and flowers. Two teahouses are open May 1–Thanksgiving. *Plains Rd. (Hwy. 2)*

*in Burlington, accessible from the Queen Elizabeth Way and Hwys.
6 and 403, tel. 905/527–1158; in Ontario and Quebec, 800/668–9449.
Admission: (summer) $4.25 adults, $3.25 senior citizens and children 5–12, $10.75 family; (winter) no charge to grounds but $2 per
visitor to the greenhouse. Main bldg. open daily 9–5; outdoor garden open daily 9:30–6. Closed Dec. 25.*

Sir Allan Napier MacNab, War of 1812 hero and Upper Canada's
pre-Confederation prime minister, built a 35-room mansion called
**Dundurn Castle** in 1832–35. It has been furnished to reflect the opulence in which MacNab lived at the height of his political career.
*Dundurn Park at York Blvd., tel. 905/546–2872. Admission: $4.50
adults, $1.75 children. Open June–Labor Day, daily 11–4; Labor
Day–May, daily 1–4. Closed Dec. 25 and Jan. 1.*

**Flamboro Downs harness racing track,** just west of Hamilton, has
matinee and evening races year-round, though not on a daily basis.
The clubhouse has two dining areas that overlook the track. *Hwy. 5.,
tel. 905/627–3561.*

**67** **Brantford,** 40 kilometers (25 miles) west of Hamilton on Highway
403, is named after Joseph Brant, the Loyalist Mohawk chief who
brought members of the Six Nations Confederacy into Canada after
the American Revolution.

King George III showed gratitude to Chief Brant and his loyal Indian subjects by building the **Mohawk Church.** In 1904, by Royal as-
sent, it was given the name His Majesty's Chapel of the Mohawks
(now changed to Her Majesty's). It is the oldest Protestant church in
Ontario and the only one that may suggest Royal in its name. The
simple, white-painted frame building has eight stained-glass windows depicting the colorful history of the Six Nations people. *291
Mohawk St., tel. 519/445–4528. Admission free. A guide is available. Open July and Aug., daily 10–6; Sept.–June, Wed.–Sat. 10–6,
Sun. 1–5.*

**Woodland Indian Cultural Educational Centre** is a museum of sorts
that aims to preserve and promote the culture and heritage of the
native people of the First Nation. The modern building contains displays and exhibits showing early Woodland Indian culture. *184 Mohawk St., near the Mohawk Chapel., tel. 519/759–2650. Open daily
10–5.*

Although Brantford is the hometown of hockey star Wayne Gretzky,
it is better known as "the Telephone City" because Alexander Graham Bell invented the device here and made the first long-distance
call from his parents' home to nearby Paris, Ontario, in 1874. The
**Bell Homestead** is now a National Historic Site. Next door is the
house of the Reverend Thomas Henderson, a Baptist minister who
left the church when he recognized the profit potential in telephones. His home was the first telephone office and now is a museum
of telephone artifacts and displays. *94 Tutela Heights Rd., tel. 519/
756–6220. Admission: $1 adults, children under 16 free. Guides
available. Open mid-Mar.–Thanksgiving, Tues.–Sun. 10–5.*

**68** About 27 kilometers (18 miles) north of Brantford by Highway 24
are the cities of **Kitchener** and **Waterloo,** which merge into each other
and are usually referred to as K–W. The region was settled around
1800 by Swiss-German Mennonites from Pennsylvania. The German
origins remain obvious: There's a huge glockenspiel downtown by
Speakers' Corner, and each October since 1967 the city has hosted
Oktoberfest. The event now draws more than 600,000 people who
swarm to more than a dozen festival halls where they dance, gorge

on German-style food, listen to oompah bands, and drink with a fervor that seems driven by an irrational fear that all Canadian breweries are about to go on strike.

There are farmers' markets all over Ontario, but the **Kitchener Market** is particularly well known. It isn't the oldest or biggest, but it's been around since 1869 and since 1986 has been housed in spacious quarters at Market Square. The block-long complex is wrapped in green-tinted glass and contains 70 shops and snack bars and an Eaton's department store. *At Frederick and Duke Sts., tel. 519/ 741-2287. Open Sat. 6-2; mid-May-mid-Oct., Thurs. 11-6.*

William Lyon Mackenzie King, who was prime minister of Canada for almost 22 of the years between 1821 and 1848, spent his teenage years in a rented 10-room house called Woodside, now **Woodside National Historic Park.** There's no particular imprint here of the bachelor prime minister whose diaries reveal his belief in mysticism, portents, and communications with the dead, but the house has been furnished to reflect the period of the King family occupancy. *528 Wellington St., tel. 519/742-5273. Admission free. Open May-Dec., daily 10-5.*

The **Seagram Museum** is a shrine to booze, and every exhibit in the enormous former barrel warehouses and new exhibition building relates to the product. Tour guides are available, and for those who develop a powerful thirst while browsing, there's a specialty liquor store that sells Seagram products and gift items. Lunch and dinner are available in a fine dining room on the premises. *57 Erb St. W, tel. 519/855-1857. Open daily 10-6.*

**Doon Heritage Crossroads** is a complete pioneer village just north of Highway 401, a few kilometers south and west of Kitchener. The village tranquilly recalls the lifestyle of a people who lived near the main highway of the early 1800s—the Huron Road. Visitors wander through tree-shaded roadways where neither automobiles nor the noises of the urban complex to the north intrude. Staff at the village wear period costumes, and some work at old-time crafts. *Tel. 519/ 748-1914. Open May-Labor Day, weekdays 10-4:30; Labor Day-Dec., weekdays 10-4:30.*

**69** The villages of **St. Jacobs** and **Elmira,** a few kilometers north of K–W, are in the heart of Mennonite and Hutterite country. These are peaceful people who live off the land, refuse to participate in wars, and have a strict moral code. They also resist modern conveniences, such as cars, electricity, and the internal combustion engine. The region is a shopper's paradise, with many stands selling all manner of fresh and preserved foods and gift items handcrafted by the Mennonites. **Crafts By Us** (tel. 519/669-8480) is one of several stores found in the Elmira Olde Town Village at the main intersection in Elmira.

**70** The city of **Stratford** is 46 kilometers (28 miles) west of Kitchener by Highways 7 and 8. It was named by homesick English settlers; all that the town would have had in common with England's Stratford was a river called Avon meandering through rolling countryside—and not even particularly similar countryside.

The **Stratford Festival** hosts music, opera, and drama annually for more than 400,000 people. (*See* The Arts and Nightlife, *below*, for details.)

**71** To reach **London** from Stratford, take Highway 7 west and turn south on Highway 4 at Elginfield. This will bring you into the city's north end and past the entrance to the University of Western Ontario. London is a quiet, provincial city where old money rules the arts and development projects. Its nickname is Forest City—it has more than 50,000 trees on city property and 1,500 acres of parks, including 1,000 acres along the Thames River. It has also become famous for its hospitals, which specialize in organ-transplant and other intricate operations. This low-key city has been called a microcosm of Canadian life; it is so "typically Canadian," it's often used as a test market for new products—if something will sell in London, it will probably sell anywhere in Canada.

The easiest way to get an overview of the town is to take a tour on a big, red, double-decker—what else?—London bus. They operate from City Hall, July 1 to Labor Day (at 10 and 2). From June through October you can get another view of London by cruising on the Thames River in a 60-passenger boat. Afternoon cruises (tel. 519/ 473–0363) depart every hour, June through August, from Storybook Gardens.

Because **Storybook Gardens** is owned and operated by the city's Public Utility Commission, this is one of the least expensive children's theme parks in the country. It's on the Thames River in the 281-acre Springbank Park. You'll see a castle, storybook characters, and a zoo with foreign and indigenous animals, including those from Old MacDonald's Farm. Children can slide down Jack and Jill's hill and the throat of Willie the Whale. *696 Headley Dr., tel. 519/661–5770. Admission: $4.50 adults, $2.50 children. Open May–Labor Day, daily 10–8; Labor Day–Thanksgiving, weekends 10–6.*

**London Regional Art and Historical Museum** is as interesting from the outside as its exhibits are on the inside. The gallery is contained in six joined, glass-covered structures whose ends are the shape of croquet hoops. *At The Forks of the Thames, tel. 519/672–4580. Open Tues.–Sun. noon–5 and holidays.*

The **London Museum of Archaeology** houses more than 40,000 native artifacts and a gallery of artists' conceptions of the lives of the Neutral, or Attawandaron, natives who lived on the Lawson site some 500 years ago. Nearby is a reconstructed multifamily longhouse on its original site. *1600 Attawandaron Rd., south of Hwy. 22., tel. 519/ 473–1360. Admission: $3.50 adults, $2.75 students and senior citizens, $1.50 children, $8 families. Open daily 10–5.*

London's oldest building is also one of its most impressive. The wrecker's ball came awfully close to the **Old Courthouse Building,** and it got one wall of the former Middlesex County Gaol. But a citizens' group prevailed, and in 1981, after a $2.5 million face-lift, the Old Courthouse, modeled after Malahide Castle in England, reopened as the home of Middlesex County council. On weekday afternoons free tours are available. *Tel. 519/434–7321.*

On the grounds of **Labatt's Brewery** is a well-researched replica of the 1828 London Brewery, which became Labatt's Brewery in 1853. Samples are not offered. *150 Simcoe St., tel. 519/663–5050. Admission free. Open June–Labor Day, Mon.–Sat. 11–5.*

## Tour 6: Sault Ste. Marie and West to Thunder Bay

*Numbers in the margin correspond to points of interest on the Upper Ontario Province map.*

**72** **Sault Ste. Marie** has always been a natural meeting place and cultural melting pot. Long before Etienne Brulé "discovered" the rapids in 1622, Ojibwa tribes gathered here. Whitefish, their staple food, could easily be caught year-round, and the rapids in the St. Marys River linking Lakes Huron and Superior were often the only open water for miles during the winter. When Father Jacques Marquette opened a mission in 1668, he named it Sainte Marie de Sault. Today everybody but tourists call it simply "the Sault," and the smaller city across the river in Michigan is called "the Soo." Different spelling, identical pronunciation.

The elegant **Ermatinger Stone House** was built by Montréal fur trader Charles Oakes Ermatinger in 1814 and is the oldest building in Canada west of Toronto. Ermatinger married Charlotte, a daughter of influential Indian chief Katawebeda, a move that didn't hurt his business. Today, costumed interpreters show visitors through the house and demonstrate cooking, baking, and crafts. *831 Queen St. E, tel. 705/759–5443. Admission: donation. Open Apr.–May, weekdays 10–5; June–Sept., daily 10–5; Oct.–Nov., weekdays 1–5.*

One of the Sault's most-touted sights is a boat tour through the **Soo Locks,** the 16th and final lift for ships bound for Lake Superior from the St. Lawrence River, 600 feet lower and 3,200 kilometers (2,000 miles) downstream. Your cruise boat will be lifted only 21 feet through one of the four locks on the U.S. side, but if you haven't been through a lock before it's an interesting experience. Two-hour tours aboard the **MV** *Chief Shingwauk* or the **MV** *Bon Soo* leave the Norgoma Dock near the Holiday Inn mid-May to mid-October, and up to eight times daily July to Labor Day. *Tel. 705/253–9850.*

The Algoma Central Railway (129 Bay St., tel. 705/254–4331) not only operates main line track between the Sault and iron mines at Hearst and Michipicoten Harbor but also runs a lucrative sideline of tour trains to and from scenic Agawa Canyon, through which their main line passes. From spring through fall the **Agawa Canyon Train Tour** runs from the Sault to Mile 114 (182 kilometers). In winter, the **Snow Train** goes to Mile 120 (192 kilometers). In summer the train stops for two hours in **Agawa Canyon,** a deep valley 19 kilometers (12 miles) long with cliff walls up to 800 feet high through which the Agawa River flows. During the stopover, passengers can lunch in a park, hike to their choice of three waterfalls, or climb to a lookout 250 feet above the train. Tour trains run daily June 5 to mid-October and on weekends only, January through March. Trains depart at 8 AM in summer and 8:30 AM in winter and return at 5 PM. Dining car service is continuous 7 AM–3:45 PM.

Gas up in the Sault before you head north on Highway 17, **The Great North Road.** There is some spectacular scenery along this route. The highway climbs through high hills, and from the top of headlands there are vistas across wide bays in Lake Superior. At the crossings of the Batchawana, Montréal, Agawa, and Michipicoten rivers, south of **Wawa** there are picnic spots. It's 225 kilometers (131 miles) from the Sault to Wawa; the last 80 kilometers (50 miles) is through **Lake Superior Provincial Park.** If you're going to Thunder Bay, 690 kilometers (400 miles) northwest, plan to stop for gas at **Wawa** or **White River.**

 **Wawa** is an Ojibwa word meaning "wild goose," and the 3,700 residents of Wawa have erected a massive goose monument at the entrance to town from Highway 17. Next door is the town's new log-cabin tourist information office.

**White River,** 90 kilometers (56 miles) north on Highway 17, is marked by a huge thermometer indicating 72 degrees below zero and a sign that advises: "White River—coldest place in Canada." The town has another claim to fame: It was the home of Winnie-the-

Pooh, the black bear immortalized in Christopher Robin children's stories by British author A. A. Milne. A 25-foot-high statue honoring Winnie was put up in 1992, and each August the town holds a three-day Winnie's Homecoming Festival, with parades, street dances, and a community barbecue.

Continue west on the Trans-Canada Highway, around the top of Lake Superior. Just past the town of Hurkett, west of Nipigon, watch for signs to **Ouimet Canyon.** This geological anomaly is a midget compared to Agawa Canyon but, because of the vantage point, it is more spectacular. At Ouimet, the visitor strolls a wide path and suddenly comes to the edge of the canyon. Viewing platforms extend over the edge so you can look straight down 329 feet. The far wall is only 492 feet away, and the chasm is only 2.4 kilometers (1.5 miles) long. Geologists believe the canyon could be a gigantic fault in the world's surface, or it could have been carved by a glacier. *The turnoff to Ouimet Park is 67 km (42 mi) northeast of Thunder Bay. Admission free. Open mid-May–Thanksgiving, daily 9–5.*

Although they amalgamated into one city of 110,000 in 1970, there are still **Port Arthur** and **Fort William** sections of **Thunder Bay.** The city is one of the world's largest grain-handling centers. It has an extraordinary ethnic mix, with 42 nationalities clearly represented, 110 churches, and the largest Finnish population outside Finland. The area has Ontario's best skiing and longest ski season, superb fishing and hunting, unlimited canoe and boating routes, and even mountain climbing. The city has an art gallery, hundreds of restaurants, nine shopping malls, and **Old Fort William** (tel. 807/577–8461), a reconstructed fur-trading fort with 42 historic buildings on a 125-acre site.

The double-decker cruise ship *Welcome* carries visitors on harbor tours and to and from Old Fort William. The harbor cruises get the visitor closer to the giant grain elevators, the ships servicing them, and the nearby islands. Visitors can take the *Welcome* to the fort and return on the cruise company's bus. In mid-summer there are three harbor tours daily, including an evening cruise. *467 Parkwood Dr., tel. 807/344–2512. Admission to harbor cruise: $12.50 adults, $11.50 senior citizens, $6.50 children 6–14, children under 6 free. Admission to Old Fort William cruise and return by bus: $15 adults, $14 senior citizens, $6.50 children 6–14, children under 6 free. Cruises run mid-May–early Oct.*

If legend is to be believed, wearing an amethyst will protect you from hangovers. Ontario's gemstone is an imperfect quartz, tinted violet or purple by the impurity of iron atoms mixing with the original liquid rock. There are five amethyst mines between Sleeping Giant Provincial Park and Ouimet Canyon, a distance of 50 kilometers (31 miles) along Highways 11 and 17 east of Thunder Bay. All are signposted from the highway, and each offers the opportunity to hand-pick some samples (you pay for them by the pound). If you don't want to drive to a mine, the stone is sold in jewelry stores, and several of the mines have shops in the city. **Thunder Bay Amethyst Mine Panorama** is closest to the city and claims to be North America's largest. Also, on the site is a gift shop and custom-jewelry store. Tours run four times daily at 11, 12:30, 3, and 5. Follow Loon Lake Road from Highways 11 and 17, east of Thunder Bay. *E. Loon Rd., tel. 807/622–6908. Admission for tours: $1. Open mid-May–June and Sept.–mid-Oct., Mon.–Sat. 10–5; July and Aug., Mon.–Sat. 10–7.*

**77** **Kakabeka Falls** on the Kaministikwia River, 40 kilometers (25 miles) northwest of Thunder Bay, drop 154 feet over a limestone ledge into a deep gorge. The falls can be seen from either side and there are large, free parking lots.

## Tour 7: East along Georgian Bay and South to Manitoulin Island

**78** **St. Joseph Island** is a sparsely settled island about 24 by 30 kilometers (16 by 20 miles) in the mouth of the St. Mary's River, 40 kilometers (25 miles) southeast of the Sault and connected by causeway and bridge to the mainland. In spring the island is a scented riot of wild lilac, and you're likely to see moose and deer along the quiet side roads. In fur-trading days, Fort St. Joseph was a British fort at the southeast tip of the island that guarded the trade route from Montréal to the upper Great Lakes. Today's visitor can wander the rounded peninsula on which the fort and commercial buildings once stood and see the outlines and a few above-ground stone ruins of the 42 building sites that have been identified. Free walking tours and a free walking-tour booklet are available at the visitor center, which is located about 30 minutes from the bridge. Call ahead for directions. *Tel. 705/246–2664. Open late May–Thanksgiving, daily 10–5.*

East of St. Joseph Island and south of **Espanola,** along Route 6, the world's largest freshwater island sits at the top of Lake Huron plugging the mouth of Georgian Bay. **Manitoulin Island** is 160 kilometers

**79** (100 miles) long and varies in width from 3 to 64 kilometers (2 to 40 miles). The island is pretty and rugged, with granite outcrops, forests, meadows, rivers, and rolling countryside. Only 20% of the land is arable, and much of the rest is used for grazing sheep and cattle. Yachtsmen rate the waters around the islands among the best in the world, and hunters and fishermen have taken advantage of the island's riches for generations. Hikes and exploration could easily turn this "side trip" into a week-long stay. This is a place that for the most part has been unravaged by time. Archaeological digs on Manitoulin Island have produced traces of human habitation that are more than 30,000 years old, making them the oldest on the North American continent. There is no interim record of people living on the island until explorer Samuel de Champlain met some island residents in 1650.

**Little Current–Howland Centennial Museum,** about 18 kilometers (12 miles) south of **Little Current,** in the village of Sheguiandah on Highway 6, displays native and pioneer artifacts. *Tel. 705/368–2367. Admission: $1.50 adults, $1 senior citizens and students, 75¢ children 5–12. Open June–mid-Sept., daily 10–4:30 and Thanksgiving weekend.*

The extreme eastern end of the island is **Wikwemikong,** 484 square kilometers (300 square miles). One of Manitoulin's most colorful events is the Wikwemikong Pow Wow, held on Civic Holiday (the first Monday in August) weekend. Dancers accompanied by drummers and singers compete for prizes while performing the steps of their ancestors.

There is another way of reaching Manitoulin Island, which is especially convenient if you are heading up the Bruce Peninsula from southern Ontario. A ferry, the **MV** *Chi-Cheemaun,* connects the picturesque town of Tobermory at the northern tip of the peninsula, with South Baymouth on the island. The trip takes 2 hours 45 minutes each way. There are four sailings in each direction daily between mid-June and Labor Day, and three during the spring and fall. *Ontario Northland Marine Services, tel. 800/265–3163. One-way fares: $10.50 adults, $9 senior citizens, $5.25 chidren 5–11, $35.25 families, plus $23 per car. Reservations advised.*

**80** Back on the mainland, about 60 kilometers (40 miles) east of Espanola, is the mining town of **Sudbury**, which used to bear the brunt of a lot of unkind jokes. After all, didn't the U.S. astronauts go there to train in the type of terrain they were likely to encounter on the moon? Today, the Greening of Sudbury, a student planting project, and other renovations have given this clean city of 110,000 a face-lift. New, imaginatively designed buildings, well-lighted streets, and a downtown anchored by a spiffy Civic Square Provincial Tower invite visitors. There are concerts in the park, art centers, and a cruise on Lake Ramsey, the largest freshwater lake inside city limits in North America.

Northern Ontario's biggest tourism magnet, **Science North,** opened in 1984. This hands-on science museum is housed in two snowflake-shape buildings that cling to a rocky ledge of the shore of Lake Ramsey. Lie on a bed of nails, create a soapstone carving, or make your own hurricane or snowstorm. At every turn there are eager museum staff to answer questions and encourage participation in the dozens of laboratories. *100 Ramsey Lake Rd., tel. 705/522–3701. Admission: $7.95 adults, $5.25 children. Open May–Oct., daily 9–5; Nov.–Apr., daily 10–4.*

The **Big Nickel,** a 30-foot replica of the Canadian 1951 commemorative coin, has been synonymous with Sudbury for almost three decades. It is the largest coin in the world and stands on a barren hillside on the west side of the city, overlooking the smokestacks of the International Nickel Company (Inco). Near the Big Nickel is the entrance to the **Big Nickel Mine.** At 23 meters (73 feet), it is one of the shallowest mines in the area. Science North (*see above*) offers tours of the mine in summer. Visitors are given hard hats, coats, and boots and lowered into the mine shaft in a "cage" elevator. In the 400-meter-long (437-yard-long) drifts, or tunnels, miners demonstrate mining techniques. *At Hwy. 17 and Big Nickel Mine Rd., tel. 705/673–5659 or 705/522–3701. Admission: $6.50 adults, $4.25 students and senior citizens. Tour runs May–June 25, daily 9–5; June 26–Labor Day, daily 9–7; Labor Day–Oct. 9, daily 9–5.*

The 2½-hour **Path of Discovery Tour** bus leaves from the Big Nickel and Science North several times daily. Visitors are taken to the spot where a railroad worker discovered copper and nickel ores 4 kilometers (2½ miles) west of the townsite in 1884. The tour also goes to the edge of the Sudbury Basin, a massive indentation in the landscape created 2 billion years ago by a meteorite, a volcanic eruption, or a combination of the two. The event created an elliptical depression 59 kilometers (40 miles) long and 27 kilometers (18 miles) wide. The tour visits Sudbury's oldest mine, historic sites in Copper Cliff, and the smelter and super stack at Inco, the world's largest integrated nickel mining, smelting, and refining complex. *Tel. 705/673–5659 or 705/522–3701. Admission: $11 adults, $7 children and senior citizens, children under 5 free. Same hrs as Science North, above.*

## Tour 8: From Cochrane to Moosonee and Moose Factory Island

**81** **82** **Moosonee** and **Moose Factory** are considered Ontario's gateway to the Arctic. Although you can fly to Moosonee (Air Creebec, tel. 705/264–9521 or 800/567–6567, has service from Timmins), Ontario Northland's *Polar Bear Express* train is the more popular and the more nostalgia-inducing option. The *Polar Bear* makes a round-trip from **Cochrane,** 300 kilometers (200 miles) south, every day of the week except Friday, from late June to Labor Day. There's train service to Cochrane from Toronto or North Bay. The *Polar Bear Express* leaves Cochrane at 8:30 AM and arrives at Moosonee just before 1 PM. It departs Moosonee at 5:15 PM and returns to Cochrane by 9:20 PM. Meals, light lunches, and snacks are available in the restaurant-snack car.

**Moose Factory Island,** one of a number in the delta of the Moose River, is 8 kilometers (5 miles) long and just over a kilometer wide. It's a 20-minute boat ride from Moosonee. Passengers then transfer to a bus or van. The island was the site of the second Hudson's Bay Company trading post, established in 1672 on what was then called Hayes Island, 24 kilometers (16 miles) up the Moose River from James Bay. It was captured by the French in 1686 and renamed Fort St. Louis. Contrary to popular myth, the holes in the floor of **St. Thomas Anglican Church** are to let floodwater *out* and to ventilate the foundation. When the church was being built in 1864, the foundation floated a short distance in a spring flood, but the church itself has never floated anywhere. The altar cloths and lectern hangings are of moose hide decorated with beads.

The Hudson's Bay Post is a modern building, and the company now goes by the name of the North West Company—after the group of fur traders who competed against the Bay in the 19th century. Beside it is the 1850 **Hudson's Bay Staff House** in which are sold animal pelts, carvings, snowshoes, gloves, slippers, and beadwork.

Some guidebooks will tell you the **Blacksmith's Shop** in Centennial Park on Moose Factory Island is the oldest wooden building in Ontario. It isn't, but the stone forge inside it may be the oldest "structure" in the province. The original shop was built in the late 1600s but moved back from the riverbank in 1820. Because the forge stones had been transported a long distance, they were disassembled and rebuilt at the present location. In summer an apprentice smithy runs the forge and explains its operation.

Moosonee is Ontario's only tidal port and, even though it's almost 20 kilometers (14 miles) from James Bay, summer tides average 5 feet. The community came into existence only in 1903, when the Revillon Frères Trading Company of France established a post to compete with the Hudson's Bay Company. It wasn't until the Ontario Northland Railway arrived in 1932 that the region's population began to catch up to that of Moose Factory. The Moosonee visitor center (tel. 705/336–2480) is in a small, one-floor office building on First Street. Next door is a theater in which free videos on wildlife and natural and cultural history are shown. Opposite the dock on Revillon Road, a small, two-story frame house has displays and artifacts recalling the heyday of the area's fur trade. Farther down Revillon Road is the modern Ministry of Natural Resources Interpretive Centre, offering exhibits of regional wildlife and of the area's geological and geographical history. During tourist season there are stalls on Revillon Road where natives sell handcrafts ranging from moccasins and buckskin vests to jewelry, beadwork, and wood and stone carvings.

Some 90 miles (144 kilometers) southwest of Cochrane is the mining center of **Timmins,** with a population of about 46,600. Timmins prides itself on being the biggest city in Canada (by area, that is, not population). Despite its vastness, there's not much to see in Timmins, except for one of Canada's few underground mine tours. Visitors dress in full mining attire for the 2½-hour tour of the old

Hollinger gold workings. Surface attractions include a headframe, a prospector's trail with a view of mineral outcrops and ore samples, and a refurbished miners' house. The road to the tour site, located near downtown Timmins, is well marked. *Timmins Underground Gold Mine Tour, tel. 705/267–6222. Tours run mid-May to late October, tours begin daily at 9:30, 10:30, noon, 1:30, and 3. From November to May, tours take place Wed.–Sun. Call ahead for precise times. Admission: $16 adults, $14 senior citizens and students, $45 families. Discount coupons are available.*

For more information about the area, or if you're interested in an overnight stay, contact **Ontario Northland** (65 Front St. W, Toronto, Ont. M5J 1E6, tel. 416/314–3750).

## What to See and Do with Children

**African Lion Safari,** Rockton, near Hamilton. Lions, tigers, cheetahs, elephants, and zebras abound in this wildlife park. You can drive your own car or take an air-conditioned tram over a 9-kilometer (6-mile) safari trail. *Off Hwy. 8, south of Cambridge, tel. 519/623–2620. Admission: $13.50 adults, $11.50 senior citizens and youths 13–17, $9.50 children 3–12. Grounds open early Apr.–Oct., daily 9–6:30; tours run weekdays 10–4, weekends 10–5.*

**Doon Heritage Crossroads,** near Kitchener (*see* Tour 5).
**Maple Leaf Village Amusement Park,** Niagara Falls (*see* Tour 5).
**Marineland,** Niagara Falls (*see* Tour 5).
**National Museum of Science and Technology,** Ottawa (*see* Tour 1).
**Old Fort William,** Thunder Bay (*see* Tour 6).
**Sainte-Marie among the Hurons,** Midland (*see* Tour 3).
**Santa's Village,** Bracebridge (*see* Tour 3).
**Science North** (*see* Tour 7).
**Storybook Gardens,** London (*see* Tour 5).
**Upper Canada Village,** Morrisburg (*see* Tour 2).

# Shopping

## Native Crafts

Ottawa, Sault Ste. Marie, Midland, and Thunder Bay have museum shops and galleries that specialize in native and Inuit crafts.

## Antiques

**John Coles** at the **Astrolabe Gallery** (90 Sparks St., tel. 613/234–2348) is a good source for 19th-century prints of Ottawa scenes or antique maps of North America. Some of the best antiques can be found at small shops in **Bayfield, Cobourg, Meaford, Peterborough, Shakespeare,** and **St. Jacobs.** Sunday flea markets in **Aberfoyle, Burlington, Grand Bend,** and **Hamilton** can be another good source of antiques.

## Shopping Centers and Malls

**Rideau Centre** at Rideau Street and Colonel By Drive in Ottawa has more than 200 stores, including The Bay, Ogilvy's, and Eaton department stores.

In Hamilton, **Hess Village** is a small area crammed with interesting boutiques, cafés, and pubs.

Windsor draws shoppers from nearby Michigan seeking British imports of china and woolens.

In Paris, try **Halls's** on the main street for Irish linens.

# Sports and Outdoor Activities

### Bicycling

**Ottawa** has 114 kilometers (65 miles) of **bicycle paths.** On Sunday, **Queen Elizabeth Drive** and **Colonel By Drive** are closed to traffic until noon for cyclists. Rent A Bike, located in the Château Laurier Hotel, rents a variety of bicycles, including tandems and children's models. There are miles of bicycle trails in and around **Toronto,** but two of the best biking spots are **Hanlan's Point Island** and **Ward's Island** in Lake Ontario, just offshore from Toronto. In summer, ferries leave the foot of Bay Street every 15 minutes. The NPC operates 55 kilometers (30 miles) of **bicycle trails** along the Niagara River between Fort Erie and Niagara-on-the-Lake. The city of **Brantford** is protected by a flood-control dam on top of which is a bicycle trail that passes most of the city's many interesting tourist attractions. Two other popular bike routes can be accessed from **Fergus,** 24 kilometers (15 miles) northwest of Guelph: One is a 32-kilometer (20-mile) tour around Lake Belwood, and the other is a 40-kilometer (25-mile) loop around Eramosa Township. There is little traffic on these scenic routes, and restaurants are few and far between, so it's advised that you take a picnic lunch along. Another scenic spot, **London's Springbank Park,** has miles of pretty bicycle trails.

### Camping

There are 261 provincial parks in Ontario and hundreds of other parks that are privately owned and operated as businesses. The provincial parks are owned, maintained, and protected by the province, and they range in size from being only a few acres to massive areas of land such as Polar Bear Provincial Park, which, at 15,000 square kilometers (9,300 square miles), is just a tad smaller than 15,498-square-kilometer (9,609-square-mile) state of Vermont. Algonquin, created in 1893, is Ontario's oldest park, and at 4,764 square kilometers (2,954 square miles), it's only 495 square kilometers (307 square miles) smaller than the combined size of the states of Rhode Island and Delaware.

Most of the provincial parks offer a variety of services for campers, from electrical outlets and sturdy, covered picnic shelters to laundry facilities and camp stores for provisions. Additionally, many sponsor educational programs that teach children wilderness survival techniques and aim to offer a better understanding of nature.

In southern Ontario most provincial parks are in full operation from mid-May until Labor Day weekend; in northern Ontario provincial parks are generally open from early June until Labor Day weekend. Even when "closed," however, the parks never completely shut down and visitors are welcome in the off-season, though few facilities are maintained. Some parks may be gated to prevent vehicular entry, but all are accessible to pedestrians from sunrise to sunset. Expect vault privies to be open, fireplace grates should be available, and fees usually will be collected through self-serve registration. Winter camping, which is becoming a popular pastime, is allowed in some provincial parks, though most are unsupervised and facilities are limited. During the fall and winter months reservations are not required at most parks.

Peak season in Ontario's parks is June through August, and it is advised that you reserve a campsite, if reservations are accepted. It's possible to request space in advance by telephone (tel. 416/963–2992 or 800/ONTARIO for reservations and availability), mail, or in person, and sites can be guaranteed by using a Visa or MasterCard credit card. However, reservations are not always accepted or necessary: All provincial parks have some sites available on a first-come, first-served basis. In an effort to avoid overcrowding on canoe routes and hiking or backpacking trails in such major canoeing parks as Algonquin, Quetico, Killarney, and Frontenac parks, daily quotas have been established governing the number of people permitted in the parks. In these parks interior permits can be reserved ahead of time.

In the four above-mentioned parks and in Lake Superior Provincial Park, cans and bottles are banned throughout, and are permitted only in the organized car campground areas. For more detailed information on parks and campgrounds in Ontario, write to Ontario Ministry of Tourism (77 Bloor St. W, Toronto, Ont. M7A 2R9) for the free catalogue.

## Dog Sledding

Dog-sledding excursions ranging from half-hour runs to overnights in wilderness outpost cabins are offered by outfitters at Shanty Bay (near Barrie), Temagami, Dorset, and Vermilion Bay. Two companies offer one- to four-day dog-sledding packages from downtown Toronto. **Harbourfront Canoe School** (283A Queen's Quay W, Toronto, Ont. M5V 1A2, tel. 416/203–2277) has a one-day dog-sled excursion to the edge of Algonquin Park for $176.55 per person, including tax, instruction, trip, and lunch and supper. **Voyageur Quest** (129 Coldstream Ave., Toronto, Ont. M5N 1X7, tel. 416/322–3605) offers a four-day combination dog-sledding/snowshoeing/cross-country skiing package to Temagami at $275 per person including all equipment, accommodation, food, and instruction. **Burton Penner** (Box 151, Vermilion Bay, Ont. P0V 2V0, tel. 807/227–5593) of Vermilion Bay, 91 kilometers (57 miles) east of Kenora, offers guided dog sled tours into the wilderness, overnighting in an outpost cabin or heated-wall tent. Rates run from $300 per person for a one-night trip to $595 per person for a three-night trip, maximum of three people per trip, everything included.

## Fishing

Ontario has about 250,000 lakes and 150,000 rivers that contain an inestimable number of species of fish. The favorite trophies of most anglers are salmon and trout but others lust after pike or muskie and still others swear that battling a frenzied black bass on light tackle is life's ultimate piscatorial challenge.

Licenses are required for fishing in Ontario and may be purchased from the Ministry of Natural Resources district offices and from most sporting goods stores, outfitters, and resorts. Seasons and catch limits change annually and some districts infringe closed seasons. Restrictions are published in *Summary of the Fishing Regula-*

*tions*, free from the Ministry of Natural Resources (Public Information Centre, Macdonald Block, Room M1-73, 900 Bay St., Toronto, Ont. M7A 1W3, tel. 416/314–2000).

**Fishing Lodges** There are about 500 fishing resorts and lodges listed in the current catalogue of fishing packages issued by the Ontario Ministry of Tourism (77 Bloor St. W, Toronto, Ont. M7A 2R9) and available free. The establishments listed are not hotels that happen to be located near bodies of water that contain fish but are businesses designed to make sport fishing available to their guests. To that end, each property offers all the accoutrements of the modern fisherman, including boats, motors, guides, float planes, and freezers.

When planning your vacation at a fishing lodge, you may be surprised by the rates: Horse racing may be the sport of kings, but modern-day sport fishing must run a close second in terms of the cost of equipment, apparel, and logistics. A good example is **Totem Lodge** (Sioux Narrows, off Lake of the Woods; Totem Lodge, Box 180, Sioux Narrows P0X 1N0, tel. 807/226–5275), 60 kilometers (37 miles) south of Kenora, with standards by which other lodges in the province may be gauged. Guests can stay in deluxe suites at the lodge or deluxe housekeeping cabins, all with air-conditioning, satellite TV, and wood-burning fireplaces. There's a store on the grounds for supplies and a dining room with no set meal hours. The lodge's fleet of fishing boats and motors is brand new each year and the boats are equipped with videographs, downriggers, depth-finders, live wells, and two-way VHF marine-band radios. Since not all fishermen want to stay on top of the stock market or office crises when the big ones are biting, cellular telephones in the boats are optional. Another option is to have your catch cleaned, packaged, and frozen, so you won't have to touch it once it's been hooked. A six-night, five-day package at Totem Lodge starts at $1,195 per person, double occupancy, and includes three meals daily, fishing boat with gas and bait, fishing license, guide, and pickup and return to Kenora.

**Ice Fishing** During the winter most of Ontario's 250,000 lakes freeze, providing good fishing for hardy souls who want to drill a hole through the ice and drop down a baited hook and line. The best ice-fishing spots in Ontario are Mitchell's Bay off Lake St. Clair, Lake Simcoe, Lake Nipissing, and lakes between and around North Bay and Temagami. Licenses are required for any fishing in Ontario, and they may be purchased from the Ministry of Natural Resources district offices, and most sporting goods stores, tourist outfitters, and resorts. Seasons and catch limits change annually and there are closed seasons in some districts. Regulations are published in the above-mentioned *Summary of the Fishing Regulations*.

## Hiking

Hiking trails are signposted along all Ontario highways, and usually there's parking, trail information, and comfort stations. A popular mini-hike in southern Ontario (part of the Grand Valley Trail) is the 5-kilometer (3-mile) pathway along the Elora Gorge between Fergus and Elora. Among the features are a whirlpool at Templin Gardens, a restored English garden, and a bridge across the gorge at Mirror Basin, where there are excellent views up and down the gorge. This hike should not be attempted in street shoes.

Other trails include the 680-kilometer (430-mile) **Bruce Trail,** which stretches along the limestone Niagara Escarpment from the orchards of the Niagara Peninsula to the cliffs and bluffs at Tobermory, at the end of the Bruce Peninsula. Contact the Bruce Trail Association (Box 857, Hamilton, Ont. L8N 3N9). Also, there's the **Grand Valley Trail,** running 128 kilometers (80 miles) between Elora and Brantford. Contact the Grand Valley Trail Association (Box 1233, Kitchener, Ont. N2G 4G8). The **Rideau Trail** runs 406 kilometers (241 miles) along the Rideau Canal from Kingston to Ottawa. Access points from the highway are marked with orange triangles. Contact Rideau Trail Association (Box 15, Kingston, K7L 4V6).

## Ice Climbing

Only one Ontario company offers ice-climbing instruction and expeditions. **Alpamayo Exploration and Adventure Services Co.** (Box 2204, Thunder Bay, Ont. P7B 5E8, tel. 807/344–9636) has one-day trips or expeditions up to five days in length in the Thunder Bay area. One-day trips with one instructor per four participants costs $75 per person including all equipment, but no meals. Five-day ice-climbing trips for beginner, intermediate, or advanced climbers cost $900 per person. Deluxe accommodations in rustic cabins or motels are provided, but meals are not included.

## Rafting

For thrills (and perhaps a few spills) few sports can beat whitewater rafting. Eastern Ontario has many rivers suitable for rafting, and a growing number of companies offer packages ranging from half-day to week-long trips between May and September. RiverRun (Box 179, Beachburg, Ont. K0J 1C0, tel. 800/267–8504), located at Beachburg, a 90-minute drive west of Ottawa, has a one-day tour on the Ottawa River for $75. A three-day outing costs around $200, depending on the days of the week. Family Float Trips (Box 29, Forester's Falls, Ont. K0J 1V0, tel. 613/646–2263) offers half-day excursions on the nearby Ottawa and Madawaska rivers.

## Skiing

Cross-country   Nordic ski trails exist just about anywhere in the province where you'll find snow and accommodations for skiers. Around Toronto, try **Caledon Ski Club** (tel. 519/927–5221) in Caledon; **Glen Eden Ski Area** (tel. 905/878–5011) near Milton; and **Hockley Valley Resort** (tel. 519/942–0754) near Orangeville. **Horseshoe Valley** (tel. 705/835–2790) near Barrie is among the few resorts that offer both Nordic and downhill skiing facilities. **Mansfield** (tel. 705/435–3838), about one hour's drive north-west of Toronto, is another. All the above ski areas are suitable for day outings from Toronto.

In southern Ontario, the Huntsville area (215 kilometers, 134 miles) north of Toronto is usually the cross-country skier's best bet for an abundance of natural snow. The region is riddled with lakes and streams, stands of virgin birch and pine, and deer and smaller forest dwellers that live along the trail. Because the area is Toronto's summer playground, too, there is no shortage of year-round resorts from such spectacular, self-contained communities as the ultra-deluxe **Deerhurst Resort** (tel. 705/789–6411) to the rustic cottages of **Norseman Restaurant** at **Walker Lake Resort** (tel. 705/635–2473), which overlook deer-feeding stations on either side of the frozen lake.

*Lodge-to-Lodge*   From the town of Haliburton, 250 kilometers (156 miles) northeast of Toronto, three- and four-night guided lodge-to-lodge cross-country ski packages are available along the Haliburton Nordic Trail system. There are groups for skiers of all levels, and the trips cover 8–25 kilometers (5–16 miles) per day, depending on the group's abilities. Eight lodges participate in the program and skiers stay and dine at a different lodge each night; by the time skiers come off the trail, luggage will be in their rooms. Packages include all meals, trail passes, and a guide. Three-night packages cost $349 single, $319 per person, double occupancy; four-night packages are $419 single, $379 per person, double occupancy.

**Downhill** Ontario has hundreds of alpine slopes, although most are under 200 meters (640 feet) in vertical drop. All major Ontario ski centers have high-tech snow-making equipment, which in average years has guaranteed good skiing from late November through early April. For a recorded snow report of most Ontario resorts call 416/314–0998.

The highest ski slopes are **Candy Mountain Resort** and Loch Lomond (tel. 807/475–7787), both just outside Thunder Bay and both with 235 meters (750 feet) of vertical. Lift tickets are interchangeable between Candy Mountain and Loch Lomond. Also close to Thunder Bay are **Big Thunder National Ski Centre** and **Mount Baldy Ski Area.** Big Thunder has a vertical drop of 200 meters (650 feet) and a 5-kilometer (3-mile) lighted trail, and is served by a double chair and T-bar. Mount Baldy Ski Area is served by a double chair and T-bar and has a vertical drop of 195 meters (650 feet).

**Blue Mountain** (tel. 705/445–0231 or 416/869–3799 in Toronto), near Collingwood north of Toronto, is the most extensively developed and heavily trafficked mountain, with a vertical drop of 216 meters (720 feet). It has 31 pistes serviced by a high-speed quad lift, three triple chairs, eight double chairs, two pomas, and a rope tow. The acclaimed **Blue Mountain Inn** (tel. 705/445–0231) with 103 rooms, indoor swimming pool, fireplaces in some rooms and an assortment of restaurants and lounges, is at the base of the ski hills.

Near Barrie, 90 kilometers (56 miles) north of Toronto, is **Horseshoe Resort,** with 22 trails serviced by a quad and two triple and three double lifts. The vertical drop is only 94 meters (309 feet), but seven of the runs are rated for advanced skiers. The popular **Inn at Horseshoe** has 102 rooms and suites on the hill, as well as an indoor swimming pool, lounges, and fine dining. Many of the suites have whirlpools and wood-burning fireplaces.

**Mount Madawaska ski area** (tel. 613/756–2931), near Barry's Bay west of Ottawa, has a vertical drop of 120 meters (400 feet).

## Snowmobiling

Ontario is crisscrossed by thousands of miles of snowmobile trails, most of which are kept groomed by enthusiastic members of dozens of snowmobile clubs. For many trails a permit must be purchased. Overnight guided excursions are available in Haliburton Highlands/Algonquin Park and out of Kenora. **C Mac Snow Tours** (R.R. 3, Walton, Ont. N0K 1Z0, tel. 519/887–6686) has five-night, four-day trips for $590–$690 per person, double occupancy. The all-inclusive excursions are in Haliburton Highlands/Algonquin Park. At Kenora, **Halley's Camps** has guided excursions on wilderness trails to outpost camps for three to six nights, starting at $595 per person. The expeditions are all-inclusive, including fishing tackle for ice fishing, cross-country skis, snowshoes, and a snowmobile with gas and oil. (Box 608, Kenora, Ont. P9N 3X6, tel. 807/224–6531 or 800/465–3325 in all provinces but B.C.)

# Dining and Lodging

## Dining

Unless otherwise noted, reservations are not necessary and dress is casual. Highly recommended restaurants in each price category are indicated by a star ★.

| Category | Cost* |
| --- | --- |
| $$$$ | over $50 |
| $$$ | $35–$50 |
| $$ | $15–$35 |
| $ | under $15 |

*per person, excluding drinks, service, 7% GST, 8% food tax, and 10% bar tax*

## Lodging

Reservations are strongly recommended anywhere in Ontario during summer months.

Generally you get what you pay for at Ontario hotels and motels, though rates are often double or more than those charged in the United States for comparable accommodation.

Bed-and-breakfast associations exist in most cities, but, again, many of those rates exceed what you'd pay for a good hotel or motel room south of the border. A comprehensive bed-and-breakfast guide listing about 200 establishments is published by the **Federation of Ontario Bed and Breakfast Accommodation** (Box 437, 253 College St., Toronto, Ont. M5T 1R5, tel. 613/782–2464).

In Niagara Falls, the closer the hotel is to the falls, or the better the view is of them, the higher the rate.

Highly recommended lodgings in each price category are indicated by a star ★.

| Category | Cost* |
| --- | --- |
| $$$$ | over $100 |
| $$$ | $75–$100 |
| $$ | $35–$75 |
| $ | under $35 |

*All prices are for a standard double room, excluding taxes.*

**Alton**
*Dining and*
*Lodging*
★

**The Millcroft Inn.** Situated about 80 kilometers (50 miles) northwest of Toronto is this former 19th-century stone knitting mill, which has been converted to an exquisite full-service country inn beside the millpond. It is one of Canada's finest hostelries and a member of the Relais & Châteaux Association. The dining room is a stage for the Millcroft's executive chef, Rob Buchannan, who with advance notice will prepare any guest's favorite dish. *John St., L0N 1A0, tel. 519/941–8111, fax 519/941–9192. 42 rooms and suites, some with fireplaces. Facilities: pool, 2 saunas, outdoor year-round whirl-*

*pool, exercise room, 2 tennis courts, dining room. Reservations advised for dining room. AE, DC, MC, V. $$$$*

**Bracebridge**
*Dining and Lodging*
★

**Inn at the Falls.** Recently redone by professional new owners, this Victorian inn and its annex of motel-style rooms command a magnificent view of the pretty Bracebridge Falls on the Muskoka River. The main dining room and pub-lounge offer food and live entertainment; there's an outdoor patio for dining and sipping as well. The innkeepers live up to their boast of "the best steak-and-kidney pie this side of the Atlantic." *17 Dominion St., Box 1139, P0B 1C0, tel. 705/645–2245, fax 705/645–5093. 17 rooms, 6 with fireplaces. Facilities: dining room, pub, dining patio, parlor, outdoor heated pool. Reservations advised for restaurant. AE, MC, V. $$$*

**Cambridge**
*Dining and Lodging*
★

**Langdon Hall.** This magnificent colonial-revival-style mansion on 40 landscaped acres has grand public rooms and huge fireplaces. It was built in 1898 as a summer home for a great-grandson of John Jacob Astor and has been sensitively converted to a grand country hotel with 13 guest rooms in the original building and 28 in a modern annex. The chef, Louise Dumel, has trained in a number of prestigious kitchens in Europe, and her menu offers variations on French and Continental dishes. *Take Exit 275 from Hwy. 401 west of Kitchener, travel south on Fountain St./Homer Watson Blvd., to Blair Rd. Go through the village of Blair to Langdon Rd. Turn at the first driveway on the left and follow the lane to Langdon Hall, RR3, N3H 4R8, tel. 519/740–2100, fax 519/740–8161. 41 rooms. Facilities: meeting rooms, conservatory and drawing room, outdoor heated pool, sauna, whirlpool, exercise equipment, billiard room, card room, canoes (for the nearby Grand River), ballooning, tennis, croquet, 24-hr room service. Reservations advised and jacket recommended in dining room. AE, MC, V. $$$$*

**Cochrane**
*Dining and Lodging*

If you plan to take the *Polar Bear Express* train, you'll probably need to stay over in Cochrane. There are seven motels in and around the town that range in size from 7 to 42 units. Only First Canada Inns and Chimo Motel have restaurant facilities, but all are geared to early wake-up calls for guests taking the *Polar Bear Express* and late check-ins for those returning from the excursion. The four largest are **Westway Motor Motel** (21 First St., tel. 705/272–4285, fax 705/272–4429); **First Canada Inns,** (200 Railway St., tel. 705/272–3500, fax 705/272–5713); **Motel Cochrane** (R. R. 2, tel. 705/272–4253, fax 705/272–4250); and **Chimo Motel,** (Box 2326, tel. 705/272–6555, fax 705/272–5666). The postal code for all four is P0L 1C0.

**Elora**
*Dining and Lodging*
★

**Elora Mill.** This is one of Canada's few remaining five-story gristmills, which has been converted to luxury accommodations and offers superb dining. There are 16 guest rooms in the 1859 mill building and 16 more rooms in four other historic stone buildings in the immediate vicinity of the mill. The inn is in the heart of a village with historic stone buildings that could have been lifted from England's Cotswolds or southern France. The cuisine is a mix of imaginative Canadian and European dishes. *77 Mill St. W, tel. 519/846–5356, fax 519/846–9180. 32 rooms. Facilities: dining lounge with live music. Reservations advised for dining room. AE, MC, V. $$$*

**Goderich**
*Dining*
★

**La Brassine.** The kitchen in this large farm home–cum–country inn produces some of the finest French cuisine west of the Québec border. It's available only to those few who have booked ahead at least 24 hours for Wednesday–Saturday dinners or daily for residents of the five double guest rooms in the inn. Everything served is created in-house; the linen-covered tables are set with crystal and silver. *Off*

*Hwy. 21, midway between Bayfield and Goderich; turn toward Lake Huron on Kitchigami Rd. (R.R. 2), N7A 3X8, tel. 519/524–6300. Reservations advised. Dress: casual (no shorts or T-shirts). MC, V accepted; cash or personal check preferred. Note: no license for beer, wine, or liquor.* $$

**Hamilton**
*Dining*

**Ancaster Old Mill.** This historic mill is just outside Hamilton and worth the trip if only to sample the bread, baked daily with flour made at the mill on millstones installed in 1863. The dining rooms are light and bright and have hanging plants. Try to get a table overlooking the mill stream and a waterfall. *548 Old Dundas Rd., Ancaster, L9G 3J4 (from Hwy. 403 west of Hamilton take Mohawk Rd. W exit to Wilson St. in Ancaster. Turn right to Montgomery Dr., turn left and follow signs), tel. 905/648–1827. Reservations advised. Dress: casual (no shorts or T-shirts). AE, DC, MC, V.* $$

*Dining and*
*Lodging*

**The Royal Connaught Hotel.** The venerable Royal Connaught Hotel in the heart of downtown Hamilton was built in 1914 and is one of those grand old places complete with ballroom. The lobby and seventh floor have recently been renovated. The indoor swimming pool has one of Canada's longest water slides. The **Grill** is the hotel's very popular dining room. Meat is broiled over an open fire of mesquite. There's a marble floor, and after you've eaten—or while you're waiting for your entrée to be flamed—you can dance in the gazebo. *112 King St. E, L8N 1A8, tel. 905/546–8111 or 800/263–8558; fax 416/546–8144. 207 rooms, 21 suites. Facilities: restaurant, lounge, comedy cabaret, sauna, whirlpool. Reservations advised. AE, MC, V.* $$$

**Kingston**
*Lodging*

**Hochelaga Inn.** This Victorian-age inn, built more than a century ago, is located in a quiet residential and historic neighborhood but is a five-minute walk from downtown. All 23 rooms have private baths, and all but one have a queen-size double bed. The inn has no bar or restaurant, but a complimentary Continental breakfast, served in a small dining room, is included in the room rate. Guests also have the use of a cozy living room. *24 Sydenham St. S, Kingston K7L 3G9, tel. and fax 613/549–5534. AE, MC, V.* $$$

**Kitchener**
*Dining and*
*Lodging*

**Valhalla Inn.** This modern hotel has a major sports complex in its basement and is connected by a glassed-in skywalk to the Market Square shopping mall and Farmers' Market. **Shatzi's**, the main restaurant, seats 75 and the attached café accommodates about 40. All three meals are served in both dining areas, but for more formal, romantic occasions the main, candlelit room—decorated in earthtones—is more suitable. Continental fare dominates the menu. *105 King St. E, N2G 3W9, tel. 519/744–4141, fax 519/578–6889. 203 rooms. Facilities: dining room, lounge, restaurant, banquet room, fitness center with indoor pool, sauna, whirlpool, miniature golf. Reservations advised in restaurant. Dress: casual (no shorts or T-shirts). AE, MC, V.* $$$

**Walper Terrace Hotel.** This rejuvenated 1893 hotel sustains a Kitchener tradition started in 1820 by Phineas Varnum, who leased land from Joseph Schneider (of packing-house fame) to build what was then called the Varnum Inn. It now features at least one piece of period cherry-wood furniture in each of the guest rooms. The wooden-trim moldings, carved marble pillars, and the ornate brass banister of the main staircase have been preserved. The **Terrace Cafe** has an art deco floor, vaulted ceilings, marble pillars, stained glass windows, and a view of one of the city's major intersections. The setting is romantic, and meals are moderately priced. *1 King St. W, N2G 1A1, tel. 519/745–4321, fax 519/745–3625. 90 rooms, 12 suites. Facilities: restaurant, lounge, mini shopping mall, ballroom. Reserva-*

*tions advised for restaurant. Dress: casual (no shorts or T-shirts). AE, MC, V. $$$*

**London**
*Dining*

**Marienbad and Chaucer's Pub.** Reasonably priced Czech fare is served in surroundings that will remind you of your Eastern European vacation (if you had one). Great goulash, schnitzels, and sauerbraten are among the choices. *122 Carling St., N6A 1H6, tel. 519/679–9940. AE, MC, V. $$*

**Michael's on the Thames.** This popular lunch and dinner spot overlooking the Thames River offers flambéed dishes and has a maître d', Jack DiCarlo, who has become something of a local celebrity with his impromptu song-and-dance acts. The Canadian and Continental cuisine includes fresh seafood, chateaubriand, and flaming desserts and coffees. *1 York St. at the Thames River, N6A 1A1, tel. 519/672–0111. Reservations advised. AE, MC, V. $$*

*Lodging*

**Idlewylde Inn.** Though an elevator was installed in this converted 1878 mansion, the architects succeeded in keeping many original features in the 27 luxurious guest rooms and suites and in the public rooms. Some rooms have a Jacuzzi. Complimentary breakfast and snacks are included in the rate. *36 Grand Ave., N6C 1L1, tel. and fax 519/433–2891. 27 rooms. AE, DC, MC, V. $$$$*

**Sheraton Armouries Hotel.** This 20-story silver-mirrored tower rises from the center of the 1905 London Armoury. The lobby is a greenhouse of vines, trees, plants, and fountains wrapped in marble and accented by rich woods and old yellow brick. The architects left as much of the original armory intact as possible. A set of steps through manicured jungle takes you to the indoor swimming pool, sauna, and whirlpool. Guest rooms are spacious and decorated in pastel shades. Suites vary in size and grandeur—for example, the Middlesex Suite has a grand piano. *325 Dundas St., N6B 1T9, tel. 519/679–6111 or 800/325–3535, fax 519/679–3957. 250 rooms and suites. Facilities: racquetball and squash courts, pool, sauna, whirlpool, entertainment, sushi restaurant, dining room. Reservations advised for dining room. AE, MC, V. $$$*

London also has a strip of motels on Wellington Road north of Highway 401 and on Dundas Street East, out toward the airport.

**Midland**
*Dining and*
*Lodging*

**The Highland Inn.** This is a completely self-contained year-round hotel/motel/resort, most of which is contained in an enormous atrium. Sunday brunches by the pool in the **Garden Cafe** are popular. There are four dining areas, honeymoon suites with heart-shape tubs or sunken Jacuzzis, meeting rooms, a tanning room, exercise and weight rooms, and a full-time fitness director. *King St. and Hwy. 12, Box 515, L4R 4L3, tel. 705/526–9307; 800/461–4265 for reservations; fax 705/526–0099. 125 rooms and suites. Facilities: dining rooms, tanning rooms, weight rooms. Reservations advised for dining room. AE, MC, V. $$*

**Moosonee**
*Dining and*
*Lodging*

In Moosonee you can choose either the **Polar Bear Lodge** or the **Moosonee Lodge,** both of which are on Revillon Street facing the Moose River. Rates are high for the caliber of accommodation, but if you want to stay, these are your choices. Both hotels serve meals, but alcohol is served only during the dinner hour, and then only to those dining at the hotel. The mailing address for both Moosonee hotels is: 65 Enterprise Rd., Rexdale, Ont. M9W 1C4. *Polar Bear Lodge: tel. 705/336–2345, fax 705/336–2185. 30 rooms. Facilities: restaurant. MC, V. $$$ Moosonee Lodge: tel. 705/336–2351, fax 705/336–2773. 21 rooms. Facilities: restaurant. MC, V. $$$*

**Niagara Falls**
*Dining*

**Capri Restaurant.** Soft chairs and a softly tinkling piano create an elegant mood here. The combination of good steak, seafood, and

Italian dishes makes this one of the better Niagara dining spots. *5438 Ferry St., tel. 905/354–7519. Reservations advised. AE, MC, V. $$*

**Queenston Heights Restaurant.** This is one of four restaurants operated by the NPC, which ensures good food at fair prices. Queenston Heights Restaurant is a few kilometers north of (downriver from) the falls, and you can have a relaxed lunch or dinner overlooking a golf course or, if you're lucky, the Niagara Gorge. This is especially recommended for its Sunday brunch. *14184 Niagara Parkway, Queenston Heights Park, tel. 905/262–4274. Reservations advised. AE, DC, MC, V. $$*

**Skylon Tower's Revolving Dining Room and Summit Suite Restaurant.** If you have just one night for dining at the falls, make a reservation at the Skylon Tower's Revolving Dining Room. It makes a full circle every hour, and the view of the illuminated falls at night—at any time of the year—is a sight long remembered. The Canadian and Continental cuisine is usually excellent. The Skylon's Summit Suite Restaurant serves buffet breakfasts, plus lunch and dinner, and it has dancing, but it doesn't revolve. *Skylon Tower, tel. 905/356–2651. Reservations advised. AE, DC, MC, V. $$*

*Lodging* **Skyline Brock Hotel, Skyline Foxhead Hotel, Skyline Village Hotel.** The former Sheraton-Foxhead Hotel is now the 232-room Skyline Brock Hotel, the 395-room Skyline Foxhead Hotel, and the 208-room Skyline Village Hotel, and all are located at 5685 Falls Avenue. The most distinguishing characteristic of these hotels is the price. The Foxhead rates start lower than those at the other two but climb to as high as $209 for some rooms. Many guest-room windows overlook the falls; some have particularly splendid views, and rates are based to some extent on the view. *5685 Falls Ave., L2E 6W7, tel. (for all 3) 905/374–4444, fax 905/337–4804. Facilities: restaurant, lounge, bar, coffee shop. AE, MC, V. $$$*

**Michael's Inn.** If you're on a first, second, third, or even fourth honeymoon, consider something fun and romantic. Michael's Inn has a number of theme rooms, all of which overlook the American falls and the gorge. Carry your mate across the threshold into deepest Africa, the Old South, or the Orient. The "Midnight at the Oasis" room has a Jacuzzi for two surrounded by mirrors, a 2-meter-high (6½-foot-high) stuffed tiger, palm-leaf wallpaper, and bamboo trees. *5599 River Rd., L2E 3H3, tel. 905/354–2727, fax 905/374–7706. 130 rooms. Facilities: indoor pool with slide, sauna, whirlpool, gift shop, lounge, dining room. AE, MC, V. $$*

**Niagara-on-the-Lake** **Queen's Landing.** Also called the Inn at Niagara-on-the-Lake, this remarkable property is a welcome addition to an old town that has
*Lodging* had no new places in a long while. The owner—who also runs the Pillar & Post—has obtained antique furnishings and installed fireplaces in 78 rooms and Jacuzzis in 44 rooms. Located at the mouth of the Niagara River, right across from historic Fort Niagara, the hotel has knockout views. The dining room has recently won some acclaim. *Melville and Bryon Sts. (Box 1180), L0S 1J0, tel. 905/468–2195, fax 905/468–2227. 137 rooms. Facilities: dining room, lounge, lap pool, indoor pool, whirlpool, exercise facilities, baby-sitting service, 24-hr room service, tennis and golf nearby. Dress for dining room: no jeans; collar and sleeves required. AE, DC, MC, V. $$$*

*Dining and* **Prince of Wales.** This hotel is a family affair. The Wiens family has
*Lodging* been doling out its gracious hospitality since 1975, turning a 16-
★ room inn into a 105-room hotel. The original section of the inn was built as Long's Hotel in 1864. The additions over the years now make the hotel a block long, but the changes (inside and out) have been so

sensitively wrought that only an expert could guess where most of the changes were made. One obvious exception is the **Patio Restaurant,** where tables are under a canopy of hanging plants and behind glass walls overlooking the main street. Guest rooms are furnished in reproduction French provincial or traditional English furniture. Guests may dine in the **Dining Room,** the **Queen's Royal Lounge,** or the **Greenhouse Patio Restaurant,** particularly popular with the local lunch crowd. *6 Picton St., L0S 1J0, tel. 905/468–3246 or 800/263–2452, fax 905/468–5521. 105 rooms and suites with bath, some with fireplaces. Facilities: 3 dining areas, lounge, indoor pool, sauna, whirlpool, health club, tennis. Reservations advised for restaurants. Dress: casual (no shorts or T-shirts). AE, MC, V. $$$$*

**Oban Inn.** This elegant, historic country inn is centrally located and has a view of Lake Ontario. For much of 1992 and 1993, after a devastating fire, the hotel was closed, but happily, it is now back in business. The respected dining room offers standard treatments of beef, duck, lobster, and steak. *160 Front St., L0S 1J0, tel. 905/468–2165, fax 905/468–4165. 23 rooms, some with fireplaces. Facilities: dining room, lounge, lap pool, indoor pool, whirlpool, exercise room. Reservations advised for dining room. Dress: casual (no shorts or T-shirts). AE, DC, MC, V. $$$*

**Ottawa** **Flippers.** As the name suggests, this is a seafood restaurant, and the
**Dining** specialties change almost daily as different kinds of fresh fish and seafoods are available. Part of the decor in the old building on Bank Street is marine artifacts and model ships. *823 Bank St., 2nd Floor, tel. 613/232–2703. Reservations advised. AE, MC, V. $$$*

**Chequers.** In this three-story, Gothic-style 1868 country inn 25 kilometers (16 miles) southwest of Ottawa, the specialties are French and Spanish haute cuisine. The service is European and so is the decor. *5816 Hazeldean Rd., Stittsville (from the Queensway, take Terry Fox Dr. south to Hazeldean Rd.—old Hwy. 7), tel. 613/836–1665. Reservations required. AE, MC, V. $$*

**Courtyard Restaurant.** Fine French cuisine is served in this lovely, historic limestone building on a quiet cul-de-sac near By Ward Market, a five-minute stroll from the Parliament Buildings. The forerunner of today's elegant dining establishment was a log tavern built in 1827, likely inspired by construction of the nearby Rideau Canal. The humble log tavern was replaced by the limestone Ottawa Hotel a decade later. Extensive renovations created Courtyard Restaurant, and its cuisine and ambience established a dedicated following. *21 George St., tel. 519/565–2611. Reservations advised. AE, MC, V. $$*

**Fresco.** This cozy Italian restaurant's dominant feature is a mural of mountains on the back wall, although the dizzying choice of menu options is quite impressive, too. Ten sauces accompany such house specialties as scallops, salmon and veal. *354 Elgin St., tel. 613/235–7541. Reservations advised. AE, MC, V. $$*

*Lodging* **Château Laurier Hotel.** Ottawa has all kinds of posh new hotels with great service and food, but this hotel is an institution. It's one of Canada's great railroad hotels, built in 1916. It now has 480 large, airy rooms; an indoor pool; a variety of dining rooms, lounges, and bars; and indoor parking. The Château, as it's known, is part of the Ottawa experience; it's also smack dab in the middle of the must-see list for Ottawa. *1 Rideau St., K1N 8S7, tel. 613/241–1414, fax 613/241–2958. 480 rooms. Facilities: restaurant, lounge, bar, indoor pool. AE, MC, V. $$$$*

**Minto Place Suite Hotel.** One- and two-bedroom suites in this 31-story hotel, which is within strolling distance of Sparks Street Mall, have full kitchen and laundry facilities. *433 Laurier Ave. W, K1R*

*7Y1, tel. 613/232–2200, fax 613/232–6962. 418 suites. Facilities: lounge, sauna, indoor pool, whirlpool, health spa, indoor parking. AE, MC, V. $$$–$$$$*

**O'Connor House Bed and Breakfast.** In the heart of downtown Ottawa, this former hotel has 34 guest rooms and family suites. Ice skates and bicycles are available to guests along with a lounge, 24-hour snacks, and a full buffet breakfast. *172 O'Connor St., K2P 1T5, tel. 613/236–4221. 34 rooms. Facilities: ice skates, bicycles. AE, MC, V. $$*

**Peterborough**
*Dining and Lodging*

**Ramada Red Oak Inn.** This 181-room hotel is connected to the city's largest downtown indoor shopping complex. Guest rooms are comfortably furnished. **Sir William's Dining Room** offers Continental fare and lighter meals, and snacks are served at the **Garden Cafe** in the pool area. There is free underground parking. *100 Charlotte St., K9J 7L4, tel. 705/743–7272, fax 705/749–0845. 181 rooms. Facilities: restaurants, indoor pool, sauna, and whirlpool, shopping, free parking. Reservations advised for dining room. AE, D, MC, V. $$$*

**Picton**
*Dining and Lodging*

**Isaiah Tubbs Resort.** A dozen kilometers west of Picton, this posh 58-room property has rooms and suites with fireplaces, 12 cottages, and 35 housekeeping cottages. There's fine dining in the **Restaurant on the Knoll Overlooking the Sandbanks at West Lake.** (That's the correct name of the restaurant and that's what it overlooks!) *RR 1, K0K 2T0, tel. 613/393–2090 or 800/267–0525, fax 613/393–1291. 58 rooms. Facilities: restaurant, indoor and outdoor swimming pools, saunas and whirlpool. AE, MC, V. $$*

*Lodging*

**Merrill Inn.** This beautiful 1870 home is a short stroll from the heart of downtown Picton. It has been converted to a cozy 15-room inn by the same folks who created Idlewyld Inn at London (*see above*). The refrigerator is stocked with soft drinks and the sideboard with croissants, muffins, tea, and coffee 24 hours a day, but no meals are served. *343 Main St. E, K0K 2T0, tel. 613/476–7451, fax 613/476–8283. 15 rooms. MC, V. $$$*

**Port Stanley**
*Dining and Lodging*
★

**Kettle Creek Inn.** This small, elegant, full-service country inn features fine food and a friendly pub ambience. Two new suites with balconies, fireplaces, and whirlpools and five new rooms with baths were installed in the original inn in 1992, and in 1990 eight rooms, three suites, and full facilities for small business meetings were added in a cleverly designed annex. Some of the new rooms have whirlpool baths and gas fireplaces. There are other nice touches, such as old-fashioned pedestal sinks, interesting local artwork, and views from all the rooms and suites of a landscaped courtyard and gazebo. Continental breakfast is included in room rates. The three dining rooms in the original inn offer daily specials, including fresh Lake Erie fish just brought ashore by the local fishing fleet. Fresh Ontario lamb and pork tenderloin are also featured. *Main St., N0L 2A0, tel. 519/782–3388, fax 519/782–4747. 10 rooms, 5 suites. Facilities: 3 dining rooms (reservations advised). AE, D, DC, MC, V. $$–$$$$*

**Rossport**
*Dining and Lodging*

**Rossport Inn.** The hamlet of Rossport on a harbor off Lake Superior is about as close as you can get to an outport on the Great Lakes. The inn was built in 1884 as a railroad hotel and now has six small guest rooms sharing two bathrooms. This is one of the nicest country inns in the province. It's cozy and down-home—the nightlife consists of swapping lies with the innkeepers and other guests about fish that got away. Breakfast is included in the room rate. The dining room's homestyle cooking of locally caught fish, as well as of steak, chicken, pork chops, and lobster is irresistible. *On Rossport Loop, ½ mi from*

*Trans-Canada Hwy., Bowman St., P0T 2R0, tel. 807/824–3213. 6 rooms with shared bath. MC, V. Closed Nov.–May. $$*

**St. Jacobs**
*Dining and Lodging*

**Benjamins.** This is a lovely re-creation of the original 1852 Farmer's Inn. Nine guest rooms on the second floor are furnished in antiques, and every bed is covered with a locally made Mennonite quilt. The licensed 120-seat restaurant has pine ceiling beams, an open-hearth fireplace, lots of greenery, and imaginative French cuisine. *17 King St., N0B 2N0, tel. 519/664–3731, fax 519/664–2218. 9 rooms, all with private bath. Reservations advised for restaurant. AE, MC, V. $$$*

**Sault Ste. Marie**
*Dining and Lodging*

**Quality Inn Bayfront.** If you're planning to take the Agawa Canyon Snow Train, try to get a room at this popular hotel. The 110 rooms (including 18 suites) are clean and modern with many creature comforts, including a sauna and in-house movies. Most important—because the train leaves at 8 AM and you should be at the station by 7:30 AM at the latest—the hotel is directly across the street from the Algoma Central Railroad station. That means you can enjoy a room-service or dining-room breakfast, stroll across the street, and leave your car parked at the hotel. When you return at night, the hotel's swimming pool and dining room await you. **Blossoms Bistro** in the hotel offers good prices, friendly service . . . and edible floral garnishes! The dining area is bright and airy with lots of brass and greenery, and reservations are suggested. *180 Bay St., P6A 6S2, tel. 705/945–9264, fax 705/945–9766. 82 rooms, 18 suites. Facilities: dining room, indoor pool, sauna, whirlpool, exercise room. Reservations advised for dining room. AE, MC, V. $$$*

**Stratford**
*Dining*

**The Church Restaurant and Belfry.** Located one block from the Avon Theatre, this property—a church—is complete with organ pipes and stained-glass windows, and has been converted into a restaurant. There's even an old pew outside the washroom. The Belfry restaurant and bar is more casual, and less expensive. *Brunswick and Waterloo Sts., tel. 519/273–3424. Reservations advised. Dress: casual (no shorts or T-shirts). AE, DC, MC, V. $$$$*

*Dining and Lodging*

**The Queen's Inn at Stratford.** In this beautifully restored 1853 hotel, guests can enjoy traditional Canadian food in the dining room while listening to tinkling music from a baby grand piano. Light fare is served in one half of the divided room, and there are also a popular pub-lounge and two function rooms. *161 Ontario St., N5A 3H3, tel. 519/271–1400, fax 519/271–7373. 30 rooms with bath. Facilities: restaurant, lounge. Reservations advised for restaurant. AE, MC, V. $$$*

**Woods Villa Bed and Breakfast.** Owner Ken Vinen has restored this elegant 1875 home of a wealthy magistrate to its original grandeur, and some of the five rooms have fireplaces. Vinen uses the public rooms to display an astonishing collection of vintage juke boxes, music boxes, and player pianos he has restored to mint condition. If he doesn't have the old favorite you want to hear, he'll sit down at one of the pianos and pound it out for you. In summer, a full breakfast is served on an outside patio beside an enormous, ceramic-tile swimming pool. Woods Villa does not accept children or pets; the latter might ruffle the feathers of Vinen's five pet macaws. *62 John St. N, Stratford, N5A 6K7, tel. 519/271–4576. 5 rooms. MC, V accepted; cash preferred. Facilities: pool. $$*

**Windsor**
*Dining*

**Brigantino's.** This popular establishment is outstanding for home-style Italian cooking and melt-in-your-mouth pasta. *851 Erie St. E, tel. 519/254–7041. Reservations advised. AE, D, DC, MC, V. $$*

**The Old Fish Market.** A wonderful ambience is created here with hanging plants and brass railings and lots of lovely woodwork. The menu lives up to the name and is heavy on seafood. It has a deserved reputation of excellence. *156 Chatham St. W, tel. 519/253–7417. Weekend reservations advised. AE, DC, MC, V. $$*

**Lodging**  **Hilton International Windsor.** Each of the 293 guest rooms in this 22-story, downtown riverbank hotel has a view of Detroit's impressive skyline and the shipping activity on the world's busiest inland waterway. The Park Terrace Restaurant and Lounge offers a wide menu and spectacular river view. In the River Runner Bar and Grill, there's music and dancing. *277 Riverside Dr. W, N9A 5K4, tel. 519/973–5555, fax 519/973–1600. 293 rooms. Facilities: indoor pool, sauna, whirlpool, meeting facilities, room service. AE, MC, V. $$$$*

# The Arts and Nightlife

**Hamilton**  Opera Hamilton holds performances in the Great Hall of Hamilton Place September through April (Summers La., opposite the Art Gallery of Hamilton, tel. 905/527–7627).

**Shaw Festival, Niagara-on-the-Lake**  A stage-struck Toronto lawyer's dream in 1961 now has an impressive track record and a world-class reputation. Brian Doherty started the festival in 1961 with a few Shaw plays produced on weekends in the old town courthouse. The performances were well received, and the company drew continuing support, mainly from Toronto. Government kicked in most of the $3 million needed to build the 863-seat Shaw Festival Theatre, which opened in 1973. This is the only festival in the world specializing in the works of George Bernard Shaw and his contemporaries. Besides the modern Festival Theatre, plays are also staged at the original Court House Theatre, and the more cozy Royal George Theatre. The festival starts at the end of April and runs through mid-November. *Tel. 800/267–4759 in Canada, 800/724–2934 in US.*

**Stratford Festival**  It all started in 1953, in a massive tent, with Sir Alec Guinness playing Richard III. The next year, musical programs were added to augment Shakespeare's plays. The venture was a huge success, and the 1957 season opened in a permanent home with 2,262 seats, none of which is more than 65 feet from the stage. The 1901-vintage, 1,107-seat Avon Theatre became a partner in the festival in 1967, and The Third Stage, seating 410, opened in 1971. Stratford Festival now starts in late April and runs into November. *For information: Stratford and Area Visitors and Convention Bureau, 38 Albert St., Stratford, Ont. N5A 3K3, tel. 519/271–5361; box office, tel. 519/273–1600.*

**Nightlife**  The brochure says **Lulu's Roadhouse** has a "warm, casual atmosphere" but doesn't try to suggest it is "cozy" or "intimate." This unique play spot, located in a former K-Mart store just south of Kitchener, is Canada's largest bar. It can seat 2,000 customers at 450 tables and on bar stools, and there's room for another 1,000 standing along the longest and second-longest bars in the world. (The world's longest bar is 333 feet; the second-longest is 310 feet.) Since Lulu's opened in 1984, it's been packing 'em in to watch performances by big-name rock-and-roll entertainers. *4263 King St. E (Hwy. 8), tel. 800/561–5858. Cover charge varies with entertainment. Open Thurs.–Sat. 4:30 PM–1 AM, sometimes Wed. for special concerts. Jeans not permitted.*

# 10 Province of Québec

By Dorothy
Guinan

Dorothy
Guinan is a
political
researcher for
the Montréal
Gazette and
is a freelance
writer.

Among the provinces of Canada, Québec is set apart by its strong French heritage, a matter not only of language but of customs, religion, and political structure. Québec covers a vast area—almost one-sixth of Canada's total—although the upper three-quarters is only sparsely inhabited. Most of the population lives in the southern cities, especially Montréal (see Chapter 3) and Québec City (see Chapter 4). Outside the cities, however, you'll find serenity and natural beauty in the province's innumerable lakes, streams, and rivers; in its farmlands and villages; in its great mountains and deep forests; and in its rugged coastline along the Gulf of St. Lawrence. Though the winters are long, there are plenty of winter sports to while away the cold months, especially in the Laurentians, with its many ski resorts.

Québec's recent threats to secede from the Canadian union are part of a long-standing tradition of independence. The first European to arrive in Québec was French explorer Jacques Cartier, in 1534; another Frenchman, Samuel de Champlain, arrived in 1603, determined to build French settlements in the region, and Jesuit missionaries followed in due course. Louis XIV of France proclaimed Canada a crown colony in 1663, and the land was allotted to French aristocrats in large grants called seigneuries. As tenants, known as habitants, settled upon farms in Québec, the Roman Catholic church took on an importance that went beyond religion. Priests and nuns also acted as doctors, educators, and overseers of business arrangements between the habitants and between French-speaking fur traders and English-speaking merchants. An important doctrine of the church in Québec was survivance, the survival of the French people and their culture. Couples were told to have large families, and they did—families with 10 or 12 children were the norm.

Although the British won control of Canada in the French and Indian War in 1763, Parliament passed the Quebec Act in 1774, which ensured the continuation of French law in Québec and left provincial authority in the hands of the Roman Catholic church. In general, the law preserved the traditional Québecois way of life. Tensions between Québec and English-speaking Canada accelerated throughout the 20th century, however, and in 1974 the province defiantly proclaimed French its national language. In 1990 a three-year attempt by the Canadian government to add Québec's signature to the Canadian Constitution failed. Québec had been willing to sign provided that it received special status to promote its French language and culture. However, two of the 10 provinces would not agree to Québec's request. The incident became known as Meech Lake. In 1992 the Canadian government came up with a new plan that would have vastly changed the 125-year-old Constitution by recognizing Québec as a distinct society and giving more powers to the provincial governments. On October 26, in a nationwide referendum, Québec and five other provinces rejected the offer, and today the problem remains unresolved.

Being able to speak French can make your visit to the province more pleasant—many locals do not speak English. If you don't speak French, arm yourself with a phrase book or at least a knowledge of some basic phrases. It's also worth your while to sample the hearty traditional Québecois cuisine, for this is a province where food is taken seriously.

# Lower Québec

James Bay

Kesagami Lake

Albanel Lake

109

Matagami

113

Lake Mistassini

Harricana R.

Lake Abitibi

La Sarre

109

QUEBEC

Parent Lake

Gouin Reservoir

167

Mistass

111

Amos

Saint-Félicien

Lake St-Jean

101

Noranda

117

Malartic

Val-d'Or

113

Louvicourt

Chambord

169

New Liskeard

La Vérendrye Prov. Park

101

155

La Pr

11

Kipawa Lake

117

Manouane

La Tuque

Mont-Tremblant Prov. Park

St-Zénon

Mauricie Nat. Park

Qué

17

Mattawa

Ottawa R.

Mont-Laurier

117

St-Donat

Trois-Rivières

11

Algonquin Prov. Park

Pembroke

105

309

St-Jovite

40

132

20

Vict

60

60

62

17

Gatineau Nat. Park

Ste-Agathe-des-Monts

Sorel

Richmond

Hawkesbury

158

Laval

Hull

17

Montréal

Sherbrooke

29

Ottawa

Dorion

10

OTTAWA

31

CANADA

15

133

55

28

62

41

Cornwall

U.S.

91

7

Rideau

401

Massena

VERMONT

Lake Simcoe

Ogdensburg

St. Regis R.

87

7

Lake Champlain

401

NEW YORK

HAM

Lake Ontario

Hudson R.

91

Niagara Falls

Rochester

Buffalo

90

90

Genesee R.

15

90

81

MASSACHUSET

# Essential Information

## Important Addresses and Numbers

**Tourist Information Québec** **Tourism Québec** (12 rue Ste. Anne, Qué., G1R 3X2, tel. 418/643–2280, toll-free from the Montréal area; from Québec, Canada, or the United States, 800/363–7777) can provide information on provincial tourist bureaus throughout the province.

*The Laurentians* The major tourist office is the **Maison du Tourisme des Laurentides** at Saint-Jérôme, just off the Autoroute des Laurentides 15 at exit 39. *14142 rue de Lachapelle, RR 1, St-Jérôme J7Z 5T4, tel. 514/436–8532. Open mid-June–Aug., daily 8:30–8; Sept.–mid-June, Sat.–Thurs 9–5, Fri. 9–7.*

You can also get information in person at **Infotouriste** (1001 Sq. Dorchester, Montréal). Year-round regional tourist offices are located in the towns of Labelle, Mont Laurier, Mont Tremblant, Saint-Antoine, Saint-Sauveur-des-Monts, Saint-Jovite, Sainte-Adèle, and Sainte-Agathe-des-Monts. Seasonal tourist offices (mid-June–Labor Day) are also located in Bois Briand, Grenville, Lachute, L'Annociation, Sainte-Marguerite-du-Lac-Masson, Notre-Dame-du-Laus, Piedmont, Saint-Adolphe-Howard, and Val David. For information about ski conditions, telephone the Maison du Tourisme des Laurentides (*see above*) and ask for the ski info-line number.

*L'Estrie* In Montréal, information about l'Estrie is available at **Infotouriste** (*see above*). Year-round regional provincial tourist offices are located in the towns of Bromont, Danville, Granby, Magog, Sherbrooke, and Sutton. Seasonal tourist offices (June–Labor Day) are also located in Ayer's Cliff, Coaticook, Knowlton, La Patrie, Lac-Mégantic, Lennoxville, Masonville, North Hatley, and Pike River. Seasonal bureaus' schedules are irregular, so contact the **Association Touristique de l'Estrie** (25 Brocage, Sherbrooke, J1L 2J4, tel. 819/820–2020) before visiting. The association also provides lodging information.

## Arriving and Departing by Plane

Most airlines fly into either of Montréal's airports (Mirabel or Dorval) or Québec City's airport (*see* Chapters 3 and 4).

## Arriving and Departing by Car, Train, and Bus

*By Car* The major highways are Autoroute des Laurentides 15, a six-lane highway from Montréal to the Laurentians; Autoroute 10 East from Montréal to l'Estrie; U.S. 91 from New England, which becomes Autoroute 55 as it crosses the border to l'Estrie; and Highway 138, which runs from Montréal along the north shore of the St. Lawrence River.

*By Train* Regular **VIA Rail** passenger service connects all the provinces with Montréal and Québec City and offers limited service to the Gaspé Peninsula.

*By Bus* Most major bus lines in the province connect with **Voyageur** (tel. 514/842–2281).

## Getting Around

**Québec Province**
*By Car*

The province has fine roads, along which drivers insist on speeding. Free road maps are available at any of the numerous seasonal or permanent Québec Tourist Offices (call 800/363–7777 for the nearest location). Major entry points are Ottawa/Hull, U.S. 87 from New York State south of Montréal, U.S. 91 from Vermont into l'Estrie area, and the Trans-Canada Highway just west of Montréal.

*By Bus*

Most bus traffic to the outer reaches of the province begins at the bus terminal in downtown Québec City (225 boul. Charest E, tel. 418/524–4692).

**The Laurentians**
*By Car*

Autoroute des Laurentides 15, a six-lane highway, and the slower but more scenic secondary road, Route 117, lead to this resort country. Try to avoid traveling to and from the region on Friday evening or Sunday afternoon, as you're likely to sit for hours in bumper-to-bumper traffic.

*By Bus*

Frequent bus service is available from the Terminus Voyageur (505 boul. de Maisonneuve E, tel. 514/842–2281) in downtown Montréal. **Limocar Laurentides'** service (tel. 514/435–8899) departs regularly for L'Annociation, Mont Laurier, Sainte-Adèle, Sainte-Agathe-des-Monts, and Saint-Jovite, among other stops en route. Limocar also has a service to the Basses Laurentides (Lower Laurentians) region, departing from the Laval bus terminal at the Métro Henri-Bourassa stop in north Montréal, stopping in many towns, and ending in Saint-Jérôme.

**L'Estrie**
*By Car*

Take Autoroute 10 East from Montréal; from New England take U.S. 91, which becomes Autoroute 55 as it crosses the border at Rock Island.

*By Bus*

Buses depart daily from the Terminus Voyageur in Montréal (505 boul. de Maisonneuve E, tel. 514/842–2281), to Granby, Lac-Mégantic, Magog, Sherbrooke, and Thetford Mines.

## Guided Tours

**Special-Interest Tours**
*Nature tours*

The **Montréal Zoological Society** (2055 rue Peel, Montréal H3A 1V4, tel. 514/845–8317) is a nature-oriented group that offers lectures, field trips, and weekend excursions. Tours include hiking and birdwatching in national parks throughout Québec, Canada, and the northern United States.

*Whale-watching*

**Croisières Navimex Canada, Inc.** (25 Pl. Marché Champlain, Suite 400, Québec City G1K 4H2, tel. 418/692–4643), offers three-hour whale-watching cruises ($30 adults, $15 children under 14) and 4½-hour dinner cruises on the Saguenay Fjord ($40 adults, $20 children under 14). Cruises depart from Baie-Ste-Catherine, Tadoussac, and Rivière du Loup (the departure from Rivière du Loup costs an additional $5 for adults).

Graduate-student marine biologists from the **Montréal Zoological Society** (*see above*) accompany whale-watching excursions in the St. Lawrence estuary, a habitat for many whale species, including the endangered beluga.

*River Excursions*

**Croisières Navimex Canada, Inc.** (*see above*) also offers a 10-hour boat trip along the St. Lawrence River between Québec and Montréal for between $100–$120. The package includes two meals, a few hours of free time at the port-of-call (Québec or Montréal, depending on the city of departure), and return bus transportation the same evening. The trip is not recommended for children under 12.

*Train Tours*  The **Choo-Choo Steam Train Company** (tel. 819/778–7246) operates a five-hour scenic excursion along the Gatineau River from Hull to Wakefield and back, daily or on weekends, depending on season. There's room for 600 passengers—68 per car—and the train makes a two-hour stopover in Wakefield, where there's a museum, a grist-mill, and craft shops. Fares are $21 for adults, $19 for students and senior citizens, and $10 for children under 13. During the month of December, there is also a "Santa Express:" the same five-hour excursion with a few surprise appearances from Santa Claus; the cost is $16 for adults and $10 for children under 13. Reservations are necessary for both trips.

# Exploring Québec

There are two major attractions beyond the city limits of Montréal: l'Estrie (formerly the Eastern Townships), where city folk retreat in summer, and Les Laurentides (the Laurentians), where they escape in winter. Les Laurentides are characterized by thousands of miles of unspoiled wilderness and world-famous ski resorts, while l'Estrie has rolling hills and farmland. As major vacation areas in both winter and summer, they offer outdoor activities on ski slopes and lakes and in their provincial parks. The two other regions worth exploring are Charlevoix, often called the Switzerland of Québec because of its landscape, and the knobby Gaspé Peninsula, where the St. Lawrence River meets the Gulf of St. Lawrence.

## Highlights for First-time Visitors

**Basilica of Ste-Anne-de-Beaupré,** Sainte-Anne-de-Beaupré, Tour 3: Charlevoix
**Bonaventure Island and its gannet colony,** off Percé, Tour 4: The Gaspé Peninsula
**Cross-country skiing** in Les Laurentides, Tour 1: Les Laurentides
**Jardin Zoologique de Granby,** Granby, Tour 2: L'Estrie
**"Sugaring off"** at a sugar shack in Les Laurentides, Dining
**Théâtre Lac Brome,** Knowlton, Tour 2: L'Estrie
**Whale-watching in the St. Lawrence Seaway,** Guided Tours and Tour 3: Charlevoix

## Tour 1: Les Laurentides

Avid skiers might call Montréal a bedroom community for the Laurentians; just 56 kilometers (35 miles) to the north, they are home to some of North America's best-known ski resorts. The Laurentian range is ancient, dating to the Precambrian era (more than 600 million years ago). These rocky hills are relatively low, worn down by glacial activity, but they include eminently skiable hills, with a few peaks above 2,500 feet. World-famous Mont Tremblant, at 3,150 feet, is the tallest.

The **P'tit Train du Nord** made it possible to easily transport settlers and cargo to the Upper Laurentians. It also opened them up to skiing by the turn of the century. Before long, trainloads of skiers replaced settlers and cargo as the railway's major trade. The Upper Laurentians soon became known worldwide as the number-one ski center in North America—a position they still hold today. Initially a winter weekend getaway for Montréalers who stayed at boarding-houses and fledgling resorts while skiing its hills, the Upper Laurentians began attracting an international clientele, especially with the advent of the Canadian National Railway's special skiers' train, begun in 1928. (Its competitor, the Canadian Pacific Railway, jumped on the bandwagon soon after, doubling the number of train runs bringing skiers to the area.)

Soon, points north of Saint-Jérôme began to develop as resort areas: Saint-Sauveur-des-Monts, Saint-Jovite, Sainte-Agathe-des-Monts, Mont Tremblant, and points in between became major ski centers. The Upper Laurentians also began to grow as a winter haven for prominent Montréalers, who traveled as far north as Sainte-Agathe-des-Monts to establish private family ski lodges. A number of these properties continue to be preserved in their rustic turn-of-the-century wilderness settings.

Accessible only by train until the 1930s, when the highway was built, these were used primarily as winter ski lodges. But once the road opened up, cottages became year-round family retreats. Today, there is an uneasy alliance between the longtime cottagers and resort-driven entrepreneurs. Both recognize the other's historic role in developing the Upper Laurentians, but neither espouses the other's cause. At the moment, commercial development seems to be winning out. A number of large hotels have added indoor pools and spa facilities, and efficient highways have brought the country closer to the city—45 minutes to Saint-Saveur, 1½–2 hours to Mont Tremblant. Montréalers can drive up to enjoy the fall foliage or engage in spring skiing and still get home before dark. The only slow periods are early October, when there is not much to do, and June, when there is plenty to do but the area is beset by blackflies.

**Les Basses Laurentides**
The Laurentians are actually divided into two major regions—les Basses Laurentides (the Lower Laurentians) and les Hautes Laurentides (the Upper Laurentians). But don't be fooled by the designations; they don't signify great driving distances.

The Lower Laurentians start almost immediately outside Montréal. Considered the birthplace of the Laurentians, this area is rich in historic and architectural landmarks. Beginning in the mid-17th century, the governors of New France, as Québec was then called, gave large concessions of land to its administrators, priests, and top-ranking military, who became known as *seigneurs*. In the Lower Laurentians, towns like Terrebonne, Saint-Eustache, Lac-des-Deux-Montagnes, and Oka are home to the manors, mills, churches, and public buildings these seigneurs had built for themselves and their *habitants*—the inhabitants of these quasi-feudal villages.

*Numbers in the margin correspond to points of interest on the Laurentians map.*

Two of the most famous seigneuries are within an hour of Montréal: ❶ **La Seigneurie de Terrebonne,** on l'Île-des-Moulins, is about 20 minutes from Montréal; La Seigneurie du Lac-des-Deux-Montagnes, in St-Scholastique, is 40 minutes from Montréal. You reach Terrebonne by taking boulevard Pie-IX in Montréal to the bridge of the same name. From the bridge take Highway 25 North. Exit at Terrebonne to Highway 440.

Governor Frontenac gave the land to Sieur André Daulier in 1673. Terrebonne was maintained by a succession of seigneurs until 1832, when Joseph Masson, the first French Canadian millionaire, bought it. He and his family were the last seigneurs de Terrebonne; their reign ended in 1883.

Today, Terrebonne offers visitors a bona fide glimpse of the past. Now run by the Corporation de l'Ile-des-Moulins rather than a French aristocrat, the seigneurie's mansions, manors, and build-

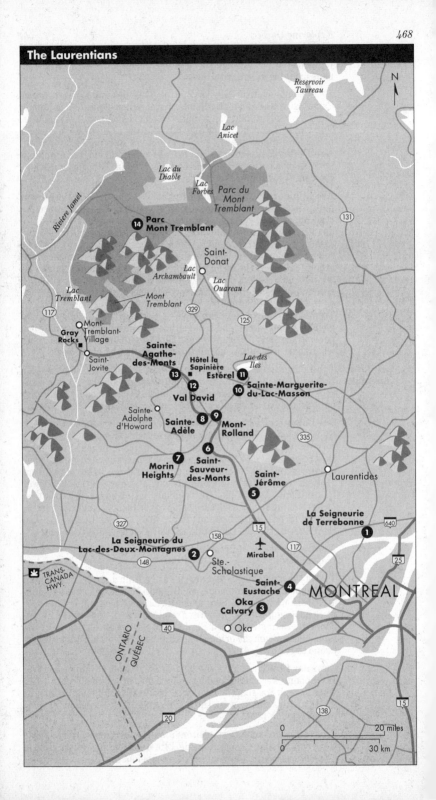

# The Laurentians

ings have all been restored. Take a walk through Terrebonne's historical center and then stop at the **Centre d'Interprétation Historique de Terrebonne Museum.** It features three exhibits: the Seigneurial Regime; the water, saw, flour, and wool mills of the region that gave the island its name; and the beginning of the Industrial Revolution in Terrebonne. The Ile-des-Moulins art gallery hosts exhibitions of works by local artists, and a theater presents plays in French as well as musical matinees and outdoor summer shows ($7 for theater; most other activities free). *Cnr. boul. des Braves and rue St-Pierre, tel. 514/471–0619. Admission free. Open mid-May–late June, Tues.–Sun. 1–5; late June–early Sept., Tues.–Sun. 10–8.*

❷ **La Seigneurie du Lac-des-Deux-Montagnes** was allotted to the Sulpician priests in 1717. Already appointed the seigneurs of the entire island of Montréal, the priests used this as the base from which to establish an Amerindian mission. To reach this mission, take Highway 13 or 15 North out of Montréal to Highway 640 West. Exit from Highway 640 West at Highway 148. Take this road into the town of Saint-Scholastique. A highlight of the seigneurie is the Sulpicians' seignorial manor on rue Belle-Rivière, erected between 1802 and 1808 in the village of Saint-Scholastique. The manor was used as part of the set for the late Claude Jutra's acclaimed film, *Kamouraska,* based on the novel by Québec's prize-winning author Anne Hébert.

❸ To promote piety among the Amerindians, the Sulpicians erected the **Oka Calvary (Stations of the Cross)** between 1740 and 1742. Three of the seven chapels are still maintained, and every September 14 since 1870, Québecois pilgrims have congregated here from across the province to participate in the half-hour ceremony that proceeds on foot to the Calvary's summit. A sense of the divine is inspired as much by the magnificent view of Lac-des-Deux-Montagnes as by religious fervor.

In 1887, the Sulpicians gave about 865 acres of their property located near the Oka Calvary to the Trappist monks, who had arrived in New France in 1880 from the Bellefontaine Abbey in France. Within 10 years they had built their monastery, the **Abbaye Cistercienne d'Oka,** and they transformed this land into one of the most beautiful domains in Québec. The abbey is one of the oldest in North America. Famous for creating Oka cheese, the Trappists established the Oka School of Agriculture, which operated until 1960. Today, the monastery is a noted prayer retreat. The gardens and chapel are open to visitors. *1600 chemin d'Oka, tel. 514/479–8361. Admission free. Chapel open daily 8– 12:15 and 1–8; gardens and boutique open weekdays 9:30–11:30 and 1–4:30, Sat. 9–4.*

Close by is the **Ferme Avicole d'Oka,** one of Québec's largest poultry farms, also developed by the Trappists. Tours of the breeding grounds for exotic pheasant, partridge, and guinea-hen fowl, as well as for the ordinary variety, are given, and there is a slide show of the transition from farm to table—an interesting encounter for city children. Fresh eggs and fowl can be bought on site. *1525 chemin d'Oka, tel. 514/479–8394. Store open weekdays 9–noon and 1–5, Sat. 9–5, Sun. 1–5.*

**Kanestake,** a Mohawk Indian reserve near Oka, made the headlines during the summer of 1990 when a 78-day armed standoff between Mohawk Warriors (the reserve's self-proclaimed peacekeeping force) and Canadian and provincial authorities took place. The Mohawks of Kanestake opposed the expansion of the Oka golf course, claiming the land was stolen from them 273 years before. When the standoff ended, the golf course was not expanded.

**④** Nearby **Saint-Eustache** is another must for history buffs. One of the most important and tragic scenes in Canadian history took place here: the 1837 Rebellion. Since the British conquest of 1760, French Canadians had been confined to preexisting territories while the new townships were allotted exclusively to the English. Adding to this insult was the government's decision to tax all imported products from England, which made them prohibitively expensive. The result? In 1834, the French Canadian Patriot party defeated the British party locally. Lower Canada, as it was then known, became a hotbed of tension between the French and English, with French resistance to the British government reaching an all-time high. Rumors of rebellion were rife, and in December 1837, some 2,000 English soldiers led by General Colborne were sent in to put down the "army" of North Shore patriots by surrounding the village of Saint-Eustache. Jean-Olivier Chénier and his 200 patriots took refuge in the local church, which Colborne's cannons bombed and set afire. Chénier and 80 of his comrades were killed during the battle, and more than 100 of the town's houses and buildings erected during the seignorial regime were looted and burned down by Colborne's soldiers. Even today, traces of the bullets fired by the English army cannons are visible on the facade of Saint-Eustache's church at 123 rue St-Louis. Most of the town's period buildings are open to the public. Note especially **Manoir Globenski** and **Moulin Légaré,** the only water mill still in operation in Canada. For a guided tour or for a free brochure that gives a good walking-tour guide, visit the town's Arts and Cultural Services Center (235 rue St-Eustache, tel. 514/ 472–4440, ext. 282). Tours are offered from April until December.

**Time Out** Before heading north, stop at **Pâtisserie Grande-Côte** (367A chemin de la Grande-Côte, tel. 514/473–7307) to sample the wares of St-Eustache's most famous bakery and pastry shop.

**Les Hautes Laurentides** Rivaling Saint-Eustache in Québec's historic folklore is **Saint-Jérôme,** founded in 1830. Today a thriving economic center and cul- **⑤** tural hub off Route 117, it first gained prominence in 1868 when Curé Antoine Labelle became pastor of this parish on the shores of Rivière du Nord. Curé Labelle devoted himself to opening up northern Québec to French Canadians. Between 1868 and 1890, he founded 20 parish towns—an impressive achievement given the harsh conditions of this vast wilderness. But his most important legacy was the famous P'tit Train du Nord railway line, which he persuaded the government to build in order to open Saint-Jérôme to travel and trade.

Follow Saint-Jérôme's **promenade,** a 4-kilometer-long (2½-mile) boardwalk alongside the Rivière du Nord from rue de Martigny bridge to rue St-Joseph bridge for a walk through the town's history. Descriptive plaques en route highlight episodes of the Battle of 1837. The **Centre d'Exposition du Vieux-Palais** housed in St-Jérôme's old courthouse has temporary exhibits of contemporary art, featuring mostly Québec artists. A music hall next door sometimes hosts concerts. *185 rue du Palais, tel. 514/432–7171. Admission free. Open Tues.–Fri. noon–5, weekends 1–5.*

Saint-Jérôme's **Parc Régional de la Rivière-du-Nord** (1051 boul. International, tel. 514/431–1676) was created as a nature retreat. Paths throughout the park lead to the spectacular Wilson Falls (*chutes,* in French). Rain or shine, the Pavillon Marie-Victorin is open daily, with summer weekend displays and workshops devoted to nature, culture, and history.

The resort vacation area truly begins at Saint-Sauveur-des-Monts (Exit 60) and extends as far north as Mont Tremblant, where it turns into a wilderness of lakes and forests best visited with an outfitter. Laurentian guides planning fishing and hunting trips are concentrated around Saint-Donat near Parc Mont Tremblant.

To the first-time visitor, the hills and resorts around Saint-Sauveur, Sainte-Marguerite Station, Morin Heights, Val Morin, and Val David, up to Sainte-Agathe, form a pleasant hodgepodge of villages, hotels, and inns that seem to blend one into another.

**❻ Saint-Sauveur-des-Monts,** exit 60 off the Autoroute, is the focal point for area resorts. It has gone from a 1970s sleepy Laurentian village of 4,000 residents that didn't even have a traffic light to a thriving year-round town attracting some 30,000 cottagers and visitors on weekends. Its main street, rue Principale, once dotted with quaint French restaurants, now boasts *brochetteries* and sushi bars, and the narrow strip is so choked in summertime by cars and tourists that it has earned the sobriquet "Crescent Street of the North," borrowing its name from the well-known, action-filled street in Montréal. Residents here once won the battle against a McDonald's opening. Now the parking lots of major franchise fast-food eateries are always packed. Despite all this development, Saint-Sauveur has managed to maintain some of its charming, rural character.

The gleaming white spires of **Saint-Sauveur Church** still dominate rue Principale, but **Saint Francis of the Birds** has not been so lucky. Built in 1951 with support from Montréal's Molson family, this sturdy, rustic log church with its fine stained-glass-window portraits of the Laurentian countryside no longer offers the worshiper or visitor a secluded and peaceful spiritual retreat. Where only a few years ago its immediate neighbors were modest chalets dotting the forest, today the empty, bankrupt Delta Hotel complex sits in the church's backyard. However, classical concerts can still be heard in the church every second Saturday evening during September and October (tel. 514/227–2423).

But for those who like their vacations—winter or summer—lively and activity-filled, Saint-Sauveur is *the* place where the action rolls nonstop. In winter, skiing is the main thing. (Mont-Saint-Sauveur, Mont Avila, Mont Gabriel, and Mont Olympia all offer special season passes and programs, and some ski-center passes can be used at more than one center in the region.) From Mont-Saint-Sauveur to Mont Tremblant, the area's ski centers (most situated in or near Saint-Sauveur, Sainte-Adèle, Sainte-Agathe, and Saint-Jovite) offer night skiing. All have ski instructors—many are members of the Canadian Ski Patrol Association.

Just outside Saint-Sauveur, the $7 million Mont Saint-Sauveur **Water Park** and tourist center (exit 58 or 60) will keep children occupied with slides, wave pools, snack bars, and more. The "Children's Island" is the park's latest attraction, with calm, shallow wading ponds designed for youngsters one to six years old. The man-made "Colorado" rafting river attracts the older, braver crowd; the nine-minute ride follows the natural contours of steep hills and requires about 12,000 gallons of water to be pumped per minute. *350 rue Saint-Denis, Saint-Sauveur-des-Monts, tel. 514/871–0101 or 800/363–2426. Admission: full day—$20 adults, $14 children 3 and over; half day (after 3 PM)—$16 adults, $12 children 3 and over; eve-*

*ning (after 5 PM)—$12 adults, $9 children 3 and over. Open mid-June–Aug., daily 10–7.*

**❼** Nearby in **Morin Heights,** there's a new spin on an old sport at **Ski Morin Heights** (exit 60, Autoroute 15 N, tel. 514/227–2020 or 800/661–3535), where snowboarding is the latest craze. Although it doesn't have overnight accommodations, Ski Morin Heights boasts a 44,000-square-foot chalet with a full range of hospitality services and sports-related facilities, eateries, après-ski activities, pubs, a health club, and a day-care center. There's also a large nursery on-site and special ski-lesson programs for children ages 2 and up.

The town's architecture and population reflect its English settlers' origins. Most residents are English-speaking. Morin Heights has escaped the overdevelopment of Saint-Sauveur but still offers the visitor a good range of restaurants, bookstores, boutiques, and crafts shops to explore. During the summer months, windsurfing, swimming, and canoeing on the area's two lakes are popular pastimes. Another popular attraction is **Théâtre Morin Heights** (tel. 514/226–1944), whose "professional amateur" productions are presented at a local elementary school during the summer months. Popular musicals, lighthearted comedies, mysteries, and children's plays are in the repertoire. Reservations are a must.

In the summer, holiday goers head for the region's golf courses (two of the more pleasant are 18-hole links at Sainte-Adèle and Mont Gabriel), campgrounds at Val David, Lacs Claude and Lafontaine, and beaches; in the fall and winter, they come for the foliage as well as alpine and Nordic skiing.

**❽** The busy town of **Sainte-Adèle** is full of gift and Québec-crafts shops, boutiques, and restaurants. It also has an active nightlife, including a few discos.

Just as much of a rave with adults as with children are the **Super Splash** waterslides. *1791 boul. Ste-Adèle, tel. 514/229–2925. 3 giant slides for adults, 3 for children. Admission: $15 adults, $10 children under 12, $40 families. Open June–Aug., daily 10–7.*

A couple of miles north on Highway 117, the reconstructed **Village de Seraphin**'s 20 small homes, grand country house, general store, and church recall the settlers who came to Sainte-Adèle in the 1840s. This award-winning historic town also features a train tour through the woods. *Tel. 514/229–4777. Admission: $8.75 adults, $6.75 children 12–17, $5.75 children 5–11. Open late May–late June and early Sept.–mid-Oct., weekends 10–5; late June–early Sept., daily 10–5.*

**❾** In **Mont Rolland, Station Touristique de Mont Gabriel** offers superb skiing, primarily for intermediate and advanced skiers. The on-site lodge, **Auberge Mont Gabriel** (*see* Lodging, *below*), has week-long and weekend packages. *Autoroute 15, exit 64, Mont Rolland J0R 1G0, tel. 514/229–3547.*

**❿** Neighboring community **Sainte-Marguerite-du-Lac-Masson** celebrated its 125th anniversary in 1990. The town's Service des Loisirs (tel. 514/228–2545) is the place to call for details about events, as well as cruises and skating on Lac-Masson.

**⓫** The permanent population of the town of **Estérel** is a mere 80 souls. But visitors to **Ville d'Estérel,** a 135-room resort at Autoroute 69, near Sainte-Marguerite Station, swell that number into the thousands. Founded in 1959 on the shores of Lac Dupuis, this 5,000-acre domain was bought by Fridolin Simard from Baron Louis Empain.

Named Estérel by the baron because it evoked memories of his native village in Provence, Ville d'Estérel soon became a household word for holiday vacationers in search of a first-class resort area. (For more details, *see* Lodging, *below*.)

**⑫** Children know **Val David** for its **Santa Claus Village.** This is Santa Claus's summer residence, where children can sit upon Santa's knee and speak to him. (He's bilingual, too: French and English.) On the grounds is a petting zoo, with goats, sheep, horses, and colorful birds. Bumper boats and games are run here, as well. *987 rue Morin, Val David, tel. 819/322–2146. Admission: $7 adults, $5.50 children 2–12. Open late May–early June, weekends 10–6; early June–late Aug., daily 10–6.*

Val David is a rendezvous for mountain climbers, ice scalers, dogsledders, hikers, and summer or winter campers. For equipment rentals and other information, contact the Maison du Tourisme des Laurentides (tel. 514/436–8532).

Val David is also a haven for artists, many of whose studios are open to the public. Most of their work is for sale. The **Atelier Bernard Chaudron, Inc.** (2449 chemin de l'Ile, tel. 819/322–3944), sells hand-shaped and hammered lead-free pewter objets d'art.

**⑬** About 96 kilometers (60 miles) from Montréal, overlooking Lac des Sables, is **Sainte-Agathe-des-Monts,** the largest commercial center for ski communities farther north. This lively resort area attracts campers to its spacious **Au Parc des Campeurs** (Rte. 329, 50 rue St. Joseph, Sainte-Agathe-des-Monts J8C 1M9, tel. 819/324–0482 or 800/324–0482), bathers to its municipal beach, and sailors to its lake cruises on the *Alouette* (tel. 819/326–3656) touring launch. Sailing is the favorite summer sport, especially during the "24 Heures de la Voile," a weekend sailing competition (tel. 819/326–0457) that takes place each year in June.

Scuba diving is also popular here. The **Service Ambulance Gilles Thibault Inc.** (124 rue Principale, tel. 819/326–4464) will refill air tanks and provide information about equipment rentals.

Perhaps the best way to view the scenery of the Upper Laurentians is to mountain climb. The **Fédération Québécoise de la Montagne** (4545 rue Pierre-de-Coubertin, C.P. 1000, Succursale M, Montréal H1V 3R2, tel. 514/252–3004) can give you information about this sport, as can the region's tourist offices.

About 1 kilometer (½ mile) north of Sainte-Agathe-des-Monts is the **Village du Mont-Castor,** an attractive re-creation of a turn-of-the-century Québecois village; more than 100 new homes have been built here in the traditional fashion of full-length logs set *pièce sur pièce* (one upon the other).

Farther north lie two of Québec's best-known ski resorts—Gray Rocks and Mont Tremblant Resort (*see* Lodging, *below*). Mont Tremblant is also car-racing country. Racing champion Jackie Stewart has called Mont Tremblant "the most beautiful racetrack in the world." The **Formula 2000 "Jim Russell Championships"** of the Canadian Car Championships (tel. 819/425–2739) take place here on weekends in June, July, August, and September.

**⑭** The mountain and the hundreds of square miles of wilderness beyond it constitute **Parc Mont Tremblant.** Created in 1894, this was once the home of the Algonquin Indians, who called this area Manitonga Soutana, meaning "mountain of the spirits." Today it is a vast wildlife sanctuary of more than 500 lakes and rivers protecting about 230 species of birds and animals, including moose, deer, bear, and beaver. In the winter, its trails are used by cross-country skiers, snowshoers, and snowmobile enthusiasts. Moose hunting is allowed in season, and camping and canoeing are the main summer activities.

## Tour 2: L'Estrie

*Numbers in the margin correspond to points of interest on the L'Estrie (Eastern Townships) and Montérégie map.*

L'Estrie (also known as the Eastern Townships) refers to the area in the southeast corner of the province of Québec, bordering Vermont and New York State. Its northern Appalachian hills, rolling down to placid lakeshores, were first home to the Abenaki natives, long before "summer people" built their cottages and horse paddocks here. The Abenaki are gone, but the names they gave to the region's recreational lakes remain— Memphremagog, Massawippi, Mégantic.

L'Estrie was initially populated by United Empire Loyalists fleeing the American War of Independence and, later, the newly created United States of America, to continue living under the English king in British North America. It's not surprising that l'Estrie is reminiscent of New England with its covered bridges, village greens, white church steeples, and country inns. The Loyalists were followed, around 1820, by the first wave of Irish immigrants—ironically, Catholics fleeing their country's union with Protestant England. Some 20 years later the potato famine sent more Irish pioneers to the townships.

The area became more Gallic after 1850, as French Canadians moved in to work on the railroad and in the lumber industry, and later to mine asbestos at Thetford. Around the turn of the century, English families from Montréal and Americans from the border states discovered the region and began summering at cottages along the lakes. During the Prohibition era, the area attracted even more cottagers from the United States. Lac Massawippi became a favorite summer resort of wealthy families whose homes have since been converted into gracious inns, including the Manoir Hovey and the Hatley Inn.

Today the summer communities fill up with equal parts French and English visitors, though the year-round residents are primarily French. Nevertheless, the locals are proud of both their Loyalist heritage and Québec roots. They boast of "Loyalist tours" and Victorian gingerbread homes and in the next breath direct visitors to the snowmobile museum in Valcourt, where, in 1937, native son Joseph-Armand Bombardier built the first *moto-neige* (snowmobile) in his garage. (Bombardier's inventions were the basis of one of Canada's biggest industries, supplying New York City and Mexico City with subway cars and other rolling stock.)

Over the past two decades, l'Estrie has developed from a series of quiet farm communities and wood-frame summer homes to a thriving all-season resort area. In winter, skiers flock to eight downhill centers and some 20 cross-country trails. By early spring, the sugar huts are busy with the new maple syrup. L'Estrie's southerly location makes this the balmiest corner of Québec, notable for its spring skiing. In summer, boating, swimming, sailing, golfing, and bicycling take over. And every fall the inns are booked solid with "leaf peepers" eager to take in the brilliant foliage.

**⑮ Granby,** about 80 kilometers (50 miles) from Montréal, is considered to be the gateway to l'Estrie. This town is best known for its zoo, the **Jardin Zoologique de Granby.** It houses some 800 animals from 225 species. Two rare snow leopards on loan from Chicago's Lincoln Park Zoo and New York's Bronx Zoo have won the zoo recognition from the International Union for the Conservation of Nature. The complex includes amusement park rides and souvenir shops as well as a playground and picnic area. *347 rue Bourget, tel. 514/372–9113. Admission: $15 adults, $13 senior citizens, $8 children 5–17 and people with disabilities, $4 children 1–4. Open late May–early Sept., daily 9:30–5; Sept., weekends 9–5.*

Granby is also gaining repute as the townships' gastronomic capital. Each October, the month-long Festival Gastronomique attracts more than 10,000 *gastronomes* who use the festival's "gastronomic passport" to sample the cuisines at several dining rooms. To reserve a passport, contact: Festival Gastronomique de Granby et Région, 650 rue Principle, Granby J2G 8L4. *Tel. 514/378–7272.*

The **Yamaska** recreation center on the outskirts of town features sailboarding, swimming, and picnicking all summer, and cross-country skiing and snowshoeing in winter.

In the past two decades, l'Estrie has developed into a scenic and increasingly popular ski center. Although it is still less crowded and commercialized than the Laurentians, it boasts ski hills on four mountains that dwarf anything the Laurentians have to offer, with the exception of lofty Mont Tremblant. And, compared with those in Vermont, ski-pass rates are still a bargain.

**⑯ Bromont,** closest to Montréal, is as lively at night as during the day. It offers the only night skiing in l'Estrie and a slope-side disco, **Le ⑰ Débarque,** where the action continues into the night après-ski. **Mont Orford,** located at the center of a provincial park, offers plenty of challenges for alpine and cross-country skiers, from novices to vet-⑱ erans. **Owl's Head** has become a mecca for skiers looking for fewer crowds on the hills. It also boasts a 4-kilometer (2.4-mile) intermediate run, the longest in l'Estrie. Aside from superb skiing, Owl's Head offers tremendous scenery. From the trails you can see nearby Vermont and Lac Memphrémagog. (You might even see the lake's legendary sea dragon, said to have been sighted around 90 times ⑲ since 1816.) As it has for decades, **Mont Sutton** attracts the same die-hard crowd of mostly Anglophone skiers from Québec. It's also one of the area's largest resorts, with trails that plunge and wander through pine, maple, and birch trees slope-side. **Sutton** itself is a well-established community with crafts shops, cozy eateries, and bars (La Paimpolaise is a favorite among skiers).

Bromont and Orford are *stations touristiques* (tourist centers), meaning that they offer a wide range of activities in all seasons—boating, camping, golf, horseback riding, swimming, tennis, water parks, trail biking, canoeing, fishing, hiking, cross-country and downhill skiing, and snowshoeing. A water-slide park (tel. 514/534–2200)—take exit 78 off Autoroute 10—and a large flea market (weekends from May to mid-November) offer pleasant additions to horseback riding. The same exit will bring you to Bromont's factory outlet shopping malls (50 rue Gaspé). There are about 30 shops that carry Canadian, American, and European designer goods at discount prices.

**⑳** Along the shore of Lac Brome is the village of **Knowlton,** a pleasant place to shop for antiques and gifts. In summer check to see what's playing at Knowlton's popular **Théâtre Lac Brome** (*see* The Arts, *be-*

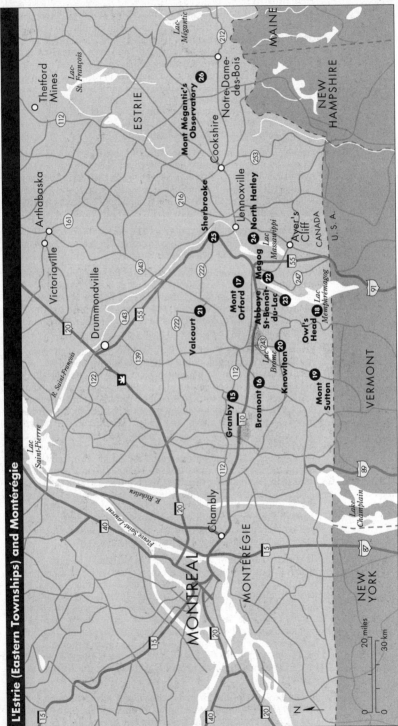

476

**L'Estrie (Eastern Townships) and Montérégie**

MAINE

NEW HAMPSHIRE

Thetford Mines

*Lac St-François*

ESTRIE

*Lac Mégantic*

Notre-Dame-des-Bois

Mont Mégantic's Observatory **26**

112

Cookshire

212

Arthabaska

161

Victoriaville

112

Sherbrooke

216

Lennoxville

North Hatley **24**

253

Ayer's Cliff

CANADA

U.S.A.

Drummondville

20

243

143

55

222

**25**

55

Mont Orford **17**

Magog

Abbaye St-Benoît-du-Lac **23**

**22**

*Lac Massawippi*

247

91

Valcourt **21**

222

Owl's Head **18**

*Lac Memphrémagog*

*R. Saint-François*

122

139

222

*Lac Brome*

Knowlton **20**

243

112

Mont Sutton **19**

VERMONT

Granby **15**

Bromont **16**

112

10

*Lac Saint-Pierre*

*R. Richelieu*

112

20

Chambly

89

MONTRÉAL

40

*Fleuve Saint-Laurent*

MONTÉRÉGIE

15

*Lake Champlain*

87

NEW YORK

20

15

40

20

N

20 miles

30 km

*low*). In winter many Montréalers come here to ski at **Glen Mountain** (off Route 243, tel. 514/243–6142).

**㉑** **Valcourt** is the birthplace of the inventor of the snowmobile, so it follows that this is a world center for the sport, with more than 1,500 kilometers (1,000-plus miles) of paths cutting through the woods and meadows. The **Musée Joseph-Armand Bombardier** displays this innovator's many inventions year-round. *1001 av. Joseph-Armand Bombardier, tel. 514/532– 5300. Admission: $5 adults, $3 students and senior citizens, children under 5 free, $13 families. Open late June– Aug., daily 10–5:30; Sept.–late June, Tues.–Sun. 10–5.*

**㉒** South of Mont Orford at the northern tip of Lac Memphrémagog, a large body of water reaching into northern Vermont, lies the bustling resort town of **Magog,** which celebrated its centenary in 1988. A once sleepy village, the town has grown into a four-season resort destination. Two sandy beaches, great bed-and-breakfasts, hotels and restaurants, boating, ferry rides, bird-watching, sailboarding, aerobics, horseback riding, and snowmobiling are just some of the activities offered.

Stroll along Magog's **rue Principale** for a look at boutiques, art galleries, and crafts shops with local artisans' work. Other shops are spread throughout downtown, where the streets are lined with century-old homes and churches, some of which have been converted into storefronts, galleries, and theaters.

Magog is lively after dark, with a variety of bars, cafés, bistros, and great restaurants to suit every taste and pocketbook. **La Lanterne** (tel. 819/843–7205) is a popular hangout. The more sedentary may find **La Source's** (tel. 819/843–0319) array of cheeses, pâtés, and Swiss chocolates irresistible.

**㉓** Near Magog is the **Abbaye St-Benoît-du-Lac.** To reach St-Benoît from Magog, take the road to Austin and then follow the signs for the side road to the abbey. This abbey's slender bell tower juts up above the trees like a fairy-tale castle. Built on a wooded peninsula in 1912 by the Benedictines, the abbey is home to some 60 monks, who sell apples and apple cider from their orchards as well as distinctive cheeses: Ermite, St-Benoît, and ricotta. Gregorian masses are held daily. Check for those open to the public (tel. 819/843–4080). The abbey was once known as a favorite retreat for some of Québec's best-known politicians; they abandoned the thrust-and-cut of their secular concerns for spiritual rejuvenation.

**㉔** **North Hatley,**the town on the tip of Lac Massawippi, is home to **The Pilsen,** Québec's earliest microbrewery. Although the beer is no longer brewed on-site, the Pilsen (tel. 819/842–2971) still serves Massawippi pale ale on tap. For those who ask, proprietor Gilles Peloquin will arrange a visit to the famous brewery, now located in nearby Lennoxville. The pub also has great food, loads of atmosphere, and a convivial crowd year-round. The avant-garde **Piggery** theater is based in North Hatley (*see* the Arts, *below*).

**㉕** The region's unofficial capital and largest city is **Sherbrooke,** named in 1818 for Canadian Governor General Sir John Coape Sherbrooke. Founded by Loyalists in the 1790s, and located along the St-François River, it boasts a number of art galleries, including the **Musée des Beaux-Arts de Sherbrooke** (174 rue du Palais, tel. 819/821–2115; admission: $2 adults, $1 students and senior citizens, Wed. evenings free; open Tues., Thurs–Sun. 1–5, Wed. 1–9). The Sherbrooke Tourist Information Center conducts city tours from late June through August. Call for reservations. (48 rue Dépôt, tel. 819/564–8331).

For a more cosmic experience, continue from Sherbrooke along Route 212 to **Mont Mégantic's Observatory.** Both amateur stargazers and serious astronomers are drawn to this site, located in a beautifully wild and mountainous part of l'Estrie. The observatory is at the summit of l'Estrie's second-highest mountain (3,601 feet), whose northern face records annual snowfalls rivaling any in North America. The observatory is a joint venture by l'Université de Montréal and l'Université Laval. Its powerful telescope allows resident scientists to observe celestial bodies 10 million times smaller than the human eye can detect. There's a welcome center on the mountain's base, where amateur stargazers can get information about the evening celestial sweep sessions, Thursday through Saturday. *Notre-Dame-des-Bois, tel. 819/888–2822. Open late June–Labor Day, daily 10–5.*

## Tour 3: Charlevoix

*Numbers in the margin correspond to points of interest on the Charlevoix map.*

Stretching along the St. Lawrence River's north shore east of Québec City from Sainte-Anne-de-Beaupré to the Saguenay River, Charlevoix embraces mountains rising from the sea and a succession of valleys, plateaus, and cliffs cut by waterfalls, brooks, and streams. The roads wind into villages of picturesque houses and huge tin-roof churches.

New France's first historian, the Jesuit priest François-Xavier de Charlevoix, gave his name to the region. Charlevoix (Sharle-vwah) was first explored by Jacques Cartier, who landed in 1535, although the first colonists didn't arrive until well into the 17th century. They developed a thriving shipbuilding industry, specializing in the sturdy schooner they called a *goelette,* which they used to haul everything from logs to lobsters up and down the coast in the days before rail and paved roads. Shipbuilding has been a vital part of the provincial economy until recent times, though wrecked and forgotten goelettes are visible from many beaches in the region.

Charlevoix begins about 33 kilometers (20 miles) east of Québec City, in the tiny town of **Sainte-Anne-de-Beaupré** (named for Québec's patron saint). Each year more than a million pilgrims visit the region's most famous religious site, the **Basilica of Sainte-Anne-de-Beaupré** (*see* Chapter 4), which is dedicated to the mother of the Virgin Mary.

Only 8 kilometers (5 miles) beyond the pilgrimage center is the **Cap Tourmente Wildlife Reserve,** where more than 100,000 greater snow geese gather every October and May. Other parts of the region offer whale-watching cruises, and you can, on occasion, spot whales, seals, and dolphins from ferries and from land, so nature-lovers are encouraged to bring their binoculars. *St-Joachim G0A 3X0, tel. 418/827–3776.*

In fact, the region is a haven for anyone who enjoys being active in the outdoors, including hikers, joggers, cyclists, and, in particular, skiers. Charlevoix has three main ski areas, with excellent facilities for both the downhill and cross-country skier. **Parc du Mont-Sainte-Anne** (*see* Chapter 4), outside Québec City, is on the World Cup downhill ski circuit; **Mont Grand Fonds** (1000 chemin des Loisirs, La Malbaie, tel. 418/665–4405) has 14 slopes and 141 kilometers (87

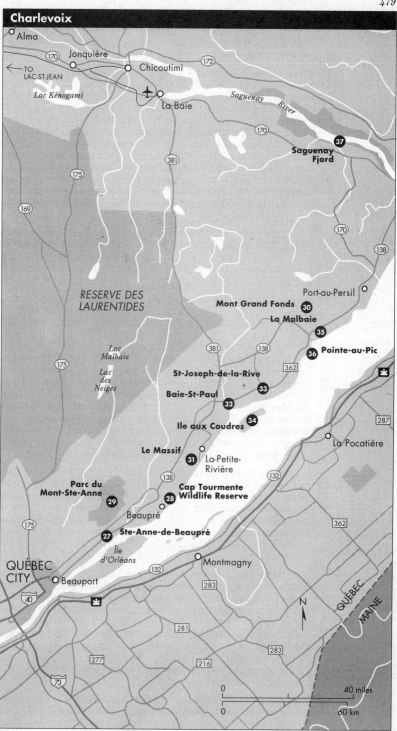

# Charlevoix

Alma

Jonquière

Chicoutimi

170

TO LAC-ST-JEAN

172

Lac Kénogami

La Baie

Saguenay River

170

170

**Saguenay Fjord** 37

381

175

138

169

170

Port-au-Persil

**RESERVE DES LAURENTIDES**

**Mont Grand Fonds** 30

**La Malbaie** 35

138

**Pointe-au-Pic** 36

Lac Malbaie

381

362

Lac des Neiges

**St-Joseph-de-la-Rive** 33

175

287

**Baie-St-Paul** 32

**Ile aux Coudres** 34

La Pocatière

**Le Massif** 31

La-Petite-Rivière

132

**Parc du Mont-Ste-Anne** 29

138

**Cap Tourmente Wildlife Reserve** 28

Beaupré

362

175

**Ste-Anne-de-Beaupré** 27

Île d'Orléans

**QUÉBEC CITY**

Beauport

132

Montmagny

283

40

QUÉBEC

MAINE

281

N

73

277

216

283

0      40 miles

0      60 km

**③¹** miles) of cross-country trails; and **Le Massif** (1350 rue Principale, C.P. 47, Petite Rivière St. François, tel. 418/632–5879) is a three-peak ski resort that boasts the province's highest vertical drop (762 meters, or 2,500 feet).

**③²** **Baie-St-Paul,** Charlevoix's earliest settlement after Beaupré, is popular with hang-gliding fans and artists. You will find artisans working in old habitant houses. Here, the high hills circle a wide plain holding the village beside the sea. Many of Québec's greatest landscapists portray the area, and their work is on display year-round at the **Centre d'Art Baie-St-Paul** (4 boul. Fafard, tel. 418/435–3681). Recently the center has garnered a reputation in North America as a major regional arts center promoting the area's own talent, as well as providing those just starting out with wider exposure while they study their crafts. At town-center, **Auberge la Maison Otis,** an 1858 stone house, has been converted into what many consider the area's finest inn-restaurant (*see* Lodging, *below*).

From Baie-St-Paul, you can take the open, scenic coastal drive (Rte. 362) or the faster Route 138 to **Pointe-au-Pic, La Malbaie,** and **Cap-à-l'Aigle.** This section of Route 362 has memorable views of rolling hills—green, white, or ablaze with fiery hues, depending on the season—meeting the broad expanse of the "sea" as the locals like to call the St. Lawrence estuary.

**③³** A secondary road leads sharply down into **St-Joseph-de-la-Rive,** with its line of old houses hugging the mountain base on the narrow shore road. The town is host to peaceful inns and inviting restaurants, such as l'Auberge sous les Pins, which means "inn under the pines." Nearby Papeterie St-Gilles produces unusual handcrafted stationery, using a 17th-century process. The small **Charlevoix Musée** commemorates the days of the St. Lawrence goelettes. From St-Joseph

**③⁴** you can catch a ferry to **Ile aux Coudres,** an island where Jacques Cartier's men gathered *les coudres* (hazelnuts) in 1535. Since then, the island has produced many a goelette, and former captains now run several small inns. Larger inns feature folk-dance evenings. Many visitors like to bike around the 16-kilometer (10-mile) island taking in inns, windmills, and old schooners, as well as boutiques selling paintings and local handcrafts, such as household linen.

**③⁵** Continuing on Route 362, you will come to one of the most elegant and historically interesting resorts in the entire province. **La Malbaie** was known as Murray Bay in an earlier era when wealthy Anglophones summered here and in the neighboring villages of Pointe-au-Pic and Cap-à-l'Aigle. The regional museum—**Musée de Charlevoix**—traces its history as a vacation spot in a series of exhibits and is developing an excellent collection of local paintings and folk art. *1 rue du Havre, Pointe-au-Pic, tel. 418/665–4411.*

**③⁶** Once called the "summer White House," this area became popular with both American and Canadian politicians in the late 1800s when Ottawa Liberals and Washington Republicans partied decorously through the summer with members of the Québec judiciary. William Howard Taft built the first of three summer residences in **Pointe-au-Pic** in 1894, when he was the American civil governor of the Philippines. He became the 27th president of the United States in 1908, and later chief justice of the Supreme Court. Locals still fondly remember the Tafts and the parties they threw in their elegant summer homes.

Now many Taft-era homes serve as handsome inns, guaranteeing an old-fashioned coddling, with such extras as breakfast in bed, gourmet meals, whirlpools, and free shuttles to the ski areas in winter.

Many serve lunch and dinner to nonresidents, so you can tour the area going from one gourmet's delight to the next. The cuisine, as elsewhere in Québec, is genuine French, rather than a hybrid invented for North Americans.

The road, the views, and the villages continue all the way up to Baie-Ste-Catherine, which shares the view up the magnificent **Saguenay Fjord** with the small town of **Tadoussac**. Jacques Cartier made a stop at this point in 1535, and it became an important meeting site for fur traders in the French Territory until the mid-19th century. Whale-watching excursions and cruises of the fjord now depart from Tadoussac, as well as from Chicoutimi, farther up the deep fjord. As the Saguenay River flows from Lake St-Jean south toward the St. Lawrence, it has a dual character: Between Alma and Chicoutimi, the once rapidly flowing river has been turned into hydroelectric power; in its lower section, it becomes wider and deeper and flows by steep mountains and cliffs, en route to the St. Lawrence. The white beluga whale breeds in the lower portion of the Saguenay in summer, and in the confluence of the fjord and the seaway are many marine species, which attract other whales, such as pilot, finback, humpback, and blues.

Sadly, the beluga is an endangered species; the whales, along with 27 species of mammals and birds and 17 species of fish, are being threatened by pollution from the St. Lawrence River. This has inspired a $100 million project funded by both the federal and provincial governments. An 800-square-kilometer (496-square-mile) marine park at the confluence of the Saguenay and St. Lawrence rivers has been created to protect its fragile ecosystem in hope of reversing some of the damage already done. Full-day and half-day cruises from Chicoutimi operate daily June–September (tel. 418/543–7630); other trips leave from Hotel Tadoussac (tel. 418/235–4421) from May through mid-October.

## Tour 4: The Gaspé Peninsula

*Numbers in the margin correspond to points of interest on the Gaspé Peninsula map.*

Jutting into the stormy Gulf of St. Lawrence like the battered prow of a ship, the Gaspé Peninsula remains an isolated region of unsurpassed wild beauty, an area where the land ends. Sheer cliffs tower above broad beaches, and tiny coastal fishing communities cling to the shoreline. Inland rise the Chic-Choc Mountains, eastern Canada's highest, the realm of woodland caribou, black bear, and moose. Townspeople in some Gaspé areas speak mainly English, though *Gaspésiens* speak slightly Acadian-accented French.

Jacques Cartier landed on the Gaspé in 1534, but it wasn't until the early 1800s that the first settlers arrived. Today, the area still seems unspoiled and timeless, a blessing for travelers dipping and soaring along the spectacular coastal highways or venturing on river-valley roads to the interior. Geographically, the peninsula is among the oldest lands on earth. A vast, mainly uninhabited forest covers the hilly hinterland. Local tourist officials can be helpful in locating outfitters and guides to fish and hunt large and small game. The Gaspé's four major parks—**Port Daniel, Forillon, Causapscal,** and **Gaspé Park**—cover a total of 2,292 square kilometers (885 square miles).

Take the Trans-Canada Highway northeast along the southern shore of the St. Lawrence River to just south of Rivière-du-Loup, where you pick up the 270-kilometer (150-mile) Route 132, which hugs the dramatic coastline. At Ste-Flavie, follow the southern leg of Route 132. Windsurfers and sailors enjoy the breezes around the Gaspé; there are windsurfing marathons in **Baie des Chaleurs** (at Carleton) each summer.

The Gaspé was on Jacques Cartier's itinerary—he first stepped ashore in North America in the town of Gaspé—but Vikings, Basques, and Portuguese fisherfolk had come long before. The area's history is told in countless towns en route. Acadians, displaced
**❸❽** by the British from New Brunswick in 1755, settled **Bonaventure**;
**❸❾** **Paspébiac** still has a gunpowder shed built in the 1770s to help defend the peninsula from American ships; and United Empire Loyal-
**❹⓿** ists settled **New Carlisle** in 1784.

The largest colony of gannets in the world summers on the Gaspé's
**❹❶** **Bonaventure Island,** off Percé. The most famous sight in the region is
**❹❷** the huge fossil-embedded rock off the town of **Percé** that the sea "pierced" thousands of years ago.

The region boasts Québec's longest ski season and highest peaks.
**❹❸** For instance, **Sainte-Anne-des-Monts,** on the north shore of the peninsula, offers the only heli-skiing east of the Rockies, with deep powder, open bowl, and glade skiing clear into June on peaks that rise to 2,700 feet. Other centers operate from mid-November through May.

### What to See and Do with Children

**Jardin Zoologique de Granby,** Tour 2: L'Estrie
**Mont Saint-Sauveur Water Park,** Tour 1: Les Laurentides
**Santa Claus Village,** Tour 1: Les Laurentides

# Shopping

When in the Laurentians, consider strolling along Saint-Sauveur-des-Monts' rue Principale with its shops, fashion boutiques, and outdoor café terraces decorated with bright awnings and flowers. Housed in a former bank, **La Voute Boutique** (239B rue Principale, tel. 514/227–1234) carries such international labels as Byblos and an up-to-the-minute all-season selection of coordinates in cotton, knits, suede, and leather, plus sequined dresses, sweaters, pants, jackets, and suits from France, Italy, and Spain. If you feel like shopping for your stomach, have a bite at **Jardin des Oliviers** (239 rue Principale, tel. 514/227–2110), a popular, moderately priced French restaurant in the middle of town.

Saint-Sauveur-des-Monts is also home to **Les Factoreries Saint-Sauveur** (100 rue Guindon, Exit 60 from Hwy. 15, tel. 514/227–1074), a factory outlet mall with 12 boutiques. Canadian, American, and European manufacturers sell a variety of goods at reduced prices, from designer clothing to exclusive household items.

Magog's rue Principale, in l'Estrie, is another interesting place to browse. The street is dotted with boutiques, art galleries, and crafts shops with local artisan's work. **Amandine** (499 rue Principale O, tel. 819/847–1346) is a lovely gift shop with unusual dishes, stemware, luxury bath items, and Belgian chocolates. When you want a rest, drop by **La Source** (420 rue Principale O, tel. 819/843–0319), a small tea room with an array of cheeses, pâtés, and Swiss chocolates. Other shops are spread throughout the town's downtown, where the streets are lined with century-old homes and churches,

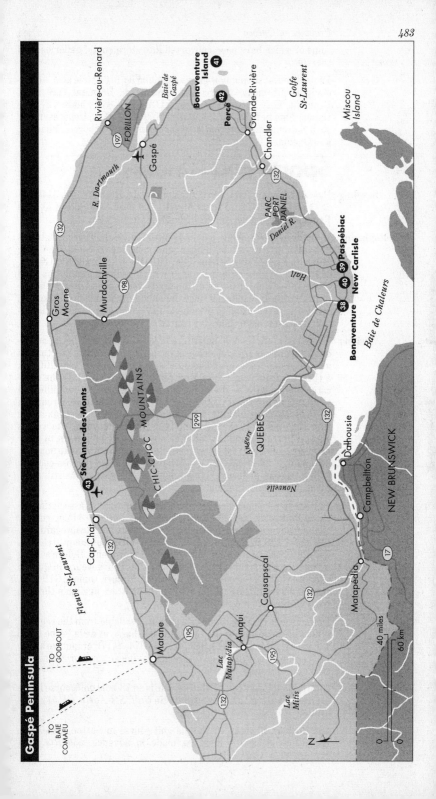

# Gaspé Peninsula

TO GODBOUT

TO BAIE COMEAU

Fleuve St-Laurent

Matane

195

132

Lac Matapédia

Amqui

195

Lac Mitis

132

Causapscal

132

Cap-Chat

132

Ste-Anne-des-Monts
43

CHIC-CHOC MOUNTAINS

299

Matapédia

132

17

Campbellton

NEW BRUNSWICK

Dalhousie

QUEBEC

Angers

Nouvelle

132

Bonaventure
38

New Carlisle
40

Paspébiac
39

Baie de Chaleurs

Hall

PARC PORT DANIEL
Daniel R.

132

Chandler

Grande-Rivière

Percé
42

Bonaventure Island
41

Golfe St-Laurent

Miscou Island

Baie de Gaspé

FORILLON

197

Rivière-au-Renard

Gaspé

R. Dartmouth

132

Murdochville

198

Gros Morne

N

0

0

40 miles

60 km

some of which have been converted into storefronts, galleries, and theaters.

Factory outlet shopping is gaining popularity in l'Estrie also—especially in Bromont, where **Les Versants de Bromont** (120 boul. Bromont, Exit 78 from Hwy. 10, tel. 819/843–8300) houses 27 boutiques. Shoppers can save between 30% and 70% on items carrying such national and international labels as Liz Claiborne, Vuarnet, and Oneida.

# Sports and Fitness

**Bicycling** **Base de Plein Air Davignon** (319 chemin Gale, Bromont, tel. 514/534–2277 or 800/363–8952) rents bicycles, as does **Vélo Sutton** (33 rue Principale N, Sutton, tel. 819/538–2561).

**Deltaplaning** If white-water rafting isn't adventure enough, there is always deltaplaning, in which human and machine become one. The **Vélidelta Free-Flying School** (C.P. 631, Mont Rolland J0R 1G0, tel. 514/229–6887) offers lessons on free-flying, flight simulation, and the more advanced tricks of the trade you'll need to earn the required deltaplane pilot's license, including flight maneuvers, speed, and turns. Equipment is provided. You can choose a one-day initiation flying lesson, or four-day course.

**Fishing** There are more than 60 outfitters (a.k.a. innkeepers) in the northern Laurentians area, where provincial parks and game sanctuaries abound. Pike, walleye, and lake and speckled trout are plentiful just a three-hour drive north of Montréal. Outfitters provide the dedicated angler with accommodations and every service wildlife and wilderness enthusiasts could possibly require. Open year-round in most cases, their lodging facilities range from the most luxurious first-class resort to the log-camp type "back of beyond." As well as supplying trained guides, all offer services and equipment to allow neophytes or experts the best possible fishing in addition to boating, swimming, river rafting, windsurfing, ice fishing, cross-country skiing, hiking, or just relaxing amid the splendor of this still spectacularly unspoiled region.

Outfitters recommended by the Laurentian tourist association include **Pourvoirie des 100 Lacs Nords** (tel. 514/444–4441), run by Claude Lavigne; **Club de Chasse et Pêche du Lac Beauregard** (tel. 819/425–7722) in Saint-Jovite; and **Pourvoirie Boismenu** (tel. 819/597–2619) at Lac-du-Cerf, run by Adrien Boismenu. Before setting off into the wilds, consult the Fédération des Pourvoyeurs du Québec (Québec Outfitters Federation, 2485 boul. Hamel, Québec G1P 2H9, tel. 418/527–5191) or ask for its list of outfitters available through tourist offices.

Don't forget: Fishing requires a permit, available from the regional offices of the Ministère du Loisir, de la Chasse et de la Pêche (6255 13ième av., Montréal H1X 3E6, tel. 514/374–2417), or inquire at any Laurentians sporting-goods store displaying an "authorized agent" sticker.

**Golf** Club de Golf Chantecler Sainte-Adèle is an 18-hole golf course in the Laurentians. *Exit 67, 2520 chemin du Golf, Ste-Adèle, tel. 514/229–3742.*

**Les Rochers Bleus** is an 18-hole golf course in Sutton, located in Estrie. Reservations must be made in advance. *550 Rte. 139, Sutton, tel. 514/538–2324.*

When in the Charlevoix region, you may want to try the 18-hole course in Pointe-au-Pic, **Club de Golf de Manoir Richelieu**. *181 av. Richelieu, Pointe-au-Pic, tel. 418/665–3703 or 800/463–2613.*

**Horseback Riding** As the former Olympic equestrian site, **Bromont** is horse country, and every year in late June and early July it holds a riding festival (tel. 514/534–3255).

**Mountain Climbing** Mountain climbing is one of the best ways to view the scenery of the Upper Laurentians. For information, contact the **Fédération Québecoise de la Montagne.** *4545 rue Pierre-de-Coubertin, C.P. 1000, Succ. M, Montréal H1V 3R2, tel. 514/252–3004.*

**River Rafting** According to expert river rafters, the Rivière Rouge in the Laurentians rates among the best in North America, so it's not surprising that this river has spawned a miniboom in the sport. Just an hour's drive north of Montréal, the Rouge cuts across the rugged Laurentians through rapids, canyons, and alongside beaches. From April through October, the adventurous can experience what traversing the region must have meant in the days of the voyageurs and *coureurs du bois*, though today's trip, by comparison, is much safer and more comfortable.

Four companies specializing in white-water rafting are on-site at the trip's departure point near Calumet. (Take Rte. 148 past Calumet; turn onto chemin de la Rivière Rouge until you see the signs for the access road to each rafter's headquarters.) **Aventures en Eau Vive** (tel. 819/242–6084), **Nouveau Monde** (tel. 819/242–7238), **Propulsion** (tel. 514/953–3300), and **W-3 Rafting** (tel. 514/334–0889) all offer four- to five-hour rafting trips. All provide transportation to and from the river site, as well as guides, helmets, life jackets, and, at the end of the trip, a much-anticipated meal. Most have facilities on-site or nearby for dining, drinking, camping, bathing, swimming, hiking, and horseback riding.

**Skiing**
*Les Laurentides* With the longest vertical drop (2,131 feet) in eastern Canada, **Mont Tremblant** (tel. 819/425–8711) offers a wide range of ski trails. Beginners favor the 5-kilometer (3-mile) Nansen trail; intermediate skiers head for the steeply sloped Flying Mile and Beauchemin runs. Experts choose the challenging Duncan and Expo runs on the mountain's north side. The Vancouver-based developers who bought the resort in 1991 promised to invest $47 million over five years in order to turn Mont Tremblant into a world-class ski and four-season resort. The speedy Duncan Express, a quadruple chair lift, is only a beginning.

**Ski Mont Gabriel** (tel. 514/229–3547) in Mont Rolland has 16 downhill trails primarily for intermediate and advanced skiers. The most popular runs are the Tamarack and the O'Connell trails for advanced skiers and Obergurgl for intermediates.

For something different, try **Ski Morin Heights** (*see* Tour 1, Les Laurentides, *above*), where snowboarding is the latest craze.

*L'Estrie* In l'Estrie the larger downhill slopes include **Mont Bromé** (tel. 514/534–2200) in Bromont (site of the 1986 World Cup) with 22 trails, **Mont Orford** (tel. 819/843–6548) with 39, **Owl's Head** (tel. 514/292–3342) with 27, and **Mont Sutton** (tel. 514/538–2339), where you pay to ski by the hour, with 53. The steepest drop, one of 853 meters (2,800 feet), is at Orford. All four resorts feature interchangeable lift tickets so skiers can test out all the major runs in the area. Call Ski East, tel. 819/820–2020.

With more than 20 cross-country sites, l'Estrie is a peaceful getaway. Trails at Bromont crisscross the site of the 1976 Olympic equestrian center. Three inns—Le Manoir Hovey, Auberge Hatley, and the Ripplecove Inn (*see* Dining and Lodging, *below*)—offer the **Skiwippi,** a week-long package of cross-country treks from one inn to another. The network covers some 32 kilometers (20 miles) of l'Estrie.

**Snowmobiling** **Point de Vue Canada** offers snowmobilers tours in the Laurentians, in Charlevoix, and as far north as the James Bay region. The group also has such adventure packages as "The Magic of the Nunavik Arctic," a week-long adventure in Québec's Grand Nord, where participants spend one night in an igloo, travel on dogsleds, and ice fish. *1227 av. St-Hubert, Suite 200, Montréal H2L 3Y8, tel. 514/843-8161.*

# Dining

Whether you enjoy a croissant and espresso at a sidewalk café or order *poutine* (a streetwise mix of homemade french fries—*frites*—and curd cheese and gravy) from a fast-food emporium, you won't soon forget your meals in Québec. There is no such thing as simply "eating out" in the province; restaurants are an integral slice of Québec life.

Outside Montréal and Québec City, you can find both good value and classic cuisine. Cooking in the province tends to be hearty, with such fare as cassoulet, *tourtières* (meat pies), onion soup, and apple pie heading up menus. In the Laurentians, chefs at some of the finer inns have attracted international followings. Local blueberries and maple syrup find their way into a surprising number of dishes.

Early reservations are essential. Monday or Tuesday is not too soon to book weekend tables at the best provincial restaurants. If you have any doubt about acceptable dress at a restaurant, call ahead. Jacket and tie are still the rule at many first-rate restaurants, even in summer.

Granby and its environs is one of Québec's foremost regions for traditional Québecois cuisine, here called *la fine cuisine estrienne*. Specialties include such mixed-game meat pies as *cipaille* and sweet, salty dishes like ham and maple syrup. Actually, maple syrup—on everything and in all its forms—is a mainstay of Québecois dishes. L'Estrie is one of Québec's main maple-sugaring regions.

In addition to maple sugar, the flavorings cloves, nutmeg, cinnamon, and pepper—spices used by the first settlers—have never gone out of style here, and local restaurants make good use of them in their distinctive dishes. The full country experience of l'Estrie includes warm hospitality at area lodges and inns.

Highly recommended restaurants in each price category are indicated by a star ★.

| Category | Cost* |
|----------|-------|
| $$$$ | over $35 |
| $$$ | $25–$35 |

| $$ | $15–$25 |
|---|---|
| $ | under $15 |

*per person, excluding drinks, service, 7% federal tax, and 4% provincial tax*

## Les Laurentides

**Ste-Adèle**    **La Clef des Champs.** This family-owned hillside restaurant, well known for its gourmet French cuisine, is a charming alternative to even the most superbly prepared hotel fare. It is tucked away among trees and faces a mountain, and it serves elegant dishes in a cozy, romantic atmosphere. Try the *noisette d'agneau en feuilleté* (lamb in pastry) or fresh poached salmon in red wine sauce. Top off your meal with the *gâteau aux deux chocolats* (two-chocolate cake). *875 chemin Ste-Marguerite, tel. 514/229–2857. Reservations advised. Dress: casual. AE, DC, MC, V. Closed Mon. Oct.–May, except on holidays. $$$$*

★ **L'Eau à la Bouche.** A consistent award winner in gastronomic circles, the restaurant has received top laurels among the Laurentians region's auberge–restaurants for its superb marriage of nouvelle cuisine and traditional Québec dishes. The care and inventiveness of chef-proprietor Anne Desjardins, who opened the Bavarian-style property a decade ago with her husband, Pierre Audette, is extraordinary. Such dishes as goat cheese tart, saddle of rabbit with onions, *baluchon* of lobster and scallops, roast partridge stuffed with oyster mushrooms and cream sauce and *pavé* of dark chocolate with English cream leave dinner guests clamoring for more. *3041 boul. Ste-Adèle, Rte. 117, tel. 514/229–2991. Reservations required. Dress: casual but neat. AE, DC, MC, V. $$$$*

**Ste-Agathe**    **Chatel Vienna.** Run by Eberhards Rado and his wife, who is also the
★ chef, this Austrian restaurant presents Viennese and other Continental dishes and serves them up in a lakeside setting. You may want to try the prize-winning home-smoked trout, served with an herb and spice butter, and garden fresh vegetables. Opt for a variety of schnitzels (veal dishes), a sauerkraut plate, or venison. Meals are accompanied by hot spiced wine, Czech pilsner beer, or dry Austrian and other international white wines. A Sunday buffet brunch tempts the palate with approximately 30 dishes, and is served from 11:30 until 2 for under $20. *6 rue Ste-Lucie, tel. 819/326–1485. Reservations advised. Dress: casual. MC, V. $$–$$$*

**Chez Girard.** Excellent French cuisine is the hallmark of this restaurant–auberge on the shores of Lac des Sables. The airy dining room has windows facing the lake and pastel colors that create a soft, romantic atmosphere. Some of the house specialties include *saumon au champagne* (salmon with champagne), lamb with cream of garlic sauce, caribou, and *feuilleté d'escargots et de pleurotes* (escargots and mushroom pastry). A Sunday brunch is offered for $16.95. *18 rue Principale O, tel. 819/326–0922. Reservations advised. Dress: casual. AE, DC, MC, V. $$–$$$*

**St-Sauveur-**    **Auberge Saint-Denis.** The distinction "Relais Gourmand" was
**des-Monts**    earned by this classic Québec inn for its fine French cuisine. Specializing in game, the artfully presented dishes are served in one of three dining rooms with a huge stone fireplace. Try the *arrivage de gibier*, an assortment of wild game with an exotic fruit sauce. *61 St-Denis, tel. 514/227–4602. Reservations advised for dinner. Dress: casual but neat. AE, DC, MC, V. $$$*

### l'Estrie

**Ayer's Cliff**    **The Ripplecove Inn.** The Ripplecove vies with the Hatley and Hovey inns (*see* Lodging, *below*) for best in the region. Its accommodations and service are consistently excellent, and the dining room is an award winner. The English-pub style dining combines classical and French cuisine in such dishes as *mousseline de rouget et truite* (mullet and trout mousse served with lobster and dill sauce), followed by *rable de lapereau* (stuffed rabbit with paprika sauce), topped off with a sublime dessert, such as *nougat glacé au coulis framboise* (nougat with raspberry sauce). The menu changes seasonally. *700 chemin Ripplecove, C.P. 246, tel. 819/838–4296. Reservations advised on weekends. Dress: casual. AE, MC, V. $$$*

**Magog**    **Auberge de l'Étoile.** This popular restaurant serves three meals a day in casual surroundings. Its somber interior, decorated in dark colors, is brightened by the windows facing Lac Memphé-Magog. House specialties include wild game and Swiss fondue. *1150 rue Principale O, tel. 819/843–6521. Reservations advised. Dress: casual. AE, DC, MC, V. $$*

**Notre-Dame-des-Bois**    **Aux Berges de l'Aurore.** Although this tiny bed-and-breakfast has spectacular views, situated as it is at the foot of Mont Mégantic, the draw here is the inn's cuisine. The award-winning restaurant features a five-course meal with ingredients supplied from the inn's huge fruit, vegetable, and herb garden, as well as wild game from the surrounding area: boar, fish, hare, and quail. It has been attractively furnished by its owners, Michel Martin and Daniel Pepin, and is closed from January until May. *51 chemin de l'Observatoire, tel. 819/888–2715. Reservations advised. Dress: casual. MC, V. $$$*

**Sherbrooke**    **Restaurant au P'tit Sabot.** On Sherbrooke's main drag, this restaurant offers a pleasant refuge from the hustle and bustle. With room for only 35 patrons, a piano in the corner, and pink decor, a romantic atmosphere prevails. This restaurant recently won an award for the best local-style eatery in the region. Among the many provincial dishes are wild boar, quail, and bison. *1410 rue King O, tel. 819/563–0262. Reservations accepted. Dress: casual. AE, DC, MC, V. $$*

---

### Charlevoix

**Baie-St-Paul**    **Auberge la Maison Otis.** Québec-oriented French cuisine is how chef Bernard Paten describes his cooking. His menu changes seasonally, and creative dishes might include *Ballotine de faisan* (pheasant), stuffed with quail and served in a venison sauce. A delicious assortment of cheeses or desserts caps off your meal. The restaurant is a 150-year-old Norman-style house, elegantly decorated in pink pastel, centered around a huge stone fireplace. *23 rue St-Jean-Baptiste, tel. 418/435–2255. Reservations advised. Dress: casual but neat. MC, V. $$$*

**Mouton Noir.** French cuisine is served amid flowers on the terrace in the summer or in a cozy rustic setting in the winter. You'll always find a varied menu, with pasta, fish, and meat, for a very reasonable price. Locals highly recommend this restaurant. *43 rue Ste-Anne, tel. 418/ 435–3075. Reservations accepted. Dress: casual. AE, MC, V. $$*

**La Malbaie**    **Auberge sur la Côte.** Simple white tablecloths, natural wood, and stone walls create a rustic setting for fine French cuisine. A house specialty is *agneau de Charlevoix*, lamb seasoned with lemon and thyme, served with fresh vegetables. Lunch is served in summer only, but the dining room is open in the evening year-round. *205* *chemin des Falaises, tel. 418/665-3972. Reservations advised. Dress: casual. AE, MC, V. $$$-$$$$*

**Pointe-au-Pic** **Auberge des 3 Canards.** This inn has made a name for itself in the region, not only for its accommodations but also for its award-winning restaurant. The menu, which changes with the seasons, may include *gratin d'escargots aux bluets* (snails with a blueberry and grapefruit sauce baked au gratin) as an appetizer, and stuffed pheasant—the breasts smothered in mustard sauce and the legs seasoned with spicy maple sauce—as a main course. Desserts are all homemade, including Pomme de l'Ile aux Coudres—cheese topped apples with a touch of honey. Meals are elegantly presented in a rustic setting. The warmth of the natural wood contrasts with the pale and deep blue touches throughout. *49 côte Bellevue, tel. 418/665-3761. Reservations advised. Dress: casual. AE, MC, V. $$$$*

### Gaspé Peninsula

**Gaspé** **La Belle Hélène.** Large windows face the bay filled with fishing boats—busy, perhaps, catching your meal. The menu specializes in regional cuisine, namely seafood and game. In the summer, the restaurant serves *crêpes bretonnes*, thin pancakes with a variety of fillings and toppings. *135A rue de la Reine, tel. 418/368-1455. Reservations in summer advised. Dress: casual. MC, V. $$*
**La Brise-Bise Bistro.** This chic bistro-bar, overlooking the Gaspé Bay, offers deluxe fast food, such as sauerkraut and sausages, a variety of imported beer, and live entertainment. *2 côte Carter, tel. 418/368-1456. Reservations accepted. Dress: casual. MC, V. $$*

**Pabos Mills** **La Sieur de Pabos.** Boasting the best seafood in the province, this rustic restaurant overlooks Pabos Bay, just outside Chandler. The chef suggests *crêpe de la signeurie*, a seafood crepe with a delicately seasoned white sauce. *325 Rte. 132, tel. 418/689-2281. Reservations accepted. AE, MC, V. $*

### Sugar Huts

Every March the combination of sunny days and cold nights causes the sap to run in the maple trees. Sugar huts (*cabanes à sucre*) go into operation boiling the sap collected from the trees in buckets (now, at some places, complicated tubing and vats do the job). The many commercial shacks scattered over the area host "sugaring offs" and tours of the operation, including the tapping of maple trees, the boiling vats, and *tire sur la neige*, when hot syrup is poured over cold snow to give it a taffy consistency just right for "pulling" and eating. A number of cabanes offer hearty meals of ham, baked beans, and pancakes, all drowned in maple syrup. It's best to call before visiting these cabanes: **Erablière Patoine** (1105 chemin Beauvoir, tel. 819/563-7455) in Fleurimont, near Sherbrooke, and **Bolduc** (525 chemin Lower, tel. 819/875-3022) in Cookshire.

# Lodging

Weary travelers have a full spectrum of accommodation options in Québec: from large resort hotels in the Laurentians and Relais et Châteaux properties in l'Estrie to shared dormitory space in rustic youth hostels near the heart of Gaspé. For information on camping in the province's private trailer parks and campgrounds, write for the free publication "Québec Camping," available from **Tourisme Qué-**

bec (12 rue Ste Anne, Québec G1X 3X2, tel. 418/643–2280). Inquiries about camping in Québec's three national parks should be directed to **Parks Canada Information Services** (3 Buade St., Box 6060, Haute Ville, Québec City G1R 4V7, tel. 418/648–4177). **Agricotours** (4545 av. Pierre de Couberten, C.P. 1000, Succursale M, Montréal H1V 3R2, tel. 514/252–3138), the Québec farm-vacation association, can provide lists of guest farms in the province.

Highly recommended lodgings in each price category are indicated by a star ★.

| Category | Cost* |
|----------|-------|
| $$$$ | over $125 |
| $$$ | $90–$125 |
| $$ | $50–$90 |
| $ | under $50 |

*Prices are for a standard double room, excluding 10% service charge, 7% federal tax, and 4% provincial tax, unless Modified American Plan (MAP) is indicated. MAP charges apply to each guest and include all meals, service charges, and taxes.*

## Charlevoix

**Baie-St-Paul**
★
**Auberge la Maison Otis.** Situated in the center of the village, this inn offers calm and romantic accommodations in three buildings, including an old stone house. Chef Bernard Paten specializes in nouvelle "Québec" cuisine—nouvelle cuisine with a regional twist—and summer lunches are served amid flowers on an outdoor terrace. Some of the 30 country-style rooms have whirlpools, fireplaces, and antique furnishings; all are air-conditioned and have private bath, TV, and radio. Skiing and ice-skating are nearby. *23 rue St-Jean-Baptiste, G0A 1B0, tel. 418/435–2255, fax 418/435–2464. 30 rooms, 4 suites. Facilities: restaurant, piano bar, lounge, indoor pool, health center, sauna. MAP optional. MC, V. $$$$*

**Cap-à-l'Aigle**
★
**Auberge la Pinsonnière.** The Pinsonnière is a member of the French association of fine country hotels, the Relais & Châteaux. Some even classify this small inn as a resort. Rooms offer a commanding view of Murray Bay on the St. Lawrence River. An atmosphere of country luxury prevails, and each room is decorated differently, some featuring fireplaces, whirlpools, and king-size four-poster beds. The weary traveler may relax in one of the three lounges within the auberge. *124 rue St-Raphael, G0T 1B0, tel. 418/665–4431, fax 418/665–7156. 22 rooms, 6 suites. Facilities: 2 restaurants, tennis court, indoor pool, sauna, private beach, mini spa. MAP. AE, MC, V. $$$$*

**Ile aux Coudres**
★
**Hôtel Cap-aux-Pièrres.** This hotel, located on Coudres Island in the St. Lawrence River, provides top-notch accommodations in both a traditionally Canadian main building and a motel section (open summer only). About a third of the rooms afford river views, and all have color TV and telephones. The restaurant serves a mix of Québec standards and nouvelle cuisine, and entertainment includes folk dancing on summer Saturday evenings. *246 rue Principale, La Baleine, G0A 2A0, tel. 418/438–2711 or 800/463–5250, fax 418/438–2127. 98 rooms. Facilities: restaurant, bar, indoor and outdoor heated pools. MAP. AE, DC, MC, V. $$*

**Pointe-au-Pic** **Hôtel Manoir Richelieu.** The Manoir Richelieu, an imposing castle nestled amid trees on a cliff overlooking the St. Lawrence River, has been offering first-class accommodations to vacationers for centuries, literally. It was founded in 1776 as a haven for wealthy travelers. Although still rich in elegance and charm, the resort has adapted to the needs of today's visitor and is now an affordable vacation spot. Guests can swim in the hotel's indoor and outdoor swimming pools and enjoy horseback riding, golf, and cross-country and downhill skiing. Whale-watching and snowmobile packages are available. *181 rue Richelieu, G0T 1M0, tel. 418/665–3703 or 800/463–2613, fax 418/665–3093. 391 rooms. Facilities: restaurant, indoor and outdoor pools, golf course, cross-country skiing, tennis courts, sauna, snowmobiling. AE, DC, MC, V. $$$$*

**St-Irenée** **Les Studios du Domaine.** This unique retreat, located at the foot of the Charlevoix Mountains facing the St. Lawrence River, is an artists' colony in the summer but is open to tourists during the winter season. Studio apartments, each with one bedroom, bathroom, and living area with fully equipped kitchenette, are available for a rather reasonable price. Although its workshops and studios make this a great setting for artists, it's also a good base for sports lovers: Golf and cross-country and downhill skiing are all nearby. *398 chemin les Bains, G0T 1V0, tel. 418/452–3535, fax 418/452–3503. 28 apartments. Facilities: 5 artists' workshops. MC, V. Closed June–Aug. $$*

## Gaspé Peninsula

**Matane** **Auberge des Gouverneurs.** This seaside motor inn, built in 1975, is well equipped with recreational facilities and offers many rooms with ocean views. The rooms are not fancy, but all are comfortable, with whirlpool baths. All rooms have telephone and color TV. Near the dock of the ferry for Baie Comeau, the auberge is a good choice for visitors who have come to ski or fish. *250 av. du Phare E, G4W 3N4, tel. 418/566–2651, fax 418/562–7365. 72 rooms, 2 suites. Facilities: restaurant, lounge, outdoor pool, tennis court, sauna, exercise room, parking. AE, DC, MC, V. $$*

**Percé** **La Normandie Hotel/Motel.** All but four rooms of this decade-old split-level motel face the ocean, with views of Percé Rock and Bonaventure Island. The location in the center of town puts shops and restaurants within walking distance. Lower floors were recently renovated, decorated in fresh pastel colors. Third-floor rooms are more spacious. *221 Rte. 132 O, C.P. 129, G0C 2L0, tel. 418/782–2112 or 800/463–0820. 45 rooms. Facilities: restaurant, lounge, exercise room, sauna, beach and municipal pool nearby. MAP optional. AE, DC, MC, V. Closed Nov.–Apr. $$–$$$*

**La Bonaventure-sur-Mer Hotel.** Though the decor is motel-standard, the waterfront location with views of Percé Rock and Bonaventure Island makes this a pleasant property. The older section is a big hotel building; some motel units offer kitchenettes. *Rte. 132, C.P. 339, G0C 2L0, tel. 418/782–2166. 90 rooms. Facilities: dining room, beach, parking. AE, MC, V. Closed Nov.–Apr. $$–$$$*

**La Côte Surprise Motor Hotel.** Most of the rooms of this recently renovated motel have views of Percé Rock and the village. Decor is standard in both motel and second-floor hotel units, but the private balconies and terraces are a plus. *Rte. 132, C.P. 339, tel. 418/782–2166, fax 418/782–5323. 36 rooms. Facilities: dining rooms, snack bar, lounge, parking. AE, MC, V. Closed Oct.–May. $$*

## Les Laurentides

**Estérel**    **Hôtel d'Estérel.** If this all-inclusive resort were in the Caribbean, it would probably be run by Club Med, given the nonstop activities. The property includes a private 18-hole golf course, beach, marina, downhill-skiing facilities, 87 kilometers of cross-country ski trails, outdoor skating rink, and sports complex. Comfortable rooms offer a view of either the lake or the beautiful flower gardens. *39 boul. Fridolin Simard, J0T 1E0, tel. 514/228–2571 or 800/363–3623, fax 514/228–4977. 135 rooms. Facilities: restaurant, disco, indoor pool, tennis courts, and gym. MAP optional. AE, DC, MC, V. $$$$*

**Mont Rolland**    **Auberge Mont Gabriel.** At this deluxe resort located on a 1,200-acre estate, choose to relax in one of the spacious, modern rooms with a view of the valley, or be close to nature in one of the cozy log cabins with fireplaces to keep you warm. The dining is superb here. Tennis, golf, and ski-week and -weekend packages are available. *Autoroute 15, Exit 64, J0R 1G0, tel. 514/229–3547, fax 514/229–7034. 120 rooms, 10 suites. Facilities: restaurant, 18-hole golf course, indoor and outdoor pools, 6 tennis courts. MAP optional. AE, DC, MC, V. $$$*

**Mont Tremblant** ★    **Station Mont Tremblant Lodge.** Only 90 minutes from Montréal, on 14-kilometer-long (9-mile-long) Lac Tremblant, this is the northernmost resort that is easily accessible in the Upper Laurentians. Accommodations include modern condo units with kitchenettes, a rustic lodge, and individual cabins. The partying is lively in winter, with lots of après-ski bars in the hotel and the immediate area. In summer, guests swim, windsurf, and sail. *3005 chemin Principale, J0T 1Z0, tel. 819/425–8711 or 800/461–8711, fax 819/681–5590. Facilities: restaurant, bar, disco, golf course, tennis courts, horseback riding, private beach. MAP optional. AE, MC, V. $$$–$$$$*

**Club Tremblant.** Across the lake from Mont Tremblant Lodge, this hotel was built as a private retreat in the 1930s by a wealthy American. The original large, log-cabin lodge is furnished in colonial style, with wooden staircases and huge stone fireplaces. The rustic but comfortable main lodge has excellent facilities and a dining room serving four-star gourmet cuisine. Both the main lodge and the deluxe condominium complex—fireplaces, private balconies, kitchenettes, and split-level design de rigueur—built just up the hill from the lodge, offer magnificent views of Mont Tremblant and its ski hills. Warm-weather activities include swimming, fishing, boating, and tennis. There is a golf course nearby. *av. Cuttle, J0T 1Z0, tel. 819/425–2731, fax 819/425–9903. 150 rooms. Facilities: restaurant, indoor pool, exercise room. MAP optional. AE, DC, MC, V. $$$–$$$$*

**Auberge Villa Bellevue.** This equally venerable and less expensive alternative to Gray Rocks (*see below*) is on Lac Ouimet, and has been run by the Dubois family for more than three generations. Supporting its reputation as a family resort, the inn invites children under 18 who share a room with their parents to stay free and pay for meals only during the summer. In winter, weekend packages include transportation to nearby Mont Tremblant. The hotel has a list of local baby-sitters, and offers a full summer program of children's activities. Accommodations range from hotel rooms to chalets and condominiums. In summer, tennis lessons for adults and children are available. Sailing, windsurfing, waterskiing, and lounging about on the outdoor lakeside terrace are other possible pastimes at Villa Bellevue. The indoor swimming pool and fitness center offer nonskiers plenty of physical activity during the winter without having to step outdoors. *845 rue Principale, J0T 1Z0, tel. 819/425–2734* *or 800/567–6763, fax 819/425–9360. 86 rooms, 14 suites. Facilities: restaurant, indoor pool, gym, tennis courts, private beach, marina. MAP optional. AE, DC, MC, V. $$$*

**Auberge du Coq de Montagne.** Owners Nino and Kay Faragalli have earned a favorable reputation for their auberge, situated on Lac Moore. The cozy, family-run inn, is touted for its friendly service, great hospitality, and modern accommodations. Kudos have also been garnered for the great Italian cuisine served up nightly, which also draws a local crowd: Reservations are a must. Year-round facilities and activities, on-site or nearby, include canoeing, kayaking, sailboarding, fishing, badminton, tennis, horseback riding, skating, and skiing. *2151 chemin Principale, C.P. 208, Lac Moore, J0T 1Z0, tel. 819/425–3380, fax 819/425–7846. 16 rooms. Facilities: restaurant, exercise room, sauna, private beach. MAP in winter, optional in summer. AE, MC, V. $$–$$$$*

**Morin Heights**

**The Auberge Swiss Inn.** Located within 4 kilometers (3 miles) of Ski Morin Heights, this moderately priced inn is a well-situated bargain. The authentic Swiss-style chalet exudes coziness, from the wood paneling and fireplace lounge to the individually decorated rooms. *796 Rte. St-Adolphe, J0R 1H0, tel. 514/226–2009, fax 514/226–5709. 10 rooms. Facilities: restaurant, canoeing, cross-country skiing, lounge. MC, V. $$*

**Pointe-du-Lac**
★

**L'Auberge du Lac Saint-Pierre.** Set on the lake near Trois Rivières, halfway between Montréal and Québec City, this modern small hotel was built in 1988 and has quickly gained the highest ratings for cuisine and accommodations. The luxurious rooms are done in soothing pastels, with television, telephones, and many whirlpool baths. Lake views from the dining room, the conservatory, and many of the guest rooms add to the tranquillity. It's an ideal stop on a tour of southern Québec. *1911 Notre-Dame (Rte. 138), Box 10, G0X 1Z0, tel. 819/377–5971, fax 819/377–5579. 30 rooms. Facilities: restaurant, heated outdoor pool, tennis court, meeting rooms for 40 and 15, business equipment rentals. MAP optional. AE, MC, V. $$$*

**Ste-Adèle**

**Le Chantecler.** This Montréaler favorite on Lac Rond is nestled at the base of a mountain with 22 downhill ski runs. Skiing is the obvious draw—trails begin almost at the hotel entrance. (It's been the official training site of the National Alpine Ski Teams.) The condominium units, hotel rooms, and chalets all have a rustic appeal, furnished with Canadian pine. Summer activities include tennis, golf, and boating. An indoor pool and spa, as well as a beach, make swimming a year-round possibility. *1474 chemin Chantecler, C.P. 1048, J0R 1L0, tel. 514/229–3555; elsewhere in Québec, 800/363–2420; fax 514/229–5593. 300 rooms, 20 suites. Facilities: restaurant, indoor pool, spa, private beach, golf course. MAP optional. AE, DC, MC, V. $$$$*

**L'Eau à la Bouche.** This 25-room auberge has received commendations for superb service and luxurious appointments, and is perfect for weekend getaways or business retreats. Its restaurant is a draw in itself (*see Dining, above*). The auberge faces Le Chantecler's ski slopes, so skiing is literally at the door. Tennis, sailing, horseback riding, and a golf course are nearby. Package rates are available. *3003 boul. Ste-Adèle, J0R 1L0, tel. 514/229–2991, fax 514/229–7573. 25 rooms. Facilities: restaurant, pool, flower garden terrace, wine cellar, facilities for people with disabilities. MAP optional. AE, MC, V. $$$–$$$$*

**Auberge aux Croissants.** Situated at the foot of the Laurentian Mountains, this inn is only a five-minute drive from Mont-Saint-Sauveur. Although most rooms have no TV or telephone, such conveniences are found in one of the two cozy lounges, and an impressive buffet-breakfast is included with the price of the room. *750 chemin Ste-Marguerite, J0R 1L0, tel. 514/229-3838. 12 rooms with private bath, 1 with whirlpool bath, 1 suite. MC, V. $$*

**Ste-Agathe** **Auberge du Lac des Sables.** A favorite with couples, this inn offers a quiet, relaxed atmosphere in a country setting with a magnificent view of Lac des Sables. Enjoy the view from your balcony or from the dining room. All rooms have contemporary decor, with queen-size beds and color TVs. A complimentary breakfast is served. *230 St-Venant, J8C 3Z7, tel. 819/ 326-3994, fax 819/326-7556. 19 rooms. Facilities: whirlpool. MC, V. $$$*

**Ste-Jovite** **Gray Rocks.** This oldest ski resort in the Laurentians has its own private mountain ribboned by 20 ski runs; a sprawling wood hotel with modern chalets and condominium units overlooks Lac Ouimet. Winter ski packages, including cross-country, are good value for the money, as are the summer tennis packages. Gray Rocks also runs the more intimate Auberge le Château with 24 rooms farther along Route 327 North. *Rte. 327 N, J0T 2H0, tel. 819/425-2771 or 800/567-6767, fax 819/425-3474. 306 rooms, 13 with shared bath. Facilities: restaurant, 22 clay tennis courts, tennis school, riding stables, marina, La Spa fitness center with hot tubs, indoor swimming pool, children's activity programs, private airstrip and seaplane anchorage. MAP optional. Ski packages available. AE, MC, V. $$–$$$$*

**Val David** **Hôtel La Sapinière.** Comfortable accommodations are offered in this homey, dark-brown frame hotel with its bright country flowers. Each room—with country-style furnishings and pastel floral accents—has its own personality, yet all rooms come with such luxurious little extras as thick terry-cloth bathrobes and hair dryers. Relax in one of several cozy lounges scattered throughout the hotel, in front of a blazing fire. The property is best known for its fine dining room and wine cellar. *1244 chemin de la Sapinière, J0T 2N0, tel. 819/322-2020 or 800/567-6635, fax 819/322-6510. 70 rooms. MAP. AE, DC, MC, V. $$$$*

## L'Estrie

**Bromont** **Le Château Bromont Resort Spa.** Massages, algotherapy, electropuncture, algae wraps, facials, and aroma therapy are just a few of the pampering services at this European-style resort spa. The Atrium houses an indoor pool, hot tubs, and a sauna, and there are also outdoor hot tubs, squash, racquetball, and badminton courts. Rooms are large and comfortable, with contemporary furniture, but those facing the Atrium are a little somber. Chef Daniel Guay creates "cuisine sauvage" at the château's dining room, Les Quatres Canards. (There is also a special spa menu offered.) L'Equestre Bar, named for Bromont's equestrian interests, has a cocktail hour and live entertainment. *90 rue Stanstead, J0E 1L0, tel. 514/534-3433, fax 514/534-0514. 147 rooms. Facilities: restaurant, bar, spa, indoor pool, sauna. MAP optional. AE, DC, MC, V. $$$–$$$$*

**Eastman** **Centre de Santé Eastman.** This four-season resort offers respite to the bone-weary and bruised skier. The 20 country-style rooms are located in three separate houses: the rustic Maison Canadienne, the country-style Volet Bleu, and the modern Pavillon Kaufman. Holistic spa treatments include massage (Swedish and shiatsu) and gentle body conditioning and stretch workouts. There's also horseback riding and cross-country skiing. Top off an already healthy day with fine vegetarian cuisine offered in the dining room. *895 chemin Dili-*

*gence, J0E 1P0, tel. 514/297–3009, fax 514/297–3370. 20 rooms. Facilities: dining room. MAP. AE, MC, V. $$$–$$$$*

**Lennoxville**  **Bishop's University.** If you are on a budget, this is a great place to stay. The prices can't be beat, and the location near Sherbrooke is good for touring. The university's grounds are lovely, with a river cutting through the campus and its golf course. Much of the architecture is reminiscent of stately New England campuses. Visit the university's 136-year-old chapel, and also look for the butternut tree, an endangered species in l'Estrie. Reservations for summer guests are accepted as early as September, so it's a good idea to book in advance. *Rue College, J1M 1Z7, tel. 819/822–9651, fax 819/822–9615. 559 beds. Facilities: sports complex with Olympic-size indoor pool, tennis courts. MC, V. Closed Sept.–early May. $*

**Magog**  **O'Berge du Village.** Half of this condo complex is on a time-share basis and half is run like a hotel. Rustic Canadian pine furniture and fireplaces adorn the condos, which accommodate from two to eight people. All units have a balcony facing the lake and a fully equipped kitchenette. If you don't feel like cooking, you can try the bistro; for those with something more elaborate in mind, enjoy dinner in the formal dining room. *261 rue Merry S, J1X 3L2, tel. 819/843–6566 or 800/567–6089, fax 819/843–2924. 117 rooms. Facilities: restaurant, bistro, wine bar, indoor and outdoor pools, games room, marina, aquatic sports, day-care service, daily activities in the summer. AE, MC, V. $$$*

**North Hatley**  **Auberge Hatley.** Gourmet cuisine is the main attraction at this country inn, whose dining room was once named the top restaurant in Québec in the annual Ordre du Mérite de la Restauration awards. After savoring chef Alain Labrie's fine cuisine, guests sleep it off in one of the 25 charmingly decorated rooms in this 1903 country manor, a member of Relais & Châteaux. *325 Virgin Rd., C.P. 330, J0B 2C0, tel. 819/842–2451, fax 819/842–2907. 25 rooms, some with Jacuzzi and fireplace. Facilities: restaurant. MAP. AE, MC, V. Closed last 2 wks in Nov. $$$$*

★  **Manoir Hovey.** Overlooking the perfectly pristine Lac Massawippi, this retreat has the ambience of a private estate, while offering the activities of a resort—boating, water skiing, mountain biking, cross-country skiing, tennis, and more. Built in 1900 as a summer home for Henry Atkinson, then owner of Georgia Power in Atlanta, Hovey Manor resembles George Washington's home at Mount Vernon, Virginia. Each wallpapered room has personality, with a mix of antiques and newer wood furniture, richly printed fabrics, and lace trimmings. Many rooms have working fireplaces and private balconies. The dining room serves exquisite Continental and French cuisine; the changing dinner menu might include warm roulades of Swiss chard with spring lamb, preserved apricots, and roasted hazelnuts; swordfish with a sabayon of leeks and pink peppercorns au gratin; or grilled tenderloin of beef marinated with juniper berries and a sauce of tarragon and horseradish. Dinner, breakfast, and most sports facilities are included in room rates. *C.P. 60, J0B 2C0, tel. 819/842–2421, fax 819/842–2248. 40 rooms and 4-bedroom cottage. Facilities: dining room, library, 2 bars, heated outdoor pool, tennis courts, 2 beaches, 2 conference rooms, water sports, mountain bikes, ice fishing, ski trails. MAP. AE, DC, MC, V. $$$$*

**Orford**  **Auberge Estrimont.** An exclusive complex in cedar combining hotel rooms, condos, and larger chalets, Auberge Estrimont is close to ski hills, riding stables, and golf courses. Every room, whether in the hotel or in an adjoining condo unit, has a fireplace and a private balcony. *44 av. de l'Auberge, C.P. 98, Orford-Magog, J1X 3W7, tel. 819/*

*843–1616 or 800/567–7320, fax 819/843–4909. 76 rooms, 7 suites. Facilities: restaurant; bar; indoor and outdoor pools; tennis, squash, racquetball courts; exercise room; sauna; Jacuzzi; cross-country ski trails. AE, DC, MC, V. $$$*

**Sutton** **Auberge la Paimpolaise.** This auberge is located right on Mont Sutton, 50 feet from the ski trails. Nothing fancy is offered, but the location is hard to beat. Rooms are simple, comfortable, and clean, with a woodsy appeal. All-inclusive weekend ski packages are available. A complimentary breakfast is served. *615 rue Maple, J0E 2K0, tel. 514/538–3213, fax 514/538–3970. 29 rooms. MAP optional. AE, MC, V. $$–$$$*

**Auberge Schweizer.** No matter what the season, this lodge is the perfect place to relax. It has its own farm, and guests feast on home-cooked meals with vegetables straight from the garden. Nearby is a pond for swimming, as well as some hiking trails and ski trails. In addition to the standard accommodations, the auberge has a two-bedroom chalet, each bedroom with private bath and powder room; a three-bedroom chalet with one bath and a playroom; and another three-bedroom/three-bathroom chalet. All the chalets have kitchens, and two have washers and dryers. *357 chemin Schweizer, J0E 2K0, tel. 514/538–2129. 11 rooms, 3 chalets with fireplace. V. $–$$*

## Montérégie

**St-Marc-** **Hostellerie Les Trois Tilleuls.** This romantic little member of the
**sur-Richelieu** Relais et Châteaux group, on a quiet country road, is a lovely spot to
**★** hole up in and investigate the surrounding Montérégie region, or to return to after a hard day exploring the big city—Montréal is 20 minutes away. The rooms are modern, conveniently arranged, and well equipped (with hair dryers and magnifying mirrors), and each has a balcony or terrace facing the lovely Rivière Richelieu just outside. Packages are available for summer theatergoers and cross-country skiers, among others. Montréalers come to savor the cuisine of chef Roger Robin—and in the hopes of taking home one of his recipes. *290 Richelieu, Saint-Marc-sur-Richelieu, Qué. J0L 2E0, tel. 514/584–2231 or 800/856–7787 in Québec, 800/263–2230 in the U.S.; fax 514/584–3146. 24 rooms with bath, 1 suite. Facilities: restaurant, bar, pool, 2 tennis courts, 6 meeting rooms. AE, DC, MC, V. $$$–$$$$*

# The Arts and Nightlife

## The Arts

**Lac Brome** Théâtre Lac Brome (tel. 514/243–0361) is an English-language theater company that stages productions of classic Broadway and West End hits. The 175-seat, air-conditioned theater is located behind Knowlton's popular pub of the same name.

**Lac** L'Association du Festival du Lac Massawippi presents an annual an-
**Massawippi** tiques and folk-arts show (tel. 819/563–4141) each July. The association also sponsors a series of classical music concerts performed at the L'Eglise Sainte Catherine in North Hatley, on Sundays starting in late April and continuing until the end of June.

**Lennoxville** Lennoxville's **Centennial Theatre** at Bishop's University (tel. 819/822–9692) presents a roster of international, Canadian, and Québecois jazz, classical, and rock concerts, as well as dance, mime, and children's theater. Jazz greats Gary Burton, Carla Bley, and

Larry Coryell have appeared here, as have such classical artists as the Amsterdam Guitar Trio and the Allegri String Quartet.

**Magog** **Théâtre le Vieux Clocher** (64 rue Merry N, tel. 819/847–0470) presents pop and rock concerts, and occasionally French plays.

**North Hatley** **The Piggery,** housed in a former pig barn in North Hatley on the shores of Lac Massawippi, reigns supreme in l'Estrie cultural life. The venue is renowned for its risk taking, often presenting new plays by Canadian playwrights and even experimenting with bilingual productions. *Box 390, North Hatley J0B 2C0, tel. 819/842–2432 or 819/842–2431. Reservations required. Season runs June–Aug.*

**Orford** Orford's regional park is the site of an annual arts festival highlighting classical music, pops, and chamber orchestra concerts. Since 1951, thousands of students have come to the **Orford Arts Center** to study and perform classical music in the summer. Canada's internationally celebrated Orford String Quartet originated here. Festival Orford has recently expanded to include jazz and folk music. *Orford Arts Center, Box 280, Magog J1X 3W8, tel. 819/843–3981; in Canada from May to Aug., 800/567–6155.*

**Sutton** Sutton is also home to the visual and performing arts. **Arts Sutton** (7 rue Academy, tel. 514/538–2563) is a long-established mecca for the visual arts.

## Nightlife

The Laurentians and l'Estrie are your best bets when looking for nightlife in Québec's outlying regions. Après-ski bars, bistros, and cafés are spread throughout the Laurentians. In Piedmont, **La Nuit Blanche** (762 rue Principale, tel. 514/227–5419) is a popular dancing spot. If live music is what you want, head to **Bourbon Street** (2045 Rte. 117, tel. 514/229–2905) in Mont Rolland. **Les Vieilles Portes** (185 rue Principale, tel. 514/227–2662) in Saint-Sauveur is a popular pub where you can relax, order your favorite beer, and have a bite to eat.

If you are looking for action in l'Estrie, visit Magog, a village that comes to life after dark. **La Lanterne** (70 rue du Lac, tel. 819/843–7205) is a popular restaurant-bar that often hosts theme nights. For information, tune in to the local radio station. **La Grosse Pomme** (270 rue Principale O, tel. 819/843–9365) is also a popular place. This multilevel complex considers itself a cinema-bar, with huge video screens, dance floors, and restaurant service. An outdoor summer terrace has live entertainment. **The Auberge Orford** (20 rue Merry S, tel. 819/843–9361) is another outdoor summer terrace that doesn't stop. Here you can enjoy live entertainment.

# 11 Nova Scotia

By Silver
Donald
Cameron

Novelist,
playwright,
and sailor,
Silver Donald
Cameron is
one of
Canada's
most versatile
authors. His
recent books
Wind, Whales
and Whisky:
A Cape
Breton
Voyage and
Sun, Sand
and
Strawberries:
An Acadian
Voyage record
cruises with
his wife and
son in
Silversark, a
27-foot
sailboat,
which they
built
themselves.

Updated by
Julie V.
Watson

"Infinite riches in a little room," said Elizabethan playwright Christopher Marlowe. Was he speaking of Nova Scotia, Canada's second-smallest province that packs an impossible variety of cultures and landscapes into a mass that's half the size of Ohio?

Nova Scotia's landscapes echo every region of Canada. Mountain clefts in Cape Breton Island could pass for crannies in British Columbia. Stretches of the Tantramar Marshes are as board-flat as the prairies. The glaciated interior, spruce-swathed and peppered with lakes, closely resembles the Canadian Shield in northern Manitoba. The apple blossoms in the Annapolis Valley are as glorious as those in Niagara, and parts of Halifax could masquerade as downtown Toronto. A massive Catholic church in a tiny French village recalls Québec. The warm salt water and long sandy beaches of Prince Edward Island are also found on the mainland side of Northumberland Strait, and the brick-red mudflats of the Bay of Fundy echo their counterparts in New Brunswick. Neil's Harbour looks just like a Newfoundland outport—and sounds like one, too, since many of its people are Newfoundlanders by origin.

As with the land, so with the people. The Micmac Indians have been here for 10,000 years. The French came to the Annapolis Basin in 1605. In the 1750s, the English settled cockneys and Irish in Halifax and "Foreign Protestants"—chiefly Germans—in Lunenburg. By then Yankees from New England were putting down roots in Liverpool, Cape Sable Island, and the Annapolis Valley. In the 1780s they were joined by thousands of "Loyalists"—many of them black—displaced by the American Revolution. Soon after, the Scots poured into northern Nova Scotia and Cape Breton, evicted from the Highlands by their landlords' preference for sheep. The last wave of immigrants, in the 1890s, became steelworkers and coal miners in Cape Breton. They came from Wales, the West Indies, Poland, the Ukraine, and the Middle East. They're all Nova Scotians, and they're all still here, eating their own foods, worshipping in their own churches, speaking in their rich, full-flavored voices.

Infinite riches abound: Gaelic street signs in Pugwash and Mabou, French masses in Cheticamp and Point de l'Eglise, black gospel choirs in Halifax, Micmac handcrafts in Eskasoni, onion-dome churches in Sydney, sauerkraut in Lunenburg, and Yankee Puritanism in Clark's Harbour.

This is a little buried nation, compact and distinctive, with a capital city the same size as Marlowe's London. Before Canada was formed in 1867, Nova Scotians were prosperous shipwrights and merchants, trading with the world. Who created Cunard Lines? A Haligonian, Samuel Cunard. Those spacious days brought democracy to the British colonies, left Victorian mansions in all the salty little ports that dot the coastline, and created a uniquely Nova Scotian outlook: worldly, approachable, sturdily independent.

"Infinite riches in a little room." Kit Marlowe would love it here.

# Essential Information

## Important Addresses and Numbers

Tourist
Information

The **Nova Scotia Department of Tourism and Culture** (Box 456, Halifax, NS B3J 2R5, tel. 902/424–5000) publishes a range of literature, including an exhaustive annual travel guide to sights, accommodations, and transportation.

*Halifax*  The **Nova Scotia Tourism Information Centre** (Old Red Store at Historic Properties, tel. 902/424–4247), and **Tourism Halifax** (City Hall, Duke and Barrington Sts., tel. 902/421–8736) are open mid-June–Labor Day, daily 9–6; Labor Day–mid-June, weekdays 9–4:30.

**Emergencies**  Dial "0" for operator in emergencies; check the front of the local phone book for specific medical services.

*Hospital*  **Victoria General** (tel. 902/428–2110) is Halifax's major hospital.

## Arriving and Departing by Plane, Car, Ferry, Train, and Bus

**By Plane**  The **Halifax International Airport** is 40 kilometers (25 miles) northeast of downtown Halifax. **Sydney Airport** is 13 kilometers (8 miles) east of Sydney.

**Air Canada** (tel. 902/429–7111 or 800/776–3000) provides regular, daily service to Halifax and Sydney, Nova Scotia, from New York, Boston, Toronto, Montréal, and St. John's, Newfoundland. **Canadian Airlines International** (tel. 800/527–8499) has service to Halifax via Toronto and Montréal. **Air Nova** (tel. 902/429–7111 or 800/776–3000) and **Air Atlantic** (tel. 800/426–7000 or 800/665–1177 in Canada) provide regional service to both airports with flights to Toronto, Montréal, and Boston.

*Between Airport and City Center*  Airport bus service to most Halifax and Dartmouth hotels costs $18 round-trip, $11 one-way. Normal taxi fare is $33 each way, but if you book in advance with **Aero Cab** (tel. 902/445–3393) the fare is $24.60 cash, slightly more by credit card (MC or V). The trip takes 30–40 minutes.

**By Car**  The Trans-Canada Highway reaches Nova Scotia through New Brunswick. Entering the province at Amherst, it becomes Highway 104. To reach Halifax, pick up Highway 102 at Truro. To reach Cape Breton, continue on Highway 104.

Highways throughout Nova Scotia, numbered from 100 to 199, are all-weather, limited-access roads, with 100 kilometers-per-hour (62.5 miles-per-hour) speed limits. The last two digits usually match the number of an older trunk highway along the same route, numbered from 1 to 99. Thus, Highway 102, between Halifax and Truro, matches the older Route 2, between the same towns. Roads numbered from 200 to 399 are secondary roads that usually link villages. Unless otherwise posted, the speed limit is 80 kilometers per hour (50 miles per hour) except on the 100-series highways.

Most highways in the province lead to Halifax-Dartmouth. Highways 3/103, 7, 2/102, and 1/101 terminate in the twin cities.

*Rental Cars*  Halifax is the most convenient place from which to begin your driving tour of the province. The following list details city and airport venues of rental-car agencies: **Avis** (5600 Sackville St., tel. 902/423–6303; airport, tel. 902/873–3523); **Budget** (1558 Hollis St., tel. 902/421–1242; airport, tel. 902/873–3509); **Hertz** (Halifax Sheraton, tel. 902/421–1763; airport, tel. 902/873–3700); **Thrifty** (6930 Lady Hammond, tel. 902/422–4455; airport, tel. 902/873–3527); **Tilden** (1130 Hollis St., tel. 902/422–4433; airport, tel. 902/873–3505).

**By Ferry**  Three car ferries connect Nova Scotia with Maine and New Brunswick. **Marine Atlantic** (tel. 800/341–7981) sails from Bar Harbor, Maine, and **Prince of Fundy Cruises** (tel. 800/341–7540) from Portland; both arrive in Yarmouth. From Saint John, New Brunswick, to

Digby, Nova Scotia, ferry service is provided by **Marine Atlantic** (tel. 800/565–9470 in New Brunswick).

Marine Atlantic also operates ferries between New Brunswick and Prince Edward Island, and between Cape Breton and Newfoundland. In Nova Scotia, call 902/794–5700; in Newfoundland, 709/772–7701.

Between May and December, **Northumberland Ferries** (tel. 902/485–6580; in Nova Scotia, 800/565–0201) operate between Caribou, Nova Scotia, and Wood Islands, Prince Edward Island.

By Train **VIA Rail** (tel. 800/561–3949) provides service from Montréal to Halifax via Moncton and Saint John, in New Brunswick; and Amherst and Truro, in Nova Scotia.

**Amtrak** (tel. 800/USA–RAIL) from New York City makes connections in Montréal.

By Bus **Greyhound Lines** (800/231–2222) from New York, and **Voyageur Inc.** (tel. 613/238–5900) from Montréal, connect with **Scotia Motor Tours** or **SMT** (tel. 506/458–6000) through New Brunswick, which links (rather inconveniently) with **Acadian Lines Limited** (tel. 902/454–8279), which provides inter-urban services within Nova Scotia.

## Getting Around

Halifax Walking and biking are excellent ways to get around and see the city, especially on weekdays when parking in the downtown area can be a problem. A pleasant alternative, however, is to take one of the rickshaws, available downtown during summer.

*By Taxi* Rates begin at about $2.40 and increase based on mileage and time. A crosstown trip should cost $4–$5, depending on traffic. Hailing a taxi can be difficult, but there are taxi stands at major hotels and shopping malls. Most Haligonians simply phone for a taxi service. Call **Aero Cab** (tel. 902/445–3393).

*By Bus* The **Metropolitan Transit Commission** (tel. 902/421–6600) bus system covers the entire Halifax-Dartmouth area. The base fare is $1.20 adults, 65¢ children 5–15; exact change only.

*By Ferry* The **Dartmouth Ferry Commission** (tel. 902/464–2336) runs two-passenger ferries from the George Street terminal in Halifax to the Portland Street terminal in Dartmouth, from 6 AM to midnight on an hourly and half-hourly schedule (during the weekday commuter rush, ferries also go to the Woodside terminal from 7–9 AM and 4–6 PM only). The fare for a single crossing is 85¢, which is well worth it considering you get an up-close view of both waterfronts.

Elsewhere in Nova Scotia You will need a car to explore the province beyond Halifax. For rental car information, *see* Rental Cars in Arriving and Departing by Car, *above.*

As you explore Nova Scotia, be on the lookout for the 10 designated "Scenic Travelways" that appear throughout the province and are easily identified by roadside signs with icons that correspond with trail names. These routes, as well as tourist literature (maps and the provincial *Travel Guide*) that has been published in accordance with this scheme, have been developed by the Nova Scotia Department of Tourism and Culture.

**Guided Tours**

Boat Tours **Murphy's on the Water** (tel. 902/420–1015) sails various vessels: *Harbour Queen I*, a paddle wheeler; *Haligonian III*, an enclosed motor launch; *Stormy Weather I*, a 40-foot Cape Islander (fishing boat); and *Mar II*, a 23-meter sailing ketch. All operate from mid-May to late October, from berths at 1751 Lower Water Street on Cable Wharf, next to the Historic Properties in Halifax. Costs vary, but a basic tour of the harbor ranges from $10–15 adults, 10% discount for children and senior citizens, children under 5 free, $30 families.

*Bluenose II* (tel. 902/422–2678 or 902/424–5000) is an exact replica of Nova Scotia's 143-foot fishing schooner *Bluenose*, the ship that was the undefeated champion in international schooner racing for nearly 20 years and is featured on the Canadian dime. *Bluenose II* departs from Privateer's Wharf three times daily on a two-hour harbor sail in summer. Fares are $14 for adults, $7 for senior citizens and children, but are subject to change.

Bus Tours Both **Gray Line Sightseeing** (tel. 902/454–8279) and **Cabana Tours** (tel. 902/423–6066) run coach tours through Halifax-Dartmouth and Peggy's Cove. **Halifax Double Decker Tours** (tel. 902/420–1155) offers two-hour tours on double-decker buses that leave daily from Historic Properties. You can also charter a bus from the **Metropolitan Transit Commission** (tel. 902/421–6600) for a narrated tour.

# Exploring Nova Scotia

## Highlights for First-Time Visitors

**Cape Breton Highlands National Park,** Tour 4: Cape Breton Island
**Fortress Louisbourg National Historic Park,** Tour 4: Cape Breton Island
**Halifax Citadel National Historic Park,** Tour 1: Halifax and Dartmouth
**Historic Annapolis Royal,** Tour 2: The South Shore and Annapolis Valley
**Historic Properties and *Bluenose II*,** Tour 1: Halifax and Dartmouth
**Lunenburg's Nautical Heritage,** Tour 2: The South Shore and Annapolis Valley
**Pictou's Scottish Heritage,** Tour 3: Northern Nova Scotia
**Sherbrooke Village,** Tour 3: Northern Nova Scotia

## Tour 1: Halifax and Dartmouth

*Numbers in the margin correspond to points of interest on the Nova Scotia and Halifax maps.*

**1** Salty and urbane, learned and plain-spoken, **Halifax** is large enough to have the trappings of a capital city, yet small enough to retain the warmth and convenience of a small town.

**2** Begin your walking tour at **Purdy's Wharf**—twin office towers shaped like milk cartons with feet, standing right in the harbor. Much of downtown Halifax is connected by overhead pedways, making it convenient for executives in Purdy's Wharf to get around without venturing outdoors. Take the pedway to the Sheraton, built low to match the historic ironstone buildings next door. If the weather is fine, try the Sheraton's outdoor bar, right on the water, and admire the schooner ***Bluenose II*** (*see* Guided Tours, *above*).

❸ Next door are the warehouses of **Historic Properties,** dating from the early 19th century when trade and war made Halifax prosperous. They were built by such raffish characters as Enos Collins, who did business in the Collins Bank building. A privateer, smuggler, and shipper whose vessels defied Napoleon's blockade to bring American supplies to the Duke of Wellington, Collins was also a prime mover into the Halifax Banking Company, which evolved into the Royal Bank of Canada, the country's largest bank. Look up and to the right: There's the Royal Bank's office tower, three blocks away. When Collins died in 1871, at 99, he was said to be the richest man in Canada. The buildings have been taken over by quality shops and restaurants, boisterous pubs, and chic offices.

Walk along the water behind the modern Law Courts to the ❹ **Dartmouth ferry terminal,** jammed with commuters during the rush hour. The terminal is home to the oldest operational salt-water ferry service in North America, which began operation in 1732. Beyond lies the Cable Wharf, so named because it was once home to the ships that laid the undersea telegraph and telephone cables to Europe. There's a fishmarket here.

Pass the offices of the federal Department of Fisheries (other government offices are in the Central Guaranty Trust tower, across the ❺ street) and you'll arrive at the **Maritime Museum of the Atlantic,** housed in a restored chandlery and warehouse. The exhibits include an assortment of small boats once used around the coast, as well as displays describing Nova Scotia's proud heritage of sail—when the province, on its own, was one of the world's foremost shipbuilding and trading nations. There's a new exhibit on the Halifax Explosion of 1917. *1675 Lower Water St., tel. 902/424-7490 or 902/424-7491. Admission charged from June 1–Oct. 15: $3 adults, 50¢ children 5–18. Open June 1–Oct. 15, Mon.–Sat. 9–5:30 (Tues. until 8 PM), Sun. 1–5:30; Oct. 16–May 30, Mon.–Sat. 9–5, Sun. 1–5.*

The wharves outside the museum are favorite berths for visiting transatlantic yachts and sail-training ships; at any time you may find South American and European square-riggers, classic yachts, and even Viking longships. The hydrographic steamer *Acadia* is moored here permanently, after a long life of charting the coasts of Labrador and the Arctic.

At the next wharf, in summer, is Canada's naval memorial, HMCS *Sackville,* the sole survivor of a fleet of doughty little corvettes (highly maneuverable warships) that escorted convoys of ships from Halifax to England during World War II. An interpretation center (open mid-June–Sept., Mon.–Sat. 10–5, Sun. 1–5), adjacent to the ship, explains that the convoys assembled in Bedford Basin, Halifax's vast inner harbor, where the first ships were launched in the early morning and others would follow in a steady stream all day long. The last ones would still be steaming out late at night.

**Time Out** Between the Maritime Museum and Cornwallis Place (the modern office building just to the south) is an open square and playground at the bottom of Sackville Street. The square is a favorite lunchtime promenade for Halifax office workers, and a setting for concerts associated with the Atlantic Jazz Festival and performances during the Busker Festival. This is a perfect people-watching or picnic spot. Coffee shops and restaurants are within a few blocks, mostly back the way we came.

❻ Just south of the square is the **tugboat terminal,** which is about to become world famous: Andrew Cochran Associates—a local film

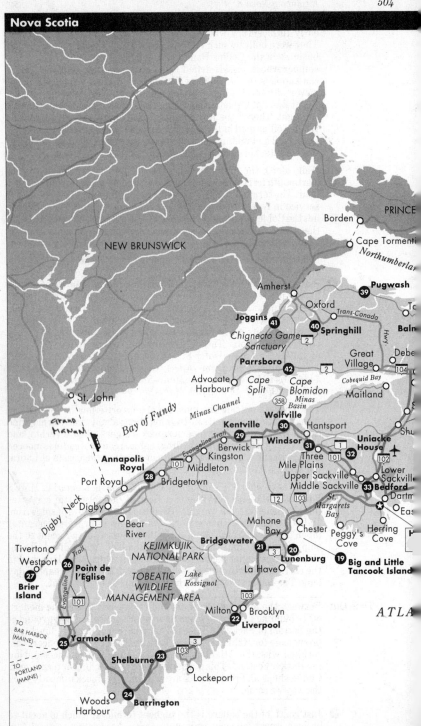

PRINCE

Borden

Cape Tormenti

*Northumberlar*

NEW BRUNSWICK

**Pugwash**

Amherst

Oxford

**39**

*Trans-Canada*

**Joggins** **41**

**40** **Springhill**

**Baln**

*Chignecto Game Sanctuary*

**2**

Great Village

Debe

**104**

**Parrsboro** **42**

**2**

*Cobequid Bay*

Advocate Harbour

*Cape Split*

*Cape Blomidon*

*Minas Basin*

Maitland

St. John

**358**

*Bay of Fundy*

*Minas Channel*

**Wolfville**

*GRAND MANAN*

**Kentville**

**30**

Hantsport

**29**

*Evangeline Trail*

Berwick

**1**

**Windsor**

**31**

**Uniacke House**

**32**

Shu

**Annapolis Royal**

Kingston

**101**

Middleton

**Bridgetown**

Three Mile Plains

**101**

Lower Sackvill

**102**

**28**

Upper Sackville

Middle Sackville

**33** **Bedford**

Port Royal

*Digby Neck*

**12**

**103**

*St. Margarets Bay*

Dartm

Digby

**1**

Bear River

Mahone Bay

Chester

Peggy's Cove

Eas

Herring Cove

H

Tiverton

Westport

**26**

*Kejimkujik National Park*

**Bridgewater**

**21**

**27**

**Brier Island**

**Point de l'Eglise**

*TOBEATIC WILDLIFE MANAGEMENT AREA*

*Lake Rossignol*

La Have

**20**

**Lunenburg**

**19** **Big and Little Tancook Island**

*Evangeline Trail*

**101**

*ATLA*

**1**

Milton

Brooklyn

TO BAR HARBOR (MAINE)

**22**

**Liverpool**

**25**

**Yarmouth**

TO PORTLAND (MAINE)

**Shelburne**

**23**

**103**

Lockeport

Woods Harbour

**24** **Barrington**

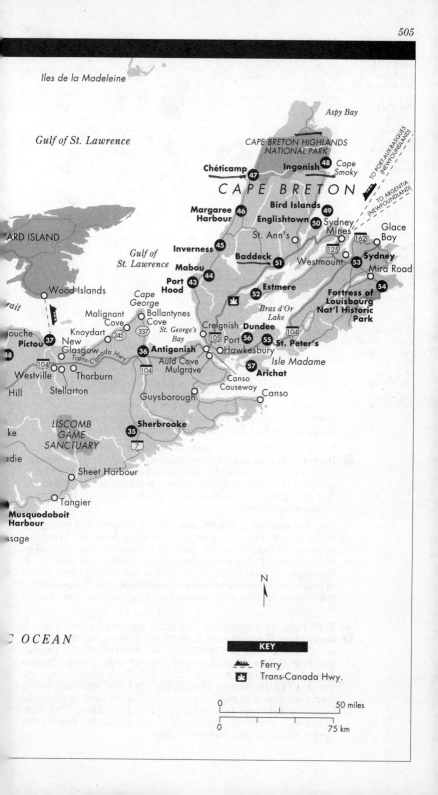

*Iles de la Madeleine*

*Gulf of St. Lawrence*

*Aspy Bay*

CAPE BRETON HIGHLANDS
NATIONAL PARK

**Chéticamp** **47**

**Ingonish** **48** *Cape
Smoky*

C A P E   B R E T O N

TO PORT-AUX-BASQUES
(NEWFOUNDLAND)

TO ARGENTIA
(NEWFOUNDLAND)

**Margaree
Harbour** **46**

**Bird Islands**

**Englishtown** **50**

**49**

Sydney
Mines

Glace
Bay

St. Ann's

**162**

**ARD ISLAND**

*Gulf of
St. Lawrence*

**Inverness** **45**

**Baddeck** **51**

Westmount

**125**

**53** **Sydney**

Mira Road

**Mabou**

**Port
Hood** **43** **44**

Wood Islands

*Cape
George*

Ballantynes
Cove

**Estmere**

**52**

*Bras d'Or
Lake*

**Dundee**

**54**

**Fortress of
Louisbourg
Nat'l Historic
Park**

Malignant
Cove

Knoydart

**245**

**337**

*St. George's
Bay*

Creignish

**105**

Port

**55** **St. Peter's**

**104**

*rait*

*ouche*

**Pictou** **37**

New
Glasgow

*Trans-Canada Hwy*

**36** **Antigonish**

**56**

Hawkesbury

*Isle Madame*

**38**

**104**

Westville

Thorburn

Auld Cove
Mulgrave

Canso
Causeway

**57**

**Arichat**

Hill

Stellarton

Guysborough

Canso

*LISCOMB
GAME
SANCTUARY*

**Sherbrooke**

**35**

**7**

*ke*

*adie*

Sheet Harbour

Tangier

**Musquodoboit
Harbour**

*ssage*

N

*C OCEAN*

| KEY | |
|---|---|
| 🚢 | Ferry |
| 🏕 | Trans-Canada Hwy. |

0                    50 miles

0                    75 km

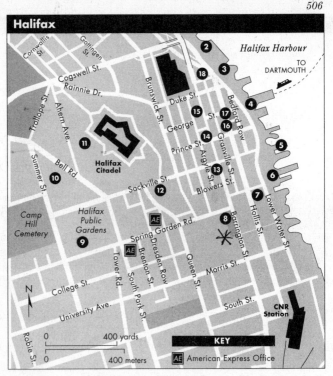

company—recently produced an animated television series called *Theodore Tugboat*, based on the ships' fictional adventures.

Leave the tugboats and walk up to Water Street and enter the ⑦ **Brewery Market,** a sprawling ironstone complex that was once Keith's Brewery (named for Alexander Keith, a 19th-century brewer) but now houses boutiques, offices, restaurants, and a Farmers' Market. This area is a favored haunt of knowledgeable Haligonians on Saturday morning.

Take the elevator at the office-end of the complex, and emerge on Hollis Street. Turn left, past several elegant Victorian townhouses—notably Keith Hall (1475 Hollis St.)—once the executive offices of the brewery. Turn right on Bishop Street and walk up to Barrington Street, Halifax's main downtown thoroughfare. Ahead of you is the **Technical University of Nova Scotia,** one of seven Halifax universities; it offers degrees in engineering, architecture, and similar fields.

Turn right on Barrington. The stone mansion on your right is ⑧ **Government House,** the official residence of Nova Scotia's Lieutenant-Governor, built in 1799 for Sir John Wentworth, the Loyalist governor of New Hampshire and his racy wife, Fanny. Thomas Raddall's novel *The Governor's Lady* tells their story. Across the street is **The Old Burying Ground,** the city's first cemetery, dating from 1749. One of its residents is General Robert Ross, leader of the attack on Baltimore in 1814 that inspired the anthem "The Star-Spangled Banner." Its Sebastopol Monument honors two Halifax heroes of the Crimean War (1853–1856).

Beyond Government House is **St. Matthew's Church** (1859), and **Maritime Centre,** a towering office block above a shopping mall. Turn left on Spring Garden Road and go past the Catholic cathedral church, **St. Mary's Basilica** (1833), with the tallest polished-granite spire in the world.

**Time Out** In the summer, the front lawn of the public library is crowded with people listening to street singers and snacking on french fries bought from **Bud the Spud,** a chip-wagon parked at the curb. Surrounding the lawn are plenty of opportunities for a more substantial take-out lunch.

**9** From the library walk west on Spring Garden Road to the South Park Street entrance of the **Halifax Public Gardens,** where the statues of Robbie Burns and Sir Walter Scott face one another from across Spring Garden Road. The gardens were first laid out in 1753, but the present design was created in 1889 by Richard Power, who had been gardener to the Duke of Devonshire. Power's descendants cared for the gardens until the 1960s. Gravel paths wind among ponds, trees, and flower beds, revealing an astonishing variety of plants from all over the world. The centerpiece is a filigreed bandstand erected in 1887 for Queen Victoria's Golden Jubilee.

**10** The **Nova Scotia Museum of Natural History,** on the South Commons, holds collections of human and natural-history artifacts and administers them to the smaller provincial museums throughout Nova Scotia. The museum is best known for its exhibits and events honoring tiny frogs known as "spring peepers." A huge fiberglass frog is mounted on the corner of the building in May and stays up until the real creatures fall silent in the autumn. *1747 Summer St., tel. 902/424–7353. Admission: $2.25 adults, 50¢ children 5–16. Open mid-May–Oct., Mon., Tues., and Thurs.–Sun. 9:30–5:30, Wed. 9:30–8; Nov.–early May, Tues. and Thurs.–Sun. 9:30–5, Wed. 9:30–8.*

**11** Between the Commons and the compact downtown rises the green bulk of **Citadel Hill,** topped by its star-shape fort. The Citadel was the heart of the city's fortifications, and was linked to smaller forts and gun emplacements on the harbor islands and on the bluffs above the entrance. It is now a National Historic Site, with kilted soldiers drilling in front of the **Army Museum,** once the barracks. A cannon is fired every day at noon. *Citadel Hill, tel. 902/426–5080. Admission: mid-June–Labor Day, $2 adults, $1 children, senior citizens free. Open July–Labor Day, daily 9–6; Labor Day–mid-June, daily 10–5.*

Most of the city's secondary fortifications have been turned into public parks. **Point Pleasant Park,** a favorite recreation spot, encompasses 186 wooded acres, veined with walking trails and seafront paths. The park was leased from the British Crown by the city for 999 years, at a shilling a year. Its major military installation is a massive round Martello tower dating from the late 18th century. Point Pleasant is about 12 blocks down South Park Street from Spring Garden Road.

The handsome four-sided **Town Clock** on Citadel Hill was given to Halifax by Prince Edward, Duke of Kent, military commander from 1794 to 1800. The prince was enamored of round buildings, of which two survive: **St. George's Church,** downtown at Brunswick and Cornwallis streets, and **Julie's Music Room,** on a knoll beside the Bedford Highway. "Julie" was the prince's French mistress, with whom he lived for more than 20 years before being summoned to marry a princess and produce an heir to the British throne. He did his duty, and the result was Queen Victoria.

Pause over the view from the Citadel, and take in the details: the spiky downtown crowded between the hilltop and the harbor; the wooded islands at the harbor's mouth; and the naval dockyard under the Angus L. MacDonald Bridge, the nearer of the two bridges connecting Halifax with its sister city of Dartmouth.

**12** From the Citadel, walk down Sackville Street toward the harbor. On your right is the **Royal Artillery Park,** with its little-known but excellent military library. The School Board building at Sackville and Brunswick streets is the old Halifax Academy, attended by author Hugh MacLennan.

**13** Farther down Sackville, where it meets Argyle Street, is the **Neptune Theatre,** Canada's first professional repertory theater, which offers full summer and winter seasons. Argyle Street is the center of the Halifax dining and nightlife scene and a lively place on a Saturday night. A block north of the theater is the **Carleton Hotel,** built of cut stone from the original Fortress of Louisbourg. The hotel, which dates from 1760, was once the home of Richard Bulkeley, one of Halifax's founders, and it later served as a Court of Admiralty.

**14** Turn left on Barrington Street. A block north is **St. Paul's Church** (1749), Canada's oldest Protestant church, Britain's first overseas cathedral, and the burial site of many colonial notables. Inside, on the north end, a piece of metal is embedded in the wall. It is a fragment of the *Mont Blanc,* one of the two ships whose collision caused the Halifax Explosion of December 6, 1917, the greatest man-made explosion prior to Hiroshima. The blast flattened a square mile of the North End and left 2,000 dead, another 2,000 seriously injured, and 6,000 homeless.

**15** Leaving St. Paul's, you will find yourself on the **Grand Parade,** facing City Hall. Musicians perform here at noon on fine summer days. From here, look uphill: The tall, stylish brick building is the **World Trade and Convention Centre** and is attached to the 10,000-seat **Halifax Metro Centre**—the site of hockey games, rock concerts, and political conventions. Farther to the right are the office towers above **Scotia Square,** the leading downtown shopping mall.

**16** Walk downhill a block, and you'll see **Province House,** "a gem of Georgian architecture," according to Charles Dickens. The provincial legislature still meets in this lovely sandstone building, erected in 1819. *Hollis St., tel. 902/424-5982. Admission free. Open weekdays 9–6, Sat. 9–4.*

**17** Across Hollis, on Cheapside—a pedestrian-way directly opposite Province House—is the **Art Gallery of Nova Scotia,** which features work by Canadian and international artists. The gallery, housed in a renovated four-story building, displays extensive collections of maritime, Canadian, and folk art, and hosts contemporary traveling exhibitions from around the world. *1741 Hollis St. at Cheapside, tel. 902/424-7542. Admission: $2.50 adults, $1.25 students and senior citizens, children under 12 free, $5.50 families. Open June–Oct., Tues, Wed., Fri., and Sat. 10–5:30, Thurs. 10–9, Sun. noon–5:30; Sept.–May, Tues–Fri. 10–5, weekends noon–5.*

Return to Province House, turn left, and go one block back to Historic Properties, where this tour began. In addition to owning the warehouses near Purdy's Wharf, Historic Properties also owns the 19th-century buildings between Granville, Duke, and Lower Water streets, at Duke. The upper floors of most of these buildings are used by the **Nova Scotia College of Art and Design** (NSCAD)—the first degree-granting arts university in Canada and a formidable influence in the world of art.

Go up the hill a block to Granville Street, past NSCAD's unobtrusive main entrance, and turn right at the Split Crow pub into the one-block **pedestrian mall** with its iron park benches, outdoor cafés, and chic shops. Near the end of the block is the **Anna Leonowens Gallery,** which belongs to NSCAD, and often shows the most challenging exhibits in Halifax. The gallery is named for the college's founder, a remarkable Victorian woman who served the King of Siam as governess and wrote a book about the experience; Rodgers and Hammerstein eventually turned it into the Broadway production of *The King and I*, starring Yul Brynner and Deborah Kerr. *1891 Granville St., tel. 902/422–7381. Admission free. Open Tues.–Fri. 11–5, Sat. noon–4.*

Turn right when you leave the gallery. At the end of the block, look toward the harbor: Just across the street is the Sheraton, *Bluenose II*, and Privateer's Warehouse. Welcome back to the beginning of the tour. From here, the tour continues on to two areas: the Northwest Arm and Dartmouth. To continue the tour it will be necessary to travel by car.

"The Arm" is Halifax's recreational secondary harbor, with a popular park, many elegant waterfront homes, and two yacht clubs. From Historic Properties, follow either Duke Street or Cogswell Street (both converge at the Commons) to Quinpool Road, a busy shopping street. Quinpool takes you to a traffic circle called the Armdale Rotary, which heads the Northwest Arm. Take the exit for Purcell's Cove Road (Rte. 253), which winds along the Arm to the pretty village of **Purcell's Cove,** and passes the Armdale Yacht Club, Flemming Park, the Royal Nova Scotia Yacht Squadron, and the historic cliff-top fortifications of York Redoubt, before ending at the tiny fishing harbor of **Herring Cove.** There is no similar shorefront drive on the Halifax side of the Arm, though several Halifax streets terminate at the Arm's shores.

**Dartmouth** is Nova Scotia's second city, but it has always been overshadowed by the capital. It was first settled by Quaker whalers from Nantucket, and boasts Canada's largest Coast Guard base and Nova Scotia's most successful industrial park, at Burnside. The 23 lakes within Dartmouth's boundaries provided the Micmacs with a canoe route to the province's interior and to the Bay of Fundy. A 19th-century canal system connected the lakes for a brief time, but today there are only ruins, which have been partially restored as heritage sites.

Halifax-Dartmouth has North America's third-largest concentration of marine scientists, mostly due to the **Bedford Institute of Oceanography,** off Windmill Road just under the A. Murray Mackay Bridge. The institute also has a substantial fleet of specialized ships and submersibles. Visitors can take self-guided walking tours of the facility, or guided tours by reservation; call ahead. *Challenger Dr., tel. 902/426–4093. Admission free. Open weekdays 9–4.*

## Tour 2: The South Shore and Annapolis Valley

Mainland Nova Scotia is a long, narrow peninsula; no point in the province is more than 56 kilometers (35 miles) from salt water. The South Shore is on the Atlantic side, the Annapolis Valley on the

Fundy side, and though they are less than an hour apart by car, the two destinations seem like different worlds.

The South Shore is rocky coast, island-dotted bays, fishing villages, and shipyards; the Valley is lumber, farms, vineyards, and orchards. The South Shore is German, French, and Yankee; the Valley is stoutly British. The South Shore is Lutheran, Catholic, and Puritan and boasts a Catholic university; the Valley university is Baptist. The sea is everywhere on the South Shore; in the Valley the sea is blocked from view by a ridge of mountains.

Highway 103, Route 3, and various secondary roads form the province's designated **Lighthouse Route,** which leads from Halifax down the South Shore. It touches the heads of several big bays and small harbors, revealing an ever-changing panorama of shoreline, inlet, and island. Charming little towns are spaced out every 50 kilometers (30 miles) or thereabouts. This tour mostly focuses on the towns along the route, but you should follow the side roads whenever the inclination strikes; the South Shore rewards slow, relaxed exploration.

Leave Halifax on Route 3 or 103—or 333, the scenic road around the shore. **St. Margaret's Bay,** just minutes from Halifax, has always been a favorite summer haunt for Haligonians and is rapidly becoming an outer suburb.

**Peggy's Cove,** on Route 333, stands at the mouth of the bay facing the open Atlantic. The cove, with its houses huddled around the narrow slit in the boulders, is probably the most photographed village in Canada. It also has the only Canadian post office located in a lighthouse (open April–November). Be careful exploring the bald, rocky shore. Incautious visitors have been swept to their deaths by the towering surf that sometimes breaks here.

**Chester,** with just over 1,100 people, is the first stop on Lunenburg County's Mahone Bay. The bay has literally hundreds of islands and, according to local claims, there is one for every day of the year. In summer Chester swells with its well-established population of U.S. visitors and Haligonians and with the sailing and yachting community. In mid-August the town celebrates **Chester Race Week,** the largest regatta in Atlantic Canada.

**⑲** A passenger-only ferry runs from the dock in Chester to **Big and Little Tancook Islands,** 8 kilometers (5 miles) out in the bay. The boat runs four times daily Monday–Thursday; six times daily Friday; and twice daily on weekend days, and costs $1 for the 45-minute trip. Reflecting its part-German heritage, Big Tancook claims to make the best sauerkraut in Nova Scotia.

Take Route 12 inland from Chester to the **Ross Farm** at New Ross. The restored 19th-century farm-cum-museum illustrates the evolution of agriculture from 1600 to 1925. *Rte. 12, New Ross, tel. 902/ 689–2210. Admission: $2.25 adults, 50¢ children 5–16, $5.50 families. Open June–mid-Oct., daily 9:30–5:30.*

The town of **Mahone Bay** presents a dramatic face to visitors: Three tall wooden churches—of different denominations—stand side by side, their images reflected in the harbor water. Once a shipbuilding community, Mahone Bay is now a crafts center and also home to the **Wooden Boat Festival,** held during the first week of August, when the works of some of Lunenburg County's top wooden-boat builders are displayed.

**㉒ Lunenburg,** about 9½ kilometers (6 miles) away, is a feast of Victorian-era architecture, wooden boats, steel draggers (a fishing boat that operates a trawl), historic inns, and good restaurants. In the center of town is a national historic district, and the fantastic old school on the hilltop is the finest remaining example of Second Empire architecture, an ornate style that began in France.

Lunenburg is also homeport to *Bluenose* and *Bluenose II* (*see* Guided Tours, *above*), the great racing schooner and its replica. Both were built at the Smith and Rhuland yard here, as was the replica of HMS *Bounty*, used in the film *Mutiny on the Bounty*.

The **Fisheries Museum of the Atlantic,** part of the Nova Scotia Museum complex, is housed in a renovated waterfront building and includes a traditional fishing schooner, the *Theresa E. Connor;* and a steel-hulled stern trawler, *Cape Sable;* as well as an aquarium; dory shop; and a wide range of displays. *Bluenose Dr., tel. 902/634–4794. Admission: $2.25 adults, 50¢ children 5–16, $5.50 families. Open June–mid-Oct., daily 9:30–5:30.*

Before leaving Lunenburg, you may want to visit the **Houston North Gallery,** which represents both trained and self-taught Nova Scotian artists and Inuit (Eskimo) soapstone carvers and printmakers. The gallery, in a large converted house, overlooks the harbor and is near the Fisheries Museum. *110 Montague St., tel. 902/634–8869. Open Feb.–Dec., Mon.–Sat. 10–6, Sun. 1–6.*

**㉑ Bridgewater,** located at the head of navigation on the La Have River, is the main market town of the South Shore. Another of those towns whose focus was shipping and shipbuilding, Bridgewater, with its more than 7,000 residents, is now sustained by the large Michelin Tire plant nearby.

Just west of Bridgewater, on Route 325, is the **Wile Carding Mill,** which was built in 1860 and retains its original machinery. The mill itself was once powered by an overshot waterwheel. *242 Victoria Rd., tel. 902/543–8233. Admission free. Open June–Sept., Mon.–Sat. 9:30–5:30, Sun. 1–5:30.*

Farther down the La Have River, at La Have on Route 331, is **Fort Point Museum,** a former lighthouse-keeper's house that's open daily in the summer.

**㉒ The Lighthouse Route winds on to **Liverpool,** on the estuary of the Mersey River. This community, settled around 1760 by New Englanders, is a fishing and paper-milling town and also serves as a convenient base for visiting the 381-square-kilometer (147-square-mile) **Kejimkujik National Park,** an inland wilderness about 45 minutes away via Route 8. The Mersey is the oldest documented canoe route on the continent; it drains Lake Rossignol, Nova Scotia's largest freshwater lake. The interior of the province here is almost entirely unsettled and is ideally explored by canoe. There is also good trout and salmon fishing. For outfitters, go into the town of Greenfield, on Route 210, off Route 8.

During the American Revolution and the War of 1812, Liverpool was a privateering center; later, it became an important shipping and trading port. In the center of town is the **Simeon Perkins House,** built in 1766, which was the former home of a prominent early settler who kept an extensive and revealing diary. The house is now part of the Queens County Museum. *109 Main St., tel. 902/354–4058. Admission free. Open June–mid-Oct., Mon.–Sat. 9:30–5:30, Sun. 1–5:30.*

The Perkins diary was used extensively by Thomas Raddall, whose internationally successful novels and stories are sometimes set in and around Liverpool. *His Majesty's Yankees* (1944) is a vivid account of a local family's deeply divided loyalties during the American Revolution, when many Nova Scotians sympathized with the rebels, not the Crown. Raddall still lives in Liverpool.

**㉓** The high noon of **Shelburne** occurred right after the Revolution, when 16,000 Loyalists briefly made it one of the largest communities in North America. Today it is a fishing and shipbuilding town situated on a superb harbor at the mouth of the Roseway River. Many of its homes date back to the Loyalists, including the **Ross-Thomson House** (9 Charlotte La., tel. 902/875–3141; open June–mid-Oct., daily 9:30–5:30), which is now a provincial museum. Also in Shelburne and worth a visit is the **Dory Shop** (Dock St.; open mid-June–mid-Sept., daily 9:30–5:30), a provincial museum property that was officially opened in 1983 by Prince Charles and Princess Diana. Dories are flat-bottom boats with flaring sides and a sharp bow, well-suited to North Atlantic waters.

South of Shelburne, from Barrington to Digby, is the most prosperous fishing region in the province. With a noticeably milder climate than the rest of Nova Scotia and easy access to the rich fishing grounds of George's Bank, fishermen can work almost year-round to bring in a rich harvest of lobster, scallops, and groundfish.

**㉔** **Barrington,** with only 349 residents, was the home of Captain Benjamin Doane, whose book *Following the Sea* is a fine, lucid account of 19th-century whaling and trading. Visit the **Barrington Woolen Mill,** built in 1884 and now a provincial museum, with the original machinery intact and exhibits on weaving wool into bolts of twills and flannels, blankets and suitings. *2368 Rte. 3, tel. 902/637–2185. Admission free. Open mid-June–Sept., Mon.–Sat. 9:30–5:30, Sun. 1:30–5:30.*

Now turn off for **Cape Sable Island,** Nova Scotia's southernmost extremity. Like Barrington, Cape Sable Island is a Yankee community, as common family names attest; everyone seems to be named "Smith" or "Nickerson." Interestingly, there is a bewildering variety of small evangelical churches, which presumably reflects the Puritan enthusiasm for irreconcilable disagreements over fine points of doctrine. The largest community on Cape Sable is **Clark's Harbour** (locally pronounced "Cla'k's Ha'bah," sounding more like a town in Massachusetts), named for Michael Swim, an early settler who could read and write. He was thus described as a clerk or, to the British, a "clark."

The famous Cape Islander fishing boat was developed here. By now you have seen hundreds of examples of them: Sitting high on the water, with its pilothouse forward and its high, flaring bow and low stern, the Cape Islander is Nova Scotia's standard inshore fishing boat. Boatbuilding (in fiberglass as well as wood) is still a thriving occupation along these shores. Successful fishermen buy new boats and sell the older ones to such less-favored regions as the Eastern Shore and Cape Breton, and many boats eventually turn up as spacious, inexpensive pleasure craft.

Upon reaching **Pubnico** you enter the Acadian milieu; from here to Digby the communities are mostly French-speaking. Favorite local fare includes *fricot*, a stew made mostly of vegetables and sometimes has rabbit meat; and rappie pie, made of meat or poultry with potatoes from which much of the starch has been removed.

You'll no doubt notice that there are no fewer than seven Pubnicos: Lower West Pubnico, Middle West Pubnico, and West Pubnico, all on the west shore of Pubnico Harbour; three East Pubnicos on the eastern shore; and just plain Pubnico, at the top of the harbor. These towns were founded by Phillipe Muis D'Entremont, and they once constituted the only barony in French Acadia. He was a prodigious progenitor: To this day, many of the people in the Pubnicos are D'Entremonts, and most of the rest are D'Eons or Amiraults.

You'll also notice the Acadian flag, tricolored with a gold star representing *stella maris*, the star of the sea. The star guides the Acadians during troubled times, which have been frequent. In 1755, after residing for a century and a half in Nova Scotia, chiefly in the Annapolis Valley, the Acadians were expelled by the British—an event that inspired Longfellow's famous *Evangeline*. Some eluded capture and others slowly crept back, and many settled in New Brunswick and along this shore of Nova Scotia.

**㉕** The next stop en route is **Yarmouth**, the largest town in southern Nova Scotia, the biggest port west of Halifax, and the point of entry for travelers arriving by ferry from Maine. Its population is relatively big, as well, with 8,500 people. The ferries are a major reason for Yarmouth's prosperity, as they pull in much revenue by providing quick, inexpensive access for merchants and consumers going to the Boston market for fish, pulpwood, boxes and barrels, knitwear, Irish moss, Christmas trees, and berries.

In the 19th century Yarmouth was an even bigger shipbuilding center than most, and its location put the port on all the early steamship routes. The award-winning **Yarmouth County Museum**, housed in a late-19th-century church, does a fine job of unraveling the region's history with its displays of period furniture, costumes, tools, and toys, as well as a significant collection of ship models and paintings. *22 Collins St., tel. 902/742–5539. Admission: $1 adults, 50¢ students, 25¢ children under 14, $2.50 families. Open June–mid-Oct., Mon.–Sat. 9–5, Sun. 1–5; mid-Oct.–May, Tues.–Sat. 2–5.*

Yarmouth has another museum that's surprisingly interesting: The **Firefighters Museum of Nova Scotia**, located one block from the waterfront, presents the evolution of fire fighting through its displays of equipment from the leather bucket to the chemical spray. *451 Main St., tel. 902/742–5525. Admission: $1 per person, $2 families. Open June, Mon.–Sat. 9–5; July and Aug., Mon.–Sat. 9–9, Sun. 10–5; Sept., Mon.–Sat. 9–5; Oct.–May, weekdays 10–noon and 2–4.*

The Lighthouse Route ends here, and the **Evangeline Trail** begins, winding along the shore of St. Mary's Bay, through a succession of Acadian villages collectively known as the French Shore. The villages blend seamlessly into one another for about 32 kilometers (nearly 20 miles), each one, it seems, with its own wharf, fish plant, and enormous Catholic church. Hence, this part of Route 1 is sometimes called "the longest main street in the world."

Along this shore and through Nova Scotia as far east as Truro are nondescript shops called Frenchy's. "Frenchy" refers to Ed Theriault of Meteghan, who hit upon the idea of importing quality used clothing in bulk from Boston and selling it at flat-rate bargain prices. Normally it costs as much to dry-clean the clothes as it does to buy them. Today, even well-heeled Nova Scotians root through the tables at Frenchy's.

**❷❻ Point de l'Eglise** (Church Point), past Meteghan River, is the site of **Université Ste-Anne,** the only French-language institution among Nova Scotia's 17 degree-granting colleges and universities. Founded in 1891, this small university is a focus of Acadian studies and culture in the province.

**St. Mary's Church** (1905) at Point de l'Eglise is the tallest and largest wooden church in North America, at 58 meters (190 feet) long and 56 meters (185 feet) high. The steeple requires 40 tons of rock ballast to keep it steady in the ocean winds. **St. Bernard,** just a few miles farther and marking the end of the French Shore, has an equally impressive granite gothic church, which seats 1,000 people. Built entirely by local people, beginning in 1910, this monument took 40 years to complete.

The other side of St. Mary's Bay is known as Digby Neck. To explore it, drive on to Digby and follow Route 217. Digby Neck is actually a long basalt peninsula extended seaward by two narrow islands, **❷❼** Long Island and **Brier Island.** On the far side is the mouth of the Bay of Fundy; ferries going between the islands have to crab sideways against the ferocious Fundy tidal streams that course back and forth through the narrow gaps. The ferries operate hourly, 24 hours a day, and are free to pedestrians ($1 for cars). One of the boats is called *Joshua Slocum* and the other is *Spray;* the former is named for Westport's most famous native, and the latter for the 11-meter (36-foot) oyster sloop, which he rebuilt and in which he became the first man to single-handedly circumnavigate the world, in 1894–96. At the southern tip of Brier Island is a cairn commemorating the voyage.

An important stop on the "Atlantic Flyway," Brier Island is an excellent spot for bird-watching; because the surrounding waters are rich in plankton they attract a variety of whales, including fins, humpbacks, minkes, and right whales, as well as harbor porpoises. Whale-watching tours are available through several companies, including **Pirate's Cove Whale Cruises** (Rte. 217, Tiverton, Long Island, tel. 902/839–2242; $33 adults, $16.50 children 6–14) which operates from June through October.

**Digby** is the terminus of the ferry service from Saint John, New Brunswick, and an important fishing port with several good restaurants and a major resort, The Pines. The town is particularly famous for its scallops and for smoked herring known as "Digby Chicks." Digby is located on the almost-landlocked Annapolis Basin, into which the Annapolis River flows after its long course through the valley that bears its name.

Swing inland to **Bear River,** a jewel of a village with a large arts-and-crafts community; or follow the shore of the Basin to the **Upper Clements Park,** a theme park that celebrates Nova Scotia's crafts and heritage and has a variety of rides and attractions, including a waterslide, carousel, and roller coaster. *Box 99, Clementsport, tel. 902/532–7557 or 800/565–PARK in Atlantic provinces. Admission free, but visitors pay for rides. Open June, weekends 10–7; July and Aug., daily 10–7; Sept., weekends 10–7.*

**❷❽** At the head of the Annapolis Basin is **Annapolis Royal,** the oldest European settlement in Canada, founded in 1605. Samuel de Champlain called it Port Royal and established his settlement 8 kilometers (5 miles) down the opposite side of the Basin; the settlement has been reconstructed and is now **Port Royal National Historic Site.** *Tel. 902/532–2898. Admission free. Open mid-May–mid-Oct., daily 9–6.*

**Fort Anne National Historic Site** was fortified in 1643; the present structures are the remains of the fourth fort erected here and garrisoned by the British as late as 1854. The officers' quarters are now a museum, with exhibits on the site's history. *On the waterfront, tel. 902/532–2397. Admission free. Open mid-May–mid-Oct., daily 9–6; mid-Oct.–mid-May, weekdays 9–6.*

Annapolis Royal was Nova Scotia's first capital and first military base. Local businesses (or the tourist information center, located in the Annapolis Royal Tidal Power Building; *see below*) can provide *Footprints with Footnotes*, a self-guided walking tour of the town; guided tours leave from the lighthouse on St. George Street, daily at 10 and 2:30.

Don't miss the **Annapolis Royal Historic Gardens,** 10 acres of magnificent theme gardens connected to the wildlife sanctuary, maintained by Ducks Unlimited. *441 St. George St., tel. 902/532–7018. Admission: $3.50 adults, $3 children and senior citizens, $9.75 families. Open mid-May–mid-Oct., daily 8–dusk.*

Located just ¼ mile from Annapolis Royal on the causeway that crosses the Annapolis River to the Granville Ferry is the **Annapolis Royal Tidal Power Project.** Designed to test the feasibility of generating electricity from tidal energy, this pilot project is the only saltwater generating station in existence. The interpretation center explains the process. *Tel. 902/532–5454. Admission free. Open mid-May–mid-June, daily 9–5:30; mid-June–Aug., daily 9–8; Sept.–mid-Oct., daily 9–5:30.*

The **Annapolis Valley** runs northeast like a huge trench, flat on the bottom, sheltered on both sides by the long ridges of the North and South mountains. Occasional roads over the South Mountain lead to the South Shore; short roads over the North Mountain lead to the Fundy shore. The rich soil of the valley bottom supports dairy herds, hay, grain, root vegetables, tobacco, grapes, plums, strawberries, peaches, pears, cherries, and apples, apples, apples. The best time to visit? Apple blossom season: late May and early June.

Like the South Shore, the Valley is punctuated with pleasant small towns, each with a generous supply of extravagant Victorian homes and churches. (Annapolis Royal is especially well supplied with imposing mansions, particularly along the upper end of St. George Street.) For most visitors, the Valley towns go by like charming milestones, among them: Bridgetown, Lawrencetown, Aylesford, Greenwood, Berwick. Each has its distinctions: the Gallery at Saratoga in **Bridgetown** features the paintings of Kenneth Tolmie, whose works reveal Valley scenes and hang in many leading galleries, including the National Gallery of Canada; **Lawrencetown** is the site of the Nova Scotia College of Geographical Sciences, which offers internationally recognized training in cartography, surveying, and various applications of high-technology to geography. **Aylesford** has a farm zoo; **Greenwood** is the home of Canada's antisubmarine aircraft squadrons; **Berwick** is the birthplace (1885) of Alfred Fuller, the original Fuller Brush man. Most of the Valley towns have small museums. But the major impression of the region is one of tranquillity: lush farmland and a settled agricultural society.

Kentville, New Minas, Greenwich, and Wolfville run into one another almost like the towns of the French Shore; their more than 12,000  residents form the Valley's largest urban cluster. At **Kentville, Agriculture Canada** (tel. 902/678–1093) maintains an important research station on horticulture and poultry; the grounds are beautiful, and free guided tours can be arranged from June through August, week-days 8–4:30.

**⓲ Wolfville,** a bucolic college town, is the seat of Acadia University. The school's **Beveridge Art Centre** (Acadia University, Highland Ave., tel. 902/542–2201; open Sept.–May, Tues.–Fri. 11–5, week-ends 1–4; June–Aug., daily noon–5) includes several works by Alex Colville, the internationally celebrated magical realist painter who lives on Wolfville's main thoroughfare and has served as Acadia's Chancellor.

At Greenwich, take Route 358 to Cape Blomidon via Port Williams and Canning for a spectacular view of the Valley and the Bay of Fundy from **The Lookoff.** Cape Blomidon itself rises 231 meters (760 feet) from the Bay. Continue to **Scots Bay,** where rock shelves contain ribbons of amethyst, jasper, and carnelian. A popular hiking trail leads from the end of Route 358 to the dramatic cliffs of Cape Split.

Beyond Wolfville is **Grand Pré,** once a major Acadian site, where a small stone church, at the Grand Pré National Historic Site (open mid-May–mid-Oct., daily 9–6), commemorates Longfellow's hero-ine Evangeline, and houses an exhibit on the 1755 deportation of the Acadians from the Valley.

**⓲ Windsor,** the last of the Valley towns, was settled in 1703 as an Aca-dian community, and **Fort Edward** (no phone; open mid-June–Labor Day, daily 10–6)—one of the assembly points for the expulsion of the Acadians—still stands as the only remaining colonial blockhouse in Nova Scotia. Flora Macdonald, the Scottish heroine who helped Bonnie Prince Charlie escape to France, spent the winter of 1779 in Windsor while her husband was posted at the fort.

Windsor is also the home of Judge Thomas Chandler Haliburton—lawyer, politician, historian, and humorist. His best-known work, *The Clockmaker*, pillories Nova Scotian follies from the viewpoint of a Yankee clockmaker. **Haliburton's Home** (Clifton Ave., tel. 902/798–2915; open mid-May–mid-Oct., Mon.–Sat. 9:30–5:30, Sun. 1–5:30), set on a manicured 25-acre estate, now belongs to the Nova Scotia Museum.

The tide's average rise and fall at Windsor is over 40 feet, and you can see the tidal bore (the leading edge of the incoming tide) rushing up the Meander River and sometimes reaching a height of 3 feet. The local tourist office (902/798–2690) can tell you estimated tide times.

Continuing along the Evangeline Trail, Halifax is only about 45 min-utes away, but one site 30 miles (18 miles) from Windsor deserves **⓲** attention: **Uniacke House,** built about 1815 for Richard John Uniacke. During the American Revolution, Uniacke, who was fight-ing on the rebel side, was captured in Cumberland County, just across the Bay of Fundy. The young Irishman was released through some hazy politics and came to Nova Scotia seeking his fortune. He eventually found it as Attorney-General and Advocate-General to the Admiralty Court, where his fees in one three-year period during the War of 1812 amounted to the stupendous sum of £50,000. Some of that money went into Uniacke House, a superb example of colonial architecture, situated on spacious grounds near a lake. The house, which is now part of the Nova Scotia Museum, is preserved in its original condition with many authentic furnishings. *758 Windsor Hwy., tel. 902/866–2560. Admission free. Open mid-May–mid-Oct., Mon.–Sat., 9:30–5:30, Sun. 1–5:30.*

Highway 101 cuts across the peninsula through gypsum hills to
**❸ Bedford,** at the head of Bedford Basin. Once a toney summer resort,
Bedford is now a favored suburb of Halifax. Follow the Bedford
Highway to Halifax, noting **Julie's Music Room** (*see* Tour 1) as you
pass through Prince's Lodge. If you take Windsor Street downtown,
you will be following the 18th-century route between Windsor and
Halifax—a proper conclusion to a memorable tour.

## Tour 3: Northern Nova Scotia

This tour takes in parts of three of the official Scenic Trails, including **Marine Drive, The Sunrise Trail,** and **The Glooscap Trail.** Any one
leg of the route could be done comfortably as an overnight trip from
Halifax; for the whole tour, allow three or four days.

Pick up Route 7 at Dartmouth. The Eastern Shore—the Atlantic
coast east of Halifax-Dartmouth—is perhaps the most scenic and
unspoiled stretch of coastline in mainland Nova Scotia. Because it is
unspoiled, of course, the Eastern Shore's facilities are relatively few
and simple. The road winds along a deeply indented, glaciated
coastline of rocky waters interspersed with pocket beaches, long
narrow fjords, and fishing villages. Take the time to prowl the side
roads and discover your own favorite rock pools and islets—there
are plenty to find.

**❸ Musquodoboit Harbour,** with about 930 residents, is a substantial
village at the mouth of the Musquodoboit River, just east of
Dartmouth. The river itself offers good trout and salmon fishing,
and the village touches on two slender and lovely harbors. One of the
Eastern Shore's best beaches, **Martinique Beach,** is about 12 kilometers (8 miles) south of the village, and other fine beaches are at Clam
Bay and Clam Harbour, several kilometers (a few miles) east of Martinique.

The pretty villages slip by: Jeddore, Salmon River, Lake Charlotte.
An increasingly important part of their economies is aquaculture:
Nearby, in **Ship Harbour,** the provincial Department of Fisheries
has developed an aquaculture **Demonstration Centre** (Rte. 7, tel.
902/845–2991; admission free; open May–Sept., weekdays 9–3),
with a small interpretive center on the hatchery, open to the public.
As you travel a bit farther, take note of the strings of white buoys in
Ship Harbour, marking North America's largest cultivated mussel
farm.

This part of the shore experienced a small gold rush during the first
part of this century, complete with a 1936 mine disaster, during
which the first live, on-the-spot radio newscasts were made throughout Canada and the world. A small local museum at **Moose River Gold
Mines,** about 30 kilometers (19 miles) north of Tangier, commemorates the period. *Rte. 224, tel. 902/384–2630. Admission free. Open
late–June–Labor Day, Tues.–Sat. 10–5, Sun. 1–6.*

**Time Out**  Don't fail to stop in Tangier for some delicious smoked salmon, eel,
or mackerel from **Willy Krauch's Danish Smokehouse** (Rte. 7, tel.
902/772–2188; open Apr.–Christmas, daily 8–7; Christmas–Apr.,
daily 8–5).

**Sheet Harbour** is the major service center for the Eastern Shore,
with a bank, hospital, accommodations, and campgrounds. Like
Musquodoboit, this town straddles two harbors, one of which ships
pulpwood to Europe.

The road winds on through a string of uniquely named villages: Necum Teuch, Ecum Secum, Marie Joseph, Spanish Ship Bay. The latter was named for a ghostly galleon, which is said to enter the harbor in flames every seven years. Just beyond, at Liscomb Mills, is Liscomb Lodge, a full-service resort with a very respectable restaurant.

 The next major center is **Sherbrooke,** which has fewer than 400 residents, but is the Shore's leading tourist center. The St. Mary's River, which flows through the hamlet, is one of Nova Scotia's best salmon rivers, and much of the village itself has been rebuilt by the Nova Scotia Museum to its late 19th-century character, with a blacksmith shop, water-powered sawmill, horse-drawn wagons, tearooms, and stores. Twenty-five buildings have been restored on their original sites for the living history village. *Tel. 902/522–2400. Admission: $2.25 adults, 50¢ children under 16. Open June–mid-Oct., daily 9:30–5:30.*

From Sherbrooke you'll have to decide in which direction you wish to go. Marine Drive continues down the shore through wild, harsh, lovely country rarely visited by tourists. To see Nova Scotia unbuttoned, as it were, follow the Drive down to **Canso,** and pick up the Trans-Canada Highway via Guysborough. You will find few tourist attractions, although Canso itself has a stirring history and a National Historic Site; in this part of the province you'll come closer to traditional Nova Scotian ways of life than you will anywhere else.

The alternative is to stay on Route 7, which turns inland up the St. Mary's River through spruce woods and rolling farmland to Antigonish, an hour's drive away. The drive takes you from the Atlantic to the Northumberland Strait, part of the Gulf of St. Lawrence: from cold water and rocky shores to warm water and broad sandy beaches. If water sports are your thing, this is your shore: there are miles of wonderful beaches all along Northumberland Strait.

**Antigonish** is the home of **St. Francis Xavier University,** a center for Gaelic studies and for the co-operative movement. Its Coady International Institute offers training to co-op and credit union workers from foreign countries. It's also a cathedral town with a population of about 5,200.

Follow Route 337, the Sunrise Trail, for a glorious drive along St. George's Bay with its many good swimming beaches, before the road abruptly climbs 1,000 feet up and over to **Cape George.**

---

**Time Out** There's a little take-out shop on the wharf at **Ballantyne's Cove,** a tiny artificial harbor near the tip of Cape George, that is said to have the best fish-and-chips in Nova Scotia. Grab an order and enjoy the views.

---

After following the Cape, high above the sea, the road runs along Northumberland Strait through lonely farmlands and tiny villages, such as Arisaig and Lismore. If, after hearing those names, you have any doubt about the Scottish origin of the people, they will be laid to rest by a stone cairn in Lismore that commemorates Bonnie Prince Charlie's Highland rebels, slaughtered by the English at Culloden in 1746.

Much of the rest of the road runs inland, but the turnoff to Merigomish leads into a maze of inlets, beaches, and islands that are well worth exploring. Either way you go, you'll eventually emerge at Highway 104, the Trans-Canada. Turn right a kilometer and a half (a mile) later, and follow the shore road to **Melmerby Beach**—a favorite local spot—and continue on to New Glasgow by a circuitous shoreside road. Alternatively, stay on the Trans-Canada to reach New Glasgow a few kilometers (2 miles) away.

**New Glasgow** is one of five industrial towns on the three rivers that flow into Pictou Harbour. Combined, the five towns have a population of nearly 30,000, making this one of the largest urban centers in the province. New Glasgow is a steel-fabricating and manufacturing center, **Trenton** manufactures railway cars, and **Westville** and **Stellarton** are coal-mining towns.

 For the visitor, the most interesting town by far is **Pictou,** somewhat sullied by a papermill across the harbor, but nevertheless one of the most engaging communities in Nova Scotia. Lining its streets are typically Scottish-style stone cottage homes and public buildings, and there's a good selection of very attractive small hotels and restaurants. Using the main highway system, Pictou can be reached in about two hours from Halifax.

In 1773, the *Hector*—the nearest thing to a Canadian *Mayflower*—came to Pictou Harbour, inaugurating the torrent of Scottish immigration that permanently altered the character of the province and the nation. A replica of the *Hector* is under construction at the *Hector Heritage Quay* (tel. 902/485–8028; admission charged).

Under the inspired leadership of such men as the pioneering educator Thomas McCulloch, Pictou quickly became a center of commerce, education, theological disputation, and radical politics. **McCulloch House,** a restored 1806 building with displays of McCulloch's scientific collection and such personal items as furniture, is preserved as part of the Nova Scotia Museum. *Old Haliburton Rd., tel. 902/485–4563. Admission free. Open June–mid-Oct., Mon.–Sat. 9:30–5:30, Sun. 11:30–5:30; mid-Oct.–May, weekdays 9–5.*

Leave Pictou on Route 6, the Sunrise Trail. The road runs beside an apparently endless string of beaches, with many summer homes plunked in the adjoining fields. **River John** is a good meal stop, especially during May, June, and July, when the community prepares lobster suppers, or in August, when chicken barbecues are on the menu.

At Brule, take Route 326, then turn right on Route 256 to reach the  water-powered gristmill at **Balmoral Mills** (1860), the oldest operating mill in Nova Scotia, and one of five that once operated on this stream. It is now a museum with milling demonstrations, and the grounds include a picnic park. *Tel. 902/657–3016. Admission free. Open June–mid-Oct., Mon.–Sat. 9:30–5:30, Sun. 1–5:30. Demonstrations 10–noon.*

Follow Route 256 to Route 311 and turn right to rejoin the Sunrise Trail. **Tatamagouche,** a market center for farmers and fishermen, is beautifully situated on a ridge overlooking a small estuarine harbor. Beyond Tatamagouche, turn right to Malagash to find **Jost Vineyards** (tel. 902/257–2636 or 800/565–4567 in Canada), one of three farm wineries in the province. Jost produces a surprisingly wide range of very acceptable wines, and offers tours at 3 PM daily, from mid-June through September.

The road continues through the small community of Wallace, on another small harbor, to **Pugwash.** This was the home of Cleveland industrialist Cyrus Eaton, at whose estate numerous Thinkers' Conferences brought together leading intellectual figures from the

West and the Soviet Union during the 1950s and 1960s. Pugwash is still Scottish terrain, as the Gaelic street signs attest. The town is also the home of **Seagull Pewter** (Durham St., tel. 902/243–2516) a husband-and-wife crafts operation that has grown into a $25-million business of exporting pewter vessels, picture frames, and other artifacts worldwide. The showroom fronts on the main highway.

From Pugwash, a half-hour drive will take you to Amherst, through rolling hills and along the edge of Amherst Marsh, part of the Tantramar Marsh. The Tantramar covers most of the Isthmus of Chignecto, the narrow neck of land that joins Nova Scotia to the rest of North America, and it is said to be the largest marsh in the world. If you have not yet had your fill of sandy beaches, however, an attractive alternative route leads through Northport, Lorneville, and Tidnish Dock.

**Amherst** stands on one of the glacial ridges that borders the Tantramar Marsh. Like New Glasgow, Truro, Oxford, and several other towns along what is now the Canadian National main line, Amherst was once a thriving manufacturing center for many products, including pianos and furnaces. During World War II, Amherst's aerospace factories (which still survive, but on a much smaller scale) built hundreds of Anson bombers. The town is historically significant for another reason: In 1917, en route from New York to Russia, the Communist leader Leon Trotsky was confined here for a month in a prisoner-of-war camp.

From Amherst, a two-hour drive via Highways 104 and 102 will return you directly to Halifax. However, the Glooscap Trail from Amherst through Parrsboro to Truro is much more interesting and takes only about an hour longer. Relatively few tourists travel the latter route, which provides some of the most striking scenery in Nova Scotia.

If you opt for the Glooscap Trail, there are several roads that connect Amherst and Parrsboro. Route 2 leads through the coal-mining
**40** town of **Springhill,** the site of the famous mine disaster immortalized in the folk song "The Ballad of Springhill" by Peggy Seeger and Ewen McColl, and hometown of singer Anne Murray, whose career is celebrated in the **Anne Murray Centre** (Main St., tel. 902/597–8614; admission $5 adults, $4 senior citizens, $3.50 children 7–12, $2 children 3–6; open May–Oct., daily 9–5). Routes 2 and 302 offer the most direct passage to Parrsboro, running through tall hills and farmland to join Route 2 at Southampton.

An alternative—and better—option is to take the Glooscap Trail,
**41** which branches off via Route 242 to **Joggins,** where coal age fossils are embedded in 150-foot sandstone cliffs. Visit the **Joggins Fossil Centre,** where you can learn about the region's geological and archaeological history. Also, guided tours of the fossil cliffs are available, but departure times depend on the tides. *30 Main St., tel. 902/ 251–2727. Admisson to center: $3.50 adults, $3 senior citizens, $2 children 5–18. Admission for tours: $10 adults, $8 senior citizens, $4 children 5–18. Open June–Sept., daily 9–6:30.*

From Joggins, the Glooscap Trail runs along the shore of Chignecto Bay through Shulie and Sand River to Apple River. You are now on the Bay of Fundy, the third coastline of this tour, where stupendous volumes of water rushing into a narrow shelving bay create the world's highest tides, which sometimes reach heights of 50 feet. **Advocate Harbour** was named by Champlain for his friend Marc Lescarbot, who was a lawyer, or "avocat." Built on flat shore land with a tall ridge backdrop and a broad harbor before it, Advocate is eerily beautiful. The road continues past the spectacular lighthouse at **Cape d'Or,** a piece of land that juts out and divides the waters of the main Bay of Fundy from the narrow enclosure of the Minas Basin. As the tides change, fierce riptides create spectacular waves. The view from the ridge down to the lighthouse is superb; the view from the lighthouse itself is almost equally magnificent, but the road down is rather primitive and should be attempted only in four-wheel drive vehicles.

Route 209 continues through the 19th-century shipbuilding communities of **Spencer's Island** and **Port Greville.** A cairn at Spencer's Island commemorates the construction of the famous *Mary Celeste*, which was found in 1872, sailing in the mid-Atlantic without a crew; she had been abandoned at sea with the table still set for dinner.

**42** **Parrsboro,** a center for rockhounds and fossil hunters, is the main town on this shore, and hosts the annual **Rockhound Roundup,** held every August. Among the exhibits and festivities are geological displays, concerts, and other special events. The **Fundy Geological Museum** (Two Island Rd., tel. 902/254–3814; $3 adults, $1 youth 12–16, 50¢ children 6–12, $6.50 families) sustains geologists' interests year-round with geology exhibits from the days of the dinosaurs to present. Parrsboro is an appropriate setting for the new museum since it's not far from the site where the world's smallest dinosaur fossils were found. These tiny fossils, now on display, are 200 million years old, and represent the grandmother and grandfather of larger dinosaurs. The museum also has displays of the amethysts and agates that wash out of nearby cliffs; hunting for them is a favorite pastime of the town's visitors. The museum offers workshops on jewelry-making by advance booking.

Fossils are Parrsboro's claim to fame, but this harbor town was also a major shipping and shipbuilding port, and its history is described at the **Ottawa House Museum-by-the-Sea.** Ottawa House, which occupies a striking location overlooking the Bay of Fundy, was the summer home of Sir Charles Tupper, a former Premier of Nova Scotia who was briefly Prime Minister of Canada. *Whitehall Rd., tel. 902/254–2376. Admission: $1. Open July–early Sept., daily 10–8.*

From Parrsboro, Route 2 runs along the shore of the Minas Basin to Truro. Almost 5 kilometers (about 3 miles) from Parrsboro is the 125-foot-high **Hidden Falls** (tel. 902/254–2505; admission free; open mid-May–Nov.). The gift shop here is a jumble of antique furniture, books, crockery, and bric-a-brac that warrants a visit.

Among the most beautiful scenic areas along Route 2 is **Five Islands,** which, according to Micmac legend, was created when the god Glooscap threw handfuls of sod at Beaver. A provincial park on the shore of Minas Bay includes a campground, a beach, hiking trails, and some interpretation of the region's unusual geology.

Route 2 rejoins the Trans-Canada (Highway 104) at **Glenholme.** From here it is a 75-minute drive to Halifax.

## Tour 4: Cape Breton Island

Allow three or four days for this meandering tour that begins by entering the island via the Canso Causeway on Highway 104; turn left at the rotary, and take Route 19, the Ceilidh Trail. The road winds along the mountainside, with fine views across St. George's Bay to Cape George. This western shoreline of Cape Breton faces the Gulf of St. Lawrence, and is famous for its sandy beaches and warm salt water.

If Halifax is the heart of Nova Scotia, Cape Breton is its soul, complete with soul music: flying fiddles, boisterous rock, velvet ballads. Cape Breton musicians—weaned on Scottish jigs and reels—are among Canada's finest, and you can hear them all over the island, all summer long, at dozens of local festivals and concerts (*see* Festivals and Seasonal Events in Chapter 1).

**43** **Port Hood,** with its fine beaches, is the first stop on this tour. Visit **Port Hood Island,** whose 17 traditional homes are now used primarily as a summer retreat by urban refugees. The island has scenic hills, rock formations on the shore, sandy beaches, and warm waters. It's accessible only by an informal ferry operated by Bertie Smith (tel. 902/787–2515), the island's last year-round resident.

**44** On the way from Port Hood to **Mabou,** the land lies low until Mabou Harbour, where it rises abruptly to the tall hills of the Mabou Highlands. Mabou itself has been called "the prettiest village in Canada," and it is also perhaps the most Scottish, with its Gaelic signs and a deep tradition of Scottish music and dancing. This is the hometown of national recording and performing artists, such as John Allan Cameron and the Rankin Family; stop at a local gift shop and pick up some tapes to play as you drive down the long fjord of Mabou Harbour to **Mabou Mines.** The mines is a place so hauntingly exquisite that you expect to meet the *sidhe,* the Scottish fairies, capering on the hillsides. Within these hills is some of the finest hiking in the province, and above the land fly bald eagles, plentiful in this region. Inquire locally or at the tourist office on Margaree Forks for information about trails. The Ceilidh Trail winds on through green wooded glens and hidden farms.

**45** The road continues through **Inverness,** a fishing port and former coal-mining town with many services, and on to **Broad Cove,** the site of one of the most venerable Cape Breton Scottish concerts, held annually in late July. The road forks at **Dunvegan,** the home of Alastair MacLeod, whose powerful short stories pierce deeply into the life of these Scottish communities. Look for his collections *The Lost Salt Gift of Blood* or *As Birds Bring Forth the Sun* for a better understanding of the region.

Take Route 219 at Dunvegan, following the coast through **Chimney Corner** and **Whale Cove.** One of the beaches near Chimney Corner has "sonorous sands": When you step on the sand or drag a foot through it, it squeaks and moans. The Ceilidh Trail joins the Cabot **46** Trail at **Margaree Harbour** at the mouth of the Margaree River, a famous salmon-fishing stream and a favorite canoe route. Stop at the schooner *Marion Elizabeth,* now the Schooner Village restaurant and free museum, with many small shops and a good selection of books about Cape Breton. On the grounds is writer Farley Mowat's schooner *Happy Adventure,* featured in his book *The Boat That Wouldn't Float.*

The Margaree River is a cultural dividing line: South of the river the settlements are Scottish, up the river they are largely Irish, and north of the river they are Acadian French. The Cabot Trail crosses the river and runs along the shore through Belle Côte and **Cap Le Moine.** Don't miss Joe Delaney's whimsical scarecrow farm and gift shop at Cap Le Moine (Cabot Trail, tel. 902/235–2108). Most of the harbors on this bold, straight coast are the estuaries of small rivers, with treacherous sandbars at their mouths. Stop at **Friar's Head** and look over the cliff: The tiny cleft in the rocks below was long used as a fishing harbor.

**47** **Chéticamp,** an Acadian community, is the best harbor and the largest settlement on the shore. With its tall silver steeple towering over the village, it stands exposed on a wide lip of flat land below a range of bald green hills, behind which lies the high plateau of the Cape Breton Highlands. Cheticamp is famous for its hooked rugs, available at many local gift shops, and for whale cruises, which depart in June, once daily; July and August, three times daily from the government wharf. **Whale Cruisers Ltd.** (tel. 902/224–3376) is one of the reliable charter companies in the area. Cruises cost $25 for adults, $10 for children 6–12.

At the outskirts of Cheticamp begins **Cape Breton Highlands National Park,** a 597-square-kilometer (370-square-mile) wilderness of wooded valleys, plateau barrens, and steep cliffs that stretches across the northern peninsula of Cape Breton from the Gulf Shore to the Atlantic. The highway through the park is magnificent, as it rises to the tops of the coastal mountains and descends through tight switchbacks to the sea. For wildlife watchers there's much to see, including moose, eagle, deer, bear, fox, and bobcat. *Tel. in summer 902/285–2535, in winter 902/285–2270. Admission June–Sept.: $5 per vehicle per day, $10 for 4-day pass, $20 for annual pass. Admission free in winter. No charge for vehicles passing through on Cabot Trail. Camping fees: $11 for tent camping, $17 for full hookup.*

**Pleasant Bay** is a tiny village in a cleft of the mountains, where the Grande Anse River reaches the sea. A spur road creeps along the cliffs to Red River, beyond which is **Gampo Abbey**—the only Tibetan Buddhist monastery in America—situated on a broad flat bench of land high above the sea. The main road climbs North Mountain, past the trail to **Lone Shieling,** a re-creation of a Scottish crofter's cottage. The cottage, about a 20-minute scenic walk from the highway, includes displays about the region's history and flora. Its name is taken from the anonymous "Canadian Boat Song," which expresses yearnings for the emigrants' lost Scottish home:

*From the lone sheiling on the misty island*
*Mountains divide us, and the waste of seas;*
*But still the blood is strong, the heart is Highland*
*And we in dreams behold the Hebrides.*

The most northerly tip of the island is not part of the National Park; turn off to discover **Bay St. Lawrence** and **Meat Cove,** set in an amphitheatre of bare green hills, and looking northward to the killer island of **St. Paul's,** site of more than 60 charted shipwrecks. Whale-watching cruises are available June through August, three times daily, through **Whale Watch Bay St. Lawrence** (tel. 902/383–2981); the cost is $22 for adults, $11 for children 6–12.

The main road reenters the park near **Cabot's Landing,** the long sandy beach in Aspy Bay where Cape Breton folks believe that John Cabot made his landfall in 1497; this theory, however, is vigorously denied in Newfoundland. Dingwall, in the center of the bay, is an archetypal fishing village; so are White Point, New Haven, and Neil's Harbour.

**48** **Ingonish,** one of the leading holiday destinations on the island, is actually several villages on two bays, divided by a long narrow peninsula called Middle Head. Each bay has a sandy beach, and Middle Head is home to the provincially owned **Keltic Lodge,** a first-class hotel and resort complex. The hamlet offers a wide range of activities, among them, downhill and cross-country skiing, golfing, swimming, and hiking. Stop at **Lynn's Craft Shop and Art Gallery** (on Hwy., tel.

902/285–2735), which offers the work of noted local artist Christopher Gorey and others.

The road serpentines up Cape Smokey and along the face of the mountains, offering spectacular views from high above the sea. **Wreck Cove** is the headquarters of *Cape Breton's Magazine,* an award-winning oral-history publication whose homespun appearance belies its essential sophistication. Look for it on newsstands throughout the island.

Notice the small islands on the far side of the mouth of St. Ann's Bay:  These are the **Bird Islands,** breeding grounds for Atlantic puffins, black guillemots, razor-billed auks, and cormorants. Boat tours are available from **Bird Islands Boat Tour** (tel. 902/674-2384) in Big Bras d'Or (landing on the islands is forbidden, however). The road descends at last to the flatlands around the mouth of the bay.

If you'd like to extend your drive, take the short ferry ride (runs 24  hours and costs 50¢) to **Englishtown,** home of the celebrated Cape Breton Giant, Angus MacAskill. A museum holds the remains of a 7'9" man. *Tel. 902/929–2875. Admission: $1 adults, 50¢ children. Open May–Oct., daily 9–6.*

This alternative route around the head of the bay brings you to **St. Ann's,** home of North America's only **Gaelic College** (tel. 902/295–3441), with the Great Hall of the Clans and a Scottish gift shop. The college offers courses in Gaelic language and literature, Scottish music, and dancing, weaving, and other Scottish arts. In the first week of August Gaelic College hosts the **Gaelic Mod,** a week-long festival of games, theater, and music.

 Turn right on Highway 105 for **Baddeck,** the most highly developed tourist center in Cape Breton, with more than 1,000 motel beds, a golf course, many fine gift shops, and numerous restaurants. Baddeck is the main town on the **Bras d'Or Lakes,** a vast, warm, almost-landlocked inlet of the sea, which occupies the entire center of Cape Breton. The coastline of the Lakes is more than 967 kilometers (600 miles) long, and yachtspeople sail from all over the world to cruise their serene, unspoiled coves and islands. Four of the largest communities along the shore are Micmac Indian reserves.

Baddeck's attractions include the **Centre Bras d'Or Festival of the Arts,** which offers live music and drama every evening during the summer, and the annual regatta of the Bras d'Or Yacht Club, held in the first week of August. Sailing tours and charters are available locally, as are bus tours along the Cabot Trail. A free ferry (passengers only) shuttles between the government wharf and the sandy beach, by the lighthouse at Kidston Island.

The **Alexander Graham Bell National Historic Site** commemorates the great inventor who spent his summers here and is buried on the mountaintop above his mansion, still owned by his family and visible from the town. The site contains displays and detailed records of Bell's research into an astonishing range of subjects. *Chebucto Rd., tel. 902/295–2069. Admission free. Open July–Sept., daily 9–9; Oct.–June, daily 9–5.*

Continue along the lake shore on Trans-Canada 105 to Exit 6 which leads to **Little Narrows,** then take the ferry (runs 24 hours and costs 25¢) to the Washabuck Peninsula. Take Route 223 to **Estmere** and **Iona,** site of the **Nova Scotia Highland Village,** set high on a mountainside, with a spectacular view of Bras d'Or Lake and the narrow Barra Strait. The village's 10 historic buildings were assembled from all over Cape Breton to depict Highland Scots' way of life from their origins in the Hebrides to the present day. Among the participants at this living-history museum are a smith in the blacksmith shop and a clerk in the store. *Rte. 233, tel. 902/725–2272. Admission: $3 adults, $2.50 senior citizens, $1 students, $6 families. Open mid-June–mid-Sept., Mon.–Sat. 9–5, Sun. 11–6.*

The newly constructed Barra Strait Bridge joins Iona to Grand Narrows. A few kilometers (about 2 miles) from the bridge, bear right toward East Bay. (If you miss this turn, don't worry; you'll have just as scenic a drive along St. Andrews Channel.) The East Bay route runs through the Micmac village of **Eskasoni,** the largest native community in the province. This is one of the friendliest villages in the province, with a fascinating cultural heritage: Find an excuse to stop and talk, perhaps at a gift shop or a general store.

**53** Farther on, East Bay becomes a prosperous outer suburb of **Sydney,** the heart of Nova Scotia's second-largest urban cluster. "Industrial Cape Breton" encompasses villages, unorganized districts, and half-a-dozen towns—most of which sprang up around the coal mines, which fed the steel plant at Sydney. These are warmhearted, interesting communities with a diverse ethnic population, including Ukraines, Welsh, Polish, Lebanese, West Indians, Italians; most residents descended from the miners and steelworkers who arrived a century ago when the area was booming. Sydney is also the only significantly industrialized district in Atlantic Canada, and it has suffered serious environmental damage.

Industrial Cape Breton has the island's only real airport, its only university, and a lively entertainment scene that specializes in Cape Breton music. The **University College of Cape Breton** offers many facilities for the public, such as a theater, art gallery, the Cape Breton Archives, and the Beaton Institute of Cape Breton Studies. The campus is located on the Sydney-Glace Bay Highway, not far from the airport.

Sydney is also a popular departure point: Fast ferries leave from North Sydney for Newfoundland, and scheduled air service to Newfoundland and the French islands of St. Pierre and Miquelon departs from Sydney Airport.

**54** Situated about 30 minutes from Sydney, on Route 22, is **Fortress of Louisbourg National Historic Park,** the most remarkable site in Cape Breton. Louisbourg tends to be chilly, so pack a warm sweater or windbreaker. After the French were forced out of mainland Nova Scotia in 1713, they established their headquarters here, in a walled and fortified town on a low point of land at the mouth of Louisbourg Harbour.

The fortress was twice captured, once by New Englanders and once by the British; after the second siege, in 1758, it was razed to the ground. Its capture essentially ended the French Empire in America. During the past 30 years, a quarter of the original town has been rebuilt on its foundation, just as it was in 1744, before the first siege. Costumed actors re-create the lives and activities of the original inhabitants; you can watch a military drill, see nails and lace being made, and eat food prepared from 18th-century recipes in the town's two inns. Plan on spending at least half a day. Tours available. *Tel. 902/733–2280. Admission: $6.25 adults, $3.25 children 5–16, senior citizens free, $16 families. Open June and Sept., daily 9:30–5; July and Aug., daily 9–6.*

While in Louisbourg, consider stopping at the railway museum at the **Sydney and Louisburg Historical Society,** or the **Atlantic**

**Statiquarium,** a marine museum devoted largely to underwater treasure. *Railway Museum: 7336 Main St., tel. 902/733–2720. Admission free. Open June–Sept., weekdays 9–5; July and Aug., daily 9–7. Statiquarium: 7523 Main St., tel. 902/733–2220. Admission: $2.50 adults, $1 children 5–16, $5 families. Open June–Sept., daily 10–8.*

To return, you must retrace your tracks, via Route 22, Highway 125, and Route 4 to East Bay; continue down the east side of the Bras d'Or Lakes.

---

**Time Out**  On your return route, you'll come to **Big Pond,** home of singer/songwriter Rita MacNeil, who operates a tearoom here. Stop for tea and oatcakes, and pick up one of her tapes. *Rte. 4. Open June, daily 10–6; July and Aug., daily 10–8; Sept. and Oct., daily 10–6.*

---

Route 4 continues along the lake, sometimes close to the shore and sometimes high in the hills. The **Chapel Island Reserve** is the site of a major Micmac spiritual and cultural celebration, which draws 5,000 visitors every year during the last weekend in July. The event combines native and Roman Catholic ceremonies, and non-natives are welcome.

From St. Peter's to Port Hawkesbury the population is largely Acadian French. At **St. Peter's** the Atlantic Ocean is connected with the Bras d'Or Lakes by the century-old St. Peter's Canal, still heavily used by pleasure craft and fishing vessels. The town is a service center for the surrounding region, and offers such amenities as a marina, hotels, restaurants, and a liquor store. From St. Peter's, Route 247 leads through the Acadian villages of Grand Greve and L'Ardoise to a fine beach at Point Michaud.

The road onward along the Bras d'Or Lakes leads through pretty Acadian villages along the twisting channel of St. Peter's Inlet, with many coves and islands, and then along the main body of the lake to **Dundee,** a large resort with a spectacular hilltop golf course overlooking the island-studded waters of West Bay. The alternative route, equally engaging, leads along the Atlantic coast, through coves and islands past River Tillard and River Bourgeois to Louisdale.

Turn off on Route 320 for Isle Madame, a 27-square-kilometer (17-square-mile) island named for Madame de Maintenon, second wife of Louis XIV. Route 320 leads through the villages of Poulamon and D'Escousse, and overlooks the protected waterway of Lennox Passage, with its spangle of islands. Route 206 meanders through the low hills to a maze of land and water at West Arichat. Together, the two routes encircle the island, meeting at Arichat, the principal town of **Isle Madame.**

**Arichat** was once the seat of the local Catholic diocese; **Notre Dame de l'Assumption church,** built in 1838, still retains the grandeur of its former cathedral status. The bishop's palace, the only one in Cape Breton, is now a law office. The two cannons overlooking the harbor were installed after the town was sacked by John Paul Jones, founder of the U.S. Navy, during the American Revolution. The town was an important shipbuilding and trading center during the 19th century, and some fine old houses from that period still remain, along with the 18th-century **LeNoir Forge** (tel. 902/226–9364; open May–Sept., weekdays 9–5, Sat. 10–3).

A dead-end road leads to the Acadian villages of Petit de Grat, Sampson's Cove, and **Little Anse;** with its rocky red bluffs, cobble shores, tiny harbor, and brightly painted houses, the latter is particularly attractive to artists and photographers.

From Louisdale, Route 104 passes through the woods and crosses the Inhabitants River to **Port Hawkesbury,** a new industrial center around the deep-water port created when, in 1955, the Canso Causeway blocked the once-fierce currents from the Gulf of St. Lawrence. Port Hawkesbury has a paper mill, an electrical generating station, a gypsum wallboard plant, and an oil trans-shipment depot. It also has all the usual services, including a number of motels.

Eight kilometers (5 miles) farther on is **Port Hastings,** at the Cape Breton end of the Canso Causeway. Crossing the Causeway, Halifax is a three-hour drive away.

# Shopping

You may claim a refund of Nova Scotia's 11% sales tax (nonrefundable on accommodations, meals, and alcohol) paid on goods you transport home. Refund claims must be filed within 90 days of leaving Nova Scotia and must be in excess of $15. (Refunds of the national Goods and Services Tax must be applied for separately; *see* Shopping in Chapter 1). For refund forms and information, contact the **Provincial Tax Commission** (Tax Refund Unit, Box 755, Halifax, NS B3J 2V4, tel. 902/424–5946 or 1/424–6708 in Nova Scotia).

**Halifax** The Spring Garden Road area has two stylish shopping malls, with shops selling everything from designer clothing to fresh pasta. **Jennifers of Nova Scotia** (5635 Spring Garden Rd., tel. 902/425–3119) sells locally made jewelry, pottery, wool sweaters, and soaps. You can also find fine crafts in Historic Properties and the Barrington Inn complex, near the waterfront, at such shops as **Pewter House** (1875 Granville St., tel. 902/423–8843) and the **Stornoway** (1873 Granville St., tel. 902/422–9507). The **Plaid Place** (1903 Barrington Pl., tel. 902/429–6872) has a dazzling array of tartans and Highland accessories. The **Wool Sweater Outlet** (1870 Hollis St., tel. 902/422–9209) offers wool and cotton sweaters at good prices.

**Elsewhere in Nova Scotia**
*Shopping Malls* Shopping malls in Nova Scotia are similar to those in other parts of Canada or in the United States. The two largest malls are the **Mic-Mac Mall** in Dartmouth, off the A. Murray Mackay Bridge; and the **Halifax Shopping Centre** on Mumford Road. On Route 4 in Sydney you'll find the **Mayflower Mall** on the way to Glace Bay.

*Specialty Shops* Antiques, gifts, and crafts are especially popular in Cape Breton, but shops selling these items appear in numbers throughout the province. You'll find everything from blacksmithing in East Dover and silversmithing in Waverley to leaded glass ornaments in Purcells Cove, hooked rugs in Cheticamp, woolens in Yarmouth, wooden toys in Middletown, pewter in Wolfville, pottery in Arichat, and apple dolls in Halifax. A good shoppers' guide is the *Buyers Guide to Art and Crafts in Nova Scotia*, from the Department of Tourism and Culture (*see* Important Addresses and Numbers in Essential Information, *above*).

# Sports and the Outdoors

The Department of Tourism and Culture (*see* Important Addresses and Numbers in Essential Information, *above*) publishes *The Nova Scotia Travel Guide*, which has an Outdoors chapter with information on aviation, diving, kayaking, river rafting, rockhounding, windsurfing, skiing, and many other sports.

**Biking** *Bicycle Tours in Nova Scotia* (C$5.00) is published by **Bicycle Nova Scotia** (5516 Spring Garden Rd., Box 3010, Halifax B3J 3G6, tel. 902/425–5450). The organization also conducts a variety of excursions around the province. **Backroads** (1516 5th St., Suite Q333, Berkeley, CA 94710, tel. 510/527–1555 or 800/245–3874) offers five- and six-day bike trips on the Evangeline Trail.

**Bird-Watching** Nova Scotia is located on the "Atlantic Flyway" and is an important staging point for migrating species. An excellent, beautifully illustrated book, *Birds of Nova Scotia*, by Robie Tufts, is a must on every ornithologist's reading list. One of the highest concentrations of bald eagles in North America—about 250 nesting pairs—is located in Cape Breton, along the Bras d'Or Lake region or in Cape Breton Highlands National Park. July and August are the best eagle-watching times. MacNabs Island, in Halifax harbor, has a large osprey population. The Bird Islands, off the coast of Cape Breton, are home to a variety of sea birds, including the rare Atlantic puffin.

**Canoeing** Nova Scotia is seamed with small rivers and lakes, by which the Micmac Indians roamed both Cape Breton and the peninsula. Especially good canoe routes are within Kejimkujik National Park (*see* National Parks, *below*). The publication *Canoe Routes of Nova Scotia* and a variety of route maps are available from the Nova Scotia Government Bookstore (Box 637, 1700 Granville St., Halifax B3J 2T3, tel. 902/424–7580).

**Fishing** Nova Scotia has more than 9,000 lakes and 100 brooks; practically all lakes and streams are open to anglers. The catch includes Atlantic salmon (June–September), brook and sea trout, bass, rainbow trout, and shad. You can get a nonresident fishing license from any Department of Natural Resources office in the province and at most sporting-goods stores.

**Golf** Nova Scotia and Cape Breton have 38 golf courses, as well as driving ranges and miniature golf courses. The 9-hole course at Parrsboro and the 18-hole links at Dundee offer spectacular views of the Minas Basin and Bras d'Or Lake, respectively. One of Canada's finest courses is at The Pines Resort Hotel, in Digby (*see* Lodging, *below*), offering 18 challenging holes amid a pine forest.

**Hiking** The province has a wide variety of trails along the rugged coastline and inland through forest glades, which enable you to experience otherwise inaccessible scenery, wildlife, and vegetation. *Hiking Trails of Nova Scotia* (C$9.95) is available through the **Canadian Hostelling Association** (5516 Spring Garden Rd., Box 3010, Halifax B3J 3G6, tel. 902/425–5450).

**Windsurfing** Wind and water conditions are often excellent for windsurfing, the fastest-growing aquatic summer sport in Nova Scotia. Lessons and equipment rentals are available from retail outlets throughout the province.

## Beaches

The province is one big seashore. The warmest beaches are found on the Northumberland Strait shore and include Heather Beach, Caribou, and Melmerby, all in provincial parks. The west coast of Cape Breton and the Bras d'Or Lakes also offer fine beaches and warm salt water.

## National Parks

Nova Scotia has two national parks: **Cape Breton Highlands National Park** (*see* Tour 4, *above*), through which the Cabot Trail runs; and **Kejimkujik National Park** (*see* Tour 2, *above*), in the interior of the western part of the province. Essentially a wilderness area with many lakes, Kejimkujik offers well-marked canoe routes into the interior, with primitive campsites. Nature trails are marked for hikers, boat rentals are available, and there's freshwater swimming. One precaution: Check for ticks after hiking in the deep woods. Kejimkujik also operates the Seaside Adjunct near Port Joli on the Atlantic shore that protects one of the last undeveloped tracts of coastline on the Eastern Seaboard. There are two mile-long beaches, both reached by hiking trails (no visitor services; day use only). *To Kejimkujik: Take Hwy. 8 from Liverpool or Annapolis Royal, Box 36, Maitland Bridge, B0T 1N0, tel. 902/682–2772. Park fee: $4 per vehicle per day, $9 for 4-day pass, $25 for annual pass. Camping fee: $8.50–$13 per day.*

# Dining and Lodging

## Dining

Many of Halifax's restaurants are set in refurbished historic homes or other restored quarters. The menus almost always center on seafood, including Malpeque oysters, Fundy lobster, and Digby scallops. Unless otherwise noted, dress is casual; only in expensive restaurants is a jacket required.

Along the main highways, your best bet for a meal will be at truck stops, particularly the **Irving Big Stops.** Expect nothing fancy, just generous helpings of plain, solid food at reasonable prices.

Highly recommended restaurants in each price category are indicated by a star ★.

| Category | Cost* |
| --- | --- |
| $$$$ | over $50 |
| $$$ | $35–$50 |
| $$ | $15–$35 |
| $ | under $15 |

*per person, excluding drinks, service, 7% GST, and 10% sales tax on meals more than $3.

## Lodging

Nova Scotia has a superb computerized system called **Check In** (tel. 800/565–0000; in Halifax-Dartmouth, 902/425–5781; in the continental U.S., 800/341–6096; in Maine, 800/492–0643), which provides information and makes reservations with more than 700 hotels, motels, inns, campgrounds, and car-rental agencies. Check In also represents most properties in Prince Edward Island and some in New Brunswick.

Several hotel and motel chains operate in Nova Scotia. **Best Western** (tel. 800/528–1234) and **Wandlyn Inns** (in eastern Canada, tel. 800/561–0000; in the U.S., 800/561–0006) are mid-range chains, quite suitable for families. **Journey's End** (tel. 800/668–4200) is a chain of new budget hotels with clean and pleasant rooms, but no facilities.

In addition to the reliable chains, Halifax-Dartmouth has a number of excellent hotels; reservations are necessary year-round, and can be made by calling Check In (*see above*). Expect to pay considerably more in the capital district than elsewhere. Those on a budget might try a hostel, country inn, or bed-and-breakfast.

Highly recommended lodgings in each price category are indicated by a star ★.

| Category | Cost* |
| --- | --- |
| $$$$ | over $80 |
| $$$ | $65–$80 |
| $$ | $45–$65 |
| $ | under $45 |

*All prices are for a standard double room, excluding 10% service charge.*

## Halifax-Dartmouth

Dining   **MacAskill's Restaurant.** Experience a continuing tradition of Nova Scotian hospitality in this romantic dining room overlooking beautiful Halifax Harbor. Award-winning chefs will delight you with a unique selection of seafood dishes prepared using only the finest, freshest fish available. Specialties include pepper steak, flambéed tableside. *88 Alderney Dr., Dartmouth Ferry Terminal Bldg., tel. 902/466–3100. AE, DC, MC, V. $$$*

**Ryan Duffy's.** Steaks are the specialty at this spot, in the Spring Garden Place shopping mall, where you can select your own cut by the ounce; other options include an array of seafood and lamb. Upstairs, corner window seats allow you to watch the world walk by from inside this brass and wood-paneled dining room. The green-and-burgundy color scheme adds to Ryan Duffy's old-time atmosphere. *5640 Spring Garden Rd., tel. 902/421–1116. Reservations advised for dining room. AE, MC, V. $$–$$$*

★  **Salty's On The Waterfront.** This restaurant gets the prize for the best location in the city: It overlooks Privateer's Wharf and the entire harbor. Request a table with a window view and choose the smoked salmon from the menu. The **Salty Dog Bar** on the ground level is less expensive, and serves lunches outside on the wharf in summer. *1869 Upper Water St., tel. 902/432–6818. Reservations advised. AE, DC, MC, V. $$–$$$*

**Da Maurizio.** This popular northern Italian restaurant and adjoining wine bar, **Baccus**, are located in the Brewery Center. Chef-owner Maurizio serves homemade pastas with olive oil, ravioli stuffed with duck or rabbit, grilled fish and meats, and the only risotto in town. The brewery has enormously high ceilings—15 and 20 feet—

and stone-and-brick walls adorned with paintings and masks of a Venetian carnival theme. Fresh flowers are placed at linen-draped tables set with gleaming silver. There's a wide wine selection by the bottle and by the glass, and food is served in the wine bar, too. *1496 Lower Water St., tel. 902/423–0859. Reservations advised. AE, MC, V. Closed Sat. lunch and Sun. $$*

★ **Old Man Morias.** Authentic Greek specialties at this turn-of-the-century Halifax town house include lamb on a spit and moussaka. Greek music, tapestries, and archways set the mood for a traditionally Greek evening, and full-flavored dishes enrich the spirit; sample the fried squid and fried cheese appetizers. *1150 Barrington St., tel. 902/422–7960. Reservations advised. AE, DC, MC, V. Closed Sun. $$*

**Scanway.** Scandinavian dishes are the specialty of this bright, pretty restaurant, decorated with pine wood and orange-and-yellow drapes. Try the *sjokreps* (Danish scampi with garlic and parsley butter). The dessert menu alone makes Scanway worth a visit: homemade ice cream, King Olav's cake (chocolate truffle torte), marzipan cake filled with fresh fruit. *1569 Dresden Row, tel. 902/422–3733. Reservations advised. AE, MC, V. $$*

**Privateer's Warehouse.** History surrounds you in this 200-year-old building, where three restaurants share the early 18th-century stone walls and hewn beams, serving food in descending order of elegance. **The Upper Deck Waterfront Fishery & Grill,** where you can experience a nautical setting with great views of the harbor, specializes in such delicacies as oysters Rockefeller, fresh Atlantic salmon, and lobster straight from their holding tank. The **Middle Deck Pasta Works & Beverage Co.** has a bistro-style, relaxed atmosphere. The varied menu features innovative pastas, specialty drinks, and traditional cuisine; a children's menu is also available. The **Lower Deck Good Time Pub** is a boisterous pub with long trestle tables, a patio, beer mugs for thumping, and lots of hand-holding and singing of traditional Maritime, Irish, and Scottish songs; fish and chips and other pub food is served. *Historic Properties, tel. 902/422–1289. AE, DC, MC, V. $–$$*

**A.K.'s Food & Beverage Emporium.** When you're hungry for the good old days, relax amidst mementos of Bogie and Bacall, Chaplin and Churchill, and dig into a hearty meal. From innovative salads to meaty sandwiches to full dinners, there is something for everyone, along with a selection of imported beers. *Brewery Market, 1496 Lower Water St., Halifax, tel. 902/492–2441. AE, DC, MC, V. Closed Sun. $*

**Satisfaction Feast.** This small, vegetarian restaurant and bakery is informal, friendly, and usually packed at lunchtime. The food is simple and wholesome; try the fresh whole-wheat bread and one of the daily curries. Smoking is not permitted. *1581 Grafton St., tel. 902/422–3540. MC, V. $*

**Lodging** **Cambridge Suites.** You can get "a suite for the price of a room" is this hotel's motto . . . and a good one it is. Choose among three suite sizes; all have sitting room and kitchenette. What makes this lodging even more desirable is its convenient location near the Citadel and the Spring Garden Road shopping district, and it's only a short walk from downtown. Complimentary Continental breakfast is served. *1583 Brunswick St., B3J 3P5, tel. 902/420–0555 or 800/565–1263 in Canada. 200 mini-suites and 1-bedrooms. Facilities: whirlpool, sauna, rooftop sundeck, exercise room. AE, MC, V. $$$$*

**Chateau Halifax.** This first-class Canadian Pacific hotel offers large, pretty rooms in a perfect location, near Scotia Square and Historic Properties. There's a good dining room and an upbeat bar with live entertainment. *1990 Barrington St., B3J 1P2, tel. 902/425–6700. 279 rooms, 21 suites. Facilities: restaurant, coffee shop, lounge, pool, sauna. AE, DC, MC, V. $$$$*

**Citadel Inn.** Situated at the base of Citadel Hill, this business-oriented hotel is still within walking distance of the action. Rooms with a harbor view are recommended, though they will cost more than those without. Free parking is an asset in car-clogged Halifax. *1960 Brunswick St., B3J 2G7, tel. 902/422–1391. 261 rooms, 6 suites. Facilities: restaurant, indoor pool, fitness center, sauna, whirlpool, and exercise room. AE, DC, MC, V. $$$$*

**Delta Barrington.** This traditional-style hotel was built in 1979 using the original facade of an entire city block. It has a prime downtown location, and the rooms are spacious. All-weather walkways connect the hotel to Scotia Square shops. *1875 Barrington St., B3J 3L6, tel. 902/429– 7410. 200 rooms, 1 suite. Facilities: restaurant, lounge, fitness center, sauna, whirlpool, and pool. AE, DC, MC, V. $$$$*

**Halliburton House Inn.** Halifax's only registered four-star heritage property, this hotel is an elegant renovation of several 19th-century town houses. Thirty comfortable rooms are furnished with period antiques, lending a homey ambience to the inn. All have private baths. Several suites with working fireplaces. Continental breakfast is included in the room rate. *5184 Morris St., B3J 1B3, tel. 902/ 420–0658, fax 902/423–2324. 24 rooms, 3 suites. Facilities: dining room, library sitting room, private garden courtyard, conference rooms. AE, DC, MC, V. $$$$*

**Holiday Inn Halifax Centre.** This first-class property overlooking Halifax Commons is 1 kilometer (½ mile) west of Scotia Square. Standard Holiday Inn decor with modern amenities. *1980 Robie St., B3H 3G5, tel. 902/423–1161. 228 rooms, 3 suites. Facilities: meeting rooms, restaurant, piano bar, indoor pool, sauna, whirlpool, exercise equipment, gift shop, free parking. AE, DC, MC, V. $$$$*

**Prince George Hotel.** The Prince George is a luxurious and understated business-oriented hotel. The contemporary mahogany furnishings include a writing desk. The building is conveniently connected by underground tunnel to the World Trade and Convention Center. *1725 Market St., B3J 3N9, tel. 902/425–1986 or 800/ 565–1567 in Canada. 208 rooms, 3 suites. Facilities: restaurant, café, 2 lounges, pub, pool, whirlpool, fitness center, concierge, children's playroom, roof deck and gardens. AE, DC, MC, V. $$$$*

**Sheraton Halifax.** The convenient location, in Historic Properties, contributes to the elegance of this waterfront hotel. Other assets include the hotel's indoor pool with a summer sun deck and spa facilities. There's also docking space for yachts. In summer you can sit on an outdoor terrace at the **Café Maritime** restaurant and eat lobster while you watch the ships go by. *1919 Upper Water St., B3J 3J5, tel. 902/ 421–1700 or 800/325–3535. 332 rooms, 24 suites. Facilities: restaurant, 24-hr room service, concierge, shops, meeting facilities, boat slips, skywalk to shopping and office complexes. AE, DC, MC, V. $$$$*

**Ramada Renaissance.** Located in Dartmouth's Burnside Industrial Park, this luxury hotel is aimed at the business traveler as well as families. There is an 108-foot indoor water slide. *240 Brownlow Ave., Dartmouth, B3B 1X6, tel. 902/468–8888 or 800/561–3733 in Canada. 178 rooms, 30 suites. Facilities: restaurant, lounge, bar, room service, pool, whirlpool, sauna, exercise room, gift shop, meeting and banquet facilities. AE, DC, MC, V. $$$$*

**Waken'n Eggs B&B.** Situated across the Common from the Citadel is this Victorian, originally built as two homes, but now a single house. The comfortable, eclectic furnishings include antiques and folk art, and the helpful service makes this a hospitable B&B. *2114 Windsor*

*St., B3K 5B4, tel. 902/422–4737. 3 rooms with 1 private, 1 shared bath. No credit cards. $$*

## Mainland Nova Scotia

**Annapolis Royal**
*Lodging*

**Wandlyn Royal Anne Motel.** This modern, no-frills motel offers clean rooms at reasonable rates. Enjoy the pleasant, quiet, country setting by taking a walk on the motel's 20 acres of land. *Box 628, B0S 1A0, tel. 902/532–2323. 30 rooms. Facilities: whirlpool, sauna, conference room. AE, DC, MC, V. $$*

**The Moorings B&B.** This tall, beautiful home overlooking Annapolis Basin, built in 1881 by sea captain Joseph Hall and the former home of author H. R. Percy, comes complete with fireplace, tin ceilings, antiques, and contemporary art. *Box 118, Granville Ferry B0S 1K0, tel. 902/532–2146. 3 rooms, 2 with half-baths, 2 with shared full baths. V. $*

**Antigonish**
*Dining*

**Lobster Treat Restaurant.** Once a two-room schoolhouse, this property has since been converted into a cozily decorated brick, pine, and stained-glass restaurant. Located on the Trans-Canada Highway, it's convenient for travelers following the Sunrise Trail. The menu features fresh seafood and vegetables year-round, as well as bread and pies baked on the premises. Because of a relaxed atmosphere and a varied menu, including a separate list for children, families enjoy coming here. *241 Post Rd., tel. 902/863–5465. Reservations advised in summer. AE, DC, MC, V. Closed Jan. $$*

**Bedford**
*Dining*

**Pictures Restaurant.** A fun place to eat with the family, this spot is also popular for business lunches. The restaurant takes its name from the collection of vintage photographs of Bedford that adorn the walls. Pasta plays a big part in the picture, and there's a special children's menu. *1516 Bedford Hwy., tel. 902/835–8082. AE, DC, MC, V. $$*

**Chester**
*Dining*

**The Galley.** Decked out in nautical bric-a-brac and providing a spectacular view of the ocean, this restaurant offers a pleasant, relaxed atmosphere. The menu features seafood: Smoked salmon and mussel dishes are the local favorites, but save room for the homemade blueberry pie. *Hwy. 3, on the Marina, tel. 902/275–4700. Reservations advised. AE, MC, V. Closed mid-Dec.–mid-Mar. $*

**Digby**
*Dining and Lodging*

**The Pines Resort Hotel.** Complete with fireplaces, sitting rooms, a bistro, dining room, and a view of Annapolis Basin, this elegant property offers myriad amenities. Seafood with a French touch is served daily in the restaurant, and the lounge is perfect for quiet relaxation. *Box 70, Shore Rd., tel. 902/245–2511 or 800/667–4637. 90 rooms in main lodge, 60 in cottages. Facilities: restaurant, lounge, fitness center with sauna, tennis, pool, golf. AE, DC, MC, V. Closed mid-Oct.–May. $$$*

**Lorneville**
*Dining and Lodging*
★

**Amherst Shore Country Inn.** This seaside country inn with a beautiful view of Northumberland Straight has comfortable rooms, suites and seaside cottages fronting 600 feet of private beach. Incredibly well-prepared four-course dinners are served at one daily seating (7:30 PM by reservation only). *32 km (20 mi) from Amherst on Rte. 366, R.R. 2, Amherst, B4H 3X9, tel. 902/661–4800. 5 rooms, suites, cottages. Facilities: restaurant. AE, DC, MC, V. Closed late Oct.–Apr. $$$*

**Lunenburg**
*Lodging*

**Bluenose Lodge.** This 130-year-old mansion has nine large bedrooms and offers a full complimentary breakfast featuring such treats as freshly baked muffins, stewed rhubarb, and quiche. The bedrooms and sitting areas are furnished with distinctive antiques. The lodge also arranges deep-sea fishing, biking, and whale-watching excursions. *Box 339, 10 Falkland St., B0J 2C0, tel. 902/634–8851. 9 rooms. MC, V. Closed Nov.–Apr. $$–$$$*

**Boscawen Inn.** Antiques and fireplaces decorate this elegant mansion built in 1888, located in the center of this National Heritage Town. The inn has views of the town's harbor. Afternoon tea is served in the drawing rooms or on the balcony. McLachlan House, an annex, has four harbour view suites which opened in 1994. *150 Cumberland St., Box 1343, B0J 2C0, tel. 902/634–3325. 17 rooms. AE, MC, V. Closed Jan.–Easter. $$–$$$*

**Masstown**
*Lodging*

**Shady Maple B&B.** Here's a unique property: a working dairy farm where you can breakfast on fresh eggs, the farm's own maple syrup, jams, and jellies. Enjoy the smoke-free rooms and sun-dried bed linen, and take a dip in the pool. One of the three rooms is a deluxe suite with a waterbed. *R.R. 1, B0M 1G0, tel. 902/662–3565. 3 rooms. Facilities: pool. MC, V. $$–$$$*

**Musquodoboit**
**Harbour**
*Lodging*

**Salmon River House.** About 35 minutes east of Dartmouth, where Route 7 crosses the Salmon River, is this unpretentious white-frame inn, situated on 30 acres and providing glorious views. The home has a licensed dining room, sun room, wheelchair-accessible guest room, and one room with a waterbed and whirlpool bath. *R.R. 2, head of Jeddore, B0J 1P0, tel. 902/889–3353 or 800/565–3353. 6 rooms with bath or shower. Facilities: dining room, canoe and boat rentals, fishing arranged. MC, V. $$–$$$*

**Pictou**
*Dining and*
*Lodging*

**The Braeside Inn.** Built in 1938, this inn, situated on a 4-acre hillside site in the center of historic Pictou, has been totally refurbished and now offers well-appointed accommodations and fine food. The Olympic-size pool is open year-round, and beaches are nearby. The dining room specializes in fresh seafood dishes. *126 Front St., Box 1810, B0K 1H0, tel. 902/485–5046, fax 902/485–1701. 20 rooms with bath. Facilities: 2 dining rooms, conference room, pool. AE, MC, V. $$–$$$*

*Lodging*

**The Walker Inn.** A hospitable and energetic Swiss couple run this downtown inn in their brick Georgian-style town house, built in 1865. Every room is different, the dining room is fully licensed, and there's a new library-conference room. A Continental breakfast buffet is included in the room rate. *34 Coleraine St., Box 629, B0K 1H0, tel. 902/485–1433. 10 rooms with bath. Facilities: restaurant, meeting room. AE, MC, V. $$*

**Wolfville**
*Dining and*
*Lodging*

**Blomidon Inn.** This 19th-century sea captain's mansion, located in the beautiful Annapolis Valley, was restored in 1981. Guestrooms are uniquely furnished, most with four poster beds. Relax over lunch or dinner in one of the dining rooms or on the terrace, enjoying the fresh fare from the valley and sea. Lobster bisque, and salmon and scallop Florentine are among the menu favorites. Afternoon tea is served daily, and there's a weekend brunch (reservations advised). *127 Main St., Box 839, B0P 1X0, tel. 902/542–2291. 26 rooms. Facilities: 2 dining rooms, terrace, conference room, tennis court, horseshoes, shuffleboard. MC, V. Closed Dec. 25. $$$*

**Yarmouth**
*Dining and*
*Lodging*

**Manor Inn.** With superior rooms and good food in pleasant surroundings, this colonial mansion on Highway 1 is a nice find. There are three settings to choose from: a lakeside cottage, the main estate, or the more secluded side wing. Steak and lobster are the specialties in the dining room; reservations are required. *Box 56, Hebron, B0W 1X0, tel. 902/742–2487. 54 rooms. Facilities: 2 dining rooms, 2 bars, whirlpool, heated pool, tennis court, fireplaces. AE, DC, MC, V. $$*

## Cape Breton Island

**Baddeck**
*Lodging*

**Inverary Inn Resort.** Choose from pleasant accommodations in a 100-year-old inn, cottages, motel units, or duplex cabins. All are situated within a waterfront complex on the island's scenic central drive. The property offers boating and swimming and close proximity to the village, but the resort remains tranquil. Families will appreciate the on-site children's playground, and most guests appreciate the wharfside restaurant. The main lodge with its paneled walls, stone fireplace, and polished horse brasses, has a strong Scottish flavor. *Box 190, B0E 1B0, tel. 902/295–2674. 137 rooms. Facilities: restaurant, chapel, indoor and outdoor pools, fitness and games room, tennis, sauna. AE, MC, V. $$$$*

**Iona**
*Dining and
Lodging*

**Highland Heights Inn.** The rural surroundings, the Scottish homestyle cooking served near the dining room's huge stone fireplace, and the unspoiled view of the lake substitute nicely for the Scottish Highlands. The inn is located on a hillside beside the Nova Scotia Highland Village, overlooking the village of Iona, where some residents still speak the Gaelic language of their ancestors. Enjoy the salmon (or any fish in season), fresh-baked oat cakes, and homemade desserts. *Box 19, Iona, tel. 902/725–2360. 26 rooms. Facilities: dining room, traditional entertainment. D, MC, V. Closed mid-Oct.–mid-May. $$*

**Margaree
Valley**
*Lodging*

**Normaway Inn.** This secluded, 1920s inn is nestled in the hills of the river valley, on 250 acres. Many of the cabins have wood-burning stoves. Take advantage of the recreation barn and the nightly traditional entertainment, including square dancing. The inn is known for its gourmet country food, all of which is prepared on the premises. The owners will organize salmon-fishing trips for interested guests. *Box 326, B0E 2C0, tel. 902/248–2987. 9 rooms, 17 cabins. Facilities: restaurant, tennis, bicycles. AE, MC, V. Closed Oct. 16–mid-June. $$*

**Northeast
Margaree**
*Lodging*

**Heart of Hart's Tourist Farm.** This 100-year-old rural farmhouse on the Cabot Trail is within walking distance of the village. The theme is "very country," with wood stove, antiques, and old-fashioned deep tubs in two of the bathrooms. Hot homemade oatmeal and Red River cereal are a favorite part of the full breakfast that is included in the room rate. Salmon and trout-fishing trips can be arranged. *On Cabot Trail, B0E 2H0, tel. 902/248–2765. 5 rooms. No credit cards. Closed Nov.–Apr. $*

**Sydney**
*Dining*

**Joe's Warehouse.** For excellent food in the heart of town, stop here, where the specialties include local seafood and prime rib. The porridge rolls and homemade scones also win rave reviews. In summer, when the patio is open, the restaurant seats 200 people. Dress is casual and the atmosphere fun. After dinner head downstairs for live music and dancing at Smooth Herman's. *424 Charlotte St., tel. 902/ 539–6686. AE, DC, MC, V. $$*

*Lodging*

**Delta Sydney.** This new hotel is located on the harbor, beside the yacht club and close to the center of town. The attractively decorated guest rooms each have a view of the harbor. The intimate dining room specializes in seafood and Continental cuisine. *300 Esplanade, B1P 6J4, tel. in Canada, 902/562–7500 or 800/268– 1133; in U.S., 800/887–1133; 152 rooms. Facilities: restaurant, lounge, indoor pool, sauna, fitness center. AE, DC, MC, V. $$$*

# The Arts and Nightlife

## The Arts

**Theater**  Canada's oldest professional repertory theater, the **Neptune Theatre** (5216 Sackville St., Halifax, tel. 902/429–7300), presents a full season each summer and winter of performances from classics to contemporary Canadian drama. The **Mulgrave Road Co-Op Theatre** (tel. 902/533–2092) is a small but active professional company performing all over the Maritime Provinces, producing original plays based on local history. **Mermaid Theatre** (tel. 902/798–5841), based in Windsor, travels the world with original children's plays that make extensive use of masks and puppets.

The **Cape Breton Summertime Revue,** based in Sydney, performs an annual original revue of music and comedy that tours Nova Scotia during June and August.

The **Atlantic Fringe Festival** presents 40 shows in eight venues during the first week of September. Dinner theaters in Halifax include the **Historic Feast Company** (tel. 902/420–1840), which presents shows set in the 19th century at Historic Properties Thursday, Friday, and Saturday evenings; and the **Grafton Street Dinner Theatre** (1741 Grafton St., tel. 902/425–1961), where shows run Wednesday through Saturday.

Parrsboro's professional **Ship's Company Theatre** (tel. 902/254–2003) offers a summer season of plays based on historical events of the region, performed aboard the MV *Kipawo,* a former Minas Basin ferry. The **Chester Summer Theatre** (tel. 902/275–2933) operates throughout the summer. Among the best of Nova Scotia's thriving amateur companies are the **Kipawa Show Boat Company** (tel. 902/542–3500), which performs in Wolfville on summer weekends, and **Theatre Antigonish** (tel. 902/867–3954), which performs at St. Francis Xavier University in Antigonish.

Many other towns have theaters that present touring shows and occasional local productions, notably Chester, Liverpool, Yarmouth, Annapolis Royal, Middle Musquodoboit, Pictou, and Sydney. Glace Bay's opulent old opera house, the **Savoy Theatre,** is the home of the summer-long Festival on the Bay.

**Music**  Live concerts and musical presentations are held in Halifax at the **Metro Centre** (Brunswick and Duke Sts., tel. 902/451–1202) and the **Rebecca Cohn Auditorium** (6101 University Ave., tel. 902/494–2646). **Symphony Nova Scotia** normally appears at "the Cohn."

**Scotia Festival of Music** (tel. 902/429–9469) presents internationally recognized classical musicians in concerts and master classes each May and June at various locations in Halifax. **Musique Royale** hosts an August series of superb Renaissance and baroque concerts in historic buildings around the province. The **Atlantic Jazz Festival** takes place in Halifax in mid-July.

Talented musicians abound in Nova Scotia, ranging from traditional fiddlers to folk singers and rock bands. They appear in clubs, concerts, dances, and a constant stream of open-air festivals. Names to watch for include The Rankin Family, The Barra MacNeills, the Minglewood Band, Sam Moon, Rita MacNeil, David MacIsaac, Scott Macmillan, and such traditional fiddlers as Buddy MacMaster, Ashley MacIsaac, Sandy MacIntyre, Lee Cremo, Jerry Holland, and Natalie MacMaster. An annual **Nova Scotia Bluegrass and**

**Oldtime Music Festival** is held in Ardoise the last weekend in July; the **Lunenburg Folk Harbour Festival,** devoted to acoustic instruments and authentic folk music, takes place in early August; many leading fiddlers appear at Cape Breton's **Big Cove Concert** in mid-July.

## Film

Halifax has a dynamic and growing film industry, which presents current work during the **Atlantic Film Festival,** held in Halifax the third week in September. The festival also showcases feature films, TV movies, and documentaries made elsewhere in the Atlantic Provinces. **Wormwood's Dog and Monkey Cinema** (2015 Gottingen St., tel. 902/422–3700) shows Canadian, foreign-language, and experimental films. Its associated video store, Critic's Choice, specializes in hard-to-find films on videotape.

## Nightlife

The multilevel entertainment center in Historic Properties, **Privateer's Warehouse** (tel. 902/422–1289), is a popular night-time hangout. At the ground-level Lower Deck tavern you can quaff a beer to Celtic music.

Other popular Halifax night spots include **Cheers** (1743 Grafton St., tel. 902/421–1655), with bands and entertainment nightly, and **O'Carroll's** (1860 Upper Water St., tel. 902/423–4405), a restaurant, oyster bar, and lounge where you can hear live Irish music nightly.

# 12 Prince Edward Island

Prince Edward Island seems too good to be true, with its crisply painted farmhouses, manicured green fields rolling down to sandy beaches, the warmest ocean water north of Florida, lobster boats in trim little harbors, and a vest-pocket capital city packed with architectural heritage.

When you experience PEI, you'll understand instantly that it was no accident that Lucy Maud Montgomery's novel of youth and innocence, *Anne of Green Gables*, was framed against this land. What may have been unexpected, however, was how the story burst on the world in 1908 and is still selling untold thousands of copies every year. After potatoes and lobsters, Anne is the island's most important product.

Anne is everywhere on the island: At the Confederation Centre of the Arts in Charlottetown you can peruse Montgomery's original handwritten manuscript; even on cars throughout the province you'll see the freckled redhead, as the government recently stamped her face on the province's license plates. But Anne's fame stretches beyond PEI and Cavendish—fondly referred to as Anne's land. She attracts international attention, especially from the Japanese, with whom she is hugely popular.

Those visitors who have come because of Anne usually leave having fallen in love with her island. Outside the tourist mecca of Cavendish, the island seems like an oasis of peace in a world of turmoil. Here you'll find fishing ports, crossroads villages, small family farms. You can choose full-service resorts and gourmet restaurants, or bed-and-breakfasts and lobster suppers. You can opt for a farm vacation or take a deep-sea fishing cruise to experience life on a working farm or fishing harbor.

Visitors often tour the island in a loop: They take the ferry from New Brunswick to Bordon, see Anne country and the PEI National Park, and depart by ferry from Wood Island to Nova Scotia. This is a good strategy; but, to more deeply experience the island's character, stray to the wooded hills of the east—to compact, bustling Montague, straddling its river; or to the estuarine maze of Murray Harbour. Or go west to the Acadian parishes of Egmont Bay and Tignish and the silver fox country around Summerside. Even if you're in a rush, it won't take long to get off the beaten path: In most places you can cross the island, north to south, in half an hour or so.

PEI is ringed by beaches, and few of them are heavily used. Ask a dozen islanders to recommend their favorites. Bothwell Beach, near Souris, says one—miles of singing sands, utterly deserted. West Point, says a second—lifeguards, restaurant nearby, showers at the provincial park. Greenwich, near St. Peter's Bay, another suggests—a half-hour walk through magnificent wandering dunes brings you to an endless empty beach.

When you're back in Charlottetown see the musical "Anne of Green Gables." Have dinner first, though—there's a great little place two blocks from the theater.

# Essential Information

## Important Addresses and Numbers

Tourist Information
For prices and information before your trip, contact the **Prince Edward Island Department of Economic Development & Tourism,** Quality Service Division (Box 940, Charlottetown, PEI C1A 7M5,

tel. 902/368–4444 or 800/463–4PEI). The department offers an excellent annual "Visitor's Guide," and maintains eight Visitor Information Centres (VICs) on the island. The main VIC is in Charlottetown (Oak Tree Pl., University Ave., tel. 902/368–4444 or 902/463–4PEI), and is open mid-May–October, daily; November—mid-May, weekdays.

**Emergencies** **Police** and **fire,** dial 0.

*Hospitals* **Queen Elizabeth Hospital,** Charlottetown, tel. 902/566–6200.

## Arriving and Departing by Plane

Charlottetown Airport is 5 kilometers (3 miles) north of town. **Air Canada** (tel. 902/892-1007 or 800/776–3000) and **Canadian Airlines International** (tel. 902/892–4581 or 800/665-1177) offer daily service to major cities in eastern Canada and the United States via Halifax. **Prince Edward Air** (tel. 902/892–5816) offers non-stop service to Moncton and Halifax from Summerside and Charlottetown. **Northwest Airlink** (tel. 902/628-6665 or 800/225–2525) operates a regular daily flight schedule between PEI and Boston.

## Arriving and Departing by Ferry

Two car-ferry services serve Prince Edward Island. **Marine Atlantic** (tel. 902/794–5700 or 902/855–2030) sails between Cape Tormentine, New Brunswick, and Borden, year-round, crossing daily between 6:30 AM and 1 AM. The crossing takes about 45 minutes and costs $18 per car round-trip and $7.25 per adult. The second service, **Northumberland Ferries** (tel. 902/566–3838; in the Maritimes, 800/565–0201), sails between Caribou, Nova Scotia, and Wood Islands, from May to mid-December. The crossing takes about 75 minutes, and the round-trip costs $26.50 per automobile and $8.25 per person (reduced price for senior citizens and children). No fares are collected inbound; you pay only on leaving the island. Neither service takes reservations.

## Getting Around

**By Car** There are more than 3,700 kilometers (2,294 miles) of paved road in the province, including the three scenic coastal drives called Lady Slipper Drive, Blue Heron Drive, and Kings Byway.

## Guided Tours

The island offers about 20 sightseeing tours, including double-decker bus tours, cycling tours, harbor cruises, and walking tours. Most tour companies are located in Charlottetown and offer excursions around the city and to the beaches.

# Exploring Prince Edward Island

The tours here divide Prince Edward Island into central Queens County, Kings County in the east, and Prince County at the western end of the island. Tour 1 is primarily a walking tour, while tours 2, 3, and 4 follow the major scenic highways—Blue Heron Drive, Kings Byway, and Lady Slipper Drive. There are plenty of chances to get out of the car, go fishing, hit the beach, collect wild flowers, or just watch the sea roll in.

## Highlights for First-Time Visitors

***Anne of Green Gables* farmhouse,** Tour 2: Blue Heron Drive
**North Cape,** Tour 4: Lady Slipper Drive
**Orwell Corner Pioneer Village,** Tour 3: Kings Byway
**Province House,** Tour 1: Charlottetown
**Seascapes and July's wild lupins near Souris,** Tour 3: Kings Byway

---

## Tour 1: Charlottetown

Sheltered on an arm of the Northumberland Strait, Prince Edward Island's only city is named for the stylish consort of King George III. Charlottetown, the largest community on the island, is a small city (population 15,800) with generous, gingerbread-clad Victorian houses and tree-shaded squares. It is often called "the Cradle of Confederation," a reference to the 1864 conference held here that led to the union of Nova Scotia, New Brunswick, Ontario, and Québec in 1867.

Charlottetown's main activities center on government, tourism, and private commerce. While new suburbs were springing up around it, the core of Charlottetown remained unchanged and the waterfront was restored to recapture the flavor of earlier eras. Today the waterfront includes the Prince Edward Hotel and Convention Centre, several informal restaurants, and handcraft and retail shops. You can easily explore the downtown by foot in a couple of hours. Irene Rogers's *Charlottetown: The Life in Its Buildings* gives much detail about the architecture and history of downtown Charlottetown.

*Numbers in the margin correspond to points of interest on the Prince Edward Island and Charlottetown maps.*

**❶**
**❷** **Charlottetown's** historic redbrick core is the setting for the modern, concrete **Confederation Centre of the Arts,** opened in 1964 as a tribute to the Fathers of Confederation. The Confederation Centre houses a 1,100-seat theater, a memorial hall, a gift shop featuring Canadian crafts, an art gallery and museum, and restaurant and catering facilities. From June to September the center's **Charlottetown Festival** offers excellent professional theater, including the annual musical adaptation of *Anne of Green Gables. Queen St., bet. Grafton and Richmond Sts., tel. 902/628–1864; box office 902/566–1267. Open July–Sept., daily 9–8; Oct.–June, Mon.–Sat. noon–5:30.*

**❸** Next door, on Richmond Street, is the Georgian-style **Province House National Historic Site,** the meeting place of the provincial legislature. The three-story sandstone building, completed in 1847, contains the Confederation Chamber, where representatives of the 19th-century provinces met to discuss creating a union. The room, restored to its 1864 condition, and the legislative chamber are open to the public. Displays and a slide presentation portray the historic meeting. *Richmond St., tel. 902/566–7626. Admission free. Open weekdays 9–5; July–Aug., daily 9–8. Reservations preferred for large groups. Note: When legislature is in session, certain rooms are closed to the public.*

**❹** Two churches near Province House are noteworthy. **St. Paul's Anglican Church** (east of Province House) was erected in 1747, making it
**❺** the oldest Protestant church on the island. **St. Dunstan's Basilica,** south of Province House on Great George Street, is the seat of the Roman Catholic diocese on the island. Known for its twin Gothic

# Prince Edward Island

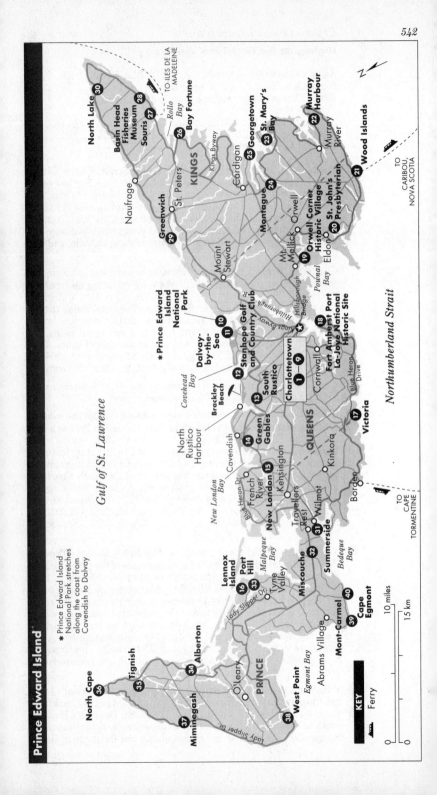

* Prince Edward Island National Park stretches along the coast from Cavendish to Dalvay

*Gulf of St. Lawrence*

*Northumberland Strait*

TO ILES DE LA MADELEINE

TO CARIBOU, NOVA SCOTIA

TO CAPE TORMENTINE

**KINGS**

**QUEENS**

**PRINCE**

North Lake ㉚
Basin Head Fisheries Museum ㉘
Souris ㉗
Bay Fortune ㉖
Greenwich ㉙
St. Peters
Naufrage
Mount Stewart
Cardigan
Georgetown ㉕
St. Mary's Bay ㉓
Murray Harbour ㉒
Murray River
Wood Islands ㉑
Montague ㉔
Orwell
Orwell Corner Historic Village ㉚
Mt. Mellick ⑲
St. John's Presbyterian ⑳
Eldon
Pownal Bay
Hillsborough Bridge
Kings Byway
Prince Edward Island National Park ⑩ ⑪
Stanhope Golf and Country Club ⑫
Dalvay-by-the-Sea
Coveheadhead Bay
Brackley Beach ⑬
North Rustico Harbour
South Rustico
Charlottetown ① – ⑨
Fort Amherst Port La-Joye National Historic Site ⑱
Cornwall
Kinkora
Blue Heron Drive
Victoria ⑰
Green Gables ⑭
Cavendish
New London ⑮
Kensington
Travellers Rest
Wilmot ㉛
Borden
French River
Blue Heron Dr.
New London Bay
Summerside ㉜
Miscouche
Malpeque Bay
Bedeque Bay
Lennox Island ⑯
Port Hill ㉝
Tyne Valley
Lady Slipper Dr.
Cape Egmont ㊵
Mont-Carmel ㊴
Abrams Village
Egmont Bay
O'Leary
Alberton ㉞
Tignish
North Cape ㊱ ㉟
Mimminegash �337
West Point ㊳
Lady Slipper Dr.

**KEY**

🚢 Ferry

0 ———— 10 miles
0 ———— 15 km

N

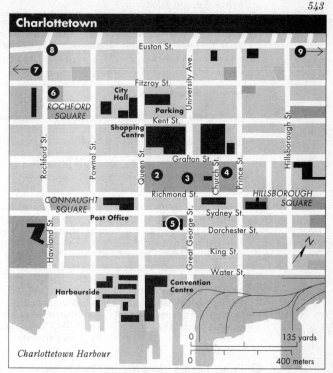

spires and fine Italian carvings, it is one of Canada's largest churches.

**Time Out**  **Kelly's** (52 Queen St., tel. 902/628–6569), located in a historic building just blocks from the waterfront, is a cozy spot for breakfast, lunch, late-afternoon tea, or a full meal. A second location recently opened on Victoria Row, Richmond Street. *AE, MC, V.*

**6**  A few blocks northeast of Province House, on Rochford Square, is **St. Peter's Cathedral.** All Saints Chapel contains murals by Robert Harris, the famous Canadian portrait painter. The chapel was designed in 1888 by his brother W. C. "Willy" Harris, the most celebrated of the island's architects, and the designer of many historic homes and buildings.

**7**  At the southern tip of the city is the beautiful 40-acre **Victoria Park,** overlooking the Charlottetown Harbour. Next to the park, on a hill between groves of white birches, is the white colonial Government House, built in 1835 as the official residence of the province's lieu-
**8**  tenant-governors. Near the park entrance, **Beaconsfield,** a gracious Harris-designed Victorian mansion with restored rooms open for touring, contains the offices of the PEI Museum and Heritage Foundation and a bookstore with publications about the island. *Park open year-round, daily sunrise–sunset.*

**9**  At the eastern end of the city is the **Charlottetown Driving Park** on Kensington Road, home of a sport that is dear to the hearts of islanders—harness racing. Standardbred horses are raised on farms throughout the island, and harness racing on the ice and on country tracks has been popular for generations. In fact, there are more horses per capita on the island than in any other province of Canada. *Kensington Rd., tel. 902/892–6823. Admission: $2 adults, 50¢ children. Year-round races are held once a week Jan.–May; three nights a week in June, July, and most of Aug.; and twice daily (except Sun.) during Old Home Week in mid-Aug.*

## Tour 2: Blue Heron Drive

Circling the island's center segment and roughly outlining Queens County, Blue Heron Drive is 190 kilometers (114 miles) long. It takes its name from the great blue heron, a stately water bird that migrates to Prince Edward Island every spring to nest in the shallow bays and marshes. You are likely to see several herons along the route. The highway marker is a white square with a blue border and a blue heron in the center.

From Charlottetown, Blue Heron Drive follows Route 15 north to the north shore, then winds along Route 6 through the north-shore fishing villages, the spectacular white sand beaches of Prince Edward Island National Park and Cabot Provincial Park, through the Anne of Green Gables country, and finally along the south shore with its red sandstone seascapes and historic sites. This drive circles some of the island's most beautiful landscapes and best beaches, but its north shore, around picturesque Cavendish and the Green Gables farmhouse, is also cluttered with tourist traps. If you're looking for unspoiled beauty, you'll have to look beyond the fried chicken joints, the tacky gift shops, King Tut's Tomb, and Ripley's Believe It Or Not, and try to keep in your mind's eye the island's simpler days.

**❿** **Prince Edward Island National Park** stretches for about 40 kilometers (25 miles) along the north shore of the island on the Gulf of St. Lawrence. The Park is blessed with nature's broadest brush strokes—sky and sea meet red sandstone cliffs, rolling dunes, and long stretches of sand. Beaches invite you to swim, picnic, or take a quiet walk. Trails lead through woodlands and along streams and ponds. Among more than 200 species of birds are the northern phalarope, Swainson's thrush, and the endangered piping plover. The park **Visitor Centres** in Cavendish and Brackley provide information on activities and events in the National Park. The 56-acre campground has toilets, showers, electrical hookups, and a laundromat. *24 km (15 mi) north of Charlottetown, tel. 902/672–6350. Park open daily; Visitor Centre open June–Oct., daily 10–6.*

**⓫** At the eastern end of the National Park is **Dalvay-by-the-Sea,** built in the 1890s as a summer home by an oil magnate. The park now operates the hotel as a resort lodge (*see* Lodging, *below*).

**Time Out**   The dining room of **Dalvay-by-the-Sea** (tel. 902/672–2048) specializes in fresh seafood and homegrown vegetables, and is known for a traditional dessert called blueberry grunt.

**⓬** A few kilometers west of Dalvay, off Route 6, along beautiful Covehead Bay, is the **Stanhope Golf and Country Club.** The 18-hole course is among the island's longest, most challenging, and most scenic.

**⓭** Moving west, you pass Brackley Beach and then come to **South Rustico,** on Route 243. Rustico is an Acadian French district, one of several on the Island. South Rustico sits on a peninsula on Rustico Bay, with a collection of Victorian houses gathered around a dainty church. One, Barachois Inn, has been lovingly restored as a bed-

and-breakfast of high reputation. One of Canada's first cooperative banks—a precursor of the credit-union movement—was founded here; it is now a National Historic Site and museum.

Continue along the shore road. As you gaze toward the sea, think of the hundreds of ships that sank in these waters including that of the famed Marco Polo, which ran aground off Cavendish. Follow the signs to **Green Gables House** in PEI National Park, the green-and-white farmhouse that is the setting for Lucy Maud Montgomery's first and most famous novel, *Anne of Green Gables*. The book was published in 1908, and it became one of the most popular children's books ever written. It's about a young orphan girl adopted by a strict but kindly brother and sister who live on a Prince Edward Island farm. The story has so caught the imagination of readers that hundreds of thousands of visitors from around the world visit Green Gables every summer. The house, once owned by Montgomery's cousins, is organized to reflect the story. *Near Cavendish, in PEI National Park, tel. 902/673-6350. Open mid-May-late June, daily 9-5; late June-Aug., daily 9-8; Sept. and Oct., daily 9-5.*

In **New London,** west of Cavendish on Route 6, is the modest white house where Lucy Maud Montgomery was born in 1874. Among memorabilia on display are the author's wedding dress and personal scrapbooks. *In New London, on Rte. 6, tel. 902/886-2596. Admission: $1 adults, 50¢ children. Open June and early Sept.-mid-Sept., daily 9-5; July and Aug., daily 9-7; mid-Sept.-mid-Oct., daily 9-5.*

The Blue Heron Drive follows the coastline south to the other side of the island through rolling farmland by the shores of Malpeque Bay, almost into Summerside. Across Malpeque Bay is **Lennox Island,** the largest Micmac Indian reserve in the province. The head of Malpeque Bay almost meets Bedeque Bay, nearly cutting the island in two. At Carleton, Blue Heron Drive intersects with Route 1, the main highway between Charlottetown and Borden and the terminus for the New Brunswick ferries.

Paralleling the coast, the drive continues past a fine Harris church at Crapaud to **Victoria,** a picturesque fishing village with antiques, art galleries, handicraft shops, and live summer theater in the historic **Victoria Playhouse** (tel. 902/658-2025 for ticket information and reservations).

The drive winds on through Argyle Shore to **Fort Amherst Port-La-Joye National Historic Site,** at the mouth of Charlottetown Harbour. This pretty spot, with its lighthouse, is the location of the first European settlement on the island, established in 1720 during French rule. You can picnic on the site while watching boats and cruise ships sail into the harbor. *32 km (20 mi) south of Charlottetown on Rte. 19 at Rocky Point, tel. 902/675-2220. Open mid-June-Labor Day, daily 10-6.*

## Tour 3: Kings Byway

The Kings Byway follows the coastline of Kings County for 375 kilometers (225 miles) on the eastern end of the island. The route passes woodlots, patchwork-quilt farms, fishing villages, and historic sites in this green and tranquil section of the province. Starting at Charlottetown, take Route 1 east and follow Kings Byway counter-clockwise.

**The Orwell Corner Historic Village** re-creates a 19th-century rural settlement in the form of a living farm museum, employing methods used by Scottish settlers in the 19th century, including the use of handsome draft horses. The village contains a beautifully restored store and post office, school, church, farmhouse, and barns. Musical evenings (ceilidhs) in the village feature traditional Scottish fiddle music by local musicians. *Tel. 902/651–2013. Admission: $3 adults, children under 12 free. Open late June–Labor Day, daily 9–5; mid-May–late June and Labor Day–late Oct., weekdays 10–3.*

**㉑** One of the island's most historic churches, **St. John's Presbyterian,** in Belfast, is just off Route 1 on Route 207. This pretty white church, on a hill against a backdrop of trees, was built by settlers from the Isle of Skye who were brought to the island in 1803 by Lord Selkirk.

**㉑** Route 1 passes **Wood Islands,** the terminus for the Northumberland Ferries service to Nova Scotia, which operates while Northumberland Strait is free of ice, generally from May through December.

**㉒** The island-dotted waters of **Murray Harbour** drain five rivers, and empty through the narrow gut between Poverty Beach and Beach Point. This favorite refuge for island yachtsmen supports a large fishing fleet.

---

**Time Out** | **Brehaut's Restaurant** (tel. 902/962–3141) in Murray Harbour village, right by the fishermen's wharf, has a take-out and café downstairs and a pleasant dining room upstairs. Tasty, wholesome food in a rustic ambience, with very pleasant service, is what you'll get here.

---

The eastern coastline is dotted with fishing villages and long uncrowded beaches. Seal-watching and bird-watching boat tours are
**㉓** available at Murray River and Montague; **St. Mary's Bay,** inside Panmure Island, offers excellent windsurfing behind a long protective beach. Three rivers enter into Cardigan Bay. Seductive
**㉔** **Montague,** on the Montague River, is the business hub of eastern
**㉕** PEI, while **Georgetown,** on a point between the Cardigan and Brudenell rivers, is a shipbuilding town with a lively summer thea-
**㉖** ter. **Bay Fortune,** a little-known scenic spot, has been a secret refuge of well-heeled Americans for two generations, and is home to the wonderful Inn at Bay Fortune (*see* Lodging, *below*) with old-time style and panache.

In early summer, you can see whole fields of blue, white, pink, and purple wild lupins sloping down to red cliffs and blue sea. The view
**㉗** from the hill overlooking the town of **Souris,** on the northeastern coast, is especially lovely. At Souris, a car-ferry links PEI with the Québec–owned Magdalen Islands. The Souris area is noted for its fine traditional musicians. An outdoor Scottish concert at Rollo Bay in July, featuring fiddling and step-dancing, attracts thousands every year.

---

**Time Out** | The **Uptown Restaurant** (tel. 902/687–4123), on the main street in Souris, is a Chinese restaurant with a difference. Ask about the silver aliwana fish—a Chinese species—in an aquarium on the wall, and try the "bumbleberry" pie.

---

**㉘** North of Souris, the **Basin Head Fisheries Museum** is located on a bluff overlooking the Atlantic Ocean. Displays include a boat shed, an aquarium, a smokehouse, a fish-box factory, a cannery, and fishermen's sheds. On the grounds is a fine beach. *Box 248, Souris, tel. 902/357–2966. Admission: $3 adults, children under 12 free. Open mid-June–Labor Day, daily 9–5; Labor Day–Sept., weekdays 9–5.*

Walk over the cast-iron bridge by the museum. The exquisite, silvery beach stretches northeast for miles, backed by high, grassy dunes. Scuff your feet in the sand: it will squeak, squawk, and purr at you. These are known locally as the "singing sands," a phenomenon found in only a few locations worldwide.

Follow the shore road (Route 16) and visit **East Point Lighthouse**; ships from many nations have wrecked on the reef running northeast from the lighthouse. An especially good stop for photographers and those interested in fishing communities is **North Lake**, several kilometers (a few miles) from Basin Head.

For even more extensive dune scenery, follow Route 2 to St. Peter's Bay, and Route 313 to **Greenwich**. The road ends among sandhills, but from here you can take a half-hour walk through beige dunes to reach the superb beach. These dunes are moving, gradually burying the nearby woods; here and there the bleached skeletons of trees thrust up through the sand like wooden ghosts.

## Tour 4: Lady Slipper Drive

This drive—named for the delicate lady slipper orchid, the province's official flower—winds along the coast of the narrow indented western end of the island through very old and very small villages, which still adhere to a traditional way of life. Many of these hamlets are inhabited by Acadians, descendants of the original French settlers. The area is known for its oysters and Irish moss, but most famously for its potato farms: The province is a major exporter of seed potatoes worldwide, and half the crop is grown here.

From Charlottetown, take Route 2 to **Summerside**, the second-largest community on the island. A self-guided walking tour of Summerside, arranged by the Summerside Tourism Office, is a pleasant excursion through the leafy streets, with their spacious houses. Some of these homes are known as "fox houses"; silver foxes were first bred in captivity in western PEI, and for several decades Summerside was the headquarters of a virtual gold rush based on fox ranching. For more history and walking-tour brochures, stop in at the **International Fox Museum and Hall of Fame**. *286 Fitzroy St., tel. 902/436–2400 or 902/436–1589. Admission free; $1 donation accepted. Open May–Sept., Mon.–Sat. 9–6.*

The eight-day **Summerside Lobster Carnival**, held every July, includes livestock exhibitions, harness racing, fiddling contests, and lobster suppers. Mid-summer **Grand Prix hydroplane races** take place in the harbor. The boats are powered by 1,500-horsepower engines and attain speeds of 150 miles (240 kilometers) per hour.

On Route 2, just west of Summerside, you will find the **Acadian Museum of Prince Edward Island,** located in **Miscouche**. The museum has a permanent exhibition on Acadian life as well as an audio-visual presentation depicting the history and culture of Island Acadian people from the first settlement of 1720 to the present. Access to 30,000 genealogical cards listing Acadian descent is available. *Rte. 2, Miscouche, tel. 902/436–6237. Admission: $2.75 adults, $1.50 students, under 6 free, $7 family. Open weekdays 9:30–5; late June–Labor Day, Sat. 9:30–5, Sun. 1–5.*

Relatively few visitors travel west of Summerside, which is unfortunate for them and fortunate for you. Route 2 travels straight as an arrow through the drab plain of the Miscouche Swamp. Avoid this route by following the Lady Slipper signs from Miscouche to **Port Hill**, about 35 kilometers (22 miles) northwest of Summerside. The

**Green Park Shipbuilding Museum and Historic House** was originally the home of shipbuilder James Yeo, Jr. This 19th-century mansion, restored and open to visitors, is topped by a cupola, from which Yeo observed his nearby shipyard through a spyglass. The modern museum building on the site details the history of the shipbuilder's craft. *Rte. 12, Port Hill, tel. 902/831–2206. Admission: $2.50 adults, children under 12 free. Open mid-June–Labor Day, daily 9–5.*

Lady Slipper Drive leads to the tiny community of **Tyne Valley,** reputed to offer some of the finest food on PEI, as well as an annual summer Oyster Festival. Lady Slipper Drive continues around ❸ Foxley Bay and Cascumpec Bay to **Alberton,** where Jacques Cartier made his first landing on the island. Oulton Island, just offshore, was the first place foxes were bred successfully in captivity and claims to be the world's first fur ranch.

❸ Follow the shore north to **Tignish,** another Acadian community. Everything in Tignish seems to be co-operative, including the supermarket, insurance company, fish plant, service station, and credit union. The imposing **parish church of St. Simon and St. Jude Parish House** (315 School St., tel. 902/882–2049), across from Dalton Square, has a superb Tracker pipe organ, one of the finest such instruments in eastern Canada, and is often used for recitals by world-renowned musicians.

The **Dalton Centre,** on Church Street, was built by the first fox-breeder, Sir Charles Dalton, a Tignish native; it now includes a museum. *Church St., tel. 902/882–2488. Admission:$1.50 adults, 75¢ children. Open mid-June–Aug., Sun.–Fri. 10–5.*

❸ Drive on to **North Cape,** where the island fades to a narrow north-pointing arrow of land with an imposing lighthouse. At low tide you can walk out onto one of the longest reefs in the world, a great spot to find tidal pools teeming with marine life. The curious structures nearby are wind turbines at the **Atlantic Wind Test Site,** set up on this breezy promontory to evaluate the feasibility of electrical generation by wind power. *Tel. 902/882–2746. Admission free. Open July–late Aug., daily 10–8.*

**Time Out** | **Wind & Reef** (tel. 902/882–3535) is a licensed restaurant that serves good seafood meals and has a breathtaking view of the Gulf of St. Lawrence and Northumberland Strait.

From the cape, Lady Slipper Drive turns almost due south along the island's western shore. Near North Cape, just off the Drive, is the very popular natural rock formation called "Elephant Rock." You may see draft horses in the fields or working in the surf. They are "moss horses," used in harvesting a versatile and valuable sea plant ❸ known as Irish moss. At **Miminegash,** visit the **Irish Moss Interpretive Centre,** and find out how much Irish moss was in your last ice-cream cone. *On Rte. 152 off Rte. 2, tel. 902/882–2920. Admission free. Open late June–Aug., weekdays 9–5.*

❸ At the southern tip of the western shore is **West Point,** with a tiny, man-made fishing harbor, provincial campsite, supervised beach, and what one recent visitor called an "insanely friendly" community. Above all, there is the **West Point Lighthouse,** 115 years old and the tallest on the island. When the lighthouse was automated, the community took over the building and converted it into an inn (you can book a room here) and museum, with a gift shop and an excellent, moderately priced restaurant attached. The area is steeped in ghostly tales and legends; ask about the Phantom Ship and the treasure that's supposed to be buried nearby. *Rte. 14, tel. 902/859–3605. Admission: $1.65 adults, $1.40 senior citizens, 85¢ children. Open mid-May–mid-Oct., daily 8–9:30.*

Lady Slipper Drive meanders back to Summerside through Région ❸❾ Evangeline, the main Acadian district of the island. At **Cape Egmont,** stop for a look at the **Bottle Houses,** the work of a retired carpenter: two tiny houses and a chapel built entirely out of glass ❹⓿ bottles mortared together like bricks. In **Mont-Carmel,** an adjoining community, is a magnificent brick church overlooking Northumberland Strait, and an **Acadian Pioneer Village** with a church, school, blacksmith shop, store, restaurant, and modern accommodations. *Rte. 11, tel. 902/854–2227. Admission to village: $2 adults, 75¢ students, children 50¢. Open mid-June–mid-Sept., daily 10–7.*

# Shopping

Prince Edward Islanders have been making beautiful homemade items since colonial days, when crafts were necessities of life. Island craftspeople excel at quilting, rug-hooking, weaving, knitting, and pottery, to name but a few crafts. Full information on outlets and types of crafts is provided by the **PEI Crafts Council** (156 Richmond St., Charlottetown C1A 1H9, tel. 902/892–5152). There are more than 100 crafts outlets throughout the island.

The **Island Crafts Shop** has a wide selection of weaving, pottery, woodwork and other items. *156 Richmond St., Charlottetown, tel. 902/892–5152. Open July and Aug., Mon.–Sat. 9–8, Sun. 11–4; Sept.–June, Mon.–Sat. 9:30–5.*

The **Wood Islands Handcraft Co-op Association Ltd.,** in southeastern Kings County, sells a large number of knitted and crocheted items and other crafts. *Murray River, Kings County, tel. 902/962–3539. Open daily 9–5; July and Aug., daily 9–6.*

Along Lady Slipper Drive look for hand-turned bird's-eye maple products at the **Leavitts' Wood Craft** in Alberton. *Alberton, tel. 902/853–2504. Open Mon.–Sat. 8–5.*

The **Dunes Studio and Gallery,** on Rte 15, near Brackley Beach, is the Island's most visually stunning shop and museum, featuring the work of leading local artists, as well as craftsmen and -women from around the world. The production pottery studio is open for viewing, as is a rooftop water garden. *Brackley Beach, tel. 902/672–2586. Open May–Oct., daily 10–6; July and Aug., daily 9–9; off-season by appointment.*

**Shoreline Sweaters,** sometimes known as Tyne Valley Studio, in Tyne Valley, is where Lesley Dubey produces sweaters with a unique Fair Isle–style lobster pattern, and sells local crafts. *Lady Slipper Dr., Tyne Valley, tel. 902/831–2950. Open mid-May–Sept., daily 9:30–5:30.*

You can buy fresh, canned, or frozen lobster and other seafood at numerous processing plants and retail stores throughout the island. Some, such as **Crabby's Seafood** in Wood Islands, will pack your purchases for travel. *Wood Islands, next to ferry, tel. 902/962–3228. Open daily 7–7.*

# Sports and Outdoor Activities

**Bicycling**  Prince Edward Island is popular with bike-touring companies for its moderately hilly roads and stunning scenery. Level areas can be found over most of the island, especially east of Charlottetown to Montague and along the north shore. However, shoulderless, narrow, secondary roads in some areas and summer's car traffic can be challenging for cyclists. An 8.7-kilometer (5.4-mile) path near Cavendish campground loops around marsh, woodland, and farmland. Cycling trips are organized throughout the province, and the Department of Tourism and Parks (*see* Important Addresses and Numbers in Essential Information, *above*) can recommend tour operators. Also, bicycles can be rented in Charlottetown and Cavendish.

**Hiking**  Hiking within the lush scenic areas of Prince Edward Island National Park and Cabot Provincial Park is encouraged with marked trails. Some of the former railway lines on the Island that have been abandoned are being upgraded to walking trails that lead to previously inaccessible areas. Many country roads are now protected as heritage roads, and provide a smooth walking surface for an uncomplicated hike. Or, pull over near a beach, take off your shoes, wiggle your toes in the sand, and listen to the sound of the surf and the cry of the gulls as you explore miles of coastal nature.

**Fishing**  PEI offers some of the best brook-trout fishing in eastern Canada, as well as excellent deep-sea fishing off the island's northeast coast. Charter boats leave daily in summer from the fishing ports of Cove Head, North Lake, and North Rustico, for very elusive tuna and rich mackerel fishing; there are more than 20 boat charters to choose from.

Clam digging is possible in many less-populated coastal areas around the island.

**Golf**  Popular with tourists, golfing in PEI is virtually hassle free: Tee-off times are easily booked any day of the week. **Stanhope Golf Course** (*see* Tour 2) is one of the more challenging courses on the island. In the western end, **Mill River Provincial Golf Course** (tel. 902/859–2238) in Mill River Provincial Park, 57 kilometers (35 miles) west of Summerside, is among the most scenic and challenging courses in eastern Canada. **Brudenell River Provincial Golf Course** (tel. 902/652–2332) at the east end of the island has hosted four national championships and three CPGAs. The latter two courses are within major resort complexes. **Green Gables Course** (tel. 902/963–2488) in Cavendish is a scenic Scottish-style "links" course. The Island's newest course, **The Links** (tel. 902/961–3274), at Crowbush Cove near Morell, is expected to be rated among the top five courses in Canada and many say it is PEI's best.

# Dining

On Prince Edward Island, plain, wholesome, home-cooked fare is a matter of course. The service is friendly—though a little laid back at times—and the setting is informal everywhere but in a few restaurants in Charlottetown. Seafood is generally good anywhere on the island, with top honors being given to lobster and any dish using local produce. Unless noted, there is no need to wear a jacket and tie.

Look for lobster suppers, offered both commercially and by church and civic groups. These meals feature lobster, rolls, salad, and mountains of sweet, home-baked goodies, and are usually presented at New London, New Glasgow, St. Ann's Church in Hope River, and Fisherman's Wharf in North Rustico. Check the local papers or the bulletin boards at local grocery stores.

Highly recommended restaurants in each price category are indicated by a star ★.

| Category | Cost* |
| --- | --- |
| $$$$ | over $35 |
| $$$ | $25–$35 |
| $$ | $15–$25 |
| $ | under $15 |

*per person, excluding drinks, service, 10% sales tax, and 7% GST*

**Bay Fortune**
★ **Inn at Bay Fortune.** Superb local fresh-caught and harvested ingredients are served in an ambiance reminiscent of a by-gone era. Dine amid antiques, many pieces collected by actress Colleen Dewhurst when she owned the Inn. This is where the movers and shakers take those they wish to impress. *Rte. 310, tel. 902/687–3745. Reservations advised. MC, V. Closed lunch and late Oct.–mid-May. $$$*

**Brackley Beach**
★ **Shaw's Hotel and Cottages.** This family-oriented hotel dating from the 1860s offers fine home cooking in an elegant, country setting. Lobster is served twice weekly, and the grand Sunday-night buffets draw people from near and far to sample fresh salmon, seafood casserole, home-baked breads, and a variety of popular desserts, such as cheesecake and fresh berries in season. Lunch is served in the tea room. *Rte. 15, tel. 902/672–2022. Reservations advised. AE, MC, V. Closed Oct.–May. $$$$*

★ **The Dunes Cafe.** This stunning café is an integral part of a pottery studio, art gallery, artisans outlet, and outdoor gardens. Elegant, soaring, wood ceilings add to a spacious setting that seats more than 80 people on two levels, as well as on an outside deck overlooking the dunes and marshlands of Covehead Bay. The chef specializes in local seafood and Island lamb, and dishes use locally-grown, fresh produce, much of which comes from the café's own gardens. *Rte. 15, tel. 902/672–2586. Reservations advised. AE, MC, V. Closed Nov.–May and weekday dinner in June, Sept., and Oct. $$*

**Cavendish**
**Fiddles 'n Vittles.** Lively, friendly, and decorated in rustic marine, with fishnets hanging in the dining room, the restaurant is true to its theme: House specialties are fresh and fried seafood. *Bay Vista Motor Inn, R.R. 1, Breadalbane, tel. 902/963–3003. AE, DC, MC, V. Closed mid-Sept.–mid-June. $*

**Charlottetown**
★ **The Griffin Room.** This cozy dining room of the Dundee Arms Inn has a working fireplace and is filled with antiques, copper, and brass. The French Continental cuisine uses only fresh, natural ingredients. Fresh seafood is served year-round, and salmon, scallops, and crab are available all winter. Specialties include rack of lamb, chateaubriand, and poached or grilled fillet of salmon in a light lime-dill sauce. *Dundee Arms Motel and Inn, 200 Pownal St., tel. 902/892–2496. Reservations advised. MC, V. $$$*

★ **Claddagh Room Restaurant.** You'll find some of the best seafood in Charlottetown here. The "Galway Bay Delight," one of the Irish owner's specialties, is a savory combination of fresh scallops and shrimp sautéed with onions and mushrooms, flambéed in Irish Mist, and doused with fresh cream. A pub upstairs features live Irish entertainment every night in summer and on weekends in winter. *131 Sydney St., tel. 902/892–9661. Reservations advised. AE, DC, MC, V. $$–$$$*

**Off Broadway.** Popular with Charlottetown's young professional set is this attractive, cozy spot located near the Confederation Centre of the Arts. It began modestly as a crêpe-and-soup joint, and indeed, you can still make a meal of the lobster or chicken crêpe and the spinach or Caesar salad that's served with it. But the restaurant also has a fairly inventive menu of such Continental entrées as the hearty mussel chowder, fillets, and salmon. The old-fashioned private booths won't reveal your indiscretions—including your penchant for one of the many desserts. *125 Sydney St., tel. 902/566–4620. Reservations advised. AE, MC, V. $$*

**Captain Scott's.** The fish-and-chips served at this spot in the Confederation Court Mall rival any found in England. *Corner of Grafton and Queen Sts., tel. 902/628–1674. No credit cards. Closed Sun. $*

**Cornwall** **Bonnie Brae.** What you'll find here is a welcoming and comfortable modern restaurant that offers well-prepared seafood and steaks. Summer's nightly all-you-can-eat lobster buffet is guaranteed to satisfy any appetite, but leave room for such desserts as Black Forest cake and raspberry cheesecake. *Trans-Canada Hwy., tel. 902/566–2241. Reservations advised. AE, DC, MC, V. $$$*

**Grand** **Dalvay-by-the-Sea.** Choose a table by the stone fireplace or dine with
**Tracadie** a lake view on the enclosed terrace. The menu at this elegant Victorian dining room, located in the Dalvay-by-the-Sea Hotel in PEI National Park, includes island lobster, curried scallops, poached halibut, peppercorn steak, and filet mignon—all served with fresh vegetables. Desserts are baked on the premises; blueberry grunt, a sweet dumpling with blueberry sauce, is the Dalvay's own traditional specialty dessert. *Rte. 6, near Dalvay Beach, tel. 902/672–2048. Reservations advised. AE, MC, V. Closed late Sept.–early June. $$$$*

# Lodging

Prince Edward Island offers a variety of accommodations at a variety of prices, from full-service resorts and luxury hotels to moderately priced motels, cottages, and lodges, to farms that take guests. Lodgings on the north coast in summer should be booked early, especially if you're planning a long stay.

Highly recommended lodgings in each price category are indicated by a star ★.

| Category | Cost* |
| --- | --- |
| $$$$ | over $75 |
| $$$ | $55–$75 |
| $$ | $40–$55 |
| $ | under $40 |

*All prices are for a standard double room, excluding 10% provincial sales tax and 7% GST.*

**Blooming** **Blue Heron Hideaways.** The MacAndrews, the owners, are a film
**Point** producer and a journalist who run these executive-style cottages, a

luxury beach-house, and a honeymoon cottage located just 15 minutes from downtown Charlottetown. The safe, private beach offers access to sand dunes and much wildlife and it's a great place for windsurfing. An outboard motorboat and gas barbecues are available for guest use. Weekly rentals only are available from early June through mid-October. *Meadowbank, R.R. 2, Cornwall, C0A 1H0, tel. 902/566–2427. One 2-bedroom cottage, two 3-bedroom cottages, one waterfront cottage with bunkhouse, one 6-bedroom oceanfront house with guest house. No credit cards. $$$$*

**Brackley Beach**
★

**Shaw's Hotel and Cottages.** Each room is unique in this 1860s hotel, with antique furnishings, floral-print wallpapers, and hardwood floors. Half the cottages have fireplaces. This country elegance doesn't come cheap; Shaw's is one of the most expensive hotels on the island. Guests can choose to include in their room rate a home-cooked breakfast and dinner in the Shaw's dining room (*see* Dining, *above*). *Rte. 15, C0A 2H0, tel. 902/672–2022. 40 units, including 18 cottages and 2 suites. Facilities: cocktail bar, sailboats, windsurfing, beach nearby. AE, MC, V. Closed late Sept.–May. $$$$*

**Cavendish**

**Bay Vista Inn.** This clean, friendly motel caters to families. Parents can sit on the outdoor deck and admire the New London Bay panorama while keeping an eye on their children in the motel's large playground. Almost all of the rooms have views of the bay. Fiddles 'n Vittles (*see* Dining, *above*) is a great place to eat with the family. *R.R.1, Breadalbane, C0A 1E0; in winter, R.R. 1, North Wiltshire C0A 1Y0, tel. 902/963–2225. 30 units, including 2 motel efficiencies. Facilities: restaurant, outdoor heated pool, playground, boating, deep-sea fishing, golf nearby. AE, MC, V. Closed late Sept.–mid-June. $$$*

**Charlottetown**

**Best Western MacLauchlan's Motor Inn.** One of the many good hotels in the Best Western chain, this one is convenient to downtown and contains 17 apartment suites with bedroom, living room, kitchen, and bathroom. A senior-citizens' program is available. *238 Grafton St., C1A 1L5, tel. 902/892–2461. 143 units. Facilities: dining room, lounge, indoor pool, sauna, Jacuzzi, gym, laundry facilities. AE, DC, MC, V. $$$$*

★

**The Charlottetown.** This five-story, redbrick hotel with white pillars and a circular driveway is just two blocks from the center of Charlottetown. The rooms and public areas offer the latest amenities but retain the hotel's old-fashioned flavor, with well-detailed, antique-reproduction furnishings. The grandeur and charm of the Confederation Dining Room will take you back to the elegance of a previous era. *Kent and Pownal Sts., Box 159, C1A 7K4, tel. 902/894–7371. 109 rooms, including 2 suites. Facilities: licensed dining room, lounge with entertainment, indoor pool, sauna, whirlpool, parking. AE, DC, MC, V. $$$$*

**Dundee Arms Inn.** Depending on your mood, you can choose to stay in either a 1960s motel or a 1904 inn. The motel is simple, modern, and neat; the inn is homey and furnished with brass and antiques. The Griffin Room (*see* Dining, *above*), the inn's dining room, serves fine French cuisine. Continental breakfast is included in motel and inn rates. *200 Pownal St., C1A 3W8, tel. 902/892–2496, fax 902/368–8532. 18 rooms, including 2 suites. Facilities: restaurant, pub. MC, V. $$$$*

★

**Prince Edward Hotel and Convention Centre.** Two-thirds of the rooms in this 10-story hotel overlook the developed Charlottetown waterfront. A member of the Canadian Pacific chain of hotels and resorts, the Prince Edward has all the comforts and luxuries of its first-rate counterparts—from Jacuzzis in some suites to a grand

ballroom and conference center. Guest rooms are modern and decorated in warm pastels. The lobby is a bright, open, two-story atrium
complete with a waterfall above the front desk. *18 Queen St., Box
2170, C1A 8B9, tel. 902/566–2222 or 800/828–7447. 211 rooms, including 33 suites. Facilities: 3 restaurants, lounge with nightly entertainment, heated indoor pool, whirlpool, sauna, Nautilus
equipment. AE, DC, MC, V. $$$$*

**Duchess of Kent Inn.** This turreted Victorian bed-and-breakfast is
packed with antiques, even in the bedrooms. It's within walking distance of Charlottetown's major sites, including the Confederation
Centre. *218 Kent St., C1A 1P2, tel. 902/566–5826. 7 rooms share 5
baths. Facilities: guest kitchen, living room with VCR, bicycle stor-
age. Closed Dec.–May. $$*

**Court Bed and Breakfast.** In a residential area 2 kilometers (1.2
miles) from downtown, this two-story bed-and-breakfast with a wel-
coming red door offers large, simple, comfortable rooms and a full,
hearty breakfast, including ham, eggs, bacon, muffins, and fresh
fruits in season. *68 Hutchinson Ct., C1A 8H7, tel. 902/894–5871. 2
rooms with shared bath. No credit cards. Closed Sept.–Apr. $*

**Sherwood Motel.** This is a small, clean, family-oriented motel about 5
kilometers (3.1 mi) north of downtown Charlottetown on Route 15.
The friendly owners offer help in reserving tickets for events and
planning day trips. Don't be daunted by the Sherwood's proximity
to the airport—the motel sees very little traffic. *R.R. 9, Winsloe
C1E 1Z3, tel. 902/892–2622 or 800/567–1622. 30 rooms with bath;
pets permitted. Facilities: kitchenettes (22 rooms), cable TV. MC,
V. $*

**Grand
Tracadie
★**

**Dalvay-by-the-Sea.** Just within the borders of the Prince Edward Is-
land National Park is this Victorian house, built in 1896 as a private
summer home. Now a popular inn and restaurant, Dalvay-by-the-
Sea offers elegant but homey rooms furnished with original antiques
and reproductions. Guests can sip drinks or tea on the porch while
admiring the inn's gardens, Dalvay Lake, or the nearby beach.
Breakfasts and dinners in the dining room, included in the room
rates, are exceptional (*see* Dining, *above*). *Rte. 6, near Dalvay
Beach. Box 8, York, C0A 1P0, tel. 902/672–2048, or 902/672–2546 in
winter. 31 rooms in main house and 2 cottages. Facilities: restau-
rant, lounge, 2 tennis courts, driving range, canoes, rowboats,
windsurfing. AE, MC, V. Closed mid-Sept.–mid-June. $$$$*

**Bay Fortune
★**

**The Inn at Bay Fortune.** The regularity with which this facility is on
"most recommended" lists confirms its reputation as an enticing,
unforgettable get-away. Formerly the summer home of a Broadway
playwright, and more recently of actress Colleen Dewhurst (Marilla
in *Anne of Green Gables*), it's now a charming inn overlooking For-
tune Harbour and Northumberland Straight, offering superb din-
ing (*see* Dining, *above*), cooking classes from a top chef, and a taste of
genteel living. A full breakfast is included in room rates. *Rte. 310,
Souris, R.R. #4, C0A 2B0, tel. 902/687–3745 or 203/633–4930 (off-
season). 11 rooms with bath, 8 with fireplace sitting areas. Closed
late Oct.–mid-May. $$$$*

**Montague**

**Lobster Shanty North.** Roses growing outside the windows of its
weathered-wood façade, and old fishnets draped around the barn-
board walls of the dining room, contribute to the truly charming
style of this motel. All rooms have picture windows and open onto a
deck that overlooks the Montague River. *Main St., Box 158, C0A
1R0, tel. 902/838–2463. 11 rooms. Facilities: restaurant, lounge,
golf, clam-digging, swimming nearby. AE, MC, V. $$*

**O'Leary**  **Rodd's Mill River Resort and Conference Centre.** With activities ranging from night skiing and tobogganing to golfing, this is truly an all-season resort. Ask about family weekend packages, offered year-round. *Box 399, C0B 1V0, tel. 902/859–3555 or 800/565–RODD. 90 rooms including 3 suites. Facilities: dining room, 2 bars, 2 heated indoor pools, golf course, pro shop, tennis court, 2 squash courts, fitness center with whirlpool and sauna, games room, gift shop, canoeing, windsurfing, bicycle rentals, ice-skating rink, toboggan run, cross-country skiing. AE, MC, V. Closed Nov.–early Dec., Apr. $$$$*

**Roseneath**  **Rodd's Brudenell River Resort.** A distinctive facility which opened in 1992, this is a great spot for the sports-minded, with it's indoor and outdoor swimming pools, 18-hole championship golf course, tennis courts, horseback riding, lawn bowling, canoeing, and two marinas. *Off Rte. 3 to Georgetown, P.O. Box 67, Cardigan C0A 1G0, tel. 902/ 652–2332 or 800/565–0207, winter 902/892–7448. 50 rooms, 38 riverside chalets. Facilities: licensed dining room, lounge, whirlpool, exercise room, saunas, gift shop. AE, MC, V. Closed Nov.–Apr. $$$$*

**Summerside**  **Loyalist Country Inn.** Located at the waterfront, this traditional inn with Victorian decor is close to the Eptek National Exhibition Centre and PEI Sports Hall of Fame, a marina, shopping mall, and outdoor summer entertainment. *195 Harbour Dr., Summerside C1N 5B2, tel. 902/436–3333, fax 902/436–4304. 42 rooms, 10 with whirlpool. Facilities: indoor pool and sauna, tennis court, outside patio, licensed dining room and lounge. AE, DC, MC, V. $$$*

**Quality Inn Garden of the Gulf.** Close to downtown Summerside, this clean motel is a convenient place to stay. The nine-hole golf course on the property slopes to Bedeque Bay. *618 Water St. E, C1N 2V5, tel. 902/436–2295 or 800/265–5551. 83 rooms, including 6 suites. Facilities: restaurant, coffee shop, lounge, heated outdoor pool, indoor pool, gift shop, 9-hole golf course. AE, DC, MC, V. $$–$$$*

**Glade Motor Inn and Cottages.** Conveniently located 10 minutes from the Borden Ferry Terminal, this property has comfortable if generic motel rooms as well as cottages. What's different about the place is that it is set on a 300-acre farm, with horseback riding and nature trails. Kids get free rides in the corral. *Box 1387, C1N 4K2, tel. 902/436–5564. 33 units. Facilities: restaurant, lounge, heated outdoor pool, horseback riding, nature trails. AE, MC, V. Closed late-Sept.–mid-June. $$*

**Tyne Valley**  **The Doctor's Inn Bed & Breakfast.** This charming, beautifully landscaped village home is a joy in summer, with its beds of herbs and flowers. The inn caters to cross-country skiers on winter weekends. There's plenty of opportunity to gather 'round the woodstove and share good conversation over a warm drink. One dining room table seats up to eight, where you can experience fine meals based on what is available from local fishermen and farmers and from the inn's own organic gardens. *1 Rte. 167, C0B 2C0, tel. 902/831–2164. 2 rooms with shared bath. V. $$*

**West Point**  **West Point Lighthouse.** This unique property is still a functioning lighthouse (though automated), situated within a provincial park. Nearby are nature trails and opportunities to clam-dig, fish, and bike. Within the lighthouse is a museum and licensed dining room and patio; outside is the beach. Two rooms have a whirlpool tub. Complimentary breakfast is served on your first morning. *R.R. 2, O'Leary, C0B 1V0, tel. 902/859–3605. 9 rooms. MC, V. Closed Oct.– early May. $$$*

# The Arts

The highlights of the island's theater season are the productions of the **Charlottetown Festival,** which takes place from June through October at the Confederation Centre of the Arts.

Special art exhibitions are offered in the Confederation Centre Gallery, one of Canada's premier museums. The permanent collection features the country's largest assemblage of paintings by Robert Harris (1848–1919), Canada's foremost portrait artist. For information and tickets to the festival, contact the **Confederation Centre of the Arts** (145 Richmond St., Charlottetown C1A 1J1, tel. 902/628–1864; box office, 902/566–1267).

**Eptek National Exhibition Centre and PEI Sports Hall of Fame,** on the waterfront properties in Summerside, displays changing history and fine arts exhibits from all parts of Canada. *Harbour Dr., Summerside C1N 5B2, tel. 902/888–8873. Admission free. Open June–Sept., daily; Oct.–May, Tues.–Sun.*

The **King's Playhouse** (tel. 902/652–2053) in Georgetown, 50 kilometers (30 miles) east of Charlottetown, offers varied entertainment from June through early September. The **Victoria Playhouse** (tel. 902/658–2025) in Victoria, a half-hour's drive west of Charlottetown, features professional repertory theater. The **Feast** (tel. 902/436–7674) dinner-theater provides rollicking entertainment and a satisfying meal, hosting productions at Brothers Two Water Street Station restaurant in Summerside, as well as at various hotels in Charlottetown. **La Cuisine a Mémé** (tel. 902/854–2227), a French dinner-theater, offers typical Acadian entertainment, such as stepdancing and fiddle music, and a buffet in Mont-Carmel.

Concerts and musical festivals abound on the island, especially in summer. Live traditional Celtic music, with fiddling and step-dancing, can be heard almost any day of the week. Best bets: the outdoor fiddle festival (tel. 902/368–5555) at Rollo Bay in late July; **The College of Piping and Celtic Performing Arts of Canada** (tel. 902/436–5377) summer concerts and highland games in Summerside; Friday night ceilidhs at the **Benevolent Irish Hall** (tel. 902/892–2367) in Charlottetown; and the Sunday concerts of classical, sacred, and traditional music at **St. Mary's Church** (tel. 902/836–3733) in Indian River, between Charlottetown and Summerside.

# 13 New Brunswick

*By Colleen Whitney Thompson*

*Updated by Ana Watts*

New Brunswick is where the great Canadian forest, sliced by sweeping river valleys and modern highways, meets the sea. It's an old place in New World terms, and the remains of a turbulent past are still in evidence in some of its quiet nooks. Near Moncton, for instance, bees gather nectar and wild strawberries perfume the air of the grassy slopes of Fort Beausejour, where, in 1755, one of the last battles for possession of Acadia took place—the English finally overcoming the French. The dual heritage of New Brunswick (35% of its population is Acadian French) provides added spice. If you decide to stay in both Acadian and Loyalist regions, a trip to New Brunswick can seem like two vacations in one.

More than half the province is surrounded by coastline—the rest nestles into Québec and Maine, creating slightly schizophrenic attitudes in border towns. The dramatic Bay of Fundy, which has the highest tides in the world, sweeps up the coast of Maine, around the enchanting Fundy Isles at the southern tip of New Brunswick and on up the province's rough and intriguing south coast. To the north and east, the gentle, warm Gulf Stream washes quiet beaches.

New Brunswick is still largely unsettled—85% of the province is forested lands. Inhabitants have chosen the easily accessible area around rivers, ocean, and lakes, leaving most of the interior to the pulp companies. For years this Cinderella province has been virtually ignored by tourists who whiz through to better-known Atlantic destinations. New Brunswick's residents can't seem to decide whether this makes them unhappy or not. Money is important in the economically depressed maritime area, where younger generations have traditionally left home for higher-paying jobs in Ontario and "the West." But no one wishes to lose the special characteristics of this still unspoiled province by the sea.

This attitude is a blessing in disguise to motorists who leave major highways to explore 2,240 kilometers (1,400 miles) of spectacular seacoast, pure inland streams, pretty towns, and historical cities. The custom of hospitality is so much a part of New Brunswick nature that tourists are perceived more as welcome visitors than paying guests. Even cities often retain a bit of naiveté. It makes for a charming vacation, but don't be deceived by ingenuous attitudes. Most residents are products of excellent school and university systems, generally travel widely, live in modern cities, and are well versed in world affairs.

# Essential Information

## Important Addresses and Numbers

**Tourist Information**
**Department of Economic Development and Tourism** (Box 6000, Fredericton E3B 5H1, tel. 506/453–2170 or 800/561–0123) can provide information on the seven provincial tourist bureaus. Also helpful are information services of the cities of: **Bathurst** (tel. 506/548–0400), **Campbellton** (tel. 506/789–2367), **Fredericton** (tel. 506/452–9500), **Moncton** (tel. 506/853–3590), and **Saint John** (tel. 506/658–2990).

**Emergencies**
Dial 911 for medical emergencies and police in New Brunswick cities and their surrounding areas. For other areas find emergency numbers inside the front cover of the local telephone directory.

*Hospitals*
**Dr. Everett Chalmers Hospital** (Priestman St., Fredericton, tel. 506/452–5400); **Moncton City Hospital** (135 MacBeath Ave., Moncton,

tel. 506/857–5111); **Dr. Georges Dumont Hospital** (330 Archibald St., Moncton, tel. 506/858–3232); **Saint John Regional Hospital** (Tucker Park Rd., Saint John, tel. 506/648–6000); **Chaleur Regional Hospital** (1750 Sunset Dr., Bathurst, tel. 506/548–8961); **Campbellton Regional Hospital** (189 Lilly Lake Rd., Campbellton, tel. 506/789–5000); **Edmundston Regional Hospital** (275 Hébert Blvd., tel. 507/739–2200); **Hôtel Dieu** (53 Lobban Ave., Chatham, tel. 506/773–4401).

## Arriving and Departing by Plane

**Canadian Airlines International** through **Air Atlantic** (tel. 800/665–1177) operates in Saint John, Fredericton, Moncton, Charlo, and Chatham and serves the Atlantic provinces, Montréal, Ottawa, and Boston. **Air Canada** and its regional carrier **Air Nova** (tel. 800/776–3000) serves New Brunswick in Saint John, Moncton, Fredericton, Bathurst, and Saint-Léonard, and serves the Atlantic provinces from Montréal, Toronto, and Boston.

## Arriving and Departing by Car Ferry, Train, and Bus

**By Car Ferry** There are car ferries from Prince Edward Island and Nova Scotia. **Marine Atlantic** (tel. 902/794–7203) has a car-and-passenger ferry from Digby, Nova Scotia, which takes 2½ hours. For reservations in the United States, call 800/341–7981.

**By Train** **VIA Rail** offers passenger service three times a week from Moncton to Montréal and Halifax. The southern route connects Montréal with Halifax by way of Fredericton Junction, Saint John, and Moncton. The northern route goes through Campbellton and on to Moncton and Halifax. Bus connections are available to Prince Edward Island and Newfoundland.

**By Bus** **SMT** (tel. 506/859–5100) within the province connects with most major bus lines.

## Getting Around

**By Car** New Brunswick has an excellent highway system with numerous facilities. The only map you'll need is the one available at the tourist information centers listed above. Major entry points are at St. Stephen, Houlton, Edmundston, and Cape Tormentine from Prince Edward Island, and Aulac from Nova Scotia.

## Guided Tours

**Boat Tours** Harbor tours are offered in Saint John by **Partridge Island Tours** (tel. 506/693–2598) and **DMK Marine Tours** (tel. 506/635–4150, fax 506/635–8714).

**City Tours** **Heritage Tour Guide Service** (856 George St., Fredericton, tel. 506/459–5950) provides guides for bus tours of Fredericton.

The **Calithumpians** theater company offers guides dressed in 18th-century costume for free historical walks from City Hall (Queen St., tel. 506/457–1975).

In Saint John free guided walking tours begin in Market Square at Barbours General Store. For information call the Saint John Tourist and Convention Center (tel. 506/658–2990).

**Special-Interest** More than 240 species of seabirds nest on Grand Manan Island, and the island is a paradise for painters, nature photographers, and hikers, not to mention whale-watchers. Any of these activities can be arranged by calling **Tourism New Brunswick** at 800/561–0123. **Covered Bridge Bicycle Tours** (Box 693, Dept. K, Main Post Office, Saint John E2L 4B3, tel. 506/849–9028) offers bike tours. **Fundy Rock and Ice School** (Box 6713, Station A, Saint John E2L 4S2, tel. 506/658–1906) leads hikes in the Fundy area.

# Exploring New Brunswick

Our exploration of New Brunswick is broken down into four areas: a tour of the city of Fredericton, a tour of the Saint John Valley ending at the city of Saint John, a tour of the Fundy Coast, and a jog north to the sunny Acadian Peninsula.

## Highlights for First-Time Visitors

**Acadian Village,** Grand Anse, Tour 4: Moncton and the Acadian Peninsula
**Beaverbrook Art Gallery,** Tour 1: Fredericton
**Campobello Island,** Tour 3: The Fundy Coast
**Fundy National Park,** Tour 3: The Fundy Coast
**Kings Landing,** Prince William, Tour 1: Fredericton
**Kouchibouguac National Park, Acadian Peninsula,** Tour 4: The Acadian Peninsula
**Market Square and Market Slip,** Saint John, Tour 2: Saint John River Valley
**Moncton's Tidal Bore and Magnetic Hill,** Tour 4: Moncton and the Acadian Peninsula

## Tour 1: Fredericton

*Numbers in the margin correspond to points of interest on the New Brunswick and Fredericton maps.*

The small inland city of **Fredericton** spreads itself on a broad point of land jutting into the Saint John River. Its predecessor, the early French settlement of St. Anne's Point, was established in 1642, during the reign of the French governor, Villebon, who made his headquarters at the junction of the Nashwaak and the Saint John rivers. Settled by Loyalists and named for Frederick, second son of George III, the city serves as the seat of government for New Brunswick's 728,500 residents. From the first town plan, the wealthy and scholarly Loyalists set out to create a gracious and beautiful place, and thus even before the establishment of the University of New Brunswick, in 1785, the town served as a center for "liberal arts and sciences."

Fredericton's streets are shaded by leafy plumes of ancient elms. Downtown Queen Street runs parallel with the river, and its blocks enclose historic sites and attractions. Most major sites are within walking distance.

**❶** The **Military Compound** (including Officer's Quarters, parade grounds, Guard House, and Soldiers' Barracks) extends two blocks along Queen Street, at the corner of Carleton Street. The buildings have been restored, and visitors are welcome to tour the Guard House and Soldier's Barracks; soldier's from the British 15th Regiment will be your guide. Redcoats stand guard; in summer a changing-of-the-guard ceremony takes place in Officer's Square at 11 and 7. *Queen St. at Carleton St., tel. 506/453–3747. Admission free.*

*Open early June–Labor Day, daily 10–6; Sept.–June, group tours by appointment.*

Within the Military Compound stands the John Thurston Clark Building—an outstanding example of Second Empire architecture. On the main floor is the **National Exhibition Centre.** You'll have fun with the scintillating displays of arts, crafts, history, science, and technology. Upstairs you'll find the Sports Hall of Fame, which celebrates the surprising array of locals who have made sports history, most notably, Ron Turcotte, who won horse racing's Triple Crown on the immortal Secretariat. The Hall of Fame's collection of original charcoal portraits of honored members is the largest of its kind in Canada. *503 Queen St., tel. 506/453–3747. Admission free. Both attractions open May 1–Labor Day, daily 10–6 or by appt.; Labor Day–end of April, Tues.–Sun. noon–5 or by appt.*

**②** Officer's Quarters houses the **York-Sunbury Museum,** a living picture of the community from the time when only natives inhabited the area, through the pioneer days, to the immediate past. It also contains the shellacked remains of one of Fredericton's legends, the puzzling Coleman Frog. This giant frog, allegedly discovered in nearby Killarney Lake by late hotelier Fred Coleman, supposedly weighed 42 pounds soaking wet at the time of its death (by a dynamite charge set by unorthodox fishermen). Coleman had the frog stuffed and displayed it for years in the lobby of his hotel. Take a look and judge for yourself—the frog just keeps on smiling. *Officer's Sq., Queen St., tel. 506/455–6041. Admission: $1 adults, 50¢ senior citizens and students, $2.50 families. Open May–Labor Day, Mon.–Sat. 10–6 (July and Aug., Tues. and Thurs. 10–9 and Sun. noon–6); Labor Day–mid-Oct., weekdays 9–5, Sat. noon–4; mid-Oct.–Apr., Mon., Wed., and Fri. 11–3 or by appt.*

Just a block or so east along the same street, at the intersection where Queen Street becomes Waterloo Row, you'll come to the **③ Christ Church Cathedral,** one of Fredericton's prides. Completed in 1853, the gray stone building is an excellent example of decorated Gothic architecture and the first new cathedral foundation built on British soil since the Norman Conquest. Inside you'll see a clock known as "Big Ben's little brother," the test-run for London's famous timepiece, designed by Lord Grimthorpe.

The late Lord Beaverbrook, former New Brunswick resident and multimillionaire British peer and newspaper magnate, showered gifts upon his native province. Near the cathedral you'll find the **④ Beaverbrook Art Gallery,** displaying works by many of New Brunswick's noted artists as well as internationally acclaimed painters. Salvador Dali's gigantic canvas *Santiago el Grande* is worth more than a passing glance. There are also canvases by Reynolds, Turner, Hogarth, Gainsborough, the Canadian Group of Seven, and even Andy Warhol. The gallery has the largest collection in any public institution of the works of Cornelius Krieghoff, famed Canadian landscape painter of the early 1800s. *703 Queen St., tel. 506/458–8545. Admission: $3 adults, $2 senior citizens, $1 students. Open July and Aug., Sun.–Wed. 10–5, Thurs.–Sat. 10–7; fall and winter, Tues.–Sat. 10–5, Sun.–Mon. noon–5.*

Beside the gallery sits **The Playhouse** (686 Queen St., tel. 506/458–8344), a gift of the Beaverbrook and Dunn Foundation to the city and province. It is the home of the professional **Theatre New Brunswick,** whose major season runs from September through May.

**⑤** Directly across the street from the gallery is the 1880 **Provincial Legislature.** The interior of the Chamber, restored in 1988, reflects

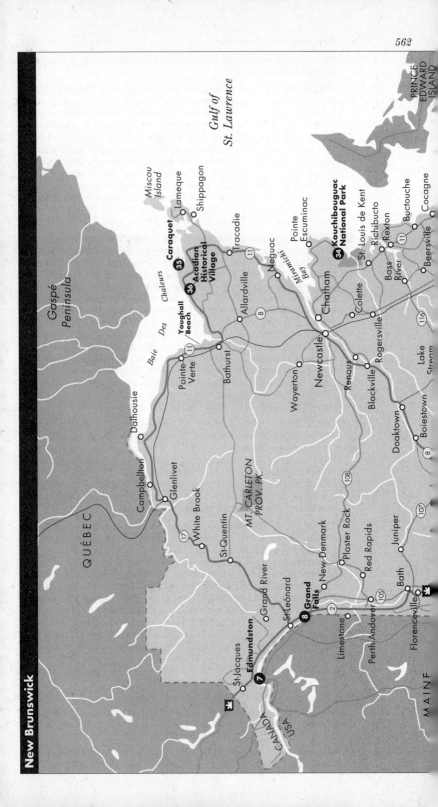

**New Brunswick**

Gulf of
St. Lawrence

PRINCE EDWARD ISLAND

Gaspé
Peninsula

QUÉBEC

Baie   Des   Chaleurs

Miscou Island

Lameque
Shippagon

**Caraquet** 35
36 **Acadian Historical Village**

Youghall Beach

Tracadie

Neguac

Pointe Escuminac

**Kouchibouguac National Park** 34

St. Louis de Kent
Richibucto
Rexton
Buctouche
Cocagne

Bass River
Beersville

11

Miramichi Bay

Chatham

Colette

Allardville

8

Pointe Verte

Bathurst

Dalhousie

Campbellton

Glenlivet

White Brook

St-Quentin

MT. CARLETON PROV. PK.

Wayerton

Newcastle

Renous

Rogersville

Lake Stream

116

11

Blackville

Doaktown

Boiestown

8

108

New Denmark

Plaster Rock

Red Rapids

Juniper

107

Grand River

St-Léonard

**Grand Falls** 8

2

New Denmark

Bath

105

Perth-Andover

Florenceville

St-Jacques

**Edmundston** 7

17

Limestone

CANADA
USA

M A I N E

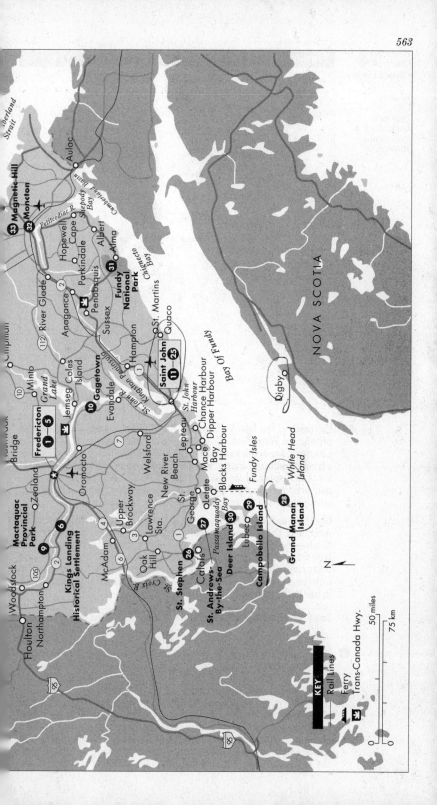

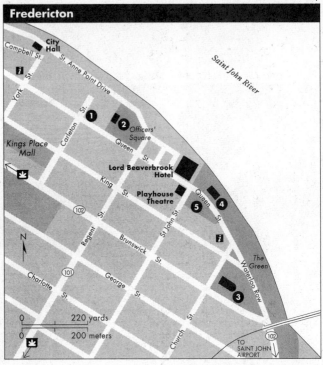

**Fredericton**

the taste of the late Victorians. The chandeliers are brass and the
prisms are Waterford. The portraits of King George III and Queen
Charlotte are replicas of paintings by Sir Joshua Reynolds. There is
a free-standing staircase, and a volume of Audubon's *Birds of America* is on display. *Queen St., tel. 506/453-2527. Admission free. Legislature tours: early-June–late Aug., daily 9–8; early Sept.–June,
weekdays 9–4. Library open year-round, weekdays 8:15–5.*

Continue east on Waterloo Row (Rte. 102), turn south at University
Avenue to the **University of New Brunswick** campus. Be prepared to
climb—the buildings are scattered over a fairly steep hill. The college was established in 1785—ancient by Canadian standards—and
was originally called the College of New Brunswick, and later Kings
College. Its Old Arts Building is the oldest university structure still
in use in the country.

## Tour 2: The Saint John River Valley to Saint John

To understand New Brunswick's background and history, visit
**⑥ Kings Landing Historical Settlement,** located about 30 kilometers
(23 miles) west of Fredericton on the Trans-Canada Highway. This
reconstructed village—more than 60 buildings, including homes,
inn, forge, store, church, school, working farms, and sawmill—illustrates life in the central Saint John River valley between 1790 and
1900. Winding country lanes, creaking wagons, old houses, and
freshly baked bread pull you back a century or more. The costumed
staff is friendly and informative. The Tap Room of Kings Head Inn is
a congenial spot to try a draft of cold beer or a mug of frosty cider;
the restaurant upstairs serves tasty, old-fashioned traveler's fare.

After a hearty meal of King George III's roast beef or Mrs. Long's chicken vegetable pie, drop by the General Store. It's the heart of the community and the genial storekeeper makes everyone feel welcome. *Box 522, Fredericton, tel. 506/363–5090. Admission: $7.50 adults, $6 senior citizens, $6 students under 18, $4.50 youth 6–18, children under 6 free, $18 families. Other discounts and group rates available. Open June–mid-Oct., daily 10–5.*

The Saint John River forms 120 kilometers (75 miles) of the border with Maine and rolls down to Saint John, New Brunswick's largest, and Canada's oldest, city. Gentle hills of rich farmland and the blue sweep of the water make this a pretty drive. The Trans-Canada Highway (Highway 2) follows the banks of the river for most of its winding, 403-kilometer (250-mile) course.

At the northern end of the valley, near the border with Québec, you will find yourself in the mythical Republic of Madawaska. In the early 1800s the narrow wedge of land was coveted by Québec on one side and New Brunswick on the other; the United States claimed it as well. Seeking to retain it for New Brunswick, Governor Sir Thomas Carleton found it easy to settle with Québec. He rolled dice all night with the governor of British North America at Québec, who happened to be his brother. Sir Thomas won at dawn—by one point. Settling with the Americans was more difficult. The border had always been disputed, and even the lumbermen engaged in combat. Finally, in 1842, the British flag was hoisted over Madawaska county. One old-timer, tired of being asked to which country he belonged, replied, "I am a citizen of the Republic of Madawaska." So began the republic, which exists today with its own flag (an independent eagle on a field of white) and a coat of arms.

❼ **Edmundston,** the unofficial capital of Madawaska, has always depended on the wealth of the deep forest around it. Even today, Edmundston looks to the Fraser Company pulp mills as the major source of employment. It was in these woods that the legend of Paul Bunyan was born. Tales spread to Maine and even to the West Coast. The Foire Brayonne festival, held annually during the last week of July, is proud to claim the title of the biggest festival outside of Québec's Winter Carnival. It is certainly one of the most lively and vibrant cultural events in New Brunswick, offering prestigious concerts by acclaimed artists as well as local musicians and entertainers who enliven the Arts & Crafts Square. In winter the whole province enjoys skiing on the slopes of Mt. Farlagne.

❽ About 50 kilometers (30 miles) downriver, at **Grand Falls,** the Saint John throws itself over a high cliff, squeezes through a narrow rocky gorge, and emerges as a wider river. The result is a magnificent cascade, whose force has worn strange round wells in the rocky bed— some as much as 16 feet in circumference and 30 feet deep. Take the Gorge Walk ($2 adults, $1 children, $5 families) where you'll see the holes and the magnificent stream up close. According to Indian legend, a young maiden named Malabeam led her Iroquois captors to their deaths over the foaming cataract rather than guide them to her village. Local history is depicted at the **Grand Falls Historical Museum.** *209 Sheriff St., tel. 506/473–5265. Admission free. Open July and Aug., Mon.–Sat. 9–5, Sun. 2–5; Sept.–June, by appt.*

Although Grand Falls is largely French-speaking, English becomes more prevalent as you move down the Saint John River valley. Stop in **Florenceville** for a look at the small but reputable Andrew and Laura McCain Gallery, which has launched the career of many a New Brunswick artist.

The Trans-Canada Highway is intriguingly scenic, but if you're looking for less crowded highways and typical small communities, cross the river to Route 105 at Hartland, via the **longest covered bridge** in the world—1,282 feet in length.

If you prefer, stay on the Trans-Canada Highway until you reach the quiet hamlet of **Woodstock** (population 4,911). The town was named for a novel by Sir Walter Scott, and is most lively during its Old Home Week celebrations, in July. Built in 1883, the **Old Courthouse**—once a coaching stop, a social hall, a political meeting place, and the seat of justice for the area—has been carefully restored.

**Time Out** | Between Woodstock and Meductic, look for good German food at **Heino's Restaurant,** in the John Gyles Motel (junction Route 2 and Trans-Canada Highway).

**⑨** Within the **Mactaquac Provincial Park** is Mactaquac pond, whose existence is attributed to the building of the hydroelectric dam, which has caused the upper Saint John River to flood as far up as Woodstock. The park has wheelchair accessible campsites. *Hwy. 105 and Mactaquac Dam, tel. 506/363–3011. 300 campsites, supervised recreation, 2 beaches, 2 marinas, 18-hole golf course, and lodge with dining room. Admission: $3.50 per vehicle in summer, free in off-season. Open May 15–Sept. 2 for camping 24 hrs; early Sept.–mid-May for day and evening activities.*

From Fredericton to Saint John you have a choice of two routes. Route 7 cuts away from the river to run straight south for its fast 109 kilometers (68 miles). Route 102 leads along the Saint John River through engaging communities. You make your decision at **Oromocto,** the site of the Canadian Armed Forces Base, **Camp Gagetown** (not to be confused with the pretty town of Gagetown farther down river), the largest military base in Canada (Prince Charles completed his helicopter training here). An interesting military museum within the base is open to the public. *Tel. 506/422–2630. Admission free. Open July and Aug., weekdays 9–5, weekends and holidays noon–5; Sept.–June, weekdays 8:30–noon and 1–4.*

**⑩** **Gagetown,** one of New Brunswick's pleasant historic communities, bustles with artisans' studios and the summer sailors who tie up at the marina. The gingerbread-trimmed **Tilley House** takes you back to Canada's beginnings. Once the home of Sir Leonard Tilley, one of the Fathers of Confederation, it is now home of the Queens County Museum. *Front St., tel. 506/488–2966. Admission: $1 adults. 25¢ students. Open mid-June–mid-Sept., daily 10–5.*

From Gagetown you can ferry to Jemseg and continue to **Grand Lake Provincial Park** (tel. 506/385–2919), which offers freshwater swimming on sandy beaches. At Evandale you can ferry to Belleisle Bay and the beautiful **Kingston Peninsula,** with its mossy Loyalist graveyards and pretty churches.

**⑪** As you travel south you'll begin to get a feeling for how old New Brunswick really is, and nowhere more so than in **Saint John.** It was the first incorporated city in Canada and has that weather-beaten quality common to so many antique seaport communities. Although sometimes termed a blue-collar town because so many of its residents work for Irving Oil, its genteel Loyalist heritage lingers; you sense it in its grand old buildings, the ladies' teas at the old Union Club, and the beautifully restored downtown harbor district.

The city has spawned many of the province's major artists—Jack Humphrey, Millar Brittain, Fred Ross—along with such Hollywood notables as Louis B. Mayer, Donald Sutherland, and Walter Pidgeon. There's also a large Irish population that emerges in a jubilant Irish Festival every March. In July, costumed residents reenact the landing of the Loyalists during the Loyalist City Festival.

In 1604, two Frenchmen, Samuel de Champlain and Sieur de Monts, landed here on Saint John the Baptist Day to trade with the natives. Nearly two centuries later, in May of 1785, 3,000 Loyalists escaping from the Revolutionary War poured off a fleet of ships to found a city amid the rocks and forests. From those beginnings Saint John has emerged as a thriving industrial port.

Up until the early 1980s, the buildings around Saint John's waterfront huddled together in forlorn dilapidation, their facades crumbling and blurred by a century of grime. A surge of civic pride sparked a major renovation project that reclaimed old warehouses as part of an enchanting waterfront development.

*Numbers in the margin correspond to points of interest on the Downtown Saint John and Greater Saint John maps.*

❷ You can easily explore Saint John's town center and harbor area on foot. Get your bearings on **King Street,** the town's old main street, whose sidewalks are paved with red brick and lit with old-fashioned ❸ lamps. King Street connects **Market Slip** on the waterfront with King Square at the center of town.

At Market Slip, where the Loyalists landed in 1783, and the adjoining ❹ **Market Square,** you can while away a morning among the shops, historic displays, and cafés (some with outdoor dining in summer). Market Slip is the site of **Barbour's General Store** (tel. 506/658–2939), a fully stocked 19th-century shop redolent of the past: Inside, the scents of tobacco, pickles, smoked fish, and peppermint sticks mingle with the tangy, unforgettable aroma of dulse, the edible seaweed. Beside the store is a 19th-century red schoolhouse, now a tourist information center. Skywalks and underground passages lead from Market Square to City Hall, the new Delta Hotel, and Brunswick Square, an adjoining shopping mall.

❺ Stroll up King Street to Germain Street, turn left, and walk up to the block-long **Old City Market,** built in 1876, which offers a variety of temptations, including red fresh-cooked lobster, great cheeses, dulse, and other inexpensive snacking along with much friendly chatter.

❻ The imposing **Old Loyalist House,** built in 1810 by Daniel David Merritt, a wealthy Loyalist merchant, is distinguished by its authentic period furniture and eight fireplaces. *120 Union St., tel. 506/652–3590. Admission: $2 adults, 25¢ children. Open June–Sept., Mon.–Sat. 10–5, Sun. 2–5, or by appt.; off-season, by appt.*

❼ Follow Union Street away from the harbor to Sydney Street and ❽ turn right to visit the **Old Loyalist Burial Grounds.** At one corner, in adjacent **King Square,** you'll find a strange mass of metal on the ground. It is actually a great lump of melted stock from a neighboring hardware store that was demolished in Saint John's Great Fire of 1877, in which hundreds of buildings were destroyed.

❾ At the corner of King and Sydney streets is the **Old Courthouse.** Its spiral staircase, built of tons of unsupported stone, ascends seemingly by miracle for three stories.

❿ Walk around the south side of King Square to visit **Trinity Church** (115 Charlotte St., tel. 506/693–8558), which dates from 1877, when it was rebuilt after the Great Fire. Inside, over the west door, note

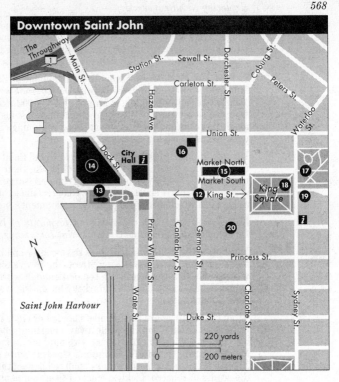

**Downtown Saint John**

the coat of arms—a symbol of the monarchy—rescued from the council chamber of the colony at Massachusetts Bay. The coat of arms was deemed a worthy refugee and given a place of honor in the church.

**㉑** If you have a car, drive north from downtown on Prince William Street to Main Street; in a park on your right you'll find **Fort Howe** (Rockland Road and Magazine Street). The reconstructed fortress sits atop a cliff overlooking the harbor and affords fine views from its walls. It is near the site of Fort LaTour, a French stronghold resolutely defended by Madame La Tour from her absent husband's fur-trading rival. Finally surrendering on the condition that the lives of her men would be spared, the unfortunate woman was betrayed and forced to watch them all put to death. She died shortly after, of a broken heart it is said—a romantic fate befitting her former profession as star of the Paris stage.

**㉒** Main Street soon crosses Douglas Avenue; turn left to reach two of the city's most notable attractions. First is the **New Brunswick Museum,** Canada's oldest continuing museum. Its exhibits reflect the history, culture and spirit of New Brunswick. Displays include fine arts, natural science, marine history, and an immense collection of historical artifacts and scientific specimens. The Museum's Discovery Centre provides hands-on science experiences for kids. *277 Douglas Ave., tel. 506/643–2300. Admission: $2 adults, $5 families, $1 students and children (4 and over). Group tours can be arranged. Open daily 10–5. Closed Good Friday and Dec. 25.*

**㉓** Continue west on Douglas Avenue to reach the **Reversing Falls Rapids,** touted by all tourist brochures as a sight no one should miss. Ac-

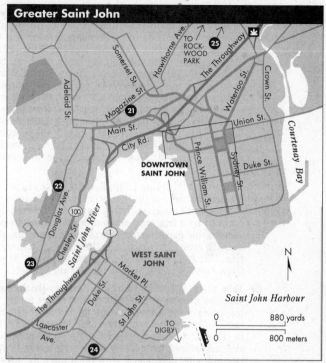

**Greater Saint John**

tually, you *should* see it, though less for its beauty than its interest: Twice daily, the strong Fundy Tides rise faster than the river can empty, and the tide water attempts to push the river water back upstream. When the tide ebbs, the river once again pours over the rock ledges and the rapids appear to reverse themselves. A pulp mill on the bank is less scenic, and the stench it occasionally sends out is one of the less-than-charming parts of a visit. To learn more about the phenomenon, see the excellent free film shown in the tourist information center on the site.

Cross the river on Bridge Road to **West Saint John.** Make a left on Lancaster Avenue at Simms Corner and proceed to Charlotte Street, where you can't miss the **Carleton Martello Tower.** Like Fort Howe, this is a great place to survey the harbor. The tower was built in 1810 as a precaution against American attack. Costumed guides point out 8-foot-thick walls and pose for photographs. *Charlotte Ext. W, tel. 506/636–4011 in season. Admission free. Open June–mid-Oct., daily 9–5.*

**Cherry Brook Zoo,** at the very northern tip of Rockwood Park, houses Siberian tigers, wildebeest, and other exotic species. *Tel. 506/634–1440. Admission: $3.25 adults, $2.25 senior citizens and students, $1.40 pre-schoolers, children under 2 free. Open daily 10–dusk. Tour rates available.*

## Tour 3: The Fundy Coast

*Numbers in the margin correspond to points of interest on the New Brunswick map.*

Bordering the chilly and powerful tidal Bay of Fundy is some of New Brunswick's loveliest coastline. A tour of the region will take you from the border town of St. Stephen, through tiny fishing villages and past rocky coves, to Fundy National Park, where the world's **26** most extreme tides rise and fall twice daily. **St. Stephen,** on the Maine border, is a mecca for chocoholics, who converge on the small town during the Chocolate Festival held the first week in August. Choctails and chocolate puddings, cakes, and complete meals should come as no surprise when you realize that it was here that the chocolate bar was invented. Sample Ganong's famed hand-dipped chocolates at the factory store, the **Ganong Chocolatier.** *73 Milltown Blvd., tel. 506/465–5611. Open July and Aug., weekdays 9–8, Sat. 9–5, Sun. noon–5; Sept.–Dec., daily 9–5; Jan.–mid-May, Mon.–Sat. 9–5.*

A small side trip along Ledge Road will take you to **Crocker Hill Studios,** on the banks of the St. Croix River. Walk down the garden path to the artist's studio with its paintings and carved decoys. It is surrounded by a fragrant, tranquil herb garden. Relax in one of the comfortable garden benches and watch the osprey and eagles soar over the river, and seals make their way upstream on the incoming tide. *Tel. 506/466–4251. Admission: $3 adults, $2 youth under 16. Open June–Sept., daily 10–5; Oct.–June by appt.*

**27** Take Route 127 off Route 1 to **St. Andrews-By-the-Sea,** one of North America's prettiest and least-spoiled resort towns. Long the summer place of the affluent (mansions ring the town), St. Andrews retains its year-round population of fishermen, and little has changed in the past two centuries. Of the town's 550 buildings 280 were erected before 1880; 14 have survived from the 1700s. Some Loyalists brought their homes with them piece by piece from Castine, Maine, across the bay, when the war didn't go their way.

Pick up a walking-tour map at the tourist information center on Water Street and follow it through the pleasant streets. Particular gems are the **Court House** and **Greenock Church.** The church owes its existence to a remark someone made at an 1822 dinner party about the "poor" Presbyterians not having a church of their own. Captain Christopher Scott, who took exception to the slur, spared no expense on the building, which is decorated with a carving of a green oak tree in honor of Scott's birthplace, Greenock, Scotland. Also along Water Street are numerous antiques shops and artists' studios. The porch of the **Shiretown Inn** (218 Water St., tel. 506/529–8877) is a perfect place for a snack and a view.

The **Ross Memorial Museum** features a fine antiques collection. *188 Montague St., tel. 506/529–1824. Admission free. Open late May–June and early October, Mon.–Sat. 10–4:30; July–Sept., Mon.–Sat. 10–4:30, Sun. 1:30–4:30; shoulder seasons, Tues.–Sat. 10–4:30.*

A drive up Joe's Point Road takes you to the **Huntsman Aquarium and Museum,** which houses marine life and displays. *Brandy Cove Rd., tel. 506/529–1202. Admission: $4 adults, $3.50 senior citizens, $2.75 youth under 18, children under 4 free; $10.70 families. Open late May–mid-Oct., Tues.–Sat. 10–4:30; July and Aug., Tues.–Sat. 10–4:30, Sun. 1:30–4:30.*

Back on Route 1 is **St. George,** a pretty town with some excellent bed-and-breakfasts, one of the oldest Protestant graveyards in Canada, and a fish ladder running up the side of a dam.

The Fundy Isles—Grand Manan, Deer Island, and Campobello—are havens of peace that have lured harried mainlanders for generations. **Grand Manan Island,** largest of the three, is also farthest away (about two hours by car-ferry from Black's Harbour); you might see spouting whales, sunning seals, or a rare puffin on the way. Circular herring weirs dot the coastal water, and fish sheds and smokehouses lie beside long wharfs that reach out to bobbing fishing boats. Place names are romantic—Swallowtail, Southern Head, Seven Days Work, and Dark Harbour. It's easy to get around—only about 32 kilometers (20 miles) of road lead from the lighthouse at Southern Head to the one at Northern Head. Grand Manan attracted John James Audubon, that living encyclopedia of birds, in 1831. The puffin is the island's symbol. Whale-watching expeditions can be booked at the Marathon Hotel and the Compass Rose, and scuba diving to old wrecks is popular.

Connected to Lubec, Maine, by an international bridge, **Campobello Island** may be approached from the other side by toll ferry from Deer Island. Neatly manicured, preening itself in the bay, Campobello Island has always had a special appeal to the wealthy and the famous. It was here that the Roosevelt family spent their summers. The home of Franklin Delano Roosevelt, former president of the United States, is now maintained as a lovely museum in his honor. Located in the center of Roosevelt International Park, a joint project of the Canadian and American governments, **President Roosevelt's home** was the setting for the movie *Sunrise at Campobello. Roosevelt Park Rd., tel. 506/752–2922. Admission free. House open late May–mid-Oct., daily 10–6; grounds open year-round.*

The island's **Herring Cove Provincial Park** has camping facilities and a nine-hole golf course.

An easy, 20-minute, free ferry ride from Letete near St. George brings you to the relaxing **Deer Island.** You'll enjoy exploring the fishing wharves, such as those at **Chocolate Cove.** You can walk through a small nature park at **Deer Point** while waiting for the toll ferry to nearby Campobello Island. If you listen carefully, you may be able to hear the sighing and snorting of "the Old Sow," the second largest whirlpool in the world. If you can't hear it, you'll be able to see it, just a few feet offshore. Exploring the island takes only a few hours; it's 12 kilometers (7½ miles) long, varying in width from almost 5 kilometers (3 miles) to a few hundred feet at some points.

After returning from the Fundy Isles to the mainland, proceed east along coastal Route 1. If you have the time, dip down to the peaceful, hidden fishing villages of **Maces Bay, Dipper,** and **Chance Harbour,** all much the same as they have been for centuries. At Dipper Harbour, you can rent sea kayaks and canoes, arrange for whale-watching and deep-sea fishing (Eastern Outdoors Marine, tel. 506/634–1530 or 800/56KAYAK), or buy a lobster roll to munch on while strolling the long sun-warmed wharf. Farther up the coast is St. Martins with a rich shipbuilding heritage, whispering caves, miles of beaches, spectacular tides, and a unique cluster of covered bridges.

Drive east through Saint John along a scenic stretch of Route 1 to Route 114, which angles south to the 129-square-kilometer (80-square-mile) **Fundy National Park.** Stand on a sandstone ledge above a dark-sand beach and watch the bay's phenomenal tide rise or fall. *Box 40, Alma E0A 1B0, tel. 506/887–2000. Admission: $5 per car in summer; free rest of the year.*

**Alma** is the small seaside town that services the national park. Here you'll find great lobster and the local specialty, sticky buns. Past Alma, the coast road to Moncton winds by covered bridges and along rocky coasts, past such photogenic spots as the wild driftwood-cluttered beach at **Cape Enragé** and **Hopewell Cape,** home of the famous giant flowerpots, rock formations carved by the Fundy Tides.

## Tour 4: Moncton and the Acadian Peninsula

A friendly town, often called the Gateway to Acadia because of its mix of English and French and its proximity to the Acadian shore, **Moncton** has a pretty downtown where wisely placed malls do a booming business.

This city has long touted two natural attractions, the Tidal Bore and the Magnetic Hill. You may be disappointed if you've read too much tourist hype. In days gone by, before the harbor mouth filled with silt, the **Tidal Bore** was indeed an incredible sight, a high wall of water that surged in through the narrow opening of the river to fill red mud banks to the brim. It still moves up the river, and the moving wave is worth waiting for, but it's nowhere near as lofty as it used to be, except sometimes in the spring when the tides are very high. Bore Park on Main Street is the best vantage point; viewing times are posted there.

**Magnetic Hill,** north of town just off the Trans-Canada Highway, creates a bizarre optical illusion. If you park your car in neutral at the designated spot, you'll seem to be coasting up hill without power. An excellent family water-theme park, **Magic Mountain,** is adjacent to the hill. *On Magnetic Hill, tel. 506/857–9283. Admission: $17.25 adults/$10.50 afternoon; $11.75 children under 12 and senior citizens/$9.50 afternoon; $53.25 for a family of 4 for a full day. Open mid-June–July and mid-Aug.–Labor Day, daily 10–6; July–mid-Aug., daily 10–8.*

Among Moncton's notable man-made attractions is the **Acadian Museum,** at the Univ. of Moncton, whose remarkable collection of artifacts reflects 300 years of Acadian life in New Brunswick. *Clement Cormier Bldg., Univ. of Moncton, tel. 506/858–4088. Admission free. Open June–Sept., weekdays 10–5, weekends 1–5; Oct.–May, Tues.–Fri. 1–4:30, weekends 1–4.*

Turn northeast along the coast from Moncton to the salty shores of such unique Acadian communities as **Shediac, Cocagne, Buctouche,** and **Rexton,** where you'll find long warm sand dunes, lobster feeds, lighthouses, weathered wharves, and sea-stained churches. The friendliness of the Acadians makes this trip a joy, and the white, dune-edged beaches of **Kouchibouguac National Park** are among the finest on the continent. *Kent County, tel. 506/876–2443. Admission: $5 per vehicle, senior citizen $4. Day and annual passes available.*

Route 11 continues north to the Miramichi River and the fabled **Miramichi region** of lumberjacks, fishermen, and "come all ye's." Celebrated for its salmon rivers and the ebullient nature of its residents (Scottish, English, Irish, and a smattering of French and Indian), this is a land of stories, folklore, and lumber kings. Pleasant towns and villages of sturdy wood homes dot the banks of Miramichi Bay at **Chatham** and **Newcastle** (where the politician and British media mogul Lord Beaverbrook grew up and is buried). At **Doaktown** (south of Newcastle on Route 8), the **Miramichi Salmon Museum** (tel. 506/365–7787) provides a look at the endangered Atlantic salmon and at life in noted fishing camps along the rivers.

The **Woodmen's Museum** of Boiestown (in the exact center of the province), with artifacts that date from the 1700s to the present, is housed in what looks like two giant logs set on more than 60 acres of land. The museum portrays a lumberman's life through its displays, but its tranquil grounds are excuse enough to visit. Picnic facilities and camping sites are also available. *Rte 8, Boiestown, tel. 506/369–7214. Admission: $5 adults, $4 senior citizens, $2 children, $12 families. Open May–mid-Sept., daily 10–5:30.*

**㉟** Return to Newcastle and swing north and east on Route 11 to **Caraquet,** on the Acadian Peninsula. The town is perched along the Baie des Chaleurs, with Québec's Gaspé Peninsula beckoning across the inlet.

**㊱** The *pièce de résistance* of the Acadian Peninsula is, without doubt, the **Acadian Historical Village,** 10 kilometers (6 miles) west of Caraquet on Route 11, near Grand Anse. As Kings Landing depicts the early English settlement, this village re-creates an early Acadian community between 1780 and 1890. Summer days are wonderfully peaceful. A chapel bell tolls, ducks waddle and quack under a footbridge, wagons creak, and the smell of hearty cooking wafts from cottage doors. Costumed staff act as guides, and a restaurant serves old-Acadian dishes. *Tel. 506/727–3467. Admission: $7.50 adults, $4.50 youth 6–18, $5.50 students over 18, $6 senior citizens, $18 families. Open June–Labor Day, daily 10–6; Sept., daily 10–5.*

# Shopping

New Brunswick is famous for its crafts, and the province's directory of craftspeople and crafts shops provides comprehensive listings of potters, weavers, glassblowers, jewelers, and carvers throughout the province. Get a copy from Tourism New Brunswick (Box 6000, Fredericton E3B 5H1, tel. 800/561–0123).

**Fredericton**  Mammoth crafts markets are held occasionally in town and every Labor Day weekend in Mactaquac Park. **The New Brunswick Craft Centre** (103 Church Street) offers all juried crafts (pottery, blown glass, pressed flowers, metal flowers, turned wood, leather, quilts) made by members of the New Brunswick Craft Council. **Aitkens Pewter** (81 Regent St.) offers beautiful pewter, goblets, belt buckles, and jewelry. **Shades of Light Studio and Gift Shop** (28 Regent St.) features stained glass and other local crafts. **Mulhouse Country Classics,** about 2 kilometers (1 mile) from downtown in Lower St. Marys across the river on the north side, is a gem for crafts and handmade furniture.

Excellent men's shoes can be bought at **Hartt's Shoe Factory** (York St.); **The Linen Closet** (King St.) sells laces, exquisite bedding, and Victorian nightgowns.

**Gagetown**  **Flo Grieg's** on Front Street carries superior pottery. **Claremont House B&B,** on Tilley Road, displays unusual batik items and copper engravings. **Loomcrofters,** just off Main Street, is a good choice for handwoven items.

**Moncton**  Five spacious malls and numerous pockets of shops in downtown Moncton make it one of the best places to shop in New Brunswick. Among the crafts to look for are the yarn portraits of La Sagouine, "the old sage" of Buctouche. The sayings of the old Acadian woman as she does her daily chores were made famous in Antonine Maillet's novel *La Sagouine.*

| | |
|---|---|
| Saint-Andrews-by-the-Sea | This "veddy British" town has many places to buy English and New Brunswick woolens, English bone china, and marvelous wool yarn, among them **The Sea Captain's Loft** (Water St.) and **Cottage Craft** (Town Sq.). On Water Street, the main shopping strip, head to **Tom Smith's Studio** (Water St.) for highly regarded oriental Raku pottery. |
| Saint John | The little antiques stores and crafts shops sprinkled around the downtown area provide the best shopping in Saint John. **Prince William Street** has interesting browsing in antiques shops and crafts boutiques; **House of Tara** (72 Prince William St.) is wonderful for fine Irish linens and woolens. Airy **Brunswick Square** has many top-quality boutiques. **Old City Market**, between Charlotte and Germain streets, bustles six days a week and always stocks delicious local specialties, such as maple syrup and lobster. |
| Saint-Léonard | A visit to the studio and store of the **Madawaska Weavers** (Main St.), whose handwoven items are known the world over, is a must. Handsome skirts, stoles, and ties are some of the items on sale. |

# Sports and Fitness

| | |
|---|---|
| Bicycling | Byroads, lanes, and rolling secondary highways run through small towns, along the ocean, and into the forest. Set out on your own, or try a guided adventure with a specialist tour operator, such as **Covered Bridge Bicycle Tours** (Dept. F, Box 693, Main Post Office, Saint John E2L 4B3, tel. 506/849–9028). Bed-and-breakfasts frequently have bicycles for hire and the Department of Economic Development and Tourism has listings and free cycling maps (*See* Important Addresses and Numbers in Essential Information, *above*). Information on competitive cycling and races is available from **Velo New Brunswick** (457 Chartersville Rd., Dieppe, NB, E1A 5H1). |
| Fishing | Dotted with freshwater lakes, crisscrossed with fish-laden rivers, and bordered by 1,129 kilometers (700 miles) of seacoast, this province is one of Canada's natural treasures. Sportspeople are drawn by the excellent bass fishing and such world-famous salmon rivers as the Miramichi, the Restigouche, and the Nashwaak. Commercial fishermen often take visitors line fishing for groundfish. An annual freshwater fishing license for out-of-province visitors costs $25 for three days; $50 for seven days; $100 for the season (plus GST). For more information, call New Brunswick Fish and Wildlife (tel. 506/453–2440). |
| Golf | There are 36 excellent golf courses in New Brunswick—many, such as the **Algonquin Golf Club** (tel. 506/529–3062) in St. Andrews and the **Gowan Brae Golf and Country Club** (tel. 506/546–2707) in Bathurst, with sparkling views of the sea. The **Fundy National Park Golf Club** (tel. 506/887–2970) at Alma is nestled near cliffs overlooking the restless Bay of Fundy; deer grazing on the course are one of its hazards. Greens fees run about $20–$25, $15 for some nine-hole courses; and visitors are generally welcome. For a list of golf courses, ask for the free "New Brunswick Activity Guide" from the Department of Economic Development and Tourism (Box 6000, Fredericton E3B 5H1). |
| Hiking | Rocky coastline and inland highland trails offer hiking opportunities for both experienced and casual trekkers. **Fundy Rock and Ice School** (Box 6713, Station A, Saint John E2L 4S2, tel. 506/658–1906) and **Miramichi Four Seasons Outfitters** (Box 705, RR 2, Newcastle E1V 3L9, tel. 506/622–0089) offer guided hiking tours. For trail information, contact Eric Hadley, of **New Brunswick Trails Council** |

(c/o Fredericton Trails Coalition, Box 3715, Station B, Fredericton E3A 5L7, tel. 506/453–3826).

**Skiing**
*Cross-Country* A perfect province for cross-country skiing, New Brunswick offers groomed trails at such provincial and national parks as Mactaquac Provincial Park near Fredericton, Fundy National Park in Alma, and Kouchibouguac National Park between Moncton and Bathurst. Many communities and small hotels offer groomed trails, but it's also possible to set off on your own in almost every section of the province.

*Downhill* New Brunswick downhill ski areas usually operate from mid-December through April. They include **Crabbe Mountain Winter Park** (tel. 506/463–8311) in Lower Hainesville (near Fredericton); **Sugarloaf Provincial Park** (tel. 506/789–2366) in Campbellton, northern New Brunswick; **Mont Farlagne** (tel. 506/735–8401) in Saint-Jacques, near Edmundston; **Poley Mountain Ski Area** (tel. 506/433–3230) in Sussex; and **Silverwood Winter Park** (tel. 506/450–3380) in Fredericton.

**Tennis** Courts are available in most city and town parks. Most are free. Many resorts and hotels have courts, as well.

**Water Sports**
*Canoeing and Kayaking* Kayaking along the coasts of Fundy and Chaleur has become very popular. A list of canoe and kayak liveries is available from the Department of Economic Development and Tourism (Box 6000, Fredericton E3B 5H1). For canoes, try **A to Z Rentals** (128 Prospect St., tel. 506/452–9758) in Fredericton and in Saint John (535 Rothesay, tel. 506/633–1919). Such outfitters as **Eastern Outdoors** (Brunswick Square, Saint John, tel. 506/634–1530 or 800/56KAYAK) offer single and double kayaks, lessons, tours, and white-water rafting on the world-famous Reversing Falls.

*Sailing* Sailboats can be chartered from many companies, including **Fundy Yacht Sales and Charter** (Dipper Harbour, Rte. 2, Lepreau E0G 2H0, tel. 506/634–1530 or 800/56KAYAK).

*Rowing* Shells can be rented at the **Kennebecasis Club** (tel. 506/849–9910) in Rothesay, and at the **Aquatic Center** (tel. 506/458–5513) in Fredericton.

**Whale-Watching** One New Brunswick experience that is difficult to forget is the sighting of a huge humpback, right whale, finback, or minke. Whale-watching tours are available from a number of operators such as **Ocean Search** (Marathon Inn, North Head, Grand Manan, tel. 506/662–8488) and **West Isles World** (Lambertville, Deer Island, tel. 506/747–2946). **Cline Marine Tours** (tel. 506/529–2287) in St. Andrews and Deer Island offers whale-watching, as well as scenic, tours. **Chaleur Phantom** (tel. 506/684–4722) in Dalhousie combines scenic tours, to observe marine life in the calmer waters around the islands, with deep-sea fishing excursions.

# Dining and Lodging

## Dining

Although there are not a lot of choices for fine dining in New Brunswick, a few good restaurants exist, and families will find plenty of quality food in many outlets. A number of gourmet restaurants have popped up in Saint John in recent years—so there is hope that the dining scene will improve throughout the province.

In the spring, once the ice has left streams and rivers, a provincial delicacy—the fiddlehead fern—is picked from the shores. Eaten as a vegetable (boiled, drenched with lemon, butter, salt, and pepper), fiddleheads have something of an artichoke taste and go well with spring's bony fish, shad, and gaspereaux. Silver salmon, once a spring staple when set nets were allowed, is still available but quite costly. Most salmon served in restaurants is farm-reared. Lobster, a favorite maritime dish, is available in most restaurants, but is not always cheap. The custom of the residents is to buy it fresh from the fishermen or shore outlets and devour it in huge quantities. Because of the cool waters, shellfish is especially tasty. Look for oysters, scallops, clams, crab, and mussels. And be sure to try the purple seaweed called dulse that the residents eat like potato chips. To be truly authentic, accompany any New Brunswick–style feast with hearty Moosehead beer, brewed in Saint John and one of the province's well-known exports.

Dress is casual everywhere except at the Expensive and Very Expensive listings, and, unless noted, no reservations are needed.

Highly recommended restaurants in each price category are indicated by a star ★.

| Category | Cost* |
| --- | --- |
| $$$$ | over $40 |
| $$$ | $20–$40 |
| $$ | $10–$20 |
| $ | under $10 |

*per person, excluding drinks, service, and 11% sales tax*

## Lodging

New Brunswick has a number of officially designated Heritage Inns—historically significant establishments built in the last century. Many have antique china and furnishings or other charming touches, and their accommodations run the gamut from elegant to homey.

Hotels and motels in and around Saint John and Fredericton are adequate and friendly. Accommodations in Saint John are at a premium in summer, so reserve ahead to ensure a place to stay.

Highly recommended lodgings in each price category are indicated by a star ★.

| Category | Cost* |
| --- | --- |
| $$$ | over $60 |
| $$ | $45–$60 |
| $ | under $45 |

*All prices are for a standard double room, excluding 10% service charge.*

**Campbellton**
*Dining and*
*Lodging*
★

**Aylesford Inn.** Truly a find, this friendly inn housed in a Victorian mansion near the Québec border and Sugarloaf Provincial Park has guest rooms handsomely furnished with Eastlake and Canadian-pine antiques. Large gardens and verandas offer views of the

Restigouche River. Excellent dinners are served to guests (quail and frogs' legs are featured entrées), and full breakfasts are included in the room rate. Nonguests are welcome for afternoon tea. *8 MacMillan Ave., E3N 1E9, tel. 506/759–7672. 6 rooms. Facilities: dining room, croquet. AE, MC, V. $$$*

**Campobello Island**
*Lodging*
★

**Owen House.** Mellow with history, this 200-year-old home was built by Admiral Owen, who fancied himself ruler of the island. Its gracious old rooms have hosted such luminaries as actress Greer Garson, who stayed here (in a room with a fireplace in the bathroom) when filming *Sunrise at Campobello*. Breakfasts are wonderful—pancakes come topped with local berries. *Welshpool, E0G 3H0, tel. 506/752–2977. 9 rooms. V. $$*

**Lupine Lodge.** Originally a vacation home built by the Adams family (friends of the Roosevelts) around the turn of the century, these three attractive log buildings set on a bluff overlooking the Bay of Fundy have been converted into a modern guest lodge. Nature trails connect it to the provincial park. The 10 available rooms occupy two of the cabins; the third houses the dining room, which specializes in simple but well-prepared local seafood. *Box 2, Welshpool, E0G 3H0, tel. 506/752–2255. 10 rooms. Facilities: restaurant, lounge. AE, MC, V. $$*

**Caraquet**
*Dining and Lodging*

**Hotel Paulin.** The word *quaint* really fits this property. The pretty rooms were redecorated in 1993. Each has its own unique look and the colors are as bright and cheerful as the seaside town. An excellent small dining room specializes in fresh fish cooked to perfection. *143 Boul. St. Pierre, tel. 506/727–9981. 10 rooms with shared bath. Facilities: restaurant. MC, V. $*

**Deer Island**
*Dining and Lodging*

**45th Parallel Motel and Restaurant.** Deer Island has only one motel, and it's clean and comfortable. A full breakfast is complimentary, and everything from lobster to pizza is available at the informal restaurant. Pets are welcome. *Fairhaven, E0G 1R0, tel. 506/747–2231. 10 rooms, 3 with kitchenette. Facilities: restaurant. AE, MC, V. $$*

**West Isles World B&B.** This white frame house overlooks the cove and offers three snug rooms with an informal country feel; the big upstairs bedroom has a water view. The owners will arrange whale-watching cruises for you. A full breakfast is included in the room rate, and other meals are served on request. *Lord's Cove, E0G 2J0, tel. 506/747–2946. 3 rooms, 1 with bath. No credit cards. $$*

**Fredericton**
*Dining*

**Luna Steakhouse.** Specialties include huge Caesar salad, garlic bread, escargots, brochettes, and Italian food. In fine weather you can dine on an outdoor terrace. Inside the restaurant, the stucco walls and dark arches make a cozy environment. *168 Dundonald St., tel. 506/455–4020. AE, DC, MC, V. $$*

**Bar B Q Barn.** Special children's menus and barbecued ribs and chicken are the standards; the blackboard lists plenty of other daily dinner specials, such as salmon, scallops, and chili. This is a popular spot for its convenient downtown location, and is great for winding down; the bar serves fine martinis. *540 Queen St., tel. 506/455–2742. AE, MC, V. $–$$*

**Pink Pearl.** This restaurant features tasty Cantonese food, with exceptional wontons and weekend buffets. *343 Queen St., tel. 506/450–8997. MC, V. $*

*Lodging*

**Auberge Wandlyn Inn.** Just off the Trans-Canada Highway, this hotel is away from the downtown area but close to three shopping malls, many restaurants, and theaters. The guest rooms are no-frills, but the family-oriented dining room was completely redecorated in 1993, and there's a cozy bar. *58 Prospect St. W, Box 214,*

*E3B 4Y9, tel. 506/452–8937 or 800/561–0000 (eastern Canada), 800/ 561–0006 (U.S.), fax 506/452–7658. 101 rooms. Facilities: restaurant, bar, indoor and outdoor pools, sauna, hot tub. AE, DC, MC, V. $$$*

**Howard Johnson Motor Lodge.** This HoJo's, located on the north side of the river and at the north end of the Princess Margaret Bridge, has a terrace bar in a pleasant interior courtyard overlooked by balconies from many of the rooms. Guest-room decor is standard for the chain. *Trans-Canada Hwy., Box 1414, E3B 5E3, tel. 506/472–0480 or 800/654–2000, fax 506/472–0170. 116 rooms. Facilities: restaurant, bar, indoor pool, fitness center, indoor tennis courts. AE, DC, MC, V. $$$*

**Sheraton Inn Fredericton.** Brand-new and within walking distance of downtown, this big hotel with elegant country decor offers modern rooms with sunset views over the river. *225 Woodstock Rd., E3B 2H8, tel. 506/457–7000 or 800/325–3535, fax 506/457–4000. 223 rooms, all with minibars. Facilities: restaurant with outdoor terrace, bar, indoor and outdoor pools. AE, DC, MC, V. $$$*

**Lord Beaverbrook Hotel.** A central location is this modern, seven-story hotel's main attraction, although 1991 renovations spruced things up a bit. Some rooms have Jacuzzis or minibars. The food in the main dining room is forgettable. There is a lively bar. *659 Queen St., E3B 5A6, tel. 506/455–3371 or 800/561–7666, fax 506/455–1441. 163 rooms. Facilities: 2 restaurants, bar, indoor pool, non-smoking rooms. AE, D, DC, MC, V. $$–$$$*

**Carriage House Inn.** This heritage mansion has lovely bedrooms furnished with Victorian antiques. Homemade breakfast, complete with home-grown maple syrup for the fluffy pancakes, is served in the solarium. *230 University Ave., E3B 4H7, tel. 506/452–9924 or 800/267–6068, fax 506/458–0799. 10 rooms, 5 with bath. MC, V. $$*

**Grand Manan Island**
*Lodging*

**Marathon Inn.** Perched on a hill overlooking the harbor, this gracious mansion built by a sea captain offers guest rooms furnished with antiques. Whale- and bird-watching cruises can be arranged for those wishing to explore. *Box 129, North Head, E0G 2M0, tel. 506/662–8488. 28 rooms, 15 with bath. Facilities: restaurant, 2 lounges, pool, tennis. MC, V. $$–$$$*

**Compass Rose.** Lovely guest rooms, with comfortable turn-of-the-century furnishings, are available in the two old houses that have been combined into this small, English-style country inn. It is conveniently near the ferry landing, and whale-watching tours can be arranged. A full English breakfast is included in the room rate. Morning and afternoon teas, lunch, and dinner are also served. *North Head, E0G 2M0, tel. 506/662–8570. 8 rooms with shared baths. V. $$*

**Ludlow**
*Lodging*

**Pond's Chalet Resort.** You'll get a traditional fishing-camp experience here, in a lodge and chalets set among trees overlooking a salmon river. *Ludlow (near Boiestown), E0C 1N0, tel. 506/369–2612. 10 rooms in lodge, 8 camps. Facilities: dining room. AE, DC, MC, V. $$$*

**Moncton**
*Dining*
★

**Cy's Seafood Restaurant.** This favorite for seafood, decorated in dark wood and brass, has been serving generous portions for decades. Though renowned for its seafood casserole, the restaurant also offers reliable scallop, shrimp, and lobster dishes. You can see the Tidal Bore from the windows. *170 Main St., tel. 506/857–0032. AE, DC, MC, V. $$*

**Fisherman's Paradise.** In spite of the enormous dining area, which seats more than 350 people, this restaurant serves memorable à la carte seafood dishes in an atmosphere of candlelight and wood furnishings. The children's menu and such down-home specials as lobster-bake make this a good spot for families. *375 Dieppe Blvd., tel. 506/859–4388. AE, DC, MC, V. $$*

*Lodging* **Hotel Beausejour.** Moncton's finest hotel is conveniently located
★ downtown. The friendly greeting in the elegant lobby is matched by the friendly service. The decor of the guest rooms and executive suites echoes the city's Loyalist and Acadian roots. L'Auberge, the main hotel restaurant, has a distinct Acadian flavor. The Windjammer dining room is more formal, modeled after the opulent luxury liners of the turn-of-the-century, and reservations are required. *750 Main St., tel. 506/854–4344 or 800/441–1414 (Canada and U.S.), 800/561–2328 (Maritimes and Québec), fax 506/858–0957. 314 rooms. Facilities: 2 restaurants, café, bar, pool, access to health club. AE, DC, MC, V. $$$*

**The Best Western Crystal Palace.** Moncton's newest hotel is unique: There are theme rooms (want to be Ali Baba for a night?) and, for families, an indoor pool and a miniature wonderland of rides, midway stalls, and coin games. Champlain Mall is just across the parking lot. *499 Paul St., tel. 506/858–8584 or 800/528–1234, fax 506/ 858–5486. 115 rooms. Facilities: restaurant, indoor pool. AE, D, DC, MC, V. $$$*

**Newcastle** **Wharf Inn.** Here in Miramichi country, the staff is friendly and the
*Dining and* restaurant serves excellent salmon dinners. This low-rise modern
*Lodging* building has two wings; guest rooms in the executive wing have extra amenities. No-smoking rooms are available. *Jane St., tel. 506/ 622–0302, fax 506/622–0354. 70 rooms. Facilities: restaurant, patio lounge, indoor pool. AE, MC, V. $$–$$$*

**Sackville** **Marshlands Inn.** In this white clapboard inn, a welcoming double liv-
*Lodging* ing room with fireplace sets the informal, country atmosphere. Bed-
★ rooms are furnished with sleigh beds or four-posters, but they also have such modern touches as air-conditioning and in-room telephones. *Box 1440, E0A 3C0, tel. 506/536–0170, fax 506/536–0721. 21 rooms, 14 with bath. Facilities: restaurant. AE, DC, MC, V. $$–$$$*

**St. Andrews** **The Algonquin Resort.** The wraparound veranda of this grand old
*Lodging* hotel overlooks wide lawns. Bellmen wear kilts. A recent addition added 50 rooms and three suites to the property; the newest rooms are larger than those in the original hotel, and have air conditioning, two queen-size beds, and kitchenettes with microwave, refrigerator, coffee maker, and toaster. The suites have huge fireplaces. Rooms in the original hotel were renovated, and all now have television. The dining room is noted for its buffets, and meals can be pleasant here if the staff is in the mood. *Rte. 127, E0G 2X0, tel. 506/ 529–8823 or 800/268–9411 (Canada), 800/828–7447 (U.S.), fax 506/529–4194. 250 rooms. Facilities: 3 restaurants (dining room, coffee shop, and veranda), 2 bars, outdoor heated pool, 2 golf courses, tennis. AE, D, DC, MC, V. Closed winter. $$$*

**L'Europe.** You may be amused by the cheerful decor in this intimate restaurant, in particular the whimsical objets d'art reflecting the tastes of the German owners. The food is European—some French, Swiss, German dishes, and so on, with particular attention given to seafood. All meals are served with delicious homemade Black Forest bread and pâté. *48 King St., E0G 2X0, tel. 506/529–3818. Reservations advised. No lunch. Closed Mon. and Oct.–early May. V. $$$*

**St. George** **Granite Town Hotel.** Although this hotel was just built in 1991, it
*Lodging* nevertheless has an old-country-inn feeling to it. The decor is subtle, with pine and washed-birch woodwork prominent. Light blues and pinks dominate in the rooms. The scenery is pleasant: one side of the

building overlooking an apple orchard, the other just atop the bank of the Maguadavic River. A Continental breakfast is served but is not included in the room rate. *15 Main St., E0G 2Y0, tel. 506/755–6415, fax 506/755–6009. 32 rooms, 2 with Jacuzzi. Facilities: restaurant, barbecue patio (summer), lounge, canoe & bicycle rentals, laundry. AE, D, DC, MC, V. $$–$$$*

**Saint John**
*Dining*

**Top of the Town.** With a spectacular view of the harbour and city, this dining room at Keddy's Fort Howe Hotel offers a sophisticated menu. Local seafood is abundant and creatively prepared; Fundy scallops are a specialty, and the Maritime Mix—mussels, herring, and lobster—is the favorite of true seafood-lovers. The poached salmon served cold with a tangy dip is delightful. There is live dinner music nightly. *Main and Portland Sts., tel. 506/657–7320. Reservations advised. AE, DC, MC, V. $$$*

**Turn of the Tide.** Overlooking the harbor, this large hotel dining room is decorated with antiques. Although the dining is pleasant at all times, the best meal of the week is the Sunday buffet, with a long table full of dishes from the exotic to the tried-and-true. *Hilton Hotel, Market Sq., tel. 506/693–8484. Reservations advised. AE, D, DC, MC, V. No lunch Sat. $$$*

**Mexicali Rosa's.** For a franchise, this restaurant has a lot of character. The decor is essentially Santa Fe–style with adobe arches and so forth. The specialty is Cali-Mex food, which is heavy on sauces, as opposed to Tex-Mex, which concentrates more on meats. Guests waiting to be seated can order one of the fine margaritas in the large lounge. The chimichangas are with good reason the most popular dish. *88 Prince William St., tel. 506/652–5252. AE, DC, MC, V. $$*

**Grannan's.** Seafood brochette with scallops, shrimp, and lobster tail sautéed at your table in a white wine and mushroom sauce, or the Captain's Platter for two with salmon, halibut, scallops, lobster, jumbo shrimp, oysters, and steamed clams and mussels, are two of the specials featured in this nautically decorated restaurant. The desserts, including Caramel Apple Granny, are memorable. Dining spills over onto the sidewalk in summer, and there are three lively bars connected to the restaurant. *Market Sq., tel. 506/634–1555. AE, DC, MC, V. No lunch Sun. $–$$*

**Incredible Edibles.** Here you can enjoy down-to-earth food—biscuits, garlic-laden hummus, salads, pastas, and desserts—in cozy rooms or, in summer, on the outdoor terrace. The menu has been expanded to include beef, chicken, and crab dishes. You'll get a good cup of coffee here, too. *42 Princess St., tel. 506/633–7554. AE, DC, MC, V. Closed Sun. $–$$*

**Reggie's.** This popular spot near Brunswick Square begins serving breakfast at 6 AM. Later in the day specialties include chowders, bagel burgers, and lobster rolls. The restaurant closes at 6 or 7 PM, so come early if you want dinner. *26 Germain St., tel. 506/657–6270. MC, V. $*

*Lodging*

**Saint John Hilton.** Part of the Market Square complex, this Hilton is furnished in Loyalist decor; guest rooms overlook the harbor or the town. Mellow antiques furnish corners of the dining room and the medieval-style Great Hall, which hosts banquets. A pedway system connects the 12-story property to uptown shops, restaurants, bars, a library, and a civic center for concerts and sporting events. *1 Market Sq., E2L 4Z6, tel. 506/693–8484 or 800/561–8282, fax 506/657–6610. 197 rooms. Facilities: restaurant, bar, pool. AE, D, DC, MC, V. $$$*

★ **Shadow Lawn Country Inn.** This charming village inn is located in an affluent suburb with tree-lined streets and palatial houses, 10 minutes from Saint John. Tennis, golf, horseback riding, and a yacht club are nearby. The inn has nine old-fashioned bedrooms, some with fireplaces. Besides being open during breakfast (for guests, included in the room rate), the dining room is open to the public for dinner by reservation only; specialties include beef Wellington and seafood brioches. Pre-dinner sherry is served in the mahogany-paneled bar. *Box 41, Rothesay Rd., E0G 2W0, tel. 506/847–7539, fax 506/849–9238. 9 rooms with bath. DC, MC, V. $$–$$$*

**Shediac**
*Dining and*
*Lodging*
★

**Chez Françoise.** This lovely old mansion with a wraparound veranda has been decorated in Victorian style, with hardwood floors and antiques; an annex across the street contains several guest rooms as well. Front rooms of the main house have water views. The dining room, open to the public for dinner, serves excellent traditional French cuisine with an emphasis on seafood. *93 Main St., tel. 506/ 532–4233. 10 rooms in main house, 6 with bath; 10 rooms in annex, 4 with bath. Facilities: restaurant. AE, MC, V. Closed Jan.–May 1. $$*

# The Arts and Nightlife

## The Arts

**Theatre New Brunswick** performs in the Playhouse in Fredericton (686 Queen St., tel. 506/458–8344) and tours the province. Top musical groups, noted professional singers, and other performers usually appear at the **Aitken Center** on the University of New Brunswick campus, at **Colosseum** in Moncton, and at the **Hilton Trade Center** in Saint John.

**Beaverbrook Art Gallery** in Fredericton is the province's major gallery, but art exhibitions are also held at the **Aitken Bicentennial Exhibition Center** (ABEC) in Saint John, at **Moncton City Hall,** and at the University of Moncton's **Acadian Museum.**

## Nightlife

**Fredericton**
The **Cosmopolitan Club** (King St.) sometimes presents great jazz and also has a back room where a younger crowd hangs out. The **Chestnut Inn,** on York Street, has dining and live country or folk music. Jazz and blues bands occasionally play at **Rye's Deli** (415 King St.), which also features hot wings and popular Montréal smoked-meat sandwiches.

**Saint John**
Taverns and lounges, usually with music of some kind, provide a lively nightlife. For quiet conversation with a "Play it again, Sam" background, try the **Brigantine,** in the Hilton (*see* Saint John Lodging, *above*).

# 14 Newfoundland and Labrador

*By Margaret*
*M. Kearney*

*Updated by*
*Ana Watts*

Newfoundland was the first place explorers John Cabot (1497) and Gaspar Corte-Real (1500) touched down in the New World. Exactly where they went no one knows, for neither survived a second voyage. But while he was here, Cabot reported that he saw fish in the water so thick you could dip your line in anywhere and catch as much as you wanted. Within a decade of the explorers' discovery, St. John's had become a crowded harbor. Fishing boats from France, England, Spain, and Portugal vied for a chance to catch Newfoundland's lucrative cod, which was to subsequently shape the province's history and geography.

At one time there were 700 hard-working settlements or "outports" dotting Newfoundland's coast, each devoted to catching, salting, and drying the world's most plentiful fish. Today, only about 600 of these settlements survive. Newfoundland's most famous resource has become so scarce that a partial fishing moratorium was declared in 1992 and extended in 1993. While the province waits for the cod to return, some 25,000 fishers and processors are going to school instead of going fishing. Still, the waters are busy with boats fishing for lobster, mackerel, herring, caplin, turbot, scallops, shrimp—and cod, too, on the west and south coasts of the island. Walk down to the wharf to find out what's being landed.

Newfoundland and Labrador became part of Canada in 1949. For almost 400 years previous, however, the government had survived perfectly well on its own, until the Great Depression forced its economy to go belly-up. After 40-some years of Confederation with Canada, the economy of the province has improved considerably, but the people are still of independent mind: Newfoundlanders regard themselves as North America's first separatists and have maintained a unique language and lifestyle as well as their own customs.

Visitors to Newfoundland find themselves straddling the centuries. Old accents and customs are common in small towns and outports, yet the major cities of St. John's on the east coast and Corner Brook on the west coast are very much part of the 20th century. Regardless of where you visit—an isolated outport or lively Water Street—you're sure to interact with some of the warmest, wittiest people in North America. Strangers have always been welcome in Newfoundland, since the days when locals brought visitors in from out of the cold, warmed them by the fire, and charmingly interrogated them for news of events outside the province.

Before you can shoot the breeze, though, you'll have to acclimate yourself to the language: It's English all right, but provincial dialects are strong and vary from place to place. Newfoundland is one of two provinces in Canada with its own dictionary. Prince Edward Island is the other, but its book has only 873 entries. The Newfoundland Dictionary has more than 5,000 words, mostly having to do with fishery, weather, and scenery. To get started, you can practice with the name of the province—it's *New'fun'l'nd*, with the accent on "land." However, only "livyers" ever get the pronunciation exactly right.

Depending on the time of year you visit, your experiences will be dramatically different. In spring icebergs float down from the north, and fin, pilot, minke, and humpback whales hunt for food along the coast. Their preferred cuisine? Caplin, a small, smeltlike fish that moves in schools and spawns on Newfoundland's many pebble beaches. During the summer, temperate days turn Newfoundland's stark cliffs, bogs, and meadows into a riot of wildflowers and greenery; and the sea is dotted with boats and buoys marking traps and nets. Fall is a favored season: The weather is usually fine; cliffs and meadows are loaded with berries; and the woods are alive with moose, elk, partridges, and rabbits, to name just a few residents. In the winter, the forest trails hum with the sound of snowmobiles and ATVs hauling wood home or taking the fishermen to their favorite lodges and lakes.

The tourist season runs from June through September, when the province is awash with festivals, fairs, concerts, plays, and crafts shows. A popular vacation plan for locals is to go gravel-pit camping: It's the tradition of parking a trailer in a handy place near a brook or pond and setting up camp. There's usually no view, but free campsites and sociable company make up for most inconveniences. Not only is camping—in a bare site or one with amenities—an inexpensive way for the family to vacation together, but it's a good way to take advantage of Newfoundland's pollution-free environment: Nice days are just that, with bright, intense sunshine, free of smog or haze. The temperature in late June through early September hovers between 75 and 85 degrees, and gently cools off in the evening, providing a good night's sleep.

# Essential Information

## Important Addresses and Numbers

Tourist Information
The **Department of Tourism and Culture** (Box 8730, St. John's, NF A1B 4K2, tel. 709/729–2830) distributes brochures and maps from its offices in the Confederation Building, West Block, St. John's. The province also maintains a tourism information line (tel. 800/563–6353), which operates year-round, 24 hours a day.

From June until Labor Day, a network of **Visitor Information Centers,** open 9–9, dots the province. These centers carry up-to-date information on events, accommodations, shopping, and crafts stores in their area. There are in-season visitor information booths at the airports in Gander and St. John's. The city of St. John's operates a complete information center in a restored railway carriage next to the harbor.

Emergencies
Dial 911 for medical emergencies and police.

*Hospitals*
**St. Clare's Mercy Hospital** (154 Le Marchant Rd., tel. 709/778–3111), **Grace Hospital** (241 Le Marchant Rd., tel. 709/778–6222), and **General Hospital** (300 Prince Philip Dr., tel. 709/737–6300) in St. John's; **George B. Cross Hospital** (tel. 709/466–3411) in Clarenville; **James Paton** (tel. 709/651–2500) in Gander; **Western Memorial** (tel. 709/637–5000) in Corner Brook; **Charles S. Curtis Memorial Hospital** (tel. 709/454–3333) in St. Anthony; and **Captain William Jackman Hospital** (410 Booth Ave., tel. 709/944–2632) in Labrador City.

## Arriving and Departing by Plane, Car Ferry, and Train

By Plane
The province's main airport for connections from all major North American and European destinations is **St. John's. Canadian Airlines International** (tel. 800/426–7000 in the U.S., 800/665–1177 in Canada) and **Air Canada** (tel. 800/776–3000 in the U.S., 709/726–7880 in Canada) fly into Newfoundland. **Air Nova** (tel. 800/776–3000 in the U.S., 800/563–5151 in Newfoundland), **Provincial Airlines** (tel. 709/576–1666), **Labrador Airways** (tel. 709/896–8113 in the U.S., 800/563–3042 in Newfoundland), and **Air Atlantic** (tel. 800/563–8359 in the U.S., 709/576–0274 in Newfoundland) are regional

connectors. Airports in Newfoundland are at Stephenville, Deer Lake, St. Anthony, Gander, and St. John's; airports in Labrador are located in Happy Valley–Goose Bay, Wabush, and Churchill Falls.

**By Car Ferry**  **Marine Atlantic** operates a car ferry from North Sydney, Nova Scotia, to Port-aux-Basques, Newfoundland (crossing time is six hours); and, from June through October, from North Sydney to Argentia, twice a week (crossing time 12–14 hours). In all cases, reservations are required. Contact **Marine Atlantic** (Box 250, North Sydney, NS B2A 3M3, tel. 902/794–5700 or 709/772–7701, TDD 902/794–8109, fax 902/564–7480). For information about getting to Labrador, *see* Tour 6, *below*.

**By Train**  Rail service (tel. 514/871–1331) is provided between Sept Isles, Québec and Labrador City by Iron Ore Canada's Québec North Shore and Labrador Railways. For more information about this train, *see* Exploring, Tour 6, *below*. There is no train on the island.

## Getting around Newfoundland

**By Bus**  **CN Roadcruiser** (tel. 709/737–5912) runs a trans-island bus service. Buses leave at 8 AM from St. John's and Port-aux-Basques. Small buses known as outport taxis connect the major centers with surrounding communities.

**By Car**  Newfoundland has an excellent highway system, and all but a handful of secondary roads are paved. The province's roads are generally uncrowded, adding to the pleasure of driving. Traveling time along the Trans-Canada Highway from Port-aux-Basques to St. John's is about 13 hours, with time out for a meal in either Gander or Grand Falls. The trip from Corner Brook to St. Anthony at the northernmost tip of the island is about five hours. The drive from St. John's to Grand Bank on the southern tip of the Burin Peninsula takes about four hours.

In winter some highways may close during and after severe snowstorms. For winter road conditions on the west coast and in Labrador, call the **Department of Works, Services, and Transportation** (in Deer Lake, tel. 709/635–2162; in Grand Falls and Central Newfoundland, tel. 709/292–4300; in Clarenville, tel. 709/466–7953; in St. John's, tel. 709/729–2391).

## Getting around Labrador

*See* Tour 6 in Exploring Newfoundland and Labrador, *below*.

## Guided Tours

**Boat Tours**  The number of boat tours has increased in recent years. South of St. John's, in Bay Bulls, **O'Brien's Bird Island Charters** (tel. 709/753–4850 or 709/334–2355) and **Gatherall's Sanctuary Boat Charters** (tel. 709/334–2355) offers a popular two-hour excursion featuring whale-watching, cod jigging, and a visit to the impressive Witless Bay Islands bird sanctuary. **Great Island Tours** (tel. (tel. 709/432—2272 or 706/432–2781) charters a 10.7-meter boat on an hourly basis, accommodating up to 18 people.

On the Trinity–Bonavista Peninsula, **Ocean Contact Limited** (tel. 709/464–3269) is an established specialist in whale-watching and whale research. Dr. Peter Beamish's book, *Dancing with Whales*, documents their interesting findings. **Ocean Watch Tours** (tel. 709/677–2327) operates near Terra Nova National Park in Burnside and features park-approved field guides and an attractive ecological program. **Island Rendezvous** (tel. 709/747–7253) offers two days of boating and an overnight stay on Woody Island, Placentia Bay. **Island View Boat Tours** (tel. 709/535–2258) promises a mussel and lobster boil-up on the beach, an island treasure hunt, and a chance to visit abandoned settlements and Indian sites in the Lewisporte area. **Twillingate Island Boat Tours** (tel. 709/884–2242) specializes in iceberg photography in the iceberg-rich waters around Twillingate.

On the west coast, 2,000-foot-high cliffs and spectacular landlocked fjords are the main attraction. **Bontours** (tel. 709/458–2730 or 709/458–2256) runs the best-known of these trips—up Western Brook Pond in Gros Morne National Park. **Tableland Boat Tours** (tel. 709/451–2101) runs tours up Trout River Pond near the southern boundary of the park. **Seal Island Boat Tours** (tel. 709/898–2525) explores St. Paul's Inlet, an area of the park rich in seals, terns, and other marine and shore life.

**Bus Tours**   **McCarthy's Party** (tel. 709/781–2244) in St. John's offers guided bus tours across Newfoundland (May through October) in addition to a variety of convention and charter services. **Fleetline Motorcoach Tours** (tel. 709/722–2608) in Holyrood and **K.P. Motorcoach Tours** (tel. 709/632–5808) in Corner Brook also offer island-wide tours. Local tours are available for Port-aux-Basques, the Codroy Valley, Corner Brook, the Bay of Islands, Gros Morne National Park, the Great Northern Peninsula, and St. John's.

**Adventure Tours**   Adventure touring in Newfoundland and Labrador is experiencing a period of rapid growth. Local adventure tour operators offer sea-kayaking, ocean-diving, canoeing, wildlife viewing, mountain biking, white-water rafting, heli-hiking, and interpretive walks in the summer. In winter, snowmobiling, heli-skiing, and caribou- and seal-watching expeditions are popular. Before choosing an operator it's advisable to contact the Department of Tourism and Culture to make sure you're calling a reputable outfit. **Eastern Edge Outfitters** (tel. 709/368–9720 or 709/782–1465) offers east coast sea-kayaking tours, as well as white-water rafting expeditions down Newfoundland's Main River. **Gros Morne Adventure Guides** (tel. 709/458–2722 or 709/686–2241) offers sea-kayaking up the fjords and land-locked ponds of Gros Morne National Park, as well as a variety of hikes and adventures in the area. **Tuckamore Lodge** (tel. 709/865–6361) in Main Brook uses its luxurious lodge on the Great Northern Peninsula as a base for viewing caribou, seabird colonies, and other wildlife. **Labrador Scenic Ltd.** (tel. 709/497–8326) in North West River organizes tours through central and northern Labrador with an emphasis on wildlife and Labrador's spectacular coast.

# Exploring Newfoundland and Labrador

Tours in this chapter divide the province into the island of Newfoundland, beginning with St. John's and the Avalon Peninsula, and move west. Labrador is considered as a whole, with suggested driving and train excursions.

## Highlights for First-Time Visitors

**Cape St. Mary's Ecological Reserve,** Tour 1: St. John's and the Avalon Peninsula

## Tour 1: St. John's and the Avalon Peninsula

*Numbers in the margin correspond to points of interest on the Newfoundland and Labrador map.*

When Sir Humphrey Gilbert sailed into St. John's to establish British colonial rule for Queen Elizabeth in 1583, he found Spanish, French, and Portuguese fishermen actively working the harbor. As early as 1627, the merchants of Water Street—then known as "the lower path"—were doing a thriving business buying fish, selling goods, and supplying booze to soldiers and sailors. Still today the city encircles the snug, punchbowl harbor that helped establish its reputation.

St. John's   True early birds can begin their tour of the area at daybreak by filling up a thermos of coffee, getting some muffins, and driving on

**❶** Route 11 to **Cape Spear,** so they can be among the first to watch the sun come up over North America. Song birds begin their chirping in the dim light of dawn and whales feed directly below the cliffs, providing an unforgettable start to the day. **Cape Spear Lighthouse** (tel. 709/772–5367), Newfoundland's oldest such beacon has been lovingly restored to its original form and furnishings and is open to visitors, daily 10–6 from early June through Labor Day.

**❷** Those who are less ambitious may wish to begin exploring **St. John's** a little later in the day, when the Tourist Chalet on the waterfront is open. This is an old converted railway caboose, staffed from May through October. *Harbor Dr., tel. 709/576–8514. Open May–Oct., daily 9–7.*

Whichever way you look—left or right—you'll see the always-fascinating array of ships that tie up along **Harbour Drive.** Walk the harborfront, a favorite route in St. John's, to **The Battery,** a tiny, still-active fishing village perched precariously on the steep cliffs between hill and harbor. A well-maintained 5-kilometer (3-mile) walking path leads along the cliff edge, through the narrows, and zigzags through **Signal Hill National Historic Park.** Alternatively, you can drive on the road that also leads to the park.

In spite of its height, Signal Hill was difficult to defend: Throughout the 1600s and 1700s it changed hands with every attacking French, English, and Dutch force. A wooden palisade encircles the summit of the hill, indicating the boundaries of the old fortifications. En route to the hill is the **Park Interpretation Centre,** with exhibits describing St. John's history. *Tel. 709/772–5367. Open Labor Day–May, daily 8:30–4:30; June–Labor Day, daily 8:30–8.*

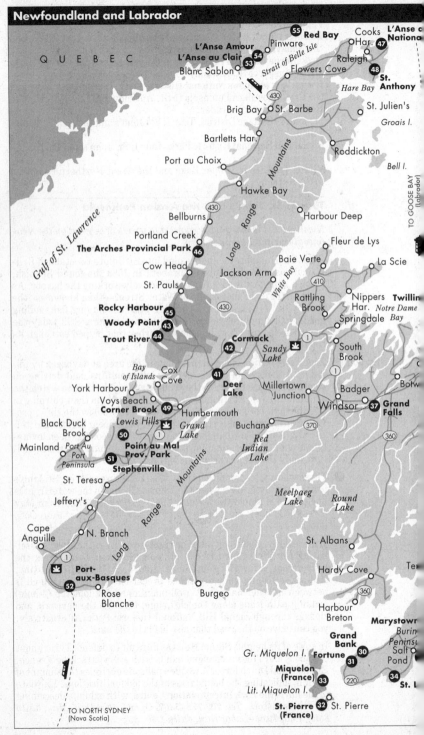

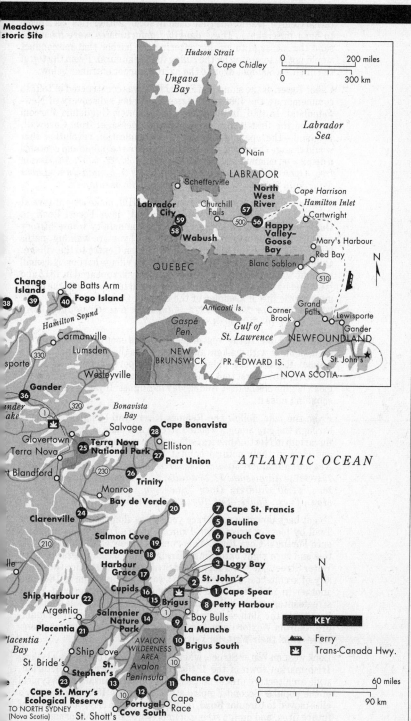

Meadows
storic Site

Hudson Strait
Cape Chidley

Ungava
Bay

200 miles

300 km

Labrador
Sea

Nain

LABRADOR

Schefferville

North
West
River

Cape Harrison
Hamilton Inlet

Labrador
City

Churchill
Falls

57

56

Cartwright

59

58

Wabush

500

Happy
Valley-
Goose
Bay

Mary's Harbour

Red Bay

QUEBEC

Blanc Sablon

510

N

Change
Islands

Joe Batts Arm

38

39

40

Fogo Island

Anticosti Is.

Corner
Brook

Grand
Falls

Lewisporte

Hamilton Sound

Gaspé
Pen.

Gulf of
St. Lawrence

Gander

Carmanville

NEWFOUNDLAND

Lumsden

330

sporte

Wesleyville

NEW
BRUNSWICK

PR. EDWARD IS.

St. John's

Gander

nder
ake

36

320

Bonavista
Bay

NOVA SCOTIA

1

Glovertown

Salvage

Cape Bonavista

Terra Nova

Terra Nova
National Park

28

Elliston

ATLANTIC OCEAN

t Blandford

25

27

Port Union

230

26

Trinity

Monroe

Clarenville

24

Bay de Verde

20

7

Cape St. Francis

5

Bauline

210

Salmon Cove

19

6

Pouch Cove

N

Ile

Carbonear

18

4

Torbay

Harbour
Grace

17

3

Logy Bay

Ship Harbour

22

Cupids

16

2

St. John's

Argentia

15

Brigus

1

Cape Spear

Salmonier
Nature
Park

14

1

8

Petty Harbour

Placentia

21

9

Bay Bulls

lacentia
Bay

Ship Cove

La Manche

10

Brigus South

St.
Stephen's

AVALON
WILDERNESS
AREA

St. Bride's

23

Avalon
Peninsula

10

Cape St. Mary's
Ecological Reserve

13

11

Chance Cove

TO NORTH SYDNEY
(Nova Scotia)

St. Shott's

10

12

Portugal
Cove South

Cape
Race

KEY

Ferry

Trans-Canada Hwy.

60 miles

90 km

**Gibbet Hill,** the rocky knob immediately to the west of the Interpretation Centre, was at one time used by local "authorities" as a place to hang miscreants. These dangling unfortunates were meant to send the message to anyone entering the harbor that misconduct would not be tolerated by the ruling fishing admiral. From the top of the hill it's a 500-foot drop to the narrow harbor entrance below.

**Cabot Tower,** at the summit of Signal Hill, was constructed in 1897 to commemorate the 400th anniversary of Cabot's discovery of Newfoundland. In 1901, in the shadow of the tower, Guglielmo Marconi received the first transatlantic wireless message, from Cornwall, England—the opening salvo in a communication revolution that would change the world. The tower is open to the public and contains a display on communications history. *Tel. 709/772–5367. Admission free. Open Labor Day–early June, daily 9–5; mid-June–Labor Day, daily 8:30–8, Weekend guides available in summer.*

If you are driving, come down from Signal Hill, make a right turn at Quidi Vidi Road, and continue to the right, down Forest Road, to **Quidi Vidi Village,** an authentic fishing community whose history goes back to the beginning of St. John's. If you are walking, paths lead from the summit and the Interpretation Centre to the village. **Quidi Vidi Battery,** near the entrance to the village harbor, is a small redoubt which has been restored to the way it appeared in 1812 and is staffed by costumed interpreters who will tell you about the hard, unromantic life of a soldier of the empire. *Quidi Vidi Village, tel. 709/729–2460 or 709/729–2977. Admission free. Open July–early Sept., daily 10–5:30; winter by appt.*

**Quidi Vidi Lake,** to the west of the village, is encircled by a leisurely path, popular with walkers and joggers. It's the site of the **St. John's Annual Regatta,** the oldest continuing sporting event in North America, which first took place in 1826. Weather permitting, the regatta begins on the first Wednesday in August: If you're in town you shouldn't miss it.

From the lake, follow the **Rennies River Trail** (4 miles) that cuts through the city along a wooded stream and ends at the only public fluvarium in North America, where you can observe spawning trout and char in their natural habitat through underwater windows. *Newfoundland Freshwater Resource Center, Pippy Park, tel. 709/754–3474. Admission: $2.75 adults, $2.25 students and senior citizens, $1.50 children. Open June–Aug., daily 9–5; Sept.–May, Mon., Tues., Thurs.–Sat. 10–4:30, Sun. noon–4:30.*

To get back downtown, retrace your steps along the Rennies River Trail by foot, or drive down Prince Phillip's Drive and turn right onto Portugal Cove Road. This runs into New Cove Road—follow this and turn right onto King's Bridge Road which intersects with Water Street. As you walk around St. John's, you'll notice the diversity of architectural styles due to two major fires: one in 1846 and another in 1892. The 1892 fire stopped where George and Water streets intersect, at **Yellowbelly Corner.** This junction was so-named because in the 19th century it was a gathering spot for Irish immigrants from Wexford who wore yellow sashes to distinguish themselves from their Waterford rivals.

Look west on Water Street, where the block still resembles a typical Irish market town of the 1840s. To the east, however, Victorian-style architecture predominates, with curved mansard roofs typical of the popular Second Empire style. After the 1892 fire the city's elite moved to **Circular Road,** in the center of the city, out of reach of future fires, and built a string of impressive and highly ornamented

Victorian mansions, which bear witness to the sizable fortunes made in the old days from the humble cod.

While you're downtown, take a look at the churches of St. John's, rich in architectural history. The **Basilica of St. John the Baptist** (Military Rd., tel. 709/754–2170), with a commanding position above Military Road, overlooks the older section of the city and the harbor. The land was granted to the church by young Queen Victoria, and the edifice was built with stones from both Ireland and Newfoundland. From here you can also see the **Anglican Cathedral of St. John the Baptist** (22 Church Hill, tel. 709/726–5677) on Church Hill, one of the finest examples of Gothic Revival architecture in North America. Nearby is the imposing **Gower Street United Church** (Grower St., tel. 709/753–7286), with its redbrick facade and green turrets. At the bottom of Military Road, adjacent to Hotel Newfoundland, is the **St. Thomas Old Garrison Church** (Military Rd., tel. 709/576–6632), where the English soldiers used to worship during the early and mid-1800s. All three churches conduct summer tours.

| | |
|---|---|
| **Time Out** | The **Commissariat House** (Kings Bridge Rd., tel. 709/729–2460 or 709/729–6730), just around the corner from the Anglican church, has been restored to the way it appeared in the 1830s. The interpreters, dressed in period costume, will show you around. |

If you have time, set aside an afternoon to visit the **Memorial University Botanical Gardens,** located at Oxen Pond on Mt. Scio Road. This 110-acre nature reserve has five attractive trails, an English cottage garden, Newfoundland heritage plants, heather and rhododendron borders, peat and woodland beds, a wildlife garden, an alpine house, rock gardens and scree, and native plant collections. The reserve also offers seasonal indoor exhibits, regular tours, and nature walks, and is heavily involved in butterfly and bat conservation. *Oxen Pond, Mt. Scio Rd., Pippy Park, tel. 709/737–8590. Admission free. Open May–Nov., Wed.–Sun. 10–5:30.*

Another beautiful spot in St. John's is **Bowring Park,** on Waterford Bridge Road. The expansive Victorian park was donated to the city by the wealthy Bowring family in 1911, and resembles the famous inner city parks of London, England, after which it was modeled. Dotting the grounds are artfully designed nooks and crannies, ponds, ducks to feed, and rustic bridges; there's also a statue of Peter Pan.

**The Avalon Peninsula** Several half-day, full-day, and two-day excursions are possible from St. John's, and in each direction a different personality of the region unfolds. On the southern half of the peninsula are small Irish hamlets separated by large tracts of wilderness. The northern half is more densely populated and still reflects its Dorset and Devon, England, origins. Here, homes are perched on narrow spits of land or tucked into the lee of cliffs.

*Coast North of St. John's* **3** You can take a leisurely half-day trip to explore the scenic coastline north of St. John's. Take Route 30 (Logy Bay Road) to Marine Drive, which winds along the coastline, passing through **Logy Bay** and its remarkable cliffs. Along the way is **Ocean Sciences Centre,** with its outdoor seal tank where you can watch the animals frolic. Large aquariums in the Discovery Room are filled with local marine life, and a Touch Tank gives everyone a chance to meet and examine many marine animals face-to-face. *Marine Lab Rd., tel. 709/737–3706. Admission $2.50 adults, $1.50 children and senior citizens, under 6 free. Tours every ½-hr late June–early Sept., 10–5.*

Follow Route 30 to **Torbay** and turn west onto Route 21 to **Bauline,** an unspoiled fishing village that overlooks Conception Bay. Continue on Route 21 to **Pouch Cove,** one of the province's oldest communities, where the adventurous should follow the unpaved road that leads to **Cape St. Francis.** On the way to the cape, there's a short coastal walk. A local legend centers around the wreck of the *Waterwitch,* which capsized in 1875 in the water at the northern edge of Pouch Cove. Alfred Moores rescued 11 people from the floundering vessel by lowering himself by rope down the cliff. A sign marks the site along the coastal walk, but you can't see the wreck.

Leave Pouch Cove on Route 20 and head straight back, or connect to Route 30, which loops around toward Logy Bay, on your return to St. John's. For one more scenic pleasure en route, take in some views at the village of **Flat Rock,** on Route 20 just past Pouch Cove.

*Coast South of St. John's* You can travel part of the peninsula's coast for a one- or two-day excursion, depending on how much time you have. Quaint coastal towns line the road, and the natural sites are beautiful.

Just south of St. John's pick up Route 10 and follow it along the southern coast toward Trepassey. Locals call this trip "going up the shore," even though it looks like you're traveling down on a map. The wildness of this coast is usually what's most striking to visitors, and La Manche and Chance Cove—both now-abandoned communities turned provincial parks—attest to the bounty of natural resources of the region.

Although a visit to many of the hamlets along the way will fill any void for prettiness, a few favorites are exceptional. **Petty Harbour, La Manche,** and **Brigus South,** have especially attractive settings and strong traditional flavors.

In springtime, between **Chance Cove** and **Portugal Cove South,** in a stretch of land about 36 miles long, hundreds of caribou gather near the road on the wide barrens with their calves. Although the graceful animals are there during other times of the year, their numbers are few and it's difficult to spot them because they blend in so well with the scenery.

Route 10 loops around the peninsula and becomes Route 90, just past **St. Stephens.**

At the intersection of Routes 90 and 91, in Salmonier, you need to decide whether to continue north toward Salmonier Nature Park and on to Conception Bay, or to head west then south to Route 100 to Cape St. Mary's Ecological Reserve (*see* Route 100: The Cape Shore, *below*). Each option takes about three hours.

If you've decided to go north, travel to **Salmonier Nature Park,** 9 miles along, where visitors can see many of the animal species that are indigenous to the province. The park is a 1,214-hectare wilderness reserve area and has an enclosed 40.5 hectare exhibit that allows up-close viewing. *Salmonier Line, Rte. 90, tel. 709/729–6974 or 709/229–7888. Admission free. Open early June–Labor Day, Thurs.–Mon., noon–7; other times by appt.*

Farther along Route 90 the road passes through the scenic Hawkes Hills, before meeting up with the Trans-Canada Highway (Route 1). Turn off at the Holyrood Junction (Route 62) and follow Route 70, which parallels **Conception Bay,** to Brigus. Meander through this beautifully restored village with winding lanes, a teahouse, and a museum set in a stone barn, where you can pick up a walking-tour brochure. *Ye Olde Stone Barn Museum, 4 Magistrate's Hill, tel. 709/*

*528–3298. Admission $1 adults, 50¢ children. Open June–Labor Day, daily 1–5; Sept. and Oct., weekends.*

Brigus was the home of many sealing captains, including Captain Bob Bartlett, who in 1909 guided Commodore Perry to within 161 kilometers (100 miles) of the North Pole. Perry abandoned Bartlett before going on the last leg so he could claim full honors for himself. The move backfired, however, for without Bartlett's testimony Perry couldn't prove that he actually made the journey.

**16** Continue on Route 70 to **Cupids,** the site of the first permanent colony in Newfoundland, which was founded in 1610 by the Bristol merchant John Guy.

Just beyond Brigus Route 70 passes by Clarke's Beach, where you should turn right and follow Route 72 along a narrow sliver of land to **Port de Grave** and **Hibbs Cove.** The **Port de Grave Fishermen's Museum, Porter House,** and **Old School House Community Museum** are actually in Hibbs Cove. Here you can learn about Newfoundland fisherman lifestyles from the 1600s until the present. *Hibbs Cove, off Rte. 72, tel. 709/786–3912 or 709/786–3900. Admission: $1 adults, 50¢ students. Open mid-June–late June, daily 1–5; July–Labor Day, Mon.–Sat. 10–noon and 1–5, Sun. 1–5.*

**17** About 10 miles farther on Route 70 is **Harbour Grace,** which once was the headquarters of Peter Easton, a 17th-century pirate. Beginning in 1919, Harbour Grace was the departure point for many attempts to fly the Atlantic. Amelia Earhart left Harbour Grace in 1932 to become the first woman to fly solo across the Atlantic. Several handsome stone churches and buildings remain as evidence of the town's former pride.

**18** Continue along Route 70 to **Carbonear,** another town with a fascinating history. In 1696 it was burned to the ground by the French, but the inhabitants retreated to a small fortified island in the harbor and successfully defended it against capture. Carbonear Island has been designated a National Historic Site to mark its colorful military past.

**19** Farther along Route 70 is picturesque **Salmon Cove,** a sheltered bay with a grassy picnic area. The road is narrow and partly unpaved, but you'll be rewarded with the finest views of Conception Bay, especially as you drive up and over Blow Me Down Head. If you plan to
**20** travel on to **Bay de Verde,** at the northern tip of the peninsula, and down the other side of the peninsula on Route 80 along Trinity Bay, consider turning in for the night at one of the several hotels or bed-and-breakfasts (*see* Lodging, *below*) in the Harbour Grace–Carbonear area. Otherwise turn around and follow the same route back.

*Route 100: The* If you opted for the Cape Shore route, from Salmonier west on Route
*Cape Shore* 91 and south on Route 100, you're headed to Avalon's Cape St. Mary's Ecological Reserve.

**21** **Placentia,** at the end of Route 91, was the French capital of Newfoundland in the 1600s. Trust the French to select a beautiful place for a capital! **Castle Hill National Historic Park,** just north of town, is located on what remains of the French fortifications. The visitor's center has a "life at Plaisance" exhibit that shows the life and hardships endured by early English and French settlers. *Off Rte. 100, tel. 709/227–2401. Admission free. Open June–Labor Day, daily 8:30–8; Labor Day–May, daily 8:30–4:30.*

**㉒** A worthwhile and nearby diversion from Placentia is **Ship Harbour,** an isolated, edge-of-the-world place that has the curious distinction of being the home of the free world. Off Route 102, amidst the splendor of Placentia Bay, an unpaved road leads to a monument marking the historic Atlantic Charter. It was on a ship in these waters where, in 1941, Roosevelt and Churchill signed the charter and formally announced the "Four Freedoms," which still shape the politics of the world's most successful democracies: freedom of speech, freedom of worship, freedom from want, and freedom from fear.

**㉓** To continue on the Cape Shore tour, double back to Route 100 and travel 24 miles to the **Cape St. Mary's Ecological Reserve** (tel. 709/729–2424), which has the second largest gannet colony in North America and is the most southerly nesting place in the world for gannets and thick-billed murres; there are about 10,000 pairs of each during the nesting season between June and August. An interpretation center is on the grounds and on-site nature guides are available during the summer. While walking out to the sanctuary, you'll experience some of the most dramatic coastal scenery in Newfoundland—that's if you are lucky enough to witness one of the cape's rare clear days. Fog is far more usual. Fortunately, the birds are close-at-hand, so you'll see and hear them no matter what the weather.

## Tour 2: Clarenville and the Bonavista and Burin Peninsulas

**㉔** **Clarenville** is about two hours from St. John's via the Trans-Canada Highway (Route 1) and is the departure point for two different excursions: the Discovery Trail and Terra Nova National Park. If you're interested in rugged terrain, golf, fishing, and camping, head
**㉕** 15 miles west along the Trans-Canada Highway to **Terra Nova National Park,** on the exposed coastline that adjoins Bonavista Bay. If you are a golfer, you can play on one of the most beautiful courses in Canada, and the only one where a licensed salmon river cuts through the 18-hole course. Call 709/543–2525, 800/461–0808 in Canada for a reservation. Fees run between $24 and $30 per person, depending on the season. The park also offers attractive campsites, whale-watching tours, and nature walks. *Tel. 709/533–2801 or 709/533–2358, fax 709/533–2706. Open daily. Vehicle permit required in summer: $5 per day per vehicle, $10 for 4-day pass, $20 for seasonal pass.*

If history and quaint towns interest you, begin the tour in Clarenville, the starting point for Route 230—the **"Discovery Trail."** The route goes as far as the town of Bonavista, one of John Cabot's reputed landing spots in 1497. On your way visit the historic
**㉖** village of **Trinity,** known as one of the jewels of Newfoundland. The village's picturesque views, winding lanes, and snug houses are the main attraction, and several homes have been turned into museums and inns. In the 1700s Trinity competed with St. John's as a center of culture and wealth. Its more contemporary claim to fame, however, is that its intricate harbor was a favorite anchorage for the British navy, and it was here that the smallpox vaccine was introduced to North America, by a local rector. An information center with costumed interpreters is open daily from July to September.

**㉗** **Port Union,** just north of Trinity on Route 230, was built as a model fishing community a century ago by the pioneer unionist Sir William Coaker. **The Port Union Museum** (contact Linda Clarke, tel. 709/464–3315) in the old railway station traces his career.

㉘ Still farther north along Route 230 is **Cape Bonavista,** a popular destination because of its association with Cabot's landing. The lighthouse on the point has been restored to the 1870 period. While here, visit the Mockbeggar Property to learn about the life of a well-to-do outport merchant in the years immediately before Confederation. *Off Rte. 230, tel. 709/729–2460 or 709/468–7444. Admission free. Open late June–early Sept., daily 10–5:30; winter, by appt.*

*Burin Peninsula* The journey down to the Burin Peninsula is a three- to four-hour drive from the intersection of Routes 230 and 1 through the sometimes incredible landscapes along Route 210. The peninsula's history is tied to the rich fishing grounds of the Grand Banks, which established this area as a center for European fishery as early as the 1500s. By the early 1900s, one of the world's largest fishing fleets was based on the Burin Peninsula. Today its inhabitants still operate the fishery in the modern trawlers that harvest the Grand Banks.

㉙ **Marystown** is the largest town on the peninsula and is its major commercial center. The town's name was changed from Mortier to Marystown by a priest during World War I, and to keep the faith a 15-foot statue of the Virgin Mary watches the town and harbor. West from here the road meets with Route 220 and passes through

㉚ **Grand Bank,** an unusually attractive community with a fascinating fishing history. This town is famous in the area as one of the most beautiful communities on the Atlantic seaboard. For details about the town's past visit the **Southern Newfoundland Seamen's Museum,** housed in a sail-shape building that was the Yugoslavian Pavilion in Expo '67. *Marine Dr., tel. 709/832–1484. Admission free. Open weekdays 9–noon, 1–5; weekends 2–5.*

㉛㉜㉝ Just south of Grand Bank is **Fortune,** where you can catch the ferry to France's only colony in North America—the islands of **St. Pierre** and **Miquelon.** These islands are the place to go if you crave French cuisine or a bottle of perfume. Shopping and eating are both popular pastimes, and if you plan to stay overnight, consider the Hotel Robert on St. Pierre. The ferry ride takes about two hours, and tourists should carry proof of citizenship. People from outside the United States and Canada will have to show valid visas and passports. Two passenger ferry companies provide service: **Lloyd G. Lake Ltd.** (tel. 709/832–2006) leaves Fortune daily at 2:15 PM from mid-June to late September. The crossing takes 55 minutes. The ferry leaves St. Pierre at 1:00 PM daily, and the round trip costs $47.95; children under 16 are free. **SPM Tours** (tel. 709/832–0429) leaves Fortune daily at 1:15 PM and leaves St. Pierre at 11 AM daily. Season and fares same as above.

㉞ Back on Route 220, you may wish to stop at **St. Lawrence,** where in 1942 one of the worst disasters befell the U.S. Navy. It was here that warships *Pollux* and *Truxton* ran aground during a February storm. Two hundred sailors perished, but the people of the area heroically pulled another 182 over the cliffs to safety. In gratitude the U.S. Navy built a hospital for the community. In the summer of 1992, some survivors of the disaster returned to renew their friendships with the people of St. Lawrence and to unveil the "Echoes of Valour" monument on the cliff overlooking the spot where the ship sank.

㉟ Following Route 220 will take you around the peninsula to the old town of **Burin,** a community amidst intricate cliffs and coves. This was an ideal setting for pirates and privateers who used to lure ships into the rocky, dead-end areas in order to escape. Captain Cook was among those who watched for smugglers from "Cook's Lookout" on a hill that still bears his name. Also in Burin is the Heritage House museum (tel. 709/891–2217, admission free, open Mon. and Tues. 9–5, Wed.–Sun. 9–9), considered one of the best community museums in Newfoundland, which gives you a sense of what life was like in the past.

## Tour 3: Gander, Grand Falls–Windsor, and Notre Dame Bay

The interior of Newfoundland is unpopulated beyond the main roads, with the towns of Gander and Grand Falls–Windsor the focal points for the region. **Gander,** a busy center with 12,000 people, is the site of the Gander International Airport. During World War II it was chosen by the Canadian and U.S. Air Forces as a major strategic air base because of its favorable weather and secure location. After the war, the airport became an international hub, and young islanders would hang around to see the stars come and go, among them Zsa Zsa Gabor and Tyrone Power. Now, like all modern airports, it's tightly secured. Gander has many hotels and still makes a good base for your travels. The **Aviation Exhibition** in the airport's Domestic Passenger's Lounge (tel. 709/729–2460; open daily) traces Newfoundland's role in the history of air travel.

**Grand Falls,** 50 minutes west of Gander along the Trans-Canada Highway (Route 1), was a paper-milling town founded by Lord Northcliffe in the early 1900s to supply newsprint for his growing newspaper empire. Within Grand Falls is the **Mary March Regional Museum,** which depicts the lives of the Beothuk Indians before they fell victim to disease and competition from early settlers. The museum is named for 23-year-old Demasduit (also named Mary March, for the month in which she was captured), one of the last Beothuks, who was captured in 1819 during a brutal encounter that resulted in the death of her husband and child. *St. Catherine St., off Rte. 1, tel. 709/489–9331. Admission free. Open weekdays 9–4:45, weekends and holidays 10–5:45.*

Using either Route 330 from Gander via the Trans-Canada Highway (Route 1) or Route 340 from Grand Falls, wander north through wooded countryside and small villages to **Twillingate.** The inhabitants of this charming old fishing village make their living from the sea and have been doing so for nearly two centuries. Every year on the last weekend in July, the town hosts the **Fish, Fun and Folk Festival,** where all different kinds of fish are cooked every kind of way. Twillingate is also one of the best places on the island to see icebergs, and is known to the locals as "Iceberg Alley." These majestic and dangerous mountains of ice are awe inspiring to see while they're grounded in early summer.

You might also be interested in taking a ferry ride to either **Change Islands** or **Fogo Island.** Branch off Route 340 to Route 335, which takes you through scenic coastal communities on the way to the ferry to either of the islands, located in Farewell. These islands give one the impression of a place frozen in time. Clapboard homes are precariously perched on rocks or built on small lots surrounded by vegetable gardens. As you walk the roads, look for moose and herds of wild Newfoundland ponies who spend their summers grazing and enjoying the warm breeze off the ocean.

## Tour 4: Deer Lake and the Great Northern Peninsula to St. Anthony

**41** **Deer Lake** was once just another small town on the Trans-Canada Highway, but the opening of Gros Morne National Park in the early '70s and a first-class paved highway passing right through to St. Anthony changed all that. Today, with an airport and car rentals available, Deer Lake is a good starting point for a fly-drive vacation.

Head north out of Deer Lake on Route 430 to Route 422 to **Sir Richard Squires Memorial Park.** This drive will take you through **42** **Cormack,** which is one of the best farming regions in the island. The park remains natural and unspoiled, and it contains one of the most interesting salmon fishing areas in Newfoundland.

Return to Route 430, and in a short while you'll be on the **Viking Trail** leading into **Gros Morne National Park** (tel. 709/458–2059). Because of its geological uniqueness and immense splendor, this park has been named a UNESCO World Heritage Site. Among the more breathtaking visions are the expanses of wild orchids in springtime. There is an excellent **Interpretation Centre** (tel. 709/458–2417) which has displays and videos about the park. Camping and hiking are popular recreations in the park, and boat tours are available. It takes at least two days to see Gros Morne properly.

Scenic **Bonne Bay,** a deep, mountainous fjord, divides the park in two. You can drive around the perimeter of the fjord on Route 430 going north.

**43** In the south of the park is **Woody Point,** a charming community of old houses and imported Lombardy poplars. Until it was bypassed by the railway, the community was the commercial capital of the West Coast. Rising behind Woody Point are the **Tablelands,** a unique rock massif that was once an ancient seabed. Its rocks are toxic to most plant life, and Ice Age conditions linger in the form of persistent snow and moving rock glaciers.

**44** Follow Route 431 to scenic **Trout River Pond** and the once isolated and still unusual community of **Trout River.** The **Green Gardens Trail,** a four- to five-hour hike, is along the way and it's one you'll remember for your lifetime, but be prepared to do a bit of climbing on your return journey. The trail passes through the Tablelands barrens and descends sharply down to a fairy-tale coastline of eroded cliffs, sea stacks, and lush green meadows.

**45** On the northern side of the park, situated along coastal Route 430, is **Rocky Harbour,** with a wide range of services and a luxurious indoor public pool—the perfect thing to soothe tired limbs after a strenuous day. The most popular attraction on the northern portion of Gros Morne is the boat tour up **Western Brook Pond,** which is reached by a leisurely 45-minute walk from the main highway through an interesting mix of bog and woods. Cliffs rise 2,000 feet on both sides of the gorge and high waterfalls tumble over ancient rocks. If you have strong legs and are in good shape, another decent attraction is the 10-mile hike up **Gros Morne Mountain,** at 2,644 feet the second-highest peak in Newfoundland. Weather permitting, your labor will be rewarded by a unique arctic landscape and spectacular views. The park's coast in the north offers visitors an unusual mix of sand beaches, rock pools, and trails through tangled dwarf forests known locally as "tuckamore." Sunsets, seen from Lobster Point Lighthouse, are spectacular. Keep an eye out for whales and visit the lighthouse museum, devoted to the history of the area.

**46** Just a short distance north of the park, on Route 430, is **The Arches Provincial Park,** a geological curiosity where the pounding sea has cut a succession of caves through a bed of dolomite.

Continuing north, parallel to the Gulf of St. Lawrence, you'll find yourself refreshingly close to the ocean and the wave-tossed beaches: Stop to breathe the fresh sea air and listen to the breakers. The Long Range Mountains to your right reminded Jacques Cartier, who saw them in 1534, of the long, rectangular-shape farm buildings of his home village in France. Small villages are interspersed with rivers where salmon and trout grow to be "liar-size." The remains of the Maritime Archaic Indians and Dorset Eskimos have been found in abundance along this coast, and there's an interesting Interpretation Centre (tel. 709/623–2601 or 709/623–2608) at Port aux Choix.

Proceed about 130 miles on Route 430, then turn onto Route 436 to **47** **L'Anse aux Meadows National Historic Site.** This UNESCO World Heritage Site was discovered in 1960 by a Norwegian team, Helge and Anne Stine Ingstad. Most believe the remains of the long sod houses here were built around 1000 as the site of Norseman Lief Erikson's colony in the New World. The Canadian Parks Service has established a marvelous **Interpretation Centre** (tel. 709/623–2601) and has meticulously reconstructed some of the sod huts. With fires burning inside and sheepskins about, one does get a sense of centuries past. *Rte. 436, tel. 709/623–2601 or 709/623–2608. Admission free. Visitor center open mid-June–Labor Day, daily 9–8.*

Return to Route 430 and about 10 miles from the junction with 430 is **48** **St. Anthony,** a beautiful town settled around a natural harbor, at the tip of the Great Northern Peninsula. Take a trip out to the lighthouse—you may see an iceberg or two floating by.

Here is also the home of the **Grenfell Mission.** The huge hospital attests to the work done by Sir Wilfred Grenfell, a British medical missionary, who established nursing stations and cooperatives and provided medical services to the scattered villages of northern Newfoundland and the south coast of Labrador in the early 1900s. The main foyer of the hospital has a decorative tile mural that's worth a visit. **Grenfell House,** the home of Sir Wilfred and Lady Grenfell, has been restored to period condition and can also be visited. *On the west side of St. Anthony on a hill overlooking the harbor, adjacent to Charles S. Curtis Memorial Hospital, tel. 709/454–3333, ext. 263. Admission: $2 adults, $1 students and senior citizens, children under 5 free. Open mid-May–mid-Oct., daily 10–8; winter, by appt.*

Don't leave without visiting the **Grenfell Handcraft** store (tel. 709/ 454–3576). Importing craftspeople to train the villagers to become self-sufficient in a harsh environment was one of Grenfell's aims. A windproof cloth that villagers turned into well-made parkas came to be known as Grenfell cloth. Beautiful clothes fashioned out of Grenfell cloth have quality and style not found anywhere else and they are available for sale here. Return to Deer Lake along Route 430.

## Tour 5: Corner Brook and the West Coast

**49** **Corner Brook** is Newfoundland's second-largest city and the hub of the west coast of the island. Mountains fringe three sides of the city and there are beautiful views of the harbor and the Bay of Islands. Corner Brook is also home to one of the largest paper mills in the world. Every July the city hosts the **Hangashore Folk Festival,**

where you can go to hear some great traditional Canadian and Newfoundland music.

If you plan to explore the west coast, Corner Brook is a convenient hub and point of departure. It is only three hours from the Port aux Basques ferry and is an attractive and active city. The town enjoys more clearly defined seasons than most of the rest of the island, and in summer there are many pretty gardens to view and enjoy. **The Marble Mountain Ski Resort** (tel. 709/639–8531 on the slopes or 709/634–2160 for the development office), just east of the city, has the highest slopes and snowfall in eastern North America and is growing rapidly as a ski center.

The north and south shores of the **Bay of Islands** have fine paved roads—Route 440 on the north shore and Route 450 on the south—and both offer a pleasant and scenic half-day drive. On both roads, farming and fishing communities exist side by side. Take a camera with you—the scenery is breathtaking, with farms, mountains, and beautiful pockets of brilliant wild flowers.

**⑤⓪**
**⑤①**
On another day, drive farther west on the Trans-Canada Highway and turn off at Route 460. Spend some time on the **Point au Mal Provincial Park** stopping at **Stephenville,** home of the old Harmon Air Force Base and now home to the annual Stephenville Arts Festival (mid-July to early August). The peninsula itself was largely settled by the French who brought their way of life and language to this small corner of Newfoundland.

**⑤②**
As you move farther down the Trans-Canada Highway toward **Port-aux-Basques,** Routes 404, 405, 406, and 407 will bring you into the small Scottish communities of the **Codroy Valley.** Nestled in the valley are some of the finest salmon rivers and most productive farms in the province, all of this against the backdrop of the Long Range Mountains and the Lewis Hills, from which gales strong enough to stop traffic hurl off the plateau and down to the coast.

## Tour 6: Labrador

Isolated from the rest of the continent, Labrador has remained one of the world's truly wild places, and yet its two main centers of Labrador City–Wabush and Happy Valley–Goose Bay offer all the amenities available in larger, urban centers. Labrador is steeped in history, a place where the past invades the present and life evolves as it did many years ago, a composite of natural phenomena, wilderness adventure, history, and culture.

Labrador's vast landscape—294,330 square kilometers (113,204 square miles) of land and 8,000 kilometers (5,000 miles) of coastline—is home to a small but richly diverse population with a history that in some cases stretches back thousands of years; in other cases, the mining towns of Labrador West for example, the history goes back less than four decades.

**Getting There** From the island of Newfoundland, you can fly to Labrador via St. John's, Gander, Deer Lake, or Stephenville. Route 500 was opened in 1992 linking Labrador City with Happy Valley–Goose Bay via Churchill Falls. If you plan on doing any extensive driving in any part of Labrador, you should contact the Department of Tourism and Culture (tel. 709/729–2830 or 800/563–6353) for advice on the best routes and road conditions.

To explore the south coast of Labrador, catch the ferry at St. Barbe on Route 430 in Newfoundland to Blanc Sablon, Québec. From here you can drive to Red Bay along Route 510. Conditions on this 439-kilometer (300-mile) unpaved wilderness road are best between June and October.

In summer, you can travel by car ferry through **Marine Atlantic** (in Lewisporte, Newfoundland, tel. 709/535–6876; in Happy Valley–Goose Bay, Labrador, 709/896–0041; or in the United States, 800/341–7981). The ship travels from Lewisporte in Newfoundland to Cartwright, on the coast of Labrador, and then through the Hamilton inlet to Happy Valley–Goose Bay. Reservations are required.

**The Straits** The trip from Blanc Sablon to Red Bay on Route 510 will take you through the small fishing communities of L'Anse au Clair, Forteau, ❸ and L'Anse au Loup. In **L'Anse au Clair,** you can walk the "Doctor's Path," where long ago Dr. Marcoux searched out herbs and medicinal plants in the days when hospitals and nursing stations were few and far between. Anglers can try their luck for trout and salmon on the scenic Forteau and Pinware rivers. The Straits were a rich hunting-and-gathering ground for the continent's earliest peoples.

The elaborate Maritime Archaic Indian burial site discovered near ❺❹ **L'Anse Amour,** about 12 miles from L'Anse au Clair, is 9,000 years old. A plaque marks the site. The L'Anse Amour lighthouse was constructed in 1857 and is the second-tallest lighthouse in Canada. During the month of August, the annual **Labrador Bakeapple Festival** in **Forteau** draws people from miles around for music, feasting, and celebration. The **Labrador Straits Museum** (Route 510, between Forteau and l'Anse-au-Loup, tel. 709/927–5659, admission $1.50, open daily during the summer) provides an interesting glimpse into the history and lifestyle of the area.

You must drive to the very end of Route 510 to visit the area's main ❺❺ attraction: **Red Bay,** the site of a 16th-century Basque whaling station and the province's newest UNESCO World Heritage Site. Basque whalers began harpooning migrating whales from flimsy boats in frigid waters a few years after Cabot's discovery of the coast in 1497. Between 1550 and 1600 Red Bay was the world's whaling capital. A new visitor center (tel. 709/920–2197, open mid-June–early Oct., Mon.–Sat. 8–8, Sun. noon–8) interprets the Basque heritage through film and artifact. Between June and October, a boat will take you on a short journey over to the actual site of excavations on Saddle Island.

**Coastal** You can tour coastal Labrador aboard Marine Atlantic's car ferry **Labrador** (*see* Arriving and Departing, *above*) from Lewisporte, Newfoundland, which also carries all sorts of food and goods for people living along the coast. The trip takes 33 hours one-way, and two regularly scheduled return trips are made weekly. A second ferry travels from Happy Valley–Goose Bay to Nain, Labrador's northernmost settlement. This trip takes two weeks to complete. As both ferries are supply boats, you'll stop at a number of summer fishing stations and coastal communities. Reservations required (tel. 709/695–7081).

❺❻ **Happy Valley–Goose Bay** is the chief service center for coastal Labrador. The town was founded in the 1940s as a top-secret air base used to ferry fleets of North American–manufactured aircraft to Europe. It is still used as a low-level flying training base by the British, Dutch, and German air forces.

❺❼ **North West River** is a pleasant, half-hour drive to the east on Route 520, and on the way you'll pass the **Snow Goose Mountain Ski Club** (tel. 709/896–5923). North West River was founded as a Hudson's

Bay trading post and is the former Labrador headquarters of the International Grenfell Association. It retains its frontier charm. Nearby **Sheshatshit** is the home of the Montagnais Innu Indians of Labrador. The spirit in which the Innu (Naskapi-Montagnais) people inhabited the interior for centuries can still be felt the moment you step outside the region's modern mining communities.

**Labrador West**     Labrador West's subarctic landscape is challenging and unforgettable. The terrain offers some of the world's best angling and wilderness adventure opportunities.

The best way to see this area is to ride the **Québec North Shore and Labrador Railway** (tel. 709/944–8205), which leaves Sept Isles, Québec, twice weekly. The 10-hour trip takes you through 419 kilometers (260 miles) of virgin forest, spectacular waterfalls, and majestic mountains. The refurbished vintage dome car is ideal for an expanded view of this breathtaking panorama. The train, though, is more than a pleasure ride—it carries iron ore from Wabush and Labrador City (site of the largest open-pit mining operation in the world) to various distribution points in Québec.

**⑤⑧ ⑤⑨**     The modern towns of **Wabush** and **Labrador City** have all the amenities of larger, urban centers, including accommodations, sports and recreational facilities, good shopping, live theater, and some of the finest hospitality you will find anywhere. Nearby are the **Smokey Mountain Alpine Skiing Center** (open mid-November–late April, tel. 709/944–3505) and the **Menihek Nordic Ski Club** (tel. 709/944–6339 or 709/944–2154), with trails and slopes for both beginners and advanced skiers.

# Shopping

The main centers of Newfoundland and Labrador—St. John's, Clarenville, Gander, Grand Falls, Corner Brook, Labrador West—all have modern shopping centers. However, the smaller communities often offer interesting crafts and native wares. Wander about—each town and village has its own country store and crafts store or general store. There are even some stores where packages are still wrapped in brown paper and tied with string.

**NONIA** (Newfoundland Outport Nurses Industrial Association), at 286 Water Street in St. John's, was started in 1923 to give Newfoundland women an opportunity to work. Throughout history, the women of Newfoundland have had a reputation for turning homespun wool into exquisite clothing. In 1923 Jubilee Guilds supplied these outport women with wool of all kinds and colors, and in this shop on Water Street, even today, you can buy their well-made knitware. Other fine crafts stores in St. John's are the **Salt Box, The Cod Jigger,** the **Devon House Craft Gallery,** and the **Newfoundland Weavery.** For antiques, **Murray's Antiques** and **Livyers** are well worth a visit.

At St. Anthony, on the northern tip of Newfoundland, browse in the **Grenfell Handcraft Store** (*see* Exploring, *above*).

Most bookstores have a prominent section devoted to local history, fiction, and memoirs. **Word Play** (221 Duckworth St., tel. 709/726–9193 or 800/563–9100) also carries a wide selection of newspapers, magazines, and books of general interest to travelers. **Fred's Records** (198 Duckworth St., tel. 709/753–9191) has the best selection of local tapes and CDs, as well as other music.

# Sports and Fitness

Many provincial and all national parks in Newfoundland have hiking and nature trails. The west coast offers opportunities for mountain climbing in the summer and skiing in the winter. There are also ski resorts near Clarenville, Labrador City, and Happy Valley–Goose Bay, and groomed cross-country ski trail systems in St. John's, Clarenville, Terra Nova National Park, Gros Morne National Park, Labrador City, and Happy Valley–Goose Bay, among other places.

Coastal and woods trails radiate from most small communities. However, you can never be sure how far the trail will go unless you ask a local. Be careful: Landmarks are few, the weather is changeable, and it is surprisingly easy to get lost. Many small communities now also have formal walking trails.

Newfoundland has 105 salmon rivers and trout streams. Angling in these unpolluted waters is a fisherman's dream. Seasonal and regulatory information can be obtained from the **Department of Tourism and Culture** (tel. 800/729–2830).

# Dining and Lodging

## Dining

John Cabot and Sir Humphrey Gilbert raved about "waters teeming with fish." Today, Newfoundland's fish are still some of the best in the world and one of the best dining bargains you will find anywhere. In Newfoundland, if you ask for "fish," you will always get cod. In season you will be treated to such local delicacies as panfried, baked, or poached cod, cod tongues, salt cod, fish and brewis (cod of course!). Fresh lobster, halibut, scallops, mussels, and Atlantic salmon are also good choices in season.

Two other foods you shouldn't leave without trying are partridgeberries and bakeapples. Partridgeberries are a small, lush-tasting relative of the cranberry and locally they are used for just about everything—pies, jams, cakes, pancakes, and even as a sauce for turkey and game. Bakeapples in the wild are a low-growing berry that looks like a yellow raspberry—you'll see them ripening in bogs in August throughout Newfoundland and Labrador. Enterprising youngsters sell them by the side of the road in jars. If the ones you buy are hard, wait a few days and they'll ripen into a rich-tasting jam. They're popular on ice cream or spread on fresh homemade bread. In Scandinavia they're known as cloudberries and are made into a liqueur.

You may also hear Newfoundlanders talk about the herb they call summer savory. Newfoundlanders are so partial to this peppery herb that they slip it into most stuffings and stews. Growers in the province ship the product all over the world, and Newfoundlanders visiting relatives living outside the province are usually asked to "bring the savory."

Only the large urban centers across the province, especially St. John's and Corner Brook, have gourmet restaurants. Fish is a safe dish to order just about everywhere—even in the lowliest take-out. You'll be agreeably surprised by the quality of the meals along the Trans-Canada Highway: Restaurants in the Irving Gas Station chain, for example, offer thick homemade soups with dumplings, and Sunday dinners that draw in local customers for miles around.

Don't be shy about trying some of the excellent meals offered in the province's expanding network of "hospitality homes," where home cooking goes hand in hand with the warm welcome for which Newfoundlanders are famous.

Dress is casual everywhere except at the Very Expensive listings.

Highly recommended restaurants in each price category are indicated by a star ★.

| Category | Cost* |
|----------|-------|
| $$$$ | over $50 |
| $$$ | $35–$50 |
| $$ | $20–$35 |
| $ | under $20 |

*per person, excluding drinks, service, and 12% sales tax*

## Lodging

Newfoundland and Labrador offer lodgings that range from modestly priced "hospitality homes" to luxury accommodations. In between, visitors can choose from affordable, basic lodging and mid-priced hotels. In remote areas, visitors should be prepared to find very basic lodgings. However, the lack of urban amenities is usually made up for by the home-cooked meals and the great hospitality that you'll encounter. Life is definitely more relaxed here: If you're expected at a "hospitality home" and you're running late, your host or hostess will leave your room key with a welcome note in the mailbox!

Highly recommended lodgings in each price category are indicated by a star ★.

| Category | Cost |
|----------|------|
| $$$ | over $100 |
| $$ | $60–$90 |
| $ | under $60 |

**Clarenville**
*Dining and Lodging*

**Holiday Inn.** There are no surprises at this chain member. Rooms are standard Holiday Inn fare. The daily buffet is plentiful and well worth the drive. *Box 967, Clarenville, A0E 1J0, tel. 709/466–7911, fax 709/466–3854. 64 rooms. AE, MC, V. $$*

**Corner Brook**
*Dining and Lodging*
★

**Best Western Mamateek Inn.** Rooms are more modern than at the Glynmill Inn (*below*). The dining room, which serves good Newfoundland home-cooked food, is known for its exquisite view of the whole city. Sunsets seen from the restaurant are remarkable. *Rte. 1, Box 787, A2H 6G7, tel. 709/639–8901, fax 709/639–7567. 55 rooms. AE, MC, V. $$*

★ **Glynmill Inn.** This charming inn has the feel of old England. It was once the staff house for the visiting top brass of the mill. Rooms are cozy and the dining room serves basic and well-prepared Newfoundland seafood, soups, and specialty desserts made with Newfoundland partridgeberries. There's also a popular steak house in the basement. *Cobb's Lane, Box 455, A2H 6E6, tel. 709/634–5106 or*

*800/563–4400 (Canada), fax 709/634–5181. 90 rooms. AE, MC, V. $$*

**Holiday Inn.** Again, there's nothing extraordinary here, aside from the convenience of being located right in town. The restaurant is average but has good seasonal fish dishes. *48 West St., A2H 2Z2, tel. 709/634–5381, fax 709/634–1723. 103 rooms. Facilities: lounge, restaurant, cable TV, minibars in some rooms, outdoor heated swimming pool. Pets allowed. AE, D, DC, MC, V. $$*

**Comfort Inn by Journey's End Motel.** This is a comfortable, modern motel (built in 1988) with an attractive interior (the dominating colors are dusty rose and blue) and beautiful views of either the city or the Bay of Islands. *41 Maple Valley Rd., Box 1142, A2H 6T2, tel. 709/639–1980, fax 709/639–1549. 81 rooms with color TV, pets allowed. AE, MC, DC, V. $–$$*

**Deer Lake**
*Dining and Lodging*
**Deer Lake Motel.** The guest rooms here are clean and comfortable, and the food in the café is basic, home-cooked fare. You'll find the seafood dishes exceptionally well prepared. *Box 820, A0K 2E0, tel. 709/635–2108, fax 709/635–3842. 54 rooms, 2 suites. AE, MC, V. $$*

**Gander**
*Dining and Lodging*
★
**Albatross Motel.** This newly renovated motel has a deserved reputation as an attractive place to stop off for a meal. Try the cod au gratin—you won't find it this good anywhere else. Rooms are basic and clean. *Box 450, A1V 1W8, tel. 709/256–3956, fax 709/651–2692. 107 rooms, 4 suites. AE, DC, MC, V. $$*

**Grand Falls**
*Dining and Lodging*
**Mount Peyton Hotel.** The rooms aren't soundproof here, but they are clean and comfortable. And the excellent Newfoundland menu makes this a great place to break up your journey across the island. *214 Lincoln Rd., A2A 1P8, tel. 709/489–2251. 150 rooms. AE, DC, MC, V. $$*

**L'Anse aux Meadows**
*Lodging*
**Valhalla Lodge Bed & Breakfast.** Located adjacent to the Viking site at L'Anse aux Meadows, this is the only game in town, but that doesn't make it any less comfortable and inviting. Note the interesting fossils in the rock fireplace in the dining room. Hot breakfasts are available, and extra meals can be had on request. *Gunner's Cove, Griquet A0K 2X0, tel. in summer, 709/623–2018; in winter, 709/896–5476. 6 rooms. V. $*

**Port-aux-Basques**
*Dining and Lodging*
**St. Christopher's Hotel.** This clean, comfortable hotel is a new addition in Port-aux-Basques that offers quiet, air-conditioned rooms and good food. *Caribou Rd., Box 2049, A0M 1C0, tel. 709/695–7034, fax 709/695–9841. 58 rooms. Facilities: banquet room, restaurant, conference room, satellite TV. AE, MC, V. $$*

**St. John's**
*Dining*
★
**The Cellar.** This restaurant situated in a historic building on the waterfront gets rave reviews for its innovative Continental cuisine featuring the best local ingredients. Menu selections include blackened fish dishes and tiramisu for dessert. *Baird's Cove, between Harbour and Water Sts., tel. 709/579–8900. Reservations advised. AE, MC, V. $$$*

★
**Stone House.** Situated in one of St. John's most historic buildings— an old restored 19th-century stone cottage—this dining room features imported game and Newfoundland specialties. *8 Kennas Hill, tel. 709/753–2380. Reservations advised. AE, D, DC, MC, V. $$$*

*Dining and Lodging*
★
**Hotel Newfoundland.** This hotel replaces an old hotel that stood on this site for many years. St. John's residents gather here for many special occasions, and it's noted for its Sunday and evening buffets, its charming rooms that overlook St. John's harbor, its atrium, and the fine cuisine of the Cabot Club. *Box 5637, A1C 5W8, tel. 709/726–4980, fax 709/726–2025. 288 rooms, 14 suites. AE, D, MC, V. $$$*

★ **Radisson Plaza Hotel.** In this new convention hotel in downtown St. John's, rooms overlook the harbor and the city. It offers two dining rooms: Brazil Square, noted for its breakfast and noon buffets; and Newman's, a secluded dining room serving elaborately presented international dishes and Newfoundland cuisine. *120 New Gower St., A1C 6K4, tel. 709/739–6404, fax 709/739–4154. 276 rooms, 9 suites. AE, D, DC, MC, V. $$–$$$*

**Journey's End Motel.** One of the newest members of the chain, this hotel overlooks St. John's harbor. Like other Journey's Ends, it offers clean, comfortable rooms at a reasonable price. The hotel's restaurant, Rumplestiltskins, has a splendid view and an unpretentious, attractive menu. *Hill O'Chips, A1C 6B1, tel. 709/754–7788, fax 709/754–5209. 161 rooms. AE, DC, MC, V. $$*

*Lodging* **Compton House Bed & Breakfast.** Housed in a charming, restored
★ historic St. John's residence in the west end of the city, this inn is professionally run and beautifully decorated. Twelve-foot ceilings and wide halls give the place a majestic feeling, and rooms done in pastels and chintzes add an air of coziness. The location, within easy walking distance of downtown St. John's, is ideal. *26 Waterford Bridge Rd., A1E 1C6, tel. 709/739–5789. 4 rooms, 2 suites. AE, MC, V. $$*

★ **Prescott House Inn.** Local art decorates the walls of this house, which has received a Heritage Award. It's the city's most popular bed-and-breakfast, made even better by a modernization that tastefully blended the new and the old. Located downtown, it's central to shopping and attractions. *17–19 Military Rd., A1C 2C3, tel. 709/ 753–6036. 6 rooms, 2 suites. MC, V. $$*

**A Gower Street House Bed & Breakfast.** This gracious former home of the late photographer Elsie Holloway has been designated by the Newfoundland Historic Trust as a point of interest. Now it is an ideal setting for paintings by prominent local artists. The downtown location is within walking distance of all the city's main attractions. Room rates include a full hot breakfast with traditional dishes as well as standard fare. *180 Gower Street, A1C 1P9, tel. 709/754–0047 or 800/563–3959. 4 rooms with bath. Facilities: access to laundry and kitchen, guest lounge. MC, V. $*

# The Arts and Nightlife

It has been a long-standing claim (since at least the 1700s) that St. John's has more bars per mile than any other city in North America. Each establishment has its own personality. Irish music, in particular, can be heard at **Erin's Pub,** Water Street, and the **Blarney Stone** on George Street. A mix of traditional folk songs and Irish music can be had at **Bridgett's,** Cookstown Road, St. John's.

George Street, in downtown St. John's, is a street of pubs and restaurants that has been beautifully restored. Open-air concerts can be heard there during the annual **George Street Festival** and on many other occasions.

Newfoundlanders love a party, and from the cities to the smallest towns they celebrate their history and unique culture throughout a summer of festivals and events. The **Newfoundland and Labrador Folk Arts Festival,** held in St. John's in early August, is the province's best-known traditional music festival. **The Newfoundland International Irish Festival** held in St. John's each July features international performers and lots of locals, too. It even includes a Leprechaun Festival for the kids. Local folk music festivals occur in every part of the province during the summer. You'll also encounter a host of community celebrations, community dinners, and church teas.

The province has an unusually active arts community, as well. Most major towns have an arts and culture center, which offers live theater presentations, ballet, and concerts by local, national, and international artists. The **Resource Centre for the Arts** (LSPU Hall), on Victoria Street (tel. 709/753–4531), is one of the country's oldest and most innovative experimental theaters. Like the arts and culture centers, it has a busy fall and winter season but is generally inactive during the summer. The **Stephenville Festival** (tel. 709/643–4982) is held throughout July and into August in Stephenville, an hour's drive south of Corner Brook. The festival is the province's major annual summer theatrical event and features a well-produced mix of light musicals and serious drama.

St. John's has a dozen commercial and public art galleries, nearly all of which feature local artists. Newfoundland's unique landscape, portrayed realistically or more experimentally, is a favorite subject. The province's largest public gallery, the **Memorial University Art Gallery** (tel. 709/737–8209), is located in the St. John's Arts and Culture Centre. The **Emma Butler Gallery** (tel. 709/739–7111) on George Street and **Christina Parker Fine Art** (tel. 709/753–0580) on Plank Road, in St. John's, offer the best selection of local fine art for sale. Several galleries specialize in reasonably priced work aimed at the visitor market.

# 15 Wilderness Canada

*by Peter Oliver*

Let it be stated as simply as possible: Life in Canada's far north is strange. Strange as in weird, strange as in wonderful, strange as in uncommon. The inherent strangeness of the world north of the 60th parallel—the latitudinal line separating Canada's provinces and the Yukon and the Northwest Territories—is perceptible in empirical, practical, and mysterious ways.

Consider examples from life in the heart of strangeness:

In what might pass for the far north's version of playing the state lottery, diamond speculators scratch around the permafrost in hopes of striking it rich, while daily life is spent in barrenland outposts protected with bear-resistant fencing. Expediters, following their own path of economic opportunism, facilitate the lives of diamond diggers, hunters, and adventurers by setting up camps for their activities. Residents of the far north drive hundreds of miles to a major city to stock up on groceries; in many cases, it is easier to hunt caribou or moose than it is to go shopping for vegetables.

Seasons become so overlapped in the few, non-winter months that summer wildflowers have not finished blooming by the time the foliage picks up its fall color. In winter, a network of highways, built entirely upon ice and hard-packed snow, opens up to automotive traffic large areas otherwise inaccessible in summer. So cold are the snow and ice that they lose their slipperiness, and thus make pretty good pavement. Bridges over rivers are also built of ice, and northerners must learn to prepare for "break-up" and "freeze-up"—the few weeks in spring and fall when ice bridges are unstable but when rivers are still too frozen for ferries to operate. Unprepared travelers will sometimes fork over $700 or more for a helicopter to sling their cars across a river. This underscores the fact that, in a region where bush pilots are held in high regard, air transport is the way to go. In a plane with pontoons, an uncountable number of lakes means an uncountable number of watery runways. As Pat McMahon, Mayor of Yellowknife, capital of the Northwest Territories puts it, "We get on planes here just like a New Yorker gets in a taxi."

If a single strange element of life in the far north stands out, it is the quality of light. In mid-summer, sunrise and sunset merge, and north of the Arctic Circle, they don't happen at all. And when night does come—so belatedly in summer that it is a way of life to draw shades tightly during sunlit evenings to simulate night— there is the mystical voodoo show of the Northern Lights.

The Yukon and the Northwest Territories make up 1,456,375 square miles, almost three times the size of Alaska and half the size of the rest of the United States. There are cities—Whitehorse and Dawson in the Yukon, and Yellowknife in the Northwest Territories being the largest—but there are many more "communities," small native settlements that more than likely are accessible only by plane.

Most of the region is geologically classified as semi-arid, much of it covered by the vast granite spread of the Canadian Shield. But because water evaporates and ice melts so slowly in Arctic climes, there is an abundance of water. That water is mostly in the form of lakes and ponds in the flatter Northwest Territories and in the form of rivers in the mountainous Yukon. A good deal of it, of course, remains ice; the glaciers of the St. Elias Mountains in the Yukon's Kluane National Park, topped by 19,850-foot Mt. Logan, create the largest non-polar ice mass in North America.

This is wilderness and the wildlife loves it. A migrating caribou herd exceeding 80,000 is not uncommon, and that's a number to keep in perspective: It represents the entire human census of the region. Indeed, people are profoundly outnumbered by non-human mammals: bears (black, grizzly, polar), Dall sheep, wolves, wolverines, moose, buffalo, and, of course, caribou. Humans are also outnumbered by fish—primarily trout, pike, grayling, whitefish, and Arctic char, and birds. Bald eagles are a common sight, as are flocks of migratory waterfowl that spend their summers here.

This is not a world intrinsically hospitable to humans, and it is certainly not easy living here given the cold and the challenge of building houses on rock and permafrost—if you can find the materials to build a house in the first place. The "treeline," marking the approximate latitudes north of which trees can't grow, bisects the region. Even south of the treeline, most of the growth is scrub.

Why would anyone want to visit such a severe environment? Most of the first people who came failed to come up with a satisfactory answer. Early expeditions seeking the Northwest Passage usually met with misery and disaster. And when a waterway finally was discovered, through the piecemeal efforts of 19th-century explorers, it was a disappointment—hardly the watery superhighway from east to west that had been envisioned. Trappers and fur traders in the 19th century managed to forge a livelihood. But it wasn't until the discovery of gold in the feeder streams of the Yukon's Klondike River in 1896 that people found a meaningful and profitable reason to settle in the north. The Klondike Gold Rush is legendary, of course, but it was relatively short-lived (even if gold continues to be mined profitably by a few companies in the Yukon). Most of the gold-rushers either packed up their money bags or abandoned exhausted claims after a few years.

Yet there are reasons to visit—good ones. Reason number one: The landscape is austere and beautiful in ways unlike anywhere else in North America. Consider the tundra plains that reach to the Arctic Ocean, the all but inaccessible ice fields of the St. Elias Mountains, white-water rivers snaking through mountain ranges and deep canyons, the glacially sculpted ranges of Baffin island. Reason number two: all of that wildlife. Fishermen regularly throw back trout weighing 10 pounds, because a fish that size is considered in these parts to be too puny.

And perhaps less obviously, reason number three: people. This is the last region of North America where native peoples have managed to sustain traditional cultures relatively undisturbed. The main tribal groups are the Dene, six nations of inland hunters, and the Inuit, who reside in the Arctic North. Many of these people still go about their lives as their ancestors did centuries before them, although helped today by such 20th-century basics as electricity and motor-driven machinery.

Government-building signs are often inscribed in as many as six languages–English, French, and various native languages. One of those languages, that of the Slavey tribe, is so difficult to learn that it was used in coding during World War II. Native people in the far north are wielding increasing influence in governmental affairs. In recent years, large tracts of land have been ceded to native groups in land-claims settlements. And in 1999, the Northwest Territories will be split in two, separating the principal lands of the Dene and the Inuit. (The new Inuit territory is to be called *Nunuvat,* or "our land.")

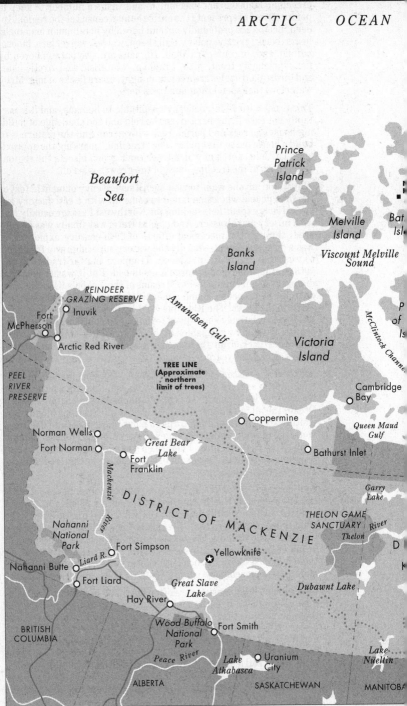

ARCTIC    OCEAN

*Beaufort
Sea*

Prince
Patrick
Island

Bat
Isl

Melville
Island

*Viscount Melville
Sound*

*Banks
Island*

*Amundsen Gulf*

REINDEER
GRAZING RESERVE

Fort
McPherson

Inuvik

*McClintock Channe*

P
of
Is

Arctic Red River

*Victoria
Island*

**TREE LINE
(Approximate
northern
limit of trees)**

PEEL
RIVER
PRESERVE

Cambridge
Bay

Coppermine

*Queen Maud
Gulf*

Norman Wells

*Great Bear
Lake*

Fort Norman

Fort
Franklin

Bathurst Inlet

*Mackenzie*

*Garry
Lake*

DISTRICT OF MACKENZIE

THELON GAME
SANCTUARY

*Thelon River*

*Nahanni
National
Park*

Fort Simpson

Yellowknife

D

Nahanni Butte

*Liard R.*

K

*River*

Fort Liard

*Great Slave
Lake*

*Dubawnt Lake*

Hay River

BRITISH
COLUMBIA

*Wood Buffalo
National
Park*

Fort Smith

*Peace River*

*Lake
Nuelin*

ALBERTA

*Lake
Athabasca*

Uranium
City

SASKATCHEWAN

MANITOB

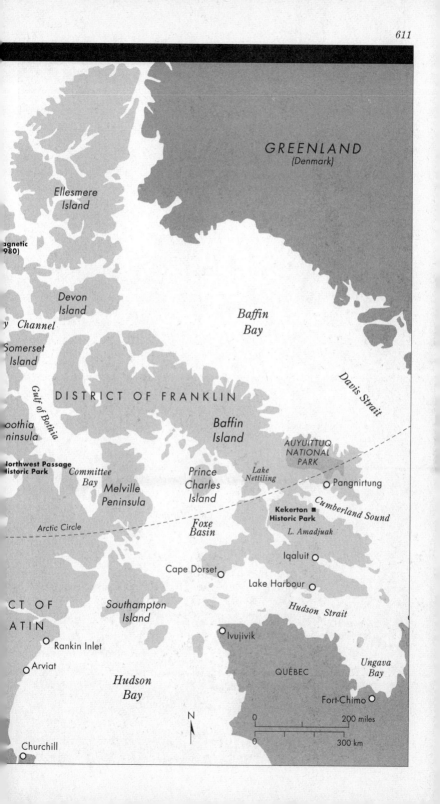

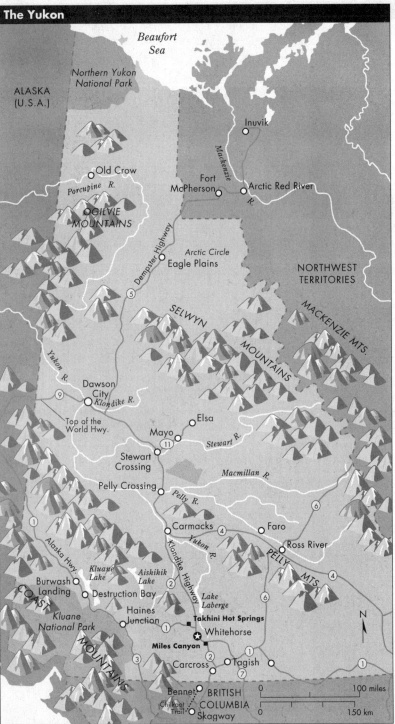

The Yukon

A visit to the far north does not happen without commitment and preparation. For starters, one must commit money. Lodging under $100 a night is the exception, unless you camp, and what you get for the price is unlikely to be fancy digs. Having to rely on planes to get from one place to the next does not come cheaply. Guides and outfitters can be expensive, too, but their fees aren't out of line with the general cost of living in the far north, and their travel packages often end up saving money.

Visitors must be willing to abide possible discomforts and inconveniences. Mosquitoes and black flies rule the north during summer and early fall, and anyone without a good insect repellent is in for big trouble. Packing gloves and insulated clothing in August might seem excessive, but such are the necessities of traveling in a world where it's not uncommon for summertime temperatures to drop from above 70°F to well below freezing in a single day. And life doesn't always proceed with clockwork precision; a frontier quality still pervades much of the far north, meaning that a lot of business is conducted on an ad-hoc, by-the-bootstraps basis.

But whatever must be put up with is well worth all that is gained: the vast expanses of true wilderness, the abundant wildlife, the undiluted native cultures. Visiting the far north can be daunting, difficult, frightening, and even dangerous, but for those who prepare themselves for the commitment, it can be nothing short of exhilarating.

# Essential Information

## Important Addresses and Numbers

**Tourist Information Northwest Territories** For general information and a copy of the Northwest Territories "Explorers' Guide," contact the **Department of Economic Development and Tourism** (Government of the Northwest Territories, Yellowknife, NT X1A 2L9, tel. 403/873-7200 or 800/661-0788). For more detailed information, regional tourist offices may be of further help.

The Northwest Territories is divided into six designated tourism regions, each with its own regional association. For the Arctic coastal region, contact the **Arctic Coast Tourism Association** (Dept. EG, Box 91, Cambridge Bay, NT X0E 0C0, tel. 403/983-2224). For Baffin and Ellesmere islands, contact the **Baffin Tourism Association** (Box 1450, Iqaluit, NT X0A 0H0, tel. 819/979-6551). For the southwest, contact the **Big River Tourism Association** (Dept. EG, Box 185, Hay River, NT X0E 0R0, tel. 403/874-2422). For the Keewatin region, which includes the western coast of Hudson Bay, contact **Travel Keewatin** (Dept. EG, Box 328, Rankin Inlet, NT X0C 0G0, tel. 819/645-2618). For the Nahanni River area and the west, contact **Nahanni-Ram Tourism Association** (Dept. EG, Box 145, Fort Simpson, NT X0E ONO, tel. 403/695-3182). For Yellowknife and the its environs, contact the **Northern Frontier Visitors Association** (Dept. EG, Box 1107, 4807 49th St., Yellowknife, NT X1A 2N8, tel. 403/873-3131). For the Great Bear Lake and McKenzie Mountain area, contact the **Sahtu Tourism Association** (Dept. EG, Box 115, Norman Wells, NT X0E 0V0, tel. 402/587-2054). For the far northwest, contact the **Western Arctic Tourism Association** (Dept. EG, Box 2600, Inuvik, NT X0E 0T0, tel. 403/979-4321).

*Yukon* **Tourism Yukon** (Box 2703, Whitehorse, YT Y1A 2C6, tel. 403/667-5340) is the central source of information for the entire area, and operates six regional information centers at **Beaver Creek** (at Kilometer 1,934, Mile 1,202 on the Alaska Highway, tel. 403/862–7321), **Carcross** (The Old Train Depot, tel. 403/821–4431), **Dawson City** (Front and King Sts., tel. 403/993–5566), **Haines Junction** (Kluane National Park Headquarters, tel. 403/634–2345), **Watson Lake** (Junction of Highways 1 and 4, tel. 403/536–7469), and **Whitehorse** (Kilometer 1,475, Mile 917 on the Alaska Highway, tel. 403/667–7545).

**Emergencies**  For emergency services in either the Northwest Territories or the Yukon, dial 0 for the operator and explain the nature of the emergency. You will then be connected with the police, fire department, or medical service, as needed. You may also call a toll-free, general emergency number, 1–667–5555, from anywhere in the Yukon.

It's a good idea when traveling in the far north—especially in remote wilderness areas and if unescorted by a guide or outfitter—to give a detailed itinerary to someone at home or to the police, to facilitate emergency rescue.

*Hospitals and*  Limited medical services, with staff on call 24 hours a day, are avail-
*Clinics*  able at nursing stations in all communities. In the Northwest Territories, the best-equipped hospital is in **Yellowknife** (Stanton Yellowknife Hospital, tel. 403/920–4111). Other hospitals are located in **Fort Smith** (Fort Smith Health Care Centre, tel. 403/872–2713), **Hay River** (H.H. Williams Memorial Hospital, tel. 403/874–6512), **Inuvik** (Inuvik General Hospital, tel. 403/979–2955), and **Iqaluit** (Baffin Regional Hospital, tel. 819/979–5231). In the Yukon, hospitals are located in **Dawson City** (Dawson Medical Clinic, tel. 403/993–5744), **Watson Lake** (Watson Lake Cottage Hospital, tel. 403/536–2541), and **Whitehorse** (Whitehorse General Hospital, tel. 403/667–8700).

*Pharmacies*  Pharmacies are located in major settlements of the Yukon and Northwest Territories, but late-night service is rarely available; after hours, contact the nearest hospital or nursing station (*see* Hospitals and Clinics, *above*). If you have a pre-existing medical condition requiring special medication, be sure you are well-supplied; getting unusual prescriptions filled can be difficult or impossible, depending on where you are.

## Arriving and Departing by Plane

**Airports and**  **Whitehorse International Airport** is the major airport for the Yukon
**Airlines**  and is located 5 kilometers (3 miles) from downtown Whitehorse. **Yellowknife Airport,** the main facility for the Northwest Territories, is 5 kilometers (3 miles) northeast of the city center. Many smaller settlements—notably Cambridge Bay, Inuvik, and Iqaluit—have regular as well as charter passenger service.

The major air carriers with connecting service from the United States to points in the Northwest Territories and the Yukon are **Air Canada** and **Canadian Airlines.** Generally speaking, Air Canada offers better connections in the east, but does not have service to the Yukon; Canadian Airlines has better connections in the west. Air Canada's service in the Northwest Territories is provided in conjunction with its affiliate, **NWT Air** (tel. 403/920–2500 or 800/661–0789). Air Canada's toll-free number for most of the United States is 800/776–3000; in Michigan and most of New York (except New York City), 800/387–2710; in Idaho and Washington, 800/663–9100.

The number for Canadian Airlines (and its affiliate, **Canadian North,** which is responsible for most of the connecting service throughout the far north) in the United States is 800/426–7000. Canadian Airlines also has a scheduling agreement with **American Airlines** (tel. 800/433–7300) for connections from the United States. For the eastern Northwest Territories, **First Air** (tel. 613/839–3340 or 800/267–1247) offers extensive service from Montréal and Ottawa.

## Arriving and Departing by Car, Train, and Bus

By Car
It hardly bears saying that getting to the Yukon or the Northwest Territories by car calls for a good deal of driving. The best route into the region is the Alaska Highway (Rte. 97 in British Columbia), accessible from Edmonton via Routes 43, 34, and 2 and from Vancouver via Route 1. After Fort Nelson, BC, Routes 7, 1, and 3 lead to Yellowknife; the Alaska Highway (Rte. 1 in the Yukon) continues on to Whitehorse. The good news is that with so few roads in the region, it's difficult to make a wrong turn. The bad news is the amount of driving required to get from one point to another. For example, the distance from Vancouver to Whitehorse is more than 2,400 kilometers (1,500 miles). Be aware that as you drive further north, gas stations are few and gas is expensive—in some cases exceeding 70 cents a liter, or roughly US$2.40 a gallon. With relatively little lodging along the way, you might want to embark on the trip in a camper or recreational vehicle. **Ambassador Motorhome & Recreational Services Ltd.** (Mile 912, Alaska Hwy., Box 4147, Whitehorse, YT Y1A 3S9, tel. 403/667–4130) offers one-way rentals between British Columbia and the Yukon.

By Train
There is no regular rail service into the Yukon or the Northwest Territories. The **White Pass & Yukon Route** (Box 435, Skagway, AK 99840, tel. 907/983–2217 or 800/343–7373) runs trains between Skagway, Alaska, and Whitehorse during the summer, primarily for the astonishing mountain scenery.

By Bus
**Greyhound Lines of Canada** (10234 103rd St., Edmonton, AB T5J 0Y9, tel. 403/421–4211) provides service from Edmonton to Hay River, Northwest Territories. Greyhound also has service from Edmonton or Vancouver to Whitehorse in the Yukon.

## Getting Around

By Car
In general, exploring by car is a more sensible idea in the Yukon than in the Northwest Territories. The only part of the Northwest Territories with any kind of highway network is the southwest, where the scenic elements—most likely waterfalls and buffalo—are glimpsed between long stretches of gravel and hardpacked dirt highways that run through the forested bush. Many highways in the Yukon, however, are paved, the scenery along the way considerable, and roadside services more extensive.

Anyone traveling by car in the far north should take precautions. Distances from one service area to the next typically exceed 160 kilometers (100 miles), so make sure to monitor your fuel gauge. At least one, good spare tire is essential, and many residents of the region carry more, especially when traveling long distances on unpaved roads. Another common practice is to cover headlights, grills, and even windshields with plastic shields or wire mesh to protect against flying gravel. It is advisable to carry extra parts (air filter, fan belt, fluids). Be sure your vehicle has good suspension, even if you plan to stick to the major highways; shifting permafrost regularly damages paved roads, and ruts and washboarding occasionally appear on unpaved roads, especially after periods of bad weather.

Winter driving requires extra precautionary measures. Many a far-north resident can tell you a tale about overnighting on the road and waiting out fierce weather. Take along emergency survival gear, including ax, shovel, plenty of matches, kindling (paper or wood) to start a fire, sleeping bag, rugged outerwear, and food. Also, you should have a properly winterized car, with light engine oil and transmission fluid, a block heater, tire chains, and good anti-freeze.

One other thing to think about: In the Northwest Territories there are several river crossings without real bridges. In summer, you ride a free ferry; in winter you cross via snow bridges. However, there are the seasons known as "freeze-up" and "break-up," in fall and spring, respectively, when snow bridges aren't solid but rivers are too frozen for ferries to run. For daily ferry reports in summer, call: for Highways 1 and 3, tel. 403/879–7799 or 800/661–0751; for the Dempster Highway, tel. 403/873–0158 or 800/661–0752. For winter road conditions, call: for Highways 1 through 7, tel. 403/873–0157 or 800/662–0750; for the Dempster Highway, tel. 403/873–0158 or 800/661–0752.

Rental agencies in both Whitehorse and Yellowknife typically rent trucks and four-wheel-drive vehicles in addition to cars. **Budget** (tel. 800/627–0700) and **Tilden** (tel. 800/387–4747) have locations at both the Whitehorse and Yellowknife airports. **Avis** (tel. 800/331–1212) rents at the Yellowknife airport; **Hertz** (tel. 800/654–3131), **Norcan** (tel. 403/668–2137), and **Thrifty** (tel. 800/367–2277) rent at the Whitehorse aiport.

Touring by camper or motorhome is a popular way to travel in the far north, especially the Yukon. **Ambassador Motor Home & Recreational Services Ltd.** (*see* Arriving and Departing by Car, *above*) is based in Whitehorse. Camper rentals are available in Yellowknife from **Frontier Rentals** (2048 Finlayson Dr., Yellowknife, NT X1A 3C7, tel. 403/873–5417).

**By Bus** **Frontier Coachlines** (328 Old Airport Rd., Yellowknife, NT X1A 3T3, tel. 403/873–4892) offers service connecting Fort Smith, Hay River, and Yellowknife. In the Yukon, **Alaskon Express** (208-G Steele St., Whitehorse, YT Y1A 2C4, tel. 403/668–3225 in summer, 800/544–2206 in winter) has service between Whitehorse and cities in Alaska from mid-May to mid-September. **Gold City Tours** (Box 960, Dawson City, YT Y0B 1G0, tel. 403/993–5175) schedules summer service for the Dempster Highway. **Norline Coaches** (Box 5237, Whitehorse, YT Y1A 4Z1, tel. 403/633–3864) provides service between Dawson City and Whitehorse.

**By Plane** Once outside the Yukon and the southwest section of the Northwestern Territories, flying is pretty much the only way to get around in wilderness Canada. **Canadian North, First Air,** and **NWT Air** (*see* Arriving and Departing by Plane, *above*) have regularly scheduled service within the territories. **Alkan Air** (tel. 403/668–2107 or 800/661-0432) and **Air North** (tel. 403/668–2228) operate primarily in the Yukon. **Air Baffin** (tel. 819/979–4318), **Buffalo Air** (tel. 403/874–3333), **North-Wright Air** (tel. 403/587–2288), and **Ptarmigan Airways** (tel. 403/873–4461) operate primarily in the Northwest Territories. All of the above also offer charter air service, an option worth considering for groups of four or more and usually the only option for getting to and from remote wilderness areas. Check with regional tourist offices for other charter services operating locally and regionally.

**Guided Tours** A number of tour operators offer general-interest tours, specialty tours, and tours combining sightseeing with such special interests as hiking or wildlife viewing. For a complete list of tour operators, contact **Yukon Tourism** or, in the Northwest Territories, the **Department of Economic Development and Tourism** (*see* Important Addresses and Numbers, *above*). For additional special-interest tours, *also see* Sports and Outdoor Activities, *below*.

**Orientation**
**Arctic Tour Co.** (181 McKenzie Rd., Box 2021, Inuvik, NT X0E 0T0, tel. 403/979–4100) offers various tours in the area of the McKenzie River Delta, between Dawson and Inuvik, and between Yellowknife and Inuvik. **Holland America Westours** (300 Elliott Ave. W, Seattle, WA 98119, tel. 206/281–3535) features bus tours through the Yukon and Alaska as well as combined cruiseship/bus tours that link in Skagway, Alaska. **Rainbow Tours** (3089 3rd Ave., Whitehorse, YT Y1A 5B3, tel. 403/668–5598 or 800/661–0468) runs tours by van throughout the Yukon. **Raven Tours** (Box 2435, Yellowknife, NT X1A 2P8, tel. 403/873–4856) offers a variety of tours in the Northwest Territories, including tours of Yellowknife and Northern Lights tours in winter. **NWT Air** (*see* Arriving and Departing by Plane, *above*), working with local operators and outfitters, also features an extensive tour program throughout the Northwest Territories.

**Special-Interest Tours**
Literally hundreds of tour operators and outfitters conduct special-interest tours in the far north. Various outdoor activities are the primary themes, although many tours include a focus on native cultures. The following are some of the largest and most reputable organizers in the region, in many cases working in conjunction with locally based outfitters. The **Department of Economic Development and Tourism** in the Northwest Territories and **Tourism Yukon** (*see* Important Important Addresses and Numbers, *above*) can provide a more complete list of outfitters. *See also* Sports and Outdoor Activities, *below*.

**Adventure Canada** (Suite 105, 227 Sterling Rd., Toronto, Ont. M6R 2B2, tel. 416/535–1197) is particularly active in arranging trips to the Arctic North, including excursions to the North Pole. Backpacking, dog-sledding, canoeing, and wildlife viewing are among the activities featured. **Arctic Edge/TransArctic Tours** (Box 4850, Whitehorse, YT Y1A 4N6, tel. 403/633–5570 or 800/661–0469 in U.S.) cover a broad spectrum of interests; Arctic Edge specializes in active adventures from cross-country skiing to canoeing, while TransArctic Tours focuses more on wildlife viewing and cultural tours. Most of the twin company's trips are in the Yukon. **Black Feather Wilderness Adventures** (1341 Wellington St. W, Ottawa, Ont. K1Y 3B8, tel. 613/722–9717) is one of the largest adventure-travel companies in Canada, leading backpacking trips in Auyuittuq National Park on Baffin Island, canoeing and hiking trips in Nahanni National Park, and canoe trips on rivers in the McKenzie Mountains. **Kluane Adventures** (Box 5396, Haines Junction, YT Y0B 1L0, tel. 403/667–1099 or 403/634–2282 in winter) specializes in backpacking, canoeing, and fly-in fishing trips in the Kluane area. The company is affiliated with **Dalton Trail Lodge** (Box 5466, Haines Junction, YT Y0B 1L0, tel. 403/667–1099 or 403/634–2282 in winter), a drive-in lodge 50 kilometers (30 miles) south of Haines Junction, which oversees fishing, horseback riding, and hunting programs. **Sub-Arctic Wilderness Adventures** (Box 685, Fort Smith, NT X0E 0P0, tel. 403/872–2467) specializes primarily in wildlife-viewing tours in the Northwest Territories, but also offers canoeing, hiking, and dog-sledding.

One tour of note is the 1,600-kilometer (1,000-mile) cruise along the Mackenzie River, from Yellowknife to Inuvik (or vice versa) aboard the **M.S.** *Norweta,* a 100-foot, 8-cabin cruise ship. The 10-day cruise includes many stops en route, as well as return air transportation to the city of departure. Contact **N.W.T. Marine Group** (5414 52nd St., Yellowknife, NT X1A 3K1, tel. 403/444–4876).

# Exploring Wilderness Canada

The idea of exploring all of Canada's far north in a single trip is an absurdity. It would be comparable to trying to visit Florida, New England, and the Rocky Mountains on the same vacation, only with far fewer roads to travel. Size is only one problem; expense is another. Food, gas, and lodging are typically priced higher than in other parts of Canada, but the big cost is transportation, especially in those vast, roadless areas where you'll need to depend on air travel. This is not to say it is difficult to get from one place to another; in fact, the number of charter plane operators and the number of expert bush pilots able to land a float plane on a little more than a mud puddle make getting around easier than you might think. But the costs of traveling by small planes can add up with dizzying speed.

Thus, the best strategy for exploring the far north is to be selective. Focus on a specific area (e.g., Baffin Island, the Nahanni region, Dawson City) and/or an activity (e.g., fishing, wildlife viewing) and plan accordingly. Specific travel plans can literally save hundreds, even thousands, of dollars.

The choices fall roughly into four categories: visiting the main cities (Dawson City, Whitehorse, Yellowknife); excursions from the main cities; adventures in the backcountry wilderness; and adventures in the Arctic north. The cities of Whitehorse and Yellowknife are probably the least interesting elements. There are points of cultural and historical interest in each—enough to hold your attention for a couple of days—and almost everyone who visits the region ends up spending some time in either Yellowknife or Whitehorse. However, it makes little sense to come this far and not venture beyond the city limits.

June through August is the high season for visiting the far north. For the other eight months of the year, many businesses and outfitters close up shop, as much for lack of business as the length of winter. However, many northerners say that April, when daylight lengthens, winter begins its recession, and such snow sports as skiing and dogsledding are still possible is a good month to visit. September is another choice month, when the fall colors are brilliant and birds (e.g., ducks and geese) and animals (e.g., caribou) begin their migrations. And as harsh—and dark—as other months are, they can be prime time for visitors fascinated by the spectral displays of the Northern Lights.

## Highlights for First-Time Visitors

**Auyuittuq National Park on Baffin Island,** Tour 7: The Arctic North
**Great Slave Lake Excursions,** Tour 6: Excursions from Yellowknife
**S.S.** *Klondike* **National Historic Site,** Tour 1: Whitehorse
**Virginia Falls in Nahanni National Park,** Tour 6: Excursions from Yellowknife
**Yukon River Canoeing,** Tour 1: Whitehorse

## Tour 1: Whitehorse

Whitehorse began as an encampment near the Whitehorse Rapids of the Yukon River. It was a logical layover point for gold rushers in the late 1890's—most coming north along the Chilkoot Trail from Alaska—headed north toward Dawson to seek their fortune. Today's city of more than 20,000 residents is the Yukon's center of commerce, communication, and transportation, and is the seat of the territorial government. It is not, however, a city of any great architectural or cultural distinction. Visitors should regard Whitehorse as a base camp, from which to venture out to explore other parts of the Yukon.

There are, however, a few points of interest in Whitehorse that can fill a well-spent day or two of exploring. The logical place to start is the **City Information Centre,** centrally located at Steele Street and Third Avenue. This is the best place to pick up information on local lodging, restaurants, shops, attractions, and special events. *Suite 101, 302 Steele St., tel. 403/667–7545. Open mid-May–mid-Sept., daily 8–8.*

From the information center, head east along Steele Street to First Avenue, and turn left to the **MacBride Museum.** The exhibits provide an historical overview of the Yukon, from early exploration to the present, covering the trapping era, the gold rush, and the construction of the Alaska Highway. *1st Ave. and Wood St., tel. 403/667–2709. Admission: $3.25 adults, $2.25 students and senior citizens, $1 children 6–12, children under 6 free, $7.50 families. Open Labor Day–May 15, Tues., Wed., and Thurs. noon–4; May 15–31, daily noon–4; June–Labor Day, daily 10–6.*

From the MacBride Museum, head south to the **Waterfront Walkway,** along the Yukon River. On your right, before you reach Rotary Park, is the **Yukon Territorial Government Building.** This is worth a quick visit to see the **Yukon Permanent Art Collection,** a display of works by Canadian artists depicting northern landscapes and lifestyles. *2nd Ave., tel. 403/667–5239. Admission free. Open weekdays 8:30–5.*

Continue through Rotary Park to the **S.S.** *Klondike,* a National Historic Site. The 71.6-meter (235-foot) sternwheeler was built in 1929, sank in 1936, and was rebuilt in 1937. In the days when the Yukon River was the transportation link between Whitehorse and Dawson, the *Klondike* was the largest boat plying the river. Today it is drydocked and has been restored to its 1930s glory. *Tel. 403/667–4511. Admission free. Daily tours mid-May–Sept.*

There are a few other points of interest just beyond the city limits. From the S.S. *Klondike* site, drive south over the Lewes Boulevard bridge and turn right on Nisultin Drive to the **Whitehorse Rapids Dam and Fish Ladder.** The best time to visit is late summer, when salmon use the ladder to bypass the dam in their annual migration. *Admission free. Open mid-July–mid-Sept., daily 8 AM–10 PM.*

Return to the S.S. *Klondike* site and drive south along the other side of the river to **Miles Canyon.** Although the dam below it now makes the canyon seem relatively tame, it was this unnavigable stretch of water that determined the location of Whitehorse as the starting point for river travel north. There is a hiking trail along the canyon, and two-hour cruises aboard the **M.V.** *Schwatka* also pass through the canyon. *Tel. 403/668–2042. Admission: $15. Open daily, June–Sept.*

Before venturing from Whitehorse, there are two final stops along the Alaska Highway, near the airport. The **Yukon Transportation Museum,** at Mile 917 of the Alaska Highway, features artifacts and exhibits of the Yukon's unusual transportation legacy, from snowshoes to cars, dogsleds to airplanes. *Mile 917, Alaska Highway, tel. 403/668–4792. Admission free. Open June, Wed.–Sun. 10–6; July and Aug., daily 10–6.*

Next door to the Transportation Museum is the **Yukon Visitor Information Centre,** an excellent source of practical information for travel throughout the territory. A 20-minute film presentation on the geology and history of the region is first-rate. *Mile 917, Alaska Hwy., tel. 407/667–2915. Open early May–Sept., daily 8–8.*

## Tour 2: Excursions from Whitehorse

The options for travelers leaving Whitehorse are: north to Dawson (see Tour 3), south to Skagway, Alaska, east to Watson Lake, and west to the Kluane region. No matter which direction you head, expect to encounter considerable bus and RV traffic during the summer; the Yukon ranks with Alaska as one of the great road-touring regions of North America.

Perhaps the least inspiring of the four options is the 450-kilometer (280-mile) trip east to **Watson Lake.** Its principal raison d'être is as gateway city to the Yukon for travelers heading northwest along the Alaska Highway. One notable point of interest, however, is **Signpost Forest;** during the construction of the Alaska Highway in 1942, a homesick U.S. soldier put up a sign indicating the name of his hometown as well as the mileage and direction. Since then, other visitors have followed suit, to the tune of more than 17,000 signs.

About 160 kilometers (100 miles) west of Whitehorse is **Haines Junction,** the main gateway to **Kluane National Park.** Kluane (pronounced kloo-AH-nee) is one of the most extraordinary national parks in the world, home to the largest non-polar ice mass in North America as well as Canada's highest mountain, Mt. Logan (5,950 meters or 19,850 feet). Glaciers up to 65 kilometers (40 miles) long, several kilometers wide, and 2 kilometers (1.6 miles) deep stretch from the huge icefields of the interior. Kluane combines with neighboring Wrangell–St. Elias National Park in Alaska to form the largest expanse of contiguous national-park land in the world.

Few visitors, other than experienced mountaineers get a full sense of Kluane's most extraordinary terrain; no roads or trails lead into the interior. **Kluane Helicopters** (Box 2128, Haines Junction, YT Y0B 1L0, tel. 403/634–2224) flies visitors in, but the privilege of a peek at the glacial spectacle is not cheap: A sightseeing fly-over costs $70 per person and a day of heli-hiking runs $350 per person. Most visitors must content themselves with exploring the front ranges, which have impressive mountains with abundant wildlife— Dall sheep, black bears, and grizzly bears are the most noteworthy species. There is also a network of hiking trails—rare in the far north—facilitating everything from half-day hikes to multi-day backpacking excursions.

Kluane visitors should start at **Kluane National Park Headquarters** (Haines Junction, YT Y0B 1L0, tel. 403/634–2251). A free, 20-minute slide presentation provides an excellent introduction to the region's geology, flora, and fauna. The Kluane mountains comprise the most earthquake-prone zone in Canada, with an average of 1,000 tremors, most barely perceptible, recorded each year.

Those who wish to hike in the park can either head south on Haines Road from the park headquarters to **Kathleen Lake,** or north on the Alaska Highway to the visitors' center at **Sheep Mountain.** (Mile 1019, Alaska Hwy., tel. 403/634–2251). Most marked hiking trails follow lake shorelines or glacially carved river basins and are relatively easy to negotiate. Day hikers should check at the Haines Junction visitors' center (*see* Important Addresses and Numbers in Essential Information, *above*) for a summer schedule of guided hikes. More ambitious hikers can backpack from the Sheep Mountain visitors' center up the Slims River valley to the toe of the Kaskawulsh Glacier, a 27-kilometer (16-mile) jaunt. Short of backcountry scrambling, this is as close as hikers can get to Kluane's glacier country. Be sure to pick up a tent-camping permit and free, food-storage canisters at the visitors' center; keep in mind that this is bear country, and all bear precautions—especially storing food in canisters—must be taken. Horsepacking trips are also possible in the Slims River valley; check at park headquarters for information on outfitters.

The last excursion from Whitehorse takes you through an interesting succession of geological zones along Route 2, which runs south out of the Yukon into British Columbia and on to Alaska. For example, 74 kilometers (46 miles) from Whitehorse near the town of **Carcross** is the "Carcross Desert," a small expanse of, indeed, desert, attesting to the aridity of the climate. But by the time the road leads over White Pass and begins descending steeply into Skagway, the landscape changes markedly to a heavily vegetated world of glacially carved fjords.

There are two alternatives to driving through this area. One is the **White Pass & Yukon Route** (Box 435, Skagway, AK 99840, tel. 907/983–2217 or 800/343–7373 in U.S. or Canada), a combined bus-and-rail trip between Whitehorse and Skagway. *Daily departures, mid-May–mid-Sept. Round-trip fare: US$92 adults, $46 children.*

The other alternative is backpacking on the 54-kilometer (33-mile) **Chilkoot Trail** between Skagway and Bennet, BC (one-way hikers' shuttles are available on the White Pass & Yukon train). Although the trail never actually reaches the Yukon, it is vitally linked with Yukon history: During the Klondike Gold Rush, prospectors trekked over Chilkoot Pass to Whitehorse, where they hopped a Yukon river steamer to Dawson.

## Tour 3: Dawson City

Dawson City was the epicenter of gold fever at the turn of the century. Preservationists have done an admirable job of not only restoring many of the city's historic buildings but also enforcing a zoning code that requires newly built structures to adopt facades conforming to a turn-of-the-century look. If it weren't for the presence of cars and camera-toting tourists strolling along Dawson's streets in summer, you might just feel like you entered the Gold Rush era.

Perhaps any tour of Dawson ought to begin where Dawson really got its start: at the gold-mining sites just east of town. Huge mounds of rock and slag along the roadside attest to the considerable amount of earth turned over in search of precious metal. The most famous of many mining sites is **Bonanza Creek,** 2 kilometers (1.6 miles) east of Dawson, which produced several million-dollar claims in the days when gold went for $16 an ounce. In fact, the creek is so rich in minerals that it is still being mined today. Those who want to try their luck at gold-panning can rent the necessary gear for $5 at

**Claim 33** (Mile 7, Bonanza Creek Rd., tel. 403/993–5303). You're guaranteed some gold, but don't expect to strike it rich.

Well worth a visit is **Dredge No. 4,** 16 kilometers (10 miles) up Bonanza Creek Road. During the summer, daily tours are conducted through the dredge, which was used to dig up the creek bed during the height of Bonanza Creek's largesse. *Contact Klondike National Historic Sites, Box 390, Dawson City, YT Y0B 1G0, tel. 403/993–5462. Admission free. Open June–Aug., daily.*

The **Visitor Reception Centre** at Front and King streets (Box 389, Dawson City, YT Y0B 1G0, tel. 403/993–5566) is an excellent source of information on everything from historical minutiae to lodging availability.

From the visitor center, head east on King Street to the **Palace Grand Theatre,** which was show-time central during the Gold Rush days, staging everything from opera to vaudeville. It was restored in the 1970s by the Canadian Parks Service, and today is the home of the **Gaslight Follies,** a musical show based on Gold Rush history. *King St. betw. 2nd and 3rd Aves., tel. 403/993–6217. Admission: $13 adults, $5.50 children under 12. Shows nightly (except Tues.) at 8, June–mid-Sept.; box office open daily noon–3:30 and 4:30–8.*

Continue east on King Street to 3rd Avenue and make a quick stop at the **Old Post Office.** The construction of a post office in 1900 was a symbolic affirmation of Dawson's permanence as a legitimate city rather than a boomtown of opportunism. The post office today effectively captures an aura of Dawson life at the turn of the century, and philatelists may want to purchase commemorative stamps. *3rd Ave. and King St. Admission free. Open June–Sept., daily noon–6.*

At 5th Avenue, turn right and go several blocks to the **Dawson City Museum,** which chronicles the Gold Rush and includes exhibits on native history and paleontology of the region. *5th Ave. betw. Mission and Turner Sts., Box 303, Dawson City, YT Y0B 1G0, tel. 403/993–5291. Admission: $3.50 adults, $2.50 senior citizens and students, children under 6 free. Open June–early Sept., daily 10–6; May and Sept., Tues., Thurs., and Sat. 1–4.*

From the museum, head east to 8th Avenue, where, within a block of one another, are the former **homes of Jack London** and **Robert Service,** the two writers most closely associated with the Yukon Territory and history. London is best known for such Yukon-inspired novels as *Call of the Wild* and *White Fang,* and Service, primarily a poet, has been dubbed "bard of the Klondike." Regular readings of the writers' works are held at each home. *Jack London Interpretive Center, 8th Ave. and 1st St., tel. 403/993–5575. Admission free. Open mid-May–mid-Sept, daily 10–6. Robert W. Service Cabin, 8th Ave. and Hanson St., tel. 403/993–5462. Admission free. Open June–mid-Sept., daily 9–5.*

Returning to Front Street, pay a visit to the **S.S. *Keno,*** one of the last sternwheelers to travel the Yukon and Stewart rivers. If you want a first-hand feel for river travel, board the ***Yukon Queen,*** docked along Front Street, which makes the 173-kilometer (108-mile) trip westward to Eagle, Alaska in approximately seven hours. One-way travelers may opt to return to Dawson by bus. *S. S. Keno: Front St. between King and Queen Sts., tel. 403/993–5599. Yukon Queen: 208G Steele St., Whitehorse, tel. 403/668-3225 or 800/628–2298. Fares: $80 adult one-way, $124 adult round-trip; $40 children one-way, $62.50 children round-trip. Open June–Sept., daily.*

## Tour 4: Excursions from Dawson

Two excursions are possible from Dawson: traveling the Top of the World Highway or the Dempster Highway. The 108-kilometer (67-mile) trip west along the **Top of the World Highway** to the Yukon/Alaska border provides expansive vistas. The road partially lives up to its name, set as it is along ridgelines and high-mountain shoulders, but the dirt-and-gravel surface (which creates plenty of dust thanks to RV traffic) can hardly be called a highway. The northernmost border crossing on land between Canada and the United States is along this route; the U.S. side is in Polar Creek, Alaska, population: two.

The 766-kilometer (476-mile) journey north to Inuvik (*see* Tour 7) on the **Dempster Highway** is a much more adventurous and ambitious undertaking. It is the only public highway in North America to cross the Arctic Circle, and passes through a landscape that is severe, tundra, mountainous, and ever-changing. In its southern extreme, the highway passes first through the rugged Tombstone Mountains and then into the more rounded ranges of the Ogilvie Mountains. The route crosses Eagle Plains (approximately halfway between Dawson and Inuvik and a good stopping point for gas and supplies) before reaching the **Arctic Circle,** where a sign marks the point of crossing, providing an obvious photo opportunity. From here, the highway passes through the Richardson Mountains and enters the flatlands surrounding the MacKenzie River delta before reaching Inuvik. This is certainly one of *the* great wilderness drives in North America, but because there are no services for 370 kilometers (230 miles) between the junction of the Dempster and Klondike highways and Eagle Plains, travelers should be prepared to cope with possible emergencies. If you prefer someone else to do the driving, contact **Gold City Tours** (Box 960, Dawson, YT tel. 403/993-5175), which has summer bus service between Dawson and Inuvik.

## Tour 5: Yellowknife

Yellowknife is not necessarily a city of great architectural, cultural, or historical distinction, but it is does provide a few elements of interest. Originally established in 1934 after the discovery of gold, Yellowknife has since grown into the hub of government, transportation, and communication in the Northwest Territories.

Start your tour with a walk through **Old Town,** where small houses and industrial buildings crowd around rocky knolls. Atop one of these knolls is the **Bush Pilots' Memorial,** which honors both the daring pilots who helped open the north and today's pilots who are vital to the north's economy. Note the many structures perched on hard granite; those who have built on less solid foundations have often seen their homes contorted or wrecked by the shifting permafrost. Keen observers might also notice around the **Float Plane Base** piles of plastic bags, which are mining samples flown in from outlying prospectors' camps; the discovery of diamonds northwest of Yellowknife in recent years has spurred a modest boom in speculation.

**Time Out** Drop in at the **Bush Pilot's Pub** (tel. 403/920-2739) on Wiley Road. The pub's bar is made from the wing of a plane, and the beer served is brewed on site by the Arctic Brewing Company.

The **Prince of Wales Northern Heritage Centre,** on the shore of Frame Lake, is just a few minutes from downtown. It houses extensive displays of northern artifacts as well as exhibits on exploration and settlement. The aviation section, documenting the north's history of flight, is especially worthwhile, as are exhibits devoted to the search for the Northwest Passage. *On Frame Lake opposite City Hall, Box 1320, Yellowknife, NT X1A 2L9, tel. 403/873–7551. Admission free. Open June–Aug., daily 10:30–5; Sept.–May, Tues.–Fri. 10:30–5, weekends noon–5.*

Yellowknife's most noteworthy geographical feature is the **Great Slave Lake.** Day trips and extended excursions on the lake are offered by a number of companies in Yellowknife. **Sail North** (*see* Sports and Outdoor Activities, *below*), offers boat rentals as well as leisurely half-day and dinner trips aboard the S.S. *Nochoa,* essentially a motorized, open-air deck on pontoons. The **M.S.** *Norweta* (*see* Special-Interest Tours in Essential Information, *above*) offers short outings as well as multiday cruises.

## Tour 6: Excursions from Yellowknife

Yellowknife is a transportation hub for outlying areas in the eastern Artic. Those with sporting inclinations will typically set out from Yellowknife for backcountry lodges on the shores of the Great Slave Lake or on one of the thousands of smaller lakes that, along with their barren rock underpinnings and scrub growth, are the principal geological constituents of the far north's interior. **Great Bear Lake,** northwest of Yellowknife, and the **MacKenzie Mountains** of the MacKenzie River, are also popular destinations for fishermen, hunters, and canoeists. *See* Sports and Outdoor Activities, *below,* or contact the **Sahtu Tourism Association** (*see* Essential Information, *above*).

For visitors wishing to make driving excursions from Yellowknife, the principal routes include passing through Wood Buffalo National Park and Fort Smith to the south, and through Fort Liard to the west. This is not, generally speaking, rousingly scenic driving. Long stretches of road cutting through the low-lying, sub-arctic bush are highlighted by occasional waterfalls or the sight of wildlife near or on the highway. Of the scenic waterfalls along the road between Yellowknife and Fort Smith, the most dramatic is **Alexandra Falls,** a few kilometers south on Route 1 at the junction of Routes 1 and 2, where the Hay River majestically drops 33 meters (108 feet) over limestone cliffs.

Perhaps the most likely area to spot wildlife is **Wood Buffalo National Park,** straddling the British Columbia/Northwest Territories border. Covering 44,807 square kilometers (17,300 square miles), this is the largest national park in Canada. Much of the terrain—a flat land of bogs, swamps, salt plains, sink holes, and meandering streams and rivers—is essentially inaccessible to visitors. This is not a world that people would think of spending much time in, but wildlife and bugs (i.e., swarms of mosquitoes and black flies) think otherwise. It is home, not surprisingly, to the world's largest free-roaming bison herd (about 5,000 total), and it is also a summer nesting ground for many bird species, including bald eagles, peregrine falcons, and the exceedingly rare whooping crane. The park's reception center in Fort Smith can provide additional information, and park rangers lead interpretive programs and hikes during July and August. *Superintendent, Wood Buffalo National Park, Box 750, Fort Smith, NT X0E 0P0, tel. 403/872–2349.*

Those interested in wildlife may want to head south from Yellowknife on Route 3 to the **MacKenzie Bison Sanctuary,** where bison are often spotted along the road. In recent years, the deadly virus, anthrax, has significantly depleted the numbers of the Mac-Kenzie herd.

The principal reason to head westward from Yellowknife is to visit **Nahanni National Park.** The MacKenzie and Liard rivers, which join forces at Fort Simpson, are the region's approximate geographical dividers, separating the low-lying bush of the east and the mountains to the west. This separation is perhaps most dramatically appreciated at **Blackstone Territorial Park,** with its views across the Liard River to the front ranges of the Nahanni Mountains. Blackstone is about as close as road-bound travelers can come to Nahanni National Park. Access to the park itself is possible only by helicopter or plane; once in the park, canoes and rafts are the principal means of travel. Perhaps the most impressive feature in the park is **Virginia Falls,** more than 125 meters (410 feet) high and about 200 meters (656 feet) wide—a thunderous wall of whitewater cascading around a central spire of rock. **Simpson Air** (Box 260, Fort Simpson, NT X0E 0N0, tel. 403/695–2505) is one of several plane and helicopter services that offers sight-seeing trips to Virginia Falls. A well-maintained park campground near the falls facilitates overnight excursions. For a complete listing of air services, contact the park headquarters. Several canoe and raft outfitters also guide trips on the Nahanni River. *See* Sports and Outdoor Activities, *below,* or contact the park headquarters for more information. *Nahanni National Park Preserve, Bag 300, Fort Simpson, NT X0E 0N0, tel. 403/695–3151.*

## Tour 7: The Arctic North

It probably goes without saying that one doesn't "tour" the Arctic North in the usual sense of the word. Rather, the concept is more expeditionary: Choose a community—such as Inuvik, Bathurst Inlet, Iqaluit, or Pangnirtung—as a base camp from which to make day or extended side trips. Lodging and transportation in the Arctic North tend to be expensive even by high-end northern standards, so that having a well-defined travel plan is critical to staying within a budget. Trip organizers and outfitters (*see* Guided Tours, *above*) can be particularly helpful in tailoring a travel program to meet particular interests and budgets. Keep in mind that the prime Arctic travel season tends to be very short: Many visitor services and tour organizers operate only in July and August.

Like Yellowknife, **Inuvik,** a commercial and transportation center of the western Arctic, is less of a destination than it is a hub from which to reach out to other Arctic points of interest. The most compelling aspects of the region, dominated by the sprawling MacKenzie River delta, are wildlife and culture. **Arctic Tour Company** (*see* Guided Tours, *above*) offers a wide range of Inuvik-based day trips as well as multi-day packages; **Western Arctic Nature Tours** (Box 1530, Inuvik, NT X0E 0T0, tel. 403/979–3300) organizes sight-seeing, fishing, and wildlife-viewing trips, as well as customized trips for small groups.

For travelers interested primarily in experiencing the culture of the north, **Tuktoyaktuk,** a small Inuit community located a short flight north of Inuvik, is the place to experience the interesting blend of ancient Inuit culture with modern influences. Tours of Tuktoyaktuk—Inuit-owned land in accordance with recent lands-claim settlements—are conducted by Inuit guides.

Although wildlife—particularly migrant birdlife—is abundant throughout the MacKenzie delta area, **Banks Island** and **Herschel Island** are destinations of particular interest. Banks Island is best known for its large herd of musk oxen. Herschel Island is today a park, although at the turn of the century it was the site of considerable whaling activity. It remains an excellent base for sighting beluga whales and is known for abundant birdlife, and wild flowers that grow from the seemingly barren tundra.

Perhaps the most popular destination in the central Arctic, particularly for ornithologists, is **Bathurst Inlet Lodge,** a lone outpost on the tundral shores of the inlet. Traveling by plane, boat, and foot from the lodge, guests typically spot musk oxen, Arctic foxes, wolves, falcons, and eagles. In late spring, as many as half a million migrating caribou pass this way. Outings from the lodge include a hike (after a short airplane transfer) to **Wilburforce Falls,** the highest waterfall north of the Arctic Circle, where the Hood River cuts spectacularly through a series of gorges. In addition to week-long naturalist tours, the lodge also outfits canoe or raft trips on nearby rivers and bays. *Bathurst Inlet Lodge, 3618 McAvoy Rd., Box 820, Yellowknife, NT X1A 2N6, tel. 403/873–2595. Fees start at about $2,300 per person for a 1-wk stay, including flights to and from Yellowknife. Open late June–early Aug.*

For experienced canoeists and kayakers, the rivers, bays, and fjords of the Arctic coast hold a wealth of possibilities. The **Coppermine River,** a fairly easy-flowing river through the tundra, is a worthy destination, if for no better reason than a visit to the **Bloody Falls,** the site of a 1771 massacre of Inuit by guides of the Northwest Passage explorer, Samuel Hearne. **Sobek Canada** (159 Main St., Unionville, ON L3R 2G8, tel. 416/479–2600) is one of several outfitters who guide trips on the Coppermine. There is also a 16-kilometer (10-mile) hiking trail along the river from the community of Coppermine to Bloody Falls.

Even northerners accustomed to the unique beauty of the Arctic wilderness speak of **Baffin Island** in tones of awe. It is a world of junctures: where mountains meet sea, where the climates of summer and winter may be experienced on the same day, where summer flowers bloom on green, tundral meadows amid ice-locked surroundings. It remains a stronghold of Inuit tradition despite the ever-increasing influences of modern culture. At least 3,000 years ago, the Thule, ancestors of the Inuit, migrated to the Canadian Arctic across the frozen Bering Sea. Later, whaling became a prime means of sustenance, both for Inuit and European hunters, and many Baffin communities have exhibits or museums that chronicle whaling life. Baffin tours start in **Iqaluit,** which, like Inuvik and Yellowknife, is a point of reference and departure rather than a destination in itself. It is the transportation, communication, and government center of Canada's eastern Arctic, and is expected to be the capital of Nunavut when the territorial division comes about in 1999.

From Iqaluit, visitors must choose a medium of travel: land or sea. In winter, of course, the land and sea merge under ice and snow, and April and May are the ideal months for those interested in cross-country skiing, dogsledding, or snowmobiling. Those who journey into the Baffin wilderness should have an adventurous spirit and a willingness to abide life in a world with virtually none of the trappings of civilization. While some tour organizers (*see below*) offer general sightseeing tours of the region, Baffin is best appreciated by those inclined (and physically fit enough) to rough it.

Sea kayaking is popular in summer in the bays and fjords of Baffin, populated by whales, narwhals, walruses, and seals. The jewel of Baffin, however, is **Auyuittuq National Park,** where rivers and glaciers have cut deep fjords and have carved out **Akshayuk Pass** (formerly Pangnirtung Pass) between Cumberland Sound to the south and Davis Strait to the north. The 60-kilometer pass is surrounded by jagged peaks exceeding 2,000 meters (6,600 feet) that jut up from glacial ice (glacial melt provides the water supply supporting the brief burst of summer wild flowers on the tundral lowlands). A marked trail leads through the pass, and in summer, backpacking groups regularly make the five- to seven-day journey. There are emergency shelters along the route, but this is still a trip only for those properly prepared and physically fit, given the length of the trip and the vagaries of climatic changes, even in mid-summer. All park visitors should sign up with a trip organizer (*see below*) and/or check in at the park headquarters in Pangnirtung for information on hiking in the park. *Auyuittuq National Park Preserve, Pangnirtung, NT X0A 0R0, tel. 819/473–8828. Park headquarters open July–Aug., weekdays 8:30–noon, 1–5, 6–10, weekends 1–5, 6–10; Sept.–June, weekdays 8:30–5.*

Even more adventurous visitors can head north from Baffin to **Ellesmere Island National Park,** above 80 degrees north latitude. Ellesmere—like Baffin, a land of mountains and glaciers—is intriguing as much for its climate as its landscape. Technically a "polar desert," the island's annual precipitation of about six centimeters (2.5 inches) makes it one of the driest places in the northern hemisphere; yet, because of the water-retaining effects of ice, parts of the island are still able to support plant and wildlife.

**Adventure Canada, Black Feather Wilderness Adventures** (*see* Special Interest Tours in Essential Information, *above*), and **Canada North Outfitting** (Box 3100, 87 Mill St., Almonte, ON K0A 1A0, tel. 613/256–4057) offer a wide range of adventure and cultural tours—by land or sea—on Baffin and Ellesmere islands.

## What to Do and See with Children

Many of the more adventurous activities in the far north are probably too strenuous for small children, not to mention many adults. River trips are especially ill-advised, given the inherent dangers of whitewater travel on remote rivers. If you do plan to bring small children on wilderness excursions, be sure to tell your outfitter or tour operator how old the children are; many trips have age limitations.

**Ndilo Cultural Village** in Yellowknife provides an excellent, hands-on opportunity for children to experience the culture and native life of the north. Village activities include leather-tanning, fish-drying, and carving, and visitors are encouraged to participate in native games and drum dances, as well as sample traditional native foods. *On the eastern end of Latham Island, Box 1287, Yellowknife, NT X1A 2N9, tel. 403/873–2869. Admission: $16 adults, $12 children 12 and under. Open May–Aug., daily.*

Ten kilometers (6 miles) north of Whitehorse off the Klondike Highway is the Takhini Hot Springs Road to **Takhini Hot Springs.** In addition to swimming in the spring-warmed water (suits and towels are available for rental), there are horseback rides and areas for picnicking. *R.R. 2, Site 19, Comp. 4, Whitehorse, YT Y1A 5A5, tel. 403/633–2706. Open daily 7 AM–10 PM.*

# Shopping

Native arts and crafts are the most compelling reason to go shopping
in the far north. (Products not made in the territories are generally
much less expensive elsewhere.) You may find that prices are best
when buying directly from artists or craftspeople in local communities; however, buying from galleries or stores in the cities provides
at least some guarantee of authenticity. Soapstone carvings, clothing, and moose- or caribou-hair tuftings are among the most popular
items to purchase. Be aware before buying, however, that some
products, such as those made from hides or materials from endangered species, may not be brought into the United States. In many
cases—such as a polar-bear rug—the import problem is obvious,
but not in all cases; for example, jewelry made of polished whale ba-
leen may be confiscated at the border.

In a world where warm clothing is essential, parkas, mukluks, cari-
bou-hide mittens, and the like are a fashion statement. **Polar Parkas**
(51st Ave. and 49th St., Box 1385, Yellowknife, tel. 403/873–3343) is
the best place in Yellowknife to buy native-made parkas. Native-
made clothing (and other products) is also available at **Yukon Native
Products** (4230 4th Ave., Whitehorse, tel. 403/668–5955).

One of the best and most reasonably priced stores for soapstone
sculpture is **Webster Gallery** (5016 48th St., Box 1597, Yellowknife,
tel. 403/873–5876), devoted exclusively to northern artists working
with northern materials (many northern artists use soapstone imported from Brazil). **Northern Images** sells a variety of native crafts
and artwork, from sculpture to moose-hair tuftings to clothing, and
has stores in several Canadian cities, including Whitehorse (4th
Ave. and Jarvis St., tel. 403/668–5739) and Yellowknife (Y K Mall,
Main Fl., tel. 403/873–5944).

**Murdoch's Gem Shop** (207 Main St., Whitehorse, tel. 403/668–7403)
is the Yukon's largest manufacturer of gold-nugget jewelry. There
are also Murdoch's outlets in Dawson, Faro, and Watson Lake.

# Sports and Outdoor Activities

Sports and outdoor activities are really the essence of visiting the
far north. In most cases, you'll have to sign up with an outfitter or
tour operator, or fly into a wilderness lodge. Even those who prefer
self-guided adventures—e.g., canoeists or backpackers—may find
the assistance of an outfitter helpful or necessary in planning an itinerary and getting transportation into and out of the wilderness.
Keep in mind that the scope of possibilities is enormous and that
most outfitters are flexible; plan ahead and use your imagination in
working with an outfitter to develop a program that best meets your
interests and physical abilities.

## Backcountry Lodges

Given the wide range of possible activities and the relatively small
number of visitors, it's not surprising that many lodge proprietors
try to be all things to all people. Not long ago, most backcountry
lodges tended to be dedicated either to fishermen or hunters, but
now wildlife viewing, hiking (often assisted by helicopter or plane),
canoeing, and winter activities are part of the mix as well. This mul-

tiple focus does have potential conflicts, and lodge proprietors avoid mixing hunters and wildlife viewers. The following lodges are among the best in the far north.

**Bathurst Inlet Lodge.** (*see* Tour 7, *above*)

**Inconnu Lodge.** Within the spectrum of rustic backcountry lodges, Inconnu Lodge is a statement in relative luxury. The fly-in lodge on the shores of Lake McEvoy, about 320 kilometers (200 miles) northeast of Whitehorse, provides accommodations in modern log cabins. The principal activities are fishing and heli-hiking, although the lodge also arranges canoe trips on nearby rivers. Wildlife is plentiful, as attested by the considerable taxidermy displayed in the lodge living room. The lodge also acts as a jumping-off point for canoe and climbing trips into Nahanni National Park. *Box 4730, Whitehorse, YT Y1A 4N6, tel. 403/667–4070. Accommodations for 20 in 5 duplex cabins. Rates for 3-day packages, including transportation to and from Whitehorse, are about $2,000 per person.*

**Nahanni Mountain Lodge.** In the front ranges of the Nahanni Mountains, this fly-in lodge lies at the edge of Little Doctor Lake. This is basically a do-it-yourself facility; while there is a full kitchen, guests bring and cook their own food. A motor boat and canoes are provided for venturing out on the lake, and hiking possibilities from the lodge are considerable. The proprietors may arrange heli-hiking services. Open year-round, the lodge is also an excellent base for cross-country skiing. *Simpson Air, Box 260, Fort Simpson, NT X0E 0N0, tel. 403/695–2505. Accommodations for 8 in 2 log cabins. Rates for 3- to 7-day packages are $500–$1,000 per person.*

**Oldsquaw Lodge.** The original lodge was built from materials salvaged from the Canol Trail by wildlife biologists. Those beginnings point to much of what the present-day lodge is all about: a place from which to access the Canol Trail, and a place dedicated primarily to wildlife viewing. The basic lodge program consists of daily hikes (in some cases helicopter assisted) on the open tundra in search of wildlife ranging from grizzly bears to falcons. The lodge also arranges mountain-biking trips on the Canol Trail and cross-country skiing in spring. Lodging is in six outlying cabins. *Bag Service 2711, Whitehorse, YT Y1A 3V5, tel. 403/668–6732. Accommodations for 12 in 6 cabins. Rates for weekly packages begin at $2,000 per person.*

## Bicycling

In a world of few roads, bicycling might not be the first sport to come to mind. Indeed, good cycling opportunities are relatively few. However, mountain biking on the Canol Trail—at least along it's western half—is becoming increasingly popular. The eastern section is rugged and rough with considerable hazards, including difficult river crossings. While some experienced backcountry cyclists do negotiate the entire route, it is not recommended. Arrangements for a cycling trip can be made through **Oldsquaw Lodge** (*see* Backcountry Lodges, *above*) or **Black Feather Wilderness Adventures** (*see* Special Interest Tours in Essential Information, *above*).

## Camping

Territorial, or public, campgrounds are found along all roads in the north, and are open from the spring thaw until the fall freeze, the exact dates varying somewhat from year to year. Visitors' centers throughout the region can provide information on specific campground locations and facilities as well as permits. Many privately-owned lodges and motels along highways of the north also have camping facilities. Fees and reservation policies vary. Note: It is advisable to boil or filter all water, even water that has been designated as "drinking water" at a campground.

## Cross-Country Skiing

In a world covered by snow eight months out of the year, cross-country skiing opportunities are obviously plentiful. The best time for skiing, however, is from mid-March until the snow melts (the precise time varying according to the latitude and elevation), when days are longer and warmer.

While short outings on skis are possible almost anywhere in the north, perhaps the most interesting extended excursions are in the Kluane area and the Arctic North. **Arctic Edge** (*see* Special Interest Tours in Essential Information, *above*) leads weekly, hut-based tours into the glacier country of Kluane between April and June. **Canadian North Outfitting** (Box 3100, 87 Mills St., Almonte, ON K0A 1A0, tel. 613/256–4057) leads six-day trips, supported by dogsleds, in the wilderness of Baffin Island.

A number of backcountry lodges have begun opening in April and May for ski-touring enthusiasts. For information on lodges that offer ski-touring packages, contact **Tourism Yukon** or the **Department of Economic Development and Tourism** in the Northwest Territories (*see* Essential Information, *above*).

## Dogsledding

Before there were planes and snowmobiles, dogsleds were the vital means of transportation in the far north. Dogsledding remains embedded in the culture of the region, particularly in the Arctic north and around Yellowknife. **Qimmiq Adventures** (Box 1181, Yellowknife, NT X1A 2N8, tel. 403/920–7533) offers both lodge-based tours and winter-camping tours in the Yellowknife area between February and April. **Arctic Odysseys** (*see* Special Interest Tours in Essential Information, *above*) leads dogsledding trips in the Baffin area from March through May.

## Fishing

Fishing in wilderness Canada is a way of life, a means of sustenance for a good many native residents. What sustains the native people of the north is also what attracts sports fishermen: fish in large quantities and of considerable proportions. Farther south on the continent, an eight-pound trout might be considered a trophy fish, but in the far north it would be rejected as not much more than a sardine. Lake trout between 30 and 70 pounds are not unusual. The most common catches in the far north are Arctic char, grayling, pike, lake trout, and whitefish.

Numerous outfitters throughout the region can guide fishermen on day trips or short excursions; your best bet is to check with a regional tourist office (*see* Essential Information, *above*) for outfitter recommendations. Day trips from Yellowknife to the Great Slave Lake are especially easy to arrange.

Some lakes and streams are accessible by road in the Yukon and in the Northwest Territories. However, the more typical fishing adventure in the far north involves flying for several days to a remote lodge. A few recommended lodges are described here, mainly to describe the type of facilities and activities to expect. For a complete listing of fly-in fishing services, contact regional tourist authorities.

**Blachford Lake Lodge.** Many fishing lodges in the far north provide a minimum of services (unless patrons request otherwise) for guests seeking to keep vacation costs down. Blachford Lake Lodge is a good example of the genre. Guests are flown to and from the remote lodge (less than a half-hour flight from Yellowknife), where they stay in cabins and have the use of boats to venture out on the small lake. Unless they request otherwise, guests are expected to bring and prepare their own food, as well as bring their own bedding and fishing tackle. The result is a cost that is generally under $120 per person per day (including the flights to and from the lodge), and less for groups—modest by fly-in fishing standards. The lodge is also open in winter for ice-fishing, snowmobiling, and dogsledding. *Box 1568, Yellowknife, NT X1A 2P2, tel. 403/873–3303. Accommodations for 14 in 6 cabins. 2- and 5-day packages begin at $110 per person.*

**Frontier Lodge.** Located on the southeastern shore of the Great Slave Lake, Frontier Lodge is typical of a full-service fishing lodge. Guests are housed in attractive, if spare, outlying cabins, and breakfast and dinner are served daily around a big table in the main lodge. Guides take guests to the best fishing waters on the Great Slave as well as adjoining rivers and lakes, and lake trout exceeding 25 pounds are landed regularly. This is a lodge strictly dedicated to fishing; aside from reading or watching wolves feeding on dinner scraps, there is not much else to do except appreciate the lakeside, wilderness setting. *5515 82 Ave., Edmonton, AB T6B 2J6, tel. 403/465–6843 (year-round) or 403/370–3501 (mid-June–mid-Sept.) Packages, including flights to and from Yellowknife, begin at $300 per day per person. Open mid-June–mid-Sept., daily.*

## Golf

Golf in the far north can be truly bizarre. For example, golfers at the Yellowknife public golf course carry mats of artificial turf with them because there are no grass fairways. Wherever your ball lands, you put down the mat, place the ball on it, and make your shot. There is also a local rule about what to do should a raven steal your ball. What this ought to tell you is that golf is not a featured reason to come to the far north, although the **Mountain View Golf Course** (Box 5883, Whitehorse, YT Y1A 5L6, tel. 403/633–6020) in Whitehorse and Dawson's **Top of the World Golf Course** (Box 130, Dawson City, YT Y0B 1G0, tel. 403/993–5443) are reasonable facsimiles of a traditional golf course, with real grass and greens. If, however, you want to take northern golf to its bizarre extreme, **Adventure Canada** (*see* Special Interest Tours in Essential Information, *above*) stages a golf "tournament" each April at the North Pole. The greens fee may be the world's highest: The cost of the eight-day trip exceeds $10,000.

## Hiking

While the landscape can be spectacular, the going can be rough. Marked trails are relatively few, and sometimes the only trails to follow are those beaten down by wild animals, such as bears and caribou. The three general areas that are best for hiking are Baffin Island, Kluane National Park, and the mountains along the Dempster Highway.

The 100-kilometer (60-mile) backpacking hike through Baffin Island's Pangnirtung Pass is a trek through a world of mountains, fjords and glaciers. **Adventure Canada** and **Black Feather Wilderness Adventures** (*see* Special-Interest Tours in Essential Information, *above*) are among the companies who sponsor guided hikes in the region. The going is rugged and remote, but at least there is a trail, something that can't be said for the region's other classic trek: the 130-kilometer (80-mile) hike from Tanquary Fjord to Lake Hazen on Ellesmere Island. The trip runs above 80 degrees north latitude, so there is considerable travel over ice plateaus and glaciers. **Ecosummer Canada Expeditions** (1516N Duranleau St., Vancouver, BC V6H 3S4, tel. 604/669–7741) leads guided backpacking trips in the area.

The trail system of Kluane National Park is the most extensive in the far north, although trails do not penetrate the park's vast, glaciated interior. The park's front ranges, however, are still spectacular country. It's possible to make a five-day backpacking trip on marked trails, with opportunities for off-trail scrambling on mountain-tops affording good views of the park's big peaks and glaciers in the distance. Be aware that Kluane is *serious* bear country, and all precautions should be strictly followed.

The opportunities for short hikes or longer backpacking trips are numerous along the Dempster Highway in the Tombstone and Ogilvie mountains. While there are no marked trails, most of the terrain is above treeline, so that finding one's way is not especially difficult. Pick a spot that looks good, pull off the highway, and go hiking.

## Hunting

Hunting is a way of life in the far north, and it is hard to find a resident who isn't a hunter. The reason is basic: In a world of few farms, game animals represent a critical food resource. For visiting sport hunters, caribou, moose, and Dall sheep are the principal game animals, and late summer and early fall is the prime hunting period. Nonresident hunters (e.g., U.S. citizens) are required to sign up with a licensed guide or outfitter. For a list of outfitters, contact **Tourism Yukon** or the **Department of Economic Development and Tourism** (*see* Essential Information, *above*) of the Northwest Territories.

For more information on bag limits, fees, and hunting regulations in the Northwest Territories, contact the **Department of Renewable Resources** (Government of the Northwest Territories, Box 1320, Yellowknife, NT X1A 2L9, tel. 403/920–8716). In the Yukon, contact the **Yukon Department of Renewable Resources** (Fish and Wildlife Branch, Box 2703, Whitehorse, YT Y1A 2C6, tel. 403/667–5221).

## Mountaineering

In the far north, the question is not so much what to climb but how to access the mountain. The major peaks of Kluane National Park, in particular, Mt. Logan, Canada's highest peak, and Mt. St. Elias, are tops in the mountaineering world but can only be reached by helicopter or plane. In addition, all climbing parties must receive authorization from the Superintendent of Kluane National Park (*see* Tour 5, *above*). The effect has been to weed out inexperienced climbers, and there have been far fewer serious accidents in Kluane than in Alaska, where many major peaks, most notably Mt. McKinley, are relatively close to public roads.

For serious rock climbers, the **Cirque of the Unclimbables,** located in Nahanni National Park, presents an obvious challenge. This breathtaking cathedral of rock towers rising as much as 3,000 vertical feet does not entirely live up to its name, but the few who have made successful ascents here can be counted among the most proficient rock climbers in the world. Perhaps the biggest problem posed by the Cirque is that it is nearly as unreachable as it is unclimbable. **Simpson Air** (Box 260, Fort Simpson, NT X0E 0N0, tel. 403/695–2505) can shuttle climbers into the Cirque from Fort Simpson. **Inconnu Lodge** (*see* Backcountry Lodges, *above*) can fly in climbers from the Yukon side; expect to pay handsomely for the service.

## Water Sports

Without question, river travel is one of the best ways to experience the wilderness of the far north; these roads of water provide access to remote areas. Canoes of various configurations are the preferred means of travel, although for some rivers—particularly those with considerable whitewater—rafts or kayaks may be used.

Trips may range in length from a half-day to over a month. Some rivers are exceedingly gentle; others rage with barely charted whitewater. The major rivers, such as the Liard, MacKenzie, and Yukon, pass through nodes of civilization, while others, such as the Keele or Mountain rivers, run through long stretches of uninhabited wilderness. If you decide on an unguided trip, outfitters can provide both the necessary gear as well as transportation to and from the river.

It would be difficult to single out one river as *the* river to run in the far north. However, the **South Nahanni** in Nahanni National Park (*see* Tour 6, *above*), as the best known, would be the logical choice. Two-week canoe trips can start from Rabbit Kettle Lake at the park's northwestern extreme, but require portage around Virginia Falls. Eight to 12-day canoe or raft trips put in below Virginia Falls. Whitewater along the way is minimal, so previous canoeing or rafting experience is not essential. Two reliable outfitters that lead guided trips are **Nahanni River Adventures** (Box 8368, Station F, Edmonton, AB T6H 4W6, tel. 403/439–1316) and **Nahanni Wilderness Adventures** (Box 4 Site 6, R.R. #1, Didsbury, AB T0M 0W0, tel. 403/637–3843).

Two other rivers that are considered classics by river runners are the **Alsek** and the **Tatsenshini,** which run primarily through the St. Elias Mountains of Alaska, although they begin in the Kluane region of the Yukon. **Mountain Travel/Sobek** (6420 Fairmount Ave., El Cerrito, CA 94539, tel. 510/527–8100 or 800/227–2384) ranks among the more reliable outfitters that lead rafting and kayaking trips.

The **Keele River** and **Natla River** run through the Mackenzie Mountains and may be preferred by canoeists seeking a more remote whitewater experience. **Black Feather Wilderness Adventures** (*see* Special Interest Tours in Essential Information, *above*) offers guided trips on both rivers. In the Yukon, **Kanoe People** (Box 5152, Whitehorse, YT Y1A 4S3, tel. 403/668–4899) arranges guided and nonguided canoe trips, from a half day to two weeks, for several rivers: The wide, turbulence-free **Yukon River** is considered one of the easiest rivers to run; the **Big Salmon,** with considerably more whitewater, is preferred by canoeists seeking more technical challenge; the **Takhini River,** with a mix of gentle stretches and whitewater, provides one of the best day trips from Whitehorse.

One other water-borne adventure to consider in the far north is sailing on **Great Slave Lake. Sail North** (Box 2497, Yellowknife, NT X1A 2P8, tel. 403/873–8019) charters 26- to 42-foot sloops, both skippered and unskippered. (For those unsure of their navigation skills, hiring a skipper is recommended, since many of the lake's small bays are still uncharted.) The lake's East Arm, a two- to three-day sail from Yellowknife, is prime cruise country, with dramatic cliffs rising from narrow bays.

## Wildlife Viewing

For many visitors to the far north, the most exciting physical activity is pressing the shutter-release button on a camera. This does not, of course, mean that one must devote a trip exclusively to wildlife viewing and photography. Chances of spotting a wide array of wildlife while participating in any of the activities listed above are, needless to say, extremely good. However, a number of lodges and tour organizers do arrange trips—in many cases targeted toward over-50 travelers—that are "naturalist" in focus, i.e., wildlife viewing is the principal activity (*see* Backcountry Lodges, and Special Interest Tours in Essential Information, *above*).

# Dining and Lodging

## Dining

Cooking in the far north rarely reaches grand epicurean standards, but it can have a distinctive character, making wide use of local foods. This means that in some places and at certain times of year, a caribou steak or a moose burger may be easier to find than a fresh salad. Once outside the main cities, be prepared for limited choices; the dining room of your hotel or lodge may well be your *only* choice. But if the far north is not necessarily a gastronomic paradise, it is surprising and certainly admirable what some chefs are able to concoct given the limitations on ingredients. Highly recommended restaurants are indicated by a star ★.

| Category | Cost* |
| --- | --- |
| $$$$ | over $25 |
| $$$ | $18–$25 |
| $$ | $10–$18 |
| $ | under $10 |

*per person, excluding drinks, service, and 7% GST*

## Lodging

Lodging prices in the far north are generally higher than you might find elsewhere in Canada. In many communities, a lodge or hotel may be the only show in town, so if you don't like the price, you don't have much choice. In addition, the shortness of the tourism season forces lodging proprietors to try to make ends meet in two or three months of active vacation business. While you might think you're paying a good chunk of change for pretty ordinary accommodations (e.g., a small room in a box-like motel), consider, too, the lack of quality building materials in many areas and the prohibitive costs of construction. That said, accommodations listed here are generally comfortable and clean, and proprietors are generally friendly and knowledgeable about things to do in the region. In months other than July and August, expect better deals—room prices reduced 50% or more—but fewer choices, since many places are closed from September to June.

Two general resources of note: **Inns North** (Arctic Cooperatives Ltd., Hotel Division, 1741 Wellington Ave., Winnipeg, MT R3H 0G1, tel. 204/786–4481) is an organization of native-operated hotels throughout the far north which may be particularly helpful to visitors planning travels in some of the region's smaller communities; the **Northern Network of Bed and Breakfasts** (Box 94-T Dawson City, YT Y0B 1G0, tel. 403/993–5648) publishes a brochure that includes more than 80 listings in the Northwest Territories and the Yukon as well as Alaska and British Columbia.

Highly recommended lodgings in each price category are indicated by a star ★.

| Category | Cost* |
|----------|-------|
| $$$$ | over $150 |
| $$$ | $120–$150 |
| $$ | $80–$120 |
| $ | under $80 |

*All prices are for a standard double room (or equivalent, where not applicable), excluding gratuities and 7% GST.*

## Northwest Territories

**Inuvik**
*Dining and Lodging*

**Finto Inn.** The Finto is typical of far-northern lodging—decent motel-style rooms in a two-story, squared-off structure resembling a big box that might have been flown in by a helicopter sling and dropped on the spot. At least the wood siding somewhat softens those harsh edges. Elegance in accommodations is not a reason to stay at the Finto, but the inn's restaurant, The Peppermill, is; it's generally considered Inuvik's best. The dining room overlooks green meadows and blue water; the menu features local foods, such as Artic char and musk ox, but the German chef lends a European influence. Home-baked breads are especially good. The inn is located on the outskirts of Inuvik, at the junction of the Marine Bypass and Mackenzie Road. *Box 1925, Inuvik, NT X0E 0T0, tel. 403/979–2647. 44 rooms with private bath, including 4 with kitchenettes. Facilities: satellite TV, restaurant, gift shop. MC, V. $$$–$$$$*

**Iqaluit**
*Dining and Lodging*

**Discovery Lodge Hotel.** The lobby area of this hotel was brightened with the installation of skylights a few years ago. An oddity here is that some rooms have trapezoidal beds, wider at the top than the bottom. The Granite Room, with its granite-slab table tops, is perhaps the best restaurant in Iqaluit, noteworthy for its use of local ingredients, including Arctic char, Baffin Island shrimp, and scallops. *Box 387, Iqaluit, NT X0A 0H0, tel. 819/979–4433. 51 rooms with private bath, 1 suite. Facilities: cable TV, dining room, lounge, laundry, airport shuttle. AE, DC, MC, V. $$$*

**Frobisher Inn.** In its brochure, the inn promotes itself as being "part of an integrated, climate-controlled, indoor shopping and highrise apartment complex." So much for the rustic charm of the far north. Rooms are boxlike and simply adorned with veneer-wood furnishings. Rooms in the front offer good views of Frobisher Bay and Iqaluit. There's no airport shuttle, but the inn will reimburse you for the taxi ride. *Box 610, Iqaluit NT X0A 0H0, tel. 819/979–2222. 48 rooms with private bath. Facilties: cable TV, valet service, dining room, lounge, laundry, pool, sauna. AE, MC, V. $$$*

**Yellowknife**
*Dining*

**The Office.** One of the tricks of life in the far north is to simulate nighttime in summer, when the sun barely sets. The Office goes a bit overboard for the cause; its downstairs location is kept so dark that it may take the eyes several minutes to adjust from the bright light of day. Upholstered swivel chairs add to that executive-office feeling. Seafood highlights the menu with dishes such as poached Arctic char topped with hollandaise; even the special steak dish, prime rib Oscar, is smothered in seafood: shrimp, crabmeat, and scallops. Soups such as char bisque are freshly made. *4915 50th St., tel. 403/ 873–3750. Dress: casual but neat. Dinner only Sat., closed Sun. AE, MC, V. $$$$*

**Bistro on Franklin.** The descent of the narrow stairs leading into the Bistro's basement setting feels vaguely ominous—more like heading down to check out the boiler room rather than going out to dinner. But the dining area brings relief: an attractive, unpretentious room with a small bar. Dinner waiters in bow ties, low lighting, and tablecloths lend a touch of formality to an otherwise casual place. Chicken and pasta dishes are excellent, including the chicken pesto pasta, a boneless breast of chicken in a pesto cream sauce, served with fettucini; fish dishes such as Arctic char are less reliable. *4910 Franklin Ave., tel. 403/873–3991. Dress: casual. AE, MC, V. $$$*

**Wildcat Cafe.** The Wildcat is an institution as much as a restaurant, the sort of place that everybody who comes to town eventually visits. It has been around since 1937, which is long enough in Yellowknife to earn it the status of an historic landmark, and the low-slung, log-structure and split-log tables and benches inside lend to the aura of life at the frontier's edge. This is a place where strangers are expected to share tables, a fact that can either be convivial or intrusive, depending on your frame of mind. The food, ranging from fresh fish to vegetarian chili to caribou burgers, is excellent and modestly priced. Many people drop in at the Wildcat for coffee and desserts—mostly fresh-baked delectables. *Doornbo's La. and Wiley Rd., tel. 403/873–8850. Dress: casual. MC, V. $$*

**Bullock's Fish and Chips.** A good alternative to the nearby Wildcat Cafe when the Wildcat becomes overcrowded, Bullock's log-cabin walls and rough-hewn furniture provide a warm, rustic atmosphere. The dining room is small—five or six tables—and the food is cooked in a kitchen that is effectively part of the dining room. As for the specialty of the house, the name tells all. *#4 Lessard Dr., tel. 403/873– 3474. Dress: casual. V. $$*

**Split Pea.** There is nothing fancy about Split Pea, primarily a take-out place on Main Street. But it's a good spot to pick up sandwiches or fresh-baked muffins for those on the go. *5000 Franklin Ave., tel. 403/873–5510. Dress: casual. No credit cards. $*

*Dining and*
*Lodging*

**Explorer Hotel.** Atop a promontory overlooking Yellowknife, the Explorer is best recommended for its views of the city and surrounding bays of the Great Slave Lake. Rooms are large and decorated with run-of-the-mill brown-veneer furniture, but they are bright and clean. The hotel's main restaurant, The Factors Club, has a big dining room highlighted by a central, circular hearth, and includes on its menu such unusual northern delicacies as musk-ox chop—but it's somewhat pricier than it ought to be. *Postal Service 7000, Yellowknife, NT X1A 2R3, tel. 403/873–3531 or 800/661–0892.*

*127 rooms with private bath, including 2 suites. Facilities: 2 restaurants, lounge, gift shop, airport shuttle bus. AE, MC, V. $$$*

**Lodging**  **Yellowknife Inn.** The Yellowknife Inn is the oldest hotel in a city where there isn't much that could be called old. It has a tradition of trying to be all things to all people, including, until the 1993 completion of a new legislative building, home to the Northwest Territories legislative assembly. Rooms in the front are preferable, with large bathrooms, pastel upholstery, and dark, varnished cabinetry. Rooms in the back are rougher around the edges, geared more toward mining speculators and the like than a mainstream tourist crowd. The hotel's MacKenzie Lounge, with dark-wood paneling that lends it a clubby feel, is a nice place to meet for a pre-dinner drink. *Box 490, Yellowknife, NT X1A 2N4, tel. 403/873-2601. 128 rooms with private bath, including 7 suites. Facilities: cable TV, restaurant, lounge, shops, airport shuttle bus, free Continental breakfast. AE, DC, MC, V. $$$*

**Igloo Inn.** Don't expect much more than a motel-style room at a decent price. Rooms are on the small side and have the basics—bed, bathroom, TV. The Igloo is a perfectly good choice for budget-minded travelers laying over for a night before heading off to more adventurous ports-of-call in the territorial outback. *Box 596, Yellowknife, NT X1A 2R3, tel. 403/873-8511. 44 rooms with private bath, including 33 with kitchenettes. Facilities: cable TV, restaurant. AE, MC, V. $$*

**Blue Raven.** There are several good bed-and-breakfast options in Yellowknife, and the Blue Raven is perhaps the best. Attractively set on a bluff at the edge of Old Town and overlooking the Great Slave Lake, this is a good place for those who like breakfast with a view. Rooms are small, modern, clean, and quiet, set apart from one another by the home's three-story configuration. *37B Otto Dr., Yellowknife, NT X1A 2T9, tel. 403/873-6328. 3 rooms with shared baths. Continental breakfast included in room price. No credit cards. $–$$*

## Yukon

**Dawson**  **Jack London Grill.** Located in the Downtown Hotel, this is one of the
**Dining**  most attractive dining rooms in Dawson. The decor evokes the urbane atmosphere of a turn-of-the-century men's club, with dark-wood siding reaching halfway up walls adorned by framed mirrors and prints. The menu highlights steaks in three sizes. For Dawson diners who want a touch of civility and formality, this is a good choice. *In the Downtown Hotel, 2nd Ave. and Queen St., tel. 403/993-5346. Dress: casual. AE, D, DC, MC, V. $$$*

**Klondike Kate's.** It's too bad that the service at Kate's gets a little harried, because the food can be extremely good. The salmon carpaccio appetizer is especially noteworthy, and the linguini pesto and smoked local king salmon stand out on the menu. A large, covered, outdoor deck offers an airy, casual spot for a meal on a warm summer's day or evening. The main decorative statement on the deck is a large map of the world, onto which guests are invited to stick pins to mark their hometowns. *3rd Ave. and King St., tel. 403/993-6527. Dress: casual. V. $$*

★ **Marina's.** You'd think that in making the effort to come this far north, you'd be inspired to order something more interesting than pizza. The fact of the matter is, Marina's thick-crusted pizzas are first-rate and reasonably priced. There might be other entrées on the menu, but it's the pizza that makes Marina's so popular with locals and visitors alike. The small dining room can fill up in a hurry, but you can always place a take-out order. *5th Ave., between Princess and Harper Sts., tel. 403/993–6800 Dress: casual. MC, V. $–$$*

**Nancy's.** For sheer caloric bang for your buck, Nancy's sourdough pancakes might be one of the best breakfast deals in North America. The flapjacks literally obscure the plate that bears them, and if you can finish two, you have accomplished a remarkable digestive feat. High ceilings, blond-wood furnishings, and big, storefront windows create an airy atmosphere. *Front and Princess Sts., tel. 403/993–5633. Dress: casual. MC, V. $*

*Lodging* **Triple J Hotel.** This "hotel" indeed comes in three parts: a main hotel, a separate motel, and several outlying cabins. The motel, little more than a large mobile home, is not worth considering. The cabins, which include kitchenettes, are the best choice. Their small porches and bright flowers out front exude a homey quality. Inside, the hominess fades: the wood veneer furnishings and cramped bathrooms come across as a bit dowdy. The rooms are also dark, though darkness can be an asset at this latitude in summer, when nighttime pretends to be daytime. *5th Ave. and Queen St., Box 359, Dawson City, YT Y0B 1G0, tel. 403/993–5323. 47 units in hotel, motel, and cabins. Facilities: satellite TV, restaurant, lounge, take-out pizza. AE, MC, V. Closed late Oct.–mid-Apr. $$*

**Westmark Inn.** Like its counterpart in Whitehorse, this Westmark is a nice hotel that suffers from tour-bus overload. Rooms are clean, modern, and spacious if not particularly distinctive. The operative concept here is to create the familiar basic-American-hotel-room comforts behind a turn-of-the-century facade dictated by Dawson zoning codes. *5th Ave. and Harper St., Box 420 Dawson City, YT Y0B 1G0, tel. 403/993–5542 or 800/544–0970 for U.S. reservations. 131 rooms. Facilities: restaurant, lounge, satellite TV, 2 rooms accessible for guests with disabilities. AE, DC, MC, V. Open mid-May–mid-Sept. $$*

**Dawson City Bunkhouse.** While accommodations in the recently built (1993) Bunkhouse are spare (e.g., no TVs or room phones), they are also comfortable and clean. Some rooms have private baths; others share public washrooms. For budget-minded travelers, this is the best deal in town. *Front and Prince Sts., Dawson, YT Y0B 1G0, tel. 403/993–6164. 32 rooms. Facilities: restaurant, satellite TV. MC, V. Open late-May–Labor Day. $*

**Haines Junction** **Cozy Corner.** The name is anything but original, yet there is a genuine coziness about this small motel and café, which is situated at the corner of the Alaska Highway and Haines Road. The rooms are unusually large—big enough for a bed and sofa bed, with plenty of room to spare—although the bathrooms are surprisingly small. Some of the rooms' small windows have views of the front ranges of Kluane National Park. As for the adjoining Cozy Corner Cafe, it's the sort of roadhouse where you order eggs for breakfast, burgers for lunch or dinner, and coffee at any time of day, served up with lots of homespun friendliness. *Box 5406, Haines Junction, YT Y0B 1L0, tel. 403/634–2511. 12 rooms. Facilities: satellite TV. AE, MC, V. $–$$*

*Dining and Lodging*

**Watson Lake** **Watson Lake Hotel.** Located on the western edge of Watson Lake, this hotel provides basic services and clean, neat guest rooms at reasonable prices, either in the hotel itself or in motel units. Log walls and exposed-stone accents add to the comfortable, rustic atmosphere. *Box 370, Watson Lake, YT Y0A 1C0, tel. 403/536–7781. 48 units with private bath, including 1 suite and 3 kitchenettes. Facilities: cable TV, lounge, dining room, sauna, laundry. AE, DC, MC, V. $$*

*Dining and Lodging*

**Whitehorse** **The Cellar.** The fact that tables are draped with tablecloths immedi-
*Dining* ately makes this restaurant high-class in the Whitehorse dining
scene. Indeed, The Cellar, in the cellar of the Edgewater Hotel,
with its high-back Victorian chairs, actually does approach the standards of an elegant dining room elsewhere in the world. While perhaps a bit overbearing in the casual far north, this atmosphere may
be appropriate for a special night on the town. Seafood, such as Alaska King Crab, highlights the menu, along with steak-and-seafood
combinations. The Gallery upstairs serves breakfast and lunch on a
much more casual basis. *101 Main St. (in the Edgewater Hotel), tel.
403/667–2572. Reservations advised. Jacket advised. AE, MC, V.
No lunch. $$$$*

★ **No Pop's.** The white-brick exterior promises all of the atmosphere of
a laundromat, but inside, the dining room—with straight-edge pine
furniture and walls adorned by the works of local artists—is downright cozy. A small terrace in back with a tree rising through the
roof adds a distinctive character to dining al fresco. This is the sort
of place where people wander in and out at all hours for take-out orders, a cup of coffee, or a full, sit-down dinner. Rack of lamb and Arctic char are among the rotating dinner specials; fresh-baked pastries
are good any time of day. *312 Steele St., tel. 403/668–3227. Dress:
casual. AE, MC, V. $$*

**Talisman Cafe.** The decor of straight-edged pine furniture may be
typical of the far north, but the menu is all over the map, from the
southeastern United States (jambalaya) to the Middle East
(taboulleh). For extra cultural spice, Tarot card readings are thrown
in from time to time. The dining experience here is comfortable and
low-key. The take-out service in the storefront next door provides
well-prepared salads and fresh-baked goods. *2112 2nd Ave., tel. 403/
667–2736. Dress: casual. AE, MC, V. $–$$*

*Lodging* **Westmark Whitehorse Hotel.** If it weren't for all the tour-bus baggage to trip over in the hallways, this would be a fine place to stay.
Rooms are attractively decorated with dark-wood furnishings and
such nice touches as in-room coffee makers. The hotel can even boast
its own vaudeville show, the Frantic Follies, a revue playing heavily
on Gold Rush themes. The restaurant can get crowded. *2nd Ave.
and Wood St., Box 4250, Whitehorse, YT Y1A 3T3, tel. 403/668–4700
or 800/544–0970 for reservations in U.S. 181 units, including 5
suites. Facilities: cable TV, gift shop, barber shop, beauty salon, art
gallery, travel agency, lounge, restaurant, accessible to people with
disabilities. AE, DC, MC, V. $$$*

**Edgewater Hotel.** This small hotel on a quiet end of Main Street is a
good alternative to the Westmark for those trying to avoid the tour-
bus bustle. The lobby is small and the passageway to the rooms is a
bit narrow and awkward, but the rooms are large, modernly fur-
nished, and quiet. They are also somewhat on the dark side, but
when daylight stretches well into the night, this might be an asset.
*101 Main St., Whitehorse, YT Y1A 2A7, tel. 403/667–2572. 30 units,
including 2 suites. Facilities: restaurant, lounge. AE, MC, V. $$*

**Yukon Inn.** The Yukon Inn is a good choice for travelers on a budget,
which is to say, it's a decent place without much distinction. Located
on the west side of town in a nondescript shopping area, the two-
story motel has clean rooms with a soft-gray color scheme and furniture that would look as appropriate in an office as a motel. Sound-
proofing is not one of the Inn's strong points. The Loose Moose Cafe,
a bright, attractive place with a tropical-inspired decor, serves decent burgers, sandwiches, and fries. *4220 4th Ave., Whitehorse, YT
Y1A 1K1, tel. 403/667–2527 or 800/661–0454 (in western Canada).
98 units, including 2 suites and 25 with kitchenettes. Facilities: ca-*

*ble TV, telephones, dining room, lounge, gift shop, hair salon. AE, MC, V. $$*

# The Arts and Nightlife

## The Arts

In Yellowknife, **Folk on the Rocks** (Society for the Encouragement of Northern Talent, Box 326, Yellowknife, NT X1A 2N3, tel. 403/920–7806) is usually held on a mid-July weekend. The event attracts folk musicians from throughout North America, as well as Dene and Inuit performers. During the summer, the **Northern Arts and Cultural Centre** (Box 1025, Yellowknife, NT X1A 2N7, tel. 403/873–3840) schedules a number of productions.

In Dawson City, the **Dawson City Music Festival** (Dawson City Music Festival Association, Box 456, Dawson City, YT Y0B 1G0, tel. 403/993–5584), featuring a variety of folk musicians from around the north, is held each July.

In Whitehorse, performances of various sorts are stage throughout the year at the **Yukon Arts Centre** (Yukon Pl., Box 5931, Whitehorse Y1A 5L6, tel. 403/667–8575).

## Nightlife

The way that many Dawson visitors spend the evening (not to mention a few dollars) is at the gambling tables of **Diamond Tooth Gertie's.** Short shows are staged throughout the evening, but gambling, with Klondike flair (croupiers are dressed in period costumes) is the main attraction. *4th Ave. and Queen St., tel. 403/993–5575. Admission: $4.50. Open mid-June–mid-Sept., Mon.–Sat. 8 PM–2 AM.*

In addition to the **Gaslight Follies** in Dawson (*see* Tour 3, *above*) and the **Frantic Follies** in Whitehorse (*see* Tour 1, *above*), **El Dorado!** at the **Gold Rush Inn** (411 Main St., Whitehorse, YT tel. 403/668–6472) is a musical revue featuring tales of the Yukon.

For a different kind of night on the town—or night *out* of town—try the dinner cruise on the Great Slave Lake aboard the **S.S. *Nochoa*** (Sail North, Box 2497, Yellowknife, NT X1A, 2P8, tel. 403/873–8019). Essentially a deck on pontoons, the *Nochoa* stops for a cookout on one of the lake's many islands. *Afternoon and evening departures. Round-trip time approx. 4 hrs. $47 per person.*

## Seasonal Events

The all-night **Summer Solstice Dance** (Frostbite Music Society, tel. 403/668–4921) in Whitehorse and **Raven Mad Daze** (Yellowknife Chamber of Commerce, tel. 403/920–4944) in Yellowknife take place during the summer solstice (the third week in June), when above the Arctic Circle the sun never sets.

The **Midnight Sun Marathon** (contact Linda Brunner, Strathcona Mineral Services Ltd., 20 Toronto St., Toronto M5C 2B8, tel. 416/869–0772) takes place in early July; it is a series of four races ranging from 10 to 84 kilometers.

A Labor Day weekend event that often draws a big crowd and the enthusiastic participation of Dawson City residents is the **Great Klondike Outhouse Race** (contact the Klondike Visitors Association, tel. 403/993–5575), in which runners pull home-built "outhouses" on wheels through the streets of Dawson.

# Index

*Escape to ancient cities and exotic*

*islands*

*with CNN Travel Guide, a*

*wealth of valuable advice. Host Valerie Voss will take you*

*to all of your favorite destinations,*

*including those off the beaten path.*

*Tune into your passport to the world.*

# CNN TRAVEL GUIDE
SATURDAY 10:00 PMpt    SUNDAY 8:30 AMet

**Personalized:**
Prepared expressly
for you.

**Up-to-the-minute:**
Includes the most current
information available.

**Your travel dates:**
Covers only days
when you will be
there.

June 1

Fodor's/Worldview presents a Travel Update for:

Mr. Gavin Lynch
201 East 50th Street
New York, New York, 10022

Fodor's
WORLDVIEW

LONDON, UK

**HIGHLIGHTS—EVENTS**

ARRIVE 23 Jun DEPART: 21 Jul

**Your Interests:**
Features only
those categories
that matter to you.

**Wimbledon Lawn Tennis Championships**
Seats for the Wimbledon championships, especiall
those for the men's and women's finals on the
Centre Court, are the hottest tickets in Lon
ummer. Each winter there is a ballot
No. 1 Court seats for the foll
nt. Through this ballot, te
ance of securing a ticket.
top matches are included
ining hotel accommodati
ailable from the tourname
NAA Events Internation

**en Air Theatre Season**
of open-air theater produ
lovely park, once the e
andies, is as much of an
adway in the Park and e
bring your largest umbrel
n interrupted by showe
for the almost 1,200-seat
e offered when perfor-
n, but refunds are no
tact Sheila Ben
ent's Pa

### Ordering is easy.

You can order a Travel Update up to a few days
before you leave. We need 48 hours to prepare
Updates, and you have to allow for delivery time.

You can also order as much as three months before
you leave. We can send your Travel Update
immediately, or if you prefer, we can hold your
order until just before you leave so that the
information is as current as possible.

There's an order form at the end of this special
section. Choose your destinations and interests; mail
or fax the completed form to us. Or if you prefer, you
can call us toll-free. We'll send out your personalized
Update within 48 hours.

**Special concerts—
who's performing
what and where**

**One-of-a-kind,
one-time-only events**

**Special interest,
in-depth listings**

## Children — Events

### Angel Canal Festival
The festivities include a children's funf[ai]
entertainers, a boat rally and displays on [the]
water. Regent's Canal. Islington. N1. Tu[be:]
Angel. Tel: 267 9100. 11:30am-5:30pm. 7/0[

### Blackheath Summer Kite Festival
Stunt kite displays with parachuting ted[dy]
bears and trade stands. Free admission. S[
BR: Blackheath. 10am. 6/27.

### Megabugs
Children will delight in this infestation [of]
giant robotic insects, including a prayi[ng]
mantis 60 times life size. Mon-Sat 10a[m-]
6pm; Sun 11am-6pm. Admission 4.[
pounds. Natural History Museum, Cromw[ell]
Road. SW7. Tube: South Kensington. T[el:]
938 9123. Ends 10/01.

### Childminders
This establishment employs only wome[n,]
providing nurses and qualified nannies to [

## Music — Jazz & Blues

### Tito Puente's Golden Men of Latin Jazz
The father of mambo and Cuban rumba king
comes to town. Royal Festival Hall. South Bank.
SE1. Tube: Waterloo. Tel: 928 8800. 8pm. 7/15.

### Georgie Fame and The New York Band
Riding a popular tide with his latest album, the
smoky-voiced Fame and his keyboard are on a
tour yet again. The Grand. Clapham Junction.
SW11. BR: Clapham Junction. Tel: 738 9000.
7:30pm. 7/07.

### Jacques Loussier Play Bach Trio
The French jazz classicist and colleagues.
Kenwood Lakeside. Hampstead Lane.
Kenwood. NW3. Tube: Golders Green, then bus
210. Tel: 413 1443. 7pm. 7/10.

### Tony Bennett and Ronnie Scott
Royal Festival Hall. South Bank. SE1. Tube:
Waterloo. Tel: 928 8800. 8pm. 7/11.

### Santana
Royal Festival Hall. South Bank. SE1. Tube[
Waterloo. Tel: 928 8800. 8pm. 7/12.

### Count Basie Orchestra and Nancy Wilson Trio
Royal Festival Hall. South Bank. SE1. Tube[
Waterloo. Tel: 928 8800. 8pm. 7/14.

### King Pleasure and the Biscuit Boys
Royal Festival Hall. South Bank. SE1. Tube[
Waterloo. Tel: 928 8800. 6:30 and 9pm. 7/16.

### Al Green and the London Community Gospel Choir
Royal Festival Hall. South Bank. SE1. Tube[
Waterloo. Tel: 928 8800. 8pm. 7/13.

### BB King and Linda Hopkins
Mother of the blues and successor to Bess[ie]
Smith, Hopkins meets up with "Blues Boy[
South Bank. SE[

## Music — Classical

### Marylebone Sinfonia
Kenneth Gowen conducts music by [
and Rossini. Queen Elizabeth Hall[
Bank. SE1. Tube: Waterloo. Tel: 92[
7:45pm. 7/16.

### London Philharmonic
Franz Welser-Moest and George [
conduct selections by Alexande[r]
Messiaen, and some of Benjamin's [
positions. Queen Elizabeth Hall. So[
SE1. Tube: Waterloo. Tel: 928 8800[

### London Pro Arte Orchestra and Fore[
Murray Stewart conducts sele[
Rossini, Haydn and Jonathan Willce[
Queen Elizabeth Hall. South B[
Tube: Waterloo. Tel: 928 8800. 7:4[

### Kensington Symphony Orchestra
[
[ ] Keeble conducts Dvorak[

# Here's what you get . . .

## Detailed information about what's going on — precisely when you'll be there.

**Reviews by local critics**

**Show openings during your visit**

**Handy pocket-size booklet**

**Exhibitions & Shows—Antique & Flower**

**Westminster Antiques Fair**
Over 50 stands with pre-1830 furniture and other Victorian and earlier items. Thu-Fri 11am-8pm; Sat-Sun 11am-6pm. Admission 4 pounds, children free. Old Royal Horticultural Hall. Vincent Square. SW1. Tel: 0444/48 25 14. 6-24 thru 6/27.

**Royal Horticultural Society Flower Show**
The show includes displays of carnations, summer fruit and vegetables. Tue 11am-7pm; Wed 10am-5pm. Admission Tue 4 pounds, Wed 2 pounds. Royal Horticultural Halls. Greycoat Street and Vincent Square. SW1. Tube: Victoria. 7/20 thru 7/21.

**mpton Court Palace International Flower Show**
Major international garden and flower show taking place in conjunction with

**eater — Musical**

**Sunset Boulevard**
In June, the four Andrew Lloyd Webber musicals which dominated London's stages in the 1980s (Cats, Starlight Express, Phantom of the Opera and Aspects of Love) are joined by the composer's latest work, a show rumored to have his best music to date. The 1950 Billy Wilder film about a helpless young writer who is drawn into the world of a possessive, aging silent screen star offers rich opportunities for Webber's evolving style. Soaring, aching melodies, lush technical effects and psychological thrills are all expected. Patti Lupone stars. Mon-Sat at 8pm; matinee Thu-Sat at 3pm. In-person sales only at the box office; credit card bookings, Tel: 344 0055. Admission 15-32.50 pounds. Adelphi Theatre. The Strand. WC2. Tube: Charing Cross. Tel: 836 7611. Starts: 6/21.

**Leonardo  A Portrait of Love**
A new musical about the great Renaissance artist and inventor comes in for a London pre-
ing tested by a brief run at Oxford's Old
. . . . . The work explores

**Spectator Sports — Other Sports**

**Greyhound Racing: Wembley Stadium**
This dog track offers good views of greyhound racing held on Mon, Wed and Fri. No credit cards. Stadium Way. Wembley. HA9. Tube: Wembley Park. Tel: 902 8833.

**Benson & Hedges Cricket Cup Final**
Lord's Cricket Ground. St. John's Wood Road. NW8. Tube: St. John's Wood. Tel: 289 1611. 11am. 7/10.

**siness-Fax & Overnight Mail**

**Post Office, Trafalgar Square Branch**
Offers a network of fax services, the Intelpost system, throughout the country and abroad. Mon-Sat 8am-8pm, Sun 9am-5pm. William IV Street. WC2. Tube: Ch

**Fodor's WORLDVIEW**
TRAVEL UPDATE

London, England
Arriving: June 23
Departing: July 21

# Interest Categories

For your personalized Travel Update, choose the categories you're most interested in from this list. Every Travel Update automatically provides you with *Event Highlights* - the best of what's happening during the dates of your trip.

| | | |
|---|---|---|
| **1.** | **Business Services** | Fax & Overnight Mail, Computer Rentals, Photocopying, Protocol, Secretarial, Messenger, Translation Services |

**Dining**

| | | |
|---|---|---|
| **2.** | **All Day Dining** | Breakfast & Brunch, Cafes & Tea Rooms, Late-Night Dining |
| **3.** | **Local Cuisine** | In Every Price Range—from Budget Restaurants to the Special Splurge |
| **4.** | **European Cuisine** | Continental, French, Italian |
| **5.** | **Asian Cuisine** | Chinese, Far Eastern, Japanese, Other |
| **6.** | **Americas Cuisine** | American, Mexican & Latin |
| **7.** | **Nightlife** | Bars, Dance Clubs, Casinos, Comedy Clubs, Ethnic, Pubs & Beer Halls |
| **8.** | **Entertainment** | Theater—Comedy, Drama, English Language, Musicals, Dance, Ticket Agencies |
| **9.** | **Music** | Country/Western/Folk, Classical, Traditional & Ethnic, Opera, Jazz & Blues, Pop, Rock |
| **10.** | **Children's Activities** | Events, Attractions |
| **11.** | **Tours** | Local Tours, Day Trips, Overnight Excursions, Cruises |
| **12.** | **Exhibitions, Festivals & Shows** | Antiques & Flower, History & Cultural, Art Exhibitions, Fairs & Craft Shows, Music & Art Festivals |
| **13.** | **Shopping** | Districts & Malls, Markets, Regional Specialities |
| **14.** | **Fitness** | Bicycling, Health Clubs, Hiking, Jogging |
| **15.** | **Recreational Sports** | Boating/Sailing, Fishing, Golf, Ice Skating, Skiing, Snorkeling/Scuba, Swimming, Tennis & Racquet |
| **16.** | **Spectator Sports** | Auto Racing, Baseball, Basketball, Boating & Sailing, Football, Golf, Horse Racing, Ice Hockey, Rugby, Soccer, Tennis, Track & Field, Other Sports |

Please note that interest category content will vary by season, destination, and length of stay.

# Destinations

The Fodor's/Worldview Travel Update covers more than 160 destinations world-wide. Choose the destinations that match your itinerary from this list. (Choose bulleted destinations only.)

## Europe
- Amsterdam
- Athens
- Barcelona
- Berlin
- Brussels
- Budapest
- Copenhagen
- Dublin
- Edinburgh
- Florence
- Frankfurt
- French Riviera
- Geneva
- Glasgow
- Istanbul
- Lausanne
- Lisbon
- London
- Madrid
- Milan
- Moscow
- Munich
- Oslo
- Paris
- Prague
- Provence
- Rome
- Salzburg
* Seville
- St. Petersburg
- Stockholm
- Venice
- Vienna
- Zurich

## United States (Mainland)
- Albuquerque
- Atlanta
- Atlantic City
- Baltimore
- Boston
* Branson, MO
* Charleston, SC
- Chicago
- Cincinnati
- Cleveland
- Dallas/Ft. Worth
- Denver
- Detroit
- Houston
* Indianapolis
- Kansas City
- Las Vegas
- Los Angeles
- Memphis

- Miami
- Milwaukee
- Minneapolis/ St. Paul
* Nashville
- New Orleans
- New York City
- Orlando
- Palm Springs
- Philadelphia
- Phoenix
- Pittsburgh
- Portland
* Reno/ Lake Tahoe
- St. Louis
- Salt Lake City
- San Antonio
- San Diego
- San Francisco
* Santa Fe
- Seattle
- Tampa
- Washington, DC

## Alaska
- Alaskan Destinations

## Hawaii
- Honolulu
- Island of Hawaii
- Kauai
- Maui

## Canada
- Quebec City
- Montreal
- Ottawa
- Toronto
- Vancouver

## Bahamas
- Abaco
- Eleuthera/ Harbour Island
- Exuma
- Freeport
- Nassau & Paradise Island

## Bermuda
- Bermuda Countryside
- Hamilton

## British Leeward Islands
- Anguilla

- Antigua & Barbuda
- St. Kitts & Nevis

## British Virgin Islands
- Tortola & Virgin Gorda

## British Windward Islands
- Barbados
- Dominica
- Grenada
- St. Lucia
- St. Vincent
- Trinidad & Tobago

## Cayman Islands
- The Caymans

## Dominican Republic
- Santo Domingo

## Dutch Leeward Islands
- Aruba
- Bonaire
- Curacao

## Dutch Windward Island
- St. Maarten/ St. Martin

## French West Indies
- Guadeloupe
- Martinique
- St. Barthelemy

## Jamaica
- Kingston
- Montego Bay
- Negril
- Ocho Rios

## Puerto Rico
- Ponce
- San Juan

## Turks & Caicos
- Grand Turk/ Providenciales

## U.S. Virgin Islands
- St. Croix
- St. John
- St. Thomas

## Mexico
- Acapulco
- Cancun & Isla Mujeres
- Cozumel
- Guadalajara
- Ixtapa & Zihuatanejo
- Los Cabos
- Mazatlan
- Mexico City
- Monterrey
- Oaxaca
- Puerto Vallarta

## South/Central America
* Buenos Aires
* Caracas
* Rio de Janeiro
* San Jose, Costa Rica
* Sao Paulo

## Middle East
* Jerusalem

## Australia & New Zealand
- Auckland
- Melbourne
* South Island
- Sydney

## China
- Beijing
- Guangzhou
- Shanghai

## Japan
- Kyoto
- Nagoya
- Osaka
- Tokyo
- Yokohama

## Pacific Rim/Other
* Bali
- Bangkok
- Hong Kong & Macau
- Manila
- Seoul
- Singapore
- Taipei

* Destinations available by 1/1/95

# Fodor's WORLDVIEW TRAVEL UPDATE **Order Form**

**THIS TRAVEL UPDATE IS FOR (Please print):**

Name

Address

| City | State | Country | ZIP |
|------|-------|---------|-----|

Tel # ( ) - Fax # ( ) -

Title of this Fodor's guide:

Store and location where guide was purchased:

**INDICATE YOUR DESTINATIONS/DATES:** You can order up to three (3) destinations from the previous page. Fill in your arrival and departure dates for each destination. <u>Your Travel Update itinerary (all destinations selected) cannot exceed 30 days from beginning to end.</u>

| | | | Month | Day | | Month | Day |
|---|---|---|---|---|---|---|---|
| (Sample) | LONDON | From: | 6 / | 21 | To: | 6 / | 30 |
| 1 | | From: | / | | To: | / | |
| 2 | | From: | / | | To: | / | |
| 3 | | From: | / | | To: | / | |

**CHOOSE YOUR INTERESTS:** Select up to eight (8) categories from the list of interest categories shown on the previous page and circle the numbers below:

**1  2  3  4  5  6  7  8  9  10  11  12  13  14  15  16**

**CHOOSE WHEN YOU WANT YOUR TRAVEL UPDATE DELIVERED (Check one):**
❑ Please send my Travel Update immediately.
❑ Please hold my order until a few weeks before my trip to include the most up-to-date information.
*Completed orders will be sent within 48 hours. Allow 7-10 days for U.S. mail delivery.*

**ADD UP YOUR ORDER HERE.** *SPECIAL OFFER FOR FODOR'S PURCHASERS ONLY!*

| | Suggested Retail Price | Your Price | This Order |
|---|---|---|---|
| First destination ordered | $ 9.95 | $ 7.95 | $ 7.95 |
| Second destination (if applicable) | $ 6.95 | $ 4.95 | + |
| Third destination (if applicable) | $ 6.95 | $ 4.95 | + |

**DELIVERY CHARGE (Check one and enter amount below)**

| | Within U.S. & Canada | Outside U.S. & Canada |
|---|---|---|
| First Class Mail | ❑ $2.50 | ❑ $5.00 |
| FAX | ❑ $5.00 | ❑ $10.00 |
| Priority Delivery | ❑ $15.00 | ❑ $27.00 |

**ENTER DELIVERY CHARGE FROM ABOVE:** + 

**TOTAL:** $ 

**METHOD OF PAYMENT IN U.S. FUNDS ONLY (Check one):**
❑ AmEx   ❑ MC   ❑ Visa   ❑ Discover   ❑ Personal Check (U. S. & Canada only)
❑ Money Order/ International Money Order
*Make check or money order payable to: Fodor's Worldview Travel Update*

Credit Card —/—/—/—/—/—/—/—/—/—/—/—/—/—/—/—/ **Expiration Date:___/___**

**Authorized Signature**

**SEND THIS COMPLETED FORM WITH PAYMENT TO:**
Fodor's Worldview Travel Update, 114 Sansome Street, Suite 700, San Francisco, CA 94104

**OR CALL OR FAX US 24-HOURS A DAY**
Telephone **1-800-799-9609** • Fax **1-800-799-9619** (From within the U.S. & Canada)
(Outside the U.S. & Canada: Telephone 415-616-9988 • Fax 415-616-9989)

(Please have this guide in front of you when you call so we can verify purchase.)
Code: FTG                                                      Offer valid until 12/31/95.